PRENTICE HALL

LITERATURE
THE AMERICAN EXPERIENCE

PRENTICE HALL
LITERATURE

COPPER

BRONZE

SILVER

GOLD

PLATINUM

THE AMERICAN EXPERIENCE

THE BRITISH TRADITION

WORLD MASTERPIECES

PRENTICE HALL

LITERATURE
THE AMERICAN EXPERIENCE

PARAMOUNT EDITION

AN EXPRESSION OF A SILKTOWN IN NEW JERSEY, c. 1915
Oscar F. Bluemner
New Jersey State Museum

PRENTICE HALL
Englewood Cliffs, New Jersey
Needham, Massachusetts

ISBN 0-13-722448-6

                9 10   02 01 00 99 98

Art credits begin on page 1205.

PRENTICE HALL
A Division of Simon & Schuster
Englewood Cliffs, New Jersey 07632

STAFF CREDITS FOR PRENTICE HALL LITERATURE

Publisher: Eileen Thompson

Editorial: Ellen Bowler, Douglas McCollum, Philip Fried, Kelly Ackley, Eric Hausmann, Lauren Weidenman

Multicultural/ESL: Marina Liapunov, Barbara T. Stone

Marketing: Mollie Ledwith, Belinda Loh

National Language Arts Consultants: Ellen Lees Backstrom, Ed.D., Craig A. McGhee, Karen Massey Riley, Vennisa Travers, Gail Witt

Permissions: Doris Robinson

Design: Susan Walrath, Carmela Pereira, Leslie Osher, AnnMarie Roselli

Visual Research: Libby Forsyth, Emily Rose, Martha Conway

Production: Suse Bell, Joan McCulley, Elizabeth Torjussen, Amy E. Fleming, Lynn Contrucci, Garret Schenck, Lorraine Moffa

Publishing Technology: Andrew Black, Deborah J. Jones, Monduane Harris, Cleasta Wilburn, Greg Myers

Pre-Press Production: Laura Sanderson, Natalia Bilash, Denise Herckenrath

Print and Bind: Rhett Conklin, Gertrude Szyferblatt

ACKNOWLEDGMENTS

Grateful acknowledgment is made to the following for permission to reprint copyrighted material:

The American Scholar
Lines from the Poem "Garden of My Childhood" by Kuangchi C. Chang. Reprinted from *The American Scholar,* Volume 26, Number 3, Summer 1957. Copyright © 1957 by the United Chapters of Phi Beta Kappa. Reprinted by permission of the publishers.

Elizabeth Barnett, Literary Executor of the estate of Norma Millay Ellis
Excerpts from "I Shall Go Back Again to the Bleak Shore" and "Recuerdo" by Edna St. Vincent Millay. Copyright 1922, 1923, 1950, 1951 by Edna St. Vincent Millay and Norma Millay Ellis. "Renascence" by Edna St. Vincent Millay. From *Collected Poems,* Harper & Row. Copyright 1912, 1940 by Edna St. Vincent Millay. Reprinted by permission.

Susan Bergholz Literary Services
"Straw Into Gold" by Sandra Cisneros. Copyright © by Sandra Cisneros 1987. First published under the title "A Writer's Voyage" in *The Texas Observer,* September 1987. Reprinted by permission of Susan Bergholz Literary Services, New York.

(Continued on page 1201.)

CONTENTS

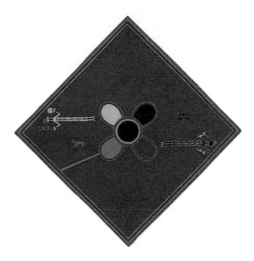

THE NEW LAND
TO 1750

INTRODUCTION 1

■ Timeline 4
■ American Voices 9
■ Reading Critically 10

Native American Voices

Delaware
  from The Walam Olum 14
Navajo
  from The Navajo Origin Legend 18
Iroquois
  from The Iroquois Constitution 21
Pima
  From the Houses of Magic 26
Chippewa
  Spring Song 29
Teton Sioux
  Song Concerning a Dream
    of the Thunderbirds 30

Cross Currents: Native American Voices
  Today 31

Explorers

Christopher Columbus
  from Journal of the First Voyage
    to America 36
Alvar Nuñez Cabeza de Vaca
  from Relation of Alvar Nuñez Cabeza
    de Vaca 38
Pedro de Casteñada
  from The Narrative of the Expedition
    of Coronado 40

Living in the New Land

John Smith
  from The General History of Virginia ... 46
William Bradford
  from Of Plymouth Plantation 54
Anne Bradstreet
  To My Dear and Loving Husband 61
  Upon the Burning of Our House 62
Edward Taylor
  Huswifery 68

Upon a Wasp Chilled with Cold 70

Jonathan Edwards
from Sinners in the Hands
    of an Angry God 74

Cotton Mather
from The Wonders of the Invisible
    World 79

YOUR WRITING PROCESS: Persuasion/
Description
Writing a Flier 84

THE REVOLUTIONARY PERIOD
1750–1800

INTRODUCTION 88

■ Timeline 90

■ American Voices 96
■ Reading Critically 97

Benjamin Franklin
from The Autobiography 100
from Poor Richard's Almanack 111

Multicultural Connection: Proverbs From
Around the World 113

Patrick Henry
Speech in the Virginia Convention 116
Thomas Paine
from The Crisis, Number 1 122
Phillis Wheatley
To His Excellency, General
    Washington 129
Thomas Jefferson
The Declaration of Independence 134

One Writer's Process: Thomas Jefferson
and the Declaration 138

Abigail Adams
Letter to Her Daughter from the New
    White House 142

Michel-Guillaume Jean de Crèvecoeur
from Letters from an American
    Farmer 148

Multicultural Connection: How America
Evolved into a Multicultural Society ... 150

Olaudah Equiano
from The Interesting Narrative of the Life
    of Olaudah Equiano 153

Cross Currents: The Statue of Liberty .. 156

YOUR WRITING PROCESS: Narration
Writing a News Story 158

COMMON SENSE;

ADDRESSED TO THE

INHABITANTS

OF

AMERICA,

On the following interesting

SUBJECTS.

I. Of the Origin and Design of Government in general,
    with concise Remarks on the English Constitution.
II. Of Monarchy and Hereditary Succession.
III. Thoughts on the present State of American Affairs.
IV. Of the present Ability of America, with some mis-
    cellaneous Reflections.

Man knows no Master save creating Heaven,
Or those whom choice and common good ordain.
THOMSON.

PHILADELPHIA;
Printed, and Sold, by R. BELL, in Third-Street.
MDCCLXXVI.

A GROWING NATION
1800–1840

INTRODUCTION 162

■ Timeline 164

■ American Voices 170
■ Reading Critically 171

Washington Irving
The Devil and Tom Walker 174
William Cullen Bryant
Thanatopsis 187

To a Waterfowl 189
Edgar Allan Poe
The Fall of the House of Usher 194
The Raven 209

One Writer's Process: Edgar Allan Poe
and "The Raven" 214

To Helen 217

Cross Currents: Alfred J. Hitchcock 218

YOUR WRITING PROCESS: Narration/
Creative Writing
Writing a First-Person Narrative 220

NEW ENGLAND RENAISSANCE
1840–1855

INTRODUCTION 224

■ Timeline 226
■ American Voices 236
■ Reading Critically 237

Ralph Waldo Emerson
from Nature 240
from Self-Reliance 242
The Snowstorm 245
Concord Hymn 247

Multicultural Connection: The American
Revolution: Supporters From Around
the World 248

The Rhodora 249
Brahma 251
Henry David Thoreau
from Walden 254
from Civil Disobedience 262

Multicultural Connection: From Walden
Pond to India and Back 263

Cross Currents: Contemporary
Thoreaus 264

Nathaniel Hawthorne
The Minister's Black Veil 268
Herman Melville
from Moby-Dick 280

New England Poets

Henry Wadsworth Longfellow
The Tide Rises, The Tide Falls 300
A Psalm of Life 302
The Arsenal at Springfield 304
Oliver Wendell Holmes
Old Ironsides 308
The Chambered Nautilus 310
James Russell Lowell
Auspex 315
The First Snowfall 316
John Greenleaf Whittier
from Snowbound 320
Hampton Beach 326
Emily Dickinson
"Hope" is the thing with feathers— 332
There's a certain Slant of light, ... 333
I Never saw a Moor— 334
A narrow Fellow in the Grass 335
Tell all the Truth but tell it slant— 336
Success is counted sweetest 336
I heard a Fly buzz—when I died— ... 337
I felt a Funeral, in my Brain, ... 338

My life closed twice before its
close— 339
The Bustle in a House 339
As imperceptibly as grief 340
Much Madness is divinest Sense— ... 340
The Soul selects her own society— .. 341
How happy is the little Stone 342
There is a solitude of space 342
This is my letter to the World 343

YOUR WRITING PROCESS: Exposition
**Writing a Comparison/Contrast
Essay** 344

DIVISION, WAR, AND RECONCILIATION
1855–1865

INTRODUCTION 348

■ Timeline 350

■ American Voices 356
■ Reading Critically 357

Spirituals
Swing Low, Sweet Chariot 360
Go Down, Moses 361
Frederick Douglass
from My Bondage and My Freedom .. 364

Multicultural Connection: The Influence
of Frederick Douglass 368

Mary Chesnut
from Mary Chesnut's Civil War 371
Robert E. Lee
Letter to His Son 378
Abraham Lincoln
The Gettysburg Address 380

One Writer's Process: Abraham Lincoln
and the Gettysburg Address 382

Civil War Voices: A First-Person Narrative
of the War 384
Chief Joseph
I Will Fight No More Forever 394

Multicultural Connection: Orators From
Many Cultures 395

Walt Whitman
from Preface to the 1855 Edition
of Leaves of Grass 398
from Song of Myself 399
Beat! Beat! Drums! 404
When I Heard the Learn'd
Astronomer 406
A Noiseless Patient Spider 407
When Lilacs Last in the Dooryard
Bloom'd 408

Cross Currents: Mathew Brady 418

YOUR WRITING PROCESS: Persuasion
Writing an Editorial 420

REALISM AND THE FRONTIER
1865–1915

INTRODUCTION 424

■ Timeline 426

■ American Voices 433
■ Reading Critically 434

Prose

Mark Twain
from Life on the Mississippi, The Boys'
Ambition 438

Multicultural Connection: Mark Twain and
African American Speech 442

The Notorious Jumping Frog
of Calaveras County 445

Bret Harte
  The Outcasts of Poker Flat 452

Cross Currents: Frederic Remington ... 460

Ambrose Bierce
  An Occurrence at Owl Creek Bridge .. 464
Kate Chopin
  The Story of an Hour 474
Willa Cather
  A Wagner Matinée 480
Jack London
  To Build a Fire 490
Stephen Crane
  The Open Boat 504

One Writer's Process: Stephen Crane and
"The Open Boat" 523

Poetry

Sidney Lanier
  Song of the Chattahoochee 527
Paul Laurence Dunbar
  We Wear the Mask 532
  Douglass 534
Edwin Arlington Robinson
  Luke Havergal 538
  Miniver Cheevy 540
  Richard Cory 542

Edgar Lee Masters
  Lucinda Matlock 546
  Fiddler Jones 548
YOUR WRITING PROCESS: Exposition
  Writing an Introduction 550

THE MODERN AGE
1915–1946

INTRODUCTION 554

■ Timeline 556

■ American Voices 565
■ Reading Critically 566

Prose

Sherwood Anderson
  Sophistication 570
Ernest Hemingway
  In Another Country 580
F. Scott Fitzgerald
  Winter Dreams 588
Katherine Anne Porter
  The Jilting of Granny Weatherall 606
Thomas Wolfe
  The Far and the Near 616
Eudora Welty
  A Worn Path 622
John Steinbeck
  Flight 630
William Faulkner
  The Bear 646

Multicultural Connection: The Bear as a
Universal Symbol 656

  Faulkner's Nobel Prize Acceptance
  Speech 658
Zora Neale Hurston
  from Dust Tracks on a Road 662

Multicultural Connection: Gathering
Folklore 667
John Dos Passos
   Tin Lizzie 670
E. B. White
   Walden 676
James Thurber
   The Night the Ghost Got In 684
Richard Wright
   from Black Boy: A Record of Childhood
    and Youth 692

Poetry

Ezra Pound
   In a Station of the Metro 700
   The River-Merchant's Wife: A Letter .. 701
   Canto 13 703
T. S. Eliot
   The Love Song of J. Alfred Prufrock .. 708
Wallace Stevens
   Disillusionment of Ten O'Clock 716
   Anecdote of the Jar 717
Amy Lowell
   Patterns 720
H. D.
   Pear Tree 726
   Heat 728
William Carlos Williams
   The Locust Tree in Flower 733

   The Red Wheelbarrow 734
   This Is Just to Say 735
Carl Sandburg
   Grass 738
   from The People, Yes 740
   Chicago 742
Edna St. Vincent Millay
   Renascence 746
Archibald MacLeish
   Ars Poetica 754
Marianne Moore
   Poetry 756
E. E. Cummings
   since feeling is first 760
   anyone lived in a pretty how town 761
   old age sticks 763
Robert Frost
   Birches 766
   Mending Wall 768
   The Death of the Hired Man 770
   "Out, Out—" 775
   Fire and Ice 777
   Nothing Gold Can Stay 777
   Stopping by Woods on a Snowy
    Evening 778
   Acquainted with the Night 779
W. H. Auden
   Who's Who 782
   The Unknown Citizen 783

Harlem Renaissance Poetry

Countee Cullen
   Any Human to Another 789
Claude McKay
   The Tropics in New York 790
Langston Hughes
   The Negro Speaks of Rivers 795

One Writer's Process: Langston Hughes
and "The Negro Speaks of Rivers" ... 796

Jean Toomer
   Storm Ending 800

Arna Bontemps
A Black Man Talks of Reaping 802
Cross Currents: Music in Harlem 803
YOUR WRITING PROCESS: Exposition
Writing a Self-Evaluation 806

CONTEMPORARY WRITERS
1946–Present

INTRODUCTION 810
■ Timeline 812
■ American Voices 817
■ Reading Critically 818

Fiction

Bernard Malamud
The First Seven Years 822
Flannery O'Connor
The Life You Save May Be
Your Own 832
James Baldwin
The Rockpile 844
John Updike
The Slump 854
Joyce Carol Oates
Journey 860
Donald Barthelme
Engineer-Private Paul Klee Misplaces an
Aircraft Between Milbertshofen and
Cambrai, March 1916 866
Anne Tyler
Average Waves in Unprotected
Waters 872
Ann Beattie
Imagined Scenes 882
Alice Walker
Everyday Use 892

Nonfiction

Carson McCullers
The Mortgaged Heart 902
Ralph Ellison
from Hidden Name and Complex
Fate 908
Joan Didion
On the Mall 916
Multicultural Connection: How People
Shop in Different Parts of the World .. 920
N. Scott Momaday
A Vision Beyond Time and Place 924
Sandra Cisneros
Straw Into Gold: The Metamorphosis
of the Everyday 930
Barry Lopez
from Arctic Dreams 936
Amy Tan
Mother Tongue 946

Poetry

Theodore Roethke
The Waking 954
Once More, the Round 956
James Dickey
The Rain Guitar 960
Denise Levertov
Merritt Parkway 962
Gwendolyn Brooks
The Explorer 966
Elizabeth Bishop
Little Exercise 968
House Guest 970
Robert Lowell
Hawthorne 974
Randall Jarrell
The Death of the Ball Turret Gunner .. 979
Losses 980
José García Villa
Be Beautiful, Noble, Like the
Antique Ant 984

Martín Espada
We Live by What We See at Night ... 986

One Writer's Process: Martín Espada and "We
Live by What We See at Night" 988

Victor Hernández Cruz
#1 Atmosphere 990
#2 Memory 990
Poem 990
Richard Wilbur
The Beautiful Changes 994
Robert Penn Warren
Gold Glade 996
Evening Hawk 998
Sylvia Plath
Mirror 1002
Robert Hayden
Frederick Douglass 1004
Those Winter Sundays 1005
William Stafford
Traveling Through the Dark 1006
Colleen McElroy
For My Children 1010

Louise Erdrich
Bidwell Ghost 1012
James Wright
Lying in a Hammock at William Duffy's
Farm in Pine Island, Minnesota ... 1014
Adrienne Rich
The Observer 1018
Simon Ortiz
Hunger in New York City 1020
Diana Chang
Most Satisfied by Snow 1022
Lawson Fusao Inada
Plucking Out a Rhythm 1026
Lorna Dee Cervantes
Freeway 280 1028
Rita Dove
This Life 1030

Drama

Arthur Miller
The Crucible 1034

Cross Currents: Aaron Copland 1120

YOUR WRITING PROCESS: Exposition/
Persuasion
Writing a Review 1122

ADDITIONAL FEATURES

Literary Map of the United States 1124
Handbook of the Writing Process 1126
**Handbook of Grammar and Revising
Strategies** 1136
**Handbook of Literary Terms and
Techniques** 1155
Glossary 1176
Index of Fine Art 1185
Index of Skills 1190
Index of Titles by Themes 1193
Index of Authors and Titles 1197
Acknowledgments (continued) 1201

PRENTICE HALL

LITERATURE
The American Experience

America is a land of wonders, in which everything is in constant motion and every change seems an improvement.
—Alexis de Tocqueville

AFTERGLOW
Martin Johnson Heade
The Chrysler Museum

THE NEW LAND
To 1750

Let England know our willingnesse,
  For that our worke is good;
Wee hope to plant a nation,
  Where none before hath stood.

Thomas Dale
Governor of the Jamestown Colony

More than a century after European explorers discovered North America, there were still no permanent settlements in the New World north of St. Augustine, Florida. By 1607, however, a small group of English settlers was struggling to survive on a marshy island in the James River in the present state of Virginia. In 1611, Thomas Dale, governor of the colony, wrote a report to the king expressing the colonists' determination to succeed. Despite disease and starvation, Jamestown did survive.

The first settlers were entranced by the presence and, to them, the strangeness of the native inhabitants. They did not at first realize that these earlier Americans, like Europeans, had cultural values and literary traditions of their own. The literature was entirely oral, for the tribes of North America had not yet developed writing systems. This extensive oral literature, along with the first written works of the colonists, forms the beginning of the American literary heritage.

THE HISTORICAL SETTING

When Christopher Columbus reached North America in 1492, the continent was already populated, though sparsely, by several hundred Native American tribes. Europeans did not encounter these tribes all at one time. Explorers from different nations came into contact with them at different times. As we now know, these widely dispersed tribes of Native Americans differed greatly from one another in language, government, social organization, customs, housing, and methods of survival.

The Native Americans

No one knows for certain when or how the first Americans arrived in what is now the United States. It may have been as recently as 12,000 years ago or as long ago as 70,000 years. Even if the shorter estimate is correct, Native Americans have been on the continent thirty times longer than the Europeans. Colonists from Europe did not begin arriving on the East Coast of North America until the late 1500's.

What were the earliest Americans doing for those many centuries? To a great extent, the answer is shrouded in mystery. As the historian Samuel Eliot Morison noted, "Even now we cannot write 'The History of America before 1492,' because history presupposes a more or less continuous and dated story." No such story of the Native Americans exists. Archeologists have deduced a great deal from artifacts, however, and folklorists have recorded a rich variety of songs, legends, and myths.

What we do know is that the Native Americans usually, but by no means always, greeted the earliest European settlers as friends. They instructed the newcomers in New World agriculture and woodcraft, introduced them to maize, beans, squash, maple sugar, snowshoes, toboggans, and birch bark canoes. Indeed, many more of the European settlers would have succumbed to the bitter Northeastern winters had it not been for the help of these first Americans.

Pilgrims and Puritans

A small group of Europeans sailed from England on the *Mayflower* in 1620. The passengers were religious reformers, Puritans who were critical of the Church of England. Having given up hope of "purifying" the church from within, they chose instead to withdraw from the church. This action earned them the name Separatists. We know them as the Pilgrims. They landed in the New World and established a settlement at what is now Plymouth, Massachusetts. With help from friendly tribes of Native Americans, the Plymouth settlement managed to survive the rigors of the New World. The colony never grew very large, however. Eventually, it was engulfed by the Massachusetts Bay Colony, the much larger settlement to the north.

Like the Plymouth Colony, the Massachusetts Bay Colony was also founded by religious reformers. These reformers, however, did not withdraw from the Church of England. Unlike the Separatists, they were Puritans who intended instead to reform the church from within. In America, the Puritans hoped to establish what John Winthrop, governor of the colony, called a "city upon a hill," a community guided in all aspects by the Bible. Their form of government would be a theocracy, a state under the immediate guidance of God.

Religion affected every aspect of Puritan life, although the Puritans were not always as stern and otherworldly as they are sometimes pictured. Their writings occasionally reveal a sense of humor, and the hardships of daily life forced them to be practical. In one sense, the Puritans were radical, since they demanded fundamental changes in the Church of England. In another sense, however, they were conservative. They preached a plain, unadorned Christianity that contrasted sharply with the cathedrals, vestments, ceremony, and hierarchy of the Church of England.

What exactly did the Puritans believe? Their beliefs were far from simple, but they agreed that human beings exist for the glory of God and that the Bible is the sole expression of God's will. They believed in predestination—John Calvin's doctrine that God has already decided who will achieve salvation and who will not. The elect, or saints, who are to be saved cannot take election for granted, however. Because of that, all devout Puritans searched their souls with great rigor and frequency for signs of grace. The Puritans believed in original sin and felt that they could accomplish good only through continual hard work and self-discipline. When people today speak of the "Puritan ethic," that is what they mean.

Puritanism was in decline throughout New England by the early 1700's, as more liberal Protestant congregations attracted followers. A reaction against this new freedom, however, set in around 1720. The Great Awakening, a series of religious revivals led by such eloquent ministers as Jonathan Edwards and George Whitefield, swept the colonies. The Great Awakening attracted thousands of converts to many Protestant groups, but it did little to revive old-fashioned Puritanism. What had been the dominant religion of New England had all but

THE BEGINNING OF NEW ENGLAND
After the Painting by Clyde O. Deland

The New Land (A.D. 1490 – A.D. 1750)

The *Mona Lisa*

Captain John Smith

The *Mayflower*

1490   **1540**   **1590**

AMERICAN EVENTS

- Native American groups first encounter European explorers.
- **Christopher Columbus** lands in the Bahamas.
  - Juan Ponce de Léon lands on the Florida peninsula.
  - Vasco Núñez de Balboa reaches the Pacific Ocean.
    - Pánfilo de Narváez lands in Florida.

- Francisco Vázquez de Coronado explores the Southwest
  - St. Augustine, Florida, first permanent settlement in U.S., founded by Pedro Menéndez.
    - English colony at Roanoke Island disappears; known as the Lost Colony.

- Iroquois Confederacy established to stop warfare among the Five Nations.
  - First permanent English settlement at Jamestown, Virginia.
  - **Captain John Smith** writes *A True Relation . . . of Virginia.*
    - House of Burgesses established in Virginia; first legislature in the New World.
    - Pilgrims land at Plymouth, Massachusetts.

WORLD EVENTS

- Italy: Leonardo da Vinci paints the *Mona Lisa.*
  - Italy: Michelangelo paints ceiling of Sistine Chapel.
    - Africa: Algiers and Tunisia founded.
    - Magellan sails around the world.
      - Spain: Chocolate introduced to Europe.
        - Mexico: Cortez conquers Aztecs.
          - Peru: Pizarro conquers Incas.

- Scotland: First golf organization founded.
  - England: Elizabeth I inherits throne.
  - England: 20,000 people die in London plague.
    - Belgium: Bruegel paints *The Wedding Dance.*
    - South America: 2 million Indians die of typhoid.
      - France: Montaigne's *Essays* published.

- England: Shakespeare completes *A Midsummer Night's Dream.*
  - Spain: Cervantes publishes Part I of *Don Quixote.*
    - Italy: Galileo builds first telescope.

Nat Bacon's
Rebellion

Woman Accused of
Witchcraft in Salem

Johann
Sebastian Bach

| 1640 | 1690 | 1740 |

- **William Bradford** begins writing *Of Plymouth Plantation*, completes it in 1651.

  - Harvard University founded in Cambridge, Massachusetts.

    - First printing press in English-speaking North America arrives in Massachusetts.

      - *Bay Psalm Book* published; first book printed in the colonies.

        - Massachusetts establishes free public schools.

          - London publication of **Anne Bradstreet's** *The Tenth Muse . . .* , a collection of poems.

            - John Eliot, Apostle to the Indians, publishes *The Indian Primer.*

- King Philip, chief of the Wampanoags, begins raiding New England frontier towns.

  - Nat Bacon's ill-fated rebellion launched against Virginia's Governor Berkeley.

    - Salem witchcraft trials result in the execution of 20 "witches."

- **Cotton Mather's** *The Wonders of the Invisible World* analyzes evidence against witches.

    - First theater in the colonies opens in Williamsburg, Virginia.

      - Smallpox epidemic breaks out in Boston; **Cotton Mather** argues for inoculation.

- John Peter Zenger acquitted of libel, furthering freedom of the press.

  - Great Awakening, a series of religious revivals, begins to sweep the colonies.

    - **Jonathan Edwards** first delivers his sermon *Sinners in the Hands of an Angry God.*

- England: John Donne publishes *Poems.*

  - Japan: All Europeans expelled.

    - India: English establish settlement at Madras.

      - Holland: Rembrandt paints *Night Watch.*

      - England: Civil War begins.

      - China: Ming Dynasty ends.

        - South Africa: First Dutch settlers arrive.

          - England: Milton publishes *Paradise Lost.*

            - France: Molière's *Tartuffe* first performed.

- China: All ports opened to foreign trade.

  - India: Calcutta founded by British.

    - England: First daily newspaper begins publication.

      - England: Daniel Defoe publishes *Robinson Crusoe.*

        - Germany: Bach composes *Brandenburg Concertos.*

          - England: Jonathan Swift publishes *Gulliver's Travels.*

            - Brazil: First coffee planted.

- France: Montesquieu publishes *The Spirit of Laws.*

  - Portugal: Sign language invented.

vanished by the time of the American Revolution. Nevertheless, Puritanism made a lasting impression on American attitudes. Its ideals of hard work, frugality, self-improvement, and self-reliance are still regarded as basic American virtues.

The Southern Planters

The Southern colonies differed from New England in climate, crops, social organization, and religion. Prosperous coastal cities grew up in the South, just as in the North, but beyond the Southern cities lay large plantations, not small farms. Despite its romantic image, the plantation was in fact a large-scale agricultural enterprise and a center of commerce. Up to a thousand people, many of them slaves, might live and work on a single planta-

tion. The first black slaves were brought to Virginia in 1619, a year before the Pilgrims landed at Plymouth. The plantation system and the institution of slavery were closely connected from the very beginning, although slavery existed in every colony, including Massachusetts.

Most of the plantation owners were Church of England members who regarded themselves as aristocrats. The first generation of owners, the men who established the great plantations, were ambitious, energetic, self-disciplined, and resourceful, just as the Puritans were. The way of life on most plantations, however, was more sociable and elegant than that of any Puritan. By 1750, Puritanism was in decline everywhere, despite the Great Awakening, while the plantation system in the South was just reaching its peak.

GOOD TIMES IN THE NEW WORLD (THE HOPE OF JAMESTOWN)
John Gadsby Chapman
Virginia Museum of Fine Art, Richmond, VA

THE EARLIEST AMERICAN LITERATURE

It was an oddly assorted group that established the foundations of American literature: the Native Americans with their oral traditions, the Puritans with their preoccupation with sin and salvation, and the Southern planters with their busy social lives. Indeed, much of the literature that the colonists read was not produced in the colonies. It came from England. Yet, by 1750, there were the clear beginnings of a native literature that would one day be honored throughout the English-speaking world.

Their Name Is on Your Waters

For a long time, Native American literature was viewed mainly as folklore. The consequence was that song lyrics, hero tales, migration legends, and accounts of the creation were studied more for their content than for their literary qualities. In an oral tradition, the telling of the tale may change with each speaker, and the words are almost sure to change over time. Thus, no fixed versions of such literary works exist. Still, in cases where the words of Native American lyrics or narratives have been captured in writing, the language is often poetic and moving. As might be expected in an oral setting, oratory was much prized among Native Americans. The names of certain orators, such as Logan and, later, Red Jacket, were widely known.

The introductory literature in this unit suggests the depth and power of those original American voices. Interestingly, you can find familiar, one-word examples of the various tribal languages simply by looking at a map or at road signs. A remarkable number of American place names, including the names of more than half of our fifty states, come from Native American words. In the nineteenth century, Lydia Sigourney wrote a popular poem called "Indian Names."

> Ye say they all have pass'd away
> That noble race and brave;
> That their light canoes have vanish'd,
> From off the crested wave;

That mid the forests where they roam'd,
There rings no hunter's shout;
But their name is on your waters,
Ye may not wash it out. . . .

"In Adam's Fall/We Sinned All"

Just as religion dominated the lives of the Puritans, it also dominated their writings, most of which would not be considered literary works by modern standards. Typically, the Puritans wrote theological studies, hymns, histories, biographies, and autobiographies. The purpose of such writing was to provide spiritual insight and instruction. When Puritans wrote for themselves, in journals or diaries, their aim was the serious kind of self-examination they practiced in other aspects of their lives. The Puritans produced neither fiction nor drama, since they regarded both as sinful.

The Puritans did write poetry, however, as a vehicle of spiritual enlightenment. Although they were less concerned with a poem's literary form than with its message, some writers were naturally more gifted than others. A few excellent Puritan poets emerged in the 1600's, among them Anne Bradstreet and Edward Taylor. Anne Bradstreet's moving, personal voice and Edward Taylor's devotional intensity shine through the conventional Puritanism of their themes.

The Puritans were highly literate, with a strong belief in education for both men and women. In 1636, they founded Harvard University to ensure a well-educated ministry. Two years later, they set up the first printing press in the colonies. In 1647, free public schools were established in Massachusetts to combat the influence of "ye ould deluder, Satan." *The New England Primer,* first published around 1690, combined instruction in spelling and reading with moralistic teachings, such as "In Adam's fall/We sinned all."

One of the first books printed in the colonies was the *Bay Psalm Book,* the standard hymnal of the time. Richard Mather, a prominent preacher, was one of its three authors. Increase Mather, Richard's youngest son, served for many years as pastor of the North Church in Boston. He was the author of some 130 books. *Cases of Conscience Concerning Evil*

THE TRIAL OF TWO "WITCHES" AT SALEM, MASSACHUSETTS, IN 1692
Illustration by Howard Pyle

ing, one in which clear statement is the highest goal. An ornate or clever style would be a sign of vanity and, as such, would not be in accordance with God's will. Despite the restrictions built into their life and literature, the Puritans succeeded in producing a small body of excellent writing.

The Planter from Westover

Considering the number of brilliantly literate statesmen who would later emerge in the South, especially in Virginia, it seems surprising that only a few notable Southern writers appeared prior to 1750. As in Puritan New England, those who were educated produced a substantial amount of writing, but it was mostly of a practical nature. Many planters spent long hours each day writing letters. Unlike the Puritans, Southerners did not oppose fiction or drama, and the first theater in America opened in Williamsburg, Virginia, in 1716.

The important literature of the pre-Revolutionary South can be summed up in one name—William Byrd. Byrd lived at Westover, a magnificent plantation on the James River bequeathed to him by his wealthy father. Commissioned in 1728 to survey the boundary line between Virginia and North Carolina, he kept a journal of his experiences. That journal served as the basis for Byrd's book, *The History of the Dividing Line,* which was circulated in manuscript form among Byrd's friends in England. Published nearly a century after Byrd's death, the book was immediately recognized as a minor humorous masterpiece. More of Byrd's papers were published later, establishing his reputation as the finest writer in the pre-Revolutionary South.

The writers whose work appears in this unit are not the great names in American literature. They are the founders, the men and women who laid the groundwork for the towering achievements that followed. The modest awakening of American literature seen in this unit had repercussions that echoed down the years.

Spirits, published in 1693, was a discourse on the Salem witchcraft trials of the previous year. The trials, conducted in an atmosphere of hysteria, resulted in the hanging of nineteen people as witches.

Increase's eldest son, Cotton Mather, far exceeded his father's literary output, publishing at least 400 works in his lifetime. Cotton Mather, like his father, is remembered in part because of his connection with the Salem witchcraft trials. Although he did not actually take part in the trials, his works on witchcraft had helped to stir up some of the hysteria. Still, Cotton Mather was one of the most learned men of his time, a power in the state, and a notable author. His theory of writing was simple (although his writing was not): The more information a work contains, the better its style.

In fact, the Puritans in general had a theory of literary style. They believed in a plain style of writ-

AMERICAN VOICES

The voice that beautifies the land,
The voice above,
The voice of the grasshopper,
Among the plants,
Again and again it sounds,—
The voice that beautifies the land.
    Navajo

This island even exceeds the others in beauty and fertility.
Groves of lofty and flourishing trees are abundant, as also
large lakes, surrounded and overhung by the foliage, in a
most enchanting manner. Everything looked as green as in
April in Andalusia.
    Christopher Columbus, *Journal of the First Voyage to America*

The sun . . . ever shineth on one part or the other [of the
Spanish dominions] we have conquered for our king.
    Captain John Smith, *Advertisements for the Unexperienced*

They knew they were pilgrims.
    William Bradford, *Of Plymouth Plantation*

Welcome, Englishmen.
    Squanto

The public must and will be served.
    William Penn, *Some Fruits of Solitude*

Resolved, never to do anything which I should be afraid to
do if it were the last hour of my life.
    Jonathan Edwards, *Seventy Resolutions*

Brother! Our lands were once large, and yours were very
small. You have now become a great people, and we have
scarcely a place left to spread our blankets. You have got
our country, but are not satisfied.
    Red Jacket, *Seneca Council Speech*

The Literature to 1750

When you read literature written during particular time periods, it is important to know the historical background.

HISTORICAL CONTEXT Before settlers came to North America, Native Americans lived lives close to the land. Their interaction with nature shows in their literature. The early settlers came from Europe seeking freedom to live and worship as they pleased. For most, their strong religious convictions sustained them as they endured the hardships of life in the New World.

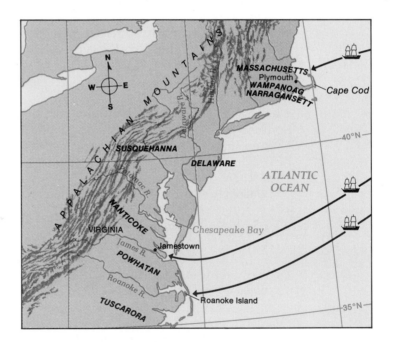

THE FIRST ENGLISH SETTLEMENTS

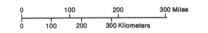

LITERARY MOVEMENTS The traditional literature of Native Americans related to their tribal knowledge, customs, and rituals. This literature consists of myths, songs, and chants in the oral tradition.

The early settlers who came from Europe brought with them their knowledge of written communication with its particular style and content. They wrote about their new experiences in forms that were familiar to them—letters, factual records, sermons, and poems.

WRITERS' TECHNIQUES Traditional Native American literature reflects the value placed on oratory in cultures that passed legends on through the spoken word. Native American orators used poetic language to capture their listeners' attention. The early settlers, on the other hand, generally used a simple, direct, unadorned style.

Native American Voices

PHILIP (METACOMET), AMERICAN WAMPANOAG INDIAN CHIEF
Colored Engraving, 1772, by Paul Revere
The Granger Collection

DELAWARE, NAVAJO

Delaware

Long before the first Europeans arrived in North America, the people of the Delaware tribe lived in parts of what is now Delaware, Pennsylvania, New York, and New Jersey. The Delaware hunted, fished, and farmed. For the most part, the Delaware lived in peace, except when threatened by their powerful enemies, the Iroquois.

In the seventeenth century, European colonists settled in Delaware territory. In 1686 the Delaware signed a treaty with William Penn, the colonial leader, but colonists took the tribe's land. During the next hundred years, eighteen treaties between the colonists and the Delaware were made and broken as the Delaware were pushed westward—eventually, to a reservation in Oklahoma. Today, there are fewer then three thousand Delaware, living primarily in Oklahoma, Wisconsin, and southern Canada.

Living close to the land as they did, the Delaware sought explanations for natural phenomena. Some of their explanations, like *The Walam Olum,* are recorded in pictographs, symbols painted on wood or stone.

Navajo

The Navajo are believed to have settled in the American Southwest between A.D. 900 and 1200. Fierce warriors and hunters, they intermarried with members of the peaceful Pueblo tribe, who taught them how to weave and raise fruits and vegetables. The Spanish gave the tribe the name "Navajo," which means "cultivator of fields," but the Navajo usually referred to themselves as Dine, "the people." After the Spanish introduced domestic animals to the Navajo, many became herders of sheep and goats.

In the early 1800's, as American settlers began establishing ranches on Navajo land, the Navajo fought to drive the ranchers away. In 1864 U.S. Army troops defeated the Navajo, and seven thousand captives were marched to New Mexico, a trek of more than three hundred miles through the desert. Four years later they were allowed to return to a reservation on their old land. The Navajo reservation, covering more than 24,000 square miles in Arizona, Utah, and New Mexico, is the largest in the United States. At more than 110,000 people, the Navajo are also the nation's biggest tribe. Today thousands of tribe members choose to live in the traditional Navajo manner, inhabiting earth and log structures as their ancestors did, and practicing their tribal religion.

GUIDE FOR INTERPRETING

from The Walam Olum;
from The Navajo Origin Legend

Literary Forms

Myths. Myths are traditional stories passed down from generation to generation, characteristically involving immortal beings. Myths attempt to explain natural phenomena; the origin of humans; the customs, institutions, or religious rites of a people; or events beyond people's control. Indirectly, myths teach the values and ideals of a culture.

The Walam Olum and *The Navajo Origin Legend* are both myths. *The Walam Olum* is the Delaware origin myth. Originally it consisted of a long series of pictographs explaining the origin of the Delaware people as a result of the actions of a manito, or spirit. At traditional ceremonies a person who had inherited the right to keep *The Walam Olum* would interpret its meaning for the other members of the tribe. *The Navajo Origin Legend,* an important part of the Navajo tradition, also explains the origin of life.

Commentary

For all Native Americans, each creature in nature contains its own power by which it maintains itself and affects others. Each tribe has a different name for this power. The early white settlers learned the Algonquian term *manitou*, or *manito*. It has many meanings: power, mystery, magic, spirit, medicine.

Manitos come in all shapes and sizes, from weak to powerful. How did the Native Americans determine the strength of the manito? Outward appearances were not thought a sure sign of power: A small animal or stone could possess great magic. However, close observation of the effects of the creature on other creatures could reveal the extent of its power, or it could be revealed in a dream or vision.

Many tribes recognize a chief manito, or Great Spirit—an invisible power that is the source of life and good for humans. The Navajo are unusual in that their great manitos are represented primarily in human rather than animal forms.

In the following selections, notice the forms and roles of the manitos. What is their power used for? What does this tell us of the cultural values of the tribe?

Focus

What events that defy explanation occur in the modern world? Are there natural phenomena, such as black holes, that you find mysterious or difficult to understand? List events that are not fully understandable and freewrite about one of them.

from **The Walam Olum**

Delaware

At first, in that place, at all times, above the earth,

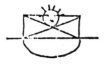

On the earth was an extended fog, and there the great Manito was.

At first, forever, lost in space, everywhere, the great Manito was.

He made the extended land and the sky.

He made the sun, the moon, the stars.

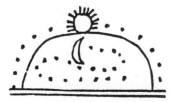

He made them all to move evenly.

Then the wind blew violently, and it cleared, and the water flowed off far and strong.

And groups of islands grew newly, and there remained.

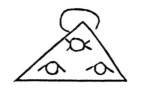

Anew spoke the great Manito, a manito to manitos,

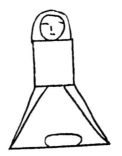

To beings, mortals, souls and all,

And ever after he was a manito to men, and their grandfather.

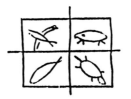

He gave the first mother, the mother of beings.

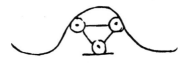

He gave the fish, he gave the turtles, he gave the beasts, he gave the birds.

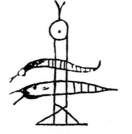

But an evil Manito made evil beings only, monsters.

from *The Walam Olum* 15

He made the flies, he made the gnats.

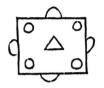 All beings were then friendly.

 Truly the manitos were active and kindly

 To those very first men, and to those first mothers; fetched them wives,

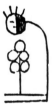 And fetched them food, when first they desired it.

 All had cheerful knowledge, all had leisure, all thought in gladness.

 But very secretly an evil being, a mighty magician, came on earth,

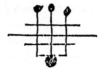 And with him brought badness, quarreling, unhappiness,

 Brought bad weather, brought sickness, brought death.

 All this took place of old on the earth, beyond the great tidewater, at the first.

RESPONDING TO THE SELECTION

Your Response

1. Describe or draw the pictograph you would use to depict the creative power in nature.

Recalling

2. List five of the great Manito's creations.
3. What did the evil Manito create?

Interpreting

4. According to *The Walam Olum,* what constitutes a happy life for the Delaware?
5. Examine the pictographs carefully. What evidence is there that the "evil Manito" and the "evil being, a mighty magician" might be the same spirit?

Applying

6. Identify three evils of the twentieth century. Provide an imaginative explanation for the origin of each of these evils.

ANALYZING LITERATURE

Recognizing Myths

Myths, like *The Walam Olum,* are ancient stories, generally involving immortal characters, that explain the mysteries of nature or the customs and religious rites of a people. For example, the excerpt from *The Walam Olum* explains how the universe was created.

1. What supernatural powers does the great Manito have?
2. According to *The Walam Olum,* how did human beings come to inhabit the earth?
3. How does *The Walam Olum* explain bad weather, sickness, and death?

CRITICAL THINKING AND READING

Inferring Cultural Values

Myths like *The Walam Olum* reveal the ideals and values of the people who created them. These ideals and values may not be stated directly, but by reading closely, you can infer them. For example, in *The Walam Olum,* when you read that the first inhabitants of the earth "all had cheerful knowledge, all had leisure, all thought in gladness," you can probably infer that the Delaware value knowledge and leisure, because the statement indicates that knowledge and leisure make people happy.

What can you infer that the Delaware valued from each of the following statements?

1. "He gave the fish, he gave the turtles, he gave the beasts, he gave the birds. . . . All beings were then friendly."
2. ". . . an evil being, a mighty magician, came on earth, And with him brought badness, quarreling, unhappiness. . . ."

from The Navajo Origin Legend
Navajo

On the morning of the twelfth day the people washed themselves well. The women dried themselves with yellow cornmeal; the men with white cornmeal. Soon after the ablutions were completed they heard the distant call of the approaching gods.[1] It was shouted, as before, four times—nearer and

---

1. the approaching gods: The four Navajo gods: White Body, Blue Body, Yellow Body, and Black Body.

THE PLACE OF EMERGENCE AND THE FOUR WORLDS
Navajo
Wheelwright Museum of the American Indian

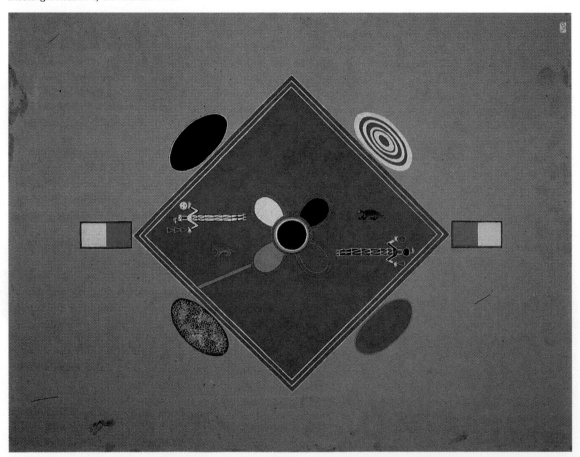

louder at each repetition—and, after the fourth call, the gods appeared. Blue Body and Black Body each carried a sacred buckskin. White Body carried two ears of corn, one yellow, one white, each covered at the end completely with grains.

The gods laid one buckskin on the ground with the head to the west; on this they placed the two ears of corn, with their tips to the east, and over the corn they spread the other buckskin with its head to the east; under the white ear they put the feather of a white eagle, under the yellow ear the feather of a yellow eagle. Then they told the people to stand at a distance and allow the wind to enter. The white wind blew from the east, and the yellow wind blew from the west, between the skins. While the wind was blowing, eight of the Mirage People[2] came and walked around the objects on the ground four times, and as they walked the

_____
2. **Mirage People:** Mirages personified.

eagle feathers, whose tips protruded from between the buckskins, were seen to move. When the Mirage People had finished their walk the upper buckskin was lifted; the ears of corn had disappeared, a man and a woman lay there in their stead.

The white ear of corn had been changed into a man, the yellow ear into a woman. It was the wind that gave them life. It is the wind that comes out of our mouths now that gives us life. When this ceases to blow we die. In the skin at the tips of our fingers we see the trail of the wind; it shows us where the wind blew when our ancestors were created.

The pair thus created were First Man and First Woman (Atsé *Hastín* and Atsé Estsán). The gods directed the people to build an enclosure of brushwood for the pair. When the enclosure was finished, First Man and First Woman entered it, and the gods said to them: "Live together now as husband and wife."

RESPONDING TO THE SELECTION

Your Response
1. The Navajos chose corn to represent the source of their civilization. What symbol would you choose for twentieth-century America?

Recalling
2. What brings First Man and First Woman to life?

Interpreting
3. Why do the Navajo associate the skin at the tips of the fingers with the trail of the wind?
4. Find evidence in the passage that suggests that four is a sacred number for the Navajo.

Applying
5. State two ways in which the wind affects the animals or plants living on the earth.

THINKING AND WRITING

Comparing and Contrasting Myths
Find a myth explaining the origin of life in another culture. Compare and contrast it with the Navajo origin myth. First, prepare a list of similarities and differences between the excerpt from *The Navajo Origin Legend* and the myth you have chosen. Organize your information into an outline, and write a thesis statement about the similarities and differences between the two myths. Then write a short essay in which you support your thesis statement with the information in your lists. When you revise, make sure that you have included corresponding points of comparison and contrast for each myth to support your thesis and that you have used appropriate transitions to show either comparison or contrast.

GUIDE FOR INTERPRETING

from The Iroquois Constitution

The **Iroquois** were a powerful tribe of Native Americans who lived in what is now the northeast United States. During the fourteenth century, an Iroquoian mystic and prophet named Dekanawidah traveled from village to village urging the Iroquoian-speaking peoples to stop fighting and to band together in peace and brotherhood. Dekanawidah's efforts led to the foundation of the Iroquois Confederation of the Five Nations, a league of five Iroquois tribes: Mohawk, Oneida, Seneca, Cayuga, and Onondaga.

Literary Forms

Constitutions. A constitution is a written or unwritten system of fundamental laws and principles governing a society. The Iroquois Constitution, which was unwritten, was first presented to confederate lords of the Five Nations in a speech by Dekanawidah. The confederate lords memorized it and recorded it in symbols on strings of shells.

In most constitutions, laws and principles are listed in a straightforward, factual manner. Because the Iroquois Constitution was spoken rather than written, it had to be presented in a way that would hold the listeners' attention. Therefore, it uses elegant phrasing and metaphors to describe the foundation of the confederation and the system by which the confederation will be governed.

Commentary

The Iroquois lived in large wooden structures called longhouses. After the confederation was established, the Iroquois called themselves the People of the Longhouse. In this longhouse the most western tribe, the Senecas, were designated the Keepers of the Western Door; and the Mohawks, the most eastern tribe, the Keepers of the Eastern Door. The other three tribes were ranged between them like families in a longhouse, each with their cooking fire. Thus they were the Confederation of the Five Fires. Later, they called the United States "the Thirteen Fires."

The Iroquois were crucial in the struggle between England and France for control of the continent. Expert diplomats and shrewd politicians, the Iroquois played off both sides, finally backing England. As you read the Iroquois Constitution, notice the system of rules it sets up and the language and metaphors it uses to do this. Would you remember the United States Constitution better if it used similar language and metaphors?

Focus

Try to imagine a society without laws and principles. What would it be like living there? Freewrite about the function of the laws and principles that govern a society.

from The Iroquois Constitution

Iroquois

I am Dekanawidah and with the Five Nations[1] confederate lords I plant the Tree of the Great Peace. I name the tree the Tree of the Great Long Leaves. Under the shade of this Tree of the Great Peace we spread the soft white feathery down of the globe thistle as seats for you, Adodarhoh, and your cousin lords.

We place you upon those seats, spread soft with the feathery down of the globe thistle, there beneath the shade of the spreading branches of the Tree of Peace. There shall you sit and watch the council fire of the confederacy of the Five Nations, and all the affairs of the Five Nations shall be transacted at this place before you.

Roots have spread out from the Tree of the Great Peace, one to the north, one to the east, one to the south and one to the west. The name of these roots is the Great White Roots and their nature is peace and strength.

If any man or any nation outside the Five Nations shall obey the laws of the Great Peace and make known their disposition to the lords of the confederacy, they may trace the roots to the tree and if their minds are clean and they are obedient and promise to obey the wishes of the confederate council, they shall be welcomed to take shelter beneath the Tree of the Long Leaves.

We place at the top of the Tree of the Long Leaves an eagle who is able to see afar. If he sees in the distance any evil approach-

RED JACKET
George Catlin
The Thomas Gilcrease Institute of American History and Art, Tulsa, Oklahoma

---

1. Five Nations: The Mohawk, Oneida, Onondaga, Cayuga, and Seneca tribes. Together, these tribes formed the Iroquois Confederation.

ing or any danger threatening he will at once warn the people of the confederacy.

The smoke of the confederate council fire shall ever ascend and pierce the sky so that other nations who may be allies may see the council fire of the Great Peace. . .

Whenever the confederate lords shall assemble for the purpose of holding a council, the Onondaga lords shall open it by expressing their gratitude to their cousin lords and greeting them, and they shall make an address and offer thanks to the earth where men dwell, to the streams of water, the pools, the springs and the lakes, to the maize and the fruits, to the medicinal herbs and trees, to the forest trees for their usefulness, to the animals that serve as food and give their pelts for clothing, to the great winds and the lesser winds, to the thunderers, to the sun, the mighty warrior, to the moon, to the messengers of the Creator who reveal his wishes and to the Great Creator who dwells in the heavens above, who gives all the things useful to men, and who is the source and the ruler of health and life.

Then shall the Onondaga lords declare the council open. . .

All lords of the Five Nations' Confederacy must be honest in all things. . . It shall be a serious wrong for anyone to lead a lord into trivial affairs, for the people must ever hold their lords high in estimation out of respect to their honorable positions.

When a candidate lord is to be installed he shall furnish four strings of shells (or wampum)[2] one span in length bound together at one end. Such will constitute the evidence of his pledge to the confederate

lords that he will live according to the constitution of the Great Peace and exercise justice in all affairs.

When the pledge is furnished the speaker of the council must hold the shell strings in his hand and address the opposite side of the council fire and he shall commence his address saying: "Now behold him. He has now become a confederate lord. See how splendid he looks." An address may then follow. At the end of it he shall send the bunch of shell strings to the opposite side and they shall be received as evidence of the pledge. Then shall the opposite side say:

"We now do crown you with the sacred emblem of the deer's antlers, the emblem of your lordship. You shall now become a mentor of the people of the Five Nations. The thickness of your skin shall be seven spans—which is to say that you shall be proof against anger, offensive actions and criticism. Your heart shall be filled with peace and good will and your mind filled with a yearning for the welfare of the people of the confederacy. With endless patience you shall carry out your duty and your firmness shall be tempered with tenderness for your people. Neither anger nor fury shall find lodgement in your mind and all your words and actions shall be marked with calm deliberation. In all of your deliberations in the confederate council, in your efforts at law making, in all your official acts, self-interest shall be cast into oblivion. Cast not over your shoulder behind you the warnings of the nephews and nieces should they chide you for any error or wrong you may do, but return to the way of the Great Law which is just and right. Look and listen for the welfare of the whole people and have always in view not only the present but also the coming generations, even those whose faces are yet beneath the surface of the ground—the unborn of the future nation."

---

2. **wampum** (wäm′ pəm) n.: Small beads made of shells.

RESPONDING TO THE SELECTION

Your Response

1. If you were the chief of another Native American nation, would this speech persuade you to join the Federation? Why or why not?
2. What do you admire about Dekanawidah, the author of the Iroquois Constitution? Explain.

Recalling

3. Describe the roots of the Tree of Great Peace.
4. What is the role of the eagle at the top of the Tree of the Long Leaves?
5. How will the Onondaga lords open each council meeting?

Interpreting

6. What does the council fire of the Five Nations represent?
7. The constitution tells the lords to "offer thanks to the earth where men dwell." What does this decree suggest about the Iroquois?
8. What conclusions can you draw about Dekanawidah from the constitution he created?

Applying

9. In the constitution, Dekanawidah outlines the qualities he expects the Iroquois lords to possess. What qualities do you think the leaders of a contemporary society should possess? Explain your answer.

ANALYZING LITERATURE

Recognizing a Constitution

A **constitution** is a written or unwritten system of fundamental principles, laws, and customs that governs a nation or union of nations. The Iroquois Constitution outlines the principles on which the union of the Five Nations is based and presents the manner in which the confederation will be governed.

1. List three principles emphasized in the Iroquois Constitution.
2. (a) What is the function of the confederate council? (b) What sort of behavior is expected of its members?

CRITICAL THINKING AND READING

Interpreting Metaphors

A **metaphor** is an implied comparison between two seemingly dissimilar things. In most constitutions the rules and principles outlined are presented in a direct manner. In contrast, many of the ideas in the Iroquois Constitution are revealed through metaphors. As a result, you must interpret the comparison being made in each metaphor. For example, Dekanawidah uses the thickness of the council lords' skin as a metaphor for their ability to resist anger and criticism.

1. For what is the planting of the Tree of Great Peace a metaphor?
2. What does Dekanawidah mean when he says that any nation outside the Five Nations that obeys the laws of the Great Peace "shall be welcomed to take shelter beneath the Tree of Long Leaves"?

THINKING AND WRITING

Comparing and Contrasting

Write a short essay contrasting the Iroquois Constitution and the United States Constitution. Carefully study both documents. In your prewriting, list the similarities and differences between the two documents. Then write a short essay in which you support a thesis statement about the contrasts between the two constitutions.

LEARNING OPTION

Language. In the constitution, Dekanawidah proposes that each candidate lord furnish a string of shells, or wampum. A Native American word brought into English by the early settlers, *wampum* is now a slang term for money. Colonists borrowed many other words from Native Americans to describe new places and new things. Using a dictionary, find the origin and meaning of these borrowed words: raccoon, Iowa, Oklahoma, husky, Missouri, opossum, Nebraska, totem, Kentucky. Can you think of any other words that may come from a Native American language?

PIMA, CHIPPEWA, SIOUX

Pima

The Pima have lived in the Gila and Salt River valleys in southern Arizona for hundreds of years. A peaceful people, the Pima were friendly to both the Spanish explorers and the American settlers who ventured into their region. In the nineteenth century, as American pioneers flooded through Pima land on their way to the new frontier, the Pima fought against only their traditional enemies, the Apaches. Today about 5,500 Pima live on reservations near the Gila and Salt rivers. Many maintain their oral literature, including songs like "From the Houses of Magic."

Chippewa

When the European settlers arrived in America, the Chippewa were a nomadic people living on the shores of Lake Superior. They sustained themselves by hunting and fishing. After the French gave them guns in exchange for furs, the Chippewa drove the Sioux and Fox tribes out of the Wisconsin area, seizing control of their land. The Chippewa's territory eventually extended from Lake Huron to central North Dakota. Today there are about 30,000 Chippewa living on reservations in North Dakota, Michigan, Wisconsin, and Minnesota, in addition to about 50,000 Chippewa living in Canada. Their early nomadic life made them sensitive to nature. This sensitivity is apparent in "Spring Song."

Teton Sioux

The Teton Sioux are the largest of three tribes in the Sioux, or Dakota, Confederation. Originally living in the northeastern and northcentral part of the country, the Teton Sioux were pushed westward to the midwestern plains by the Chippewa. Like the other tribes of the plains, the Teton Sioux were nomadic hunters who lived in tepees and depended on buffalo for food. In 1874, after gold was discovered on Teton Sioux land, the Teton Sioux became involved in conflicts with the United States Army with increasing frequency. In June of 1876, an army of Sioux defeated General Custer at the Battle of the Little Bighorn. In the months following the battle, the American forces began an intensive campaign that led to the final defeat of the Sioux at Wounded Knee, South Dakota, in 1890. Today 40,000 Sioux live on reservations in Minnesota, Nebraska, Montana, North Dakota, and South Dakota.

GUIDE FOR INTERPRETING

From the Houses of Magic; Spring Song; Song Concerning a Dream of the Thunderbirds

Literary Forms

The Oral Tradition. The oral tradition refers to the process of passing down sayings, songs, tales, and myths from one generation to the next by word of mouth. Native Americans did not have a written language, though they occasionally recorded myths or historical events in pictographs engraved on wood or hide or in symbols painted on strings of beads. Therefore, members of a tribe memorized the tribal literature and communicated it orally to the next generations. In some tribes, the person who had the best memory became the "keeper" of the tribe's history, songs, and myths.

Native American poetry began as songs chanted to a regular beat. Sometimes complicated melodies accompanied the words. To help the singer remember the poem or song, lines were often repeated, sometimes with a slight variation in the second line. Each line usually contained the same number of accented syllables or beats. Certain images and comparisons were also used so often that the listeners expected to hear them in tribal songs.

Commentary

The prose and poetry of Native Americans differ in purpose, form, and content. Prose stories, rhythmically intoned, tell the adventures of humans, animals, or supernatural beings; they recount ancient times, when the world was new. In this way information, beliefs, and values necessary for the survival of the tribe are passed on.

For Native Americans every thing in the world has its life and purpose, and every event is significant. Poetry attempts to use the magical power of language to connect with this mysterious world. Poems were used only on special occasions and usually dealt with mystical experiences or the symbolic meanings of things or events. They were sung or chanted rhythmically, usually to the accompaniment of drums or other instruments.

To understand the following poems, chant or sing them aloud, noticing the effects of rhythm and repetitions. Do any popular songs use rhythm and repetition in the same way and for the same effects? Explain.

Focus

The lyrics of songs often stand out in our memories. What qualities make lyrics memorable? Freewrite about the feelings you associate with one of your favorite songs and the qualities that make the lyrics easy to remember.

From the Houses of Magic

Pima

1

Down from the houses of magic,
Down from the houses of magic;
Blow the winds, and from my antlers
And my ears, they stronger gather.

5   Over there I ran trembling,
Over there I ran trembling,
For bows and arrows pursued me,
Many bows were on my trail.

2

I ran into the swamp confused,
10   There I heard the tadpoles singing.
I ran into the swamp confused,
Where the bark-clothed tadpoles sang.

In the west the dragonfly wanders,
Skimming the surfaces of the pools,
15   Touching only with his tail. He skims
With flapping and rustling wings.

Thence I ran as the darkness gathers,
Wearing cactus flowers in my hair.
Thence I ran as the darkness gathers,
20   In fluttering darkness to the singing-place.

3

At the time of the white dawning,
At the time of the white dawning,
I arose and went away,
At Blue Nightfall I went away.

INDIAN VILLAGE, RIVER GILA
Seth Eastman
Rhode Island School of Design Museum of Art

4

25   The evening glow yet lingers,
    The evening glow yet lingers:
    And I sit with my gourd rattle
    Engaged in the sacred chant.
    As I wave the eagle feathers
30   We hear the magic sounding.

    The strong night is shaking me,
    Just as once before he did
    When in spirit I was taken
    To the great magician's house.

5

35   Pitiable harlot though I am,
    My heart glows with the singing
    While the evening yet is young.
    My heart glows with the singing.

6

    Now the swallow begins his singing;
40   Now the swallow begins his singing;
    And the women who are with me,
    The poor women commence to sing.

    The swallows met in the standing cliff;
    The swallows met in the standing cliff;
45   And the rainbows arched above me,
    There the blue rainbow-arches met.

7

    In the reddish glow of the nightfall,
    In the reddish glow of the nightfall.
    I return to my burrow
50   About which the flowers bloom.

    With the four eagle feathers,
    With the four eagle feathers,
    I stir the air. When I turn
    My magic power is crossed.

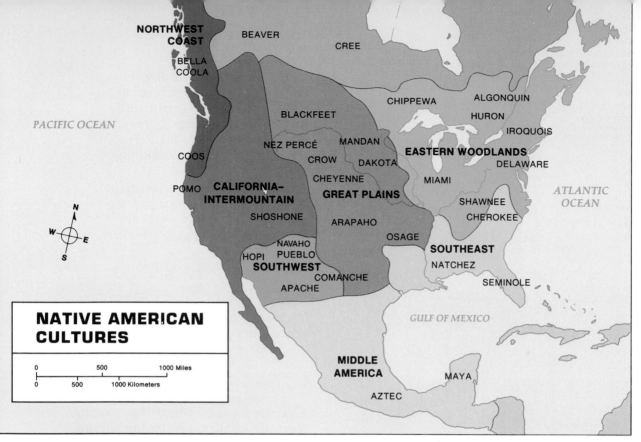

NATIVE AMERICAN CULTURES

| 0 | 500 | 1000 Miles |
| 0 | 500 | 1000 Kilometers |

RESPONDING TO THE SELECTION

Your Response

1. What aspects of nature do you find magical? Why?

Recalling

2. Summarize the narrator's movements in stanzas 1–3.
3. (a) What does the narrator hear while waving eagle feathers? (b) What does the narrator do with the feathers at the end of the song?

Interpreting

4. (a) What time of day is described in the poem? (b) What details indicate the time?
5. List three emotions or feelings that the song conveys. How are they conveyed?

Applying

6. The Pima, as well as many other Native American tribes, considered the deer to be a sacred animal. (a) What qualities of deer make them appropriate for being considered sacred?
(b) How does the way in which most people today regard deer differ from the Pima view? (c) What does this difference suggest about the contrasts between Pima society and today's society?

ANALYZING LITERATURE

Understanding the Oral Tradition

The **oral tradition** is the process of passing down literature from generation to generation. Poems and songs were an important part of the Native American oral tradition. Because they had to be memorized, various techniques, such as repeated lines and images and the use of lines with the same number of accented syllables, or beats, were used to make them easier to remember. For example, many lines in "From the Houses of Magic" are repeated.

1. What one image, or word picture, is repeated several times in the song?
2. Aside from the use of repetition, in what way are many of the lines similar?

Spring Song

Chippewa

As my eyes
search
the prairie
I feel the summer
in the spring.

RESPONDING TO THE SELECTION

Your Response
1. How does this poem make you feel?

Interpreting
2. What type of weather does the speaker of the poem seem to be experiencing?
3. What is meant by the statement "I feel the summer in the spring"?

Applying
4. What seasonal change do you consider to be the most dramatic? Why?

LEARNING OPTION

Speaking and Listening. In "Spring Song," the Chippewa convey their deep reverence for nature. Locate an anthology of Native American poetry and find a song or prayer of another Native American group that similarly exemplifies what author N. Scott Momaday calls the "gift of seeing truly, with wonder and delight, into the natural world." Share your choice by reading it aloud to classmates.

Song Concerning a Dream of the Thunderbirds

Teton Sioux

Friends, behold!
Sacred I have been made.
Friends, behold!
In a sacred manner
5 I have been influenced
At the gathering of the clouds.
Sacred I have been made,
Friends, behold!
Sacred I have been made.

THE MYSTIC
William R. Leigh
The Thomas Gilcrease Institute of American History and Art,
Tulsa, Oklahoma

RESPONDING TO THE SELECTION

Your Response

1. What associations does this poem evoke? Why?

Interpreting

2. (a) To what does the "gathering of the clouds" refer? (b) How does it relate to the title of the poem?
3. How does the pattern of the song add emphasis to lines 4–6?

Applying

4. In many ancient cultures, thunderstorms inspired fear and awe. (a) Why did the people of these cultures react this way? (b) What other natural occurrences might have inspired such emotions in these cultures?

THINKING AND WRITING

Writing a Song

Today's songwriters often use some of the same techniques when writing lyrics that the Native American tribes did. Try some of these techniques as you compose a song. First decide on a topic you might like to write a song about and an audience for the song. Brainstorm for ideas about your topic and select some that might work for your audience. Then review your notes about song lyrics and look over the Native American songs once again, taking note of the qualities that make them easy to remember. Once you have a topic and an audience, write a song using the techniques you observed in the songs of the Native American tribes and other songwriters. Then revise your song, making sure that it is appropriate for your audience, and prepare a final draft.

Native American Voices Today

The coming of white settlers to North America in the seventeenth century resulted in almost complete destruction of the Native American societies there. Whole tribes were nearly wiped out in battles or by diseases brought by the Europeans. Survivors were forced off their lands and herded indiscriminately into designated reservations, where many more died. Those left were soon surrounded and controlled by a society they had little knowledge of and no place in.

The land on which each tribe lived was central and sacred to their life. It fed and clothed them. Just as important, the land contained the bones of their ancestors and therefore the knowledge and power of the past, of the Old Ones. Separated from this power and obliged to learn the white man's ways to survive, Native Americans were in danger of losing forever their identity, language, and traditions. Fortunately, through dedicated work by determined tribal members and some enlightened whites, the Native Americans and the United States have not completely lost this heritage.

A REBIRTH OF NATIVE AMERICAN LITERATURE

Recently, Native American voices are once again heard in the land. Some are angry, some sorrowful, others wryly comic—all are powerful. Native Americans are again telling stories and composing poems of their past and present, attempting to create connections between them. Many of their books have become best-sellers.

The one book most credited with beginning the current "rebirth" of Native American literature is N. Scott Momaday's Pulitzer Prize-winning novel, *House Made of Dawn*, published in 1969. Momaday (page 922) was quickly followed by such writers as Leslie Marmon Silko (Laguna Pueblo), Simon Ortiz (Acoma Pueblo), and James Welch (Blackfeet/Gros Ventre).

All these writers vividly portray the struggle of Native Americans to keep hold of their past, live in the present, and create a future. None of the authors romanticize either the past or the present, as many nineteenth-century writers did. The characters in their novels, like themselves, are often only part Native American and must relearn what their grandparents grew up knowing. At the same time, they are living in a modern society where traditional ways of living do not seem possible.

Louise Erdrich

The tragic—and comic—elements of these characters' lives are vividly portrayed by author Louise Erdrich. Erdrich is a member of the Turtle Mountain Chippewa Reservation in North Dakota, where her grandparents lived. She now lives in New Hampshire with her husband, Michael Dorris, a professor of Native American literature at Dartmouth College.

Erdrich has published three novels, two volumes of poetry, and numerous short stories. Her novels are set in the vicinity of the Chippewa territory and are peopled with sev-

eral generations of various Native American families. *Love Medicine*, published in 1984, and *The Beet Queen*, published in 1986, cover roughly the same time period—from 1934 to 1984. *Tracks*, however, published in 1988, precedes the other two chronologically; its events occur between 1912 and 1924. In all three novels, many of the same characters occur but at different points in their lives. The result is a fascinating intertwining of lives and events.

Tracks describes the early twentieth-century struggles of the Native Americans with epidemics, famine, and the dwindling of their lands. In this novel the mysterious, mythic forces of the Chippewa gods are felt strongly through a central character with supernatural powers. This situation is the background for *Love Medicine* and *The Beet Queen*. In these two novels, we meet the families—parents who fight to stay on the grandparents' land and the children who are dislocated between the ways of the reservation and the modern world. Most of the youngest generation have disappeared to Chicago or Minneapolis, but some still recognize their needs for the bonds of family and tradition.

At the end of *Love Medicine*, one of the young men sums up their common situation: "I'd heard that this river was the last of an ancient ocean, miles deep, that once had covered the Dakotas and solved all our problems. It was easy to still imagine us beneath them vast unreasonable waves, but the truth is we live on dry land." His is the voice of the contemporary Native American, struggling to reconcile his place in the modern world with his heritage.

Explorers

COLUMBUS LANDING IN THE NEW WORLD

BIOGRAPHIES

Christopher Columbus (1451–1506)

Not much is known about the early life of history's most famous explorer, Christopher Columbus. Evidently he left his home in Genoa, Italy, and went to sea at a young age. At age 25 he was shipwrecked off the coast of Portugal. Columbus studied mapmaking and navigation; he learned Latin and read Marco Polo's account of the riches of Asia. Within ten years he embraced the idea that led to his lifelong goal: reaching the fabled cities of Asia by sailing westward around the world. King Ferdinand and Queen Isabella of Spain agreed to finance the voyage in 1492.

Columbus set sail on August 3. On October 12 he reached one of the Bahama islands, which he mistook for an island off India. Columbus named the island San Salvador; then he continued to explore the Caribbean. Over the next twelve years, he made three more transatlantic voyages, ever convinced that he had reached Asia and always hopeful of finding Marco Polo's fabled cities.

Alvar Nuñez Cabeza de Vaca (1490?–1557?)

In 1528 Pánfilo de Narváez and 300 Spanish soldiers landed at what is now Tampa Bay and set out to explore Florida's west coast. Alvar Nuñez Cabeza de Vaca was second in command.

Foolishly, Narváez attacked the native Seminoles, who mounted a successful defense. Beset by hostile natives, illness, and the prospect of starvation, Narváez and his men set sail for Mexico in five flimsy boats. He and most of the men drowned. Cabeza de Vaca and a party of about sixty reached the Texas shore near present-day Galveston.

Shipwrecked without supplies, only fifteen of the group lived through the winter. In the end, only Cabeza de Vaca and three others survived. In 1536, after an eighteen-month walk across the Texas plains, the survivors reached Mexico City.

Pedro de Casteñeda (1510?–1570?)

Back in Mexico, Cabeza de Vaca contributed to rumors of cities of incredible wealth north of the Rio Grande. In response, conquistador Francisco Vásquez de Coronado in 1540 led an expedition into what is now New Mexico.

Pedro de Casteñeda, a contemporary of Coronado, lived in northwestern Mexico at the time the expedition was formed. Twenty years later he recorded an account of Coronado's journey.

from Journal of the First Voyage to America; *from* Relation of Alvar Nuñez Cabeza de Vaca; *from* The Narrative of the Expedition of Coronado

Literary Forms

Journals. History shows that events sometimes have totally unexpected results. In 1453 the Turks announced a new tax on Europe's profitable overland trade with India. The announcement led Portugal and Spain, the world's leading maritime nations, to look for an alternate route to India by sea. By pure chance their search brought Europe into contact with the Americas. Within a century much of these two vast continents and most of their 10 million people would come under European control.

The European encounter with and conquest of the Americas are recorded in the journals of the explorers. A **journal,** or diary, is an individual's day-by-day account of events and personal reactions. As a firsthand account of events, a journal provides valuable details that can be supplied only by a participant or an eyewitness. As a record of personal reactions, a journal reveals much about the writer.

While offering insight into the life and times of the writer, a journal is not a totally reliable record of facts. The writer's impressions color the telling of events, particularly when he or she is a participant. Journals written for publication rather than private use are even less likely to be objective. This is true of the selections you are about to read.

The following selections trace three important expeditions in the Americas: Columbus's in San Salvador, Cabeza de Vaca's in northern Florida, and Coronado's in southwestern United States. Written for public record, each account presents the version of events that the writer wanted published. Columbus's account is taken from the journal he sent back to Ferdinand and Isabella. Cabeza de Vaca's account is taken from his official report upon his return to Mexico. Casteñeda's account is taken from a book he wrote for publication.

The original manuscript of Columbus's journal has been lost. The account that follows comes from the transcript of the manuscript made in the 1500's by Bartolomé de las Casas, a Spanish priest and historian.

Focus

What experiences have you had that you regard as adventures? Brainstorm a list of possibilities. Then freewrite about one adventure. Jot down what you did and how you felt about it. Do you think there are any similarities between your adventures and those of these early explorers?

from Journal of the First Voyage to America

Christopher Columbus

This account begins nine days after Columbus landed on San Salvador.

Sunday, Oct. 21st [1492]. At 10 o'clock, we arrived at a cape of the island,[1] and anchored, the other vessels in company. After having dispatched a meal, I went ashore, and found no habitation save a single house, and that without an occupant; we had no doubt that the people had fled in terror at our approach, as the house was completely furnished. I suffered nothing to be touched, and went with my captains and some of the crew to view the country. This island even exceeds the others in beauty and fertility. Groves of lofty and flourishing trees are abundant, as also large lakes, surrounded and overhung by the foliage, in a most enchanting manner. Everything looked as green as in April in Andalusia.[2] The melody of the birds was so exquisite that one was never willing to part from the spot, and the flocks of parrots obscured the heavens. The diversity in the appearance of the feathered tribe from those of our country is extremely curious. A thousand different sorts of trees, with their fruit were to be met with, and of a wonderfully delicious odor. It was a great affliction to me to be ignorant of their natures, for I am very certain they are all valuable; specimens of them and of the plants I have preserved. Going round one of these lakes, I saw a snake, which we killed, and I have kept the skin for your Highnesses; upon being discovered he took to the water, whither[3] we followed him, as it was not deep, and dispatched him with our lances; he was seven spans[4] in length; I think there are many more such about here. I discovered also the aloe tree, and am determined to take on board the ship tomorrow, ten quintals[5] of it, as I am told it is valuable. While we were in search of some good water, we came upon a village of the natives about half a league from the place where the ships lay; the inhabitants on discovering us abandoned their houses, and took to flight, carrying off their goods to the mountain. I ordered that nothing which they had left should be taken, not even the value of a pin. Presently we saw several of the natives advancing towards our party, and one of them came up to us, to whom we gave some hawk's bells and glass beads, with which he was delighted. We asked him in return, for water, and after I

---

1. **the island:** San Salvador.
2. **Andalusia** (an' də loo' zhə): A region of Spain.
3. **whither:** To which place.
4. **spans** *n.*: A span is a unit of measure equal to about nine inches.
5. **quintals** (kwint' lz) *n.*: Units of weight, each equal to 100 kilograms, or 220.46 pounds.

had gone on board the ship, the natives came down to the shore with their calabashes[6] full, and showed great pleasure in presenting us with it. I ordered more glass beads to be given them, and they promised to return the next day. It is my wish to fill all the water casks of the ships at this place, which being executed, I shall depart immediately, if the weather serve, and sail round the island, till I succeed in meeting with the king, in order to see if I can acquire any of the gold, which I hear he possesses. Afterwards I shall set sail for another very large island which I believe to be *Cipango*,[7] according to the indications I receive from the Indians on board. They call the Island *Colba*,[8] and say there are many large ships, and sailors there. This other island they name *Bosio*,[9] and inform me that it is very large; the others which lie in our course, I shall examine on the passage, and according as I find gold or spices in abundance, I shall determine what to do; at all events I am determined to proceed on to the continent, and visit the city of *Guisay*[10] where I shall deliver the letters of your Highnesses to the *Great Can*,[11] and demand an answer, with which I shall return.

----

6. calabashes (kal′ ə bash′ əz) *n.*: Dried, hollow shells of gourds, used as cups or bowls.
7. Cipango (si paŋ′ gō): Old name for a group of islands east of Asia, probably what is now Japan.

8. Colba (Kôl′ bə): Cuba.
9. Bosio (bō′ sē ō): Probably the island on which the Dominican Republic and Haiti are now located.
10. Guisay (gē sā′): The City of Heaven, the name given by Marco Polo to the residence of Kublai Khan (kōō′ blı kän), the ruler of China from A.D. 1260–1294.
11. Great Can: Kublai Khan.

▌RESPONDING TO THE SELECTION

Your Response
1. Based on his journal entries, what is your impression of Christopher Columbus?
2. If you had sponsored Columbus's voyage, how would you feel upon reading this account?

Interpreting
3. How can you tell that Columbus was struck by the beauty of the island?
4. What appears to have been Columbus's primary consideration in choosing "specimens" to send back to Spain?

Applying
5. How might this account be different if it were written by a crew member? Explain.

▌ANALYZING LITERATURE

Understanding Journals
A **journal** is an individual's day-by-day account of events and personal reactions. Although most journals are kept solely as personal records, Columbus chronicled his voyage to the Americas for his investors, the King and Queen of Spain.

1. Why do you think Columbus often refers to the monetary value of things he has seen?
2. What impression of the Americas does Columbus seem to be trying to convey?

▌CRITICAL THINKING AND READING

Appreciating Cultural Perspectives
The story of Columbus's discovery of the Americas is generally told from a European point of view. Even the use of the word *discovery* reflects a European perspective, because Native Americans were obviously first to see the land.

How might this account be different if it were written by a Native American observing the activities of the crew members?

▌THINKING AND WRITING

Writing a Continuation
Put yourself in the place of Columbus or one of his crew members. Then pick up where Columbus left off and write a journal entry in which you describe your thoughts and feelings as you continue exploring the islands of the Caribbean.

from *Journal of the First Voyage to America*   **37**

from Relation of Alvar Nuñez Cabeza de Vaca

Alvar Nuñez Cabeza de Vaca

The events in this account take place in June of 1528, as Cabeza de Vaca and his party explored northern Florida.

In this Province are many maize fields; and the houses are scattered as are those of the Gelves.[1] There are deer of three kinds, rabbits, hares, bears, lions and other wild beasts. Among them we saw an animal with a pocket on its belly, in which it carries its young until they know how to seek food; and if it happen that they should be out feeding and any one come near, the mother will not run until she has gathered them in together.

The country is very cold. It has fine pastures for herds. Birds are of various kinds. Geese in great numbers. Ducks, mallards, royal-ducks, fly-catchers, night-herons and partridges abound. We saw many falcons, gerfalcons, sparrow-hawks, merlins, and numerous other fowl.

Two hours after our arrival at Apalachen, the Indians who had fled from there came in peace to us, asking for their women and children, whom we released; but the detention of a cacique[2] by the Governor produced great

---

1. Gelves (hēl' vās): Gelves was the ancient name of the island of Chebra, off the coast of Tunisia.

2. cacique (kə sēk'): A local chief.

SEARCH FOR GOLD IN AN APPALACHIAN POND
Theodore de Bry and Lemoyne de Morgues
Service Historique de la Marine

excitement, in consequence of which they returned for battle early the next day [June 26], and attacked us with such promptness and alacrity that they succeeded in setting fire to the houses in which we were. As we sallied they fled to the lakes near by, because of which and the large maize fields, we could do them no injury, save in the single instance of one Indian, whom we killed. The day following, others came against us from a town on the opposite side of the lake, and attacked us as the first had done, escaping in the same way, except one who was also slain.

We were in the town twenty-five days [July 19], in which time we made three incursions, and found the country very thinly peopled and difficult to travel for the bad passages, the woods and lakes. We inquired of the cacique we kept and the natives we brought with us, who were the neighbors and enemies of these Indians, as to the nature of the country, the character and condition of the inhabitants, of the food and all other matters concerning it. Each answered apart from the rest, that the largest town in all that region was Apalachen; the people beyond were less numerous and poorer, the land little occupied, and the inhabitants much scattered; that thenceforward were great lakes, dense forests, immense deserts and solitudes. We then asked touching the region towards the south, as to the towns and subsistence in it. They said that in keeping such a direction, journeying nine days, there was a town called Aute, the inhabitants whereof had much maize, beans and pumpkins, and being near the sea, they had fish, and that those people were their friends.

In view of the poverty of the land, the unfavorable accounts of the population and of everything else we heard, the Indians making continual war upon us, wounding our people and horses at the places where they went to drink, shooting from the lakes with such safety to themselves that we could not retaliate, killing a lord of Tescuco,[3] named Don Pedro,[4] whom the Commissary brought with him, we determined to leave that place and go in quest of the sea, and the town of Aute of which we were told. . . .

___

3. Tescuco: Tezcoco (təz cō′ cō): Now Mexico City.
4. Don Pedro (dön pä′ drō): Believed to be the brother of an heir to the throne of the Aztecs, a native people of Mexico. After being banished by his father, Don Pedro commanded an army allied with the Spaniards in the battle of Mexico City.

RESPONDING TO THE SELECTION

Your Response
1. What do you find most interesting about this first-person account? Explain.

Recalling
2. Why do the Native Americans attack the Spanish forces on June 26?
3. What reasons does Cabeza de Vaca give for leaving the region of Apalachen for Aute?

Interpreting
4. What impression of Apalachen do you get from this account?
5. What impression of the natives do you get from this account?

Applying
6. In what ways is this account similar to Columbus's account of the exploration of San Salvador? Explain.

THINKING AND WRITING

Exploring Another Point of View
How might this account be different if it were written by a Native American? Describe the exploration of Apalachen from the point of view of a Seminole warrior. You might focus on the battle of June 26, using details from the selection to explain both how and why you attacked the Spanish "exploration party."

from **The Narrative of the Expedition of Coronado**

Pedro de Casteñada

Coronado and his men set off to find the fabled Native American city of Quivira, in the southwestern plains. Their guide, Turk, a plains Indian who cooperated with the Spanish in exchange for a promise of freedom, leads them far off course into central Texas.

The general started from the ravine with the guides that the Teyas[1] had given him. He appointed the alderman Diego Lopez his army-master, and took with him the men who seemed to him to be most efficient, and the best horses. . . .

The general arrived—I mean, the guides ran away during the first few days and Diego Lopez had to return to the army for guides, bringing orders for the army to return to Tiguex[2] to find food and wait there for the general. The Teyas, as before, willingly furnished him with new guides. The army waited for its messengers and spent a fortnight here, preparing jerked beef to take with them. It was estimated that during this fortnight they killed 500 bulls.[3] The number of these that were there without any cows was something incredible. Many fellows were lost at this time who went out hunting and did not get back to the army for two or three days, wandering about the country as if they were crazy, in one direction or another, not knowing how to get back where they started from, although this ravine extended in either direction so that they could find it. Every night they took account of who was missing, fired guns and blew trumpets and beat drums and built great fires, but yet some of them went off so far and wandered about so much that all this did not give them any help, although it helped others. The only way was to go back where they had killed an animal and start from there in one direction and another until they struck the ravine or fell in with somebody who could put them on the right road. It is worth noting that the country there is so level that at midday, after one has wandered about in one direction and another in pursuit of game, the only thing to do is to stay near the game quietly until sunset, so as to see where it goes down, and even then they have to be men who are practiced to do it. Those who are not, had to trust themselves to others.

The general followed his guides until he reached Quivira, which took forty-eight days' marching, on account of the great detour they had made toward Florida. He was received peacefully on account of the guides

---

1. Teyas (tā′ yäs): The Spanish name for the natives they encountered in Texas.
2. Tiguex (tē gyōō′): A region in what is now New Mexico.
3. bulls: Buffalo.

whom he had. They asked the Turk why he had lied and had guided them so far out of their way. He said that his country was in that direction and that, besides this, the people at Cicuye[4] had asked him to lead them off on to the plains and lose them, so that the horses would die when their provisions gave out, and they would be so weak if they ever returned that they would be killed without any trouble, and thus they could take revenge for what had been done to them.[5] This was the reason why he had led them astray, supposing that they did not know how to hunt or to live without corn, while as for the gold, he did not know where there was any of it. He said this like one who had given up hope and who found that he was being persecuted, since they had begun to believe Ysopete[6] who had guided them better than he had, and fearing lest those who were there might give some advice by which some harm would come to him. . . .

The messengers whom the army had sent to the general returned, as I said, and then, as they brought no news except what the alderman had delivered, the army left the ra-

vine and returned to the Teyas, where they took guides who led them back by a more direct road. They readily furnished these, because these people are always roaming over this country in pursuit of the animals and so know it thoroughly. They keep their road in this way: In the morning they notice where the sun rises and observe the direction they are going to take, and then shoot an arrow in this direction. Before reaching this they shoot another over it, and in this way they go all day toward the water where they are to end the day. In this way they covered in 25 days what had taken them 37 days going, besides stopping to hunt cows on the way. They found many salt lakes on this road, and there was a great quantity of salt. There were thick pieces of it on top of the water bigger than tables, as thick as four or five fingers. Two or three spans[7] down under water there was salt which tasted better than that in the floating pieces, because this was rather bitter. It was crystalline. All over these plains there were large numbers of animals like squirrels[8] and a great number of their holes.

On its return the army reached the Cicuye river more than 30 leagues[9] below

---

4. Cicuye: (sē ko͞o′ yā): A Plains Indian village in what is now Texas.
5. What had been done to them: The Spanish had used force to subdue the Pueblo Indians.
6. Ysopete: (ē sō′ pā tā′): A Plains Indian found in captivity with the Pueblo Indians.

7. spans *n.*: A span is a unit of measure equal to nine inches.
8. animals like squirrels: Prairie dogs.
9. leagues (lēgz) *n.*: A league is a unit of measure equal to about three miles.

from *The Narrative of the Expedition of Coronado*   41

there—I mean below the bridge they had made when they crossed it, and they followed it up to that place. In general, its banks are covered with a sort of rose bushes, the fruit of which tastes like muscatel grapes. They grow on little twigs about as high up as a man. It has the parsley leaf. There were unripe grapes and currants and wild marjoram. The guides said this river joined that of Tiguex more than 20 days from here, and that its course turned toward the east. It is believed that it flows into the mighty river of the Holy Spirit[10] which the men with Don Hernando de Soto[11] discovered in Florida. A painted Indian woman ran away from Juan de Saldibar and hid in the ravines about this time, because she recognized the country of Tiguex where she had been a slave. She fell into the

hands of some Spaniards who had entered the country from Florida to explore it in this direction. After I got back to New Spain[12] I heard them say that the Indian told them that she had run away from other men like them nine days, and that she gave the names of some captains; from which we ought to believe that we were not far from the region they discovered, although they said they were more than 200 leagues inland. I believe the land at that point is more than *600 leagues* across from sea to sea.

As I said, the army followed the river up as far as Cicuye, which it found ready for war and unwilling to make any advances toward peace or to give any food to the army. From there they went on to Tiguex where several villages had been reinhabited, but the people were afraid and left them again.

10. **the mighty river of the Holy Spirit:** The Mississippi.
11. **Don Hernando** (hər nan′ dō) **de Soto** (di sōt′ ō): A Spanish explorer who discovered the Mississippi River.

12. **New Spain:** A former Spanish colony that included, at its height, Mexico, the southwestern United States, and Central America north of Panama.

RESPONDING TO THE SELECTION

Your Response

1. With whom do your sympathies lie, the Plains Indian who misled the Spanish or the group of soldiers who followed him onto the Great Plains? Explain.

Recalling

2. What do the soldiers camped at the ravine do as they waited for orders?
3. On the way back to Tiguex, what system do the Native American guides use for marking the route?

Interpreting

4. Why would the army be eager to accompany Coronado to Quivira?
5. Why did so many soldiers get lost in the plains?

Applying

6. Coronado and other Spanish explorers came to the Americas in search of gold and glory. What do you think motivates people who explore new frontiers today?

THINKING AND WRITING

Writing a Narrative

What risks have you taken in search of adventure? Based on the notes you jotted down before reading these selections, write a first-person account of one of your adventures. First, tell about your fears and expectations; then describe the experience itself. Use vivid details to communicate your impressions to the reader.

LEARNING OPTION

Cross-curricular Connection. Like Francisco de Coronado, Hernando de Soto and Juan Cabrillo each headed north across the Rio Grande between 1539 and 1542. Investigate the expeditions of one of these explorers. What did he hope to find? What did he find instead? Share your findings in a short oral or written report.

Living in the New Land

THE ARRIVAL OF THE ENGLISHMEN IN VIRGINIA
Colored Line Engraving, 1590, by Theodor de Bry

JOHN SMITH

1580–1631

John Smith was a leader in the settlement of Jamestown, Virginia, the first successful English colony in America, and was one of England's most famous New World explorers. The stories of his adventures, often embellished by his own pen, fascinated European readers of his day and continue to provide a wealth of details about the early exploration and colonization of America.

The son of a farmer, Smith was born in Lincolnshire, England. He left home at the age of sixteen to become a soldier. During the next ten years, Smith traveled throughout Europe and the Near East, fought in numerous battles, and was promoted to captain. Then, in 1606, a year after his return to England, Smith led a group of colonists across the Atlantic to establish a settlement in the New World. The group landed in Virginia in 1607 and founded Jamestown.

As president of the colony from 1608 to 1609, Smith helped assure the colony's success, obtaining food, enforcing discipline, and dealing with the native tribes who inhabited the region. In 1608 Smith published *A True Relation of Virginia,* the first English book describing life in America. In 1609, after being burned in a gunpowder accident and involved in disputes with other colonists, Smith traveled back to England.

Smith made two more voyages to America in 1614 and 1615, exploring and mapping the coast of the region he named New England. Then Smith returned to England, settling in London, where he lived for the remainder of his life. During his later years, he published his two most famous works, *A Description of New England* (1616) and *The General History of Virginia, New England, and the Summer Isles* (1624).

Smith was at heart a traveler. He made several determined attempts to reach North America again before reluctantly settling in London. Bad weather, lack of money, and (once) pirates stopped him. Although he was not sympathetic with Puritans, he offered to lead the group sailing on the *Mayflower* in 1620. They did not accept his offer but were happy to use his maps.

In *The General History of Virginia,* which describes the founding of Jamestown, Smith attempts to dispel English misconceptions about America and encourages others to settle in the New World. The book also includes an account of what has become Smith's most famous adventure. According to his story, Smith was captured by the Native Americans and faced execution until the chief's daughter Pocahontas saved him from death. This episode, along with the other experiences Smith describes, provides an understanding and appreciation of what the early colonists' lives were like.

GUIDE FOR INTERPRETING

from The General History of Virginia

History. A history is a factual account of events in the life or development of a people, nation, institution, or culture. Histories, which usually recount events chronologically, often include analysis and explanation. Some histories are firsthand accounts by people who lived through the events. Other histories are secondhand, or secondary, accounts by people who have researched the events but did not live through them.

Firsthand accounts are likely to be subjective because of the writer's personal involvement with the events. Also, they sometimes lack accuracy because the writer often wrote to persuade or entertain the audiences of the time. For example, John Smith often exaggerates events in *The General History of Virginia*. At the same time, firsthand accounts often capture the flavor of living through those events.

All his adventurous life, Smith was in trouble with authority, sometimes because he was more capable than his superiors. The private trading company in England that financed the expedition knew little about the wilderness conditions of the North American continent and was unrealistic in its expectations of material gain from the colony. Smith's practical survival skills saved the settlement, but even that did not keep him from censure and near imprisonment.

It is not surprising, then, that he tried to give his version of the story in his writings. (Although Pocahontas was a real person, Smith's adventure with her is doubtful, since he did not mention it in two earlier accounts of the same events.)

In the following selection, Smith describes, seventeen years later, the hard times in 1607 when the settlers fought to survive until a supply ship could arrive from England. Notice his vivid and detailed description of life then. Notice also when he interprets or explains events or gives his own opinion and when he perhaps exaggerates. Can we ever depend on a history to be completely accurate and unbiased? Could you and another student agree on an account of what happened in class yesterday and why?

The early American settlers faced a great number of hardships. List the problems you think the colonists faced. Then freewrite about how you would have dealt with each of these hardships if you had been in their situation.

from The General History of Virginia

John Smith

What Happened Till the First Supply

Being thus left to our fortunes, it fortuned[1] that within ten days, scarce ten amongst us could either go[2] or well stand, such extreme weakness and sickness oppressed us. And thereat none need marvel if they consider the cause and reason, which was this: While the ships stayed, our allowance was somewhat bettered by a daily proportion of biscuit which the sailors would pilfer to sell, give, or exchange with us for money, sassafras,[3] or furs. But when they departed, there remained neither tavern, beer house, nor place of relief but the common kettle.[4] Had we been as free from all sins as gluttony and drunkenness we might have been canonized for saints, but our President[5] would never have been admitted for engrossing to his private,[6] oatmeal,

sack,[7] oil, aqua vitae,[8] beef, eggs, or what not but the kettle; that indeed he allowed equally to be distributed, and that was half a pint of wheat and as much barley boiled with water for a man a day, and this, having fried some twenty-six weeks in the ship's hold, contained as many worms as grains so that we might truly call it rather so much bran than corn; our drink was water, our lodgings castles in the air.

With this lodging and diet, our extreme toil in bearing and planting palisades so strained and bruised us and our continual labor in the extremity of the heat had so weakened us, as were cause sufficient to have made us as miserable in our native country or any other place in the world.

From May to September, those that escaped lived upon sturgeon and sea crabs. Fifty in this time we buried; the rest seeing the President's projects to escape these miseries in our pinnace[9] by flight (who all this time had neither felt want nor sickness) so

---

1. **fortuned:** Happened.
2. **go:** Be active.
3. **sassafras:** A tree, the root of which was valued for its supposed medicinal qualities.
4. **common kettle:** Communal cooking pot.
5. **President:** Wingfield, the leader of the colony.
6. **engrossing to his private:** Taking for his own use.

---

7. **sack** n.: A type of white wine.
8. **aqua vitae** (ak′wə vīt′ē): Brandy.
9. **pinnace** (pin′ is) n.: A small sailing ship.

moved our dead spirits as we deposed him and established Ratcliffe in his place . . .

But now was all our provision spent, the sturgeon gone, all helps abandoned, each hour expecting the fury of the savages; when God, the patron of all good endeavors, in that desperate extremity so changed the hearts of the savages that they brought such plenty of their fruits and provision as no man wanted.

And now where some affirmed it was ill done of the Council[10] to send forth men so badly provided, this incontradictable reason will show them plainly they are too ill advised to nourish such ill conceits: First, the fault of our going was our own; what could be thought fitting or necessary we had, but what we should find, or want, or where we should be, we were all ignorant and supposing to make our passage in two months, with victual to live and the advantage of the spring to work; we were at sea five months where we both spent our victual and lost the opportunity of the time and season to plant, by the unskillful presumption of our ignorant transporters that understood not at all what they undertook.

Such actions have ever since the world's beginning been subject to such accidents, and everything of worth is found full of difficulties, but nothing so difficult as to establish a commonwealth so far remote from men and means and where men's minds are so untoward[11] as neither do well themselves nor suffer others. But to proceed.

The new President and Martin, being little beloved, of weak judgment in dangers, and less industry in peace, committed the managing of all things abroad[12] to Captain Smith, who, by his own example, good words, and fair promises, set some to mow, others to bind thatch, some to build houses, others to thatch them, himself always bearing the greatest task for his own share, so that in short time he provided most of them lodgings, neglecting any for himself . . .

Leading an expedition on the Chickahominy River, Captain Smith and his men are attacked by Indians, and Smith is taken prisoner.

When this news came to Jamestown, much was their sorrow for his loss, few expecting what ensued.

Six or seven weeks those barbarians kept him prisoner, many strange triumphs and conjurations they made of him, yet he so demeaned himself amongst them, as he not only diverted them from surprising the fort, but procured his own liberty, and got himself and his company such estimation amongst them, that those savages admired him.

The manner how they used and delivered him is as followeth:

The savages having drawn from George Cassen whither Captain Smith was gone, prosecuting that opportunity they followed him with three hundred bowmen, conducted by the King of Pamunkee,[13] who in divisions searching the turnings of the river found Robinson and Emry by the fireside; those they shot full of arrows and slew. Then finding the Captain, as is said, that used the savage that was his guide as his shield (three of them being slain and divers[14] others so galled),[15] all the rest would not come near him. Thinking thus to have returned to his boat, regarding them, as he marched, more than his way, slipped up to the middle in an oozy creek and his savage with him; yet dared they not come to him till being near dead with cold he threw away his

10. **Council:** The seven persons in charge of the expedition.
11. **untoward:** Stubborn.
12. **abroad:** Outside the palisades.

13. **Pamunkee:** The Pamunkee River.
14. **divers** (dī′ vərz) *adj.*: Several.
15. **galled:** Wounded.

arms. Then according to their composition[16] they drew him forth and led him to the fire where his men were slain. Diligently they chafed his benumbed limbs.

He demanding for their captain, they showed him Opechancanough, King of Pamunkee, to whom he gave a round ivory double compass dial. Much they marveled at the playing of the fly and needle,[17] which they could see so plainly and yet not touch it because of the glass that covered them. But when he demonstrated by that globe-like jewel the roundness of the earth and skies, the sphere of the sun, moon, and stars, and how the sun did chase the night round about the world continually, the greatness of the land and sea, the diversity of nations, variety of complexions, and how we were to them antipodes[18] and many other such like matters, they all stood as amazed with admiration.

Nothwithstanding, within an hour after, they tied him to a tree, and as many as could stand about him prepared to shoot him, but the King holding up the compass in his hand, they all laid down their bows and arrows and in a triumphant manner led him to Orapaks where he was after their manner kindly feasted and well used. . . .

At last they brought him to Werowocomoco, where was Powhatan, their Emperor. Here more than two hundred of those grim courtiers stood wondering at him, as he had been a monster, till Powhatan and his train had put themselves in their greatest braveries. Before a fire upon a seat like a bedstead, he sat covered with a great robe made of raccoon skins and all the tails hanging by. On either hand did sit a young wench of sixteen or eighteen years and along on each side the house, two rows of men and behind them as many women, with all their heads and shoulders painted red, many of their heads bedecked with the white down of birds, but every one with something, and a great chain of white beads about their necks.

At his entrance before the King, all the people gave a great shout. The Queen of Appomattoc was appointed to bring him water to wash his hands, and another brought him a bunch of feathers, instead of a towel, to dry them; having feasted him after their best barbarous manner they could, a long consultation was held, but the conclusion was, two great stones were brought before Powhatan; then as many as could, laid hands on him, dragged him to them, and thereon laid his head and being ready with their clubs to beat out his brains, Pocahontas, the King's dearest daughter, when no entreaty could prevail, got his head in her arms and laid her own upon his to save him from death; whereat the Emperor was contented he should live to make him hatchets, and her bells, beads, and copper, for they thought him as well of all occupations as themselves.[19] For the King himself will make his own robes, shoes, bows, arrows, pots; plant, hunt, or do anything so well as the rest.

Two days after, Powhatan, having disguised himself in the most fearfulest manner he could, caused Captain Smith to be brought forth to a great house in the woods and there upon a mat by the fire to be left alone. Not long after, from behind a mat that divided the house, was made the most dolefulest noise he ever heard; then Powhatan more like a devil than a man, with some two hundred more as black as himself, came unto him and told him now they were friends, and presently he should go to Jamestown to send him two great guns and a grindstone for which he would give him the country of Capahowasic and forever esteem him as his son Nantaquond.

---

16. **composition:** Ways.
17. **fly and needle:** Parts of a compass.
18. **antipodes** (an tip′ ə dēz′): On the opposite side of the globe.

---

19. **as well . . . themselves:** Capable of making them just as well as they could themselves.

FOUNDING OF THE FIRST PERMANENT ENGLISH SETTLEMENT
IN AMERICA
A. C. Warren
New York Public Library

So to Jamestown with twelve guides Powhatan sent him. That night they quartered in the woods, he still expecting (as he had done all this long time of his imprisonment) every hour to be put to one death or other, for all their feasting. But almighty God (by His divine providence) had mollified the hearts of those stern barbarians with compassion. The next morning betimes they came to the fort, where Smith having used the savages with what kindness he could, he showed Rawhunt, Powhatan's trusty servant, two demiculverins[20] and a millstone to carry Powhatan; they found them somewhat too heavy, but when they did see him discharge them, being loaded with stones, among the boughs of a great tree loaded with icicles, the ice and branches came so tumbling down that the poor savages ran away

---

20. demiculverins (dem′ ē kul′ vər inz): Large cannons.

from *The General History of Virginia*   49

half dead with fear. But at last we regained some conference with them and gave them such toys and sent to Powhatan, his women, and children such presents as gave them in general full content.

Now in Jamestown they were all in combustion,[21] the strongest preparing once more to run away with the pinnace; which, with the hazard of his life, with saker falcon[22] and musket shot, Smith forced now the third time to stay or sink.

Some, no better than they should be, had plotted with the President the next day to have him put to death by the Levitical law,[23] for the lives of Robinson and Emry; pretending the fault was his that had led

---

21. combustion: Tumult.
22. saker falcon: Small cannon.
23. Levitical law: "He that killeth man shall surely be put to death" (Leviticus 24:17).

them to their ends; but he quickly took such order with such lawyers that he laid them by their heels till he sent some of them prisoners for England.

Now every once in four or five days, Pocahontas with her attendants brought him so much provision that saved many of their lives, that else for all this had starved with hunger.

His relation of the plenty he had seen, especially at Werowocomoco, and of the state and bounty of Powhatan (which till that time was unknown), so revived their dead spirits (especially the love of Pocahontas) as all men's fear was abandoned.

Thus you may see what difficulties still crossed any good endeavor; and the good success of the business being thus oft brought to the very period of destruction; yet you see by what strange means God hath still delivered it.

RESPONDING TO THE SELECTION

Your Response
1. Is John Smith someone you would have liked to know? Why or why not?
2. Do you agree or disagree with Smith's statement that "everything of worth is found full of difficulties"? Explain.

Recalling
3. (a) What hardships do the colonists face during their first several months in the New World? (b) What assistance do they receive?
4. (a) What criticisms does Smith make of the new president and colonist Martin? (b) What does Smith praise?

Interpreting
5. What impression of Smith do you get from this account?
6. What seems to be Smith's attitude toward the Native Americans?
7. Why does Smith write in the third person, referring to himself as "he" instead of "I"?

Applying
8. Describe some situations in which people today are coping with great hardships.

ANALYZING LITERATURE

Understanding a History
A **history** is a nonfiction account of events that occurred to a people, a nation, an institution, or a culture. Histories may be either firsthand accounts, written by someone who was involved with the events, or secondhand accounts, written by someone who was not involved in the events. Firsthand accounts, which sometimes lack factual accuracy, tend to be subjective, but they often capture the flavor of the time. For example, while *The General History of Virginia* conveys a sense of life in the Jamestown settlement, most historians consider Smith's account of his rescue by Pocahontas to be greatly exaggerated.
1. Find two examples in which Smith displays subjectivity in recounting events.
2. List three details that capture the flavor of life in Jamestown.

CRITICAL THINKING AND READING

Recognizing Author's Purpose

While the **purpose** of most secondhand historical accounts is to inform, many firsthand accounts are written to entertain or persuade. For example, Smith's primary purpose in writing *The General History of Virginia* was probably to encourage other English men and women to settle in the New World.

1. In what way is the primary purpose of *The General History of Virginia* made apparent?
2. What other purposes does Smith appear to have had?

THINKING AND WRITING

Writing a Historical Account

During our lifetime we all live through or are in some way a part of important events. Think of an important historical event that occurred during your lifetime or of an event in your community. Brainstorm to recall details of the event, and, if necessary, research the event in your library. Then, after listing the details in chronological order, write a brief secondhand account. Try to be as objective as possible. When you revise, make sure you have included enough information to inform thoroughly a reader who has no prior knowledge of the event. Try to remove any subjective details you may have included. At this point, you might decide to include tables or maps to make your information clearer.

Founding of the Colonies

Colony/Date Founded	Leader	Reasons Founded
New England Colonies		
Massachusetts		
Plymouth/1620	William Bradford	Religious freedom
Massachusetts Bay/1630	John Winthrop	Religious freedom
New Hampshire/1623	Ferdinando Gorges John Mason	Profit from trade and fishing
Connecticut		
Hartford/1636	Thomas Hooker	Expand trade; religious and political
New Haven/1639		freedom
Rhode Island/1636	Roger Williams	Religious freedom
Middle Colonies		
New York/1625	Peter Minuit	Expand trade
Delaware/1638	Swedish settlers	Expand trade
New Jersey/1664	John Berkeley George Carteret	Profit from land sales; religious and political freedom
Pennsylvania/1682	William Penn	Profit from land sales; religious and political freedom
Southern Colonies		
Virginia/1607	John Smith	Trade and farming
Maryland/1632	Lord Baltimore	Profit from land sales; religious and political freedom
The Carolinas/1663	Group of eight proprietors	Trade and farming; religious freedom
North Carolina/1712		
South Carolina/1712		
Georgia/1732	James Oglethorpe	Profit, home for debtors; buffer against Spanish Florida

WILLIAM BRADFORD

1590–1657

Thirteen years after the first permanent English settlement was established in Jamestown, another group of colonists, known as the Pilgrims, landed on the shore of what is now Massachusetts. William Bradford, one of their leaders, recorded the experiences of these early settlers in a factually accurate account.

Bradford was born in Yorkshire, England. Having developed a strong devotion to religion early in life, Bradford joined a group of Puritan extremists, who felt that the Church of England was corrupt and wished to separate themselves from it entirely. In the face of stiff persecution, Bradford's group eventually fled to Leyden, Holland, where Bradford worked as a weaver. Later Bradford and many other group members left Holland to establish a settlement in the New World.

After a difficult voyage aboard the *Mayflower,* a small ship with a cracked beam, the Pilgrims reached North America in November 1620. They landed not in Virginia as intended but much farther north, on the tip of Cape Cod in Massachusetts. Searching the coast in a small boat, they decided to settle in what is now Plymouth. It was mid-December before they could build shelters and all move ashore. During those dreary weeks on the ship, facing an unknown wilderness, Bradford's wife, Dorothy, fell overboard and was drowned.

Once ashore, the Pilgrims encountered not only the hardships experienced by Jamestown's first settlers but also a harsh New England winter. Added to that were disagreements about the validity of the rules of their charter, since it was for Virginia. To silence the argument, Bradford and the other leaders drew up the "Mayflower Compact." This was the first agreement for self-government made in the New World and served as a model for following settlements.

After the death of their first governor, John Carver, the Pilgrims elected William Bradford as their leader. Bradford was reelected governor thirty times. During his tenure as governor, he organized the repayment of debts to financial backers, encouraged new immigration, and established good relations with the Native Americans, without whose help the colony never would have survived.

In 1630 Bradford began writing *Of Plymouth Plantation,* an account of the Pilgrims' voyage to the New World, the founding of Plymouth Plantation, and the Pilgrims' experiences during the early years of the colony's existence. Bradford's work, which was not published until 1856, provides a firsthand view of the Pilgrims' struggle to endure and the courage and unbending religious faith that helped them survive. Written in the simple language that has come to be known as Puritan plain style, *Of Plymouth Plantation* stands as a tribute to the fortitude of Bradford and the other Pilgrim settlers.

GUIDE FOR INTERPRETING

from Of Plymouth Plantation

Literary Forms

Modes of Discourse. Prose is often classified into four modes, or forms, of discourse: narration, description, exposition, and persuasion. Narration is writing that relates a story. The subject may be fictional, as in novels and short stories, or factual, as in historical accounts and biographies. Description presents the details of something, often through appeal to one or more of the five senses—sight, sound, taste, smell, and touch. Exposition uses logical patterns, such as comparison and contrast or definition, to inform or explain. Grammar textbooks and repair manuals are two examples of books containing expository writing. The fourth mode of discourse is persuasion, writing that attempts to convince readers to adopt an opinion or act in a certain way. Examples of persuasion include television advertisements and newspaper editorials.

Most often, the author's main purpose determines which of these categories a work best fits into. However, an author usually uses more than one form of discourse. For example, when writing a narrative, an author is likely to include descriptions of people and places and information about historical events.

Focus

The belief that we should be thankful for what we have, regardless of how difficult our circumstances may be, is often associated with the Pilgrims. What associations do you normally have when you think of the Pilgrims? Write a journal entry in which you discuss the ideas you associate with the Pilgrims.

Primary Source

In Book I of *Of Plymouth Plantation,* Bradford describes his little group of Puritan Separatists as they left the Dutch city of Leyden, headed for England and from there to North America. It is this passage that gave them the name "Pilgrims": "So they left that goodly and pleasant city which had been their resting place near twelve years; but they knew they were pilgrims, and looked not much on those things, but lift up their eyes to the heavens, their dearest country, and quieted their spirits."

Bradford describes their first wintry view of North America as they searched "an unknown coast" for a landing place: ". . . what could they see but a hideous and desolate wilderness, full of wild beasts and wild men—and what multitudes there might be of them they knew not . . . If they looked behind them, there was the mighty ocean . . . to separate them from all the civil parts of the world."

from Of Plymouth Plantation

William Bradford

Of Their Voyage and How They Passed the Sea; and of Their Safe Arrival at Cape Cod

After they had enjoyed fair winds and weather for a season, they were encountered many times with cross winds and met with many fierce storms with which the ship was shroudly[1] shaken, and her upper works made very leaky; and one of the main beams in the midships was bowed and cracked, which put them in some fear that the ship could not be able to perform the voyage. So some of the chief of the company, perceiving the mariners to fear the sufficiency of the ship as appeared by their mutterings, they entered into serious consultation with the master and other officers of the ship, to consider in time of the danger, and rather to return than to cast themselves into a desperate and inevitable peril. And truly there was great distraction and difference of opinion amongst the mariners themselves; fain would they do what could be done for their wages' sake (being now near half the seas over) and on the other hand they were loath to hazard their lives too desperately. But in examining of all opinions, the master and others affirmed they knew the ship to be strong and firm under water; and for the buckling of the main beam, there was a great iron screw the passengers brought out of Holland, which would raise the beam into his place; the which being done, the carpenter and master affirmed that with a post put under it, set firm in the lower deck and otherways bound, he would make it sufficient. And as for the decks and upper works, they would caulk them as well as they could, and though with the working of the ship they would not long keep staunch, yet there

THE COMING OF THE MAYFLOWER
N. C. Wyeth
From the Collection of the Metropolitan Life Insurance Company, New York City

---

1. shroudly: Wickedly.

would otherwise be no great danger, if they did not overpress her with sails. So they committed themselves to the will of God and resolved to proceed.

In sundry of these storms the winds were so fierce and the seas so high, as they could not bear a knot of sail, but were forced to hull[2] for divers days together. And in one of them, as they thus lay at hull in a mighty storm, a lusty young man called John Howland, coming upon some occasion above the gratings was, with a seel[3] of the ship, thrown into sea; but it pleased God that he

_____

2. **hull:** Drift with the wind.
3. **seel:** Rolling.

caught hold of the topsail halyards[4] which hung overboard and ran out at length. Yet he held his hold (though he was sundry fathoms under water) till he was hauled up by the same rope to the brim of the water, and then with a boat hook and other means got into the ship again and his life saved. And though he was something ill with it, yet he lived many years after and became a profitable member both in church and commonwealth. In all this voyage there died but one of the passengers, which was William Butten, a youth, servant to Samuel Fuller, when they drew near the coast.

But to omit other things (that I may be brief) after long beating at sea they fell with that land which is called Cape Cod; the which being made and certainly known to be it, they were not a little joyful. After some deliberation had amongst themselves and with the master of the ship, they tacked about and resolved to stand for the southward (the wind and weather being fair) to find some place about Hudson's River for their habitation. But after they had sailed that course about half the day, they fell amongst dangerous shoals and roaring breakers, and they were so far entangled therewith as they conceived themselves in great danger; and the wind shrinking upon them withal,[5] they resolved to bear up again for the Cape and thought themselves happy to get out of those dangers before night overtook them, as by God's good providence they did. And the next day they got into the Cape Harbor[6] where they rid in safety.

Being thus arrived in a good harbor, and brought safe to land, they fell upon their knees and blessed the God of Heaven who had brought them over the vast and furious ocean, and delivered them from all the perils and miseries thereof, again to set their feet on the firm and stable earth, their proper element.

_____

4. **halyards** *n.*: Ropes for raising or lowering sails.
5. **withal:** Also.
6. **Cape Harbor:** Now Provincetown Harbor.

from *Of Plymouth Plantation*   55

THE LANDING OF THE PILGRIMS AT PLYMOUTH, MASSACHUSETTS, December 22nd, 1620
Currier & Ives, 1876
Museum of the City of New York

The Starving Time

But that which was most sad and lamentable was, that in two or three months' time half of their company died, especially in January and February, being the depth of winter, and wanting houses and other comforts; being infected with the scurvy[7] and other diseases which this long voyage and their inaccommodate[8] condition had brought upon them. So as there died sometimes two or three of a day in the foresaid time, that of one hundred and odd persons, scarce fifty remained. And of these, in the time of most distress, there was but six or seven sound persons who to their great commendations, be it spoken, spared no pains night or day, but with abundance of toil and hazard of their own health, fetched them wood, made them fires, dressed them meat, made their beds, washed their loathsome clothes, clothed and unclothed them. In a word, did all the homely[9] and necessary offices for them which dainty and queasy stomachs cannot endure to hear named; and all this

---

7. scurvy *n.*: A disease caused by vitamin C deficiency.
8. inaccommodate *adj.*: Unfit.

9. homely *adj.*: Domestic.

willingly and cheerfully, without any grudging in the least, showing herein their true love unto their friends and brethren; a rare example and worthy to be remembered. Two of these seven were Mr. William Brewster, their reverend Elder, and Myles Standish, their Captain and military commander, unto whom myself and many others were much beholden in our low and sick condition. And yet the Lord so upheld these persons as in this general calamity they were not at all infected either with sickness or lameness. And what I have said of these I may say of many others who died in this general visitation,[10] and others yet living; that whilst they had health, yea, or any strength continuing, they were not wanting to any that had need of them. And I doubt not but their recompense is with the Lord.

But I may not here pass by another remarkable passage not to be forgotten. As this calamity fell among the passengers that were to be left here to plant, and were hasted ashore and made to drink water that the seamen might have the more beer, and one[11] in his sickness desiring but a small can of beer, it was answered that if he were their own father he should have none. The disease began to fall amongst them also, so as almost half of their company died before they went away, and many of their officers and lustiest men, as the boatswain, gunner, three quartermasters, the cook and others. At which the Master was something strucken and sent to the sick ashore and told the Governor he should send for beer for them that had need of it, though he drunk water homeward bound.

But now amongst his company there was far another kind of carriage[12] in this misery than amongst the passengers. For they that before had been boon[13] companions in drinking and jollity in the time of their health and welfare, began now to desert one another in this calamity, saying they would not hazard their lives for them, they should be infected by coming to help them in their cabins; and so, after they came to lie by it, would do little or nothing for them but, "if they died, let them die." But such of the passengers as were yet aboard showed them what mercy they could which made some of their hearts relent, as the boatswain (and some others) who was a proud young man and would often curse and scoff at the passengers. But when he grew weak, they had compassion on him and helped him; then he confessed he did not deserve it at their hands, he had abused them in word and deed. "Oh!" (saith he) "you, I now see, show your love like Christians indeed one to another, but we let one another lie and die like dogs." Another lay cursing his wife, saying if it had not been for her he had never come this unlucky voyage, and anon cursing his fellows, saying he had done this and that for some of them; he had spent so much and so much amongst them, and they were now weary of him and did not help him, having need. Another gave his companion all he had, if he died, to help him in his weakness; he went and got a little spice and made him a mess[14] of meat once or twice. And because he died not so soon as he expected, he went amongst his fellows and swore the rogue would cozen[15] him, he would see him choked before he made him any more meat; and yet the poor fellow died before morning.

Indian Relations

All this while the Indians came skulking about them, and would sometimes show themselves aloof off, but when any approached near them, they would run away; and once they stole away their tools where they had been at work and were gone to dinner. But about the sixteenth of March, a certain Indian came boldly amongst them and

---

10. **visitation** n.: Affliction.
11. **one:** William Bradford.
12. **carriage** n.: Behavior.
13. **boon** adj.: Close.

14. **mess** n.: Meal.
15. **cozen** (kuz' n) v.: Cheat.

spoke to them in broken English, which they could well understand but marveled at it. At length they understood by discourse with him, that he was not of these parts, but belonged to the eastern parts where some English ships came to fish, with whom he was acquainted and could name sundry of them by their names, amongst whom he had got his language. He became profitable to them in acquainting them with many things concerning the state of the country in the east parts where he lived, which was afterwards profitable unto them; as also of the people here, of their names, number and strength, of their situation and distance from this place, and who was chief amongst them. His name was Samoset. He told them also of another Indian whose name was Squanto, a native of this place, who had been in England and could speak better English than himself.

Being, after some time of entertainment and gifts dismissed, a while after he came again, and five more with him, and they brought again all the tools that were stolen away before, and made way for the coming of their great Sachem,[16] called Massasoit. Who, about four or five days after, came with the chief of his friends and other attendance, with the aforesaid Squanto. With whom, after friendly entertainment and some gifts given him, they made a peace with him

---

16. **Sachem** (sā′ chəm): Chief.

(which hath now continued this twenty-four years) in these terms:

1. That neither he nor any of his should injure or do hurt to any of their people.
2. That if any of his did hurt to any of theirs, he should send the offender, that they might punish him.
3. That if anything were taken away from any of theirs, he should cause it to be restored; and they should do the like to his.
4. If any did unjustly war against him, they would aid him; if any did war against them, he should aid them.
5. He should send to his neighbors confederates to certify them of this, that they might not wrong them, but might be likewise comprised in the conditions of peace.
6. That when their men came to them, they should leave their bows and arrows behind them.

After these things he returned to his place called Sowams, some 40 miles from this place, but Squanto continued with them and was their interpreter and was a special instrument sent of God for their good beyond their expectation. He directed them how to set their corn, where to take fish, and to procure other commodities, and was also their pilot to bring them to unknown places for their profit, and never left them till he died.

RESPONDING TO THE SELECTION

Your Response

1. How did reading this selection affect your impressions of the Pilgrims?
2. What is your opinion of the terms of the peace agreement between the settlers and the Native Americans?

Recalling

3. What hardships do the Pilgrims endure during their trip across the Atlantic?
4. What hardships do they encounter during their first winter at Plymouth?

Interpreting

5. How would you characterize the Pilgrims' reactions to the hardships they encountered during their first winter in Plymouth?
6. Find two statements by Bradford that convey the Pilgrims' belief that they were being guided and protected by God.
7. (a) What change occurs in Bradford's attitude toward the Native Americans? (b) How does the Native Americans' attitude toward the Pilgrims change? (c) Based on Bradford's descriptions, what do you think brought about these changes in attitude?

Applying

8. Do you feel that the changing attitudes of the settlers toward the Native Americans and of the Native Americans toward the settlers reflect typical experiences with newcomers? Why or why not?

ANALYZING LITERATURE

Using Modes of Discourse

Prose is often classified into four modes of discourse: narration, description, exposition, and persuasion. Most often, the author's main purpose determines into which of these modes a work is best classified. However, a writer rarely uses only one form of discourse in a work. For example, while *Of Plymouth Plantation* is primarily a narrative, because Bradford's main purpose is to tell about a series of event, the work contains many descriptive passages.

1. Find at least two examples of Bradford's use of description.
2. Find two examples of Bradford's use of a third form of discourse.

CRITICAL THINKING AND READING

Making Inferences About Attitudes

Many narratives, such as *Of Plymouth Plantation,* reveal the attitudes and values of the people being portrayed. However, in most cases, cultural attitudes and values are revealed indirectly. As a result, you must make inferences, or draw conclusions, by carefully examining the characters' actions, thoughts, and comments. For example, from Bradford's statement that the Pilgrims "committed themselves to the will of God," you can conclude that the Pilgrims had a strong faith in God.

What inferences can you make about the Pilgrims' attitudes and values from each of the following passages?

1. ". . . there was but six or seven sound persons who . . . did all the homely and necessary offices for them [sick Pilgrims] . . . willingly and cheerfully, without any grudging in the least. . . ."
2. "The boatswain . . . would often curse and scoff at the passengers. But when he grew weak, they had compassion on him and helped him. . . ."

THINKING AND WRITING

Comparing and Contrasting Accounts

Write an essay comparing and contrasting *The General History of Virginia* and *Of Plymouth Plantation* in such areas as style, purpose, objectivity, accuracy, and content. First, prepare a list of similarities and differences, and then organize your information into an outline or map. In the essay, use specific examples and passages from both works to support your thesis. When you revise, make sure your essay is well organized and includes supporting information.

GUIDE FOR INTERPRETING

To My Dear and Loving Husband; Upon the Burning of Our House

Anne Bradstreet (1612–1672) was born in Northampton, England, and raised as a Puritan. In 1630 she and her husband, Simon Bradstreet, left England and settled in the Massachusetts Bay Colony. Bradstreet endured the hardships of life in the New World and raised eight children. In 1650 a collection of her scholarly poems, *The Tenth Muse Lately Sprung Up in America, By a Gentlewoman of Those Parts,* was published in England. Bradstreet's later poems, like "To My Dear and Loving Husband," are more personal, expressing her feelings about the joyful but difficult and sometimes tragic experiences of everyday Puritan life.

Literary Forms

Lyric Poetry. Lyric poems, or lyrics, are brief poems that express the writer's personal feelings and thoughts. These poems, which in ancient Greece were sung to the accompaniment of a stringed instrument called a lyre, tend to be melodic and focus on producing a single, unified effect.

Although Bradstreet's early poetry consisted of scholarly poems on such subjects as physics, history, and philosophy, most of her later poems are lyrics. As she became more deeply immersed in her life in the New World, Bradstreet expressed her personal feelings about her family and the difficulties of colonial life.

Commentary

For the Puritans the sole purpose of literature was moral instruction. They were aware of the emotional power of poetry but approved of it only if, like the Psalms, it "moved hearts to righteousness." There were many writers of verse in Puritan times, but few of them were women. Bradstreet was aware that writing was considered unacceptable behavior for women, but she persevered nonetheless.

Her poetry reflects the Puritans' knowledge of the stories and language of the Bible and their awareness of the relationship between earthly and heavenly life. At the same time, she read the French and English poets of her day and was influenced by their use of comparisons and paradox. Finally, she was among the first American writers—and the first woman—to speak of and thus try to find a place for individual feelings within the context of Puritanism. Notice these different elements as you read her poems.

Focus

Like most other Puritans, Bradstreet was very devoted to her family. List ways in which people may demonstrate such devotion to others.

To My Dear and Loving Husband

Anne Bradstreet

If ever two were one, then surely we.
If ever man were lov'd by wife, then thee;
If ever wife was happy in a man,
Compare with me ye women if you can.
5   I prize thy love more than whole mines of gold,
Or all the riches that the East doth hold.
My love is such that rivers cannot quench,
Nor ought[1] but love from thee, give recompense.
Thy love is such I can no way repay,
10 The heavens reward thee manifold, I pray.
Then while we live, in love let's so persevere,
That when we live no more, we may live ever.

---

1. **ought:** Anything whatever.

READING WOMAN
Terborch

RESPONDING TO THE SELECTION

Your Response
1. Are you moved by the poem? Why or why not?
2. What is your image of Anne Bradstreet after reading this poem?

Interpreting
3. What does Bradstreet mean by the apparent paradox in the last two lines: ". . . let's so persevere / That when we live no more, we may live ever"?
4. What ideas about heaven and the afterlife does the poem convey?

Applying
5. Do you think personal devotion is as much esteemed today as it was in Anne Bradstreet's day? Support your answer.

ANALYZING LITERATURE

Understanding Lyric Poetry
A **lyric poem** expresses the personal thoughts and feelings of the poet in lively, musical language. For example, "To My Dear and Loving Husband" is a lyric poem that conveys the poet's happiness.
1. What is the main feeling Bradstreet expresses?
2. What other thoughts or feelings does Bradstreet express?
3. How do Bradstreet's repetition and images help to convey the strength of the emotion being expressed?

Upon the Burning of Our House

July 10th, 1666

Anne Bradstreet

In silent night when rest I took
For sorrow near I did not look
I wakened was with thund'ring noise
And piteous shrieks of dreadful voice.

THE PARSON BARNARD HOUSE
Henry Marsh
North Andover Historical Society

5   That fearful sound of "Fire!" and "Fire!"
Let no man know is my desire.
I, starting up, the light did spy,
And to my God my heart did cry
To strengthen me in my distress
10   And not to leave me succorless.
Then, coming out, beheld a space
The flame consume my dwelling place.
And when I could no longer look,
I blest His name that gave and took,
15   That laid my goods now in the dust.
Yea, so it was, and so 'twas just.
It was His own, it was not mine,
Far be it that I should repine;
He might of all justly bereft

20   But yet sufficient for us left.
      When by the ruins oft I past
      My sorrowing eyes aside did cast,
      And here and there the places spy
      Where oft I sat and long did lie:
25   Here stood that trunk, and there that chest,
      There lay that store I counted best.
      My pleasant things in ashes lie,
      And them behold no more shall I.
      Under thy roof no guest shall sit,
30   Nor at thy table eat a bit.
      No pleasant tale shall e'er be told,
      Nor things recounted done of old.
      No candle e'er shall shine in thee,
      Nor bridegroom's voice e'er heard shall be.
35   In silence ever shall thou lie,
      Adieu, Adieu,[1] all's vanity.
      Then straight I 'gin my heart to chide,
      And did thy wealth on earth abide?
      Didst fix thy hope on mold'ring dust?
40   The arm of flesh didst make thy trust?
      Raise up thy thoughts above the sky
      That dunghill mists away may fly.
      Thou hast an house on high erect,
      Framed by that mighty Architect,
45   With glory richly furnished,
      Stands permanent though this be fled.
      It's purchased and paid for too
      By Him who hath enough to do.
      A price so vast as is unknown
50   Yet by His gift is made thine own:
      There's wealth enough, I need no more,
      Farewell, my pelf,[2] farewell my store.
      The world no longer let me love,
      My hope and treasure lies above.

      _____

      1. adieu (ə dyoo'): "Farewell" (French).
      2. pelf *n.*: Money or wealth regarded with contempt.

RESPONDING TO THE SELECTION

Your Response

1. If you lived in Puritan New England, how might you have reacted to the burning of your house? Explain.

Recalling

2. What does the speaker see whenever she passes by her house?
3. In the end, where does the speaker's "hope and treasure" lie?

Interpreting

4. Why does the speaker bless God as her house is burning down?
5. (a) With what emotions is the speaker filled when she passes by the ruins of her house? (b) How does she react to these emotions?
6. To what is the speaker referring when she speaks of the "house on high" in line 43?
7. (a) On the basis of this poem, what generalization would you make about the Puritan attitude toward worldly goods? (b) What seems to be the theme of the poem?

Applying

8. Do you think the contemporary attitude toward worldly goods is similar to or different from that expressed in this poem? Explain your answer.

ANALYZING LITERATURE

The Puritan Plain Style

The writing style of the Puritans reflected the plain style of their lives—spare, simple, and straightforward, with a focus on the essentials of life, not on frivolities. Short words, direct statements, and references to ordinary, everyday objects—these were the characteristics of the style. Anne Bradstreet writes mainly in this plain style; however, she does occasionally allow herself some strong, vivid images to present her ideas.

1. Point out three basic, plain words referring to everyday items.
2. Point out three examples of more vivid, colorful words.

3. Find a line that is an example of a direct statement of her Puritan beliefs.

CRITICAL THINKING AND READING

Appreciating Connotations

The **connotation** of a word refers to the suggestions or associations evoked by it—beyond its literal meaning. For example, the word *sky* literally refers to the upper atmosphere or the appearance of this atmosphere. However, *sky* has the connotation of soaring, extreme height. Therefore, when Bradstreet writes "raise up thy thoughts above the sky," in line 41, she is reminding herself of God's province—the highest attainment.

Explain the connotation of the italicized word in each of the following lines.

1. "And did thy *wealth* on earth abide?"
2. "Didst fix thy hope on *mold'ring* dust?"

THINKING AND WRITING

Writing About Lyric Poetry

In her lyrics Anne Bradstreet conveys important Puritan beliefs and concerns. Reread "Upon the Burning of Our House" carefully, noting concerns expressed in the poem. What seems to be her major concern ? Write an essay in which you show how this one concern seems to dominate the poem. Include passages from the poem to support your thesis. Once you have finished writing a draft, revise your paper where needed, and prepare a final copy.

LEARNING OPTION

Art. Like most Puritan women, Anne Bradstreet was skilled at needlework. At an early age, she undoubtedly learned to make samplers by cross-stitching mottoes or patterns on canvas. Design a sampler for the Bradstreet home. Include a motto that expresses Bradstreet's beliefs and concerns as reflected in her poetry. You might choose to let Bradstreet speak for herself by using a line or two from one of her poems.

EDWARD TAYLOR

1642–1729

Edward Taylor is now generally regarded as the best of the colonial poets. Yet, because Taylor thought of his poetry as a form of personal religious worship, he permitted only two stanzas from one of his poems to be printed while he was alive, and he instructed his heirs not to have any more of his poetry published. As a result, few people knew about his work until his poems were first published more than two centuries after his death.

Before the English government's lack of tolerance for his Puritan beliefs prompted him to emigrate to America, Taylor worked as a teacher in England. After arriving in Boston in 1668, Taylor entered Harvard College and graduated in 1671. Taylor was then asked to serve as the minister and physician of the small farming community of Westfield, Massachusetts. After accepting the position, Taylor walked more than one hundred miles, partly through knee-deep snow, to get to his new home.

Taylor spent the rest of his life in Westfield. It was a life filled with hardships. Because of the fierce battles between the Native Americans and the colonists, Taylor and the other people of Westfield lived in a state of constant fear. Taylor also experienced many personal tragedies. Five of the eight children he had with his first wife died in infancy, and his first wife died while still a young woman. He married a second time, however, and had five or six more children. (Biographers differ on the exact number.)

In spite of the difficulties of his life and the demands of his position, Taylor wrote a considerable amount of poetry. He appears to have been interested in writing poems most of his life. He tried his hand at a great variety of poetic forms: elegies on the deaths of public figures, lyric poems in the style of Elizabethan songs, and a long "debate" poem. Most popular today, however, are what he called "Preparatory Meditations"—short poems written to "unwind" and express the emotional force of the sermon he was preparing for the next day.

Taylor's grandson, to whom Taylor left his poems, described his grandfather as "A man of small stature but firm: of quick Passions— yet serious and grave." In a time when the power of Puritanism was waning, Taylor held intellectually and emotionally to the original doctrines. Nearly all of his poems are expressions of his extremely conservative religious beliefs. Taylor believed that only a select few people were predestined to escape eternal damnation. His poems convey the intensity of the conservative Puritans' devotion to God and the strength of their desire for salvation perhaps better than any of the other poetry of his day.

GUIDE FOR INTERPRETING

Huswifery; Upon a Wasp Chilled with Cold

Figurative Language. Figurative language is language that is not intended to be interpreted literally. To interpret figurative language, you must examine the suggestions and associations it evokes. Writers use figurative language for strength and freshness of expression, to illustrate similarities between things that are seemingly quite different, or to express abstract ideas with concrete images, or word pictures. For example, the statement that a character's "thoughts were like scattered leaves" is figurative. In suggesting that the character's thoughts lacked focus, the phrase creates a concrete picture of an abstract idea and presents an interesting and unusual comparison.

Conceits. One kind of figurative language is a conceit, an elaborate and unusual comparison between two startlingly different subjects. Conceits are often lengthy and intricate, frequently developing through a series of shorter, less elaborate comparisons into the framework for an entire poem. Like the seventeenth-century English poets such as John Donne and George Herbert, whose work he greatly admired, Edward Taylor often used extended conceits in his writing. Yet, while Donne and Herbert used conceits primarily to surprise or shock readers, Taylor used conceits to emphasize the close relationship between God and the natural world.

Preachers and poets have much in common. They both appeal to the minds and emotions of their audience. They both use images and examples from everyday life to express abstract or complex concepts. Also, sermons use the rhythm and repetition common in poetry.

The Puritan habit of seeing God's teachings everywhere in nature provided preachers with a ready store of concrete images. For his frontier congregation, Taylor, the preacher, had to keep his comparisons simple. But Taylor the poet, influenced by the conceits of the metaphysical poets and writing for himself, developed ingenious and elaborate comparisons. In the following poems, notice the comparisons that Taylor develops and his purpose in each. Do you ever use comparisons to explain a difficult idea?

When figurative language is used to express abstract ideas through concrete images, it often adds to our understanding and appreciation of these ideas. Taylor uses figurative language in the poems you will read. List five abstract words, such as *love* and *sorrow*. Then brainstorm about concrete images that illustrate each of these ideas, and record each image beside the idea that it is intended to express.

Huswifery

Edward Taylor

Make me, O Lord, Thy spinning wheel complete.
    Thy holy word my distaff[1] make for me.
Make mine affections[2] Thy swift flyers[3] neat
    And make my soul Thy holy spoole to be.
5   My conversation make to be Thy reel
    And reel the yarn thereon spun of Thy wheel.

Make me Thy loom then, knit therein this twine:
    And make Thy holy spirit, Lord, wind quills:[4]

---

1. distaff *n.*: A staff on which flax or wool is wound
for use in spinning.
2. affections: Emotions.
3. flyers *n.*: The part of a spinning wheel which
twists fibers into yarn.
4. quills *n.*: A weaver's spindles or bobbins.

Then weave the web Thyself. The yarn is fine.
10   Thine ordinances[5] make my fulling mills.[6]
     Then dye the same in heavenly colors choice,
     All pinked[7] with varnished flowers of paradise.

     Then clothe therewith mine understanding, will,
        Affections, judgment, conscience, memory
15   My words, and actions, that their shine may fill
        My ways with glory and Thee glorify.
        Then mine apparel shall display before Ye
        That I am clothed in holy robes for glory.

_____
5. ordinances: Sacraments.
6. fulling mills _n._: Mills used for cleaning and
thickening cloth.
7. pinked: Decorated.

■ RESPONDING TO THE SELECTION

Your Response
1. Given the title, were you surprised by the content of this poem? Explain.
2. Do you think "Huswifery" is a poem or a prayer? Explain.

Recalling
3. To what is the speaker compared in the first two stanzas?

Interpreting
4. What does the poem suggest about the speaker's attitude toward God?
5. (a) What seems to be the poem's overall purpose? (b) How do the final two lines convey Taylor's belief that religious grace comes as a gift from God, rather than as a result of a person's efforts?

Applying
6. What process might Taylor have described if he had written the poem today?

■ ANALYZING LITERATURE

Noting Figurative Language and Conceits
   Figurative language is language that is not meant to be interpreted literally. To grasp the meaning of figurative language, you must examine the suggestions and associations it evokes. For example, the first line of "Huswifery"—"Make me, O Lord, Thy spinning wheel complete"—suggests that the speaker is asking to be made an instrument or agent of God.

   A **conceit** is an elaborate, often lengthy comparison between two startlingly different subjects. For example, in "Huswifery," Taylor creates an intricate, extended comparison between the making of cloth and the granting of God's grace.
1. What do each of the following lines from "Huswifery" suggest?
   a. "And make my soul Thy holy spoole to be."
   b. "That I am clothed in holy robes for glory."
2. Taylor believed that the granting of grace involved the transformation of a person from a flawed and imperfect state of being to a state of purity and perfection. How does Taylor's conceit express this belief?
3. What does Taylor's comparison of a common household task with the granting of grace suggest about his beliefs concerning the relationship between God and the earthly world?

Upon a Wasp Chilled with Cold

Edward Taylor

The bear[1] that breathes the northern blast
Did numb, torpedo-like,[2] a wasp
Whose stiffened limbs encramped, lay bathing
In Sol's[3] warm breath and shine as saving,
5 Which with her hands she chafes and stands
Rubbing her legs, shanks, thighs, and hands.
Her petty[4] toes, and fingers' ends
Nipped with this breath, she out extends
Unto the sun, in great desire
10 To warm her digits at that fire.
Doth hold her temples in this state
Where pulse doth beat, and head doth ache.
Doth turn, and stretch her body small,
Doth comb her velvet capital.[5]
15 As if her little brain pan were
A volume of choice precepts clear.
As if her satin jacket hot
Contained apothecary's shop[6]
Of Nature's receipts,[7] that prevails
20 To remedy all her sad ails,[8]
As if her velvet helmet high
Did turret[9] rationality.
She fans her wing up to the wind
As if her petticoat were lined,
25 With reason's fleece, and hoists sails
And humming flies in thankful gails
Unto her dun curled[10] palace hall
Her warm thanks offering for all.

---

1. The bear: The constellation of Ursa Major, commonly called the Big Dipper.
2. torpedo-like: Capable of producing a strong electrical charge.
3. Sol: Personification of the sun.
4. petty: Small.
5. capital: Head.
6. apothecary's shop: Shop where medicines are prepared and sold.
7. nature's receipts: Natural remedies.
8. ails: Ailments.
9. turret: Contain.
10. dun curled: Dark curved.

Lord clear my misted sight that I
30 May hence view thy divinity.
Some sparks whereof thou up dost hasp[11]
Within this little downy wasp
In whose small corporation[12] we
A school and a schoolmaster see
35 Where we may learn, and easily find
A nimble spirit bravely mind
Her work in every limb: and lace
It up neat with a vital grace,
Acting each part though ne'er so small
40 Here of this fustian[13] animal.
Till I enravished climb into
The godhead[14] on this lather do.
Where all my pipes inspired upraise
An heavenly music furred with praise.

---

11. hasp: Fasten.
12. corporation: Here, body.
13. fustian: Coarsely coated.
14. godhead: Paradise.

RESPONDING TO THE SELECTION

Your Response

1. In what aspect of nature do you see a higher power? Why?
2. What do you think can be learned from observing a wasp?

Recalling

3. (a) What human features does Taylor use in describing the wasp? (b) How does the wasp warm itself? (c) What does the wasp do after it has warmed itself?

Interpreting

4. In the first stanza, the speaker creates a comparison between the warming of the wasp and the granting of God's grace. (a) What does the manner in which the wasp is warmed suggest about Taylor's beliefs concerning the granting of God's grace? (b) To what can the actions of the wasp in lines 23–28 be compared?

Applying

5. In this poem, the wasp serves as an example for the speaker. List two other insects or animals you feel could serve as an example for humans, and explain what you think we could learn from them.

THINKING AND WRITING

Writing a Conceit

Think of two seemingly different processes that are in some way similar to each other. Then list the stages of each process and try to think of vivid images, or word pictures, to describe each stage. Write a poem in which you develop an extended conceit by directly comparing each of the corresponding stages of the two processes. Your poem does not need to have rhythm or a definite structure. When you revise, make sure that the comparison you are making is clear and that you have used vivid imagery in your descriptions.

JONATHAN EDWARDS

1703–1758

Though he also wrote extensively, Jonathan Edwards is remembered mainly as one of the most powerful and persuasive Puritan preachers of colonial New England.

Born in East Windsor, Connecticut, Edwards grew up in an atmosphere of devout Puritan discipline. As a young boy, he is said to have demonstrated his religious devotion by preaching sermons to his playmates from a makeshift pulpit he built behind his home. Edwards also displayed academic brilliance at an early age. By the time he was twelve, he had learned to speak Latin, Greek, and Hebrew and had written numerous philosophical and scientific essays. Edwards entered Yale at the age of thirteen and graduated four years later as the valedictorian of his class. Edwards went on to earn his master's degree in theology.

In 1727 Edwards became the assistant to his grandfather, Solomon Stoddard, who was the pastor of the church at Northampton, Massachusetts, one of the largest and wealthiest congregations in the Puritan world. Edwards became the church pastor two years later when his grandfather died, and he also began preaching as a visiting minister throughout New England. Strongly desiring a return to the simplicity and orthodoxy of the Puritan past, Edwards became one of the leaders of the Great Awakening, a religious revival that swept the colonies in the 1730's and 1740's.

The Great Awakening did not last long, however, and in 1750 Edwards was dismissed from his position after many members of his congregation had become displeased with his conservative beliefs. Edwards then moved to Stockbridge, Massachusetts, where he preached to the Native Americans and wrote a number of theological works. In 1757 Edwards became the president of the College of New Jersey (now Princeton University), but he died shortly after taking office.

Although in most of his sermons, books, and essays Edwards appeals to reason and logic, his highly emotional "fire and brimstone" sermon *Sinners in the Hands of an Angry God* is by far his most famous work. This sermon, which was delivered to a congregation in Enfield, Connecticut, in 1741, and is said to have caused listeners to rise from their seats in a state of hysteria, demonstrates Edwards's tremendous powers of persuasion and captures the religious fervor of the Great Awakening.

GUIDE FOR INTERPRETING

from Sinners in the Hands of an Angry God

Literary Forms

Persuasive Speeches. A persuasive speech attempts to convince listeners to think or act in a certain way. The effectiveness of a persuasive speech depends to a large extent on the audience's perception of the speaker, the speaker's consideration of the audience and setting, and the choice of persuasive techniques.

The Speaker's Qualifications. A speaker must establish his or her qualifications to speak on the subject. In many cases the speaker's reputation alone convinces an audience of his or her qualifications. In other cases the speaker must gain the audience's trust by displaying knowledge of the subject or presenting his or her credentials.

Audience. It is also important for the speaker to be aware of the audience he or she is addressing. The writer must take into account the backgrounds, ages, interests, and beliefs of the audience.

Occasion. The time and place at which a speech is presented will also affect its content. The speaker may include references to current events or examples that will appeal to current interests.

Technique. Finally, the speaker must decide which persuasive techniques will best serve his or her purpose. A speaker may choose to present a logical argument or may appeal to past traditions or to the audience's emotions or sense of reason, or he or she may use a variety of other techniques.

Focus

Some of the factors that determine the effectiveness of a television commercial are similar to the factors that determine the effectiveness of a persuasive speech. Brainstorm about television commercials that you consider effective. Then list them and jot down the reasons why you think each one is effective.

Primary Source

In *Jonathan Edwards, Pastor,* Patricia Tracy discusses how Edwards achieved the "terrifying effects" of his sermon:

"Although it conveys the reek of brimstone, the sermon does not say that God will hurl man into everlasting fires—on the contrary, doom will come from God's indifference . . . He holds man above the pit as by a spider's thread, and should He become weary of protecting worthless man, that abominable insect will *drop of his own weight.* Man's preservation lay in God's whim of mercy, and the terror of this message derived from the insecurity of being temporarily protected by an all-powerful being who had an infinite anger. (Was the control of such strong feelings something that Edwards's audience found difficult to understand or to trust?)"

from Sinners in the Hands of an Angry God

Jonathan Edwards

This is the case of every one of you that are out of Christ:[1] That world of misery, that lake of burning brimstone, is extended abroad under you. There is the dreadful pit of the glowing flames of the wrath of God; there is Hell's wide gaping mouth open; and you have nothing to stand upon, nor anything to take hold of; there is nothing between you and Hell but the air; it is only the power and mere pleasure of God that holds you up.

You probably are not sensible of this; you find you are kept out of Hell, but do not see the hand of God in it; but look at other things, as the good state of your bodily constitution, your care of your own life, and the means you use for your own preservation. But indeed these things are nothing; if God should withdraw his hand, they would avail no more to keep you from falling than the thin air to hold up a person that is suspended in it.

Your wickedness makes you as it were heavy as lead, and to tend downwards with great weight and pressure towards Hell; and if God should let you go, you would immediately sink and swiftly descend and plunge into the bottomless gulf, and your healthy constitution, and your own care and prudence, and best contrivance, and all your righteousness, would have no more influence to uphold you and keep you out of Hell, than a spider's web would have to stop a fallen rock. Were it not for the sovereign

pleasure of God, the earth would not bear you one moment . . . The world would spew you out, were it not for the sovereign hand of Him who hath subjected it in hope. There are black clouds of God's wrath now hanging directly over your heads, full of the dreadful storm, and big with thunder; and were it not for the restraining hand of God, it would immediately burst forth upon you. The sovereign pleasure of God, for the present, stays[2] his rough wind; otherwise it would come with fury, and your destruction would come like a whirlwind, and you would be like the chaff of the summer threshing floor.

The wrath of God is like great waters that are dammed for the present; they increase more and more, and rise higher and higher, till an outlet is given; and the longer the stream is stopped, the more rapid and mighty is its course, when once it is let loose. It is true, that judgment against your evil works has not been executed hitherto; the floods of God's vengeance have been withheld; but your guilt in the meantime is constantly increasing, and you are every day treasuring up more wrath; the waters are constantly rising, and waxing more and more mighty; and there is nothing but the mere pleasure of God, that holds the waters back, that are unwilling to be stopped, and press hard to go forward. If God should only withdraw his hand from the floodgate, it would immediately fly open, and the fiery floods of the fierceness and wrath of God,

---

1. out of Christ: Not in God's grace.

2. stays: Restrains.

would rush forth with inconceivable fury, and would come upon you with omnipotent power; and if your strength were ten thousand times greater than it is, yea, ten thousand times greater than the strength of the stoutest, sturdiest devil in Hell, it would be nothing to withstand or endure it.

The bow of God's wrath is bent, and the arrow made ready on the string, and justice bends the arrow at your heart, and strains the bow, and it is nothing but the mere pleasure of God, and that of an angry God, without any promise or obligation at all, that keeps the arrow one moment from being made drunk with your blood. Thus all you that never passed under a great change of heart, by the mighty power of the spirit of God upon your souls; all you that were never born again, and made new creatures, and raised from being dead in sin, to a state of new, and before altogether unexperienced light and life, are in the hands of an angry God. However you may have reformed your life in many things, and may have had religious affections, and may keep up a form of religion in your families and closets,[3] and in the house of God, it is nothing but His mere pleasure that keeps you from being this moment swallowed up in everlasting destruction. However unconvinced you may now be of the truth of what you hear, by and by you will be fully convinced of it.

Those that are gone from being in the like circumstances with you, see that it was so with them; for destruction came suddenly upon most of them; when they expected nothing of it, and while they were saying, peace and safety: now they see, that those things on which they depended for peace and safety, were nothing but thin air and empty shadows.

The God that holds you over the pit of Hell, much as one holds a spider, or some loathsome insect over the fire, abhors you, and is dreadfully provoked: his wrath towards you burns like fire; he looks upon you as worthy of nothing else, but to be cast

---

3. **closets** *n.*: Small, private rooms for meditation.

THE PURITAN
Frank E. Schoonover
Collection of the Brandywine River Museum

into the fire; he is of purer eyes than to bear to have you in his sight; you are ten thousand times more abominable in his eyes, than the most hateful venomous serpent is in ours. . . .

O sinner! Consider the fearful danger you are in: it is a great furnace of wrath, a wide and bottomless pit, full of the fire of wrath, that you are held over in the hand of that God, whose wrath is provoked and incensed as much against you, as against many of the damned in Hell. You hang by a slender thread, with the flames of divine wrath flashing about it, and ready every moment to singe it, and burn it asunder; and you have no interest in any mediator, and nothing to lay hold of to save yourself, noth-

from *Sinners in the Hands of an Angry God* 75

ing to keep off the flames of wrath, nothing of your own, nothing that you ever have done, nothing that you can do, to induce God to spare you one moment. . . .

When God beholds the ineffable extremity of your case, and sees your torment to be so vastly disproportioned to your strength, and sees how your poor soul is crushed, and sinks down, as it were, into an infinite gloom; he will have no compassion upon you, he will not forbear the executions of his wrath, or in the least lighten his hand; there shall be no moderation or mercy, nor will God then at all stay his rough wind; he will have no regard to your welfare, nor be at all careful lest you should suffer too much in any other sense, than only that you shall *not suffer beyond what strict justice requires.* . . .

God stands ready to pity you; this is a day of mercy; you may cry now with some encouragement of obtaining mercy. But once the day of mercy is past, your most lamentable and dolorous cries and shrieks will be in vain; you will be wholly lost and thrown away of God, as to any regard to your welfare. God will have no other use to put you to, but to suffer misery; you shall be continued in being to no other end; for you will be a vessel of wrath fitted to destruction; and there will be no other use of this vessel, but to be filled full of wrath. . . .

Thus it will be with you that are in an unconverted state, if you continue in it; the infinite might, and majesty, and terribleness of the omnipotent God shall be magnified upon you, in the ineffable strength of your torments. You shall be tormented in the presence of the holy angels, and in the presence of the Lamb,[4] and when you shall be in this state of suffering, the glorious inhabitants of Heaven shall go forth and look on the awful spectacle, that they may see what the wrath and fierceness of the Almighty is; and when they have seen it, they will fall down and adore that great power and majesty. . . .

---

4. the Lamb: Jesus.

It would be dreadful to suffer this fierceness and wrath of Almighty God one moment; but you must suffer it to all eternity. There will be no end to this exquisite horrible misery. When you look forward, you shall see a long forever, a boundless duration before you, which will swallow up your thoughts and amaze your soul; and you will absolutely despair of ever having any deliverance, any end, any mitigation, any rest at all. . . .

How dreadful is the state of those that are daily and hourly in the danger of this great wrath and infinite misery! But this is the dismal case of every soul in this congregation that has not been born again, however moral and strict, sober and religious, they may otherwise be. Oh that you would consider it, whether you be young or old! . . . Those of you that finally continue in a natural condition, that shall keep you out of Hell longest will be there in a little time! Your damnation does not slumber; it will come swiftly, and, in all probability, very suddenly upon many of you. You have reason to wonder that you are not already in Hell. It is doubtless the case of some whom you have seen and known, that never deserved Hell more than you, and that heretofore appeared as likely to have been now alive as you. Their case is past all hope; they are crying in extreme misery and perfect despair; but here you are in the land of the living and in the house of God, and have an opportunity to obtain salvation. What would not those poor damned hopeless souls give for one day's opportunity such as you now enjoy!

And now you have an extraordinary opportunity, a day wherein Christ has thrown the door of mercy wide open, and stands in calling and crying with a loud voice to poor sinners; a day wherein many are flocking to him, and pressing into the kingdom of God. Many are daily coming from the east, west, north and south; many that were very lately in the same miserable condition that you are in, are now in a happy state, with their hearts filled with love to him who has loved them, and washed them from their sins in his own blood, and rejoicing in hope of the glory of God. How awful is it to be left behind at such a day! To see so many others feasting, while you are pining and perishing! To see so many rejoicing and singing for joy of heart, while you have cause to mourn for sorrow of heart, and howl for vexation of spirit! . . .

Therefore, let everyone that is out of Christ, now awake and fly from the wrath to come. The wrath of Almighty God is now un-doubtedly hanging over a great part of this congregation: let everyone fly out of Sodom.[5] "Haste and escape for your lives, look not behind you, escape to the mountain, lest you be consumed."[6]

---

5. Sodom: In the Bible, a city destroyed by fire because of the sinfulness of its people.
6. "Haste . . . consumed": From Genesis 19:17, the angels' warning to the only virtuous man in Sodom, Lot, to flee the city before they destroy it.

RESPONDING TO THE SELECTION

Your Response

1. What images in this sermon do you find particularly striking? Why?
2. How do you think you would have reacted if you had heard Edwards deliver this sermon?

Recalling

3. According to the opening paragraph, what keeps sinners from falling into Hell?
4. Toward the end of the selection, what does Edwards say the sinners can obtain?

Interpreting

5. Why do you think Edwards begins his sermon with a vivid description of Hell?
6. (a) State two comparisons Edwards uses to describe God's wrath. (b) How do these comparisons add to the speech's impact?
7. (a) At what point is there a change in Edwards's tone and emphasis? (b) How is this change related to the purpose of the sermon?

Applying

8. Would the approach Edwards takes in this sermon be effective in today's society?

ANALYZING LITERATURE

Understanding Persuasive Speeches

A **persuasive speech** attempts to convince an audience to think or act in a certain way. For example, in this excerpt from *Sinners in the Hands of an Angry God,* Edwards tries to convince members of a church congregation who "are out of Christ" that they must dedicate their lives to God to escape eternal damnation. The effectiveness of Edwards's sermon depended to a large extent on the listeners' perception of him, his consideration of the audience and setting, and his choice of persuasive techniques.

1. Why would this sermon have been less effective if Edwards had not had a reputation as a brilliant spiritual leader?
2. In what ways does Edwards exhibit his understanding of the people he is addressing?
3. What emotion does Edwards appeal to? Considering Edwards's purpose, why is this an appropriate choice?
4. This sermon was delivered during the midst of the Great Awakening, a religious revival during which thousands of people converted to Puritanism. Toward the end of his sermon, how does Edwards draw on the occasion to support his argument?

THINKING AND WRITING

Evaluating Persuasive Techniques

Write an essay in which you explain why Edwards's choice of persuasive techniques was appropriate for his audience, setting, and purpose. Carefully reread Edwards's sermon, keeping in mind his audience, setting, and purpose, and taking note of the persuasive techniques he uses. Then take some time to think about the relationship between his choice of persuasive techniques and the other factors. After developing a thesis statement, write your essay, making sure that you include passages from the sermon to support your thesis.

GUIDE FOR INTERPRETING

from The Wonders of the Invisible World

Cotton Mather (1663–1728), a descendant of a prominent family of Puritan church leaders, was born in Boston. After receiving two degrees from Harvard College, Mather entered the ministry. He devoted his life to preaching and writing and produced more than four hundred books and pamphlets. His books include *Memorable Providences, Relating to Witchcraft and Possessions* (1689) and *The Wonders of the Invisible World* (1693), a report of the testimony at the Salem witchcraft trials.

Writers' Techniques

Style. Style refers to the manner in which a writer puts his or her thoughts into words. It involves the characteristics of a literary selection that concern form of expression—the choice and arrangement of words, the length and structure of sentences, the relationship between sentences and paragraphs, and the use of literary devices—rather than the ideas conveyed.

Cotton Mather's style is usually characterized by his use of ornate, elegant language and his frequent use of allusions—short references to literary works or figures, places, or events from history, religion, or mythology. In *The Wonders of the Invisible World,* however, Mather used a plain, direct, journalistic style. Mather's choice of words clearly indicates his biased point of view. Mather's purpose in writing the report was to justify the outcome of the trials, and he was careful to choose language that served this purpose.

Commentary

Cotton Mather felt that his generation was falling away from the original vision and purpose of the Puritan immigrants to North America. In the introduction to his account of the witchcraft trials, he reminds his readers that "New Englanders are a people of God settled in those, which were once the devil's territories." Now, warns Mather, the Devil is making a last, forceful attempt to drive them out.

Even though long interested in witchcraft as evidence of the Devil's work, Mather did not take part in the trials. Nor, however, did he speak out against them, even though he became skeptical of some of the evidence offered. In the following selection, notice how Mather's style indicates both his belief in witches and his skeptical attitude as a historian. Who do you think *could* have written the most objective account of the witchcraft trials?

Focus

What sort of impressions do you have of the Salem witchcraft trials? Freewrite about the witchcraft trials, describing the causes of the trials and the lessons we can learn from them.

from The Wonders of the Invisible World

Cotton Mather

The Trial of Martha Carrier at the Court of Oyer and Terminer,[1] Held by Adjournment at Salem, August 2, 1692

I. Martha Carrier was indicted for the bewitching of certain persons, according to the form usual in such cases, pleading not guilty to her indictment. There were first brought in a considerable number of the bewitched persons who not only made the court sensible[2] of an horrid witchcraft committed upon them, but also deposed that it

---

1. Court of Oyer and Terminer: A court authorized to hear (oyer) and determine (terminer) cases.

2. sensible: Aware.

was Martha Carrier, or her shape, that grievously tormented them by biting, pricking, pinching and choking of them. It was further deposed that while this Carrier was on her examination before the magistrates, the poor people were so tortured that everyone expected their death upon the very spot, but that upon the binding of Carrier they were eased. Moreover the look of Carrier then laid the afflicted people for dead; and her touch, if her eye at the same time were off them, raised them again; which things were also now seen upon her trial. And it was testified that upon the mention of some having their necks twisted almost round, by the shape of this Carrier, she replied, "It's no matter though their necks had been twisted quite off."

II. Before the trial of this prisoner several of her own children had frankly and fully confessed not only that they were witches themselves, but that this, their mother, had made them so. This confession they made with great shows of repentance and with much demonstration of truth. They related place, time, occasion; they gave an account of journeys, meetings, and mischiefs by them performed, and were very credible in what they said. Nevertheless, this evidence was not produced against the prisoner at the bar,[3] inasmuch as there was other evidence enough to proceed upon.

III. Benjamin Abbot gave his testimony that last March was a twelvemonth this Carrier was very angry with him upon laying out some land near her husband's. Her expressions in this anger were that she would stick as close to Abbot as the bark stuck to the tree, and that he should repent of it afore seven years came to an end, so as Doctor Prescot should never cure him. These words were heard by others besides Abbot himself, who also heard her say she would hold his nose as close to the grindstone as ever it was held since his name was Abbot. Presently af-

ter this, he was taken with a swelling in his foot, and then with a pain in his side, and exceedingly tormented. It bred into a sore, which was lanced by Doctor Prescot, and several gallons of corruption ran out of it. For six weeks it continued very bad, and then another sore bred in the groin, which was also lanced by Doctor Prescot. Another sore then bred in his groin, which was likewise cut, and put him to very great misery. He was brought unto death's door and so remained until Carrier was taken and carried away by the constable, from which very day he began to mend and so grew better every day and is well ever since.

Sarah Abbot also, his wife, testified that her husband was not only all this while afflicted in his body, but also that strange, extraordinary, and unaccountable calamities befell his cattle, their death being such as they could guess at no natural reason for.

IV. Allin Toothaker testified that Richard, the son of Martha Carrier, having some difference with him, pulled him down by the hair of the head. When he rose again he was going to strike at Richard Carrier but fell down flat on his back to the ground and had not power to stir hand or foot until he told Carrier he yielded, and then he saw the shape of Martha Carrier go off his breast.

This Toothaker had received a wound in the wars, and he now testified that Martha Carrier told him he should never be cured. Just afore the apprehending of Carrier, he could thrust a knitting needle into his wound four inches deep; but presently after her being seized, he was thoroughly healed.

He further testified that when Carrier and he sometimes were at variance she would clap her hands at him and say he should get nothing by it; whereupon he several times lost his cattle by strange deaths, whereof no natural causes could be given.

V. John Rogger also testified that upon the threatening words of this malicious Carrier his cattle would be strangely bewitched, as was more particularly then described.

---

3. bar: Court.

VI. Samuel Preston testified that about two years ago, having some difference with Martha Carrier, he lost a cow in a strange, preternatural, unusual manner; and about a month after this, the said Carrier, having again some difference with him, she told him he had lately lost a cow, and it should not be long before he lost another; which accordingly came to pass; for he had a thriving and well-kept cow which without any known cause quickly fell down and died.

VII. Phebe Chandler testified that about a fortnight before the apprehension of Martha Carrier, on a Lord's day while the psalm was singing in the Church, this Carrier then took her by the shoulder and, shaking her, asked her where she lived. She made her no answer, although as Carrier, who lived next door to her father's house, could not in reason but know who she was. Quickly after this, as she was at several times crossing the fields, she heard a voice that she took to be Martha Carrier's, and it seemed as if it was over her head. The voice told her she should within two or three days be poisoned. Accordingly, within such a little time, one half of her right hand became greatly swollen and very painful, as also part of her face, whereof she can give no account how it came. It continued very bad for some days, and several times since she has had a great pain in her breast and been so seized on her legs that she has hardly been able to go. She added that lately, going well to the house of God, Richard, the son of Martha Carrier, looked very earnestly upon her; and immediately her hand, which had formerly been poisoned, as is abovesaid, began to pain her greatly, and she had a strange burning at her stomach; but was then struck deaf so that she could not hear any of the prayer or singing till the two or three last words of the psalm.

VIII. One Foster, who confessed her own share in the witchcraft for which the prisoner stood indicted, affirmed that she had seen the prisoner at some of their witch meetings, and that it was this Carrier who persuaded her to be a witch. She confessed that the devil carried them on a pole to a witch meeting; but the pole broke, and she hanging about Carrier's neck, they both fell down, and she then received an hurt by the fall, whereof she was not at this very time recovered.

IX. One Lacy, who likewise confessed her share in this witchcraft, now testified that she and the prisoner were once bodily present at a witch meeting in Salem village, and that she knew the prisoner to be a witch and to have been at a diabolical sacrament, and that the prisoner was the undoing of her and her children by enticing them into the snare of the devil.

X. Another Lacy, who also confessed her share in this witchcraft, now testified that the prisoner was at the witch meeting in Salem village, where they had bread and wine administered unto them.

XI. In the time of this prisoner's trial, one Susanna Sheldon in open court had her hands unaccountably tied together with a wheel band[4] so fast that without cutting it it could not be loosed. It was done by a specter, and the sufferer affirmed it was the prisoner's.

Memorandum. This rampant hag, Martha Carrier, was the person of whom the confessions of the witches and of her own children among the rest agreed that the devil had promised her she should be queen of Hell.

---

4. wheel band: A band or strap that goes around a wooden wheel.

Commentary

Three hundred years later, the Salem witch hunt still fascinates and horrifies us. Though the trials and hangings in Salem ended in 1692, the urge to hunt "witches" has certainly not ended. However, the term *witch hunt* has taken on a new meaning. Today a witch hunt is a campaign taken on to uncover alleged disloyalty or subversive activity. In 1953 the American playwright Arthur Miller vividly dramatized the Salem trials in his play *The Crucible* (page 1034). Using historical records of the proceedings, Miller imagined the personal suffering of John and Elizabeth Proctor, both accused of witchcraft.

The play was written and produced during a modern witch hunt: the loyalty hearings of the House Un-American Activities Committee, led by Senator Joseph McCarthy. The hearings were to investigate suspected Communist activity in the federal government. Like the Salem judges, McCarthy used his authority to play on public fear and patriotism and caused many innocent people to be blacklisted, lose their jobs, or be sent to jail. Miller himself was called before the committee in 1956 and, like John Proctor, refused to testify against his colleagues.

RESPONDING TO THE SELECTION

Your Response

1. With whom does your sympathy lie, Martha Carrier or the "bewitched persons"? Why?
2. What do you think of Cotton Mather's account of the trials?
3. What do you think of Cotton Mather after reading his account?

Recalling

4. For what is Martha Carrier indicted?
5. Who is brought in to testify against her?
6. To what had Carrier's children confessed prior to the trial?
7. According to Benjamin Abbot's testimony, what happened to Abbot after Martha Carrier became angry with him?
8. (a) According to Phoebe Chandler's testimony, what did Martha Carrier do to Chandler "on a Lord's day"? (b) What happened "quickly after" this incident?
9. What information does Mather present in his "memorandum" at the end of the excerpt?

Interpreting

10. What detail in Abbot's description of his physical ailments is clearly exaggerated?
11. What does Chandler's testimony that she heard a voice above her head "that she took to be Martha Carrier's" imply about Carrier?

Applying

12. Do you think witnesses might have been likely to fabricate their testimony during the Salem witchcraft trials? Explain your answer.

ANALYZING LITERATURE

Recognizing a Writer's Style

Style refers to the way in which a writer expresses his or her thoughts. For example, in *The Wonders of the Invisible World,* Cotton Mather writes in a plain, direct, journalistic style.

1. How does Mather's style make his report of the trial seem like an objective, factual account?
2. Why would the report be less effective if it had been written in the elaborate, elegant style Mather used in his other works?

CRITICAL THINKING AND READING

Recognizing Author's Bias

Bias means "partiality" or "an inclination toward a certain position." Although Mather's report is supposedly an objective account of the trial, his choice of words makes it clear that in reality his report is written from a biased point of view. For example, his reference to Martha Carrier as a "rampant hag" clearly indicates his negative attitude toward her.

1. How does Mather's statement that "a number of bewitched persons" were brought in to testify against Carrier reveal his bias?
2. Find two other examples of language that clearly indicates Mather's bias.
3. Do you think it possible for a person to be completely free of bias? Explain your answer.

THINKING AND WRITING

Writing a Journal Entry

Write a journal entry in which you describe the trial of Martha Carrier from Carrier's point of view. Reread the selection, thinking about how Martha Carrier might have viewed the proceedings. Then write your journal entry, using a plain, journalistic style similar to Mather's. When you revise, make sure your entry is simple and clear.

LEARNING OPTION

Speaking and Listening. Now it can be told. Produce a television exposé to reveal the truth about the witchcraft hysteria in Salem Village in 1692. Do some research to find out what historians have to say. Recruit classmates to help you present your findings in a half-hour program. You might focus on the trial of Martha Carrier and include interviews with "descendants" of Salem citizens who testified against the woman Cotton Mather describes as a "rampant hag." Keep in mind that you want to both entertain and inform viewers.

YOUR WRITING PROCESS

WRITING A FLIER

"Hear ye! Hear ye! Opportunities in the New World!" Imagine that it is the seventeenth century and that you've been hired to write a one-page flier intended to entice Europeans to the North American colonies. What words and images will you use to persuade people to leave their homelands and to endure a long sea journey?

> **Focus**
> **Assignment:** Write a description of what life is like in colonial America for prospective colonists.
> **Purpose:** Persuade people to come to America.
> **Audience:** Seventeenth-century Europeans who may want to emigrate to America.

Prewriting

1. Skim the selections. As you look back at the selections in this unit, make a list of the passages you find most appealing. Put a star beside those that you think could be included in a flier.

2. Explore travel brochures with other writers. How do modern writers make places sound alluring to travelers? What kinds of writing techniques do they use? How and when do they use full sentences, phrases, and even single words? With a partner or small group, jot down some observations.

3. Think like your audience. Freewrite in the voice of a European who is thinking about coming to America. Then look for ways to appeal to the hopes and fears of such a person. For example, a European might think, "It's hard to earn a living here; sometimes I would just like to start all over somewhere new." You might attract this person to the New World by stressing the financial opportunities available in America and the lack of opportunities in Europe.

4. Organize your ideas. After deciding how to appeal to your audience, outline your arguments in an effective way. Will you begin by scaring your readers or by enticing them?

Drafting

1. Use strong language. Make your writing vivid by using specific nouns; lively, active verbs; and punchy, powerful adjectives. See how much emotional and persuasive mileage you can get out of your words, phrases, and sentences.

2. Use more than one tactic. How is the New World appealing physically? Financially? Emotionally? For adventurers? For romantics? For families? Use a variety of reasons to make your audience an offer they can't refuse.

> ### Student Model
>
> The New World offers vast and fertile farmland, lakes and rivers teeming with fish, and forests crowded with game—enough to feed your family and get rich, too! In addition, the New World offers scenes of spectacular beauty.

3. Choose a point of view that serves you best. Consider how the various points of view used in this unit affected you as a reader. A first-person point of view, for example, conveys a personal and individual appeal (as in William Byrd's journal). With the second-person point of view, you will directly address readers, asking them to imagine themselves in the place you describe (as in parts of Jonathan Edwards's sermon). By using a third-person point of view, you can make the New World seem accessible to anyone.

Revising and Editing

1. Delete what is weak. Try to be honest about which words, phrases, and sentences are strong and effective and which are not.

2. Have a peer editor read your draft aloud. Ears can often hear what eyes will miss: an awkward repetition, a clumsy phrase, an unnecessary sentence. After you and your peer editor listen to the draft, discuss both its strengths and its weaknesses.

3. Proofread for consistent tense and point of view. Notice how the following draft was improved when the writer eliminated inconsistencies in tense and point of view.

> ### Student Model
>
> The New World is a safe and free place to raise your children. The land ~~will be~~ *is* lovely and unspoiled, ~~Out my window I see~~ a playground of rolling green hills.

4. Use the buddy system to proofread. We're all better at spotting someone else's spelling, grammar, or mechanics errors than we are at finding our own. Remember that your goal is to have error-free final copy.

Writer's Hint
Mark Twain once admitted that he used adjectives only when he couldn't find the right noun. It's a good rule. For example, why use the standard adjective-noun combination *fast-paced life* when you can use the expressive noun *hustle*?

Options for Publishing
• Ask someone who is not in your class to read your description and to tell you what is most persuasive about it.
• Read your description aloud to your classmates.
• Combine your "copy" with a strong photograph or picture, creating a one-page flier for display on a bulletin board.
• Distribute your descriptions to a history class studying the colonial period; ask them which ones they consider most persuasive and why.

Reviewing Your Writing Process
1. How did you choose a point of view for your flier? Are you satisfied with your choice? Explain.
2. Did you listen to a peer editor read your draft aloud? If so, did this editing strategy help you identify awkward passages? Why or why not?

THE SIGNING OF THE CONSTITUTION, 1787
Howard Chandler Christy

THE REVOLUTIONARY PERIOD
1750–1800

Yesterday the greatest question was decided which ever was debated in America; and a greater perhaps never was, nor will be, decided among men. A resolution was passed without one dissenting colony, that these united colonies are, and of right ought to be, free and independent states.

John Adams

John Adams, who was to become the second President of the United States, wrote these sentences in a letter to his wife Abigail on the eve of the adoption of the Declaration of Independence. The momentous event of July 4, 1776, capped more than a decade of controversy between England and the American colonies. More than a decade of struggle to establish the new nation followed. During those years—indeed, during the entire second half of the eighteenth century— American literature was largely political. So dominant was the question of our relationship to England, and so talented and literate were the statesmen of the emerging nation, that some of the most notable writers of the period were the founders of the republic.

THE HISTORICAL SETTING

It is easy to forget how long the thirteen original states had been colonies. By 1750, there were fourth- and fifth-generation Americans of European descent living in Virginia and New England. These people were English subjects, and, on the whole, they were well satisfied with that status. Royal governors irritated them from time to time, but the colonial assemblies were locally elected and exercised considerable power, particularly over money. Year by year, decade by decade, Americans acquired experience in the art of self-government. As late as the early 1760's, however, few Americans had given much thought to the prospect of independence.

Between the mid-1760's and the mid-1770's, however, attitudes changed dramatically. King George III and Parliament imposed a number of unwise regulations that threatened the liberties of the colonists. With each succeeding measure, the outrage in America grew, finally erupting into war. As one Revolutionary veteran put it, "We always had governed ourselves, and we always meant to."

The Age of Reason

Great upheavals in history occur when circumstances are ripe. The American Revolution was such an upheaval, and the groundwork for it had been laid by European writers and thinkers as well as by the English king and Parliament. The eighteenth century is often characterized as the Age of Reason, or the Enlightenment. Spurred by the work of seventeenth-century scientists such as Galileo and Sir Isaac Newton, the writers and thinkers of the Enlightenment valued reason over faith. Unlike the Puritans, they had little interest in the hereafter, believing instead in the power of reason and science to further human progress. They spoke of a social contract that forms the basis of government. Above all, they believed that people are by nature good, not evil. A perfect society seemed to them to be more than just an idle dream.

Among the most influential figures of the Enlightenment were the French writer Voltaire, the French philosopher Jean Jacques Rousseau, the English political theorist John Locke, and the Scottish historian David Hume. Educated readers in the American colonies were familiar with the writings of these men.

The American statesmen of the Revolutionary period were themselves figures of the Enlightenment. No history of the period would be complete without mention of the thought and writings of Benjamin Franklin, Thomas Paine, and Thomas Jefferson. These Americans not only expressed the ideas of the Age of Reason, but they also helped to put them spectacularly into practice.

Toward a Clash of Arms

The American Revolution was preceded by the French and Indian War, a struggle between England and France for control of North America. The conflict broke out in the colonies in 1754 and continued for nearly a decade. British forces won the decisive battle of the war at the city of Quebec, Canada, in 1759. When the French and Indian War officially ended in 1763, France gave up its claims to North American territory. There was general jubilation in the thirteen English colonies.

The good feelings were short-lived, however. The British government, wanting to raise revenue in the colonies to pay its war debt, passed the Stamp Act in 1765. This was the first tax other than customs duties ever imposed on the colonists by

EMBOSSED TAX STAMP ISSUED BY THE
BRITISH GOVERNMENT IN 1765 FOR
USE IN THE AMERICAN COLONIES

Great Britain. The act required buying and affixing stamps to each of fifty-four kinds of items, including newspapers, playing cards, legal documents, licenses, and almanacs. Colonial reaction to the Stamp Act was swift and bitter. Stamps were burned. Stamp distributors were beaten and their shops destroyed. No blood was shed, but the hated stamps were withdrawn within six months, and the Stamp Act was repealed.

Other acts and reactions followed. The Townshend Acts of 1767 taxed paper, paint, glass, lead, and tea. When the colonists organized a boycott, the British dissolved the Massachusetts legislature and sent two regiments of British troops to Boston. In 1770, these Redcoats fired into a taunting mob, causing five fatalities. This so-called Boston Massacre further inflamed passions. Parliament repealed the Townshend duties except for the tax on tea, but a separate Tea Act soon greeted the colonists. The Tea Act gave an English company a virtual monopoly of the American tea trade. Furious, a group of Bostonians dressed as Mohawks dumped a shipment of tea into Boston harbor. As punishment for this Boston Tea Party, the English Parliament passed the Coercive Acts. Colonists immediately dubbed them the Intolerable Acts.

The situation had in fact become intolerable to both the colonists and the British. Colonial leaders, although not speaking openly of independence, met in Philadelphia for the First Continental Congress. The British, their authority slipping away, appointed General Thomas Gage governor of Massachusetts. The stage was set for war.

"The World Turned Upside Down"

On the night of April 18, 1775, General Gage sent a detail of about 700 British troops from Boston to destroy colonial munitions at Concord. The next morning, these troops met a drawn-up line of some seventy colonial Minutemen on the Lexington green. A musket shot was fired (from which side, no one knows), and the firing became widespread. Before it was over, eight Americans lay dead.

The British continued marching west to Concord, where another skirmish took place. Two more Americans fell, but so did three Redcoats. The British commander ordered a retreat to Boston. American snipers fired on the British troops all the way back, causing a total of 273 casualties.

The encounters at Lexington and Concord, a landmark in American history, have been referred to as "the shot heard round the world." The American revolution had begun, and there would be no turning back. In June, the Americans killed or wounded more than a thousand British soldiers at the Battle of Bunker Hill. Although all the fighting up to this point had taken place in Massachusetts, the revolt involved all the colonies. Two days before Bunker Hill, the Second Continental Congress, meeting in Philadelphia, had named a commander in chief of the official American army. He was George Washington of Virginia.

More than a year would pass before the colonies declared their independence. More than six years would pass before the war ended, although the Battle of Saratoga, in the fall of 1777, marked a turning point. At Saratoga, in upstate New York, the British were surrounded and forced to surrender more than 5,000 men. When news of this American victory reached Paris, the government of France formally recognized the independence of

The Revolutionary Period
(A.D. 1750 – A.D. 1800)

Benjamin Franklin
Conducts His
Experiment

Colonists
Protest
Stamp Act

Phillis
Wheatley

| 1750 | 1760 | 1770 |

AMERICAN EVENTS

- **Benjamin Franklin** conducts his kite and key experiment with lightning.
  - French and Indian War begins.
    - *Poor Richard's Almanack* sold to new owner after 25 years under **Benjamin Franklin.**

- France gives up claims to North American territory.
  - Stamp Act passed by British Parliament; colonists protest bitterly.
    - Townshend Acts impose new taxes, angering colonists further.
    - First American play, Thomas Godfrey's *The Prince of Parthia,* produced.

- **Benjamin Franklin** begins his *Autobiography.*
  - Parliament's Tea Act prompts Boston Tea Party.
- **Phillis Wheatley's** *Poems on Various Subjects* published in England.
  - First Continental Congress meets in Philadelphia.
    - **Patrick Henry** gives his "liberty or death" speech.
    - The American Revolution begins.
      - Second Continental Congress adopts Declaration of Independence.
        - France recognizes U.S. independence and signs treaty of alliance.

WORLD EVENTS

- England: Thomas Gray completes "Elegy Written in a Country Churchyard."
  - England: Samuel Johnson publishes *Dictionary of the English Language.*
    - England: Robert Clive defeats native army at Plassey, India.
      - France: Voltaire publishes *Candide,* satirizing optimism of Rousseau.

- France: Jean Jacques Rousseau states his political philosophy in *The Social Contract.*
  - Seven Years War ends.
    - Scotland: James Watt invents an improved steam engine.
      - England: Richard Arkwright invents a frame for spinning; helps bring about factory system.

- Germany: Goethe begins 50 years of work on the dramatic poem *Faust.*
- Germany: Ludwig von Beethoven is born.
  - Poland: First of three major partitions of Poland gives land to Russia, Prussia, and Austria.
  - England: Joseph Priestley discovers oxygen, named later by Lavoisier.
    - England: Captain James Cook becomes first European to see Hawaii.
      - South Africa: First of many Kaffir Wars between blacks and whites breaks out.

The British
Surrender at
Yorktown

Napoleon
Bonaparte

James Boswell

1780   **1790**   **1800**

- General Cornwallis surrenders British army to George Washington at Yorktown.
  - **Michel-Guillaume Jean de Crèvecoeur's** *Letters From an American Farmer* published in London.
    - Noah Webster's *Spelling Book* first appears; 60 million copies would be sold.
  - Revolutionary War ends.
    - Constitutional Convention meets in Philadelphia to draft Constitution.
      - George Washington elected first President of United States.

- Eli Whitney invents cotton gin.
  - University of North Carolina opens as America's first state university.

- **Thomas Jefferson**, principal author of Declaration of Independence, elected President.

- England: William Herschel discovers planet Uranus.
  - France: Jean-Pierre Blanchard makes first balloon crossing of English Channel.
    - Scotland: Robert Burns is widely acclaimed for his first book of poems.
    - Austria: Wolfgang Amadeus Mozart creates the comic opera *The Marriage of Figaro*.
      - France: Storming of Bastille in Paris sets off French Revolution.

- England: James Boswell publishes *The Life of Samuel Johnson*.
  - France: King Louis XVI and Marie Antoinette executed.
    - England: Edward Jenner develops smallpox vaccine.
      - England: William Wordsworth and Samuel Taylor Coleridge publish *Lyrical Ballads*.
        - Spain: Goya creates *Los Caprichos* etchings.
        - France: Napoleon Bonaparte comes to power in France.

- Germany: Ludwig von Beethoven composes *First Symphony*.

THE BATTLE OF LEXINGTON AT THE BEGINNING OF THE COMBAT
Line Engraving, 1832, by Amos Doolittle and John W. Barber

the United States. Soon afterward, France began to commit troops to aid the American cause.

The war finally came to an end at Yorktown, Virginia, on October 19, 1781. Aided by the French army and the French navy, General Washington bottled up the 8,000-man British force under General Cornwallis. Seeing that escape was impossible, Cornwallis surrendered. After the British regiments had stacked their arms, they marched back to camp between rows of American and French soldiers. The British bands played a number of tunes during this ceremony. One of them was an old English song that seemed appropriate to the American troops: "The World Turned Upside Down."

The New Nation

One of the most impressive aspects of the American Revolution is that its original aims were realized. The revolt did not end in a bloodbath, or a military dictatorship, or a regime worse than the one overthrown. Thomas Jefferson recognized the danger of this in 1776 when he warned that "should a bad government be instituted for us in the future, it had been as well to have accepted . . . the bad one offered to us from beyond the water. . . ."

The path to self-government was not always smooth. After the Revolution, the Articles of Confederation established a "league of friendship" among the new states. This arrangement did not work well, however. The federal Constitution that replaced the Articles required many compromises and was ratified only after a long fight. Even then, a Bill of Rights had to be added to placate those who feared the centralized power that the Constitution conferred.

The old revolutionaries, by and large, remained true to their principles and continued their public duties. George Washington became the nation's first President. John Adams, a signer of the Decla-

GEORGE WASHINGTON
ADDRESSING THE SECOND
CONTINENTAL CONGRESS
*Contemporary Colored
Line Engraving*

ration of Independence, succeeded him in that office. Then, in 1800, Americans elected as their President the brilliant statesman who had drafted the Declaration, one of the heroes of the Enlightenment, Thomas Jefferson.

LITERATURE IN A TIME OF CRISIS

Like the Puritans in New England, educated Americans in the Age of Reason did a great deal of writing. Unlike the private soul-searching of the Puritans, however, much of what was produced during the Revolutionary period was public writing. By the time of the War for Independence, nearly fifty newspapers had been established in the coastal cities. At the time of Washington's inauguration, there were nearly forty magazines. Almanacs were popular from Massachusetts to Georgia.

During this period, the mind of the nation was on politics. Journalists and printers provided a forum for the expression of ideas. After 1763, those ideas were increasingly focused on relations with

Great Britain and, more broadly, on the nature of government. The writing of permanent importance from the Revolutionary era is mostly political writing.

Politics as Literature

The public writing and speaking of American statesmen in two tumultuous decades, the 1770's and 1780's, helped to reshape not only the nation but also the world. James Otis of Massachusetts defended colonial rights vigorously in speeches and pamphlets. Otis, an eloquent speaker, is credited with giving Americans their rallying cry: "Taxation without representation is tyranny."

Another spellbinder was Patrick Henry, whose speech against the Stamp Act in the Virginia House of Burgesses brought cries of "Treason!" Ten years later, his electrifying speech to the Virginia Convention expressed the rising sentiment for independence.

One man was more influential than any other in swaying public opinion in favor of independence. He was Thomas Paine, and his pamphlet

PATRICK HENRY SPEAKING AGAINST THE STAMP ACT IN THE VIRGINIA HOUSE OF BURGESSES IN 1765
Colored Line Engraving, 19th Century

Common Sense, published in January 1776, created an immediate sensation. It swept the colonies, selling 100,000 copies in three months. George Washington praised its "sound doctrine and unanswerable reasoning," as did countless other readers. "Independence rolls in on us like a torrent," said John Adams, who set forth his own ideas in *Thoughts on Government,* published in 1776.

The Declaration of Independence was first drafted by Thomas Jefferson in June 1776. The finished document is largely his work, although a committee of five, including Benjamin Franklin, was involved in its creation. The Declaration, despite some exaggerated charges against King George III, is well reasoned and superbly written. It is one of the most influential political statements ever made.

Another document written by committee that has stood the test of time is the Constitution of the United States, drafted in 1787. The framers, whose new nation contained about four million people, hoped that the Constitution would last a genera-

tion. It still survives, amended many times, as the political foundation of a superpower of fifty states and nearly 230 million people. Not everyone in 1787 was pleased with the Constitution. Alexander Hamilton called it a "weak and worthless fabric," and Benjamin Franklin supported it only because "I expect no better."

The doubts of the framers were reflected in the controversy over ratification. Delaware ratified the Constitution within three months, thus becoming the first state in the Union. But the ratification of nine states was necessary before the document could go into effect. The last few states proved difficult. The contest between supporters and opponents was especially hard-fought in New York. Alexander Hamilton, whose opinion of the Constitution was none too high, nevertheless wanted to see it pass in his home state. With James Madison and John Jay, he wrote a series of essays that were first published as letters to three New York newspapers. These essays, collected as *The Federalist,* served their immediate purpose. New York ratified the Constitution by a vote of 30 to 27. Over time, they have also come to be recognized as authoritative statements on the principles of American government.

The Cultural Scene

While politics dominated the literature of the Revolutionary period, not every writer of note was a statesman. Verse appeared in most of the newspapers, and numerous broadside ballads were published. (A broadside is a single sheet of paper, printed on one or both sides, dealing with a current topic.) One of the most popular broadside ballads was called "The Dying Redcoat," supposedly written by a British sergeant mortally wounded in the Revolution. The sergeant in the ballad realizes too late that his sympathy lies with the American cause:

> Fight on, America's noble sons,
> Fear not Britannia's thundering guns:
> Maintain your cause from year to year,
> God's on your side, you need not fear.

One poet of the time whose works were more sophisticated than the broadside ballads was Philip Freneau, a 1771 graduate of Princeton. A journalist and newspaper editor by profession, Freneau wrote

TITLE PAGE OF VOLUME 1 OF *THE FEDERALIST*, NEW YORK, 1788

poetry throughout his life. A few of his poems, such as "The Wild Honeysuckle" and "The Indian Burying Ground," earned his reputation as America's earliest important lyric poet.

Two other poets of the day were Joel Barlow and Phillis Wheatley. Barlow, a 1778 Yale graduate, is best remembered for "The Hasty Pudding," a mock-heroic tribute to cornmeal mush. Phillis Wheatley, born in Africa and brought to Boston in early childhood as a slave, showed signs of literary genius. A collection of her poems was published in England while she was still a young woman.

One writer of the Revolutionary period recorded his impressions of everyday American life. He was Michel-Guillaume Jean de Crèvecoeur. Born of an aristocratic French family, Crèvecoeur became a soldier of fortune, a world traveler, and a farmer. For fifteen years he owned a plantation in Orange County, New York, and his impressions of life there were published in London in 1782 as *Letters from an American Farmer*.

Perhaps the best-known writing of the period outside the field of politics was done by Benjamin Franklin. His *Poor Richard's Almanack* became familiar to most households in the colonies. A states-man, printer, author, inventor, and scientist, Franklin was a true son of the Enlightenment. His *Autobiography,* covering only his early years, is regarded as one of the finest autobiographies in any language.

During this period, America began to establish a cultural identity of its own. Theaters were built from New York to Charleston. A number of new colleges were established after the war, especially in the South. Several outstanding painters were at work in the colonies and the young republic. Among them were John Singleton Copley, Gilbert Stuart, John Trumbull, and Charles Willson Peale. Patience Wright, famous in the colonies as a sculptor of wax portraits, moved to London before the war. While there, she acted as a Revolutionary spy. In music, William Billings produced *The New England Psalm-Singer* and a number of patriotic hymns. This was a turbulent time, a time of action, and its legacy was cultural as well as political.

American Literature at Daybreak

By the early 1800's, America could boast a small body of national literature. The Native Americans had contributed haunting poetry and legends through their oral traditions. The Puritans had written a number of powerful, inward-looking works. The statesmen of the Revolutionary period had produced political documents for the ages. A few poets and essayists had made a permanent mark on the literature of the young republic. There were, however, no American novels or plays of importance. The modern short story had yet to be invented.

The raw materials for a great national literature were at hand, waiting to be used. The nation stood on the threshold of a territorial and population explosion unique in the history of the world. It would take almost exactly a century to close the frontier on the vast and varied continent beyond the Appalachians. During that century, American literature would burst forth with a vitality that might have surprised even the farsighted founders of the nation. The colonial age ended with a narrow volume of memorable literature. The nineteenth century would close with a library of works that form a major part of America's literary heritage.

Quotations by Prominent Figures of the Period

Experience keeps a dear school, but fools will learn in
no other.
  Benjamin Franklin, *Poor Richard's Almanack*

We must all hang together, or assuredly we shall all hang
separately.
  Benjamin Franklin at signing of Declaration of Independence

Caesar had his Brutus: Charles the First his Cromwell; and
George the Third ["Treason!" cried the Speaker] *may profit
by their example.* If *this* be treason, make the most of it.
  Patrick Henry, Speech on the Stamp Act, Virginia House of Burgesses

He that would make his own liberty secure must guard even
his enemy from oppression.
  Thomas Paine, *Dissertation on First Principles of Government*

For bright Aurora now demands my song.
   Aurora, hail, and all the thousand dyes,
Which deck thy progress through the vaulted skies.
  Phillis Wheatley, "An Hymn to the Morning"

The tree of liberty must be refreshed from time to time with
the blood of patriots and tyrants.
  Thomas Jefferson, Letter to William Stevens Smith

It is not in the still calm of life, or the repose of a pacific
station, that great characters are formed. . . . All history
will convince you of this. . . . Great necessities call out
great virtues.
  Abigail Adams, Letter to her son, John Quincy Adams

What then is the American, this new man?
  Michel-Guillaume Jean de Crèvecoeur, *Letters from an American Farmer*

Thus briefly sketched the sacred RIGHTS OF MAN,
How inconsistent with the ROYAL PLAN!
  Philip Freneau, "On Mr. Paine's *Rights of Man*"

READING CRITICALLY

The Literature of 1750–1800

During the years from 1750 to 1800, almost all writing in America was influenced by the revolutionary spirit or the spirit of the new nation. Recognizing this spirit and the ideas of this period will enable you to better understand the purpose and techniques of the writers of the period.

HISTORICAL CONTEXT It was during these years that the American colonists reached the point where they were no longer able to tolerate British rule. The colonies united and took a stand against Britain. The Revolution was successful, and a proud and practical new nation emerged.

LITERARY MOVEMENTS This was the Age of Reason. Logic and discipline prevailed in the writing of the time. Because the attention of the nation was focused on the events surrounding the Revolution, the literature was mostly political. There was some personal writing such as poetry and letters, but most writing was public—pamphlets, speeches, and other documents—advocating and supporting a break with England.

WRITERS' TECHNIQUES Logical reasoning was the major technique used by the writers of this period. Public writing offered sound, clear arguments in support of the causes. Personal writing, too, showed the reasoning process.

BENJAMIN FRANKLIN

1706–1790

No other colonial American better embodied the promise of America than Benjamin Franklin. Through hard work, dedication, and ingenuity, Franklin was able to rise out of poverty to become a wealthy, famous, and influential person. Although he never received a formal education, Franklin made important contributions in a variety of fields, including literature, journalism, science, diplomacy, education, and philosophy.

Franklin was born in Boston, one of seventeen children. After leaving school at the age of ten, Franklin spent two years working for his father, before becoming an apprentice to his older brother, who was a printer. When he was seventeen, Franklin left Boston and traveled to Philadelphia, hoping to open his own print shop. Once he established himself as a printer, Franklin began producing a newspaper and an annual publication called *Poor Richard's Almanack,* which contained information, observations, and advice. The *Almanack,* which Franklin published from 1732 through 1757, was very popular and earned Franklin a reputation as a talented writer.

When Franklin was forty-two, he retired from the printing business to devote himself to science. Franklin proved to be as successful a scientist as he had been a printer. Over the course of his lifetime, he was responsible for inventing the lightning rod, bifocals, and a new type of stove; confirming the laws of electricity; and contributing to the scientific understanding of earthquakes and ocean currents.

In spite of his other contributions, Franklin probably is remembered by most as a statesman and diplomat. Franklin played an important role in drafting the Declaration of Independence, enlisting French support during the Revolutionary War, negotiating a peace treaty with Britain, and drafting the United States Constitution.

Franklin, the diplomat and inventor, became an international figure who "played with lightning and the French court." He spent several years in London and nine years in France near Paris. For the French court, the seventy-year-old Franklin played the role of the simple, noble rustic, wearing plain clothes and a frontiersman's fur hat. At the same time, he wrote and published satirical essays, witty "letters," and clever verses. The French idolized him, and he was much sought after as a brilliant storyteller and conversationalist. Franklin's sense of humor, clever wit, and knowledge of European and classical literature are evident in all he wrote.

Though it was never completed, Franklin's *Autobiography,* filled with his opinions and suggestions about self-discipline and moral perfection, provides not only a record of his achievements but also an understanding of his character.

GUIDE FOR INTERPRETING

from The Autobiography

Literary Forms

Autobiography. An autobiography is a person's account of his or her life. Generally written in the first person, with the author speaking as "I," autobiographies present life events as the writer views them. As a result, the author's portrayals are colored by his or her attitudes, thoughts, and feelings. Thus, they can provide unique insights into the beliefs and perceptions of the author.

People write autobiographies because they feel that their lives are interesting or important or can in some way serve as an example for others. The autobiography has been a popular literary form in America.

Commentary

Franklin wrote the first section of his *Autobiography* in 1771 at the age of sixty-five while vacationing in England. At the urging of friends, he wrote three more sections, the last shortly before his death, but only brought the account of his life to the years 1757–1759, before his diplomatic successes.

The first section is written as a letter to his son, William, then aged forty and Governor of New Jersey. Franklin begins by suggesting that William may be interested in how he rose from poverty to his current state of affluence. This "letter of fatherly advice" is a way for Franklin to tell his remarkable "rags to riches" story without seeming to flaunt his accomplishments.

One of the best known parts of the *Autobiography* is Franklin's description of his earnest attempts to improve himself. This "project for arriving at moral perfection" has sometimes been cited as an example of Franklin's perhaps simplistic faith in the perfectibility of man and the powers of human reason. Franklin, however, writing at the age of seventy-nine, seems to be smiling a little at his youthful vanities and enthusiasm. (In some ways, his methods are not much different from those recommended in popular self-improvement books of today.)

As you read the *Autobiography*, note how you feel about both the young and the older Franklin. Is the idea of "moral perfection" hopelessly old-fashioned, or have you ever thought of trying something similar? What virtues would you list?

Focus

What experiences would you choose to write about if you were preparing your own autobiography? List the experiences that you would be most likely to include.

from The Autobiography

Benjamin Franklin

My brother had in 1720 or '21, begun to print a newspaper. It was the second that appeared in America and was called the *New England Courant.* The only one before it was *the Boston News Letter.* I remember his being dissuaded by some of his friends from the undertaking, as not likely to succeed, one newspaper being in their judgment enough for America. At this time (1771) there are not less than five-and-twenty. He went on, however, with the undertaking, and after having worked in composing the types and printing off the sheets, I was employed to carry the papers through the streets to the customers. He had some ingenious men among his friends who amused themselves by writing little pieces for this paper, which gained it credit and made it more in demand, and these gentlemen often visited us. Hearing their conversations and their accounts of the approbation their papers were received with, I was excited to try my hand among them; but, being still a boy, and suspecting that my brother would object to printing anything of mine in his paper if he knew it to be mine, I contrived to disguise my hand, and writing an anonymous paper, I put it in at night under the door of the printing house. It was found in the morning and communicated to his writing friends when they called in as usual. They read it, commented on it in my hearing, and I had the exquisite pleasure of finding it met with their approbation, and that, in their different guesses at the author, none were named but men of some character among us for learning and ingenuity. I suppose now that I was rather lucky in my judges, and that per-

haps they were not really so very good ones as I then esteemed them.

Encouraged however by this, I wrote and conveyed in the same way to the press several more papers, which were equally approved; and I kept my secret till my small fund of sense for such performances was pretty well exhausted, and then I discovered[1] it, when I began to be considered a little more by my brother's acquaintance, and in a manner that did not quite please him, as he thought, probably with reason, that it tended to make me too vain. And perhaps this might be one occasion of the differences that we began to have about this time. Though a brother, he considered himself as my master, and me as his apprentice, and accordingly expected the same services from me as he would from another; while I thought he demeaned me too much in some he required of me, who from a brother expected more indulgence. Our disputes were often brought before our father, and I fancy I was either generally in the right or else a better pleader, because the judgment was generally in my favor. But my brother was passionate and had often beaten me, which I took extremely amiss; and, thinking my apprenticeship very tedious, I was continually wishing for some opportunity of shortening it, which at length offered in a manner unexpected.

One of the pieces in our newspaper, on some political point which I have now forgotten, gave offense to the assembly. He was taken up, censured and imprisoned for a

---

1. discovered: Revealed.

month, by the speaker's warrant, I suppose because he would not discover his author. I too was taken up and examined before the council; but though I did not give them any satisfaction, they contented themselves with admonishing me, and dismissed me, considering me perhaps as an apprentice who was bound to keep his master's secrets.

During my brother's confinement, which I resented a good deal, notwithstanding our private differences, I had the management of the paper; and I made bold to give our rulers some rubs in it, which my brother took very kindly, while others began to consider me in an unfavorable light, as a young genius that had a turn for libeling and satire. My brother's discharge was accompanied with an order of the House (a very odd one) "that James Franklin should no longer print the paper called the *New England Courant.*"

There was a consultation held in our printing house among his friends what he should do in this case. Some proposed to evade the order by changing the name of the paper; but my brother seeing inconveniences in that, it was finally concluded on as a better way to let it be printed for the future under the name of Benjamin Franklin. And to avoid the censure of the Assembly that might fall on him as still printing it by his apprentice, the contrivance was that my old indenture should be returned to me with a full discharge on the back of it, to be shown on occasion; but to secure to him the benefit of my service, I was to sign new indentures for the remainder of the term, which were to be kept private. A very flimsy scheme it was; however, it was immediately executed, and the paper went on accordingly under my name for several months.

At length a fresh difference arising between my brother and me, I took upon me to assert my freedom, presuming that he would not venture to produce the new indentures. It was not fair in me to take this advantage, and this I therefore reckon one of the first errata[2] of my life; but the unfairness of it

BIRTHPLACE OF FRANKLIN IN MILK STREET
J. H. Buffords
Metropolitan Museum of Art

weighed little with me when under the impressions of resentment for the blows his passion too often urged him to bestow upon me, though he was otherwise not an ill-natured man: perhaps I was too saucy and provoking.

When he found I would leave him, he took care to prevent my getting employment in any other printing house of the town by going round and speaking to every master, who accordingly refused to give me work. I then thought of going to New York as the nearest place where there was a printer; and I was the rather inclined to leave Boston when I reflected that I had already made myself a little obnoxious to the governing party, and, from the arbitrary proceedings of the Assembly in my brother's case, it was likely I might if I stayed soon bring myself into scrapes. I determined on the point, but my

---

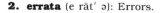

2. errata (e rät′ ə): Errors.

father now siding with my brother, I was sensible that if I attempted to go openly, means would be used to prevent me. My friend Collins, therefore, undertook to manage a little for me. He agreed with the captain of a New York sloop for my passage. So I sold some of my books to raise a little money, was taken on board privately, and as we had a fair wind, in three days I found myself in New York near three hundred miles from home, a boy of but seventeen, without the least recommendation to, or knowledge of, any person in the place, and with very little money in my pocket.

My inclinations for the sea were by this time worn out, or I might now have gratified them. But, having a trade, and supposing myself a pretty good workman, I offered my service to the printer in the place, old Mr. William Bradford, who had been the first printer in Pennsylvania, but removed from thence upon the quarrel of George Keith. He could give me no employment, having little to do and help enough already; but, says he, "My son at Philadelphia has lately lost his principal hand, Aquila Rose, by death. If you go thither I believe he may employ you." Philadelphia was one hundred miles farther. I set out, however, in a boat for Amboy,[3] leaving my chest and things to follow me round by sea. In crossing the bay we met with a squall that tore our rotten sails to pieces, prevented our getting into the kill,[4] and drove us upon Long Island. . . .

When we drew near the island, we found it was at a place where there could be no landing, there being a great surf on the stony beach. So we dropped anchor and swung round towards the shore. Some people came down to the water edge and hallowed[5] to us, as we did to them. But the wind was so high and the surf so loud, that we could not hear so as to understand each other. There were canoes on the shore, and we made signs and hallowed that they should fetch us, but they either did not understand us, or thought it impracticable. So they went away, and night coming on, we had no remedy but to wait till the wind should abate; and in the meantime the boatman and I concluded to sleep if we could, and so crowded into the scuttle,[6] and the spray beating over the head of our boat, leaked through to us. In this manner we lay all night with very little rest. But the wind abating the next day, we made a shift to reach Amboy before night, having been thirty hours on the water without victuals or any drink but a bottle of filthy rum, the water we sailed on being salt.

In the evening I found myself very feverish, and went in to bed. But having read somewhere that cold water drank plentifully was good for a fever, I followed the prescription, sweat plentifully most of the Night; my Fever left me, and in the morning crossing the ferry, I proceeded on my journey, on foot, having fifty miles to Burlington, where I was told I should find boats that would carry me the rest of the way to Philadelphia.

It rained very hard all day, I was thoroughly soaked, and by noon a good deal tired; so I stopped at a poor inn where I stayed all night, beginning now to wish I had never left home. I cut so miserable a figure, too, that I found by the questions asked me I was suspected to be some runaway servant, and in danger of being taken up on that suspicion. However I proceeded the next day and got in the evening to an inn within eight to ten miles of Burlington, kept by one Dr. Brown.

He entered into conversation with me while I took some refreshment, and finding I had read a little, became very sociable and friendly. Our acquaintance continued as long as he lived. . . .

At his house I lay that night, and the next morning reached Burlington, but had

---

3. **Amboy:** A town on the New Jersey coast.
4. **kill** *n*.: Channel.
5. **hallooed:** Called.

6. **scuttle** *n*.: A small, covered opening or hatchway in the outer hull or deck of a ship.

the mortification to find that the regular boats were gone a little before my coming and no other expected to go till Tuesday, this being Saturday. Wherefore I returned to an old woman in the town of whom I had bought gingerbread to eat on the water and asked her advice. She invited me to lodge at her house till a passage by water should offer, and, being tired with my foot traveling, I accepted the invitation. She, understanding I was a printer, would have had me stay at that town and follow my business, being ignorant of the stock necessary to begin with. She was very hospitable, gave me a dinner of oxcheek with great good will, accepting only a pot of ale in return; and I thought myself fixed till Tuesday should come. However, walking in the evening by the side of the river, a boat came by, which I found was going towards Philadelphia with several people in her. They took me in, and as there was no wind, we rowed all the way; and about midnight not having yet seen the city, some of the company were confident we must have passed it, and would row no farther; the others knew not where we were; so we put towards the shore, got into a creek, landed near an old fence, with the rails of which we made a fire, the night being cold in October, and there we remained till daylight. Then one of the company knew the place to be Cooper's Creek, a little above Philadelpia, which we saw as soon as we got out of the creek, and arrived there about eight or nine o'clock on the Sunday morning, and landed at the Market Street Wharf.

I have been the more particular in this description of my journey, and shall be so of

DELAWARE RIVER FRONT, PHILADELPHIA
Thomas Birch
Museum of Fine Arts, Boston

my first entry into that city, that you may in your mind compare such unlikely beginnings with the figure I have since made there. I was in my working dress, my best clothes being to come round by sea. I was dirty from my journey; my pockets were stuffed out with shirts and stockings; I knew no soul, nor where to look for lodging. I was fatigued with traveling, rowing, and want of rest; I was very hungry; and my whole stock of cash consisted of a Dutch dollar and about a shilling in copper. The latter I gave the people of the boat for my passage, who at first refused it, on account of my rowing; but I insisted on their taking it, a man being sometimes more generous when he has but a little money than when he has plenty, perhaps through fear of being thought to have but little.

Then I walked up the street, gazing about, till near the markethouse I met a boy with bread. I had made many a meal on bread, and inquiring where he got it, I went immediately to the baker's he directed me to in Second Street, and asked for biscuit, intending such as we had in Boston; but they, it seems, were not made in Philadelphia. Then I asked for a threepenny loaf and was told they had none such. So, not considering or knowing the difference of money and the greater cheapness nor the names of his bread, I bade him give me threepenny worth of any sort. He gave me, accordingly, three great puffy rolls. I was surprised at the quantity, but took it, and, having no room in my pockets, walked off with a roll under each arm and eating the other. Thus I went up Market Street as far as Fourth Street, passing by the door of Mr. Read, my future wife's father; when she, standing at the door, saw me and thought I made, as I certainly did, a most awkward, ridiculous appearance. Then I turned and went down Chestnut Street and part of Walnut Street, eating my roll all the way, and, coming round, found myself again at Market Street Wharf, near the boat I came in, to which I went for a draft of the river water; and, being filled with one of my rolls,

gave the other two to a woman and her child that came down the river in the boat with us and were waiting to go farther.

Thus refreshed, I walked again up the street, which by this time had many clean-dressed people in it, who were all walking the same way. I joined them, and thereby was led into the great meetinghouse of the Quakers near the market. I sat down among them, and, after looking round awhile and hearing nothing said, being very drowsy through labor and want of rest the preceding night, I fell fast asleep, and continued so till the meeting broke up, when one was kind enough to rouse me. This was therefore the first house I was in, or slept in, in Philadelphia.

The following excerpt relates events that occurred several years later.

It was about this time I conceived the bold and arduous project of arriving at moral perfection. I wished to live without committing any fault at any time; I would conquer all that either natural inclination, custom, or company might lead me into. As I knew, or thought I knew, what was right and wrong, I did not see why I might not always do the one and avoid the other. But I soon found I had undertaken a task of more difficulty than I had imagined. While my care was employed in guarding against one fault, I was often surprised by another; habit took the advantage of inattention; inclination was sometimes too strong for reason. I concluded, at length, that the mere speculative conviction that it was our interest to be completely virtuous was not sufficient to prevent our slipping; and that the contrary habits must be broken, and good ones acquired and established, before we can have any dependence on a steady, uniform rectitude of conduct. For this purpose I therefore contrived the following method.

In the various enumerations of the moral virtues I had met with in my reading, I found the catalog more or less numerous, as dif-

QUAKER MEETING
British, fourth quarter 18th century or first quarter 19th century
Museum of Fine Arts, Boston

ferent writers included more or fewer ideas under the same name. Temperance, for example, was by some confined to eating and drinking, while by others it was extended to mean the moderating every other pleasure, appetite, inclination, or passion, bodily or mental, even to our avarice and ambition. I proposed to myself, for the sake of clearness, to use rather more names, with fewer ideas annexed to each, than a few names with more ideas; and I included under thirteen names of virtues all that at that time oc-

curred to me as necessary or desirable, and annexed to each a short precept, which fully expressed the extent I gave to its meaning.

These names of virtues, with their precepts, were:

1. TEMPERANCE Eat not to dullness; drink not to elevation.

2. SILENCE Speak not but what may benefit others or yourself; avoid trifling conversation.

3. ORDER Let all your things have their places; let each part of your business have its time.

4. RESOLUTION Resolve to perform what you ought; perform without fail what you resolve.

5. FRUGALITY Make no expense but to do good to others or yourself; *i.e.,* waste nothing.

6. INDUSTRY Lose no time; be always employed in something useful; cut off all unnecessary actions.

7. SINCERITY Use no hurtful deceit; think innocently and justly, and, if you speak, speak accordingly.

8. JUSTICE Wrong none by doing injuries, or omitting the benefits that are your duty.

9. MODERATION Avoid extremes; forebear resenting injuries so much as you think they deserve.

10. CLEANLINESS Tolerate no uncleanliness in body, clothes, or habitation.

11. TRANQUILLITY Be not disturbed at trifles, or at accidents common or unavoidable.

12. CHASTITY

13. HUMILITY Imitate Jesus and Socrates.[7]

My intention being to acquire the *habitude* of all these virtues, I judged it would be well not to distract my attention by attempting the whole at once but to fix it on one of them at a time; and, when I should be master of that, then to proceed to another, and so on, till I should have gone through the thirteen; and, as the previous acquisition of some might facilitate the acquisition of certain others, I arranged them with that view,

as they stand above. *Temperance* first, as it tends to procure that coolness and clearness of head, which is so necessary where constant vigilance was to be kept up, and guard maintained against the unremitting attraction of ancient habits and the force of perpetual temptations. This being acquired and established, *Silence* would be more easy; and my desire being to gain knowledge at the same time that I improved in virtue, and considering that in conversation it was obtained rather by the use of the ears than of the tongue, and therefore wishing to break a habit I was getting into of prattling, punning, and joking, which only made me acceptable to trifling company, I gave *Silence* the second place. This and the next, *Order,* I expected would allow me more time for attending to my project and my studies. *Resolution,* once become habitual, would keep me firm in my endeavors to obtain all the subsequent virtues; *Frugality* and *Industry* freeing me from my remaining debt and producing affluence and independence, would make more easy the practice of *Sincerity* and *Justice,* etc., etc. Conceiving then, that, agreeably to the advice of Pythagoras[8] in his *Golden Verses,* daily examination would be necessary, I contrived the following method for conducting that examination.

I made a little book, in which I allotted a page for each of the virtues. I ruled each page with red ink, so as to have seven columns, one for each day of the week, marking each column with a letter for the day. I crossed these columns with thirteen red lines, marking the beginning of each line with the first letter of one of the virtues, on which line and in its proper column I might mark, by a little black spot, every fault I found upon examination to have been committed respecting that virtue upon that day.

I determined to give a week's strict attention to each of the virtues successively.

7. **Socrates** (säk′ rə tēz′): Ancient Greek philosopher and teacher (470?–399 B.C.).

8. **Pythagoras** (pi thag′ ər əs): An ancient Greek philosopher and mathematician who lived in the sixth century B.C.

Thus, in the first week, my great guard was to avoid every[9] the least offense against *Temperance*, leaving the other virtues to their ordinary chance, only marking every evening the faults of the day. Thus, if in the first week I could keep my first line, marked *T*, clear of spots, I supposed the habit of that virtue so much strengthened, and its opposite weakened, that I might venture extending my attention to include the next, and for the following week keep both lines clear of spots. Proceeding thus to the last, I could go through a course complete in thirteen weeks, and four courses in a year. And like him who, having a garden to weed, does not attempt to eradicate all the bad herbs at once, which would exceed his reach and his strength, but works on one of the beds at a time, and, having accomplished the first, proceeds to a second, so I should have, I hoped, the encouraging pleasure of seeing on my pages the progress I made in virtue, by clearing successively my lines of their spots, till in the end, by a number of courses, I should be happy in viewing a clean book, after a thirteen weeks' daily examination . . .

The precept of *Order* requiring that *every part of my business should have its allotted time*, one page in my little book contained the following scheme of employment for the twenty-four hours of a natural day.

THE MORNING. *Question.* What good shall I do this day?	5 6	Rise, wash, and address *Powerful Goodness!* Contrive day's business, and take the resolution of the
	7	day; prosecute the present study, and breakfast.
	8 9 10 11	Work.
NOON.	12 1	Read, or overlook my accounts, and dine.
	2 3 4 5	Work.
EVENING. *Question.* What good have I done today?	6 7 8 9	Put things in their places. Supper. Music or diversion, or conversation. Examination of the day.
	10 11 12	
NIGHT.	1 2 3 4	Sleep.

---

9. every: Even.

I entered upon the execution of this plan for self-examination, and continued it with occasional intermissions for some time. I was surprised to find myself so much fuller of faults than I had imagined; but I had the satisfaction of seeing them diminish. To avoid the trouble of renewing now and then my little book, which, by scraping out the marks on the paper of old faults to make room for new ones in a new course, became full of holes, I transferred my tables and precepts to the ivory leaves of a memorandum book, on which the lines were drawn with red ink that made a durable stain, and on those lines I marked my faults with a black-lead pencil, which marks I could easily wipe out with a wet sponge. After a while I went through one course only in a year, and afterward only one in several years, till at length I omitted them entirely, being employed in voyages and business abroad, with a multiplicity of affairs that interfered; but I always carried my little book with me.

My scheme of *Order* gave me the most trouble; and I found that, though it might be practicable where a man's business was such as to leave him the disposition of his time, that of a journeyman printer, for instance, it was not possible to be exactly observed by a master, who must mix with the world and often receive people of business at their own hours. *Order*, too, with regard to places for things, papers, etc., I found extremely difficult to acquire. I had not been early accustomed to it, and, having an exceeding good memory, I was not so sensible of the inconvenience attending want of method. This article, therefore, cost me so much painful attention, and my faults in it vexed me so much, and I made so little progress in amendment, and had such frequent relapses, that I was almost ready to give up the attempt, and content myself with a faulty character in that respect, like the man who, in buying an ax of a smith, my neighbor, desired to have the whole of its surface as bright as the edge. The smith consented to grind it bright for him if he would turn the wheel; he turned, while the smith pressed the broad face of the ax hard and heavily on the stone, which made the turning of it very fatiguing. The man came every now and then from the wheel to see how the work went on, and at length would take his ax as it was, without farther grinding. "No," said the smith, "turn on, turn on; we shall have it bright by and by; as yet, it is only speckled." "Yes," says the man, *"but I think I like a speckled ax best."* And I believe this may have been the case with many, who, having, for want of some such means as I employed, found the difficulty of obtaining good and breaking bad habits in other points of vice and virtue, have given up the struggle, and concluded that *"a speckled ax was best"*; for something, that pretended to be reason, was every now and then suggesting to me that such extreme nicety as I exacted of myself might be a kind of foppery in morals, which, if it were known, would make me ridiculous; that a perfect character might be

attended with the inconvenience of being envied and hated; and that a benevolent man should allow a few faults in himself, to keep his friends in countenance.

In truth, I found myself incorrigible with respect to *Order;* and now I am grown old, and my memory bad, I feel very sensibly the want of it. But, on the whole, though I never arrived at the perfection I had been so ambitious of obtaining, but fell far short of it, yet I was, by the endeavor, a better and a happier man than I otherwise should have been if I had not attempted it; as those who aim at perfect writing by imitating the engraved copies, though they never reached the wished-for excellence of those copies, their hand is mended by the endeavor, and is tolerable while it continues fair and legible.

It may be well my posterity should be informed that to this little artifice, with the blessing of God, their ancestor owed the constant felicity of his life, down to his seventy-ninth year in which this is written. What reverses may attend the remainder is in the hand of Providence; but, if they arrive, the reflection on past happiness enjoyed ought to help his bearing them with more resignation. To *Temperance* he ascribes his long-continued health, and what is still left to him of a good constitution; to *Industry* and *Frugality*, the early easiness of his circumstances and acquisition of his fortune, with all that knowledge that enabled him to be a useful citizen, and obtained for him some degree of reputation among the learned; to *Sincerity* and *Justice*, the confidence of his country, and the honorable employs it conferred upon him; and to the joint influence of the whole mass of the virtues, even in the imperfect state he was able to acquire them, all that evenness of temper, and that cheerfulness in conversation, which makes his company still sought for, and agreeable even to his younger acquaintance. I hope, therefore, that some of my descendants may follow the example and reap the benefit.

RESPONDING TO THE SELECTION

Your Response

1. What do you think of Benjamin Franklin's behavior toward his brother? Explain your reaction.
2. What is your opinion of Franklin's plan for moral perfection? Can you imagine ever undertaking a similar plan?

Recalling

3. Why does Franklin choose not to sign the first papers he submits for publication?
4. (a) Why does Franklin leave Boston? (b) How old is Franklin when he leaves?
5. What is Franklin's condition when he arrives in Philadelphia?
6. (a) What thirteen virtues does Franklin feel are necessary for moral perfection? (b) How successful is Franklin in carrying out his plan?

Interpreting

7. (a) What characteristics does Franklin display in his dealings with his brother? (b) What qualities does he display during his trip to Philadelphia?
8. (a) What does Franklin's plan for moral perfection reveal about him? (b) Why is it surprising that the virtue of order gives him the most trouble?
9. (a) Find five examples of self-analysis in the selection. (b) How does Franklin's character change as he grows older?

Applying

10. How can analyzing behavior contribute to personal growth?

ANALYZING LITERATURE

Understanding an Autobiography

An **autobiography** is the story of a person's life written by that person. Because the author's attitudes, thoughts, and feelings color the self-portrayal as well as the portrayal of other people and events, the autobiography is subjective. How-

ever, for this same reason, autobiographies often provide insights into the beliefs and perceptions of the author. For example, Franklin's sense of morality is revealed in the excerpt from his *Autobiography.*

1. What impression does Franklin convey of himself as a young man?
2. How might the account of Franklin's early years be different if it had been written by his brother or his father?

CRITICAL THINKING AND READING

Making Inferences About the Author

Because an autobiographical account is colored by the author's viewpoint, you can make **inferences,** or draw conclusions, about the author's personality by examining the manner in which the self, other people, and events are portrayed. For example, one of the inferences that you might make from Franklin's portrayal of himself is that he was a very proud man.

1. What inference can you make about Franklin from his portrayal of his brother? Explain the evidence that supports your inferences.
2. What inference can you make about Franklin from his description of his journey to Philadelphia? Explain the evidence that supports your inference.

THINKING AND WRITING

Writing an Autobiographical Account

Examine the list of experiences you wrote before reading this selection. Decide which one you think others would find most interesting. Outline the events that led up to the experience, and think about what it taught you. Then write an autobiographical account, relating events in chronological order and including descriptive details that will help bring the experience to life for your readers. When you finish writing, revise your account and prepare a final copy.

GUIDE FOR INTERPRETING

from Poor Richard's Almanack

Literary Forms

Aphorisms. An aphorism is a short, concise statement expressing a wise or clever observation or a general truth. A variety of devices make aphorisms easy to remember. Some aphorisms contain rhymes or repeated words or sounds; others contain two phrases that use the same grammatical structure to present contrasting ideas. For example, the contemporary aphorism "when the going gets tough, the tough get going" contains repeated words and contrasting ideas.

Most of Benjamin Franklin's aphorisms are adapted from proverbs, or anonymous traditional sayings. Franklin, who believed that clarity and brevity were two of the most important characteristics of good prose, rewrote the traditional sayings, making them short, direct, and witty.

Franklin put an aphorism at the top or bottom of most pages in his almanacs. The aphorisms allowed Franklin to include many moral messages in very little space. Because readers found them entertaining, Franklin's aphorisms contributed to the popularity of *Poor Richard's Almanack.*

Focus

People often use aphorisms or proverbs in everyday speech. What sayings do you use or hear others use? Brainstorm for such sayings, and list as many as you can.

Primary Source

In the almanac of 1758, Richard Saunders, the author/editor created by Franklin and called Poor Richard, claims to overhear a speech made by white-haired Father Abraham to a crowd in front of a store. This speech is made up of most of Poor Richard's aphorisms on prudence and hard work. It was published separately as "The Way to Wealth" and was a tremendous success. By the end of the eighteenth century alone, it was reprinted at least 145 times in seven different languages.

What is Father Abraham's advice? Father Abraham says "plough deep, while Sluggards sleep, and you shall have Corn to sell and to keep . . . If you would have your Business done, go; if not, send . . . And now to conclude, Experience keeps a dear School, but Fools will learn in no other, and scarce in that; for it is true, we may give Advice, but we cannot give Conduct . . . However, remember this, They that won't be counselled, can't be helped, as Poor Richard says: And farther, that if you will not hear Reason, she'll rap your Knuckles."

Poor Richard then comments, "The People heard it, and approved the Doctrine, and immediately practiced the contrary, just as if it had been a common Sermon."

from Poor Richard's Almanack

Benjamin Franklin

Hunger is the best pickle.

He that lives upon hope will die fasting.

Fish and visitors smell in three days.

Keep thy shop, and thy shop will keep thee.

If your head is wax, don't walk in the sun.

Necessity never made a good bargain.

Love your neighbor; yet don't pull down your hedge.

A slip of the foot you may soon recover, but a slip of the tongue you may never get over.

Early to bed, early to rise, makes a man healthy, wealthy, and wise.

God helps them that help themselves.

Three may keep a secret if two of them are dead.

Fools make feasts, and wise men eat them.

God heals and the doctor takes the fee.

The rotten apple spoils his companions.

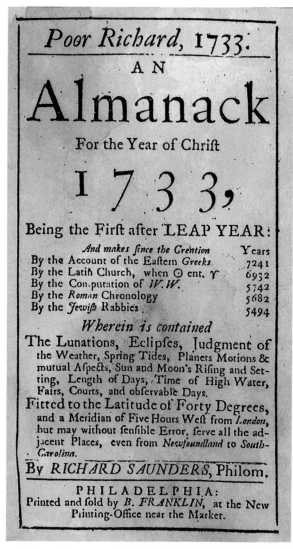

POOR RICHARD'S ALMANACK

If you would know the value of money,
try to borrow some.

A small leak will sink a great ship.

Drive thy business; let it not drive thee.

Dost thou love life? Then do not
squander time; for that's the stuff life
is made of.

Genius without education is like silver
in the mine.

The cat in gloves catches no mice.

RESPONDING TO THE SELECTION

Your Response

1. If Benjamin Franklin were a guest on a talk show today, would you be sure to tune in? Why or why not?
2. Based on his works, do you admire Franklin? Do you like him? Explain your response.

Interpreting

3. In what way are the ninth and eighteenth aphorisms related to each other?
4. How are the fourteenth and sixteenth aphorisms related?
5. Which aphorisms express Franklin's belief in the need for self-discipline and self-motivation? Explain why.

Applying

6. Which aphorisms would Franklin apply to business? Which to education? Explain your answers.

ANALYZING LITERATURE

Recognizing Aphorisms

Aphorisms are brief statements expressing wise observations or general truths. A variety of techniques, such as rhymes or repeated words or sounds, are used to make aphorisms easy to remember. For example, in his aphorism "Keep thy shop, and thy shop will keep thee," Franklin uses word repetition to make his saying memorable.

1. Identify Franklin's techniques in each of the following aphorisms, and list them. Then state the meaning of each aphorism, and explain why the aphorisms have more of an impact than the simple statements of their meaning.
   a. "A slip of the foot you may soon recover, but a slip of the tongue you may never get over."
   b. "Early to bed and early to rise, makes a man healthy, wealthy, and wise."
   c. "Fools make feasts, and wise men eat them."
2. Using Franklin's techniques, write three aphorisms for contemporary life.

THINKING AND WRITING

Responding to a Statement About Style

In his essay "On Literary Style," Franklin states that good writing must be "smooth, clear, and short." Examine the excerpt from Franklin's *Autobiography* and the aphorisms from *Poor Richard's Almanack*. Does Franklin's writing meet his own requirements? List passages that support your opinion. Organize your information into an outline. Then write a thesis statement and an essay in which you use transitions to link your ideas, and support your argument with examples of Franklin's writing. When you revise, make sure that your paper meets Franklin's requirements for good writing.

MULTICULTURAL CONNECTION

Proverbs From Around the World

Ben Franklin adapted many of his aphorisms from folk sayings, or proverbs. Such proverbs can have many purposes and are used in different types of situations—to amuse, to educate, to sanction or shame, to make a point, or to add color to ordinary conversation. They state basic principles of folk wisdom, draw from the daily experiences of a group of people, and are an essential element of daily speech in all societies.

Proverbs reflect a particular culture's view of the world, expressing feelings about fate, the seasons, the natural world, work and effort, love, death, and other universal experiences. Sometimes these feelings are contradictory, as can be seen from the following two English proverbs: "Absence makes the heart grow fonder" and "Out of sight, out of mind."

A common viewpoint. Although each culture has its own proverbs, there are many examples of a common viewpoint among the proverbs of different cultures. Similarities may even reflect the ways in which different cultures borrow from one another.

Following are English, Russian, and Mexican proverbs that express similar attitudes about haste.

"Haste makes waste." (English)
"The slower you go, the further you get." (Russian)
"Slowly, one goes far." (Mexican)

A Swahili proverb says that "A cow does not know the value of its tail until it is cut off." Versions of the same proverb, with very little variation, exist in several other cultures.

Clearly, judging from the following three proverbs from different countries, procrastinating is common to many cultures.

"When God says today, the devil says tomorrow." (German)
"Life is made up of tomorrows." (French)
"One of these days is none of these days." (English)

Different surroundings, different sayings. It is interesting to observe how sayings and proverbs reflect different surroundings. One does not "argue apples and oranges" when mangoes and guavas are growing in one's orchard! Also, a saying like "Save something for a rainy day" would not make much sense in a country with little or no rainfall, but it is often used in England, where it frequently rains.

Activity

Here is a sampling of proverbs from around the world. As you read them, think about what they mean and try to paraphrase them. You may also want to discuss them in class or share other proverbs with your classmates.

"Better a red face than a black heart." (Portuguese)
"A new broom sweeps clean, but the old one knows all the corners." (Irish)
"Experience is a comb that nature gives us when we are bald." (Chinese)
"Ten men, ten minds." (Japanese)
"The dogs bark, but the caravan moves on." (Arabian)
"Be first at the feast and last at the fight." (Indian)
"When money falls from heaven, there is no sack; when there is a sack, money does not fall." (Russian)

PATRICK HENRY

1736–1799

Remembered most for his fiery battle cry, "Give me liberty or give me death," Patrick Henry is considered the most powerful orator of the American Revolution. Using his talents as a speaker, Henry helped to inspire colonists to unite in an effort to win their independence.

Born on his father's plantation in Hanover County, Virginia, Henry attended school only until the age of ten, though his father continued his schooling at home. After unsuccessfully attempting to run a store with his brother, Henry married at the age of eighteen and took up farming. When his farm was destroyed by a fire several years later, Henry found himself deeply in debt, with several children to support. He then began studying law, and in 1760 he received his license to practice. His talent as a speaker contributed to his reputation as an excellent lawyer.

In 1765 Henry was elected to the Virginia House of Burgesses. Shortly after his election, Henry delivered one of his most powerful speeches, declaring his opposition to the Stamp Act. At the end of his speech, Henry mentioned two kings who had been killed for political reasons and declared that King George III of Britain might "profit by their example." According to legend, this shocked the members of the audience so much that they accused Henry of treason. To this accusation, Henry is reported to have replied, "If this be treason, make the most of it!"

Whatever his actual words may have been, they were effective. Over the protests of some of the most influential members, the Virginia House adopted Henry's resolutions. Virginia thus became the first colony officially to protest the Stamp Act.

Henry rapidly became the leader of Virginia's opposition to British policy. When the royal governor closed the port of Boston in 1774 and dissolved the Virginia legislature, Henry organized a small group of the legislators, who met in a Williamsburg tavern. From there they invited the other colonies to send delegates to what became the First Continental Congress.

In 1775, after he had served as a member of the First Continental Congress, Henry delivered his most famous speech at the Virginia Provincial Convention. While most of the speakers that day argued that the colony should seek a compromise with the British, Henry boldly and dramatically urged armed resistance to England. Henry's speech had a powerful impact on the audience, reinforcing the revolutionary spirit that led to the signing of the Declaration of Independence. In the years that followed, Henry continued to be an important political leader, serving as the governor of Virginia and as a member of the Virginia General Assembly. It was this speech that secured him a place in American history.

GUIDE FOR INTERPRETING

Speech in the Virginia Convention

Literary Forms

Oratory. Oratory is the art of skilled, eloquent public speaking. Throughout history talented orators have used their skills to spread messages, gain support, and sway opinions. Oratory has always played an important role in American politics. In fact, to a great extent, America owes its independence to gifted speakers such as Patrick Henry who were responsible for influencing colonists to resist British rule.

An effective orator uses a variety of devices to emphasize important points. Four of these devices are rhetorical questions, restatement, repetition, and parallelism.

Rhetorical questions are questions that the speaker does not expect people to answer verbally. Because people generally will try to answer the questions in their mind, however, the questions force them to think actively about what the speaker is saying.

Restatement, repetition, and parallelism are methods used to highlight important points. A speaker uses restatement to state an idea in a variety of ways. When a speaker uses repetition, he or she restates an idea using the same words. Parallelism involves the use of a repeated grammatical structure.

Commentary

Patrick Henry's ability to rise to his feet and, in a few words and gestures, totally command his audience was extraordinary. This ability, coupled with an intelligent mind, led to his rise to political prominence from rather lowly beginnings.

The Virginia House of Burgesses was largely controlled by men from aristocratic families, wealthy and usually college educated. Henry had little schooling and that mostly informal, but he made good use of it in his speeches. After failing at storekeeping and farming, he studied law on his own and, to everyone's surprise, passed the oral exams.

In 1763 Virginia was again disputing with Britain the right to set prices and taxes in the colony. The case seemed lost for the colonists when Henry rose to speak. Casually, even poorly dressed, rather awkward and unpolished, Henry won the case for Virginia against the king. He was twenty-seven years old. Two years later, he was elected to the House of Burgesses, one of its youngest members.

As you read his "Speech in the Virginia Convention," see and hear him. Notice how he builds logically and emotionally to his famous conclusion.

Focus

What were the main reasons the colonies rebelled against British rule? Spend five minutes brainstorming about the causes of the American Revolution, and list them.

Speech in the Virginia Convention

Patrick Henry

Mr. President: No man thinks more highly than I do of the patriotism, as well as abilities, of the very worthy gentlemen who have just addressed the house. But different men often see the same subject in different lights; and, therefore, I hope it will not be thought disrespectful to those gentlemen, if, entertaining, as I do, opinions of a character very opposite to theirs, I shall speak forth my sentiments freely and without reserve. This is no time for ceremony. The question before the house is one of awful moment[1] to this country. For my own part, I consider it as nothing less than a question of freedom or slavery. And in proportion to the magnitude of the subject ought to be the freedom of the debate. It is only in this way that we can hope to arrive at truth, and fulfill the great responsibility which we hold to God and our country. Should I keep back my opinions at such a time, through fear of giving offense, I should consider myself as guilty of treason toward my country, and of an act of disloyalty toward the Majesty of Heaven, which I revere above all earthly kings.

Mr. President, it is natural to man to indulge in the illusions of hope. We are apt to shut our eyes against a painful truth, and listen to the song of that siren till she transforms us into beasts.[2] Is this the part of wise men, engaged in a great and arduous struggle for liberty? Are we disposed to be of the number of those who having eyes see not, and having ears hear not,[3] the things which so nearly concern their temporal salvation? For my part, whatever anguish of spirit it may cost, I am willing to know the whole truth; to know the worst and to provide for it.

I have but one lamp by which my feet are guided, and that is the lamp of experience. I know of no way of judging of the future but by the past. And judging by the past, I wish to know what there has been in the conduct of the British ministry for the last ten years to justify those hopes with which gentlemen have been pleased to solace themselves and the house? Is it that insidious smile with which our petition has been lately received? Trust it not, sir; it will prove a snare to your feet. Suffer not yourselves to be betrayed with a kiss.[4] Ask yourselves how this gracious reception of our petition comports with those warlike preparations which cover our waters and darken our land. Are fleets and armies necessary to a work of love and reconciliation? Have we shown ourselves so unwilling to be reconciled that force must be called in to win back our love? Let us not deceive ourselves, sir. These are the implements of war and subjugation—the last arguments to which kings resort.

I ask gentlemen, sir, what means this martial array, if its purpose be not to force

---

1. moment: Importance.
2. listen . . . beasts: In Homer's *Odyssey* the enchantress Circe transforms men into swine after charming them with her singing.

3. having eyes . . . hear not: In Ezekiel 12:2 those "who have eyes to see, but see not, who have ears to hear, but hear not" are addressed.
4. betrayed with a kiss: In Luke 22:47–48 Jesus is betrayed with a kiss.

PATRICK HENRY BEFORE THE VIRGINIA HOUSE OF BURGESSES
Peter F. Rothermel
Red Hill, The Patrick Henry National Memorial

Speech in the Virginia Convention 117

us to submission? Can gentlemen assign any other possible motive for it? Has Great Britain any enemy in this quarter of the world, to call for all this accumulation of navies and armies? No, sir, she has none. They are meant for us: they can be meant for no other. They are sent over to bind and rivet upon us those chains which the British ministry have been so long forging.

And what have we to oppose to them? Shall we try argument? Sir, we have been trying that for the last ten years. Have we anything new to offer upon the subject? Nothing. We have held the subject up in every light of which it is capable; but it has been all in vain. Shall we resort to entreaty and humble supplication? What terms shall we find which have not been already exhausted? Let us not, I beseech you, sir, deceive ourselves longer.

Sir, we have done everything that could be done to avert the storm which is now coming on. We have petitioned; we have remonstrated; we have supplicated; we have prostrated ourselves before the throne, and have implored its interposition[5] to arrest the tyrannical hands of the ministry and Parliament. Our petitions have been slighted; our remonstrances have produced additional violence and insult; our supplications have been disregarded; and we have been spurned with contempt from the foot of the throne! In vain, after these things, may we indulge the fond[6] hope of peace and reconciliation. There is no longer any room for hope. If we wish to be free, if we mean to preserve inviolate those inestimable privileges for which we have been so long contending, if we mean not basely to abandon the noble struggle in which we have been so long engaged, and which we have pledged ourselves never to abandon until the glorious object of our contest shall be obtained—we must fight! I repeat it, sir, we must fight! An appeal to arms and to the God of Hosts is all that is left us!

They tell us, sir, that we are weak—unable to cope with so formidable an adversary. But when shall we be stronger? Will it be the next week, or the next year? Will it be when we are totally disarmed, and when a British guard shall be stationed in every house? Shall we gather strength by irresolution and inaction? Shall we acquire the means of effectual resistance by lying supinely on our backs and hugging the delusive phantom of hope until our enemies shall have bound us hand and foot? Sir, we are not weak, if we make a proper use of those means which the God of nature hath placed in our power. Three millions of people, armed in the holy cause of liberty, and in such a country as that which we possess, are invincible by any force which our enemy can send against us. Besides, sir, we shall not fight our battles alone. There is a just God who presides over the destinies of nations and who will raise up friends to fight our battles for us. The battle, sir, is not to the strong alone;[7] it is to the vigilant, the active, the brave. Besides, sir, we have no election.[8] If we were base enough to desire it, it is now too late to retire from the contest. There is no retreat but in submission and slavery! Our chains are forged! Their clanging may be heard on the plains of Boston! The war is inevitable—and let it come! I repeat it, sir, let it come!

It is in vain, sir, to extenuate the matter. Gentlemen may cry, "Peace, peace"—but there is no peace. The war is actually begun! The next gale that sweeps from the north[9] will bring to our ears the clash of resounding arms! Our brethren are already in the field! Why stand we here idle? What is it that gentlemen wish? What would they have? Is life so dear, or peace so sweet, as to be purchased at the price of chains and slavery? Forbid it, Almighty God! I know not what course others may take; but as for me, give me liberty or give me death!

---

5. interposition: Intervention.
6. fond: Foolish.

7. The battle . . . alone: "The race is not to the swift, nor the battle to the strong." (Ecclesiastes 9:11).
8. election: Choice.
9. The next gale . . . north: In Massachusetts some colonists had already shown open resistance to the British.

RESPONDING TO THE SELECTION

Your Response

1. What is your impression of Patrick Henry? Based on this speech, do you think his reputation as a powerful orator was deserved? Explain.
2. If you were an American colonist, would Henry's speech sway you to join the revolutionaries? Why or why not?
3. Henry implies that death is preferable to life without liberty. Do you agree?

Recalling

4. How does Henry say that he judges the future?
5. (a) What does Henry say is the reason for the British military buildup in America? (b) What course of action must the colonists take?
6. What does Henry say "the next gale that sweeps from the north" will bring?

Interpreting

7. Why do you think Henry begins by stating his opinions of the previous speakers?
8. Why does Henry believe that compromise with the British is not a workable solution?
9. How does Henry answer the objection that the colonists are not ready to fight?
10. To what does Henry compare the colonists' situation?

Applying

11. What occasion or situation might prompt a statesman to deliver such a formal, dramatic speech today?

ANALYZING LITERATURE

Recognizing Oratory

Oratory is the art of formal public speaking. A skilled orator uses such devices as rhetorical questions, restatement, repetition, and parallelism to emphasize points.

1. (a) Find one instance where Henry answers a possible objection to his argument with a series of rhetorical questions. (b) What purpose does this series of questions serve?

2. List two ideas that Henry repeats using different words.
3. Find one example of parallelism.

CRITICAL THINKING AND READING

Understanding Persuasive Techniques

An effective orator may use a number of persuasive techniques to try to convince an audience to think or act in a certain way. For example, Patrick Henry uses a blend of logical arguments and emotional appeals in his speech.

1. Considering the purpose of Henry's speech, why do you feel these two techniques were appropriate?
2. Why do you think Henry chose to end his speech with an emotional appeal?
3. Rational thought is thinking based on reason. (a) What is the difference between rational thought and rationalization? (b) Which characterizes Henry's speech? Explain.

THINKING AND WRITING

Writing a Speech

Imagine that you are speaker in the Virginia Provincial Convention and you do not agree with Patrick Henry. Write a speech in which you rebut each of Henry's points.

LEARNING OPTIONS

1. **Speaking and Listening.** Part of what made Patrick Henry's speech successful was his dramatic delivery. Practice reading the speech aloud, carefully pronouncing each word. Emphasize important points by using appropriate hand gestures and varying the pitch and loudness of your voice. When you are ready, deliver the speech to classmates.
2. **Writing.** Imagine that you are a member of the Virginia House of Burgesses in March 1775. You have just heard Henry's powerful speech. Are you ready to go to war? Write a diary entry in which you record your feelings.

THOMAS PAINE

1737–1809

Though he did not become a journalist until he was in his late thirties, Thomas Paine was the most effective American political writer of the Revolution. Throughout the war, Paine's pamphlets convinced people of the justness of the American cause and helped to inspire faltering American troops.

Born in Thetford, England, Paine left school at thirteen and worked unsuccessfully as a teacher, corset maker, sailor, and grocer. After meeting Benjamin Franklin in London, Paine decided to emigrate to the colonies to start a new life. With a letter of introduction from Franklin, Paine came to America in 1774 and began a career in journalism.

In January 1776, less than two years after his arrival in America, Paine published *Common Sense,* a pamphlet in which he accused the English king of tyranny and argued that Americans had no choice but to fight for their independence. *Common Sense,* which sold more than 500,000 copies in three months, had a powerful effect on the American public. Less than six months after the pamphlet's publication, America declared its independence.

After enlisting in the American army toward the end of 1776, Paine wrote the first of a series of sixteen essays called *The American Crisis.* Paine joined Washington's troops after they had retreated from the British in New York. Suffering from the cold weather and a shortage of provisions, the soldiers were extremely disheartened. As the troops prepared to leave Valley Forge to fight the British at Trenton, General Washington had the first of Paine's inspirational essays read to the men to raise their spirits.

In 1787, several years after the end of the Revolution, Paine traveled to Europe and became involved with the French Revolution. Though Paine supported the revolutionary cause in *The Rights of Man* (1791–1792), the French revolutionaries imprisoned him for pleading against the execution of the overthrown French king. While in prison, he began writing *The Age of Reason* (1784–1785), a sharp attack on organized religion.

When he returned to America in 1802, Paine was treated harshly by the American public for supporting the French Revolution and criticizing religion. Paine died in New York in 1809, an unhappy man, not to be recognized as an American revolutionary hero until years after his death.

GUIDE FOR INTERPRETING

from The Crisis, Number I

Writers' Techniques

Aphorisms. An aphorism is a short, pointed statement expressing a wise or clever observation or a general truth. Though aphorisms may appear by themselves, they can also be used as a part of a longer work. Because aphorisms capture our attention and are easy to remember, writers may use them to express or emphasize important points.

Thomas Paine uses aphorisms throughout *The American Crisis* to make his argument strong and memorable. By defending the American cause through a series of statements expressing general truths, Paine creates the impression that the American forces are fighting not only for their own independence but also for the cause of liberty and justice for all humankind.

Commentary

This first of the sixteen *Crisis* papers was often called "The American Crisis." Paine wrote it while retreating with Washington's army across New Jersey during the first, dark winter of the Revolutionary War. The army had just been crushingly defeated at Fort Lee by the British, who had taken the fort and many prisoners. Only about 3,000 men remained with Washington's forces. Washington had the paper read to his troops before they crossed the Delaware River from Philadelphia, where they then defeated the Hessians at Trenton.

Paine's words were inspiring and encouraging, both for the cold, tired, defeated soldiers and for the colonists who read them in December of 1776. The ideas he presents are simple, and they can be clearly and therefore forcefully stated. Sometimes, it is true, he oversimplified an idea or situation to gain force. But he passionately believed in the need to arouse the colonists to immediate rebellion. He knew to whom he was speaking and writing, and made his words easily understood by the average person. He once wrote, "It is my design to make those who can scarcely read understand."

As you read this *Crisis* paper, notice how Paine is speaking personally and directly both to the individual, discouraged soldier standing listening in the cold and to all the colonists. If you were a tired soldier, a resentful colonist, *or* a colonist who supported the British, how would you respond to Paine? How does he logically and emotionally affect you?

Focus

What inspirational sayings or slogans from the American Revolution can you think of? Spend five minutes brainstorming about revolutionary sayings and slogans, and list them.

from The Crisis, Number I

Thomas Paine

These are the times that try men's souls. The summer soldier and the sunshine patriot will in this crisis, shrink from the service of his country; but he that stands it NOW, deserves the love and thanks of man and woman. Tyranny, like hell, is not easily conquered; yet we have this consolation with us, that the harder the conflict, the more glorious the triumph. What we obtain too cheap, we esteem too lightly; 'tis dearness only that gives everything its value. Heaven knows how to put a proper price upon its goods; and it would be strange indeed, if so celestial an article as FREEDOM should not be highly rated. Britain, with an army to enforce her tyranny, has declared that she has a right (not only to TAX) but "to BIND us in ALL CASES WHATSOEVER," and if being bound in that manner, is not slavery, then is there not such a thing as slavery upon earth. Even the expression is impious, for so unlimited a power can belong only to God . . .

I have as little superstition in me as any man living, but my secret opinion has ever been, and still is, that God Almighty will not give up a people to military destruction, or leave them unsupportedly to perish, who have so earnestly and so repeatedly sought to avoid the calamities of war, by every decent method which wisdom could invent. Neither have I so much of the infidel in me, as to suppose that he has relinquished the government of the world, and given us up to the care of devils; and as I do not, I cannot see on what grounds the king of Britain can look up to heaven for help against us: a common murderer, a highwayman, or a housebreaker, has as good a pretense as he . . .

I once felt all that kind of anger, which a man ought to feel, against the mean[1] principles that are held by the Tories:[2] a noted one, who kept a tavern at Amboy, was standing at his door, with as pretty a child in his hand, about eight or nine years old, as I ever saw, and after speaking his mind as freely as he thought was prudent, finished with this unfatherly expression, *"Well! give me peace in my day."* Not a man lives on the continent but fully believes that a separation must some time or other finally take place, and a generous parent should have said, *"If there must be trouble let it be in my day, that my child may have peace";* and this single reflection, well applied, is sufficient to awaken every man to duty. Not a place upon earth might be so happy as America. Her situation is remote from all the wrangling world, and she has nothing to do but to trade with them. A man can distinguish himself between temper and principle, and I am as confident, as I am that God governs the world, that America will never be happy

---

1. mean *adj.*: Here, small-minded.
2. Tories: Colonists who remained loyal to Great Britain.

RECRUITING FOR THE CONTINENTAL ARMY
William T. Ranney
Munson-Williams-Proctor Institute

till she gets clear of foreign dominion. Wars, without ceasing, will break out till that period arrives, and the continent must in the end be conqueror; for though the flame of liberty may sometimes cease to shine, the coal can never expire . . .

I turn with the warm ardor of a friend to those who have nobly stood, and are yet determined to stand the matter out: I call not upon a few, but upon all; not on *this* state or *that* state, but on *every* state; up and help us; lay your shoulders to the wheel; better

have too much force than too little, when so great an object is at stake. Let it be told to the future world, that in the depth of winter, when nothing but hope and virtue could survive, that the city and the country, alarmed at one common danger, came forth to meet and to repulse it. Say not that thousands are gone, turn out your tens of thousands; throw not the burden of the day upon Providence, but *"show your faith by your works,"* that God may bless you. It matters not where you live, or what rank of life you hold, the evil or the blessing will reach you all. The far and the near, the home counties and the back, the rich and the poor, will suffer or rejoice alike. The heart that feels not now, is dead: the blood of his children will curse his cowardice, who shrinks back at a time when a little might have saved the whole, and made *them* happy. (I love the man that can smile at trouble; that can gather strength from distress, and grow brave by reflection.) 'Tis the business of little minds to shrink; but he whose heart is firm, and whose conscience approves his conduct, will pursue his principles unto death. My own line of reasoning is to myself as straight and clear as a ray of light. Not all the treasures of the world, so far as I believe, could have induced me to support an offensive war, for I think it murder; but if a thief breaks into my house, burns and destroys my property, and kills or threatens to kill me, or those that are in it, and to "*bind me in all cases whatsoever*," to his absolute will, am I to suffer it? What signifies it to me, whether he who does it is a king or a common man; my countryman, or not my countryman; whether it be done by an individual villain or an army of them? If we reason to the root of things we shall find no difference; neither can any just cause be assigned why we should punish in the one case and pardon in the other.

RESPONDING TO THE SELECTION

Your Response

1. Which of Thomas Paine's arguments or statements do you find most powerful?
2. Do you agree with Paine that the colonists' situation was like slavery? Why or why not?
3. Paine remarks on the necessity of pursuing one's principles "unto death." What principles do you believe are worth dying for?

Recalling

4. (a) According to the first paragraph, who will "shrink from the service of his country"? (b) What will the people who do not shrink from service deserve?
5. According to the first paragraph, what has Britain declared?

6. Of what is Paine confident in the third paragraph?
7. What opinion of offensive wars does Paine express in the final paragraph?

Interpreting

8. What does Paine mean when he refers to "the summer soldier" and "the sunshine patriot"?
9. What is the point of Paine's story about the tavernkeeper at Amboy?
10. Name two emotions to which Paine appeals in his essay.
11. (a) What is the main idea of this essay? (b) How does Paine support his main idea?

Applying

12. How might a colonist who had remained loyal to the British react to Paine's argument?

ANALYZING LITERATURE

Using Aphorisms

An **aphorism** is a brief, pointed statement expressing a wise or clever observation or a general truth. Sometimes writers use aphorisms in their works to express or emphasize important points. For example, Paine uses the aphorism "the harder the conflict, the more glorious the triumph" to express his belief that hardships faced by the American forces during the war will make their eventual victory more meaningful.

1. Find three more aphorisms used in Paine's essay.
2. What point does each of these aphorisms emphasize or express?

CRITICAL THINKING AND READING

Understanding the Effect of Aphorisms

Aphorisms can make a work more forceful and memorable. Because aphorisms express general truths, they can create the impression that the specific argument being presented has a more general application. For example, Paine's use of aphorisms helps to convey his belief that the American Revolution is a part of a greater struggle aimed at attaining liberty and justice for all humankind.

1. Why does the universal application of Paine's argument add to the essay's value as a work of literature?
2. What other historical situations can you think of for which Paine's essay would have been appropriate?

THINKING AND WRITING

Writing About Revolutionary Literature

Read the "Speech in the Virginia Convention," "The Declaration of Independence," and the excerpt from *The Crisis, Number 1,* taking notes that will help you to write an essay discussing the common purpose of revolutionary speeches and documents and the various methods used to achieve this purpose. Organize your notes into an outline and prepare a thesis statement. Then write your essay, being sure to include passages that demonstrate the different methods and arguments used by revolutionary writers to achieve their purpose. When you finish writing, revise your essay and prepare a final copy.

LEARNING OPTIONS

1. **Cross-curricular Connection.** An unsuccessful teacher, corset maker, sailor, and grocer, Thomas Paine seems to be an unlikely candidate for a revolutionary war hero. What led him to become a spokesperson for revolution? Locate a biography and read about Paine's early years. Be prepared to share your impressions in a class discussion.
2. **Art.** In *The Crisis, Number 1,* Paine calls on all colonists to support their comrades in arms. Design a war poster to help him enlist support for the revolutionary war effort. In your poster you might appeal to the colonists' patriotism or to their fear of the British. Like Paine, you might also deride "the summer soldier and the sunshine patriot."
3. **Writing.** December 1776 was a low point for George Washington as well as for the American forces. In a letter to his brother, he wrote, "I am wearied to death. I think the game is pretty near up." How do you think Washington felt after reading Paine's words? Take the part of George Washington and write either a letter to your brother or a note to Thomas Paine expressing your feelings.
4. **Cross-curricular Connection.** Thomas Paine's exalted words helped spur American troops on to victory. So did the less exalted words of the song "Yankee Doodle Dandy." At one point British General Gage supposedly said, "I hope I shall never hear that tune again!" Investigate the surprising origin of the song. Share your findings with classmates.

PHILLIS WHEATLEY

1753[?]–1784

Although she was a black slave whose native language was not English, Phillis Wheatley achieved success as a poet at an early age and went on to become a highly regarded American poet in the Revolutionary period.

Born in West Africa, she was brought to America on a slave ship when she was about eight years old. She was purchased by the Wheatley family of Boston, who gave her their name and converted her to Christianity. Recognizing her extraordinary intelligence, the Wheatleys taught her to read and write. Wheatley learned quickly and was soon reading the Bible, the Latin and Greek classics, and the works of the contemporary English poets. Wheatley also began writing poetry, and when she was thirteen her first poem was published.

In 1770, when she published a poem about the death of George Whitehead, a celebrated English clergyman, Wheatley became famous. Two years later, she accompanied the Wheatley's son on a trip to England, where she was introduced to a number of British aristocrats who were impressed by her poetry and helped to have *Poems on Various Subjects: Religious and Moral* published in London in 1773.

In a foreword to this volume, the publisher claimed that persons who had read the poems felt that "Numbers would be ready to suspect they were not really the Writings of Phillis." Therefore he offered an "attestation" to their authorship, which was signed by eighteen prominent Massachusetts men, among them John Hancock. She was well received by London society, and Benjamin Franklin visited her there. However, *Poems on Various Subjects* was not published in the United States until 1786, two years after her death.

After returning to Boston in the fall of 1773, Wheatley continued to write poetry. During the Revolutionary War, she wrote several poems supporting the American cause, including a poem addressed to George Washington, the commander of the American forces. Washington was so impressed with this poem, "To His Excellency, George Washington," that he invited her to visit him at his headquarters.

Though she was freed in 1778 when John Wheatley died, the last several years of Wheatley's life were filled with hardships. She married John Peters, a free black man, but Peters had trouble maintaining a job and was eventually imprisoned for failing to pay his debts. They had three children, but two of them died in infancy. In addition, Wheatley fell into obscurity as a poet. Though she assembled a second collection of her poetry, the manuscript was lost before it could be published. With her husband in jail and her fame having faded, Phillis Wheatley died alone and impoverished in 1784.

GUIDE FOR INTERPRETING

To His Excellency, General Washington

Personification. Personification is the attribution of human powers and characteristics to something that is not human, such as an object, an aspect of nature, or an abstract idea. For instance, in the sentence, "The angry wind mercilessly pounded the walls," the wind is personified with two human qualities: anger and lack of mercy.

Throughout history, personification has fulfilled people's need to understand the world in human terms. In ancient religions, gods personified elements of the universe and the natural world. For example, the Greek god Poseidon and the Roman god Neptune were personifications of the ocean. Today, personification is often used as a part of everyday speech. In fact, certain personifications, such as "the screaming of the siren" and "the sighing of the wind," are so common that we do not even think of them as personifications.

In eighteenth-century English literature, poets often drew upon the traditions of the ancient Greek and Roman religions, personifying abstract ideas and elements of the natural world as gods or goddesses. Phillis Wheatley was greatly influenced by the work of the eighteenth-century English poets. This influence is reflected in Wheatley's personification of both America and Great Britain as goddesses in "To His Excellency, General Washington."

Focus

Brainstorm for examples of personification in everyday language, listing your examples.

Primary Source

In October of 1775, when Washington was at his headquarters in Cambridge near Boston, Phillis Wheatley sent him a short letter and the poem addressed to him. Several months later Washington responded.

> I thank you most sincerely for your polite notice of me in the elegant lines you enclosed; and however undeserving I may be of such encomium [high praise] and panegyric [tribute], the style and manner exhibit a striking proof of your poetical talents; in honor of which, and as a tribute justly due you, I would have published the poem, had I not been apprehensive that, while I only meant to give the world this new instance of your genius, I might have incurred the imputation of vanity. This, and nothing else, determined me not to give it a place in the public prints.
>
> If you should ever come to Cambridge, or near headquarters, I shall be happy to see a person so favored by the Muses, and to whom nature has been so beneficent in her dispensations.

GEORGE WASHINGTON AT THE BATTLE OF PRINCETON
Charles Wilson Peale
Yale University Art Gallery

To His Excellency, General Washington

Phillis Wheatley

Celestial choir! enthron'd in realms of light,
  Columbia's[1] scenes of glorious toils I write.
While freedom's cause her anxious breast alarms,
She flashes dreadful in refulgent arms.
5 See mother earth her offspring's fate bemoan,
And nations gaze at scenes before unknown!
See the bright beams of heaven's revolving light
Involved in sorrows and the veil of night!
  The goddess comes, she moves divinely fair,
10 Olive and laurel binds her golden hair:
Wherever shines this native of the skies,
Unnumber'd charms and recent graces rise.
  Muse![2] bow propitious while my pen relates
How pour her armies through a thousand gates,
15 As when Eolus[3] heaven's fair face deforms,
Enwrapp'd in tempest and a night of storms;
Astonish'd ocean feels the wild uproar,
The refluent surges beat the sounding shore;
Or thick as leaves in Autumn's golden reign,
20 Such, and so many, moves the warrior's train.
In bright array they seek the work of war,
Where high unfurl'd the ensign[4] waves in air.
Shall I to Washington their praise recite?
Enough thou know'st them in the fields of fight.
25 Thee, first in peace and honors,—we demand
The grace and glory of thy martial band.
Fam'd for thy valor, for thy virtues more,
Hear every tongue thy guardian aid implore!
  One century scarce perform'd its destined round,
30 When Gallic[5] powers Columbia's fury found;

---

1. Columbia: America personified as a goddess.
2. Muse: The goddess who presides over poetry; one of nine muses presiding over literature, the arts, and the sciences.
3. Eolus (ē′ ə ləs): The Greek god of the winds.
4. ensign (en′ s'n): Flag.
5. Gallic (găl′ ik): French. The colonists, led by Washington, defeated the French in the French and Indian War (1754–1763).

And so may you, whoever dares disgrace
The land of freedom's heaven-defended race!
Fix'd are the eyes of nations on the scales,
For in their hopes Columbia's arm prevails.
35 Anon Britannia[6] droops the pensive head,
While round increase the rising hills of dead.
Ah! cruel blindness to Columbia's state!
Lament thy thirst of boundless power too late.
   Proceed, great chief, with virtue on thy side,
40 Thy ev'ry action let the goddess guide.
A crown, a mansion, and a throne that shine,
With gold unfading, WASHINGTON! be thine.

---

6. Britannia: England.

Commentary

From a young age, Phillis Wheatley attracted considerable attention. Her learning and social grace were truly impressive, made more so by the fact that she was a woman, a slave, and a black. In Boston she was "the sooty prodigy"; in London she was all the rage as the "Sable Muse."

Her poetry, although well done, follows the neoclassical conventions of the times. Thomas Jefferson did not think highly of her as a poet: In his *Notes on the State of Virginia* (1784–1785) he writes, "Religion indeed has produced a Phillis Wheatley; but it could not produce a poet." Many equally illustrious persons came to her defense. A college president responded, "I will demand of Mr. Jefferson, or of any other man who is acquainted with American planters, how many of those masters could have written poems equal to those of Phillis Wheatley?"

Although she was largely forgotten by the public in her last years, the abolition movement of the 1830's and 1840's revived her writings, this time as evidence for abolishing slavery. In 1838 in Boston, her poems and those of another slave were published as *Memoir and Poems of Phillis Wheatley, a Native African and a Slave; Also, Poems by a Slave*. Shortly before the end of the Civil War there appeared *The Letters of Phillis Wheatley, the Negro-Slave Poet of Boston*.

Wheatley herself in her poems was not concerned with freedom from slavery but with freedom for all people, an issue of concern in the years before the Revolution.

RESPONDING TO THE SELECTION

Your Response

1. Whom would you choose for the subject of a poetic tribute? Why?
2. How would you personify the spirit of the United States today?

Recalling

3. What images does Wheatley use to describe Columbia?
4. Why does the poet cut short her praise of Columbia's armies?
5. What hope does the poet express in lines 31–32?
6. According to line 39, what does Washington have on his side?

Interpreting

7. (a) Find three instances in which Wheatley indicates a relationship between God and the American cause. (b) What is the nature of this relationship?
8. What does Wheatley suggest about the American forces in comparisons made in lines 13–20?
9. (a) What are the "scales" Wheatley refers to in line 33? (b) Why are eyes fixed on them?
10. What do the last two lines indicate about the influence of the British social and political systems on American thinking?

Applying

11. What does this poem suggest about Wheatley's feelings regarding her country?

ANALYZING LITERATURE

Recognizing Personification

Personification is the attribution of human powers to something that is not human, such as an inanimate object or an abstract idea. For example, in "To His Excellency, General Washington," Phillis Wheatley personifies America as the goddess Columbia.

1. How does Wheatley characterize Columbia?
2. What details does she use in describing Columbia's physical appearance?

3. What is the significance of the physical details Wheatley uses in describing Columbia?
4. What does the god Eolus (line 15) personify?
5. How does Wheatley personify Britain?

CRITICAL THINKING AND READING

Evaluating the Effect of Personification

Personification makes it possible for us to understand a subject in human terms. For example, in "To His Excellency, General Washington," we are able to view American ideals and beliefs as character traits of the goddess Columbia.

1. Explain how Wheatley's use of personification makes us sympathize more readily with the American cause.
2. Compare and contrast Wheatley's personification of America as the goddess Columbia with the common personification of the United States as Uncle Sam.

THINKING AND WRITING

Developing a Personification

What type of person would best personify America today? Prepare to write a poem or several paragraphs in which you personify America. First, develop a list of character traits that express the ideals and beliefs of today's society. Think of how you would describe the physical appearance of a man or woman who personifies America, and think about how this person would behave. Then develop your personification of America as a man or woman through your description of his or her appearance, behavior, and character traits. When you finish writing, revise your poem or paragraphs and prepare a final copy.

LEARNING OPTION

Art. Phillis Wheatley was the first poet to personify America as the goddess Columbia. The image caught on and it frequently appeared in patriotic paintings. Find an illustration of Columbia or draw a picture of the figure you would use to represent the United States today. How does it compare to Wheatley's Columbia?

THOMAS JEFFERSON

1743–1826

Thomas Jefferson is one of the most widely respected and admired figures in American history. A gifted writer, diplomat, political leader, inventor, architect, philosopher, and educator, with an intense belief in equal rights and individual freedoms, Jefferson played a significant role in the creation and shaping of America.

Born into a wealthy Virginia family, Jefferson received a thorough classical education as a boy. After graduating from the College of William and Mary in 1762, Jefferson spent five years studying law. In 1769, two years after Jefferson received his license to practice law, he was elected to the Virginia House of Burgesses. While serving in the House, Jefferson became an outspoken defender of American rights. After Jefferson displayed his persuasive abilities in his pamphlet *A Summary View of the Rights of British America* (1774), he was chosen to draft the Declaration of Independence at the Second Continental Congress in 1776.

When the Revolutionary War ended, Jefferson served as the American minister to France for several years. He then became America's first Secretary of State in 1789. In 1801, after he served as Vice President under John Adams, Jefferson became the third American President. While in office, Jefferson nearly doubled the size of the nation by authorizing the purchase of the Louisiana Territory from France.

In 1809 Jefferson retired to Monticello, the Virginia home he had designed, and devoted his time to reading, conducting scientific experiments, collecting paintings, and playing the violin. Jefferson also helped to found the University of Virginia, designing the campus and planning the curriculum.

We owe many further aspects of American life to Jefferson's extremely varied interests and talents. He began collecting an immense library that eventually became the basis of the Library of Congress. He outlined our public school system and proposed the decimal system for American money. He commissioned the Lewis and Clark expedition to find a land route to the Pacific through the then largely unmapped West.

Among his most important legacies to us today are his belief in an aristocracy based on moral character and ability—not on wealth and family name—and his deep faith in the small farmer, the "common man," as the basis of democratic life. "Those who labor in the earth," he wrote, "are the chosen people of God." He wrote eloquently against a belief then current in Europe that in the wilderness life of North America, people would degenerate morally and socially.

On July 4, 1826, the fiftieth anniversary of the Declaration of Independence, Thomas Jefferson died.

GUIDE FOR INTERPRETING

The Declaration of Independence

Parallelism. Parallelism refers to the repeated use of phrases, clauses, or sentences that are similar in structure or meaning. Writers use this technique to emphasize important ideas, create rhythm, and make their writing forceful and direct. In the Declaration of Independence, Thomas Jefferson uses parallelism when listing the reasons that Americans felt compelled to declare their independence. Jefferson's use of parallelism makes his argument grow stronger with each reason he presents.

At the Second Continental Congress, Jefferson was elected to join Benjamin Franklin, John Adams, Roger Sherman, and Robert Livingston in drafting a declaration of independence for the colonies. The draft that the committee sent to the Congress was primarily Jefferson's work.

Congress, however, to Jefferson's disappointment, made further changes before approving the final document. They dropped Jefferson's condemnation of the British people for tolerating a corrupt parliament and king, and struck out a strong statement against slavery.

The document finally signed and sent to George III was clearly treasonous. The penalty for treason against the Crown was death— a fact all the delegates were well aware of. Therefore, the two opening paragraphs, preceding the list of grievances, were very important in justifying this act of treason. As you read them and the rest of the Declaration, imagine that you are one of the delegates, and the time has come to sign. What are your chances of *not* being tried and beheaded for treason?

What does freedom mean to you? Prepare a journal entry in which you discuss your ideas about the concept of freedom. Include specific examples.

The Declaration of Independence

Thomas Jefferson

When in the course of human events, it becomes necessary for one people to dissolve the political bands which have connected them with another, and to assume among the powers of the earth, the separate and equal station to which the laws of nature and of nature's God entitle them, a decent respect to the opinions of mankind requires that they should declare the causes which impel them to the separation.

We hold these truths to be self-evident: that all men are created equal; that they are endowed by their Creator with certain unalienable rights; that among these are life, liberty and the pursuit of happiness; that to secure these rights, governments are instituted among men, deriving their just powers from the consent of the governed; that whenever any form of government becomes destructive of these ends, it is the right of the people to alter or to abolish it, and to institute new government, laying its foundation on such principles and organizing its powers in such form, as to them shall seem most likely to effect their safety and happiness. Prudence, indeed, will dictate that governments long established should not be changed for light and transient causes; and accordingly all experience hath shown, that mankind are more disposed to suffer while evils are sufferable than to right themselves by abolishing the forms to which they are accustomed. But when a long train of abuses and usurpations, pursuing invariably the same object, evinces a design to reduce them under absolute despotism,[1] it is their right, it is their duty, to throw off such government, and to provide new guards for their future security. Such has been the patient sufferance of these colonies; and such is now the necessity which constrains[2] them to alter their former systems of government. The history of the present king of Great Britain is a history of repeated injuries and usurpations, all having in direct object the establishment of an absolute tyranny over these states. To prove this, let facts be submitted to a candid world.

He has refused his assent to laws the most wholesome and necessary for the public good.

He has forbidden his governors to pass laws of immediate and pressing importance, unless suspended in their operation till his assent should be obtained; and when so suspended, he has utterly neglected to attend to them.

He has refused to pass other laws for the accommodation of large districts of people, unless those people would relinquish the right of representation in the legislature, a right inestimable to them and formidable to tyrants only.

He has called together legislative bodies at places unusual, uncomfortable, and distant from the depository of their public rec-

---

1. **despotism** (des' pə tiz'm) *n.*: Tyranny.
2. **constrains** *v.*: Forces.

THE DECLARATION OF INDEPENDENCE
John Trumbull
Yale University Art Gallery

ords, for the sole purpose of fatiguing them into compliance with his measures.

He has dissolved representative houses repeatedly, for opposing with manly firmness his invasions on the rights of the people.

He has refused for a long time after such dissolutions to cause others to be elected, whereby the legislative powers, incapable of annihilation, have returned to the people at large for their exercise, the state remaining in the mean time exposed to all the dangers of invasion from without, and convulsions within.

He has endeavored to prevent the population of these states; for that purpose obstructing the laws for naturalization of foreigners, refusing to pass others to encourage their migration hither, and raising the conditions of new appropriations of lands.

He has obstructed the administration of justice, by refusing his assent to laws for establishing judiciary powers.

He has made judges dependent on his will alone, for the tenure of their offices, and the amount and payment of their salaries.

He has erected a multitude of new offices, and sent hither swarms of officers to harass our people and eat out their substance.

He has kept among us in times of peace standing armies without the consent of our legislatures.

He has affected to render the military independent of, and superior to, the civil power.

He has combined with others to subject us to a jurisdiction foreign to our constitution and unacknowledged by our laws, giving his assent to their acts of pretended legislation: for quartering large bodies of armed troops among us; for protecting them by a mock trial from punishment for any murders which they should commit on the inhabitants of these states; for cutting off our trade with all parts of the world; for imposing taxes on us without our consent; for depriving us, in many cases, of the benefits of trial by jury; for transporting us beyond seas to be tried for pretended offenses; for abolishing the free system of English laws in a neighboring province,[3] establishing therein an arbitrary government, and enlarging its boundaries, so as to render it at once an example and fit instrument for introducing the same absolute rule into these colonies; for taking away our charters, abolishing our most valuable laws, and altering fundamentally the forms of our governments; for suspending our own legislatures, and declaring themselves invested with power to legislate for us in all cases whatsoever.

He has abdicated government here, by declaring us out of his protection and waging war against us.

He has plundered our seas, ravaged our coasts, burned our towns, and destroyed the lives of our people.

He is at this time transporting large armies of foreign mercenaries to complete the works of death, desolation, and tyranny, already begun with circumstances of cruelty and perfidy scarcely paralleled in the most barbarous ages, and totally unworthy the head of a civilized nation.

He has constrained our fellow citizens taken captive on the high seas to bear arms against their country, to become the executioners of their friends and brethren, or to fall themselves by their hands.

He has excited domestic insurrections amongst us, and has endeavored to bring on the inhabitants of our frontiers, the merciless Indian savages, whose known rule of warfare is an undistinguished destruction of all ages, sexes, and conditions.

In every stage of these oppressions we have petitioned for redress in the most humble terms. Our repeated petitions have been answered only by repeated injury.

A prince whose character is thus marked by every act which may define a tyrant is unfit to be the ruler of a free people.

Nor have we been wanting in attentions to our British brethren. We have warned them from time to time of attempts by their legislature to extend an unwarrantable jurisdiction over us. We have reminded them of the circumstances of our emigration and settlement here. We have appealed to their native justice and magnanimity and we have conjured[4] them by the ties of our common kindred to disavow these usurpations which would inevitably interrupt our connections and correspondence. They too have been deaf to the voice of justice and of consanguinity. We must therefore acquiesce in the necessity which denounces[5] our separation and hold them, as we hold the rest of mankind, enemies in war, in peace friends.

We, therefore, the representatives of the United States of America in general congress assembled, appealing to the Supreme Judge of the world for the rectitude of our intentions, do in the name and by authority of the good people of these colonies, solemnly publish and declare that these united colonies are and of right ought to be free and independent states; that they are absolved from all allegiance to the British Crown, and that all political connection between them and the state of Great Britain is and ought to be totally dissolved; and that as free and independent states, they have full power to levy war, conclude peace, contract alliances, establish commerce, and to do all other acts and things which independent states may of right do.

And for the support of this declaration, with a firm reliance on the protection of divine providence, we mutually pledge to each other our lives, our fortunes and our sacred honor.

---

3. **neighboring province:** Quebec.

4. **conjured:** Solemnly appealed to.
5. **denounces:** Here, announces.

RESPONDING TO THE SELECTION

Your Response

1. What feelings does this document evoke? After reading it, do you feel proud to be an American? Why or why not?
2. What do you consider "unalienable rights"?

Recalling

3. What are the three "unalienable rights" listed in the second paragraph?
4. (a) According to Jefferson, what is the purpose of a government? (b) When should a government be abolished?
5. List three of the statements Jefferson presents to support his claim that the king's objective is "the establishment of an absolute tyranny over these states."
6. (a) What does Jefferson claim the colonists have done at "every stage of these oppressions"? (b) How has the king responded to the colonists' actions?
7. What pledge is made in the last paragraph?

Interpreting

8. What effect does Jefferson's long list of specific grievances have on his argument?
9. Why does Jefferson focus his attack on King George III rather than on the British Parliament or people?
10. How is the eighteenth-century faith in reason reflected in the Declaration?

Applying

11. Considering Jefferson's views concerning the purpose of a government, to what governments in today's world might he object?

ANALYZING LITERATURE

Recognizing Parallelism

Parallelism refers to the repeated use of phrases, clauses, or sentences that are similar in structure or meaning. For example, Jefferson lists the colonists' grievances in a series of sentences with the same structure.

1. Find another example of Jefferson's use of parallel structure.

2. In what ways does Jefferson's use of parallelism strengthen his argument?

CRITICAL THINKING AND READING

Recognizing Charged Words

In presenting an argument, a writer may appeal to emotions indirectly through the use of emotionally charged words. **Charged words** are words with strong connotations beyond their literal meanings that are likely to produce an emotional response. For example, the word *tyranny* evokes a feeling of fear. It suggests living in a state of terror, afraid of being jailed or executed for disagreeing with governmental policies.

What associations are evoked by these words from the Declaration of Independence?

1. liberty   2. justice   3. honor

THINKING AND WRITING

Comparing and Contrasting Arguments

The Declaration of Independence and Patrick Henry's "Speech in the Virginia Convention" are both powerful arguments for American independence. In what ways are the two arguments similar? In what ways are they different? Reread both documents carefully and list similarities and differences in format, content, and persuasive techniques. Review your notes to help you develop your thesis statement; then prepare an outline. When you write your essay, make sure that you include passages from both selections to support your argument. After you finish writing, review your essay, making sure you have included enough information to support your thesis.

LEARNING OPTION

Writing. Become a student activist. Use the Declaration of Independence as a model in drawing up a petition to redress something you would like to see corrected at your school. Begin with a statement of rights followed by a list of wrongs. You might work with a committee to draft your petition. When you have finished, you might present your petition to the student council.

ONE WRITER'S PROCESS

Thomas Jefferson and the Declaration of Independence

PREWRITING

A Call to Action By June 1776 relations between the American colonies and the British crown had reached an all-time low. In open rebellion against the British crown, the colony of South Carolina had already created its own constitution. Other colonies began to follow its example.

Now the time was ripe for even bolder measures. At the Continental Congress in Philadelphia on the seventh of June, Richard Henry Lee of Virginia rose to make a daring resolution: "*Resolved.* That these United Colonies are, and of right ought to be, free and independent states; that they are absolved from all allegiance to the British Crown. . . ."

Four days later the delegates took concrete action. A five-member committee was appointed to prepare the Declaration of Independence.

Finding the Right Voice Of the five members of the committee, John Adams, eloquent advocate of the revolutionary cause, seemed the most likely choice to write the Declaration. Adams, however, turned the job down. Because some members of Congress deplored his bold ideas and aggressive tactics, he was afraid they might oppose the Declaration if he were its author. Adams recommended Thomas Jefferson, whom he respected as a writer and as a scholar of Greek and Roman literature. Jefferson had already written passionately about colonial political rights. He also came from the influential colony of Virginia, the most populous state in the union.

DRAFTING

Toward an "American Mind" While Adams argued daily for independence in Congress, Jefferson shut himself up on the second floor of a quiet house in Philadelphia. Over a period of eleven days, he drafted the Declaration on a portable writing box of his own design. He strove for perfect phrasing of the document. He wanted it to serve as a voice for all Americans rather than as a model of sophisticated political theory. In order for the Declaration to win the full support of the people, Jefferson thought it had to be "an expression of the American mind." The proof of his success is that more than 200 years later, we are using such phrases from the document as "life, liberty, and the pursuit of happiness" to discuss the ideals of this country.

In the first section of the first draft of the document, Jefferson established the idea that Americans were a single people with their own identity, not merely an extension of the British crown. He did this by speaking of the colonies as "a people" with a natural right to an "equal & independent station." The middle section listed twenty-seven charges against King George III. These charges seemed to build naturally to a conclusion, which declared the colonies to be "free & independent states."

REVISING

Adding New Voices Jefferson's first draft is one of the most eloquent documents of American political writing. Although its ideas were derived from the writings of some of the

West's greatest political thinkers, the Declaration is clear and understandable. Nevertheless, the Declaration of Independence had to go through a lengthy editing process before it was finally approved by the Congress.

The first of Jefferson's peers to edit the document was senior statesman Benjamin Franklin, who, at the age of seventy, was a highly experienced writer and editor. Franklin seems to have been a diplomatic and easygoing peer editor. He made few changes to the document. At this stage he was unconcerned with Jefferson's many misspellings, such as "independant" for "independent" and "unacknoleged" for "unacknowledged." Nor at this point did he raise objections to Jefferson's habit of beginning sentences with a lowercase letter. Two specific word changes in the first paragraph, however, strengthened its original intent. Where Jefferson referred to Americans as "a people" in the first sentence, Franklin changed the phrase to "one people," thus imparting a stronger sense of unity and a separate identity for Americans. Whereas Jefferson had written of the need for a "change" at the end of the first paragraph, Franklin spoke of "separation," which referred more specifically to the break with Britain.

Jefferson next showed the document to Adams, who made very few changes. Wisely, he chose not to offend Jefferson by being overly critical.

The sixty members of Congress were the harshest critics. They scrutinized and debated every paragraph of the document for twelve hours. This part of the editing process was especially painful for Jefferson. Anyone who has labored over a piece of writing will understand why he was so upset. Jefferson sat silently as his peers attacked phrases he had rewritten countless times. Sometimes their ideas were defeated by Adams, and the wording of a line remained the same. At other times their changes were adopted. For example, to please the slave-owning colonies of South Carolina and Georgia, a passage condemning the king for promoting slavery was deleted.

Most of the changes made by Congress had the effect of making the document briefer and less emotional. For example, look at this original version of paragraph 10 of the Declaration, which is part of the complaint against the king. The handwritten changes replacing the deleted lines were made by Congress in the final edit of the document.

He has ~~suffered~~ *obstructed* the administration of justice ~~totally to cease in some of these~~ ~~states~~ *by* refusing his assent to laws for establishing judiciary powers.

PUBLISHING

Writing Read Around the World The final version of the Declaration of Independence was printed by Philadelphia printer John Dunlap. Apparently no member of the five-person drafting committee came to Dunlap's shop to proofread the document after it was typeset, because it contains errors of punctuation, capitalization, and spelling.

Despite these errors copies were sent out to all the colonies on July 5 and 6. This document was destined to stay in print and to change the course of American history.

THINKING ABOUT THE PROCESS

1. How did shortening the Declaration of Independence make it more suitable for its audience and purpose?
2. **Cooperative Activity** With a partner, read aloud the edited version of the Declaration presented here. Discuss the changed phrases. Do you agree or disagree with the changes? Why?

ABIGAIL SMITH ADAMS

1744–1818

Abigail Smith Adams, the wife of John Adams, the second President of the United States, and the mother of John Quincy Adams, the sixth President, was one of the most important and influential American women of her time. A dedicated supporter of women's rights and the American Revolutionary movement, Adams wrote many letters to her husband and other members of her family expressing her opinions. In these letters Adams included vivid descriptions that capture the essence of life in early America.

Abigail Smith was born in Weymouth, Massachusetts. At the age of twenty, she married John Adams. The couple had four sons and one daughter, and Abigail made sure that her daughter received a thorough education—something few American girls received at the time.

Although her father was a well-to-do minister and her mother from an upper-class family, Abigail herself had no formal schooling of any kind. John, of a much more modest social position, was a Harvard graduate. Abigail often excused her lack of schooling by saying that she was frequently ill as a child. However, in later years, she made observations such as this in a letter of 1778: "Every assistance and advantage which can be procured is afforded to the Sons, whilst the daughters are wholly neglected in point of Literature." (By "Literature" she means the liberal arts.)

In 1774, when John left home to serve as a member of the Continental Congress, Abigail assumed the responsibility of managing the family farm in what is now Quincy, Massachusetts. Because of John's political involvement, John and Abigail were separated from each other for most of the next ten years. During this period Abigail became an avid letter writer. In her letters Abigail provided her husband with information about British troops and ships in the Boston area, stressed the importance of women's rights, and voiced her opposition to slavery.

When John Adams was elected President of the United States, John and Abigail Adams became the first couple to live in the White House. Among the letters Abigail wrote while living there is one to her daughter describing her temporary home. This letter and the others she wrote during this period provide an interesting view of life in the new nation.

Abigail Adams died in 1818, after spending the last seventeen years of her life at the Adams family home in Massachusetts. In 1840 a volume of her letters was published, and since then three more volumes have been published. Today Abigail Adams is widely recognized as a writer and a pioneer of the American women's movement.

GUIDE FOR INTERPRETING

Writers' Techniques

Letter to Her Daughter from the New White House

Description. Descriptive writing creates an impression of a person, place, or thing through the use of details appealing to one or more of the five senses—sight, sound, taste, smell, and touch. In a description, a writer includes enough details to enable us to visualize the subject. Because a writer cannot use all the details of the subject in a description, he or she selects those details that create a desired impression.

Abigail Adams lived in the days before cameras were invented. Her descriptions provided the equivalent of snapshots. In passages in her letters, she described for her daughter what the White House looked like and what it was like to live there. When we read Adams's letter, the contrast between her description of the White House and our perceptions of today's White House makes the impression created by Adams even more striking.

Focus

What details would you include in a description of your city hall? List its most significant and striking details.

Primary Source

The letters of Abigail Adams reveal a well-read and politically sensitive writer, well aware of the decisions facing the country. In August 1774, while John was at the Continental Congress in Philadelphia, Massachusetts was in near rebellion. Abigail wrote him, comparing the colonies' position to that of Sparta, a city of ancient Greece, and commenting on the desire for "peace in our time":

Uncertainty and expectation leave the mind great Scope. Did ever any Kingdom or State regain their Liberty, when once it was invaded without Blood shed? I cannot think of it without horror.

Yet we are told that all the Misfortunes of Sparta were occasioned by their too great Sollicitude for present tranquility, and by an excessive love of peace they neglected the means of making it sure and lasting. They ought to have reflected says Polibius [a Greek historian] that as there is nothing more desirable, or advantageous than peace, when founded in justice and honour, so there is nothing more shameful and at the same time more pernicious when attained by bad measures, and purchased at the price of liberty.

Letter to Her Daughter from the New White House

Abigail Adams

Washington, 21 November, 1800

My Dear Child:

I arrived here on Sunday last, and without meeting with any accident worth noticing, except losing ourselves when we left Baltimore and going eight or nine miles on the Frederick road, by which means we were obliged to go the other eight through woods, where we wandered two hours without finding a guide or the path. Fortunately, a straggling black came up with us, and we engaged him as a guide to extricate us out of our difficulty; but woods are all you see from Baltimore until you reach *the city*, which is only so in name. Here and there is a small cot, without a glass window, interspersed amongst the forests, through which you travel miles without seeing any human being. In the city there are buildings enough, if they were compact and finished, to accommodate Congress and those attached to it; but as they are, and scattered as they are, I see no great comfort for them. The river, which runs up to Alexandria,[1] is in full view of my window, and I see the vessels as they pass and repass. The house is upon a grand and superb scale, requiring about thirty servants to attend and keep the apartments in proper order, and perform the ordinary business of the house and stables; an establishment very well proportioned to the President's salary. The lighting of the apartments, from the kitchen to parlors and chambers, is a tax indeed; and the fires we are obliged to keep to secure us from daily agues is another very cheering comfort. To assist us in this great castle, and render less attendance necessary, bells are wholly wanting, not one single one being hung through the whole house, and promises are all you can obtain. This is so great an inconvenience, that I know not what to do, or how to do. The ladies from Georgetown[2] and in the city have many of them visited me. Yesterday I returned fifteen visits—but such a place as Georgetown appears—why, our Milton is beautiful. But no comparisons—if they will put me up some bells and let me have wood enough to keep fires, I design to be pleased. I could content myself almost anywhere three months; but, surrounded with forests, can you believe that wood is not to be had because people cannot be found to cut and cart it? Briesler entered into a contract with a man to supply him with wood. A small part, a few cords only, has he been able to get. Most of that was expended to dry the walls of the house before we came in, and yesterday the man told him it was impossible for him to procure it to be cut and carted. He has had recourse to coals; but we cannot get grates made and set. We have, indeed, come into a *new country.*

---

1. **Alexandria:** A city in northeastern Virginia.

2. **Georgetown:** A section of Washington, D.C.

BUILDING THE FIRST WHITE HOUSE

WASHINGTON D.C. 1798

You must keep all this to yourself, and, when asked how I like it, say that I write you the situation is beautiful, which is true. The house is made habitable, but there is not a single apartment finished, and all within-side, except the plastering, has been done since Briesler came. We have not the least fence, yard, or other convenience, without, and the great unfinished audience room I make a drying-room of, to hang up the clothes in. The principal stairs are not up, and will not be this winter. Six chambers are made comfortable; two are occupied by the President and Mr. Shaw; two lower rooms, one for a common parlor, and one for a levee room. Upstairs there is the oval room, which is designed for the drawing room, and has the crimson furniture in it. It is a very handsome room now; but, when completed, it will be beautiful. If the twelve years, in which this place has been considered as the future seat of government, had been improved, as they would have been if in New England, very many of the present inconveniences would have been removed. It is a beautiful spot, capable of every improvement, and, the more I view it, the more I am delighted with it.

Since I sat down to write, I have been called down to a servant from Mount Vernon,[3] with a billet[4] from Major Custis, and a haunch of venison, and a kind, congratulatory letter from Mrs. Lewis, upon my arrival in the city, with Mrs. Washington's love, inviting me to Mount Vernon, where, health permitting, I will go before I leave this place.

Affectionately, your mother,
Abigail Adams

---

3. Mount Vernon: Home of George Washington, located in northern Virginia.
4. billet (bil' it) *n.*: A brief letter.

RESPONDING TO THE SELECTION

Your Response
1. Based on this letter, what is your impression of Abigail Adams?
2. What details in the letter did you find most interesting? Why?

Recalling
3. By what is Washington, D.C., surrounded?
4. (a) Why are the Adamses "obliged to keep" a fire burning in the fireplace? (b) Why is there very little firewood?
5. Describe the state of the living quarters in the White House.
6. At the end of her letter, what invitation does Adams mention receiving?

Interpreting
7. What do you think is Adams's attitude toward living in the White House? Explain how her selection of details conveys this attitude.
8. Why do you think Adams tells her daughter to keep her complaints about the White House to herself?

Applying
9. Name two contrasts between Adams's description of the White House and Washington, D.C., and the appearance of the building and the city today.

ANALYZING LITERATURE

Recognizing Descriptive Writing
Descriptive writing creates an impression of a person, place, or thing through details that appeal to one or more of the five senses. For example, one of the details Abigail Adams includes

in her description of the surroundings of the White House is "the river, which runs up to Alexandria."

1. Name four details, including some that appeal to senses other than sight, that Adams includes in her description of the interior of the White House.
2. What impression of the White House does Adams's description create?
3. How does her description of the area surrounding the White House add to this impression?

CRITICAL THINKING AND READING

Inferring a Writer's Attitude

Writers often convey their attitude toward a subject through their description of it. Though in some cases the writer's attitude may be directly stated, most often you have to make inferences, or draw conclusions, about the writer's attitude by examining his or her choice of words or details. For example, from Adams's statement that "woods are all you see from Baltimore until you reach the city, which is so only in name," you can infer that Adams felt that Washington, D.C., was isolated and undeveloped.

What inference can you make from each of the following passages from the "Letter to Her Daughter"?

1. "In the city there are buildings enough, if they were compact and finished, to accommodate Congress and those attached to it; but as they are, and scattered as they are, I see no great comfort for them."
2. "The house is upon a grand and superb scale. . . ."
3. "We have not the least fence, yard, or other convenience, without . . . ."

THINKING AND WRITING

Writing a Description

Review your list of details about your city hall. Selecting appropriate details from your list, write a description of some aspect of your city hall, such as the exterior. Write a description, presenting your details in spatial order. When you revise try to think about how someone who has never seen your city hall would respond to your description. Have you included enough details to enable a person to visualize it? Have you included too many for a brief description?

LEARNING OPTIONS

1. **Language.** Upon arriving in Washington, Adams reports that she and her party wandered around in the woods for two hours before they found someone to "extricate" them. The word *extricate* comes from the Latin *extricare* meaning "to disentangle." Use a dictionary that provides etymologies, or word histories, to find the original source of the following words from Adams's letter: interspersed, superb, apartment, furniture, congratulatory.
2. **Cross-curricular Connection.** As Adams describes it, Washington, D.C., is a wilderness. Why did Congress choose a site in the middle of nowhere for our nation's capital? Investigate the politics that went into the decision. Share your findings in a brief oral or written report.
3. **Writing.** Imagine that picture postcards were available in 1800. Develop a line of postcards of Washington and the White House to sell to tourists. Write detailed directions for an artist or draw pictures that are based on Adams's vivid description.

MICHEL-GUILLAUME JEAN DE CRÈVECOEUR

1735–1813

The first writer to compare America to a melting pot, Michel-Guillaume Jean de Crèvecoeur chronicled his experiences and observations as a European immigrant adjusting to life in America. His idealistic descriptions confirmed many people's vision of America as a land of great promise.

Born into a wealthy French aristocratic family, Crèvecoeur emigrated to Canada at the age of nineteen and served for several years as a member of the French army in Quebec. After his military career ended in 1759, Crèvecoeur spent ten years traveling throughout the colonies as a surveyor and an Indian trader. In 1769 Crèvecoeur married and settled on a 120-acre farm in Orange County, New York. While living on his farm, which he named Pine Hill, Crèvecoeur began writing about his experiences in America.

Because his position during the Revolutionary War was ambiguous, Crèvecoeur was at one point forced by the revolutionaries to leave his farm; another time he was imprisoned for several months by the British. In 1780 Crèvecoeur sailed to London, where his *Letters from an American Farmer* was published two years later. The book, which was translated into several languages, was successful and made Crèvecoeur famous.

Meanwhile France was moving toward its own revolution. While there, Crèvecoeur prepared an expanded French edition of his *Letters . . .*, which was received with wild enthusiasm. He found himself a popular hero who confirmed the evils of the Old World and extolled the promises of the New.

In 1783 he returned to America as the French Consul to New York, New Jersey, and Connecticut. He was so popular that various cities gave him honorary citizenship; St. Johnsbury, Vermont, took its name from the name he used in America, J. Hector St. John.

His good fortune, however, was mixed with bad. On his return he discovered that his farm had been burned, his wife killed, and his children sent to live with foster parents in Boston. When the French Revolution began in 1789, he was obliged to return to Paris. He never came back to America.

With the outbreak of the Reign of Terror in 1793, Crèvecoeur fled Paris for his family home in Normandy. There he wrote another book about New York and Pennsylvania, which was published in 1801. France and the rest of Europe, however, were by then absorbed in the wars of Napoleon and no longer interested in stories of America.

Crèvecoeur spent the last twelve years of his life largely forgotten amid the political turmoil of Europe.

GUIDE FOR INTERPRETING

from Letters from an American Farmer

Epistles. An epistle, or literary letter, is a formal composition written in the form of a letter addressed to a distant person or group of people. Unlike common personal letters, which tend to be conversational and private compositions, epistles are carefully crafted works of literature, intended for a general audience.

The epistle has been a popular literary form throughout history. In ancient Greece and Rome, philosophers recorded their thoughts in epistle form. Centuries later the epistle form was used in the New Testament. During the eighteenth century, European writers frequently composed their works—poems, essays, and novels—using the epistle form.

Influenced by the eighteenth-century European writers, Crèvecoeur chose the epistle form for his essays about life in America. Crèvecoeur's letters are supposedly written by an American farmer named "James" to his friend "Mr. F. B.," but in reality they are intended for a general audience. By presenting his essays in this form, Crèvecoeur is able to maintain a personal tone, while attempting to convince the general public to accept his ideas and opinions.

A careful reader of Crèvecoeur's twelve *Letters* will see that life in the New World is not totally idyllic, but that is not what Europe wanted to hear. Although he did not intend to write a piece of immigrant propaganda, luring people to North America, Crèvecoeur does boast in his last letter that he has "caused upwards of a hundred and twenty families to remove thither."

The new country needed hard workers, so it is no wonder that some of its leaders were worried about the popularity of Crèvecoeur's glowing descriptions. Washington called the *Letters* "rather too flattering," but it was up to the wise and witty Ben Franklin to write and publish (first in France) in 1784 *Advice to Such As Would Remove to America*. He begins by warning that even though "there are in that country few people so miserable as the poor of Europe," neither are there many rich. "America is a land of labor," he continues, and what it needs are laborers, farmers, mechanics, and skilled artisans. Gentlemen need not apply.

As you read the selection, note what seems probably true about North America at the time and what seems perhaps wishful exaggeration by Crèvecoeur. Do you *want* to believe him? Why or why not?

What does being an American mean to you? Freewrite about what you associate with being an American.

from Letters from an American Farmer

Michel-Guillaume Jean de Crèvecoeur

In this great American asylum, the poor of Europe have by some means met together, and in consequence of various causes; to what purpose should they ask one another what countrymen they are? Alas, two thirds of them had no country. Can a wretch who wanders about, who works and starves, whose life is a continual scene of sore affliction or pinching penury, can that man call England or any other kingdom his country? A country that had no bread for him, whose fields procured him no harvest, who met with nothing but the frowns of the rich, the severity of the laws, with jails and punishments; who owned not a single foot of the extensive surface of this planet? No! Urged by a variety of motives, here they came. Everything has tended to regenerate them; new laws, a new mode of living, a new social system; here they are become men: in Europe they were as so many useless plants, wanting vegetative mold[1] and refreshing showers; they withered, and were mowed down by want, hunger, and war; but now by the power of transplantation, like all other plants they have taken root and flourished! Formerly they were not numbered in any civil lists[2] of their country, except in those of the poor; here they rank as citizens. By what invisible power has this surprising metamorphosis been performed? By that of the laws and that of their industry. The laws, the indulgent laws, protect them as they arrive, stamping on them the symbol of adoption; they receive ample rewards for their labors; these accumulated rewards procure them lands; those lands confer on them the title of freemen, and to that title every benefit is affixed which men can possibly require. This is the great operation daily performed by our laws. From whence proceed these laws? From our government. Whence the government? It is derived from the original genius and strong desire of the people ratified and confirmed by the crown. . . .

What attachment can a poor European emigrant have for a country where he had nothing? The knowledge of the language, the love of a few kindred as poor as himself, were the only cords that tied him: his country is now that which gives him land, bread, protection, and consequence: *Ubi panis ibi patria*[3] is the motto of all emigrants. What then is the American, this new man? He is either a European, or the descendant of a European, hence that strange mixture of blood, which you will find in no other country. I could point out to you a family whose grandfather was an Englishman, whose wife was Dutch, whose son married a French woman, and whose present four sons have now four wives of different nations. *He* is an American, who, leaving behind him all his ancient prejudices and manners, receives

---

1. **vegetative mold:** Enriched soil.
2. **civil lists:** Lists of distinguished persons.

3. ***Ubi . . . patria:*** "Where there is bread, there is one's fatherland" (Latin).

new ones from the new mode of life he has embraced, the new government he obeys, and the new rank he holds. He becomes an American by being received in the broad lap of our great *Alma Mater.*[4] Here individuals of

all nations are melted into a new race of men, whose labors and posterity will one day cause great changes in the world. Americans are the western pilgrims, who are carrying along with them that great mass of arts, sciences, vigor, and industry which began long since in the east; they will finish the great circle. The Americans were once scattered all over Europe; here they are incorporated into one of the finest systems of population

---

4. *Alma Mater* (al′ mə mä′ tər): "Fostering mother." Here, referring to America; usually used in reference to a school or college.

INDEPENDENCE (SQUIRE JACK PORTER) 1858
Frank Blackwell Mayer
National Museum of American Art, Smithsonian Institution

from *Letters from an American Farmer* 149

which has ever appeared, and which will hereafter become distinct by the power of the different climates they inhabit. The American ought therefore to love this country much better than that wherein either he or his forefathers were born. Here the rewards of his industry follow with equal steps the progress of his labor; his labor is founded on the basis of nature, *self-interest;* can it want a stronger allurement? Wives and children, who before in vain demanded of him a morsel of bread, now, fat and frolicsome, gladly help their father to clear those fields whence exuberant crops are to arise to feed and to clothe them all; without any part being claimed, either by a despotic prince, a rich abbot,[5] or a mighty lord. Here religion demands but little of him; a small voluntary salary to the minister, and gratitude to God; can he refuse these? The American is a new man, who acts upon new principles; he must therefore entertain new ideas, and form new opinions. From involuntary idleness, servile dependence, penury, and useless labor, he has passed to toils of a very different nature, rewarded by ample subsistence—This is an American.

---

5. abbot *n.*: The head of a monastery.

MULTICULTURAL CONNECTION

How America Evolved Into a Multicultural Society

Crèvecoeur's letter indicates that even in Colonial times, immigrants were coming to America from a variety of countries. During the 1600's and 1700's, settlers came to the Thirteen Colonies from England, Germany, Holland, Ireland, Wales, Scotland, and France. At that time, the Southwest was owned by Spain, and colonists from that country settled there and later established large ranches. Finally, many enslaved Africans were brought to America as unwilling "immigrants."

"Waves" of immigration. After this early period, America experienced several great waves of immigration. In the 1840's, a potato famine in Ireland drove one and a half million people westward to our shores. Also, large numbers of Chinese immigrants arrived in California hoping to strike it rich in the Gold Rush of 1849.

A second great wave of immigration took place in the 1870's. Millions of immigrants came from northern Europe—mostly from Germany and Scandinavia. Some were farmers who settled on the Great Plains; others were skilled workers who entered the rapidly growing industries of the East.

The third wave of immigration lasted from the 1880's until the outbreak of World War I in 1914. It brought as many immigrants to America's shores as both earlier waves combined. These new immigrants were from southern and eastern Europe. They included Czechs, Hungarians, Poles, Greeks, and southern Italians, as well as Russians and Turks.

Bar the gate or keep it open? By 1929, laws had reduced the annual quota of immigrants to 150,000. Immigration laws eased up after World War II, as new prosperity made Americans more generous.

Today, immigrants are as likely to come from Mexico, Vietnam, and Korea as from Europe. The United States continues to be a nation of immigrants.

Exploring on Your Own

When and from where did your family first come to the United States? Find out what immigration was like for them, and share your information with the class in an oral presentation.

RESPONDING TO THE SELECTION

Your Response
1. In your opinion, what is an American?
2. Do you recognize the America and the American that Crèvecoeur describes? How has the country and its people changed?
3. Do you agree with Crèvecoeur that self-interest is a valuable quality? Why or why not?

Recalling
4. What has "tended to regenerate" Europeans who have immigrated to America?
5. According to Crèvecoeur, what effect will the "new race of men" created in America ultimately have on the world?

Interpreting
6. (a) What is the logic of Crèvecoeur's arguments? (b) What are his premises? (c) What is his support?
7. (a) How would you summarize Crèvecoeur's definition of an American? (b) Why does he refer to an American as a "new man"?
8. (a) Find two examples of exaggeration in Crèvecoeur's description of life in America. (b) Why does he use exaggeration?

Applying
9. Do you think Crèvecoeur would have written his epistle today? If so, what has stayed essentially the same? If not, what are the important differences?

ANALYZING LITERATURE

Understanding Epistles
An **epistle,** or literary letter, is a formal composition written in the form of a letter addressed to a distant person or group of people. Crèvecoeur's essays in *Letters from an American Farmer* are written in epistle form. The letters are addressed to a fictional character named Mr. F. B., though in reality they are intended for a general audience.

One way that Crèvecoeur establishes a personal tone is to use the pronoun *you* in address-ing his audience. How does the epistle form allow him to maintain a personal tone while attempting to convince the general public to accept his ideas and opinions? Support your answer with passages from the selection.

CRITICAL THINKING AND READING

Supporting Opinions
A **fact** can be proved true or false. An **opinion** is a personal belief, attitude, or judgment that cannot be proved. However, an opinion that is supported by facts we call well-grounded or sound.

Identify the facts Crèvecoeur uses to back up each of the following opinions.
1. ". . . here they are become men: in Europe they were so many useless plants . . ."
2. "The American ought therefore to love this country much better than that wherein either he or his forefathers were born."

THINKING AND WRITING

Writing an Epistle
What does it mean to be an American today? Review your freewriting about being an American. Spend some time brainstorming about the people who live in the United States, the opportunities they have, and the difficulties they may face. Record your thoughts so that you can write an epistle discussing what it means to be an American today. Address your letter to a fictional person in a foreign country. Then write your letter, using examples to support your opinions. Try to maintain a personal tone. When you revise, make sure that your letter is well organized and that your opinions are stated clearly.

LEARNING OPTION

Art. What, then, is an American? Respond to Crèvecoeur's question in any way you choose. For example, you might write a poem, create a photo montage, interpret a piece of music, or perform a dance. Share your idea of what an American is.

GUIDE FOR INTERPRETING

from The Interesting Narrative of the Life of Olaudah Equiano

Olaudah Equiano (1745–1797) was eleven years old when he and his sister were kidnapped from their home in West Africa and sold to British slave traders. Separated from his sister, Equiano was taken first to the West Indies, then to Virginia, where he was purchased by a British captain and employed at sea.

Renamed Gustavus Vassa, Equiano was enslaved for nearly ten years. After buying his freedom, he continued to work as a seaman. In later years he settled in England and devoted himself to the abolition of slavery. To publicize the plight of slaves, he wrote his two-volume autobiography, *The Interesting Narrative.*

Published in 1789, Equiano's autobiography created a sensation. It brought polite society face to face with the cruelties of slavery and contributed to the banning of the slave trade in both the United States and England.

Literary Forms

Slave Narrative. In the following excerpt, Equiano describes crossing the Atlantic in a slave ship. Called "the middle passage," this nightmarish voyage was the middle part of the Africans' journey from freedom to slavery. For six to ten weeks, Africans were crammed below deck in spaces sometimes less than 5 feet high. Families were torn apart, men and women placed in separate holds. Men were often shackled together in pairs.

Confinement in the hot, poorly ventilated holds was torturous. Overcrowding, disease, and despair claimed many lives. Some Africans mutinied. Others tried to starve themselves or jump overboard, as Equiano describes. Historians estimate that nearly 2 million Africans died before reaching the West Indies.

Equiano's account of the middle passage is an early example of a slave narrative. An American literary genre, a **slave narrative** is an autobiographical account of life as a slave. Often written to expose the horrors of human bondage, it documents a slave's experiences from his or her own point of view.

Encouraged by abolitionists, many former slaves published narratives in the years before the Civil War. Others told their stories in the first part of the twentieth century. Henry Louis Gates, Jr., professor of English and African American studies, notes that "no other group of slaves anywhere, at any other period in history, has left such a large repository of testimony about the horror of becoming the legal property of another human being."

Focus

Imagine you have been kidnapped and taken to a foreign country to perform forced labor. What would you miss most? How would you maintain your memories of home? Respond in a journal entry.

from The Interesting Narrative of the Life of Olaudah Equiano

Olaudah Equiano

In the first several chapters, Vassa describes how he and his sister were kidnapped from their home in West Africa by slave traders and transported to the African coast. During this six- or seven-month journey, Vassa was separated from his sister and held at a series of way stations. After reaching the coast, Vassa was shipped with other slaves to the New World. The following account describes this horrifying journey.

At last when the ship we were in, had got in all her cargo, they made ready with many fearful noises, and we were all put under deck, so that we could not see how they managed the vessel. But this disappointment was the least of my sorrow. The stench of the hold while we were on the coast was so intolerably loathsome, that it was dangerous to remain there for any time, and some of us had been permitted to stay on the deck for the fresh air; but now that the whole ship's cargo were confined together, it became absolutely pestilential. The closeness of the place, and the heat of the climate, added to the number in the ship, which was so crowded that each had scarcely room to turn himself, almost suffocated us. This produced copious perspirations, so that the air soon became unfit for respiration, from a variety of loathsome smells, and brought on a sickness among the slaves, of which many died—thus falling victims to the improvident avarice, as I may call

it, of their purchasers. This wretched situation was again aggravated by the galling of the chains, now become insupportable, and the filth of the necessary tubs, into which the children often fell, and were almost suffocated. The shrieks of the women, and the groans of the dying, rendered the whole a scene of horror almost inconceivable. Happily perhaps, for myself, I was soon reduced so low here that it was thought necessary to keep me almost always on deck; and from my extreme youth I was not put in fetters.[1] In this situation I expected every hour to share the fate of my companions, some of whom were almost daily brought upon deck at the point of death, which I began to hope would soon put an end to my miseries. Often did I think many of the inhabitants of the deep much more happy than myself. I envied them the freedom they enjoyed, and as often

---

1. fetters (fet′ ərz) *n.*: Chains.

SLAVES BELOW DECK (detail)
Lt. Francis Meynell
National Maritime
Museum, Greenwich

wished I could change my condition for theirs. Every circumstance I met with, served only to render my state more painful, and heightened my apprehensions, and my opinion of the cruelty of the whites.

One day they had taken a number of fishes; and when they had killed and satisfied themselves with as many as they thought fit, to our astonishment who were on deck, rather than give any of them to us to eat, as we expected, they tossed the remaining fish into the sea again, although we begged and prayed for some as well as we could, but in vain; and some of my countrymen, being pressed by hunger, took an opportunity, when they thought no one saw them, of trying to get a little privately; but they were discovered, and the attempt procured them some very severe floggings. One day, when we had a smooth sea and moderate wind, two of my wearied countrymen who were chained together (I was near them at the time), preferring death to such a life of misery, somehow made through the nettings and jumped into the sea; immediately, another quite dejected fellow, who, on account of his illness, was suffered to be out of irons, also followed their example; and I believe many more would very

soon have done the same, if they had not been prevented by the ship's crew, who were instantly alarmed. Those of us that were the most active, were in a moment put down under the deck; and there was such a noise and confusion amongst the people of the ship as I never heard before, to stop her, and get the boat out to go after the slaves. However, two of the wretches were drowned, but they got the other, and afterwards flogged him unmercifully, for thus attempting to prefer death to slavery. In this manner we continued to undergo more hardships than I can now relate, hardships which are inseparable from this accursed trade. Many a time we were near suffocation from the want of fresh air, which we were often without for whole days together. This, and the stench of the necessary tubs, carried off many.

During our passage, I first saw flying fishes, which surprised me very much; they used frequently to fly across the ship, and many of them fell on the deck. I also now first saw the use of the quadrant;[2] I had often with

---

2. **quadrant** (kwä′ drənt) *n*.: An instrument used by navigators to determine the position of a ship.

astonishment seen the mariners make observations with it, and I could not think what it meant. They at last took notice of my surprise; and one of them, willing to increase it, as well as to gratify my curiosity, made me one day look through it. The clouds appeared to me to be land, which disappeared as they passed along. This heightened my wonder; and I was now more persuaded than ever, that I was in another world, and that every thing about me was magic. At last, we came in sight of the island of Barbados, at which the whites on board gave a great shout, and made many signs of joy to us. We did not know what to think of this; but as the vessel drew nearer, we plainly saw the harbor, and other ships of different kinds and sizes, and we soon anchored amongst them, off Bridgetown.[3] Many merchants and planters now came on board, though it was in the evening. They put us in separate parcels,[4] and examined us attentively. They also made us jump,

and pointed to the land, signifying we were to go there. We thought by this, we should be eaten by these ugly men, as they appeared to us; and, when soon after we were all put down under the deck again, there was much dread and trembling among us, and nothing but bitter cries to be heard all the night from these apprehensions, insomuch, that at last the white people got some old slaves from the land to pacify us. They told us we were not to be eaten, but to work, and were soon to go on land, where we should see many of our country people. This report eased us much. And sure enough, soon after we were landed, there came to us Africans of all languages.

We were conducted immediately to the merchant's yard, where we were all pent up together, like so many sheep in a fold, without regard to sex or age. . . . We were not many days in the merchant's custody, before we were sold after their usual manner, which is this: On a signal given (as the beat of a drum), the buyers rush at once into the yard where the slaves are confined, and make choice of that parcel they like best. . . .

---

3. Bridgetown: The capital of Barbados.
4. parcels (pär′ səlz) *n.*: Groups.

RESPONDING TO THE SELECTION

Your Response
1. What do you find most disturbing about this selection? Explain.
2. Based on his narrative, what is your impression of Equiano?

Interpreting
3. Why does Equiano blame the illness aboard the ship on the "improvident avarice" of the traders?
4. How can you tell that Equiano has a great zest for life despite his assertion that he wanted to die? Provide examples from the selection.

Applying
5. Equiano graphically describes the effects of the slave trade on the enslaved. How do you think the slave traders were affected by their business activities? Explain.

ANALYZING LITERATURE

Slave Narrative
A **slave narrative** is an autobiographical account of life as a slave. In describing significant events in his or her life, the writer often documents the horrors of slavery. This selection from Equiano's narrative provides a sobering description of the middle passage and the operation of the slave trade.
1. Cite two examples of the slave traders' cruelty to the slaves.
2. Cite two examples that show the traders' concern for the slaves' well-being.
3. What might have motivated the traders' behavior toward their human cargo? Explain.

from *The Interesting Narrative of the Life of Olaudah Equiano* 155

The Statue of Liberty

In early July 1986, the nation's attention was on New York Harbor, where festivities were in progress celebrating the centennial of the Statue of Liberty. The Centennial Year of Liberty, proclaimed by President Reagan, climaxed on October 28 with a rededication of the statue, exactly one hundred years after its unveiling by President Cleveland.

The immense statue was a gift from the people of France to the people of America commemorating the signing of the Declaration of Independence. The gift was an expression of the friendship and the ideal of liberty shared by both nations.

The friendship between the United States and France began in the Revolutionary Period. The help of France had been crucial to the colonists' victory over Great Britain. The French people—and even some of the French aristocracy, such as the Marquis de Lafayette—saw in the American Revolution not only a revolt against a powerful ruler but the successful establishment of a constitutional government with leadership based on ability, not on wealth or family. This ideal motivated France. The victory of the American colonists in 1776 directly influenced the outbreak of revolution in France eight years later. The friendship between the nations remained strong over the next century. When the Statue of Liberty was dedicated in 1886, it was offered as a memorial to the alliance between France and the American colonists who had fought for independence in the Revolutionary War.

THE STATUE'S HISTORY

In Paris in the late 1860's, two men—Édouard-René Lafebvre de Laboulaye, a pro-

fessor of law, and Frédéric Bartholdi, a young sculptor—conceived the plan of a monument to the ideal of liberty. They greatly admired the United States and felt that such a monument would honor the successful establishment in America of a representative government—something still not achieved and dearly desired in France. France's own revolution had yet to achieve its goals of "Liberty, Equality, Fraternity."

The "Monument to American Independence: Liberty Enlightening the World," as it was officially called, was laboriously built of 350 thin sheets of copper, hammered over wooden molds. By 1885 the completed statue, 150 feet high, towered over the Parisian skyline, waiting to be shipped to the United States.

Meanwhile, in the United States, money was being raised for a suitable pedestal for the statue, which was to be placed in New York Harbor. The fund-raising committee asked a young Jewish poet, Emma Lazarus, to write a poem to aid their efforts. Lazarus, who was a tireless crusader for the immigrants who came through New York Harbor, wrote a poem that ends with these lines:

> . . . Give me your tired, your poor,
> Your huddled masses yearning to
>   breathe free,
> The wretched refuse of your teeming
>   shore.
> Send these, the homeless, tempest-
>   tossed to me
> I lift my lamp beside the golden door.

A WORLDWIDE SYMBOL

Since its dedication the statue has come to symbolize far more than the ideal of lib-

erty to which it was dedicated. Standing in New York Harbor, it has welcomed multitudes of immigrants, promising hope and opportunity. Emma Lazarus's poem added to Liberty's stern gaze and outstretched arm the voice of a protective mother. In 1903 the poem was engraved on a bronze plaque and affixed to the interior of the pedestal. The large numbers of immigrants linked the statue with the poem's image as "Mother of Exiles."

Over the years, the Lady With the Torch has become a worldwide symbol of human equality and personal liberty. In May 1989, Chinese students demonstrating for freedom in Beijing's Tiananmen Square carried and raised a Goddess of Democracy as a symbol of their goals. This goddess closely resembled the Statue of Liberty. Her well-known image made a statement that words could not.

YOUR WRITING PROCESS

WRITING A NEWS STORY

Colonists relied on newspapers for information about current events because there was no television or radio. Imagine that you are a reporter for a colonial press and that you've been assigned to cover an important event during the Revolutionary period.

Focus

Assignment: Write a news story about an important event associated with the Revolution.
Purpose: Inform readers of what has happened.
Audience: People living in the Thirteen Colonies.

Prewriting

1. Do some research. Look through American history books to brainstorm for story ideas. Choose three to five topics that interest you. Then focus on one of these and take notes from as many sources as possible.

2. Ask questions. Good reporters use six basic types of questions—*who?, what?, where?, why?, when?,* and *how?*—to explore their topics. Write these categories across the top of a page and, under each, list appropriate questions. Work with another writer to make your questions as probing as possible.

3. Look at models with other classmates. Get together in small groups and study a current newspaper, noting the content and style of news stories. For example, observe how the following lead, or opening paragraph, captures a reader's attention while conveying essential information:

> What could be the 27th Amendment to the Constitution was ratified by the necessary 38th state today. But it is unclear whether this measure, which won its first state ratification in 1789, will ever take effect.

Drafting

1. Outline first. Some writers like formal outlines; others prefer rough lists. Whatever you choose, prepare the outline before you begin to draft. Plan how many paragraphs your news story will include and what information each paragraph will contain.

2. Write a good lead. Make sure that your opening paragraph includes the most essential information, so that it draws the reader into the story. Then include the details in a decreasing order of importance, as reflected in the following diagram of an inverted pyramid:

Lead ——— Most important details
- Least important details

3. Grab your readers' attention with a headline. Use the key words of your report to write a headline that will grab your readers' attention. For example, try some alliteration or a punchy noun or verb.

Revising and Editing

1. Whittle your language down to its bones. Be ruthless. Ask yourself whether every word is doing its fair share of the work. One student improved her lead by taking out unnecessary words and using more specific verbs and nouns.

Student Model

On the evening of December 16, 1773, a group of 40
to 50 colonists looking like *disguised as* Indians threw *dumped* the entire
contents of 342 containers *chests* of good tea into the water
of Boston Harbor.

---

2. Write questions for your peer editor. Ask your editor specific questions. For example, if parts of your story don't seem quite right, ask your peer editor about them. Maybe he or she can suggest ways to improve them. Use questions like the following to prompt your classmate:
• Does this quotation seem relevant to the story?
• Do you think this paragraph is necessary?
• Is this list of reasons too long to be clear?
• Is my account of events fair and objective?

3. Read your draft aloud. Your eyes may skip over a mistake or fill in a missing word, but you'll catch such errors if you're reading aloud. You may also hear the clumsiness of a sentence that looks just fine on the page.

4. Check pronoun-antecedent agreement. It's helpful to repeat key names and words throughout your report, but you will also find yourself using pronouns to refer to key people, places, and things that you mention in your first paragraph. As you edit, check pronoun-antecedent agreement carefully (gender, number, and case).

Writer's Hint

Here are some headline-writing guidelines:
• Put the story's main idea in the headline.
• Use mostly short words.
• Avoid beginning a headline with a verb, so that the reader doesn't have to ask, "Who did it?"
• Omit articles—*a, an, the*—except where necessary.

Options for Publishing

• Show your news story to adults you know and ask them what they like best about it.
• Share your news story with a history class that is studying the Revolution. Ask them for their reactions to it.
• Together with your classmates, create an edition of the *Colonial News*, complete with a masthead, bylines, and graphics.

Reviewing Your Writing Process

1. Did looking at newspaper stories help you with this assignment? Why or why not?
2. Did your peer editor give you helpful suggestions when you questioned him or her? Explain.

NIAGARA FALLS, ABOUT 1832–1840
Thomas Chambers
Wadsworth Atheneum, Hartford

A GROWING NATION
1800–1840

America is a land of wonders, in which everything is in constant motion and every change seems an improvement. . . . No natural boundary seems to be set to the efforts of man; and in his eyes what is not yet done is only what he has not yet attempted to do.

Alexis de Tocqueville

In 1831, Alexis de Tocqueville, a young Frenchman, journeyed to the United States to report on the American penitentiary system for his government. He observed far more than prisons during his stay, however. His observations were compiled in a monumental four-volume work, *Democracy in America,* that is considered a classic of political literature. While Tocqueville was impressed by the bustle and optimism that he noted, he was not as impressed by American literature. "America has produced very few writers of distinction," he wrote, adding that the literary output of England "still darts its rays into the forests of the New World."

Tocqueville had perhaps arrived a few years too soon. At the very time he was in the United States, a number of writers of distinction were at work. Among them were Washington Irving, James Fenimore Cooper, William Cullen Bryant, and Edgar Allan Poe, all of whom would achieve fame and acceptance far beyond "the forests of the New World."

LOUISIANA PURCHASE CEREMONY AT
NEW ORLEANS, 20 DECEMBER 1803
Thor de Thulstrup

THE HISTORICAL SETTING

When Thomas Jefferson was elected President in 1800, three new states, Vermont, Kentucky, and Tennessee, had joined the original thirteen. Then, in 1803, at the stroke of a pen, the Louisiana Purchase doubled the nation's territory. By 1837, when Michigan became a state, more than half the present-day fifty states were in the Union.

The rapid growth of the nation brought with it an upsurge of national pride and identity. Improved transportation helped bind the old and the new states together. Canals, turnpikes, and railroads boomed during this period. Steamboats and sailing packets helped speed people and goods to their destinations. The westward expansion of the United States and its explosive growth in population had profound effects on American life and literature.

Old New York

By 1800, the country's frontier had moved far away from the East Coast. Yet there were other kinds of national frontiers. In the early 1800's, New York, the city that Washington Irving called "Gotham," was becoming a sort of American literary frontier.

New York City had a population of 60,000 in 1800, making it the second largest city in the nation after Philadelphia. A decade later, it passed Philadelphia and was never again challenged for population leadership. By 1840, the population of New York City was 312,000, or about the size of Philadelphia and Boston combined.

The earliest Dutch settlement on Manhattan Island had been at the very southern tip. In 1820, the built-up area extended north to 14th Street and was advancing rapidly up the island. The commercial buildings of the day were low, three or four stories at most.

Despite New York's prosperity, it was not looked upon as a cultural capital. Tocqueville saw it as a center of "all our greatest vices, without any of those interests which counteract their baneful influence." In many people's eyes, Philadelphia remained "the Athens of America," but that was changing. New York, cultivated or not, was attracting America's first professional writers. All four authors represented in this section—Irving,

Cooper, Bryant, and Poe—spent important parts of their careers in New York City.

The Growth of Democracy

When Tocqueville looked at American cities such as New York, he foresaw problems. A firm believer in democratic ideals, Tocqueville was concerned about the possible excesses of democracy in urban areas. He thought that cities were too likely to put power "in the hands of a populace carrying out its own impulses."

In fact, the people of the United States had already moved toward giving themselves more direct power over government. The election in 1828 of Andrew Jackson, "the People's President," ushered in the era of the common man. Property re-

quirements for voting began to be eliminated. Presidential electors were increasingly chosen by popular vote, rather than by state legislatures.

Not everyone shared in the triumph of the common man, however. Despite early stirrings of feminism, little political attention was paid to women. The majority of blacks were still slaves, and each slave counted as three fifths of a person for purposes of congressional representation. Still, this period saw the beginnings of the feminist and anti-slavery movements.

One of the tragic aspects of the Jackson era was "Indian removal," the forcible seizure of tribal lands. In the South, many thousands of Native Americans were uprooted and moved to open lands in the West. The most publicized removal was that of the Cherokees from northwestern Georgia to the Indian Territory, now Oklahoma. This 1838 "Trail

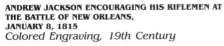

ANDREW JACKSON ENCOURAGING HIS RIFLEMEN AT THE BATTLE OF NEW ORLEANS, JANUARY 8, 1815
Colored Engraving, 19th Century

A Growing Nation (A.D. 1800–A.D. 1840)

The Lewis and
Clark Expedition

Jane Austen

The Battle of New Orleans

1800   **1810**

AMERICAN EVENTS

- Louisiana Purchase extends nation's territory to Rocky Mountains.
  - Lewis and Clark begin expedition exploring and mapping vast region of West.
    - Robert Fulton's steamboat makes first trip from New York City to Albany.
      - *A History of New York . . .* by Diedrich Knickerbocker brings recognition to **Washington Irving.**

- U.S. declares war on Great Britain; early battles in War of 1812 are at sea.
  - Bombardment of Fort McHenry inspires Francis Scott Key to write "The Star-Spangled Banner."
  - Battle of New Orleans occurs after war is officially over.
  - **William Cullen Bryant** publishes early draft of "Thanatopsis" in a Boston magazine.
  - Spain relinquishes claims to Florida for $5 million.

WORLD EVENTS

- England: Samuel Taylor Coleridge finishes writing "Kubla Khan."
  - France: Napoleon Bonaparte proclaims himself emperor.
  - Germany: Friedrich von Schiller gives Swiss their national festival play, *William Tell.*
  - Germany: Ludwig von Beethoven breaks formal musical conventions with *Third Symphony.*
    - England: William Wordsworth completes "Ode on Intimations of Immortality."

- France: Napoleon suffers disastrous military defeat in Russia.
  - England: Jane Austen publishes *Pride and Prejudice.*
  - Belgium: French army under Napoleon routed at Waterloo.
  - Austria: Congress of Vienna redraws map of Europe following Napoleon's downfall.
    - England: Mary Wollstonecraft Shelley creates a legend with *Frankenstein.*
    - England: John Keats writes "Ode to a Nightingale" and "Ode on a Grecian Urn."
    - France: René Laënnec invents the stethoscope.

Alfred, Lord
Tennyson

Samuel Morse

The "Trail of Tears"

| 1820 | 1830 | 1840 |

- **Washington Irving's** *Sketch Book* begins to appear serially in U.S.
- Missouri Compromise bans slavery in some parts of new territories.
  - First women's college in United States founded.
    - James Fenimore Cooper publishes *The Pioneers*.
      - Completion and success of Erie Canal spurs canal building throughout the nation.
        - **Edgar Allan Poe** publishes *Tamerlane,* his first collection of poems.

- Peter Cooper builds *Tom Thumb,* America's first steam-driven locomotive.
  - Cyrus McCormick invents mechanical reaper.
    - Battles at the Alamo and San Jacinto fought while Texas is a republic.
      - Samuel F. B. Morse patents electromagnetic telegraph.
        - U.S. Army marches Cherokees of Georgia on long "Trail of Tears" to Oklahoma.

- **Edgar Allan Poe's** "The Fall of the House of Usher" first appears in print.
  - James Fenimore Cooper's *Leatherstocking Tales* resume with *The Pathfinder*.

- England: Percy Bysshe Shelley publishes the four-act drama *Prometheus Unbound*.
  - Mexico: Mexico gains independence from Spain.
    - Germany: Jakob and Wilhelm Grimm have *Grimm's Fairy Tales* translated into English.
      - Hawaii: King Kamehameha III, who favors U.S. interests, ascends the throne.
        - Russia: Decembrist uprising crushed by czarist forces.

- England: George Stephenson perfects a steam locomotive for Liverpool-Manchester Railway.
  - France: Victor Hugo publishes *Notre Dame de Paris,* popularly called *The Hunchback of Notre Dame*.
    - England: Alfred, Lord Tennyson completes "The Lady of Shalott."
      - France: Eugène Delacroix paints *Women of Algiers*.
        - Denmark: Hans Christian Andersen publishes his first book of fairy tales.

- England: Charles Dickens achieves great success with *Oliver Twist*.
  - England: Elizabeth Barrett Browning adds to her fame with *The Seraphim and Other Poems*.

of Tears" took the lives of about 4,000 of the 15,000 Cherokees who began the long trek.

Despite all this, the first four decades of the 1800's were, on the whole, hopeful ones. The young republic seemed able to weather any storm.

America on the World Stage

One of the storms to be weathered was the War of 1812. This two-and-a-half-year conflict was fought to settle a number of grievances against Great Britain, including the impressment of American seamen by the Royal Navy. Although neither side gained or lost, the war created a number of American military heroes. The bombardment of Fort McHenry in Baltimore Harbor inspired Francis Scott Key to write "The Star-Spangled Banner." After the war, there was a feeling of solidarity in the United States. In addition, the war convinced Europeans that the United States was on the world stage to stay.

That fact was emphasized again in 1823 with the Monroe Doctrine. President James Monroe, fearing European intervention in the newly free nations of Latin America, stated that "the American continents . . . are henceforth not to be considered as subjects for future colonization by any European powers." Monroe's statement attracted little attention at the time. As the United States gained strength and prestige, however, European nations were not eager to challenge it.

Florida and the Southwest raised special problems for the young nation. As late as 1818, Florida was still a Spanish province. Border troubles created tension, and some Americans were killed. The resulting invasion by Andrew Jackson's Tennessee militia convinced Spain to sell Florida rather than have it seized. In 1819, the United States purchased all of Spain's land east of the Mississippi for $5 million.

The situation in Texas was more complicated. Originally a part of Mexico, Texas seceded from Mexico in 1835. The following year, the Mexican army made its famous assault on the Alamo, where every Texan defender was killed. President Jackson recognized the Republic of Texas in 1837. Although Texas wanted to be annexed by the United States, it was not admitted to the Union until

LAST STAND AT THE ALAMO
N. C. Wyeth

1845. The annexation brought about war between Mexico and the United States. The American victory in this war added further territory in the West and Southwest to the United States.

AMERICAN LITERATURE COMES OF AGE

In 1783, when the Peace of Paris ended the American Revolution, an eleventh child was born into the family of a wealthy merchant in New York City. The child, Washington Irving, would become the first professional author of the new nation and the first American literary figure to win an international reputation. Other notable writers appeared on the scene in the early nineteenth century. By 1840, Americans could offer convincing answers to British writer Sydney Smith's taunt from twenty years earlier: "In the four quarters of the globe, who reads an American book, or goes to an American play, or looks at an American picture or statue?"

The Professionals

From early colonial times, there were journalists who wrote and edited for a living. Their works were meant for the moment and did not survive as literature. The important literary figures who do survive from those days were outstanding writers, but none made writing his profession. Thomas Jefferson, for example, was a statesman, and Benjamin Franklin was a printer, inventor, and statesman.

America's cultural independence did not come easily. For nearly 200 years, American readers had been looking to Europe, mainly Great Britain, for most of their reading material other than the Bible, almanacs, newspapers, magazines, and broadsides. Susanna Rowson, raised in Massachusetts but living in England, wrote America's first best-selling novel, *Charlotte Temple*. It was published in London in 1791 and reprinted in Philadelphia in 1794.

In the early nineteenth century, two Scottish writers, Robert Burns and Sir Walter Scott, were popular in the United States. So, too, were three young English poets, Lord Byron, Percy Bysshe Shelley, and John Keats. In addition, classic English works dating back hundreds of years were in print. Tocqueville observed, "There is hardly a pioneer's hut that does not contain a few odd volumes of Shakespeare."

Most American writers of the time could not compete in that company. The names of dozens of writers in the early national period, familiar in their own time, are all but forgotten today. Charles Brockden Brown, James Paulding, Fitz-Greene Halleck, Caroline Kirkland, and N. P. Willis achieved substantial reputations in the early 1800's. All lived in or near New York City, except Kirkland, who was born in New York but moved to frontier Michigan, where she wrote realistic sketches of backwoods life.

A New York Biblical scholar, Clement Clarke Moore, gained more lasting fame with a poem he wrote for his family, with no thought of publication. A relative of Moore's gave a copy of the poem to a newspaper editor in Troy, New York. The poem, popularly known as "'Twas the Night Before Christmas," thus made its first appearance in 1823.

One writer who had a national reputation was William Gilmore Simms of Charleston, South Carolina. As a young man, Simms lived briefly in New York City and published his first novel, *Martin Faber*, there in 1833. His reputation rests mainly on the romantic novels set in South Carolina that he wrote after returning to Charleston.

The major American authors of the day have already been mentioned. Washington Irving achieved his first great success in 1809 with the satiric *History of New York*, supposedly written by Diedrich Knickerbocker. James Fenimore Cooper introduced his frontier hero Natty Bumppo in *The Pioneers*, published in 1823. William Cullen Bryant, born in Massachusetts, wrote the first draft of his famous poem "Thanatopsis" when he was 17. Edgar Allan Poe, today the most widely read of the four, was a tormented genius. Poe's life, though brief and tragic, produced poems, stories, and criticism that have had a powerful influence on the course of American literature.

Knickerbocker and Leatherstocking

The North American continent offered a vast and exciting vista for American writers, whether in the settled regions or on the advancing edge of settlement. The first who took artistic advantage of this view in any sustained way were New Yorkers, members of two informal literary and artistic groups.

One was the Knickerbocker Group, led by Washington Irving. A notable member of this group was William Cullen Bryant, who moved to New York City in 1825. He remained a dominant literary figure in the city for the rest of his eighty-four years. Other members of stature were James Paulding and Fitz-Greene Halleck. Many Knickerbocker members were of lesser talent. Edgar Allan Poe ridiculed them in a critical review, *The Literati of New York City*, as writers with grand pretensions but limited abilities.

The second New York group, whose leader was James Fenimore Cooper, was called the Bread and Cheese Club. Basically a social club, its members' interests were not restricted to literature. Samuel F. B. Morse, renowned as both a painter and the inventor of the telegraph, was a member. So, too, was William Dunlap, an artist, the founder of the National Academy of Design, and the first professional American playwright and producer.

Not only were these groups located in New York, but the subject matter of their members' work was often local. Irving's *History of New York* and some of the stories in *The Sketch Book* (particularly "Rip Van Winkle" and "The Legend of Sleepy Hollow") make vivid use of local scenes and events. Irving, a world traveler, also used many European settings. The sketches in *The Alhambra*, for example, all involve Spain. Even so, Irving's use of regional materials sparked an interest in American locales, especially the Hudson River valley.

James Fenimore Cooper's fearless, straight-shooting frontier hero enthralled readers here and abroad. Natty Bumppo, a man of complete moral integrity, established the pattern for countless western heroes to come (although Bumppo himself was not a westerner). Four of the novels about Natty Bumppo, which are collectively known as *The Leatherstocking Tales,* are set on the upstate New York frontier, which was already a dim memory in Cooper's time.

Cooper, like Irving, was a world traveler, and some of his novels have European settings. Yet Cooper, too, found much near at hand to write about, helping to focus attention on the varied literary wellsprings within the new nation.

In 1831, while Irving was in London and Cooper was in Paris, Samuel Francis Smith, a Boston Baptist clergyman, wrote new words for the British song "God Save the King." Smith's words, simple and stirring, expressed the national mood in a timeless hymn: "My country, 'tis of thee,/Sweet land of liberty,/Of thee I sing."

ILLUSTRATION FROM AN 1872 EDITION OF JAMES FENIMORE COOPER'S *THE LAST OF THE MOHICANS*
Felix Octavius Carr Darley

From Reason to Romance

The Puritans were religious fundamentalists who sought salvation. The founders of the republic were political realists who pursued reason. So, then, how can the writers of the early nineteenth century—Irving, Cooper, Bryant, and Poe—be described? Despite unmistakable differences among them, they were all Romantics.

That name can be misleading, because the Romantics do not necessarily write about love. Romanticism can be viewed as an artistic movement, or a state of mind, or both. Romantic writers favor the imagination over reason, intuition over facts. Irving's *History of New York* is not a dry account of actual events; it is a rollicking history that ignores and alters facts at will. Cooper's *The Deerslayer*, the first in the *Leatherstocking* plot sequence, is not a realistic novel of life on the New York frontier. It is a mythical tale of the "natural" man and of lost innocence, of nature versus civilization.

There are other aspects of Romanticism. One is its intense interest in and reverence for nature. The poems of William Cullen Bryant are nearly perfect examples of this characteristic of Romanticism. Most of Bryant's best-known poems exalt the virtues of nature, whatever the poems' individual themes may be. Their titles show this emphasis: "The Yellow Violet," "A Forest Hymn," "Green River," "Summer Wind," and "The Prairies."

KINDRED SPIRITS
Asher B. Durand
New York Public Library

Another aspect of Romanticism is its accent on mystery—on the strange and fantastic aspects of human experience. In this realm, Edgar Allan Poe stands supreme. Poe wrote forty-eight brilliantly original lyric poems and a number of short stories whose characters, in the words of a biographer, "are either grotesques or the inhabitants of another world than this."

Not all Romantics were writers. Romanticism pervaded all the arts in this time of America's youth. Of special note were the landscape painters who came to be known as the Hudson River School. The most influential of this New York group was English-born Thomas Cole. His haunting and dramatic views of the Hudson River and Catskill Mountains have often been compared to Irving's word images. Perhaps the most famous Hudson River School painting is Asher B. Durand's *Kindred Spirits,* in which Thomas Cole and

William Cullen Bryant stand on a jutting rock overlooking a picturesque valley.

Seedtime in New England

Although many of the significant literary accomplishments from 1800 to 1840 occurred in New York, cultural activity was by no means limited to that city. Small groups of writers could be found in most major cities on the East Coast, notably Philadelphia, Richmond, and Charleston. After 1840, as New York writing lost its preeminence, an impressive burst of literary activity took place in and around Boston. By that date, the movement that one critic has called "the flowering of New England" had already begun. In the next fifteen years, it would produce an array of important writers and enduring literary works.

Quotations by Prominent Figures of the Period

How convenient it would be to many of our great men and great families of doubtful origin, could they have the privilege of the heroes of yore, who, whenever their origin was involved in obscurity, modestly announced themselves descended from a god.
> **Washington Irving,** *A History of New York*

To see him striding along the profile of a hill on a windy day, with his clothes bagging and fluttering about him, one might have mistaken him for the genius of famine descending upon the earth, or some scarecrow eloped from a cornfield.
> **Washington Irving,** "The Legend of Sleepy Hollow"

I am always at a loss to know how much to believe of my own stories.
> **Washington Irving,** *Tales of a Traveler*

All is contradiction in the settlements, while all is concord in the woods. Forts and churches almost always go together, and yet they're downright contradictions, churches being for peace and forts for war.
> **James Fenimore Cooper,** *The Deerslayer*

Ignorance and superstition ever bear a close, and even a mathematical, relationship to each other.
> **James Fenimore Cooper,** *Jack Tier*

Loveliest of lovely things are they,
On earth, that soonest pass away.
> **William Cullen Bryant,** "A Scene on the Banks of the Hudson"

These are the gardens of the Desert, these
The unshorn fields, boundless and beautiful,
For which the speech of England has no name—
The Prairies.
> **William Cullen Bryant,** "The Prairies"

True!—nervous—very, very dreadfully nervous I had been and am; but why *will* you say that I am mad?
> **Edgar Allan Poe,** "The Tell-Tale Heart"

READING CRITICALLY

The Literature of 1800–1840

During the years from 1800 to 1840, the new nation grew and expanded at a rapid pace. During this time the country began developing its own distinctive literary tradition. Because the United States was now an established nation, writers were able to turn from the subject of politics and create literature equal in quality to the work of European writers.

HISTORICAL CONTEXT In 1803 President Jefferson completed the Louisiana Purchase, extending the American boundary to the Rocky Mountains. During the years that followed, many Americans traveled westward, seeking new homes and new opportunities. At the same time, the eastern cities grew rapidly, as the United States developed into an industrialized and self-sufficient nation.

LITERARY MOVEMENTS Following the turn of the century, an artistic movement that had originated in Europe swept through the United States. This movement, which came to be known as Romanticism, grew out of a reaction against the dominant attitudes and approaches of the eighteenth century. Unlike the eighteenth-century writers, who emphasized reason, logic, and scientific observation, the Romantics stressed the examination of inner feelings and emotions and the use of the imagination. The Romantic movement was also characterized by an interest in nature and the supernatural, a strong belief in democracy, and a deep awareness of the past.

WRITERS' TECHNIQUES The attitudes, concerns, and interests of the Romantics are reflected in the themes of the majority of the literary works written between 1800 and 1840. Writers explored the mysteries of nature and the inner self and the relationship between nature and the human imagination. With the establishment of the American identity, writers also began focusing on distinctively American themes and delving into the history of the young nation.

WASHINGTON IRVING

1783–1859

Named after the first American President, Washington Irving became the first American writer to achieve an international reputation.

Born into a wealthy New York family, Irving began studying law at the age of sixteen. He had little interest in his studies, however, and spent much time traveling throughout Europe and New York's Hudson Valley and reading European literature. Irving also wrote satirical essays using the pen name Jonathan Oldstyle. When Irving was twenty-four, he and his brother began publishing an anonymous magazine, *Salmagundi* (the name of a spicy appetizer), which carried humorous sketches and essays about New York society.

In 1809 Irving published his first major work, *A History of New York from the Beginning of the World to the End of the Dutch Dynasty,* using the pseudonym Diedrich Knickerbocker. The *History,* a humorous examination of New York during colonial times, was popular and made Irving famous.

From 1815 to 1832, Irving lived in Europe, traveling extensively and learning about European customs, traditions, and folklore. Inspired by the European folk heritage, Irving created two of his most famous stories, "The Legend of Sleepy Hollow" and "Rip Van Winkle," transforming two traditional German tales into distinctly American stories set in the Hudson Valley. When Irving published these two stories in *The Sketch Book* (1820) under the pseudonym Geoffrey Crayon, writers and critics throughout Europe and the United States responded enthusiastically.

Irving produced other books while living in Europe, including *Bracebridge Hall* (1822), *Tales of a Traveller* (1824), and *The Alhambra* (1832). Another of Irving's more famous stories, "The Devil and Tom Walker," an American adaptation of a German legend about a man who sells his soul to the devil, appeared in *Tales of a Traveller*.

Irving's lengthy stay in Europe prompted some to question his loyalty to his native land. Irving responded, "I am endeavoring to serve my country. Whatever I have written has been written with the feelings and published as the writing of an American. Is that renouncing my country? How else am I to serve my country—by coming home and begging an office of it: which I should not have the kind of talent or the business habits requisite to fill?—If I can do any good in this world it is with my pen."

Although Irving continued to write after returning to the United States in 1832, he is remembered mainly for a few of the stories he wrote while in Europe. Like the folk tales from which they were adapted, these stories have remained popular for generations, becoming an important part of the American literary heritage.

GUIDE FOR INTERPRETING

The Devil and Tom Walker

Literary Forms

Folk Tales. Folk tales are stories handed down orally among the common people of a particular culture. These stories often relate events that are unrealistic or unlikely to happen in the real world in order to teach a lesson or express a general truth about life. The characters in folk tales tend to be stereotypes or stock characters embodying a single human trait, quality, or emotion. For example, a character in a folk tale may embody hatred or greed.

Washington Irving created "The Devil and Tom Walker" by reshaping a German folk tale about a man who sells his soul to the devil. Irving makes the tale distinctly American by setting it in New England during the late 1720's—a time when Puritanism, especially the belief that a person's life should be devoted to God, was being replaced by commercialism and the desire for personal gain. Like the tale from which it was adapted, Irving's story relates a series of unlikely events, involves stereotyped characters, and teaches an important lesson about life. Because Irving's story is grounded in a specific time and place, it also reveals a great deal about life in New England in the 1720's.

Focus

Do you think that some people today sometimes become so concerned with acquiring money and power that they forget to be sympathetic and compassionate toward other people? Freewrite about your thoughts regarding this question.

Primary Source

In "The Devil and Tom Walker," Irving dramatizes the colonists' attitudes toward Native Americans in a number of passages. Irving commented on the attitudes of colonial Americans in an essay called "Traits of Indian Character." These attitudes were reflected in their treatment of the Indians and in the way early American writers portrayed them in their works. The Indians were "doubly wronged by the white men. They have been dispossessed of their hereditary possessions by mercenary and frequently wanton warfare; and their characters have been traduced by bigoted and interested writers. The colonist has often treated them like beasts of the forest; and the author has endeavored to justify him in his outrages. The former found it easier to exterminate than to civilize; the latter to vilify than to discriminate. The appellations of savage and pagan were deemed sufficient to sanction the hostilities of both; and thus the poor wanderers of the forest were persecuted and defamed, not because they were guilty, but because they were ignorant."

The Devil and Tom Walker

Washington Irving

A few miles from Boston in Massachusetts, there is a deep inlet, winding several miles into the interior of the country from Charles Bay, and terminating in a thickly wooded swamp or morass. On one side of this inlet is a beautiful dark grove; on the opposite side the land rises abruptly from the water's edge into a high ridge, on which grow a few scattered oaks of great age and immense size. Under one of these gigantic trees, according to old stories, there was a great amount of treasure buried by Kidd the pirate.[1] The inlet allowed a facility to bring the money in a boat secretly and at night to the very foot of the hill; the elevation of the place permitted a good look-out to be kept that no one was at hand; while the remarkable trees formed good landmarks by which the place might easily be found again. The old stories add, moreover, that the Devil presided at the hiding of the money, and took it under his guardianship; but this it is well known he always does with buried treasure, particularly when it has been ill-gotten. Be that as it may, Kidd never returned to recover his wealth; being shortly after seized at Boston, sent out to England, and there hanged for a pirate.

About the year 1727, just at the time that earthquakes were prevalent in New England, and shook many tall sinners down upon their knees, there lived near this place a meager, miserly fellow, of the name of Tom Walker. He had a wife as miserly as himself: they were so miserly that they even conspired to cheat each other. Whatever the woman could lay hands on, she hid away; a hen could not cackle but she was on the alert to secure the new-laid egg. Her husband was continually prying about to detect her secret hoards, and many and fierce were the conflicts that took place about what ought to have been common property. They lived in a forlorn-looking house that stood alone, and had an air of starvation. A few straggling savin trees, emblems of sterility, grew near it; no smoke ever curled from its chimney; no traveler stopped at its door. A miserable horse, whose ribs were as articulate as the bars of a gridiron, stalked about a field, where a thin carpet of moss, scarcely covering the ragged beds of puddingstone, tantalized and balked his hunger; and sometimes he would lean his head over the fence, look piteously at the passerby, and seem to petition deliverance from this land of famine.

The house and its inmates had altogether a bad name. Tom's wife was a tall termagant, fierce of temper, loud of tongue, and strong of arm. Her voice was often heard in wordy warfare with her husband; and his face sometimes showed signs that their conflicts were not confined to words. No one ventured, however, to interfere between them. The lonely wayfarer shrunk within himself at the horrid clamor and clapperclawing;[2] eyed the den of discord askance; and hurried on his way, rejoicing, if a bachelor, in his celibacy.

One day that Tom Walker had been to a

---

1. **Kidd the pirate:** Captain William Kidd (1645–1701).

2. **clapperclawing** (klap′ ər klô′ ing): Clawing or scratching.

distant part of the neighborhood, he took what he considered a shortcut homeward, through the swamp. Like most shortcuts, it was an ill-chosen route. The swamp was thickly grown with great gloomy pines and hemlocks, some of them ninety feet high, which made it dark at noonday, and a retreat for all the owls of the neighborhood. It was full of pits and quagmires, partly covered with weeds and mosses, where the green surface often betrayed the traveler into a gulf of black, smothering mud; there were also dark and stagnant pools, the abodes of the tadpole, the bullfrog, and the watersnake; where the trunks of pines and hemlocks lay half-drowned, half-rotting, looking like alligators sleeping in the mire.

Tom had long been picking his way cautiously through this treacherous forest; stepping from tuft to tuft of rushes and roots, which afforded precarious footholds among deep sloughs; or pacing carefully, like a cat, along the prostrate trunks of trees; startled now and then by the sudden screaming of the bittern, or the quacking of a wild duck, rising on the wing from some solitary pool. At length he arrived at a piece of firm ground, which ran out like a peninsula into the deep bosom of the swamp. It had been one of the strongholds of the Indians during their wars with the first colonists. Here they had thrown up a kind of fort, which they had looked upon as almost impregnable, and had used as a place of refuge for their squaws and children. Nothing remained of the old Indian fort but a few embankments, gradually sinking to the level of the surrounding earth, and already overgrown in part by oaks and other forest trees, the foliage of which formed a contrast to the dark pines and hemlocks of the swamp.

It was late in the dusk of evening when Tom Walker reached the old fort, and he paused there awhile to rest himself. Anyone but he would have felt unwilling to linger in this lonely, melancholy place, for the common people had a bad opinion of it, from the stories handed down from the time of the In-

dian wars; when it was asserted that the savages held incantations here, and made sacrifices to the evil spirit.

Tom Walker, however, was not a man to be troubled with any fears of the kind. He reposed himself for some time on the trunk of a fallen hemlock, listening to the boding cry of the tree toad, and delving with his walking staff into a mound of black mold at his feet. As he turned up the soil unconsciously, his staff struck against something hard. He raked it out of the vegetable mold, and lo! a cloven skull, with an Indian tomahawk buried deep in it, lay before him. The rust on the weapon showed the time that had elapsed since this deathblow had been given. It was a dreary memento of the fierce struggle that had taken place in this last foothold of the Indian warriors.

"Humph!" said Tom Walker, as he gave it a kick to shake the dirt from it.

"Let that skull alone!" said a gruff voice. Tom lifted up his eyes, and beheld a great black man seated directly opposite him, on the stump of a tree. He was exceedingly surprised, having neither heard nor seen anyone approach; and he was still more perplexed on observing, as well as the gathering gloom would permit, that the stranger was neither Negro nor Indian. It is true he was dressed in a rude half-Indian garb, and had a red belt or sash swathed round his body; but his face was neither black nor copper color, but swarthy and dingy, and begrimed with soot, as if he had been accustomed to toil among fires and forges. He had a shock of coarse black hair, that stood out from his head in all directions, and bore an ax on his shoulder.

He scowled for a moment at Tom with a pair of great red eyes.

"What are you doing on my grounds?" said the black man, with a hoarse growling voice.

"Your grounds!" said Tom with a sneer, "no more your grounds than mine; they belong to Deacon Peabody."

"Deacon Peabody be d——d," said the

stranger, "as I flatter myself he will be, if he does not look more to his own sins and less to those of his neighbors. Look yonder, and see how Deacon Peabody is faring."

Tom looked in the direction that the stranger pointed, and beheld one of the great trees, fair and flourishing without, but rotten at the core, and saw that it had been nearly hewn through, so that the first high wind was likely to blow it down. On the bark of the tree was scored the name of Deacon Peabody, an eminent man, who had waxed wealthy by driving shrewd bargains with the Indians. He now looked round, and found most of the tall trees marked with the name of some great man of the colony, and all more or less scored by the ax. The one on which he had been seated, and which had evidently just been hewn down, bore the

name of Crowninshield; and he recollected a mighty rich man of that name, who made a vulgar display of wealth, which it was whispered he had acquired by buccaneering.

"He's just ready for burning!" said the black man, with a growl of triumph. "You see I am likely to have a good stock of firewood for winter."

"But what right have you," said Tom, "to cut down Deacon Peabody's timber?"

"The right of a prior claim," said the other. "This woodland belonged to me long before one of your white-faced race put foot upon the soil."

"And pray, who are you, if I may be so bold?" said Tom.

"Oh, I go by various names. I am the wild huntsman in some countries; the black miner in others. In this neighborhood I am known by the name of the black woodsman. I am he to whom the red men consecrated this spot, and in honor of whom they now and then roasted a white man, by way of sweet-smelling sacrifice. Since the red men have been exterminated by you white savages, I amuse myself by presiding at the persecutions of Quakers and Anabaptists;[3] I am the great patron and prompter of slave dealers, and the grandmaster of the Salem witches."

"The upshot of all which is, that, if I mistake not," said Tom, sturdily, "you are he commonly called Old Scratch."

"The same, at your service!" replied the black man, with a half-civil nod.

Such was the opening of this interview, according to the old story; though it has almost too familiar an air to be credited. One would think that to meet with such a singular personage, in this wild, lonely place, would have shaken any man's nerves; but Tom was a hard-minded fellow, not easily daunted, and he had lived so long with a termagant wife, that he did not even fear the Devil.

It is said that after this commencement they had a long and earnest conversation together, as Tom returned homeward. The black man told him of great sums of money buried by Kidd the pirate, under the oak trees on the high ridge, not far from the morass. All these were under his command, and protected by his power, so that none could find them but such as propitiated his favor. These he offered to place within Tom Walker's reach, having conceived an especial kindness for him; but they were to be had only on certain conditions. What these conditions were may easily be surmised, though Tom never disclosed them publicly. They must have been very hard, for he required time to think of them, and he was not a man to stick at trifles where money was in view. When they had reached the edge of the swamp, the stranger paused—"What proof have I that all you have been telling me is true?" said Tom. "There is my signature," said the black man, pressing his finger on Tom's forehead. So saying, he turned off among the thickets of the swamp, and seemed, as Tom said, to go down, down, down, into the earth, until nothing but his head and shoulders could be seen, and so on, until he totally disappeared.

When Tom reached home, he found the black print of a finger, burnt, as it were, into his forehead, which nothing could obliterate.

The first news his wife had to tell him was the sudden death of Absalom Crowninshield, the rich buccaneer. It was announced in the papers with the usual flourish, that "A great man had fallen in Israel."[4]

Tom recollected the tree which his black friend had just hewn down, and which was ready for burning. "Let the freebooter roast," said Tom, "who cares!" He now felt convinced that all he had heard and seen was no illusion.

He was not prone to let his wife into his confidence; but as this was an uneasy secret, he willingly shared it with her. All her avarice was awakened at the mention of hidden gold, and she urged her husband to comply with the black man's terms and secure what would make them wealthy for life. However Tom might have felt disposed to sell himself to the Devil, he was determined not to do so to oblige his wife; so he flatly refused, out of the mere spirit of contradiction. Many and bitter were the quarrels they had on the subject, but the more she talked, the more resolute was Tom not to be damned to please her.

At length she determined to drive the bargain on her own account, and if she succeeded, to keep all the gain to herself. Being of the same fearless temper as her husband, she set off for the old Indian fort towards the close of a summer's day. She was many hours absent. When she came back, she was reserved and sullen in her replies. She spoke something of a black man, whom she had met about twilight, hewing at the root of a tall tree. He was sulky, however, and would not come to terms: she was to go again with a propitiatory offering, but what it was she forbore to say.

3. **Quakers and Anabaptists:** Two religious groups that were persecuted for their beliefs.

4. **A . . . Israel:** A reference to II Samuel 3:38 in the Bible. The Puritans often called New England "Israel."

The next evening she set off again for the swamp, with her apron heavily laden. Tom waited and waited for her, but in vain; midnight came, but she did not make her appearance: morning, noon, night returned, but still she did not come. Tom now grew uneasy for her safety, especially as he found she had carried off in her apron the silver teapot and spoons, and every portable article of value. Another night elapsed, another morning came; but no wife. In a word, she was never heard of more.

What was her real fate nobody knows, in consequence of so many pretending to know. It is one of those facts which have become confounded by a variety of historians. Some asserted that she lost her way among the tangled mazes of the swamp, and sank into some pit or slough; others, more uncharitable, hinted that she had eloped with the household booty, and made off to some other province; while others surmised that the tempter had decoyed her into a dismal quagmire, on the top of which her hat was found lying. In confirmation of this, it was said a great black man, with an ax on his shoulder, was seen late that very evening coming out of the swamp, carrying a bundle tied in a checked apron, with an air of surly triumph.

The most current and probable story, however, observes, that Tom Walker grew so anxious about the fate of his wife and his property, that he set out at length to seek them both at the Indian fort. During a long summer's afternoon he searched about the gloomy place, but no wife was to be seen. He called her name repeatedly, but she was nowhere to be heard. The bittern alone responded to his voice, as he flew screaming by; or the bullfrog croaked dolefully from a neighboring pool. At length, it is said, just in the brown hour of twilight, when the owls began to hoot, and the bats to flit about, his attention was attracted by the clamor of carrion crows hovering about a cypress tree. He looked up, and beheld a bundle tied in a checked apron, and hanging in the branches of the tree, with a great vulture perched hard

by, as if keeping watch upon it. He leaped with joy; for he recognized his wife's apron, and supposed it to contain the household valuables.

"Let us get hold of the property," said he, consolingly to himself, "and we will endeavor to do without the woman."

As he scrambled up the tree, the vulture spread its wide wings, and sailed off screaming into the deep shadows of the forest. Tom seized the checked apron, but woeful sight! found nothing but a heart and liver tied up in it!

Such, according to the most authentic old story, was all that was to be found of Tom's wife. She had probably attempted to deal with the black man as she had been accustomed to deal with her husband; but though a female scold is generally considered a match for the Devil, yet in this instance she appears to have had the worst of it. She must have died game, however; for it is said Tom noticed many prints of cloven feet deeply stamped about the tree, and found handfuls of hair, that looked as if they had been plucked from the coarse black shock of the woodsman. Tom knew his wife's prowess by experience. He shrugged his shoulders, as he looked at the signs of a fierce clapperclawing. "Egad," said he to himself, "Old Scratch must have had a tough time of it!"

Tom consoled himself for the loss of his property, with the loss of his wife, for he was a man of fortitude. He even felt something like gratitude towards the black woodsman, who, he considered, had done him a kindness. He sought, therefore, to cultivate a further acquaintance with him, but for some time without success; the old blacklegs played shy, for whatever people may think, he is not always to be had for calling for: he knows how to play his cards when pretty sure of his game.

At length, it is said, when delay had whetted Tom's eagerness to the quick, and prepared him to agree to anything rather than not gain the promised treasure, he met the black man one evening in his usual woodsman's dress, with his ax on his shoulder, sauntering along the swamp, and humming a tune. He affected to receive Tom's advances with great indifference, made brief replies, and went on humming his tune.

By degrees, however, Tom brought him to business, and they began to haggle about the terms on which the former was to have the pirate's treasure. There was one condition which need not be mentioned, being generally understood in all cases where the Devil grants favors; but there were others about which, though of less importance, he was inflexibly obstinate. He insisted that the money found through his means should be employed in his service. He proposed, therefore, that Tom should employ it in the black traffic; that is to say, that he should fit out a slave ship. This, however, Tom resolutely refused: he was bad enough in all conscience, but the Devil himself could not tempt him to turn slave-trader.

Finding Tom so squeamish on this point, he did not insist upon it, but proposed, instead, that he should turn usurer; the Devil being extremely anxious for the increase of usurers, looking upon them as his peculiar[5] people.

To this no objections were made, for it was just to Tom's taste.

"You shall open a broker's shop in Boston next month," said the black man.

"I'll do it tomorrow, if you wish," said Tom Walker.

"You shall lend money at two per cent a month."

---

5. peculiar: Particular, special.

"Egad, I'll charge four!" replied Tom Walker.

"You shall extort bonds, foreclose mortgages, drive the merchant to bankruptcy——"

"I'll drive him to the D——l," cried Tom Walker.

"You are the usurer for my money!" said the blacklegs with delight. "When will you want the rhino?"[6]

"This very night."

"Done!" said the Devil.

"Done!" said Tom Walker. So they shook hands and struck a bargain.

A few days' time saw Tom Walker seated behind his desk in a countinghouse in Boston.

His reputation for a ready-moneyed man, who would lend money out for a good consideration, soon spread abroad. Everybody remembers the time of Governor Belcher,[7] when money was particularly scarce. It was a time of paper credit. The country had been deluged with government bills; the famous Land Bank[8] had been established; there had been a rage for speculating; the people had run mad with schemes for new settlements, for building cities in the wilderness; land jobbers[9] went about with maps of grants, and townships, and El Dorados,[10] lying nobody knew where, but which everybody was ready to purchase. In a word, the great speculating fever which breaks out every now and then in the country, had raged to an alarming degree, and everybody was dreaming of making sudden fortunes from nothing. As usual the fever had subsided; the dream had gone off, and the imaginary for-

tunes with it; the patients were left in doleful plight, and the whole country resounded with the consequent cry of "hard times."

At this propitious time of public distress did Tom Walker set up as usurer in Boston. His door was soon thronged by customers. The needy and adventurous, the gambling speculator, the dreaming land jobber, the thriftless tradesman, the merchant with cracked credit, in short, everyone driven to raise money by desperate means and desperate sacrifices, hurried to Tom Walker.

Thus Tom was the universal friend of the needy, and acted like a "friend in need"; that is to say, he always exacted good pay and good security. In proportion to the distress of the applicant was the hardness of his terms. He accumulated bonds and mortgages; gradually squeezed his customers closer and closer, and sent them at length, dry as a sponge, from his door.

In this way he made money hand over hand, became a rich and mighty man, and exalted his cocked hat upon 'Change.[11] He built himself, as usual, a vast house, out of ostentation; but left the greater part of it unfinished and unfurnished, out of parsimony. He even set up a carriage in the fullness of his vainglory, though he nearly starved the horses which drew it; and as the ungreased wheels groaned and screeched on the axletrees, you would have thought you heard the souls of the poor debtors he was squeezing.

As Tom waxed old, however, he grew thoughtful. Having secured the good things of this world, he began to feel anxious about those of the next. He thought with regret on the bargain he had made with his black friend, and set his wits to work to cheat him out of the conditions. He became, therefore, all of a sudden, a violent churchgoer. He prayed loudly and strenuously, as if heaven were to be taken by force of lungs. Indeed, one might always tell when he had sinned most during the week, by the clamor of his Sunday devotion. The quiet Christians who

---

6. rhino (rī′ nō): Slang term for money.

7. Governor Belcher: Jonathan Belcher, the governor of Massachusetts Bay Colony from 1730 through 1741.

8. Land Bank: A bank that financed transactions in real estate.

9. land jobbers: People who bought and sold undeveloped land.

10. El Dorados (el′ də rä′ dōz): Places that are rich in gold or opportunity. El Dorado was a legendary country in South America sought by early Spanish explorers for its gold and precious stones.

11. 'Change: The exchange, where bankers and merchants did business.

had been modestly and steadfastly traveling Zionward,[12] were struck with self-reproach at seeing themselves so suddenly outstripped in their career by this new-made convert. Tom was as rigid in religious as in money matters; he was a stern supervisor and censurer of his neighbors, and seemed to think every sin entered up to their account became a credit on his own side of the page. He even talked of the expediency of reviving the persecution of Quakers and Anabaptists. In a word, Tom's zeal became as notorious as his riches.

Still, in spite of all this strenuous attention to forms, Tom had a lurking dread that the Devil, after all, would have his due. That he might not be taken unawares, therefore, it is said he always carried a small Bible in his coat pocket. He had also a great folio Bible on his countinghouse desk, and would frequently be found reading it when people called on business; on such occasions he would lay his green spectacles in the book, to mark the place, while he turned round to drive some usurious bargain.

Some say that Tom grew a little crack-brained in his old days, and that fancying his end approaching, he had his horse newly shod, saddled and bridled, and buried with his feet uppermost; because he supposed that at the last day the world would be turned upside down, in which case he should find his horse standing ready for mounting, and he was determined at the worst to give his old friend a run for it. This, however, is probably a mere old wives' fable. If he really did take such a precaution, it was totally superfluous; at least so says the authentic old legend, which closes his story in the following manner.

One hot summer afternoon in the dog days, just as a terrible black thunder-gust was coming up, Tom sat in his counting-house in his white linen cap and India silk morning gown. He was on the point of foreclosing a mortgage, by which he would complete the ruin of an unlucky land speculator

for whom he had professed the greatest friendship. The poor land jobber begged him to grant a few months' indulgence. Tom had grown testy and irritated, and refused another day.

"My family will be ruined and brought upon the parish," said the land jobber. "Charity begins at home," replied Tom; "I must take care of myself in these hard times."

"You have made so much money out of me," said the speculator.

Tom lost his patience and his piety— "The Devil take me," said he, "if I have made a farthing!"

Just then there were three loud knocks at the street door. He stepped out to see who was there. A black man was holding a black horse, which neighed and stamped with impatience.

"Tom, you're come for," said the black fellow, gruffly. Tom shrunk back, but too late. He had left his little Bible at the bottom of his coat pocket, and his big Bible on the desk buried under the mortgage he was about to foreclose: never was sinner taken more unawares. The black man whisked him like a child into the saddle, gave the horse the lash, and away he galloped, with Tom on his back, in the midst of the thunderstorm. The clerks stuck their pens behind their ears, and stared after him from the windows. Away went Tom Walker, dashing down the streets, his white cap bobbing up and down, his morning gown fluttering in the wind, and his steed striking fire out of the pavement at every bound. When the clerks turned to look for the black man he had disappeared.

Tom Walker never returned to foreclose the mortgage. A countryman who lived on the border of the swamp, reported that in the height of the thunder-gust he had heard a great clattering of hoofs and a howling along the road, and running to the window caught sight of a figure, such as I have described, on a horse that galloped like mad across the fields, over the hills and down into the black hemlock swamp towards the

---

12. Zionward (zī′ ən wôrd): Toward heaven.

old Indian fort; and that shortly after a thunderbolt falling in that direction seemed to set the whole forest in a blaze.

The good people of Boston shook their heads and shrugged their shoulders, but had been so much accustomed to witches and goblins and tricks of the Devil, in all kind of shapes from the first settlement of the colony, that they were not so much horror struck as might have been expected. Trustees were appointed to take charge of Tom's effects. There was nothing, however, to administer upon. On searching his coffers all his bonds and mortgages were found reduced to cinders. In place of gold and silver his iron chest was filled with chips and shavings; two skeletons lay in his stable instead of his half-starved horses, and the very next day his great house took fire and was burned to the ground.

Such was the end of Tom Walker and his ill-gotten wealth. Let all griping money brokers lay this story to heart. The truth of it is not to be doubted. The very hole under the oak trees, whence he dug Kidd's money, is to be seen to this day; and the neighboring swamp and old Indian fort are often haunted in stormy nights by a figure on horseback, in morning gown and white cap, which is doubtless the troubled spirit of the usurer. In fact, the story has resolved itself into a proverb, and is the origin of that popular saying, so prevalent throughout New England, of "The Devil and Tom Walker."

RESPONDING TO THE SELECTION

Your Response

1. What do you like best about this story? What do you like least? Why?
2. How do you feel about the fate of Tom Walker? Explain.
3. What lessons could you learn from this story?

Recalling

4. Describe Tom Walker's first encounter with the devil.
5. In all likelihood, what was the fate of Tom's wife?
6. (a) What bargain does Tom finally strike with the devil? (b) What does he do when he begins to regret his bargain?

Interpreting

7. What does Irving's description of the Walkers' house and the surrounding land indicate about the kind of people they are?
8. What details indicate that while Tom Walker's condition changes during the story his nature remains the same?
9. (a) What does Irving mean when he says that Walker became "a *violent* churchgoer"? (b) How is the manner in which Walker approaches religion similar to the way he approaches his financial dealings?

Applying

10. Would this story be effective if it were set in contemporary America? Why or why not?

ANALYZING LITERATURE

Recognizing Folk Tales

Folk tales are stories passed down from generation to generation in a particular culture. These stories usually relate unlikely or unrealistic events, involve stereotypes or stock characters, and teach a lesson or express a general truth about life.

1. What trait does Tom Walker embody?
2. What trait does Tom Walker's wife embody?
3. What general truth about life does the story express?

CRITICAL THINKING AND READING

Inferring Cultural Attitudes

"The Devil and Tom Walker" reveals many of the attitudes of the people living in New England in the late 1720's and early 1730's. Because these attitudes are revealed indirectly, you must make inferences, or draw conclusions, about them by examining the evidence presented in the story. For example, when describing the old Indian fort, Irving states that "the stories handed down from the time of the Indian wars . . . asserted that the savages held incantations here, and made sacrifices to the evil spirit." From this passage you can infer that the colonists had a suspicious attitude toward the Native Americans and a firm belief in the devil.

What inferences about the cultural attitudes of the New Englanders of this period can you make from each of the following passages?

1. ". . . the great speculating fever which breaks out every now and then in the country had raged to an alarming degree, and everybody was dreaming of making sudden fortunes from nothing."
2. "The quiet Christians who had been moving modestly and steadfastly traveling Zionward were struck with self-reproach at seeing themselves so suddenly outstripped of their career by this new-made convert."

THINKING AND WRITING

Adapting a Folk Tale

In your library, find a folk tale that interests you, perhaps the tale of John Henry, for example. In what ways would this tale be different if it were set in twentieth-century America? Think about how you can reshape the characters and events to make them fit into a contemporary setting. List the qualities that each character in your adaptation will embody, prepare an outline of events, and decide what lesson your tale will teach. When you write your tale, include details of the setting that will ground it in time and place. After you finish writing, revise your tale and prepare a final copy.

WILLIAM CULLEN BRYANT

1794–1878

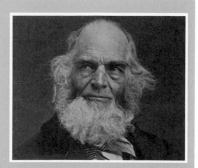

During William Cullen Bryant's long life, America emerged from its infancy to become a large and powerful nation, and American literature blossomed, earning its place among the world's literature. As a journalist and political activist, Bryant fought to make sure that industrialization and rapid growth did not obscure the democratic values and principles upon which the country was built. As a poet Bryant helped to establish an American literary tradition by producing a number of poems that could be matched against the work of the European poets of his day.

Bryant, a descendant of idealistic Puritans, was born in a rural area in western Massachusetts. His father, a country doctor with a deep interest in nature, encouraged him to explore the surrounding wilderness. Bryant's father also taught his son Greek and Latin and urged him to become an avid reader. As a boy he read the work of eighteenth-century English poets, and during his teens he developed a strong interest in the work of the nineteenth-century English Romantic poets. Bryant began writing poetry at the age of nine, and at nineteen he wrote the first version of "Thanatopsis," his most famous poem. When "Thanatopsis" was published in the *North American Review* in 1817, it was greeted with great enthusiasm. In spite of the poem's success, however, Bryant decided to revise it several years later.

Finding that pursuing a full-time career as a poet was economically impossible, Bryant earned a law degree and practiced law for ten years, continuing to write poetry in his spare time. In 1825 Bryant moved to New York City and began a new career as a journalist. By 1829 he had become editor-in-chief and part owner of the New York *Evening Post,* one of the most highly regarded newspapers in the country. In this position Bryant became an influential and enthusiastic defender of human rights and personal freedoms. He supported such causes as women's rights, freedom of speech and religion, and the abolition of slavery.

Though Bryant did not produce a great quantity of poetry, he was the first American poet to win worldwide critical acclaim. Like the European poets of his day, Bryant explored the connection between nature and humanity in his poetry. His work played a major role in establishing the Romantic movement in American literature and influenced the next generation of American poets.

GUIDE FOR INTERPRETING

Writers' Techniques

Thanatopsis; To a Waterfowl

Blank Verse. Though "Thanatopsis" is not written in rhyme, its lines do have a regular rhythm, that is, a recurring pattern of stressed and unstressed syllables, known as meter. The basic unit of meter is the foot. Usually a *foot* consists of one stressed syllable and one or more unstressed syllables. The most frequently used foot in American and English verse is the *iamb,* which consists of one unstressed syllable followed by a stressed syllable. When the lines in a poem consist of five iambs, as in "Thanatopsis," the poem is written in iambic pentameter. Verse consisting of unrhymed lines of iambic pentameter is called *blank verse.* Below is an example of blank verse from "Thanatopsis." The unstressed syllables are marked with ˘; the stressed syllables with ′.

> Yet not to thine eternal resting place
> Shalt thou retire alone, nor couldst thou wish

Because it effectively re-creates the smooth natural flow of everyday speech in English, blank verse is one of the most common metrical patterns in American and English poetry. However, when poets use blank verse, they often introduce slight variations in the rhythm to avoid monotony.

Literary Movement

Romanticism. Romanticism was a major literary and cultural movement that emerged from the revolutionary spirit of the late 1700's. Although Romantic writers had different concerns and approaches, they generally shared a desire to discard the dominant ideas and techniques of the eighteenth century and to forge a new type of literature.

The Romantics favored emotion over reason, intuition over intellect, the subjective over the objective. They celebrated the creative spirit of the individual and the use of the imagination to arrive at spiritual truth. Their writings reflect a deepened appreciation of nature, a preoccupation with self-knowledge, an interest in the common people and folklore, and a love of the mysterious and exotic. An early Romantic, poet William Cullen Bryant helped to establish the movement in American literature with his reflections on nature.

Focus

What thoughts does nature bring to your mind? Freewrite about nature, considering the relationship between humanity and nature.

VERNAL FALLS, YOSEMITE VALLEY
Thomas Moran

Thanatopsis

William Cullen Bryant

To him who in the love of Nature holds
Communion with her visible forms, she speaks
A various language; for his gayer hours
She has a voice of gladness, and a smile
5 And eloquence of beauty, and she glides
Into his darker musings, with a mild
And healing sympathy, that steals away
Their sharpness, ere[1] he is aware. When thoughts
Of the last bitter hour come like a blight
10 Over thy spirit, and sad images
Of the stern agony, and shroud, and pall,
And breathless darkness, and the narrow house,[2]
Make thee to shudder, and grow sick at heart—
Go forth, under the open sky, and list
15 To Nature's teachings, while from all around—
Earth and her waters, and the depths of air—
Comes a still voice—Yet a few days, and thee
The all-beholding sun shall see no more
In all his course; nor yet in the cold ground,
20 Where thy pale form was laid, with many tears,
Nor in the embrace of ocean, shall exist
Thy image. Earth, that nourished thee, shall claim
Thy growth, to be resolved to earth again,
And, lost each human trace, surrendering up
25 Thine individual being, shalt thou go
To mix forever with the elements,
To be a brother to the insensible rock
And to the sluggish clod, which the rude swain[3]
Turns with his share,[4] and treads upon. The oak
30 Shall send his roots abroad, and pierce thy mold.

Yet not to thine eternal resting place
Shalt thou retire alone, nor couldst thou wish
Couch[5] more magnificent. Thou shalt lie down
With patriarchs of the infant world—with kings,
35 The powerful of the earth—the wise, the good,
Fair forms, and hoary seers of ages past,
All in one mighty sepulcher. The hills
Rock-ribbed and ancient as the sun—the vales

---

1. ere: Before.
2. narrow house: coffin.
3. swain: A country youth.
4. share: Plowshare.
5. couch: Bed.

Stretching in pensive quietness between;
40 The venerable woods—rivers that move
In majesty, and the complaining brooks
That make the meadows green; and, poured round all,
Old Ocean's gray and melancholy waste—
Are but the solemn decorations all
45 Of the great tomb of man. The golden sun,
The planets, all the infinite host of heaven,
Are shining on the sad abodes of death,
Through the still lapse of ages. All that tread
The globe are but a handful to the tribes
50 That slumber in its bosom. Take the wings
Of morning,[6] pierce the Barcan[7] wilderness,
Or lose thyself in the continuous woods
Where rolls the Oregon,[8] and hears no sound,
Save his own dashings—yet the dead are there:
55 And millions in those solitudes, since first
The flight of years began, have laid them down
In their last sleep—the dead reign there alone.
So shalt thou rest, and what if thou withdraw
In silence from the living, and no friend
60 Take note of thy departure? All that breathe
Will share thy destiny. The gay will laugh
When thou art gone, the solemn brood of care
Plod on, and each one as before will chase
His favorite phantom; yet all these shall leave
65 Their mirth and their employments, and shall come
And make their bed with thee. As the long train
Of ages glide away, the sons of men,
The youth in life's green spring, and he who goes
In the full strength of years, matron and maid,
70 The speechless babe, and the gray-headed man—
Shall one by one be gathered to thy side,
By those, who in their turn shall follow them.

    So live, that when thy summons comes to join
The innumerable caravan, which moves
75 To that mysterious realm, where each shall take
His chamber in the silent halls of death,
Thou go not, like the quarry-slave at night,
Scourged to his dungeon, but, sustained and soothed
By an unfaltering trust, approach thy grave,
80 Like one who wraps the drapery of his couch
About him, and lies down to pleasant dreams.

---

6. Take . . . morning: An allusion to Psalm 139:9.
7. Barcan (bär′ kən): Referring to Barca, a desert region in North Africa.
8. Oregon: A river flowing between Oregon and Washington, now known as the Columbia River.

To a Waterfowl

William Cullen Bryant

Whither, midst falling dew,
While glow the heavens with the last steps of day,
Far, through their rosy depths, dost thou pursue
   Thy solitary way?

5   Vainly the fowler's[1] eye
Might mark thy distant flight to do thee wrong,
As, darkly seen against the crimson sky,
   Thy figure floats along.

_____

1. fowler's: Referring to a hunter.

Seek'st thou the plashy brink
10 Of weedy lake, or marge[2] of river wide,
Or where the rocking billows rise and sink
On the chafed ocean-side?

There is a Power whose care
Teaches thy way along that pathless coast—
15 The desert and illimitable air—
Lone wandering, but not lost.

All day thy wings have fanned,
At that far height, the cold, thin atmosphere,
Yet stoop not, weary, to the welcome land,
20 Though the dark night is near.

And soon that toil shall end;
Soon shalt thou find a summer home, and rest,
And scream among thy fellows; reeds shall bend
Soon, o'er thy sheltered nest.

25 Thou'rt gone, the abyss of heaven
Hath swallowed up thy form; yet, on my heart
Deeply has sunk the lesson thou hast given,
And shall not soon depart.

He who, from zone to zone,
30 Guides through the boundless sky thy certain flight,
In the long way that I must tread alone,
Will lead my steps aright.

---

2. marge: Edge or border.

RESPONDING TO THE SELECTION

Your Response
1. What is your reaction to each poem? Explain.
2. What aspect of nature do you find comforting?

Recalling
3. In "Thanatopsis" Bryant turns to nature to come to an understanding of death. (a) What kind of support does nature offer? (b) What is the fate of the "individual being"? (c) Who shares the individual's destiny?
4. In "To a Waterfowl," Bryant ponders a mystery of nature. (a) What guides the weary waterfowl in its flight? (b) What does the poet learn from observing it?

Interpreting
5. In "Thanatopsis" what enables the poet to come to terms with death?
6. In "To a Waterfowl," how does the speaker's interest in the waterfowl contrast with the fowler's concern with the bird?

Applying
7. How do you think Bryant's conservative Puritan ancestors would have reacted to each poem? Explain.

ANALYZING LITERATURE

Recognizing Blank Verse

Blank verse is composed of unrhymed lines of iambic pentameter. In iambic pentameter there are five feet, or beats, per line, and every second syllable is stressed. Below is an example of blank verse from "Thanatopsis."

Shall one by one be gathered to thy side,

By those, who in their turn shall follow them.

1. Find four more lines of blank verse in "Thanatopsis."
2. Find two lines in which the rhythm is varied. Is there any apparent reason why the rhythm is varied besides to break the monotony?

Understanding Romanticism

Romanticism was an artistic movement that grew out of a reaction against the dominant attitudes and approaches of the eighteenth century. The Romantics stressed the examination of inner feelings and emotions and the use of the imagination, rather than the use of reason and logic. They were interested in nature and its mysteries and even in the supernatural. Often, the Romantics sought inspiration and understanding through the observation and contemplation of nature. The Romantics also turned to legends and folklore for inspiration.

1. "To a Waterfowl" focuses on the migration of birds, a subject that scientists still cannot fully explain. Why is this an appropriate subject for a Romantic poem?
2. How does the speaker's approach to understanding the waterfowl's flight reflect the concerns of the Romantics?
3. Unlike the writers of the eighteenth century, the Romantics were concerned with specific experiences of individuals, rather than with general, universal experiences. How is this concern reflected in Bryant's poem?
4. In writing about the concerns of the Romantic movement, some writers capitalize *Nature.* Explain why this would be appropriate.

THINKING AND WRITING

Responding to Criticism

In discussing "To a Waterfowl," Edgar Allan Poe commented that the poem's main strength is its "completeness," adding that the poem's "rounded and didactic termination has done wonders." Write an essay in which you discuss the poem in relation to this comment. Reread the poem, keeping Poe's comment in mind. Do you think his statement is accurate? Why or why not? When writing your essay, use evidence from the poem to support your argument. When you finish writing, revise your essay, making sure it supports your opinion of the quotation. Proofread your essay and prepare a final draft.

LEARNING OPTIONS

1. **Speaking and Listening.** In poetry, sound contributes to sense. To hear the leisurely flow of sound and follow the poet's train of thought in "Thanatopsis," read it aloud to yourself. Pay close attention to the poem's basic iambic rhythm and its variations. Use the punctuation as a guide in deciding where to pause. When you are ready, read aloud a portion of the poem to classmates.
2. **Cross-curricular Connection.** How do migrating birds find their way to their destination? In "To a Waterfowl," Bryant provides a mystical explanation. What rational explanation do scientists provide? Investigate the migratory habits and patterns of birds. Share your findings in a brief written report.
3. **Art.** Asher B. Durand's painting *Kindred Spirits* reproduced on page 169 pays tribute to the friendship between Bryant and landscape painter Thomas Cole. Learn more about Thomas Cole, founder of the Hudson River School. In what sense can he claim kinship with Bryant? In an oral report, analyze one of Cole's landscapes, comparing his view of nature with Bryant's.

EDGAR ALLAN POE

1809–1849

Throughout the years following Edgar Allan Poe's death, there have been disagreements among writers and critics concerning the quality of his work. In spite of these disagreements, Poe has remained the most influential and widely read American writer of his time.

Poe was born in Boston in 1809, the son of impoverished traveling actors. Shortly after Poe's birth, his father deserted the family. A year later, Poe's mother died. Young Edgar was taken in, though never formally adopted, by the family of John Allan, a wealthy Virginia merchant. The Allans provided for Poe's education, and in 1826 Poe entered the University of Virginia. However, when he contracted large gambling debts which his stepfather refused to pay, Poe was forced to leave the school.

In 1827, after joining the army under an assumed name, Poe published his first volume of poetry, *Tamerlane and Other Poems,* and in 1829 he published a second volume, *Al Aaraaf.* The following year Poe's stepfather helped him to win an appointment to the United States Military Academy at West Point. Poe was expelled for academic violations within a year, however, and his dismissal resulted in an irreparable break with his stepfather.

During the second half of his life, Poe pursued a literary career in New York, Richmond, Philadelphia, and Baltimore, barely supporting himself by writing and working as an editor for a number of magazines. After his third volume of poetry, *Poems* (1831), failed to bring him either money or acclaim, he turned from poetry to fiction and literary criticism. Five of his short stories were published in newspapers in 1832, and in 1838 he published his only novel, *The Narrative of Arthur Gordon Pym.* Though Poe's short stories gained him some recognition and his poem "The Raven" (1845) was greeted with enthusiasm, he was never able to escape from poverty. In 1849, two years after the death of his beloved wife Virginia, Poe died alone and unhappy.

In the years since his death, Poe's work has received much attention. Some writers and critics have harshly criticized Poe's writing. Others have praised his use of vivid imagery and sound effects and his exploration of altered mental states and the dark side of human nature. Despite Poe's uncertain status among writers and critics, however, his work has remained extremely popular among generations of American readers.

GUIDE FOR INTERPRETING

The Fall of the House of Usher

Writers' Techniques

The Single Effect. More than any other writer, Edgar Allan Poe is responsible for the emergence of the short story as a popular and respected literary form. Poe was the first writer to classify and define the short story as a distinct literary genre and argue that the short story deserved the same status as such other genres as the poem and the novel. In his definition, which first appeared in his review of Nathaniel Hawthorne's *Twice-Told Tales,* Poe asserted that a story should be constructed to achieve "a certain unique or single effect." Poe believed that every character, detail, and incident in a story should contribute to this effect, commenting that "in the whole composition there should be no word written, of which the tendency, direct or indirect, is not to the one preestablished design." Poe even stated that if a writer's "very initial sentence tend not to the outbringing of this effect, then he has failed in his first step."

Focus

What sorts of characters, events, and details make a book or movie terrifying? Brainstorm about terrifying books you have read or movies you have seen. Then compose a list of the characters, events, and details that contributed to the effect of these books or movies.

Primary Source

Poe restated his views about the single effect on more than one occasion. Describing the aims and methods of his writing in *The Philosophy of Composition,* he wrote,

> I prefer commencing with the consideration of an *effect.* Keeping originality *always* in view—for he is false to himself who ventures to dispense with so obvious and so easily attainable a source of interest—I say to myself, in the first place, "Of the innumerable effects, or impressions, of which the heart, the intellect, or (more generally) the soul is susceptible, what one shall I, on the present occasion, select?" Having chosen a novel, first, and secondly a vivid effect, I consider whether it can be best wrought by incident or tone—whether by ordinary incidents and peculiar tone, or the converse, or by peculiarity both of incident and tone—afterward looking about me (or rather within) for such combinations of event, or tone, as shall best aid me in the construction of the effect.

The Fall of the House of Usher

Edgar Allan Poe

Son cœur est un luth suspendu;
Sitôt qu'on le touche il résonne.[1]

During the whole of a dull, dark, and soundless day in the autumn of the year, when the clouds hung oppressively low in the heavens, I had been passing alone, on horseback, through a singularly dreary tract of country, and at length found myself, as the shades of evening drew on, within view of the melancholy House of Usher. I know not how it was—but, with the first glimpse of the building, a sense of insufferable gloom pervaded my spirit. I say insufferable; for the feeling was unrelieved by any of that half-pleasurable, because poetic, sentiment, with which the mind usually receives even the sternest natural images of the desolate or terrible. I looked upon the scene before me—upon the mere house, and the simple landscape features of the domain—upon the bleak walls—upon the vacant eyelike windows—upon a few rank sedges[2]—and upon a few white trunks of decayed trees—with an utter depression of soul, which I can compare to no earthly sensation more properly than to the afterdream of the reveler upon opium—the bitter lapse into everyday life—the hideous dropping off of the veil. There was an iciness, a sinking, a sickening of the heart—an unredeemed dreariness of thought which no goading of the imagina-tion could torture into aught[3] of the sublime. What was it—I paused to think—what was it that so unnerved me in the contemplation of the House of Usher? It was a mystery all insoluble; nor could I grapple with the shadowy fancies that crowded upon me as I pondered. I was forced to fall back upon the unsatisfactory conclusion, that while, beyond doubt, there *are* combinations of very simple natural objects which have the power of thus affecting us, still the analysis of this power lies among considerations beyond our depth. It was possible, I reflected, that a mere different arrangement of the particulars of the scene, of the details of the picture, would be sufficient to modify, or perhaps to annihilate its capacity for sorrowful impression; and, acting upon this idea, I reined my horse to the precipitous brink of a black and lurid tarn[4] that lay in unruffled luster by the dwelling, and gazed down—but with a shudder even more thrilling than before—upon the remodeled and inverted images of the gray sedge, and the ghastly tree stems, and the vacant and eyelike windows.

Nevertheless, in this mansion of gloom I now proposed to myself a sojourn of some weeks. Its proprietor, Roderick Usher, had been one of my boon companions in boyhood; but many years had elapsed since our last meeting. A letter, however, had lately reached me in a distant part of the country—a letter from him—which, in its wildly im-

---

1. Son . . . résonne: "His heart is a suspended lute; as one touches it, it resounds." From "Le Rufus" by Pierre Jean de Béranger (1780–1857).
2. sedges (sej′ ez) *n.*: Grasslike plants.

3. aught (ôt): Anything.
4. tarn (tärn) *n.*: A small lake.

"I AT LENGTH . . . ," EDGAR ALLAN POE'S TALES OF MYSTERY AND IMAGINATION
Arthur Rackham
New York Public Library, Astor, Lenox and Tilden Foundations

The Fall of the House of Usher 195

portunate nature, had admitted of no other than a personal reply. The MS.[5] gave evidence of nervous agitation. The writer spoke of acute bodily illness—of a mental disorder which oppressed him—and of an earnest desire to see me, as his best and indeed his only personal friend, with a view of attempting, by the cheerfulness of my society, some alleviation of his malady. It was the manner in which all this, and much more, was said—it was the apparent *heart* that went with his request—which allowed me no room for hesitation; and I accordingly obeyed forthwith what I still considered a very singular summons.

Although, as boys, we had been even intimate associates, yet I really knew little of my friend. His reserve had been always excessive and habitual. I was aware, however, that his very ancient family had been noted, time out of mind, for a peculiar sensibility of temperament, displaying itself, through long ages, in many works of exalted art, and manifested, of late, in repeated deeds of munificent yet unobtrusive charity, as well as in a passionate devotion to the intricacies, perhaps even more than to the orthodox and easily recognizable beauties, of musical science. I had learned, too, the very remarkable fact, that the stem of the Usher race, all time-honored as it was, had put forth, at no period, any enduring branch; in other words, that the entire family lay in the direct line of descent, and had always, with very trifling and very temporary variations, so lain. It was this deficiency, I considered, while running over in thought the perfect keeping of the character of the premises with the accredited character of the people, and while speculating upon the possible influence which the one, in the long lapse of centuries, might have exercised upon the other—it was this deficiency, perhaps of collateral issue,[6] and the consequent undeviating transmission, from sire to son, of the patrimony[7] with the name, which had, at length, so identified the two as to merge the original title of the estate in the quaint and equivocal appellation of the "House of Usher"—an appellation which seemed to include, in the minds of the peasantry who used it, both the family and the family mansion.

I have said that the sole effect of my somewhat childish experiment—that of looking down within the tarn—had been to deepen the first singular impression. There can be no doubt that the consciousness of the rapid increase of my superstition—for why should I not so term it?—served mainly to accelerate the increase itself. Such, I have long known, is the paradoxical law of all sentiments having terror as a basis. And it might have been for this reason only, that, when I again uplifted my eyes to the house itself, from its image in the pool, there grew in my mind a strange fancy—a fancy so ridiculous, indeed, that I but mention it to show the vivid force of the sensations which oppressed me. I had so worked upon my imagination as really to believe that about the whole mansion and domain there hung an atmosphere peculiar to themselves and their immediate vicinity—an atmosphere which had no affinity with the air of heaven, but which had reeked up from the decayed trees, and the gray wall, and the silent tarn—a pestilent and mystic vapor, dull, sluggish, faintly discernible and leaden-hued.

Shaking off from my spirit what *must* have been a dream, I scanned more narrowly the real aspect of the building. Its principal feature seemed to be that of an excessive antiquity. The discoloration of ages had been great. Minute fungi overspread the whole exterior, hanging in a fine tangled web-work from the eaves. Yet all this was apart from any extraordinary dilapidation. No portion of the masonry had fallen; and there appeared to be a wild inconsistency between its still perfect adaptation of parts, and the crum-

---

5. MS.: Manuscript.
6. collateral (kə lat′ ər əl) **issue** *adj.*: Decended from the same ancestors, but in a different line.

7. patrimony (pat′ rə mō′ nē) *n.*: Property inherited from one's father.

bling condition of the individual stones. In this there was much that reminded me of the specious totality of old woodwork which has rotted for long years in some neglected vault, with no disturbance from the breath of the external air. Beyond this indication of extensive decay, however, the fabric gave little token of instability. Perhaps the eye of a scrutinizing observer might have discovered a barely perceptible fissure, which, extending from the roof of the building in front, made its way down the wall in a zigzag direction, until it became lost in the sullen waters of the tarn.

Noticing these things, I rode over a short causeway to the house. A servant in waiting took my horse, and I entered the Gothic[8] archway of the hall. A valet, of stealthy step, then conducted me, in silence, through many dark and intricate passages in my progress to the *studio* of his master. Much that I encountered on the way contributed, I know not how, to heighten the vague sentiments of which I have already spoken. While the objects around me—while the carvings of the ceilings, the somber tapestries of the walls, the ebon blackness of the floors, and the phantasmagoric[9] armorial trophies which rattled as I strode, were but matters to which, or to such as which, I had been accustomed from my infancy—while I hesitated not to acknowledge how familiar was all this—I still wondered to find how unfamiliar were the fancies which ordinary images were stirring up. On one of the staircases, I met the physician of the family. His countenance, I thought, wore a mingled expression of low cunning and perplexity. He accosted me with trepidation and passed on. The valet now threw open a door and ushered me into the presence of his master.

The room in which I found myself was very large and lofty. The windows were long, narrow, and pointed, and at so vast a distance from the black oaken floor as to be altogether inaccessible from within. Feeble gleams of encrimsoned light made their way through the trellised panes, and served to render sufficiently distinct the more prominent objects around; the eye, however, struggled in vain to reach the remoter angles of the chamber, or the recesses of the vaulted and fretted[10] ceiling. Dark draperies hung upon the walls. The general furniture was profuse, comfortless, antique, and tattered. Many books and musical instruments lay scattered about, but failed to give any vitality to the scene. I felt that I breathed an atmosphere of sorrow. An air of stern, deep, and irredeemable gloom hung over and pervaded all.

Upon my entrance, Usher arose from a sofa on which he had been lying at full length, and greeted me with a vivacious warmth which had much in it, I at first thought, of an overdone cordiality—of the constrained effort of the *ennuyé*[11] man of the world. A glance, however, at his countenance convinced me of his perfect sincerity. We sat down; and for some moments, while he spoke not, I gazed upon him with a feeling half of pity, half of awe. Surely, man had never before so terribly altered, in so brief a period, as had Roderick Usher! It was with difficulty that I could bring myself to admit the identity of the wan being before me with the companion of my early boyhood. Yet the character of his face had been at all times remarkable. A cadaverousness of complexion; an eye large, liquid, and luminous beyond comparison; lips somewhat thin and very pallid, but of a surpassingly beautiful curve; a nose of a delicate Hebrew model, but with a breadth of nostril unusual in similar formations; a finely molded chin, speaking, in its want of prominence, of a want of moral energy; hair of a more than weblike softness and tenuity—these features, with an inordinate expansion above the regions of the temple, made up altogether a countenance not easily to be forgotten. And now in the mere

---

8. Gothic: High and ornate.
9. phantasmagoric (fan taz′ mə gôr′ ik) *adj.*: Fantastic or dreamlike.

10. fretted: Ornamented.
11. ennuyé (än′ wē ā′): Bored (French).

exaggeration of the prevailing character of these features, and of the expression they were wont to convey, lay so much of change that I doubted to whom I spoke. The now ghastly pallor of the skin, and the now miraculous luster of the eye, above all things startled and even awed me. The silken hair, too, had been suffered to grow all unheeded, and as, in its wild gossamer texture, it floated rather than fell about the face, I could not, even with effort, connect its Arabesque[12] expression with any idea of simple humanity.

In the manner of my friend I was at once struck with an incoherence—an inconsistency; and I soon found this to arise from a series of feeble and futile struggles to overcome an habitual trepidancy—an excessive nervous agitation. For something of this nature I had indeed been prepared, no less by his letter than by reminiscences of certain boyish traits, and by conclusions deduced from his peculiar physical conformation and temperament. His action was alternately vivacious and sullen. His voice varied rapidly from a tremulous indecision (when the animal spirits seemed utterly in abeyance) to that species of energetic concision—that abrupt, weighty, unhurried, and hollow-sounding enunciation—that leaden, self-balanced, and perfectly modulated guttural utterance, which may be observed in the lost drunkard, or the irreclaimable eater of opium, during the periods of his most intense excitement.

It was thus that he spoke of the object of my visit, of his earnest desire to see me, and of the solace he expected me to afford him. He entered, at some length, into what he conceived to be the nature of his malady. It was, he said, a constitutional and a family evil and one for which he despaired to find a remedy—a mere nervous affection,[13] he immediately added, which would undoubtedly soon pass off. It displayed itself in a host of

unnatural sensations. Some of these, as he detailed them, interested and bewildered me; although, perhaps, the terms and the general manner of their narration had their weight. He suffered much from a morbid acuteness of the senses; the most insipid food was alone endurable; he could wear only garments of certain texture; the odors of all flowers were oppressive; his eyes were tortured by even a faint light; and there were but peculiar sounds, and these from stringed instruments, which did not inspire him with horror.

To an anomalous species of terror I found him a bounden slave. "I shall perish," said he, "I *must* perish in this deplorable folly. Thus, thus, and not otherwise, shall I be lost. I dread the events of the future, not in themselves, but in their results. I shudder at the thought of any, even the most trivial, incident, which may operate upon this intolerable agitation of soul. I have, indeed, no abhorrence of danger, except in its absolute effect—in terror. In this unnerved, in this pitiable, condition I feel that the period will sooner or later arrive when I must abandon life and reason together, in some struggle with the grim phantasm, FEAR."

I learned, moreover, at intervals, and through broken and equivocal hints, another singular feature of his mental condition. He was enchained by certain superstitious impressions in regard to the dwelling which he tenanted, and whence, for many years, he had never ventured forth—in regard to an influence whose supposititious[14] force was conveyed in terms too shadowy here to be restated—an influence which some peculiarities in the mere form and substance of his family mansion had, by dint of long sufferance, he said, obtained over his spirit—an effect which the physique of the gray walls and turrets, and of the dim tarn into which they all looked down, had at length, brought about upon the morale of his existence.

---

12. Arabesque (ar′ ə besk′) *n*.: Of complex and elaborate design.
13. affection: Affliction.

14. supposititious (sə päz′ ə tish′ əs) *adj*.: Supposed.

He admitted, however, although with hesitation, that much of the peculiar gloom which thus afflicted him could be traced to a more natural and far more palpable origin—to the severe and long-continued illness—indeed to the evidently approaching dissolution—of a tenderly beloved sister, his sole companion for long years, his last and only relative on earth. "Her decease," he said, with a bitterness which I can never forget, "would leave him (him, the hopeless and the frail) the last of the ancient race of the Ushers." While he spoke, the lady Madeline (for so was she called) passed through a remote portion of the apartment, and, without having noticed my presence, disappeared. I regarded her with an utter astonishment not unmingled with dread; and yet I found it impossible to account for such feelings. A sensation of stupor oppressed me as my eyes followed her retreating steps. When a door, at length, closed upon her, my glance sought instinctively and eagerly the countenance of the brother; but he had buried his face in his hands, and I could only perceive that a far more than ordinary wanness had overspread the emaciated fingers through which trickled many passionate tears.

The disease of the lady Madeline had long baffled the skill of her physicians. A settled apathy, a gradual wasting away of the person, and frequent although transient affections of a partially cataleptical[15] character were the unusual diagnosis. Hitherto she had steadily borne up against the pressure of her malady, and had not betaken herself finally to bed; but on the closing in of the evening of my arrival at the house, she succumbed (as her brother told me at night with inexpressible agitation) to the prostrating power of the destroyer; and I learned that the glimpse I had obtained of her person would thus probably be the last I should obtain—that the lady, at least while living, would be seen by me no more.

For several days ensuing, her name was unmentioned by either Usher or myself; and during this period I was busied in earnest endeavors to alleviate the melancholy of my friend. We painted and read together, or I listened, as if in a dream, to the wild improvisations of his speaking guitar. And thus, as a closer and still closer intimacy admitted me more unreservedly into the recesses of his spirit, the more bitterly did I perceive the futility of all attempt at cheering a mind from which darkness, as if an inherent positive quality, poured forth upon all objects of the moral and physical universe in one unceasing radiation of gloom.

I shall ever bear about me a memory of the many solemn hours I thus spent alone with the master of the House of Usher. Yet I should fail in any attempt to convey an idea of the exact character of the studies, or of the occupations, in which he involved me, or led me the way. An excited and highly distempered ideality[16] threw a sulfureous[17] luster over all. His long improvised dirges will ring forever in my ears. Among other things, I hold painfully in mind a certain singular perversion and amplification of the wild air of the last waltz of von Weber.[18] From the paintings over which his elaborate fancy brooded, and which grew, touch by touch, into vaguenesses at which I shuddered the more thrillingly, because I shuddered knowing not why—from these paintings (vivid as their images now are before me) I would in vain endeavor to educe more than a small portion which should lie within the compass of merely written words. By the utter simplicity, by the nakedness of his designs, he arrested and overawed attention. If ever mortal painted an idea, that mortal was Roderick Usher. For me at least, in the circumstances then surrounding me, there arose out of the pure abstractions which the hypochondriac contrived to throw upon his

---

15. cataleptical (kat′ 'l ep′ tik 'l) *adj.*: In a state in which consciousness and feeling are suddenly and temporarily lost and the muscles become rigid.

16. ideality (ī′ dē al′ ə tē) *n.*: Something that is ideal and has no reality.
17. sulfureous (sul fyoor′ ē əs) *adj.*: Greenish-yellow.
18. von Weber: Karl Maria von Weber (1786–1826), a German Romantic composer.

canvas, an intensity of intolerable awe, no shadow of which felt I ever yet in the contemplation of the certainly glowing yet too concrete reveries of Fuseli.[19]

One of the phantasmagoric conceptions of my friend, partaking not so rigidly of the spirit of abstraction, may be shadowed forth, although feebly, in words. A small picture presented the interior of an immensely long and rectangular vault or tunnel, with low walls, smooth, white and without interruption or device. Certain accessory points of the design served well to convey the idea that this excavation lay at an exceeding depth below the surface of the earth. No outlet was observed in any portion of its vast extent, and no torch or other artificial source of light was discernible; yet a flood of intense rays rolled throughout, and bathed the whole in a ghastly and inappropriate splendor.

I have just spoken of that morbid condition of the auditory nerve which rendered all music intolerable to the sufferer, with the exception of certain effects of stringed instruments. It was, perhaps, the narrow limits to which he thus confined himself upon the guitar which gave birth, in great measure, to the fantastic character of his performances. But the fervid facility of his impromptus could not be so accounted for. They must have been, and were, in the notes, as well as in the words of his wild fantasias (for he not unfrequently accompanied himself with rhymed verbal improvisations), the result of that intense mental collectedness and concentration to which I have previously alluded as observable only in particular moments of the highest artificial excitement. The words of one of these rhapsodies I have easily remembered. I was, perhaps, the more forcibly impressed with it as he gave it because, in the under or mystic current of its meaning, I fancied that I perceived, and for the first time, a full consciousness on the part of Usher of the tottering of his lofty reason upon her throne. The verses, which were entitled "The Haunted Palace," ran very nearly, if not accurately, thus:

I

In the greenest of our valleys,
  By good angels tenanted,
Once a fair and stately palace—
  Radiant palace—reared its head.
In the monarch Thought's dominion—
  It stood there!
Never seraph[20] spread a pinion
  Over fabric half so fair.

II

Banners yellow, glorious, golden,
  On its roof did float and flow
(This—all this—was in the olden
  Time long ago)
And every gentle air that dallied,
  In that sweet day,
Along the ramparts plumed and
  pallid,
  A winged odor went away.

III

Wanderers in that happy valley
  Through two luminous windows saw
Spirits moving musically
  To a lute's well-tunèd law;
Round about a throne, where sitting
  (Porphyrogene!)[21]
In state his glory well befitting,
  The ruler of the realm was seen.

IV

And all with pearl and ruby glowing
  Was the fair palace door,
Through which came flowing, flowing,
  flowing
  And sparkling evermore,

---

19. Fuseli: Johann Heinrich Fuseli (1742–1825), a Swiss-born painter who lived in England and was noted for his work in the supernatural.

20. seraph (ser′ əf): Angel.
21. Porphyrogene (pôr fər ō jēn′): Born to royalty or "the purple."

A troop of Echoes whose sweet duty
  Was but to sing,
In voices of surpassing beauty,
  The wit and wisdom of their king.

V

But evil things, in robes of sorrow,
  Assailed the monarch's high estate;
(Ah, let us mourn, for never morrow
  Shall dawn upon him, desolate!)
And, round about his home, the glory
  That blushed and bloomed
Is but a dim-remembered story
  Of the old time entombed.

VI

And travelers now within that valley,
  Through the red-litten[22] windows see
Vast forms that move fantastically
  To a discordant melody;
While, like a rapid ghastly river,
  Through the pale door,
A hideous throng rush out forever,
  And laugh—but smile no more.

I well remember that suggestions arising from this ballad led us into a train of thought wherein there became manifest an opinion of Usher's which I mention not so much on account of its novelty (for other men have thought thus), as on account of the pertinacity with which he maintained it. This opinion, in its general form, was that of the sentience of all vegetable things. But, in his disordered fancy the idea had assumed a more daring character, and trespassed, under certain conditions, upon the kingdom of inorganization.[23] I lack words to express the full extent, or the earnest abandon of his persuasion. The belief, however, was connected (as I have previously hinted) with the gray stones of the home of his forefathers. The conditions of the sentience had been here, he imagined, fulfilled in the method of collocation of these stones—in the order of their arrangement, as well as in that of the many fungi which overspread them, and of the decayed trees which stood around—above all, in the long undisturbed endurance of this arrangement, and in its reduplication in the still waters of the tarn. Its evidence—the evidence of the sentience—was to be seen, he said (and I here started as he spoke), in the gradual yet certain condensation of an atmosphere of their own about the waters and the walls. The result was discoverable, he added, in that silent yet importunate and terrible influence which for centuries had molded the destinies of his family, and which made him what I now saw him—what he was. Such opinions need no comment, and I will make none.

Our books—the books which, for years, had formed no small portion of the mental existence of the invalid—were, as might be supposed, in strict keeping with this character of phantasm. We pored together over such works as the *Ververt et Chartreuse*[24] of Gresset; the *Belphegor* of Machiavelli; the *Heaven and Hell* of Swedenborg; the *Subterranean Voyage of Nicholas Klimm* by Holberg; the *Chiromancy* of Robert Flud, of Jean D'Indaginé and of De la Chambre; the *Journey into the Blue Distance* of Tieck; and the *City of the Sun* of Campanella. One favorite volume was a small octavo edition of the *Directorium Inquisitorium*, by the Dominican Eymeric de Gironne; and there were passages in Pomponius Mela, about the old African Stayrs and Œgipans, over which Usher would sit dreaming for hours. His chief delight, however, was found in the perusal of an exceedingly rare and curious book in quarto Gothic—the manual of a forgotten church—the *Vigiliæ Mortuorum secundum Chorum Ecclesiae Maguntinae.*

I could not help thinking of the wild ritual of this work, and of its probable influence upon the hypochondriac, when, one evening, having informed me abruptly that the lady Madeline was no more, he stated his

---

22. litten: Lighted.
23. inorganization: Inanimate objects.

24. Ververt et Chartreuse, etc.: All of the books listed deal with magic or mysticism.

intention of preserving her corpse for a fort-night (previously to its final interment), in one of the numerous vaults within the main walls of the building. The worldly reason, however, assigned for this singular proceeding, was one which I did not feel at liberty to dispute. The brother had been led to his resolution (so he told me) by consideration of the unusual character of the malady of the deceased, of certain obtrusive and eager inquiries on the part of her medical men, and of the remote and exposed situation of the burial ground of the family. I will not deny that when I called to mind the sinister countenance of the person whom I met upon the staircase, on the day of my arrival at the house, I had no desire to oppose what I regarded as at best but a harmless, and by no means an unnatural precaution.

At the request of Usher, I personally aided him in the arrangements for the temporary entombment. The body having been encoffined, we two alone bore it to its rest. The vault in which we placed it (and which had been so long unopened that our torches, half smothered in its oppressive atmosphere, gave us little opportunity for investigation) was small, damp, and entirely without means of admission for light; lying, at great depth, immediately beneath that portion of the building in which was my own sleeping apartment. It had been used, apparently, in remote feudal times, for the worst purposes of a donjon-keep, and, in later days, as a place of deposit for powder, or some other highly combustible substance, as a portion of its floor, and the whole interior of a long archway through which we reached it, were carefully sheathed with copper. The door, of massive iron, had been, also, similarly protected. Its immense weight caused an unusually sharp, grating sound, as it moved upon its hinges.

Having deposited our mournful burden upon trestles within this region of horror, we partially turned aside the yet unscrewed lid of the coffin, and looked upon the face of the tenant. A striking similitude between the brother and sister now first arrested my attention; and Usher, divining, perhaps, my thoughts, murmured out some few words from which I learned that the deceased and himself had been twins, and that sympathies of a scarcely intelligible nature had always existed between them. Our glances, however, rested not long upon the dead—for we could not regard her unawed. The disease which had thus entombed the lady in the maturity of youth, had left, as usual in all maladies of a strictly cataleptical character, the mockery of a faint blush upon the bosom and the face, and that suspiciously lingering smile upon the lip which is so terrible in death. We replaced and screwed down the lid, and, having secured the door of iron, made our way, with toil, into the scarcely less gloomy apartments of the upper portion of the house.

And now, some days of bitter grief having elapsed, an observable change came over the features of the mental disorder of my friend. His ordinary manner had vanished. His ordinary occupations were neglected or forgotten. He roamed from chamber to chamber with hurried, unequal, and objectless step. The pallor of his countenance had assumed, if possible, a more ghastly hue—but the luminousness of his eye had utterly gone out. The once occasional huskiness of his tone was heard no more; and a tremulous quaver, as if of extreme terror, habitually characterized his utterance. There were times, indeed, when I thought his unceasingly agitated mind was laboring with some oppressive secret, to divulge which he struggled for the necessary courage. At times, again, I was obliged to resolve all into the mere inexplicable vagaries[25] of madness, for I beheld him gazing upon vacancy for long hours, in an attitude of the profoundest attention, as if listening to some imaginary sound. It was no wonder that his condition terrified—that it infected me. I felt creeping

---

25. vagaries (və ger′ ēz) *n.*: Odd, unexpected actions or notions.

upon me, by slow yet uncertain degrees, the wild influences of his own fantastic yet impressive superstitions.

It was, especially, upon retiring to bed late in the night of the seventh or eighth day after the placing of the lady Madeline within the donjon, that I experienced the full power of such feelings. Sleep came not near my couch—while the hours waned and waned away. I struggled to reason off the nervousness which had dominion over me. I endeavored to believe that much, if not all of what I felt, was due to the bewildering influence of the gloomy furniture of the room—of the dark and tattered draperies, which, tortured into motion by the breath of a rising tempest, swayed fitfully to and fro upon the walls, and rustled uneasily about the decorations of the bed. But my efforts were fruitless. An irrepressible tremor gradually pervaded my frame; and, at length, there sat upon my very heart an incubus[26] of utterly causeless alarm. Shaking this off with a gasp and a struggle, I uplifted myself upon the pillows, and, peering earnestly within the intense darkness of the chamber, hearkened—I know not why, except that an instinctive spirit prompted me—to certain low and indefinite sounds which came, through the pauses of the storm, at long intervals, I knew not whence. Overpowered by an intense sentiment of horror, unaccountable yet unendurable, I threw on my clothes with haste (for I felt that I should sleep no more during the night), and endeavored to arouse myself from the pitiable condition into which I had fallen by pacing rapidly to and fro through the apartment.

I had taken but few turns in this manner, when a light step on an adjoining staircase arrested my attention. I presently recognized it as that of Usher. In an instant afterward he rapped, with a gentle touch, at my door, and entered, bearing a lamp. His countenance was, as usual, cadaverously wan—but, moreover, there was a species of mad hilarity in his eyes—an evidently restrained hysteria in his whole demeanor. His air appalled me—but anything was preferable to the solitude which I had so long endured, and I even welcomed his presence as a relief.

"And you have not seen it?" he said abruptly, after having stared about him for some moments in silence—"you have not then seen it?—but, stay! you shall." Thus speaking, and having carefully shaded his lamp, he hurried to one of the casements, and threw it freely open to the storm.

The impetuous fury of the entering gust nearly lifted us from our feet. It was, indeed, a tempestuous yet sternly beautiful night, and one wildly singular in its terror and its beauty. A whirlwind had apparently collected its force in our vicinity; for there were frequent and violent alterations in the direction of the wind; and the exceeding density of the clouds (which hung so low as to press upon the turrets of the house) did not prevent our perceiving the lifelike velocity with which they flew careering from all points against each other, without passing away into the distance. I say that even their exceeding density did not prevent our perceiving this—yet we had no glimpse of the moon or stars, nor was there any flashing forth of the lightning. But the under surfaces of the huge masses of agitated vapor, as well as all terrestrial objects immediately around us, were glowing in the unnatural light of a faintly luminous and distinctly visible gaseous exhalation which hung about and enshrouded the mansion.

"You must not—you shall not behold this!" said I, shuddering, to Usher, as I led him, with a gentle violence, from the window to a seat. "These appearances, which bewilder you, are merely electrical phenomena not uncommon—or it may be that they have their ghastly origin in the rank miasma[27] of

---

26. incubus (iŋ′ kyə bəs) *n*.: Something nightmarishly burdensome.

27. miasma (mī az′ mə) *n*.: An unwholesome atmosphere.

the tarn. Let us close this casement;—the air is chilling and dangerous to your frame. Here is one of your favorite romances. I will read, and you shall listen:—and so we will pass away this terrible night together."

The antique volume which I had taken up was the *Mad Trist* of Sir Launcelot Canning;[28] but I had called it a favorite of Usher's more in sad jest than in earnest; for, in truth, there is little in its uncouth and unimaginative prolixity which could have had interest for the lofty and spiritual ideality of my friend. It was, however, the only book immediately at hand; and I indulged a vague hope that the excitement which now agitated the hypochondriac, might find relief (for the history of mental disorder is full of similar anomalies) even in the extremeness of the folly which I should read. Could I have judged, indeed, by the wild overstrained air of vivacity with which he hearkened, or apparently hearkened, to the words of the tale, I might well have congratulated myself upon the success of my design.

I had arrived at that well-known portion of the story where Ethelred, the hero of the Trist, having sought in vain for peaceable admission into the dwelling of the hermit, proceeds to make good an entrance by force. Here, it will be remembered, the words of the narrative run thus:

"And Ethelred, who was by nature of a doughty heart, and who was now mighty withal, on account of the powerfulness of the wine which he had drunken, waited no longer to hold parley with the hermit, who, in sooth, was of an obstinate and maliceful turn, but feeling the rain upon his shoulders, and fearing the rising of the tempest, uplifted his mace outright, and, with blows, made quickly room in the plankings of the door for his gauntleted hand; and now pulling therewith sturdily, he so cracked, and ripped, and tore all asunder, that the noise of the dry and hollow-sounding wood alar-

---

28. *Mad Trist* of Sir Launcelot Canning: A fictional book and author.

umed and reverberated throughout the forest."

At the termination of this sentence I started and, for a moment, paused; for it appeared to me (although I at once concluded that my excited fancy had deceived me)—it appeared to me that, from some very remote portion of the mansion, there came, indistinctly to my ears, which might have been, in its exact similarity of character, the echo (but a stifled and dull one certainly) of the very cracking and ripping sound which Sir Launcelot had so particularly described. It was, beyond doubt, the coincidence alone which had arrested my attention; for, amid the rattling of the sashes of the casements, and the ordinary commingled noises of the still increasing storm, the sound, itself, had nothing, surely, which should have interested or disturbed me. I continued the story:

"But the good champion Ethelred, now entering within the door, was sore enraged and amazed to perceive no signal of the maliceful hermit; but, in the stead thereof, a dragon of a scaly and prodigious demeanor, and of a fiery tongue, which sate in guard before a palace of gold, with a floor of silver; and upon the wall there hung a shield of shining brass with this legend enwritten—

Who entereth herein, a conqueror
*   hath bin;*
Who slayeth the dragon, the
*   shield he shall win.*

And Ethelred uplifted his mace, and struck upon the head of the dragon, which fell before him, and gave up his pesty breath, with a shriek so horrid and harsh, and withal so piercing, that Ethelred had fain to close his ears with his hands against the dreadful noise of it, the like whereof was never before heard."

Here again I paused abruptly, and now with a feeling of wild amazement—for there could be no doubt whatever that, in this instance, I did actually hear (although from what direction it proceeded I found it impossible to say) a low and apparently distant, but harsh, protracted, and most unusual screaming or grating sound—the exact counterpart of what my fancy had already conjured up for the dragon's unnatural shriek as described by the romancer.

Oppressed, as I certainly was, upon the extraordinary coincidence, by a thousand conflicting sensations, in which wonder and extreme terror were predominant, I still retained sufficient presence of mind to avoid exciting, by an observation, the sensitive nervousness of my companion. I was by no means certain that he had noticed the sounds in question; although, assuredly, a strange alteration had, during the last few minutes, taken place in his demeanor. From a position fronting my own, he had gradually brought round his chair; so as to sit with his face to the door of the chamber; and thus I could but partially perceive his features, although I saw that his lips trembled as if he were murmuring inaudibly. His head had dropped upon his breast—yet I knew that he was not asleep, from the wide and rigid opening of the eye as I caught a glance of it in profile. The motion of his body, too, was at variance with this idea—for he rocked from side to side with a gentle yet constant and uniform sway. Having rapidly taken notice of all this, I resumed the narrative of Sir Launcelot, which thus proceeded:

"And now, the champion, having escaped from the terrible fury of the dragon, bethinking himself of the brazen shield, and of the breaking up of the enchantment which was upon it, removed the carcass from out of the way before him, and approached valorously over the silver pavement of the castle to where the shield was upon the wall; which in sooth tarried not for his full coming, but fell down at his feet upon the silver floor, with a mighty great and terrible ringing sound."

No sooner had these syllables passed my lips, than—as if a shield of brass had indeed, at the moment, fallen heavily upon a floor of silver—I became aware of a distinct, hollow, metallic, and clangorous, yet apparently muffled, reverberation. Completely unnerved, I leaped to my feet; but the measured rocking movement of Usher was undisturbed. I rushed to the chair in which he sat. His eyes were bent fixedly before him, and throughout his whole countenance there reigned a stony rigidity. But, as I placed my hand upon his shoulder, there came a strong shudder over his whole person; a sickly smile quivered about his lips; and I saw that he spoke in a low, hurried, and gibbering murmur, as if unconscious of my presence. Bending closely over him I at length drank in the hideous import of his words.

"Not hear it?—yes, I hear it, and have heard it. Long—long—long—many minutes, many hours, many days, have I heard it—yet I dared not—oh, pity me, miserable wretch that I am!—I dared not—I *dared* not speak! *We have put her living in the tomb!* Said I not that my senses were acute? I *now* tell you that I heard her first feeble movement in the hollow coffin. I heard them—many, many days ago—yet I dared not—*I dared not speak!* and now—tonight—Ethelred—ha! ha!—the breaking of the hermit's door, and the death cry of the dragon, and the clangor of the shield—say, rather, the rending of her coffin, and the grating of the iron hinges of her prison, and her struggles within the coppered archway of the vault! Oh! wither shall I fly? Will she not be here anon? Is she not hurrying to upbraid me for my haste? Have I not heard her footstep on the stair? Do I not distinguish that heavy and horrible beating of her heart? Madman!"—here he sprang furiously to his feet, and shrieked out his syllables, as if in the effort he were giving up his soul—*"Madman! I tell you that she now stands without the door!"*

As if in the superhuman energy of his utterance there had been found the potency of a spell, the huge antique panels to which the speaker pointed threw slowly back, upon the instant, their ponderous and ebony jaws. It was the work of the rushing gust—but then without those doors there *did* stand the lofty and enshrouded figure of the lady Madeline of Usher. There was blood upon her white robes, and the evidence of some bitter struggle upon every portion of her emaciated frame. For a moment she remained trembling and reeling to and fro upon the threshold—then, with a low moaning cry, fell heavily inward upon the person of her brother, and in her violent and now final death agonies, bore him to the floor a corpse, and a victim to the terrors he had anticipated.

From that chamber, and from that mansion, I fled aghast. The storm was still abroad in all its wrath as I found myself crossing the old causeway. Suddenly there shot along the path a wild light, and I turned to see whence a gleam so unusual could have issued; for the vast house and its shadows were alone behind me. The radiance was that of the full, setting, and blood-red moon, which now shone vividly through that once barely discernible fissure, of which I have before spoken as extending from the roof of the building, in a zigzag direction, to the base. While I gazed, this fissure rapidly widened—there came a fierce breath of the whirlwind—the entire orb of the satellite burst at once upon my sight—my brain reeled as I saw the mighty walls rushing asunder—there was a long tumultuous shouting sound like the voice of a thousand waters—and the deep and dank tarn at my feet closed sullenly and silently over the fragments of the *"House of Usher."*

RESPONDING TO THE SELECTION

Your Response

1. What was your mood at the beginning of the story? midway through the story? at the end of the story? Why?
2. What images from the story linger in your mind? Why?
3. Would you enjoy seeing a film version of "The Fall of the House of Usher"? Why or why not?

Recalling

4. (a) What is the narrator's first impression of the House of Usher? (b) Why has he come to the house?
5. (a) When the narrator meets Usher, what startles him most about Usher's appearance? (b) What strikes him about Usher's behavior?
6. (a) According to Usher, what is "the nature of his malady"? (b) To what is Usher a "bounden slave"?
7. (a) Why is the narrator "forcibly impressed" with Usher's performance of "The Haunted Palace"? (b) What opinion does Usher offer following his performance?
8. (a) What does the narrator assist Usher with following the death of Usher's sister, Madeline? (b) What does the narrator notice when he and Usher turn aside the cover of Madeline's coffin?
9. (a) What noises does the narrator hear in the midst of reading the *Mad Trist?* (b) How does Usher explain these noises? (c) What happens immediately after Usher finishes his explanation?
10. What happens to the House of Usher at the end of the story?

Interpreting

11. (a) How is the physical appearance of the interior of the House of Usher related to the condition of Usher's mind? (b) How is it related to his physical appearance?
12. What details early in the story foreshadow, or hint at, the ending?
13. Critics have argued that Madeline and Roderick are not only twins but are physical and mental components of the same being. What evidence is there in the story to support this claim?
14. What is the significance of the fact that, rather than helping Usher, the narrator finds himself becoming infected by Usher's condition?
15. Explain the two meanings of the story's title.

16. (a) In what way is the ending of the story ambiguous? (b) What do you think has happened?

Applying

17. Poe's story may suggest that the human imagination is capable of producing false perceptions of reality. Do you agree with this suggestion? Why or why not?

ANALYZING LITERATURE

Understanding the Single Effect

In his definition of a short story, Edgar Allan Poe asserted that a story should be constructed to achieve a single effect and that every word, detail, character, and incident in a story should contribute to this effect. Carefully constructed to create a growing sense of terror, "The Fall of the House of Usher" is a perfect illustration of Poe's theory.

How do each of the following events or details contribute to the growing sense of terror in "The Fall of the House of Usher"?
1. The description of the House of Usher
2. The description of Usher's painting
3. The entombment of Madeline
4. Storms and other natural phenomena
5. Madeline's appearance at the end of the story

CRITICAL THINKING AND READING

Supporting Statements of Theme

In his definition of the short story, Poe went on to state that "truth is often, and in very great degree, the aim" of the short story. In other words, in addition to being constructed to achieve a single effect, short stories are often written to make a point or express a general truth about life. The general truth a story expresses is the story's **theme.** There have been many different interpretations of the theme of "The Fall of the House of Usher." Find evidence from the story to support each of the following statements of possible themes.
1. In the absence of contact with the real world, the human imagination can produce a distorted perception of reality.
2. When isolated from the real world, a person can be infected by another person's fears and false perceptions of reality.
3. If artists (many critics believe that Roderick Usher represents a typical creative artist) completely turn away from the external world and become drawn into the internal world of their imaginations, they ultimately destroy their capacity to create and may eventually destroy themselves.

THINKING AND WRITING

Supporting a Statement of Theme

Develop one of your answers from the Critical Thinking and Reading exercise into an essay. Review the story to see if there is additional evidence you can use to support the theme statement. Take note of specific passages from the story that you can use in your essay. Organize your support into an outline. Develop the statement of theme into a thesis statement. When you write your essay, use transitions to link your ideas. When you revise make sure that your argument is well organized and clearly presented.

LEARNING OPTIONS

1. **Writing.** The death of the illustrious Roderick Usher would undoubtedly rate space in the local newspaper. Elaborate on details from the story to write his obituary. Be sure to include the circumstances of his death, a brief biographical sketch, and information about funeral arrangements. You might use the obituary of a prominent person from your community as a model.
2. **Art.** Design the set for a local production of "The Fall of the House of Usher." Reread Poe's description of the "mansion of doom" and choose a few scenes to design. Then draw a picture, create a model, or describe in detail the set you would use for each.

GUIDE FOR INTERPRETING

The Raven

Writers' Techniques

Sound Devices. Alliteration, consonance, and assonance are three sound devices that poets use to give their writing a musical quality. Alliteration is the repetition of similar sounds, usually consonants, at the beginnings of words or accented syllables. Notice the repetition of the *n* sound in the following line from "The Raven": "While I nodded, nearly napping, suddenly there came a tapping." Consonance is the repetition of consonant sounds at the ends of words or accented syllables. For example, Poe ends several stanzas of "The Raven" with a line containing a repeated *v* sound: "Quoth the Raven, 'Nevermore.' " Assonance is the repetition of vowel sounds. For example, the *ur* sound is repeated in line 13 of "The Raven": "And the silken, sad, uncertain rustling of each purple curtain."

The repetition of similar sounds in poetry pleases the ear and reinforces meaning by emphasizing important words. Poe's use of alliteration, consonance, and assonance throughout "The Raven" creates a hypnotic effect that draws us into the speaker's irrational world. As a result, we are persuaded temporarily to abandon our conception of reality and accept the speaker's vision as reality. At the same time, the repetition of sounds emphasizes certain words that contribute to the mood and reinforce the meaning of the poem.

Focus

Describe a creature that you find frightening or mysterious. Try to use descriptive details that convey the fear or uncertainty that you associate with this creature.

Primary Source

In *The Philosophy of Composition,* Poe described how he used the repetition of the Raven's response, "Nevermore":

> I saw that I could make the first query propounded by the lover—the first query to which the Raven should reply "Nevermore"—that I could make this first query a commonplace one—the second less so—the third still less, and so on—until at length the lover, startled from his original *nonchalance* by the melancholy character of the word itself—by its frequent repetition—and by a consideration of the ominous reputation of the fowl that uttered it—is at length excited to superstition, and wildly propounds queries of a far different character—. . . because he experiences a frenzied pleasure in so modeling his questions as to receive from the *expected* "Nevermore" the most delicious because the most intolerable of sorrow.

ILLUSTRATION TO E. A. POE'S
THE RAVEN
Edouard Manet
Courtesy, Museum of Fine Arts, Boston

The Raven

Edgar Allan Poe

Once upon a midnight dreary, while I pondered, weak and weary,
Over many a quaint and curious volume of forgotten lore,
While I nodded, nearly napping, suddenly there came a tapping,
As of someone gently rapping, rapping at my chamber door.
5 " 'Tis some visitor," I muttered, "tapping at my chamber door—
                Only this, and nothing more."

Ah, distinctly I remember it was in the bleak December,
And each separate dying ember wrought its ghost upon the floor.
Eagerly I wished the morrow—vainly I had tried to borrow
10 From my books surcease[1] of sorrow—sorrow for the lost Lenore—
For the rare and radiant maiden whom the angels name Lenore—
                Nameless here for evermore.

And the silken, sad, uncertain rustling of each purple curtain
Thrilled me—filled me with fantastic terrors never felt before;
15 So that now, to still the beating of my heart, I stood repeating
" 'Tis some visitor entreating entrance at my chamber door—
Some late visitor entreating entrance at my chamber door—
                This it is and nothing more."

---

1. surcease (sʉr sēs'): End.

Presently my soul grew stronger; hesitating then no longer,
20   "Sir," said I, "or Madam, truly your forgiveness I implore;
But the fact is I was napping, and so gently you came rapping,
And so faintly you came tapping, tapping at my chamber door,
That I scarce was sure I heard you"—here I opened wide the door—
                              Darkness there, and nothing more.

25   Deep into that darkness peering, long I stood there wondering,
          fearing,
Doubting, dreaming dreams no mortal ever dared to dream before;
But the silence was unbroken, and the darkness gave no token,
And the only word there spoken was the whispered word, "Lenore!"
This *I* whispered, and an echo murmured back the word, "Lenore!"
30   Merely this, and nothing more.

Then into the chamber turning, all my soul within me burning,
Soon I heard again a tapping somewhat louder than before.
"Surely," said I, "surely that is something at my window lattice;
Let me see, then, what thereat is, and this mystery explore—
35   Let my heart be still a moment and this mystery explore—
                              'Tis the wind, and nothing more!"

Open here I flung the shutter, when, with many a flirt and flutter,
In there stepped a stately raven of the saintly days of yore;
Not the least obeisance made he; not an instant stopped or stayed
          he;
40   But, with mien of lord or lady, perched above my chamber door—
Perched upon a bust of Pallas² just above my chamber door—
                              Perched, and sat, and nothing more.

Then this ebony bird beguiling my sad fancy into smiling,
By the grave and stern decorum of the countenance it wore,
45   "Though thy crest be shorn and shaven, thou," I said, "art sure no
          craven,
Ghastly grim and ancient raven wandering from the Nightly
          shore—
Tell me what thy lordly name is on the Night's Plutonian³ shore!"
                              Quoth the raven, "Nevermore."

Much I marveled this ungainly fowl to hear discourse so plainly,
50   Though its answer little meaning—little relevancy bore;
For we cannot help agreeing that no sublunary being
Ever yet was blessed with seeing bird above his chamber door—
Bird or beast upon the sculptured bust above his chamber door,
                              With such name as "Nevermore."

---

2. Pallas (pal′ əs): Pallas Athena, the ancient Greek goddess of
wisdom.
3. Plutonian (ploo tō′ nē ən) *adj.*: Referring to Pluto, the Greek and
Roman god of the underworld.

55 But the raven, sitting lonely on the placid bust, spoke only
That one word, as if his soul in that one word he did outpour.
Nothing farther then he uttered—not a feather then he fluttered—
Till I scarcely more than muttered, "Other friends have flown
before—
On the morrow *he* will leave me, as my hopes have flown before."
60 Quoth the raven, "Nevermore."

Wondering at the stillness broken by reply so aptly spoken,
"Doubtless," said I, "what it utters is its only stock and store,
Caught from some unhappy master whom unmerciful Disaster
Followed fast and followed faster—so, when Hope he would adjure,
65 Stem Despair returned, instead of the sweet Hope he dared
adjure—
That sad answer, "Nevermore!"

But the raven still beguiling all my sad soul into smiling,
Straight I wheeled a cushioned seat in front of bird, and bust, and
door;
Then upon the velvet sinking, I betook myself to linking
70 Fancy unto fancy, thinking what this ominous bird of yore—

ILLUSTRATION TO E. A. POE'S *THE RAVEN*
Edouard Manet
Courtesy, Museum of Fine Arts, Boston

What this grim, ungainly, ghastly, gaunt, and ominous bird of yore
                    Meant in croaking "Nevermore."

This I sat engaged in guessing, but no syllable expressing
To the fowl whose fiery eyes now burned into my bosom's core;
75 This and more I sat divining, with my head at ease reclining
On the cushion's velvet lining that the lamplight gloated o'er,
But whose velvet violet lining with the lamplight gloating o'er,
                    She shall press, ah, nevermore!

Then, methought, the air grew denser, perfumed from an unseen
    censer
80 Swung by angels whose faint foot-falls tinkled on the tufted floor.
"Wretch," I cried, "thy God hath lent thee—by these angels he hath
    sent thee
Respite—respite and nepenthe[4] from thy memories of Lenore!
Let me quaff this kind nepenthe and forget this lost Lenore!"
                    Quoth the raven, "Nevermore."

85 "Prophet!" said I, "thing of evil!—prophet still, if bird or devil!—
Whether Tempter sent, or whether tempest tossed thee here
    ashore,
Desolate, yet all undaunted, on this desert land enchanted—
On this home by Horror haunted—tell me truly, I implore—
Is there—*is* there balm in Gilead?[5]—tell me—tell me, I implore!"
90   Quoth the raven, "Nevermore."

"Prophet!" said I, "thing of evil!—prophet still, if bird or devil!
By that Heaven that bends above us—by that God we both adore—
Tell this soul with sorrow laden if, within the distant Aidenn,[6]
It shall clasp a sainted maiden whom the angels name Lenore—
95 Clasp a rare and radiant maiden whom the angels name Lenore."
                    Quoth the raven, "Nevermore."

"Be that word our sign of parting, bird or fiend!" I shrieked,
    upstarting—
"Get thee back into the tempest and the Night's Plutonian shore!
Leave no black plume as a token of that lie thy soul hath spoken!
100 Leave my loneliness unbroken!—quit the bust above my door!
Take thy beak from out my heart, and take thy form from off my
    door!"
                    Quoth the raven, "Nevermore."

----

4. nepenthe (ni pen′ thē) *n.*: A drug that the ancient Greeks
believed could relieve sorrow.
5. balm in Gilead (gil′ ē əd): In the Bible, a healing ointment was
made in Gilead, a region of ancient Palestine.
6. Aidenn (ā′den): Arabic for *Eden* or *heaven.*

And the raven, never flitting, still is sitting, still is sitting
On the pallid bust of Pallas just above my chamber door;
105 And his eyes have all the seeming of a demon that is dreaming,
And the lamplight o'er him streaming throws his shadow on the
    floor;
And my soul from out that shadow that lies floating on the floor
                                                Shall be lifted—nevermore!

RESPONDING TO THE SELECTION

Your Response

1. What effect does the poem have on you? Why?
2. What actor or speaker would you like to hear read the poem? Explain.

Recalling

3. How does the speaker respond to the noise he hears?
4. What does the speaker want to forget?
5. How does the raven get into the chamber?
6. (a) What does the speaker ask the raven? (b) What is its response? (c) What does the speaker order the raven to do?

Interpreting

7. (a) What is the mood? (b) How is the mood established in the first two stanzas?
8. (a) During the course of the poem, what changes occur in the speaker's attitude toward the raven? (b) What brings about each of these changes? (c) What does the raven finally come to represent?
9. (a) How does the speaker's emotional state change during the poem? (b) How are these changes related to the changes in his attitude toward the raven?
10. How is the word spoken by the raven related to the speaker's emotional state at the end of the poem?

Applying

11. "The Raven" has been popular for well over one hundred years. What do you think accounts for its continuing appeal?

ANALYZING LITERATURE

Using Sound Devices

Alliteration, consonance, and **assonance** are three sound devices used in poetry. Alliteration is the repetition of similar sounds, usually consonants, at the beginnings of words or accented syllables (for example, "surcease of sorrow," line 10). Consonance is the repetition of consonant sounds at the ends of words or accented syllables (for example, "chamber door," line 14). Assonance is the repetition of vowel sounds (for example, "weak and weary," line 1).

Find three more examples of each of these techniques in "The Raven." Explain how each contributes to the poem's hypnotic effect.

THINKING AND WRITING

Responding to a Statement

Poe stated, "A poem, in my opinion, is opposed to a work of science by having, for its *immediate* object, pleasure, not truth. . . ." Review the poem, considering how Poe's use of sound devices and his choice of subject relate to the poem's *immediate* purpose. Try to determine the general truth, or theme, the poem expresses. Think about how the theme relates to the poem's *overall* purpose. Then, after deciding how you will respond to Poe's statement, find passages from the poem to support your response. Start your essay with Poe's statement, followed by your response. Then develop an argument supporting your response. When you finish writing, revise your essay and prepare a final copy.

Edgar Allan Poe and "The Raven"

PREWRITING

Explaining Poe's Method As much as we enjoy many great poems from the past, we seldom have an opportunity to learn about how they were created. Homer gave no newspaper interviews to explain how the *Odyssey* came into being. Nor did Dante appear on television to discuss the origins of the *Divine Comedy*.

We are lucky, then, that Poe left a detailed account of how he composed "The Raven." In an essay called "The Philosophy of Composition," the author set out not only his ideas about the goals of poetry, but a step-by-step account of how his most famous poem was written.

No Accidents Often, poets will point out how "accidents" or sudden impulses contribute to their poetry. Poe, however, insisted that there was nothing accidental about his poem: "The work proceeded, step by step, to its completion with the precision and rigid consequence of a mathematical problem."

What were these steps? According to Poe, he first chose a proper length for his poem. Poe thought a poem should be relatively short in order to retain its intensity. "If any literary work is too long to be read at one sitting," he wrote, "we must be content to dispense with the immensely important effect derivable from unity of impression."

Taking such thoughts into account, Poe soon made his decision: "I reached at once what I conceived the proper length for my intended poem—a length of about one hundred lines. It is, in fact, a hundred and eight."

"The Choice of an Impression" Poe's next step was to choose "an impression, or effect, to be conveyed." Before Poe even selected a character, setting, or voice for his poem, he decided which philosophical effect he wanted the poem to have upon its readers. "The Raven," he decided, would aim for neither Truth nor Passion. Instead he set his sights on Beauty, which he defined as an "intense and pure elevation of the soul." (Do you think that Poe achieved his goal? Did any truth or passion slip in by accident?) Having chosen beauty as his effect, Poe also settled on a specific tone—sadness. "Beauty of whatever kind," he wrote, "in its supreme development, invariably excites the sensitive soul to tears."

"The Nature of My Refrain" Next, the poet began to consider actual words—or at least one word. Can you guess which word in "The Raven" Poe considered first of all?

If you guessed "Nevermore," you were right. Poe quickly decided that his poem would benefit from a refrain—that is, a word or phrase that is repeated regularly throughout. Because this refrain would be the closing line of each stanza, it would have to be a forceful, memorable word. "That such a close . . . must be sonorous and susceptible of protracted emphasis," Poe wrote, "admitted no doubt: and these considerations inevitably led me to the long *o* as the most sonorous vowel, in connection with *r* as the most producible consonant." Once Poe had decided on these sounds, it was a short leap to "Nevermore."

Strictly for the Birds Poe now had his refrain: "Nevermore." But he wondered whether any human being would credibly repeat the word "so continuously or monotonously." He soon hit upon a solution: "Here, then, immediately arose the idea of a non-reasoning creature capable of speech; and, very naturally, a parrot, in the first instance, suggested itself, but was superseded forthwith by a Raven, as equally capable of speech, and infinitely more in keeping with the intended tone."

Poe now had his refrain and his "ebony bird beguiling"—the Raven. These elements combined to generate the poem's situation: "a lover lamenting his deceased mistress." The poet was ready, finally, to start writing.

DRAFTING

Beginning at the End Poe began with the last stanza. "Here then," he wrote, "the poem may be said to have its beginning—at the end, where all works of art should begin."

According to Poe, the final stanza should produce a poem's moment of climax. The preceding stanzas should merely inch toward this level of intensity, and if necessary, the poet should deliberately water down his or her work. "Had I been able, in the subsequent composition, to construct more vigorous stanzas, I should, without scruple, have purposely enfeebled them, so as not to interfere with the climacteric effect."

The Meter Is Running As he composed this final stanza, Poe also made decisions about the meter of his poem. As always, he sought to be original. Looking over the history of poetry, Poe felt that originality was in short supply: "Admitting that there is little possibility of variety in mere rhythm, it is still clear that the possible varieties of meter and stanza are absolutely infinite—and yet, for centuries, no man, in verse, has ever done, or ever seemed to think of doing, an original thing."

Needless to say, Poe was exaggerating, and as he was quick to point out, the trochaic meter of "The Raven" broke no new ground. Nevertheless, the poet did obtain an original effect by combining lines of different lengths within each stanza. "Each of these lines, taken individually, has been employed before," Poe pointed out, "and what originality 'Raven' has, is in their combination into stanzas; nothing even remotely resembling this combination has ever been attempted."

For some readers these varying line lengths produce a feeling of unpredictability, which mirrors in turn the confusion of the narrator. What effect do these varying line lengths have on you as you read the poem?

PUBLISHING

Breaking Into Print Poe wrote nothing in his essay about publication; he was concerned entirely with the process of poetic composition. At least once, however, he mentioned the audience at which he was aiming his poem. In his discussion of the proper length for "The Raven," he wrote of his wish to satisfy "that degree of excitement which I deemed not above the popular, while not below the critical, taste." In other words Poe wanted to satisfy both critics and a large audience.

In this he succeeded. You may be interested to know that "The Raven" first appeared in 1845 in a newspaper, *The New York Mirror.* The poem made Poe's reputation, and his new fame enabled him to get a job at yet another newspaper, the *Broadway Journal.* Here he wrote essays, stories, and poems, for which he was paid at the rate of $1.00 per newspaper column!

THINKING ABOUT THE PROCESS

1. To some people Poe's writing process may seem to operate backward—that is, he decided on the sounds in the word "Nevermore" before hitting upon the word itself. How do you think this kind of process could be helpful to a writer?
2. Do you agree with Poe that a poem must be short to be effective?
3. **Writing** Try writing a single line of poetry, and then use it for the first line of one poem and the last line of another. How did you use the line differently in each case?

GUIDE FOR INTERPRETING

To Helen

Allusions. An **allusion** is a reference to another literary work or a figure, a place, or an event from history, religion, or mythology. For example, in the first stanza of "To Helen," Poe alludes to Helen of Troy, a legendary Greek woman known for her incomparable beauty.

The theme or central idea of "To Helen"—that the purest, most enduring form of beauty is spiritual beauty rather than physical beauty—is revealed through the progression of allusions Poe uses in the poem. By interpreting the meaning of each allusion, we can see how the poet forms his conception of beauty as an ideal.

What does beauty mean to you? Freewrite about the thoughts and feelings you associate with the concept of beauty.

What accounts for Poe's strange imagination? In "The Cabinet of Edgar Allan Poe," Angela Carter imagines the childhood of the young Poe, whose parents were actors in the theater.

Consider the theatrical illusion with special reference to this impressionable child, who was exposed to it at an age when there is no reason for anything to be real.

He must often have toddled onto the stage when the theater was empty and the curtains down. . . .

Here he will find a painted backdrop of, say, an antique castle—a castle! such as they don't build here; a Gothic castle all complete with owls and ivy. The flies are painted with segments of trees, massy oaks or something like that, all in two dimensions. Artificial shadows fall in all the wrong places. Nothing is what it seems. You knock against a gilded throne or horrid rack that looks perfectly solid, thick, immovable, and you kick it sideways, it turns out to be made of papier mâché, it is as light as air—a child, you yourself, could pick it up and carry it off with you and sit in it and be a king or lie in it and be in pain.

A creaking, an ominous rattling scares the little wits out of you; when you jump round to see what is going on behind your back, why, the very castle is in mid-air! Heave-ho and up she rises, amid the inarticulate cries and muttered oaths of the stagehands, and down comes Juliet's tomb or Ophelia's sepulcher, and a super scuttles in, clutching Yorrick's skull.

To Helen
Edgar Allan Poe

Helen, thy beauty is to me
    Like those Nicéan barks[1] of yore,
That gently, o'er a perfumed sea,
    The weary, way-worn wanderer bore
5   To his own native shore.

On desperate seas long wont to roam,
    Thy hyacinth[2] hair, thy classic face,
Thy Naiad airs have brought me home
    To the glory that was Greece,
10   And the grandeur that was Rome.

Lo! in yon brilliant window-niche
    How statue-like I see thee stand,
The agate lamp within thy hand!
    Ah, Psyche, from the regions which
15   Are Holy Land!

---

1. Nicéan (nī sē′ ən) **barks:** Boats from the
shipbuilding city of Nicea in Asia Minor.
2. hyacinth (hī′ ə sinth′) *adj.*: Wavy; lustrous.

PROSERPINE
Dante Gabriel Rossetti
The Tate Gallery, London

RESPONDING TO THE SELECTION

Your Response
1. What is your impression of the Helen of the poem? Do you think she is an actual woman or an idealized woman? Explain.
2. To whom or to what would you address a poem about beauty? Explain.

Interpreting
3. What effect does Helen's beauty have on the "weary, way-worn" wanderer?
4. During the course of the poem, Helen is transformed from a person into a statue of a goddess. What does this tell you about the poet's concept of beauty?

Applying
5. What do you think is the purest form of beauty? Explain your answer.

ANALYZING LITERATURE

Recognizing Allusions
An **allusion** is a reference to another literary work or a figure, a place, or an event from history, religion, or mythology. For example, in the first stanza, Poe alludes to Helen of Troy, a woman known for her incomparable beauty.
1. Identify the meaning of each of the following allusions.
    a. Naiad   b. Psyche
2. How do these allusions relate to the overall meaning of the poem?

Alfred J. Hitchcock (1899–1980)

"At sixteen I discovered the work of Edgar Allan Poe," recalled Alfred Hitchcock, the great director of horror and suspense films. "When I came home from the office where I worked I went straight to my room, took the cheap edition of his *Tales of the Grotesque and Arabesque*, and began to read. I still remember my feelings when I finished 'The Murders in the Rue Morgue.' I was afraid, but this fear made me discover something I've never forgotten since: Fear, you see, is an emotion people like to feel when they know they're safe."

In his more than fifty-year career of film making, Alfred Hitchcock has given viewers

plenty of opportunity to experience fear. He began directing films during the silent era, and by the 1930's he had established his reputation as a director of suspense thrillers. By the time he directed *Vertigo* (1958), *Psycho* (1960), and *The Birds* (1963), he had moved beyond suspense into terror.

POE'S INFLUENCE

Hitchcock learned much from Edgar Allan Poe, the master of terror and suspense. Poe's influence is evident in Hitchcock's vision of a morally ambiguous world in which the seemingly ordinary person is susceptible to madness and corruption. Like the characters Poe created, Hitchcock's characters frequently must cope with the hallucinatory effects of guilt, paranoia, and loss of identity. A character in *Psycho* seems to capture Hitchcock's view of the world when he says, "We all go a little mad from time to time."

THEMES AND TECHNIQUES

Hitchcock's psychological thrillers explore many of the themes and ideas that Poe used in his stories and poems. Most striking is the recurring conflict between appearance and reality. Many of Hitchcock's films examine the way the human mind can distort the world, resulting in a life of fantasy bordering on insanity. To illustrate obsession and mental distortion, he often focused his films through a single character's consciousness, as in *Suspicion*. Poe used a narrator to create the same effect. Sometimes, notably in *Rear Window*, Hitchcock allowed the viewer

to observe secretly the private lives of others to emphasize how claustrophobic and perverse the mind in isolation becomes.

Another Hitchcock theme that recalls Poe is the power of the dead over the living. This idea is examined in such films as *Rebecca* and *Vertigo*.

The techniques with which Hitchcock created his effects resemble those Poe used in his tales of horror and suspense. In the typical Hitchcock film, the plot is less important than the development of character and theme, so the viewer is drawn deeply into the moral world of the film. Hitchcock also used the technique of beginning with apparently normal and safe settings that slide almost imperceptibly into depravity and nightmare.

As a result, everyday objects and familiar things—staircases, rooms, birds—become the machinery of terror.

Like Poe, Hitchcock was interested in the black humor of the macabre; he intermixed humor with horror, as if to lure the audience into a false mood of security and nervous relief. For Hitchcock as for Poe, the world was one in which disorder and death lurked beneath the surface of everyday life. And the audience for both loves to experience the fear and terror that exists in this world.

YOUR WRITING PROCESS

WRITING A FIRST-PERSON NARRATIVE

"The pattern of the thing precedes the thing. I fill in the gaps of the crossword at any spot I happen to choose. These bits I write on index cards until the novel is done."

Vladimir Nabokov

"The Devil and Tom Walker" and "The Fall of the House of Usher" are two stories that describe strange or dreamlike meetings with unusual characters. Perhaps you have told similar stories to your friends, trying to evoke feelings of mystery and fear. Whom or what have you visited—in reality or in your dreams—that would make a good subject for such a tale?

> **Focus**
>
> **Assignment:** Write a first-person narrative about a visit to an unusual person or place.
> **Purpose:** To convey a sense of mystery or uniqueness.
> **Audience:** A good friend.

Prewriting

1. Cluster to find possible topics. Make a cluster diagram around the words "unique people" and another one around "strange places" just to get ideas. Allow your memory to wander and your imagination to roam.

2. Brainstorm imagery. Once you've chosen a topic or two, brainstorm word images that you associate with each. Try to include images that appeal to all five senses. Remember that appealing to the senses of touch, taste, and smell can be very effective in making a description vivid.

3. Create a timeline. When writing a story, it may be helpful to draw a timeline to organize its events. First, decide how much time will pass: an hour? a day? a year? Draw a horizontal line to represent the span of time you have chosen. Then, decide on the key events of your narrative and locate them on your timeline.

4. Freewrite about characters. Get to know your characters—all of them—by freewriting separately about each. What are their likes and dislikes? How do they spend their time? How old are they? What do they look like? You'll discover details that will be useful in your story.

Drafting

1. Dialogue. One of the best ways to bring characters and actions to life is through dialogue. Try to make yours believable and lively. Make every word contribute to the mood you are trying to create.

> ## Student Model
>
> The cave looked like the black mouth of a monster. "Let's go," Hillary whispered.
>
> "No," I answered quickly, as she stepped into the shadow. Then, I called, "Wait!" and ran in behind her.

2. Add details from your imagination. If you've chosen a topic from a real experience, don't hold yourself to facts. Let your imagination go; enhance your story with some exaggeration, whimsy, or an out-and-out lie. Make the unique person or place even more unforgettable for readers.

Revising and Editing

1. Use transitions to show time relationships. Some paragraphs of your story may be organized spatially, but most will follow a chronological order. Use transitional words and phrases such as the following to clarify the time relationships between events: meanwhile, at the same time, a few hours later, the following Saturday.

2. Have a peer editor look at your modifiers. Use modifiers only if they genuinely contribute to your story. Ask a peer editor to read your draft and to bracket the modifiers that are not necessary. As you read the following passage, see whether or not you agree with the peer editor's suggestions for removing the bracketed words.

> ## Student Model
>
> Sean McCole was [actually] missing [his] two front teeth. A horse [that he'd been shoeing] had kicked them [right] out of his mouth, he told [the five of] us one [sunny summer] afternoon while he pounded his [heavy] anvil on the [hot, red] iron, bending it [as he talked] into the [U-] shape of a [horse's] hoof.

3. Use a variety of sentences. Don't settle for the first way you write a sentence; try various combinations of clauses and phrases and choose the one that best suits your subject and style. Also, weave together long and short sentences to keep readers interested.

Writer's Hint

In reading Washington Irving and Edgar Allan Poe, you will see many clues for varying sentences:

• Use an **appositive phrase:** "A few straggling savin trees, *emblems of sterility,* grew near it . . . (page 174).

• Begin a sentence with a **prepositional phrase:** "*At the request of Usher,* I personally aided him in the arrangements . . ." (page 202).

• Break up a sentence with a **relative clause:** "These appearances, *which bewilder you,* are merely electrical phenomena . . ." (page 203).

Options for Publishing

• Have someone you know who draws or paints illustrate your story.

• With a small group, give a dramatic reading of your story for the class. Tape-record the reading for posterity!

• Submit your story to a local newspaper or magazine.

• Enter your narrative in a short story contest.

Reviewing Your Writing Process

1. Did you have a hard time creating dialogue for your characters? Why or why not?

2. As you revised your story, what strategy did you use to increase the variety of your sentences? Would you use this strategy again? Explain.

BOSTON HARBOR
Fitz Hugh Lane
Museum of Fine Arts, Boston

NEW ENGLAND RENAISSANCE

1840–1855

One man's justice is another's injustice; one man's beauty
another's ugliness; one man's wisdom another's folly.

Ralph Waldo Emerson

By 1840, it was clear that the American experiment in democracy had succeeded. England, rebuffed in the "Second American War for Independence," was no longer a threat to the survival of the republic. Andrew Jackson, the first "People's President," had served two tempestuous terms in office. New states were entering the Union: Arkansas had come in as the twenty-fifth state in 1836, and Michigan was soon to follow. Despite the Panic of 1837, the mood in America was buoyant; the best was yet to come. Alexis de Tocqueville, a French traveler in the 1830's, observed that Americans had "a lively faith in the perfectibility of man," and they "admit that what appears to them today to be good may be superseded by something better tomorrow."

Although the great early presidents of the Virginia and Massachusetts dynasties had passed from the scene, a bright new galaxy of statesmen could be seen in Washington, D.C.: Daniel Webster from Massachusetts, Henry Clay from Kentucky, Thomas Hart Benton from Missouri, and John C. Calhoun from South Carolina. As these men struggled with political issues that would ultimately break the nation apart, American literature blossomed suddenly and brilliantly in the New England states, particularly in Massachusetts, and specifically in Boston, Concord, Salem, Pittsfield, and Amherst. Historians have called this brief, sunlit era in American cultural history a "flowering," a "renaissance," and a "golden day." Its guiding spirit was Ralph Waldo Emerson, a Unitarian minister who in 1832 had left the pulpit of the Second Church of Boston for a broader stage. Wrote one historian, "The year 1836, when Emerson published his essay on *Nature,* may be taken as the focus of a period in American thought corresponding to 1776 in American politics."

HUB OF THE SOLAR SYSTEM

When the New England literary group burst into flower, Boston was a vibrant, expanding city of nearly 100,000 people. Then, as now, it was the metropolis of the region, a cosmopolitan city whose clipper ships were known from Liverpool to Singapore. Oliver Wendell Holmes, a Boston physician and man of letters, said, tongue in cheek, "Boston State House is the hub of the solar system."

Certainly, Boston's four-story Tremont House, with 170 guest rooms, was at mid-century one of the finest hotels in America. In 1842, Charles Dickens, twenty-nine years old and already a world-famous author, stayed at the Tremont House. As a climax to his visit, the Young Men of Boston staged a great dinner in his honor, scarcely imagining that some of their close friends would one day have international literary reputations to rival that of Dickens.

Just as the city of Boston, a center of culture and commerce, was growing, so were a great many Massachusetts factory and mill towns. Of the 1,200 cotton factories in the United States in 1840, two thirds were located in New England. Francis C. Lowell, who developed the first American power loom, devised a plan to attract conscientious workers. He hired high-principled young women, most of them from nearby farms, to work in the textile mills of Lowell, Waltham, Lawrence, and other towns on the Merrimack River. These so-called "Lowell factory girls" lived in boarding houses under strict supervision, and worked from 5:00 A.M. to 7:30 P.M., with two half-hour breaks for meals. While the Lowell plan was far from typical, the factory system in general was an economic success. Textile companies prospered. The town of Lowell mushroomed from 200 people in 1820 to over 30,000 by 1845.

If New England was growing and changing, so was the rest of the country. The factory system, with its mass production, would eventually change the face of America, but that change was mostly in the future. America was still an agricultural nation. More often than not, the Lowell factory girls returned to their family farms after a few years, more mature, ready to marry, and by no means part of an urban American underclass. City populations were growing throughout the United States, but so was the number of American farms. The nation as a whole experienced a period of spectacular growth during these years of New England's literary prime. Cities, farms, factories—all were booming.

CORNELL FARM
Edward Hicks

The Way West

In one sense, the entire course of American history since 1607 can be seen as a pageant of continuous westward movement. The first white settlers sailed west from Europe, establishing their homes on the East Coast of the New World. All thirteen original states were on the eastern seaboard, hemmed in by mountain barriers blocking easy access to the interior. As late as 1845, the most western state in the Union was Texas. The last of the fifty states, Hawaii, lying far away to the west of the North American continent, was at that time an independent kingdom.

During the years in which New England literature flowered, American transportation was steadily changing and improving. The Erie Canal, completed in the state of New York in 1825, set off a wave of frenzied canal building in the Northeast. Throughout the 1840's, American railroads competed not only with canals but also with plank roads. A plank road, usually constructed of hemlock boards, was strong enough to support heavy wagons and stagecoaches. Built by private turnpike companies, plank roads enjoyed a brief flurry of popularity in the 1840's. By 1855, however, it was obvious that railroads had clear-cut advantages over plank roads, and in many places railroads had already rendered canals unprofitable. As the Civil War approached, the golden age of railroading was about to begin.

New England Renaissance

(A.D. 1840 – A.D. 1855)

Abraham
Lincoln

First
Postage
Stamps

Charlotte
Brontë

1840	1843	1846

AMERICAN EVENTS

- The Transcendentalist magazine, *The Dial,* begins publication.
  - **Ralph Waldo Emerson** publishes *Essays.*
  - Brook Farm, the Transcendental community, established near Boston.
  - **Henry Wadsworth Longfellow** publishes "The Skeleton in Armor."

- **John Greenleaf Whittier** publishes *Lays of My Home and Other Poems.*
  - First telegraph message sent.
  - **Ralph Waldo Emerson** publishes *Essays: Second Series.*
    - Texas admitted to the Union.

- Anesthesia first used for medical purposes.
- Mexican War begins
- **Oliver Wendell Holmes** publishes *Poems.*
  - **Abraham Lincoln** first elected to Congress.
  - First adhesive postage stamps issued.
    - Mexican War ends; United States expands borders.
    - California gold rush begins.
    - Women's Rights Convention held.

WORLD EVENTS

- Canada: Upper and Lower Canada united.
- Antarctica: First explored by Englishman James Ross.
- South Pacific: New Zealand becomes a British colony.
  - Asia: Hong Kong becomes a British colony.
  - England: Alfred, Lord Tennyson publishes *Poems.*

- England: Charles Dickens publishes *A Christmas Carol.*
  - Germany: Heinrich Heine publishes *Germany: A Winter's Tale.*
  - France: Alexandre Dumas publishes *The Three Musketeers.*
    - Ireland: Famine results from failure of potato crop.

- Russia: Fyodor Dostoyevsky publishes *Poor Folk.*
  - Italy: Verdi's opera *Macbeth* first performed.
  - England: Charlotte Brontë publishes *Jane Eyre.*
  - England: Emily Brontë publishes *Wuthering Heights.*
    - Belgium: Karl Marx and Friedrich Engels publish *The Communist Manifesto.*
    - England: Women first admitted to University of London.

California
Gold Rush

Women's Rights
Convention

Henry David
Thoreau

1849   **1852**   **1855**

- **Ralph Waldo Emerson** publishes *Representative Man*.
  - **Nathaniel Hawthorne** publishes *The Scarlet Letter*.
  - California admitted to the Union.
    - **Herman Melville** publishes *Moby-Dick*.
    - **Nathaniel Hawthorne** publishes *The House of Seven Gables*.
    - *The New York Times* begins publication.

- **Harriet Beecher Stowe** publishes *Uncle Tom's Cabin*.
- **Nathaniel Hawthorne** publishes *The Blithedale Romance*.
  - Arizona and New Mexico purchased from Mexico.
    - **Henry David Thoreau** publishes *Walden*.
    - Republican Party organized.

- **Henry Wadsworth Longfellow** publishes *The Song of Hiawatha*.

- France: Life insurance introduced.
- England: Elizabeth Barrett Browning publishes *Sonnets From the Portuguese*.
- England: Charles Dickens publishes *David Copperfield*.
- Germany: Wagner's opera *Lohengrin* first performed.
- China: Taiping Rebellion begins.
  - Australia: Gold discovered in New South Wales.
  - Norway: Henrik Ibsen writes *Norma*.

- Russia: Leo Tolstoy publishes *Childhood*.
- France: Louis Napoleon proclaims himself emperor.
- Europe: Crimean War begins.
  - England: Charles Dickens publishes *Hard Times*.
  - Japan: Ports opened to trade.

- England: Robert Browning publishes *Men and Women*.

Advances in agriculture followed advances in technology. John Deere, a native of Vermont, developed the steel plow out in Illinois. Cyrus McCormick, a Virginian, invented the reaper. These two inventions contributed immensely to the settlement of the prairies and later the Great Plains, for they helped make farming practical on the vast, sod-covered grasslands. Another invention of the time, the telegraph, had far-reaching effects, enabling people to communicate almost instantly across great distances. Inventor Samuel F. B. Morse's message from Washington to Baltimore in 1844 could serve as the motto for this era of innovation: "What hath God wrought!"

Clouds in a Summer Sky

"In this refulgent summer," wrote Emerson, "it has been a luxury to draw the breath of life. The grass grows, the buds burst, the meadow is spotted

HARRIET BEECHER STOWE, 1853
Alanson Fisher

with fire and gold in the tint of flowers. The air is full of birds, and sweet with the breath of pine, the balm-of-Gilead, and the new hay. . . . One is constrained to respect the perfection of this world in which our senses converse."

Ever the optimist, Emerson, as one critic said, "counted on things to take care of themselves. He could not be angry, he could not be sad." Yet it was evident to even the most cheerful observer that the United States, in the middle of the nineteenth century, faced growing problems as well as shining promises. The factories and mills that were building prosperity did not always offer the clean boarding houses, matronly chaperons, and pleasant camaraderie of Lowell at its best. More often the factory system brought increasingly fierce competition, which sometimes led to "those dark Satanic mills" of the English poet William Blake's grim vision, in which child labor, low wages, long hours, and unsafe working conditions combined to produce a situation that cried for reform.

In the anthracite mines of Pennsylvania, boys as young as seven or eight spent long days working as slate pickers in cavernous coal breakers. These boys, blackened by coal dust, supplemented the income of their fathers, whose own twelve to fourteen hours of labor brought in too little money to support the family. Their plight was worse than most, but in time even the Lowell factory girls lost many of their benefits, saw their wages slashed, and began to think about striking.

Most other women at mid-century were also living in less than idyllic circumstances. In many states, women could not vote, make a will, or file a lawsuit. A woman's property was under the absolute control of her husband, making her, as one woman wrote, "a ward, an appendage." The 1840's and 1850's saw an outburst of energy directed toward increasing the rights of women. One of the pivotal events in the women's movement, the Seneca Falls Convention, organized by Lucretia Mott and Elizabeth Cady Stanton, took place in 1848. Susan B. Anthony, a superb organizer and tireless campaigner, soon joined the movement. Women were active in other reform movements as well. Dorthea Dix crusaded for better treatment of the mentally ill, while Julia Ward Howe and Harriet Beecher Stowe attacked the institution of slavery.

135,000 SETS, 270,000 VOLUMES SOLD.

UNCLE TOM'S CABIN

FOR SALE HERE.

AN EDITION FOR THE MILLION, COMPLETE IN 1 Vol. PRICE 37 1-2 CENTS.
" " IN GERMAN. IN 1 Vol. PRICE 50 CENTS.
" " IN 2 Vols. CLOTH, 6 PLATES, PRICE $1.50.
SUPERB ILLUSTRATED EDITION, IN 1 Vol. WITH 153 ENGRAVINGS.
PRICES FROM $2.50 TO $5.00.

The Greatest Book of the Age.

AMERICAN BOOKSELLER'S ANNOUNCEMENT FOR *UNCLE TOM'S CABIN*, 1852

Sarah and Angelina Grimké advocated women's rights and freedom for the slaves, as did Lucy Stone and the eloquent Sojourner Truth, who had been born a slave.

Utopias and Lyceums

"What a fertility of projects for the salvation of the world!" exclaimed Emerson. With reform in the air, it is little wonder that utopias, or "perfect communities," were on many people's minds. One of the most famous of these utopias was Brook Farm, located only nine miles from Boston. Brook Farm was established in 1841 by George Ripley, an ex-Unitarian minister like Emerson, and strongly influenced by Emerson's views. The community attracted a number of prominent writers, including Nathaniel Hawthorne. It soon fell under the influence of Fourierism, a communal system promoted by New York journalist Arthur Brisbane. Since Fourierism held scant appeal for the gentle Bostonians who had established the community, Brook Farm gradually withered away. Meanwhile, three other utopias had been founded in New England: Hopedale, Fruitlands, and Northampton. All failed.

Indeed, very few utopian communities anywhere ever prospered. Among the few that did were seven small Amana colonies, settled in 1855 near the Iowa River in east central Iowa. The woolen goods from Amana, especially blankets, became commercially popular, and today the colonies still survive, their quaint villages attracting many tourists. The 700-member Amana Church Society is virtually all that remains today of the utopian fever that swept America in the 1840's and 1850's.

Another trend of that era, also idealistic in its aims, was the movement for better public and private education. By 1850, most people in the United States seemed to agree that free public elementary and secondary schools should be provided for all children and that higher education should be available for students who were able to pay. Adult education had its advocates, too. The lyceum movement, which originated in Millbury, Massachusetts, gained great momentum during these years. A lyceum (like the chautauqua that eventually replaced it) was a popular society established for literary and scientific study. One of the most famous lyceums was Boston's Lowell Institute, founded in 1839. Lyceums offered lectures, debates, scientific demonstrations, and other entertainments. Many authors of the period, including those of the New England renaissance, appeared frequently as paid lyceum speakers.

THE NOTCH OF THE WHITE MOUNTAINS (CRAWFORD NOTCH), 1839
Thomas Cole
National Gallery of Art, Washington, D.C.

LITERATURE IN FULL FLOWER

Elaborate theories have been devised to explain why sudden outbursts of creativity occur at certain places and times. The facts are often more fascinating than the theories—and easier to comprehend. In New England between 1840 and 1855, and mostly around Boston, an array of writers, now world-famous, produced a remarkable body of work that bulks large in the American literary tradition.

Goodbye, Courtly Muses

Ralph Waldo Emerson published his first essay anonymously in 1836. The next year he delivered his famous oration, *The American Scholar*, before the Phi Beta Kappa Society of Harvard, a speech that attracted widespread attention. Oliver Wendell Holmes called the address "our intellectual Declaration of Independence," which is precisely what Emerson had in mind. Emerson believed that American writers "had listened too long to the courtly muses of Europe" and should begin to interpret their own culture in new, and not borrowed, ways. Emerson named no names, but few readers could deny that Washington Irving and James Fenimore Cooper sometimes sounded like transplanted Englishmen. Edgar Allan Poe never did, but not all American critics, then or later, took Poe seriously—"three-fifths genius," James Russell Lowell, a Bostonian, called him, "and two-fifths sheer fudge."

Critics would be much kinder to the writers who arose in New England in the 1840's and early

1850's. There was the sanguine Emerson himself, whose essays, poems, journals, and letters hold a permanent place in our literature. There was Henry David Thoreau, fourteen years younger than Emerson and something of a protégé, although a very individualistic one, who lived in the Emerson household for two years. Thoreau's classic work, *Walden*, appeared in 1854. On the darker side there was Nathaniel Hawthorne, whose powerful, sometimes enigmatic style reached its peak in *The Scarlet Letter*, published in 1850. Then there was a volatile New Yorker living in Pittsfield, the ex-sailor of the South Seas, Herman Melville, whose masterpiece, *Moby-Dick*, met with indifference at first and lavish praise later. In Amherst, living quietly and publishing almost nothing in her lifetime, was the young, brilliantly gifted poet, Emily Dickinson.

Those were the giants, or so they seem to us today. In 1850, the reading public in the United States might have pointed more quickly to four other New England writers. Henry Wadsworth Longfellow, a Harvard professor until 1854 and a tremendously popular poet, was a leading figure among New England intellectuals. So was Oliver Wendell Holmes, the unofficial poet laureate of the group. Two other celebrated writers of the day were John Greenleaf Whittier, who came from a hardworking Quaker farm family, and James Russell Lowell, born to wealth and position. Both Whittier and Lowell were antislavery crusaders as well as poets.

Transcendentalism

Most, if not all, of these writers of the period were influenced by the Transcendental movement then flourishing in New England. Emerson and Thoreau were the best-known Transcendentalists, but the ferment of Transcendental ideas affected many other writers, some of whom hovered on the fringes of the movement, some of whom opposed it.

Transcendentalism demands careful definition, yet it is very hard to define. It has many facets, many sources, and encompasses a range of beliefs whose specific principles depend on the individual writer or thinker. The term itself and some of the ideas came from the German philosopher Immanuel Kant. In his *Critique of Practical Reason*, published in 1788, Kant refers to the "transcendental," which to him meant the knowledge or understanding a person gains intuitively, although it lies beyond direct physical experience. New England Transcendentalism drew on other philosophical theories besides Kant's. These included Plato's as well as those of Pascal, the French mathematician and moralist, and Swedenborg, the Swedish scientist and mystic. In addition, it drew on Buddhist thought.

The movement was not essentially religious, but there were religious overtones. Even though a hundred years had passed since Jonathan Edwards, a Calvinist minister in Northampton, Massachusetts, had preached that human beings can share directly in the divine light, Edwards's idea continued to exert influence in the mid-nineteenth century. More recently, William Ellery Channing, minister of the Federal Street Church, Boston, had broken with the Calvinism of his day to become the apostle of Unitarianism. Channing's sermons and essays, promoting more tolerant religious attitudes and various social causes, reflected his own optimism and idealism. The inscription on a statue of him in the Boston Public Garden reads, "He breathed into theology a humane spirit."

Beyond that, Channing helped to lay the groundwork for New England's Transcendentalism. His influence on American literature was substantial; Emerson, Longfellow, Lowell, and Holmes all acknowledged their debt to him. To a remarkable degree, his views became their views. Seven years before Emerson's *American Scholar* address, Channing's *Remarks on American Literature* had called for American writers to cease imitating British models and to find their inspiration closer to home.

Philosophy, religion, literature—all merged in New England Transcendentalism, producing a native blend that was romantic, intuitive, mystical, and considerably easier to recognize than to explain. Emerson, believing in the divinity of human nature, embodied the spirit of Transcendentalism. Thoreau, in *Walden*, provided it with its most sustained expression. Yet Transcendentalism was, and is, hard to pin down. To some in the luminous literary group in Boston and its environs, whose members met from time to time—a group which outsiders came to call the "Transcendental Club"—the movement meant intense individualism and self-reliance. To others it meant practically the opposite and was considered a single-minded commitment to improving the lot of the poor and oppressed. The Transcendentalists could accept such differences, for theirs was a democracy of intellect. They recognized few absolutes beyond an all-encompassing belief in the unity of God and the world. Even self-contradictions might be necessary, as Emerson stated in a much-quoted sentence: "A foolish consistency is the hobgoblin of little minds."

For Transcendentalists the point was that the real truths, the fundamental truths, lay outside the experience of the senses, residing instead in the "Over-Soul . . . a universal and benign omnipresence . . . a God known to men only in moments of mystic enthusiasm, whose visitations leave them altered, self-reliant, and purified of petty aims."

If that seems a bit obscure, as it did to many people in the United States, and often to the press, so did the essays in *The Dial,* the quarterly magazine of New England Transcendentalism, which grew out of the informal and sporadic meetings of the Transcendentalists. Published from 1840 to 1844, *The Dial*'s first editor was Margaret Fuller, a dominant personality and zealous feminist, whose book *Woman in the Nineteenth Century* was the first serious American exploration of feminism. Margaret Fuller, astonishingly erudite, was accepted as the intellectual equal, or even superior, of the most honored members of the circle. Under her editorship, however, *The Dial,* like Transcendentalism, seemed to lack a clear focus and may have bewildered as many people as it enlightened.

Nodding Fields and Walden Pond

If the Transcendentalists, and Emerson himself, lacked a well-defined philosophy, there were certain basic areas of agreement. The Transcendentalists revered nature. Emerson titled his first major work *Nature,* and although the essay deals with many topics—beauty, discipline, idealism, spirit, and others—Nature (with a capital N) provides its

unifying theme. "The fields and woods," wrote Emerson, "nod to me, and I to them." This essay is considered the first full-scale expression of American Transcendentalism.

Both of Henry David Thoreau's important works, *Walden* and the earlier *A Week on the Concord and Merrimack Rivers,* emphasize the central importance of nature. *Walden* begins, "When I wrote the following pages, or rather the bulk of them, I lived alone, in the woods, a mile from any neighbor, in a house which I had built myself, on the shore of Walden Pond, in Concord, Massachusetts, and earned my living by the labor of my hands only." The book comprises eighteen essays that deal with matters ranging from the pickerel in Walden Pond to a battle between red and black ants. Nature is the central subject, and from its development emerges Thoreau's philosophy of individualism, simplicity, and passive resistance to injustice.

Brook Farm, as a kind of back-to-nature venture, reflected the Transcendentalists' interest in putting theories into practice. Nathaniel Hawthorne, partly at the urging of Elizabeth Peabody, a Transcendentalist and a friend of Margaret Fuller, bought two shares of stock in Brook Farm and took up residence there in 1841. He hated it. "It is my opinion," he wrote to his fiancée, "that a man's soul may be buried and perish under a dungheap or in a furrow of the field just as well as under a pile of money." Hawthorne, who never shared the optimism of Emerson and Thoreau, found nothing at Brook Farm to alter his view that the world is more complex and less perfectible than the Transcendentalists believed.

The Possibility of Evil

Although the Transcendentalists were widely influential, their view of life seemed far too rosy to many writers. If Emerson and Thoreau can be conveniently paired as Transcendentalists, Nathaniel Hawthorne and Herman Melville can be paired as Anti-Transcendentalists. They were writers who, in Hawthorne's words, "burrowed into the depths of our common nature" and found the area not always shimmering, but often "dusky."

Just as the younger Thoreau was an apprentice, in a sense, in Emerson's household, so Melville, fifteen years younger than Hawthorne, sought the counsel and friendship of the older and more widely acclaimed Hawthorne. It happened almost by accident. Melville, in his early thirties, had moved from New York City to Pittsfield in western Massachusetts, where, on a farm he called "Arrowhead," he wrote his monumental book *Moby-Dick*. It was published in 1851, a year after Hawthorne's *The Scarlet Letter* appeared. Although *Moby-Dick* would be recognized as a great work only after Melville's death, *The Scarlet Letter* achieved immediate fame in both the United States and England.

Meanwhile, Hawthorne had moved to Lenox, Massachusetts, in the Berkshires, a few miles south of Pittsfield. There he was working on the manuscript of *The House of the Seven Gables*. Melville, pessimistic about *Moby-Dick*—"the product is a final hash," he wrote, "and all my books are botches"—approached Hawthorne, seeking solace. According to a biographer, the young Melville was in "a state of exhaustion and hyper-excitability"; his "impetuous soul rushed out to embrace Hawthorne's . . . in headlong and absolute devotion." Hawthorne may have been surprised by this adulation, but he and Melville became and remained friends.

Their visions, however, while equally dark, were very different. Hawthorne's Puritan heritage, which included an ancestor who was a judge at the Salem witchcraft trials, was never far from his consciousness. *The Scarlet Letter* is a historical romance set in Puritan Boston in the middle of the seventeenth century. In it Hawthorne deals with sin and concealed guilt, with hypocrisy and humility, in a dark tale that shows his insight into the Puritan conscience. In *The House of the Seven Gables,* he delves into seventeenth-century witchcraft, insanity, and a legendary curse. These unhappy themes do not reflect the easy optimism of the Transcendentalists, and yet Hawthorne, despite a tendency toward solitude, was stable and self-possessed, absorbed by questions of evil and moral responsibility, yet a shrewd man without illusions.

THE WHALE FISHERY—THE SPERM WHALE IN A FLURRY
Undated Lithograph by Currier and Ives

Melville, by contrast, was a maelstrom of emotions, a man at odds with the world, a tortured and cryptic personality. He was an artist raging against the fates, much like Captain Ahab was in *Moby-Dick*, when he unleashed his fury against the white whale that had torn away his leg. Melville dedicated *Moby-Dick* to Nathaniel Hawthorne "in token of my admiration for his genius." Melville was a genius, too, but an embittered one, a great writer rejected by the public. Only in his later years, with the short novel *Billy Budd*, did he affirm that the cruelties of existence might be overcome by the strength and nobility of the human spirit. Perhaps by then, after long years of obscurity as a customs inspector in New York, he had acquired in his personal life some of the serenity of Hawthorne.

When Poetry Was in Bloom

During the flowering of New England, Americans were avid readers of poetry. Newspapers and magazines published poems, and books of poetry sold briskly. Longfellow was acclaimed as the American bard; Whittier's eightieth birthday was marked by a national celebration; Holmes's comic verse made him a celebrity here and abroad. Today, when poetry is widely written but not so widely read, it may be hard to picture a time in which the

HIAWATHA, c. 1871
Thomas Eakins
Hirshhorn Museum and Sculpture Garden, Smithsonian Institution

names and works of poets were part of the national consciousness. "Poets," said the English poet Shelley in 1821, "are the unacknowledged legislators of the world." In the 1840's and 1850's, there were Americans who still believed this.

Among the Transcendentalists, Emerson wrote poetry of an exceptionally high quality. Thoreau declared, "My life has been the poem I would have writ," but in fact he produced some fine poetry on paper as well. Hawthorne concentrated on prose, but Melville in his later years wrote a number of noteworthy poems, especially during the Civil War.

The popular poets of the day, though, were a group commonly known as the Fireside Poets: Longfellow, Whittier, Holmes, Lowell, and a few lesser-known writers. Working separately—they had no "club" as the Transcendentalists did—the Fireside Poets created verse that the average reader could understand and appreciate. Some of their poems were on inspiring or patriotic themes; others dealt with love, nature, home, family, and children. At their best, the Fireside Poets appealed to well-educated, highly literate readers as well as to the less sophisticated. Longfellow, in particular, had a towering reputation in his own time, and is the only American with a bust in the Poet's Corner of Westminster Abbey in London.

Later critics have tended to rank these poets below Emerson, Thoreau, Hawthorne, and Melville in the literary pantheon. Many of their works are still read, however, and the Fireside Poets appear to have earned a permanent place in the hearts of Americans. They lived in New England and were part of its literary blossoming, but they are no longer considered to have been its finest blooms. Even so, their output of memorable poetry helped to build an American myth that still survives and enriches our culture.

At Home in Amherst

At the time Charles Dickens visited Boston and met its emerging literary figures, a young girl was growing up in the valley town of Amherst, Massachusetts. She was not yet writing poetry, at least not seriously, but when she did begin to write, her achievements would catapult her (although not in her lifetime) into the company of the greatest poets in American literature.

Emily Dickinson cannot be easily assigned to any literary category. Her gem-like poetry is unique, just as her life was unique. A recluse for the last twenty-five years of her life, she did not write for publication, or even for her family. Only a few of her poems appeared in print during her lifetime, and those were released without her consent. Why, then, did she write? She may have done so partly to resolve the questions about death, immortality, and the soul that orthodox Calvinism raised but, to her inquiring mind, did not satisfactorily answer.

Since her poems were not published until 1890, and since a definitive edition of them did not appear until 1955, it is hard to pigeonhole Emily Dickinson, even historically. She was not a Transcendentalist. She wrote many of her poems during the Civil War, but she was wholly uninfluenced by the conflict. Since she was a New Englander, and since her remarkable poetry with its dazzling brevity and breathtaking images adds a special luster to the New England literary renaissance, her work appears in this unit rather than a later one.

Beyond the Flowering

The renaissance did not end abruptly in 1855, of course, but as the storm clouds of war gathered, the great sunburst of creativity in the Northeast did subside. Americans increasingly turned their attention to the coming struggle, and antislavery writers, such as Emerson, Melville, Whittier, and Lowell, strongly supported the northern war effort. Thoreau and Hawthorne died before the last shot was fired. Oliver Wendell Holmes, energetic and cheerful, lived on, outlasting all the rest of that renowned generation of writers, thus becoming "the last leaf upon the tree," to quote his own words. Holmes had written his well-known poem, "The Last Leaf," about Herman Melville's grandfather, "a venerable relic of the Revolution." The poem had been published sixty-three years earlier, in 1831, back when Holmes was a young man and before New England had even begun to bloom.

Quotations by Prominent Figures of the Period

Hitch your wagon to a star.
Ralph Waldo Emerson, "Society and Solitude," *from Civilization*

Any man more right than his neighbor constitutes a
majority of one.
Henry David Thoreau, *Civil Disobedience*

The mass of men lead lives of quiet desperation.
Henry David Thoreau, *Walden*

If a man does not keep pace with his companions, perhaps
it is because he hears a different drummer. Let him step to
the music which he hears, however measured or far away.
Henry David Thoreau, *Walden*

Life is made up of marble and mud.
Nathaniel Hawthorne, *The House of Seven Gables*

Call me Ishmael.
Herman Melville, *Moby-Dick*

I 'spect I growed. Don't think nobody ever made me.
Harriet Beecher Stowe, *Uncle Tom's Cabin*

If we could read the secret history of our enemies, we
should find in each man's life sorrow and suffering enough
to disarm all hostility.
Henry Wadsworth Longfellow, *Driftwood*

Put not your trust in money, but your money in trust.
Oliver Wendell Holmes, *The Autocrat of the Breakfast Table*

And what is so rare as a day in June?
    Then, if ever, come perfect days.
James Russell Lowell, *The Vision of Sir Launfal*

If I feel physically as if the top of my head were taken off, I
know that is poetry.
Emily Dickinson, *Life and Letters of Emily Dickinson*

READING CRITICALLY

The Literature of 1840–1855

During the years from 1840 to 1855, the United States continued to expand rapidly. A steady flow of American pioneers traveled westward, settling in the new frontier. At the same time, a group of writers in New England brought about a literary renaissance that earned the country a place among the world's great literary traditions.

HISTORICAL CONTEXT The rapid growth and expansion of the United States helped bring about scientific advances that established the United States as one of the most technologically advanced nations in the world. New agricultural machines were invented, new roads, canals, and railroads were built, and telegraph lines were put into place. These developments brought about an overwhelming sense of optimism about the country's future.

LITERARY MOVEMENTS The sense of optimism that dominated many people's thoughts during this period was reflected in the ideas of the Transcendentalists, the members of one of the main intellectual and artistic movements of the period. Possessing a deep faith in human potential, the Transcendentalists believed that all forms of being are spiritually united through a shared universal soul. In contrast, two major writers who have come to be known as Anti-Transcendentalists espoused a much darker vision of the world, believing that the truths of existence tend to be elusive and disturbing. A third group of writers known as the Fireside Poets also made important contributions during this period. By creating poetry that was inspiring and easy to read, these poets helped to establish poetry as a popular literary form among the American public.

WRITERS' TECHNIQUES Focusing on popular themes such as love and nature, the Fireside Poets wrote poetry using traditional poetic forms and techniques. Although Ralph Waldo Emerson, the founder of the Transcendentalists, also wrote poetry, the Transcendentalists are remembered mainly for their essays expressing their ideas and beliefs. The Anti-Transcendentalists, on the other hand, expressed their beliefs through the themes of their novels and short stories, often using symbols to convey their themes.

RALPH WALDO EMERSON

1803–1882

Ralph Waldo Emerson was an essayist, a poet, an orator, and, more than anything else, a philosopher. Throughout the course of his life, Emerson's mind was constantly in motion, bringing forth new ideas and refining and redefining his view of the world. As a result, Emerson's philosophy was reflected in all of his work—his essays, his poems, and his lectures.

Emerson was born in Boston, the son of a Unitarian minister. When Emerson was eight, his father died, leaving the family in a state of poverty. Despite his family's financial difficulties, Emerson received a thorough education. At the age of fourteen, he entered Harvard, where he began recording his ideas in a journal. After his graduation, Emerson taught for several years before deciding to become a minister. In 1825 Emerson entered Harvard Divinity School. Four years later, he became the pastor of the Second Church of Boston.

Saddened by the death of his young wife, Ellen, and dissatisfied with the spiritual restrictions of Unitarianism, Emerson resigned his ministry in 1832. Following his resignation, Emerson traveled to Europe, where he met English poets William Wordsworth and Samuel Taylor Coleridge. When Emerson returned to America, he settled in Concord, Massachusetts, remarried, and began his lifelong career of writing and lecturing.

Emerson's second wife, Lydia Jackson of Plymouth, provided a supportive and secure family life. Emerson was now receiving money from his first wife's legacy. For the first time in his life, he was not living in poverty. The Emerson household, which for a while included Henry David Thoreau, welcomed a slowly widening circle of friends and admirers.

During the 1830's and 1840's, Emerson and a small group of intellectuals gathered regularly to discuss philosophy, religion, and literature. This group, which came to be known as the Transcendental Club, developed a philosophical system that stressed intuition, individuality, and self-reliance. In 1836 Emerson—the group's most influential member—published *Nature,* a lengthy essay that became the Transcendental Club's unofficial statement of belief.

Emerson first achieved national fame in 1841 when he published *Essays,* a collection of essays based on material from his journals and lectures. Emerson went on to publish several more volumes of essays, including *Essays, Second Volume* (1844), *Representative Men* (1849), and *The Conduct of Life* (1860). Though Emerson was known mostly for his essays and lectures, he also published two successful volumes of poetry, *Poems* (1847) and *May-Day and Other Pieces* (1867).

GUIDE FOR INTERPRETING

from Nature; *from* Self-Reliance

Transcendentalism. Transcendentalism was an intellectual movement that directly or indirectly affected most of the writers of the New England Renaissance. The Transcendentalists, led by Ralph Waldo Emerson, believed that the human senses can know only physical reality. The fundamental truths of being and the universe lie outside the reach of the senses and can be grasped only through intuition. As a result, in their quest for understanding, the Transcendentalists focused their attention on the human spirit. The Transcendentalists were also interested in the natural world and its relationship to humanity. They felt that if they explored nature thoroughly, they would come to know themselves and the universal truths better. Through this exploration, they discovered that the human spirit is reflected in nature. This led them to the conclusion that formed the heart of their beliefs: All forms of being—God, nature, and humanity—are spiritually united through a shared universal soul, or Over-Soul.

Emerson was a quiet, soft-spoken, sober man, given neither to physical nor emotional excesses. His ideas, however, were neither cautious nor conventional. They often shocked conservative believers. His speech to the graduating class of the Harvard Divinity School in 1838 aroused a tremendous furor. He was accused of speaking against established tenets of Christianity. As a result, he was not invited to speak again at Harvard for thirty years.

His ideas were deeply and fervently held, and his training as a preacher helped him effectively express them. He saw himself as a seer and poet rather than a coolly objective philosopher with a logically developed argument. Many of his lectures and essays were put together from notes from his extensive journals.

His writings abound in these insights, expressed in vivid statements, which are then developed in a paragraph. Here are some examples: "To go into solitude, a man needs to retire as much from his chamber as from society" and "A man is a god in ruins" (from *Nature*); "The civilized man has built a coach, but has lost the use of his feet" (from "Self-Reliance"); and "Books are the best of things, well used; abused, among the worst" (from "The American Scholar").

Emerson writes about the effect of nature on him. What do *you* enjoy about nature? What effect does the natural world have on you? Freewrite about your perceptions of the natural world and its effect on you.

from **Nature**

Ralph Waldo Emerson

Nature is a setting that fits equally well a comic or a mourning piece. In good health, the air is a cordial of incredible virtue. Crossing a bare common,[1] in snow puddles, at twilight, under a clouded sky, without having in my thoughts any occurrence of special good fortune, I have enjoyed a perfect exhilaration. I am glad to the brink of fear. In the woods, too, a man casts off his years, as the snake his slough, and at what period soever of life is always a child. In the woods is perpetual youth. Within these plantations of God, a decorum and sanctity reign, a perennial festival is dressed, and the guest sees not how he should tire of them in a thousand years. In the woods, we return to reason and faith. There I feel that nothing can befall me in life—no disgrace, no calamity (leaving me my eyes), which nature cannot repair. Standing on the bare ground—my head bathed by the blithe air and uplifted into infinite space—all mean egotism vanishes. I become a transparent eyeball; I am nothing; I see all; the currents of the Universal Being circulate through me; I am part or parcel of God. The name of the nearest friend sounds then foreign and accidental: to be brothers, to be acquaintances, master or servant, is then a trifle and a disturbance. I am the lover of uncontained and immortal beauty. In the wilderness, I find something more dear and connate than in the streets or villages. In the tranquil landscape, and especially in the distant line of the horizon, man beholds somewhat as beautiful as his own nature.

The greatest delight which the fields and

---

1. common: Piece of open public land.

SUNSET
Frederick E. Church
Munson-Williams-Proctor Institute
Museum of Art, Utica, New York

woods minister is the suggestion of an oc-cult relation between man and the vegetable. I am not alone and unacknowledged. They nod to me, and I to them. The waving of the boughs in the storm is new to me and old. It takes me by surprise, and yet is not un-known. Its effect is like that of a higher thought or a better emotion coming over me, when I deemed I was thinking justly or doing right.

Yet it is certain that the power to pro-duce this delight does not reside in nature, but in man, or in a harmony of both. It is necessary to use these pleasures with great temperance. For nature is not always tricked[2] in holiday attire, but the same scene which yesterday breathed perfume and glit-tered as for the frolic of the nymphs is over-spread with melancholy today. Nature always wears the colors of the spirit. To a man la-boring under calamity, the heat of his own fire hath sadness in it. Then there is a kind of contempt of the landscape felt by him who has just lost by death a dear friend. The sky is less grand as it shuts down over less worth in the population.

───────────

2. tricked: Dressed.

RESPONDING TO THE SELECTION

Your Response

1. Do you agree with Emerson's ideas about na-ture? Why or why not?
2. Which of your experiences have "made you glad to the brink of fear"?

Recalling

3. According to Emerson, where can we "return to reason and faith"?
4. What happens to Emerson when he stands on the bare ground with his head "uplifted into in-finite space"?
5. What is "the greatest delight which the fields and woods minister"?
6. What "colors" does nature wear?

Interpreting

7. What does Emerson mean when he comments that in the woods "a man casts off his years"?
8. What does Emerson mean when he describes himself as a "transparent eyeball"?

Applying

9. In what ways is Emerson's attitude toward na-ture different from a scientist's attitude?

ANALYZING LITERATURE

Understanding Transcendentalism

Transcendentalism was an intellectual movement that held that knowledge of funda-mental reality was derived through intuition rather than through sensory experience. This movement focused on the human spirit and the spiritual re-lationship between humanity and nature. The Transcendentalists ultimately reached the con-clusion that all forms of being are spiritually united through a shared universal soul, or Over-Soul.

Emerson's essay *Nature,* published in 1836, was the Transcendentalists' unofficial statement of belief.

1. What does *Nature* reveal about the Transcen-dentalists' attitude toward nature?
2. What does *Nature* reveal about the Transcen-dentalists' perceptions of human nature?
3. How does the essay convey the Transcenden-talists' belief in the Over-Soul?
4. Do you find any evidence of Transcendentalist beliefs in today's poetry and song lyrics? Ex-plain.

LEARNING OPTION

Art. Emerson is noted for his "choice and pith of language," his "eye for a fine, telling phrase." Choose a vivid phrase from this essay and illus-trate it in any way you choose. You might draw a picture, write a poem, interpret a piece of music, or perform a dance.

from Self-Reliance

Ralph Waldo Emerson

There is a time in every man's education when he arrives at the conviction that envy is ignorance; that imitation is suicide; that he must take himself for better, for worse, as his portion; that though the wide universe is full of good, no kernel of nourishing corn can come to him but through his toil bestowed on that plot of ground which is given to him to till. The power which resides in him is new in nature, and none but he knows what that is which he can do, nor does he know until he has tried. Not for nothing one face, one character, one fact makes much impression on him, and another none. This sculpture in the memory is not without preestablished harmony. The eye was placed where one ray should fall, that it might testify of that particular ray. We but half express ourselves, and are ashamed of that divine idea which each of us represents. It may be safely trusted as proportionate and of good issues, so it be faithfully imparted, but God will not have his work made manifest by cowards. A man is relieved and gay when he has put his heart into his work and done his best; but what he has said or done otherwise, shall give him no peace. It is a deliverance which does not deliver. In the attempt his genius deserts him; no muse befriends; no invention, no hope.

Trust thyself: every heart vibrates to that iron string. Accept the place the divine providence has found for you; the society of your contemporaries, the connection of events. Great men have always done so and confided themselves childlike to the genius of their age, betraying their perception that the absolutely trustworthy was stirring at their heart, working through their hands, predominating in all their being. And we are now men, and must accept in the highest mind the same transcendent destiny; and not minors and invalids in a protected corner, but guides, redeemers, and benefactors, obeying the Almighty effort and advancing on Chaos and the Dark. . . .

Society everywhere is in conspiracy against the manhood of every one of its members. Society is a joint-stock company in which the members agree for the better securing of his bread to each shareholder, to surrender the liberty and culture of the eater. The virtue in most request is conformity. Self-reliance is its aversion. It loves not realities and creators, but names and customs.

Whoso would be a man must be a nonconformist. He who would gather immortal palms must not be hindered by the name of goodness, but must explore if it be goodness. Nothing is at last sacred but the integrity of your own mind. Absolve you to yourself, and you shall have the suffrage of the world. . . .

A foolish consistency is the hobgoblin of little minds, adored by little statesmen and philosophers and divines. With consistency a great soul has simply nothing to do. He may as well concern himself with his shadow on the wall. Speak what you think now in hard words and tomorrow speak what tomorrow thinks in hard words again, though it contradict everything you said today. "Ah, so you shall be sure to be misunderstood?"—Is it so bad, then, to be misunderstood? Pythagoras was misunderstood, and Socrates, and Jesus, and Luther, and Copernicus, and Galileo, and Newton,[1] and every pure and wise spirit that ever took flesh. To be great is to be misunderstood. . . .

---

1. Pythagoras . . . Newton: Individuals who made major contributions to scientific, philosophical, or religious thinking.

RESPONDING TO THE SELECTION

Your Response
1. Based on his essay, what is your impression of Ralph Waldo Emerson?
2. Which of Emerson's statements from this essay, if any, would you choose as a guideline for personal conduct? Explain.

Recalling
3. According to the first paragraph, at what conviction does every person arrive?
4. According to the second paragraph, what must every person accept?
5. How does Emerson describe society?

Interpreting
6. What does he mean when he comments, "no kernel of nourishing corn can come to him but through his toil bestowed on that plot of ground which is given to him to till"?
7. Why, according to Emerson, should people trust themselves?
8. How does Emerson believe people should be affected by the way others perceive them?
9. How does Emerson support his claim that "to be great is to be misunderstood"?

Applying
10. Toward the end of the essay, Emerson writes, "Speak what you think now in hard words and tomorrow speak what tomorrow thinks in hard words again, though it contradict everything you said today." Explain your reaction to this view.

THINKING AND WRITING

Writing About Conformity
What are the advantages of conforming to society's expectations? Of not conforming? Make notes about your thoughts on the subject. Then take a stand and present your ideas in an essay. Begin by writing a draft explaining your reasons. Conclude by indicating your agreement or disagreement with Emerson's ideas on conformity. Revise your essay so that your points are clear and supported.

LEARNING OPTIONS

1. **Speaking and Listening.** What message would Ralph Waldo Emerson have for young people today? Drawing from the philosophy Emerson expresses in "Self-Reliance," produce a public service message in Emerson's name for a mock radio broadcast. Enlist classmates to help you write the message. Then assume the role of Emerson and record the message or deliver it to your class.

2. **Art.** Emerson's Transcendental Club met regularly to discuss philosophy, religion, and literature. Get together with several classmates to form a similar club. Then work together to create a poster that will convince other students to join your club. Come up with a name for the club that would appeal to fellow students, and try to make it sound as interesting and exciting as possible.

3. **Cross-curricular Connection.** According to Emerson, the misunderstood individual is in good company. He or she joins the ranks of Pythagoras, Socrates, Jesus, Joan of Arc, Luther, Copernicus, Galileo, and Newton. Choose one of these "great souls." Do research to find out why each was misunderstood. Share your findings with classmates.

GUIDE FOR INTERPRETING

The Snowstorm; Concord Hymn; The Rhodora; Brahma

Writers' Techniques

Apostrophe. Apostrophe is a literary device in which a writer directly addresses an inanimate object, an abstract idea, or an absent person. A writer may address a person who is no longer living, an ocean, or a season. For example, the English poet Shelley addresses the wind in these lines: "O Wind,/If Winter comes, can Spring be far behind?"

The Transcendentalists believed that all living things were spiritually united through a shared universal soul, or Over-Soul. In "The Rhodora" Emerson uses apostrophe to express this spiritual unity, directly addressing a flower as if it were a person.

Focus

Freewrite, describing a scene that suggests the majesty of nature. Explore your thoughts and reactions to this scene.

Primary Source

Emerson was keeping journals and writing poetry well before the publication of *Nature,* and he continued both activities to the end of his life. Despite his success as a speaker and an essayist, he always regarded himself as a poet. He described his vocation to his fiancée, Lydia Jackson, in a letter explaining why he could not live in her hometown of Plymouth.

> Under this morning's severe but beautiful light I thought dear friend that hardly should I get away from Concord. I must win you to love it. I am born a poet, of a low class without doubt yet a poet. That is my nature & vocation. My singing be sure is very "husky," & is for the most part in prose. Still am I a poet in the sense of a perceiver & dear lover of the harmonies that are in the soul & in matter, & specially of the correspondences between these and those. A sunset, a forest, a snowstorm, a certain river-view, are more to me than many friends & do ordinarily divide my day with my books. Wherever I go therefore I guard & study my rambling propensities with a care that is ridiculous to people, but to me is the care of my high calling. Now Concord is only one of a hundred towns in which I could find these necessary objects but Plymouth I fear is not one. Plymouth is streets; I live in the wide [countryside].

FARM YARD, WINTER
George Henry Durrie
Courtesy of the New York Historical Society

The Snowstorm

Ralph Waldo Emerson

Announced by all the trumpets of the sky,
Arrives the snow, and, driving o'er the fields,
Seems nowhere to alight: the whited air
Hides hills and woods, the river, and the heaven,
5 And veils the farmhouse at the garden's end.
The sled and traveler stopped, the courier's feet
Delayed, all friends shut out, the housemates sit
Around the radiant fireplace, enclosed
In a tumultuous privacy of storm.

10   Come see the north wind's masonry.
        Out of an unseen quarry evermore
        Furnished with tile, the fierce artificer
        Curves his white bastions with projected roof
        Round every windward stake, or tree, or door.
15   Speeding, the myriad-handed, his wild work
        So fanciful, so savage, nought cares he
        For number or proportion. Mockingly,
        On coop or kennel he hangs Parian¹ wreaths;
        A swan-like form invests the hidden thorn;
20   Fills up the farmer's lane from wall to wall,

        Maugre² the farmer's sighs; and at the gate
        A tapering turret overtops the work.
        And when his hours are numbered, and the world
        Is all his own, retiring, as he were not,
25   Leaves, when the sun appears, astonished Art
        To mimic in slow structures, stone by stone,
        Built in an age, the mad wind's nightwork,
        The frolic architecture of the snow.

_____

1. Parian (per′ē ən) *adj.*: Referring to a fine, white marble of the Greek city Paros.
2. Maugre (mô′ gər) *prep.*: In spite of.

▌RESPONDING TO THE SELECTION

Your Response

1. What did you picture as you read this poem?
2. How does your attitude toward snow compare with Emerson's?

Recalling

3. What announces the storm's arrival?
4. What does "the whited air" hide?
5. What does the speaker describe in the second stanza?
6. According to lines 25–28, what has the storm left behind "when the sun appears"?

Interpreting

7. What mood does Emerson establish in the first stanza?

8. Explain what Emerson means when he refers to the "tumultuous privacy of the storm" in line 9.
9. In this poem Emerson compares the storm and an artist at work. (a) How does he develop this comparison in the second stanza? (b) How does he extend the comparison in the final stanza? (c) How does this comparison express Emerson's belief in a spiritual unity between humanity and nature?

Applying

10. Emerson expresses a favorable attitude toward the snowstorm. Why might some people living in northern climates not share Emerson's attitude?

Concord Hymn

Sung at the Completion of the Battle Monument, April 19, 1836

Ralph Waldo Emerson

This poem was written for the unveiling of a monument commemorating the Minute Men, who fought the British in the first two battles of the Revolutionary War at Lexington and Concord, Massachusetts, in April of 1775.

By the rude bridge that arched the flood,
    Their flag to April's breeze unfurled,
Here once the embattled farmers stood,
    And fired the shot heard round the world.

5   The foe long since in silence slept;
    Alike the conqueror silent sleeps;
And Time the ruined bridge has swept
    Down the dark stream which seaward creeps.

On this green bank, by this soft stream,
10   We set today a votive[1] stone;
That memory may their deed redeem,
    When, like our sires, our sons are gone.

Spirit, that made those heroes dare
    To die, and leave their children free,
15   Bid Time and Nature gently spare
    The shaft we raise to them and thee.

---

1. votive (vōt′ iv) *adj.*: Dedicated in fulfillment of a vow or pledge.

RESPONDING TO THE SELECTION

Your Response

1. What feelings does this poem evoke in you?
2. Do you think it is important to build war monuments? Why or why not?

Recalling

3. What event took place "by the rude bridge"?
4. What has since happened to the bridge?
5. What may redeem the farmers' deed?

Interpreting

6. (a) What is meant by "the shot heard round the world"? (b) In what way was this shot heard round the world?
7. How does Emerson express his belief in a shared universal soul in the final stanza?

Applying

8. What aspects of this poem would be appropriate for the dedication of other war monuments?

CRITICAL THINKING AND READING

Understanding Cause and Effect

"Concord Hymn" commemorates a historical event. To understand history, you must understand causes and effects, or the reasons behind actions and the results of these actions.

Do some library research on the Revolutionary War. What caused the battles at Lexington and Concord? What were the results of these battles? Present your findings to your classmates.

THINKING AND WRITING

Writing About History

History is all around us. Wherever you live, your town or county or state may have been the site for some important historical event. Interview people in your town to find out about a local historical event. Use this information to write a short poem commemorating this event.

MULTICULTURAL CONNECTION

The American Revolution: Supporters From Around the World

Emerson says in the "Concord Hymn" that the first shot of the Revolutionary War was "heard round the world." He might also have added that those who fought for America came from around the world.

African Americans in the Revolution. Although it is not widely known, one of the first Americans to die in the cause for American independence was a former slave named Crispus Attucks. He was shot in the Boston Massacre of 1770, a small protest against British troops that ended violently.

Thousands of African Americans eventually took part in the war. At first, the Colonial army refused to let them enlist, but when the British began offering freedom to any enslaved African who would fight with them, the American army reversed its policy.

Notable valor. Approximately 5,000 African Americans, some free and some enslaved, fought for American independence. Four all-black units were formed; the rest of the black volunteers fought alongside the white troops. Their bravery was mentioned by both sides in the war. Among the more notable volunteers was Mark Starlin, a former slave who became captain of the Virginian ship *The Patriot*.

Foreign volunteers. Many foreigners also fought for the American side, including thousands of French troops. Foreign commanders fought with the American troops as well, including the French Marquis de Lafayette, the Polish nobleman Casimir Pulaski and the Prussian Baron von Steuben.

Exploring On Your Own

Find out more about the role of African Americans and volunteers from other countries in the Revolution. Share findings with your classmates.

The Rhodora

On Being Asked,
Whence is the Flower?

Ralph Waldo Emerson

In May, when sea winds pierced our solitudes,
I found the fresh Rhodora in the woods,
Spreading its leafless blooms in a damp nook,
To please the desert and the sluggish brook.
5 The purple petals, fallen in the pool,
Made the black water with their beauty gay;
Here might the red-bird come his plumes to cool,
And court the flower that cheapens his array.
Rhodora! if the sages ask thee why
10 This charm is wasted on the earth and sky,

Tell them, dear, that if eyes were made for seeing,
Then Beauty is its own excuse for being;
Why thou wert there, O rival of the rose!
I never thought to ask, I never knew;
15 But, in my simple ignorance, suppose
The self-same Power that brought me there brought you.

RESPONDING TO THE SELECTION

Your Response
1. Which line in the poem is most memorable? Why?
2. What mysteries of nature do you wonder about?

Recalling
3. (a) Where in the woods does the speaker find the rhodora? (b) Who besides the speaker sees it there?
4. (a) According to the speaker, what question might the sages ask the rhodora? (b) How does he suggest the rhodora might respond?
5. In the final line, how does the speaker explain the rhodora's existence?

Interpreting
6. What larger concept does the rhodora represent?
7. (a) How is the sages' attitude toward nature different from the speaker's attitude? (b) Which attitude seems to produce a more meaningful understanding of nature? Explain your answer.
8. What is unexpected about the speaker's reference to his "simple ignorance" in line 15?
9. How does the final line express Emerson's belief in a spiritual unity among all living things?

Applying
10. At another time Ralph Waldo Emerson wrote, "Though we travel the world over to find the beautiful, we must carry it with us or we find it not." Explain the view of beauty Emerson expresses here. How is it similar to or different from the view of beauty expressed in "The Rhodora"?

ANALYZING LITERATURE

Understanding Apostrophe
Apostrophe is a literary device in which a writer directly addresses an inanimate object, an abstract idea, or an absent person. Emerson directly addresses a flower in "The Rhodora."
1. What is the effect of the use of apostrophe?
2. How does Emerson's use of apostrophe reinforce the meaning of the poem?

LEARNING OPTIONS

1. **Cross-curricular Connection.** Is Emerson's image of the rhodora accurate? Use an encyclopedia or a book of horticulture to learn more about the flower. Then describe it as a scientist would. Tell what it looks like and where it grows. Share your findings with classmates.
2. **Writing.** From the age of sixteen, Emerson conscientiously recorded his impressions and observations in a journal. Spend an afternoon in a place that is special to you and record your impressions and observations in a journal entry.

Brahma[1]

Ralph Waldo Emerson

If the red slayer think he slays,
    Or if the slain think he is slain,
They know not well the subtle ways
    I keep, and pass, and turn again.

5   Far or forgot to me is near;
    Shadow and sunlight are the same;
The vanished gods to me appear;
    And one to me are shame and fame.

They reckon ill who leave me out;
10   When me they fly, I am the wings;
I am the doubter and the doubt,
    And I the hymn the Brahmin[2] sings.

The strong gods pine for my abode,
    And pine in vain the sacred Seven;[3]
15 But thou, meek lover of the good!
    Find me, and turn thy back on heaven.

---

1. **Brahma** (brä′ mə): In Hindu religion, the supreme and eternal essence or spirit of the universe.
2. **Brahmin:** A Hindu priest.
3. **sacred Seven:** The most sacred Hindu saints.

RESPONDING TO THE SELECTION

Your Response
1. What is your impression of the speaker of the poem?

Recalling
2. In the first stanza, the speaker suggests that death is an illusion. According to the speaker, why do neither the red slayer nor the slain recognize this?
3. (a) Who can find Brahma? (b) Who cannot?

Interpreting
4. Who is the speaker of the poem?
5. Who is "the red slayer"?
6. In the sacred Hindu writings, Brahma is the supreme essence, or spirit, of the universe. What does this poem reveal about Brahma's powers?
7. How does Emerson use the concept of Brahma to express his belief that the fundamental truths of the universe lie beyond the reach of our senses?

Applying
8. In what way is the Hindu belief in Brahma similar to the Transcendentalist belief in a universal soul, or Over-Soul?

CRITICAL THINKING AND READING

Understanding a Paradox
A **paradox** is a statement that seems contradictory but in reality contains a possible truth. In "Brahma" Emerson explores the subject of death from a Hindu perspective. In doing so he presents a series of paradoxes—apparent contradictions that are resolved in the higher reality, or the universal truth, of Brahma. For example, the paradox, "Far . . . is near," is presented in line 5. That something can be both far and near seems contradictory, but in the speaker's context, there is truth in the statement.
1. List six paradoxes that are presented in the poem.
2. Who can resolve these contradictions?

HENRY DAVID THOREAU

1817–1862

When Henry David Thoreau died of tuberculosis at the age of forty-four, his work had received little recognition. Yet he had achieved an inner success that few others have experienced. Speaking at Thoreau's funeral, Ralph Waldo Emerson commented, "The country knows not yet, or in the least part, how great a son it has lost. . . . But he, at least, is content. His soul was made for the noblest society; he had in a short life exhausted the capabilities of this world; wherever there is knowledge, wherever there is virtue, wherever there is beauty, he will find a home."

Thoreau was born and raised in Concord, Massachusetts. After graduating from Harvard, Thoreau became a teacher. When his objection to corporal punishment forced him to quit his first job, he and his older brother John opened their own school. The school was quite successful, but they had to close it when John became ill.

In 1842 Thoreau moved into Emerson's house. He lived there for two years, performing odd jobs to pay for his room and board. Thoreau became Emerson's close friend and devoted disciple. Deciding not to go back to teaching and refusing to pursue another career, Thoreau dedicated himself to testing the Transcendentalist philosophy through experience. By simplifying his needs, Thoreau was able to devote the rest of his life to exploring and writing about the spiritual relationship between humanity and nature and supporting his political and social beliefs.

For two years (1845–1847) Thoreau lived alone in a cabin he built himself at Walden Pond. Thoreau's experiences during this period provided him with the material for his masterwork, *Walden* (1854). Condensing his experiences at Walden Pond into one year, Thoreau used the four seasons as a structural framework for the book. A unique blend of natural observation, social criticism, and philosophical insight, *Walden* is now generally regarded as the supreme work of Transcendentalist literature.

Thoreau wrote throughout his life; however, only *A Week on the Concord and Merrimack Rivers* and some poems were published—and at Thoreau's own expense—during his lifetime. *The Maine Woods, Cape Cod,* and *A Yankee in Canada* were published posthumously. Carefully and deliberately crafted, Thoreau's work reflects the economy for which he strove throughout his life and about which he wrote in *Walden*.

Thoreau's reputation has steadily grown since his death. His work has inspired and influenced writers, environmentalists, and social and political leaders. It has made generations of readers aware of the possibilities of the human spirit and the limitations of society.

GUIDE FOR INTERPRETING

from Walden; from Civil Disobedience

Writers' Techniques

Style. Style refers to the manner in which a writer puts his or her thoughts into words. In *Walden* Thoreau's style is closely related to his purpose, which is to encourage us to examine the way we live and think. To achieve his purpose, Thoreau constructs paragraphs so that the sentences build to a climax.

Historical Context

The Mexican War. The Mexican War was a conflict between Mexico and the United States that took place from 1846 to 1848. The war was caused by a dispute over the boundary between Texas and Mexico and Mexico's refusal to discuss selling California and New Mexico to the United States. Believing that President Polk intentionally provoked the conflict before having congressional approval, Thoreau and many other Americans strongly objected to the war. To demonstrate his disapproval, Thoreau refused to pay taxes. His gesture led to his arrest, and he was forced to spend a night in jail.

Focus

How do you think you would respond to living alone in the wilderness? Write about how you think you would manage.

Primary Source

In 1954 E. B. White, a well-known author of essays and children's books *(Charlotte's Web),* wrote an article in honor of the one-hundredth anniversary of the publication of *Walden*.

> *Walden* is an oddity in American letters. It may very well be the oddest of our distinguished oddities . . . . Many think it a sermon; many set it down as an attempt to rearrange society; some think it an exercise in nature-loving; some find it a rather irritating collection of inspirational puffballs by an eccentric show-off. I think it none of these. It still seems to me the best youth's companion yet written by an American, for it carries a solemn warning against the loss of one's valuables, it advances a good argument for traveling light and trying new adventures, it rings with the power of positive adoration, it contains religious feeling without religious images, and it steadfastly refuses to record bad news. . . . Thoreau, very likely without knowing quite what he was up to, took man's relation to nature and man's dilemma in society and man's capacity for elevating his spirit and he beat all these matters together, in a wild free interval of self-justification and delight, and produced an original omelette from which people can draw nourishment in a hungry day. *Walden* is one of the first of the vitamin-enriched American dishes.

from Walden

Henry David Thoreau

from Where I Lived, and What I Lived For

At a certain season of our life we are accustomed to consider every spot as the possible site of a house. I have thus surveyed the country on every side within a dozen miles of where I live. In imagination I have bought all the farms in succession, for all were to be bought, and I knew their price. I walked over each farmer's premises, tasted his wild apples, discoursed on husbandry[1] with him, took his farm at his price, at any price, mortgaging it to him in my mind; even put a higher price on it—took everything but a deed of it—took his word for his deed, for I dearly love to talk—cultivated it, and him too to some extent, I trust, and withdrew when I had enjoyed it long enough, leaving him to carry it on. This experience entitled me to be regarded as a sort of real-estate broker by my friends. Wherever I sat, there I might live, and the landscape radiated from me accordingly. What is a house but a *sedes*, a seat?—better if a country seat. I discovered many a site for a house not likely to be soon improved, which some might have thought too far from the village, but to my eyes the village was too far from it. Well, there I might live, I said; and there I did live, for an hour, a summer and a winter life; saw how I could let the years run off, buffet the winter through, and see the spring come in. The future inhabitants of this region, wherever they may place their houses, may be sure that they have been anticipated. An afternoon sufficed to lay out the land into orchard woodlot and pasture, and to decide what fine oaks or pines should be left to stand before the door, and whence each blasted tree could be seen to the best advantage; and then I let it lie, fallow[2] perchance, for a man is rich in proportion to the number of things which he can afford to let alone.

My imagination carried me so far that I even had the refusal of several farms—the refusal was all I wanted—but I never got my fingers burned by actual possession. The nearest that I came to actual possession was when I bought the Hollowell Place, and had begun to sort my seeds, and collected materials with which to make a wheelbarrow to carry it on or off with; but before the owner gave me a deed of it, his wife—every man has such a wife—changed her mind and wished to keep it, and he offered me ten dollars to release him. Now, to speak the truth, I had but ten cents in the world, and it surpassed my arithmetic to tell, if I was that man who had ten cents, or who had a farm, or ten dollars, or all together. However, I let him keep the ten dollars and the farm too, for I had

---

1. **husbandry** (huz′ bən drē) *n.*: Farming.

2. **fallow** (fal′ō) *adj.*: Left uncultivated or unplanted.

carried it far enough; or rather, to be generous, I sold him the farm for just what I gave for it, and, as he was not a rich man, made him a present of ten dollars, and still had my ten cents, and seeds, and materials for a wheelbarrow left. I found thus that I had been a rich man without any damage to my poverty. But I retained the landscape, and I have since annually carried off what it yielded without a wheelbarrow. With respect to landscapes:

"I am monarch of all I *survey*,
  My right there is none to dispute."[3]

I have frequently seen a poet withdraw, having enjoyed the most valuable part of a farm, while the crusty farmer supposed that he had got a few wild apples only. Why, the owner does not know it for many years when a poet has put his farm in rhyme, the most admirable kind of invisible fence, has fairly impounded it, milked it, skimmed it, and got all the cream, and left the farmer only the skimmed milk.

The real attractions of the Hollowell farm, to me, were: its complete retirement, being about two miles from the village, half a mile from the nearest neighbor, and separated from the highway by a broad field; its bounding on the river, which the owner said protected it by its fogs from frosts in the spring, though that was nothing to me; the gray color and ruinous state of the house and barn, and the dilapidated fences, which put such an interval between me and the last occupant; the hollow and lichen-covered apple trees, gnawed by rabbits, showing what kind of neighbors I should have; but above all, the recollection I had of it from my earliest voyages up the river, when the house was concealed behind a dense grove of red maples, through which I heard the house-dog bark. I was in haste to buy it, before the proprietor finished getting out some rocks, cut-

ting down the hollow apple trees, and grubbing up some young birches which had sprung up in the pasture, or, in short, had made any more of his improvements. To enjoy these advantages I was ready to carry it on; like Atlas,[4] to take the world on my shoulders—I never heard what compensation he received for that—and do all those things which had no other motive or excuse but that I might pay for it and be unmolested in my possession of it; for I knew all the while that it would yield the most abundant crop of the kind I wanted if I could only afford to let it alone. But it turned out as I have said.

All that I could say, then, with respect to farming on a large scale (I have always cultivated a garden) was that I had had my seeds ready. Many think that seeds improve with age. I have no doubt that time discriminates between the good and the bad; and when at last I shall plant, I shall be less likely to be disappointed. But I would say to my fellows, once for all, As long as possible live free and uncommitted. It makes but little difference whether you are committed to a farm or the county jail.

Old Cato,[5] whose "De Re Rustica" is my "Cultivator," says, and the only translation I have seen makes sheer nonsense of the passage, "When you think of getting a farm, turn it thus in your mind, not to buy greedily; nor spare your pains to look at it, and do not think it enough to go round it once. The oftener you go there the more it will please you, if it is good." I think I shall not buy greedily, but go round and round it as long as I live, and be buried in it first, that it may please me the more at last. . . .

I do not propose to write an ode to dejection, but to brag as lustily as chanticleer[6] in the morning, standing on his roost, if only to wake my neighbors up.

---

3. "I am . . . dispute.": From William Cowper's *Verses Supposed to Be Written by Alexander Selkirk*.

4. Atlas (at′ ləs): From Greek mythology, a Titan who supported the heavens on his shoulders.

5. Old Cato: Roman statesman (234–149 B.C.). "De Re Rustica" is Latin for "Of Things Rustic."

6. chanticleer (chan′ tə klir′) *n*.: A rooster.

When first I took up my abode in the woods, that is, began to spend my nights as well as days there, which, by accident, was on Independence Day, or the fourth of July, 1845, my house was not finished for winter, but was merely a defense against the rain, without plastering or chimney, the walls being of rough weatherstained boards, with wide chinks, which made it cool at night. The upright white hewn studs and freshly planed door and window casings gave it a clean and airy look, especially in the morning, when its timbers were saturated with dew, so that I fancied that by noon some sweet gum would exude from them. To my imagination it retained throughout the day more or less of this auroral[7] character, reminding me of a certain house on a mountain which I had visited the year before. This was an airy and unplastered cabin, fit to entertain a traveling god, and where a goddess might trail her garments.The winds which passed over my dwelling were such as sweep over the ridges of mountains, bearing the broken strains, or celestial parts only, of ter-

---

7. auroral (ô rôr′ əl) *adj.*: Resembling the dawn.

restrial music. The morning wind forever blows, the poem of creation is uninterrupted; but few are the ears that hear it. Olympus[8] is but the outside of the earth everywhere. . . .

I went to the woods because I wished to live deliberately, to front only the essential facts of life, and see if I could not learn what it had to teach, and not, when I came to die, discover that I had not lived. I did not wish to live what was not life, living is so dear; nor did I wish to practice resignation, unless it was quite necessary. I wanted to live deep and suck out all the marrow of life, to live so sturdily and Spartanlike[9] as to put to rout all that was not life, to cut a broad swath and shave close, to drive life into a corner, and reduce it to its lowest terms, and, if it proved to be mean, why then to get the whole and genuine meanness of it, and publish its meanness to the world; or if it were sublime, to know it by experience, and be able to give a true account of it in my next excursion. For most men, it appears to me, are in a strange uncertainty about it, whether it is of the devil or of God, and have *somewhat hastily* concluded that it is the chief end of man here to "glorify God and enjoy him forever."[10]

Still we live meanly, like ants; though the fable tells us that we were long ago changed into men; like pygmies we fight with cranes;[11] it is error upon error, and clout upon clout, and our best virtue has for its occasion a superfluous and evitable wretchedness. Our life is frittered away by detail. An honest man has hardly need to count more than his ten fingers, or in extreme cases he may add his ten toes, and lump the rest. Simplicity, simplicity, simplicity! I say, let your affairs be as two or three, and not a hundred or a thousand; instead of a million count half a dozen, and keep your accounts on your thumbnail. In the midst of this chopping sea of civilized life, such are the clouds and storms and quicksands and thousand-and-one items to be allowed for, that a man has to live, if he would not founder and go to the bottom and not make his port at all, by dead reckoning,[12] and he must be a great calculator indeed who succeeds. Simplify, simplify. Instead of three meals a day, if it be necessary eat but one; instead of a hundred dishes, five; and reduce other things in proportion. Our life is like a German Confederacy,[13] made up of petty states, with its boundary forever fluctuating, so that even a German cannot tell you how it is bounded at any moment. The nation itself, with all its so-called internal improvements, which, by the way, are all external and superficial, is just such an unwieldy and overgrown establishment, cluttered with furniture and tripped up by its own traps, ruined by luxury and heedless expense, by want of calculation and a worthy aim, as the million households in the land; and the only cure for it as for them is in a rigid economy, a stern and more than Spartan simplicity of life and elevation of purpose. It lives too fast. Men think that it is essential that the *Nation* have commerce, and export ice, and talk through a telegraph, and ride thirty miles an hour, without a doubt, whether *they* do or not; but whether we should live like baboons or like men, is a little uncertain. If we do not get out sleepers,[14] and forge rails, and devote days and nights to the work, but go to tinkering upon our *lives* to improve *them*, who will build railroads? And if railroads are not

---

8. Olympus (ō lim′ pəs): In Greek mythology, the home of the gods.

9. Spartanlike: Like the people of Sparta, an ancient Greek state, whose citizens were known to be hardy, stoical, simple, and highly disciplined.

10. "glorify . . . forever.": The answer to the question "What is the chief end of man?" in the Westminster catechism.

11. like . . . cranes: In the *Iliad*, the Trojans are compared to cranes fighting against pygmies.

12. dead reckoning: Navigating without the assistance of stars.

13. German Confederacy: At the time, Germany was a loose union of thirty-eight independent states, with no common government.

14. sleepers (slē′ pərz) *n.*: Ties supporting railroad tracks.

built, how shall we get to heaven in season? But if we stay at home and mind our business, who will want railroads? We do not ride on the railroad; it rides upon us. . . .

Time is but the stream I go a-fishing in. I drink at it; but while I drink I see the sandy bottom and detect how shallow it is. Its thin current slides away, but eternity remains. I would drink deeper; fish in the sky, whose bottom is pebbly with stars. I cannot count one. I know not the first letter of the alphabet. I have always been regretting that I was not as wise as the day I was born. The intellect is a cleaver; it discerns and rifts its way into the secret of things. I do not wish to be any more busy with my hands than is necessary. My head is hands and feet. I feel all my best faculties concentrated in it. My instinct tells me that my head is an organ for burrowing, as some creatures use their snout and forepaws, and with it I would mine and burrow my way through these hills. I think that the richest vein is somewhere hereabouts; so by the divining rod[15] and thin rising vapors I judge; and here I will begin to mine. . . .

from The Conclusion

I left the woods for as good a reason as I went there. Perhaps it seemed to me that I had several more lives to live, and could not spare any more time for that one. It is remarkable how easily and insensibly we fall into a particular route, and make a beaten track for ourselves. I had not lived there a week before my feet wore a path from my door to the pondside; and though it is five or six years since I trod it, it is still quite distinct. It is true, I fear that others may have fallen into it, and so helped to keep it open. The surface of the earth is soft and impress-

---

15. divining rod: A forked branch or stick alleged to reveal underground water or minerals.

ible by the feet of men; and so with the paths which the mind travels. How worn and dusty, then, must be the highways of the world, how deep the ruts of tradition and conformity! I did not wish to take a cabin passage, but rather to go before the mast and on the deck of the world, for there I could best see the moonlight amid the mountains. I do not wish to go below now.

I learned this, at least, by my experiment; that if one advances confidently in the direction of his dreams, and endeavors to live the life which he has imagined, he will meet with a success unexpected in common hours. He will put some things behind, will pass an invisible boundary; new, universal, and more liberal laws will begin to establish themselves around and within him; or the old laws be expanded, and interpreted in his favor in a more liberal sense, and he will live with the license of a higher order of beings. In proportion as he simplifies his life, the laws of the universe will appear less complex, and solitude will not be solitude, nor poverty poverty, nor weakness weakness. If you have built castles in the air, your work need not be lost; that is where they should be. Now put the foundations under them. . . .

Why should we be in such desperate haste to succeed, and in such desperate enterprises? If a man does not keep pace with his companions, perhaps it is because he hears a different drummer. Let him step to the music which he hears, however measured or far away. It is not important that he should mature as soon as an apple tree or an oak. Shall he turn his spring into summer? If the condition of things which we were made for is not yet, what were any reality which we can substitute? We will not be shipwrecked on a vain reality. Shall we with pains erect a heaven of blue glass over ourselves, though when it is done we shall be sure to gaze still at the true ethereal heaven far above, as if the former were not?. . . .

However mean your life is, meet it and live it; do not shun it and call it hard names.

It is not so bad as you are. It looks poorest when you are richest. The faultfinder will find faults even in paradise. Love your life, poor as it is. You may perhaps have some pleasant, thrilling, glorious hours, even in a poorhouse. The setting sun is reflected from the windows of the almshouse[16] as brightly as from the rich man's abode; the snow melts before its door as early in the spring. I do not see but a quiet mind may live as contentedly there, and have as cheering thoughts, as in a palace. The town's poor seem to me often to live the most independent lives of any. Maybe they are simply great enough to receive without misgiving. Most think that they are above being supported by the town; but it oftener happens that they are not above supporting themselves by dishonest means, which should be more disreputable. Cultivate poverty like a garden herb, like sage. Do not trouble yourself much to get new things, whether clothes or friends. Turn the old; return to them. Things do not change; we change. Sell your clothes and keep your thoughts. God will see that you do not want society. If I were confined to a corner of a garret[17] all my days, like a spider, the world would be just as large to me while I had my thoughts about me. The philosopher said: "From an army of three divisions one can take away its general, and put it in disorder; from the man the most abject and vulgar one cannot take away his thought." Do not seek so anxiously to be developed, to subject yourself to many influences to be played on; it is all dissipation. Humility like darkness reveals the heavenly lights. The shadows of poverty and meanness gather around us, "and lo! creation widens to our view."[18] We are often reminded that if there were bestowed on us the wealth of Croesus,[19] our aims must still be the same, and our means essentially the same. Moreover, if you are restricted in your range by poverty, if you cannot buy books and newspapers, for instance, you are but confined to the most significant and vital experiences; you are compelled to deal with the material which yields the most sugar and the most starch. It is life near the bone where it is sweetest. You are defended from being a trifler. No man loses ever on a lower level by magnanimity on a higher. Superfluous wealth can buy superfluities only. Money is not required to buy one necessary of the soul. . . .

The life in us is like the water in the river. It may rise this year higher than man has ever known it, and flood the parched uplands; even this may be the eventful year, which will drown out all our muskrats. It was not always dry land where we dwell. I see far inland the banks which the stream anciently washed, before science began to record its freshets. Everyone has heard the story which has gone the rounds of New England, of a strong and beautiful bug which came out of the dry leaf of an old table of apple-tree wood, which had stood in a farmer's kitchen for sixty years, first in Connecticut, and afterward in Massachusetts— from an egg deposited in the living tree many years earlier still, as appeared by counting the annual layers beyond it; which was heard gnawing out for several weeks, hatched perchance by the heat of an urn. Who does not feel his faith in a resurrection and immortality strengthened by hearing of this? Who knows what beautiful and winged life, whose egg has been buried for ages under many concentric layers of woodenness in

---

16. **almshouse** *n.*: A home for people too poor to support themselves.
17. **garret** (gar′ it) *n.*: Attic.
18. **"and . . . view":** From the sonnet "To Night" by British poet Joseph Blanco White (1775–1841).

---

19. **Croesus** (krē′ səs): The King of Lydia (d. 546 B.C.), believed to be the wealthiest person of his time.

the dead dry life of society, deposited at first in the alburnum[20] of the green and living tree, which has been gradually converted into the semblance of its well-seasoned tomb—heard perchance gnawing out now for years by the astonished family of man, as they sat round the festive board—may unexpectedly come forth from amidst society's most trivial and handselled furniture, to enjoy its perfect summer life at last!

I do not say that John or Jonathan[21] will realize all this; but such is the character of that morrow which mere lapse of time can never make to dawn. The light which puts out our eyes is darkness to us. Only that day dawns to which we are awake. There is more day to dawn. The sun is but a morning star.

---

20. alburnum (al bur′ nəm) n.: Soft wood between the bark and the heartwood where water is conducted.

21. John or Jonathan: The average person.

RESPONDING TO THE SELECTION

Your Response

1. Henry David Thoreau experienced life through his imagination. What experiences or ideas have you imagined?
2. Where would you go to "live deep and suck out all the marrow of life"?

Recalling

3. What does Thoreau imagine doing?
4. (a) Why does Thoreau go to live in the woods? (b) Why does he eventually leave?
5. What does he learn from his "experiment"?
6. What advice does Thoreau offer to those who live in poverty?

Interpreting

7. What does Thoreau mean by this comment: "It makes but little difference whether you are committed to a farm or the county jail"?
8. (a) How does Thoreau's description of the wind convey the Transcendentalist belief in a shared universal soul, or Over-Soul? (b) What does he suggest about people's awareness of the Over-Soul?
9. Why does Thoreau believe that living in the woods will enable him to "live deep and suck all the marrow out of life"?
10. Considering the attitude toward commitments that Thoreau expresses in his discussion of farms, why is it not surprising that he decides to leave Walden?
11. In your own words, describe Thoreau's attitude toward individuality and conformity.
12. Why, according to Thoreau, are people better off being poor than wealthy?
13. (a) What does the story of the "beautiful bug" reveal about our capacity to experience a spiritual awakening? (b) What does Thoreau believe we can do to help bring about this type of rebirth?

Applying

14. Explain why you either do or do not believe that it would be possible for Thoreau to conduct his "experiment" in today's society.

ANALYZING LITERATURE

Understanding Style

Style refers to the way in which a writer expresses his or her thoughts. For example, Thoreau writes in a powerfully excessive style, constantly reinforcing his main points.

1. How does the paragraph on simplicity (page 257) demonstrate Thoreau's tendency to make sentences build to a climax? Find one other paragraph that is structured in this manner.
2. Thoreau often starts a paragraph by discussing specific incidents or examples. He then applies them to a larger truth. Find one paragraph in which he uses this technique.

CRITICAL THINKING AND READING

Evaluating the Effect of Style

Some critics have argued that Thoreau overstates his main points in *Walden*. Thoreau, however, felt that it was impossible to overstate the truth about human potential. He deliberately repeated his main ideas to reinforce what he was saying.

Examine the paragraph on simplicity. Explain whether or not the structure of the paragraph contributes to its effectiveness.

THINKING AND WRITING

Comparing and Contrasting Essays

Write an essay in which you compare and contrast the excerpt from *Walden* with the excerpt from Emerson's *Nature* (page 240). Start by carefully rereading the two selections. Take notes on the ideas expressed in each selection. Organize your notes according to corresponding points of contrast. Then draft your essay, supporting your points with passages from each selection. When you revise, make sure that you have varied the length and structure of your sentences and connected your ideas with transitions. Proofread and prepare a final draft.

from Walden 261

from Civil Disobedience

Henry David Thoreau

I heartily accept the motto, "That government is best which governs least";[1] and I should like to see it acted up to more rapidly and systematically. Carried out, it finally amounts to this, which also I believe: "That government is best which governs not at all"; and when men are prepared for it, that will be the kind of government which they will have. Government is at best but an expedient; but most governments are usually, and all governments are sometimes, inexpedient. The objections which have been brought against a standing army, and they are many and weighty, and deserve to prevail, may also at last be brought against a standing government. The standing army is only an arm of the standing government. The government itself, which is only the mode which the people have chosen to execute their will, is equally liable to be abused and perverted before the people can act through it. Witness the present Mexican war, the work of comparatively a few individuals using the standing government as their tool; for in the outset, the people would not have consented to this measure.

This American government—what is it but a tradition, though a recent one, endeavoring to transmit itself unimpaired to posterity, but each instant losing some of its integrity? It has not the vitality and force of a single living man; for a single man can bend it to his will. It is a sort of wooden gun to the people themselves; and, if ever they should use it in earnest as a real one against each other, it will surely split. But it is not the less necessary for this; for the people must have some complicated machinery or other, and hear its din, to satisfy that idea of government which they have. Governments show thus how successfully men can be imposed on, even impose on themselves, for their own advantage. It is excellent, we must all allow; yet this government never of itself furthered any enterprise, but by the alacrity with which it got out of its way. *It* does not keep the country free. *It* does not settle the West. *It* does not educate. The character inherent in the American people has done all that has been accomplished; and it would have done somewhat more, if the government had not sometimes got in its way. For government is an expedient by which men would fain succeed in letting one another alone; and, as has been said, when it is most expedient, the governed are most let alone by it. Trade and commerce, if they were not made of India rubber,[2] would never manage to bounce over the obstacles which legislators are continually putting in their way; and, if one were to judge these men wholly by the effects of their actions, and not partly by their intentions, they would deserve to be classed and punished with those mischievous persons who put obstructions on the railroads.

But, to speak practically and as a citizen, unlike those who call themselves no government men, I ask for, not at once no government, but *at once* a better government. Let every man make known what kind of government would command his respect, and that will be one step toward obtaining it. . . .

---

1. **"That . . . least":** The motto of the *United States Magazine and Democratic Review,* a literary-political journal.

2. **India rubber:** A form of crude rubber.

Your Response

1. What kind of government commands your respect? Why?

Recalling

2. What motto does Thoreau heartily accept?
3. How does Thoreau suggest people can contribute toward improving the government?

Interpreting

4. (a) How would you summarize Thoreau's attitude concerning the role of the government? (b) In what ways does he believe the American government has failed?

Applying

5. (a) What current government policies do you think Thoreau would object to? (b) What policies would he endorse?

ANALYZING LITERATURE

Understanding Historical Context

Thoreau wrote *Civil Disobedience* after spending a night in jail for refusing to pay his taxes in protest of the Mexican War and slavery. In the essay he urged people to resist governmental policies with which they disagree.

1. In this excerpt who does Thoreau suggest is responsible for the Mexican War?
2. What does he imply are his reasons for disapproving of the war?
3. How does he use the war to support his argument concerning the role of the government?

THINKING AND WRITING

Writing a Report

Write a brief report about the Mexican War. Start by researching the war in encyclopedias and history books. Organize your information. Then write your report, making sure that you mention each of the important events related to the war.

MULTICULTURAL CONNECTION

From Walden Pond to India and Back

The influence of Thoreau on Gandhi. Thoreau's concept of civil disobedience greatly influenced Indian leader Mohandas Karamchand Gandhi in his campaign against British rule in his homeland.

Drawing on Thoreau's ideas, Gandhi formulated his philosophy of Satyagraha ("The Devotion to Truth" or "Truthful Force" in Sanskrit, an ancient Indian language) in 1906. His purpose was to oppose laws that discriminated against Asians in South Africa, where he practiced law, and his philosophy relied on peaceful noncooperation.

Back home, Gandhi successfully used Satyagraha as a weapon against the colonial power and its unfair policies. He called for massive boycotts of British goods and British-run institutions in India that treated Indians unfairly. Thousands of Gandhi's supporters and Gandhi himself repeatedly went to prison without resistance. When Gandhi's protests helped India win its independence in 1947, it was largely due to Gandhi's nonviolent protests.

The influence of Gandhi on Martin Luther King, Jr. Gandhi's ideas later helped shape the civil rights movement in the United States from the 1950's to the 1970's. Martin Luther King, one of the leaders of the movement, was committed to the concept of civil disobedience and helped to organize boycotts, marches, and sit-ins, which brought about important social changes.

For Discussion.

What are some other examples of civil disobedience? Discuss these with your classmates and debate the pros and cons of this type of protest.

Contemporary Thoreaus

During Henry David Thoreau's lifetime, his writings were known only by a small group of friends and acquaintances. Soon after his death, however, his reputation began spreading, until today it is worldwide.

Thoreau's account of his "experiment" at Walden Pond has inspired many people to do the same. They have retreated to such places as snowbound cabins, hill farms, and mountain huts. Some have written reflective accounts of their experiences. Among these modern-day Thoreaus are two American writers, Annie Dillard and Edward Abbey.

Both Dillard and Abbey followed Thoreau's recommendation to go to nature to "explore thyself." In their books they accurately record and vividly describe the natural world, seeking its spiritual meanings. Yet each writer's experience and account of living alone is unique.

ANNIE DILLARD

Annie Dillard spent a year in a small cabin next to Tinker Creek in Virginia, her only company a goldfish named Ellery Channing. She described her life and thoughts there in the award-winning book *Pilgrim at Tinker Creek*, published in 1974.

"I propose," she tells us in the first chapter, "to keep here what Thoreau called 'a meteorological journal of the mind,' telling some tales and describing some of the sights of this rather tamed valley, and exploring, in fear and trembling, some of the unmapped dim reaches and unholy fastnesses to which those tales and sights so dizzyingly lead." Her exploration leads her to horrifying scenes and joyous moments in the natural world around her.

Dillard has a mystical vision of nature, expressed with intense emotional lyricism. She seeks and sees the face of God and of the unknown in the trees, water, and changing seasons of Tinker Creek. A few years later on an island in Puget Sound, she wrote *Holy the Firm* (published in 1978), a theological meditation on the ultimate meaning of life.

EDWARD ABBEY

Edward Abbey's retreat was a small government-issue trailer at Arches National Monument, where he spent several summers as a park ranger. His account of his experiment, *Desert Solitaire: A Season in the Wilderness*, was published in 1968. As Thoreau did in *Walden*, Abbey compresses the events of several seasons into one.

The harsh and delicate beauty of the Utah desert inspires him: "I am twenty miles or more from the nearest fellow human, but instead of loneliness I feel loveliness. Loveliness and a quiet exultation." The desert and its inhabitants, both animal and human, also bring many doubts and questions about his and all humans' purpose on earth.

It is, however, Thoreau as skeptical observer and critic of society that seems most to attract Abbey. Even more than Thoreau, he is outspoken, witty, sometimes sarcastic in his criticisms of dubious "improvements" made in the land by individuals and government agencies. He is often irreverent and outrageous in condemning the ignorance and greed he sees destroying the last vestiges of wildness. His purpose, like Thoreau's, is to wake up his neighbors before it is too late.

Fiercely against mechanization, Abbey is proud to be a "river rat." In the fall of 1980, he floated down the canyons of the Green and Colorado rivers. With him he took "a worn and greasy paperback copy of a book called *Walden, or Life in the Woods*." He described this trip in "Down the River with Henry Thoreau," first published in 1981.

"Thoreau's mind has been haunting mine for most of my life," he admits. Throughout the river trip he quotes from, talks about, and argues with Thoreau.

At the last rapid, before returning to "civilization, such as it is," Abbey concludes, "Henry thou should be with us now. . . . Wherever there are deer and hawks, wherever there is liberty and danger, wherever there is wilderness, wherever there is a living river, Henry Thoreau will find his eternal home."

NATHANIEL HAWTHORNE

1804–1864

Despite his admiration for Ralph Waldo Emerson, Nathaniel Hawthorne found it impossible to accept the optimistic world view of the Transcendentalists. Haunted by the intolerance and cruelty of his Puritan ancestors, Hawthorne viewed evil as one of the dominant forces in the world. As a result, his works express a gloomy vision of the world, which contrasts sharply with the positive view of the Transcendentalists.

Hawthorne was born in Salem, Massachusetts, a descendant of a prominent Puritan family. His ancestors included a judge known for his persecution of the Quakers and a judge who played an important role in the Salem witchcraft trials. Though Hawthorne himself was not a Puritan, he was deeply aware of the actions of his ancestors, and his character was shaped by a sense of inherited guilt.

After graduating from Bowdoin College in Maine in 1825, Hawthorne lived in seclusion in his mother's house in Salem for twelve years, devoting his energy to developing his skills as a writer. Hawthorne's self-imposed isolation lasted until 1837, when he published his first collection of stories, *Twice-Told Tales.* The book sold poorly, but it established him as a respected writer.

After moving out of his mother's house, Hawthorne lived briefly at Brook Farm, the Transcendentalist commune. Then, in 1842, he married Sophia Peabody and moved to the Old Manse at Concord, Massachusetts, where Emerson had lived. While living in Concord, he became a friend of both Emerson and Thoreau and published a second collection of stories, *Mosses from an Old Manse* (1846).

When he received a political appointment at the Salem customhouse, he moved back to Salem. A change of administrations forced him out of office, and Hawthorne once again focused on his writing. In 1850 he published *The Scarlet Letter,* a powerful novel about sin and guilt among early Puritans. *The Scarlet Letter* was extremely successful, earning Hawthorne international fame. During the next two years, Hawthorne published two more novels, *The House of the Seven Gables* (1851) and *The Blithedale Romance* (1852).

When his college friend Franklin Pierce became President, Hawthorne was made the American consul at Liverpool, England. After spending several years in England and Italy, Hawthorne returned to Massachusetts. Hawthorne's experiences in Italy provided him with the material for his final novel, *The Marble Faun* (1860). Four years after the book's publication, Hawthorne died in his sleep while on a walking tour in New Hampshire.

GUIDE FOR INTERPRETING

The Minister's Black Veil

Literary Movements

Anti-Transcendentalism. Anti-Transcendentalism was a literary movement that essentially consisted of only two writers. Yet these two writers, Nathaniel Hawthorne and Herman Melville, were easily the greatest fiction writers of their time. They focused on the limitations and potential destructiveness of the human spirit rather than on its possibilities.

Writers' Techniques

Allegory. An allegory is a work of literature in which events, characters, and details of setting have a symbolic meaning. For example, a character in an allegory may represent a single human trait, such as jealousy, greed, or compassion. Allegories are used to teach or explain moral principles and universal truths.

Commentary

The truths Hawthorne suggests in his allegories were often themselves mysterious and dimly seen. He was seeking them in the innermost workings of the human heart and mind, an area largely unexplored even today. Ordinary humans as well as the natural world around us, he felt, contained dark places that the cold light of reason alone could not penetrate—at least not without risking one's peace of mind. Truths lay in the shadows, in the time between sleeping and waking, in the world transformed by moonlight.

To entice his readers into this almost dreamlike world, Hawthorne used the voice of the storyteller, the humble teller of folk tales, which we know are not strictly "true" but nevertheless fascinate us. He always called his stories "tales" and his novels "romances," and he explained what he meant.

Rather than sticking closely to the ordinary reality of the novel, he said, the romance writer could best "present the truth of the human heart" by using his artistic imagination to create a rich, shadowy atmosphere or mood. He can, Hawthorne continues, then manage this atmosphere so "as to bring out or mellow the lights and deepen and enrich the shadows of the picture." Finally, in a tale or romance, he can "mingle the Marvelous" with the ordinary and the legendary past with the present.

As you read the following story, listen for the voice of the storyteller speaking directly to you. Notice how Hawthorne creates an atmosphere by mingling not only real and unreal and past and present, but also light and dark and good and evil. Can people or events today be both good and bad, ordinary and marvelous, or a mingling of other opposites?

Focus

Freewrite about how a person's physical appearance can isolate him or her from other people.

The Minister's Black Veil

Nathaniel Hawthorne

A Parable

The sexton[1] stood in the porch of Milford meetinghouse, pulling busily at the bell rope. The old people of the village came stooping along the street. Children, with bright faces, tripped merrily beside their parents, or mimicked a graver gait, in the conscious dignity of their Sunday clothes. Spruce bachelors looked sidelong at the pretty maidens, and fancied that the Sabbath sunshine made them prettier than on weekdays. When the throng had mostly streamed into the porch, the sexton began to toll the bell, keeping his eye on the Reverend Mr. Hooper's door. The first glimpse of the clergyman's figure was the signal for the bell to cease its summons.

"But what has good Parson Hooper got upon his face?" cried the sexton in astonishment.

All within hearing immediately turned about, and beheld the semblance of Mr. Hooper, pacing slowly his meditative way towards the meetinghouse. With one accord they started, expressing more wonder than if some strange minister were coming to dust the cushions of Mr. Hooper's pulpit.

"Are you sure it is our parson?" inquired Goodman[2] Gray of the sexton.

"Of a certainty it is good Mr. Hooper," replied the sexton. "He was to have exchanged pulpits with Parson Shute, of Westbury; but Parson Shute sent to excuse himself yesterday, being to preach a funeral sermon."

The cause of so much amazement may appear sufficiently slight. Mr. Hooper, a gentlemanly person, of about thirty, though still a bachelor, was dressed with due clerical neatness, as if a careful wife had starched his band, and brushed the weekly dust from his Sunday's garb. There was but one thing remarkable in his appearance. Swathed about his forehead, and hanging down over his face, so low as to be shaken by his breath, Mr. Hooper had on a black veil. On a nearer view it seemed to consist of two folds of crape,[3] which entirely concealed his features, except the mouth and chin, but probably did not intercept his sight, further than to give a darkened aspect to all living and inanimate things. With this gloomy shade before him, good Mr. Hooper walked onward, at a slow and quiet pace, stooping somewhat, and looking on the ground, as is customary with abstracted men, yet nodding kindly to those of his parishioners who still waited on the meetinghouse steps. But so wonderstruck were they that his greeting hardly met with a return.

"I can't really feel as if good Mr. Hooper's face was behind that piece of crape," said the sexton.

"I don't like it," muttered an old woman, as she hobbled into the meetinghouse. "He has changed himself into something awful, only by hiding his face."

"Our parson has gone mad!" cried Goodman Gray, following him across the threshold.

---

1. **sexton** (seks' tən) n.: A person in charge of the maintenance of a church.
2. **Goodman:** A title of respect similar to "Mister."

3. **crape** (krāp) n.: A piece of black cloth worn as a sign of mourning.

WINTER SUNDAY IN NORWAY, MAINE
Unidentified Artist
New York State Historical Association, Cooperstown

preacher, but not an energetic one: he strove to win his people heavenward by mild, persuasive influences, rather than to drive them thither by the thunders of the Word. The sermon which he now delivered was marked by the same characteristics of style and manner as the general series of his pulpit oratory. But there was something, either in the sentiment of the discourse itself, or in the imagination of the auditors, which made it greatly the most powerful effort that they had ever heard from their pastor's lips. It was tinged, rather more darkly than usual, with the gentle gloom of Mr. Hooper's temperament. The subject had reference to secret sin, and those sad mysteries which we hide from our nearest and dearest, and would fain conceal from our own consciousness, even forgetting that the Omniscient[4] can detect them. A subtle power was breathed into his words. Each member of the congregation, the most innocent girl, and the man of hardened breast, felt as if the preacher had crept upon them, behind his awful veil, and discovered their hoarded iniquity of deed or thought. Many spread their clasped hands on their bosoms. There was nothing terrible in what Mr. Hooper said, at least, no violence; and yet, with every tremor of his melancholy voice, the hearers quaked. An unsought pathos came hand in hand with awe. So sensible were the audience of some unwonted attribute in their minister, that they longed for a breath of wind to blow aside the veil, almost believing that a stranger's visage would be discovered, though the form, gesture, and voice were those of Mr. Hooper.

At the close of the services, the people hurried out with indecorous confusion, eager to communicate their pent-up amazement, and conscious of lighter spirits the moment they lost sight of the black veil. Some gathered in little circles, huddled closely together, with their mouths all whispering in the center; some went homeward alone, wrapt in silent meditation; some talked loudly, and profaned the Sabbath day with ostentatious laughter. A few shook their sagacious heads, intimating that they could penetrate the mystery; while one or two affirmed that there was no mystery at all, but only that Mr. Hooper's eyes were so weakened by the midnight lamp, as to require a shade. After a brief interval, forth came good Mr. Hooper also, in the rear of his flock. Turning his veiled face from one group to another, he paid due reverence to the hoary heads, saluted the middle-aged with kind dignity as their friend and spiritual guide, greeted the young with mingled authority and love, and laid his hands on the little children's heads to bless them. Such was always his custom on the Sabbath day. Strange and bewildered looks repaid him for his courtesy. None, as on former occasions, aspired to the honor of walking by their pastor's side. Old Squire Saunders, doubtless by an accidental lapse of memory, neglected to invite Mr. Hooper to his table, where the good clergyman had been wont to bless the food, almost every Sunday since his settlement. He returned, therefore, to the parsonage, and, at the moment of closing the door, was observed to look back upon the people, all of whom had their eyes fixed upon the minister. A sad smile gleamed faintly from beneath the black veil, and flickered about his mouth, glimmering as he disappeared.

"How strange," said a lady, "that a simple black veil, such as any woman might wear on her bonnet, should become such a terrible thing on Mr. Hooper's face!"

"Something must surely be amiss with Mr. Hooper's intellects," observed her husband, the physician of the village. "But the strangest part of the affair is the effect of this vagary, even on a sober-minded man like myself. The black veil, though it covers only our pastor's face, throws its influence over his whole person, and makes him ghostlike from head to foot. Do you not feel it so?"

"Truly do I," replied the lady; "and I would not be alone with him for the world. I wonder he is not afraid to be alone with himself!"

---

4. Omniscient (äm nish' ent): All-knowing God.

"Men sometimes are so," said her husband.

The afternoon service was attended with similar circumstances. At its conclusion, the bell tolled for the funeral of a young lady. The relatives and friends were assembled in the house, and the more distant acquaintances stood about the door, speaking of the good qualities of the deceased, when their talk was interrupted by the appearance of Mr. Hooper, still covered with his black veil. It was now an appropriate emblem. The clergyman stepped into the room where the corpse was laid, and bent over the coffin, to take a last farewell of his deceased parishioner. As he stooped, the veil hung straight down from his forehead, so that, if her eyelids had not been closed forever, the dead maiden might have seen his face. Could Mr. Hooper be fearful of her glance, that he so hastily caught back the black veil? A person who watched the interview between the dead and living, scrupled not to affirm, that, at the instant when the clergyman's features were disclosed, the corpse had slightly shuddered, rustling the shroud and muslin cap, though the countenance retained the composure of death. A superstitious old woman was the only witness of this prodigy. From the coffin Mr. Hooper passed into the chamber of the mourners, and thence to the head of the staircase; to make the funeral prayer. It was a tender and heart-dissolving prayer, full of sorrow, yet so imbued with celestial hopes, that the music of a heavenly harp, swept by the fingers of the dead, seemed faintly to be heard among the saddest accents of the minister. The people trembled, though they but darkly understood him when he prayed that they, and himself, and all of mortal race, might be ready, as he trusted this young maiden had been, for the dreadful hour that should snatch the veil from their faces. The bearers went heavily forth, and the mourners followed, saddening all the street, with the dead before them, and Mr. Hooper in his black veil behind.

"Why do you look back?" said one in the procession to his partner.

"I had a fancy," replied she, "that the minister and the maiden's spirit were walking hand in hand."

"And so had I, at the same moment," said the other.

That night, the handsomest couple in Milford village were to be joined in wedlock. Though reckoned a melancholy man, Mr. Hooper had a placid cheerfulness for such occasions, which often excited a sympathetic smile where livelier merriment would have been thrown away. There was no quality of his disposition which made him more beloved than this. The company at the wedding awaited his arrival with impatience, trusting that the strange awe, which had gathered over him throughout the day, would now be dispelled. But such was not the result. When Mr. Hooper came, the first thing that their eyes rested on was the same horrible black veil, which had added deeper gloom to the funeral, and could portend nothing but evil to the wedding. Such was its immediate effect on the guests that a cloud seemed to have rolled duskily from beneath the black crape, and dimmed the light of the candles. The bridal pair stood up before the minister. But the bride's cold fingers quivered in the tremulous hand of the bridegroom, and her deathlike paleness caused a whisper that the maiden who had been buried a few hours before was come from her grave to be married. If ever another wedding were so dismal, it was that famous one where they tolled the wedding knell.[5] After performing the ceremony, Mr. Hooper raised a glass of wine to his lips, wishing happiness to the new-married couple in a strain of mild pleasantry that ought to have brightened the features of the guests, like a cheerful gleam from the hearth. At that instant, catching a glimpse of his figure in the looking glass, the black veil involved his own spirit in the horror with which it overwhelmed all others. His frame shuddered, his lips grew white, he

---

5. If . . . knell: A reference to Hawthorne's short story "The Wedding Knell." A *knell* is the slow ringing of a bell, as at a funeral.

spilt the untasted wine upon the carpet, and rushed forth into the darkness. For the Earth, too, had on her Black Veil.

The next day, the whole village of Milford talked of little else than Parson Hooper's black veil. That, and the mystery concealed behind it, supplied a topic for discussion between acquaintances meeting in the street, and good women gossiping at their open windows. It was the first item of news that the tavernkeeper told to his guests. The children babbled of it on their way to school. One imitative little imp covered his face with an old black handkerchief, thereby so affrighting his playmates that the panic seized himself, and he well nigh lost his wits by his own waggery.

It was remarkable that of all the busybodies and impertinent people in the parish, not one ventured to put the plain question to Mr. Hooper, wherefore he did this thing. Hitherto, whenever there appeared the slightest call for such interference, he had never lacked advisers, nor shown himself averse to be guided by their judgment. If he erred at all, it was by so painful a degree of self-distrust that even the mildest censure would lead him to consider an indifferent action as a crime. Yet, though so well acquainted with this amiable weakness, no individual among his parishioners chose to make the black veil a subject of friendly remonstrance. There was a feeling of dread, neither plainly confessed nor carefully concealed, which caused each to shift the responsibility upon another, till at length it was found expedient to send a deputation of the church, in order to deal with Mr. Hooper about the mystery, before it should grow into a scandal. Never did an embassy so ill discharge its duties. The minister received them with friendly courtesy, but became silent, after they were seated, leaving to his visitors the whole burden of introducing their important business. The topic, it might be supposed, was obvious enough. There was the black veil swathed round Mr. Hooper's forehead, and concealing every fea-

ture above his placid mouth, on which, at times, they could perceive the glimmering of a melancholy smile. But that piece of crape, to their imagination, seemed to hang down before his heart, the symbol of a fearful secret between him and them. Were the veil but cast aside, they might speak freely of it, but not till then. Thus they sat a considerable time, speechless, confused, and shrinking uneasily from Mr. Hooper's eye, which they felt to be fixed upon them with an invisible glance. Finally, the deputies returned abashed to their constituents, pronouncing the matter too weighty to be handled, except by a council of the churches, if, indeed, it might not require a general synod.[6]

But there was one person in the village unappalled by the awe with which the black veil had impressed all beside herself. When the deputies returned without an explanation, or even venturing to demand one, she, with the calm energy of her character, determined to chase away the strange cloud that appeared to be settling round Mr. Hooper, every moment more darkly than before. As his plighted wife,[7] it should be her privilege to know what the black veil concealed. At the minister's first visit, therefore, she entered upon the subject with a direct simplicity, which made the task easier both for him and her. After he had seated himself, she fixed her eyes steadfastly upon the veil, but could discern nothing of the dreadful gloom that had so overawed the multitude: it was but a double fold of crape, hanging down from his forehead to his mouth, and slightly stirring with his breath.

"No," said she aloud, and smiling, "there is nothing terrible in this piece of crape, except that it hides a face which I am always glad to look upon. Come, good sir, let the sun shine from behind the cloud. First lay aside your black veil: then tell me why you put it on."

Mr. Hooper's smile glimmered faintly.

6. synod (sin′ əd) *n.*: A high governing body in certain Christian churches.
7. plighted wife: Fiancée.

"There is an hour to come," said he, "when all of us shall cast aside our veils. Take it not amiss, beloved friend, if I wear this piece of crape till then."

"Your words are a mystery, too," returned the young lady. "Take away the veil from them, at least."

"Elizabeth, I will," said he, "so far as my vow may suffer me. Know, then, this veil is a type and a symbol, and I am bound to wear it ever, both in light and darkness, in solitude and before the gaze of multitudes, and as with strangers, so with my familiar friends. No mortal eye will see it withdrawn. This dismal shade must separate me from the world: even you, Elizabeth, can never come behind it!"

"What grievous affliction hath befallen you," she earnestly inquired, "that you should thus darken your eyes forever?"

"If it be a sign of mourning," replied Mr. Hooper, "I, perhaps, like most other mortals, have sorrows dark enough to be typified by a black veil."

"But what if the world will not believe that it is the type of an innocent sorrow?" urged Elizabeth. "Beloved and respected as you are, there may be whispers that you hide your face under the consciousness of secret sin. For the sake of your holy office, do away this scandal!"

The color rose into her cheeks as she intimated the nature of the rumors that were already abroad in the village. But Mr. Hooper's mildness did not forsake him. He even smiled again—that same sad smile, which always appeared like a faint glimmering of light, proceeding from the obscurity beneath the veil.

"If I hide my face for sorrow, there is cause enough," he merely replied; "and if I cover it for secret sin, what mortal might not do the same?"

And with this gentle, but unconquerable obstinacy did he resist all her entreaties. At length Elizabeth sat silent. For a few moments she appeared lost in thought, considering, probably, what new methods might be tried to withdraw her lover from so dark a fantasy, which, if it had no other meaning, was perhaps a symptom of mental disease. Though of a firmer character than his own, the tears rolled down her cheeks. But in an instant, as it were, a new feeling took the place of sorrow: her eyes were fixed insensibly on the black veil, when, like a sudden twilight in the air, its terrors fell around her. She arose, and stood trembling before him.

"And do you feel it then, at last?" said he mournfully.

She made no reply, but covered her eyes with her hand, and turned to leave the room. He rushed forward and caught her arm.

"Have patience with me, Elizabeth!" cried he, passionately. "Do not desert me, though this veil must be between us here on earth. Be mine, and hereafter there shall be no veil over my face, no darkness between our souls! It is but a mortal veil—it is not for eternity! O! you know not how lonely I am, and how frightened, to be alone behind my black veil. Do not leave me in this miserable obscurity forever!"

"Lift the veil but once, and look me in the face," said she.

"Never! It cannot be!" replied Mr. Hooper.

"Then farewell!" said Elizabeth.

She withdrew her arm from his grasp, and slowly departed, pausing at the door, to give one long shuddering gaze, that seemed almost to penetrate the mystery of the black veil. But, even amid his grief, Mr. Hooper smiled to think that only a material emblem had separated him from happiness, though the horrors, which it shadowed forth, must be drawn darkly between the fondest of lovers.

From that time no attempts were made to remove Mr. Hooper's black veil, or, by a direct appeal, to discover the secret which it was supposed to hide. By persons who claimed a superiority to popular prejudice, it was reckoned merely an eccentric whim, such as often mingles with the sober actions of men otherwise rational, and tinges them all with its own semblance of insanity. But

CEMETERY
Peter McIntyre
Courtesy of the artist

with the multitude, good Mr. Hooper was irreparably a bugbear.[8] He could not walk the street with any peace of mind, so conscious was he that the gentle and timid would turn aside to avoid him, and that others would make it a point of hardihood to throw themselves in his way. The impertinence of the latter class compelled him to give up his customary walk at sunset to the burial ground; for when he leaned pensively over the gate, there would always be faces behind the gravestones, peeping at his black veil. A fable went the rounds that the stare of the dead people drove him thence. It grieved him, to the very depth of his kind heart, to observe how the children fled from his approach, breaking up their merriest sports, while his melancholy figure was yet afar off. Their instinctive dread caused him to feel more strongly than aught else, that a preternatu-

ral[9] horror was interwoven with the threads of the black crape. In truth, his own antipathy to the veil was known to be so great that he never willingly passed before a mirror, nor stooped to drink at a still fountain, lest, in its peaceful bosom, he should be affrighted by himself. This was what gave plausibility to the whispers, that Mr. Hooper's conscience tortured him for some great crime too horrible to be entirely concealed, or otherwise than so obscurely intimated. Thus, from beneath the black veil, there rolled a cloud into the sunshine, an ambiguity of sin or sorrow, which enveloped the poor minister, so that love or sympathy could never reach him. It was said that ghost and fiend consorted with him there. With self-shudderings and outward terrors, he walked continually in its shadow, groping

---

8. bugbear *n.*: Something causing needless fear.

9. preternatural (prēt′ ər naċh′ ər əl) *adj.*: Supernatural.

darkly within his own soul or gazing through a medium that saddened the whole world. Even the lawless wind, it was believed, respected his dreadful secret, and never blew aside the veil. But still good Mr. Hooper sadly smiled at the pale visages of the worldly throng as he passed by.

Among all its bad influences, the black veil had the one desirable effect, of making its wearer a very efficient clergyman. By the aid of his mysterious emblem—for there was no other apparent cause—he became a man of awful power over souls that were in agony for sin. His converts always regarded him with a dread peculiar to themselves, affirming, though but figuratively, that, before he brought them to celestial light, they had been with him behind the black veil. Its gloom, indeed, enabled him to sympathize with all dark affections. Dying sinners cried aloud for Mr. Hooper, and would not yield their breath till he appeared; though ever, as he stooped to whisper consolation, they shuddered at the veiled face so near their own. Such were the terrors of the black veil, even when Death had bared his visage! Strangers came long distances to attend service at his church, with the mere idle purpose of gazing at his figure, because it was forbidden them to behold his face. But many were made to quake ere they departed! Once, during Governor Belcher's[10] administration, Mr. Hooper was appointed to preach the election sermon. Covered with his black veil, he stood before the chief magistrate, the council, and the representatives, and wrought so deep an impression that the legislative measures of that year were characterized by all the gloom and piety of our earliest ancestral sway.

In this manner Mr. Hooper spent a long life, irreproachable in outward act, yet shrouded in dismal suspicions; kind and loving, though unloved, and dimly feared; a man apart from men, shunned in their health and joy, but ever summoned to their aid in mortal anguish. As years wore on, shedding their snows above his sable veil, he acquired a name throughout the New England churches, and they called him Father Hooper. Nearly all his parishioners, who were of mature age when he was settled, had been borne away by many a funeral: he had one congregation in the church, and a more crowded one in the churchyard; and having wrought so late into the evening, and done his work so well, it was now good Father Hooper's turn to rest.

Several persons were visible by the shaded candlelight, in the death chamber of the old clergyman. Natural connections[11] he had none. But there was the decorously grave, though unmoved physician, seeking only to mitigate the last pangs of the patient whom he could not save. There were the deacons, and other eminently pious members of his church. There, also, was the Reverend Mr. Clark, of Westbury, a young and zealous divine, who had ridden in haste to pray by the bedside of the expiring minister. There was the nurse, no hired handmaiden of death, but one whose calm affection had endured thus long in secrecy, in solitude, amid the chill of age, and would not perish, even at the dying hour. Who, but Elizabeth! And there lay the hoary head of good Father Hooper upon the death pillow, with the black veil still swathed about his brow, and reaching down over his face, so that each more difficult gasp of his faint breath caused it to stir. All through life that piece of crape had hung between him and the world: it had separated him from cheerful brotherhood and woman's love, and kept him in that saddest of all prisons, his own heart; and still it lay upon his face, as if to deepen the gloom of his darksome chamber, and shade him from the sunshine of eternity.

For some time previous, his mind had been confused, wavering doubtfully between the past and the present, and hovering forward, as it were, at intervals, into the indis-

---

10. **Governor Belcher:** Jonathan Belcher (1682–1757), the royal governor of the Massachusetts Bay Colony from 1730 through 1741.

---

11. **natural connections:** Relatives.

tinctness of the world to come. There had been feverish turns, which tossed him from side to side, and wore away what little strength he had. But in his most convulsive struggles, and in the wildest vagaries of his intellect, when no other thought retained its sober influence, he still showed an awful solicitude lest the black veil should slip aside. Even if his bewildered soul could have forgotten, there was a faithful woman at his pillow, who, with averted eyes, would have covered that aged face, which she had last beheld in the comeliness of manhood. At length the death-stricken old man lay quietly in the torpor of mental and bodily exhaustion, with an imperceptible pulse, and breath that grew fainter and fainter, except when a long, deep, and irregular inspiration seemed to prelude the flight of his spirit.

The minister of Westbury approached the bedside.

"Venerable Father Hooper," said he, "the moment of your release is at hand. Are you ready for the lifting of the veil that shuts in time from eternity?"

Father Hooper at first replied merely by a feeble motion of his head; then, apprehensive, perhaps, that his meaning might be doubtful, he exerted himself to speak.

"Yea," said he, in faint accents, "my soul hath a patient weariness until that veil be lifted."

"And is it fitting," resumed the Reverend Mr. Clark, "that a man so given to prayer, of such a blameless example, holy in deed and thought, so far as mortal judgment may pronounce; is it fitting that a father in the church should leave a shadow on his memory, that may seem to blacken a life so pure? I pray you, my venerable brother, let not this thing be! Suffer us to be gladdened by your triumphant aspect as you go to your reward. Before the veil of eternity be lifted, let me cast aside this black veil from your face!"

And thus speaking, the Reverend Mr. Clark bent forward to reveal the mystery of so many years. But, exerting a sudden energy, that made all the beholders stand aghast, Father Hooper snatched both his hands from beneath the bedclothes, and pressed them strongly on the black veil, resolute to struggle, if the minister of Westbury would contend with a dying man.

"Never!" cried the veiled clergyman. "On earth, never!"

"Dark old man!" exclaimed the affrighted minister, "with what horrible crime upon your soul are you now passing to the judgment?"

Father Hooper's breath heaved; it rattled in his throat; but, with a mighty effort, grasping forward with his hands, he caught hold of life, and held it back till he should speak. He even raised himself in bed; and there he sat, shivering with the arms of death around him, while the black veil hung down, awful, at that last moment, in the gathered terrors of a lifetime. And yet the faint, sad smile, so often there, now seemed to glimmer from its obscurity, and linger on Father Hooper's lips.

"Why do you tremble at me alone?" cried he, turning his veiled face round the circle of pale spectators. "Tremble also at each other! Have men avoided me, and women shown no pity, and children screamed and fled, only for my black veil? What, but the mystery which it obscurely typifies, has made this piece of crape so awful? When the friend shows his inmost heart to his friend; the lover to his best beloved; when man does not vainly shrink from the eye of his Creator, loathsomely treasuring up the secret of his sin; then deem me a monster, for the symbol beneath which I have lived, and die! I look around me, and, lo! on every visage a Black Veil!"

While his auditors shrank from one another, in mutual affright, Father Hooper fell back upon his pillow, a veiled corpse, with a faint smile lingering on the lips. Still veiled, they laid him in his coffin, and a veiled corpse they bore him to the grave. The grass of many years has sprung up and withered on that grave, the burial stone is moss-grown, and good Mr. Hooper's face is dust; but awful is still the thought that it moldered beneath the Black Veil!

RESPONDING TO THE SELECTION

Your Response

1. If you were a member of Mr. Hooper's congregation, how do you think you might have reacted to his black veil?
2. What lesson could you learn from this parable?

Recalling

3. How do the parishioners initially react to the minister's black veil?
4. (a) What is different about Parson Hooper's sermon on the first day he wears the veil? (b) What is the subject of the sermon?
5. How does Elizabeth react when Parson Hooper refuses to remove the veil?
6. What is its "one desirable effect"?
7. (a) What happens when Reverend Clark tries to remove the veil? (b) What does Parson Hooper suggest makes the veil so awful?

Interpreting

8. (a) How does the veil affect Parson Hooper's perception of the world? (b) In what way does it isolate him? (c) Why does it make him a more effective minister?
9. What does Parson Hooper mean when he tells Elizabeth, "There is an hour to come . . . when all of us shall cast aside our veils"?
10. (a) Why does the black veil have such a powerful effect on people? (b) What do you think it represents?
11. Why do you think Hawthorne chooses not to reveal the reason that Parson Hooper begins wearing the veil?

Applying

12. Hawthorne suggests that all people have certain secrets that they choose not to reveal to anyone. Explain why you either do or do not agree with this suggestion.

ANALYZING LITERATURE

Understanding Anti-Transcendentalism

In "The Minister's Black Veil" Hawthorne conveys a dark vision of the world that is characteristic of **Anti-Transcendentalist** writing.

1. In what way does the story reflect the Anti-Transcendentalists' belief that people possess the potential for both good and evil?
2. The Anti-Transcendentalists believed that the truths of existence tend to be elusive and disturbing. What disturbing truth does Hawthorne convey through Parson Hooper and his black veil?
3. How does the parishioners' inability to grasp the meaning of Parson Hooper's veil reflect the Anti-Transcendentalists' belief in the elusiveness of truth?

CRITICAL THINKING AND READING

Recognizing the Author's Attitudes

Hawthorne had a gloomy vision that was possibly shaped by his awareness of the intolerance and cruelty of his Puritan ancestors. Therefore, he was unable to accept the optimistic views of the Transcendentalists.

Like a number of Hawthorne's other works, "The Minister's Black Veil" is set in Puritan New England. Judging from the story, do you think Hawthorne had a negative attitude toward the Puritans? Support your answer.

THINKING AND WRITING

Comparing and Contrasting Attitudes

Write an essay in which you compare and contrast the attitude toward human nature expressed in "The Minister's Black Veil" with the attitude expressed by the Transcendentalists. Start by reviewing the discussions of Transcendentalism and Anti-Transcendentalism on pages 239 and 267. Take note of the beliefs characterizing each movement. Then review "The Minister's Black Veil," noting the attitudes it expresses. Organize your notes by corresponding points of comparison and contrast. When you write your essay, make sure you support your argument with passages from the story. When you revise, make sure that you have clearly expressed the two attitudes being compared and contrasted.

HERMAN MELVILLE

1819–1891

Herman Melville is one of America's great novelists. Unfortunately, his work was never fully appreciated during his lifetime, and he lived a life that was often filled with frustration and despair.

Melville was born in New York City, the son of a wealthy merchant. His family's financial situation changed drastically in 1830, however, when his father's import business failed. Two years later his father died, leaving the family in debt. Forced to leave school, Melville spent the rest of his childhood working as a clerk, a farmhand, and a teacher to help support his family.

After becoming a sailor at the age of nineteen, Melville spent several years exploring the South Pacific. Working on a number of different whaling ships, he visited many exotic places and even spent several weeks living among natives in the Marquesas Islands. He did not return to the United States until 1844, after a brief period of service in the navy.

Using his adventures in the South Pacific as material for his novels, Melville started a new career as a writer. He quickly established himself as a popular writer with two successful novels, *Typee* (1846) and *Omoo* (1847), both set in the Pacific islands. His readers found his third novel, *Mardi* (1849), confusing, however, and his fame rapidly faded.

Using the profits from his novels, Melville bought a farm near Pittsfield, Massachusetts. He became a close friend of Nathaniel Hawthorne, who lived in a neighboring village. Encouraged by Hawthorne's interest and influenced by his reading of Shakespeare, Melville's work became more sophisticated.

In 1851 he published his masterpiece *Moby-Dick*, under the title *The Whale*. *Moby-Dick* is a novel with several layers of meaning. On the surface it is the story of the fateful voyage of a whaling ship. On another level, it is the story of a bitter man's quest for vengeance and search for truth. On still another level, it is a philosophical examination of humanity's relationship to the natural world.

Unable to appreciate the novel's depth, readers responded unfavorably to *Moby-Dick*. They also reacted negatively to Melville's next two novels, *Pierre* (1852) and *The Confidence Man* (1857). As a result, Melville fell into debt and was forced to accept a job as an inspector at the New York customshouse.

Disillusioned and bitter, Melville turned away from writing fiction during the latter part of his life. He produced only a handful of short stories and a powerful novella, *Billy Budd*. He died in 1891, unnoticed and unappreciated. In the 1920's, his work was rediscovered by scholars, and he finally received the recognition he deserved.

GUIDE FOR INTERPRETING

from Moby-Dick

Writers' Techniques

Symbolism. A symbol is a person, place, or thing that has a meaning in itself and also represents something larger than itself. For example a flag symbolizes the character, attitude, and values of a country.

While some symbols are easy to interpret, others are complex, having a number of possible meanings. The white whale in Melville's *Moby-Dick* is an example of an extremely complex symbol. Only by examining all of the meanings suggested by its appearance and behavior do we realize that the whale ultimately represents all that is paradoxical, unexplainable, and uncontrollable in nature. Like nature, Moby-Dick is massive and threatening but beautiful and awe-inspiring. Moby-Dick is nourishing and destructive, powerful and graceful. Moby-Dick is unpredictable and mindless, yet it is controlled by natural laws. Like nature, Moby-Dick seems indestructible and immortal and at the same time indifferent to human mortality.

Another quality that contributes to the whale's symbolism is its color. Like the other aspects of the whale's appearance, its whiteness conveys contradictions. It suggests purity and goodness but at the same time signifies emptiness and death. Because of the whale's blank whiteness, each crew member attaches a different meaning to the whale—just as each person attaches a different meaning to the mysteries of nature.

Focus

Determination is often considered a positive characteristic. Freewrite, exploring how it can also be a negative characteristic.

Primary Source

In *Melville and His World,* the biographer Gay Wilson Allen describes Melville's early sailing adventures on the whaling ship *Acushnet.* Then he continues:

> Throughout this trip, and even long before he had signed on the *Acushnet,* Melville frequently heard tall tales about a fabulous white whale variously known as 'Mocha Dick,' or 'Moby Dick.' In 1834 Emerson had heard of him as 'Old Tom, who rushed upon the boats which attacked him and crushed the boats to small chips in his jaws, the men generally escaping by jumping overboard and being picked up . . .'
>
> The monstrous albino whale with a scar on his head had already become a myth in whaling folklore before Melville began his voyage. But some of the stories of a whale chewing up rowboats, or ramming a whale ship, were based on fact. An English ship had such an experience in July 1840, and a Russian ship a month later.

from **Moby-Dick**

Herman Melville

Moby-Dick is the story of a man's obsession with the dangerous and mysterious white whale that years before had taken off one of his legs. The man, Captain Ahab, guides the Pequod, a whaling ship, and its crew in relentless pursuit of this whale, Moby-Dick. Among the more important members of the crew are Starbuck, the first mate; Stubb, the second mate; Flask, the third mate; Queequeg, Tashtego, and Daggoo, the harpooners; and Ishmael, the young sailor who narrates the book.

In the following excerpt, Ishmael and Queequeg sample some famous chowder before their voyage.

Chowder

It was quite late in the evening when the little Moss came snugly to anchor, and Queequeg and I went ashore; so we could attend to no business that day, at least none but a supper and a bed. The landlord of the Spouter Inn had recommended us to his cousin Hosea Hussey of the Try Pots, whom he asserted to be the proprietor of one of the best kept hotels in all Nantucket,[1] and moreover he had assured us that Cousin Hosea, as he called him, was famous for his chowders. In short, he plainly hinted that we could not possibly do better than try potluck at the Try Pots. But the directions he had given us about keeping a yellow warehouse on our starboard[2] hand till we opened a white church to the larboard, and then keeping that on the larboard hand till we made a corner three points to the starboard, and

that done, then ask the first man we met where the place was; these crooked directions of his very much puzzled us at first, especially as, at the outset, Queequeg insisted that the yellow warehouse—our first point of departure—must be left on the larboard hand, whereas I had understood Peter Coffin to say it was on the starboard. However, by dint of beating about a little in the dark, and now and then knocking up a peaceful inhabitant to inquire the way, we at last came to something which there was no mistaking.

Two enormous wooden pots painted black, and suspended by ass's ears, swung from the crosstrees of an old topmast, planted in front of an old doorway. The horns of the crosstrees were sawed off on the other side, so that this old topmast looked not a little like a gallows. Perhaps I was oversensitive to such impressions at the time, but I could not help staring at this gallows with a vague misgiving. A sort of crick was in my neck as I gazed up to the two remaining horns; yes, *two* of them, one for Queequeg, and one for me. It's ominous, thinks I.

---

1. Nantucket (nan tuk′ it): An island off the coast of Massachusetts.
2. Starboard *adj.*: The right-hand side of a ship. Larboard refers to the left-hand side.

A coffin my innkeeper upon landing in my first whaling port; tombstones staring at me in the whalemen's chapel; and here a gallows! and a pair of prodigious black pots too! Are these last throwing out oblique hints touching Tophet?[3]

I was called from these reflections by the sight of a freckled woman with yellow hair and a yellow gown, standing in the porch of the inn, under a dull red lamp swinging there, that looked much like an injured eye, and carrying on a brisk scolding with a man in a purple woolen shirt.

"Get along with ye," said she to the man, "or I'll be combing ye!"

"Come on, Queequeg," said I, "all right. There's Mrs. Hussey."

And so it turned out; Mr. Hosea Hussey being from home, but leaving Mrs. Hussey entirely competent to attend to all his affairs. Upon making known our desires for a supper and a bed, Mrs. Hussey, postponing further scolding for the present, ushered us into a little room, and seating us at a table spread with the relics of a recently concluded repast, turned round to us and said "clam or cod?"

"What's that about cods, ma'am?" said I, with much politeness.

---

3. **Tophet** (tō' fĭt): Hell.

"Clam or cod?" she repeated.

"A clam for supper? a cold clam; is *that* what you mean, Mrs. Hussey?" says I! "but that's a rather cold and clammy reception in the winter time, ain't it, Mrs. Hussey?"

But being in a great hurry to resume scolding the man in the purple shirt who was waiting for it in the entry, and seeming to hear nothing but the word "clam," Mrs. Hussey hurried towards an open door leading to the kitchen, and bawling out "clam for two," disappeared.

"Queequeg," said I, "do you think that we can make a supper for us both on one clam?"

However, a warm savory steam from the kitchen served to belie[4] the apparently cheerless prospect before us. But when that smoking chowder came in, the mystery was delightfully explained. Oh! sweet friends, hearken to me. It was made of small juicy clams, scarcely bigger than hazel nuts, mixed with pounded ship biscuits, and salted pork cut up into little flakes! The whole enriched with butter, and plentifully seasoned with pepper and salt. Our appetites being sharpened by the frosty voyage, and in particular, Queequeg seeing his favorite fishing food before him, and the chowder being surpassingly excellent, we dispatched it with great expedition: when leaning back a moment and bethinking me of Mrs. Hussey's clam and cod announcement, I thought I would try a little experiment. Stepping to the kitchen door, I uttered the word "cod" with great emphasis, and resumed my seat. In a few moments the savory steam came forth again, but with a different flavor, and in good time a fine cod chowder was placed before us.

We resumed business; and while plying our spoons in the bowl, thinks I to myself, I wonder now if this here has any effect on the head? What's that stultifying saying about chowder-headed people? "But look, Quee-queg, ain't that a live eel in your bowl? Where's your harpoon?"

Fishiest of all fishy places was the Try Pots, which well deserved its name; for the pots there were always boiling chowders. Chowder for breakfast, and chowder for dinner, and chowder for supper, till you began to look for fish bones coming through your clothes. The area before the house was paved with clam shells. Mrs. Hussey wore a polished necklace of codfish vertebra; and Hosea Hussey had his account books bound in superior and old shark-skin. There was a fishy flavor to the milk, too, which I could not at all account for, till one morning happening to take a stroll along the beach among some fishermen's boats, I saw Hosea's brindled[5] cow feeding on fish remnants, and marching along the sand with each foot in a cod's decapitated head, looking very slipshod, I assure ye.

Supper concluded, we received a lamp, and directions from Mrs. Hussey concerning the nearest way to bed; but, as Queequeg was about to precede me up the stairs, the lady reached forth her arm, and demanded his harpoon; she allowed no harpoon in her chambers. "Why not?" said I; "every true whaleman sleeps with his harpoon—but why not?" "Because it's dangerous," says she. "Ever since young Stiggs coming from that unfort'nt v'y'ge of his, when he was gone four years and a half, with only three barrels of *ile*,[6] was found dead in my first floor back, with his harpoon in his side; ever since then I allow no boarders to take sich dangerous weepons in their rooms at night. So, Mr. Queequeg" (for she had learned his name), "I will just take this here iron, and keep it for you till morning. But the chowder; clam or cod tomorrow for breakfast, men?"

"Both," says I, "and let's have a couple of smoked herring by way of variety."

---

4. belie (bi li´) *v.*: Prove false.

5. brindled (brin´ d'ld) *adj.*: Having a gray or tawny coat with streaks of darker color.
6. ile (ile): Oil.

When the crew signed aboard the Pequod, the voyage was to be nothing more than a business venture. However, early in the voyage, Ahab makes clear to the crew that his purpose is to seek revenge against Moby-Dick.

from The Quarter-Deck

One morning shortly after breakfast, Ahab, as was his wont, ascended the cabin gangway to the deck. There most sea captains usually walk at that hour, as country gentlemen, after the same meal, take a few turns in the garden.

Soon his steady, ivory stride was heard, as to and fro he paced his old rounds, upon planks so familiar to his tread, that they were all over dented, like geological stones, with the peculiar mark of his walk. Did you fixedly gaze, too, upon that ribbed and dented brow; there also, you would see still stranger footprints—the footprints of his one unsleeping, ever-pacing thought.

But on the occasion in question, those dents looked deeper, even as his nervous step that morning left a deeper mark. And, so full of his thought was Ahab, that at every uniform turn that he made, now at the mainmast and now at the binnacle,[7] you could almost see that thought turn in him as he turned, and pace in him as he paced; so completely possessing him, indeed, that it all but seemed the inward mold of every outer movement.

"D'ye mark him, Flask?" whispered Stubb; "the chick that's in him pecks the shell. 'Twill soon be out."

The hours wore on—Ahab now shut up within his cabin; anon, pacing the deck, with the same intense bigotry of purpose[8] in his aspect.

It drew near the close of day. Suddenly he came to a halt by the bulwarks, and inserting his bone leg into the auger hole there, and with one hand grasping a shroud, he ordered Starbuck to send everybody aft.

"Sir!" said the mate, astonished at an order seldom or never given on shipboard except in some extraordinary case.

"Send everybody aft," repeated Ahab. "Mastheads, there! come down!"

When the entire ship's company were assembled, and with curious and not wholly unapprehensive faces, were eyeing him, for he looked not unlike the weather horizon when a storm is coming up, Ahab, after rapidly glancing over the bulwarks, and then darting his eyes among the crew, started from his standpoint; and as though not a soul were nigh him resumed his heavy turns upon the deck. With bent head and half-slouched hat he continued to pace, unmindful of the wondering whispering among the men; till Stubb cautiously whispered to Flask, that Ahab must have summoned them there for the purpose of witnessing a pedestrian feat. But this did not last long. Vehemently pausing, he cried:

"What do ye do when ye see a whale, men?"

"Sing out for him!" was the impulsive rejoinder from a score of clubbed voices.

"Good!" cried Ahab, with a wild approval in his tones; observing the hearty animation into which his unexpected question had so magnetically thrown them.

"And what do ye next, men?"

"Lower away, and after him!"

"And what tune is it ye pull to, men?"

"A dead whale or a stove[9] boat!"

More and more strangely and fiercely glad and approving, grew the countenance of the old man at every shout; while the mariners began to gaze curiously at each other, as if marveling how it was that they them-

---

7. binnacle (bin' ə k'l) *n.*: The case enclosing the ship's compass.
8. bigotry of purpose: Complete singlemindedness.

9. stove: Broken, smashed.

selves became so excited at such seemingly purposeless questions.

But, they were all eagerness again, as Ahab, now half-revolving in his pivot hole, with one hand reaching high up a shroud,[10] and tightly, almost convulsively grasping it, addressed them thus:

"All ye mastheaders have before now heard me give orders about a white whale. Look ye! d'ye see this Spanish ounce of gold?"—holding up a broad bright coin to the sun—"it is a sixteen-dollar piece, men. D'ye see it? Mr. Starbuck, hand me yon topmaul."

While the mate was getting the hammer, Ahab, without speaking, was slowly rubbing the gold piece against the skirts of his jacket, as if to heighten its luster, and without using any words was meanwhile lowly humming to himself, producing a sound so strangely muffled and inarticulate that it seemed the mechanical humming of the wheels of his vitality in him.

Receiving the topmaul from Starbuck, he advanced towards the mainmast with the hammer uplifted in one hand, exhibiting the gold with the other, and with a high raised voice exclaiming: "Whosoever of ye raises me a white-headed whale with a wrinkled brow and a crooked jaw; whosoever of ye raises me that white-headed whale, with three holes punctured in his starboard fluke[11]—look ye,

---

10. **shroud** *n.*: A set of ropes from a ship's side to the masthead.

11. **starboard fluke** (flōōk) *n.*: The right half of a whale's tail.

whosoever of ye raises me that same white whale, he shall have this gold ounce, my boys!"

"Huzza! huzza!" cried the seamen, as with swinging tarpaulins they hailed the act of nailing the gold to the mast.

"It's a white whale, I say," resumed Ahab, as he threw down the topmaul: "a white whale. Skin your eyes for him, men; look sharp for white water; if ye see but a bubble, sing out."

All this while Tashtego, Daggoo, and Queequeg had looked on with even more intense interest and surprise than the rest, and at the mention of the wrinkled brow and crooked jaw they had started as if each was separately touched by some specific recollection.

"Captain Ahab," said Tashtego, "that white whale must be the same that some call Moby-Dick."

"Moby-Dick?" shouted Ahab. "Do ye know the white whale then, Tash?"

"Does he fantail[12] a little curious, sir, before he goes down?" said the Gay-Header deliberately.

"And has he a curious spout, too," said Daggoo, "very bushy, even for a parmacetty,[13] and mighty quick, Captain Ahab?"

"And he have one, two, tree—oh! good many iron in him hide, too, Captain," cried Queequeg disjointedly, "all twiske-tee betwisk, like him—him—" faltering hard for a word, and screwing his hand round and round as though uncorking a bottle—"like him—him——"

"Corkscrew!" cried Ahab, "aye, Queequeg, the harpoons lie all twisted and wrenched in him; aye, Daggoo, his spout is a big one, like a whole shock of wheat, and white as a pile of our Nantucket wool after the great annual sheepshearing; aye, Tashtego, and he fantails like a split jib in a

squall. Death and devils! men, it is Moby-Dick ye have seen—Moby-Dick—Moby-Dick!"

"Captain Ahab," said Starbuck, who, with Stubb and Flask, had thus far been eyeing his superior with increasing surprise, but at last seemed struck with a thought which somewhat explained all the wonder. "Captain Ahab, I have heard of Moby-Dick—but it was not Moby-Dick that took off thy leg?"

"Who told thee that?" cried Ahab; then pausing, "Aye, Starbuck; aye, my hearties all round; it was Moby-Dick that dismasted me; Moby-Dick that brought me to this dead stump I stand on now. Aye, aye," he shouted with a terrific, loud, animal sob, like that of a heart-stricken moose; "Aye, aye! it was that accursed white whale that razeed me; made a poor pegging lubber[14] for me forever and a day!" Then tossing both arms, with measureless imprecations he shouted out: "Aye, aye! and I'll chase him round Good Hope, and round the Horn, and round the Norway Maelstrom, and round perdition's flames before I give him up. And this is what ye have shipped for, men! to chase that white whale on both sides of land, and over all sides of earth, till he spouts black blood and rolls fin out. What say ye, men, will ye splice hands on it, now? I think ye do look brave."

"Aye, aye!" shouted the harpooneers and seamen, running closer to the excited old man: "A sharp eye for the white whale; a sharp lance for Moby-Dick!"

"God bless ye," he seemed to half sob and half shout. "God bless ye, men. Steward! go draw the great measure of grog. But what's this long face about, Mr. Starbuck; wilt thou not chase the white whale? art not game for Moby-Dick?"

"I am game for his crooked jaw, and for the jaws of Death too, Captain Ahab, if it fairly comes in the way of the business we follow; but I came here to hunt whales, not my commander's vengeance. How many bar-

---

12. fantail: To spread the tail like a fan.
13. parmacetty: Dialect for *spermaceti*, a waxy substance taken from a sperm whale's head and used to make candles.

---

14. lubber (lub′ ər) *n.*: A slow, clumsy person.

rels will thy vengeance yield thee even if thou gettest it, Captain Ahab? it will not fetch thee much in our Nantucket market."

"Nantucket market! Hoot! But come closer, Starbuck; thou requirest a little lower layer. If money's to be the measurer, man, and the accountants have computed their great countinghouse the globe, by girdling it with guineas, one to every three parts of an inch; then, let me tell thee, that my vengeance will fetch a great premium *here*!"

"He smites his chest," whispered Stubb, "what's that for? methinks it rings most vast, but hollow."

"Vengeance on a dumb brute!" cried Starbuck, "that simply smote thee from blindest instinct! Madness! To be enraged with a dumb thing, Captain Ahab, seems blasphemous."

"Hark ye yet again—the little lower layer. All visible objects, man, are but as pasteboard masks. But in each event—in the living act, the undoubted deed—there, some unknown but still reasoning thing puts forth the moldings of its features from behind the unreasoning mask. If man will strike, strike through the mask! How can the prisoner reach outside except by thrusting through the wall? To me, the white whale is that wall, shoved near to me. Sometimes I think there's naught beyond. But 'tis enough. He tasks me; he heaps me; I see in him outrageous strength, with an inscrutable malice sinewing it. That inscrutable thing is chiefly what I hate; and be the white whale agent, or be the white whale principal, I will wreak that hate upon him. Talk not to me of blasphemy, man; I'd strike the sun if it insulted me. For could the sun do that, then could I do the other; since there is ever a sort of fair play herein, jealousy presiding over all creations. But not my master, man, is even that fair play. Who's over me? Truth hath no confines. Take off thine eye! more intolerable than fiends' glarings is a doltish stare! So, so; thou reddenest and palest; my heat has melted thee to anger-glow. But look ye, Starbuck, what is said in heat, that thing unsays itself. There are men from whom warm words are small indignity. I meant not to incense thee. Let it go. Look! see yonder Turkish cheeks of spotted tawn—living, breathing pictures painted by the sun. The pagan leopards—the unrecking and unworshiping things, that live, and seek, and give no reasons for the torrid life they feel! The crew, man, the crew! Are they not one and all with Ahab, in this matter of the whale? See Stubb! he laughs! See yonder Chilean! he snorts to think of it. Stand up amid the general hurricane, thy one tossed sapling cannot, Starbuck! And what is it? Reckon it. 'Tis but to help strike a fin; no wondrous feat for Starbuck. What is it more? From this one poor hunt, then, the best lance out of all Nantucket, surely he will not hang back, when every foremasthand has clutched a whetstone. Ah! constrainings seize thee; I see! the billow lifts thee! Speak, but speak!— Aye, aye! thy silence, then, *that* voices thee. (*Aside*) Something shot from my dilated nostrils, he has inhaled it in his lungs. Starbuck now is mine; cannot oppose me now, without rebellion."

"God keep me!—keep us all!" murmured Starbuck, lowly.

But in his joy at the enchanted, tacit acquiescence of the mate, Ahab did not hear his foreboding invocation; nor yet the low laugh from the hold; nor yet the presaging vibrations of the winds in the cordage; nor yet the hollow flap of the sails against the masts, as for a moment their hearts sank in. For again Starbuck's downcast eyes lighted up with the stubbornness of life; the subterranean laugh died away; the winds blew on; the sails filled out; the ship heaved and rolled as before. Ah, ye admonitions and warnings! why stay ye not when ye come? But rather are ye predictions than warnings, ye shadows! Yet not so much predictions from without, as verifications of the foregoing things within. For with little external to constrain us, the innermost necessities in our being, these still drive us on.

"The measure! the measure!" cried Ahab.

Receiving the brimming pewter, and turning to the harpooneers, he ordered them to produce their weapons. Then ranging them before him near the capstan,[15] with their harpoons in their hands, while his three mates stood at his side with their lances, and the rest of the ship's company formed a circle round the group; he stood for an instant searchingly eyeing every man of his crew. But those wild eyes met his, as the bloodshot eyes of the prairie wolves meet the eye of their leader, ere he rushes on at their head in the trail of the bison; but, alas! only to fall into the hidden snare of the Indian.

"Drink and pass!" he cried, handing the heavy charged flagon to the nearest seamen. "The crew alone now drink. Round with it, round! Short drafts—long swallows, men; 'tis hot as Satan's hoof. So, so; it goes round excellently. It spiralizes in ye; forks out at the serpent-snapping eye. Well done; almost drained. That way it went, this way it comes. Hand it me—here's a hollow! Men, ye seem the years; so brimming life is gulped and gone. Steward, refill!

"Attend now, my braves. I have mustered ye all round this capstan; and ye mates, flank me with your lances; and ye harpooneers, stand there with your irons; and ye, stout mariners, ring me in, that I may in some sort revive a noble custom of my fishermen fathers before me. O men, you will yet see that— Ha! boy, come back? bad pennies come not sooner. Hand it me. Why, now, this pewter had run brimming again, wer't not thou St. Vitus' imp[16]—away, thou ague![17]

"Advance, ye mates! cross your lances full before me. Well done! Let me touch the axis." So saying, with extended arm, he grasped the three level, radiating lances at their crossed center; while so doing, sud-denly and nervously twitched them; meanwhile glancing intently from Starbuck to Stubb; from Stubb to Flask. It seemed as though, by some nameless, interior volition, he would fain have shocked into them the same fiery emotion accumulated within the Leyden jar[18] of his own magnetic life. The three mates quailed before his strong, sustained, and mystic aspect. Stubb and Flask looked sideways from him; the honest eye of Starbuck fell downright.

"In vain!' cried Ahab; "but, maybe, 'tis well. For did ye three but once take the full-forced shock, then mine own electric thing, *that* had perhaps expired from out me. Perchance, too, it would have dropped ye dead. Perchance ye need it not. Down lances! And now, ye mates, I do appoint ye three cup-bearers to my three pagan kinsmen there— yon three most honorable gentlemen and noblemen, my valiant harpooneers. Disdain the task? What, when the great Pope washes the feet of beggars, using his tiara for ewer? Oh, my sweet cardinals! your own condescension, *that* shall bend ye to it. I do not order ye; ye will it. Cut your seizings and draw the poles, ye harpooneers!"

Silently obeying the order, the three harpooneers now stood with the detached iron part of their harpoons, some three feet long, held, barbs up, before him.

"Stab me not with that keen steel! Cant them; cant them over! know ye not the goblet end? Turn up the socket! So, so; now, ye cup-bearers, advance. The irons! take them; hold them while I fill!" Forthwith, slowly going from one officer to the other, he brimmed the harpoon sockets with the fiery waters from the pewter.

"Now, three to three, ye stand. Commend the murderous chalices! Bestow them, ye who are now made parties to this indissoluble league. Ha! Starbuck! but the deed is

---

15. capstan (kap′ stən) *n.*: A large cylinder, turned by hand, around which cables are wound.
16. St. Vitus' imp: Offspring of St. Vitus. Saint Vitus is the patron saint of people stricken with the nervous disorder chorea, characterized by irregular, jerking movements.
17. ague (ā′ gyoo) *n.*: A chill or fit of shivering.

18. Leyden (līd′'n) **jar** *n.*: A glass jar coated inside and out with tinfoil with a metal rod passing through the lid and connected to the inner lining; used to store condensed static electricity.

done! Yon ratifying sun now waits to sit upon it. Drink, ye harpooneers! drink and swear, ye men that man the deathful whale-boat's bow— Death to Moby-Dick! God hunt us all, if we do not hunt Moby-Dick to his death!" The long, barbed steel goblets were lifted; and to cries and maledictions against the white whale, the spirits were simultaneously quaffed down with a hiss. Starbuck paled, and turned, and shivered. Once more, and finally, the replenished pewter went the rounds among the frantic crew; when, waving his free hand to them, they all dispersed; and Ahab retired within his cabin.

After Moby-Dick has been sighted in the Pacific Ocean, the Pequod's boats pursue the whale for two days. One of the boats has been sunk, and Ahab's ivory leg has been broken off. However, as the next day dawns, the chase continues.

The Chase–Third Day

The morning of the third day dawned fair and fresh, and once more the solitary night man at the foremasthead was relieved by crowds of the daylight lookouts, who dotted every mast and almost every spar.

"D'ye see him?" cried Ahab; but the whale was not yet in sight.

"In his infallible wake, though; but follow that wake, that's all. Helm there; steady, as thou goest, and hast been going. What a lovely day again! were it a new-made world, and made for a summerhouse to the angels, and this morning the first of its throwing open to them, a fairer day could not dawn upon that world. Here's food for thought, had Ahab time to think; but Ahab never thinks; he only feels, feels, feels; *that's* tingling enough for mortal man! to think's audacity. God only has that right and privilege. Thinking is, or ought to be, a coolness and a calmness; and our poor hearts throb, and our poor brains beat too much for that. And yet, I've sometimes thought my brain was very calm—frozen calm, this old skull cracks so, like a glass in which the contents turned to ice, and shiver it. And still this hair is growing now; this moment growing, and heat must breed it; but no, it's like that sort of common grass that will grow anywhere, between the earthy clefts of Greenland ice or in Vesuvius lava. How the wild winds blow it; they whip it about me as the torn shreds of split sails lash the tossed ship they cling to. A vile wind that has no doubt blown ere this through prison corridors and cells, and wards of hospitals, and ventilated them, and now comes blowing hither as innocent as fleeces.[19] Out upon it!—it's tainted. Were I the wind, I'd blow no more on such a wicked, miserable world. I'd crawl somewhere to a cave, and slink there. And yet, 'tis a noble and heroic thing, the wind! who ever conquered it? In every fight it has the last and bitterest blow. Run tilting at it, and you but run through it. Ha! a coward wind that strikes stark-naked men, but will not stand to receive a single blow. Even Ahab is a braver thing—a nobler thing than *that*. Would now the wind but had a body but all the things that most exasperate and outrage mortal man, all these things are bodiless, but only bodiless as objects, not as agents. There's a most special, a most cunning, oh, a most malicious difference! And yet, I say again, and swear it now, that there's something all glorious and gracious in the wind. These warm trade winds, at least, that in the clear heavens blow straight on, in strong and steadfast, vigorous mildness; and veer not from their mark, however the baser currents of the sea may turn and tack, and mightiest Mississippis of the land swift and swerve about, uncertain where to go at last. And by the eternal poles! these same trades that so directly blow my good ship on; these trades, or something like them—something so unchangeable, and full as strong, blow my keeled soul along! To it! Aloft there! What d'ye see?"

"Nothing, sir."

---

19. fleeces (flēs′ əz) *n*.: Sheep.

"Nothing! and noon at hand! The doubloon[20] goes a-begging! See the sun! Aye, aye, it must be so. I've oversailed him. How, got the start? Aye, he's chasing *me* now; not I, *him*—that's bad; I might have known it, too. Fool! the lines—the harpoons he's towing. Aye, aye, I have run him by last night. About! about! Come down, all of ye, but the regular lookouts! Man the braces!"

Steering as she had done, the wind had been somewhat on the *Pequod*'s quarter, so that now being pointed in the reverse direction, the braced ship sailed hard upon the breeze as she rechurned the cream in her own white wake.

"Against the wind he now steers for the open jaw," murmured Starbuck to himself, as he coiled the new-hauled main brace upon the rail. "God keep us, but already my bones feel damp within me, and from the inside wet my flesh. I misdoubt me that I disobey my God in obeying him!"

"Stand by to sway me up!" cried Ahab, advancing to the hempen basket.[21] "We should meet him soon."

"Aye, aye, sir," and straightway Starbuck did Ahab's bidding, and once more Ahab swung on high.

A whole hour now passed; gold-beaten out to ages. Time itself now held long breaths with keen suspense. But at last, some three points off the weather bow, Ahab descried the spout again, and instantly from the three mastheads three shrieks went up as if the tongues of fire had voiced it.

"Forehead to forehead I meet thee, this third time, Moby-Dick! On deck there!—brace sharper up; crowd her into the wind's eye. He's too far off to lower yet, Mr. Starbuck. The sails shake! Stand over that helmsman with a topmaul! So, so; he travels fast, and I must down. But let me have one more good round look aloft here at the sea; there's

time for that. An old, old sight, and yet somehow so young; aye, and not changed a wink since I first saw it, a boy, from the sand hills of Nantucket! The same!—the same!—the same to Noah as to me. There's a soft shower to leeward. Such lovely leewardings! They must lead somewhere—to something else than common land, more palmy than the palms. Leeward! the white whale goes that way; look to windward, then; the better if the bitterer quarter. But good-bye, good-bye, old masthead! What's this?—green? aye, tiny mosses in these warped cracks. No such green weather stains on Ahab's head! There's the difference now between man's old age and matter's. But aye, old mast, we both grow old together; sound in our hulls, though, are we not, my ship? Aye, minus a leg, that's all. By heaven this dead wood has the better of my live flesh every way. I can't compare with it; and I've known some ships made of dead trees outlast the lives of men made of the most vital stuff of vital fathers. What's that he said? he should still go before me, my pilot; and yet to be seen again? But where? Will I have eyes at the bottom of the sea, supposing I descend those endless stairs? and all night I've been sailing from him, wherever he did sink to. Aye, aye, like many more thou told'st direful truth as touching thyself, O Parsee; but, Ahab, there thy shot fell short. Good-bye, masthead—keep a good eye upon the whale, the while I'm gone. We'll talk tomorrow, nay, tonight, when the white whale lies down there, tied by head and tail."

He gave the word; and still gazing round him, was steadily lowered through the cloven blue air to the deck.

In due time the boats were lowered; but as standing in his shallop's stern, Ahab just hovered upon the point of the descent, he waved to the mate—who held one of the tackle ropes on deck—and bade him pause.

"Starbuck!"

"Sir?"

"For the third time my soul's ship starts upon this voyage, Starbuck."

---

20. doubloon (du bloon') *n.*: The gold coin Ahab offered as reward to the first man to spot the whale.
21. hempen basket: A rope basket constructed earlier by Ahab, in which he could be raised, by means of a pulley device, to the top of the mainmast.

"Aye, sir, thou wilt have it so."

"Some ships sail from their ports, and ever afterwards are missing, Starbuck!"

"Truth, sir: saddest truth."

"Some men die at ebb tide; some at low water; some at the full of the flood—and I feel now like a billow that's all one crested comb, Starbuck. I am old—shake hands with me, man."

Their hands met; their eyes fastened; Starbuck's tears the glue.

"Oh, my captain, my captain!—noble heart—go not—go not!—see, it's a brave man that weeps; how great the agony of the persuasion then!"

"Lower away!"—cried Ahab, tossing the mate's arm from him. "Stand by the crew!"

In an instant the boat was pulling round close under the stern.

"The sharks! the sharks!" cried a voice from the low cabin window there; "O master, my master, come back!"

But Ahab heard nothing; for his own voice was high-lifted then; and the boat leaped on.

Yet the voice spake true; for scarce had he pushed from the ship, when numbers of sharks, seemingly rising from out the dark waters beneath the hull, maliciously snapped at the blades of the oars, every time they dipped in the water; and in this way accompanied the boat with their bites. It is a thing not uncommonly happening to the whaleboats in those swarming seas; the sharks at times apparently following them in the same prescient way that vultures hover over the banners of marching regiments in the east. But these were the first sharks that had been observed by the *Pequod* since the White Whale had been first descried; and whether it was that Ahab's crew were all such tiger-yellow barbarians, and therefore their flesh more musky to the senses of the sharks—a matter sometimes well known to affect them—however it was, they seemed to follow that one boat without molesting the others.

"Heart of wrought steel!" murmured Starbuck gazing over the side, and following with his eyes the receding boat—"canst thou yet ring boldly to that sight?—lowering thy keel among ravening sharks, and followed by them, open-mouthed to the chase; and this the critical third day?—For when three days flow together in one continuous intense pursuit; be sure the first is the morning, the second the noon, and the third the evening and the end of that thing—be that end what it may. Oh! my God! what is this that shoots through me, and leaves me so deadly calm, yet expectant—fixed at the top of a shudder! Future things swim before me, as in empty outlines and skeletons; all the past is somehow grown dim. Mary, girl; thou fadest in pale glories behind me; boy! I seem to see but thy eyes grown wondrous blue.[22] Strangest problems of life seem clearing; but clouds sweep between—Is my journey's end coming? My legs feel faint; like his who has footed it all day. Feel thy heart—beats it yet? Stir thyself, Starbuck!—stave it off—move, move! speak aloud!—Masthead there! See ye my boy's hand on the hill?—Crazed—aloft there!—keep thy keenest eye upon the boats—mark well the whale!—Ho! again!—drive off that hawk! see! he pecks—he tears the vane"—pointing to the red flag flying at the maintruck—"Ha, he soars away with it!—Where's the old man now? see'st thou that sight, oh Ahab!—shudder, shudder!"

The boats had not gone very far, when by a signal from the mastheads—a downward pointed arm, Ahab knew that the whale had sounded; but intending to be near him at the next rising, he held on his way a little sideways from the vessel; the becharmed crew maintaining the profoundest silence, as the head-beat waves hammered and hammered against the opposing bow.

"Drive, drive in your nails, oh ye waves! to their uttermost heads drive them in! ye but strike a thing without a lid; and no coffin and no hearse can be mine:—and hemp only can kill me! Ha! ha!"

Suddenly the waters around them slowly

---

22. Mary . . . blue.: A reference to Starbuck's wife and son.

swelled in broad circles; then quickly up-heaved, as if sideways sliding from a submerged berg of ice, swiftly rising to the surface. A low rumbling sound was heard; a subterraneous hum; and then all held their breaths; as bedraggled with trailing ropes, and harpoons, and lances, a vast form shot lengthwise, but obliquely from the sea. Shrouded in a thin drooping veil of mist, it hovered for a moment in the rainbowed air; and then fell swamping back into the deep. Crushed thirty feet upwards, the waters flashed for an instant like heaps of fountains, then brokenly sank in a shower of flakes, leaving the circling surface creamed like new milk round the marble trunk of the whale.

"Give way!" cried Ahab to the oarsmen, and the boats darted forward to the attack; but maddened by yesterday's fresh irons that corroded in him, Moby-Dick seemed combinedly possessed by all the angels that fell from heaven. The wide tiers of welded tendons overspreading his broad white forehead, beneath the transparent skin, looked knitted together; as head on, he came churning his tail among the boats; and once more flailed them apart; spilling out the irons and lances from the two mates' boats, and dashing in one side of the upper part of their bows, but leaving Ahab's almost without a scar.

While Daggoo and Queequeg were stopping the strained planks; and as the whale swimming out from them, turned, and showed one entire flank as he shot by them again; at that moment a quick cry went up. Lashed round and round to the fish's back; pinioned in the turns upon turns in which, during the past night, the whale had reeled the involutions of the lines around him, the half-torn body of the Parsee was seen; his sable raiment frayed to shreds; his distended eyes turned full upon old Ahab.

The harpoon dropped from his hand.

"Befooled, befooled!"—drawing in a long lean breath—"Aye, Parsee! I see thee again—Aye, and thou goest before; and this, *this* then is the hearse that thou didst promise.

But I hold thee to the last letter of thy word. Where is the second hearse? Away, mates, to the ship! those boats are useless now; repair them if ye can in time, and return to me; if not, Ahab is enough to die—Down, men! the first thing that but offers to jump from this boat I stand in, that thing I harpoon. Ye are not other men, but my arms and my legs; and so obey me—Where's the whale? gone down again?"

But he looked too nigh the boat; for as if bent upon escaping with the corpse he bore, and as if the particular place of the last encounter had been but a stage in his leeward voyage, Moby-Dick was now again steadily swimming forward; and had almost passed the ship—which thus far had been sailing in the contrary direction to him, though for the present her headway had been stopped. He seemed swimming with his utmost velocity, and now only intent upon pursuing his own straight path in the sea.

"Oh! Ahab," cried Starbuck, "not too late is it, even now, the third day, to desist. See! Moby-Dick seeks thee not. It is thou, thou, that madly seekest him!"

Setting sail to the rising wind, the lonely boat was swiftly impelled to leeward, by both oars and canvas. And at last when Ahab was sliding by the vessel, so near as plainly to distinguish Starbuck's face as he leaned over the rail, he hailed him to turn the vessel about, and follow him, not too swiftly, at a judicious interval. Glancing upwards he saw Tashtego, Queequeg, and Daggoo, eagerly mounting to the three mastheads; while the oarsmen were rocking in the two staved boats which had just been hoisted to the side, and were busily at work in repairing them. One after the other, through the portholes, as he sped, he also caught flying glimpses of Stubb and Flask, busying themselves on deck among bundles of new irons and lances. As he saw all this; as he heard the hammers in the broken boats; far other hammers seemed driving a nail into his heart. But he rallied. And now marking that the vane or flag was gone from the main masthead, he shouted to Tashtego, who had just gained that perch, to descend again for another flag, and a hammer and nails, and so nail it to the mast.

Whether fagged by the three days' running chase, and the resistance to his swimming in the knotted hamper he bore; or whether it was some latent deceitfulness and malice in him: whichever was true, the White Whale's way now began to abate, as it seemed, from the boat so rapidly nearing him once more; though indeed the whale's last start had not been so long a one as before. And still as Ahab glided over the waves the unpitying sharks accompanied him; and so pertinaciously stuck to the boat; and so continually bit at the plying oars, that the blades became jagged and crunched, and left small splinters in the sea, at almost every dip.

"Heed them not! those teeth but give new rowlocks to your oars. Pull on! 'tis the better rest, the sharks' jaw than the yielding water."

"But at every bite, sir, the thin blades grow smaller and smaller!"

"They will last long enough! pull on!—But who can tell"—he muttered—"whether these sharks swim to feast on the whale or on Ahab?—But pull on! Aye, all alive, now—we near him. The helm! take the helm! let me pass"—and so saying, two of the oarsmen helped him forward to the bows of the still flying boat.

At length as the craft was cast to one side, and ran ranging along with the White Whale's flank, he seemed strangely oblivious of its advance—as the whale sometimes will—and Ahab was fairly within the smoky mountain mist, which, thrown off from the whale's spout, curled round his great Monadnock[23] hump; he was even thus close to him; when, with body arched back, and both arms lengthwise high-lifted to the poise, he darted his fierce iron, and his far fiercer curse into the hated whale. As both steel and

curse sank to the socket, as if sucked into a morass, Moby-Dick sidewise writhed; spasmodically rolled his nigh flank against the bow, and, without staving a hole in it, so suddenly canted the boat over, that had it not been for the elevated part of the gunwale to which he then clung, Ahab would once more have been tossed into the sea. As it was, three of the oarsmen—who foreknew not the precise instant of the dart, and were therefore unprepared for its effects—these were flung out; but so fell, that, in an instant two of them clutched the gunwale again, and rising to its level on a combing wave, hurled themselves bodily inboard again; the third man helplessly dropping astern, but still afloat and swimming.

Almost simultaneously, with a mighty volition of ungraduated, instantaneous swiftness, the White Whale darted through the weltering sea. But when Ahab cried out to the steersman to take new turns with the line, and hold it so; and commanded the crew to turn round on their seats, and tow the boat up to the mark; the moment the treacherous line felt that double strain and tug, it snapped in the empty air!

"What breaks in me? Some sinew cracks!—'tis whole again; oars! oars! Burst in upon him!"

Hearing the tremendous rush of the sea-crashing boat, the whale wheeled round to present his blank forehead at bay; but in that evolution, catching sight of the nearing black hull of the ship; seemingly seeing in it the source of all his persecutions; bethinking it—it may be—a larger and nobler foe; of a sudden, he bore down upon its advancing prow, smiting his jaws amid fiery showers of foam.

Ahab staggered; his hand smote his forehead. "I grow blind; hands! stretch out before me that I may yet grope my way. Is't night?"

"The whale! The ship!" cried the cringing oarsmen.

"Oars! oars! Slope downwards to thy depths, O sea that ere it be forever too late,

---

23. **Monadnock** (mə nad′ näk): A mountain in New Hampshire.

Ahab may slide this last, last time upon his mark! I see: the ship! the ship! Dash on, my men! will ye not save my ship?"

But as the oarsmen violently forced their boat through the sledge-hammering seas, the before whale-smitten bow-ends of two planks burst through, and in an instant almost, the temporarily disabled boat lay nearly level with the waves; its half-wading, splashing crew, trying hard to stop the gap and bale out the pouring water.

Meantime, for that one beholding instant, Tashtego's masthead hammer remained suspended in his hand; and the red flag, half wrapping him as with a plaid, then streamed itself straight out from him, as his own forward-flowing heart; while Starbuck and Stubb, standing upon the bowsprit beneath, caught sight of the down-coming monster just as soon as he.

"The whale, the whale! Up helm, up helm! Oh, all ye sweet powers of air, now hug me close! Let not Starbuck die, if die he must, in a woman's fainting fit. Up helm I say—ye fools, the jaw! the jaw! Is this the end of all my bursting prayers? all my life-long fidelities? Oh, Ahab, Ahab, lo, thy work. Steady! helmsman, steady. Nay, nay! Up helm again! He turns to meet us! Oh, his unappeasable brow drives on towards one, whose duty tells him he cannot depart. My God, stand by me now!"

from *Moby-Dick*   293

"Stand not by me, but stand under me, whoever you are that will now help Stubb; for Stubb, too, sticks here. I grin at thee, thou grinning whale! Who ever helped Stubb, or kept Stubb awake, but Stubb's own unwinking eye? And now poor Stubb goes to bed upon a mattress that is all too soft; would it were stuffed with brushwood! I grin at thee, thou grinning whale! Look ye, sun, moon, and stars! I call ye assassins of as good a fellow as ever spouted up his ghost. For all that, I would yet ring glasses with thee, would ye but hand the cup! Oh, oh! oh, oh! thou grinning whale, but there'll be plenty of gulping soon! Why fly ye not, O Ahab! For me, off shoes and jacket to it; let Stubb die in his drawers! A most moldy and oversalted death, though—cherries! cherries! cherries! Oh, Flask, for one red cherry ere we die!"

"Cherries? I only wish that we were where they grow. Oh, Stubb, I hope my poor mother's drawn my part-pay ere this; if not, few coppers will now come to her, for the voyage is up."

From the ship's bows, nearly all the seamen now hung inactive; hammers, bits of plank, lances, and harpoons, mechanically retained in their hands, just as they had darted from their various employments; all their enchanted eyes intent upon the whale, which from side to side strangely vibrating his predestinating head, sent a broad band of overspreading semicircular foam before him as he rushed. Retribution, swift vengeance, eternal malice were in his whole aspect, and spite of all that mortal man could do, the solid white buttress of his forehead smote the ship's starboard bow, till men and timbers reeled. Some fell flat upon their faces. Like dislodged trucks, the heads of the harpooneers aloft shook on their bull-like necks. Through the breach, they heard the waters pour, as mountain torrents down a flume.

"The ship! The hearse!—the second hearse!" cried Ahab from the boat; "its wood could only be American!"

Diving beneath the settling ship, the whale ran quivering along its keel; but turning under water, swiftly shot to the surface again, far off the other bow, but within a few yards of Ahab's boat, where, for a time, he lay quiescent.

"I turn my body from the sun. What ho, Tashtego! let me hear thy hammer. Oh! ye three unsurrendered spires of mine; thou uncracked keel; and only god-bullied hull; thou firm deck, and haughty helm, and Pole-pointed prow—death-glorious ship! must ye then perish, and without me? Am I cut off from the last fond pride of meanest shipwrecked captains? Oh, lonely death on lonely life! Oh, now I feel my topmost greatness lies in my topmost grief. Ho, ho! from all your furthest bounds, pour ye now in, ye bold billows of my whole foregone life, and top this one piled comber of my death! Towards thee I roll, thou all-destroying but unconquering whale; to the last I grapple with thee; from hell's heart I stab at thee; for hate's sake I spit my last breath at thee. Sink all coffins and all hearses to one common pool! and since neither can be mine, let me then tow to pieces, while still chasing thee, though tied to thee, thou damned whale! *Thus*, I give up the spear!"

The harpoon was darted; the stricken whale flew forward; with igniting velocity the line ran through the groove;—ran foul. Ahab stooped to clear it; he did clear it; but the flying turn caught him round the neck, and voicelessly as Turkish mutes bowstring their victim, he was shot out of the boat, ere the crew knew he was gone. Next instant, the heavy eye splice in the rope's final end flew out of the stark-empty tub, knocked down an oarsman, and smiting the sea, disappeared in its depths.

For an instant, the tranced boat's crew stood still; then turned. "The ship? Great God, where is the ship?" Soon they through dim, bewildering mediums saw her sidelong fading phantom, as in the gaseous fata morgana,[24] only the uppermost masts out of

---

24. fata morgana: A mirage seen at sea.

water; while fixed by infatuation, or fidelity, or fate, to their once lofty perches, the pagan harpooneers still maintained their sinking lookouts on the sea. And now, concentric circles seized the lone boat itself, and all its crew, and each floating oar, and every lance pole, and spinning, animate and inanimate, all round and round in one vortex, carried the smallest chip of the *Pequod* out of sight.

But as the last whelmings intermixingly poured themselves over the sunken head of the Indian at the mainmast, leaving a few inches of the erect spar yet visible, together with long streaming yards of the flag, which calmly undulated, with ironical coincidings, over the destroying billows they almost touched—at that instant, a red arm and a hammer hovered backwardly uplifted in the open air, in the act of nailing the flag faster and yet faster to the subsiding spar. A sky hawk that tauntingly had followed the main-truck downwards from its natural home among the stars, pecking at the flag, and incommoding Tashtego there: this bird now chanced to intercept its broad fluttering wing between the hammer and the wood; and simultaneously feeling that ethereal thrill, the submerged savage beneath, in his deathgasp, kept his hammer frozen there; and so the bird of heaven, with archangelic shrieks, and his imperial beak thrust upwards, and his whole captive form folded in the flag of Ahab, went down with his ship, which, like Satan, would not sink to hell till she had dragged a living part of heaven along with her, and helmeted herself with it.

Now small fowls flew screaming over the yet yawning gulf; a sullen white surf beat against its steep sides; then all collapsed, and the great shroud of the sea rolled on as it rolled five thousand years ago.

▌RESPONDING TO THE SELECTION

Your Response

1. What is your impression of Captain Ahab? Do you admire, despise, or pity him? Explain.
2. How do you feel about the fate of Ahab and his crew? Explain.

Recalling

3. What makes the narrator feel uncomfortable at the entrance to the Try Pots?
4. (a) What does Ahab offer to the man who spots Moby-Dick? (b) How do the men respond to his offer?
5. (a) Why is Ahab obsessed with killing Moby-Dick? (b) How does Starbuck interpret Ahab's obsession?
6. (a) What does Ahab tell Starbuck just before his whaleboat is lowered into the water? (b) What follows Ahab's boat as it pulls away from the ship?
7. (a) What happens to Ahab at the end of the novel? (b) What happens to Moby-Dick? (c) What happens to the *Pequod*?

Interpreting

8. How does the narrator's impression of the entrance to the Try Pots foreshadow the outcome of the novel?
9. (a) What does Ahab's obsession with Moby-Dick reveal about his character? (b) In what ways is Starbuck different from Ahab? (c) Why does Starbuck obey Ahab even though he disagrees with him? (d) Why does the rest of the crew join Ahab without hesitation in his quest?
10. On the morning of the third day of the chase, Ahab comments, "Thinking is, or ought to be, a coolness and a calmness; and our poor hearts throb, and our brains beat too much for that." (a) How does this comment apply to Ahab's behavior? (b) How does it apply to the crew?
11. (a) What do Ahab's comments about the wind (page 288) at the beginning of "The Chase—Third Day" indicate about his attitude toward nature? (b) How has his obsession with Moby-Dick shaped his attitude?
12. (a) What omens appear as Ahab's whaleboat

pulls away from the ship? When Moby-Dick surfaces? (b) How does Ahab respond to these omens?

13. What is the significance of the fact that Moby-Dick seems "strangely oblivious" to the advance of Ahab's boat?

14. What does the final paragraph indicate about the relationship between humanity and nature?

Applying

15. In his speech at the beginning of "The Chase—Third Day," Ahab expresses his belief that people are guided by instinct and intuition rather than reason. React to Ahab's view.

16. (a) How can obsession with achieving a goal affect a person's ability to reach that goal? (b) What types of goals do you think many people are obsessed with reaching in today's world?

ANALYZING LITERATURE

Recognizing a Symbol

A **symbol** is a person, place, or thing that has a meaning in itself and also represents something larger than itself. For example, the crew of the *Pequod,* which includes representatives from many of the world's races and cultures, symbolizes humanity.

1. Given the fact that the crew of the *Pequod* symbolizes humanity, and Moby-Dick symbolizes everything in nature that is paradoxical, unexplainable, and uncontrollable, what do you think the voyage of the *Pequod* symbolizes?

2. Considering the symbolic meaning and the outcome of the journey, what do you think is the theme, or central idea, of the novel?

CRITICAL THINKING AND READING

Analyzing the Meaning of a Symbol

Analyzing Ahab's comments is one effective way to understand the meaning of Moby-Dick as a symbol.

Explain how the following passage from one of Ahab's speeches supports the interpretation of Moby-Dick as a symbol of the mysteries of existence.

"All visible objects, man, are but pasteboard masks. But in each event—in the living act, the undoubted deed—there, some unknown but still reasoning thing puts forth the moldings of its features from behind the unreasoning mask. If man will strike, strike through the mask! How can the prisoner reach outside except by thrusting through the wall? To me, the white whale is that wall, shoved near me."

THINKING AND WRITING

Writing About Symbolism and Theme

Write an essay in which you discuss how the theme, or central idea, of *Moby-Dick* is revealed through Melville's use of symbolism. Start by re-reading the excerpt, noting passages in which the meaning of any of the primary symbols in the novel is suggested. Define the meaning of each symbol in your own words. Prepare a chart showing the relationship between the symbols and the theme. Write a thesis statement. Then write your essay. Include enough passages from the novel to support your thesis. When you revise, make sure that your ideas are well-organized and clearly stated.

LEARNING OPTIONS

1. **Writing.** Ishmael, the young sailor who narrates *Moby-Dick,* is the sole survivor of the ill-fated *Pequod.* Write the eulogy that he might have delivered at a memorial service for his shipmates. In your eulogy make special mention of Ishmael's friend Queequeg.

2. **Cross-curricular Connection.** Hunted for their meat, bones, and oil, several species of whales are endangered. Find out which species face possible extinction and what efforts are being made to save them. Present your findings in a brief oral or written report.

New England Poets

AFTER THE FIRST SNOW IN WINTER IN VERMONT
Charles Hughes

HENRY WADSWORTH LONGFELLOW

1807–1882

Henry Wadsworth Longfellow once wrote, "Music is the universal language of mankind—poetry their universal pastime and delight." During the latter half of the nineteenth century, Longfellow's poetry certainly was a "universal pastime and delight." His work, which was translated into two dozen foreign languages, was read and enjoyed by millions of readers throughout Europe and the United States.

Born in Portland, Maine, Longfellow attended Bowdoin College, where Nathaniel Hawthorne was one of his classmates. After graduating in 1825, Longfellow spent four years in Europe before returning to Bowdoin as a professor of modern languages. He taught at Bowdoin for five years. Then, after spending another year in Europe, he accepted a position at Harvard University in Cambridge, Massachusetts, which he held for eighteen years.

Longfellow suffered the tragic deaths of two wives. In 1831 when he was twenty-four and a professor at Bowdoin, he married Mary Potter, the attractive and educated daughter of a Portland judge. While traveling in Europe in 1835, Mary, already in delicate health and exhausted by the hardships of traveling, suffered a miscarriage and died of the resulting infection.

Eight years later, after a long courtship, Longfellow married Frances Appleton of Boston. It was an extremely happy but not a long marriage. In 1861 Frances was fatally burned in a household accident. Longfellow's attempts to put out the flames left him badly burned. He had always been cleanshaven, but now the scars on his face made it difficult, if not impossible, to shave. Thus resulted the portrait with the long flowing beard, once so familiar to generations of Americans.

During his years as a professor at Bowdoin and Harvard, Longfellow had a long and successful career as a poet, publishing his first collection of poems, *Voices of the Night,* in 1839. Writing poems that appealed to a general audience, Longfellow established himself as the most popular American poet of his time.

Recognizing the need to maintain a connection to the past, Longfellow found subjects for his poetry in American history. His narrative poems, such as *Evangeline* (1847), *The Song of Hiawatha* (1855), *The Courtship of Miles Standish* (1858), and "Paul Revere's Ride" (1861), gave readers a romanticized view of America during its infancy and expressed the democratic ideals of the young nation.

Longfellow's poetry has been criticized for being overly optimistic and sentimental; yet it was Longfellow's optimism that made him so popular. By writing poetry that soothed and encouraged readers, Longfellow became the first American poet to reach a wide audience and create a national interest in poetry.

GUIDE FOR INTERPRETING

The Tide Rises, The Tide Falls; A Psalm of Life; The Arsenal at Springfield

Writers' Techniques

Stanza Forms. A stanza is a unit of poetry consisting of two or more lines arranged in a pattern according to rhyme and meter, or rhythm. Like paragraphs in prose, stanzas organize ideas into units. Unlike paragraphs in prose, however, stanzas in a poem are generally of a fixed length and share the same pattern of rhyme and meter.

Stanza forms are described in terms of rhyme scheme and length. Rhyme scheme is indicated by assigning a different letter of the alphabet to each new rhyming sound in a stanza. For example, in a stanza in which every other line rhymes, the rhyme scheme is *abab*. Length is determined by the number of lines in a stanza. The following are common stanza lengths:

the couplet	(2 lines)
the tercet	(3 lines)
the quatrain	(4 lines)
the cinquain	(5 lines)
the sestet	(6 lines)
the octave	(8 lines)

Focus

What do the ocean and the constant motion of the tide suggest to you? List the ideas you associate with the ocean and the rising and falling of the tide.

Primary Source

In his poems Longfellow returned again and again to the wooded shores and restless sea of his Maine childhood. In the following excerpts from "My Lost Youth," written when he was forty-eight, he vividly describes Portland:

Often I think of the beautiful town
   That is seated by the sea;
Often in thought go up and down
The pleasant streets of that dear old town,
   And my youth comes back to me.
      . . .
I remember the black wharves and the slips,
   And the sea-tides tossing free;
And Spanish sailors with bearded lips,
And the beauty and mystery of the ships,
   And the magic of the sea.

The Tide Rises, The Tide Falls

Henry Wadsworth Longfellow

The tide rises, the tide falls,
The twilight darkens, the curlew[1] calls;
Along the sea sands damp and brown
The traveler hastens toward the town,
5   And the tide rises, the tide falls.

Darkness settles on roofs and walls,
But the sea, the sea in the darkness calls;
The little waves, with their soft, white hands,
Efface the footprints in the sands,
10   And the tide rises, the tide falls.

The morning breaks; the steeds in their stalls
Stamp and neigh, as the hostler[2] calls;
The day returns, but nevermore
Returns the traveler to the shore,
15   And the tide rises, the tide falls.

---

1. curlew (kʉr′ lōo) *n.*: A large, long-legged wading bird whose call is associated with the evening.
2. hostler (häs′ lər) *n.*: A person who tends horses at an inn or stable.

THE RETURN ALONE
Eugene Higgins
The Phillips Collection, Washington, D.C.

RESPONDING TO THE SELECTION

Your Response

1. How does this poem make you feel? Explain.

Recalling

2. What is the setting of the poem?
3. What do the "little waves" do in lines 8–9?
4. What happens in the third stanza?

Interpreting

5. (a) What details of the setting in the first stanza suggest that the traveler is nearing death? (b) What details in the second stanza suggest that the traveler has died?
6. What does the poem suggest about the relationship between humanity and nature?
7. (a) What is the effect of the refrain, or repeated line? (b) How does the rhythm of the refrain contribute to its meaning?
8. What do the details in lines 11–13 suggest about Longfellow's attitude toward death?

Applying

9. (a) What is the significance of the fact that Longfellow wrote "The Tide Rises, The Tide Falls" near the end of his life? (b) How might the poem have been different if he had written it earlier in life?

LEARNING OPTIONS

1. **Performance.** Writer Edgar Allan Poe described poetry as "music . . . combined with a pleasurable idea." Listen to the beat of "The Tide Rises, The Tide Falls" as you read it aloud to yourself. Then find or create a piece of music or choreograph a modern dance or ballet to accompany the poem. Try to capture the mood and the message of the poem in your musical interpretation or choreography. Play the music or perform the dance for classmates.
2. **Multicultural Activity.** In his 1845 anthology, *The Poets and Poetry of Europe,* Longfellow translated non-English poetry for American readers. Locate a copy of the anthology and choose a poem to share with classmates. Which poem might have inspired "The Tide Rises, The Tide Falls"?

Commentary

Longfellow was very influential, both as a teacher and a poet, in acquainting the American public with European literature. At the same time, he actively worked to establish an American literature equal to that of Europe.

While a student at Bowdoin, he showed great aptitude for languages. He began teaching at Bowdoin in 1829, leaving there in 1835 for a professorship at Harvard.

In the early years, he taught languages, writing and publishing his own textbooks since there were none available. At the same time, he was writing and publishing essays on European literature and prose sketches based on his travels in Europe. Firmly American in his point of view, he hoped to create a national literature by giving Americans their rich European heritage. His anthology, *The Poets and Poetry of Europe*, published in 1845, was very popular and accomplished his goal of bringing non-English poetry to the ordinary American reader. Longfellow himself supplied many of the translations.

Translation of foreign literature, especially poetry, was very important to him. For many years his translations greatly outnumbered his original poems. Although he began translating to provide materials for his college students, it is clear that he also found in the foreign poetry inspiration and models for his own work.

A Psalm of Life

Henry Wadsworth Longfellow

Tell me not, in mournful numbers,[1]
　　Life is but an empty dream!—
For the soul is dead that slumbers,
　　And things are not what they seem.

5　Life is real! Life is earnest!
　　And the grave is not its goal;
Dust thou art, to dust returnest,
　　Was not spoken of the soul.

Not enjoyment, and not sorrow,
10　　Is our destined end or way;
But to act, that each tomorrow
　　Find us farther than today.

Art is long, and Time is fleeting,
　　And our hearts, though stout and brave,
15　Still, like muffled drums, are beating
　　Funeral marches to the grave.

In the world's broad field of battle,
　　In the bivouac of Life,
Be not like dumb, driven cattle!
20　　Be a hero in the strife!

Trust no Future, howe'er pleasant!
　　Let the dead Past bury its dead!
Act—act in the living Present!
　　Heart within, and God o'erhead!

25　Lives of great men all remind us
　　We can make our lives sublime,
And, departing, leave behind us
　　Footprints on the sands of time;

Footprints, that perhaps another,
30　　Sailing o'er life's solemn main,[2]
A forlorn and shipwrecked brother,
　　Seeing, shall take heart again.

---

1. numbers: Verses.
2. main: The open sea.

Let us, then, be up and doing,
　　With a heart for any fate;
35　Still achieving, still pursuing,
　　Learn to labor and to wait.

RESPONDING TO THE SELECTION

Your Response
1. What "footprints" would you like to leave "on the sands of time"?
2. Would you like to meet the speaker of this poem? Why or why not?

Recalling
3. What opinion about life does the speaker express in line 5?
4. What comment concerning time does the speaker make in line 13?
5. (a) What advice does the speaker offer in the fifth stanza? (b) What advice does he offer in the sixth stanza?
6. According to the speaker, what can we learn from the "lives of great men"?
7. What advice is offered in the final stanza?

Interpreting
8. Summarize the speaker's view of life.
9. How would you describe the speaker's attitude concerning individuality and self-reliance?
10. How does the speaker think our lives can influence future generations?

Applying
11. Give your opinion of the speaker's view of life.

LEARNING OPTIONS

1. **Writing.** Can we leave behind us "footprints on the sands of time"? In a brief composition, contrast the views presented in "A Psalm of Life" and "The Tide Rises, The Tide Falls." Which view of life do you prefer? Explain.
2. **Cross-curricular Connection.** Find a piece of music that reflects the view of life expressed in "A Psalm of Life" and one that captures the view presented in "The Tide Rises, The Tide Falls." Bring in and share the two pieces. Discuss how each conveys the appropriate view and note the contrasts between the pieces.

The Arsenal at Springfield

Henry Wadsworth Longfellow

This is the Arsenal. From floor to ceiling,
    Like a huge organ, rise the burnished arms;
But from their silent pipes no anthem pealing
    Startles the villages with strange alarms.

5 Ah! what a sound will rise, how wild and dreary,
    When the death angel touches those swift keys!
What loud lament and dismal Miserere[1]
    Will mingle with their awful symphonies!

I hear even now the infinite fierce chorus,
10   The cries of agony, the endless groan,
Which, through the ages that have gone before us,
    In long reverberations reach our own.

On helm and harness rings the Saxon hammer,
    Through Cimbric[2] forest roars the Norseman's song,
15 And loud, amid the universal clamor,
    O'er distant deserts sounds the Tartar[3] gong.

I hear the Florentine, who from his palace
    Wheels out his battle bell with dreadful din,
And Aztec priests upon their teocallis[4]
20   Beat the wild war drums made of serpent's skin;

The tumult of each sacked and burning village;
    The shout that every prayer for mercy drowns;
The soldiers' revels in the midst of pillage;
    The wail of famine in beleaguered towns;

---

1. Miserere (miz′ ə rer′ ē): The 51st Psalm of the Bible (50th in the Douay Version) beginning, "Have mercy upon me, O God."
2. Cimbric (sim′ brik): Pertaining to Germanic people of central Europe who invaded Italy and were defeated by the Romans in 101 B.C.
3. Tartar: Refers to the Tartars, who ruled a region of Asia and eastern Europe in the thirteenth and fourteenth centuries.
4. teocallis (tē′ ə ka′ lis) n.: Ancient temples erected by Aztec Indians of Mexico and Central America.

25   The bursting shell, the gateway wrenched asunder,
       The rattling musketry, the clashing blade:
   And ever and anon, in tones of thunder
       The diapason of the cannonade.

   Is it, O man, with such discordant noises,
30   With such accursed instruments as these,
   Thou drownest Nature's sweet and kindly voices,
       And jarrest the celestial harmonies?

   Were half the power that fills the world with terror,
       Were half the wealth bestowed on camps and courts,
35   Given to redeem the human mind from error,
       There were no need of arsenals or forts:

   The warrior's name would be a name abhorrèd!
       And every nation, that should lift again
   Its hand against a brother, on its forehead
40   Would wear forevermore the curse of Cain!

   Down the dark future, through long generations,
       The echoing sounds grow fainter and then cease;
   And like a bell, with solemn, sweet vibrations,
       I hear once more the voice of Christ say, "Peace!"

45   Peace! and no longer from its brazen portals
       The blast of War's great organ shakes the skies!
   But beautiful as songs of the immortals,
       The holy melodies of love arise.

RESPONDING TO THE SELECTION

Your Response

1. What is your opinion about arms control? Did reading this poem affect the way you feel? Explain.

Recalling

2. To what does the speaker first compare the arms in the arsenal?

3. (a) What discordant sounds of war does the speaker hear? (b) What would he hear if there "were no need of arsenals or forts"?

Interpreting

4. What is the effect of the historical and cultural references in the poem?

5. What is the effect of the extended comparison between music and war?

6. How would you summarize the speaker's attitude toward war?

Applying

7. Explain whether you think the speaker's attitude toward war is realistic.

ANALYZING LITERATURE

Describing Stanza Forms

A **stanza** is a unit of poetry consisting of two or more lines arranged according to rhyme and meter. Describe the stanza form of the Longfellow poems you have read in terms of rhyme scheme and length.

OLIVER WENDELL HOLMES

1809–1894

An extraordinarily energetic man with a variety of talents and interests, Oliver Wendell Holmes made important contributions to both literature and medicine. In addition to serving as a professor of anatomy at Harvard University for thirty-five years and writing numerous professional articles, Holmes wrote three novels and several volumes of poems and essays.

Holmes, a descendant of seventeenth-century poet Anne Bradstreet (page 60), was born in Cambridge, Massachusetts. He attended Harvard University, where he was named class poet in 1829. Following his graduation Holmes entered Harvard Law School. While there, he wrote the poem "Old Ironsides" to protest the planned demolition of the battleship *Constitution,* nicknamed "Old Ironsides" because of its ability to withstand the attacks of British warships during the War of 1812. The poem, which aroused such protest that the ship was preserved as a national monument, earned Holmes national recognition as a poet.

After abandoning the study of law, Holmes studied medicine in Paris for several years. Then, in 1836, he returned to Harvard to complete his medical degree. In that same year Holmes also published his first collection of poetry, *Poems.*

In 1847 Holmes began his lengthy teaching career at Harvard. During his years there, he established himself as a leading medical researcher. At the same time, he continued his literary pursuits with energy and enthusiasm. Along with James Russell Lowell, Holmes helped to found the *Atlantic Monthly,* a literary magazine that is still published today. Holmes published many of his best-known works in the *Atlantic Monthly,* including his poem "The Chambered Nautilus" and a series of humorous essays eventually collected in *The Autocrat of the Breakfast-Table* (1858), his most popular book.

Holmes was known for his wise and witty conversation, which was preserved in *The Autocrat of the Breakfast-Table*. The Autocrat, the speaker in the essays, presides over the conversation among a variety of characters: a divinity student, the landlady, a Poor Relation, and later a School Teacher and two aspects of Holmes himself, the Poet and the Professor. The dramatic interplay among the various personalities provided a perfect excuse for humorous exaggeration, colorful expressions, and quotable quotes. Further essays were collected in *The Professor at the Breakfast-Table* (1860), *The Poet at the Breakfast-Table* (1872), and *Over the Teacups* (1891).

Retiring from medicine in 1882, Holmes devoted the final years of his life to writing and lecturing. He died in 1894, the last member of America's first generation of highly regarded writers.

GUIDE FOR INTERPRETING

Old Ironsides; The Chambered Nautilus

Writers' Techniques

Meter and Scansion. Meter is a systematic arrangement of stressed and unstressed syllables in poetry. The basic unit of meter is the foot. Usually a foot consists of one stressed syllable and one or more unstressed syllables. The most common foot in American and English verse is the iamb, which is made up of one unstressed syllable followed by a stressed syllable. Other common feet include the trochee, a stressed syllable followed by an unstressed syllable; the anapest, two unstressed syllables followed by a stressed syllable; and the dactyl, a stressed syllable followed by two unstressed syllables.

Meter is determined by combining the type of foot with the number of feet per line: monometer (one foot), dimeter (two feet), trimeter (three feet), tetrameter (four feet), pentameter (five feet), hexameter (six feet). For example, the following line from "The Chambered Nautilus" is written in iambic pentameter:

Its webs of living gauze no more unfurl;

Often, writers vary the number of feet per line in a poem. For example, a poet may alternate lines of iambic pentameter with lines of iambic trimeter. A poet may also introduce slight variations in the metrical pattern to avoid monotony or emphasize important words. For example, a poem written in iambic trimeter may contain several lines that end with two stressed syllables.

The analysis of the meter of poetry is called **scansion**. To scan a line of poetry, you divide it into feet and mark the stressed and unstressed syllables. You determine the meter by taking note of the type of foot being used and counting the number of feet in each line.

Commentary

Like the rhythm of music, the rhythm of poetry is caused by light and heavy beats, like the beating of a drum. The pattern, or meter, should be just regular enough to establish it but not become monotonous. When the poet wants to change the speed of a line or emphasize a word or phrase, he or she does it by altering the rhythm. The best way both to hear the rhythm and to understand a poem is to read it aloud— several times—as if you were saying it to someone. Try that with the following poems, using the punctuation to help with both rhythm and meaning. Do you ever use the rhythm of a sentence to persuade or command?

Focus

Holmes's poem "Old Ironsides" aroused strong public opinion about a current issue. Make a list of social and political issues about which you have strong opinions.

Guide for Interpreting 307

U.S. FRIGATE CONSTITUTION, 1823
Nicholas Cammilliri
The Mariner's Museum, Newport News, Virginia

Old Ironsides

Oliver Wendell Holmes

Ay, tear her tattered ensign down!
    Long has it waved on high,
And many an eye has danced to see
    That banner in the sky;
5 Beneath it rung the battle shout,
    And burst the cannons roar—
The meteor of the ocean air
    Shall sweep the clouds no more.

Her deck, once red with heroes' blood,
10   Where knelt the vanquished foe,
When winds were hurrying o'er the flood,
    And waves were white below,
No more shall feel the victor's tread,
    Or know the conquered knee—

15 The harpies[1] of the shore shall pluck
       The eagle of the sea!

   Oh, better that her shattered hulk
       Should sink beneath the wave;
   Her thunders shook the mighty deep,
20   And there should be her grave;
   Nail to the mast her holy flag,
       Set every threadbare sail,
   And give her to the god of storms,
       The lightning and the gale!

---

1. harpies (här′ pēz): In Greek mythology, hideous, filthy winged monsters with the head and trunk of a woman and the tail, legs, and talons of a bird. Here, the word refers to relentless, greedy, or grasping people.

■ RESPONDING TO THE SELECTION

Your Response

1. If you were alive in 1830, how would you have responded to Holmes's plea to save "Old Ironsides"? Explain.

Recalling

2. (a) In the first stanza, how does the speaker describe the ship's banner during battle? (b) What does he call the ship at the end of the second stanza?

3. What does the speaker suggest might be a more fitting end for the ship?

Interpreting

4. Consider what Holmes meant by referring to "Old Ironsides" as "the eagle of the sea." What did "Old Ironsides" seem to represent to him?

5. How does Holmes appeal in the poem to the American sense of patriotism?

Applying

6. When "Old Ironsides" was published, it aroused such protest that the ship was saved.

Do you believe that a poem could have such a powerful effect on the American public today? Why or why not?

■ THINKING AND WRITING

Writing a Poem in Support of a Cause

Review your list of social and political issues. Decide which issue is most important to you. List the reasons you feel so strongly about this issue. Think of some descriptive details that convey your feelings, and come up with some concrete images, or word pictures, related to the issue. Decide on the audience you would like to persuade to accept your opinion. Then use your list of details and images to write a poem expressing your opinion. Keep your audience in mind as you write. Do not worry about rhyme or rhythm. Focus on the content of your poem. When you revise, make sure that you have included enough concrete images to allow your audience to visualize your subject.

The Chambered Nautilus

Oliver Wendell Holmes

This is the ship of pearl, which, poets feign,
    Sails the unshadowed main—
    The venturous bark that flings
On the sweet summer wind its purpled wings
5 In gulfs enchanted, where the Siren[1] sings,
    And coral reefs lie bare,
Where the cold sea-maids rise to sun their streaming hair.

Its webs of living gauze no more unfurl;
    Wrecked is the ship of pearl!
10   And every chambered cell,
Where its dim dreaming life was wont to dwell,
As the frail tenant shaped his growing shell,
    Before thee lies revealed—
Its irised[2] ceiling rent, its sunless crypt unsealed!

---

1. Siren (sī′ rən): In Greek mythology, one of several sea nymphs
who lured sailors to their deaths by singing enchanting songs.
2. irised *adj.*: Rainbow colored.

15 Year after year beheld the silent toil
        That spread his lustrous coil;
        Still, as the spiral grew,
  He left the past year's dwelling for the new,
  Stole with soft step its shining archway through,
20   Built up its idle door,
  Stretched in his last-found home, and knew the old no more.

  Thanks for the heavenly message brought by thee,
        Child of the wandering sea,
        Cast from her lap, forlorn!
25 From thy dead lips a clearer note is born
  Than ever Triton[3] blew from wreathèd horn!
        While on mine ear it rings,
  Through the deep caves of thought I hear a voice that sings:

  Build thee more stately mansions, O my soul,
30   As the swift seasons roll!
        Leave thy low-vaulted past!
  Let each new temple, nobler than the last,
  Shut thee from heaven with a dome more vast,
        Till thou at length art free,
35 Leaving thine outgrown shell by life's unresting sea!

---

3. Triton (trīt' 'n) *n.*: A Greek sea god with the body of a man and
the tail of a fish, who usually carried a conch-shell trumpet.

RESPONDING TO THE SELECTION

Your Response

1. What do you think can be learned from observing the snail-like chambered nautilus?

Recalling

2. (a) What has happened to the nautilus the speaker is describing? (b) What did the nautilus do as "the spiral grew"?
3. What message does the nautilus bring?

Interpreting

4. Each year throughout the course of its life, the nautilus creates a new chamber of shell to house its growing body. How does Holmes compare this process to the development of the human soul?

Applying

5. What is it about the chambered nautilus that makes it appropriate for Holmes's message?
6. What can you learn from the life of the chambered nautilus?

ANALYZING LITERATURE

Using Meter and Scansion

    Meter is a systematic arrangement of stressed and unstressed syllables in poetry. **Scansion** is the process of analyzing meter.

1. Scan each line in the first stanza of "The Chambered Nautilus."
2. Identify the meter in each line.

JAMES RUSSELL LOWELL

1819–1891

James Russell Lowell may have been the most talented of the Fireside Poets. His literary career was disrupted by personal tragedies, however, and he was never able to fulfill his early promise as a poet. Still, Lowell did make many important contributions to the world of literature as a poet, editor, and critic.

Lowell was born in Cambridge, Massachusetts, the descendant of a prominent family. He graduated from Harvard Law School but quickly lost interest in practicing law. Instead, Lowell decided to pursue a career in literature, publishing his first book of poetry, *A Year's Life,* in 1841. While continuing to write poetry and essays, Lowell also supported the abolitionist movement. He frequently wrote editorials attacking slavery, thereby establishing himself as one of the country's leading abolitionist journalists.

In 1848 Lowell's literary career reached its peak. During that year he published three of his best works: *A Fable for Critics,* a satire of other American writers of his time; *The Biglow Papers,* a collection of poems and letters; and *The Vision of Sir Launfal,* an epic poem about medieval knighthood. All three works were very successful, earning him international fame.

These works, published when Lowell was only twenty-nine, demonstrate his varied interests. *The Vision of Sir Launfal* is the climax of his poetic romanticism. Inspired by the Arthurian legends, it teaches ethical lessons. For years it was regularly found in school texts. In *A Fable for Critics,* Lowell humorously criticizes his contemporaries, among them such established figures as Emerson and Hawthorne, and himself as well. In *The Biglow Papers* Lowell successfully used Yankee dialect and humor in a satire of American imperialism and Southern greed for slave territory.

Unfortunately, Lowell's literary success was overshadowed by tragic events in his personal life. Three of his four children died in infancy, and he lost his beloved wife, Maria, in 1853. Following Maria's death, Lowell lost his focus as a writer, and he found himself unable to produce poems or essays that matched his earlier work.

During the second half of his life, Lowell gradually turned away from writing toward other interests. In 1855 he succeeded Longfellow as professor of languages at Harvard, and he remained there until 1875. Lowell also helped to found the *Atlantic Monthly,* a respected literary magazine, and served as its first editor. Later Lowell became co-editor of the *North American Review,* another distinguished literary magazine. Then, in 1877, Lowell began a career in diplomacy, serving for a number of years as the American ambassador to Spain and, later, Great Britain.

GUIDE FOR INTERPRETING

Auspex; The First Snowfall

Tone. Tone refers to the writer's attitude toward his or her subject, characters, or audience. The tone of a work of literature is revealed through the writer's choice of words and portrayal of characters and events. For example, in a work with a humorous tone a writer might use witty language and include amusing descriptions of characters and events.

Tone can dramatically affect the way you respond to the subject and characters in a literary work. For example, if a writer expresses a sympathetic attitude toward a character, you are also likely to be sympathetic toward that character. In contrast, if the writer expresses contempt for a character, you are likely to have a negative response to that character.

Your awareness of tone can be important to your understanding of a literary work, because tone is often closely related to the theme, or central idea. For example, a work written to convey the cruelty and destructiveness of war is likely to have a solemn or despairing tone.

These two poems by Lowell deal with emotional reactions to some aspect of a season. People often have strong emotional reactions to the first snowstorm of each winter. Describe your typical response to a change of season—either the end of one or the beginning of another.

Lowell's early poetry ranks among the best America has. Although he did not develop this early promise in his later work, Lowell always felt himself to be more than anything else a poet. In a letter to a fellow journalist before beginning work on some Abolition writing, Lowell wrote: "If I have any vocation, it is the making of verse. When I take my pen for that, the world opens itself ungrudgingly before me, everything seems clear and easy, as it seems sinking to the bottom would be as one leans over the edge of his boat in one of those dear coves at Fresh Pond. But, when I do prose, . . . I feel as if I were wasting time and keeping back my message. My true place is to serve the cause as a poet. Then my heart leaps on before me into the conflict."

His engaging sincerity and earnestness are again evident when, in a critical essay, he later writes: ". . . all great poetry must smack of the soil, for it must be rooted in it, must suck life and substance from it, . . . but it must do so with the aspiring instinct of the pine that climbs forever toward diviner air, and not in the groveling fashion of the potato."

LOW BRANCH, 1968
Scarlett
Courtesy New York Graphic Society

Auspex[1]

James Russell Lowell

My heart, I cannot still it,
Nest that had song birds in it;
And when the last shall go,
The dreary days, to fill it,
5   Instead of lark or linnet,
Shall whirl dead leaves and snow.

Had they been swallows only,
Without the passion stronger
That skyward longs and sings—
10   Woe's me, I shall be lonely
When I can feel no longer
The impatience of their wings!

A moment, sweet delusion,
Like birds the brown leaves hover;
15   But it will not be long
Before their wild confusion
Fall wavering down to cover
The poet and his song.

---

1. Auspex (ôs´ peks) *n.*: In ancient Rome,
someone who watched for omens in the flight
of birds.

RESPONDING TO THE SELECTION

Your Response

1. How are you affected by changes of season? Between which seasons, if any, do you feel a sense of loss?
2. What do you associate with songbirds? With swallows? With autumn leaves? Why?

Recalling

3. What will take the place of the songbirds that nest in the speaker's heart?
4. What is the "sweet delusion" the speaker refers to in lines 13–14?

Interpreting

5. In this poem Lowell compares songbirds to poetry or poetic inspiration. What happens to the poet when the songbirds leave?
6. If larks and linnets represent poetry, what do swallows represent?
7. What does the image of the leaves falling and covering the poet suggest?
8. What statement do you think Lowell is making about poetry?

Applying

9. What type of event in Lowell's life might have prompted him to write this poem?

The First Snowfall

James Russell Lowell

The snow had begun in the gloaming,
    And busily all the night
Had been heaping field and highway
    With a silence deep and white.

5   Every pine and fir and hemlock
    Wore ermine too dear for an earl,
And the poorest twig on the elm tree
    Was ridged inch deep with pearl.

From sheds new-roofed with Carrara[1]
10   Came Chanticleer's[2] muffled crow,
The stiff rails softened to swan's-down,
    And still fluttered down the snow.

I stood and watched by the window
    The noiseless work of the sky,
15 And the sudden flurries of snowbirds,
    Like brown leaves whirling by.

I thought of a mound in sweet Auburn[3]
    Where a little headstone stood;
How the flakes were folding it gently,
20   As did robins the babes in the wood.

Up spoke our own little Mabel,
    Saying, "Father, who makes it snow?"
And I told of the good All-Father
    Who cares for us here below.

25 Again I looked at the snowfall,
    And thought of the leaden sky
That arched o'er our first great sorrow,
    When that mound was heaped so high.

---

1. Carrara (kə rä′ rə) *n.*: Fine, white marble.
2. Chanticleer's (chan′ tə klirz′): Referring to
a rooster.
3. Auburn: Mt. Auburn Cemetery in Cambridge,
Massachusetts.

I remembered the gradual patience
30   That fell from that cloud like snow,
     Flake by flake, healing and hiding
          The scar that renewed our woe.

     And again to the child I whispered,
          "The snow that husheth all,
35   Darling, the merciful Father
          Alone can make it fall!"

     Then, with eyes that saw not, I kissed her;
          And she, kissing back, could not know
     That *my* kiss was given to her sister,
40   Folded close under deepening snow.

RESPONDING TO THE SELECTION

Your Response
1. How does this poem make you feel? Explain.
2. What natural events trigger personal memories for you?

Recalling
3. Of what does the snowstorm make the speaker think?
4. (a) What question does the speaker's daughter ask him? (b) How does he respond at first? (c) What does he later add to his response?
5. What does the speaker's daughter not know when he kisses her?

Interpreting
6. (a) How does the speaker imply that "our first great sorrow" is the death of his daughter? (b) Why does the snowfall remind him of the death of his daughter?
7. To what does the speaker compare the process of recovering from his sorrow (lines 29–32)?
8. What does the speaker's comment to his daughter suggest about the source of emotional healing?
9. In your own words, describe the tone of "The First Snowfall."

Applying
10. This poem suggests that a natural event, such as a snowstorm, can both remind us of sorrow and help to heal it. Explain why you do or do not agree with this suggestion.

THINKING AND WRITING

Comparing and Contrasting Tones
Write an essay in which you compare and contrast the tones of "Auspex" and "The First Snowfall." Start by rereading the two poems, taking note of the similarities and differences in tone and the way in which the tone is revealed. Look over your notes and sum up the similarities and differences in a topic sentence. Then write your essay, using passages from each poem for support. When you finish writing, revise your essay and prepare a final copy.

JOHN GREENLEAF WHITTIER

1807–1892

John Greenleaf Whittier stands apart from the other Fireside Poets in several ways. Unlike Longfellow, Holmes, and Lowell, Whittier was born in poverty and received virtually no formal education. He was also more deeply involved with the social issues of his time than were the other poets. Finally, because of his devotion to the abolitionist movement, Whittier, unlike the other poets, did not gain national prominence as a poet until late in his life.

Whittier was born and raised on a farm near Haverhill, Massachusetts. His parents were Quakers, who taught him to believe in hard work, simplicity, pacifism, religious devotion, and social justice. Because he worked long hours on the debt-ridden family farm, Whittier suffered from poor health throughout much of his childhood. Though he was able to attend school for only one year, he educated himself by reading—primarily the Bible and other religious writings and the poetry of Scottish poet Robert Burns. During his teens he began writing poetry, and when he was eighteen his first poem was published in a local newspaper.

As a young man, Whittier became deeply committed to the abolitionist movement. He worked as a writer and editor for antislavery newspapers, wrote a large number of antislavery poems, spoke at abolitionist rallies, and became active in politics, serving a term in the Massachusetts legislature. Unfortunately, Whittier's dedication to abolitionism prevented him from gaining national recognition as a poet until after the Civil War.

His abolitionist work, however, did bring him recognition as a speaker and journalist—as well as personal danger. On a speaking tour in New Hampshire in 1835, he and a British abolitionist were attacked by a hostile mob. Driving their carriage through a hail of bullets, they somehow escaped with their lives.

When the war ended, Whittier turned away from politics, focused his attention on writing poetry, and established himself as one of the country's leading poets. He earned national fame in 1866, when he published his most highly regarded work, *Snowbound*. In this poem and in many later poems, Whittier vividly depicts the warmth and simplicity of life in rural New England.

As the way of life depicted in his poetry disappeared, the popularity of Whittier's poems grew. By the time of his death, Whittier had enjoyed more than twenty-five years of success as a poet. Yet he never allowed his success to affect his warmth, simplicity, and modesty, and he remained faithful at all times to his social and spiritual convictions.

GUIDE FOR INTERPRETING

from Snowbound; Hampton Beach

Writers' Techniques

Imagery. Imagery refers to words or phrases that create mental pictures, or images, that appeal to one or more of the five senses—sight, hearing, touch, smell, or taste. Most often, images appeal to the reader's sense of sight. For example, when Whittier writes, "The sun . . . rose cheerless over hills of gray," he creates a visual picture. Sometimes, however, images present sensations that cannot be visualized. For example, when Whittier refers to "a hard, dull bitterness of cold," he presents an image that you can feel but cannot see. A single image may also appeal to more than one sense. Whittier creates an image that you can both see and feel when he writes, "Unwarmed by any sunset light the gray day darkened into night."

Focus

What images come to mind when you envision the morning after a snowstorm? What images do you associate with the beach? List the images that come to mind when you think of each of these scenes.

Primary Source

During 1864 and 1865 Whittier worked on *Snowbound.* He wrote a prefatory note for the edition of 1892. From it we can see that he drew on the oral history, stories, and folk tales of New England, his memories of family and neighbors, and his Quaker religious mysticism.

> The inmates of the family at the Whittier homestead who are referred to in the poem were my father, mother, my brother and two sisters, and my uncle and aunt both unmarried.
>
> In my boyhood, in our lonely farmhouse, we had scanty sources of information; . . . Under such circumstances storytelling was a necessary resource in the long winter evenings. My father when a young man had traversed the wilderness of Canada, and could tell us of his adventures with Indians and wild beasts, and of his sojourn in the French villages. . . . My mother, who was born in the Indian-haunted region of Somersworth, New Hampshire, . . . told us of the inroads of the savages, and the narrow escape of her ancestors. She described strange people who lived on the [rivers], among whom was Bantam the sorcerer. I have in my possession the wizard's 'conjuring book,' which he solemnly opened when consulted. . . .

A quotation from the "conjuring book" ends ". . . as the celestial Fire drives away dark spirits, so also this our Fire of Wood doth the same." Whittier then finishes his note with the first stanza of Emerson's poem "The Snowstorm."

from Snowbound

John Greenleaf Whittier

A Winter Idyll

The sun that brief December day
Rose cheerless over hills of gray,
And, darkly circled, gave at noon
A sadder light than waning moon.
5   Slow tracing down the thickening sky
Its mute and ominous prophecy,
A portent seeming less than threat,
It sank from sight before it set.
A chill no coat, however stout,
10   Of homespun stuff could quite shut out,
A hard, dull bitterness of cold,
That checked, mid-vein, the circling race
Of lifeblood in the sharpened face,
The coming of the snowstorm told.
15   The wind blew east; we heard the roar
Of Ocean on his wintry shore,
And felt the strong pulse throbbing there
Beat with low rhythm our inland air.

Meanwhile we did our nightly chores—
20   Brought in the wood from out of doors,
Littered the stalls, and from the mows
Raked down the herd's-grass for the cows:
Heard the horse whinnying for his corn;
And, sharply clashing horn on horn,
25   Impatient down the stanchion[1] rows
The cattle shake their walnut bows;
While, peering from his early perch
Upon the scaffold's pole of birch,
The cock his crested helmet bent
30   And down his querulous challenge sent.

Unwarmed by any sunset light
The gray day darkened into night,
A night made hoary with the swarm
And whirl-dance of the blinding storm,

---

1. stanchion (stan′ chən): A restraining device fitted around the neck of a cow to confine it to its stall.

35 As zigzag, wavering to and fro,
    Crossed and recrossed the wingèd snow:
    And ere the early bedtime came
    The white drift piled the window frame,
    And through the glass the clothesline posts
40 Looked in like tall and sheeted ghosts.

    So all night long the storm roared on:
    The morning broke without a sun;
    In tiny spherule[2] traced with lines
    Of Nature's geometric signs,
45 In starry flake, and pellicle,[3]
    All day the hoary meteor fell;
    And, when the second morning shone,
    We looked upon a world unknown,
    On nothing we could call our own.
50 Around the glistening wonder bent
    The blue walls of the firmament,
    No cloud above, no earth below—
    A universe of sky and snow!
    The old familiar sights of ours
55 Took marvelous shapes; strange domes and towers
    Rose up where sty or corncrib stood,
    Or garden wall, or belt of wood;
    A smooth white mound the brush pile showed,
    A fenceless drift what once was road;
60 The bridle post an old man sat
    With loose-flung coat and high cocked hat;
    The wellcurb had a Chinese roof;
    And even the long sweep,[4] high aloof,
    In its slant splendor, seemed to tell
65 Of Pisa's leaning miracle.[5]

    A prompt, decisive man, no breath
    Our father wasted: "Boys, a path!"
    Well pleased (for when did farmer boy
    Count such a summons less than joy?)
70 Our buskins[6] on our feet we drew;
    With mittened hands, and caps drawn low,
    To guard our necks and ears from snow,
    We cut the solid whiteness through.
    And, where the drift was deepest, made

---

2. spherule (sfer' o͞ol): A small sphere.
3. pellicle (pel' i k'l): A thin film.
4. sweep: A pole with a bucket at one end, used for raising water from a well.
5. Pisa's leaning miracle: The famous leaning tower of Pisa in Italy.
6. buskins: High-cut shoes.

75 A tunnel walled and overlaid
With dazzling crystal: we had read
Of rare Aladdin's[7] wondrous cave,
And to our own his name we gave,
With many a wish the luck were ours
80 To test his lamp's supernal powers.
We reached the barn with merry din,
And roused the prisoned brutes within,
The old horse thrust his long head out,
And grave with wonder gazed about;
85 The cock his lusty greeting said,
And forth his speckled harem led;
The oxen lashed their tails, and hooked,
And mild reproach of hunger looked;
The hornèd patriarch of the sheep,
90 Like Egypt's Amun[8] roused from sleep,
Shook his sage head with gesture mute,
And emphasized with stamp of foot.

All day the gusty north wind bore
The loosening drift its breath before;
95 Low circling round its southern zone,
The sun through dazzling snow-mist shone.
No church bell lent its Christian tone
To the savage air, no social smoke
Curled over woods of snow-hung oak.
100 A solitude made more intense
By dreary-voicèd elements,
The shrieking of the mindless wind,
The moaning tree boughs swaying blind,
And on the glass the unmeaning beat
105 Of ghostly fingertips of sleet.
Beyond the circle of our hearth
No welcome sound of toil or mirth
Unbound the spell, and testified
Of human life and thought outside.
110 We minded that the sharpest ear
The buried brooklet could not hear,
The music of whose liquid lip
Had been to us companionship,
And, in our lonely life, had grown
115 To have an almost human tone.

As night drew on, and, from the crest
Of wooded knolls that ridged the west,

---

7. Aladdin's: Referring to Aladdin, a boy in *The Arabian Nights* who found a magic lamp and through its powers discovered a treasure in a cave.
8. Amun: An Egyptian god with a ram's head.

OLD HOLLEY HOUSE, COS COB
John Henry Twachtman
Cincinnati Art Museum

The sun, a snow-blown traveler, sank
From sight beneath the smothering bank,
120 We piled, with care, our nightly stack
Of wood against the chimney back—
The oaken log, green, huge, and thick,
And on its top the stout backstick;
The knotty forestick laid apart,

from *Snowbound*   323

125 And filled between with curious art
The ragged brush; then, hovering near,
We watched the first red blaze appear,
Heard the sharp crackle, caught the gleam
On whitewashed wall and sagging beam,
130 Until the old, rude-furnished room
Burst, flowerlike, into rosy bloom;
While radiant with a mimic flame
Outside the sparkling drift became,
And through the bare-boughed lilac tree
135 Our own warm hearth seemed blazing free.
The crane and pendent trammels[9] showed,
The Turks' heads[10] on the andirons glowed;
While childish fancy, prompt to tell
The meaning of the miracle,
140 Whispered the old rhyme: "*Under the tree,*
When fire outdoors burns merrily,
There the witches are making tea."

The moon above the eastern wood
Shone at its full; the hill range stood
145 Transfigured in the silver flood,
Its blown snows flashing cold and keen,
Dead white, save where some sharp ravine
Took shadow, or the somber green
Of hemlocks turned to pitchy black
150 Against the whiteness at their back.
For such a world and such a night
Most fitting that unwarming light,
Which only seemed where'er it fell
To make the coldness visible.

155 Shut in from all the world without,
We sat the clean-winged hearth[11] about,
Content to let the north wind roar
In baffled rage at pane and door,
While the red logs before us beat
160 The frost line back with tropic heat;
And ever, when a louder blast
Shook beam and rafter as it passed,
The merrier up its roaring draft
The great throat of the chimney laughed;
165 The house dog on his paws outspread

---

9. trammels: Adjustable pothooks hanging from the movable arm, or crane, attached to the hearth.
10. Turks' heads: Turbanlike knots at the top of the andirons.
11. clean-winged hearth: A turkey wing was used for the hearth broom.

Laid to the fire his drowsy head,
The cat's dark silhouette on the wall
A couchant tiger's seemed to fall:
And, for the winter fireside meet,
170   Between the andirons' straddling feet,
The mug of cider simmered slow,
The apples sputtered in a row,
And, close at hand, the basket stood
With nuts from brown October's wood.

RESPONDING TO THE SELECTION

Your Response

1. What are your favorite images from the poem? Why?
2. How would you respond if, like the narrator and his family, you were "shut in from all the world without" by a snowstorm or another act of nature?

Recalling

3. (a) What weather conditions forewarn the speaker of the approaching snowstorm? (b) How does the coming storm affect the family's nightly routine?
4. How long does the storm last?
5. (a) After the storm has ended, what does the speaker's father tell the boys to do? (b) How do the boys respond to the request?

Interpreting

6. What does the family's response to the coming of the storm suggest about their relationship with nature?
7. What descriptive details in lines 47–80 convey the speaker's sense of wonder and amazement upon viewing the snow-covered landscape?
8. What descriptive details in lines 93–115 convey a sense of solitude?
9. What details in the final stanza convey a sense of warmth and security?

Applying

10. Though for the most part snowstorms no longer isolate people as they did in Whittier's time, we sometimes experience a similar sense of isolation during power failures. In what ways do you think the response of today's families to a blackout is similar to and different from the family's response to their forced isolation in *Snowbound*?

ANALYZING LITERATURE

Understanding Imagery

Imagery appeals to one or more of the five senses. For example, when Whittier writes, "The sun . . . sank from sight beneath the smothering bank," he creates an image that appeals to your sense of sight.

Select three images in this excerpt from *Snowbound*. Explain to which sense each image appeals.

CRITICAL THINKING AND READING

Evaluating the Effect of Imagery

Because we all share the same capacity for physical sensations, imagery provides a natural link between the writer's observations, ideas, and experiences and our own imaginations. When used effectively, imagery allows us to picture each place and event the writer describes—even places and events unlike any we have actually seen. In *Snowbound,* for example, Whittier's imagery makes it possible for us to visualize his yard the morning after the snowstorm.

1. Explain what makes the imagery Whittier uses in describing the snowstorm effective.
2. Explain what makes the imagery used in describing the scene inside his house the night after the storm effective.

Hampton Beach

John Greenleaf Whittier

The sunlight glitters keen and bright,
   Where, miles away,
Lies stretching to my dazzled sight
A luminous belt, a misty light,
5 Beyond the dark pine bluffs and wastes of sandy gray.

The tremulous shadow of the sea!
   Against its ground
Of silvery light, rock, hill, and tree,
Still as a picture, clear and free,
10 With varying outline mark the coast for miles around.

On—on—we tread with loose-flung rein
   Our seaward way,
Through dark-green fields and blossoming grain,
Where the wild brier-rose skirts the lane,
15 And bends above our heads the flowering locust spray.

Ha! like a kind hand on my brow
   Comes this fresh breeze,
Cooling its dull and feverish glow,
While through my being seems to flow
20 The breath of a new life, the healing of the seas!

Now rest we, where this grassy mound
   His feet hath set
In the great waters, which have bound
His granite ankles greenly round
25 With long and tangled moss, and weeds with cool spray wet.

Good-bye to pain and care! I take
   Mine ease today:
Here where these sunny waters break,
And ripples this keen breeze, I shake
30 All burdens from the heart, all weary thoughts away.

I draw a freer breath, I seem
   Like all I see—
Waves in the sun, the white-winged gleam
Of sea birds in the slanting beam
35 And far-off sails which flit before the south wind free.

QUODDY HEAD
John Marin

So when time's veil shall fall asunder,
　　The soul may know
No fearful change, nor sudden wonder,
Nor sink the weight of mystery under,
40　But with the upward rise, and with the vastness grow.

　　And all we shrink from now may seem
　　　No new revealing;
　　Familiar as our childhood's stream,
　　Or pleasant memory of a dream,
45　The loved and cherished past upon the new life stealing.

　　Serene and mild the untried light
　　　May have its dawning;
　　And, as in summer's northern night
　　The evening and the dawn unite,
50　The sunset hues of time blend with the soul's new morning.

　　I sit alone; in foam and spray
　　　Wave after wave
　　Breaks on the rocks which, stern and gray,
　　Shoulder the broken tide away,
55　Or murmurs hoarse and strong through mossy cleft and cave.

　　What heed I of the dusty land
　　　And noisy town?
　　I see the mighty deep expand
　　From its white line of glimmering sand
60　To where the blue of heaven on bluer waves shuts down!

　　In listless quietude of mind,
　　　I yield to all
　　The change of cloud and wave and wind;
　　And passive on the flood reclined,
65　I wander with the waves, and with them rise and fall.

　　But look, thou dreamer! wave and shore
　　　In shadow lie;
　　The night-wind warns me back once more
　　To where, my native hilltops o'er,
70　Bends like an arch of fire the glowing sunset sky.

　　So then, beach, bluff, and wave, farewell!
　　　I bear with me
　　No token stone nor glittering shell,
　　But long and oft shall memory tell
75　Of this brief thoughtful hour of musing by the sea.

RESPONDING TO THE SELECTION

Your Response

1. Would you like to spend some time at the place described in the poem? Why or why not?
2. What place evokes the same feelings for you as Hampton Beach does for the narrator? Explain.

Recalling

3. As the speaker sits by the sea, what does he vow to "shake" from his heart?
4. What does the speaker do "In listless quietude of mind"?
5. (a) What "warns" the speaker to start heading home? (b) What does he "bear with" him when he leaves?

Interpreting

6. What details in the first three stanzas convey the beauty of the coast?
7. (a) In the fifth stanza, how does the speaker personify, or attribute human qualities to, the bluff on which he settles? (b) How does this help to convey his sense of oneness with nature?
8. (a) What do you think might be the "burdens" from which the sea helps the speaker to escape? (b) What does the speaker mean when he says that he seems like the waves, sea birds, and far-off sails?
9. (a) What event is the speaker describing when he writes, "when time's veil shall fall asunder"? (b) How does he feel his respite by the sea helps to prepare him for this event?
10. Why does the speaker need "no token stone nor glittering shell" to remind him of his afternoon by the sea?

Applying

11. Whittier suggests that the ocean has the power to heal and soothe. Do you agree? Why or why not?

THINKING AND WRITING

Writing a Poem Using Imagery

Using the images you have already listed, write a poem describing either a beach or a landscape the morning after a snowstorm. Start by trying to come up with new images that you can add to your list. Try to include a number of images appealing to senses other than sight. Use vivid adjectives in your images to make them clear and effective. When you finish developing your list, focus your subject and write your poem. Imagine that your readers have never seen a scene similar to the one you are describing. When you finish writing, revise and add details to make your description thorough and clear.

LEARNING OPTIONS

1. **Art.** In "Hampton Beach" Whittier creates vivid images, or word pictures, of what the speaker sees and feels at Hampton Beach. Choose an especially striking image and create a drawing to illustrate it. Use the written image as the caption for your drawing.
2. **Cross-curricular Connection.** Whittier was known as the "Quaker Poet" for his gentle verses about rural New England. Yet he was fierce in his fight against slavery. Consult an encyclopedia entry about the poet and read about his political activities between 1833 and 1863. Find out how Whittier served the abolitionist cause. Be prepared to share your findings in a classroom discussion.
3. **Art.** Join the staff of the New England Visitors Bureau in designing a literary tour that focuses on the poets of the New England Renaissance. Work with a group of classmates to create a map of sites to visit. Present the map to the class and point out the highlights of the tour.

EMILY DICKINSON

1830–1886

During her life, Emily Dickinson wrote at least 1,775 poems. Yet only seven of these were published—anonymously—in her lifetime. Dickinson was a private person, extremely reluctant to reveal herself and her work to the public. As a result, few people outside her family and small circle of friends were aware of her poetic genius until after her death. Today, however, she is generally regarded as one of the greatest American poets.

Dickinson was born in Amherst, Massachusetts, the daughter of a prominent lawyer. Though she traveled to Boston, Washington, and Philadelphia to visit friends when she was young, she rarely left her home town as she grew older. In fact, during the last ten years of her life, she refused to leave her house and garden. Her circle of friends grew smaller and smaller, and she communicated with her remaining friends mainly through notes and fragments of poems. She dressed only in white and would not allow her neighbors or any strangers to see her. When her health failed, she permitted her doctor to examine her only by observing her from a distance. In 1886, after fighting illness for two years, Dickinson died in the same house in which she was born.

Though she chose to live most of her life in virtual isolation, Emily Dickinson was a very intense, energetic person. Having a clear sense of purpose, she devoted most of her energy to her poetry. Yet, because she shared her work with few people, she sometimes doubted her abilities. In 1862 she sent four poems to Thomas Wentworth Higginson, an influential literary critic, and asked him to tell her if her verse was "alive." Like the editors who first published her work after her death, Higginson sought to change her unconventional style—her eccentric use of punctuation and her irregular use of meter and rhyme. He did not realize that Dickinson crafted her poetry with great precision and that her unique style was an important element of her poetry. Still, he did recognize her talent and encouraged her to keep writing.

The extent of Dickinson's talent was not widely recognized until 1955, when a complete, unedited edition of her poems was published. Viewing her work in its original form, writers and critics could see that Dickinson was unlike the other poets of her time. For the first time, Dickinson's unique style, her concrete imagery, and her simple but forceful language were appreciated. Dickinson's work was compared with that of the modern poets, and she was acknowledged as a poet who was truly ahead of her time.

GUIDE FOR INTERPRETING

Emily Dickinson's Poetry

Writers' Techniques

Style. Style refers to the manner in which a writer puts his or her ideas into words. It involves the characteristics that concern form of expression rather than the thoughts conveyed. In poetry, for example, style is determined by such factors as choice and arrangement of words, length and arrangement of lines, stanza length and format, use of punctuation and capitalization, and use of literary devices.

Emily Dickinson's unique style distinguishes her poetry from that of any other American poet. The most striking characteristics of her style are her unconventional use of punctuation and capitalization and the brevity of most of her lines and stanzas. Most of her poetry is written in quatrains, or four-line stanzas. In her quatrains she usually rhymes only the second and fourth lines, and she often uses slant rhymes, or partial rhymes—rhymes in which the final sounds of the words are similar but not identical. For the most part, she uses iambic rhythm—rhythm in which every second syllable is stressed—but she includes frequent variations in rhythm.

Another notable characteristic of Dickinson's style is her tendency to use figurative language—language that is not intended to be interpreted literally—to convey her ideas. Her use of figurative language adds depth to her poetry.

Commentary

Emily Dickinson's poems should not be considered only as coded messages to be deciphered for their meaning. It is true that in many poems she struggles with difficult questions of existence and death. In others, however, she paints, in quick, vivid strokes, moments from our everyday world. Dickinson sees her surroundings with the clear-eyed, sometimes mischievous, wonder of a child and breathlessly tells us about them. Sometimes she just wants us to see; other times she searches for the meaning in what she sees.

As you read her poems, notice when she is speaking only of what she is describing and when she is perhaps also speaking of what it signifies or suggests. Do you experience the world in both ways—when you watch a sunset or see a rainbow, for example?

Focus

Most people associate certain emotions with each of the four seasons. Freewrite about the emotions you associate with winter.

"Hope" is the thing with feathers—

Emily Dickinson

"Hope" is the thing with feathers—
That perches in the soul—
And sings the tune without the words—
And never stops—at all—

5 And sweetest—in the Gale—is heard—
And sore must be the storm—
That could abash the little Bird
That kept so many warm—

I've heard it in the chillest land—
10 And on the strangest Sea—
Yet, never, in Extremity,
It asked a crumb—of Me.

RESPONDING TO THE SELECTION

Your Response
1. What kind of bird did you picture as you read this poem?

Recalling
2. (a) Where does "Hope" perch? (b) What kind of song does it sing? (c) When and where is it heard?

Interpreting
3. Throughout the poem Dickinson develops a comparison between hope and a "little Bird." What is the effect of this comparison?
4. (a) What qualities does the "little Bird" possess? (b) What does this suggest about the characteristics of hope?
5. In what way do the final two lines suggest that hope is something that we cannot consciously control?
6. What does this poem suggest about the human ability to endure hardships?

Applying
7. (a) What does hope mean to you? (b) In what situations do you think of hope?

LEARNING OPTION

Writing. If hope is "the thing with feathers," what are despair, trust, and desire? Choose one of these feelings and consider how the poet might describe it. Together with classmates, brainstorm a list of things to which it might be compared. Then, using "'Hope' is the thing with feathers—" as a model, write a poem in which you develop the comparison.

There's a certain Slant of light,

Emily Dickinson

FEBRUARY 1890–1900
John Henry Twachtman
Museum of Fine Arts, Boston

There's a certain Slant of light,
Winter Afternoons—
That oppresses, like the Heft
Of Cathedral Tunes—

5   Heavenly Hurt, it gives us—
We can find no scar,
But internal difference,
Where the Meanings, are—

None may teach it—Any—
10   'Tis the Seal Despair—
An imperial affliction
Sent us of the Air—

When it comes, the Landscape listens—
Shadows—hold their breath—
15   When it goes, 'tis like the Distance
On the look of Death—

RESPONDING TO THE SELECTION

Your Response
1. Emily Dickinson captures the essence of winter in "a certain Slant of light." What single image or moment defines winter for you?

Recalling
2. According to the speaker, how does "a certain Slant of light" affect us?
3. How does it affect the Landscape and Shadows?

Interpreting
4. What mood does the "Slant of light" create?

5. (a) What is paradoxical, or self-contradictory, about Dickinson's reference to "Heavenly Hurt" (line 5)? (b) What does this paradox suggest about suffering?
6. What does the third stanza suggest about the source of despair?
7. What does the last stanza suggest about the relationship between the natural world and humanity?
8. What does the "Slant of light" seem to represent to the speaker?

Applying
9. Why do you think that weather conditions have such a powerful effect on our moods?

NEAR HARLECH, NORTH WALES
Benjamin William Leader

I never saw a Moor—

Emily Dickinson

I never saw a Moor—
I never saw the Sea—
Yet know I how the Heather looks
And what a Billow[1] be.

5   I never spoke with God
Nor visited in Heaven—
Yet certain am I of the spot
As if the Checks[2] were given—

---

1. Billow: Large wave.
2. Checks: Colored seat checks indicating the destinations of passengers on a train after their tickets have been collected.

▌RESPONDING TO THE SELECTION

Your Response
1. What is your reaction to this poem?
2. At this point, what are your impressions of Emily Dickinson?

Recalling
3. List three things the speaker knows.

Interpreting
4. (a) How might the speaker have acquired the knowledge she claims to possess in the first stanza? (b) In what way is the knowledge presented in the second stanza different from that of the first stanza? (c) How might she have acquired the knowledge presented in the second stanza?
5. How does the information in the first stanza affect your reaction to the second stanza?

Applying
6. What things do you think you know through intuition rather than through experience?

A narrow Fellow in the Grass

Emily Dickinson

A narrow Fellow in the Grass
Occasionally rides—
You may have met Him—did you not
His notice sudden is—

5 The Grass divides as with a Comb—
A spotted shaft is seen—
And then it closes at your feet
And opens further on—

He likes a Boggy Acre
10 A Floor too cool for Corn—
Yet when a Boy, and Barefoot—
I more than once at Noon

Have passed, I thought, a Whip lash
Unbraiding in the Sun
15 When stooping to secure it
It wrinkled, and was gone—

Several of Nature's People
I know, and they know me—
I feel for them a transport
20 Of cordiality—

But never met this Fellow
Attended, or alone
Without a tighter breathing
And Zero at the Bone—

RESPONDING TO THE SELECTION

Your Response

1. Did you like this poem? Why or why not?
2. At what point did you identify the subject?
3. When have you felt "a tighter breathing / and Zero at the bone"?

Recalling

4. (a) Where is the "narrow Fellow" found? (b) How does he make his presence known?

Interpreting

5. (a) What is the "narrow Fellow"? (b) Why do you think Dickinson does not name her subject?
6. In line 11 Dickinson indicates that the speaker of the poem is male. Why do you think she uses a male speaker?
7. (a) What is the speaker's attitude toward nature in general? (b) What is his attitude toward the "narrow Fellow"?

Applying

8. What is your own attitude toward the subject of the poem?

ANALYZING LITERATURE

Understanding Style

   Style refers to the way in which a writer expresses his or her thoughts. Though writers often write about similar subjects, each writer has his or her own distinctive style. As a result, we can often distinguish the work of different writers by examining style. For example, we can easily identify Emily Dickinson's poetry once we are familiar with some of the unique characteristics of her style.

1. What is unusual about Dickinson's use of punctuation?
2. What is unusual about her use of capitalization?
3. What are two other characteristics of her style revealed in this poem?

Tell all
the Truth
but tell
it slant—

Emily Dickinson

Tell all the Truth but tell it slant—
Success in Circuit lies
Too bright for our infirm Delight
The Truth's superb surprise
5 As Lightning to the Children eased
With explanation kind
The Truth must dazzle gradually
Or every man be blind—

Success
is counted
sweetest

Emily Dickinson

Success is counted sweetest
By those who ne er succeed.
To comprehend a nectar
Requires sorest need.

5 Not one of all the purple Host
Who took the Flag today
Can tell the definition
So clear of Victory

As he defeated—dying—
10 On whose forbidden ear
The distant strains of triumph
Burst agonized and clear!

RESPONDING TO THE SELECTION

Your Response

1. Do you agree with the message of each poem? Why or why not?
2. Which phrases or comparisons do you find most striking?
3. What do you feel more deeply, success or failure? Explain.

Interpreting

4. What does Dickinson mean when she advises us to "Tell all the Truth but tell it slant"?
5. The poet suggests that truth is blinding. To what type of truth do you think she is referring?
6. (a) Why, according to Dickinson, is success most important to "those who ne'er succeed"? (b) Explain lines 3–4 of her poem "Success is counted sweetest."
7. How does the example presented in the second and third stanzas of "Success . . ." support the main idea stated in the first two lines?
8. In line 10 of "Success . . . ," the poet refers to the "forbidden ear" of the dying man. What is forbidden to his ear?
9. What, according to Dickinson, is the relationship between success and failure?

Applying

10. To what types of truths do you think people have to be led gradually? Explain.
11. What is your definition of success, and how does it compare with Dickinson's?

I heard a Fly buzz— when I died—

Emily Dickinson

I heard a Fly buzz—when I died—
The Stillness in the Room
Was like the Stillness in the Air—
Between the Heaves of Storm—

5   The Eyes around—had wrung them dry—
And Breaths were gathering firm
For that last Onset—when the King
Be witnessed—in the Room—

I willed my Keepsakes—Signed away
10 What portion of me be
Assignable—and then it was
There interposed a Fly—

With Blue—uncertain stumbling Buzz—
Between the light—and me—
15 And then the Windows failed—and then
I could not see to see—

ROOM WITH A BALCONY
Adolph von Menzel
Staattiche Museen Preubischer Kulturbesitz, Nationgalerie, Berlin

---

RESPONDING TO THE SELECTION

Your Response

1. If you were describing a deathbed scene from the perspective of the dying person, would you mention the buzzing of a fly? Why or why not?
2. What is your reaction to this poem?

Interpreting

3. (a) Describe the atmosphere of the death-room. (b) What is the effect of the buzzing fly?
4. (a) Describe the activities of the onlookers. (b) What did they await?

5. Explain what happens to the speaker in the last two stanzas. (a) How can you tell that she was preparing herself for death? (b) What happens at the last moment?
6. What statement about death and dying do you think Dickinson makes in this poem?

Applying

7. Explain how Dickinson's attitude toward death is similar to and different from the attitude of another writer whose work you have read.

I felt a Funeral, in my Brain,

Emily Dickinson

I felt a Funeral, in my Brain,
And Mourners to and fro
Kept treading—treading—till it seemed
That Sense was breaking through—

5   And when they all were seated,
A Service, like a Drum—
Kept beating—beating—till I thought
My Mind was going numb—

And then I heard them lift a Box
10   And creak across my Soul
With those same Boots of Lead, again,
Then Space—began to toll,

As all the Heavens were a Bell,
And Being, but an Ear,
15   And I, and Silence, some strange Race
Wrecked, solitary, here—

And then a Plank in Reason, broke,
And I dropped down, and down—
And hit a World, at every plunge,
20   And Finished knowing—then—

RESPONDING TO THE SELECTION

Your Response

1. What do you think the speaker is describing, death or madness? Explain.

Recalling

2. Describe the sensations that the speaker experiences. (a) What does she feel? (b) What does she hear?

Interpreting

3. (a) What do you think the "Mourners" might represent? (b) How do the images in the second and third stanzas convey the speaker's growing sense of despair? (c) How do the images in the fourth stanza convey the speaker's sense of isolation?

Applying

4. Many of Emily Dickinson's poems grew out of reactions to events in her personal life. What type of event do you think might have led her to write this poem?

My life closed twice before its close—

Emily Dickinson

My life closed twice before its close—
It yet remains to see
If Immortality unveil
A third event to me,

5   So huge, so hopeless to conceive
As these that twice befell.
Parting is all we know of heaven,
And all we need of hell.

The Bustle in a House

Emily Dickinson

The Bustle in a House
The Morning after Death
Is solemnest of industries
Enacted upon Earth—

5   The Sweeping up the Heart
And putting Love away
We shall not want to use again
Until Eternity.

RESPONDING TO THE SELECTION

Your Response
1. What images come to mind when you read each poem?
2. What might make you feel as if your life had "closed"?

Interpreting
3. (a) What type of event caused the speaker's life to close "twice before its close"? (b) What line provides a clue to the nature of the events "that twice befell"?
4. (a) What is the third event to which the speaker refers in "My life closed twice"? (b) How is it related to the first two events?
5. (a) What is paradoxical, or contradictory, about Dickinson's description of parting? (b) How do you explain the paradox?
6. What does "The Bustle in a House" suggest about people's attempts to cope with the death of a loved one?

Applying
7. It has been claimed that the true beginnings of modern American poetry can be traced to Emily Dickinson and Walt Whitman. What do modern and contemporary poems that you have read have in common with Dickinson's poetry?

THINKING AND WRITING

Responding to Criticism
A critic has stated that Emily Dickinson's poetry "is exploration on a variety of levels of the ultimate meaning of life itself and equally important of the depths and heights of her own inner nature." Using evidence from the poems you have just read, write an essay supporting this statement. Reread the poems, looking for evidence to support the critic's comment. Organize your notes into an outline; then write your essay. When you finish writing, revise and proofread your essay.

As imperceptibly as grief

Emily Dickinson

As imperceptibly as grief
The summer lapsed away,—
Too imperceptible, at last,
To seem like perfidy.

5 A quietness distilled,
As twilight long begun,
Or Nature, spending with herself
Sequestered afternoon.

The dusk drew earlier in,
10 The morning foreign shone,—
A courteous, yet harrowing grace,
As guest that would be gone.

And thus, without a wing,
Or service of a keel,
15 Our summer made her light escape
Into the beautiful.

Much Madness is divinest Sense—

Emily Dickinson

Much Madness is divinest Sense—
To a discerning Eye—
Much Sense—the starkest Madness—
'Tis the Majority
5 In this, as All, prevail—
Assent—and you are sane—
Demur—you're straightway dangerous—
And handled with a Chain—

RESPONDING TO THE SELECTION

Your Response

1. What is your reaction to each poem?
2. Dickinson defines madness as "divinest Sense." How would you define it?
3. How did "As imperceptibly as grief" make you feel?

Interpreting

4. (a) What is paradoxical, or contradictory, about the poet's contention "Much Madness is divinest Sense"? (b) How can this paradox be true?
5. (a) According to the speaker of "Much Madness is divinest Sense—," how does society de- fine sanity? (b) How does it define madness?
6. Explain the comparison Dickinson makes be- tween grief and summer in "As imperceptibly as grief."
7. (a) In the second and third stanzas of "As im- perceptibly as grief," what changes associated with the passage of summer does the poet de- scribe? (b) What comparisons does she make?
8. What do you think the last two lines of "As im- perceptibly as grief" mean?

Applying

9. Contemporary poet Theodore Roethke wrote, "What's madness but Divinest sense at odds with circumstance?" Compare Roethke's words with those of Dickinson.

The Soul selects her own Society—

Emily Dickinson

The Soul selects her own Society—
Then—shuts the Door—
To her divine Majority—
Present no more—

5   Unmoved—she notes the Chariots—pausing—
At her low Gate—
Unmoved—an Emperor be kneeling
Upon her Mat—

I've known her—from an ample nation—
10 Choose One—
Then—close the Valves of her attention—
Like Stone—

![R]ESPONDING TO THE SELECTION

Your Response
1. Do you think it's possible to have more than one soul mate, or someone with whom you can share every thought? Why or why not?

Recalling
2. (a) What happens after the soul makes her choice? (b) What leaves the soul unmoved?

Interpreting
3. (a) What is the soul's "divine Majority"? (b) Of how many people does the soul's "Society" actually consist?
4. How would you describe the soul's attitude toward the rest of the world?
5. What does line 9 suggest about the speaker's relationship to the soul?

Applying
6. In real life people select a wide variety of different "societies." List as many as you can. What do you think this tendency indicates about human nature?

How happy is the little Stone

Emily Dickinson

How happy is the little Stone
That rambles in the Road alone,
And doesn't care about Careers
And Exigencies never fears—
5 Whose Coat of elemental Brown
A passing Universe put on,
And independent as the Sun
Associates or glows alone,
Fulfilling absolute Decree
10 In casual simplicity—

There is a solitude of space

Emily Dickinson

There is a solitude of space
A solitude of sea
A solitude of death, but these
Society shall be
5 Compared with that profounder site
That polar privacy
A soul admitted to itself—
Finite Infinity.

TWILIGHT IN THE WILDERNESS
Frederick E. Church
The Cleveland Museum of Art

This is my letter to the World

Emily Dickinson

This is my letter to the World
That never wrote to Me—
The simple News that Nature told—
With tender Majesty

5 Her Message is committed
To Hands I cannot see—
For love of Her—Sweet—countrymen—
Judge tenderly—of Me

RESPONDING TO THE SELECTION

Your Response

1. After reading these poems, what are your impressions of Dickinson?
2. Which poem can best be applied to your life? Why?
3. Do you think that people should seek solitude? Why or why not?

Interpreting

4. In "How happy is the little Stone," Dickinson sees the little stone as a model for human behavior. (a) What qualities does she attribute to the stone? (b) Why do these qualities make it an appropriate model?
5. In "There is a solitude of space," the poet contrasts the solitude of a "soul admitted to itself" with three other forms of solitude. (a) What is a "soul admitted to itself"? (b) How does its solitude differ from the solitude of space, sea, and death?
6. In "This is my letter to the World," the poet writes to those who will read her poetry. (a) How does Dickinson allude to her secluded life? (b) Whom does she credit with giving her inspiration? (c) What is the basis of her plea to be judged "tenderly"?

Applying

7. What makes "This is my letter to the World" an appropriate introduction to a collection of Dickinson's poetry?

THINKING AND WRITING

Responding to Dickinson's Poetry

Respond to Dickinson's letter to the world by writing a letter to her in which you express your personal reactions to her poetry. Review her poems and record your response to them. Then think about your reaction to her poetry. How does it affect you emotionally? Do you find it difficult to understand? If so, why? Do you find that it helps you to understand yourself? Start your letter by summing up your reaction. Then support your reactions with specific examples from several of her poems. When you finish writing, revise your letter and prepare a final copy.

YOUR WRITING PROCESS

WRITING A COMPARISON/ CONTRAST ESSAY

"As for style of writing, if one has anything to say, it drops from him simply and directly, as a stone falls to the ground."

Henry David Thoreau

"In a poem the words should be as pleasing to the ear as the meaning is to the mind."

Marianne Moore

Movies, TV programs, music, ideas: These are just a few of the things that bring you and your friends together. On the other hand, you are each unique individuals with your own hopes and fears. Similarly, the poets in this unit are both alike and unique. For instance, the Fireside Poets appealed to a large audience, but they didn't all write in the same way. Choose two poems from this unit that were written by different poets. How are they alike? Different?

> ### Focus
> **Assignment:** Compare and contrast two poems from this unit.
> **Purpose:** To show how poems by poets of the same era and region are alike yet different.
> **Audience:** Readers of a poetry journal for students.

Prewriting

1. Gather in a small group and listen to the poems. Read the poems aloud, have someone else read them, or listen to them on audiocassette. Then discuss the readings with members of your group. In many cases, you'll pick up meanings that you might miss when you read the poems silently.

2. Research the lives of the poets. Poems often grow out of direct experience. Knowing about the poets' lives may give you insight into their poems for comparisons and contrasts.

3. Brainstorm to find similarities and differences. After you've researched the poems and the poets, brainstorm to generate a list of similarities and differences that you can add to throughout the assignment. Consider points such as these: the poems' subject matter, imagery, and tone.

4. Develop a preliminary thesis statement. Before you begin to draft, write a one-sentence summary or generalization comparing and contrasting two poems. Remember that your thesis can change as you progress. Also remember that each detail in your essay should support the thesis.

Student Model

Both Emily Dickinson and James Russell Lowell use birds as metaphors of poetic inspiration, but Lowell's poem is pessimistic whereas Dickinson's is optimistic.

5. Outline your essay. A comparison/contrast essay can cover one topic completely and then discuss the other (AAABBB), or it can alternate between the two (ABABAB). Before you begin to draft, plan the structure of your essay. Also plan how the various parts of your essay will connect, as in the following flow-chart diagram.

Student Model

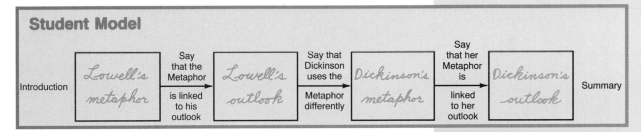

Drafting

1. Include quotations. By weaving short quotations into your sentences, you will be illustrating your points *and* providing evidence for them.

Student Model

For both poets, the birdsong is incessant, at least as long as they live. Lowell writes, "I cannot still it," and Dickinson claims that it "never stops—at all—."

2. Remember your audience. Your tone should be informal enough to capture the attention of your readers but not so casual that it puts them off. Consider looking at student literary magazines to get a sense of the appropriate tone.

Revising and Editing

1. Let your draft cool overnight. Try to give yourself time to step away from your draft. Reading it at another time will help you be more objective.

2. Punctuation with quotations. Review the rules governing direct quotations from literary sources. Remember that a misplaced comma or an omitted quotation mark can completely muddle a sentence.

3. Peer proofreading. How do you know that you have misspelled a word if you don't know how to spell it? Trade papers with another writer and act as proofreaders.

Grammar Tip

When quoting from poetry in your writing, use slash marks (/) to indicate the line divisions if the quotation extends beyond one line of poetry. Indent quotations that are longer than four lines, and place line references in parentheses immediately after the closing quotation marks, for example,

"Announced by all the trumpets of the sky,/Arrives the snow, . . ." (lines 1–2)

Options for Publishing

- Submit your essay to your school literary magazine.
- Publish your essay, with those of your classmates, in a class anthology.
- Read your essay to the class and invite comments.

Reviewing Your Writing Process

1. Was it helpful to listen to the poems before writing about them? Why or why not?

2. Do you find it helpful to use a diagram, like a flow chart, to outline your writing? Explain.

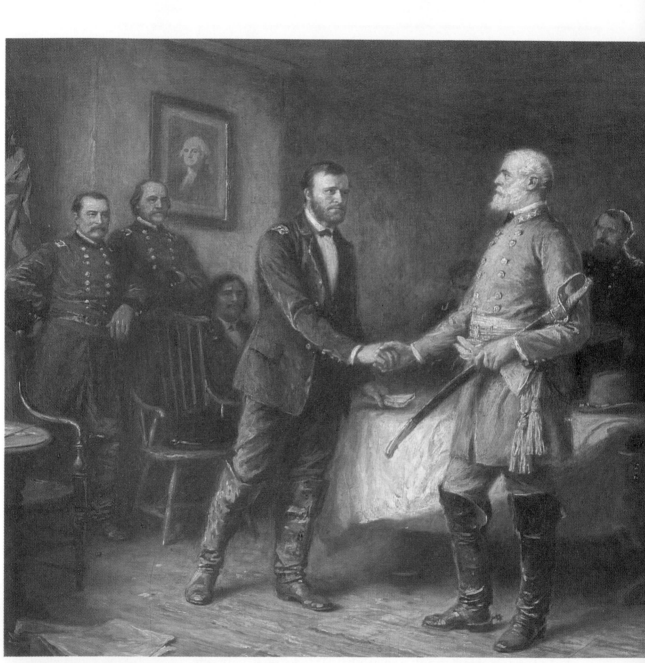

LET US HAVE PEACE (GRANT AND LEE)
J. L. G. Ferris

DIVISION, WAR, AND RECONCILIATION

1855–1865

Skimming lightly, wheeling still,
The swallows fly low
Over the fields in clouded days,
The forest-field of Shiloh—
Herman Melville

The Civil War moved Herman Melville to write a volume of sensitive poetry that treated incidents of the war in a quiet, mournful tone. His poem about the Battle of Shiloh is called "A Requiem," since it was written to honor the soldiers who had died there. The battle, fought in western Tennessee in April 1862, was one of the bloodiest contests of the American Civil War. With more than 10,000 casualties on each side, Shiloh was a decisive event. It proved that the war, begun the previous spring with cheering, flag-waving, and brave rhetoric, would be a long and bitter struggle.

Like the Revolution before it, the Civil War, or the War Between the States, absorbed the creative energies of the nation. Notable speeches, songs, letters, memoirs, and journals appeared, but little in the way of memorable fiction. Many writers became involved with the war, and some of the most important wartime literature was produced by the leaders from both sides. One towering literary figure did emerge during the wartime era, however—the poet Walt Whitman.

THE HISTORICAL SETTING

Opposition to slavery did not begin with the Civil War. Thomas Jefferson's first draft of the Declaration of Independence described the slave trade as a "cruel war against human nature itself, violating its most sacred rights of life and liberty." This language did not find its way into the final document, however. Slavery eventually disappeared in the North, where it had never been very profitable. In the South, however, slavery became the foundation of the plantation system.

The Missouri Compromise in 1820 and the Compromise of 1850 held off confrontations between slave states and free states for many years. But nothing short of secession from the Union (which the South often threatened) or freedom for the enslaved Africans (which many in the North demanded) could finally end the controversy. The northern and southern states entered the 1850's on a collision course. Would the new territories in the West enter the Union as free states or as slave states? Walt Whitman later saw this continuing conflict not as a "struggle between two distinct and separate peoples" but rather as one between "the passions and paradoxes" within the United States.

Passions and Paradoxes

The North and South had clearly developed along very different lines. In the North, commerce, not cotton, was king. The Industrial Revolution and cheap transportation had helped turn northern towns and cities into centers of bustling activity. Education, banking, science, and reform movements—all were topics of interest and concern. Immigration, too, was changing the face of the North. A rising tide of Irish and Germans, among others, were seeking a new life in the United States. Most of these newcomers landed at seaports between Boston and Baltimore and settled in the northern states.

The South, by contrast, was a slower-paced region of plantations and small farms. There were cities, to be sure, but the area was most truly defined by its cotton plantations, large and small. Sugar, rice, and tobacco were also important crops. The march of technological progress, with its hotly debated social issues and problems, had little impact on the prewar South.

One issue, however, made an indelible impression. That issue was slavery. The South believed its lifeblood to depend on the "peculiar institution" of slavery. Statesmen might make tactical compromises on such matters as free states or slave states being carved from the new territories, but there could be no compromise on the legality of slavery.

Firebrands on the other side of the issue, mostly northerners, were just as adamant. William Lloyd Garrison published an abolitionist weekly, *The Liberator,* that demanded immediate, uncompensated freedom for all enslaved Africans. His first issue proclaimed: "I am in earnest—I will not equivocate—I will not excuse—I will not retreat a single inch—*and I will be heard.*" Few people in the antislavery movement were as extreme as Garrison. Their basic goal was, nonetheless, unacceptable to most southerners.

The controversy between North and South came to a head in 1860. In that year, Abraham Lincoln was elected President of the United States

in a bitter four-way race. Lincoln had once said, "If slavery is not wrong, nothing is wrong." The national paradoxes and passions that Walt Whitman observed could no longer be contained by compromise.

The Union Is Dissolved

Even before Lincoln was inaugurated, the legislature of South Carolina had declared unanimously that "the union now subsisting between South Carolina and other States . . . is hereby dissolved." Other southern states soon followed South Carolina's lead. In February 1861, delegates from seven states met in Montgomery, Alabama, to establish the Confederate States of America.

Some northerners were willing to accept secession, but President Lincoln was not. Once he had made his position clear, war seemed inevitable. The fighting began on April 12, 1861, when Confederate artillery fired on Union troops holding Fort Sumter, in Charleston Harbor. Three days later, Lincoln issued a call for 75,000 Union volunteers to put down the rebellion. Two days after that, Virginia seceded from the Union, and its militia seized the United States Naval yard at Norfolk. The Civil War was on.

Most people in the North expected the Union to win a quick, decisive victory over the Confederacy. It was not to be. Even with the North's

Division, War, and Reconciliation (A.D. 1855 – A.D. 1865)

John Brown

Frederick Douglass

Charles Darwin

1855   1857   1859

AMERICAN EVENTS

- **Walt Whitman** publishes first edition of *Leaves of Grass.*
- *My Bondage and My Freedom,* **Frederick Douglass's** second autobiography, makes its appearance.

- **Oliver Wendell Holmes** publishes *The Autocrat of the Breakfast-Table.*
- Lincoln-Douglas debates help make **Abraham Lincoln** a national figure.

- John Brown raids federal arsenal at Harpers Ferry; he is hanged for treason.
  - Essays by **Ralph Waldo Emerson** published as *The Conduct of Life.*
  - Henry Timrod's *Poems* appears; his only collection published during his lifetime.

WORLD EVENTS

- England: Alfred, Lord Tennyson publishes his long poem *Maud.*
  - England: Bessemer steel process makes modern steelmaking possible.

- France: Gustave Flaubert completes *Madame Bovary,* classic novel of realism.
- India: Start of doomed Sepoy Rebellion; native soldiers fight British rule.

- England: Charles Darwin introduces theory of evolution in *Origin of Species.*
- England: Charles Dickens adds to his fame with *A Tale of Two Cities.*
  - England: Florence Nightingale founds Nightingale School for training nurses.

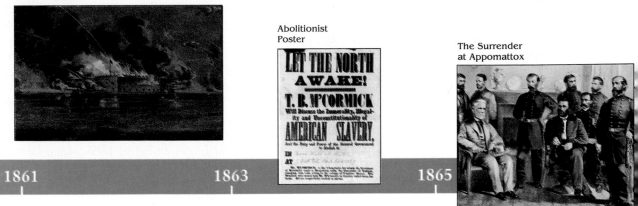

Bombardment
of Fort Sumter

Abolitionist
Poster

LET THE NORTH
AWAKE!
T. B. M'CORMICK
With Discuss the Immorality, Illegal-
ity and Unconstitutionality of
AMERICAN SLAVERY,

The Surrender
at Appomattox

1861   **1863**   **1865**

- **Lincoln** inaugurated in March; Civil War begins in April with firing on Fort Sumter.

  - Major battles are fought at Shiloh, Antietam, and Fredericksburg.
  - Julia Ward Howe writes "The Battle Hymn of the Republic."

- After Antietam, **Lincoln** issues the Emancipation Proclamation.
- Union forces lose at Chancellorsville, but win at Gettysburg and Vicksburg.

  - War nears an end with battles of the Wilderness, Atlanta, and Nashville.

- **General Robert E. Lee** surrenders to General Ulysses S. Grant at Appomattox Court House.
- Within days of Lee's surrender, **President Lincoln** is assassinated.

- England: George Eliot (Mary Ann Evans) publishes her popular novel *Silas Marner*.

  - France: Louis Pasteur proposes modern germ theory of disease.
  - Russia: Ivan Turgenev publishes *Fathers and Sons,* his masterpiece.

- Mexico: French occupy Mexico City and establish Maximilian as emperor of Mexico.

  - England: *Dramatis Personae* by Robert Browning appears.

- England: Lewis Carroll completes *Alice's Adventures in Wonderland*.

formidable economic, industrial, and numerical advantages, four years of war lay ahead. The South's one main advantage over the Union was its superior military leadership. In the end, however, not even the incomparable General Robert E. Lee could prevail against the much larger Union force under General Ulysses S. Grant. Battles raged as far north as Pennsylvania, as far south as Georgia and Florida, and throughout the Mississippi Valley. The names of the major battles are carved on countless Civil War monuments across the United States: Bull Run, Fort Donelson, Shiloh, Antietam, Fredericksburg, Chancellorsville, Gettysburg, Vicksburg, Chattanooga, Atlanta, Petersburg, and, finally, Appomattox Court House.

The Civil War was the first American war in which black troops fought in large numbers. By the end of the war, there were some 180,000 black soldiers in more than a hundred Union regiments. On the Confederate side, both slaves and free blacks accompanied the army as cooks, teamsters, and laborers. A few Native American regiments served the Union cause on the frontier. Women's contributions to the war effort, North and South, were monumental. Clara Barton, organizer of the American Red Cross, became known as the "Angel of the Battlefield" for her tireless work as a nurse in army camps and hospitals.

The war finally ended in 1865, when General Lee surrendered to General Grant at Appomattox. Although the nation was reunited, deep wounds had been opened that would take decades to heal. Unfortunately, the nation's unity had to be restored without the leadership of President Lincoln. Lincoln was assassinated just days after Lee's surrender.

TIDINGS FROM THE FRONT
Gilbert Gaul

EPIC IN BLUE AND GRAY

Literature deals with conflict, and there was plenty of real-life conflict in the United States between 1855 and 1865. The antislavery and proslavery forces, North and South, argued vehemently in public and in private. Other notable struggles pitted the United States Army against Native Americans, open-range ranchers against settlers, wage-earners against powerful new corporations, reformers against a host of real or imagined evils. All these conflicts would eventually find their way into American literature. For quite some time, however, the attention of writers was riveted on the immediate, cataclysmic event—the Civil War, its causes, clashes, and consequences.

Oh, Freedom!

When white Europeans came to America, they usually arrived with hope and the promise of a better life. Black Africans arrived as slaves, facing a life of bondage. Yet not all of them remained enslaved. Some slaves, in the North and the South, were freed even before the Revolution. By the time of the Civil War, there were a great many free blacks in the United States, including a large number in the South.

Of the blacks who remained in slavery in the 1850's, more than half worked on cotton plantations. On these plantations and elsewhere, the slaves developed a unique style of music, the black spiritual. Spirituals fused traditional African music with other familiar materials—the Bible, Protestant hymns, and the popular music of the day. To the slave, spirituals were more than just deeply moving expressions of faith. They were also work songs in the fields and mills, rowing and hauling songs, war songs, laments, lullabies, and funeral dirges.

Among the best-known spirituals are "Roll, Jordan, Roll" and "Poor Rosy." Lucy McKim, a nineteenth-century collector of spirituals, quotes a slave woman who claimed that "Poor Rosy" could be sung only with "a full heart and a troubled spirit." McKim qualifies as an unsung heroine herself. Her *Slave Songs of the United States,* published in 1867, is a valuable source of music that might otherwise have been lost forever.

Not all the black voices of the period surfaced in spirituals. One of the great black abolitionist leaders was Frederick Douglass, born into slavery in Maryland. Douglass escaped as a young man and settled in the North, where he became a persuasive orator against slavery. Later he founded and published the *North Star,* a weekly antislavery newspaper. In his autobiography, *Narrative of the Life of Frederick Douglass,* Douglass agreed with the slave woman who spoke to Lucy McKim. "The songs of the slave," he wrote, "represent the sorrows of his heart; and he is relieved by them only as an aching heart is relieved by its tears."

When the Civil War broke out, the familiar spirituals went into battle. They were joined by new songs born of the conflict, such as "Many Thousand Gone" and "Oh, Freedom!" The words of these songs were still sad, but they often expressed a new-found hope:

> Oh, freedom! Oh, freedom!
> Oh, freedom over me;
> And before I'll be a slave,
> I'll be buried in my grave,
> And go home to my Lord, and be free.

According to one historian, the spiritual "made it possible for human beings to accept their fate when they could do nothing else, and it summoned them to a sustained protest against that same fate whenever the hour struck."

Wartime Voices

In a symbolic sense, the hour struck in September 1862 for all the slaves who lived in the Confederate States of America. It was then, in the midst of war, that Lincoln signed the Emancipation Proclamation. This proclamation declared that as of January 1, 1863, slaves in the Confederacy would be "then, thenceforward, and forever free." In order for the promise to be kept, however, the Union had to win the war.

Abraham Lincoln is generally regarded as one of America's greatest presidents. His fame rests largely on his deeds, but his words could be equally impressive. No American statesman is more often quoted. Lincoln's two inaugural addresses, his letters, and his brief, inspiring speech at Gettysburg have earned him a permanent place in American literature.

FAITHFUL TROOPS CHEER GENERAL LEE, 1865
N. C. Wyeth
U. S. Naval Academy Museum

Perhaps surprisingly, Lincoln's two most able commanders—Ulysses S. Grant and William T. Sherman—produced memoirs that are still regarded as models of their kind. In fact, the quality of writing done by high-ranking officers on both sides is remarkable. Also noteworthy were the diaries of ordinary soldiers and civilians. One of the most perceptive diarists was Mary Boykin Chesnut, wife of a Confederate officer. Her vivid, close-up views of wartime life in Charleston, South Carolina, were published as *A Diary from Dixie*.

A great many patriotic songs were written and sung during the war. Among the most popular ones in the North were "The Battle Cry of Freedom" and "Tenting Tonight on the Old Campground." "Taps," composed by General Daniel Butterfield, was first played in July 1862. The most famous Union song of all is probably Julia Ward Howe's stirring "The Battle Hymn of the Republic." Among southerners, "The Bonny Blue Flag" and "The Yellow Rose of Texas" were favorites, as was the well-known "Dixie."

Countless novels have been written about the Civil War, but few of any consequence were written until many decades later. One original novel of the Confederacy, *Macaria, or Altars of Sacrifice,* by Augusta Jane Wilson, was published in Richmond in 1864. Another novel, written from the Union viewpoint, was John W. DeForest's *Miss Ravenel's Conversion from Secession to Loyalty,* published in 1867.

Many of the northern writers who were active before the war continued to write during it. William Cullen Bryant, Ralph Waldo Emerson, Henry Wadsworth Longfellow, John Greenleaf Whittier, Oliver Wendell Holmes, James Russell Lowell, Herman Melville, and Emily Dickinson all produced wartime works. Only Melville, however, wrote memorably of the war itself. In the South, Henry Timrod composed poems that led some to call him "the laureate of the Confederacy." Born in Charleston, he developed a diamond-clear style combined with lyrical power. Illness forced Timrod's discharge from the Confederate Army. He died of tuberculosis two years after the war ended. Poets throughout the nation lamented his death, believing that his promise had been largely unfulfilled.

The Good Gray Poet

A northern poet who wrote about the war unforgettably was Walt Whitman, one of the giants of American literature. A New Yorker, Whitman worked as a journalist and editor of various newspapers, including the *Brooklyn Eagle*. In his youth, Whitman was something of a dandy, with a neatly trimmed beard, well-tailored clothes, and a spruce cane. He later acquired the better-known image of "the good gray poet"—shaggy beard, rough workman's clothes, large felt hat, and red shirt open at the collar.

Leaves of Grass, the first collection of Whitman's poems, originally appeared in 1855. Although the book achieved little public success, it was well received critically. In a letter to Whitman, Ralph Waldo Emerson hailed the work. "I greet you at the beginning of a great career," he wrote. Whitman continued to revise and expand *Leaves of Grass* throughout his life, producing several expanded editions.

After the Civil War broke out, Whitman's younger brother George enlisted in the Union army. When George was wounded at the Battle of Fredericksburg, Whitman went to Virginia to care for him. He remained in Washington, DC, for the rest of the war, working as a volunteer in military hospitals. Out of this experience came such masterful poems as "Cavalry Crossing a Ford," "By the Bivouac's Fitful Flame," and "Beat! Beat! Drums!" Upon the assassination of Lincoln, Whitman wrote the much-quoted "O Captain! My Captain" and the classic elegy "When Lilacs Last in the Dooryard Bloom'd."

Whitman's poetry, unusual in both content and style, exalted democracy and the common man. No one had seen anything quite like it before. It was, said one critic, "impossible to transfix with a phrase or a theory." *Leaves of Grass* has been called the most influential volume of poetry in the history of American literature.

My brother sitting on the tree of life,
And he heard when Jordan roll,
    Roll, Jordan, roll, Jordan!
    Roll, Jordan, roll!
    Black Spiritual

"A house divided against itself cannot stand." I believe this
government cannot endure permanently half slave and half
free.
    Abraham Lincoln in a speech at the Republican State Convention, 1858

With malice toward none; with charity for all; with firmness
in the right, as God gives us to see the right, let us strive on
to finish the work we are in. . . .
    Abraham Lincoln, Second Inaugural Address

I felt so tall within—I felt as if the power of the nation was
with me.
    Frederick Douglass, *Life and Times of Frederick Douglass*

Mine eyes have seen the glory
    Of the coming of the Lord,;
He is trampling out the vintage
    Where the grapes of wrath are stored.
    Julia Ward Howe, "The Battle Hymn of the Republic"

I hear America singing, the varied carols I hear.
    Walt Whitman, "I Hear America Singing," *Leaves of Grass*

I say we are no better than our judges in the North, and no
worse. We are human beings of the nineteenth century, and
slavery has to go, of course.
    Mary Boykin Chesnut, *A Diary from Dixie*

Christmas won't be Christmas without any presents.
    Louisa May Alcott, *Little Women*

READING CRITICALLY

The Literature of 1855–1865

Nearly all of the literary activity that occurred during the years from 1855 to 1865 was in some way related to the Civil War. By reading the literature of the period, you can gain a better understanding of the causes of the war and the ways in which it affected the American people.

HISTORICAL CONTEXT During the early part of the nineteenth century, industrialization swept through the northern states, while the southern states clung to their traditional rural lifestyle. The division between the North and South became more and more pronounced, and a great deal of controversy developed over the issue of slavery. As a movement to abolish slavery gained force in the North, southerners, who believed that their economy depended on slavery, became increasingly concerned. This concern reached its peak when Abraham Lincoln, an opponent of slavery, was elected president in 1860. Following Lincoln's election, the southern states began seceding from the Union, and on April 12, 1861, the Civil War began. The conflict lasted four years, taking thousands of lives and causing a tremendous amount of pain and suffering among the American people.

LITERARY MOVEMENTS In the literary world, the decade between 1855 and 1865 was a period of transition during which no new movements developed. However, the wartime era did produce one of the most important and influential poets in the history of American literature, Walt Whitman. While the country was being torn apart by war, Whitman was reaffirming the principles upon which the country was founded by expressing American democratic ideals in his poetry.

WRITERS' TECHNIQUES A number of notable speeches, songs, letters, memoirs, and journals were written by people who were directly or indirectly involved with the Civil War. At the same time, a new type of poetry was created by Walt Whitman—a type of poetry in which traditional poetic forms were abandoned in favor of free verse.

SPIRITUALS

Spirituals are folk songs that originated among enslaved Africans in America. They served as an important means of communication and a way of expressing the slaves' desire for freedom and religious salvation. At the same time, the songs helped to replace their lost African religious traditions and allowed them to maintain a connection to their musical heritage.

Spirituals were inspired by the religious hymns of the white revivalists of the early nineteenth century and shaped by memories of traditional African music. Because of their religious content, most slave owners openly accepted these songs. Many of the spirituals had a double meaning, however, conveying not only the slaves' religious faith but also their desire to escape from their bondage. In fact, some of the songs were used to transmit secret messages that their masters and overseers would be unable to understand. For example, the spiritual "Follow the Drinking Gourd" advised runaway slaves to follow the Big Dipper, which points to the north.

Many spirituals were work songs that the slaves made up while they harvested cotton or sugar cane or loaded and unloaded ships. Many others were directly based on Methodist hymns, which the slaves turned into entirely new songs by adding a strong rhythm and depth of feeling. Many of these work and church songs followed a call-and-response form in which individuals made up new verses and were answered by the group, which acted like a chorus.

Most spirituals included references to people, places, or events in the Bible. They frequently referred to Moses, who in the Old Testament led the Jews out of slavery in Egypt. The black slaves compared their own enslavement with the plight of the ancient Jews. In spirituals such as "Swing Low, Sweet Chariot" and "Go Down, Moses," the black slaves expressed their hope that they would someday escape to their own "promised land" just as the Israelites had escaped to ancient Israel.

Spirituals were almost unknown outside the South until after the Civil War. In 1867 a collection of black music called *Slave Songs of the United States* was published. A few years later, in 1871, a group of black singers, the Jubilee Singers from Fisk University, traveled throughout the United States and to England and Germany singing spirituals to raise money for their school. Students from other schools followed their example and helped popularize the spiritual.

GUIDE FOR INTERPRETING

Swing Low, Sweet Chariot;
Go Down, Moses

Writers' Techniques

Refrain. A refrain is a word, phrase, line, or group of lines repeated at regular intervals in a poem or song. For example, the line "Coming for to carry me home" is repeated throughout "Swing, Low, Sweet Chariot."

Most spirituals include at least one, and sometimes more than one, refrain. The refrain emphasizes the most important ideas and establishes the rhythm. In a spiritual the refrain was usually sung by a chorus, with the other words being sung by a soloist. Because spirituals were passed orally from person to person and group to group, the words apart from the refrain often changed. In fact, soloists often improvised, creating new lyrics while singing. Since the refrains were frequently repeated, however, they were easy to remember and rarely changed. As a result, there is little variation in the refrain among different versions of a spiritual.

Focus

Why does music often produce a strong emotional response in people? Freewrite about the emotional impact of music. Try to include examples.

Primary Source

Frederick Douglass (1817?–1895) escaped from slavery at the age of twenty-one and went on to become one of the nation's foremost orators. In his autobiography he gave his explanation for why the enslaved Africans sang spirituals as they worked.

> Slaves are generally expected to sing as well as to work. A silent slave is not liked by masters or overseers. *"Make a noise, make a noise,"* and *"bear a hand,"* are the words usually addressed to the slaves when there is silence amongst them. This may account for the almost constant singing heard in the southern states. There was, generally, more or less singing among the teamsters, as it was one means of letting the overseer know where they were, . . .
>
> The remark is not unfrequently made, that slaves are the most contented and happy laborers in the world. They dance and sing, and make all manner of joyful noises—so they do; but it is a great mistake to suppose them happy because they sing. The songs of the slave represent the sorrows rather than the joys, of his heart; and he is relieved by them, only as an aching heart is relieved by its tears.

Swing Low, Sweet Chariot

Spiritual

Swing low, sweet chariot,
Coming for to carry me home,
Swing low, sweet chariot,
Coming for to carry me home.

5   I looked over Jordan and what did I see
Coming for to carry me home,
A band of angels coming after me,
Coming for to carry me home.

If you get there before I do,
10 Coming for to carry me home,
Tell all my friends I'm coming too,
Coming for to carry me home.

Swing low, sweet chariot,
Coming for to carry me home,
15 Swing low, sweet chariot,
Coming for to carry me home.

RESPONDING TO THE SELECTION

Your Response

1. What images does this spiritual bring to mind?

Interpreting

2. (a) If you interpret this spiritual as a religious song, what does the chariot represent? (b) What does home represent? (c) What is the subject of the song?

3. (a) If you interpret this spiritual as an expression of the enslaved Africans' desire for freedom, what does the chariot represent? (b) What does home represent? (c) What does Jordan, the river that formed the boundary to the promised land of the ancient Israelites, represent? (d) What does the band of angels represent?

Applying

4. (a) For what types of events and situations do people write protest songs today? (b) Name two recent protest songs. (c) What messages do these two songs convey?

LEARNING OPTION

Humanities. Express the desire for freedom in song. Following in the tradition of enslaved Africans and church soloists, improvise with a classmate and create two new verses to "Swing Low, Sweet Chariot." Maintain the rhythm of the spiritual by keeping the refrain.

Go Down, Moses

Spiritual

Go down, Moses,
Way down in Egypt land
Tell old Pharaoh
To let my people go.

5   When Israel was in Egypt land
Let my people go
Oppressed so hard they could not stand
Let my people go.

Go down, Moses,
10   Way down in Egypt land
Tell old Pharaoh
"Let my people go."

"Thus saith the Lord," bold Moses said,
"Let my people go;
15   If not I'll smite your first-born dead
Let my people go."

Go down, Moses,
Way down in Egypt land,
Tell old Pharaoh,
20   "Let my people go!"

RESPONDING TO THE SELECTION

Your Response
1. How would you describe the mood of this spiritual?
2. What feelings does the spiritual evoke in you? Explain.
3. To what type of music would you choose to set the spiritual?

Interpreting
4. In this song a comparison is developed between the captivity of the ancient Israelites in Egypt and the enslavement of the blacks in America. Egypt represents the South and Moses represents a leader helping blacks escape from slavery. (a) Whom does the old Pharaoh represent? (b) Whom do the people of Israel represent?

Applying
5. Harriet Tubman led other black slaves out of bondage to freedom in the North. Known by the code name of Moses, she once said, "We got to go free or die. And freedom's not bought with dust." What other American heroes can you think of who would agree with her words? Explain your choices.

ANALYZING LITERATURE

Recognizing a Refrain
A **refrain** is a word, phrase, line, or group of lines repeated at regular intervals in a poem or song.
1. What refrain is used in the song?
2. Explain how this refrain conveys the main idea.

THINKING AND READING

Writing About the Role of Spirituals
Write an essay in which you discuss what made spirituals such an important part of slave life. Prepare a list of reasons for the spirituals' importance. Then find passages in "Swing Low, Sweet Chariot" and "Go Down, Moses" that support your reasons. Prepare an outline and a thesis statement. Then write your essay. When you revise, eliminate any unnecessary information and make sure that your essay is coherent and well organized.

LEARNING OPTION

Cross-curricular Connection. Harriet Tubman, the woman known as Moses, went down South nineteen times and led more than 300 black slaves to freedom. Find out more about Tubman and her role in the underground railroad. Share your findings with classmates in a brief oral or written report.

FREDERICK DOUGLASS

1817[?]–1895

Frederick Douglass rose out of slavery to become one of the most gifted writers and orators of his time. Using these talents, he dedicated his life to fighting for the abolition of slavery and for black civil rights. Douglass's life served as an inspiration and example for both blacks and whites throughout the country.

Douglass was born on a Maryland plantation. When he was eight, he was sent to live with the family of Hugh Auld in Baltimore. There, he learned to read and write, at first with the encouragement of Mrs. Auld and later despite her objections. When his desire for freedom was fueled by his reading, Douglass escaped from slavery at the age of twenty-one.

In 1841, three years after his escape, Douglass was asked to speak at a convention of the Massachusetts Anti-Slavery Society. Though he had never spoken in public before, Douglass delivered a tremendously powerful, moving speech. Impressed by his eloquence, the society immediately hired him as a lecturer.

Although he lived in constant fear of being arrested as a fugitive slave, Douglass spent the next four years lecturing throughout the Northeast. In 1845 he published his autobiography, *Narrative of the Life of Frederick Douglass*. Fearing the book's publication would lead to his re-enslavement, Douglass fled to England, where he spent two years trying to gain British support for the abolitionist cause.

After several of his English friends raised money finally to buy his freedom, Douglass returned to the United States. Upon his return, he established the *North Star,* a newspaper for blacks, and began lecturing again. In 1855 he published *My Bondage and My Freedom,* an updated version of his autobiography.

During the Civil War, Douglass helped to recruit black soldiers for the Union army. After the war ended and slavery was abolished, he fought for black civil rights. He also held several government positions such as the marshal and recorder of deeds of the District of Columbia and the United States minister to Haiti.

In 1883, speaking as a vigorous fighter for civil rights, Douglass commented that the American people "must learn, or neglect to do so at their own peril, . . . that 'Equal Manhood means Equal Rights,' and that further, that the American people must stand each for all and all for each, without respect to color or race. . . . I expect to see the colored people of this country enjoying the same freedom, voting at the same ballot-box, using the same cartridge-box, going to the same schools, attending the same churches, . . . proud of the same country, fighting the same foe, and enjoying the same peace and all its advantages. . . ."

GUIDE FOR INTERPRETING

from My Bondage and My Freedom

Literary Forms

Autobiography. An autobiography is a person's account of his or her own life. In an autobiography the writer presents a continuous narrative of what he or she feels are the most significant events in his or her life. Because the writer's life is presented as he or she views it, the portrayal of people and events is colored by the author's feelings and beliefs. In fact, some of the writer's attitudes and beliefs may be directly stated.

Usually, the writers of autobiographies believe that their lives are interesting or important or can in some way serve as examples for others. Frederick Douglass, for instance, wrote his autobiography because he believed that his life proved that blacks were no less perceptive, intelligent, and capable than whites. Written in a plain and direct style that was also fluent and forceful, Douglass's autobiography demonstrated not only that blacks were capable of overcoming great hardships and achieving success but also that they could express themselves eloquently.

Focus

Frederick Douglass's life served as an example for both blacks and whites throughout the country. Prepare a list of other men and women whose lives have served as an example for other people.

Primary Source

In 1879, when Frederick Douglass was in his sixties, the *Rochester Democrat and Chronicle* described him as "among the greatest men, not only of this city, but of the nation as well . . ." It went on to say:

> Frederick Douglass can hardly be said to have risen to greatness on account of the opportunities which the republic offers to self-made men, and concerning which we are apt to talk with an abundance of self-gratulation. To him, the republic offered no opportunities. It sought to fetter his mind equally with his body. . . . So far as he was concerned, freedom was a mockery, and law was the instrument of tyranny. . . . There is no sadder commentary upon American slavery than the life of Frederick Douglass. He put it under his feet and stood erect in the majesty of his intellect; but how many intellects as brilliant and as powerful as his it stamped upon and crushed no mortal can tell. . . . Not alone did his voice proclaim emancipation. Eloquent as was that voice, his life, in its pathos and in its grandeur, was more eloquent still. . . .

from **My Bondage and My Freedom**

Frederick Douglass

I lived in the family of Master Hugh, at Baltimore, seven years, during which time—as the almanac makers say of the weather—my condition was variable. The most interesting feature of my history here, was my learning to read and write, under somewhat marked disadvantages. In attaining this knowledge, I was compelled to resort to indirections by no means congenial to my nature, and which were really humiliating to me. My mistress—who had begun to teach me—was suddenly checked in her benevolent design, by the strong advice of her husband. In faithful compliance with this advice, the good lady had not only ceased to instruct me, herself, but had set her face as a flint against my learning to read by any means. It is due, however, to my mistress to say, that she did not adopt this course in all its stringency at the first. She either thought it unnecessary, or she lacked the depravity indispensable to shutting me up in mental darkness. It was, at least, necessary for her to have some training, and some hardening, in the exercise of the slaveholder's prerogative, to make her equal to forgetting my human nature and character, and to treating me as a thing destitute of a moral or an intellectual nature. Mrs. Auld—my mistress—was, as I have said, a most kind and tenderhearted woman; and, in the humanity of her heart, and the simplicity of her mind, she set out, when I first went to live with her, to treat me as she supposed one human being ought to treat another.

It is easy to see, that, in entering upon the duties of a slaveholder, some little experience is needed. Nature has done almost nothing to prepare men and women to be either slaves or slaveholders. Nothing but rigid training, long persisted in, can perfect the character of the one or the other. One cannot easily forget to love freedom; and it is as hard to cease to respect that natural love in our fellow creatures. On entering upon the career of a slaveholding mistress, Mrs. Auld was singularly deficient; nature, which fits nobody for such an office, had done less for her than any lady I had known. It was no easy matter to induce her to think and to feel that the curly-headed boy, who stood by her side, and even leaned on her lap; who was loved by little Tommy, and who loved little Tommy in turn; sustained to her only the relation of a chattel. I was *more* than that, and she felt me to be more than that. I could talk and sing; I could laugh and weep; I could reason and remember; I could love and hate. I was human, and she, dear lady, knew and felt me to be so. How could she, then, treat me as a brute, without a mighty struggle with all the noble powers of her own soul. That struggle came, and the will and power of the husband was victorious. Her noble soul was overthrown; but, he that overthrew it did not, himself, escape the consequences.

He, not less than the other parties, was injured in his domestic peace by the fall.

When I went into their family, it was the abode of happiness and contentment. The mistress of the house was a model of affection and tenderness. Her fervent piety and watchful uprightness made it impossible to see her without thinking and feeling—"that woman is a Christian." There was no sorrow nor suffering for which she had not a tear, and there was no innocent joy for which she did not a smile. She had bread for the hungry, clothes for the naked, and comfort for every mourner that came within her reach. Slavery soon proved its ability to divest her of these excellent qualities, and her home of its early happiness. Conscience cannot stand much violence. Once thoroughly broken down, *who* is he that can repair the damage? It may be broken toward the slave, on Sunday, and toward the master on Monday. It cannot endure such shocks. It must stand entire, or it does not stand at all. If my condition waxed bad, that of the family waxed not better. The first step, in the wrong direction, was the violence done to nature and to conscience, in arresting the benevolence that would have enlightened my young mind. In ceasing to instruct me, she must begin to justify herself *to* herself; and, once consenting to take sides in such a debate, she was riveted to her position. One needs very little knowledge of moral philosophy, to see *where* my mistress now landed. She finally became even more violent in her opposition to my learning to read, than was her husband himself. She was not satisfied with simply doing as *well* as her husband had commanded her, but seemed resolved to better his instruction. Nothing appeared to make my poor mistress—after her turning toward the downward path—more angry, than seeing me, seated in some nook or corner, quietly reading a book or a newspaper. I have had her rush at me, with the utmost fury, and snatch from my hand such newspaper or book, with something of the wrath

and consternation which a traitor might be supposed to feel on being discovered in a plot by some dangerous spy.

Mrs. Auld was an apt woman, and the advice of her husband, and her own experience, soon demonstrated, to her entire satisfaction, that education and slavery are incompatible with each other. When this conviction was thoroughly established, I was most narrowly watched in all my movements. If I remained in a separate room from the family for any considerable length of time, I was sure to be suspected of having a book, and was at once called upon to give an account of myself. All this, however, was entirely *too late*. The first, and never to be retraced, step had been taken. In teaching me the alphabet, in the days of her simplicity and kindness, my mistress had given me the "inch," and now, no ordinary precaution could prevent me from taking the "ell."[1]

Seized with a determination to learn to read, at any cost, I hit upon many expedients to accomplish the desired end. The plea which I mainly adopted, and the one by which I was most successful, was that of using my young white playmates, with whom I met in the street, as teachers. I used to carry, almost constantly, a copy of Webster's spelling book in my pocket; and, when sent on errands, or when play time was allowed me, I would step, with my young friends, aside, and take a lesson in spelling. I generally paid my *tuition fee* to the boys, with bread, which I also carried in my pocket. For a single biscuit, any of my hungry little comrades would give me a lesson more valuable to me than bread. Not everyone, however, demanded this consideration, for there were those who took pleasure in teaching me, whenever I had a chance to be taught by them. I am strongly tempted to give the names of two or three of those little boys, as a slight testimonial of the gratitude and af-

---

1. **ell** *n.*: A former English measure of length, equal to forty-five inches.

fection I bear them, but prudence forbids; not that it would injure me, but it might, possibly, embarrass them; for it is almost an unpardonable offense to do anything, directly or indirectly, to promote a slave's freedom, in a slave state. It is enough to say, of my warm-hearted little play fellows, that they lived on Philpot Street, very near Durgin & Bailey's shipyard.

Although slavery was a delicate subject, and very cautiously talked about among grownup people in Maryland, I frequently talked about it—and that very freely—with the white boys. I would, sometimes, say to them, while seated on a curbstone or a cellar door, "I wish I could be free, as you will be when you get to be men." "You will be free, you know, as soon as you are twenty-one, and can go where you like, but I am a slave for life. Have I not as good a right to be free as you have?" Words like these, I observed, always troubled them; and I had no small satisfaction in wringing from the boys, occasionally, that fresh and bitter condemnation of slavery, that springs from nature, unseared and unperverted. Of all consciences let me have those to deal with which have not been bewildered by the cares of life. I do not remember ever to have met with a *boy*, while I was in slavery, who defended the slave system; but I have often had boys to console me, with the hope that something would yet occur, by which I might be made free. Over and over again, they have told me, that "they believed *I* had as good a right to be free as *they* had"; and that "they did not believe God ever made anyone to be a slave." The reader will easily see, that such little conversations with my play fellows, had no tendency to weaken my love of liberty, nor to render me contented with my condition as a slave.

When I was about thirteen years old, and had succeeded in learning to read, every increase of knowledge, especially respecting the free states, added something to the almost intolerable burden of the thought—"I am a slave for life." To my bondage I saw no end. It was a terrible reality, and I shall never be able to tell how sadly that thought chafed my young spirit. Fortunately, or unfortunately, about this time in my life, I had made enough money to buy what was then a very popular schoolbook, the *Columbian Orator.* I bought this addition to my library, of Mr. Knight, on Thames street, Fell's Point, Baltimore, and paid him fifty cents for it. I was first led to buy this book, by hearing some little boys say they were going to learn some little pieces out of it for the Exhibition. This volume was, indeed, a rich treasure, and every opportunity afforded me, for a time, was spent in diligently perusing it. . . . The dialogue and the speeches were all redolent of the principles of liberty, and poured floods of light on the nature and character of slavery. As I read, behold! the very discontent so graphically predicted by Master Hugh, had already come upon me. I was no longer the light-hearted, gleesome boy, full of mirth and play, as when I landed first at Baltimore. Knowledge had come. . . . This knowledge opened my eyes to the horrible pit, and revealed the teeth of the frightful dragon that was ready to pounce upon me, but it opened no way for my escape. I have often wished myself a beast, or a bird—anything, rather than a slave. I was wretched and gloomy, beyond my ability to describe. I was too thoughtful to be happy. It was this everlasting thinking which distressed and tormented me; and yet there was no getting rid of the subject of my thoughts. All nature was redolent of it. Once awakened by the silver trump[2] of knowledge, my spirit was roused to eternal wakefulness. Liberty! the inestimable birthright of every man, had, for me, converted every object into an asserter of this great right. It was heard in every sound, and beheld in every object. It was ever present, to torment me with a sense of my

---

2. **trump:** Trumpet.

from *My Bondage and My Freedom*   367

wretched condition. The more beautiful and charming were the smiles of nature, the more horrible and desolate was my condition. I saw nothing without seeing it, and I heard nothing without hearing it. I do not exaggerate, when I say, that it looked from every star, smiled in every calm, breathed in every wind, and moved in every storm.

I have no doubt that my state of mind had something to do with the change in the treatment adopted, by my once kind mistress toward me. I can easily believe, that my leaden, downcast, and discontented look, was very offensive to her. Poor lady! She did not know my trouble, and I dared not tell her. Could I have freely made her acquainted with the real state of my mind, and given her the reasons therefor, it might have been well for both of us. Her abuse of me fell upon me like the blows of the false prophet upon his ass; she did not know that an *angel* stood in the way;[3] and—such is the relation of master

---

3. blows . . . the way: An allusion to a biblical tale (Numbers 22 : 21–35) about an ass that cannot move, though she is beaten by her master, because her path is blocked by an angel.

and slave—I could not tell her. Nature had made us *friends;* slavery made us *enemies.* My interests were in a direction opposite to hers, and we both had our private thoughts and plans. She aimed to keep me ignorant; and I resolved to know, although knowledge only increased my discontent. My feelings were not the result of any marked cruelty in the treatment I received; they sprung from the consideration of my being a slave at all. It was *slavery*—not its mere *incidents*—that I hated. I had been cheated. I saw through the attempt to keep me in ignorance. . . . The feeding and clothing me well, could not atone for taking my liberty from me. The smiles of my mistress could not remove the deep sorrow that dwelt in my young bosom. Indeed, these, in time, came only to deepen my sorrow. She had changed; and the reader will see that I had changed, too. We were both victims to the same overshadowing evil—*she,* as mistress, *I,* as slave. I will not censure her harshly; she cannot censure me, for she knows I speak but the truth, and have acted in my opposition to slavery, just as she herself would have acted, in a reverse of circumstances.

MULTICULTURAL CONNECTION

The Influence of Frederick Douglass

His influence on African Americans. Frederick Douglass was perhaps the most prominent black American leader of the nineteenth century, and his influence is still felt by African Americans today. As a battler for human rights, Douglass served as a role model for African American leaders like Booker T. Washington and W.E.B. DuBois. In our own time, the record of Douglass's struggle against segregation influenced the civil rights movement. Douglass anticipated by many years the causes and struggles of this movement. As a young man, he protested segregated seating on trains by sitting in cars reserved for whites until the au-

thorities dragged him out. Later, he actively fought job discrimination against African Americans and protested segregation in the schools.

A model for all who struggle. Frederick Douglass did not limit himself to fighting for African Americans' civil rights. He also helped the suffragists in their battle to win the vote. Douglass felt very strongly that every citizen deserved the right to vote. Because he did not segregate his causes, Douglass is a model for all who struggle against injustice.

Exploring and Sharing

Research and discuss how Frederick Douglass's actions anticipated the civil rights movement of the 1950's and 1960's.

RESPONDING TO THE SELECTION

Your Response

1. What are your impressions of Frederick Douglass? Explain.
2. Comment on Douglass's observation that "conscience cannot stand much violence."
3. Do you think that it was possible to be a good slaveowner? Why or why not?

Recalling

4. (a) How long does Douglass live with the Aulds? (b) What is the "most interesting" aspect of his history with the Aulds?
5. Explain the change in Mrs. Auld's attitude toward Douglass.
6. (a) What does Douglass pay the boys who give him lessons in spelling? (b) What is their attitude toward slavery?
7. (a) What popular schoolbook does Douglass buy? (b) How does reading this book affect him?

Interpreting

8. Why does Douglass view slaveholders as well as slaves as victims of slavery?
9. Why is education incompatible with slavery?
10. Why do you think the white children's attitude toward slavery is different from that of their parents?
11. How would you describe Douglass's attitude toward Mrs. Auld?
12. Douglass writes, "My feelings were not the result of any marked cruelty in the treatment I received; they sprung from the consideration of my being a slave at all. It was *slavery*—not its mere *incidents*—that I hated." Explain the difference between *slavery* and the *incidents* of slavery. Why does the first have a so much stronger effect on the emotions?

Applying

13. Mahatma Gandhi wrote, "The moment the slave resolves that he will no longer be a slave, his fetters fall." React to this statement. Then explain whether or not you feel Douglass was free even while in bondage.

ANALYZING LITERATURE

Recognizing an Autobiography

An **autobiography** is a person's account of his or her own life. Most autobiographies convey many of the writer's attitudes and beliefs. In his autobiography Frederick Douglass expresses his attitude toward slavery.

1. Find a passage in which Douglass directly states his attitude toward slavery.
2. Find one passage in which Douglass conveys his opposition to slavery through his description of events.
3. How do you think this account would be different if it had been written by Mrs. Auld?

CRITICAL THINKING AND READING

Analyzing the Effect of Style

My Bondage and My Freedom is written in a plain but eloquent style. Douglass describes events in a straightforward, factual manner, offering little interpretation of the significance of the events. He lets the facts speak for themselves and allows readers to draw their own conclusions.

Considering that Douglass wrote his autobiography because he believed that his life could serve as an example, why do you think that his style is effective?

THINKING AND WRITING

Writing an Autobiography

College applications frequently ask prospective students to write a brief autobiographical sketch describing an important experience. Imagine that you are filling out an application that includes this request. Think about the type of impression you want to make on the admissions committee. Then decide on the experience that you want to describe. Make a list of the important details related to the experience. When you write your sketch, describe the ways in which the experience affected you and what you think it reveals about your personality. When you revise, try to think about how the members of the admissions committee would be likely to respond to your sketch.

GUIDE FOR INTERPRETING

from Mary Chesnut's Civil War

Mary Boykin Chesnut (1823–1886) was the daughter of a United States senator from South Carolina, and she was brought up in an aristocratic family in Charleston, South Carolina. When she was seventeen, Mary Boykin married James Chesnut, Jr., a wealthy lawyer, who was later elected to the Senate. The cruelty of the war deeply disturbed her. Through her journal we can share firsthand the joy and sorrow of the people of the South in victory and defeat.

Literary Forms

Journals. A journal, or diary, is a personal record of events, conversations, thoughts, feelings, and observations. Written on a day-to-day basis, journals allow writers to record their most immediate responses to their experiences. Usually, writers keep journals for their own personal use, not intending to have them published. As a result, journals tend to be written in an informal, personal style and capture the writer's innermost thoughts and feelings.

Commentary

Many people keep journals, but few journals have as widespread interest as that of Mary Chesnut. What kind of woman was Chesnut? What qualities did she bring to her role as journal writer?

According to one historian, Chesnut had unusual qualifications as a diarist. "[S]he was well informed; she knew most, if not all the leaders of the Confederate Government, and of the Confederate Army; she knew the way of life of the well-born and the wealthy southern planter; she knew a little about the way of life of poorer white people; and she knew the Negro." She was also intelligent and articulate, "expressing herself easily and clearly." Finally, "she was an interesting individual, a devoted wife and a loyal friend without being blind to the faults of her husband, or of her friends—or of herself. She had a bluntness which must have dealt many wounds, and a warmth which must have made it easy to forgive her blunt speech."

What great events might a journal writer describe today? What special qualities would be important for the writer to have in order to make the events interesting to others?

Focus

Freewrite about books you have read and movies you have seen about the Civil War. Discuss what the books and movies reveal about how the war changed people's lives. Also explain what you think the American people learned from the conflict.

from Mary Chesnut's Civil War

Mary Chesnut

April 7, 1861. Today things seem to have settled down a little.

One can but hope still. Lincoln or Seward[1] have made such silly advances and then far sillier drawings back. There may be a chance for peace, after all.

Things are happening so fast.

My husband has been made an aide-de-camp[2] of General Beauregard.

Three hours ago we were quietly packing to go home. The convention has adjourned.

Now he tells me the attack upon Fort Sumter[3] may begin tonight. Depends upon Anderson and the fleet outside. The *Herald* says that this show of war outside of the bar is intended for Texas.

John Manning came in with his sword and red sash. Pleased as a boy to be on Beauregard's staff while the row goes on. He has gone with Wigfall to Captain Hartstene with instructions.

Mr. Chesnut is finishing a report he had to make to the convention.

Mrs. Hayne called. She had, she said, "but one feeling, pity for those who are not here."

Jack Preston, Willie Alston—"the take-life-easys," as they are called—with John Green, "the big brave," have gone down to the island—volunteered as privates.

Seven hundred men were sent over. Ammunition wagons rumbling along the streets all night. Anderson burning blue lights—signs and signals for the fleet outside, I suppose.

Today at dinner there was no allusion to things as they stand in Charleston Harbor. There was an undercurrent of intense excitement. There could not have been a more brilliant circle. In addition to our usual quartet (Judge Withers, Langdon Cheves, and Trescot) our two governors dined with us, Means and Manning.

These men all talked so delightfully. For once in my life I listened.

That over, business began. In earnest, Governor Means rummaged a sword and red sash from somewhere and brought it for Colonel Chesnut, who has gone to demand the surrender of Fort Sumter.

And now, patience—we must wait.

---

1. Seward: William Henry Seward (1801–1872), U.S. Secretary of State from 1861 through 1869.
2. aide-de-camp: An officer serving as assistant and confidential secretary to a superior.
3. Fort Sumter: A fort in Charleston Harbor, South Carolina. At the time, the fort was occupied by Union troops commanded by Major Robert Anderson.

Why did that green goose Anderson go into Fort Sumter? Then everything began to go wrong.

Now they have intercepted a letter from him, urging them to let him surrender. He paints the horrors likely to ensue if they will not.

He ought to have thought of all that before he put his head in the hole.

April 12, 1861. Anderson will not capitulate.

Yesterday was the merriest, maddest dinner we have had yet. Men were more audaciously wise and witty. We had an unspoken foreboding it was to be our last pleasant meeting. Mr. Miles dined with us today. Mrs. Henry King rushed in: "The news, I come for the latest news—all of the men of the King family are on the island"—of which fact she seemed proud.

While she was here, our peace negotiator—or envoy—came in. That is, Mr. Chesnut returned—his interview with Colonel Anderson had been deeply interesting—but was not inclined to be communicative, wanted his dinner. Felt for Anderson. Had telegraphed to President Davis[4] for instructions.

What answer to give Anderson, etc., etc. He has gone back to Fort Sumter with additional instructions.

When they were about to leave the wharf, A. H. Boykin sprang into the boat, in great excitement; thought himself ill-used. A likelihood of fighting—and he to be left behind!

I do not pretend to go to sleep. How can I? If Anderson does not accept terms—at four—the orders are—he shall be fired upon.

I count four—St. Michael chimes. I begin to hope. At half-past four, the heavy booming of a cannon.

I sprang out of bed. And on my knees—prostrate—I prayed as I never prayed before.

There was a sound of stir all over the house—pattering of feet in the corridor—all seemed hurrying one way. I put on my double gown and a shawl and went, too. It was to the housetop.

The shells were bursting. In the dark I heard a man say "waste of ammunition."

I knew my husband was rowing about in a boat somewhere in that dark bay. And that the shells were roofing it over—bursting toward the fort. If Anderson was obstinate—he was to order the forts on our side to open fire. Certainly fire had begun. The regular roar of the cannon—there it was. And who could tell what each volley accomplished of death and destruction.

The women were wild, there on the housetop. Prayers from the women and imprecations from the men, and then a shell would light up the scene. Tonight, they say, the forces are to attempt to land.

The *Harriet Lane*[5] had her wheelhouse[6] smashed and put back to sea.

We watched up there—everybody wondered. Fort Sumter did not fire a shot.

Today Miles and Manning, colonels now—aides to Beauregard—dined with us. The latter hoped I would keep the peace. I give him only good words, for he was to be under fire all day and night, in the bay carrying orders, etc.

Last night—or this morning truly—up on the housetop I was so weak and weary I sat down on something that looked like a black stool.

"Get up, you foolish woman—your dress is on fire," cried a man. And he put me out.

---

4. President Davis: Jefferson Davis (1808–1889), president of the Confederacy (1861–1865).

5. The *Harriet Lane*: A federal steamer that had brought provisions to Fort Sumter.
6. wheelhouse *n*.: An enclosed place on the upper deck of a ship, in which the helmsman stands while steering.

THE HOUSETOPS IN CHARLESTON DURING THE BOMBARDMENT OF FORT SUMTER
Harper's Weekly, May 4, 1861
Library of Congress

from *Mary Chesnut's Civil War*   373

It was a chimney, and the sparks caught my clothes. Susan Preston and Mr. Venable then came up. But my fire had been extinguished before it broke out into a regular blaze.

Do you know, after all that noise and our tears and prayers, nobody has been hurt. Sound and fury, signifying nothing.[7] A delusion and a snare. . . .

Somebody came in just now and reported Colonel Chesnut asleep on the sofa in General Beauregard's room. After two such nights he must be so tired as to be able to sleep anywhere. . . .

April 13, 1861. Nobody hurt, after all. How gay we were last night.

Reaction after the dread of all the slaughter we thought those dreadful cannons were making such a noise in doing.

Not even a battery[8] the worse for wear.

Fort Sumter has been on fire. He has not yet silenced any of our guns. So the aides—still with swords and red sashes by way of uniform—tell us.

But the sound of those guns makes regular meals impossible. None of us go to table. But tea trays pervade the corridors, going everywhere.

Some of the anxious hearts lie on their beds and moan in solitary misery. Mrs. Wigfall and I solace ourselves with tea in my room.

These women have all a satisfying faith.

April 15, 1861. I did not know that one could live such days of excitement.

They called, "Come out—there is a crowd coming."

A mob indeed, but it was headed by Colonels Chesnut and Manning.

The crowd was shouting and showing these two as messengers of good news. They were escorted to Beauregard's headquarters. Fort Sumter had surrendered.

Those up on the housetop shouted to us, "The fort is on fire." That had been the story once or twice before.

When we had calmed down, Colonel Chesnut, who had taken it all quietly enough—if anything, more unruffled than usual in his serenity—told us how the surrender came about.

Wigfall was with them on Morris Island when he saw the fire in the fort, jumped in a little boat and, with his handkerchief as a white flag, rowed over to Fort Sumter. Wigfall went in through a porthole.

When Colonel Chesnut arrived shortly after and was received by the regular entrance, Colonel Anderson told him he had need to pick his way warily, for it was all mined.

As far as I can make out, the fort surrendered to Wigfall.

But it is all confusion. Our flag is flying there. Fire engines have been sent to put out the fire.

Everybody tells you half of something and then rushes off to tell something else or to hear the last news. . . .

---

7. Sound . . . nothing: From Shakespeare's *Macbeth*, Act V, Scene v, lines 27–28. Macbeth is contemplating the significance of life and death, after learning of his wife's death.
8. battery *n*.: Artillery unit.

RESPONDING TO THE SELECTION

Your Response

1. What details in Mary Chesnut's diary did you find most interesting? Explain.
2. Based on Chesnut's diary entries, what are your impressions of the way people on the home front reacted to the war?

Recalling

3. (a) Why does Colonel Chesnut go to Fort Sumter on April 7? (b) How does Mary Chesnut react to the attack on Fort Sumter on April 12?
4. (a) When do the Union troops at Fort Sumter surrender to the Confederate forces? (b) Who explains how the surrender came about?

Interpreting

5. What does this excerpt reveal about Mary Chesnut's attitude toward the war?
6. What does this excerpt reveal about Mary Chesnut's attitude toward the Confederacy?

Applying

7. In what ways do you think this excerpt would be different if it had been written by someone actively involved in the attack on Fort Sumter?
8. In what ways do you think this excerpt would have been different if Mary Chesnut had been from the North?

ANALYZING LITERATURE

Understanding a Journal

A **journal** is a personal record of events, conversations, thoughts, feelings, and observations. In *Mary Chesnut's Civil War,* Mary Chesnut's journal from the war years, for example, Chesnut records her personal responses to the important events and people of the Civil War.

1. Mary Chesnut's descriptions are often colored by her dislike for the war. What evidence is there in Chesnut's description of the attack on Fort Sumter and the events preceding it that she dreaded the coming of the war?
2. Name two characteristics of Mary Chesnut's personality that are revealed in her journal.

CRITICAL THINKING AND READING

Recognizing Main Ideas

When reading a journal, it is important to recognize the main ideas being expressed and the main events being described. One of the main ideas expressed in Mary Chesnut's journal entry for April 12, for example, is that her husband believes that the attack on Fort Sumter may begin that night.

List three other main ideas and events in the excerpt from *Mary Chesnut's Civil War.*

THINKING AND WRITING

Writing a Summary

Write a summary of the events described in the excerpt from *Mary Chesnut's Civil War.* Reread the selection. Then look at your list of main ideas and events from the Critical Thinking and Reading exercise, making sure that you have not omitted any. Write your summary in chronological order, using transitions to link ideas and indicate the order of events. When you revise, make sure that your summary is clear and concise.

LEARNING OPTIONS

1. **Writing.** Mary Chesnut's journal entry for April 12, 1861, includes a subjective account of the Confederate attack on Fort Sumter. Present a more objective account. As a correspondent for *Harper's Weekly,* provide detailed, on-the-spot coverage. You may wish to research additional details of the bombardment.
2. **Cross-curricular Connection.** When Abraham Lincoln was nominated as the Republican candidate for United States President in May 1860, a delegate from Kentucky declared, "Gentlemen, we are on the brink of a great civil war." Investigate the election of 1860 and find out what Lincoln's victory meant to southerners. Create a timeline of events leading to the opening shots of the Civil War on April 12, 1861.

BIOGRAPHIES

Robert E. Lee (1807–1870)

A descendant of a number of distinguished patriots and statesmen, Robert E. Lee was born into a respected family in Virginia. He attended the United States Military Academy at West Point, graduating with high honors in 1829. During the Mexican War, he earned a reputation as one of the country's finest military leaders. In fact, he was so highly regarded that when the Civil War began, President Lincoln offered Lee command of the Union forces.

Although he opposed secession, Lee refused Lincoln's offer. Determined not to harm his native state, Lee resigned his commission in the United States Army. In his letter of resignation, Lee vowed never to draw his sword again except in the defense of Virginia.

Lee was soon called upon to defend Virginia. He served first as commander of the army of northern Virginia, then as general-in-chief of all the Confederate armies. His fame rests on his military accomplishments against overwhelming odds as well as on his devotion to principle regardless of the personal cost.

An avid letter writer, Lee frequently wrote to family members, explaining his actions and expressing his feelings. Lee's letters not only provide insight into important historical events, but also reveal the personality of one of the greatest military leaders in American history.

Abraham Lincoln (1809–1865)

Serving as president during one of the most tragic periods in American history, Abraham Lincoln fought to reunite a nation torn apart by war. His courage, strength, and dedication in the face of an overwhelming national crisis have made him one of the most admired and respected American presidents.

A man of humble origins, Lincoln developed an early interest in politics. He served in the Illinois state legislature and the United States Congress, where he earned a reputation as a champion of emancipation. In 1858 he ran for the United States Senate against Stephen Douglas. Lincoln lost the election, but his heated debates with Douglas brought him national recognition and helped him win the presidency in 1860.

Shortly after his election, the Civil War erupted. Throughout the war Lincoln showed great strength and courage. He also demonstrated his gift for oratory. In October 1863, he was invited to make "a few appropriate remarks" at a November dedication of the battlefield at Gettysburg as a national cemetery. The world has long remembered what he said there.

GUIDE FOR INTERPRETING

THEME:
AMERICA IN
CRISIS

Letter to His Son; The Gettysburg Address

Historical Context

The Civil War. When Abraham Lincoln, a vocal opponent of slavery, won the Republican nomination for president in 1860, many southern leaders urged the southern states to withdraw from the Union if Lincoln should win the election. Many southerners believed Lincoln would abolish slavery, and they felt that their economy would collapse if he were to do so. People from the North generally opposed slavery, however, and with their support Lincoln won the election.

In December of 1860, shortly after Lincoln was elected, South Carolina became the first state to secede from the Union. A month later five more states—Mississippi, Florida, Alabama, Georgia, and Louisiana—withdrew. In February of 1860, the six states established the Confederate States of America.

The Civil War began on April 12, 1861, when Confederate forces fired on Fort Sumter, a Union military post in Charleston, South Carolina. Shortly after the attack, five more states—Virginia, Arkansas, North Carolina, Tennessee, and Texas—joined the Confederacy. The war lasted for four years, ending on April 9, 1865. During the course of the conflict, more than 620,000 soldiers were killed.

Robert E. Lee's "Letter to His Son" was written on January 23, 1861, before his home state of Virginia seceded from the Union. More than two years later—four months after the bloody battle of Gettysburg—Abraham Lincoln delivered "The Gettysburg Address."

Writers' Techniques

Diction. Diction refers to a writer's choice of words. An important aspect of style, diction must be appropriate to the subject, audience, occasion, and literary form. For example, if a writer is preparing an essay describing a mountain range for people who have never been there, he or she must use vivid, concrete language that enables the reader to visualize what is being described.

Focus

"The Gettysburg Address" is regarded as one of the most important speeches in American history because it captured the sorrow and determination of the war-torn nation. Freewrite about the Civil War and its effect on the American people.

Guide for Interpreting 377

Letter to His Son

Robert E. Lee

January 23, 1861

I received Everett's[1] *Life of Washington* which you sent me, and enjoyed its perusal. How his spirit would be grieved could he see the wreck of his mighty labors! I will not, however, permit myself to believe, until all ground of hope is gone, that the fruit of his noble deeds will be destroyed, and that his precious advice and virtuous example will so soon be forgotten by his countrymen. As far as I can judge by the papers, we are between a state of anarchy and civil war. May God avert both of these evils from us! I fear that mankind will not for years be sufficiently Christianized to bear the absence of restraint and force. I see that four states[2] have declared themselves out of the Union; four more will apparently follow their example. Then, if the border states are brought into the gulf of revolution, one half of the country will be arrayed against the other. I must try

---

1. Everett's: Referring to Edward Everett (1794–1865), an American scholar and orator who made a long speech at Gettysburg before Lincoln delivered his famous address.

2. four states: South Carolina, Mississippi, Florida, and Alabama.

THE BATTLE ABBEY MURALS: THE FOUR SEASONS OF THE CONFEDERACY, THE SUMMER MURAL, *Charles Hoffbauer*
The Virginia State Historical Society

and be patient and await the end, for I can do nothing to hasten or retard it.

The South, in my opinion, has been aggrieved by the acts of the North, as you say. I feel the aggression and am willing to take every proper step for redress. It is the principle I contend for, not individual or private benefit. As an American citizen, I take great pride in my country, her prosperity and institutions, and would defend any state if her rights were invaded. But I can anticipate no greater calamity for the country than a dissolution of the Union. It would be an accumulation of all the evils we complain of, and I am willing to sacrifice everything but honor for its preservation. I hope, therefore, that all constitutional means will be exhausted before there is a resort to force. Secession is nothing but revolution. The framers of our Constitution never exhausted so much labor, wisdom, and forbearance in its formation, and surrounded it with so many guards and securities, if it was intended to be broken by every member of the Confederacy at will. It was intended for "perpetual union," so expressed in the preamble, and for the establishment of a government, not a compact, which can only be dissolved by revolution or the consent of all the people in convention assembled. It is idle to talk of secession. Anarchy would have been established, and not a government, by Washington, Hamilton, Jefferson, Madison, and the other patriots of the Revolution. . . . Still, a Union that can only be maintained by swords and bayonets, and in which strife and civil war are to take the place of brotherly love and kindness, has no charm for me. I shall mourn for my country and for the welfare and progress of mankind. If the Union is dissolved, and the government disrupted, I shall return to my native state and share the miseries of my people; and, save in defense, will draw my sword on none.

RESPONDING TO THE SELECTION

Your Response
1. Based on this letter, what is your opinion of Robert E. Lee? Do you think he deserves the respect of both northerners and southerners? Explain.
2. After the Civil War, Lee applied for a complete pardon. If you were a member of Congress, would you have voted to grant it? Why or why not?

Interpreting
3. (a) In your own words, summarize Lee's argument against secession. (b) How does Lee link his acknowledgment of his son's gift to his argument?

Applying
4. In what ways do you think Lee's attitudes might have been different if he had been from the North?

ANALYZING LITERATURE

Knowing Historical Context
Lee wrote "Letter to His Son" as the tension leading to the Civil War was mounting. At the time Lee felt torn between his devotion to his country and his deep attachment to his native state. How does he convey this feeling?

THINKING AND WRITING

Writing a Letter
Write a letter to a friend in which you express your feelings about a current event. Start by listing ideas and opinions about an event that concerns you. Then begin your letter, writing in a casual, informal style. Mention the important details of the event. When you revise, check to see that your opinions are clearly expressed, and make sure there are no errors in spelling, grammar, or punctuation.

The Gettysburg Address

Abraham Lincoln

Four score and seven years ago our fathers brought forth on this continent, a new nation, conceived in Liberty, and dedicated to the proposition that all men are created equal.

Now we are engaged in a great civil war, testing whether that nation, or any nation so conceived and so dedicated, can long endure. We are met on a great battlefield of that war. We have come to dedicate a portion of that field, as a final resting place for those who here gave their lives that that nation might live. It is altogether fitting and proper that we should do this.

But, in a larger sense, we can not dedicate—we cannot consecrate—we cannot hallow—this ground. The brave men, living and dead, who struggled here, have consecrated it, far above our poor power to add or detract. The world will little note, nor long remember what we say here, but it can never forget what they did here. It is for us the living, rather, to be dedicated here to the unfinished work which they who fought here have thus far so nobly advanced. It is rather for us to be here dedicated to the great task remaining before us—that from these honored dead we take increased devotion to that cause for which they gave the last full measure of devotion—that we here highly resolve that these dead shall not have died in vain—that this nation, under God, shall have a new birth of freedom—and that government of the people, by the people, for the people, shall not perish from the earth.

ABRAHAM LINCOLN'S ADDRESS AT THE DEDICATION OF THE GETTYSBURG NATIONAL CEMETERY, 19 NOVEMBER 1863

RESPONDING TO THE SELECTION

Your Response

1. What do you think are the most memorable phrases in "The Gettysburg Address"? Why?
2. Why do you think the world still remembers what was said at Gettysburg?
3. If you had been at Gettysburg, how might you have responded to Lincoln's words? Explain.

Interpreting

4. (a) Why does Lincoln believe that the war will have an impact on the entire world? (b) How does he convey this belief in his speech? (c) How does it add to the impact of the speech?
5. Beyond dedicating a portion of the battlefield as a cemetery, what do you think is the purpose of Lincoln's speech?
6. Lincoln begins his speech by describing the birth of the nation and ends it by describing his vision of the nation's eventual rebirth. Considering Lincoln's purpose, why is this an effective way of structuring his speech?

Applying

7. (a) In what ways is Lincoln's speech different from the presidential addresses you have heard or seen on television? (b) How do you explain these differences?

ANALYZING LITERATURE

Understanding Diction

Diction refers to the writer's choice of words. Diction may be formal or informal, abstract or concrete. For example, "The Gettysburg Address" is written in formal, dignified language.

1. Find five words or phrases in "The Gettysburg Address" that contribute to its formal, dignified diction.
2. What words or phrases do you think Lincoln might have used in place of the five you chose in question 1 if the speech had been written using informal language?
3. The Shakespearean scholar A. L. Rowse has noted that many of Lincoln's speeches could easily be put into blank verse. In what ways do you find the language of "The Gettysburg Address" similar to the language of a poem?

CRITICAL THINKING AND READING

Analyzing Appropriateness of Diction

A writer must use language that is appropriate to the subject, audience, occasion, and literary form. For example, in writing "The Gettysburg Address," Lincoln used formal language because he felt it best suited the subject and occasion.

1. Why is Lincoln's diction appropriate?
2. Would the speech have been less effective if it had been written using informal language? Why?

THINKING AND WRITING

Comparing and Contrasting Speeches

Write an essay in which you compare and contrast the Gettysburg Address with Patrick Henry's "Speech in the Virginia Convention." Start by rereading both speeches, taking note of similarities and differences in purpose, directness, forcefulness, tone (the writer's attitude toward his or her subject), diction, structure, and methods of persuasion. Arrange your notes according to the points of contrast. Prepare a thesis statement. Then write your essay, focusing each of your body paragraphs on a single point of contrast. When you revise, make sure that you have varied the lengths and structures of your sentences and used transitions to link your ideas. Proofread your essay and prepare a final draft.

LEARNING OPTION

Writing. The immediate reactions to Lincoln's remarks at Gettysburg were mixed. Lincoln called his speech "a flat failure" and claimed that "the people are disappointed." Keynote speaker Edward Everett disagreed. In a note to Lincoln, he wrote, "I should be glad if I could flatter myself that I came as near to the central idea of the occasion in two hours as you did in two minutes." What do you think? Imagine that you are a newspaper columnist sent to cover Lincoln's address. Write a column in which you share your reaction to his speech.

ONE WRITER'S PROCESS

Abraham Lincoln and the Gettysburg Address

PREWRITING

The Occasion One day in early November 1863, President Abraham Lincoln received an invitation. The same invitation had been sent to many other northern politicians. Lincoln and the other politicians were invited to attend dedicatory ceremonies for a military cemetery at the Civil War battlefield at Gettysburg, Pennsylvania, the site of a major battle and an important Union victory.

The Assignment The famous orator Edward Everett, a distinguished politician, teacher, and former president of Harvard University, had already been scheduled to deliver the main speech of the ceremony. The commission organizing the event now had to decide what Lincoln's role in the ceremonies would be. If the President of the United States was going to be onstage with other dignitaries, shouldn't he also be invited to speak?

In an attempt to solve this problem, commission representative David Wills wrote to Lincoln, "It is the desire that after the oration, you, as chief executive of the nation, formally set apart these grounds to their sacred use by a few appropriate remarks."

Lincoln's first step was the same as any student's would be—he had to understand the terms of the assignment. He concluded that because the subject of his speech was the dedication of a military burial ground, his address would have to be brief and solemn.

DRAFTING

Only Two Weeks to Write From the time Lincoln received the invitation, he had about two weeks to complete his speech. Exactly how and when he actually wrote it remains, for the most part, a mystery. One report from a friend of Lincoln indicates that the President had drafted at least part of the speech sometime during the week before the ceremonies. It is said that this part covered merely a piece of foolscap paper, which measures 13 by 16 inches. However much Lincoln had written during the previous week, he did not have a finished draft on November 18, the day before the scheduled ceremonies. When he boarded the train that would take him from Washington to Gettysburg, he had much work yet to do.

Lincoln spent the night before the ceremonies at the home of one of Gettysburg's leading citizens. Sometime between arriving there from the train station and going to bed, he finished the speech.

Thoughts From Long Ago Scholars are fond of pointing out the similarities between Lincoln's address and certain classical Greek texts, most notably the speech given by the Athenian general Pericles as tribute to the Greek soldiers who had died in the Peloponnesian War in the fifth century B.C. Though Lincoln probably did not have Pericles' speech in front of him as he wrote, he was doubtlessly familiar with it.

In his address Pericles had pointed to the vanity of trying to honor the dead with words. Referring to dead patriots, Pericles said, "famous men have the whole earth as their memorial: it is not only the inscriptions on their graves in their own country that mark them out . . ." More than two thousand years later, Lincoln would express a similar sentiment by writing these words:

"But, in a larger sense, we cannot dedicate—we cannot consecrate—we cannot hallow—this ground. The brave men, living and dead, who struggled here, have consecrated it, far above our poor power to add or detract.

"The world will little note, nor long remember what we say here, but it can never forget what they did here."

REVISING

Invisible Editing During the week before the Gettysburg ceremonies, Lincoln is reported to have read part of a rough draft to Ward Hill Lamon, a close friend. According to Lamon, Lincoln was dissatisfied with the speech and complained about not having enough time to work on it. Between that occasion and the completion of the draft the night of November 18 in Gettysburg, Lincoln probably thought a great deal about what he wanted his short speech to accomplish. It is most likely that he did some editing and revising in his head until he could find the time to sit down with pencil and paper.

Another report claims that Lincoln showed his final draft to his Secretary of State William Henry Seward, who had traveled to Gettysburg with Lincoln to attend the ceremonies. What changes, if any, Seward made in the speech are not known.

Revising While Speaking Lincoln continued making revisions in his speech even as he delivered it. The words he held in his hand and to which he referred while speaking differed from what he actually said at several points. For example, toward the end of the speech, Lincoln said, " . . . that this nation, under God, shall have a new birth of freedom . . ." The original version did not contain the phrase "under God." Lincoln added the phrase as he spoke and also included it in subsequent copies of the speech. This seemingly small change has both sub-

tle and important effects, implying that the United States and its goals of freedom have divine approval. Being an experienced speaker, Lincoln would have been well aware of the positive effects this change would have on his audience.

PUBLISHING

A "few appropriate remarks" Lincoln had several good reasons for wanting to deliver an effective speech at Gettysburg. First, he had gathered before him a number of important politicians, including many northern governors. Their allegiance to the Union cause was vital for a Union victory, especially in 1863, when the outcome of the war was still far from certain. He also had, according to various reports, between fifteen and thirty thousand American citizens standing on the site of a recent battle in which thousands had died. Lincoln no doubt understood that this was an emotional occasion as well as an opportunity to gain public support for the Union's cause.

He used the opportunity to further another cause as well, one that was fairly subversive in 1863. He wasted no time in making this idea public. The concept of equality among races was not popular in 1863, and few people remembered that it was one of the principles upon which the United States had been founded. That men and women of all color believe in equality today can be attributed at least in part to Lincoln and his "few appropriate remarks" at Gettysburg.

THINKING ABOUT THE PROCESS

1. What might cause a speaker to add or omit words and phrases from a speech once he or she has begun addressing the audience?
2. **Speechmaking** Read aloud to friends or relatives an essay or report of which you are particularly proud. As you read, feel free to change words or phrases as you feel appropriate.

CIVIL WAR VOICES

A First-Person Narrative of the War

The Civil War was one of the most painful chapters of American history. It was a long, bloody conflict that tore the nation apart and caused the deaths of more Americans than in all other wars combined. The following letters, journals, and songs tell the story of this tragic conflict as seen through the eyes of people who experienced it firsthand.

A Call to Arms

The war erupted on April 12, 1861, when Confederate troops fired on Fort Sumter, a Union military post in Charleston, South Carolina. In the weeks that followed, thousands of people from both sides volunteered to fight. Among the early enlistees was Warren Lee Goss of Massachusetts, who conveys his feelings and describes his early experiences as a soldier in the following account.

Recollections of a Private
Warren Lee Goss

"Cold chills" ran up and down my back as I got out of bed after the sleepless night, and shaved preparatory to other desperate deeds of valor. I was twenty years of age, and when anything unusual was to be done, like fighting or courting, I shaved.

With a nervous tremor convulsing my system, and my heart thumping like muffled drumbeats, I stood before the door of the recruiting office, and before turning the knob to enter read and reread the advertisement for recruits posted thereon, until I knew all its peculiarities. The promised chances for "travel and promotion" seemed good, and I thought I might have made a mistake in considering war so serious after all. "Chances for travel!" I must confess now, after four years of soldiering, that the "chances for travel" were no myth; but "promotion" was a little uncertain and slow.

I was in no hurry to open the door. Though determined to enlist, I was half inclined to put if off awhile; I had a fluctuation of desires; I was fainthearted and brave; I wanted to enlist, and yet—Here I turned the knob, and was relieved. . . .

My first uniform was a bad fit: My trousers were too long by three or four inches; the flannel shirt was coarse and unpleasant, too large at the neck and too short elsewhere. The forage cap[1] was an ungainly bag with pasteboard top and leather visor; the blouse was the only part which seemed decent; while the overcoat made me feel like a little nubbin of corn in a large preponderance of husk. Nothing except "Virginia mud" ever took down my ideas of military pomp quite so low.

After enlisting I did not seem of so much consequence as I had expected. There was not so much excitement on account of my military appearance as I deemed justly my due. I was taught my facings, and at the time I thought the drillmaster needlessly fussy about shouldering, ordering, and presenting arms. At this time men were often drilled in

---

1. forage cap: Cap worn by infantry soldiers.

company and regimental evolutions long before they learned the manual of arms, because of the difficulty of obtaining muskets. These we obtained at an early day, but we would willingly have resigned them after carrying them a few hours. The musket, after an hour's drill, seemed heavier and less ornamental than it had looked to be.

The first day I went out to drill, getting tired of doing the same things over and over, I said to the drill sergeant: "Let's stop this fooling and go over to the grocery." His only reply was addressed to a corporal: "Corporal, take this man out and drill him"; and the corporal did! I found that suggestions were not so well appreciated in the army as in private life, and that no wisdom was equal to a drillmaster's "Right face," "Left wheel," and "Right, oblique, march." It takes a raw recruit some time to learn that he is not to think or suggest, but obey. Some never do learn. I acquired it at last, in humility and mud, but it was tough. Yet I doubt if my patriotism, during my first three weeks' drill, was quite knee high. Drilling looks easy to a spectator, but it isn't. After a time I had cut down my uniform so that I could see out of it, and had conquered the drill sufficiently to see through it. Then the word came: On to Washington! . . .

YOUNG SOLDIER. SEPARATE STUDY OF A SOLDIER GIVING WATER TO A WOUNDED COMPANION, 1861
Winslow Homer
Cooper-Hewitt, National Museum of Design

Early Victories for the South

Although the North had superior resources and a substantially larger army, the war began with a series of Confederate victories. The first Southern victory took place in July, 1861, just outside of Washington, D.C., near a small stream named Bull Run. The hero of the Battle of Bull Run was Confederate General Thomas "Stonewall" Jackson. In the following letter to his wife, Jackson recounts the battle.

An Account of the Battle of Bull Run
Stonewall Jackson

My precious pet,
Yesterday we fought a great battle and gained a great victory, for which all the glory is due to God alone. Although under a heavy fire for several continuous hours, I received only one wound, the breaking of the longest finger of my left hand; but the doctor says the finger can be saved. It was broken about midway between the hand and knuckle, the ball passing on the side next [to] the forefinger. Had it struck the center, I should have lost the fin-

ger. My horse was wounded, but not killed. Your coat got an ugly wound near the hip, but my servant, who is very handy, has so far repaired it that it doesn't show very much. My preservation was entirely due, as was the glorious victory, to our God, to whom be all the honor, praise and glory. The battle was the hardest that I have ever been in, but not near so hot in its fire. I commanded the center more particularly, though one of my regiments extended to the right for some distance. There were other commanders on my right and left. Whilst great credit is due to other parts of our gallant army, God made my brigade more instrumental than any other in repulsing the main attack. This is for your information only—say nothing about it. Let others speak praise, not myself.

Songs of War

The war inspired many patriotic songs. Probably the best-known and most enduring of these is "Battle Hymn of the Republic," written early in the war by abolitionist Julia Ward Howe.

Battle Hymn of the Republic
Julia Ward Howe

Mine eyes have seen the glory of
the coming of the Lord;
He is trampling out the vintage
where the grapes of wrath are stored;
He hath loosed the fateful lightning
of His terrible swift sword,
   His truth is marching on.

I have seen Him in the watch-fires
of a hundred circling camps;
They have builded Him an altar
in the evening dews and damps;
I can read His righteous sentence
by the dim and flaring lamps,
   His day is marching on.

I have read a fiery gospel, writ in
burnished rows of steel:
"As ye deal with my contemners,[1] so
with you my grace shall deal;
Let the Hero, born of woman, crush the serpent
with his heel,
   Since God is marching on."

He has sounded forth the trumpet
that shall never call retreat;
He is sifting out the hearts of men
before His judgment-seat;
Oh, be swift, my soul, to answer Him!
be jubilant, my feet!
   Our God is marching on.

In the beauty of the lilies Christ was born
across the sea,
With a glory in His bosom that
transfigures you and me:
As He died to make men holy, let us die
to make men free,
   While God is marching on.

---

1. contemners (kən tem' nərz) n.: People who treat or think of others with contempt or scorn.

Cries of Freedom

On September 22, 1862, President Lincoln issued the Emancipation Proclamation, declaring that all slaves in states still in rebellion would be free as of January 1, 1863. Because those states were not under Union control at the time, no slaves were set free on that day. Yet the Emancipation Proclamation changed the purpose of the war. It became a war both to restore the Union and to end slavery. The Proclamation also prompted a wave of support for the Union from free blacks. In the following account, Reverend Henry M. Turner, a free-born black living in Washington, D.C., describes his people's reaction to the news of the Proclamation.

Reaction to the Emancipation Proclamation
Reverend Henry M. Turner

READING THE EMANCIPATION PROCLAMATION
Artist Unknown

Seeing such a multitude of people in and around my church, I hurriedly sent up to the office of the first paper in which the proclamation of freedom could be printed, known as the *Evening Star,* and squeezed myself through the dense crowd that was waiting for the paper. The first sheet run off with the proclamation in it was grabbed for by three of us, but some active young man got possession of it and fled. The next sheet was grabbed for by several, and was torn into tatters. The third sheet from the press was grabbed for by several, but I succeeded in procuring so much of it as contained the proclamation, and off I went for life and death. Down Pennsylvania Avenue I ran as for my life, and when the people saw me coming with the paper in my hand they raised a shouting cheer that was almost deafening. As many as could get around me lifted me to a great platform, and I started to read the proclamation. I had run the best end of a mile, I was out of breath, and could not read. Mr. Hinton, to whom I handed the paper, read it with great force and clearness. While he was reading every kind of demonstration and gesticulation was going on. Men squealed, women fainted, dogs barked, white and colored people shook hands, songs were sung, and by this time cannons began to fire at the navy yard, and follow in the wake of the roar that had for some time been going on behind the White House. . . . Great processions of colored and white men marched to and fro and passed in front of the White House and congratulated President Lincoln on his proclamation. The President came to the window and made responsive bows, and thousands told him, if he would come out of that palace, they would hug him to death. . . . It was indeed a time of times, and nothing like it will ever be seen again in this life.

African American Troops Join the Fighting

Shortly before President Lincoln issued the Emancipation Proclamation, Congress passed a law allowing blacks to join the army. This prompted the enlistment of thousands of blacks—both Northern blacks and freed slaves from the South. The following account describes the heroic efforts of a regiment of ex-slaves from Louisiana during a pivotal battle on May 27, 1863, in the struggle for control of the Mississippi River. It is taken from a letter from Union General Nathaniel P. Banks to General H. W. Halleck in Washington, D.C.

Praising an African American Regiment
General Nathaniel P. Banks

The fight lasted on this line until 4 o'clock, and was very severely contested. The enemy was driven into his works, and our troops moved up to the fortifications. On the extreme right of our line I posted the first and third regiments of Negro troops. The First Regiment of Louisiana Engineers, composed exclusively of colored men, excepting the officers, was also engaged in the operations of the day. The position occupied by these troops was one of importance, and called for the utmost steadiness and bravery in those to whom it was confided.

It gives me pleasure to report that they answered every expectation. Their conduct was heroic. No troops could be more determined or more daring. They made, during the day, three charges upon the batteries of the enemy, suffering very heavy losses, and holding their position at nightfall with the other troops on the right of our line. The highest commendation is bestowed upon them by all the officers in command on the right. Whatever doubt may have existed before as to the efficiency of organizations of this character, the history of this day proves conclusively to those who were in a condition to observe the conduct of these regiments, that the Government will find in this class of troops effective supporters and defenders.

The severe test to which they were subjected, and the determined manner in which they encountered the enemy, leave upon my mind no doubt of their ultimate success.

The Tide Turns

From July 1 to July 3, 1863, Union and Confederate troops fought outside the small town of Gettysburg, Pennsylvania. After Union troops gained control of the hills surrounding the town, the Confederate troops commanded by Robert E. Lee launched a risky attack on the strongest Union position. The Confederate troops were pushed back and forced to retreat, and more than 40,000 soldiers were killed or wounded. The battle marked a major turning point in the war, because it was the first time that troops under Lee's command had been defeated. In the following account from his diary, Confederate soldier Randolph McKim describes the final day of the battle.

A Confederate Account of the Battle of Gettysburg
Randolph McKim

Then came General Ewell's order to assume the offensive and assail the crest of Culp's Hill, on our right. . . . The works to be stormed ran almost at right angles to those we occupied. Moreover, there was a double line of entrenchments, one above the other, and each filled with troops. In moving to the attack we were exposed to enfilading fire[1] from the woods on our left flank, besides the double line of fire which we had to face in front, and a battery of artillery posted on a hill to our left rear opened upon us at short range. . . .

On swept the gallant little brigade, the Third North Carolina on the right of the line, next the Second Maryland, then the three Virginia regiments (10th, 23d, and 37th), with the First North Carolina on the extreme left. Its ranks had been sadly thinned, and its energies greatly depleted by those six fearful hours of battle that morning; but its nerve and spirit were undiminished. Soon, however, the left and center were checked and then repulsed, probably by the severe flank fire from the woods; and the small remnant of the Third North Carolina, with the stronger Second Maryland (I do not recall the banners of any other regiment), were far in advance of the rest of the line. On they pressed to within about twenty or thirty paces of the works—a small but gallant band of heroes daring to attempt what could not be done by flesh and blood.

The end soon came. We were beaten back to the line from which we had advanced with terrible loss, and in much confusion, but the enemy did not make a countercharge. By the strenuous efforts of the officers of the line and of the staff, order was restored, and we re-formed in the breastworks[2] from which we had emerged, there to be again exposed to an artillery fire exceeding in violence that of the early morning. It remains only to say that, like Pickett's men[3] later in the day, this single brigade was hurled unsupported against the enemy's works. Daniel's brigade remained in the breastworks during and after the charge, and neither from that command nor from any other had we any support. Of course it is to be presumed that General Daniel acted in obedience to orders. We remained in this breastwork after the charge about an hour before we finally abandoned the Federal entrenchments and retired to the foot of the hill.

---

1. enfilading fire: Gunfire directed along the length of a column or line of troops.

2. breastworks: Low walls put up quickly as a defense in battle.

3. Pickett's men: General George Pickett was a Confederate leader who led the unsuccessful attack on the Union position.

On the Home Front

Women offered invaluable support to both sides during the war. One of the ways in which they contributed to the war effort was by volunteering to care for wounded soldiers. The well-known novelist Louisa May Alcott was among the many women who volunteered to serve as a nurse. In the following passage, Alcott describes the conditions in the Washington hospital in which she worked.

Description of the Conditions in a Military Hospital
Louisa May Alcott

There they were! "Our brave boys," as the papers justly call them, for cowards could hardly have been so riddled with shot and shell, so torn and shattered, nor have borne suffering for which we have no name, with an uncomplaining fortitude, which made one glad to cherish each as a brother. In they came, some on stretchers, some in men's arms, some feebly staggering along propped on rude crutches, and one lay stark and still with covered face, as a comrade gave his name to be recorded before they carried him away to the dead house. All was hurry and confusion; the hall was full of these wrecks of humanity, for the most exhausted could not reach a bed till duly ticketed and registered; the walls were lined with rows of such as could sit, the floor covered with the more disabled, the steps and doorways filled with helpers and lookers-on; the sound of many feet and voices made that usually quiet hour as noisy as noon; and, in the midst of it all, the matron's motherly face brought more comfort to many a poor soul than the cordial draughts she administered, or the cheery words that welcomed all, making of the hospital a home.

The End Draws Near

By the winter of 1865, the Southern army was in disarray, and the Confederacy was on the verge of collapse. On April 4, Union commander Ulysses S. Grant and his troops captured Richmond, Virginia, the Confederate capital. Lee and his troops had evacuated the city before the Union troops arrived, but only a few days later, on April 9, they were forced to surrender. The following account by Union officer R. B. Prescott describes the capture of Richmond.

An Account of the Fall of Richmond
R. B. Prescott

Every moment the light we had seen over Richmond on starting became more and more brilliant. Above it hung great clouds of heavy smoke, and as we drew nearer there arose a confused murmur now swelling into a loud roar and then subsiding, and again swelling into a great tumult of excited voices, while at frequent intervals short, sharp explosions were heard as of the discharge of field artillery. Weary, breathless, hungry, begrimed with dust and perspiration, but eager and excited, we pushed on, and at half-past six o'clock in the morning I stood with about two thirds of my men on the summit of a hill and looked down upon the grandest and most appalling sight that my eyes ever beheld. Richmond was literally a sea of flame, out of which the church steeples could be seen protruding here and there, while over all hung a canopy of dense black smoke, lighted up now and then by the bursting shells from the numerous arsenals scattered throughout the city. . . .

The constant explosion of ammunition in the arsenals seemed almost like a battle. Many citizens were killed by the flying fragments. Many were burned to death. In one house seventeen people perished from the flames. The sick, the aged, helpless and infirm, left to themselves in the general panic, could only pray for deliverance, which came to them when the flames had stifled their prayers in death.

Seven hundred and fifty thousand loaded shells in the arsenals, exploding from the heat, tore their way through houses, ploughed up the streets and the gardens, and spread death and destruction on every hand.

The whole city jarred and vibrated with horrid sounds, while warehouses, stores, mills, bridges, depots, and dwellings went down by scores and hundreds. The streets leading to the railroad stations were filled with a frantic mob, pushing, struggling, cursing, trampling each other without mercy in their efforts to get away with what plunder they could carry. No troops of either army were in sight, only rebel stragglers, whose long familiarity with similar scenes rendered them, no doubt, the only cool-headed and indifferent spectators of these appalling sights. Over and above all the terrible roar of the conflagration, as it leaped from building to building, from street to street, filled the whole city with its scorching breath, and lent added horrors to the scene.

The Long Struggle Begins

Although the war brought an end to slavery, the struggle against racial discrimination was just beginning. In the following letter, written on October 1, 1865, the former slave and well-known abolitionist Sojourner Truth describes an encounter with racism months after the war ended.

An Account of an Experience with Discrimination
Sojourner Truth

A few weeks ago I was in company with my friend Josephine S. Griffing, when the conductor of a streetcar refused to stop his car for me, although [I was] closely following Josephine and holding on to the iron rail. They dragged me a number of yards before she succeeded in stopping them. She reported the conductor to the president of the City Railway, who dismissed him at once, and told me to take the number of the car whenever I was mistreated by a conductor or driver. On the 13th I had occasion to go for necessities for the patients in the Freedmen's Hospital where I have been doing and advising for a number of months. I thought now I would get a ride without trouble as I was in company

with another friend, Laura S. Haviland of Michigan. As I ascended the platform of the car, the conductor pushed me, saying "Go back—get off here." I told him I was not going off, then "I'll put you off" said he furiously, clenching my right arm with both hands, using such violence that he seemed about to succeed, when Mrs. Haviland told him he was not going to put me off. "Does she belong to you?" said he in a hurried angry tone. She replied, "She does not belong to me, but she belongs to humanity." The number of the car was noted, and conductor dismissed at once upon the report to the president, who advised his arrest for assault and battery as my shoulder was sprained by his effort to put me off. Accordingly I had him arrested and the case tried before Justice Thompson. My shoulder was very lame and swollen, but is better. It is hard for the old slaveholding spirit to die. But die it must. . . .

CHIEF JOSEPH

1840[?]–1904

Chief Joseph was born in the Wallowa Valley in what is now Oregon. His father, who was one of the chiefs of the Nez Percé tribe, converted to Christianity around the time of Joseph's birth, and he sent Joseph to a school run by missionaries.

In 1871 Joseph became a chief, succeeding his father. At that time the United States Government was trying to force the Nez Percé to relocate in Idaho. The Nez Percé had signed a treaty in 1863 giving the government control of the tribe's land, but Chief Joseph felt that the treaty was illegal and refused to recognize it. Chief Joseph tried to negotiate with the government, but his attempts failed, and in June of 1877 the dispute erupted into a war. Hoping to join forces with the Sioux, Joseph led his people on a long march through Idaho and Montana toward the Canadian border. During the march the Nez Percé frequently clashed with federal troops and managed to win several battles. The tribe was heavily outnumbered by the government troops, however, and the Indians were forced to endure great hardships during the course of their retreat. Chief Joseph was forced to surrender on October 5, after being defeated in a battle in the Bear Paw Mountains in Montana.

Several Nez Percé leaders were responsible for the strategies of the military campaign and its early successes. However, because of the widespread attention that Chief Joseph's surrender speech received, he became in the public's mind a symbol for the heroic Nez Percé and their tragic plight. During his lifetime he was sometimes referred to as the "Indian Napoleon."

After a period of imprisonment, Chief Joseph went to live in the Indian territory in what is now Oklahoma. Inadequate shelter, fall rains, and winter cold resulted in the deaths of many of the Nez Percé. In 1885 Chief Joseph and the remainder of his people moved to the Colville Reservation in Washington. During his later years, he tirelessly campaigned for American Indian rights, contributing several essays to magazines and making a memorable series of public appearances in Washington, D.C.

Chief Joseph never gave up his dream that his people might someday return to the Wallowa Valley. Toward the end of his life, he visited the valley several times, hoping to convince the settlers to sell land to the Indian Bureau for his people. All his requests were refused.

Chief Joseph's speech of surrender is powerful and moving, conveying his sense of utter hopelessness and despair. The following excerpt includes some of the most memorable lines in the speech.

GUIDE FOR INTERPRETING

I Will Fight No More Forever

Writers' Techniques

Tone. Tone refers to the writer's attitude toward his or her subject, characters, or audience. The tone of a nonfiction work may be revealed through the writer's choice of words and the portrayal of people and events. In a speech, tone may also be conveyed through the tone of the speaker's voice and through the speaker's facial expressions and hand gestures.

The tones of some works are obvious and clearly defined. For example, a work may clearly have an angry tone or a humorous tone. The tones of other works, however, are less obvious and more complex. For example, in "Letter to His Son" Robert E. Lee conveys an attitude of devotion and disillusionment toward the Union.

Focus

Native American tribes such as the Nez Percé lived close to the land, adapting their lives to their environments. As the United States grew and developed, many tribes, including the Nez Percé, were forced off their land and relocated in different areas. Freewrite about your thoughts concerning the forced relocation of Native American tribes.

Primary Source

A young soldier, C.E.S. Wood, recorded the scene as Chief Joseph surrendered. At about 2 o'clock in the afternoon, Chief Joseph took his rifle and mounted his horse. Five warriors followed on foot as he rode slowly up a hill to meet the army commanders. Wood, who stood behind the commanders, noticed bullet scars on Joseph's forehead, wrist, and back. He recorded that

> Joseph's hair hung in two braids on either side of his face. He wore a blanket—I do not remember the color—I would say gray with a black stripe. . . . He wore moccasin leggings. His rifle was across the pommel in front of him. When he dismounted he picked up the rifle, pulled his blanket closer about him, and walked to General Howard and offered him the rifle. Howard waved him to Miles. He then walked to Miles and handed him the rifle. Then he stepped back, adjusted his blanket to leave his right arm free, and began his speech.

Wood recalled that as he surrendered, Chief Joseph "held himself very erect and with a quiet pride, not exactly defiance." When Chief Joseph had finished his speech, the officers present were so touched that they could not speak. Chief Joseph then pulled his blanket over his head, ending the war.

I Will Fight No More Forever

Chief Joseph

Tell General Howard I know his heart. What he told me before, I have in my heart. I am tired of fighting. Our chiefs are killed. Looking Glass is dead. Toohoolhoolzote is dead. The old men are all dead. It is the young men who say yes and no. He who led on the young men is dead. It is cold and we have no blankets. The little children are freezing to death. My people, some of them, have run away to the hills and have no blankets, no food; no one knows where they are—perhaps freezing to death. I want to have time to look for my children and see how many I can find. Maybe I shall find them among the dead. Hear me, my chiefs. I am tired; my heart is sick and sad. From where the sun now stands I will fight no more forever.

CHIEF JOSEPH'S SURRENDER TO COLONEL NELSON A. MILES
Olaf C. Seltzer
Thomas Gilcrease Institute of American History and Art, Tulsa, Oklahoma

Your Response

1. Which lines of Chief Joseph's speech do you find particularly striking? Why?
2. If you were an American soldier who fought against the Nez Percé, how do you think you would have responded to this speech?

Interpreting

3. Chief Joseph's speech is composed mostly of short sentences with the same type of structure. (a) How does his repeated use of short, simple sentences contribute to the impact of his speech? (b) In what way does the simplicity of the language contribute to the impact?
4. What does this speech convey about Chief Joseph's relationship to his people?
5. Although Chief Joseph delivered his speech to notify the federal troops of his tribe's surrender, the speech had a greater purpose. What do you think this purpose was?

Applying

6. In what ways do you think Chief Joseph's delivery of his speech might have added to its impact?

ANALYZING LITERATURE

Understanding Tone

Tone refers to the writer's attitude toward his or her subject. For example, a work of literature may have a sad tone or an indifferent tone.

1. How would you describe the tone of "I Will Fight No More Forever"?
2. How is the tone revealed?
3. Is this tone appropriate for its subject? Explain.

THINKING AND WRITING

Writing a Speech

Write a speech in which you express your thoughts concerning an important current event. Start by listing the details of the event and the reasons that the event affects you as it does. Organize your notes into an outline. Then write your speech. Make sure that your attitude toward your subject is clear. When you revise, add transitions to link your ideas. When you finish revising your speech, deliver it to your classmates.

MULTICULTURAL CONNECTION

Orators From Many Cultures

The United States is a country that has long boasted of its oratory. Although nineteenth-century Americans believed that their writers could not equal those of England, they were confident that they could out-talk any people in history. Oratory flourished at revival meetings, in churches, at political rallies and debates, and in courts of law.

Great American orators have come from a variety of backgrounds and cultures. Some of the greatest speakers in American history have been Native Americans, among them Chief Joseph. Not only did Chief Joseph's surrender speech receive widespread attention, but his later appeals for justice also added to his legend as a public speaker.

Another great orator who represented the cause of his people was an African American, Frederick Douglass. He spoke to huge audiences in the United States and abroad, calling for justice for all oppressed people.

Although women did not have the same opportunities as men in nineteenth-century America, two women who rivaled male orators were Sarah and Angelina Grimké. Key figures in the antislavery movement, they began a speaking tour on behalf of this cause in 1837. At first they addressed only women in "parlor meetings." Their powerful oratory, however, soon attracted crowds, and their meetings were relocated to churches and large halls.

Investigating Other American Orators

Find out more about prominent figures from different cultural groups that are known for their public speaking. Then present the results of your research to the class.

WALT WHITMAN

1819–1892

In the preface to his first volume of poetry, the 1855 edition of *Leaves of Grass,* Walt Whitman wrote, "The proof of a poet is that his country absorbs him as affectionately as he absorbed it." Unfortunately, Whitman's poetry did not gain the acceptance he had hoped for during his lifetime. Today, however, Whitman is widely recognized as one of the most gifted poets this country has produced.

Whitman was born on Long Island and raised in Brooklyn, New York. When he was twenty-seven, he became the editor of the Brooklyn *Eagle,* a respected newspaper, but the paper discharged him in 1848 because of his strong opposition to slavery. After accepting a position on a paper in New Orleans, Whitman traveled across the country for the first time, observing the diversity of the American landscapes and people.

In 1850 Whitman withdrew from journalism to devote his energy to writing poetry. When his first edition of *Leaves of Grass* was published five years later, the book provoked both positive and negative reactions. Ralph Waldo Emerson responded to the book with great enthusiasm, remarking that the collection was "the most extraordinary piece of wit and wisdom that America has yet contributed." Others, however, responded negatively, strongly objecting to the absence of rhyme and meter in Whitman's poetry. John Greenleaf Whittier, for example, disliked Whitman's poetry so much that he threw his copy of the book into the fireplace.

Throughout the remainder of his life, Whitman continually revised, reshaped, and expanded *Leaves of Grass.* Whitman viewed the work as one long poem, expressing his evolving vision of the world. His poetry conveyed his belief in democracy, equality, and the spiritual unity of all forms of life and celebrated the potential of the human spirit. Though Whitman's philosophy grew out of the ideas of the Transcendentalists, his poetry was mainly shaped by his unique ability to absorb and comprehend everything he observed. In the 383 poems included in the final edition of *Leaves of Grass* (1897), Whitman captures the diversity of the American people and conveys the energy and intensity of all forms of life.

In the years following Whitman's death, *Leaves of Grass* has become one of the most highly regarded collections of poetry ever written. Millions of readers have enjoyed the book, and it has influenced several generations of poets. There is little doubt that, according to his own definition, Whitman has proven himself as a poet.

GUIDE FOR INTERPRETING

Writers' Techniques

Walt Whitman's Poetry

Style. Style refers to the manner in which a writer puts his or her thoughts into words. It involves forms of expression rather than the thoughts conveyed.

Two of the most important aspects of Whitman's style are his frequent use of catalogs—the piling up of images or concrete details—and parallelism—the repeated use of phrases, clauses, or sentences that are similar in structure or meaning. For example, Whitman creates a catalog of concrete details in "Song of Myself" when he writes, "My tongue, every atom of my blood, formed from this soil, this air/Born here of parents born here from parents the same, and their parents the same" (lines 6–7). Whitman's catalogs were intended to represent the spiritual unity among all forms of being. Similarly, Whitman's use of parallelism helps to create a sense of unity within his poetry. It also provides a structure, creates a rhythm, and emphasizes important ideas in his poetry.

Free Verse. Another important characteristic of Whitman's style is his use of free verse—verse that has irregular meter and line length. Though free verse lacks regular meter, it does not lack rhythm. Free verse is structured to recreate the rising and falling cadences of natural speech, with the lengths of lines being varied according to intended emphasis.

Although free verse had first been used centuries earlier in the Psalms of the Bible, Whitman was the first American poet to use it. For Whitman, who valued freedom and individuality, free verse proved to be the most appropriate form, because it allowed him to express himself without restraint.

Focus

Prepare a list of concrete details or images that express your associations with a natural element such as grass, the ocean, the sun, or the moon.

Primary Source

In his later years, Walt Whitman developed a close friendship with Canadian doctor Richard Maurice Bucke. In describing Whitman Bucke once wrote, "Perhaps . . . no man who ever lived liked so many things and disliked so few as Walt Whitman. All natural objects seemed to have a charm for him. All sights and sounds seemed to please him. He appeared to like (and I believe he did like) all the men, women, and children he saw . . . I never knew him to argue or dispute, and he never spoke of money. . . . He never spoke deprecatingly of any nationality or class of men. . . . He never complained or grumbled, either at the weather, pain, illness, or anything else. . . ."

from Preface to the 1855 Edition of *Leaves of Grass*

Walt Whitman

America does not repel the past or what it has produced under its forms or amid other politics or the idea of castes or the old religions. . . . accepts the lesson with calmness . . . is not so impatient as has been supposed that the slough still sticks to opinions and manners and literature while the life which served its requirements has passed into the new life of the new forms . . . perceives that the corpse is slowly borne from the eating and sleeping rooms of the house . . . perceives that it waits a little while in the door . . . that it was fittest for its days . . . that its action has descended to the stalwart and well-shaped heir who approaches . . . and that he shall be fittest for his days.

The Americans of all nations at any time upon the earth have probably the fullest poetical nature. The United States themselves are essentially the greatest poem. In the history of the earth hitherto the largest and most stirring appear tame and orderly to their ampler largeness and stir. Here at last is something in the doings of man that corresponds with the broadcast doings of the day and night. Here is not merely a nation but a teeming nation of nations. Here is action untied from strings necessarily blind to particulars and details magnificently moving in vast masses. Here is the hospitality which forever indicates heroes. . . . Here are the roughs and beards and space and ruggedness and nonchalance that the soul loves. Here the performance disdaining the trivial unapproached in the tremendous audacity of its crowds and groupings and the push of its perspective spreads with crampless and flowing breadth and showers its prolific and splendid extravagance. One sees it must indeed own the riches of the summer and winter, and need never be bankrupt while corn grows from the ground or the orchards drop apples or the bays contain fish or men beget children upon women. . . .

RESPONDING TO THE SELECTION

Your Response

1. Do you recognize the America that Whitman describes? What has happened to "the roughs and the beards and space and ruggedness" that he commends?

Interpreting

2. What is Whitman's view of the past?
3. What does Whitman cite as evidence to support his statement "The United States themselves are essentially the greatest poem"?
4. What does Whitman mean when he comments that the United States "is not merely a nation but a teeming nation of nations"?
5. In your own words, describe Whitman's attitude toward America.

Applying

6. What is your definition of an American? Provide examples to clarify your definition.

from Song of Myself

Walt Whitman

1

I celebrate myself, and sing myself,
And what I assume you shall assume,
For every atom belonging to me as good belongs to you.

I loaf and invite my soul,
5   I lean and loaf at my ease observing a spear of summer
        grass.

My tongue, every atom of my blood, formed from this soil,
        this air,
Born here of parents born here from parents the same, and
        their parents the same,
I, now thirty-seven years old in perfect health begin,
Hoping to cease not till death.

10 Creeds and schools in abeyance,
Retiring back a while sufficed at what they are, but never
        forgotten,
I harbor for good or bad, I permit to speak at every hazard,
Nature without check with original energy.

6

A child said *What is the grass?* fetching it to me with full
        hands,
How could I answer the child? I do not know what it is any
        more than he.

I guess it must be the flag of my disposition, out of hopeful
        green stuff woven.

Or I guess it is the handkerchief of the Lord,
5   A scented gift and remembrancer[1] designedly dropped,
Bearing the owner's name someway in the corners, that we
        may see and remark, and say *Whose?*

                                · · ·

What do you think has become of the young and old men?
And what do you think has become of the women and
        children?

---

1. remembrancer: Reminder.

They are alive and well somewhere,
10   The smallest sprout shows there is really no death,
     And if ever there was it led forward life, and does not wait
        at the end to arrest it,
     And ceas'd the moment life appear'd.
     All goes onward and outward, nothing collapses,
     And to die is different from what anyone supposed, and
        luckier.

9

     The big doors of the country barn stand open and ready,
     The dried grass of the harvest-time loads the slow-drawn
        wagon,

The clear light plays on the brown gray and green
    intertinged,
The armfuls are pack'd to the sagging mow.

5   I am there, I help, I came stretch'd atop of the load,
I felt its soft jolts, one leg reclined on the other,
I jump from the crossbeams and seize the clover and
    timothy,
And roll head over heels and tangle my hair full of wisps.

14

The wild gander leads his flock through the cool night,
Ya-honk he says, and sounds it down to me like an
    invitation,
The pert may suppose it meaningless, but I listening close,
Find its purpose and place up there toward the wintry sky.

5   The sharp-hoof'd moose of the north, the cat on the house-
    sill, the chickadee, the prairie dog,
The litter of the grunting sow as they tug at her teats,
The brood of the turkey hen and she with her half-spread
    wings,
I see in them and myself the same old law.

The press of my foot to the earth springs a hundred
    affections,
10   They scorn the best I can do to relate them.

I am enamor'd of growing outdoors,
Of men that live among cattle or taste of the ocean or
    woods,
Of the builders and steerers of ships and the wielders of
    axes and mauls, and the drivers of horses,
I can eat and sleep with them week in and week out.

15   What is commonest, cheapest, nearest, easiest, is Me,
Me going in for my chances, spending for vast returns,
Adorning myself to bestow myself on the first that will take
    me,
Not asking the sky to come down to my good will,
Scattering it freely forever.

17

These are really the thoughts of all men in all ages and
    lands, they are not original with me,

If they are not yours as much as mine they are nothing, or
    next to nothing,
If they are not the riddle and the untying of the riddle they
    are nothing,
If they are not just as close as they are distant they are
    nothing.
5 This is the grass that grows wherever the land is and the
    water is,
This is the common air that bathes the globe.

51

The past and present wilt—I have fill'd them, emptied them,
And proceed to fill my next fold of the future.

Listener up there! what have you to confide to me?
Look in my face while I snuff the sidle of evening,[2]
5 (Talk honestly, no one else hears you, and I stay only a
    minute longer.)

Do I contradict myself?
Very well then I contradict myself,
(I am large, I contain multitudes.)

I concentrate toward them that are nigh,[3] I wait on the
    door-slab.

10 Who has done his day's work? who will soonest be through
    with his supper?
Who wishes to walk with me?

Will you speak before I am gone? will you prove already too
    late?

52

The spotted hawk swoops by and accuses me, he complains
    of my gab and my loitering.

I too am not a bit tamed, I too am untranslatable,
I sound my barbaric yawp over the roofs of the world.

---

2. snuff . . . evening: Put out the hesitant last light of day, which
is moving sideways across the sky.
3. nigh: Near.

The last scud[4] of day holds back for me,
5   It flings my likeness after the rest and true as any on the
    shadow'd wilds,
  It coaxes me to the vapor and the dusk.

  I depart as air, I shake my white locks at the runaway sun,
  I effuse my flesh in eddies, and drift it in lacy jags.

  I bequeath myself to the dirt to grow from the grass I love,
10   If you want me again look for me under your boot soles.

  You will hardly know who I am or what I mean,
  But I shall be good health to you nevertheless,
  And filter and fiber your blood.

  Failing to fetch me at first keep encouraged,
15   Missing me one place search another,
  I stop somewhere waiting for you.

---

4. scud: Low, dark, wind-driven clouds.

RESPONDING TO THE SELECTION

Your Response

1. In section 52 Walt Whitman proudly characterizes his poetry as "barbaric yawp." How would you describe it?

Interpreting

2. In section 1 how does Whitman suggest that he celebrates (a) his individual self and (b) a representative and universal self?
3. What do lines 6–14 of section 6 reveal about the speaker's attitude concerning death?
4. How do the images of grass and air in section 17 convey the speaker's belief in the spiritual unity and equality of all forms of being?
5. In the final section, what does the speaker suggest will happen to his spirit and message once he is gone?

Applying

6. In what ways is your own attitude toward nature similar to and different from the attitude conveyed in "Song of Myself"?

ANALYZING LITERATURE

Recognizing Style

Style refers to the way in which a writer expresses his or her thoughts. Each writer has his or her own distinctive style. Two important characteristics of Whitman's style are his use of catalogs and parallelism. For example, in the first stanza of section 9, Whitman uses parallelism to create a catalog of concrete images.

1. Find another example of a catalog in "Song of Myself."
2. Find two more examples of parallelism.

CRITICAL THINKING AND READING

Recognizing the Author's Attitudes

Whitman's poetry reveals a great deal about his attitudes and beliefs. For example, in "Song of Myself" (section 14, lines 11–14), Whitman reveals his affection for people who work outdoors.

Find two other passages in which Whitman expresses his attitudes or beliefs. What attitude or belief does each passage reveal?

Beat! Beat! Drums!

Walt Whitman

This poem was written in response to the defeat of the Union army by Confederate forces in the battle of Bull Run in 1861. The Confederate victory shocked many people who felt that the Union would easily win the war and made it clear that a long and bloody struggle lay ahead.

Beat! beat! drums!—blow! bugles! blow!
Through the windows—through doors—burst like a ruthless
    force,
Into the solemn church, and scatter the congregation,
Into the school where the scholar is studying;
5   Leave not the bridegroom quiet—no happiness must he
    have now with his bride,
Nor the peaceful farmer any peace, ploughing his field or
    gathering his grain,
So fierce you whirr and pound you drums—so shrill you
    bugles blow.

Beat! beat! drums!—blow! bugles! blow!
Over the traffic of cities—over the rumble of wheels in the
    streets;
10 Are beds prepared for sleepers at night in the houses? no
    sleepers must sleep in those beds,
No bargainers' bargains by day—no brokers or speculators—
    would they continue?
Would the talkers be talking? would the singer attempt to
    sing?
Would the lawyer rise in the court to state his case before
    the judge?
Then rattle quicker, heavier drums—you bugles wilder blow.

15 Beat! beat! drums!—blow! bugles! blow!
Make no parley—stop for no expostulation,
Mind not the timid—mind not the weeper or prayer,
Mind not the old man beseeching the young man,
Let not the child's voice be heard, nor the mother's
    entreaties,
20 Make even the trestles to shake the dead where they lie
    awaiting the hearses,
So strong you thump O terrible drums—so loud you bugles
    blow.

THE WOUNDED DRUMMER BOY
Eastman Johnson
The Union League Club, New York City

RESPONDING TO THE SELECTION

Your Response

1. What did you see and hear as you read this poem?
2. Would you describe the poem as a call to arms, a call for peace, or something else? Explain.

Recalling

3. (a) What activities do the drums and bugles interrupt? (b) What does the speaker instruct them to ignore?
4. What do the drums and bugles represent?
5. What does this poem suggest about the effect of war on people's everyday lives?
6. (a) How does the rhythm and repetition of lines 1, 8, and 15 add to the impact of the poem? (b) How does Whitman's use of parallelism reinforce the meaning of the poem?

Applying

7. At the beginning of the Civil War, Whitman was a staunch supporter of the Union cause. Do you think this poem shows a change in attitude? Explain.

LEARNING OPTION

Writing. Imagine that it is 1871, the year that the edition of *Leaves of Grass* that included "Beat! Beat! Drums!" was published. The book's publisher has organized a book-signing party, and you are invited. What might Whitman write in your copy of his book? Write the inscription that he addresses to you. Keep in mind Whitman's flair for self-promotion.

When I Heard the Learn'd Astronomer

Walt Whitman

When I heard the learn'd astronomer,
When the proofs, the figures, were ranged in columns
   before me,
When I was shown the charts and diagrams, to add, divide
   and measure them,
When I sitting heard the astronomer where he lectured with
   much applause in the lecture room,
5   How soon unaccountable I became tired and sick,
Till rising and gliding out I wander'd off by myself,
In the mystical moist night air, and from time to time,
Look'd up in perfect silence at the stars.

THE LAWRENCE TREE, 1929
Georgia O'Keeffe
Wadsworth Atheneum, Hartford

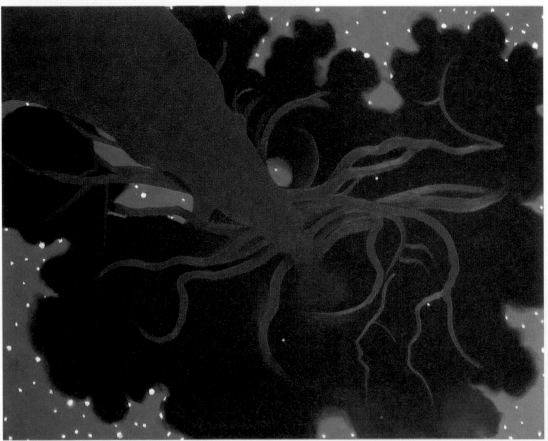

A Noiseless Patient Spider

Walt Whitman

A noiseless patient spider,
I mark'd where on a little promontory it stood isolated,
Mark'd how to explore the vacant vast surrounding,
It launch'd forth filament, filament, filament, out of itself,
5   Ever unreeling them, ever tirelessly speeding them.

And you O my soul where you stand,
Surrounded, detached, in measureless oceans of space,
Ceaselessly musing, venturing, throwing, seeking the
     spheres to connect them,
Till the bridge you will need be form'd, till the ductile
     anchor hold,
10   Till the gossamer thread you fling catch somewhere, O my
     soul.

RESPONDING TO THE SELECTION

Your Response
1. What is your reaction to each poem?
2. Do you think that Whitman is fair to the astronomer in "When I Heard the Learn'd Astronomer"? Why or why not?
3. How do you view the "noiseless patient spider"?

Interpreting
4. In "When I Heard the Learn'd Astronomer," how does the speaker's attitude toward the stars differ from the astronomer's?
5. (a) What is the theme, or message, of "When I Heard the Learn'd Astronomer"? (b) How does the use of parallelism in lines 1–4 reinforce the theme?
6. In "A Noiseless Patient Spider," what similarities does the speaker see between his soul and the spider?

Applying
7. Like the Transcendentalists, Whitman believed that the human spirit was mirrored in the world of nature. How does "A Noiseless Patient Spider" reflect this belief?

ANALYZING LITERATURE

Recognizing Free Verse
Free verse has irregular meter and line length. Whitman's use of free verse reflects his belief in freedom, democracy, and individuality.
1. Considering the theme of "When I Heard a Learn'd Astronomer," what makes free verse an appropriate form for the poem?
2. How would the poem be different if it had a regular meter and line length?

THINKING AND WRITING

Writing a Poem in Free Verse
Use the list you prepared before reading Whitman's poetry and write a poem in free verse that expresses your associations with something in nature. Structure your verse to re-create the rising and falling cadences of natural speech, and vary the lengths of the lines for emphasis. After revising, share your poem with classmates.

When Lilacs Last in the Dooryard Bloom'd

Walt Whitman

1

When lilacs last in the dooryard bloom'd,
And the great star early droop'd in the western sky in the
    night,
I mourn'd, and yet shall mourn with ever-returning spring.

Ever-returning spring, trinity sure to me you bring,
5 Lilac blooming perennial and drooping star in the west,
And thought of him I love.

2

O powerful western fallen star!
O shades of night—O moody, tearful night!
O great star disappear'd—O the black murk that hides the
    star!
10 O cruel hands that hold me powerless—O helpless soul of
    me!
O harsh surrounding cloud that will not free my soul.

3

In the dooryard fronting an old farmhouse near the white-
    wash'd palings,
Stands the lilac bush tall-growing with heart-shaped leaves
    of rich green,
With many a pointed blossom rising delicate, with the
    perfume strong I love,
15 With every leaf a miracle—and from this bush in the
    dooryard,
With delicate-color'd blossoms and heart-shaped leaves of
    rich green,
A sprig with its flower I break.

4

In the swamp in secluded recesses,
A shy and hidden bird is warbling a song.
20 Solitary the thrush,

The hermit withdrawn to himself, avoiding the settlements,
Sings by himself a song.

Song of the bleeding throat,
Death's outlet song of life, (for well dear brother I know,
25 If thou wast not granted to sing thou would'st surely die.)

5

Over the breast of the spring, the land, amid cities,
Amid lanes and through old woods, where lately the violets
    peep'd from the ground, spotting the gray debris,
Amid the grass in the fields each side of the lanes, passing
    the endless grass,
Passing the yellow-spear'd wheat, every grain from its
    shroud in the dark-brown fields uprisen,
30 Passing the apple-tree blows¹ of white and pink in the
    orchards,
Carrying a corpse to where it shall rest in the grave,
Night and day journeys a coffin.

6

Coffin that passes through lanes and streets,
Through day and night with the great cloud darkening the
    land,
35 With the pomp of the inloop'd flags with the cities draped
    in black,
With the show of the states themselves as of crape-veil'd
    women standing,
With processions long and winding and the flambeaus² of
    the night,
With the countless torches lit, with the silent sea of faces
    and the unbared heads,
With the waiting depot, the arriving coffin, and the somber
    faces,
40 With dirges through the night, with the thousand voices
    rising strong and solemn,
With all the mournful voices of the dirges pour'd around
    the coffin,
The dim-lit churches and the shuddering organs—where
    amid these you journey,
With the tolling tolling bells' perpetual clang,
Here, coffin that slowly passes,
45 I give you my sprig of lilac.

---

1. **blows:** Blossoms.
2. **flambeaus** (flam′ bōz): Torches.

7

(Nor for you, for one alone,
Blossoms and branches green to coffins all I bring,
For fresh as the morning, thus would I chant a song for
  you O sane and sacred death.

All over bouquets of roses,
50 O death, I cover you over with roses and early lilies,
But mostly and now the lilac that blooms the first,
Copious I break, I break the sprigs from the bushes,
With loaded arms I come, pouring for you,
For you and the coffins all of you O death.)

8

55 O western orb sailing the heaven,
Now I know what you must have meant as a month since I
  walk'd,
As I walk'd in silence the transparent shadowy night,
As I saw you had something to tell as you bent to me night
  after night,

THE FUNERAL OF PRESIDENT LINCOLN, NEW YORK, APRIL 25, 1865
Currier & Ives
Anne S. K. Brown Military Collection, Brown University Library

As you droop'd from the sky low down as if to my side
    (while the other stars all look'd on,)
60   As we wander'd together the solemn night (for something I
    know not what kept me from sleep,)
As the night advanced, and I saw on the rim of the west
    how full you were of woe,
As I stood on the rising ground in the breeze in the cool
    transparent night,
As I watch'd where you pass'd and was lost in the
    netherward[3] black of the night,
As my soul in its trouble dissatisfied sank, as where you
    sad orb,
65   Concluded, dropt in the night, and was gone.

9

Sing on there in the swamp,
O singer bashful and tender, I hear your notes, I hear your
    call,

---

3. netherward *adj.:* Moving downward.

I hear, I come presently, I understand you,
But a moment I linger, for the lustrous star has detain'd
  me,
70 The star my departing comrade holds and detains me.

10

O how shall I warble myself for the dead one there I loved?
And how shall I deck my song for the large sweet soul that
  has gone?
And what shall my perfume be for the grave of him I love?

Sea winds blown from east and west,
75 Blown from the eastern sea and blown from the western
  sea, till there on the prairies meeting,
These and with these and the breath of my chant,
I'll perfume the grave of him I love.

11

O what shall I hang on the chamber walls?
And what shall the pictures be that I hang on the walls,
80 To adorn the burial house of him I love?

Pictures of growing spring and farms and homes,
With the fourth-month[4] eve at sundown, and the gray
  smoke lucid and bright,
With floods of the yellow gold of the gorgeous, indolent,
  sinking sun, burning, expanding the air,
With the fresh sweet herbage[5] under foot, and the pale
  green leaves of the trees prolific,
85 In the distance the flowing glaze, the breast of the river,
  with a wind-dapple here and there,
With ranging hills on the banks, with many a line against
  the sky, and shadows,
And the city at hand with dwellings so dense, and stacks of
  chimneys,
And all the scenes of life and the workshops, and the
  workmen homeward returning.

12

Lo, body and soul—this land,
90 My own Manhattan with spires, and the sparkling and
  hurrying tides, and the ships,
The varied and ample land, the South and the North in the

---

4. fourth-month: April.
5. herbage: Grass.

light, Ohio's shores and flashing Missouri,
And ever the far-spreading prairies cover'd with grass and
    corn.

Lo, the most excellent sun so calm and haughty,
The violet and purple morn with just-felt breezes,
95 The gentle soft-born measureless light,
The miracle spreading bathing all, the fulfill'd noon,
The coming eve delicious, the welcome night and the stars,
Over my cities shining all, enveloping man and land.

13

Sing on, sing on you gray-brown bird,
100 Sing from the swamps, the recesses, pour your chant from
    the bushes,
Limitless out of the dusk, out of the cedars and pines.

Sing on dearest brother, warble your reedy song,
Loud human song, with voice of uttermost woe.

O liquid and free and tender!
105 O wild and loose to my soul!—O wondrous singer!
You only I hear—yet the star holds me, (but will soon
    depart,)
Yet the lilac with mastering odor holds me.

14

Now while I sat in the day and look'd forth,
In the close of the day with its light and the fields of
    spring, and the farmers preparing their crops,
110 In the large unconscious scenery of my land with its lakes
    and forests,
In the heavenly aerial beauty (after the perturb'd winds and
    the storms,)
Under the arching heavens of the afternoon swift passing,
    and the voices of children and women,
The many-moving sea tides, and I saw the ships how they
    sail'd,
And the summer approaching with richness, and the fields
    all busy with labor,
115 And the infinite separate houses, how they all went on,
    each with its meals and minutia[6] of daily usages,
And the streets how their throbbings throbb'd, and the
    cities pent—lo, then and there,

---

6. minutia (mi nü′ shē ə) *n.*: Small and trivial detail.

ABRAHAM LINCOLN
William Willard
National Portrait Gallery, Smithsonian Institution

Falling upon them all and among them all, enveloping me
    with the rest,
Appear'd the cloud, appear'd the long black trail,
And I knew death, its thought, and the sacred knowledge of
    death.

120   Then with the knowledge of death as walking one side of
    me,
And the thought of death close-walking the other side of
    me,
And I in the middle as with companions, and as holding
    the hands of companions,
I fled forth to the hiding receiving night that talks not,
Down to the shores of the water, the path by the swamp in
    the dimness,
125   To the solemn shadowy cedars and ghostly pines so still.

And the singer so shy to the rest receiv'd me,
The gray-brown bird I know receiv'd us comrades three,
And he sang the carol of death, and a verse for him I love.

From deep secluded recesses,
130 From the fragrant cedars and the ghostly pines so still,
Came the carol of the bird.

And the charm of the carol rapt me,
As I held as if by their hands my comrades in the night,
And the voice of my spirit tallied[7] the song of the bird.

135 *Come lovely and soothing death,*
Undulate[8] round the world, serenely arriving, arriving,
In the day, in the night, to all, to each,
Sooner or later delicate death.

Prais'd be the fathomless universe,
140 *For life and joy, and for objects and knowledge curious,*
And for love, sweet love—but praise! praise! praise!
For the sure-enwinding arms of cool-enfolding death.

Dark mother always gliding near with soft feet,
Have none chanted for thee a chant of fullest welcome?
145 *Then I chant it for thee, I glorify thee above all,*
I bring thee a song that when thou must indeed come,
    come unfalteringly.

Approach strong deliveress,
When it is so, when thou hast taken them I joyously sing
    the dead,
Lost in the loving floating ocean of thee,
150 *Laved[9] in the flood of thy bliss O death.*

From me to thee glad serenades,
Dances for thee I propose saluting thee, adornments and
    feastings for thee,
And the sights of the open landscape and the high-spread
    sky are fitting,
And life and the fields, and the huge and thoughtful
    night.

155 *The night in silence under many a star,*
The ocean shore and the husky whispering wave whose
    voice I know,
And the soul turning to thee O vast and well-veil'd death,
And the body gratefully nestling close to thee,
Over the treetops I float thee a song.

---

7. tallied: Corresponded with.
8. undulate *v.*: To move in waves.
9. laved *v.*: Washed.

160   *Over the rising and sinking waves, over the myriad fields*
        and the prairies wide,
     Over the dense-pack'd cities all and the teeming wharves
        and ways,
     I float this carol with joy, with joy to thee O death.

15

     To the tally of my soul,
     Loud and strong kept up the gray-brown bird,
165   With pure deliberate notes spreading filling the night.

     Loud in the pines and cedars dim,
     Clear in the freshness moist and the swamp perfume,
     And I with my comrades there in the night.

     While my sight that was bound in my eyes unclosed,
170   As to long panoramas of visions.

     And I saw askant[10] the armies,
     I saw as in noiseless dreams hundreds of battle flags,
     Borne through the smoke of the battles and pierc'd with
         missiles I saw them,
     And carried hither and yon through the smoke, and torn
         and bloody,
175   And at last but a few shreds left on the staffs (and all in
         silence,)
     And the staffs all splinter'd and broken.

     I saw battle corpses, myriads of them,
     And the white skeletons of young men, I saw them,
     I saw the debris and debris of all the slain soldiers of the
         war,
180   But I saw they were not as was thought,
     They themselves were fully at rest, they suffer'd not,
     The living remain'd and suffer'd, the mother suffer'd,
     And the wife and the child and the musing comrade
         suffer'd,
     And the armies that remain'd suffer'd.

16

185   Passing the visions, passing the night,
     Passing, unloosing the hold of my comrades' hands,
     Passing the song of the hermit bird and the tallying song of
         my soul,

---

10. askant: Askance; with a sideways glance.

Victorious song, death's outlet song, yet varying ever-
    altering song,
As low and wailing, yet clear the notes, rising and falling,
    flooding the night,
190 Sadly sinking and fainting, as warning and warning, and
    yet again bursting with joy,
Covering the earth and filling the spread of the heaven,
As that powerful psalm in the night I heard from recesses,
Passing, I leave thee lilac with heart-shaped leaves,
I leave thee there in the dooryard, blooming, returning with
    spring.

195 I cease from my song for thee,
From my gaze on thee in the west, fronting the west,
    communing with thee,
O comrade lustrous with silver face in the night.

Yet each to keep and all, retrievements out of the night,
The song, the wondrous chant of the gray-brown bird,
200 And the tallying chant, the echo arous'd in my soul,
With the lustrous and drooping star with the countenance
    full of woe,
With the holders holding my hand nearing the call of the
    bird,
Comrades mine and I in the midst, and their memory ever
    to keep, for the dead I loved so well,
For the sweetest, wisest soul of all my days and lands—and
    this for his dear sake,
205 Lilac and star and bird twined with the chant of my soul,
There in the fragrant pines and the cedars dusk and dim.

RESPONDING TO THE SELECTION

Your Response
1. What do you associate with lilacs in bloom?
2. What insights about life and death have you
   gained from reading this poem?

Interpreting
3. In sections 1–4 the speaker sets the scene.
   What happened when "Lilacs Last in the Dooryard Bloom'd"?
4. In sections 5–9 the speaker describes the journey of the coffin through the land. Why do you
   think the speaker places lilacs on the coffin?
5. In sections 10–13 how does the speaker suggest paying tribute to "the dead one"?

6. What does the speaker learn from his visions
   in section 15?

Applying
7. Whitman composed this poem to lament Abraham Lincoln's death. Why do you suppose he
   did not mention the President by name?

THINKING AND WRITING

Writing an Elegy
   Whitman's poem is an example of an elegy—
a lyric poem that expresses mourning, usually
upon the death of an individual. Write an elegy
mourning the death of a historical figure whom
you greatly admire.

Mathew Brady (1823–1896)

In 1839 photography in its earliest form—the Daguerreotype—was introduced. Many Americans were quick to see its commercial and artistic possibilities. A few others, among them Mathew Brady, also recognized the role it might play in recording history.

BRADY OF BROADWAY

Mathew Brady was born in upstate New York, the son of poor Irish farmers. By the early 1840's, he had moved to New York City where he studied daguerreotyping with Samuel F. B. Morse. Sometime in 1844 he opened his first portrait studio on New York's busy lower Broadway. By the late 1850's, with numerous operators and chemists in his employ, he was known as "Brady of Broadway," the most fashionable portraitist of his time.

Brady was a businessman, but early in his career he recognized that photography could be more than a commercial enterprise, that the camera could be the "eye of history." In 1845 he began work on a project of preserving for future generations the portraits of distinguished Americans. He began to seek out the great people of his time, cajoling them into visiting his studios. During his career almost all the great politicians, scientists, writers, thinkers, actors, and actresses of his era posed before his cameras.

THE CIVIL WAR

The outbreak of the Civil War filled Brady with a sense of mission. Here was truly an opportunity to preserve history. Using his friendships with government leaders, he secured authorization to enter combat zones and hurried to the front with his cameramen.

Brady and his assistants worked under difficult conditions. They traveled to the scene of battle over rough country roads in heavy wagons containing darkroom tents, hundreds of fragile glass plates, and sensitive chemicals. Once there they often remained crouched for minutes on end in their fragile darkrooms delicately processing plates while outside the earth shook with battle.

Yet Brady and his cameramen were able to photograph almost every phase of the war—battlefields, ruins, officers, men, artil-

lery, ships, railroads. Brady's photographs brought home the grim reality of the war—dead men as they had fallen, dead horses and smashed guns as they lay after a murderous assault, ravaged towns and homesteads, the loneliness of camp life. By the end of the war, Brady and his assistants had created more than 7,000 photographic images.

LATER YEARS

Brady's work was little appreciated in the later years of his life. After the Civil War, people were eager to forget the conflict. To pay the debts he incurred to finance his Civil War crews, Brady was forced to sell his negatives for a fraction of their value. He spent his last years in ill health and poverty.

Brady's photography has given us a lasting record of an era. Today the camera is recognized as an important and relatively convenient tool for the preservation of history. Vast improvements in camera technology have enabled modern photographers to record events in ever greater and often more horrifying detail. But Brady's work remains important for the way it confirmed the camera's early promise as a tool for transforming transitory events into lucid, permanent images.

YOUR WRITING PROCESS

WRITING AN EDITORIAL

The period between 1855 and 1865 was a time of contrasting dreams. Men such as Abraham Lincoln and Robert E. Lee had different visions for America's future and persuaded others to believe in their goals. Perhaps you have a dream, or the beginnings of one, for your school community. How can you explain your dream and then convince others to make it come true?

Focus

Assignment: Write an editorial presenting a dream for your school community.
Purpose: Persuade others to help fulfill your dream.
Audience: Fellow students, teachers, and school administrators.

Prewriting

1. Find the problems. Have you ever had a day at school when everything seemed to go wrong, from early morning to dismissal time? Recalling that day may give you a clue to things about your school that you would like changed.

2. Speak to your classmates. By speaking to several classmates, you can see whether they agree with you about what is wrong and how it can be fixed. If they do not share your concern about a problem, it may not be as important as you think. Your classmates may also give you new ideas to use in your editorial.

3. Think of solutions. Jot down some solutions to the problems you have found. Remember that these solutions, and your dream, must appeal to teachers and administrators as well as to other students. You may want to ask several classmates whether your solutions will win such acceptance.

4. Imagine living your dream. Relax for a moment and let yourself daydream. What would your school be like if your wishes came true? Write down words that capture the feelings you would have.

Drafting

1. Grab your listeners' attention. The opening of your editorial should make your listeners eager to hear what you have to say. You might want to give a dramatic presentation of the problems that trouble you and your audience.

2. Make your solutions sound appealing. In describing your dream for the school, use language that stirs your listeners' emotions. In the Gettysburg Address, for instance, Lincoln used emotionally charged words like "liberty," "brave," and "devotion." You may find such language in the notes you made when you imagined living your dream. Also, consider organizing your editorial by repeating a word or phrase with special meaning for your audience, perhaps a refrain from a popular song.

3. Do not write too much or too little. Remember that you are limited to the length of an average editorial, or about 8 to 10 brief paragraphs. You may want to look at editorials in your school and local newspapers to get a sense of their length.

Revising and Editing

1. Read your editorial to classmates. By reading your editorial to several classmates, you can tell where it flows easily and where it sounds awkward. Pay special attention to their body language as they listen. A yawn, for instance, may show that you need to revise a passage. When you have finished, have them answer the questions in the following Peer Revision Checklist:

- Did my editorial catch your attention? Why or why not?
- How can I better persuade you that my dream is worth realizing and is possible to accomplish?
- How can I make my dream more appealing to teachers, administrators, or students?
- Were there any passages that did not flow smoothly?

2. Proofread your editorial. Make sure that the final version of your editorial is free of errors in grammar, usage, and mechanics.

Grammar Tip

You can add interest to your editorial by using **parallelism:** the placement of equal ideas in words, phrases, or clauses of similar types. For example, at the end of the Gettysburg Address, Abraham Lincoln expresses his hope that "government *of the people, by the people, for the people,* shall not perish from the earth." By using three parallel phrases, he makes his statement more emphatic. Also, if he had merely said, "that democratic government shall not perish from the earth," his words would not have been as memorable.

Options for Publishing

- Submit the editorial to the school newspaper.
- Read the editorial aloud to your class.
- Give your editorial to school administrators.
- Help create a class looseleaf volume that contains everyone's editorials.

Reviewing Your Writing Process

1. Did speaking with classmates help you to identify problems that you wanted to solve? Explain.

2. Do you plan to work further on the issues that you raised in your editorial? Why or why not?

THE ADIRONDACK GUIDE
Winslow Homer
Museum of Fine Arts, Boston

REALISM AND THE FRONTIER
1865–1915

The Palace Hotel at Fort Romper was painted a light blue, a shade that is on the legs of a kind of heron, causing the bird to declare its position against any background. The Palace Hotel, then, was always screaming and howling in a way that made the dazzling winter landscape of Nebraska seem only a gray swampish hush.

Stephen Crane

One of the characters in Stephen Crane's story "The Blue Hotel," published in 1899, is a half-mad Swede who has arrived by train in the tiny town of Fort Romper, Nebraska. Another character guesses that the Swede "has been reading dime novels, and he thinks he's right out in the middle of it—the shootin' and stabbin' and all." A visiting cowboy wonders how the man could be so mistaken, since, as he says, "this ain't Wyoming ner none of them places. This is Nebrasker."

A few years earlier, Nebraska would have been the Wild West, but no longer. America was changing dramatically in the late nineteenth and early twentieth centuries. The Civil War, although devastating to the South, was more and more becoming a hazy memory. The American frontier, which had once seemed so vast, no longer existed by 1915. (This in no way stemmed the tide of western migration, however.) A number of railroads bridged the continent. The Wright Brothers took their first aircraft aloft at Kitty Hawk, North Carolina, in 1903. Science and industry were making great leaps forward.

So was literature. After the relative quiet of the immediate postwar years, an impressive array of writers began to appear. The prewar Romantic writers were still widely read, but most of the emerging writers were not Romantics. These new writers wanted to portray life as it was lived, not sentimentally or in flights of fancy. Their goal was Realism, or Naturalism, or Regionalism.

THE HISTORICAL SETTING

American writers were gaining a large and increasingly diverse audience. Between 1865 and 1915, the population of the United States grew by more than 42 million people. This number was

IN SEARCH OF THE LAND OF MILK AND HONEY
Harvey Dunn
Hazel L. Meyer Memorial Library, De Smet, South Dakota

larger than the entire population of the United States at the end of the Civil War. This huge population increase stemmed in part from new immigration. Before the 1880's, most immigrants came from western Europe and the Scandinavian countries. In the 1880's, immigrants began arriving from southern and eastern Europe, from Italy, Greece, Poland, and Russia. Many of the new immigrants settled in eastern cities, but some joined the relentless western march.

The populations of older cities like Boston and Baltimore tripled or quadrupled during these decades. The populations of large midwestern cities like Chicago and Detroit also skyrocketed. Major new cities sprang up almost overnight. In 1858, Denver had consisted of sixty crude log cabins. Three years later, as a result of the Pikes Peak gold rush, 3,000 people lived there. By 1890, the population of Denver exceeded 100,000.

A Nation on the Move

In many ways, the American experience has been shaped by advances in transportation. European settlers reached the shores of North America as a result of improvements in oceangoing ships. Once here, the settlers advanced westward by stagecoach, and then by railroad. Long journeys that would have been difficult for early writers of the republic were commonplace for Mark Twain. As a journeyman printer, Twain made his way from Hannibal, Missouri, to St. Louis, then New York, then Philadelphia, and back to Keokuk, Iowa. Later he went to New Orleans as a steamboat pilot, to Virginia City, Nevada, as a newspaperman, and to San Francisco as a writer and foreign correspondent. Eventually, he settled in Hartford, Connecticut. This kind of mobility helped to shape both the subject matter and the attitudes of writers in this period.

Mark Twain's *Roughing It* records his experiences in the Far West, including his days in Virginia City, Nevada. In this period, for the first time, a number of writers represented the Midwest or Far West. Some of these writers, like Bret Harte and Willa Cather, were born in the East or South, but later moved west. Harte moved as a young man from New York to California. Cather moved as a child from Virginia to Nebraska. One of the few

native California writers was Jack London, born in San Francisco and raised in Oakland. Interestingly, London's first successful stories were not set in California, but farther north and west—in the Klondike, on the Alaskan-Canadian border. London had gone to this region in 1897 to prospect for gold.

The Frontier Experience

In 1827, President John Quincy Adams's secretary of war had predicted that it would take 500 years to fill the American West. By 1890, the superintendent of the census could report that the nation's "unsettled area had been so broken into by isolated bodies of settlement that there can hardly be said to be a frontier line." To many Americans this came as quite a surprise. They had imagined that free, or at least cheap, land would always be available.

The frontier was gone, but its legacy lived on. Frontier dwellers had always been generally mobile, practical, inventive, democratic, and optimistic. Those traits colored the national character and affected American writing. Mark Twain, in his early life and writing, showed all five traits. Yet the frontier itself offered no idyllic existence. It could be lonely and cruel, as in Jack London's "To Build a Fire" or Willa Cather's "A Wagner Matinée." The

THE MINERS DURING THE GOLD RUSH, 1849, IN CALIFORNIA
Frank Tenny Johnson

Realism and the Frontier

(A.D. 1865 – A.D. 1915)

Mark Twain

Inauguration
of Statue of
Liberty

Blizzard of 1888

1865   **1875**   **1885**

AMERICAN EVENTS

- **Mark Twain** wins recognition with "The Notorious Jumping Frog of Calaveras County."
  - United States purchases Alaska from Russia for two cents an acre.
    - Louisa May Alcott's *Little Women* becomes an immediate children's favorite.
      - Transcontinental railroad completed.
        - Women in Wyoming Territory are first to win right to vote.
          - **Bret Harte** publishes *The Luck of Roaring Camp and Other Stories.*

- Alexander Graham Bell patents a telephone and transmits speech over it.
  - The Sioux wipe out General George A. Custer's cavalry at Battle of the Little Bighorn.
    - Thomas A. Edison invents electric light bulb.
      - **Mark Twain** publishes *Life on the Mississippi.*
      - Brooklyn Bridge opens.
        - **Mark Twain's** *The Adventures of Huckleberry Finn* appears.

- Statue of Liberty dedicated in New York Harbor.
  - Great mid-March blizzard in eastern United States piles 30-foot drifts in New York's Herald Square.
    - First volume of **Emily Dickinson's** poems is released.
    - Last major battle between U.S. troops and Native Americans fought at Wounded Knee, South Dakota.
      - **Ambrose Bierce** publishes *Can Such Things Be?*

WORLD EVENTS

- Russia: Fyodor Dostoyevsky publishes *Crime and Punishment.*
  - Russia: Leo Tolstoy completes *War and Peace.*
  - France: Jules Verne publishes *Twenty Thousand Leagues Under the Sea.*
    - Germany: End of Franco-Prussian War establishes German empire.
      - France: Claude Monet gathers Impressionist painters for first exhibition.

- France: People in France begin raising money to build U.S. Statue of Liberty.
  - Norway: Henrick Ibsen writes *A Doll's House.*
    - Russia: Fyodor Dostoyevsky publishes *The Brothers Karamazov.*
      - England: Robert Louis Stevenson publishes *Treasure Island.*

- Germany: Karl Benz builds first automobile powered by internal combustion engine.
  - Russia: Leo Tolstoy completes "The Death of Ivan Ilyich."
    - England: Thomas Hardy publishes *The Mayor of Casterbridge.*
      - England: Thomas Hardy publishes *Tess of the D'Urbervilles.*

First Flight at
Kitty Hawk

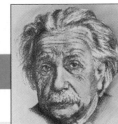
Albert Einstein

Ford Model T

1895   1905   1915

- **Kate Chopin's** *Bayou Folk* published.
  - **Paul Laurence Dunbar** publishes *Lyrics of Lowly Life.*
  - *The Country of the Pointed Firs,* Sarah Orne Jewett's masterpiece, appears.
    - President William McKinley shot in Buffalo; succeeded by Theodore Roosevelt.
      - **Jack London** publishes *The Call of the Wild.*
      - Boston Red Sox and Pittsburgh Pirates play in first World Series.
      - Wright Brothers stay aloft for 582 feet in their airplane at Kitty Hawk, North Carolina.

- **Willa Cather** publishes *The Troll Garden.*
- Edith Wharton's *The House of Mirth* appears.
  - Strong earthquake in San Francisco is followed by devastating fire.
    - Ford introduces the Model T.
      - Admiral Robert E. Peary reaches the North Pole.
      - National Association for the Advancement of Colored People (NAACP) founded.

- Sino-Japanese War breaks out; Japanese army easily defeats Chinese.
  - Germany: Wilhelm Roentgen discovers X-rays.
    - France: Pierre Curie and Marie Sklodowska Curie discover radium.
    - South Africa: Boer War breaks out between British and Dutch in South Africa.
      - Austria: Sigmund Freud publishes *The Interpretation of Dreams.*
      - China: Chinese nationalists begin Boxer Rebellion to expel foreigners.

- Spain: Pablo Picasso paints *The Old Guitarist.*
  - Russo-Japanese War begins.
  - Germany: Albert Einstein proposes his relativity theory.
    - Mexico: Francisco Madero begins revolution that overthrows dictator Porfirio Díaz.
      - Europe: World War I begins.

great majority of Americans never lived on the frontier. American life and literature have nonetheless been enriched by those who did.

Unresolved Challenges

The Civil War and its aftermath spurred the headlong growth of industry in the North. Yet even before the Civil War, writers had observed that industrial growth created hardships as well as benefits. Along with rapid industrial expansion came urban slums, farm problems, and labor unrest. By the 1880's, some of the abuses were bringing insistent demands for reform. Back in 1873, Mark Twain and Charles Dudley Warner had published *The Gilded Age*. This novel dealt with unrestrained greed in a time of financial speculation and uncertain moral values. Around the turn of the century, a group of journalists took up this same theme. Theodore Roosevelt called them "muckrakers," because they uncovered only the muck, or dirt, of American life. Among the leading muckrakers were Ida Tarbell and Lincoln Steffens. Tarbell exposed unethical business practices, while Steffens attacked corruption in city and state governments.

A further challenge facing the nation was its great and increasing diversity. Despite the Depression of 1893, the country as a whole rejoiced in economic good times. Not everyone shared in the prosperity, however. Farmers faced falling agricultural prices, high interest rates for bank loans, and unequal railroad shipping charges. After centuries of conflict, the Native American tribes had been defeated. The slaves had been freed but had not been made full participants in American democracy. Restrictive immigration laws prohibited Chinese workers from entering the United States after 1882; European immigrants often worked long hours in sweatshops and lived in slums; and women were not allowed to vote in national elections.

The literature of the time was as diverse as the nation itself. It reflected both the promise and the problems of the frontier and of the dynamic expansion of industry.

LOUISIANA INDIANS WALKING ALONG A BAYOU
Alfred Boisseau
New Orleans Museum of Art

THE BOWERY AT NIGHT, 1895
W. Louis Sonntag, Jr.
Museum of the City of New York

REALISM IN AMERICAN LITERATURE

The Civil War and its aftermath left Americans less certain about the future than ever before, diminishing their belief in a unity of national purpose. The buoyant spirits of Emerson and the wild imaginings of Poe seemed out of date to many, especially to young writers. In the South, the Jeffersonian dream of a nation of farmers lay shattered like the land itself. The South would have to rebuild on a different foundation, and it would be a long, arduous task.

Under the circumstances, it is small wonder that writers turned away from the Romanticism that had been so popular before the war. The hopes

of idealists, these new writers felt, would have to wait. Even the visions of Hawthorne and the extravagances of Melville did not fit the mood of the times. In place of Romanticism came Realism, a literary movement that sought to portray ordinary life as real people live it and attempted to show characters and events in an objective, almost factual way.

The Realistic Movement

Realistic fiction remains popular today, and it may seem strange that it was once controversial. Yet it was. Realistic writers saw themselves as being in revolt against Romanticism. Mark Twain wrote an amusing essay whose target was the Romantic writer James Fenimore Cooper. In *The Deerslayer*,

Twain claimed, Cooper "has scored 114 offenses against literary art out of a possible 115." One of these offenses, according to Twain, is that "the personages of a tale shall confine themselves to possibilities and let miracles alone; or, if they venture a miracle, the author must plausibly set it forth to make it look possible and reasonable."

Eugene Field, a Chicago journalist, held the opposite view. Field took humorous aim at the new Realistic writers, Hamlin Garland in particular. "Mr. Garland's heroes sweat and do not wear socks," Field wrote. "His heroines eat cold huckleberry pie."

How did Realism originate? There had been Realistic writers in France for some time, notably Honoré de Balzac, Stendhal, and Gustave Flaubert. Although these writers and others had great influence, American Realism had roots in this country, in the experiences of war, on the frontier, and in the cities. Science played a part as well. The objectivity of science struck many writers as a worthy goal for literature. Just as important, perhaps, was a general feeling that Romanticism was wearing thin. Students still recited Romantic poetry and read Romantic novels, but many writers believed these works to be old-fashioned.

One in particular who held that belief was William Dean Howells. Howells held prestigious edi-torial posts at the *Atlantic Monthly* and *Harper's* and knew virtually every important writer of the day. Although his early works were not Realistic, in the 1880's he began to champion Realism. His best Realistic novel, *The Rise of Silas Lapham,* was published in 1885. Many people considered Howells, a self-educated man, to be the leading literary figure of the time. He often advised his friend Mark Twain and encouraged many younger authors, among them Hamlin Garland and Stephen Crane. In 1891, Howells described his theories about Realism in a book called *Criticism and Fiction.*

Howells and others were aware that Realistic writers ran the risk of becoming boring. A Romantic was limited only by his or her imagination, but a Realist had to find meaning in the commonplace. To do this, the Realist had to be acutely observant and to lay bare to readers the hidden meanings behind familiar words and actions. On the other hand, Realistic writers could deal honestly with characters that a Romantic writer would either avoid or gloss over: factory workers, bosses, politicians, gunfighters. This emphasis did not always please the critics, however. One journalist wrote of Willa Cather's stories: "If the writers of fiction who use western Nebraska as material would look up now and then and not keep their eyes and noses in the cattle yards, they might be more agreeable company." Despite such complaints, Realism held sway, and it remains dominant to the present day.

Naturalism

Some writers of the period went one step beyond Realism. Influenced by the French novelist Émile Zola, a literary movement known as Naturalism developed. According to Zola, a writer must examine people and society objectively and, like a scientist, draw conclusions from what is observed. In line with this belief, Naturalistic writers viewed reality as the inescapable working out of natural forces. One's destiny, they said, is decided by heredity and environment, physical drives, and economic circumstances. Because they believed people have no control over events, Naturalistic writers tended to be pessimistic.

Only a few major American writers embraced Naturalism. One who did was Stephen Crane. His first novel, *Maggie: A Girl of the Streets,* published in 1893, is the earliest Naturalistic novel by an American writer. Jack London's "To Build a Fire" presents one of the recurring themes of Naturalism, man at the mercy of the brutal forces of nature. Another Naturalistic writer of the time was Frank Norris. *The Octopus,* his best-known novel, concerns the struggle between wheat growers and an all-powerful railroad in the San Joaquin Valley of California.

RABBIT STEW
Gary Niblett
Photograph Courtesy of the Gerald Peters Gallery; Santa Fe, New Mexico, and Dallas, Texas

Regionalism

The third significant literary movement that developed during the latter part of the nineteenth century was Regionalism, or the "local color movement." Through the use of regional dialect and vivid descriptions of the landscape, the Regionalists sought to capture the essence of life in the various regions of the growing nation.

At its very best, Regional writing transcends the region and becomes part of the national literature. No one today would call Mark Twain a Regionalist or a local colorist. Yet his early short story "The Notorious Jumping Frog of Calaveras County" fits the category. Bret Harte, on the other hand, is generally regarded as the founder of the local color movement. Harte's stories, such as "The Outcasts of Poker Flat," have many of the same elements as Twain's. George Washington Cable, another leader in the local color movement, wrote sketches and novels of Creole life in Louisiana. His writings have charm and style but are seldom read today.

Various reasons have been given to explain the popularity of the local color movement. Perhaps it was the desire of people throughout the reunited nation to learn more about one another after the discord of the Civil War. Whatever its cause, the outpouring of local color was remarkable. Besides Twain, Harte, and Cable, there was Edward Eggleston. Eggleston's novel *The Hoosier Schoolmaster,* portraying the backwoods country of Indiana, became a bestseller in its day. A more critically acclaimed book was Sarah Orne Jewett's *The Country of the Pointed Firs.* Many critics regard this as the finest work of fiction about nineteenth-century rural New England. Mary Wilkins Freeman, too, wrote memorably about rural New England. Kate Chopin, a Louisiana writer, produced outstanding tales of Creole and Cajun life.

Poets and Popular Writers

The poets of this period cannot be easily classified, for each of them speaks in a clear, individual voice. Stephen Crane's poems are short, spare, and untitled. Sometimes they resemble fables and some-times riddles. Sidney Lanier, whose health was shattered as a Confederate prisoner of war, fused musical and poetical principles. Among the best of his poems are "Song of the Chattahoochee" and "The Marshes of Glynn." Paul Laurence Dunbar, the son of former slaves, used black dialect and folklore in his poetry.

In 1897, one of the finest of all volumes of American poems appeared, Edwin Arlington Robinson's *The Children of the Night.* This volume contains unforgettable psychological portraits of people, including "Luke Havergal" and "Richard Cory." Fifteen years later, the *Spoon River Anthology* by Edgar Lee Masters made that poet's name a household word.

One of the famous short story writers of the time was William Sydney Porter, better known as O. Henry. Sometimes classified as a local colorist, O. Henry portrayed New York City vividly. His stories use the surprise ending to great effect. Like many bestselling authors then and now, O. Henry wrote to formula. In other words, he worked within a customary plot structure with certain familiar character types, settings, and situations.

Rarely do formula stories survive as literature, but they can have lasting influence. One type of writing that emerged during this period, the Western, has at times dominated the popular arts. Earlier, James Fenimore Cooper had created an American frontier hero. The settlement of the American West now called for a new breed of hero more closely tied to the Great Plains. Dime-novel westerns introduced this new hero and developed the modern western formula. Most of the elements of this formula were firmly fixed in Owen Wister's *The Virginian,* published in 1902.

In addition to the poets already named, a number of popular poets were at work during this period. James Whitcomb Riley, using a rustic Hoosier dialect, wrote "Little Orphant Annie," "Knee-Deep in June," and other favorites. Eugene Field, the Denver journalist, wrote "Little Boy Blue" and "Wynken, Blynken, and Nod." Two poets from Oregon also enjoyed a brief popularity: Edwin Markham, whose best-known poem is "The Man with the Hoe," and Joaquin Miller, who wrote "Columbus."

AMERICAN VOICES

Quotations by Prominent Figures of the Period

But I reckon I got to light out for the territory ahead of the rest, because Aunt Sally says she's going to adopt me and sivilize me, and I can't stand it. I been there before.
Mark Twain, *The Adventures of Huckleberry Finn*

The reports of my death are greatly exaggerated.
Mark Twain, Cable from London to the Associated Press, 1897

Bore: a person who talks when you wish him to listen. *Prejudice:* a vagrant opinion without visible means of support.
Ambrose Bierce, *The Devil's Dictionary*

The road was new to me, as roads always are, going back.
Sarah Orne Jewett, *The Country of the Pointed Firs*

The voice of the sea speaks to the soul.
Kate Chopin, *The Awakening*

There are only two or three human stories, and they go on repeating themselves as fiercely as if they had never happened before.
Willa Cather, *O Pioneers!*

Buck did not read the newspapers, or he would have known that trouble was brewing not alone for himself, but for every tidewater dog, strong of muscle and with warm, long hair, from Puget Sound to San Diego.
Jack London, *The Call of the Wild*

The red sun was pasted in the sky like a wafer.
Stephen Crane, *The Red Badge of Courage*

Silence may be as variously shaded as speech.
Edith Wharton, *The Reef*

We wear the mask that grins and lies.
It hides our cheeks and shades our eyes—
Paul Laurence Dunbar, "We Wear the Mask"

I shall have more to say when I am dead.
Edwin Arlington Robinson, "John Brown"

READING CRITICALLY

The Literature of 1865–1915

When you read literature, it is important to place it in its historical context. Doing so will help you interpret the literary movements that were prevalent during the period and appreciate the techniques that writers used to convey the ideas of the movement.

HISTORICAL CONTEXT During 1865 to 1915 the population of the United States grew dramatically, with many people moving westward and settling on the frontier. Travel from one part of the country to another became common as a result of new advances in transportation and of the desire of people in various parts of the country to learn more about each other. During his youth, Mark Twain traveled from Hannibal, Missouri, to St. Louis; New York; Philadelphia; New Orleans; Virginia City, Nevada; and San Francisco. As a result of the westward movement and increased travel, more and more of our literature became centered on the Midwest and the Far West.

LITERARY MOVEMENTS During this period writers turned away from Romanticism and strove to portray life as it was actually lived. The major movements of the period were Realism, Naturalism, and Regionalism. **Realism** attempted to present "a slice of life," whereas **Naturalism** went one step further, showing life as the inexorable working out of natural forces beyond our power to control. **Regionalism,** in contrast, was in some ways a blending of Realism and Romanticism. It emphasized locale, or place, and the elements that create local color—customs, dress, speech, and other local differences.

WRITERS' TECHNIQUES During this period the short story emerged as a popular literary form. In their stories writers used specific details to create a sense of realism and to capture local color. In addition, they tended to draw their characters from the mass of humanity and had them speak in dialect, capturing the flavor and rhythms of common speech.

Prose

TURN HIM LOOSE, BILL
Frederic Remington

MARK TWAIN

1835–1910

Mark Twain earned international fame early in his career by writing humorous tales that captured the local color of the West. He then went on to establish himself as one of the greatest writers in the history of American literature by transforming his childhood observations and experiences into the classic American novels *The Adventures of Tom Sawyer* (1876) and *The Adventures of Huckleberry Finn* (1884). So great was the influence of this later novel, in fact, that Ernest Hemingway wrote, "All modern American literature comes from one book by Mark Twain called *Huckleberry Finn.*"

Twain, who was born Samuel Langhorne Clemens, grew up in the Mississippi River town of Hannibal, Missouri. When he was eleven, his father died, and he left school to become a printer's apprentice. Though he disliked the profession, Twain worked as a printer in a number of different cities before deciding to pursue a career as a riverboat pilot at the age of twenty-one.

When the Civil War closed the Mississippi River, Twain traveled west to Nevada. There he supported himself as a journalist and lecturer, and he developed the entertaining writing style that made him famous. In 1865, when he published "The Notorious Jumping Frog of Calaveras County," his version of a tall tale he had heard in a mining camp, he became an international celebrity.

Following the publication of *The Innocents Abroad* (1869), a successful book of humorous travel letters, Twain moved to Hartford, Connecticut, where he lived for the rest of his life. There, Twain began using his past experiences as the raw material for his books. In *Roughing It* (1872), he drew on his experiences in the western mining regions. He turned to his childhood experiences in writing *The Adventures of Tom Sawyer, Life on the Mississippi* (1883), and *The Adventures of Huckleberry Finn*. In *Huckleberry Finn,* his masterpiece, he delved into the realities of the prewar South, portraying the adventures of a young white orphan and a runaway slave.

During his later years, Twain was unable to reproduce the balance between pessimism and humor that he had captured in *Huckleberry Finn*. In works such as *A Connecticut Yankee in King Arthur's Court* (1889), *Pudd'nhead Wilson* (1894), and *The Man That Corrupted Hadleyburg* (1900), he expressed an increasingly pessimistic vision of society and human nature. However, Twain displayed the same masterful command of language that had already established him as the finest American fiction writer of his time. It was this command of language that compelled the twentieth-century poet T. S. Eliot to write that in Twain he had "discovered a new way of writing . . . a literary language based on American colloquial speech."

The Boys' Ambition

Literary Forms

Narration. Narration is writing that tells a story. The story being related may be fictional, as in novels and short stories, or factual, as in historical accounts, autobiographies, and biographies. However, the distinction between fictional narration and factual narration is not always clear. Fictional narratives are often inspired by or based on real-life events. For example, *The Adventures of Huckleberry Finn,* Mark Twain's finest novel, grew out of Twain's boyhood observations and experiences. Similarly, in some factual narratives certain events and details are fictionalized or exaggerated. For example, in *Life on the Mississippi,* Twain's account of his own experiences as a boy and young man living on the Mississippi River, Twain embellishes certain events and magnifies the traits of certain people.

Commentary

Mark Twain grew up to become a famous and prosperous author. As a grown man, did he still retain his childhood wish to become a riverboat pilot? He claimed that he did—under certain conditions.

In 1880 a twelve-year-old boy named David Watter Bowser wrote Twain a letter. He had chosen Twain as the living man with whom he would most like to change places. In his letter and in a school composition that he enclosed, he explained that Twain had "everything a man could have." Twain was "jolly," "happy," and rich. Would Mr. Twain, Bowser asked, be willing to become a boy again while he, Bowser, settled into Mr. Twain's life?

The boy received an interesting response. Yes, answered Twain, he would be willing to change places, but only if certain conditions were fulfilled. "The main condition should be, that I should emerge from boyhood as a 'cub pilot' on a Mississippi boat, and that I should by and by become a pilot, and remain one." Twain's other conditions included an endless summer filled with blooming oleanders, friends to talk and sing with, and a crew that would never die. The now well-known author also called for fame as a pilot. "And when strangers were informed that I was the celebrated 'Master Pilot of the Mississippi,' . . . and exclaimed, 'O, I know *that* name very well!' I should feel a pleasurable emotion tricking down my spine and know I had not lived in vain."

With what famous writer would you want to change places? How do you think the writer might respond to your request?

Focus

In "The Boys' Ambition," Mark Twain discusses his boyhood ambition to become a steamboatman. Freewrite for five minutes about your ambitions.

from Life on the Mississippi

Mark Twain

The Boys' Ambition

When I was a boy, there was but one permanent ambition among my comrades in our village[1] on the west bank of the Mississippi River. That was, to be a steamboatman. We had transient ambitions of other sorts, but they were only transient.

When a circus came and went, it left us all burning to become clowns; the first Negro minstrel show that came to our section left us all suffering to try that kind of life; now and then we had a hope that if we lived and were good, God would permit us to be pirates. These ambitions faded out, each in its turn; but the ambition to be a steamboatman always remained.

Once a day a cheap, gaudy packet[2] arrived upward from St. Louis, and another downward from Keokuk.[3] Before these events, the day was glorious with expectancy; after them, the day was a dead and empty thing. Not only the boys, but the whole village, felt this. After all these years I can picture that old time to myself now, just as it was then: the white town drowsing in the sunshine of a summer's morning; the streets empty, or pretty nearly so; one or two clerks sitting in front of the Water Street stores, with their splint-bottomed chairs tilted back against the wall, chins on breasts, hats slouched over their faces, asleep—with shingle shavings enough around to show what broke them down; a sow and a litter of pigs loafing along the sidewalk, doing a good business in watermelon rinds and seeds; two or three lonely little freight piles scattered about the levee;[4] a pile of skids[5] on the slope of the stone-paved wharf, and the fragrant town drunkard asleep in the shadow of them; two or three wood flats[6] at the head of the wharf, but nobody to listen to the peaceful lapping of the wavelets against them; the great Mississippi, the majestic, the magnificent Mississippi, rolling its mile-wide tide along, shining in the sun; the dense forest away on the other side; the point above the town, and the point below, bounding the river-glimpse and turning it into a sort of sea, and withal a very still and brilliant and lonely one. Presently a film of dark smoke appears above one of those remote points; instantly a Negro drayman,[7] famous for his quick eye and prodigious voice, lifts up the cry, "S-t-e-a-m-boat a-comin'!" and the scene changes! The town drunkard stirs, the clerks wake up, a furious clatter of drays follows, every house and store pours out a human contribution, and all in a twinkling the dead town is alive and moving. Drays, carts, men, boys, all go hurrying from many quarters to a common center, the wharf. Assembled there, the people fasten their eyes upon the coming boat as upon a wonder they are seeing for the first time.

---

1. **our village:** Hannibal, Missouri.
2. **packet** n.: A boat that travels a regular route, carrying passengers, freight, and mail.
3. **Keokuk** (kē′ ə kuk′): A town in southeastern Iowa.
4. **levee** (lev′ ē) n.: A landing place along the bank of a river.
5. **skids** n.: Low, movable wooden platforms.
6. **flats** n.: Small flat-bottomed boats.
7. **drayman** n.: The driver of a dray, a low cart with detachable sides.

And the boat *is* rather a handsome sight, too. She is long and sharp and trim and pretty; she has two tall, fancy-topped chimneys, with a gilded device of some kind swung between them; a fanciful pilothouse, all glass and gingerbread, perched on top of the texas deck[8] behind them; the paddle-boxes are gorgeous with a picture or with gilded rays above the boat's name; the boiler deck, the hurricane deck, and the texas deck are fenced and ornamented with clean white railings; there is a flag gallantly flying from the jackstaff;[9] the furnace doors are open and the fires glaring bravely; the upper decks are black with passengers; the captain stands by the big bell, calm, imposing, the envy of all; great volumes of the blackest smoke are rolling and tumbling out of the chimneys—a husbanded grandeur created with a bit of pitch pine just before arriving at a town; the crew are grouped on the forecastle;[10] the broad stage is run far out over the port bow, and an envied deckhand stands picturesquely on the end of it with a coil of rope in his hand; the pent steam is screaming through the gauge cocks; the captain lifts his hand, a bell rings, the wheels stop; then they turn back, churning the water to foam, and the steamer is at rest. Then such a scramble as there is to get aboard, and to get ashore, and to take in freight and to discharge freight, all at one and the same time; and such a yelling and cursing as the mates facilitate it all with! Ten minutes later the steamer is under way again, with no flag on the jackstaff and no black smoke issuing from the chimneys. After ten more minutes the town is dead again, and the town drunkard asleep by the skids once more.

8. texas deck: The deck adjoining the officers' cabins, the largest cabins on the ship.

9. jackstaff *n.*: A small staff at the bow of a ship for flying flags.

10. forecastle *n.*: The front part of the upper deck.

My father was a justice of the peace, and I supposed he possessed the power of life and death over all men and could hang anybody that offended him. This was distinction enough for me as a general thing; but the desire to be a steamboatman kept intruding, nevertheless. I first wanted to be a cabin boy, so that I could come out with a white apron on and shake a tablecloth over the side, where all my old comrades could see me; later I thought I would rather be the deckhand who stood on the end of the stage plank with the coil of rope in his hand, because he was particularly conspicuous. But these were only daydreams—they were too heavenly to be contemplated as real possibilities. By and by one of our boys went away. He was not heard of for a long time. At last he turned up as apprentice engineer or striker on a steamboat. This thing shook the bottom out of all my Sunday-school teachings. That boy had been notoriously worldly, and I just the reverse; yet he was exalted to this eminence, and I left in obscurity and misery. There was nothing generous about this fellow in his greatness. He would always manage to have a rusty bolt to scrub while his boat tarried at our town, and he would sit on the inside guard and scrub it, where we could all see him and envy him and loathe him. And whenever his boat was laid up he would come home and swell around the town in his blackest and greasiest clothes, so that nobody could help remembering that he was a steamboatman; and he used all sorts of steamboat technicalities in his talk, as if he were so used to them that he forgot common people could not understand them. He would speak of the labboard[11] side of a horse in an easy, natural way that would make one wish he was dead. And he was always talking about "St. Looey" like an old citizen; he would refer casually to occasions when he "was coming down Fourth Street," or when he was "passing by the Planter's House," or when there was a

fire and he took a turn on the brakes of "the old Big Missouri"; and then he would go on and lie about how many towns the size of ours were burned down there that day. Two or three of the boys had long been persons of consideration among us because they had been to St. Louis once and had a vague general knowledge of its wonders, but the day of their glory was over now. They lapsed into a humble silence, and learned to disappear when the ruthless cub engineer approached. This fellow had money, too, and hair oil. Also an ignorant silver watch and a showy brass watch chain. He wore a leather belt and used no suspenders. If ever a youth was cordially admired and hated by his comrades, this one was. No girl could withstand his charms. He cut out every boy in the village. When his boat blew up at last, it diffused a tranquil contentment among us such as we had not known for months. But when he came home the next week, alive, renowned, and appeared in church all battered up and bandaged, a shining hero, stared at and wondered over by everybody, it seemed to us that the partiality of Providence for an undeserving reptile had reached a point where it was open to criticism.

This creature's career could produce but one result, and it speedily followed. Boy after boy managed to get on the river. The minister's son became an engineer. The doctor's and the postmaster's sons became mud clerks; the wholesale liquor dealer's son became a barkeeper on a boat; four sons of the chief merchant, and two sons of the county judge, became pilots. Pilot was the grandest position of all. The pilot, even in those days of trivial wages, had a princely salary—from a hundred and fifty to two hundred and fifty dollars a month, and no board to pay. Two months of his wages would pay a preacher's salary for a year. Now some of us were left disconsolate. We could not get on the river— at least our parents would not let us.

So by and by I ran away. I said I never would come home again till I was a pilot and could come in glory. But somehow I could not manage it. I went meekly aboard a few of

---

11. labboard: Larboard, the left-hand side of a ship.

the boats that lay packed together like sardines at the long St. Louis wharf, and very humbly inquired for the pilots, but got only a cold shoulder and short words from mates and clerks. I had to make the best of this sort of treatment for the time being, but I had comforting daydreams of a future when I should be a great and honored pilot, with plenty of money, and could kill some of these mates and clerks and pay for them.

RESPONDING TO THE SELECTION

Your Response

1. If you had lived during Twain's time, would you have been interested in becoming a steamboat pilot? Why or why not?
2. What are your ambitions? Explain.

Recalling

3. What is the one permanent ambition of Twain and his boyhood friends?
4. How do the people of Hannibal respond to the daily arrival of the steamboat?
5. Why was the boy who became an apprentice engineer "cordially hated and admired by his comrades"?
6. (a) What happens to the young apprentice's boat? (b) How do the other boys respond?
7. Why does Twain run away from home?

Interpreting

8. What impression of the town of Hannibal, Missouri, is conveyed through Twain's description of the town and its response to the steamboat's arrival?
9. How does Twain's description of the steamboat reflect his boyhood desire to be a steamboatman?
10. How would you describe the attitude of the boys toward the young apprentice engineer?
11. (a) What seems to be Twain's attitude toward himself as a boy? (b) What details in the selection convey his attitude?

Applying

12. Although Twain never earned fame as a steamboat pilot, he did become a famous writer. How do you think Twain's love for the Mississippi River and riverboats contributed to his success as a writer?

ANALYZING LITERATURE

Recognizing Narration

Narration is writing that tells a story. A narrative may be factual or fictional. Yet the distinction between factual narration and fictional narration is not always clear. For example, *Life on the Mississippi* is a factual narrative account of Twain's experiences while growing up on the Mississippi River, but certain details and events in the book are fictionalized or exaggerated.

1. Which details in "The Boys' Ambition" may be exaggerated? Support your answer.
2. What do you think might have been Twain's reasons for fictionalizing some of the details?

THINKING AND WRITING

Writing a Statement of Ambition

On many college applications, there is an essay question in which applicants are asked to discuss their main ambition in life. Prepare to answer this question by reviewing your freewriting concerning your ambitions. Decide what your main ambition is. Then list the reasons for your decision. When you write your essay, make sure you include enough reasons to support your statement of ambition. When you finish writing, revise your essay and prepare a final copy.

LEARNING OPTION

Writing. The author never forgot his boyhood ambition. He reminded others of it by taking a pen name, Mark Twain, from the steamboatman's cry for a sounding of two fathoms ("by the mark, twain"). Choose a pen name for yourself that reflects either a childhood or a current ambition. Try it out as a byline on your next writing assignment.

MULTICULTURAL CONNECTION
Mark Twain and African American Speech

Mark Twain is famous for introducing everyday regional speech into American literature. Most of the writers before Twain used more formal, standard English. Twain's characters, however, spoke the way people in America actually spoke—in down-to-earth language, with colorful images unique to the region of the country in which they lived.

African American speech and *Huckleberry Finn.* Recently, scholars gained a new understanding of Twain's mastery of speech patterns. It was previously believed that the speech of Huckleberry Finn, the young hero of Twain's greatest novel, had been inspired by Tom Blankenship, a poor white boy Twain once knew in his hometown of Hannibal, Missouri. A scholar named Shelley Fisher Fishkin, however, has claimed that Twain based Huck's speech on the language of a ten-year-old African American named Jimmy.

Twain wrote an article about the boy entitled "Sociable Jimmy," which appeared in the November 29, 1874 issue of *The New York Times.* In this article, Twain called Jimmy "the most artless, sociable and exhaustless talker I ever came across." According to Twain, Jimmy did not say "a single remarkable thing or one that was worth remembering, and yet he was himself so interested in his small marvels, and they flowed so naturally and comfortably from his lips that his talk got the upper hand of my interest, too, and I listened as one who receives a revelation."

This newspaper article was known to scholars but not considered important. Ms. Fishkin, who rediscovered it, argues that listening to Jimmy triggered Twain's memories "of black speakers in his own childhood."

HUCK FINN
E. W. Kemble

Jimmy and Huck. Following are some key similarities between Sociable Jimmy and Huckleberry Finn:

Speech
Both use the adjective "powerful" as an adverb.
Both use "drownded" for "drowned."
Both repeat the words and pepper their speech with present participles.

SOCIABLE JIMMY.

BY MARK TWAIN.

[I sent the following home in a private letter, some time ago, from a certain little village. It was in the days when I was a public lecturer. I did it because I wished to preserve the memory of the most artless, sociable, and exhaustless talker I ever came across. He did not tell me a single remarkable thing, or one that was worth remembering; and yet he was himself so interested in his small marvels, and they flowed so naturally and comfortably from his lips that his talk got the upper hand of my interest, too, and I listened as one who receives a revelation. I took down what he had to say, just as he said it—without altering a word

"We ain't got no cat heah, 'bout dis hotel. Bill he don't like 'em. He can't stan' a cat no way. Ef he was to ketch one he'd slam it outen de winder in a minute. Yes he would. Bill's down on cats. So is de gals—waiter gals. When dey ketches a cat bumming 'roun' heah, dey jis' *scoops* him—'deed dey do. Dey snake him into de cistern—dey's been cats drownded in dat water dat's in n yo' pitcher. I seed a cat in dare yistiddy—all swelled up like a pudd'n. I bet you dem gals done dat. Ma says if dey was to drownd a cat for *her*, de fust one of 'em she ketched she'd jam her into de cistern 'long wid de cat. Ma wouldn't *do* dat, I don't rekon, but 'deed an' double, she *said* she would. I can't kill a chicken—well, I kin wring its neck off, cus dat don't make 'em no sufferin scarcely; but I can't take and chop dey heads off, like some people kin. It makes me feel so—so—well, I kin see dat chicken nights so's I can't

Background

Both boys come from a family with an alcoholic father and no mother.
Neither boy is upset by dead animals.
Both are captivated by a particular clock.

Some controversy. Not everyone agrees with Ms. Fishkin's theories. One scholar, for instance, declares that a single article in a newspaper is not a strong enough basis for the claim that Huck's speech is modeled on that of African Americans.

Other scholars, however, support Ms. Fishkin's claims and welcome the thought that the white hero of an American classic in many ways speaks like an African American. One of these scholars declared, "What could be more valuable to a proper and appropriate understanding of multiculturalism than the realization that an individual writer or a figure within his work can be intrinsically multicultural?"

Exploring on Your Own

What are some of the characteristics of the speech that you hear around you? In a journal, record some of the slang words and ways of talking that you hear in your school. Then compare notes with a friend from another school to see whether he or she uses the same expressions. If you were writing a novel about your school, which of these words would you include in the dialogue?

GUIDE FOR INTERPRETING

The Notorious Jumping Frog of Calaveras County

Writers' Techniques

Humor. In literature, humor refers to writing that is intended to evoke laughter. To accomplish this purpose, writers must have the ability to perceive the ridiculous, comical, or ludicrous aspects of an incident, situation, or personality and to depict them in an amusing manner.

Humorists use a variety of techniques to make their work amusing. For example, the western humorists, including Mark Twain, made extensive uses of exaggeration in their writing. Certain incidents and details were exaggerated to such a great extent that they became comical. Usually, the exaggerated incidents or events were described by a narrator or storyteller in a very serious tone. This tone made the tale more humorous, because it created the impression that the storyteller was unaware of the ridiculousness of what he or she was describing.

Regional dialects—the colloquial languages of people living in certain areas—were another important element of western humor. The use of regional dialects helped to capture local color and made the characters more interesting and amusing. For example, Simon Wheeler's use of regional dialect in "The Notorious Jumping Frog of Calaveras County" helps make him a very entertaining character, and his frequent use of unexpected words adds to the humor of the story.

Commentary

According to one of Mark Twain's biographers, Twain first heard the story that was to become "The Notorious Jumping Frog of Calaveras County" in the barroom of a rundown tavern in Angel's Camp, California, while he himself was prospecting for gold. The storyteller was a former Illinois River pilot named Ben Coon, "a solemn, fat-witted person, who dozed by the stove, or told slow, endless stories, without point or application." Twain found it "soothing and comfortable to listen to his endless narratives, told in that solemn way, with no suspicion of humor."

Like the jumping frog story, many of Twain's stories were based on stories heard in bars, on the trail, or around campfires. To what extent should writers be given credit for stories they merely retell? What do writers need to bring to retold stories to make them their own?

Focus

Think of a humorous story you have heard in which exaggeration was used. Then briefly discuss why you think the use of exaggeration in the story makes it amusing.

The Notorious Jumping Frog of Calaveras County

Mark Twain

In compliance with the request of a friend of mine, who wrote me from the East, I called on good-natured, garrulous old Simon Wheeler, and inquired after my friend's friend, Leonidas W. Smiley, as requested to do, and I hereunto append the result. I have a lurking suspicion that *Leonidas W.* Smiley is a myth; that my friend never knew such a personage; and that he only conjectured that if I asked old Wheeler about him, it would remind him of his infamous *Jim* Smiley, and he would go to work and bore me to death with some exasperating reminiscence of him as long and as tedious as it should be useless to me. If that was the design, it succeeded.

I found Simon Wheeler dozing comfortably by the barroom stove of the dilapidated tavern in the decayed mining camp of Angel's, and I noticed that he was fat and bald-headed, and had an expression of winning gentleness and simplicity upon his tranquil countenance. He roused up, and gave me good day. I told him a friend of mine had commissioned me to make some inquiries about a cherished companion of his boyhood named *Leonidas W.* Smiley—*Rev. Leonidas W.* Smiley, a young minister of the Gospel, who he had heard was at one time a resident of Angel's Camp. I added that if Mr. Wheeler could tell me anything about this Rev. Leonidas W. Smiley, I would feel under many obligations to him.

Simon Wheeler backed me into a corner and blockaded me there with his chair, and then sat down and reeled off the monotonous narrative which follows this paragraph. He never smiled, he never frowned, he never changed his voice from the gentle-flowing key to which he tuned his initial sentence, he never betrayed the slightest suspicion of enthusiasm; but all through the interminable narrative there ran a vein of impressive earnestness and sincerity, which showed me plainly that, so far from his imagining that there was anything ridiculous or funny about his story, he regarded it as a really important matter, and admired its two heroes as men of transcendent genius in *finesse.* I let him go on in his own way, and never interrupted him once.

"Rev. Leonidas W. H'm, Reverend Le—well, there was a feller here once by the name of *Jim* Smiley, in the winter of '49—or maybe it was the spring of '50—I don't recollect exactly, somehow, though what makes me think it was one or the other is because I remember the big flume[1] warn't finished when he first come to the camp; but anyway, he was the curiousest man about always betting on anything that turned up you ever see, if he could get anybody to bet on the other side; and if he couldn't he'd change sides. Any way that suited the other man would suit *him*—any way just so's he got a bet, *he* was satisfied. But still he was lucky, uncommon lucky; he most always come out winner. He was always ready and laying for a chance; there couldn't be no solit'ry thing

---

1. flume (flo͞om) *n.*: An artificial channel for carrying water to provide power and transport objects.

mentioned but that feller'd offer to bet on it, and take ary side you please, as I was just telling you. If there was a horse race, you'd find him flush or you'd find him busted at the end of it; if there was a dogfight, he'd bet on it; if there was a cat fight, he'd bet on it; if there was a chicken fight, he'd bet on it; why, if there was two birds setting on a fence, he would bet you which one would fly first; or if there was a camp meeting,[2] he would be there reg'lar to bet on Parson Walker, which he judged to be the best exhorter about here and so he was too, and a good man. If he even see a straddle bug[3] start to go anywheres, he would bet you how long it would take him to get to—to wherever he was going to, and if you took him up, he would foller that straddle bug to Mexico but what he would find out where he was bound for and how long he was on the road. Lots of the boys here has seen that Smiley, and can tell you about him. Why, it never made no difference to *him*—he'd bet on *any* thing—the dangdest feller. Parson Walker's wife laid very sick once, for a good while, and it seemed as if they warn't going to save her; but one morning he come in, and Smiley up and asked him how she was, and he said she was considable better—thank the Lord for his inf'nite mercy—and coming on so smart that with the blessing of Prov'dence she'd get well yet; and Smiley, before he thought, says, 'Well, I'll resk two-and-a-half she don't anyway.'

Thish-yer Smiley had a mare—the boys called her the fifteen-minute nag, but that was only in fun, you know, because of course she was faster than that—and he used to win money on that horse, for all she was so slow and always had the asthma, or the distemper, or the consumption, or something of that kind. They used to give her two or three hundred yards start, and then pass her under way; but always at the fag end[4] of the race she'd get excited and desperate like, and come cavorting and straddling up, and scattering her legs around limber, sometimes in the air, and sometimes out to one side among the fences, and kicking up m-o-r-e dust and raising m-o-r-e racket with her coughing and sneezing and blowing her nose—and *always* fetch up at the stand just about a neck ahead, as near as you could cipher it down.

And he had a little small bull-pup, that to look at him you'd think he warn't worth a cent but to set around and look ornery and lay for a chance to steal something. But as soon as money was up on him he was a different dog; his under-jaw'd begin to stick out like the fo'castle[5] of a steamboat, and his teeth would uncover and shine like the furnaces. And a dog might tackle him and bullyrag him, and bite him, and throw him over his shoulder two or three times, and Andrew Jackson—which was the name of the pup—Andrew Jackson would never let on but what *he* was satisfied, and hadn't expected nothing else—and the bets being doubled and doubled on the other side all the time, till the money was all up; and then all of a sudden he would grab that other dog jest by the j'int of his hind leg and freeze to it—not chaw, you understand, but only just grip and hang on till they throwed up the sponge, if it was a year. Smiley always come out winner on that pup, till he harnessed a dog once that didn't have no hind legs, because they'd been sawed off in a circular saw, and when the thing had gone along far enough, and the money was all up, and he come to make a snatch for his pet holt,[6] he see in a minute how he'd been imposed on, and how the other dog had him in the door, so to speak, and he 'peared surprised, and then he looked sorter discouraged-like, and didn't try no more to win the fight, and so he got shucked out bad. He give Smiley a look, as much as to say his heart was broke, and it

2. **camp meeting:** A religious gathering at the mining camp.
3. **straddle bug:** An insect with long legs.
4. **fag end:** Last part.

5. **fo'castle** (fōk's'l) *n*.: Forecastle; the forward part of the upper deck.
6. **holt:** Hold.

was *his* fault, for putting up a dog that hadn't no hind legs for him to take holt of, which was his main dependence in a fight, and then he limped off a piece and laid down and died. It was a good pup, was that Andrew Jackson, and would have made a name for hisself if he'd lived, for the stuff was in him and he had genius—I know it, because he hadn't no opportunities to speak of, and it don't stand to reason that a dog could make such a fight as he could under them circumstances if he hadn't no talent. It always makes me feel sorry when I think of that last fight of his'n, and the way it turned out.

Well, thish-yer Smiley had rat terriers,[7] and chicken cocks,[8] and tomcats and all them kind of things, till you couldn't rest, and you couldn't fetch nothing for him to bet on but he'd match you. He ketched a frog one day, and took him home, and said he cal'lated to educate him; and so he never done nothing for three months but set in his back yard and learn that frog to jump. And you bet you he *did* learn him, too. He'd give him a little punch behind, and the next minute you'd see that frog whirling in the air like a doughnut—see him turn one summerset, or maybe a couple, if he got a good start, and come down flatfooted and all right, like a cat. He got him up so in the matter of ketching flies, and kep' him in practice so constant, that he'd nail a fly every time as fur as he could see him. Smiley said all a frog wanted was education, and he could do 'most anything—and I believe him. Why, I've seen him set Dan'l Webster down here on this floor—Dan'l Webster was the name of the frog—and sing out, "Flies, Dan'l, flies!" and quicker'n you could wink he'd spring straight up and snake a fly off'n the counter there, and flop down on the floor ag'in as solid as a gob of mud, and fall to scratching the side of his head with his hind foot as indifferent as if he hadn't no idea he'd been doin' any more'n any frog might do. You never see a frog so modest and straightfor'ard as he was, for all he was so gifted. And when it come to fair and square jumping on a dead level, he could get over more ground at one straddle than any animal of his breed you ever see. Jumping on a dead level was his strong suit, you understand; and when it come to that, Smiley would ante up money on him as long as he had a red.[9] Smiley was monstrous proud of his frog, and well he might be, for fellers that had traveled and been everywheres all said he laid over any frog that ever *they* see.

Well, Smiley kep' the beast in a little lattice box, and he used to fetch him downtown sometimes and lay for a bet. One day a feller—a stranger in the camp, he was—come acrost him with his box, and says:

'What might it be that you've got in the box?'

And Smiley says, sorter indifferent-like, 'It might be a parrot, or it might be a canary, maybe, but it ain't—it's only just a frog.'

And the feller took it, and looked at it careful, and turned it round this way and that, and says, 'H'm—so 'tis. Well, what's *he* good for?'

'Well,' Smiley says, easy and careless, 'he's good enough for *one* thing, I should judge—he can outjump any frog in Calaveras county.'

The feller took the box again, and took another long, particular look, and give it back to Smiley, and says, very deliberate, 'Well,' he says, 'I don't see no p'ints about that frog that's any better'n any other frog.'

'Maybe you don't,' Smiley says. 'Maybe you understand frogs and maybe you don't understand 'em; maybe you've had experience, and maybe you ain't only a amature, as it were. Anyways, I've got *my* opinion, and I'll resk forty dollars that he can outjump any frog in Calaveras county.'

And the feller studied a minute, and then says, kinder sad like, 'Well, I'm only a

---

7. rat terriers: Dogs skilled in catching rats.
8. chicken cocks: Roosters trained to fight.

9. a red: A red cent.

**MARK TWAIN (SAMUEL L. CLEMENS) RIDING
THE CELEBRATED JUMPING FROG**
*An English Caricature
by Frederic Waddy, 1872*

stranger here, and I ain't got no frog; but if I had a frog, I'd bet you.'

And then Smiley says, 'That's all right—that's all right—if you'll hold my box a minute, I'll go and get you a frog.' And so the feller took the box, and put up his forty dollars along with Smiley's, and set down to wait.

So he set there a good while thinking and thinking to hisself, and then he got the frog out and prized his mouth open and took a teaspoon and filled him full of quail-shot[10]—filled him pretty near up to his chin—and set him on the floor. Smiley he went to the swamp and slopped around in the mud for a long time, and finally he ketched a frog, and fetched him in, and give him to this feller, and says:

'Now, if you're ready, set him alongside of Dan'l, with his forepaws just even with Dan'l's, and I'll give the word.' Then he says, 'One—two—three—*git!*' and him and the feller touched up the frogs from behind, and the new frog hopped off lively, but Dan'l give a heave, and hysted up his shoulders—so—

like a Frenchman, but it warn't no use—he couldn't budge; he was planted as solid as a church, and he couldn't no more stir than if he was anchored out. Smiley was a good deal surprised, and he was disgusted too, but he didn't have no idea what the matter was, of course.

The feller took the money and started away; and when he was going out at the door, he sorter jerked his thumb over his shoulder—so—at Dan'l, and says again, very deliberate, 'Well,' he says, '*I* don't see no p'ints about that frog that's any better'n any other frog.'

Smiley he stood scratching his head and looking down at Dan'l a long time, and at last he says, 'I do wonder what in the nation that frog throw'd off for—I wonder if there ain't something the matter with him—he 'pears to look mighty baggy, somehow.' And he ketched Dan'l by the nap of the neck, and hefted him, and says, 'Why blame my cats if he don't weigh five pound!' and turned him upside down and he belched out a double handful of shot. And then he see how it was, and he was the maddest man—he set the frog down and took out after that feller, but he never ketched him. And——"

Here Simon Wheeler heard his name called from the front yard, and got up to see what was wanted. And turning to me as he moved away, he said: "Just set where you are, stranger, and rest easy—I ain't going to be gone a second."

But, by your leave, I did not think that a continuation of the history of the enterprising vagabond *Jim* Smiley would be likely to afford me much information concerning the Rev. *Leonidas W.* Smiley, and so I started away.

At the door I met the sociable Wheeler returning, and he buttonholed me and recommenced:

"Well, thish-yer Smiley had a yaller one-eyed cow that didn't have no tail, only just a short stump like a bannanner, and—"

However, lacking both time and inclination, I did not wait to hear about the afflicted cow, but took my leave.

---

10. quailshot: Small lead pellets used for shooting quail.

RESPONDING TO THE SELECTION

Your Response

1. Twain called this story "the best humorous sketch America has produced." What is your opinion?
2. If Mark Twain were a stand-up comic today, would you buy a ticket to his one-man show? Why or why not?

Recalling

3. What happens when the narrator asks Simon Wheeler about Leonidas W. Smiley?
4. Why is Jim Smiley described as "infamous"?
5. (a) How did Smiley's mare win races? (b) How did Smiley's bull-pup win fights? (c) What happened during the pup's last fight?
6. (a) How did Smiley educate his frog? (b) How did a stranger outsmart Smiley?

Interpreting

7. (a) Based on his language, how would you describe the anonymous narrator? (b) How would you describe Simon Wheeler? (c) Of the two narrators, why do you think Twain chose Wheeler to tell the story of Jim Smiley?
8. How does the contrast between the anonymous narrator and Simon Wheeler add to the effectiveness of the story?
9. What do you think is most absurd about Wheeler's description of (a) the bull-pup Andrew Jackson and (b) the frog Dan'l Webster?

Applying

10. Why do you think people enjoy telling and listening to tall tales such as the one told by Simon Wheeler?

ANALYZING LITERATURE

Recognizing Humor

In literature, **humor** refers to writing intended to evoke laughter. To accomplish this purpose, western humorists made extensive use of exaggeration and regional dialects in their writing. For example, in "The Notorious Jumping Frog of Calaveras County," westerner Simon Wheeler exaggerates when describing the frog's talents. He describes the frog as if it were intelligent and

thoughtful, commenting, "You never see a frog so modest and straightfor'ard as he was, for all he was so gifted."

1. (a) Find two more examples of exaggeration in the story. (b) Explain why each of these examples is amusing.
2. Why would the story be less effective if Wheeler spoke in standard English?
3. In "How to Tell a Story" Mark Twain wrote, "The humorous story may be spun out to great length, and may wander around as much as it pleases, and arrive nowhere in particular. . . ." Explain how this technique is evident in this tale.
4. Twain continued, "The humorous story is told gravely; the teller does his best to conceal the fact that he even dimly suspects there is anything funny about it." Explain how this technique is evident in this tale.

CRITICAL THINKING AND READING

Appreciating Dialect

Part of what makes Wheeler's use of **dialect** amusing is his frequently unexpected or unusual choice of words. For example, Wheeler's use of the word *monstrous* to describe the extent of Smiley's pride in his frog is unusual.

What is unexpected or unusual about the choice of words in each of the following passages from the story?

1. "And a dog might tackle him and bullyrag him, . . ."
2. "Now if you're ready, set him alongside of Dan'l, with his forepaws just even with Dan'l's, . . ."

THINKING AND WRITING

Writing a Story Using Dialect

Imagine that your school literary magazine has asked you to write a story in which the characters speak in a regional dialect. Think of a region in which people speak in a distinctive manner. Then develop a story in which you capture the local color of this region through the use of dialect and vivid descriptions of the setting. When you finish writing, revise your story and share it with your classmates.

BRET HARTE

1836–1902

Though relatively few of his stories were successful, Bret Harte played an important role in creating a vivid, lasting portrait of the old West. Harte's stories, filled with intriguing characters and colorful dialogue, provided much of post-Civil War America with its first glimpse into western life and established the old West as a popular literary setting.

Harte was born and raised in Albany, New York. In 1854, when he was eighteen, he traveled across the country to California. During his first few years in California, a land in a turbulent period of rapid growth brought about by the discovery of gold in 1848, Harte worked as a schoolteacher, tutor, messenger, clerk, and prospector. While Harte's life seemed to have little direction at the time, his observations of the rugged, often violent life in the mining camps and the towns and cities of the new frontier provided him with the inspiration for his most successful short stories.

After working as a typesetter and writer for two California periodicals and publishing two books of verse, *Outcroppings* (1865) and *The Lost Galleon* (1867), Harte became the editor of the *Overland Monthly,* a new literary magazine, in 1868. When Harte published his story "The Luck of Roaring Camp" in the magazine's second issue, he immediately became famous, as the American public, eager to learn about life in the new frontier, responded to the story with enthusiasm. Over the next two years, Harte published "The Outcasts of Poker Flat" and several other similar stories in the *Overland Monthly,* and his popularity grew at a rapid pace.

Following the publication of *The Luck of Roaring Camp and Other Sketches* in 1870, Harte's popularity reached its peak. In 1871 the *Atlantic Monthly,* a distinguished literary magazine, contracted to pay Harte $10,000 for any twelve sketches or stories he contributed over the next year. Harte returned to the East to fulfill his contract, but the stories he wrote were flat and disappointing compared with his earlier work, and his celebrity waned almost as quickly as it had grown.

Harte continued to publish stories, short novels, and plays during the next twenty years, but for the most part, his later work was unsuccessful. From 1878 to 1885, he was a diplomat in Germany and Scotland. He then retired to London, where he lived for the remainder of his life.

GUIDE FOR INTERPRETING

The Outcasts of Poker Flat

Literary Movements

Regionalism. The habits, speech, appearance, customs, and beliefs of people from one geographical region often differ from those of people from other areas. Regional literature captures the essence of life in a particular area, the "local color" of a region, by accurately depicting the distinctive qualities of its people and including vivid, realistic descriptions of the physical appearance of the environment.

During the nineteenth century, the United States grew at a rapid rate. New regions developed as a steady flow of immigrants settled across the land, and as a result the American population became more and more diverse. As the country grew and became more diversified, the American public became curious about the people and the style of life in different parts of the country. Regional literature like "The Outcasts of Poker Flat" satisfied their curiosity.

Commentary

As you read "The Outcasts of Poker Flat," you may wonder how true-to-life Mr. Oakhurst, a gambler and the story's main character, is. Mr. Oakhurst, a generous, genial man who is seemingly nonchalant in the face of danger, is the hero of two of Harte's stories.

Contemporary historian C. W. Haskins supported Harte's description of Mr. Oakhurst. California gamblers, he wrote, "were usually from New Orleans, Louisville, Memphis, Richmond, or St. Louis. Not infrequently they were well-born and well-educated, and among them were as many good, honest, square-dealing men as could be found in any other business; and they were, as a rule, more charitable and more ready to help those in distress."

Harte's biographer Henry Childs Merwin described a gambler named Lucky Bill who demonstrated traits similar to Mr. Oakhurst's. According to Merwin, Lucky Bill "was noted for his generosity, and, though finally hanged by a vigilance committee, he made a 'good end,' for, on the scaffold, he exhorted his son who was among the spectators, to avoid bad company, to keep away from saloons, and to lead an industrious and honest life."

What characteristics do you associate with frontier gamblers? How closely do these characteristics match those described by C. W. Haskins and Henry Childs Merwin?

Focus

Brainstorm for several minutes about films, books, and other sources of your impressions of the old West. Then make a list of typical characters, clothing, speech, situations, and scenic details that you associate with the old West.

The Outcasts of Poker Flat

Bret Harte

As Mr. John Oakhurst, gambler, stepped into the main street of Poker Flat on the morning of the twenty-third of November, 1850, he was conscious of a change in its moral atmosphere since the preceding night. Two or three men, conversing earnestly together, ceased as he approached, and exchanged significant glances. There was a Sabbath lull in the air which, in a settlement unused to Sabbath influences, looked ominous.

Mr. Oakhurst's calm, handsome face betrayed small concern in these indications. Whether he was conscious of any predisposing cause was another question. "I reckon they're after somebody," he reflected; "likely it's me." He returned to his pocket the handkerchief with which he had been whipping away the red dust of Poker Flat from his neat boots, and quietly discharged his mind of any further conjecture.

In point of fact, Poker Flat was "after somebody." It had lately suffered the loss of several thousand dollars, two valuable horses, and a prominent citizen. It was experiencing a spasm of virtuous reaction, quite as lawless and ungovernable as any of the acts that had provoked it. A secret committee had determined to rid the town of all improper persons. This was done permanently in regard of two men who were then hanging from the boughs of a sycamore in the gulch, and temporarily in the banishment of certain other objectionable characters. I regret to say that some of these were ladies. It is but due to the sex, however, to state that their impropriety was professional, and it was only in such easily established standards of evil that Poker Flat ventured to sit in judgment.

Mr. Oakhurst was right in supposing that he was included in this category. A few of the committee had urged hanging him as a possible example, and a sure method of reimbursing themselves from his pockets of the sums he had won from them. "It's agin justice," said Jim Wheeler, "to let this yer young man from Roaring Camp—an entire stranger—carry away our money." But a crude sentiment of equity residing in the breasts of those who had been fortunate enough to win from Mr. Oakhurst overruled this narrower local prejudice.

Mr. Oakhurst received his sentence with philosophic calmness, none the less coolly that he was aware of the hesitation of his judges. He was too much of a gambler not to accept Fate. With him life was at best an uncertain game, and he recognized the usual percentage in favor of the dealer.

A body of armed men accompanied the deported wickedness of Poker Flat to the outskirts of the settlement. Besides Mr. Oakhurst, who was known to be a coolly desperate man, and for whose intimidation the armed escort was intended, the expatriated party consisted of a young woman familiarly known as the "Duchess"; another, who had won the title of "Mother Shipton";[1] and "Uncle Billy," a suspected sluice robber[2] and

---

1. **"Mother Shipton":** An English woman who lived in the sixteenth century and was suspected of being a witch.
2. **sluice robber:** A person who steals gold from sluices, long troughs used for sifting gold.

EDGE OF TOWN
Charles Burchfield
Collection of the Kelson-Atkins Museum of Art, Kansas City

confirmed drunkard. The cavalcade provoked no comments from the spectators, nor was any word uttered by the escort. Only, when the gulch which marked the uttermost limit of Poker Flat was reached, the leader spoke briefly and to the point. The exiles were forbidden to return at the peril of their lives.

As the escort disappeared, their pent-up feelings found vent in a few hysterical tears from the Duchess, some bad language from Mother Shipton, and a Parthian volley of expletives[3] from Uncle Billy. The philosophic Oakhurst alone remained silent. He listened calmly to Mother Shipton's desire to cut somebody's heart out, to the repeated state-ments of the Duchess that she would die in the road, and to the alarming oaths that seemed to be bumped out of Uncle Billy as he rode forward. With the easy good humor characteristic of his class, he insisted upon exchanging his own riding horse, "Five Spot," for the sorry mule which the Duchess rode. But even this act did not draw the party into any closer sympathy. The young woman readjusted her somewhat draggled plumes with a feeble, faded coquetry; Mother Shipton eyed the possessor of "Five Spot" with malevolence, and Uncle Billy included the whole party in one sweeping anathema.

The road to Sandy Bar—a camp that, not having as yet experienced the regenerating influences of Poker Flat, consequently seemed to offer some invitation to the emigrants—lay over a steep mountain range. It was distant a day's severe travel. In that advanced season, the party soon passed out of

---

3. Parthian . . . expletives: Hostile remarks made while leaving. The Parthians were an ancient society whose cavalrymen usually shot at the enemy while retreating or pretending to retreat.

the moist, temperate regions of the foothills into the dry, cold, bracing air of the Sierras.[4] The trail was narrow and difficult. At noon the Duchess, rolling out of her saddle upon the ground, declared her intention of going no farther, and the party halted.

The spot was singularly wild and impressive. A wooded amphitheater, surrounded on three sides by precipitous cliffs of naked granite, sloped gently toward the crest of another precipice that overlooked the valley. It was, undoubtedly, the most suitable spot for a camp, had camping been advisable. But Mr. Oakhurst knew that scarcely half the journey to Sandy Bar was accomplished, and the party were not equipped or provisioned for delay. This fact he pointed out to his companions curtly, with a philosophic commentary on the folly of "throwing up their hand before the game was played out." But they were furnished with liquor, which in this emergency stood them in place of food, fuel, rest, and prescience. In spite of his remonstrances, it was not long before they were more or less under its influence. Uncle Billy passed rapidly from a bellicose state into one of stupor, the Duchess became maudlin, and Mother Shipton snored. Mr. Oakhurst alone remained erect, leaning against a rock calmly surveying them.

Mr. Oakhurst did not drink. It interfered with a profession which required coolness, impassiveness, and presence of mind, and, in his own language, he "couldn't afford it." As he gazed at his recumbent fellow exiles, the loneliness begotten of his pariah trade, his habits of life, his very vices, for the first time seriously oppressed him. He bestirred himself in dusting his black clothes, washing his hands and face, and other acts characteristic of his studiously neat habits, and for a moment forgot his annoyance. The thought of deserting his weaker and more pitiable companions never perhaps occurred to him. Yet he could not help feeling the want of that excitement which singularly

enough, was most conducive to that calm equanimity for which he was notorious. He looked at the gloomy walls that rose a thousand feet sheer above the circling pines around him; at the sky, ominously clouded; at the valley below, already deepening into shadow. And, doing so, suddenly he heard his own name called.

A horseman slowly ascended the trail. In the fresh, open face of the newcomer Mr. Oakhurst recognized Tom Simson, otherwise known as the "Innocent" of Sandy Bar. He had met him some months before over a "little game," and had, with perfect equanimity, won the entire fortune—amounting to some forty dollars—of that guileless youth. After the game was finished, Mr. Oakhurst drew the youthful speculator behind the door and thus addressed him: "Tommy, you're a good little man, but you can't gamble worth a cent. Don't try it over again." He then handed him his money back, pushed him gently from the room, and so made a devoted slave of Tom Simson.

There was a remembrance of this in his boyish and enthusiastic greeting of Mr. Oakhurst. He had started, he said, to go to Poker Flat to seek his fortune. "Alone?" No, not exactly alone; in fact (a giggle), he had run away with Piney Woods. Didn't Mr. Oakhurst remember Piney? She that used to wait on the table at the Temperance House? They had been engaged a long time, but old Jake Woods had objected, and so they had run away, and were going to Poker Flat to be married, and here they were. And they were tired out, and how lucky it was they had found a place to camp and company. All this the Innocent delivered rapidly, while Piney, a stout, comely damsel of fifteen, emerged from behind the pine tree, where she had been blushing unseen, and rode to the side of her lover.

Mr. Oakhurst seldom troubled himself with sentiment, still less with propriety; but he had a vague idea that the situation was not fortunate. He retained, however, his presence of mind sufficiently to kick Uncle Billy, who was about to say something, and

---

4. **Sierras** (sē er' əz): Mountains in eastern California, also called the Sierra Nevadas.

Uncle Billy was sober enough to recognize in Mr. Oakhurst's kick a superior power that would not bear trifling. He then endeavored to dissuade Tom Simson from delaying further, but in vain. He even pointed out the fact that there was no provision, nor means of making a camp. But, unluckily, the Innocent met this objection by assuring the party that he was provided with an extra mule loaded with provisions and by the discovery of a rude attempt at a log house near the trail. "Piney can stay with Mrs. Oakhurst," said the Innocent, pointing to the Duchess, "and I can shift for myself."

Nothing but Mr. Oakhurst's admonishing foot saved Uncle Billy from bursting into a roar of laughter. As it was, he felt compelled to retire up the canyon until he could recover his gravity. There he confided the joke to the tall pine trees, with many slaps of his leg, contortions of his face, and the usual profanity. But when he returned to the party, he found them seated by a fire—for the air had grown strangely chill and the sky overcast—in apparently amicable conversation. Piney was actually talking in an impulsive, girlish fashion to the Duchess, who was listening with an interest and animation she had not shown for many days. The Innocent was holding forth, apparently with equal effect, to Mr. Oakhurst and Mother Shipton, who was actually relaxing into amiability. "Is this yer a d—d picnic?" said Uncle Billy with inward scorn as he surveyed the sylvan[5] group, the glancing firelight, and the tethered animals in the foreground. Suddenly an idea mingled with the alcoholic fumes that disturbed his brain. It was apparently of a jocular nature, for he felt impelled to slap his leg again and cram his fist into his mouth.

As the shadows crept slowly up the mountain, a slight breeze rocked the tops of the pine trees, and moaned through their long and gloomy aisles. The ruined cabin, patched and covered with pine boughs, was set apart for the ladies. As the lovers parted, they unaffectedly exchanged a kiss, so honest and sincere that it might have been heard above the swaying pines. The frail Duchess and the malevolent Mother Shipton were probably too stunned to remark upon this last evidence of simplicity, and so turned without a word to the hut. The fire was replenished, the men lay down before the door, and in a few minutes were asleep.

Mr. Oakhurst was a light sleeper. Toward morning he awoke benumbed and cold. As he stirred the dying fire, the wind, which was now blowing strongly, brought to his cheek that which caused the blood to leave it—snow!

He started to his feet with the intention of awakening the sleepers, for there was no time to lose. But turning to where Uncle Billy had been lying, he found him gone. A suspicion leaped to his brain and a curse to his lips. He ran to the spot where the mules had been tethered; they were no longer there. The tracks were already rapidly disappearing in the snow.

The momentary excitement brought Mr. Oakhurst back to the fire with his usual calm. He did not waken the sleepers. The Innocent slumbered peacefully, with a smile on his good-humored, freckled face; the virgin Piney slept beside her frailer sisters as sweetly as though attended by celestial guardians; and Mr. Oakhurst, drawing his blanket over his shoulders, stroked his mustaches and waited for the dawn. It came slowly in a whirling mist of snowflakes that dazzled and confused the eye. What could be seen of the landscape appeared magically changed. He looked over the valley, and summed up the present and future in two words—"snowed in!"

A careful inventory of the provisions, which, fortunately for the party, had been stored within the hut and so escaped the felonious fingers of Uncle Billy, disclosed the fact that with care and prudence they might last ten days longer. "That is," said Mr. Oakhurst, sotto voce[6] to the Innocent, "if you're willing to board us. If you ain't—and

---

5. sylvan (sil´ vən) *adj.*: Characteristic of the forest.

6. sotto voce (sät´ ō vō´ c̄hē): In an undertone.

perhaps you'd better not—you can wait till Uncle Billy gets back with provisions." For some occult reason, Mr. Oakhurst could not bring himself to disclose Uncle Billy's rascality, and so offered the hypothesis that he had wandered from the camp and had accidentally stampeded the animals. He dropped a warning to the Duchess and Mother Shipton, who of course knew the facts of their associate's defection. "They'll find out the truth about us *all* when they find out anything," he added, significantly, "and there's no good frightening them now."

Tom Simson not only put all his worldly store at the disposal of Mr. Oakhurst, but seemed to enjoy the prospect of their enforced seclusion. "We'll have a good camp for a week, and then the snow'll melt, and we'll all go back together." The cheerful gaiety of the young man, and Mr. Oakhurst's calm, infected the others. The Innocent with the aid of pine boughs extemporized a thatch for the roofless cabin, and the Duchess directed Piney in the rearrangement of the interior with a taste and tact that opened the blue eyes of that provincial maiden to their fullest extent. "I reckon now you're used to fine things at Poker Flat," said Piney. The Duchess turned away sharply to conceal something that reddened her cheeks through its professional tint, and Mother Shipton requested Piney not to "chatter." But when Mr. Oakhurst returned from a weary search for the trail, he heard the sound of happy laughter echoed from the rocks. He stopped in some alarm, and his thoughts first naturally reverted to the whisky, which he had prudently cached.[7] "And yet it don't somehow sound like whisky," said the gambler. It was not until he caught sight of the blazing fire through the still-blinding storm and the group around it that he settled to the conviction that it was "square fun."

Whether Mr. Oakhurst had cached his cards with the whisky as something debarred the free access of the community, I cannot say. It was certain that, in Mother Shipton's words, he "didn't say cards once" during that evening. Haply the time was beguiled by an accordion, produced somewhat ostentatiously by Tom Simson from his pack. Notwithstanding some difficulties attending the manipulation of this instrument, Piney Woods managed to pluck several reluctant melodies from its keys, to an accompaniment by the Innocent on a pair of bone castanets. But the crowning festivity of the evening was reached in a rude camp-meeting hymn, which the lovers, joining hands, sang with great earnestness and vociferation. I fear that a certain defiant tone and Covenanter's[8] swing to its chorus, rather than any devotional quality, caused it speedily to infect the others, who at last joined in the refrain:

"I'm proud to live in the service
  of the Lord,
And I'm bound to die in
  His army."[9]

The pines rocked, the storm eddied and whirled above the miserable group, and the flames of their altar leaped heavenward as if in token of the vow.

At midnight the storm abated, the rolling clouds parted, and the stars glittered keenly above the sleeping camp. Mr. Oakhurst, whose professional habits had enabled him to live on the smallest possible amount of sleep, in dividing the watch with Tom Simson somehow managed to take upon himself the greater part of that duty. He excused himself to the Innocent by saying that he had "often been a week without sleep." "Doing what?" asked Tom. "Poker!" replied Oakhurst, sententiously; "when a man gets a streak of luck, he don't get tired. The luck gives in first. Luck," continued the gambler, reflectively, "is a mighty queer thing. All you know about it for certain is

---

7. cached (kasht) *v.*: Hidden.

8. Covenanter's (kuv' ə nan' tərz): Seventeenth-century Scottish Presbyterians who resisted the rule of the Church of England.
9. "I'm . . . army": Lines from the early American spiritual "Service of the Lord."

that it's bound to change. And it's finding out when it's going to change that makes you. We've had a streak of bad luck since we left Poker Flat—you come along, and slap you get into it, too. If you can hold your cards right along you're all right. For," added the gambler, with cheerful irrelevance,

> " 'I'm proud to live in the service
>   of the Lord,
> And I'm bound to die in
>   His army.' "

The third day came, and the sun, looking through the white-curtained valley, saw the outcasts divide their slowly decreasing store of provisions for the morning meal. It was one of the peculiarities of that mountain climate that its rays diffused a kindly warmth over the wintry landscape, as if in regretful commiseration of the past. But it revealed drift on drift of snow piled high around the hut—a hopeless, uncharted, trackless sea of white lying below the rocky shores to which the castaways still clung. Through the marvelously clear air the smoke of the pastoral village of Poker Flat rose miles away. Mother Shipton saw it, and from a remote pinnacle of her rocky fastness hurled in that direction a final malediction. It was her last vituperative attempt, and perhaps for that reason was invested with a certain degree of sublimity. It did her good, she privately informed the Duchess. "Just you go out there and cuss, and see." She then set herself to the task of amusing "the child," as she and the Duchess were pleased to call Piney. Piney was no chicken, but it was a soothing and original theory of the pair thus to account for the fact that she didn't swear and wasn't improper.

When night crept up again through the gorges, the reedy notes of the accordion rose and fell in fitful spasms and long-drawn gasps by the flickering campfire. But music failed to fill entirely the aching void left by insufficient food, and a new diversion was proposed by Piney—storytelling. Neither Mr. Oakhurst nor his female companions caring to relate their personal experiences, this plan would have failed too but for the Innocent. Some months before he had chanced upon a stray copy of Mr. Pope's[10] ingenious translation of the *Iliad*.[11] He now proposed to narrate the principal incidents of that poem—having thoroughly mastered the argument and fairly forgotten the words—in the current vernacular of Sandy Bar. And so for the rest of that night the Homeric demigods again walked the earth. Trojan bully and wily Greek wrestled in the winds, and the great pines in the canyon seemed to bow to the wrath of the son of Peleus.[12] Mr. Oakhurst listened with quiet satisfaction. Most especially was he interested in the fate of "Ash-heels," as the Innocent persisted in denominating the "swift-footed Achilles."

So with small food and much of Homer and the accordion, a week passed over the heads of the outcasts. The sun again forsook them, and again from leaden skies the snowflakes were sifted over the land. Day by day closer around them drew the snowy circle, until at last they looked from their prison over drifted walls of dazzling white that towered twenty feet above their heads. It became more and more difficult to replenish their fires, even from the fallen trees beside them, now half-hidden in the drifts. And yet no one complained. The lovers turned from the dreary prospect and looked into each other's eyes, and were happy. Mr. Oakhurst settled himself coolly to the losing game before him. The Duchess, more cheerful than she had been, assumed the care of Piney. Only Mother Shipton—once the strongest of the party—seemed to sicken and fade. At midnight on the tenth day she called Oakhurst to her side. "I'm going," she said, in a voice of querulous weakness, "but don't say anything about it. Don't waken the kids. Take the bundle from under my head and open

---

10. Mr. Pope: English poet Alexander Pope (1688–1744).
11. Iliad (il' ē əd): Greek epic poem written by Homer that tells the story of the Trojan War.
12. son of Peleus (pēl' o͞os): Achilles (ə kil' ēz), the Greek warrior hero in the *Iliad*.

it." Mr. Oakhurst did so. It contained Mother Shipton's rations for the last week, untouched. "Give 'em to the child," she said, pointing to the sleeping Piney. "You've starved yourself," said the gambler. "That's what they call it," said the woman, querulously, as she lay down again and, turning her face to the wall, passed quietly away.

The accordion and the bones were put aside that day, and Homer was forgotten. When the body of Mother Shipton had been committed to the snow, Mr. Oakhurst took the Innocent aside, and showed him a pair of snowshoes, which he had fashioned from the old pack saddle. "There's one chance in a hundred to save her yet," he said, pointing to Piney; "but it's there," he added, pointing toward Poker Flat. "If you can reach there in two days she's safe." "And you?" asked Tom Simson. "I'll stay here," was the curt reply.

The lovers parted with a long embrace. "You are not going, too?" said the Duchess as she saw Mr. Oakhurst apparently waiting to accompany him. "As far as the canyon," he replied. He turned suddenly, and kissed the Duchess, leaving her pallid face aflame and her trembling limbs rigid with amazement.

Night came, but not Mr. Oakhurst. It brought the storm again and the whirling snow. Then the Duchess, feeding the fire, found that someone had quietly piled beside the hut enough fuel to last a few days longer. The tears rose to her eyes, but she hid them from Piney.

The women slept but little. In the morning, looking into each other's faces, they read their fate. Neither spoke; but Piney, accepting the position of the stronger, drew near and placed her arm around the Duchess's waist. They kept this attitude for the rest of the day. That night the storm reached its greatest fury, and, rending asunder the protecting pines, invaded the very hut.

Toward morning they found themselves unable to feed the fire, which gradually died away. As the embers slowly blackened, the Duchess crept closer to Piney, and broke the silence of many hours: "Piney, can you pray?" "No, dear," said Piney, simply. The Duchess, without knowing exactly why, felt relieved, and, putting her head upon Piney's shoulder, spoke no more. And so reclining, the younger and purer pillowing the head of her soiled sister upon her virgin breast, they fell asleep.

The wind lulled as if it feared to waken them. Feathery drifts of snow, shaken from the long pine boughs, flew like white-winged birds, and settled about them as they slept. The moon through the rifted clouds looked down upon what had been the camp. But all human stain, all trace of earthly travail, was hidden beneath the spotless mantle mercifully flung from above.

They slept all that day and the next, nor did they waken when voices and footsteps broke the silence of the camp. And when pitying fingers brushed the snow from their wan faces, you could scarcely have told from the equal peace that dwelt upon them which was she that had sinned. Even the law of Poker Flat recognized this, and turned away, leaving them still locked in each other's arms.

But at the head of the gulch, on one of the largest pine trees, they found the deuce of clubs pinned to the bark with a bowie knife. It bore the following, written in pencil, in a firm hand:

†

BENEATH THIS TREE

LIES THE BODY

OF

JOHN OAKHURST,

WHO STRUCK A STREAK OF BAD LUCK

ON THE 23D OF NOVEMBER, 1850,

AND

HANDED IN HIS CHECKS

ON THE 7TH DECEMBER, 1850.

†

And pulseless and cold, with a Derringer[13] by his side and a bullet in his heart, though still calm as in life, beneath the snow lay he who was at once the strongest and yet the weakest of the outcasts of Poker Flat.

---

13. Derringer: A small pistol.

RESPONDING TO THE SELECTION

Your Response

1. How closely does Harte's description of Poker Flat match your image of an 1850's mining town? Explain.
2. Would you like to be transported back in time to the western frontier that Harte depicts?

Recalling

3. At the opening of the story, what has the secret committee of Poker Flat decided?
4. Who joins the outcasts at their camp?
5. What does Mr. Oakhurst discover when he awakens after his first night at the camp?
6. What does Mother Shipton do with her rations?
7. What does the rescue party discover?

Interpreting

8. (a) What does Harte's statement that Poker Flat "was experiencing a spasm of virtuous reaction, quite as lawless as the acts that provoked it" suggest about his attitude toward the secret committee's decision? (b) What motivates the committee to take action against Mr. Oakhurst?
9. (a) How is Oakhurst's occupation reflected in his attitude toward life? (b) What does Harte mean when he writes that Oakhurst "was at once the strongest and yet the weakest of the outcasts of Poker Flat"?
10. How do Mother Shipton and the Duchess change over the course of the story?

Applying

11. Though the characters in this story have little in common, they band together. What situations tend to draw people together in real life?

ANALYZING LITERATURE

Understanding Regional Literature

Regional literature captures the distinctive atmosphere, or "local color," of a particular area by accurately depicting the habits, speech, appearance, customs, and beliefs of its people and vividly describing its appearance.
1. What specific details does Harte use to create a portrait of the California landscape?

2. Find three examples of western dialect.
3. Explain why the story would not be effective if the setting were changed, for example, to New England.

CRITICAL THINKING AND READING

Making Inferences About Attitudes

Cultural attitudes and customs are important aspects of local color. In most cases, however, the distinctive attitudes and customs in regional literature are not explicitly stated by the author. As a result, you must make inferences, or draw conclusions, about the attitudes and customs being depicted by examining the characters' actions, thoughts, and comments.

What inferences about the attitudes and customs of the people of Poker Flat can you make from each of the following passages?
1. "A few of the committee had urged hanging him as a possible example, and a sure method of reimbursing themselves from his pocket of the sums he had won from them."
2. "'It's a fine justice,' said Jim Wheeler, 'to let this yer young man—an entire stranger—carry away our money.'"

THINKING AND WRITING

Comparing and Contrasting Characters

Think of a character from a western movie, novel, or television series who is in some ways similar to John Oakhurst. In your prewriting, list the similarities and differences between Oakhurst and the character you have chosen. After preparing a thesis statement, write an essay comparing and contrasting the two characters.

LEARNING OPTION

Creative Response. Imagine that you have been hired as casting director for a television production of "The Outcasts of Poker Flat." Assemble a staff and brainstorm a list of actors for the major roles. Be prepared to justify your choices.

Frederic Remington (1861–1909)

By the time Frederic Remington began his career as an artist in the 1880's, the frontier had almost ceased to exist. Yet, Remington's work provided the images that most strongly represented the old West in late nineteenth and early twentieth-century America.

EARLY YEARS

Remington is considered the best, and was certainly the most popular, painter and sculptor of the old West. Born in New York State, he first traveled west—to Montana in 1881—not as an artist but to seek his for-

THE BRONCO BUSTER
Frederic Remington
Amon Carter Museum, Fort Worth, Texas

tune, possibly in gold mining. In 1883 he traveled west again to try his hand at sheep ranching in Kansas. Later he tried to make his fortune as part owner of a Kansas City saloon. All these ventures met with failure.

During these trips Remington made sketches of landscapes and people. He sold a few of them to popular magazines, and by 1885 he had decided to make art his profession.

Remington's success as an artist came quickly. By 1888 he was one of the nation's most popular magazine illustrators. His sketches of cowboys, soldiers, gunfights, and Indian scenes fed a seemingly unquenchable popular interest in the West. At the same time, Remington began creating paintings. In the 1890's he also turned to sculpture.

REMINGTON'S WEST

Remington's West, the West that gripped the popular imagination through his work, was not the world of the homesteader, of farming and raising families, of small towns and railroading. His West was filled with conflict and action. It was a world of freedom and rugged individualism, of escape from the strictures of society—a world that was quickly passing into history.

Remington's art focused on people, often "wild riders"—cowboys and soldiers on horseback—and his figures usually projected great strength of spirit and physical energy. His work rarely featured generals, chiefs, or ranch owners and instead focused on hardworking, average individuals in a way that made them appear larger-than-life. Remington's frontier had no specific location. For him the landscape functioned mainly as a backdrop for human action. Nature, when it

THE OUTLIER
Frederic Remington
The Brooklyn Museum

played any part in his art, was often a remorseless killer.

CHRONICLER OF A ROMANTICIZED PAST

During Remington's lifetime most of the country viewed the "taming" of the West as positive and necessary. For Remington it was a tragic loss. During most of his career, he made annual trips to the West, spending a month or two each year riding with the cavalry or observing cowboys, Mexican *va-queros*, and Indians. But the West changed rapidly before his eyes, and on one trip he wrote that he would "never come west again. It is all brick buildings—derby hats and blue overalls—it spoils my early illusions."

Remington built his art on his "early illusions," on a romantic view of the West that became more and more distant from reality. As the United States became increasingly industrialized, his work fueled the fantasies of many people who longed for a simpler, less complicated time. While time marched on, Remington's art crystallized a way of life that had vanished forever.

AMBROSE BIERCE

1842–1914[?]

Both Ambrose Bierce's literary career and his philosophy of life were shaped by his career as a Union officer in the Civil War. His experiences provided the material for his best short stories and helped determine the unsentimental, cynical, pessimistic view of the world he expressed in his writing.

Bierce was born in Ohio and raised on a farm in Indiana. Having educated himself by reading his father's books, Bierce left the farm during his late teens to attend a military academy in Kentucky. A year later the Civil War broke out, and he enlisted in the Union army. He fought in several important battles and rose from private to major. Toward the end of the conflict, he was seriously wounded, but he returned to battle a few months later.

When the war ended, Bierce settled in San Francisco as a journalist. His column, the "Prattler," which appeared in *The Argonaut* (1877–1879), the *Wasp* (1880–1886), and the *San Francisco Sunday Examiner* (1887–1896), was a mixture of biting political and social satire, literary reviews, and gossip. Bierce also published many of his finest short stories in his column. Bierce's journalistic barbs angered many key political and business figures, yet his reputation as "the wickedest man in San Francisco" only added to his personal popularity. He was a handsome, magnetic figure who charmed those around him despite the malice of his words.

In the early 1890's, Bierce published two collections of his stories: *Tales of Soldiers and Civilians* (1891) and *Can Such Things Be?* (1893). The concise, carefully plotted stories in these collections, set for the most part in the Civil War, capture the cruelty and futility of war and the indifference of death and reflect Bierce's cynical view of human existence. Bierce's pessimistic outlook is also reflected in *The Devil's Dictionary* (1906), a book of humorous and cynical definitions.

Writer George Sterling wrote of Bierce, his longtime friend, that he "never troubled to conceal his justifiable contempt of humanity . . . Bierce was a 'perfectionist,' a quality that in his case led to an intolerance involving merciless cruelty. He demanded in all others, men or women, the same ethical virtues that he found essential to his own manner of life . . . [T]o deviate from his point of view, indeed, to disagree with him even in slight particulars, was the unpardonable sin."

Although Bierce enjoyed a successful career as a writer, his personal life was filled with tragedy and despair. His marriage ended in divorce and his two sons both died at an early age. In 1913 the lonely and disillusioned writer traveled into Mexico, a country in the midst of a bloody civil war, and never returned. The circumstances of his death are still unknown.

GUIDE FOR INTERPRETING

An Occurrence at Owl Creek Bridge

Writers' Techniques

Point of View. Point of view refers to the vantage point or perspective from which a narrative is told. Most stories are told from either a first-person or third-person point of view. In a narrative with a first-person point of view, one of the characters tells the story in his or her own words, using the first-person pronoun *I*. In a narrative with a third-person point of view, the narrator does not participate in the story and refers to characters using the third-person pronouns *he* and *she*. A third-person narrator may be either limited or omniscient. A third-person limited narrator focuses on the thoughts and feelings of only one character. A third-person omniscient narrator conveys the thoughts and feelings of all the characters.

The portrayal of characters and events in a story is often shaped by the point of view. In stories with first-person or limited third-person narrators, the portrayal of characters and events may be colored by the attitudes and feelings of the character from whose point of view the story is being told.

Focus

It has often been suggested that people's lives flash before their eyes as they near death. Freewrite about the thoughts and feelings that you imagine people experience during their final moments.

Primary Source

In "An Occurrence at Owl Creek Bridge," the improbable plays a key role, at least briefly. In his essay "The Short Story," Bierce expressed his view of the value of probability in fiction:

> Probability? Nothing is so improbable as what is true. It is the unexpected that occurs; but that is not saying enough; it is also the unlikely—one might almost say the impossible. John, for example, meets and marries Jane. John was born in Bombay of poor but detestable parents; Jane, the daughter of a gorgeous hidalgo, on a ship bound from Vladivostok to Buenos Aires. Will some gentlemen . . . have the goodness to figure out what, at their birth, were the chances that John would meet and marry Jane? Not one in a thousand— not one in a million—not one in a million million! . . .
>
> Fiction has nothing to say to probability; the capable writer gives it not a moment's attention, except to make what is related *seem* probable in the reading—*seem* true. Suppose he relates the impossible; what then? Why, he has but passed over the line into the realm of romance . . . the land of the poets, the home of all that is good and lasting in the literature of the imagination. . . .

An Occurrence at Owl Creek Bridge

Ambrose Bierce

I

A man stood upon a railroad bridge in northern Alabama, looking down into the swift water twenty feet below. The man's hands were behind his back, the wrists bound with a cord. A rope closely encircled his neck. It was attached to a stout cross timber above his head and the slack fell to the level of his knees. Some loose boards laid upon the sleepers[1] supporting the metals of the railway supplied a footing for him and

---

1. **sleepers** *n.*: Ties supporting a railroad track.

his executioners—two private soldiers of the Federal army, directed by a sergeant who in civil life may have been a deputy sheriff. At a short remove upon the same temporary platform was an officer in the uniform of his rank, armed. He was a captain. A sentinel at each end of the bridge stood with his rifle in the position known as "support," that is to say, vertical in front of the left shoulder, the hammer resting on the forearm thrown straight across the chest—a formal and unnatural position, enforcing an erect carriage of the body. It did not appear to be the duty of these two men to know what was occur-

THE RED BRIDGE
Julian Alden Weir
The Metropolitan Museum of Art

ring at the center of the bridge; they merely blockaded the two ends of the foot planking that traversed it.

Beyond one of the sentinels nobody was in sight; the railroad ran straight away into a forest for a hundred yards, then, curving, was lost to view. Doubtless there was an outpost farther along. The other bank of the stream was open ground—a gentle acclivity topped with a stockade of vertical tree trunks, loopholed for rifles, with a single embrasure through which protruded the muzzle of a brass cannon commanding the bridge. Midway of the slope between bridge and fort were the spectators—a single company of infantry in line, at "parade rest," the butts of the rifles on the ground, the barrels inclining slightly backward against the right shoulder, the hands crossed upon the stock. A lieutenant stood at the right of the line, the point of his sword upon the ground, his left hand resting upon his right. Excepting the group of four at the center of the bridge, not a man moved. The company faced the bridge, staring stonily, motionless. The sentinels, facing the banks of the stream, might have been statues to adorn the bridge. The captain stood with folded arms, silent, observing the work of his subordinates, but making no sign. Death is a dignitary who when he comes announced is to be received with formal manifestations of respect, even by those most familiar with him. In the code of military etiquette silence and fixity are forms of deference.

The man who was engaged in being hanged was apparently about thirty-five years of age. He was a civilian, if one might judge from his habit, which was that of a planter. His features were good—a straight nose, firm mouth, broad forehead, from which his long, dark hair was combed straight back, falling behind his ears to the collar of his well-fitting frock coat. He wore a mustache and pointed beard, but no whiskers; his eyes were large and dark gray, and had a kindly expression which one would hardly have expected in one whose neck was

in the hemp. Evidently this was no vulgar assassin. The liberal military code makes provision for hanging many kinds of persons, and gentlemen are not excluded.

The preparations being complete, the two private soldiers stepped aside and each drew away the plank upon which he had been standing. The sergeant turned to the captain, saluted and placed himself immediately behind that officer, who in turn moved apart one pace. These movements left the condemned man and the sergeant standing on the two ends of the same plank, which spanned three of the crossties of the bridge. The end upon which the civilian stood almost, but not quite, reached a fourth. This plank had been held in place by the weight of the captain; it was now held by that of the sergeant. At a signal from the former the latter would step aside, the plank would tilt and the condemned man go down between two ties. The arrangement commended itself to his judgment as simple and effective. His face had not been covered nor his eyes bandaged. He looked a moment at his "unsteadfast footing," then let his gaze wander to the swirling water of the stream racing madly beneath his feet. A piece of dancing driftwood caught his attention and his eyes followed it down the current. How slowly it appeared to move! What a sluggish stream!

He closed his eyes in order to fix his last thoughts upon his wife and children. The water, touched to gold by the early sun, the brooding mists under the banks at some distance down the stream, the fort, the soldiers, the piece of drift—all had distracted him. And now he became conscious of a new disturbance. Striking through the thought of his dear ones was a sound which he could neither ignore nor understand, a sharp, distinct, metallic percussion like the stroke of a blacksmith's hammer upon the anvil; it had the same ringing quality. He wondered what it was, and whether immeasurably distant or near by—it seemed both. Its recurrence was regular, but as slow as the tolling of a death knell. He awaited each stroke with impatience and—he knew not why—apprehension. The intervals of silence grew progressively longer; the delays became maddening. With their greater infrequency the sounds increased in strength and sharpness. They hurt his ear like the thrust of a knife; he feared he would shriek. What he heard was the ticking of his watch.

He unclosed his eyes and saw again the water below him. "If I could free my hands," he thought, "I might throw off the noose and spring into the stream. By diving I could evade the bullets and, swimming vigorously, reach the bank, take to the woods and get away home. My home, thank God, is as yet outside their lines; my wife and little ones are still beyond the invader's farthest advance."

As these thoughts, which have here to be set down in words, were flashed into the doomed man's brain rather than evolved from it the captain nodded to the sergeant. The sergeant stepped aside.

II

Peyton Farquhar was a well-to-do planter, of an old and highly respected Alabama family. Being a slave owner and like other slave owners a politician he was naturally an original secessionist and ardently devoted to the Southern cause. Circumstances of an imperious nature, which it is unnecessary to relate here, had prevented him from taking service with the gallant army that had fought the disastrous campaigns ending with the fall of Corinth, and he chafed under the inglorious restraint, longing for the release of his energies, the larger life of the soldier, the opportunity for distinction. That opportunity, he felt, would come, as it comes to all in war time. Meanwhile he did what he could. No service was too humble for him to perform in aid of the South, no adventure too perilous for him to undertake if consistent with the character of a civilian who was at heart a soldier, and who in good faith and without too much qualification assented to

at least a part of the frankly villainous dictum that all is fair in love and war.

One evening while Farquhar and his wife were sitting on a rustic bench near the entrance to his grounds, a gray-clad soldier rode up to the gate and asked for a drink of water. Mrs. Farquhar was only too happy to serve him with her own white hands. While she was fetching the water her husband approached the dusty horseman and inquired eagerly for news from the front.

"The Yanks are repairing the railroads," said the man, "and are getting ready for another advance. They have reached the Owl Creek bridge, put it in order and built a stockade on the north bank. The commandant has issued an order, which is posted everywhere, declaring that any civilian caught interfering with the railroad, its bridges, tunnels or trains will be summarily hanged. I saw the order."

"How far is it to the Owl Creek bridge?" Farquhar asked.

"About thirty miles."

"Is there no force on this side the creek?"

"Only a picket post[2] half a mile out, on the railroad, and a single sentinel at this end of the bridge."

"Suppose a man—a civilian and student of hanging—should elude the picket post and perhaps get the better of the sentinel," said Farquhar, smiling, "what could he accomplish?"

The soldier reflected. "I was there a month ago," he replied. "I observed that the flood of last winter had lodged a great quantity of driftwood against the wooden pier at this end of the bridge. It is now dry and would burn like tow.[3]

The lady had now brought the water, which the soldier drank. He thanked her ceremoniously, bowed to her husband and rode away. An hour later, after nightfall, he re-

---

2. picket post: Troops sent ahead with news of a surprise attack.

3. tow n.: The coarse and broken fibers of hemp or flax before spinning.

passed the plantation, going northward in the direction from which he had come. He was a Federal scout.

III

As Peyton Farquhar fell straight downward through the bridge he lost consciousness and was as one already dead. From this state he was awakened—ages later, it seemed to him—by the pain of a sharp pressure upon his throat, followed by a sense of suffocation. Keen, poignant agonies seemed to shoot from his neck downward through every fiber of his body and limbs. These pains appeared to flash along well-defined lines of ramification and to beat with an inconceivably rapid periodicity. They seemed like streams of pulsating fire heating him to an intolerable temperature. As to his head, he was conscious of nothing but a feeling of fullness—of congestion. These sensations were unaccompanied by thought. The intellectual part of his nature was already effaced; he had power only to feel, and feeling was torment. He was conscious of motion. Encompassed in a luminous cloud, of which he was now merely the fiery heart, without material substance, he swung through unthinkable arcs of oscillation, like a vast pendulum. Then all at once, with terrible suddenness, the light about him shot upward with the noise of a loud plash; a frightful roaring was in his ears, and all was cold and dark. The power of thought was restored; he knew that the rope had broken and he had fallen into the stream. There was no additional strangulation; the noose about his neck was already suffocating him and kept the water from his lungs. To die of hanging at the bottom of a river!—the idea seemed to him ludicrous. He opened his eyes in the darkness and saw above him a gleam of light, but how distant, how inaccessible! He was still sinking, for the light became fainter and fainter until it was a mere glimmer. Then it began to grow and brighten, and he knew that he was rising toward the surface—knew it with reluctance, for he was now very comfortable. "To be hanged and drowned," he thought, "that is not so bad; but I do not wish to be shot. No; I will not be shot; that is not fair."

He was not conscious of an effort, but a sharp pain in his wrist apprised him that he was trying to free his hands. He gave the struggle his attention, as an idler might observe the feat of a juggler, without interest in the outcome. What splendid effort!—what magnificent, what superhuman strength! Ah, that was a fine endeavor! Bravo! The cord fell away; his arms parted and floated upward, the hands dimly seen on each side in the growing light. He watched them with a new interest as first one and then the other pounced upon the noose at his neck. They tore it away and thrust it fiercely aside, its undulations resembling those of a water-snake. "Put it back, put it back!" He thought he shouted these words to his hands, for the undoing of the noose had been succeeded by the direst pang that he had yet experienced. His neck ached horribly; his brain was on fire; his heart, which had been fluttering faintly, gave a great leap, trying to force itself out at his mouth. His whole body was racked and wrenched with an insupportable anguish! But his disobedient hands gave no heed to the command. They beat the water vigorously with quick, downward strokes, forcing him to the surface. He felt his head emerge; his eyes were blinded by the sunlight; his chest expanded convulsively, and with a supreme and crowning agony his lungs engulfed a great draft of air, which instantly he expelled in a shriek!

He was now in full possession of his physical senses. They were, indeed, preternaturally keen and alert. Something in the awful disturbance of his organic system had so exalted and refined them that they made record of things never before perceived. He felt the ripples upon his face and heard their separate sounds as they struck. He looked at the forest on the bank of the stream, saw the individual trees, the leaves and the veining of each leaf—saw the very insects upon them: the locusts, the brilliant-bodied flies, the gray spiders stretching their webs from twig to twig. He noted the prismatic colors in all the dewdrops upon a million blades of grass. The humming of the gnats that danced above the eddies of the stream, the beating of the dragonflies' wings, the strokes of the water spiders' legs, like oars which had lifted their boat—all these made audible music. A fish slid along beneath his eyes and he heard the rush of its body parting the water.

He had come to the surface facing down the stream; in a moment the visible world seemed to wheel slowly round, himself the pivotal point, and he saw the bridge, the fort, the soldiers upon the bridge, the captain, the sergeant, the two privates, his executioners. They were in silhouette against the blue sky. They shouted and gesticulated, pointing at him. The captain had drawn his pistol, but did not fire; the others were unarmed. Their movements were grotesque and horrible, their forms gigantic.

Suddenly he heard a sharp report and something struck the water smartly within a few inches of his head, spattering his face with spray. He heard a second report, and saw one of the sentinels with his rifle at his shoulder, a light cloud of blue smoke rising from the muzzle. The man in the water saw the eye of the man on the bridge gazing into his own through the sights of the rifle. He observed that it was a gray eye and remembered having read that gray eyes were keenest, and that all famous marksmen had them. Nevertheless, this one had missed.

A counterswirl had caught Farquhar and turned him half round; he was again looking into the forest on the bank opposite the fort. The sound of a clear, high voice in a monotonous singsong now rang out behind him and came across the water with a distinctness that pierced and subdued all other sounds, even the beating of the ripples in his ears. Although no soldier, he had frequented camps enough to know the dread signifi-

cance of that deliberate, drawling, aspirated chant; the lieutenant on shore was taking a part in the morning's work. How coldly and pitilessly—with what an even, calm intonation, presaging, and enforcing tranquillity in the men—with what accurately measured intervals fell those cruel words:

"Attention, company! . . . Shoulder arms! . . . Ready! . . . Aim! . . . Fire!"

Farquhar dived—dived as deeply as he could. The water roared in his ears like the voice of Niagara, yet he heard the dulled thunder of the volley and, rising again toward the surface, met shining bits of metal, singularly flattened, oscillating slowly downward. Some of them touched him on the face and hands, then fell away, continuing their descent. One lodged between his collar and neck; it was uncomfortably warm and he snatched it out.

As he rose to the surface, gasping for breath, he saw that he had been a long time under water; he was perceptibly farther down stream—nearer to safety. The soldiers had almost finished reloading; the metal ramrods flashed all at once in the sunshine as they were drawn from the barrels, turned in the air, and thrust into their sockets. The two sentinels fired again, independently and ineffectually.

The hunted man saw all this over his shoulder; he was now swimming vigorously with the current. His brain was as energetic as his arms and legs; he thought with the rapidity of lightning.

"The officer," he reasoned, "will not make that martinet's[4] error a second time. It is as easy to dodge a volley as a single shot. He has probably already given the command to fire at will. God help me, I cannot dodge them all!"

An appalling plash within two yards of him was followed by a loud, rushing sound, *diminuendo*,[5] which seemed to travel back

---

4. martinet *n.*: A very strict military disciplinarian.
5. *diminuendo* (də min′ yōō wen′ dō): A musical term used to describe a gradual reduction in volume.

through the air to the fort and died in an explosion which stirred the very river to its deeps! A rising sheet of water curved over him, fell down upon him, blinded him, strangled him! The cannon had taken a hand in the game. As he shook his head free from the commotion of the smitten water he heard the deflected shot humming through the air ahead, and in an instant it was cracking and smashing the branches in the forest beyond.

"They will not do that again," he thought; "the next time they will use a charge of grape.[6] I must keep my eye upon the gun; the smoke will apprise me—the report arrives too late; it lags behind the missile. That is a good gun."

Suddenly he felt himself whirled round and round—spinning like a top. The water, the banks, the forests, the now distant bridge, fort and men—all were commingled and blurred. Objects were represented by their colors only; circular horizontal streaks of color—that was all he saw. He had been caught in a vortex and was being whirled on with a velocity of advance and gyration that made him giddy and sick. In a few moments he was flung upon the gravel at the foot of the left bank of the stream—the southern bank—and behind a projecting point which concealed him from his enemies. The sudden arrest of his motion, the abrasion of one of his hands on the gravel, restored him, and he wept with delight. He dug his fingers into the sand, threw it over himself in handfuls and audibly blessed it. It looked like diamonds, rubies, emeralds; he could think of nothing beautiful which it did not resemble. The trees upon the bank were giant garden plants; he noted a definite order in their arrangement, inhaled the fragrance of their blooms. A strange, roseate light shone through the spaces among their trunks and the wind made in their branches the music

of aeolian harps.[7] He had no wish to perfect his escape—was content to remain in that enchanting spot until retaken.

A whiz and rattle of grapeshot among the branches high above his head roused him from his dream. The baffled cannoneer had fired him a random farewell. He sprang to his feet, rushed up the sloping bank, and plunged into the forest.

All that day he traveled, laying his course by the rounding sun. The forest seemed interminable; nowhere did he discover a break in it, not even a woodman's road. He had not known that he lived in so wild a region. There was something uncanny in the revelation.

By night fall he was fatigued, footsore, famishing. The thought of his wife and children urged him on. At last he found a road which led him in what he knew to be the right direction. It was as wide and straight as a city street, yet it seemed untraveled. No fields bordered it, no dwelling anywhere. Not so much as the barking of a dog suggested human habitation. The black bodies of the trees formed a straight wall on both sides, terminating on the horizon in a point, like a diagram in a lesson in perspective. Overhead, as he looked up through this rift in the wood, shone great golden stars looking unfamiliar and grouped in strange constellations. He was sure they were arranged in some order which had a secret and malign significance. The wood on either side was full of singular noises, among which—once, twice, and again, he distinctly heard whispers in an unknown tongue.

His neck was in pain and lifting his hand to it he found it horribly swollen. He knew that it had a circle of black where the rope had bruised it. His eyes felt congested; he could no longer close them. His tongue was swollen with thirst; he relieved its fever by thrusting it forward from between his teeth into the cold air. How softly the turf

---

6. grape: A cluster of small iron balls that disperse once fired from a cannon.

7. aeolian (ē ō′ lē ən) **harps:** Harps with strings that produce music when air blows over them.

SEAT OF JOHN JULIUS PRINGLE, 1800
Charles Fraser
Carolina Art Association, Gibbes Art Gallery

had carpeted the untraveled avenue—he could no longer feel the roadway beneath his feet!

Doubtless, despite his suffering, he had fallen asleep while walking, for now he sees another scene—perhaps he has merely recovered from a delirium. He stands at the gate of his own home. All is as he left it, and all bright and beautiful in the morning sunshine. He must have traveled the entire night. As he pushes open the gate and passes up the wide white walk, he sees a flutter of female garments; his wife, looking fresh and cool and sweet, steps down from the veranda to meet him. At the bottom of the steps she stands waiting, with a smile of ineffable joy, an attitude of matchless grace and dignity. Ah, how beautiful she is! He springs forward with extended arms. As he is about to clasp her he feels a stunning blow upon the back of the neck; a blinding white light blazes all about him with a sound like the shock of a cannon—then all is darkness and silence!

Peyton Farquhar was dead; his body, with a broken neck, swung gently from side to side beneath the timbers of the Owl Creek bridge.

RESPONDING TO THE SELECTION

Your Response

1. Do you feel sympathy or contempt for Peyton Farquhar, the condemned man? Explain.
2. Farquhar believed that "all is fair in love and war." What do you think?

Recalling

3. Describe the condemned man's background.
4. (a) What do Farquhar and his wife learn from the visitor? (b) What do you learn about the visitor after he leaves?
5. (a) What sensation does Farquhar experience "with terrible suddenness" after he has been hanged? (b) How does he interpret this sensation?
6. What is Farquhar's fate?

Interpreting

7. In Part I, Bierce includes few details about the condemned man and does not reveal why he is being hanged. How does this help to create suspense?
8. (a) In what ways are the condemned man's perceptions of time and motion distorted as he is waiting to be hanged? (b) Why are his distorted perceptions important?
9. (a) Considering the outcome of the story, what is ironic, or surprising, about Farquhar's longing for "the larger life of a soldier"? (b) What is ironic about the fact that Farquhar assents to the "dictum that all is fair in love and war"?
10. (a) What details in Part III suggest that Farquhar's journey occurs in his mind? (b) How is his journey connected with the plan of escape that occurs to him moments before he is hanged?

Applying

11. Explain whether you think the portrayal of Farquhar's final thoughts is realistic.

ANALYZING LITERATURE

Recognizing Point of View

Point of view refers to the vantage point from which a narrative is told.

1. Why is a limited third-person point of view appropriate for this story?
2. Why would a first-person point of view have been inappropriate?
3. How might the story be different if Bierce had used an omniscient third-person narrator?

CRITICAL THINKING AND READING

Understanding the Sequence of Events

Writers frequently do not present all of the events in a story in chronological order. For example, in "An Occurrence at Owl Creek Bridge," Bierce presents a flashback in which he describes some of the events that led up to Farquhar's hanging.

How does Bierce's use of the flashback technique contribute to the effectiveness of the story?

THINKING AND WRITING

Exploring a Different Point of View

Imagine that your school literary magazine is having a contest in which students are asked to retell "An Occurrence at Owl Creek Bridge" from the point of view of one of the Union soldiers or the Federal scout. Start by thinking about how the character you choose might have felt about the hanging of Peyton Farquhar and what he would have known about the reasons for the hanging. List the events that led up to the hanging and some details you could use in describing these events. Then, after deciding on the order in which you want to present the events, write your story. Remember to focus on the thoughts and feelings of the character you have chosen. When you finish writing, revise your story and prepare a final copy.

LEARNING OPTION

Writing. When Farquhar closes his eyes to "fix his last thoughts upon his wife and children," images of an escape and a reunion with his wife flash through his brain. If your life were to pass before your eyes, what would you see? Describe the images and explain why they are important to you.

KATE CHOPIN

1851–1904

Despite her conservative, aristocratic upbringing, Kate O'Flaherty Chopin became one of the most powerful and controversial writers of her time. In her stories, sketches, and novels, she not only captured the local color of Louisiana but also boldly explored the role of women in society.

Kate O'Flaherty was born in St. Louis, Missouri, the daughter of a wealthy businessman. When she was nineteen, she married Oscar Chopin, a Louisiana cotton trader. The couple settled in New Orleans, where they lived for ten years before moving to a plantation in rural northwestern Louisiana. In 1883 Chopin's husband died, leaving her to raise her six children on her own. Chopin carried on the work of the plantation alone for more than a year, using her knowledge of finance and developing skills as a businesswoman. However, in 1884, she yielded to her mother's urgings, sold most of her holdings, and returned to St. Louis with her children. Her mother's sudden death in 1885 left her in deep sorrow. It was at the suggestion of her family doctor, who was concerned about her emotional state, that Chopin began writing fiction. Chopin kept St. Louis as her home for the rest of her life, devoting much of her energy to writing.

Influenced by American Regionalists such as Sarah Orne Jewett and fascinated by the mixture of cultures in Louisiana, Chopin focused on capturing the essence of life in Louisiana in her writing. Like most of her other works, her first novel, *At Fault* (1890), was set in a small Louisiana town inhabited by Creoles, descendants of the original French and Spanish settlers, and Cajuns, descendants of French Canadian settlers. Through her vivid descriptions and use of dialect, Chopin captured the local color of the region. In her stories, published in *Bayou Folk* (1894) and *Acadie* (1897), she exhibited her deep understanding of the different attitudes and concerns of the Louisiana natives. Yet her charming portraits of Louisiana life often obscured the fact that she explored themes considered radical at the time: the nature of marriage, racial prejudice, and women's desire for social, economic, and political equality.

Her finest novel, *The Awakening* (1899), is a psychological account of a woman's search for independence and fulfillment. Because the novel explored the issue of infidelity, it aroused a storm of protest. The book was severely attacked by critics and eventually banned, and Chopin's reputation was badly damaged. As a result, Chopin's work was virtually ignored for several decades after her death. Today, however, she is widely respected for her intense understanding of female psychology and her ability to capture local color.

GUIDE FOR INTERPRETING

The Story of an Hour

Irony. Irony is a contrast between what is stated and what is meant, or between what is expected to happen and what actually happens. A number of different types of irony are used in literature. Situational irony occurs when the actual result of an action or situation is quite different from the expected result. For example, in "An Occurrence at Owl Creek Bridge," when you are told that Peyton Farquhar assents to the "dictum that all is fair in love and war," you are led to expect that he may become involved in some type of covert or deceptive activity. As it turns out, however, Farquhar himself is the one who is deceived, when he is tricked by a Federal scout who pretends to be a Confederate soldier. Dramatic irony occurs when readers perceive something that a character in a literary work does not know. For example, in Shakespeare's *Romeo and Juliet,* Romeo poisons himself after being told that his beloved Juliet is dead. Yet the audience is aware that in reality Juliet has only been pretending to be dead as part of an elaborate plan to be united with Romeo.

Imagine an instance in which you or someone you know receives a piece of news that has a powerful effect. Then imagine that the news turns out not to be true. Describe how the news and the discovery that the news was false would affect you.

In "The Story of an Hour," you will meet a married woman who longs for freedom and independence. In this story and others, Kate Chopin recognized that the perfect wife of her time was submissive to her husband in all matters, that "the lack of self-assertion" was a sign of "the perfection of womanliness." Yet Chopin, who never remarried after her husband's death, had another vision of the marriage relationship, which she described in her early story "A Point of Issue":

> [The couple decided] to be governed by no precedential methods. Marriage was to be a form, that while fixing legally their relation to each other, was in no wise to touch the individuality of either; that was to be preserved intact. Each was to remain a free integral of humanity, responsible to no dominating exactions of so-called marriage laws. And the element that was to make possible such a union was trust in each other's love, honor, courtesy, tempered by the reserving clause of readiness to meet the consequences of reciprocal liberty.

The Story of an Hour

Kate Chopin

Knowing that Mrs. Mallard was afflicted with a heart trouble, great care was taken to break to her as gently as possible the news of her husband's death.

It was her sister Josephine who told her, in broken sentences; veiled hints that revealed in half concealing. Her husband's friend Richards was there, too, near her. It was he who had been in the newspaper office when intelligence of the railroad disaster was received, with Brently Mallard's name leading the list of "killed." He had only taken the time to assure himself of its truth by a second telegram, and had hastened to forestall any less careful, less tender friend in bearing the sad message.

She did not hear the story as many women have heard the same, with a paralyzed inability to accept its significance. She wept at once, with sudden, wild abandonment, in her sister's arms. When the storm of grief had spent itself she went away to her room alone. She would have no one follow her.

There stood, facing the open window, a comfortable, roomy armchair. Into this she sank, pressed down by a physical exhaustion that haunted her body and seemed to reach into her soul.

She could see in the open square before her house the tops of trees that were all aquiver with the new spring life. The delicious breath of rain was in the air. In the street below a peddler was crying his wares. The notes of a distant song which someone was singing reached her faintly, and countless sparrows were twittering in the eaves.

There were patches of blue sky showing here and there through the clouds that had met and piled one above the other in the west facing her window.

She sat with her head thrown back upon the cushion of the chair, quite motionless, except when a sob came up into her throat and shook her, as a child who has cried itself to sleep continues to sob in its dreams.

She was young, with a fair, calm face, whose lines bespoke repression and even a certain strength. But now there was a dull stare in her eyes, whose gaze was fixed away off yonder on one of those patches of blue sky. It was not a glance of reflection, but rather indicated a suspension of intelligent thought.

There was something coming to her and she was waiting for it, fearfully. What was it? She did not know; it was too subtle and elusive to name. But she felt it, creeping out of the sky, reaching toward her through the sounds, the scents, the color that filled the air.

Now her bosom rose and fell tumultuously. She was beginning to recognize this thing that was approaching to possess her, and she was striving to beat it back with her will—as powerless as her two white slender hands would have been.

When she abandoned herself, a little whispered word escaped her slightly parted lips. She said it over and over under her breath: "free, free, free!" The vacant stare and the look of terror that had followed it went from her eyes. They stayed keen and bright. Her pulses beat fast, and the cours-

WOMAN WITH A BLACK TIE
Amedeo Modigliani
Private Collection

ing blood warmed and relaxed every inch of her body.

She did not stop to ask if it were or were not a monstrous joy that held her. A clear and exalted perception enabled her to dismiss the suggestion as trivial.

She knew that she would weep again when she saw the kind, tender hands folded in death; the face that had never looked save with love upon her, fixed and gray and dead. But she saw beyond that bitter moment a long procession of years to come that would belong to her absolutely. And she opened and spread her arms out to them in welcome.

There would be no one to live for her during those coming years; she would live for herself. There would be no powerful will bending hers in that blind persistence with which men and women believe they have a right to impose a private will upon a fellow creature. A kind intention or a cruel intention made the act seem no less a crime as she looked upon it in that brief moment of illumination.

And yet she had loved him—sometimes. Often she had not. What did it matter! What could love, the unsolved mystery, count for in face of this possession of self-assertion which she suddenly recognized as the strongest impulse of her being!

"Free! Body and soul free!" she kept whispering.

Josephine was kneeling before the closed door with her lips to the keyhole, imploring for admission. "Louise, open the door! I beg; open the door—you will make yourself ill.

What are you doing, Louise? For heaven's sake open the door."

"Go away. I am not making myself ill." No; she was drinking in a very elixir of life[1] through that open window.

Her fancy was running riot along those days ahead of her. Spring days, and summer days, and all sorts of days that would be her own. She breathed a quick prayer that life might be long. It was only yesterday she had thought with a shudder that life might be long.

She arose at length and opened the door to her sister's importunities. There was a feverish triumph in her eyes, and she carried herself unwittingly like a goddess of Victory. She clasped her sister's waist, and together they descended the stairs. Richards stood waiting for them at the bottom.

Someone was opening the front door with a latchkey. It was Brently Mallard who entered, a little travel-stained, composedly carrying his gripsack[2] and umbrella. He had been far from the scene of accident, and did not know there had been one. He stood amazed at Josephine's piercing cry; at Richards's quick motion to screen him from the view of his wife.

But Richards was too late.

When the doctors came they said she had died of heart disease—of joy that kills.

---

1. **elixir of life** (i lik′ sər) *n.*: An imaginary substance thought by medieval alchemists to prolong life indefinitely.
2. **gripsack** (grip′ sak) *n.*: A small bag for holding clothes.

RESPONDING TO THE SELECTION

Your Response

1. What was your reaction to the ending of the story? Explain.
2. What is your opinion of Mrs. Mallard? Explain.
3. How might Mrs. Mallard's life have been different if the story were set in the late twentieth century?

Recalling

4. (a) How does Mrs. Mallard first react to the news of her husband's death? (b) How does her reaction change?
5. (a) Who opens the front door toward the end of the story? (b) How does Mrs. Mallard react when she sees him?

Interpreting

6. At the beginning of the story, when Chopin states that Mrs. Mallard "was afflicted with a heart trouble," she seems to be referring to a medical problem. Considering Mrs. Mallard's response to her husband's death, what other meaning do you think this statement might have?
7. How do the details of the scene outside Mrs. Mallard's room foreshadow the feelings that gradually sweep over Mrs. Mallard as she sits in her armchair?
8. What has Mrs. Mallard apparently resented about her marriage?
9. Why do you think Chopin chooses to reveal little about Mrs. Mallard's personality aside from her feelings concerning her marriage, her husband, and her independence?
10. What do you think is the actual reason for Mrs. Mallard's death?
11. What do you think is the significance of the story's title?

Applying

12. Mrs. Mallard realizes, "There would be no one to live for her during those coming years; she would live for herself." Do you think that it is important for people to live for themselves? Explain your answer.

ANALYZING LITERATURE

Recognizing Irony

Irony is a contrast between what is stated and what is meant, or between what is expected to happen and what actually happens. Situational irony and dramatic irony are two of the types of irony used in literature. An example of situational irony occurs in "The Story of an Hour," when, after you have been led to believe that Mrs. Mallard is deeply disturbed by the news of her husband's death, she is actually overcome by a sense of joy.

1. Why is Mrs. Mallard's sudden death also an example of situational irony?
2. Why is the diagnosis of the cause of Mrs. Mallard's death an example of dramatic irony?

CRITICAL THINKING AND READING

Recognizing Details of Irony

A writer creates situational irony by including details that create certain expectations. For example, in "The Story of an Hour," Chopin leads you to believe that Mrs. Mallard has been upset by the news of her husband's death by mentioning that Josephine and Richards took great care to break the news to her as gently as possible.

Find two details that help create the situational irony of Mrs. Mallard's death.

THINKING AND WRITING

Writing About Irony

Write an essay in which you discuss the role of irony in "The Story of an Hour." Reread the story focusing on Chopin's use of irony. Develop a thesis statement. When you write your essay, use evidence from the story to support your thesis. When you revise your essay, make sure you have not included any unnecessary information.

LEARNING OPTIONS

1. **Writing.** What might Mrs. Mallard have made of her life if her husband had not returned? Imagine that the story ends with Mrs. Mallard descending the stairs with her sister. Revisit the widow ten years later. Have the years fulfilled their promise? Does Mrs. Mallard still wish for a long life? In a paragraph or two, describe Mrs. Mallard's life and thoughts.
2. **Multicultural Activity.** "The Story of an Hour" offers a glimpse of what life was like for American women in the late 1800's. What is life like for women around the world today? Pick a culture or country that interests you and prepare a brief oral presentation on women's roles there. How do the roles of women in that country or culture compare with those of women in the United States?

WILLA CATHER

1873–1947

Willa Cather was born in a small town in western Virginia. When she was ten, her family moved to a farm near the frontier town of Red Cloud, Nebraska. Here, many of Cather's new neighbors were immigrants—Swedes, Germans, Slavs, and Russians—struggling to build a life for themselves in their new land and determined to preserve the culture of the land they left behind. Through her interaction with this diverse group of people, Cather developed an awareness of certain qualities shared not only by people of the frontier but by people from all over the world. She also gained a rich cultural background, studying foreign languages, history, and classical music and opera. She wrote of her childhood: "On Sundays we could drive to a Norwegian church and listen to a sermon in that language, or to a Danish or Swedish church. We could go to a French Catholic settlement or into the Bohemian township and hear one in Czech, or we could go to the church with the German Lutherans."

After graduating from the University of Nebraska in 1895, Cather worked as an editor for a Pittsburgh newspaper, while writing poems and short stories in her spare time. Her first collection of stories, *The Troll Garden,* was published in 1905. The following year she moved to New York, where she worked as the managing editor for *McClure's Magazine.* In 1912, the year after she published her first novel, *Alexander's Bridge,* she left the magazine to devote all her energy to writing. During the next several years, she produced three novels: *O Pioneers!* (1913); *The Song of the Lark* (1915); and *My Antonia* (1918), which captured the flavor of life in the midwestern prairies. In 1923 she won the Pulitzer Prize for her novel *One of Ours* (1922).

Cather shifted her attention from the Midwest to the Southwest in *Death Comes for the Archbishop* (1927) and to seventeenth-century Quebec in *Shadows on the Rock* (1931). She also published two collections of short stories: *Youth and the Bright Medusa* (1920) and *Obscure Destinies* (1932); and a collection of critical essays and recollections of earlier writers: *Not Under Forty.*

In her work Cather displayed her admiration for the courage and spirit of the immigrants and other settlers of the frontier while at the same time conveying an intense awareness of the loss felt by some of the pioneers as well as the loneliness and isolation from which they suffered. In "A Wagner Matinée" Cather captures this sense of loneliness and isolation by contrasting the stark realities of frontier life with the possibilities of life in a more cultured world.

GUIDE FOR INTERPRETING

A Wagner Matinée

Writers' Techniques

Characterization. Characterization is the means by which a writer reveals a character's personality. Writers generally develop a character through one of the following methods: direct statements about the character, physical descriptions of the character, the character's actions, the character's thoughts and comments, or other characters' reactions to or comments about the character.

In the late 1800's and early 1900's, writers began turning to the first-person and third-person limited points of view. When a writer limits the point of view to one character, as Cather does in "A Wagner Matinée," most of what is revealed about the characters is shaped by the thoughts of the character from whose point of view the story is being told.

Focus

Ralph Waldo Emerson wrote, "[Music] takes us out of the actual and whispers to us dim secrets that startle us to wonder as to who we are, and for what, whence, and whereth." Discuss the meaning of this quotation. Think about the powerful effect music often has on people's memories and emotions. Recall a piece of music—one that has no lyrics—that can produce a strong effect on your memories and emotions. Then freewrite about it.

Primary Source

As you read "A Wagner Matinée," you will notice Willa Cather's harsh portrayal of the Midwest. Although this portrayal incensed many members of Cather's family, Edith Lewis, a close friend, found herself agreeing with it. Here Lewis recalls how she felt during one trip she took with Cather to Red Cloud, Nebraska.

> A new convention had to be created for [Nebraska]; a convention that had nothing to do with woods and water-falls, streams and valleys and picturesque architecture. . . . There it lay; and it was as new, as unknown to art as it was to the pioneer.
>
> Although I had grown up in Nebraska, I remember how lost in the prairies Red Cloud seemed to me . . . as if the hot wind that so much of the time blew over it went on and left it behind, isolated, forgotten by the rest of the world. It seemed flattened down against the sea of earth as a boat of ship-wrecked men is flattened down, almost imperceptible, among the waves. And I felt again that forlornness, that terrible restlessness that comes over young people born in small towns in the middle of the continent; the sense of being cut off from all the great currents of life and thought.

A Wagner Matinée

Willa Cather

I received one morning a letter written in pale ink, on glassy, blue-lined notepaper, and bearing the postmark of a little Nebraska village. This communication, worn and rubbed, looking as though it had been carried for some days in a coat pocket that was none too clean, was from my Uncle Howard. It informed me that his wife had been left a small legacy by a bachelor relative who had recently died, and that it had become necessary for her to come to Boston to attend to the settling of the estate. He requested me to meet her at the station, and render her whatever services might prove necessary. On examining the date indicated as that of her arrival, I found it no later than tomorrow. He had characteristically delayed writing until, had I been away from home for a day, I must have missed the good woman altogether.

The name of my Aunt Georgiana called up not alone her own figure, at once pathetic and grotesque, but opened before my feet a gulf of recollections so wide and deep that, as the letter dropped from my hand, I felt suddenly a stranger to all the present conditions of my existence, wholly ill at ease and out of place amid the surroundings of my study. I became, in short, the gangling farmer boy my aunt had known, scourged with chilblains and bashfulness, my hands cracked and raw from the corn husking. I felt the knuckles of my thumb tentatively, as though they were raw again. I sat again before her parlor organ, thumbing the scales with my stiff, red hands, while she beside me made canvas mittens for the huskers.

The next morning, after preparing my landlady somewhat, I set out for the station. When the train arrived I had some difficulty in finding my aunt. She was the last of the passengers to alight, and when I got her into the carriage she looked not unlike one of those charred, smoked bodies that firemen lift from the *débris* of a burned building. She had come all the way in a day coach; her linen duster[1] had become black with soot and her black bonnet gray with dust during the journey. When we arrived at my boardinghouse the landlady put her to bed at once, and I did not see her again until the next morning.

Whatever shock Mrs. Springer experienced at my aunt's appearance she considerately concealed. Myself, I saw my aunt's misshapen figure with that feeling of awe and respect with which we behold explorers who have left their ears and fingers north of Franz Josef Land,[2] or their health somewhere along the upper Congo.[3] My Aunt Georgiana had been a music teacher at the Boston Conservatory, somewhere back in the latter sixties. One summer, which she had spent in the little village in the Green Mountains[4] where her ancestors had dwelt for generations, she had kindled the callow fancy of the most idle and shiftless of all the village lads, and had conceived for this Howard Carpenter one of those absurd and extravagant passions which a handsome

---

1. duster *n.*: A short, loose smock worn to protect clothing from dust.
2. Franz Josef Land: A group of islands in the Arctic Ocean.
3. Congo: River in central Africa.
4. Green Mountains: Mountains in Vermont.

country boy of twenty-one sometimes inspires in a plain, angular, spectacled woman of thirty. When she returned to her duties in Boston, Howard followed her; and the upshot of this inexplicable infatuation was that she eloped with him, eluding the reproaches of her family and the criticism of her friends by going with him to the Nebraska frontier. Carpenter, who of course had no money, took a homestead in Red Willow County,[5] fifty miles from the railroad. There they measured off their eighty acres by driving across the prairie in a wagon, to the wheel of which they had tied a red cotton handkerchief, and counting its revolutions. They built a dugout in the red hillside, one of those cave dwellings whose inmates usually reverted to the conditions of primitive savagery. Their water they got from the lagoons where the buffalo drank, and their slender stock of provisions was always at the mercy of bands of roving Indians. For thirty years my aunt had not been farther than fifty miles from the homestead.

But Mrs. Springer knew nothing of all this, and must have been considerably shocked at what was left of my kinswoman. Beneath the soiled linen duster, which on her arrival was the most conspicuous feature of her costume, she wore a black stuff dress whose ornamentation showed that she had surrendered herself unquestioningly into the hands of a country dressmaker. My poor aunt's figure, however, would have presented astonishing difficulties to any dressmaker. Her skin was yellow from constant exposure to a pitiless wind, and to the alkaline water which transforms the most transparent cuticle into a sort of flexible leather. She wore ill-fitting false teeth. The most striking thing about her physiognomy, however, was an incessant twitching of the mouth and eyebrows, a form of nervous disorder resulting from isolation and monotony, and from frequent physical suffering.

---

5. **Red Willow County:** County in southwestern Nebraska that borders on Kansas.

In my boyhood this affliction had possessed a sort of horrible fascination for me, of which I was secretly very much ashamed, for in those days I owed to this woman most of the good that ever came my way, and had a reverential affection for her. During the three winters when I was riding herd for my uncle, my aunt, after cooking three meals for half a dozen farmhands, and putting the six children to bed, would often stand until midnight at her ironing board, hearing me at the kitchen table beside her recite Latin declensions and conjugations, and gently shaking me when my drowsy head sank down over a page of irregular verbs. It was to her, at her ironing or mending, that I read my first Shakespeare; and her old textbook of mythology was the first that ever came into my empty hands. She taught me my scales and exercises, too, on the little parlor organ which her husband had bought her after fifteen years, during which she had not so much as seen any instrument except an accordion, that belonged to one of the Norwegian farmhands. She would sit beside me by the hour, darning and counting, while I struggled with the "Harmonious Blacksmith"; but she seldom talked to me about music, and I understood why. She was a pious woman; she had the consolation of religion; and to her at least her martyrdom was not wholly sordid. Once when I had been doggedly beating out some passages from an old score of "Euryanthe" I had found among her music books, she came up to me and, putting her hands over my eyes, gently drew my head back upon her shoulder, saying tremulously, "Don't love it so well, Clark, or it may be taken from you. Oh! dear boy, pray that whatever your sacrifice be it is not that."

When my aunt appeared on the morning after her arrival, she was still in a semi-somnambulent state. She seemed not to realize that she was in the city where she had spent her youth, the place longed for hungrily for half a lifetime. She had been so wretchedly trainsick throughout the journey that she had no recollection of anything but her discomfort, and, to all intents and purposes, there were but a few hours of nightmare between the farm in Red Willow County and my study on Newbury Street. I had planned a little pleasure for her that afternoon, to repay her for some of the glorious moments she had given me when we used to milk together in the straw-thatched cowshed, and she, because I was more than usually tired, or because her husband had spoken sharply to me, would tell me of the splendid performance of Meyerbeer's *Les Huguenots*[6] she had seen in Paris in her youth. At two o'clock the Boston Symphony Orchestra was to give a Wagner[7] program, and I intended to take my aunt, though as I conversed with her I grew doubtful about her enjoyment of it. Indeed, for her own sake, I could only wish her taste for such things quite dead, and the long struggle mercifully ended at last. I suggested our visiting the Conservatory and the Common[8] before lunch, but she seemed altogether too timid to wish to venture out. She questioned me absently about various changes in the city, but she was chiefly concerned that she had forgotten to leave instructions about feeding half-skimmed milk to a certain weakling calf, "Old Maggie's calf, you know, Clark," she explained, evidently having forgotten how long I had been away. She was further troubled because she had neglected to tell her daughter about the freshly opened kit of mackerel in the cellar, that would spoil if it were not used directly.

I asked her whether she had ever heard any of the Wagnerian operas, and found that she had not, though she was perfectly familiar with their respective situations and had once possessed the piano score of *The Flying Dutchman.* I began to think it would have been best to get her back to Red Willow County without waking her, and regretted having suggested the concert.

From the time we entered the concert hall, however, she was a trifle less passive and inert, and seemed to begin to perceive her surroundings. I had felt some trepidation lest one might become aware of the absurdities of her attire, or might experience some painful embarrassment at stepping suddenly into the world to which she had been dead for a quarter of a century. But again I found how superficially I had judged her. She sat looking about her with eyes as impersonal, almost as stony, as those with which the granite Ramses[9] in a museum watches the froth and fret that ebbs and flows about his pedestal, separated from it by the lonely stretch of centuries. I have seen this same aloofness in old miners who drift into the Brown Hotel at Denver, their pockets full of bullion, their linen soiled, their haggard faces unshorn, and who stand in the thronged corridors as solitary as though they were still in a frozen camp on the Yukon, or in the yellow blaze of the Arizona desert, conscious that certain experiences have isolated them from their fellows by a gulf no haberdasher could conceal.

The audience was made up chiefly of women. One lost the contour of faces and figures, indeed any effect of line whatever, and there was only the color contrast of bodices past counting, the shimmer and shading of fabrics soft and firm, silky and sheer, resisting and yielding: red, mauve, pink, blue, lilac, purple, ecru, rose, yellow, cream, and white, all the colors that an impressionist finds in a sunlit landscape, with here and there the dead black shadow of a frock coat. My Aunt Georgiana regarded them as though they had been so many daubs of tube paint on a palette.

---

6. Les Huguenots (hyoo′ gə nät′): Opera written in 1836 by Giacomo Meyerbeer (1791–1864).

7. Wagner (väg′ nər): Richard Wagner (1813–1883), a great German composer who is responsible for the development of the musical drama.

8. Common: Boston Common, a small park in Boston.

---

9. Ramses (ram′ sēz): Egyptian kings who ruled from c.1315 to c.1090 B.C.

When the musicians came out and took their places, she gave a little stir of anticipation, and looked with quickening interest down over the rail at that invariable grouping; perhaps the first wholly familiar thing that had greeted her eye since she had left old Maggie and her weakling calf. I could feel how all those details sank into her soul, for I had not forgotten how they had sunk into mine when I came fresh from plowing forever and forever between green aisles of corn, where, as in a treadmill, one might walk from daybreak to dusk without perceiving a shadow of change in one's environment. I reminded myself of the impression made on me by the clean profiles of the musicians, the gloss of their linen; the dull black of their coats, the beloved shapes of the instruments, the patches of yellow light thrown by the green-shaded stand-lamps on the smooth, varnished bellies of the cellos and the bass viols in the rear, the restless, wind-tossed forest of fiddle necks and bows; I recalled how, in the first orchestra I had ever heard, those long bow strokes seemed to draw the soul out of me, as a conjuror's stick reels out paper ribbon from a hat.

The first number was the Tannhäuser overture. When the violins drew out the first strain of the Pilgrims' chorus, my Aunt Georgiana clutched my coat sleeve. Then it was that I first realized that for her this singing of basses and stinging frenzy of lighter strings broke a silence of thirty years, the inconceivable silence of the plains. With the battle between the two motifs, with the bitter frenzy of the Venusberg[10] theme and its ripping of strings, came to me an overwhelming sense of the waste and wear we are so powerless to combat. I saw again the tall, naked house on the prairie, black and grim as a wooden fortress; the black pond where I had learned to swim, the rain-gullied clay about the naked house; the four dwarf

ash seedlings on which the dishcloths were always hung to dry before the kitchen door. The world there is the flat world of the ancients; to the east, a cornfield that stretched to daybreak; to the west, a corral that stretched to sunset; between, the sordid conquests of peace, more merciless than those of war.

The overture closed. My aunt released my coat sleeve, but she said nothing. She sat staring at the orchestra through a dullness of thirty years, through the films made, little by little, by each of the three hundred and sixty-five days in every one of them. What, I wondered, did she get from it? She had been a good pianist in her day, I knew, and her musical education had been broader than that of most music teachers of a quarter of a century ago. She had often told me of Mozart's operas and Meyerbeer's, and I could remember hearing her sing, years ago, certain melodies of Verdi. When I had fallen ill with a fever she used to sit by my cot in the evening, while the cool night wind blew in through the faded mosquito netting tacked over the window, and I lay watching a bright star that burned red above the cornfield, and sing "Home to our mountains, oh, let us return!" in a way fit to break the heart of a Vermont boy near dead of homesickness already.

I watched her closely through the prelude to *Tristan and Isolde*, trying vainly to conjecture what that warfare of motifs, that seething turmoil of strings and winds, might mean to her. Had this music any message for her? Did or did not a new planet swim into her ken? Wagner had been a sealed book to Americans before the sixties. Had she anything left with which to comprehend this glory that had flashed around the world since she had gone from it? I was in a fever of curiosity, but Aunt Georgiana sat silent upon her peak in Darien.[11] She preserved

---

10. Venusberg (vē′ nəs bʉrg′): A legendary mountain in Germany where Venus, the Roman goddess of love, held court.

11. peak in Darien (der′ ē ən): The mountain on the Isthmus of Panama. From "On First Looking at Chapman's Homer" by English poet John Keats (1795–1821).

AT THE OPERA
Mary Stevenson Cassatt
Museum of Fine Arts, Boston

this utter immobility throughout the numbers from the *Flying Dutchman*, though her fingers worked mechanically upon her black dress, as though of themselves they were recalling the piano score they had once played. Poor old hands! They were stretched and pulled and twisted into mere tentacles to hold, and lift, and knead with; the palms unduly swollen, the fingers bent and knotted, on one of them a thin worn band that had once been a wedding ring. As I pressed and gently quieted one of those groping hands, I remembered, with quivering eyelids, their services for me in other days.

Soon after the tenor began the "Prize Song," I heard a quick-drawn breath, and turned to my aunt. Her eyes were closed, but the tears were glistening on her cheeks, and I think in a moment more they were in my eyes as well. It never really dies, then, the soul? It withers to the outward eye only, like that strange moss which can lie on a dusty shelf half a century and yet, if placed in water, grows green again. My aunt wept gently throughout the development and elaboration of the melody.

During the intermission before the second half of the concert, I questioned my aunt and found that the "Prize Song" was not new to her. Some years before there had drifted to the farm in Red Willow County a young German, a tramp cow puncher who had sung in the chorus at Bayreuth,[12] when he was a boy, along with the other peasant boys and girls. Of a Sunday morning he used to sit on his blue gingham-sheeted bed in the hands' bedroom, which opened off the kitchen, cleaning the leather of his boots and saddle, and singing the "Prize Song," while my aunt went about her work in the kitchen. She had hovered about him until she had prevailed upon him to join the country church, though his sole fitness for this step, so far as I could gather, lay in his boyish face and his possession of this divine melody. Shortly afterward he had gone to town on the Fourth of July, lost his money at a faro[13] table, ridden a saddled Texas steer on a bet, and disappeared with a fractured collarbone.

"Well, we have come to better things than the old *Trovatore* at any rate, Aunt Georgie?" I queried, with well-meant jocularity.

Her lip quivered and she hastily put her handkerchief up to her mouth. From behind it she murmured, "And you've been hearing this ever since you left me, Clark?" Her question was the gentlest and saddest of reproaches.

"But do you get it, Aunt Georgiana, the astonishing structure of it all?" I persisted.

"Who could?" she said, absently; "why should one?"

The second half of the program consisted of four numbers from the *Ring*. This was followed by the forest music from *Siegfried*[14] and the program closed with Siegfried's funeral march. My aunt wept quietly, but almost continuously. I was perplexed as to what measure of musical comprehension was left to her, to her who had heard nothing for so many years but the singing of gospel hymns in Methodist services at the square frame schoolhouse on Section Thirteen. I was unable to gauge how much of it had been dissolved in soapsuds, or worked into bread, or milked into the bottom of a pail.

The deluge of sound poured on and on; I never knew what she found in the shining current of it; I never knew how far it bore her, or past what happy islands, or under what skies. From the trembling of her face I could well believe that the *Siegfried* march, at least, carried her out where the myriad graves are, out into the gray, burying grounds of the sea; or into some world of death vaster yet, where, from the beginning of the world, hope has lain down with hope, and dream with dream and, renouncing, slept.

The concert was over; the people filed out of the hall chattering and laughing, glad to relax and find the living level again, but my kinswoman made no effort to rise. I spoke gently to her. She burst into tears and sobbed pleadingly, "I don't want to go, Clark, I don't want to go!"

I understood. For her, just outside the door of the concert hall, lay the black pond with the cattle-tracked bluffs, the tall, unpainted house, naked as a tower, with weather-curled boards; the crook-backed ash seedlings where the dishcloths hung to dry, the gaunt, moulting turkeys picking up refuse about the kitchen door.

---

12. Bayreuth (bī roit'): A city in Germany known for its annual Wagnerian music festivals.

13. faro (fer' ō): A gambling game in which players bet on the cards to be turned up from the top of the dealer's deck.

14. Siegfried (sēg' frēd): An opera based on the adventures of Siegfried, a legendary hero in medieval German literature.

RESPONDING TO THE SELECTION

Your Response

1. What do you think of Cather's depictions of Boston and Nebraska? Do you think that she is fair to her home state? Why or why not?
2. How do you feel about Aunt Georgiana? Do you admire her or pity her? Explain.
3. What do you think of Clark?

Recalling

4. (a) Why is Clark's Aunt Georgiana coming to visit? (b) Explain his reaction to the news of her visit.
5. (a) Why does Clark take Aunt Georgiana to the Wagner matinée? (b) Why does he grow doubtful that she will enjoy it?
6. Describe three ways in which Aunt Georgiana indulged her love of music while living on the frontier.

Interpreting

7. (a) What impression is conveyed through the physical descriptions of Red Willow County? (b) Contrast the impression of life in Red Willow County with life in Boston.
8. What does Aunt Georgiana mean when she comments, "Don't love it so well, Clark, or it may be taken from you"?
9. (a) Why does the opera have such a powerful effect on Aunt Georgiana? (b) In what way does the effect of the music on Aunt Georgiana in turn awaken Clark?

Applying

10. (a) How can environment shape character? (b) How can people shape their environment?

ANALYZING LITERATURE

Understanding Characterization

Characterization is the means by which an author reveals a character's personality. Because of Cather's use of a first-person narrator, much of what we learn about Aunt Georgiana comes from Clark's thoughts and feelings regarding her.

1. What is revealed about Aunt Georgiana through descriptions of her appearance?
2. What does Aunt Georgiana's reaction to the opera reveal about her personality?
3. What is revealed about Clark's personality through his thoughts and feelings regarding his aunt?
4. How does the fact that much of what we learn about Aunt Georgiana is revealed through Clark's thoughts and feelings shape our impressions of her?

THINKING AND WRITING

Supporting an Opinion

Review the freewriting assignment you completed earlier. Do you think music is a valuable component of daily life? Write a short essay for your teacher discussing whether or not music adds to the quality of life. In your prewriting, list evidence from daily life. Then, after organizing your evidence into an outline, write your essay using your evidence to support your argument. Use transitions to link your ideas, and vary your sentence structure. When you revise, make sure that you have included enough evidence to adequately support your argument.

LEARNING OPTIONS

1. **Writing.** For the most part, Clark cannot gauge the effect of the music on his aunt. He states that he "never knew what she found in the shining current of it;" he "never knew how far it bore her." Let Aunt Georgiana speak for herself. Write a diary entry in which you record her reactions to the Wagner matinée. Keep in mind that this is her first concert in thirty years.
2. **Cross-curricular Connection.** Together with several classmates, organize a Wagner matinée. Locate recordings of two or more of the operas by Wagner. Introduce and play the music for the class.
3. **Cross-curricular Connection.** At the beginning of the story, Clark describes how Aunt Georgiana and Uncle Howard took a homestead on the Nebraska frontier. Find out how the Homestead Act of 1862 opened the frontier for settlement. Does Cather present an accurate portrait of life on a homestead? Share your findings in a class discussion.

JACK LONDON

1876–1916

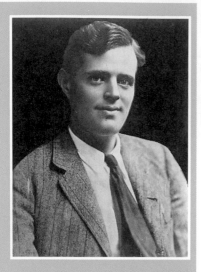

Jack London endured more hardships during the first twenty-one years of his life than most people experience in a lifetime. Yet he was able to learn from his experiences and use them as the inspiration for his successful career as a writer.

Born in San Francisco, London grew up in extreme poverty. At an early age, he left school to support himself through a variety of menial jobs. He worked as a paper boy, in bowling alleys, on ice wagons, and in canneries and mills. These jobs gave him a strong sympathy for the working class and a lasting dislike of drudgery. At the same time, he was constantly reading, borrowing books of adventure and travel from the public library. London also left San Francisco a number of times, sailing to Japan as part of a sealing expedition and participating in a protest march across the country with a group of unemployed men.

After being arrested for vagrancy near Buffalo, New York, London decided to educate himself and reshape his life. He quickly completed high school, then enrolled in the University of California. London remained in college for only one semester, however, before abandoning his studies and traveling to Alaska in search of gold.

Although he experienced no success as a miner, London's experiences in Alaska taught him about the human desire for wealth and power and about humankind's inability to control nature. Shortly after returning to California, London began transforming his Alaskan adventures into short stories and novels. In 1903 he earned national fame when he published the popular novel *The Call of the Wild*. He soon became the highest paid and most industrious writer in the country. During the course of his career, he produced more than fifty books and earned more than a million dollars. Though many of his works are no longer highly regarded by critics, several of his novels, including *The Call of the Wild (1903), The Sea-Wolf* (1904), and *White Fang* (1906), have become American classics.

London's friend Oliver Madox Huefer recalled that London "was the ideal yarnspinner—his spoken stories were even better than his written—and one reason why I think him likely to be numbered as among the writers of real mark was that he was perfectly unconscious of it. Like Peter Pan, he never grew up, and he lived in his own stories with such intensity that he ended by believing them himself."

Many of London's best short stories and novels depict a person's struggle for survival against the powerful forces of nature. For example, "To Build a Fire" tells the story of a man's fight to survive the harsh cold of the Alaskan winter.

GUIDE FOR INTERPRETING

To Build a Fire

Writers' Techniques

Conflict. Conflict, a struggle between two opposing forces or characters, plays a vital role in the plot development of a literary work. The events of a work are all related to the conflict as the plot develops. Frequently the conflict is resolved by the end of the work, though in many modern and contemporary works the conflict is left unresolved.

Conflict may be internal or external. An internal conflict is a struggle between conflicting thoughts and emotions within a character. For example, in "The Story of an Hour," Mrs. Mallard struggles between her desire for freedom and her grief at hearing of her husband's death. An external conflict is a struggle between a character and an outside force, such as another character, society, nature, or fate. For example, in *Moby-Dick* Ahab struggles against a great white whale, Moby-Dick.

Focus

Think of an incident in which you witnessed or were confronted with the tremendous power of nature. For example, you may have lived through a hurricane or tornado or experienced extremely hot or cold weather. Briefly describe your responses to this incident and how it shaped your impressions of nature.

Primary Source

The discovery in 1896 of a rich lode of gold in the Yukon led to the Klondike stampede of 1897–1898. Thousands of prospectors headed for the arctic cold of the North where they mined for gold in perpetually frozen ground.

Jack London was among the first of the stampeders. What made him join the Klondike gold rush? He once commented, "I had let career go hang and was on the adventure-path again in quest of fortune." Elsewhere he commented, "True, the new territory was mostly barren; but its several hundred thousand square miles of frigidity at least gave breathing space to those who else would have suffocated at home."

London's contemporary, writer Hamlin Garland, who also made the trip to the Klondike, probably reflected London's feelings when he made the following comments:

> I believed that I was about to see and take part in a most picturesque and impressive movement across the wilderness. I believed it to be the last march of the kind which could ever come in America, so rapidly were the wild places being settled up. . . . I wished to return to the wilderness also, to forget books and theories of art and social problems, and come again face to face with the great free spaces of woods and skies and streams.

To Build a Fire

Jack London

Day had broken cold and gray, exceedingly cold and gray, when the man turned aside from the main Yukon[1] trail and climbed the high earth-bank, where a dim and little-traveled trail led eastward through the fat spruce timberland. It was a steep bank, and he paused for breath at the top, excusing the act to himself by looking at his watch. It was nine o'clock. There was no sun nor hint of sun, though there was not a cloud in the sky. It was a clear day, and yet there seemed an intangible pall over the face of things, a subtle gloom that made the day dark, and that was due to the absence of sun. This fact did not worry the man. He was used to the lack of sun. It had been days since he had seen the sun, and he knew that

---

1. **Yukon** (yoo′ kän): Territory in northwestern Canada, east of Alaska. Also a river.

a few more days must pass before that cheerful orb, due south, would just peep above the skyline and dip immediately from view.

The man flung a look back along the way he had come. The Yukon lay a mile wide and hidden under three feet of ice. On top of this ice were as many feet of snow. It was all pure white, rolling in gentle undulations where the ice jams of the freeze-up had formed. North and south, as far as his eye could see, it was unbroken white, save for a dark hairline that curved and twisted from around the spruce-covered island to the south, and that curved and twisted away into the north, where it disappeared behind another spruce-covered island. This dark hairline was the trail—the main trail—that led south five hundred miles to the Chilcoot Pass, Dyea,[2] and salt water; and that led north seventy miles to Dawson, and still on to the north a thousand miles to Nulato,[3] and finally to St. Michael on Bering Sea, a thousand miles and half a thousand more.

But all this—the mysterious, far-reaching hairline trail, the absence of sun from the sky, the tremendous cold, and the strangeness and weirdness of it all—made no impression on the man. It was not because he was long used to it. He was a newcomer in the land, a *chechaquo*,[4] and this was his first winter. The trouble with him was that he was without imagination. He was quick and alert in the things of life, but only in the things, and not in the significances. Fifty degrees below zero meant eighty-odd degrees of frost. Such fact impressed him as being cold and uncomfortable, and that was all. It did not lead him to meditate upon his frailty as a creature of temperature, and upon man's frailty in general, able only to live within certain narrow limits of heat and cold; and from there on it did not lead him to the conjectural field of

immortality and man's place in the universe. Fifty degrees below zero stood for a bite of frost that hurt and that must be guarded against by the use of mittens, earflaps, warm moccasins, and thick socks. Fifty degrees below zero was to him just precisely fifty degrees below zero. That there should be anything more to it than that was a thought that never entered his head.

As he turned to go on, he spat speculatively. There was a sharp, explosive crackle that startled him. He spat again. And again, in the air, before it could fall to the snow, the spittle crackled. He knew that at fifty below spittle crackled on the snow, but this spittle had crackled in the air. Undoubtedly it was colder than fifty below—how much colder he did not know. But the temperature did not matter. He was bound for the old claim on the left fork of Henderson Creek, where the boys were already. They had come over across the divide from the Indian Creek country, while he had come the roundabout way to take a look at the possibilities of getting out logs in the spring from the islands in the Yukon. He would be in to camp by six o'clock; a bit after dark, it was true, but the boys would be there, a fire would be going, and a hot supper would be ready. As for lunch, he pressed his hand against the protruding bundle under his jacket. It was also under his shirt, wrapped up in a handkerchief and lying against the naked skin. It was the only way to keep the biscuits from freezing. He smiled agreeably to himself as he thought of those biscuits, each cut open and sopped in bacon grease, and each enclosing a generous slice of fried bacon.

He plunged in among the big spruce trees. The trail was faint. A foot of snow had fallen since the last sled had passed over, and he was glad he was without a sled, traveling light. In fact, he carried nothing but the lunch wrapped in the handkerchief. He was surprised, however, at the cold. It certainly was cold, he concluded, as he rubbed his numb nose and cheekbones with his mittened hand. He was a warm-whiskered

---

2. Dyea (dī′ ā): A former town in Alaska at the start of the Yukon trail.
3. Dawson and **Nulato:** Former goldmining villages in the Yukon.
4. *chechaquo* (che̊ chå′ kwō): Slang for newcomer.

man, but the hair on his face did not protect the high cheekbones and the eager nose that thrust itself aggressively into the frosty air.

At the man's heels trotted a dog, a big native husky, the proper wolf dog, gray-coated and without any visible or temperamental difference from its brother, the wild wolf. The animal was depressed by the tremendous cold. It knew that it was no time for traveling. Its instinct told it a truer tale than was told to the man by the man's judgment. In reality, it was not merely colder than fifty below zero; it was colder than sixty below, than seventy below. It was seventy-five below zero. Since the freezing point is thirty-two above zero, it meant that one hundred and seven degrees of frost obtained. The dog did not know anything about thermometers. Possibly in its brain there was no sharp consciousness of a condition of very cold such as was in the man's brain. But the brute had its instinct. It experienced a vague but menacing apprehension that subdued it and made it slink along at the man's heels, and that made it question eagerly every unwonted movement of the man as if expecting him to go into camp or to seek shelter somewhere and build a fire. The dog had learned fire, and it wanted fire, or else to burrow under the snow and cuddle its warmth away from the air.

The frozen moisture of its breathing had settled on its fur in a fine powder of frost, and especially were its jowls, muzzle, and eyelashes whitened by its crystalled breath. The man's red beard and mustache were likewise frosted, but more solidly, the deposit taking the form of ice and increasing with every warm, moist breath he exhaled. Also, the man was chewing tobacco, and the muzzle of ice held his lips so rigidly that he was unable to clear his chin when he expelled the juice. The result was that a crystal beard of the color and solidity of amber was increasing its length on his chin. If he fell down it would shatter itself, like glass, into brittle fragments. But he did not mind the appendage. It was the penalty all tobacco-chewers paid in that country, and he had been out before in two cold snaps. They had not been so cold as this, he knew, but by the spirit thermometer[5] at Sixty Mile he knew they had been registered at fifty below and at fifty-five.

He held on through the level stretch of woods for several miles, crossed a wide flat, and dropped down a bank to the frozen bed of a small stream. This was Henderson Creek, and he knew he was ten miles from the forks. He looked at his watch. It was ten o'clock. He was making four miles an hour, and he calculated that he would arrive at the forks at half past twelve. He decided to celebrate that event by eating his lunch there.

The dog dropped in again at his heels, with a tail drooping discouragement, as the man swung along the creek bed. The furrow of the old sled trail was plainly visible, but a dozen inches of snow covered the marks of the last runners. In a month no man had come up or down that silent creek. The man held steadily on. He was not much given to thinking, and just then particularly he had nothing to think about save that he would eat lunch at the forks and that at six o'clock he would be in camp with the boys. There was nobody to talk to; and, had there been, speech would have been impossible because of the ice-muzzle on his mouth. So he continued monotonously to chew tobacco and to increase the length of his amber beard.

Once in a while the thought reiterated itself that it was very cold and that he had never experienced such cold. As he walked along he rubbed his cheekbones and nose with the back of his mittened hand. He did this automatically, now and again changing hands. But rub as he would, the instant he stopped his cheekbones went numb, and the following instant the end of his nose went numb. He was sure to frost his cheeks; he knew that, and experienced a pang of regret that he had not devised a nose strap of the

---

5. spirit thermometer: A thermometer, containing alcohol, used in extreme cold.

sort Bud wore in cold snaps. Such a strap passed across the cheeks, as well, and saved them. But it didn't matter much, after all. What were frosted cheeks? A bit painful, that was all; they were never serious.

Empty as the man's mind was of thoughts, he was keenly observant, and he noticed the changes in the creek, the curves and bends and timber jams, and always he sharply noted where he placed his feet. Once, coming around a bend, he shied abruptly, like a startled horse, curved away from the place where he had been walking, and retreated several paces back along the trail. The creek he knew was frozen clear to the bottom—no creek could contain water in that arctic winter—but he knew also that there were springs that bubbled out from the hillsides and ran along under the snow and on top the ice of the creek. He knew that the coldest snaps never froze these springs, and he knew likewise their danger. They were traps. They hid pools of water under the snow that might be three inches deep, or three feet. Sometimes a skin of ice half an inch thick covered them, and in turn was covered by the snow. Sometimes there were alternate layers of water and ice skin, so that when one broke through he kept on breaking through for a while, sometimes wetting himself to the waist.

That was why he had shied in such panic. He had felt the give under his feet and heard the crackle of a snow-hidden ice skin. And to get his feet wet in such a temperature meant trouble and danger. At the very least it meant delay, for he would be forced to stop and build a fire, and under its protection to bare his feet while he dried his socks and moccasins. He stood and studied the creek bed and its banks, and decided that the flow of water came from the right. He reflected awhile, rubbing his nose and cheeks, then skirted to the left, stepping gingerly and testing the footing for each step. Once clear of the danger, he took a fresh chew of tobacco and swung along at his four-mile gait.

In the course of the next two hours he came upon several similar traps. Usually the snow above the hidden pools had a sunken, candied apppearance that advertised the danger. Once again, however, he had a close call; and once, suspecting danger, he compelled the dog to go on in front. The dog did not want to go. It hung back until the man shoved it forward, and then it went quickly across the white, unbroken surface. Suddenly it broke through, floundered to one side, and got away to firmer footing. It had wet its forefeet and legs, and almost immediately the water that clung to it turned to ice. It made quick efforts to lick the ice off its legs, then dropped down in the snow and began to bite out the ice that had formed between the toes. This was a matter of instinct. To permit the ice to remain would mean sore feet. It did not know this. It merely obeyed the mysterious prompting that arose from the deep crypts of its being. But the man knew, having achieved a judgment on the subject, and he removed the mitten from his right hand and helped tear out the ice particles. He did not expose his fingers more than a minute, and was astonished at the swift numbness that smote them. It certainly was cold. He pulled on the mitten hastily, and beat the hand savagely across his chest.

At twelve o'clock the day was at its brightest. Yet the sun was too far south on its winter journey to clear the horizon. The bulge of the earth intervened between it and Henderson Creek, where the man walked under a clear sky at noon and cast no shadow. At half-past twelve, to the minute, he arrived at the forks of the creek. He was pleased at the speed he had made. If he kept it up, he would certainly be with the boys by six. He unbuttoned his jacket and shirt and drew forth his lunch. The action consumed no more than a quarter of a minute, yet in that brief moment the numbness laid hold of the exposed fingers. He did not put the mitten on, but, instead, struck the fingers a dozen sharp smashes against his leg. Then he sat down on a snow-covered log to eat. The sting that followed upon the striking of his fingers against his leg ceased so quickly that he was startled. He had had no chance to take a bite of biscuit. He struck the fingers repeatedly and returned them to the mitten, baring the other hand for the purpose of eating. He tried to take a mouthful, but the ice muzzle prevented. He had forgotten to build a fire and thaw out. He chuckled at his foolishness, and as he chuckled he noted the numbness creeping into the exposed fingers. Also, he noted that the stinging which had first come to his toes when he sat down was already passing away. He wondered whether the toes were warm or numb. He moved them inside the moccasins and decided that they were numb.

He pulled the mitten on hurriedly and stood up. He was a bit frightened. He stamped up and down until the stinging returned into the feet. It certainly was cold, was his thought. That man from Sulphur Creek had spoken the truth when telling how cold it sometimes got in the country. And he had laughed at him at the time! That showed one must not be too sure of things. There was no mistake about it, it *was* cold. He strode up and down, stamping his feet and threshing his arms, until reassured by the returning warmth. Then he got out matches and proceeded to make a fire. From the undergrowth, where high water of the previous spring had lodged a supply of seasoned twigs, he got his firewood. Working carefully from a small beginning, he soon had a roaring fire, over which he thawed the ice from his face and in the protection of which he ate his biscuits. For the moment the cold of space was outwitted. The dog took satisfaction in the fire, stretching out close enough for warmth and far enough away to escape being singed.

When the man had finished, he filled his pipe and took his comfortable time over a smoke. Then he pulled on his mittens, settled the earflaps of his cap firmly about his ears, and took the creek trail up the left fork. The dog was disappointed and yearned back toward the fire. This man did not know cold. Possibly all the generations of his ancestry had been ignorant of cold, of real cold, of cold one hundred and seven degrees below freezing point. But the dog knew; all its ancestry knew, and it had inherited the knowledge. And it knew that it was not good to walk abroad in such fearful cold. It was the time to lie snug in a hole in the snow and wait for a curtain of cloud to be drawn across the face of outer space whence this cold came. On the other hand, there was no keen intimacy between the dog and the man. The one was the toil slave of the other, and the only caresses it had ever received were the caresses of the whiplash and of harsh and menacing throat sounds that threatened the whiplash. So the dog made no effort to communicate its apprehension to the man. It was not concerned in the welfare of the man; it was for its own sake that it yearned back toward the fire. But the man whistled, and spoke to it with the sound of whiplashes, and the dog swung in at the man's heels and followed after.

The man took a chew of tobacco and proceeded to start a new amber beard. Also, his moist breath quickly powdered with white his mustache, eyebrows, and lashes. There did not seem to be so many springs on the left fork of the Henderson, and for half an hour the man saw no signs of any. And then it happened. At a place where there were no signs, where the soft, unbroken snow seemed to advertise solidity beneath, the man broke through. It was not deep. He wet himself halfway to the knees before he floundered out to the firm crust.

He was angry, and cursed his luck aloud. He had hoped to get into camp with the boys at six o'clock, and this would delay him an hour, for he would have to build a fire and dry out his footgear. This was imperative at that low temperature—he knew that much; and he turned aside to the bank, which he climbed. On top, tangled in the underbrush about the trunks of several small spruce trees, was a high-water deposit of dry firewood—sticks and twigs, principally, but also larger portions of seasoned branches and fine, dry, last year's grasses. He threw down several large pieces on top of the snow. This served for a foundation and prevented the young flame from drowning itself in the snow it otherwise would melt. The flame he got by touching a match to a small shred of birch bark that he took from his pocket. This burned even more readily than paper. Placing it on the foundation, he fed the young flame with wisps of dry grass and with the tiniest dry twigs.

He worked slowly and carefully, keenly aware of his danger. Gradually, as the flame grew stronger, he increased the size of the twigs with which he fed it. He squatted in the snow, pulling the twigs out from their entanglement in the brush and feeding directly to the flame. He knew there must be no failure. When it is seventy-five below zero, a man must not fail in his first attempt to build a fire—that is, if his feet are wet. If his feet are dry, and he fails, he can run along the trail for half a mile and restore his circulation. But the circulation of wet and freezing feet cannot be restored by running when it is seventy-five below. No matter how fast he runs, the wet feet will freeze the harder.

All this the man knew. The old-timer on Sulphur Creek had told him about it the previous fall, and now he was appreciating the advice. Already all sensation had gone out of his feet. To build the fire he had been forced to remove his mittens, and the fingers had quickly gone numb. His pace of four miles an hour had kept his heart pumping blood to the surface of his body and to all the extremities. But the instant he stopped, the action of the pump eased down. The cold of space smote the unprotected tip of the planet, and he, being on that unprotected tip, received the full force of the blow. The blood of his body recoiled before it. The blood was alive, like the dog, and like the dog it wanted to hide away and cover itself up from the fearful cold. So long as he walked four miles an hour, he pumped that blood, willy-nilly, to the surface; but now it ebbed away and sank down into the recesses of his body. The extremities were the first to feel its absence. His wet feet froze the faster, and his exposed fingers numbed the faster, though they had not yet begun to freeze. Nose and cheeks were already freezing, while the skin of all his body chilled as it lost its blood.

But he was safe. Toes and nose and cheeks would be only touched by the frost, for the fire was beginning to burn with strength. He was feeding it with twigs the size of his finger. In another minute he would be able to feed it with branches the size of his wrist, and then he could remove his wet foot-gear, and, while it dried, he could keep his naked feet warm by the fire, rubbing them at first, of course, with snow. The fire was a success. He was safe. He remembered the advice of the old-timer on Sulphur Creek, and smiled. The old-timer had been very serious in laying down the law that no man must travel alone in the Klondike after fifty below. Well, here he was; he had had the accident; he was alone; and he had saved himself. Those old-timers were rather womanish, some of them, he thought. All a man had to do was to keep his head, and he was all right. Any man who was a man could travel alone. But it was surprising, the rapidity with which his cheeks and nose were freezing. And he had not thought his fingers could go lifeless in so short a time. Lifeless they were, for he could scarcely make them move together to grip a twig, and they seemed remote from his body and from him. When he touched a twig, he had to look and see whether or not he had hold of it. The wires were pretty well down between him and his finger ends.

All of which counted for little. There was the fire, snapping and crackling and promising life with every dancing flame. He started to untie his moccasins. They were coated with ice; the thick German socks were like sheaths of iron halfway to the knees; and the moccasin strings were like rods of steel all

To Build a Fire   495

twisted and knotted as by some conflagration. For a moment he tugged with his numb fingers, then, realizing the folly of it, he drew his sheath-knife.

But before he could cut the strings, it happened. It was his own fault or, rather, his mistake. He should not have built the fire under the spruce tree. He should have built it in the open. But it had been easier to pull the twigs from the brush and drop them directly on the fire. Now the tree under which he had done this carried a weight of snow on its boughs. No wind had blown for weeks, and each bough was fully freighted. Each time he had pulled a twig he had communicated a slight agitation to the tree—an imperceptible agitation, so far as he was concerned, but an agitation sufficient to bring about the disaster. High up in the tree one bough capsized its load of snow. This fell on the boughs beneath, capsizing them. This process continued, spreading out and involving the whole tree. It grew like an avalanche, and it descended without warning upon the man and the fire, and the fire was blotted out! Where it had burned was a mantle of fresh and disordered snow.

The man was shocked. It was as though he had just heard his own sentence of death. For a moment he sat and stared at the spot where the fire had been. Then he grew very calm. Perhaps the old-timer on Sulphur Creek was right. If he had only had a trail mate he would have been in no danger now. The trail mate could have built the fire. Well, it was up to him to build the fire over again, and this second time there must be no failure. Even if he succeeded, he would most likely lose some toes. His feet must be badly frozen by now, and there would be some time before the second fire was ready.

Such were his thoughts, but he did not sit and think them. He was busy all the time they were passing through his mind. He made a new foundation for a fire, this time in the open, where no treacherous tree could blot it out. Next, he gathered dry grasses and tiny twigs from the high-water flotsam. He could not bring his fingers together to pull them out, but he was able to gather them by the handful. In this way he got many rotten twigs and bits of green moss that were undesirable, but it was the best he could do. He worked methodically, even collecting an armful of the larger branches to be used later when the fire gathered strength. And all the while the dog sat and watched him, a certain yearning wistfulness in its eyes, for it looked upon him as the fire provider, and the fire was slow in coming.

When all was ready, the man reached in his pocket for a second piece of birch bark. He knew the bark was there, and, though he could not feel it with his fingers, he could hear its crisp rustling as he fumbled for it. Try as he would, he could not clutch hold of it. And all the time, in his consciousness, was the knowledge that each instant his feet were freezing. This thought tended to put him in a panic, but he fought against it and kept calm. He pulled on his mittens with his teeth, and threshed his arms back and forth, beating his hands with all his might against his sides. He did this sitting down, and he stood up to do it; and all the while the dog sat in the snow, its wolf brush of a tail curled around warmly over its forefeet, its sharp wolf ears pricked forward intently as it watched the man. And the man, as he beat and threshed with his arms and hands, felt a great surge of envy as he regarded the creature that was warm and secure in its natural covering.

After a time he was aware of the first faraway signals of sensation in his beaten fingers. The faint tingling grew stronger till it evolved into a stinging ache that was excruciating, but which the man hailed with satisfaction. He stripped the mitten from his right hand and fetched forth the birch bark. The exposed fingers were quickly going numb again. Next he brought out his bunch of sulphur matches. But the tremendous cold had already driven the life out of his fingers. In his effort to separate one match from the others, the whole bunch fell in the snow. He tried to pick it out of the snow, but failed. The dead fingers could neither touch nor clutch. He was very careful. He drove the thought of his freezing feet, and nose, and cheeks, out of his mind, devoting his whole soul to the matches. He watched, using the sense of vision in place of that of touch, and when he saw his fingers on each side the bunch, he closed them—that is, he willed to close them, for the wires were down, and the fingers did not obey. He pulled the mitten on the right hand, and beat it fiercely against his knee. Then, with both mittened hands, he scooped the bunch of matches, along with much snow, into his lap. Yet he was no better off.

After some manipulation he managed to get the bunch between the heels of his mittened hands. In this fashion he carried it to his mouth. The ice crackled and snapped when by a violent effort he opened his mouth. He drew the lower jaw in, curled the

upper lip out of the way, and scraped the bunch with his upper teeth in order to separate a match. He succeeded in getting one, which he dropped on his lap. He was no better off. He could not pick it up. Then he devised a way. He picked it up in his teeth and scratched it on his leg. Twenty times he scratched before he succeeded in lighting it. As it flamed he held it with his teeth to the birch bark. But the burning brimstone went up his nostrils and into his lungs, causing him to cough spasmodically. The match fell into the snow and went out.

The old-timer on Sulphur Creek was right, he thought in the moment of controlled despair that ensued: after fifty below, a man should travel with a partner. He beat his hands, but failed in exciting any sensation. Suddenly he bared both hands, removing the mittens with his teeth. He caught the whole bunch between the heels of his hands. His arm muscles not being frozen enabled him to press the hand heels tightly against the matches. Then he scratched the bunch along his leg. It flared into flame, seventy sulphur matches at once! There was no wind to blow them out. He kept his head to one side to escape the strangling fumes, and held the blazing bunch to the birch bark. As he so held it, he became aware of sensation in his hand. His flesh was burning. He could smell it. Deep down below the surface he could feel it. The sensation developed into pain that grew acute. And still he endured it, holding the flame of the matches clumsily to the bark that would not light readily because his own burning hands were in the way, absorbing most of the flame.

At last, when he could endure no more, he jerked his hands apart. The blazing matches fell sizzling into the snow, but the birch bark was alight. He began laying dry grasses and the tiniest twigs on the flame. He could not pick and choose, for he had to lift the fuel between the heels of his hands. Small pieces of rotten wood and green moss clung to the twigs, and he bit them off as well as he could with his teeth. He cherished the flame carefully and awkwardly. It meant life, and it must not perish. The withdrawal of blood from the surface of his body now made him begin to shiver, and he grew more awkward. A large piece of green moss fell squarely on the little fire. He tried to poke it out with his fingers, but his shivering frame made him poke too far, and he disrupted the nucleus of the little fire, the burning grasses and tiny twigs separating and scattering. He tried to poke them together again, but in spite of the tenseness of the effort, his shivering got away with him, and the twigs were hopelessly scattered. Each twig gushed a puff of smoke and went out. The fire provider had failed. As he looked apathetically about him, his eyes chanced on the dog, sitting across the ruins of the fire from him, in the snow, making restless, hunching movements, slightly lifting one forefoot and then the other, shifting its weight back and forth on them with wistful eagerness.

The sight of the dog put a wild idea into his head. He remembered the tale of the man, caught in a blizzard, who killed a steer and crawled inside the carcass, and so was saved. He would kill the dog and bury his hands in the warm body until the numbness went out of them. Then he could build another fire. He spoke to the dog, calling it to him; but in his voice was a strange note of fear that frightened the animal, who had never known the man to speak in such way before. Something was the matter, and its suspicious nature sensed danger—it knew not what danger, but somewhere, somehow, in its brain arose an apprehension of the man. It flattened its ears down at the sound of the man's voice, and its restless, hunching movements and the liftings and shiftings of its forefeet became more pronounced; but it would not come to the man. He got on his hand and knees and crawled toward the dog. This unusual posture again excited suspicion, and the animal sidled mincingly away.

The man sat up in the snow for a moment and struggled for calmness. Then he pulled on his mittens, by means of his teeth, and got upon his feet. He glanced down at first in order to assure himself that he was really standing up, for the absence of sensation in his feet left him unrelated to the earth. His erect position in itself started to drive the webs of suspicion from the dog's mind; and when he spoke peremptorily, with the sound of whiplashes in his voice, the dog rendered its customary allegiance and came to him. As it came within reaching distance, the man lost his control. His arms flashed out to the dog, and he experienced genuine surprise when he discovered that his hands could not clutch, that there was neither bend nor feeling in the fingers. He had forgotten for the moment that they were frozen and that they were freezing more and more. All this happened quickly, and before the animal could get away, he encircled its body with his arms. He sat down in the snow, and in this fashion held the dog, while it snarled and whined and struggled.

But it was all he could do, hold its body encircled in his arms and sit there. He realized that he could not kill the dog. There was no way to do it. With his helpess hands he could neither draw nor hold his sheath-knife nor throttle the animal. He released it, and it plunged wildly away, with tail between its legs, and still snarling. It halted forty feet away and surveyed him curiously, with ears sharply pricked forward. The man looked down at his hands in order to locate them, and found them hanging on the ends of his arms. It struck him as curious that one should have to use his eyes in order to find out where his hands were. He began threshing his arms back and forth, beating the mittened hands against his sides. He did this for five minutes, violently, and his heart pumped enough blood up to the surface to put a stop to his shivering. But no sensation was aroused in the hands. He had an impression that they hung like weights on the ends of his arms, but when he tried to run the impression down, he could not find it.

A certain fear of death, dull and oppressive, came to him. This fear quickly became poignant as he realized that it was no longer a mere matter of freezing his fingers and toes, or of losing his hands and feet, but that it was a matter of life and death with the chances against him. This threw him into a panic, and he turned and ran up the creek-bed along the old, dim trail. The dog joined in behind and kept up with him. He ran blindly, without intention, in fear such as he had never known in his life. Slowly, as he plowed and floundered through the snow, he began to see things again—the banks of the creek, the old timber jams, the leafless aspens, and the sky. The running made him feel better. He did not shiver. Maybe, if he ran on, his feet would thaw out; and, anyway, if he ran far enough, he would reach camp and the boys. Without doubt he would lose some fingers and toes and some of his face; but the boys would take care of him, and save the rest of him when he got there. And at the same time there was another thought in his mind that said he would never get to the camp and the boys; that it was too many miles away, that the freezing had too great a start on him, and that he would soon be stiff and dead. This thought he kept in the background and refused to consider. Sometimes it pushed itself forward and demanded to be heard, but he thrust it back and strove to think of other things.

It struck him as curious that he could run at all on feet so frozen that he could not feel them when they struck the earth and took the weight of his body. He seemed to himself to skim along above the surface, and to have no connection with the earth. Somewhere he had once seen a winged Mercury,[6] and he wondered if Mercury felt as he felt when skimming over the earth.

His theory of running until he reached camp and the boys had one flaw in it: he lacked the endurance. Several times he stumbled, and finally he tottered, crumpled up, and fell. When he tried to rise, he failed.

---

6. Mercury: From Roman mythology, the wing-footed messenger of the gods.

He must sit and rest, he decided, and next time he would merely walk and keep on going. As he sat and regained his breath, he noted that he was feeling quite warm and comfortable. He was not shivering, and it even seemed that a warm glow had come to his chest and trunk. And yet, when he touched his nose or cheeks, there was no sensation. Running would not thaw them out. Nor would it thaw out his hands and feet. Then the thought came to him that the frozen portions of his body must be extending. He tried to keep this thought down, to forget it, to think of something else; he was aware of the panicky feeling that it caused, and he was afraid of the panic. But the thought asserted itself, and persisted, until it produced a vision of his body totally frozen. This was too much, and he made another wild run along the trail. Once he slowed down to a walk, but the thought of the freezing extending itself made him run again.

And all the time the dog ran with him, at his heels. When he fell down a second time, it curled its tail over its forefeet and sat in front of him, facing him, curiously eager and intent. The warmth and security of the animal angered him, and he cursed it till it flattened down its ears appeasingly. This time the shivering came more quickly upon the man. He was losing in his battle with the frost. It was creeping into his body from all sides. The thought of it drove him on, but he ran no more than a hundred feet, when he staggered and pitched headlong. It was his last panic. When he had recovered his breath and control, he sat up and entertained in his mind the conception of meeting death with dignity. However, the conception did not come to him in such terms. His idea of it was that he had been making a fool of himself, running around like a chicken with its head cut off—such was the simile that occurred to him. Well, he was bound to freeze anyway, and he might as well take it decently. With this new-found peace of mind came the first glimmerings of drowsiness. A

good idea, he thought, to sleep off to death. It was like taking an anaesthetic. Freezing was not so bad as people thought. There were lots worse ways to die.

He pictured the boys finding his body next day. Suddenly he found himself with them, coming along the trail and looking for himself. And, still with them, he came around a turn in the trail and found himself lying in the snow. He did not belong with himself any more, for even then he was out of himself; standing with the boys and looking at himself in the snow. It certainly was cold, was his thought. When he got back to the States he could tell the folks what real cold was. He drifted on from this to a vision of the old-timer on Sulphur Creek. He could see him quite clearly, warm and comfortable, and smoking a pipe.

"You were right, old hoss; you were right," the man mumbled to the old-timer of Sulphur Creek.

Then the man drowsed off into what seemed to him the most comfortable and satisfying sleep he had ever known. The dog sat facing him and waiting. The brief day drew to a close in a long, slow twilight. There were no signs of a fire to be made, and, besides, never in the dog's experience had it known a man to sit like that in the snow and make no fire. As the twilight drew on, its eager yearning for the fire mastered it, and with a great lifting and shifting of forefeet, it whined softly, then flattened its ears down in anticipation of being chidden[7] by the man. But the man remained silent. Later, the dog whined loudly. And still later it crept close to the man and caught the scent of death. This made the animal bristle and back away. A little longer it delayed, howling under the stars that leaped and danced and shone brightly in the cold sky. Then it turned and trotted up the trail in the direction of the camp it knew, where were the other food providers and fire providers.

---

7. chidden: Scolded.

RESPONDING TO THE SELECTION

Your Response

1. How did you feel after reading the first paragraph? Did your feelings change at all during the course of the story? Why or why not?
2. Which character from the story would you prefer as a traveling companion, the man or the dog? Explain.

Recalling

3. Why does the tremendous cold "make no impression" on the man?
4. How is the dog's awareness of the cold different from the man's awareness?
5. (a) What "traps" is the man careful to avoid? (b) How does he get wet?
6. (a) What careless mistake does the man make when he tries to build a fire to thaw out his feet? (b) What prevents him from rebuilding the fire?
7. (a) What happens to the man at the end of the story? (b) How does the dog react?

Interpreting

8. (a) How would you characterize the man's relationship with his dog? (b) How is the man's relationship with nature different from the dog's relationship with nature? (c) Which is better equipped to survive in nature? Explain your answer.
9. How do the man's recollections of his conversation with the old man from Sulphur Creek foreshadow the end of the story?
10. At one point in the story, the man gets angry and curses his fate. Do you think the outcome of the story is due to fate or to something within the man? Explain your answer.
11. Why do you think London chose not to give the man in this story a name?
12. What does the story suggest about humanity's place in nature?

Applying

13. Many of the provisions for coping with the cold that exist today did not exist when the story was written. Explain whether the outcome of the story might be different if it were set today.

ANALYZING LITERATURE

Recognizing Types of Conflict

In literature **conflict** refers to a struggle between opposing forces or characters. Conflict may be internal, occurring within a character's mind, or external, occurring between two characters, between a character and society, between a character and nature, or between a character and fate.

1. What type of conflict is central to the plot of "To Build a Fire"?
2. How does the conflict intensify as the plot develops?
3. How is the conflict resolved?

CRITICAL THINKING AND READING

Relating Conflict to Theme

The conflict of a literary work is often closely related to the theme, or general idea. For example, the **theme** of a story in which the **conflict** is between a character and fate might be that people are unable to control their own destinies.

1. What do you think is the theme of "To Build a Fire"?
2. How is the story's conflict related to this theme?

THINKING AND WRITING

Writing About Conflict and Theme

Write an essay in which you discuss the relationship between the conflict and the theme of "To Build a Fire." Review your answers from the Analyzing Literature and Critical Thinking and Reading activities. Then develop a thesis statement and begin writing your essay. Use evidence from the story to support your argument. When you revise, make sure you have varied the length and structure of your sentences. Proofread your essay and prepare a final draft.

LEARNING OPTION

Speaking and Listening. Is dog man's best friend? Consider the relationship between the man and the dog in the story, and take a stand. Be prepared to defend your view in an informal class debate.

STEPHEN CRANE

1871–1900

Stephen Crane died of tuberculosis at the age of twenty-eight. Yet during his short life he established himself as one of the leaders of the Naturalist movement and one of the most highly regarded writers of his time.

The youngest of fourteen children, Crane was born and reared in New Jersey. After briefly attending Syracuse University, where he spent more energy playing baseball than studying, he moved to New York City and found work as a journalist. Inspired by his observations and experiences as a newspaper writer, Crane completed his first novel, *Maggie: A Girl of the Streets* (1893), which he had begun to write while at Syracuse. A grimly realistic depiction of life in the slums of New York City, the novel was so frank and shocking that Crane was unable to find a publisher. He eventually borrowed money and published it at his own expense, but despite praise from a number of writers and critics, the book did not sell.

Crane continued to write, however, and in 1895 he published his second novel, *The Red Badge of Courage: An Episode of the American Civil War*. A psychological exploration of a young soldier's reactions under fire, the novel was a success and earned Crane international acclaim at the age of twenty-four. Readers and critics applauded the book for its convincing descriptions of the young soldier's thoughts and feelings and its realistic depictions of Civil War battles. Yet Crane had neither experienced nor observed military combat. Before writing the novel, however, he had interviewed Civil War veterans and had studied photographs, battle plans, and biographical accounts of military leaders.

Crane soon had the opportunity to view the realities of war first-hand, when he served as a newspaper correspondent during the Greco-Turkish War in 1897 and the Spanish-American War in 1898. His observations convinced him of the accuracy of his depiction of war in *The Red Badge of Courage* and provided material for *War Is Kind* (1899), his second collection of poetry. Crane's experiences as a correspondent also took their toll on his health. During the final months of his life, his physical condition rapidly deteriorated, and he died in Germany shortly after the turn of the century.

Like other Naturalists, Crane depicted characters who were manipulated by forces of society and nature that were beyond their understanding and control. In his story "The Open Boat," for example, the characters are trapped in a tiny lifeboat, floating helplessly in the vast, mysterious, and tremendously powerful Atlantic Ocean. Inspired by a similar real-life experience, the story is one of the most vivid expressions of Crane's Naturalist beliefs.

GUIDE FOR INTERPRETING

The Open Boat

Realism. Realism was a literary movement that emerged as a reaction against Romanticism. Unlike the Romantic writers, who often portrayed improbable situations and events, the Realists sought to depict real life as faithfully and accurately as possible. Generally, they attempted to present "a slice of life" by delving deeply into the everyday realities of a small group of people or a small portion of the world. The Realists focused on the lives of ordinary people, often writing about lower-class and middle-class characters. In depicting the lives of people faced with poverty and other hardships, the Realists confronted many of the harsh realities of American society, often presenting pessimistic visions of the world dramatically different from the optimistic visions that dominated Romantic literature.

Naturalism. Naturalism, another major literary movement of the late nineteenth and early twentieth centuries, grew out of the Realism movement. Like the Realists, the Naturalists focused on the lives of ordinary people and attempted to depict life truthfully and accurately. Yet, while the Realists searched for the truths of existence by delving beneath the surface of everyday life, the Naturalists already possessed a well-defined, scientific view of the universe that they imposed on their works. The Naturalists believed that a person's fate is determined by environment, heredity, and chance. As a result, Naturalist writers frequently depicted characters whose lives were shaped by forces of nature or society they could not understand or control. However, despite their underlying powerlessness, the characters in Naturalist works generally conduct themselves with strength and dignity in the face of adversity, thereby affirming the significance of their existence. For example, in Crane's novel *The Red Badge of Courage,* a young soldier's experiences in a war he can neither comprehend nor control make him aware of his courage and inner strength and in doing so give his life new meaning.

Focus

Try to imagine what it would be like to be placed in a life-threatening situation, such as being stranded on a lifeboat in the middle of the ocean. Then freewrite about the situation, keeping the following questions in mind: How do you think you might react? What aspects of your personality might the situation bring out? How do you think the situation would affect your interactions with other people? If you survived the situation, how do you think it might alter the way you live your life?

The Open Boat

Stephen Crane

**A TALE INTENDED TO BE AFTER THE FACT. BEING THE
EXPERIENCE OF FOUR MEN FROM THE SUNK STEAMER *COMMODORE***

I

None of them knew the color of the sky. Their eyes glanced level, and were fastened upon the waves that swept toward them. These waves were of the hue of slate, save for the tops, which were of foaming white, and all of the men knew the colors of the sea. The horizon narrowed and widened, and dipped and rose, and at all times its edge was jagged with waves that seemed thrust up in points like rocks.

Many a man ought to have a bathtub larger than the boat which here rode upon the sea. These waves were most wrongfully and barbarously abrupt and tall, and each froth top was a problem in small boat navigation.

The cook squatted in the bottom and looked with both eyes at the six inches of gunwale which separated him from the ocean. His sleeves were rolled over his fat forearms, and the two flaps of his unbuttoned vest dangled as he bent to bail out the boat. Often he said: "Gawd! That was a narrow clip." As he remarked it he invariably gazed eastward over the broken sea.

The oiler,[1] steering with one of the two oars in the boat, sometimes raised himself suddenly to keep clear of water that swirled in over the stern. It was a thin little oar and it seemed often ready to snap.

The correspondent, pulling at the other oar, watched the waves and wondered why he was there.

The injured captain, lying in the bow, was at this time buried in that profound dejection and indifference which comes, temporarily at least, to even the bravest and most enduring when, willy nilly, the firm fails, the army loses, the ship goes down. The mind of the master of a vessel is rooted deep in the timbers of her, though he command for a day or a decade, and this captain had on him the stern impression of a scene in the grays of dawn of seven turned faces, and later a stump of a topmast with a white ball on it that slashed to and fro at the waves, went low and lower, and down. Thereafter there was something strange in his voice. Although steady, it was deep with mourning, and of a quality beyond oration or tears.

"Keep 'er a little more south, Billie," said he.

" 'A little more south,' sir," said the oiler in the stern.

A seat in this boat was not unlike a seat upon a bucking bronco, and, by the same token, a bronco is not much smaller. The craft pranced and reared, and plunged like an an-

---

1. oiler: The person responsible for oiling machinery in the engine room of a ship.

imal. As each wave came, and she rose for it, she seemed like a horse making at a fence outrageously high. The manner of her scramble over these walls of water is a mystic thing, and, moveover, at the top of them were ordinarily these problems in white water, the foam racing down from the summit of each wave, requiring a new leap, and a leap from the air. Then, after scornfully bumping a crest, she would slide, and race, and splash down a long incline and arrive bobbing and nodding in front of the next menace.

A singular disadvantage of the sea lies in the fact that after successfully surmounting one wave you discover that there is another behind it just as important and just as nervously anxious to do something effective in

BENARES
Marshall Johnson
Peabody Museum of Salem

the way of swamping boats. In a ten-foot dinghy one can get an idea of the resources of the sea in the line of waves that is not probable to the average experience, which is never at sea in a dinghy. As each slaty wall of water approached, it shut all else from the view of the men in the boat, and it was not difficult to imagine that this particular wave was the final outburst of the ocean, the last effort of the grim water. There was a terrible grace in the move of the waves, and they came in silence, save for the snarling of the crests.

In the wan light, the faces of the men must have been gray. Their eyes must have glinted in strange ways as they gazed steadily astern. Viewed from a balcony, the whole thing would doubtlessly have been weirdly picturesque. But the men in the boat had no time to see it, and if they had had leisure there were other things to occupy their minds. The sun swung steadily up the sky, and they knew it was broad day because the color of the sea changed from slate to emerald-green, streaked with amber lights, and the foam was like tumbling snow. The process of the breaking day was unknown to them. They were aware only of this effect upon the color of the waves that rolled toward them.

In disjointed sentences the cook and the correspondent argued as to the difference between a lifesaving station and a house of refuge. The cook had said: "There's a house of refuge just north of the Mosquito Inlet Light, and as soon as they see us, they'll come off in their boat and pick us up."

"As soon as who see us?" said the correspondent.

"The crew," said the cook.

"Houses of refuge don't have crews," said the correspondent. "As I understand them, they are only places where clothes and grub are stored for the benefit of shipwrecked people. They don't carry crews."

"Oh, yes, they do," said the cook.

"No, they don't," said the correspondent.

"Well, we're not there yet, anyhow," said the oiler, in the stern.

"Well," said the cook, "perhaps it's not a house of refuge that I'm thinking of as being near Mosquito Inlet Light. Perhaps it's a life-saving station."

"We're not there yet," said the oiler, in the stern.

II

As the boat bounced from the top of each wave, the wind tore through the hair of the hatless men, and as the craft plopped her stern down again the spray slashed past them. The crest of each of these waves was a hill, from the top of which the men surveyed, for a moment, a broad tumultuous expanse, shining and wind-riven. It was probably splendid. It was probably glorious, this play of the free sea, wild with lights of emerald and white and amber.

"Bully good thing it's an on-shore wind," said the cook. "If not, where would we be? Wouldn't have a show."

"That's right," said the correspondent.

The busy oiler nodded his assent.

Then the captain, in the bow, chuckled in a way that expressed humor, contempt, tragedy, all in one. "Do you think we've got much of a show, now, boys?" said he.

Whereupon the three were silent, save for a trifle of hemming and hawing. To express any particular optimism at this time they felt to be childish and stupid, but they all doubtless possessed this sense of the situation in their mind. A young man thinks doggedly at such times. On the other hand, the ethics of their condition was decidedly against any open suggestion of hopelessness. So they were silent.

"Oh, well," said the captain, soothing his children, "we'll get ashore all right."

But there was that in his tone which

made them think, so the oiler quoth: "Yes! If this wind holds!"

The cook was bailing. "Yes! If we don't catch hell in the surf."

Canton flannel[2] gulls flew near and far. Sometimes they sat down on the sea, near patches of brown seaweed that rolled over the waves with a movement like carpets on a line in a gale. The birds sat comfortably in groups, and they were envied by some in the dinghy, for the wrath of the sea was no more to them than it was to a covey of prairie chickens a thousand miles inland. Often they came very close and stared at the men with black beadlike eyes. At these times they were uncanny and sinister in their unblinking scrutiny, and the men hooted angrily at them, telling them to be gone. One came, and evidently decided to alight on the top of the captain's head. The bird flew parallel to the boat and did not circle, but made short sidelong jumps in the air in chicken-fashion. His black eyes were wistfully fixed upon the captain's head. "Ugly brute," said the oiler to the bird. "You look as if you were made with a jackknife." The cook and the correspondent swore darkly at the creature. The captain naturally wished to knock it away with the end of the heavy painter,[3] but he did not dare do it, because anything resembling an emphatic gesture would have capsized this freighted boat, and so with his open hand, the captain gently and carefully waved the gull away. After it had been discouraged from the pursuit the captain breathed easier on account of his hair, and others breathed easier because the bird struck their minds at this time as being somehow gruesome and ominous.

In the meantime the oiler and the correspondent rowed. And also they rowed.

They sat together in the same seat, and each rowed an oar. Then the oiler took both oars; then the correspondent took both oars;

then the oiler; then the correspondent. They rowed and they rowed. The very ticklish part of the business was when the time came for the reclining one in the stern to take his turn at the oars. By the very last star of truth, it is easier to steal eggs from under a hen than it was to change seats in the dinghy. First the man in the stern slid his hand along the thwart and moved with care, as if he were of Sèvres.[4] Then the man in the rowing seat slid his hand along the other thwart. It was all done with the most extraordinary care. As the two sidled past each other, the whole party kept watchful eyes on the coming wave, and the captain cried: "Look out now! Steady there!"

The brown mats of seaweed that appeared from time to time were like islands, bits of earth. They were traveling, apparently, neither one way nor the other. They were, to all intents, stationary. They informed the men in the boat that it was making progress slowly toward the land.

The captain, rearing cautiously in the bow, after the dinghy soared on a great swell, said that he had seen the lighthouse at Mosquito Inlet. Presently the cook remarked that he had seen it. The correspondent was at the oars, then, and for some reason he too wished to look at the lighthouse, but his back was toward the far shore and the waves were important, and for some time he could not seize an opportunity to turn his head. But at last there came a wave more gentle than the others, and when at the crest of it he swiftly scoured the western horizon.

"See it?" said the captain.

"No," said the correspondent, slowly, "I didn't see anything."

"Look again," said the captain. He pointed. "It's exactly in that direction."

At the top of another wave, the correspondent did as he was bid, and this time

---

2. Canton flannel: A thick cotton fabric.
3. painter: A rope attached to the bow of a boat.

4. Sèvres (sev′ rə): A type of fine French porcelain.

his eyes chanced on a small still thing on the edge of the swaying horizon. It was precisely like the point of a pin. It took an anxious eye to find a lighthouse so tiny.

"Think we'll make it, Captain?"

"If this wind holds and the boat don't swamp, we can't do much else," said the captain.

The little boat, lifted by each towering sea, and splashed viciously by the crests, made progress that in the absence of sea-weed was not apparent to those in her. She seemed just a wee thing wallowing, miraculously, top-up, at the mercy of five oceans. Occasionally, a great spread of water, like white flames, swarmed into her.

"Bail her, cook," said the captain, serenely.

"All right, Captain," said the cheerful cook.

III

It would be difficult to describe the subtle brotherhood of men that was here established on the seas. No one said that it was so. No one mentioned it. But it dwelt in the boat, and each man felt it warm him. They were a captain, an oiler, a cook, and a correspondent, and they were friends, friends in a more curiously iron-bound degree than may be common. The hurt captain, lying against the water jar in the bow, spoke always in a low voice and calmly, but he could never command a more ready and swiftly obedient crew than the motley three of the dinghy. It was more than a mere recognition of what was best for the common safety. There was surely in it a quality that was personal and heartfelt. And after this devotion to the commander of the boat there was this comradeship that the correspondent, for instance, who had been taught to be cynical of men, knew even at the time was the best experience of his life. But no one said that it was so. No one mentioned it.

"I wish we had a sail," remarked the captain. "We might try my overcoat on the end of an oar and give you two boys a chance to rest." So the cook and the correspondent held the mast and spread wide the overcoat. The oiler steered, and the little boat made good way with her new rig. Sometimes the oiler had to scull sharply to keep a sea from breaking into the boat, but otherwise sailing was a success.

Meanwhile the lighthouse had been growing slowly larger. It had now almost assumed color, and appeared like a little gray shadow on the sky. The man at the oars could not be prevented from turning his head rather often to try for a glimpse of this little gray shadow.

At last, from the top of each wave the men in the tossing boat could see land. Even as the lighthouse was an upright shadow on the sky, this land seemed but a long black shadow on the sea. It certainly was thinner than paper. "We must be about opposite New Smyrna,"[5] said the cook, who had coasted this shore often in schooners. "Captain, by the way, I believe they abandoned that life-saving station there about a year ago."

"Did they?" said the captain.

The wind slowly died away. The cook and the correspondent were not now obliged to slave in order to hold high the oar. But the waves continued their old impetuous swooping at the dinghy, and the little craft, no longer under way, struggled woundily over them. The oiler or the correspondent took the oars again.

Shipwrecks are apropos of nothing. If men could only train for them and have them occur when the men had reached pink condition, there would be less drowning at sea. Of the four in the dinghy none had slept any time worth mentioning for two days and two nights previous to embarking in the dinghy, and in the excitement of clambering

---

5. New Smyrna: New Smyrna Beach, a town on the Florida coast, about fifteen miles south of Daytona Beach.

about the deck of a foundering ship they had also forgotten to eat heartily.

For these reasons, and for others, neither the oiler nor the correspondent was fond of rowing at the time. The correspondent wondered ingenuously how in the name of all that was sane could there be people who thought it amusing to row a boat. It was not an amusement; it was a diabolical punishment, and even a genius of mental aberrations could never conclude that it was anything but a horror to the muscles and a crime against the back. He mentioned to the boat in general how the amusement of rowing struck him, and the weary-faced oiler smiled in full sympathy. Previously to the foundering, by the way, the oiler had worked double watch in the engine room of the ship.

"Take her easy, now, boys," said the captain. "Don't spend yourselves. If we have to run a surf you'll need all your strength, because we'll sure have to swim for it. Take your time."

Slowly the land arose from the sea. From a black line it became a line of black and a line of white—trees and sand. Finally, the captain said that he could make out a house on the shore. "That's the house of refuge, sure," said the cook. "They'll see us before long, and come out after us."

The distant lighthouse reared high. "The keeper ought to be able to make us out now, if he's looking through a glass," said the captain. "He'll notify the lifesaving people."

"None of those other boats could have got ashore to give word of the wreck," said the oiler, in a low voice. "Else the lifeboat would be out hunting us."

Slowly and beautifully the land loomed out of the sea. The wind came again. It had veered from the northeast to the southeast. Finally, a new sound struck the ears of the men in the boat. It was the low thunder of the surf on the shore. "We'll never be able to make the lighthouse now," said the captain. "Swing her head a little more north, Billie."

" 'A little more north,' sir," said the oiler.

Whereupon the little boat turned her nose once more down the wind, and all but the oarsman watched the shore grow. Under the influence of this expansion doubt and direful apprehension was leaving the minds of the men. The management of the boat was still most absorbing, but it could not prevent a quiet cheerfulness. In an hour, perhaps, they would be ashore.

Their backbones had become thoroughly used to balancing in the boat and they now rode this wild colt of a dinghy like circus men. The correspondent thought that he had been drenched to the skin, but happening to feel in the top pocket of his coat, he found therein eight cigars. Four of them were soaked with sea water; four were perfectly scatheless. After a search, somebody produced three dry matches, and thereupon the four waifs rode impudently in their little boat, and with an assurance of an impending rescue shining in their eyes, puffed at the big cigars and judged well and ill of all men. Everybody took a drink of water.

IV

"Cook," remarked the captain, "there don't seem to be any signs of life about your house of refuge."

"No," replied the cook. "Funny they don't see us!"

A broad stretch of lowly coast lay before the eyes of the men. It was of dunes topped with dark vegetation. The roar of the surf was plain, and sometimes they could see the white lip of a wave as it spun up the beach. A tiny house was blocked out black upon the sky. Southward, the slim lighthouse lifted its little gray length.

Tide, wind, and waves were swinging the dinghy northward. "Funny they don't see us," said the men.

The surf's roar was here dulled, but its tone was, nevertheless, thunderous and mighty. As the boat swam over the great rollers, the men sat listening to this roar. "We'll swamp sure," said everybody.

It is fair to say here that there was not a lifesaving station within twenty miles in either direction, but the men did not know this fact and in consequence they made dark and opprobrious remarks concerning the eyesight of the nation's lifesavers. Four scowling men sat in the dinghy and surpassed records in the invention of epithets.

"Funny they don't see us."

The light-heartedness of a former time had completely faded. To their sharpened minds it was easy to conjure pictures of all kinds of incompetency and blindness and, indeed, cowardice. There was the shore of the populous land, and it was bitter and bitter to them that from it came no sign.

"Well," said the captain, ultimately, "I suppose we'll have to make a try for ourselves. If we stay out here too long, we'll none of us have strength left to swim after the boat swamps."

And so the oiler, who was at the oars, turned the boat straight for the shore. There was a sudden tightening of muscles. There was some thinking.

"If we don't all get shore—" said the captain. "If we don't all get ashore, I suppose you fellows know where to send news of my finish?"

They then briefly exchanged some addresses and admonitions. As for the reflections of the men, there was a great deal of rage in them. Perchance they might be formulated thus: "If I am going to be drowned—if I am going to be drowned—if I am going to be drowned, why, in the name of the seven mad gods[6] who rule the sea, was I allowed to come thus far and contemplate sand and trees? Was I brought here merely to have my nose dragged away as I was about to nibble the sacred cheese of life? It is preposterous. If this old ninny-woman, Fate, cannot do better than this, she should be deprived of the management of men's fortunes. She is an old hen who knows not her intention. If she has decided to drown me, why did she not do it in the beginning and save me all this trouble. The whole affair is absurd. . . . But, no, she cannot mean to drown me. She dare not drown me. She cannot drown me. Not after all this work." Afterward the man might have had an impulse to shake his fist at the clouds. "Just you drown me, now, and then hear what I call you!"

The billows that came at this time were more formidable. They seemed always just about to break and roll over the little boat in a turmoil of foam. There was a preparatory and long growl in the speech of them. No mind unused to the sea would have concluded that the dinghy could ascend these sheer heights in time. The shore was still afar. The oiler was a wily surfman. "Boys," he said, swiftly, "she won't live three minutes more and we're too far out to swim. Shall I take her to sea again, Captain?"

"Yes, Go ahead!" said the captain.

This oiler, by a series of quick miracles, and fast and steady oarsmanship, turned the boat in the middle of the surf and took her safely to sea again.

There was a considerable silence as the boat bumped over the furrowed sea to deeper water. Then somebody in gloom spoke. "Well, anyhow, they must have seen us from the shore by now."

The gulls went in slanting flight up the wind toward the gray desolate east. A squall, marked by dingy clouds, and clouds brick-red, like smoke from a burning building, appeared from the southeast.

"What do you think of those lifesaving people? Ain't they peaches?"

"Funny they haven't seen us."

"Maybe they think we're out here for sport! Maybe they think we're fishin'. Maybe they think we're fools."

It was a long afternoon. A changed tide tried to force them southward, but wind and

---

6. seven mad gods: A reference to the ancient Greek gods.

CALIFORNIA SUITE
Vivian Caldwell

wave said northward. Far ahead, where coastline, sea, and sky formed their mighty angle, there were little dots which seemed to indicate a city on the shore.

"St. Augustine?"[7]

The captain shook his head. "Too near Mosquito Inlet."

And the oiler rowed, and then the correspondent rowed. Then the oiler rowed. It was a weary business. The human back can become the seat of more aches and pains than are registered in books for the composite anatomy of a regiment. It is a limited area, but it can become the theater of innumerable muscular conflicts, tangles, wrenches, knots, and other comforts.

"Did you ever like to row, Billie?" asked the correspondent.

"No," said the oiler. "Hang it."

When one exchanged the rowing seat for a place in the bottom of the boat, he suffered a bodily depression that caused him to be careless of everything save an obligation to wiggle one finger. There was cold sea water swashing to and fro in the boat, and he lay in it. His head, pillowed on a thwart, was within an inch of the swirl of a wave crest, and sometimes a particularly obstreperous sea came inboard and drenched him once more. But these matters did not annoy him. It is almost certain that if the boat had capsized he would have tumbled comfortably out upon the ocean as if he felt sure that it was a great soft mattress.

"Look! There's a man on the shore!"

"Where?"

"There! See 'im? See 'im?"

"Yes, sure! He's walking along."

"Now he's stopped. Look! He's facing us!"

"He's waving at us!"

"So he is! By thunder!"

"Ah, now, we're all right! Now we're all right! There'll be a boat out here for us in half an hour."

7. St. Augustine: A town on the Florida coast, approximately sixty-five miles north of New Smyrna Beach.

"He's going on. He's running. He's going up to that house there."

The remote beach seemed lower than the sea, and it required a searching glance to discern the little black figure. The captain saw a floating stick and they rowed to it. A bath towel was by some weird chance in the boat, and, tying this on the stick, the captain waved it. The oarsman did not dare turn his head, so he was obliged to ask questions.

"What's he doing now?"

"He's standing still again. He's looking, I think. . . . There he goes again. Toward the house. . . . Now he's stopped again."

"Is he waving at us?"

"No, not now! he was, though."

"Look! There comes another man!"

"He's running."

"Look at him go, would you."

"Why, he's on a bicycle. Now he's met the other man. They're both waving at us. Look!"

"There comes something up the beach."

"What the devil is that thing?"

"Why, it looks like a boat."

"Why, certainly it's a boat."

"No, it's on wheels."

"Yes, so it is. Well, that must be the lifeboat. They drag them along shore on a wagon."

"That's the lifeboat, sure."

"No, by——, it's—it's an omnibus."

"I tell you it's a lifeboat."

"It is not! It's an omnibus. I can see it plain. See? One of those big hotel omnibuses."

"By thunder, you're right. It's an omnibus, sure as fate. What do you suppose they are doing with an omnibus? Maybe they are going around collecting the life crew, hey?"

"That's it, likely. Look! There's a fellow waving a little black flag. He's standing on the steps of the omnibus. There come those other two fellows. Now they're all talking together. Look at the fellow with the flag. Maybe he ain't waving it!"

"That ain't a flag, is it? That's his coat.

Why, certainly, that's his coat."

"So it is. It's his coat. He's taken it off and is waving it around his head. But would you look at him swing it!"

"Oh, say, there isn't any lifesaving station there. That's just a winter resort hotel omnibus that has brought over some of the boarders to see us drown."

"What's that idiot with the coat mean? What's he signaling, anyhow?"

"It looks as if he were trying to tell us to go north. There must be a lifesaving station up there."

"No! He thinks we're fishing. Just giving us a merry hand. See? Ah, there, Willie."

"Well, I wish I could make something out of those signals. What do you suppose he means?"

"He don't mean anything. He's just playing."

"Well, if he'd just signal us to try the surf again, or to go to sea and wait, or go north, or go south, or go to hell—there would be some reason in it. But look at him. He just stands there and keeps his coat revolving like a wheel. The ass!"

"There come more people."

"Now there's quite a mob. Look! Isn't that a boat?"

"Where? Oh, I see where you mean. No, that's no boat."

"That fellow is still waving his coat."

"He must think we like to see him do that. Why don't he quit it. It don't mean anything."

"I don't know. I think he is trying to make us go north. It must be that there's a lifesaving station there somewhere."

"Say, he ain't tired yet. Look at 'im wave."

"Wonder how long he can keep that up. He's been revolving his coat ever since he caught sight of us. He's an idiot. Why aren't they getting men to bring a boat out. A fishing boat—one of those big yawls—could come out here all right. Why don't he do something?"

"Oh, it's all right, now."

"They'll have a boat out here for us in less than no time, now that they've seen us."

A faint yellow tone came into the sky over the low land. The shadows on the sea slowly deepened. The wind bore coldness with it, and the men began to shiver.

"Holy smoke!" said one, allowing his voice to express his impious mood, "if we keep on monkeying out here! If we've got to flounder out here all night!"

"Oh, we'll never have to stay here all night! Don't you worry. They've seen us now, and it won't be long before they'll come chasing out after us."

The shore grew dusky. The man waving a coat blended gradually into this gloom, and it swallowed in the same manner the omnibus and the group of people. The spray, when it dashed uproariously over the side, made the voyagers shrink and swear like men who were being branded.

"I'd like to catch the chump who waved the coat. I feel like soaking him one, just for luck."

"Why? What did he do?"

"Oh, nothing, but then he seemed so cheerful."

In the meantime the oiler rowed, and then the correspondent rowed, and then the oiler rowed. Gray-faced and bowed forward, they mechanically, turn by turn, plied the leaden oars. The form of the lighthouse had vanished from the southern horizon, but finally a pale star appeared, just lifting from the sea. The streaked saffron in the west passed before the all-merging darkness, and the sea to the east was black. The land had vanished, and was expressed only by the low and drear thunder of the surf.

"If I am going to be drowned—if I am going to be drowned—if I am going to be drowned, why, in the name of the seven mad gods who rule the sea, was I allowed to come thus far and contemplate sand and trees? Was I brought here merely to have my nose dragged away as I was about to nibble the sacred cheese of life?"

The patient captain, drooped over the

water jar, was sometimes obliged to speak to the oarsman.

"Keep her head up! Keep her head up!"

" 'Keep her head up,' sir." The voices were weary and low.

This was surely a quiet evening. All save the oarsman lay heavily and listlessly in the boat's bottom. As for him, his eyes were just capable of noting the tall black waves that swept forward in a most sinister silence, save for an occasional subdued growl of a crest.

The cook's head was on a thwart, and he looked without interest at the water under his nose. He was deep in other scenes. Finally he spoke. "Billie," he murmured, dreamfully, "what kind of pie do you like best?"

V

"Pie," said the oiler and the correspondent, agitatedly. "Don't talk about those things, blast you!"

"Well," said the cook, "I was just thinking about ham sandwiches, and——"

A night on the sea in an open boat is a long night. As darkness settled finally, the shine of the light, lifting from the sea in the south, changed to full gold. On the northern horizon a new light appeared, a small bluish gleam on the edge of the waters. These two lights were the furniture of the world. Otherwise there was nothing but waves.

Two men huddled in the stern, and distances were so magnificent in the dinghy that the rower was enabled to keep his feet partly warmed by thrusting them under his companions. Their legs indeed extended far under the rowing seat until they touched the feet of the captain forward. Sometimes, despite the efforts of the tired oarsman, a wave came piling into the boat, an icy wave of the night, and the chilling water soaked them anew. They would twist their bodies for a moment and groan, and sleep the dead sleep once more, while the water in the boat gurgled about them as the craft rocked.

The plan of the oiler and the correspondent was for one to row until he lost the ability, and then arouse the other from his sea-water couch in the bottom of the boat.

The oiler plied the oars until his head drooped forward, and the overpowering sleep blinded him. And he rowed yet afterward. Then he touched a man in the bottom of the boat, and called his name. "Will you spell me for a little while?" he said, meekly.

"Sure, Billie," said the correspondent, awakening and dragging himself to a sitting position. They exchanged places carefully, and the oiler, cuddling down in the sea water at the cook's side, seemed to go to sleep instantly.

The particular violence of the sea had ceased. The waves came without snarling. The obligation of the man at the oars was to keep the boat headed so that the tilt of the rollers would not capsize her, and to preserve her from filling when the crests rushed past. The black waves were silent and hard to be seen in the darkness. Often one was almost upon the boat before the oarsman was aware.

In a low voice the correspondent addressed the captain. He was not sure that the captain was awake, although this iron man seemed to be always awake. "Captain, shall I keep her making for that light north, sir?"

The same steady voice answered him. "Yes. Keep it about two points off the port bow."

The cook had tied a life belt around himself in order to get even the warmth which this clumsy cork contrivance could donate, and he seemed almost stovelike when a rower, whose teeth invariably chattered wildly as soon as he ceased his labor, dropped down to sleep.

The correspondent, as he rowed, looked down at the two men sleeping under foot. The cook's arm was around the oiler's shoulders, and, with their fragmentary clothing and haggard faces, they were the babes of the sea, a grotesque rendering of the old babes in the wood.

Later he must have grown stupid at his work, for suddenly there was a growling of water, and a crest came with a roar and a swash into the boat, and it was a wonder that it did not set the cook afloat in his life belt. The cook continued to sleep, but the oiler sat up, blinking his eyes and shaking with the new cold.

"Oh, I'm awful sorry, Billie," said the correspondent, contritely.

"That's all right, old boy," said the oiler, and lay down again and was asleep.

Presently it seemed that even the captain dozed, and the correspondent thought that he was the one man afloat on all the oceans. The wind had a voice as it came over the waves, and it was sadder than the end.

There was a long, loud swishing astern of the boat, and a gleaming trail of phosphorescence, like blue flame, was furrowed on the black waters. It might have been made by a monstrous knife.

Then there came a stillness, while the correspondent breathed with the open mouth and looked at the sea.

Suddenly there was another swish and another long flash of bluish light, and this time it was alongside the boat, and might almost have been reached with an oar. The correspondent saw an enormous fin speed like a shadow through the water, hurling the crystalline spray and leaving the long glowing trail.

The correspondent looked over his shoulder at the captain. His face was hidden, and he seemed to be asleep. He looked at the babes of the sea. They certainly were asleep. So, being bereft of sympathy, he leaned a little way to one side and swore softly into the sea.

But the thing did not then leave the vicinity of the boat. Ahead or astern, on one side or the other, at intervals long or short, fled the long sparkling streak, and there was to be heard the whiroo of the dark fin. The speed and power of the thing was greatly to be admired. It cut the water like a gigantic and keen projectile.

The presence of this biding thing did not affect the man with the same horror that it would if he had been a picnicker. He simply looked at the sea dully and swore in an undertone.

Nevertheless, it is true that he did not wish to be alone with the thing. He wished one of his companions to awaken by chance and keep him company with it. But the captain hung motionless over the water jar and the oiler and the cook in the bottom of the boat were plunged in slumber.

VI

"If I am going to be drowned—if I am going to be drowned—if I am going to be drowned, why, in the name of the seven mad gods who rule the sea, was I allowed to come thus far and contemplate sand and trees?"

During this dismal night, it may be remarked that a man would conclude that it was really the intention of the seven mad gods to drown him, despite the abominable injustice of it. For it was certainly an abominable injustice to drown a man who had worked so hard, so hard. The man felt it would be a crime most unnatural. Other people had drowned at sea since galleys swarmed with painted sails, but still——

When it occurs to a man that nature does not regard him as important, and that she feels she would not maim the universe by disposing of him, he at first wishes to throw bricks at the temple, and he hates deeply the fact that there are no bricks and no temples. Any visible expression of nature would surely be pelleted with his jeers.

Then, if there be no tangible thing to hoot he feels, perhaps, the desire to confront a personification and indulge in pleas,

bowed to one knee, and with hands suppli-
cant, saying: "Yes, but I love myself."

A high cold star on a winter's night is
the word he feels that she says to him.
Thereafter he knows the pathos of his situation.

The men in the dinghy had not discussed these matters, but each had, no
doubt, reflected upon them in silence and
according to his mind. There was seldom
any expression upon their faces save the
general one of complete weariness. Speech
was devoted to the business of the boat.

To chime the notes of his emotion, a
verse mysteriously entered the correspondent's head. He had even forgotten that he
had forgotten this verse, but it suddenly was
in his mind.

A soldier of the Legion[8] lay dying in
    Algiers,
There was lack of woman's nursing,
    there was dearth of woman's tears;
But a comrade stood beside him, and
    he took that comrade's hand,
And he said: "I never more shall see
    my own, my native land."[9]

In his childhood, the correspondent had
been made acquainted with the fact that a
soldier of the Legion lay dying in Algiers, but
he had never regarded it as important. Myri-
ads of his schoolfellows had informed him of
the soldier's plight, but the dinning had naturally ended by making him perfectly indifferent. He had never considered it his affair
that a soldier of the Legion lay dying in Algiers, nor had it appeared to him as a matter
for sorrow. It was less to him than the breaking of a pencil's point.

Now, however, it quaintly came to him as
a human, living thing. It was no longer

merely a picture of a few throes in the breast
of a poet, meanwhile drinking tea and warming his feet at the grate; it was an actuality—
stern, mournful, and fine.

The correspondent plainly saw the soldier. He lay on the sand with his feet out
straight and still. While his pale left hand
was upon his chest in an attempt to thwart
the going of his life, the blood came between
his fingers. In the far Algerian distance, a
city of low square forms was set against a
sky that was faint with the last sunset hues.
The correspondent, plying the oars and
dreaming of the slow and slower movements
of the lips of the soldier, was moved by a profound and perfectly impersonal comprehension. He was sorry for the soldier of the
Legion who lay dying in Algiers.

The thing which had followed the boat
and waited had evidently grown bored at the
delay. There was no longer to be heard the
slash of the cutwater, and there was no
longer the flame of the long trail. The light in
the north still glimmered, but it was apparently no nearer to the boat. Sometimes the
boom of the surf rang in the correspondent's
ears, and he turned the craft seaward then
and rowed harder. Southward, someone had
evidently built a watch fire on the beach. It
was too low and too far to be seen, but it
made a shimmering, roseate reflection upon
the bluff back of it, and this could be discerned from the boat. The wind came
stronger, and sometimes a wave suddenly
raged out like a mountain cat and there was
to be seen the sheen and sparkle of a broken
crest.

The captain, in the bow, moved on his
water jar and sat erect. "Pretty long night,"
he observed to the correspondent. He looked
at the shore. "Those lifesaving people take
their time."

"Did you see that shark playing
around?"

"Yes, I saw him. He was a big fellow, all
right."

"Wish I had known you were awake."

<hr>

8. the Legion: The French Foreign Legion.
9. A soldier . . . native land: An incorrectly quoted
passage from the poem "Bingen on the Rhine" (1883)
by Caroline E. S. Norton.

Later the correspondent spoke into the bottom of the boat.

"Billie!" There was a slow and gradual disentanglement. "Billie, will you spell me?"

"Sure," said the oiler.

As soon as the correspondent touched the cold comfortable sea water in the bottom of the boat, and had huddled close to the cook's life belt he was deep in sleep, despite the fact that his teeth played all the popular airs. This sleep was so good to him that it was but a moment before he heard a voice call his name in a tone that demonstrated the last stages of exhaustion. "Will you spell me?"

"Sure, Billie."

The light in the north had mysteriously vanished, but the correspondent took his course from the wide-awake captain.

Later in the night they took the boat farther out to sea, and the captain directed the cook to take one oar at the stern and keep the boat facing the seas. He was to call out if he should hear the thunder of the surf. This plan enabled the oiler and the correspondent to get respite together. "We'll give those boys a chance to get into shape again," said the captain. They curled down and, after a few preliminary chatterings and trembles, slept once more the dead sleep. Neither knew they had bequeathed to the cook the company of another shark, or perhaps the same shark.

As the boat caroused on the waves, spray occasionally bumped over the side and gave them a fresh soaking, but this had no power to break their repose. The ominous slash of the wind and the water affected them as it would have affected mummies.

"Boys," said the cook, with the notes of every reluctance in his voice, "she's drifted in pretty close. I guess one of you had better take her to sea again." The correspondent, aroused, heard the crash of the toppled crests.

As he was rowing, the captain gave him some whiskey and water, and this steadied the chills out of him. "If I ever get ashore and anybody shows me even a photograph of an oar——"

At last there was a short conversation. "Billie. . . . Billie, will you spell me?"

"Sure," said the oiler.

VII

When the correspondent again opened his eyes, the sea and the sky were each of the gray hue of the dawning. Later, carmine and gold was painted upon the waters. The morning appeared finally, in its splendor, with a sky of pure blue, and the sunlight flamed on the tips of the waves.

On the distant dunes were set many little black cottages, and a tall white windmill reared above them. No man, nor dog, nor bicycle appeared on the beach. The cottages might have formed a deserted village.

The voyagers scanned the shore. A conference was held in the boat. "Well," said the captain, "if no help is coming, we might better try a run through the surf right away. If we stay out here much longer we will be too weak to do anything for ourselves at all." The others silently acquiesced in this reasoning. The boat was headed for the beach. The correspondent wondered if none ever ascended the tall wind tower, and if then they never looked seaward. This tower was a giant, standing with its back to the plight of the ants. It represented in a degree, to the correspondent, the serenity of nature amid the struggles of the individual—nature in the wind, and nature in the vision of men. She did not seem cruel to him then, nor beneficent, nor treacherous, nor wise. But she was indifferent, flatly indifferent. It is, perhaps, plausible that a man in this situation, impressed with the unconcern of the universe, should see the innumerable flaws of his life and have them taste wickedly in his mind and wish for another chance. A distinction between right and wrong seems absurdly

WORSENING WEATHER
Anton Otto Fischer
U.S. Coast Guard Museum
New London, Connecticut

clear to him, then, in this new ignorance of the grave-edge, and he understands that if he were given another opportunity he would mend his conduct and his words, and be better and brighter during an introduction, or at a tea.

"Now, boys," said the captain. "she is going to swamp sure. All we can do is to work her in as far as possible, and then when she swamps, pile out and scramble for the beach. Keep cool now, and don't jump until she swamps sure."

The oiler took the oars. Over his shoulders he scanned the surf. "Captain," he said, "I think I'd better bring her about, and keep her head-on to the seas and back her in."

"All right, Billie," said the captain. "Back her in." The oiler swung the boat then and, seated in the stern, the cook and the correspondent were obliged to look over their shoulders to contemplate the lonely and indifferent shore.

The monstrous inshore rollers heaved the boat high until the men were again enabled to see the white sheets of water scudding up the slanted beach. "We won't get in very close," said the captain. Each time a man could wrest his attention from the rollers, he turned his glance toward the shore, and in the expression of the eyes during this contemplation there was a singular quality. The correspondent, observing the others, knew that they were not afraid, but the full meaning of their glances was shrouded.

As for himself, he was too tired to grapple fundamentally with the fact. He tried to coerce his mind into thinking of it, but the mind was dominated at this time by the muscles, and the muscles said they did not care. It merely occurrred to him that if he should drown it would be a shame.

There were no hurried words, no pallor, no plain agitation. The men simply looked at the shore. "Now, remember to get well clear of the boat when you jump," said the captain.

Seaward the crest of a roller suddenly fell with a thunderous crash, and the long white comber came roaring down upon the boat.

"Steady now," said the captain. The men were silent. They turned their eyes from the shore to the comber and waited. The boat slid up the incline, leaped at the furious top, bounced over it, and swung down the long back of the wave. Some water had been shipped and the cook bailed it out.

But the next crest crashed also. The tumbling boiling flood of white water caught the boat and whirled it almost perpendicular. Water swarmed in from all sides. The correspondent had his hands on the gunwale at this time, and when the water entered at that place he swiftly withdrew his fingers, as if he objected to wetting them.

The little boat, drunken with this weight of water, reeled and snuggled deeper into the sea.

"Bail her out, cook! Bail her out," said the captain.

"All right, Captain," said the cook.

"Now, boys, the next one will do for us, sure," said the oiler. "Mind to jump clear of the boat."

The third wave moved forward, huge, furious, implacable. It fairly swallowed the dinghy, and almost simultaneously the men tumbled into the sea. A piece of life belt had lain in the bottom of the boat, and as the correspondent went overboard he held this to his chest with his left hand.

The January water was icy, and he reflected immediately that it was colder than he had expected to find it off the coast of Florida. This appeared to his dazed mind as a fact important enough to be noted at the time. The coldness of the water was sad; it was tragic. This fact was somehow so mixed and confused with his opinion of his own situation that it seemed almost a proper reason for tears. The water was cold.

When he came to the surface he was conscious of little but the noisy water. Afterward he saw his companions in the sea. The oiler was ahead in the race. He was swimming strongly and rapidly. Off to the correspondent's left, the cook's great white and corked back bulged out of the water, and in the rear the captain was hanging with his one good hand to the keel of the overturned dinghy.

There is a certain immovable quality to a shore, and the correspondent wondered at it amid the confusion of the sea.

It seemed also very attractive, but the correspondent knew that it was a long journey, and he paddled leisurely. The piece of life preserver lay under him, and sometimes he whirled down the incline of a wave as if he were on a hand sled.

But finally he arrived at a place in the sea where travel was beset with difficulty. He did not pause swimming to inquire what manner of current had caught him, but there his progress ceased. The shore was set before him like a bit of scenery on a stage, and he looked at it and understood with his eyes each detail of it.

As the cook passed, much farther to the left, the captain was calling to him, "Turn over on your back, cook! Turn over on your back and use the oar."

"All right, sir." The cook turned on his back, and, paddling with an oar, went ahead as if he were a canoe.

Presently the boat also passed to the left of the correspondent with the captain clinging with one hand to the keel. He would have appeared like a man raising himself to look over a board fence, if it were not for the extraordinary gymnastics of the boat. The correspondent marveled that the captain could still hold to it.

They passed on, nearer to shore—the oiler, the cook, the captain—and following them went the water jar, bouncing gaily over the seas.

The correspondent remained in the grip

of this strange new enemy—a current. The shore, with its white slope of sand and its green bluff, topped with little silent cottages, was spread like a picture before him. It was very near to him then, but he was impressed as one who in a gallery looks at a scene from Brittany[10] or Holland.

He thought: "I am going to drown? Can it be possible? Can it be possible? Can it be possible?" Perhaps an individual must consider his own death to be the final phenomenon of nature.

But later a wave perhaps whirled him out of this small deadly current, for he found suddenly that he could again make progress toward the shore. Later still, he was aware that the captain, clinging with one hand to the keel of the dinghy, had his face turned away from the shore and toward him, and was calling his name. "Come to the boat! Come to the boat!"

In his struggle to reach the captain and the boat, he reflected that when one gets properly wearied, drowning must really be a comfortable arrangement, a cessation of hostilities accompanied by a large degree of relief, and he was glad of it, for the main thing in his mind for some moments had been horror of the temporary agony. He did not wish to be hurt.

Presently he saw a man running along the shore. He was undressing with most remarkable speed. Coat, trousers, shirt, everything flew magically off him.

"Come to the boat," called the captain.

"All right, Captain." As the correspondent paddled, he saw the captain let himself down to bottom and leave the boat. Then the correspondent performed his one little marvel of the voyage. A large wave caught him and flung him with ease and supreme speed completely over the boat and far beyond it. It struck him even then as an event in gymnastics, and a true miracle of the sea. An overturned boat in the surf is not a plaything to a swimming man.

The correspondent arrived in water that reached only to his waist, but his condition did not enable him to stand for more than a moment. Each wave knocked him into a heap, and the undertow pulled at him.

Then he saw the man who had been running and undressing, and undressing and running, come bounding into the water. He dragged ashore the cook, and then waded toward the captain, but the captain waved him away, and sent him to the correspondent. He was naked, naked as a tree in winter, but a halo was about his head, and he shone like a saint. He gave a strong pull, and a long drag, and a bully heave at the correspondent's hand. The correspondent, schooled in the minor formulae, said: "Thanks, old man." But suddenly the man cried: "What's that?" He pointed a swift finger. The correspondent said: "Go."

In the shallows, face downward, lay the oiler. His forehead touched sand that was periodically, between each wave, clear of the sea.

The correspondent did not know all that transpired afterward. When he achieved safe ground he fell, striking the sand with each particular part of his body. It was as if he had dropped from a roof, but the thud was grateful to him.

It seems that instantly the beach was populated with men with blankets, clothes, and flasks, and women with coffeepots and all the remedies sacred to their minds. The welcome of the land to the men from the sea was warm and generous, but a still and dripping shape was carried slowly up the beach, and the land's welcome for it could only be the different and sinister hospitality of the grave.

When it came night, the white waves paced to and fro in the moonlight, and the wind brought the sound of the great sea's voice to the men on shore, and they felt that they could then be interpreters.

---

10. Brittany (brit′ 'n ē): A former province of northwestern France.

RESPONDING TO THE SELECTION

Your Response

1. Did this story hold your attention? Why or why not?
2. How do you think you would react if you were in the place of one of the characters in the story? Explain.
3. Like the correspondent, do you think it's possible for the worst experience of your life to be, in some way, the best experience? Explain.

Recalling

4. (a) What happens when the men first attempt to row to the shore? (b) What happens when they are spotted by a man on the shore? (c) How do these two incidents affect the men's mood?
5. What happens when the men make their final run toward the shore?

Interpreting

6. (a) Why are the men upset by the presence of the gulls? (b) What do the gulls seem to represent to the men?
7. (a) Why do you think that the men felt that it would be "childish and stupid" to "express any particular optimism"? (b) What does Crane mean when he writes that "the ethics of their condition was decidedly against any open suggestion of hopelessness"?
8. (a) At the beginning of Part III, Crane comments that a "subtle brotherhood" had been established among the four men. How do the men's interactions in the first two parts support this observation? (b) Why did this brotherhood develop among the men? (c) What indications are there that the bond among the men remains strong throughout the story?
9. What parallels between the four men in the dinghy and the seafarers of ancient times are suggested by the allusions to the "seven mad gods who rule the sea"?
10. When the shark first appears, why does the correspondent wish that one of his companions would awaken to "keep him company with it"?

11. (a) Considering each man's physical condition, what is ironic, or surprising, about the fate of the oiler? (b) How does the oiler's fate emphasize the forcefulness and unpredictability of nature?
12. Throughout the story, Crane frequently personifies, or attributes human qualities to, the ocean. (a) How does he generally characterize the ocean in these personifications? (b) How do the personifications add to the impact of the story?

Applying

13. Explain whether you think that the men's behavior in this story represents a typical response to a highly stressful situation.
14. Explain whether you think that the outcome of the story would be different if the setting were changed to the present.

ANALYZING LITERATURE

Understanding Realism and Naturalism

Realism was a literary movement that emphasized the faithful, accurate portrayal of ordinary life. The Realists attempted to present "a slice of life," focusing on the realities of a small portion of the world. For example, in "The Open Boat" Crane focuses on the plight of four men.

Naturalism was a literary movement in which people were generally portrayed as being manipulated by forces of society and nature beyond their understanding or control. For example, in "The Open Boat" the characters are at the mercy of the powerful and unpredictable Atlantic Ocean.

1. Crane's story is filled with detailed descriptions of the ocean, the shore, and the men's movements in the boat. How do these descriptions contribute to the realistic quality of the story?
2. How do you think the fact that the story is based on a real-life experience might have contributed to the story's realistic quality?
3. Considering what you have read about the Naturalists' beliefs, why do you think that "The Open Boat" might be viewed as a classic example of a Naturalist story?

CRITICAL THINKING AND READING

Recognizing Important Passages

If you examine the story closely, you will find that at times Crane directly conveys his belief that nature is indifferent to the struggles of humanity. For example, he writes, "When it occurs to a man that nature does not regard him as important, and that she feels she would not maim the universe by disposing of him, he at first wishes to throw bricks at the temple, and he hates deeply the fact that there are no bricks and no temples."

Find two other passages in which Crane directly conveys his belief in nature's indifference to the problems of humanity.

THINKING AND WRITING

Responding to Criticism

A literary critic has commented, "The Naturalist often describes his characters as though they are conditioned and controlled by environment, heredity, instinct, or chance. But he also suggests a compensating humanistic value in his characters or their fates which affirms the significance of the individual and of his life."

Write a composition in which you respond to this statement based on your reading of "The Open Boat." Begin by reviewing the story, keeping the critic's comment in mind. Then organize your ideas, and start writing your composition, using passages from the story for support. After you have finished writing, revise your composition, making sure you have presented your ideas in a logical order.

LEARNING OPTIONS

1. **Cross-curricular Connection.** The narrator speaks for all the men in the boat when he rails against Fate and "the seven mad gods who rule the sea." Who are these seven deities? Explore which gods ruled the waters in Greek mythology and why their conduct might be described as "mad." Share your findings with the class.

2. **Writing.** After the Captain voices concern that they all may not get ashore, the four men exchange addresses. Take the part of any one of the survivors of the open boat and use the address Billie gave to send news of his death to his next of kin. In your letter be sure to describe Billie's exemplary behavior and your sense of loss on his death.

Primary Source

"The Open Boat" provides a good illustration of Crane's use of irony. For example, when Crane describes how picturesque the little boat would have looked to an outsider, he is being ironic. Even before he wrote "The Open Boat," Crane had a strong sense of irony in viewing the sea. Nine months before he himself was shipwrecked and spent time on the open ocean in a small boat, he published a brief poem about the sea, which presents a clear irony of perspective. Consider how this poem is appropriate to the situation in "The Open Boat."

To the maiden
The sea was blue meadow,
Alive with little froth-people
Singing.

To the sailor, wrecked,
The sea was dead gray walls,
Superlative in vacancy,
Upon which nevertheless at fateful time
Was written
The grim hatred of nature.

ONE WRITER'S PROCESS

Stephen Crane and "The Open Boat"

Experience With a Vengeance Writers often base their work on their own experience. In the case of Stephen Crane's "The Open Boat," however, the experience that inspired the story almost killed the author!

On January 1, 1897, Crane was aboard the steamship *Commodore* when it sank not far off the Florida coast. The ship was bound for Cuba, carrying arms and ammunition for the Cubans in their war against the Spanish. Crane was sailing as a foreign correspondent and had been planning to cover the fighting for the *New York Press,* a popular newspaper of the day.

A 10-foot Dinghy Shortly before the *Commodore* sank, Crane and three companions, including the ship's captain, Edward Murphy, climbed into a 10-foot dinghy and started rowing for shore. Thirty hours later, the men made a run for the coast, but the tiny boat was soon overturned in the rough surf. One of the men drowned; Crane and the others safely made it to land.

PREWRITING

Preliminary Notes On January 7th, Crane's account of the experience appeared on the front page of the *New York Press.* This account included the following tantalizing sentence: "The history of life in an open boat for thirty hours would no doubt be instructive for the young, but none is to be told here and now."

Soon after the story appeared, Crane began to fulfill the promise of that sentence by writing "The Open Boat." In a very real sense, the newspaper article served as a set of preliminary notes for that story.

DRAFTING

From Fact to Fiction When he began actually drafting "The Open Boat," Crane used some of the details and passages he had included in his newspaper account. He did, however, change these passages in important ways. The following paragraphs indicate some of those changes.

> **From the newspaper story:**
>
> John Kitchell of Daytona came running down the beach, and as he ran the air was filled with clothes. If he had pulled a single lever and undressed, even as the dire horses harness, he could not seem to me to have stripped with more speed. He dashed into the water and dragged the cook. Then he went after the captain, but the captain sent him to me, and then it was that he saw Billy Higgins lying with his forehead on sand that was clear of the water, and he was dead.
>
> **From "The Open Boat":**
>
> Then he saw the man who had been running and undressing, and undressing and running, come bounding into the water. He dragged ashore the cook, and then waded toward the captain; but the captain waved him away and sent him to the correspondent. He was naked—naked as a tree in winter; but a halo was about his head, and he shone like a saint. He gave a strong pull, and a long drag, and a bully heave at the correspondent's hand. The correspondent, schooled in the minor formulae, said, "Thanks, old man." But suddenly the man cried, "What's that?" He pointed a swift finger. The correspondent said, "Go."
>
> In the shallows, face downward, lay the oiler. His forehead touched sand that was periodically, between each wave, clear of the sea.

John Kitchell Becomes a Nameless Saint In the newspaper account, the man running down the beach is clearly identified as "John Kitchell of Daytona," and the oiler, Billy Higgins, is directly reported to be dead. In the story, however, the rescuer becomes a nameless saint with a halo about his head, and the reader is left to infer the fate of the sailor whose head rests in the sand.

A Moment Fraught With Symbolism, Drama, and Mystery Notice also that Crane added dialogue to the story, making the experience more personal and immediate. By adding certain details and taking out others, he changed the objective account of the newspaper article into a moment fraught with symbolism, drama, and mystery.

REVISING

Writing as Quickly as Possible Crane's large output suggests that he wrote quickly. Certainly, toward the end of his life, Crane did not spend too much time revising, as he was deeply in debt and writing as much and as quickly as possible for sales to magazines and newspapers.

Getting It Right This is not to imply that Crane was a lazy writer or one who never revised. In fact, we do have a fascinating, first-person account of Crane's method of revising "The Open Boat." This account can be found in R. W. Stallman's *Stephen Crane: A Biography:*

> Crane wrote "The Open Boat" in waterfront cafes, at the St. James Hotel, and at the Hotel de Dream [all of these were in Jacksonville, Florida], where in order to find out whether he had his facts right he read his story aloud to Captain Edward Murphy. He was overheard by Ralph Paine and Ernest McCready, who were having dinner in one of the private dining rooms, and Paine recorded their conversation in his *Roads of Adventure:*
>
> "Listen, Ed. I want to have this *right,* from your point of view. How does it sound so far?" "You've got it, Steve"—said the other man, "That is just how it happened, and how we felt. Read me some more of it."

The Advice of Eyewitnesses Reports indicate that Crane's wife Cora read over his stories after they were completed. In fact, Crane even collaborated with her on several newspaper articles. For "The Open Boat," however, he seems to have wanted only the advice of those who had firsthand experience, namely, the captain who had been with him in the dinghy.

PUBLISHING

Publication in a Popular Magazine While writing "The Open Boat," Crane doubtless had every intention of selling it to a magazine. As it turned out, the story appeared in the June 1897 issue of *Scribner's Magazine,* a leading literary journal of the day.

Standing the Test of Time A year later, the story appeared with others in a collection entitled *The Open Boat and Other Tales of Adventure.* In the May 1, 1898 edition of *The New York Times,* an enthusiastic reviewer of this volume declared: "No living English prose writer of his years approaches his wonderful gift of original and penetrating observation . . ."

Only Three Years Stephen Crane lived for only three more years after writing this story. Unfortunately, most of what he wrote before his death of tuberculosis was done out of desperation for money, and many critics believe that he never surpassed the achievement of "The Open Boat."

THINKING ABOUT THE PROCESS

1. In "The Open Boat" and in much of his best writing, Crane paid special attention to details that help readers visualize each scene. How can you gather details to help readers visualize your descriptions?
2. **Writing.** Look at some recent writing you have done. Is it as vivid as it could be? Do descriptions and scenes include precise details that help the reader see what is going on? Revise those sentences you think are weak to make them as exact and vivid as possible. Then read both the earlier version and the revision to classmates and see which they prefer.

Poetry

THE GRAND CANYON OF THE YELLOWSTONE, 1893–1901
Thomas Moran

GUIDE FOR INTERPRETING

Song of the Chattahoochee

Writers' Techniques

Sidney Lanier (1842–1881) was a talented musician as well as a gifted poet. He had a strong interest in the relationship between music and poetry. As a result, he abandoned conventional poetic structures and sought to create a musical rhythm in his poetry. Born in Macon, Georgia, Lanier entered Oglethorpe University, where he studied poetry and music. In 1880 he published *The Science of English Verse.* In his book Lanier stated his belief that poetry should have the natural rhythm and fluidity of music and that the sound of a poem should reinforce its meaning.

Sound Devices. Poets use a variety of sound devices to give their writing a musical quality. Four of the most frequently used sound devices are alliteration, consonance, assonance, and internal rhyme.

Alliteration is the repetition of similar sounds, usually consonants, at the beginnings of words or accented syllables. Notice the repetition of the *l* and *t* sounds in the following line from "Song of the Chattahoochee": "The *l*aving *l*aurel *t*urned my *t*ide."

Consonance is the repetition of consonant sounds at the ends of words or accented syllables. For example, the *l* sound is repeated in the following line from "Song of the Chattahoochee": "Vei*l*ing the va*ll*eys of Ha*ll*."

Assonance is the repetition of vowel sounds. For example, the long *a* sound is repeated in the following line: "Av*ai*l: I am f*ai*n for to water the pl*ai*n."

Rhyme refers to the repetition of similar or identical sounds in the accented syllables of two or more words appearing close to each other in a poem. Internal rhyme is rhyme that occurs within a line. An example of internal rhyme appears in the following line from "Song of the Chattahoochee": "With a lover's *pain* to at*tain* the *plain.*"

Focus

In "Song of the Chattahoochee" Lanier personifies, or attributes human characteristics to, a river. Think of another element of nature that a writer might personify. Then prepare a list of human qualities that could be attributed to this element.

Primary Source

Sidney Lanier's ideas about poetry influenced many late nineteenth- and early twentieth-century writers. Among them was American poet and author Hamlin Garland, who wrote, "That he was an immense force in my life . . . I gladly bear witness. He taught me freedom within law. His lines flowed down the printed page like rills of water rippling into whorls of rhyme, pleasantly, unexpectedly, and so easily as to be hardly more confining than prose."

Song of the Chattahoochee[1]

Sidney Lanier

    Out of the hills of Habersham,
    Down the valleys of Hall,[2]
I hurry amain to reach the plain,
Run the rapid and leap the fall,
5 Split at the rock and together again,
Accept my bed, or narrow or wide,
And flee from folly on every side
With a lover's pain to attain the plain
      Far from the hills of Habersham,
10   Far from the valleys of Hall.

---

1. Chattahoochee (c̆hat′ ə hōō′ c̆hē): A river in western Georgia.
2. Habersham . . . Hall: Two counties through which the Chattahoochee flows.

HARPERS FERRY FROM JEFFERSON ROCK, 1857
Edward Beyer
Virginia State Library

All down the hills of Habersham,
All through the valleys of Hall,
The rushes cried *Abide, Abide,*
The willful waterweeds held me thrall,
15   The laving laurel turned my tide,
The ferns and the fondling grass said *Stay,*
The dewberry dipped for to work delay,
And the little reeds sighed *Abide, abide,*
        Here in the hills of Habersham,
20   *Here in the valleys of Hall.*

        High o'er the hills of Habersham,
        Veiling the valleys of Hall,
The hickory told me manifold
Fair tales of shade, the poplar tall
25   Wrought me her shadowy self to hold,
The chestnut, the oak, the walnut, the pine,
Overleaning, with flickering meaning and sign,
Said, *Pass not, so cold, these manifold*
        Deep shades of the hills of Habersham,
30   *These glades in the valleys of Hall.*

        And oft in the hills of Habersham,
        And oft in the valleys of Hall,
The white quartz shone, and the smooth brook-stone
Did bar me of passage with friendly brawl,
35   And many a luminous jewel lone
—Crystals clear or a-cloud with mist,
Ruby, garnet and amethyst—
Made lures with the lights of streaming stone
        In the clefts of the hills of Habersham,
40   In the beds of the valleys of Hall.

        But oh, not the hills of Habersham,
        And oh, not the valleys of Hall
Avail: I am fain for to water the plain.
Downward the voices of Duty call—
45   Downward, to toil and be mixed with the main,
The dry fields burn, and the mills are to turn,
And a myriad flowers mortally yearn,
And the lordly main from beyond the plain
        Calls o'er the hills of Habersham,
50   Calls through the valleys of Hall.

RESPONDING TO THE SELECTION

Your Response

1. What did you hear as you read this poem? What did you see?
2. What are the "voices of Duty" in your life? How does your response to their call compare with the river's?

Recalling

3. (a) Toward what is the river racing? (b) What is attempting to delay the river in its course? (c) What calls the water forward?

Interpreting

4. Who is the speaker in this poem?
5. In this poem Lanier presents an extended personification of the Chattahoochee River. Name three other elements of nature that Lanier personifies in the poem.
6. Consider Lanier's use of personification in describing the river's flow. (a) What do you think the course of the river symbolizes? (b) What do the forces that try to delay the river represent? (c) What are "the voices of Duty"?

Applying

7. Do you think this poem is as effective today as it was when it was written? Why?

ANALYZING LITERATURE

Recognizing Sound Devices

Alliteration, consonance, assonance, and internal rhyme are four sound devices used in poetry. **Alliteration** is the repetition of similar sounds, usually consonants, at the beginnings of words or accented syllables (for example, "*R*un the *r*apid," line 4). **Consonance** is the repetition of consonant sounds at the ends of words or accented syllables (for example, "va*ll*eys of Ha*ll*"). **Assonance** is the repetition of vowel sounds (for example, "w*i*th fl*i*ckering," line 27). **Internal rhyme** is rhyme that occurs within a line (for example, "I hurry a*main* to reach the *plain*," line 3).

1. Find two more examples of each of these techniques in "Song of the Chattahoochee."
2. How do these examples convey the natural movement of the river?

CRITICAL THINKING AND READING

Analyzing the Effect of Sound Devices

Sidney Lanier believed that the sound of a poem should help to reinforce its meaning. In "Song of the Chattahoochee" he used sound devices to imitate the natural flowing of a river. For example, his use of alliteration in the line "And *f*lee *f*rom *f*olly on every side" captures the river's dancing, winding movement.

Do you agree with Lanier's contention? Support your answer.

THINKING AND WRITING

Writing an Extended Personification

What would a mountain say if it could speak? What message would the ocean give to humankind? What would a tornado say as it left behind a trail of destruction?

Write a poem or a short narrative essay in which you present an extended personification of an element of nature. Start by reviewing the list of human qualities you have already prepared. Add any other qualities you think of. Then write your personification using the element you are personifying as your speaker or narrator.

LEARNING OPTIONS

1. **Cross-curricular Connection.** Investigate the relationship between music and nature. Locate a recording of a musical composition that brings to life some force of nature, such as a river or a storm. Give the piece a new title, for example, "The Mississippi Mambo," and play the recording for classmates.
2. **Speaking and Listening.** Do you think Lanier's poem gives voice to the Chattahoochee River? To hear the sound of the water as it swirls downstream to the ocean, read the poem aloud to yourself. Listen to how the alliteration in the first stanza speeds your reading, while the alliteration in succeeding stanzas slows you down. How successful was Lanier in imitating the river's sound?

PAUL LAURENCE DUNBAR

1872–1906

The first black American to support himself entirely by writing, Paul Laurence Dunbar displayed great versatility as a writer throughout his short career. Dunbar wrote poems, both in a formal, elegant style and in black dialect, and he wrote several novels and numerous short stories.

Dunbar was born in Dayton, Ohio, the son of former slaves. Encouraged by his mother, he began writing poetry at an early age. During high school, Dunbar, who was the only black student in his class, frequently recited his poetry before school assemblies. He also served as the president of the literary society, as class poet, and as editor of the school newspaper.

Following his graduation, he supported himself by working as an elevator operator while continuing to write. He first earned recognition among writers and critics in 1892, when he gave a poetry reading during a meeting of the Western Association of Writers. A year later he published his first collection of poetry, *Oak and Ivy.* In 1895 he published a second collection, *Majors and Minors* (1895), which was received by critics with great enthusiasm. In fact, William Dean Howells, the leading critic of the day, was so impressed with the book that he wrote an introduction for Dunbar's next collection, *Lyrics of a Lowly Life* (1896), which sold over twelve thousand copies and established Dunbar as a widely read and admired American poet.

Dunbar went on to write three more volumes of poetry, four novels, and four volumes of short stories. Dunbar's fiction often focused on daily life in the lost world of the southern plantation. Sometimes, however, it revolved around social problems facing black people in midwestern towns and urban ghettos. His characters included farmers, politicians, preachers, traders, entertainers, and professional people.

Dunbar, however, thought of himself primarily as a poet. He gave readings throughout the United States and Europe. Unfortunately, his life was cut short by tuberculosis in 1906. By the end of his life, his poetry was so popular that he was able to write from Florida, "Down here one finds my poems recited everywhere." One biographer has commented that "young blacks recited his poems and saw in turn what was possible for them."

Despite his success as a poet, Dunbar was disillusioned by the critics' tendency to focus on his poetry written in black dialect, while virtually ignoring his more formal verse. In poems such as "Douglass" and "We Wear the Mask," Dunbar demonstrates a command of the English language that was often overlooked, capturing the despair of black people in a dignified, graceful manner.

GUIDE FOR INTERPRETING

We Wear the Mask; Douglass

Literary Forms

The Sonnet. A sonnet is a fourteen-line lyric poem, usually written in rhymed iambic pentameter—verse with five feet per line, each foot consisting of an unstressed syllable followed by a stressed syllable. A sonnet usually expresses a single complete idea or theme.

The two most common types of sonnets are *English sonnets,* or *Shakespearean sonnets* (named after English playwright William Shakespeare), and *Italian sonnets,* or *Petrarchan sonnets* (named after the fourteenth-century Italian poet Francesco Petrarch). English sonnets are composed of three quatrains (four-line stanzas) followed by a couplet (two rhyming lines), with the rhyme scheme *abab cdcd efef gg.* In most English sonnets, the main idea is presented and developed in the three quatrains, and the couplet offers a conclusion. Italian sonnets consist of an octave (eight lines) followed by a sestet (six lines), usually rhyming *abbaabba cdecde* or *abbaabba cdcdcd.* In some Italian sonnets, a question is raised in the octave and the answer is presented in the sestet. In other Italian sonnets, a single idea is presented in the octave and either developed or contradicted in the sestet.

Focus

In "Douglass" Paul Laurence Dunbar addresses the deceased black leader Frederick Douglass and expresses his people's feelings of despair and their need for Douglass's guidance and comfort. Review the excerpt from Douglass's autobiography (pages 364–368). Then list reasons why Dunbar might have chosen to address his poem to Douglass.

Primary Source

Paul Laurence Dunbar wrote against a backdrop of grave racial injustice. In a July 1903 letter, he used ironic commentary about Independence Day to express his feelings about the situation of black people. Parts of the letter follow.

> [W]e have celebrated the Nation's birthday. Yes, and we black folks have celebrated. . . .
> Like a dark cloud, pregnant with terror and destruction, disenfranchisement has spread its wings over our brethren of the South. Like the same dark cloud, industrial prejudice glooms above us in the North. . . . And yet we celebrate. . . .
> [W]ith bleeding hands uplifted, still sore and smarting from long beating at the door of opportunity, we raise our voices and sing, "My Country, 'Tis of Thee"; . . . while from the four points of the compass comes our brothers' unavailing cry, and so we celebrate.

We Wear the Mask

Paul Laurence Dunbar

We wear the mask that grins and lies,
It hides our cheeks and shades our eyes—
This debt we pay to human guile;
With torn and bleeding hearts we smile,
5   And mouth with myriad subtleties.

Why should the world be overwise,
In counting all our tears and sighs?
Nay, let them only see us, while
    We wear the mask.

10   We smile, but, O great Christ, our cries
To thee from tortured souls arise.
We sing, but oh the clay is vile
Beneath our feet, and long the mile;
But let the world dream otherwise,
15   We wear the mask!

RESPONDING TO THE SELECTION

Your Response

1. What emotions does this poem evoke in you? Why?
2. What effect do you think a mask can have on the person who wears it?

Interpreting

3. (a) Who is the speaker of the poem? (b) How would you describe the speaker's emotional state?
4. What does the mask symbolize?
5. (a) Whom does the mask deceive? (b) Why do you think the speaker chooses not to reveal what is hidden beneath the mask?
6. What is the theme of the poem?

Applying

7. Like the speaker in this poem, most people at times hide their true feelings. Why do you think this is so? Explain your answer.

LEARNING OPTIONS

1. **Multicultural Activity.** People throughout the world have made and used masks since the Stone Age. Explore the types of masks used in various cultures. Choose a culture that interests you. Create a replica or drawing of a mask used in that culture.
2. **Cross-curricular Connection.** In "We Wear the Mask," Dunbar expresses the pain experienced by African Americans in the post-Civil War years. In the letter excerpted on page 531, he comments specifically about disenfranchisement in the South and industrial prejudice in the North. Find out how pervasive racial discrimination was in the United States during Dunbar's lifetime (1872–1906). How were northern blacks excluded from industry? How did southern blacks lose political and social rights? Share your findings with the class.

Commentary

In 1970 Maya Angelou published her autobiography, *I Know Why the Caged Bird Sings,* drawing the title from the Paul Laurence Dunbar poem "Sympathy."

I know why the caged bird sings, ah me,
   When his wing is bruised and his bosom
      sore,—
When he beats his bars and he would be
     free;
It is not a carol of joy or glee,
   But a prayer that he sends from his
     heart's deep core,
But a plea, that upward to Heaven he
     flings—
I know why the caged bird sings!

Dunbar's "sympathy" for the caged bird grew out of his experience as a black writer forced by circumstances to write for a predominantly white audience. Caged by the expectations of the marketplace, most of Dunbar's poetry and fiction avoided questions of critical importance to him, questions having to do with ending discrimination and racial hatred. Dunbar was the caged bird who sang to keep from shouting out his grief, who laughed to keep from crying.

As a girl Maya Angelou absorbed much of Dunbar's poetry. Like Dunbar, she grew up in a setting that seemed to cage her with discrimination. In her autobiography she detailed how in her rural Arkansas town "whitefolks could[n't] be talked to at all without risking one's life."

Angelou defied discrimination to become a successful writer. She dedicated her autobiography to her son and "all the strong black birds of promise who defy the odds and gods and sing their songs."

FREDERICK DOUGLASS

Douglass
Paul Laurence Dunbar

Ah, Douglass,[1] we have fall'n on evil days,
    Such days as thou, not even thou didst know,
    When thee, the eyes of that harsh long ago
Saw, salient, at the cross of devious ways,
5 And all the country heard thee with amaze.
    Not ended then, the passionate ebb and flow,
    The awful tide that battled to and fro;
We ride amid a tempest of dispraise.

Now, when the waves of swift dissension swarm,
10   And Honor, the strong pilot, lieth stark,
Oh, for thy voice high-sounding o'er the storm,
    For thy strong arm to guide the shivering bark,[2]
The blast-defying power of thy form,
    To give us comfort through the lonely dark.

---

1. Douglass: Frederick Douglass, an American abolitionist (1817?–1895).
2. bark: Boat.

RESPONDING TO THE SELECTION

Your Response

1. Why do you think the poet chose to address Frederick Douglass?
2. What historical figure would you choose as a role model? Why? What would you say to or request of him or her?

Interpreting

3. Summarize the main idea of the poem.
4. (a) To what does the speaker compare the plight of the black people? (b) What role does the speaker propose Douglass take?
5. What apparently prompted Dunbar to write this poem?

Applying

6. How do you think Dunbar might characterize the present times?
7. (a) What black leaders might the speaker have called on had the poem been written today? (b) How do their efforts on behalf of African Americans compare with Douglass's?

ANALYZING LITERATURE

Recognizing a Sonnet

A **sonnet** is a fourteen-line lyric poem. Sonnets are usually written in rhymed iambic pentameter and express a single, complete thought. The two most common types of sonnets are the English sonnet, or Shakespearean sonnet, and the Italian sonnet, or Petrarchan sonnet. "Douglass" is an example of an Italian sonnet.

1. What is the theme expressed in "Douglass"?
2. At what point in the poem does Dunbar present the main idea?
3. How is the main idea developed in the sestet?
4. How does Dunbar's use of the sonnet form contribute to the poem's effectiveness?

THINKING AND WRITING

Writing a Sonnet

Write a sonnet in which you address an important historical figure, as Dunbar does in "Douglass." Start by thinking of a historical figure who had an important impact on American society. For example, you might select Martin Luther King, Jr., Abraham Lincoln, or Abigail Adams. How would this person respond to contemporary life? Then write a sonnet focusing on issues concerning contemporary society that would be of interest to this person. When you finish writing, revise your sonnet and share it with your classmates.

Commentary

Frederick Douglass was aware of Paul Laurence Dunbar's poetry and once commented to a friend, "He is very young but there is no doubt he is a poet." Dunbar for his part was a youthful admirer of Douglass. The two met in 1893.

At that time Douglass, then almost eighty, was commissioner in charge of the Haitian Pavilion at the World's Columbian Exposition in Chicago—the first world's fair. He hired Dunbar to be a clerk, paying him out of his own pocket.

Douglass's interest and encouragement helped Dunbar at a key moment in his life. At the Exposition he met other black people active in the arts or in the pursuit of civil rights. His newfound friends included poets and performers.

Dunbar wrote two poems about Douglass, the one you just read and one titled "Frederick Douglass." In this earlier poem, Dunbar celebrated Douglass as a man who was "no soft-tongued apologist." The poem noted, "His heart, his talents, and his hands were free / To all who truly needed aught of him."

EDWIN ARLINGTON ROBINSON

1869–1935

Edwin Arlington Robinson's poetry bridged the gap between two literary eras. Like most nineteenth-century poetry, his work was traditional in form. Yet like the work of modern poets, his poetry was innovative in content, probing beneath the surface of human behavior and exploring the psychological realities of the inner self.

Robinson was raised in Gardiner, Maine, a small town that served as the model for Tilbury Town, the fictional setting of many of his finest poems. When his father, a successful lumber merchant, died, Robinson's family suddenly found itself living in poverty. Robinson attended Harvard for two years before his family's financial problems forced him to leave. He returned to Gardiner and began writing poetry, depending on friends and patrons for financial support. During his four years in Gardiner, Robinson drew back inside himself. He took little interest in the world outside and, instead, read voluminously. He missed the friendships he had made at Harvard and sensed that he was seen as a failure. Despite the despair Robinson experienced during these years, he came through them with a sense of himself as a poet who could speak the truth.

Just before the turn of the century, Robinson published two unsuccessful collections of poetry, *The Torrent and the Night Before* (1896) and *Children of the Night* (1897), at his own expense. Hoping to improve his financial situation, he moved to New York. As it turned out, his situation did improve when President Theodore Roosevelt appointed him to a post at a New York customshouse. Robinson also discovered success as a poet when his fourth volume of poetry, *The Town Down the River* (1910), sold well and received much critical acclaim.

Robinson went on to become a highly regarded poet. His collections *The Man Against the Sky* (1916), *Avon's Harvest* (1922), and *Collected Poems* (1921) were very successful, as was his trilogy of long narrative poems based on the legends of King Arthur: *Merlin, Lancelot,* and *Tristram*. During the 1920's Robinson received more recognition than any other American poet, winning the Pulitzer Prize three times, in 1922, 1925, and 1928.

Growing out of his childhood observations in Gardiner, most of Robinson's best poems focus on people's inner struggles. His poems paint portraits of impoverished characters whose lives are filled with frustration and despair, characters who see their lives as trivial and meaningless, and characters who long to live in another time and place. Yet despite their pessimistic outlook, his poems always possess a certain dignity, resulting from his traditional style, his command of language, and his imagination and wit.

GUIDE FOR INTERPRETING

Luke Havergal; Miniver Cheevy; Richard Cory

Irony. Irony is a contrast between what is stated and what is meant, or between what is expected to happen and what actually happens. Three types of irony used in literature are verbal irony, situational irony, and dramatic irony. Verbal irony occurs when the literal meaning of a word or statement is different from the intended meaning. Situational irony occurs when the actual result of an action or a situation is different from the expected result. Dramatic irony occurs when the audience perceives something that a character in a literary work does not know.

Irony is an important element in many of Edwin Arlington Robinson's poems. Robinson possessed an intense awareness of the ironies of everyday life—the contrasts between reality and people's perceptions, between results and expectations, and between the way people view themselves and how they are seen by others—and he sought to capture these ironies in his harshly realistic poetry.

People are always in search of happiness, but what is happiness? William Saroyan once wrote, "The greatest happiness you can have is knowing that you do not necessarily require happiness." Freewrite, exploring the meaning of this quotation.

In describing Edwin Arlington Robinson's work, poet James Dickey has written:

> It is through people that Robinson found the hints and gleams of the universal condition that he could not help trying to solve. . . . Robinson has been perhaps the only American poet—certainly the only one of major status—interested *exclusively* in human beings as subject matter for poetry—in the psychological, motivational aspects of living, in the inner life as it is projected upon the outer. His work is one vast attempt to tell the stories that no man can really tell, for no man can know their real meaning, their real intention, or even whether such exists. . . . In all Robinson's people the Cosmos seems to be brooding in one way or another. . . .
>
> No poet ever understood loneliness or separateness better than Robinson or knew the self-consuming furnace that the brain can become in isolation. . . . He understood loneliness in all its many forms and depths. . . .

Luke Havergal

Edwin Arlington Robinson

Go to the western gate, Luke Havergal,
There where the vines cling crimson on the wall,
And in the twilight wait for what will come.
The leaves will whisper there of her, and some,
5 Like flying words, will strike you as they fall;
But go, and if you listen she will call.
Go to the western gate, Luke Havergal—
Luke Havergal.

No, there is not a dawn in eastern skies
10 To rift the fiery night that's in your eyes;
But there, where western glooms are gathering,
The dark will end the dark, if anything:
God slays Himself with every leaf that flies,
And hell is more than half of paradise.
15 No, there is not a dawn in eastern skies—
In eastern skies.

THE ARTIST'S GARDEN, c. 1880
Ralph Albert Blakelock
National Gallery of Art

Out of a grave I come to tell you this,
Out of a grave I come to quench the kiss
That flames upon your forehead with a glow
20   That blinds you to the way that you must go.
Yes, there is yet one way to where she is,
Bitter, but one that faith may never miss.
Out of a grave I come to tell you this—
To tell you this.

25   There is the western gate, Luke Havergal,
There are the crimson leaves upon the wall.
Go, for the winds are tearing them away,—
Nor think to riddle the dead words they say,
Nor any more to feel them as they fall;
30   But go, and if you trust her she will call.
There is the western gate, Luke Havergal—
Luke Havergal.

R ESPONDING TO THE SELECTION

Your Response

1. What did you hear as you read this poem? What did you see?
2. How does this poem make you feel?

Recalling

3. Why should Luke Havergal go to the western gate?
4. From where has the speaker come to deliver his message?

Interpreting

5. What do you think was Luke's relationship to the woman referred to in the poem?
6. (a) Considering that the sun sets in the west and considering the details used in describing the western gate, what do you think the western gate symbolizes? (b) What does the "dawn in eastern skies" symbolize?
7. The speaker may actually be part of Luke Havergal's inner self. If this is so, what does the poem reveal about Luke Havergal's state of mind?
8. Considering Luke's state of mind and the action he is being urged to take, what do you think the speaker means when he comments, "The dark will end the dark"?
9. Robinson's use of repetition in the poem creates a hypnotic effect. How is this effect related to the meaning of the poem?

Applying

10. This poem suggests that a person can never replace a loved one whom he or she has lost. Discuss this view.

L EARNING OPTION

Writing. Who exactly is Luke Havergal? What is the tragedy of his life? Fill in the missing details. Write a biographical sketch of the Tilbury Town resident who is the subject of Robinson's poem. In your sketch you might recount the central events of Havergal's life and present your interpretation of the events.

Miniver Cheevy

Edwin Arlington Robinson

Miniver Cheevy, child of scorn,
    Grew lean while he assailed the seasons;
He wept that he was ever born,
    And he had reasons.

5   Miniver loved the days of old
    When swords were bright and steeds were prancing;
The vision of a warrior bold
    Would set him dancing.

Miniver sighed for what was not,
10   And dreamed, and rested from his labors;
He dreamed of Thebes[1] and Camelot,[2]
    And Priam's[3] neighbors.

Miniver mourned the ripe renown
    That made so many a name so fragrant;
15 He mourned Romance, now on the town,[4]
    And Art, a vagrant.

Miniver loved the Medici,[5]
    Albeit he had never seen one;
He would have sinned incessantly
20   Could he have been one.

Miniver cursed the commonplace
    And eyed a khaki suit with loathing;
He missed the medieval grace
    Of iron clothing.

25 Miniver scorned the gold he sought,
    But sore annoyed was he without it;
Miniver thought, and thought, and thought,
    And thought about it.

---

1. Thebes (thēbz): A city-state in ancient Greece.
2. Camelot (kam' ə lät'): The legendary English town where King Arthur's court and Round Table were located.
3. Priam (prī' əm): King of Troy during the Trojan War.
4. on the town: On public assistance.
5. Medici (med' ə chē): A rich, powerful family of Florence, Italy, in the fourteenth, fifteenth, and sixteenth centuries.

Miniver Cheevy, born too late,
30 Scratched his head and kept on thinking;
Miniver coughed, and called it fate,
  And kept on drinking.

RESPONDING TO THE SELECTION

Your Response

1. What is your opinion of Miniver Cheevy? Do you sympathize with him or "scorn" him? Explain.
2. What advice would you give Cheevy if he were a friend of yours?

Recalling

3. What is Miniver Cheevy's basic problem?
4. What does the final line reveal about how Miniver Cheevy copes with his unhappiness?

Interpreting

5. The word *miniver* refers to a white fur used for trimming ceremonial robes during the Middle Ages. Why is this an appropriate name for the character in the poem?
6. How does the speaker suggest that Cheevy does not have a realistic image of the past?
7. Why do you think Cheevy "scorned the gold he sought"?

Applying

8. Like Miniver Cheevy, people often try to escape from their problems, rather than confronting them and trying to find a solution. Why is this an ineffective way of dealing with problems?

ANALYZING LITERATURE

Understanding Irony

Irony is a contrast between what is stated and what is meant, or between what is expected to happen and what actually happens. Three types of irony used in literature are verbal irony, situational irony, and dramatic irony.

1. In line 2 the speaker comments that Cheevy "assailed the seasons." (a) How is this image related to Cheevy's visions of the past? (b) Why is this image ironic considering Cheevy's life?
2. What is ironic about Cheevy missing "the medieval grace" of iron clothing?
3. Explain how the use of irony affects your attitude toward Cheevy.

LEARNING OPTIONS

1. **Writing.** Help Miniver Cheevy fulfill his dreams. Transport the failed romantic to ancient Thebes, Camelot, or Troy. How does he fare in the world of Hercules, King Arthur, or King Priam? Add a stanza or two to Robinson's poem to describe Cheevy's experiences.
2. **Art.** Imagine that you have been commissioned by the publisher to illustrate a collection of Edwin Arlington Robinson's Tilbury Town poems. How would you illustrate "Miniver Cheevy"? Capture Cheevy's personality in a picture. You might find a painting, draw a portrait, or write detailed directions for an artist. Share your picture or your description with classmates.

Richard Cory

Edwin Arlington Robinson

Whenever Richard Cory went down town,
We people on the pavement looked at him:
He was a gentleman from sole to crown,
Clean favored, and imperially slim.

5 And he was always quietly arrayed,
And he was always human when he talked;
But still he fluttered pulses when he said,
"Good-morning," and he glittered when he walked.

THE THINKER
(Portrait of Louis N. Kenton, 1900)
Thomas Eakins
The Metropolitan Museum of Art

542   *Realism and the Frontier*

And he was rich—yes, richer than a king—
10 And admirably schooled in every grace:
In fine, we thought that he was everything
To make us wish that we were in his place.

So on we worked, and waited for the light,
And went without the meat, and cursed the bread;
15 And Richard Cory, one calm summer night,
Went home and put a bullet through his head.

RESPONDING TO THE SELECTION

Your Response

1. What was your reaction to the last two lines of the poem?
2. Would you like to read Edwin Arlington Robinson's poems about other residents of Tilbury Town? Why or why not?

Recalling

3. Why was Richard Cory envied by the townspeople?
4. What does Richard Cory do "one calm summer night"?

Interpreting

5. (a) Who is the speaker of the poem? (b) In what ways is the speaker different from Richard Cory?
6. What do the words "crown" (line 3) and "imperially" (line 4) suggest about the speaker's impression of Richard Cory?
7. Why would the poem be less forceful if the speaker had used the pronoun "I" instead of "we"? Explain your answer.
8. What makes the poem's final line surprising?
9. What do you think is the theme of the poem?

Applying

10. (a) Why do you think a person like Richard Cory, who seemingly has every reason to be happy, might in fact be miserable? (b) What do you think are the keys to a person's happiness?
11. The French writer Colette wrote, "What a wonderful life I've had! I only wish I'd realized it sooner." Discuss the meaning of this quotation.

CRITICAL THINKING AND READING

Recognizing Attitudes

This poem points out that each person has a different outlook on life and that it is often difficult for people to perceive or understand the outlooks of others. In the poem we are presented with the speaker's view of Richard Cory, which leads us to expect Cory to be happy. As a result, we are shocked by the ending of the poem and forced to realize that the speaker's impressions were false. The ending also forces us to contemplate Cory's perceptions of himself and the speaker and to think about how they are different from the speaker's perceptions.

1. Considering the outcome of the poem, how do you think Cory's attitude toward himself differs from the speaker's attitude toward him?
2. What do you think might have been Richard Cory's attitude toward the townspeople?

LEARNING OPTION

Writing. Richard Cory is the mystery man, Miniver Cheevy, the failed romantic, and Luke Havergal, the star-crossed lover. Who else might have lived in Tilbury Town? Together with classmates, write poems about characters who could have lived in Tilbury Town. Try to assign each character a name that provides insight into his or her character.

EDGAR LEE MASTERS

1868–1950

Edgar Lee Masters is primarily remembered for one volume of his poetry. Yet this volume, *Spoon River Anthology,* is widely regarded as one of the finest collections of poetry ever produced by an American poet.

Masters was born in Kansas but grew up in rural southern Illinois—the area where Abraham Lincoln had spent his early years. After briefly attending Knox College, Masters studied law in his father's law office and eventually passed the bar exam. In 1891 he moved to Chicago, where he became a successful criminal lawyer. During his spare time, he wrote poems, plays, and essays, and he published some of his poems in the highly regarded Chicago magazine *Poetry.*

Masters's early poems, which were traditional in form, received little attention. In 1914, however, Masters's direction as a poet changed dramatically when a friend gave him a copy of *Selected Epitaphs from the Greek Anthology.* This collection included many concise, interconnected epitaphs that each captured the essence of a person's life. Using this structure and abandoning conventional rhyme and meter for free verse, Masters wrote a series of poems about the lives of people in rural southern Illinois. Published under the title *Spoon River Anthology* in 1915, the series provoked strong reactions among critics and became a best seller.

Spoon River Anthology consists of 244 epitaphs for characters buried in the mythical Spoon River cemetery. The dead themselves serve as the speakers of the poems, often revealing secrets they kept hidden throughout their lifetimes. Many types of people are represented, including storekeepers, housewives, and murderers. Some of the characters had lived happy lives, but many more had lived lives filled with frustration and despair. Presented together the epitaphs paint a vivid portrait of the loneliness and isolation with which people living in the Midwest at the time were often confronted.

Poet May Swenson has commented that in *Spoon River Anthology,* Masters gave "outlet to all his grudges, beliefs, indignations, insights, prophesies, discoveries of glaring injustice, revelations of life's mysteries and paradoxes—and his own eccentric philosophy. Miraculously he also created and bequeathed to us a world in microcosm, new in form, timeless in essence."

Several years after *Spoon River Anthology* was published, Masters gave up his law practice to devote all of his energy to writing. Yet, while he was able to produce many other volumes of poetry in addition to novels, biographies, and his autobiography, *Across Spoon River,* he was never able to match the success of *Spoon River Anthology.*

GUIDE FOR INTERPRETING

Lucinda Matlock; Fiddler Jones

The Speaker. The speaker is the voice of a poem. Although the speaker is often the poet, the speaker could be a fictional character, or an inanimate object, or another type of nonhuman entity. For example, the speakers in the poems in Edgar Lee Masters's *Spoon River Anthology* are fictional characters who are buried in the mythical Spoon River cemetery. By using the characters themselves as the speakers, Masters is able to delve deeply into the characters' minds. In each poem a different speaker discusses his or her own life intimately and honestly, candidly expressing his or her most profound thoughts, feelings, and emotions.

Many of the characters are based on people Masters observed or was acquainted with during his childhood. For example, Lucinda Matlock, one of the most forceful speakers, represents Masters's own grandmother.

In *Spoon River Anthology,* Edgar Lee Masters paints portraits of a variety of characters based on people he observed during his childhood. Think of an interesting or amusing character from a book, a movie, or in the news. Then list details describing this person's appearance, personality, and behavior.

In his essay "The Genesis of Spoon River," Edgar Lee Masters described experiences from his youth in the Illinois towns of Petersburg and Lewiston that contributed to his writing of *Spoon River Anthology.* He then went on to describe his state of mind as he neared completion of the Spoon River poems in December 1914:

> I was nearing exhaustion of body. . . . The flame had now become so intense that it could not be seen, by which I mean that the writing of the pieces did not seem to involve any effort whatever; and yet I should have known that I was being sapped rapidly. I had no auditory or visual experiences which were not the effect of actuality; but I did feel that somehow, by these months of exploring the souls of the dead, by this unlicensed revelation of their secrets, I had convoked about my head swarms of powers and beings who were watching me and protesting and yet inspiring me to go on.
>
> I do not mean by this that I believed that I was so haunted; I only mean I had that sensation, as one in a lonely and eyrie room might suddenly feel that someone was in the next room spying upon him.

Lucinda Matlock

Edgar Lee Masters

I went to the dances at Chandlerville,
And played snap-out[1] at Winchester.
One time we changed partners,
Driving home in the moonlight of middle June,
5 And then I found Davis.
We were married and lived together for seventy years,
Enjoying, working, raising the twelve children,
Eight of whom we lost
Ere I had reached the age of sixty.

---

1. snap-out: A game often referred to as "crack-the whip," in which
a long line of players who are holding hands spin around in a circle,
causing the players on the end to be flung off by centrifugal force.
Note about art: Anna Mary Robertson Moses (1860–1961) began painting
in old age and became known as "Grandma" Moses. She painted country
landscapes and scenes remembered from her childhood.

10 I spun, I wove, I kept the house, I nursed the sick,
    I made the garden, and for holiday
    Rambled over the fields where sang the larks,
    And by Spoon River gathering many a shell,
    And many a flower and medicinal weed—
15 Shouting to the wooded hills, singing to the green valleys.
    At ninety-six I had lived enough, that is all,
    And passed to a sweet repose.
    What is this I hear of sorrow and weariness,
    Anger, discontent and drooping hopes?
20 Degenerate sons and daughters,
    Life is too strong for you—
    It takes life to love Life.

RESPONDING TO THE SELECTION

Your Response

1. What is your opinion of Lucinda Matlock? Is she someone you would strive to emulate? Why or why not?
2. What do you think of Lucinda's criticism of the sons and daughters she addresses? Explain.

Interpreting

3. (a) How would you characterize Lucinda Matlock's life? (b) What seems to be Lucinda Matlock's attitude concerning her life?
4. (a) Who are the "sons and daughters" Lucinda addresses in this poem? (b) What is her attitude toward them? (c) How is their attitude toward life different from her own? (d) What is the meaning of her message to them?

Applying

5. Explain whether you agree or disagree with Lucinda Matlock's message.
6. As this poem suggests, the general attitude toward life of one generation is often quite different from that of other generations. What do you think causes these differences?
7. How do you think Lucinda Matlock would respond to people who complain that life today is too complex and confusing?

THINKING AND WRITING

Writing an Epitaph

Imagine that you have entered a contest being held by your school literary magazine in which you are asked to write an epitaph in the style of Edgar Lee Masters. Start by reviewing the list of details you prepared that describe an interesting or amusing person. Try to decide which details best capture the essence of the person's life. Then decide what message about life the epitaph should convey. When you write the epitaph, use free verse and try to capture the flavor of the person's life in a limited number of lines. When you finish writing, put your epitaph aside for one day. Then reread it and make any necessary revisions.

LEARNING OPTION

Writing. If Edgar Lee Masters were to write your epitaph, what message about life would it convey? Sum up your philosophy in a single sentence. You might write an original statement or use a quotation that expresses your point of view.

Fiddler Jones

Edgar Lee Masters

The earth keeps some vibration going
There in your heart, and that is you.
And if the people find you can fiddle,
Why, fiddle you must, for all your life.
5   What do you see, a harvest of clover?
Or a meadow to walk through to the river?
The wind's in the corn; you rub your hands
For beeves hereafter ready for market;
Or else you hear the rustle of skirts
10   Like the girls when dancing at Little Grove.
To Cooney Potter a pillar of dust
Or whirling leaves meant ruinous drouth;[1]
They looked to me like Red-Head Sammy
Stepping it off, to "Toor-a-Loor."
15   How could I till my forty acres
Not to speak of getting more,
With a medley of horns, bassoons and piccolos
Stirred in my brain by crows and robins
And the creak of a windmill—only these?
20   And I never started to plow in my life
That someone did not stop in the road
And take me away to a dance or picnic.
I ended up with forty acres;
I ended up with a broken fiddle—
25   And a broken laugh, and a thousand memories,
And not a single regret.

---

1. drouth: Drought.

RESPONDING TO THE SELECTION

Your Response

1. What do you think of Fiddler Jones's life? Was he a success or a failure? Explain.
2. How do you suppose Fiddler Jones would see a glass filled halfway with water—half-empty or half-full? Explain.
3. Would you like to read Edgar Lee Masters's epitaphs for other citizens of Spoon River? Why or why not?

Recalling

4. According to Fiddler Jones, what must you do if "the people find you can fiddle"?
5. What are two explanations Fiddler Jones offers for his failures as a farmer?
6. What regrets does Fiddler Jones have about the way he lived his life?

Interpreting

7. What does Fiddler Jones mean when he comments, "The earth keeps some vibration going / There in your heart, and that is you"?
8. What examples does Fiddler Jones use to point out that there are many different ways of viewing the world?
9. How is Fiddler Jones's view of life different from that of other farmers?
10. Explain the last three lines of the poem.

Applying

11. How might you apply the lesson taught by the story of Fiddler Jones to your own life?

ANALYZING LITERATURE

Identifying the Speaker

The **speaker** is the voice of a poem. The speaker may be the poet himself or herself, or it may be a fictional character or even an inanimate object or another type of nonhuman entity. The speaker in "Fiddler Jones" is Fiddler Jones himself.

1. How would "Fiddler Jones" be different if Masters had used a different speaker?
2. Fiddler Jones and the other speakers of the poems in *Spoon River Anthology* are dead. Why might this allow them to discuss their lives more openly than if they were alive?

THINKING AND WRITING

Comparing and Contrasting Writers

Write an essay in which you compare and contrast Edwin Arlington Robinson's poetry with that of Edgar Lee Masters. Start by rereading the poems by Robinson and Masters in this book, noting similarities and differences in style, theme, and choice of subjects. Reread the biographies of Robinson and Masters, again noting similarities and differences between the two writers. Review your notes and prepare a thesis statement. Organize your notes according to corresponding points of contrast. Then begin writing your essay, using passages from the poems to support your argument. When you revise, make sure you have included enough supporting information.

Commentary

Spoon River Anthology shocked many critics and readers at the time of its publication. What accounted for its reception?

One factor, certainly, was its portrayal of small-town life and people. Although the subjects of many of the poems were admirable individuals, a large number were people whose lives were dominated by greed, religious narrow-mindedness, frustration, or inhumanity toward others. This negative view of small-town life and people ran contrary to popular views.

A second factor was the scandalous portrayal of some of the characters. Numerous readers found these poems distasteful and unwholesome.

Finally, Masters wrote his poems in unadorned free verse. Many critics found the poems overly blunt and graceless.

YOUR WRITING PROCESS

WRITING THE INTRODUCTION TO A DOCUMENTARY

The settling of the American frontier is the subject of countless novels, documentaries, films, and studies. What makes this period of history so appealing? It's your turn to answer that question. You have been hired to write the opening of a television documentary about the American frontier.

> ### Focus
>
> **Assignment:** Write an introduction about the frontier for a television documentary on the American West.
> **Purpose:** To highlight important aspects of frontier life and persuade viewers to watch the program.
> **Audience:** Television viewers across the nation.

Prewriting

1. See how it's done. View the beginning of a historical documentary or recall one you have seen. How long is the introduction? How does it create interest?

2. Diagram your ideas. Make a sunburst diagram and place the word *frontier* in the center of it. Flip through the selections in this unit for ideas and images and add more of your own personal associations. After you have finished, look at your diagram and choose the ideas you want to use. Number them to show the order in which they will be discussed.

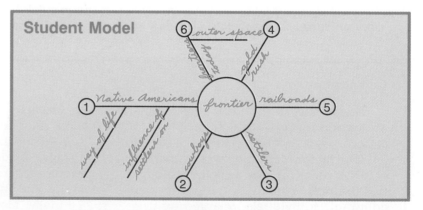

Student Model

3. Quote some eyewitnesses. Find a few spicy quotations from the period, perhaps from the selections in this unit. Choose ones that convey important aspects and that are entertaining to listen to. Keep them short.

Drafting

1. Grab viewers with your opening. Write an opening that will make viewers listen and want to see more. Ask them a question, intrigue them with a quotation, inspire them with an idea, or paint a vivid picture.

2. Follow your blueprint. Use the numbered items on your diagram as a guide for your writing. However, don't be afraid to head off in a new direction if you feel inspired.

3. Focus on sound. Since you are writing to appeal to listeners, not readers, the sound of your words is important. Play with sound devices such as alliteration and repetition.

Revising and Editing

1. Simple sentences say it best. It's much easier to listen to short, simple sentences than long, complex ones. Keep your viewers in mind as you edit and whittle your sentences down to their essential elements. Rely on strong words, not lots of words, to make your points.

> **Student Model**
>
> For some people who went to the west, the frontier life could be a somewhat uncomfortable, even a lonely place. Settlers on the frontier often had to ride on horses or wagons for several hours or even more just to see another person like themselves. *soul*

2. Tape-record your draft. Listen, as your audience will, to your words. Hear the music of your language. What words are pleasant? Strong? Harsh? Which sentences are too long to follow? Which are clumsy?

3. Weaving with words. Pay particular attention to coherence as you revise, making sure that you have fully developed each idea and that each follows from the one before. Don't leave an incomplete thought dangling like a loose thread.

4. Get a second opinion. As always, have a peer editor comment on your draft. It may help to ask your editor questions like the following:
- What is the strongest image in my introduction?
- Which sentence or passage is the weakest?
- What overall impression do I give of the frontier?

Writer's Hint

Many writers believe that the end of a piece of writing should echo, or even contain, its beginning. Making a piece of writing come full circle creates a sense of unity and coherence. If you begin with a strong image, try to remind your audience of that image at the end. For example, the first phrase of "The Story of an Hour" introduces "heart trouble" and the last line tells us that the protagonist "died of heart disease." Don't rely on simple repetition, but work to amplify the meaning of an image or build upon a word or phrase.

Options for Publishing

Contribute your introduction to a class looseleaf volume entitled Introducing the Frontier.
- Read your piece to several classmates and ask them if they would watch the program it introduces.
- Choose a piece of music to accompany your introduction and tape-record both to share with your classmates.

Reviewing Your Writing Process

1. How did you find quotations to add spice to your writing?
2. How is writing an essay that will be read silently different from writing one that will be read aloud?

CITY ROOFS, 1932
Edward Hopper
Courtesy of Kennedy Galleries, Inc., New York

THE MODERN AGE
1915–1946

We asked the cyclone
to go around our barn
but it didn't hear us.
Carl Sandburg
from *The People, Yes*

Carl Sandburg served as a soldier in the Spanish-American War (1898) and wrote his first novel after the Second World War (1948). In the years between, he was a day laborer, a journalist, a salesman, an advertising manager, a world-renowned poet, and a Pulitzer Prize-winning biographer. The focus of Sandburg's writing, like that of Walt Whitman, was America.

The America that Sandburg observed was a nation achieving world dominance, but at the same time losing some of its youthful innocence and brash confidence. Two world wars, a dizzying decade of prosperity, and a devastating worldwide depression marked this era. With these events came a new age in American literature. The upheavals of the early twentieth century ushered in a period of artistic experimentation and lasting literary achievement.

THE HISTORICAL SETTING

The years immediately preceding World War I were characterized by an overwhelming sense of optimism. Numerous technological advances occurred, dramatically affecting people's lives, and creating a sense of promise concerning the future. While a number of serious social problems still existed, reforms aimed at solving these prob-

ARMISTICE DAY, 1918
Gifford Beal
Indiana University Art Museum

lems began to be instituted. When World War I broke out in 1914, however, President Woodrow Wilson was forced to turn his attention away from the troubles at home and focus on the events in Europe.

War in Europe

World War I was one of the bloodiest and most tragic conflicts ever to occur. When the initial advances of the German forces were stalled, the conflict was transformed into a trench war. The introduction of the machine gun made it virtually impossible for one side to launch a successful attack on its opponents' trenches, however, and the war dragged on for several years with little progress being made by either side. Each unsuccessful attack resulted in the deaths of thousands of soldiers, and the war ultimately claimed almost an entire generation of European men.

President Wilson wanted the United States to remain neutral in the war, but that proved impossible. In 1915, a German submarine sank the *Lusitania*, pride of the British merchant fleet. More than 1,200 people on board lost their lives, including 128 Americans. After the sinking, American public opinion tended to favor the Allies—England, France, Italy, and Russia. When Germany resumed

THE CITY FROM GREENWICH VILLAGE, 1922
John Sloan
National Gallery of Art, Washington, D.C.

The Modern Age
(A.D. 1915 – A.D. 1945)

James Joyce

Langston Hughes

Nineteenth
Amendment
Adopted

1915 ——————————————— **1925**

AMERICAN EVENTS

- *Chicago Poems* by **Carl Sandburg** appears.
  - United States enters World War I.
    - Prohibition becomes law; law repealed in 1933.
  - **Sherwood Anderson** publishes *Winesburg, Ohio.*
    - Nineteenth Amendment to Constitution gives U.S. women the right to vote.
      - **T. S. Eliot** publishes *The Waste Land.*
        - **Wallace Stevens** publishes *Harmonium.*

- **F. Scott Fitzgerald** publishes *The Great Gatsby.*
  - **Langston Hughes** publishes *The Weary Blues.*
  - **Ernest Hemingway** publishes *The Sun Also Rises.*
    - Charles Lindbergh flies solo and nonstop from New York to Paris.
      - Stock market crashes in October, followed by Great Depression of 1930's.
        - **Katherine Anne Porter** publishes *Flowering Judas.*
          - President Roosevelt closes banks; Congress passes New Deal laws.

WORLD EVENTS

- Russia: Bolsheviks seize control of Russia in October Revolution.
  - Worldwide influenza epidemic kills as many as 20 million people.
    - France: Treaty of Versailles ends World War I.
      - England: D. H. Lawrence publishes *Women in Love.*
        - Ireland: James Joyce publishes *Ulysses.*
          - Germany: Thomas Mann publishes *The Magic Mountain.*

- England: Virginia Woolf publishes *Mrs. Dalloway.*
  - China: Chiang Kai-shek becomes head of Nationalist government.
  - Germany: Kurt Weill and Bertolt Brecht write and produce *The Threepenny Opera.*
    - India: Mahatma Gandhi leads famous march to the sea to protest British tax on salt.
      - Spain: Salvador Dali paints *Persistence of Memory.*
        - Germany: Adolf Hitler becomes German chancellor.

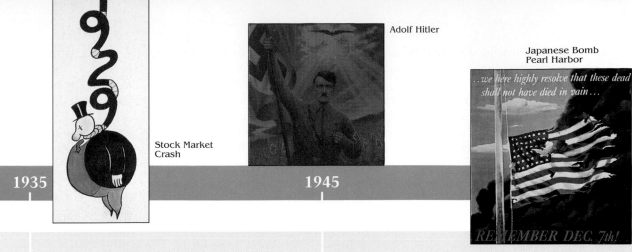

Stock Market Crash

Adolf Hitler

Japanese Bomb Pearl Harbor

...we here highly resolve that these dead shall not have died in vain...

REMEMBER DEC. 7th!

1935

1945

- Thornton Wilder's play *Our Town* opens.
  - **John Steinbeck** publishes *The Grapes of Wrath*.
  - United States declares neutrality as World War II breaks out in Europe.
    - **Richard Wright** publishes *Native Son.*
      - *A Curtain of Green* by **Eudora Welty** appears.
      - Japanese bomb American naval base at Pearl Harbor, bringing U.S. into World War II.

- World War II ends after U.S. drops two atomic bombs on Japan.

- USSR: Stalin starts Great Purge to rid government and armed forces of opposition.
- Spain: Spanish Civil War begins.
  - Poland: German blitzkrieg invasion of Poland sets off World War II.
    - France surrenders to Germany.
      - France: Albert Camus completes *The Stranger.*

- United Nations Charter signed at end of World War II.

unrestricted submarine warfare two years later, the United States abandoned neutrality and joined the Allied cause.

At first the reality of war did not sink in. Americans were confident and carefree as the troops set off overseas. That cheerful mood soon passed. A number of famous American writers saw the war firsthand and learned of its horror. E. E. Cummings, Ernest Hemingway, and John Dos Passos served as ambulance drivers. Hemingway later served in the Italian infantry and was seriously wounded. Other, less famous writers fought and died in France. Among them were the poets Joyce Kilmer, who wrote "Trees," and Alan Seeger, who wrote "I Have a Rendezvous with Death."

Prosperity and Depression

The end of the Great War in November 1918 brought little peace to Woodrow Wilson. His dream of the United States joining the League of Nations to prevent future wars failed. The war's end brought little peace to the big cities of America either. In 1919, Prohibition made the sale of liquor illegal, leading to bootlegging, speakeasies, widespread lawbreaking, and sporadic warfare among competing gangs.

Throughout the 1920's, the nation seemed on a binge. After a brief recession in 1920 and 1921, the economy boomed. New buildings rose everywhere, creating new downtown sections in many cities—Omaha, Des Moines, and Minneapolis among them. Radio arrived, and so did jazz. Movies became big business, and spectacular movie palaces sprang up across the country. Fads abounded: raccoon coats, flagpole sitting, the Charleston. The great literary interpreter of the Roaring Twenties was F. Scott Fitzgerald. In *The Beautiful and Damned* and *The Great Gatsby* Fitzgerald showed both the glamorous and the pitiful sides of the American dream.

During the 1920's, artists and writers flocked to Greenwich Village in New York City. Older buildings in the area, including barns, stables, and houses, were converted to studios, nightclubs, theaters, and shops. In 1923, playwright Eugene O'Neill founded the Greenwich Village Theatre, where experimental dramas were performed. Thomas Wolfe taught English at New York University in the Village while writing his autobiographical novel, *Look Homeward, Angel*.

In late October 1929, the stock market crashed, marking the beginning of the Great Depression. By mid-1932, about 12 million people, or one quarter of the work force, were out of work. Even as bread lines formed and the numbers of unemployed grew, most business leaders remained optimistic. But the situation continued to worsen. In the presidential election of 1932, New York's Governor Franklin D. Roosevelt defeated incumbent President Herbert Hoover. Roosevelt embarked on a far-reaching program, the New Deal, to turn the economic tide. He won reelection in 1936 and again in 1940. While circumstances had improved by then, prosperity did not begin to equal that of the 1920's.

World War II

Only twenty years after the Treaty of Versailles had ended the First World War, the German invasion of Poland touched off the Second World War. As in the earlier war, most Americans wanted to remain neutral. Even after the fall of France in 1940, the dominant mood in the United States was one of isolationism. But when the Japanese attacked Pearl Harbor in Hawaii on December 7, 1941, America could stay neutral no longer. The United States declared war on the Axis powers—Japan, Germany, and Italy.

After years of bitter fighting on two fronts, the Allies—including the United States, Great Britain, the Soviet Union, and France—defeated Nazi Germany. Japan surrendered three months later, after the United States had dropped atomic bombs on two Japanese cities. Peace, and the atomic age, had arrived.

THE BIRTH OF MODERNISM

The devastation of World War I brought about an end to the sense of optimism that had characterized the years immediately preceding the war.

LIBRARY
Bernard Boruch Zakheim
Coit Tower Mural (WPA)
San Francisco Art Commission

Many people were left with a feeling of uncertainty, disjointedness, and disillusionment. No longer trusting the ideas and values of the world out of which the war had developed, people sought to find new ideas that were more applicable to twentieth-century life. The quest for new ideas extended into the world of literature, and a major literary movement known as Modernism was born.

The Modernists experimented with a wide variety of new approaches and techniques, producing a remarkably diverse body of literature. Yet, the Modernists shared a common purpose. They sought to capture the essence of modern life in the form and content of their work. To reflect the fragmentation of the modern world, the Modernists constructed their works out of fragments, omitting the expositions, transitions, resolutions, and explanations used in traditional literature. In poetry, they abandoned traditional forms in favor of free verse. The themes of their works were usually implied, rather than directly stated, creating a sense of uncertainty and forcing readers to draw their own conclusions. In general, Modernist works demanded more from readers than the works of earlier American writers. At the same time, however, the Modernists helped to earn America a place among the world's great literary traditions.

Imagism

The Modernist movement was ushered in by a poetic movement known as Imagism. This movement, which lasted from 1909 to 1917, attracted

CONCEPTION SYNCHROMY, 1914
Stanton MacDonald-Wright
Hirshhorn Museum and Sculpture Garden, Smithsonian Institution

followers in both the United States and England. The Imagists rebelled against the sentimentality of nineteenth-century poetry. They demanded instead hard, clear expression, concrete images, and the language of everyday speech. Their models came from Greek and Roman classics, Chinese and Japanese poetry, and the free verse of the French poets of their day. The early leader of the Imagist movement was Ezra Pound. When Pound abandoned Imagism, other Imagists assumed leadership, among them the poet H. D. (Hilda Doolittle). Amy Lowell, a Massachusetts poet, led the Imagist movement in the United States in its final years.

The Expatriates

The postwar disenchantment led a number of American writers to become expatriates, or exiles. Many of these writers settled in Paris, where they were influenced by Gertrude Stein. The writer who coined the phrase "lost generation" to describe those who were disillusioned by the First World War, Stein lived in Paris from 1902 until her death in 1946. Stein's home attracted many major authors, including Sherwood Anderson, F. Scott Fitzgerald, and Ernest Hemingway.

Fitzgerald and Hemingway are the best known of the expatriates, but they are by no means the only ones. Ezra Pound spent most of his adult life in England, France, and Italy. T. S. Eliot, born in St. Louis, went to Europe in 1914 and did not return to the United States until 1932. Eliot's long, despairing poem *The Waste Land* appeared in 1922. Some have called it the most important poem of the century.

Most of the lost generation saw very little in their civilization to praise or even accept. Archibald MacLeish, an expatriate from 1923 to 1928, wrote several volumes of verse expressing the chaos and hopelessness of those years. MacLeish eventually broke with the expatriates, however. He returned to the United States in the 1930's and became increasingly concerned about the rise of dictatorships. A supporter of President Roosevelt's New Deal, he served as Librarian of Congress during the Second World War.

New Approaches

During the years between the two world wars, writers in both the United States and Europe explored new literary territories. Influenced by developments in modern psychology, writers began using the stream-of-consciousness technique, attempting to re-create the natural flow of a character's thoughts. Named by psychologist William James, the stream-of-consciousness technique involves the presentation of a series of thoughts, memories, and insights, connected only by a character's natural associations. The landmark stream-of-consciousness novel is *Ulysses,* published in 1922 by the Irish writer James Joyce. A number of American novelists soon adopted the technique, most notably William Faulkner in *The Sound and the Fury.*

The three novels in John Dos Passos's *U.S.A.* use stream-of-consciousness narration. They include some other unusual devices for a fictional work, such as brief biographies of well-known Americans and quotations from newspapers and magazines. Katherine Anne Porter's short stories also employ stream of consciousness.

Poets, no less than novelists and short story writers, sought to stretch the old boundaries. E. E. Cummings's poems attracted special attention because of their wordplay, unique typography, and special punctuation. These devices are more than mere oddities in Cummings's poetry. They are vital to its intent and its meaning.

Other poets found new devices to express their meaning. William Carlos Williams, a New Jersey physician and poet, called his poetry "objectivist." In his view, a poem is an object that presents its case by the form it assumes. So spare and cryptic are some of Williams's poems that one cannot say for sure what they "mean." This obscurity of meaning did not bother Williams. Likewise, it did not concern other poets who shared Archibald MacLeish's belief that "a poem should not mean but be."

Writers of International Renown

The Modernists dramatically altered the complexion of American literature. At the same time, many of these writers earned international acclaim that equaled that of their European literary contemporaries.

The Nobel Prize for Literature is an international award. It was established in 1901 from funds left by Alfred Nobel, the Swedish inventor of dynamite. The first American to win the Nobel Prize for Literature was Sinclair Lewis. A native of Sauk Center, Minnesota, Lewis fictionalized his hometown as Gopher Prairie in his first important novel, *Main Street*. Lewis, one of the great satirists of his era, wrote two more classics within the next few years. *Babbitt* was about an American businessman, while *Arrowsmith* dealt with the medical profession.

Lewis's Nobel Prize in 1930 was the first of many for American writers. In 1936, the prize went to Eugene O'Neill, ranked by most critics as America's greatest playwright. Among his best-known plays are *Desire under the Elms, The Iceman Cometh,* and *Long Day's Journey into Night*. O'Neill's plays are sometimes autobiographical, generally tragic, and often experimental. His *Strange Interlude,* produced in 1928, uses stream-of-consciousness asides to reveal the inner feelings of characters. These feelings often contrast with their actual spoken words.

In 1938, the Nobel Prize for Literature went to Pearl S. Buck, an American who spent her early years in China. Buck wrote about that country with

ROOM IN BROOKLYN
Edward Hopper
Museum of Fine Arts, Boston

deep understanding and compassion. *The Good Earth* is considered her finest work.

T. S. Eliot, who had become a British subject in 1927, won the award in 1948. William Faulkner won it the following year. Most of Faulkner's novels and short stories are set in mythical Yoknapatawpha County, Mississippi, which closely resembled the area of Mississippi where Faulkner lived. In addition to *The Sound and the Fury,* Faulkner wrote such enduring works as *Light in August* and *The Hamlet.*

In later years, Ernest Hemingway and John Steinbeck also won Nobel Prizes for Literature. Hemingway's clipped style of writing, evident in such novels as *The Sun Also Rises* and *A Farewell to Arms,* influenced a generation of young writers. His best writing deals with the First World War and its aftermath. Steinbeck's works depict the Depression, especially as it affected migrant workers and dust-bowl farmers. Two of Steinbeck's most memorable novels are *Of Mice and Men* and *The Grapes of Wrath.*

The Harlem Renaissance

A new literary age was dawning not only in Greenwich Village and among expatriates in Paris but also in northern Manhattan, in Harlem. African American writers, mostly newcomers from the South, were creating their own renaissance there. It began in 1921 with the publication of Countee Cullen's "I Have a Rendezvous with Life (with apologies to Alan Seeger)." Another poem by a black youth—"The Negro Speaks of Rivers," by Langston Hughes—followed six months later.

What occurred thereafter was a burst of creative activity by black writers, few of whom, other than Cullen, had been born in New York City. Most of them moved there during the renaissance. Claude McKay, for example, was from Jamaica. His most famous book was *Harlem Shadows,* a collection of poems published in 1922. A year later came Jean Toomer's *Cane,* a collection of stories, verses, and a play.

The Harlem Renaissance was publicly recognized in March 1924, when young African American writers met the literary editors of the city. Carl Van Doren, editor of the *Century,* noted that black writers, long "oppressed and handicapped . . . have gathered stores of emotion and are ready to burst forth with a new eloquence."

The Harlem phenomenon continued throughout the 1920's and into the 1930's. Arna Bontemps, born in Louisiana, published his first novel, *God Sends Sunday,* in 1931. The writers of this renaissance belonged to no single school of literature, but they did form a coherent group. They saw themselves as being part of a new and exciting movement. As well as producing their own exceptional works, they opened the door for African American writers who would follow them.

Flashes of Wit and Humor

So much of the outstanding writing between the wars echoed disenchantment and despair that the bright, cheery voices of the period tend to be forgotten. The best-known humorist of the time was Will Rogers, the "Cowboy Philosopher" from Oklahoma. He earned that nickname with his homespun humor and wry comments on politics and current events. Rogers died in a 1935 plane crash along with noted American aviator Wiley Post.

The drama critic and popular humorist Robert Benchley wrote clever works with amusing titles. James Thurber was one of a number of humorous writers associated with *The New Yorker* magazine. Thurber, who was also a cartoonist, showed real psychological insight into the odd characters in his works. Another *New Yorker* writer was E. B. White, a subtle humorist and brilliant stylist. White later wrote *Charlotte's Web* and several other stories for children..

The Second World War did not end the literary revival that had begun after the First World War. Many of the older writers continued to produce novels, short stories, plays, and poems. Meanwhile, a new generation of writers arose after the war to keep American literature at the leading edge of the world's artistic achievement.

JUKE BOX
Jacob Lawrence
Detroit Institute of Arts

AMERICAN VOICES

Quotations by Prominent Figures of the Period

All modern American literature comes from one book by Mark Twain called *Huckleberry Finn*.
Ernest Hemingway, *Green Hills of Africa*

In a real dark night of the soul it is always three o'clock in the morning.
F. Scott Fitzgerald, *The Crack-up*

His name is George F. Babbitt. He was . . . nimble in the calling of selling houses for more than people could afford to pay.
Sinclair Lewis, *Babbitt*

Well, if I called the wrong number, why did you answer the 'phone?
James Thurber, Cartoon caption

No more war, no more plague, only the dazed silence that follows the ceasing of the heavy guns. . . .
Katherine Ann Porter, *Pale Horse, Pale Rider*

You Can't Go Home Again
Thomas Wolfe, Title of novel

The storm had rolled away to faintness like a wagon crossing a bridge.
Eudora Welty, "A Piece of News"

Time is dead as long as it is being clicked off by little wheels; only when the clock stops does time come to life.
William Faulkner, *The Sound and the Fury*

This old anvil laughs at many broken hammers.
There are men who can't be bought.
Carl Sandburg, *The People, Yes*

Literature is news that *stays* news.
Ezra Pound, *ABC of Reading*

April is the cruellest month.
T. S. Eliot, "The Waste Land"

READING CRITICALLY

The Literature of 1915–1946

World War I had a tremendous impact on the attitudes and outlook of the American people. This impact is reflected in the literature of the modern age. To fully appreciate modern literature, you must understand how the nation was affected by its involvement in World War I.

HISTORICAL CONTEXT Prior to World War I, the mood of American society was confident and optimistic. This mood was shattered by the horrifying realities of American involvement in World War I—a war that caused the death of hundreds of thousands of Americans and Europeans. When the war ended, many people were left with a feeling of distrust toward the ideas and values of the past. People saw the need for change, but they were unsure about the sort of changes that were needed. There was a growing sense of uncertainty, disjointedness, and disillusionment among certain members of American society.

LITERARY MOVEMENTS In the aftermath of World War I, a major literary movement known as Modernism developed. Abandoning many traditional forms and techniques, the Modernists sought to capture the essence of modern life in both the form and content of their work. To reflect the disjointedness of modern life, they constructed their works out of fragments, omitting the expositions, resolutions, interpretations, transitions, and summaries often used in traditional works. The Modernists also frequently expressed their views about modern life in the themes of their works, often focusing on such themes as the uncertainty, bewilderment, and apparent meaninglessness of modern life.

WRITERS' TECHNIQUES Because they believed that modern life lacked certainty, the Modernists generally suggested rather than asserted meaning in their works. The theme of a typical Modernist work is implied, not stated, forcing readers to draw their own conclusions. Often, the Modernists used symbols and allusions to suggest themes. They also generally used a limited point of view in their works, because they believed that reality is shaped by people's perceptions. Finally, the Modernists experimented with a number of new literary techniques, including shifting points of view and the stream-of-consciousness technique.

Prose

ANDERSON

MAN WITH A HORN
Oliver Johnson
Courtesy of the Artist

SHERWOOD ANDERSON

1876–1941

Sherwood Anderson was one of the most influential writers of the modern age. Born and raised in a small town in Ohio, Anderson used his boyhood observations and experiences as material for his unified collection of short stories, *Winesburg, Ohio* (1919). In this work, from which "Sophistication" is taken, Anderson presents a portrait of small-town life that is strikingly different from those portraits presented in most earlier works of literature. He captures the sense of isolation and despair hidden beneath the surface of the characters' seemingly uneventful lives. He also uses simple, everyday language to capture the true flavor of his characters—a technique that influenced such later twentieth-century writers as Ernest Hemingway. Although Anderson's reputation rests mainly on this single work, he also published several other books, including *Windy McPherson's Sons* (1916), *Triumph of the Egg* (1921), *Horses and Men* (1923), and *Death in the Woods and Other Stories* (1933).

In writing the first of the *Winesburg* stories, Anderson experienced what he called "the most absorbingly interesting and exciting moment in any writer's life . . . the moment when he, for the first time, knows that he is a real writer." Twenty years later he described the experience in a letter:

> . . . I walked along a city street in the snow. . . . I was ill, discouraged, broke. I was living in a cheap rooming house. I remember that I went upstairs and into the room. It was very shabby. I had no relatives in the city and few enough friends. I remember how cold the room was. On that afternoon I had heard that I was to lose my job.
>
> . . . There was some paper on a small kitchen table I had bought and brought up into the room. I turned on a light and began to write. I wrote, without looking up—I never changed a word of it afterwards—a story called "Hands." It was and is a very beautiful story.
>
> I wrote the story and then got up from the table at which I had been sitting, I do not know how long, and went down into the city street. I thought that the snow had suddenly made the city very beautiful. . . . It must have been several hours before I got the courage to return to my room and read my own story.
>
> It was all right. It was sound. It was real. I went to sit by my desk. A great many others have had such moments. I wonder what they did. For the moment I thought the world very wonderful, and I thought also that there was a great deal of wonder in me.

GUIDE FOR INTERPRETING

Sophistication

Writers' Techniques

Character. Characters in a literary work may be described in terms of their complexity. When a character is well developed and possesses a variety of traits, he or she is referred to as a **round character.** Like Aunt Georgiana in "A Wagner Matinée," round characters are complex; they resemble real people. In contrast **flat characters** are one-dimensional caricatures. Like Tom Walker in "The Devil and Tom Walker," a flat character embodies a single trait or quality.

In the prologue to his *Winesburg* stories, Sherwood Anderson introduces a unique kind of flat character: the **grotesque.** According to Anderson, people become grotesques by living by and for only one truth, value, or assumption. Here is his explanation of grotesquerie:

> That in the beginning when the world was young there were a great many thoughts but no such thing as a truth. Man made the truths himself and each truth was a composite of a great many vague thoughts. All about in the world were the truths and they were all beautiful.
>
> . . . And then the people came along. Each as he appeared snatched up one of the truths and some who were quite strong snatched up a dozen of them.
>
> It was the truths that made the people grotesques. . . . [T]he moment one of the people took one of the truths to himself, called it his truth, and tried to live his life by it, he became a grotesque and the truth he embraced became a falsehood.

Commentary

In his introduction to Anderson's book, Malcolm Cowley shares his understanding of the role of the grotesques in the *Winesburg* stories:

> George Willard [the main character in the *Winesburg* stories] is growing up in a friendly town full of solitary persons; the author calls them "grotesques." Their lives have been distorted not, as Anderson tells us in his prologue, by their each having seized upon a single truth, but rather by their inability to express themselves. Since they cannot truly communicate with others, they have all become emotional cripples. Most of the grotesques are attracted one by one to George Willard; they feel that he might be able to help them.

Focus

In "Sophistication" George Willard learns how it feels to be a grown man. What new thoughts and feelings might he be experiencing? Share your emotions on approaching adulthood.

Sophistication

Sherwood Anderson

It was early evening of a day in the late fall and the Winesburg County Fair had brought crowds of country people into town. The day had been clear and the night came on warm and pleasant. On the Trunion Pike, where the road after it left town stretched away between berry fields now covered with dry brown leaves, the dust from passing wagons arose in clouds. Children, curled into little balls, slept on the straw scattered on wagon beds. Their hair was full of dust and their fingers black and sticky. The dust rolled away over the fields and the departing sun set it ablaze with colors.

In the main street of Winesburg crowds filled the stores and the sidewalks. Night came on, horses whinnied, the clerks in the stores ran madly about, children became lost and cried lustily, an American town worked terribly at the task of amusing itself.

Pushing his way through the crowds in Main Street, young George Willard concealed himself in the stairway leading to Doctor Reefy's office and looked at the people. With feverish eyes he watched the faces drifting past under the store lights. Thoughts kept coming into his head and he did not want to think. He stamped impatiently on the wooden steps and looked sharply about. "Well, is she going to stay with him all day? Have I done all this waiting for nothing?" he muttered.

George Willard, the Ohio village boy, was fast growing into manhood and new thoughts had been coming into his mind. All that day, amid the jam of people at the Fair, he had gone about feeling lonely. He was about to leave Winesburg to go away to some city where he hoped to get work on a city newspaper and he felt grown up. The mood that had taken possession of him was a thing known to men and unknown to boys. He felt old and a little tired. Memories awoke in him. To his mind his new sense of maturity set him apart, made of him a half-tragic figure. He wanted someone to understand the feeling that had taken possession of him after his mother's death.

There is a time in the life of every boy when he for the first time takes the backward view of life. Perhaps that is the moment when he crosses the line into manhood. The boy is walking through the street of his town. He is thinking of the future and of the figure he will cut in the world. Ambitions and regrets awake within him. Suddenly something happens; he stops under a tree and waits as for a voice calling his name. Ghosts of old things creep into his consciousness; the voices outside of himself whisper a message concerning the limitations of life. From being quite sure of himself and his future he becomes not at all sure. If he be an imaginative boy a door is torn open and for the first time he looks out upon the world, seeing, as though they marched in procession before him, the countless figures of men who before his time have come out of nothingness into the world, lived their lives and again disappeared into nothingness. The sadness of sophistication

WEST TISBURY FAIR
Thomas Hart Benton
Collection Mr. Arthur Levitte, Jr., New York

has come to the boy. With a little gasp he sees himself as merely a leaf blown by the wind through the streets of his village. He knows that in spite of all the stout talk of his fellows he must live and die in uncertainty, a thing blown by the winds, a thing destined like corn to wilt in the sun. He shivers and looks eagerly about. The eighteen years he has lived seem but a moment, a breathing space in the long march of humanity. Already he hears death calling. With all his heart he wants to come close to some other human, touch someone with his hands, be touched by the hand of another. If he prefers that the other be a woman, that is because he believes that a woman will be gentle, that she will understand. He wants, most of all, understanding.

When the moment of sophistication came to George Willard his mind turned to Helen White, the Winesburg banker's daughter.

Always he had been conscious of the girl growing into womanhood as he grew into manhood. Once on a summer night when he was eighteen, he had walked with her on a country road and in her presence had given way to an impulse to boast, to make himself appear big and significant in her eyes. Now he wanted to see her for another purpose. He wanted to tell her of the new impulses that had come to him. He had tried to make her think of him as a man when he knew nothing of manhood and now he wanted to be with her and to try to make her feel the change he believed had taken place in his nature.

As for Helen White, she also had come to a period of change. What George felt, she in her young woman's way felt also. She was no longer a girl and hungered to reach into the grace and beauty of womanhood. She had come home from Cleveland, where she was attending college, to spend a day at the Fair. She also had begun to have memories. During the day she sat in the grandstand with a young man, one of the instructors from the college, who was a guest of her mother's. The young man was of a pedantic turn of mind and she felt at once he would not do for her purpose. At the Fair she was glad to be seen in his company as he was well dressed and a stranger. She knew that the fact of his presence would create an impression. During the day she was happy, but when night came on she began to grow restless. She wanted to drive the instructor away, to get out of his presence. While they sat together in the grandstand and while the eyes of former schoolmates were upon them, she paid so much attention to her escort that he grew interested. "A scholar needs money. I should marry a woman with money," he mused.

Helen White was thinking of George Willard even as he wandered gloomily through the crowds thinking of her. She remembered the summer evening when they had walked together and wanted to walk with him again. She thought that the months she had spent in the city, the going to theaters and the see-ing of great crowds wandering in lighted thoroughfares, had changed her profoundly. She wanted him to feel and be conscious of the change in her nature.

The summer evening together that had left its mark on the memory of both the young man and woman had, when looked at quite sensibly, been rather stupidly spent. They had walked out of town along a country road. Then they had stopped by a fence near a field of young corn and George had taken off his coat and let it hang on his arm. "Well, I've stayed here in Winesburg—yes—I've not yet gone away but I'm growing up," he had said. "I've been reading books and I've been thinking. I'm going to try to amount to something in life.

"Well," he explained, "that isn't the point. Perhaps I'd better quit talking."

The confused boy put his hand on the girl's arm. His voice trembled. The two started to walk back along the road toward town. In his desperation George boasted, "I'm going to be a big man, the biggest that ever lived here in Winesburg," he declared. "I want you to do something. I don't know what. Perhaps it is none of my business. I want you to try to be different from other women. You see the point. It's none of my business, I tell you. I want you to be a beautiful woman. You see what I want."

The boy's voice failed and in silence the two came back into town and went along the street to Helen White's house. At the gate he tried to say something impressive. Speeches he had thought out came into his head, but they seemed utterly pointless. "I thought—I used to think—I had it in my mind you would marry Seth Richmond. Now I know you won't," was all he could find to say as she went through the gate and toward the door of her house.

On the warm fall evening as he stood in the stairway and looked at the crowd drifting through Main Street, George thought of the talk beside the field of young corn and was ashamed of the figure he had made of himself. In the street the people surged up and down like cattle confined in a pen. Buggies and wagons almost filled the narrow thoroughfare. A band played and small boys raced along the sidewalk, diving between the legs of men. Young men with shining red faces walked awkwardly about with girls on their arms. In a room above one of the stores, where a dance was to be held, the fiddlers tuned their instruments. The broken sounds floated down through an open window and out across the murmur of voices and the loud blare of the horns of the band. The medley of sounds got on young Willard's nerves. Everywhere, on all sides, the sense of crowding, moving life closed in about him. He wanted to run away by himself and think. "If she wants to stay with that fellow she may. Why should I care? What difference does it make to me?" he growled and went along Main Street and through Hern's Grocery into a side street.

George felt so utterly lonely and dejected that he wanted to weep but pride made him walk rapidly along, swinging his arms. He came to Wesley Moyer's livery barn and stopped in the shadows to listen to a group of men who talked of a race Wesley's stallion, Tony Tip, had won at the Fair during the afternoon. A crowd had gathered in front of the barn and before the crowd walked Wesley, prancing up and down and boasting. He held a whip in his hand and kept tapping the ground. Little puffs of dust arose in the lamplight. "Quit your talking," Wesley explained. "I wasn't afraid, I knew I had 'em beat all the time. I wasn't afraid."

Ordinarily George Willard would have been intensely interested in the boasting of Moyer, the horseman. Now it made him angry. He turned and hurried away along the street. "Old windbag," he sputtered. "Why does he want to be bragging? Why don't he shut up?"

George went into a vacant lot and, as he hurried along, fell over a pile of rubbish. A nail protruding from an empty barrel tore his trousers. He sat down on the ground and swore. With a pin he mended the torn place and then arose and went on. "I'll go to Helen White's house, that's what I'll do. I'll walk right in. I'll say that I want to see her. I'll walk right in and sit down, that's what I'll do," he declared, climbing over a fence and beginning to run.

On the veranda of Banker White's house Helen was restless and distraught. The instructor sat between the mother and daughter. His talk wearied the girl. Although he had also been raised in an Ohio town, the instructor began to put on the airs of the city. He wanted to appear cosmopolitan. "I like the chance you have given me to study the background out of which most of our girls come," he declared. "It was good of you, Mrs. White, to have me down for the day." He turned to Helen and laughed. "Your life is still bound up with the life of this town?" he asked. "There are people here in whom you are interested?" To the girl his voice sounded pompous and heavy.

Helen arose and went into the house. At the door leading to a garden at the back she stopped and stood listening. Her mother began to talk. "There is no one here fit to associate with a girl of Helen's breeding," she said.

Helen ran down a flight of stairs at the back of the house and into the garden. In the darkness she stopped and stood trembling. It seemed to her that the world was full of meaningless people saying words. Afire with eagerness she ran through a garden gate and, turning a corner by the banker's barn, went into a little side street. "George! Where are you, George?" she cried, filled with nervous excitement. She stopped running, and leaned against a tree to laugh hysterically. Along the dark little street came George Willard, still saying words. "I'm going to walk right into her house. I'll go right in and sit down," he declared as he came up to her. He stopped and stared stupidly. "Come on," he said and took hold of her hand. With hanging heads they walked away along the street under the trees. Dry leaves rustled under foot. Now that he had found her George wondered what he had better do and say.

At the upper end of the Fair Ground, in Winesburg, there is a half decayed old grandstand. It has never been painted and the boards are all warped out of shape. The Fair Ground stands on top of a low hill rising out of the valley of Wine Creek and from the grandstand one can see at night, over a cornfield, the lights of the town reflected against the sky.

George and Helen climbed the hill to the Fair Ground, coming by the path past Waterworks Pond. The feeling of loneliness and isolation that had come to the young man in the crowded streets of his town was both broken and intensified by the presence of Helen. What he felt was reflected in her.

In youth there are always two forces fighting in people. The warm unthinking little animal struggles against the thing that reflects and remembers, and the older, the more sophisticated thing had possession of George Willard. Sensing his mood, Helen walked beside him filled with respect. When they got to the grandstand they climbed up under the roof and sat down on one of the long bench-like seats.

There is something memorable in the experience to be had by going into a fair ground that stands at the end of a Middle Western town on a night after the annual fair has been held. The sensation is one never to be forgotten. On all sides are ghosts, not of the dead, but of living people. Here, during the day just passed, have come the people pouring in from the town and the country around. Farmers with their wives and children and all the people from the hundreds of little frame houses have gathered within these board walls. Young girls have laughed and men with beards have talked of the affairs of their lives. The place has been filled to overflowing with life. It has itched and squirmed with life and now it is night and the life has all gone away. The silence is almost terrifying. One conceals oneself standing silently beside the trunk of a tree and what there is of a reflective tendency in his nature is intensified. One shudders at the thought of the meaninglessness of life while at the same instant, and if the people of the town are his people, one loves life so intensely that tears come into the eyes.

In the darkness under the roof of the grandstand, George Willard sat beside Helen White and felt very keenly his own insignificance in the scheme of existence. Now that he had come out of town where the presence of the people stirring about, busy with a multitude of affairs, had been so irritating, the irritation was all gone. The presence of Helen renewed and refreshed him. It was as though her woman's hand was assisting him to make some minute readjustment of the machinery of his life. He began to think of the people in the town where he had always lived with something like reverence. He had reverence for Helen. He wanted to love and to be loved by her, but he did not want at the moment to be confused by her womanhood. In the darkness he took hold of her hand and when she crept close put a hand on her shoulder. A wind began to blow and he shivered. With all his strength he tried to hold and to understand the mood that had come upon him. In that high place in the darkness the two oddly sensitive human atoms held each other tightly and waited. In the mind of each was the same thought. "I have come to this lonely place and here is this other," was the substance of the thing felt.

In Winesburg the crowded day had run itself out into the long night of the late fall. Farm horses jogged away along lonely country roads pulling their portion of weary people. Clerks began to bring samples of goods in off the sidewalks and lock the doors of stores. In the Opera House a crowd had gathered to see a show and further down Main Street the fiddlers, their instruments tuned, sweated and worked to keep the feet of youth flying over a dance floor.

AFTER THE SHOW, 1933
Waldo Peirce
Whitney Museum of American Art

In the darkness in the grandstand Helen White and George Willard remained silent. Now and then the spell that held them was broken and they turned and tried in the dim light to see into each other's eyes. They kissed but that impulse did not last. At the upper end of the Fair Ground a half dozen men worked over horses that had raced during the afternoon. The men had built a fire and were heating kettles of water. Only their legs could be seen as they passed back and forth in the light. When the wind blew the little flames of the fire danced crazily about.

George and Helen arose and walked away into the darkness. They went along a path past a field of corn that had not yet been cut. The wind whispered among the dry corn blades. For a moment during the walk back into town the spell that held them was broken. When they had come to the crest of Waterworks Hill they stopped by a tree and George again put his hands on the girl's shoulders. She embraced him eagerly and then again they drew quickly back from that impulse. They stopped kissing and stood a little apart. Mutual respect grew big in them. They were both embarrassed and to relieve their embarrassment dropped into the animalism of youth. They laughed and began to pull and haul at each other. In some way chastened and purified by the mood they had been in, they became, not man and woman, not boy and girl, but excited little animals.

It was so they went down the hill. In the darkness they played like two splendid young things in a young world. Once, running swiftly forward, Helen tripped George and he fell. He squirmed and shouted. Shaking with laughter, he rolled down the hill. Helen ran after him. For just a moment she stopped in the darkness. There is no way of knowing what woman's thoughts went through her mind but, when the bottom of the hill was reached and she came up to the boy, she took his arm and walked beside him in dignified silence. For some reason they could not have explained they had both got from their silent evening together the thing needed. Man or boy, woman or girl, they had for a moment taken hold of the thing that makes the mature life of men and women in the modern world possible.

RESPONDING TO THE SELECTION

Your Response

1. To George sophistication is a source of sadness. What feelings do you associate with sophistication?
2. In what ways are George's experiences with growing up similar to your own?

Recalling

3. How does George feel among the crowds at the Winesburg County Fair?
4. Why do George and Helen White want to see each other?
5. What evening stands out in both George's and Helen's memory?
6. (a) Where do George and Helen go after they meet? (b) What do they do? (c) What do they get from their evening together?

Interpreting

7. What overall impression does Anderson convey of Winesburg and its inhabitants?
8. (a) What internal conflict do both George and Helen experience? (b) How are their actions in this story related to the conflict?
9. (a) What generalizations does Anderson make about the passage from childhood to adulthood? (b) How do George's and Helen's actions support these generalizations?

10. What is the story's theme, or insight into life?
11. (a) What is the "sadness of sophistication"? (b) Look up the origin of the word *sophistication* in a dictionary. Then explain the meaning of the title.

Applying

12. Do you agree with the generalizations that Anderson makes about the passage from childhood to adulthood? Why or why not?
13. The French biologist and writer Jean Rostand has written, "To be adult is to be alone." How do you think George Willard would react to this comment? Explain your answer.

ANALYZING LITERATURE

Understanding Character

In narrative fiction a complex character is called **round,** whereas a simple character is called **flat.** Many of the simpler characters in the *Winesburg* stories are **grotesques:** people who latch onto a single truth, emotion, idea, or ambition and try to live by it.

1. Are George and Helen round characters or flat characters? Explain.
2. Which characters in "Sophistication," if any, might be considered grotesques? Explain.

CRITICAL THINKING AND READING

Understanding a Character's Motivation

In portraying any type of character, a writer must provide a motivation, or a stated or implied reason for the character's actions, to make the character's behavior believable. For example, Anderson directly states that the college instructor's comments on the veranda of Banker White's house are motivated by his desire "to appear cosmopolitan."

1. What motivates George and Helen to find each other?
2. How does Anderson reveal their motivations?

THINKING AND WRITING

Writing About Theme

How would you define the turning point between youth and maturity? Write a brief essay in which you discuss what maturity means to you. Start by listing your thoughts about maturity. Organize your notes into an outline. Prepare a thesis statement. Then write your essay. When you finish writing, revise your essay, making sure you have used vivid examples from life to support your central idea. Finally, proofread your essay and share it with your classmates.

LEARNING OPTION

Writing. How might George's passage to adulthood be different if the story were set in your hometown today instead of Winesburg, Ohio, at the turn of the century? Brainstorm with a small group of classmates. Then together write a story outline for a revised version of "Sophistication." Briefly describe the setting, the main character, and the moment when he crosses into adulthood.

ERNEST HEMINGWAY

1899–1961

In his short stories and novels, Ernest Hemingway vividly and forcefully expressed the sentiments of many members of the post-World War I generation. Using a concise, direct style, he wrote about people's struggles to maintain a sense of dignity while living in a seemingly hostile and confusing world.

Hemingway was born and raised in Oak Park, Illinois. After graduating from high school, he got a job as a reporter for the Kansas City *Star*. He was eager to serve in World War I, and in 1918 he joined the Red Cross ambulance corps and was sent to the Italian front. Shortly after his arrival, he was severely wounded, and he spent several months recovering in a hospital in Milan. His experiences during the war shaped his views and provided material for his writing.

After the war Hemingway had a difficult time readjusting to life in the United States. Hoping to find personal contentment and establish himself as a writer, he went to Paris where he became friends with Ezra Pound, F. Scott Fitzgerald, Gertrude Stein, and other expatriate writers and artists. His new friends provided him with valuable advice, helped to develop his style, and encouraged his interest in writing.

In 1925 Hemingway published his first major work, *In Our Time,* a series of loosely connected short stories. A year later he published *The Sun Also Rises,* a novel about a group of British and American expatriates searching for sensations that would enable them to forget the pain and disillusionment they associate with life in the modern world. The novel earned him international acclaim, and he remained famous throughout the rest of his life. Yet he was almost as well known for his lifestyle as he was for his writing. Constantly pursuing adventure, he traveled the world, hunting in Africa, deep-sea fishing in the Caribbean, and skiing in Idaho and Europe.

Despite his thirst for adventure, Hemingway remained a productive and successful writer, transforming his observations and experiences into novels and short stories. His novels *A Farewell to Arms* (1929), based on his experiences during World War I, and *For Whom the Bell Tolls* (1940), based on his observations as a war correspondent during the Spanish Civil War, have become American classics. *The Old Man and the Sea* (1952), the story of an old fisherman's struggle to maintain dignity in the face of defeat, won the Pulitzer Prize and helped earn him the Nobel Prize for Literature in 1954.

In 1958 Hemingway defined realism in his art: "From things that have happened and from things as they exist and from all the things that you know and all those that you cannot know, you make something through your invention that is not a representation but a whole new thing truer than any thing true and alive."

GUIDE FOR INTERPRETING

In Another Country

Literary Movements

Modernism. Following World War I there was a growing sense of uncertainty, disjointedness, and disillusionment among certain members of American society. Many people came to distrust the ideas and values of the past and sought to find new ideas that seemed more applicable to twentieth-century life. Similarly, writers began turning away from the style, form, and content of nineteenth-century literature and began experimenting with new themes and techniques. A new literary movement, known as Modernism, was born.

The Modernists attempted to capture the essense of modern life in both the form and the content of their work. The uncertainty, bewilderment, and apparent meaninglessness of life were common themes in modern literature. These themes were generally implied, rather than directly stated, to reflect a sense of uncertainty and to enable readers to draw their own conclusions. For similar reasons fiction writers began abandoning the traditional plot structure, omitting the expositions and resolutions that in the past had clarified the work for the reader. Instead, stories and novels were structured to reflect the fragmentation and uncertainty of human experience. A typical modern story or novel seems to begin arbitrarily and to end without a resolution, leaving the reader with possibilities, not solutions.

Focus

Most of Hemingway's stories and novels were based on his observations and experiences. "In Another Country," for example, grew out of his observations during his hospitalization in Milan. Prepare a list of your own observations and experiences that you could use as topics for narratives.

Primary Source

Hemingway's style has been described as simple, objective, and spare. In *Death in the Afternoon* (1932) he wrote,

> If a writer of prose knows enough about what he is writing about he may omit things that he knows and the reader, if the writer is writing truly enough, will have a feeling of those things as strongly as though the writer had stated them. The dignity of movement of an iceberg is due to only one-eighth of it being above water. A writer who omits things because he does not know them only makes hollow places in his writing. A writer who appreciates the seriousness of writing so little that he is anxious to make people see he is formally educated, cultured, or well-bred is merely a popinjay. And this too remember; a serious writer is not to be confounded with a solemn writer. . . .

In Another Country

Ernest Hemingway

In the fall the war[1] was always there, but we did not go to it any more. It was cold in the fall in Milan[2] and the dark came very early. Then the electric lights came on, and it was pleasant along the streets looking in the windows. There was much game hanging outside the shops, and the snow powdered in the fur of the foxes and the wind blew their tails. The deer hung stiff and heavy and empty, and small birds blew in the wind and the wind turned their feathers. It was a cold fall and the wind came down from the mountains.

We were all at the hospital every afternoon, and there were different ways of walking across the town through the dusk to the hospital. Two of the ways were alongside canals, but they were long. Always, though, you crossed a bridge across a canal to enter the hospital. There was a choice of three bridges. On one of them a woman sold roasted chestnuts. It was warm, standing in front of her charcoal fire, and the chestnuts were warm afterward in your pocket. The hospital was very old and very beautiful, and you entered through a gate and walked across a courtyard and out a gate on the other side. There were usually funerals starting from the courtyard. Beyond the old hospital were the new brick pavilions, and there we met every afternoon and were all very polite and interested in what was the matter, and sat in the machines that were to make so much difference.

The doctor came up to the machine where I was sitting and said: "What did you like best to do before the war? Did you practice a sport?"

I said: "Yes, football."

"Good," he said. "You will be able to play football again better than ever."

My knee did not bend and the leg dropped straight from the knee to the ankle without a calf, and the machine was to bend the knee and make it move as in riding a tricycle. But it did not bend yet, and instead the machine lurched when it came to the bending part. The doctor said: "That will all pass. You are a fortunate young man. You will play football again like a champion."

In the next machine was a major who had a little hand like a baby's. He winked at me when the doctor examined his hand, which was between two leather straps that bounced up and down and flapped the stiff fingers, and said: "And will I too play football, captain-doctor?" He had been a very great fencer, and before the war the greatest fencer in Italy.

The doctor went to his office in a back room and brought a photograph which showed a hand that had been withered almost as small as the major's, before it had taken a machine course, and after was a little larger. The major held the photograph with his good hand and looked at it very carefully. "A wound?" he asked.

"An industrial accident," the doctor said.

"Very interesting, very interesting," the major said, and handed it back to the doctor.

---

1. **the war:** World War I (1914–1918).
2. **Milan** (mi lan'): A city in northern Italy.

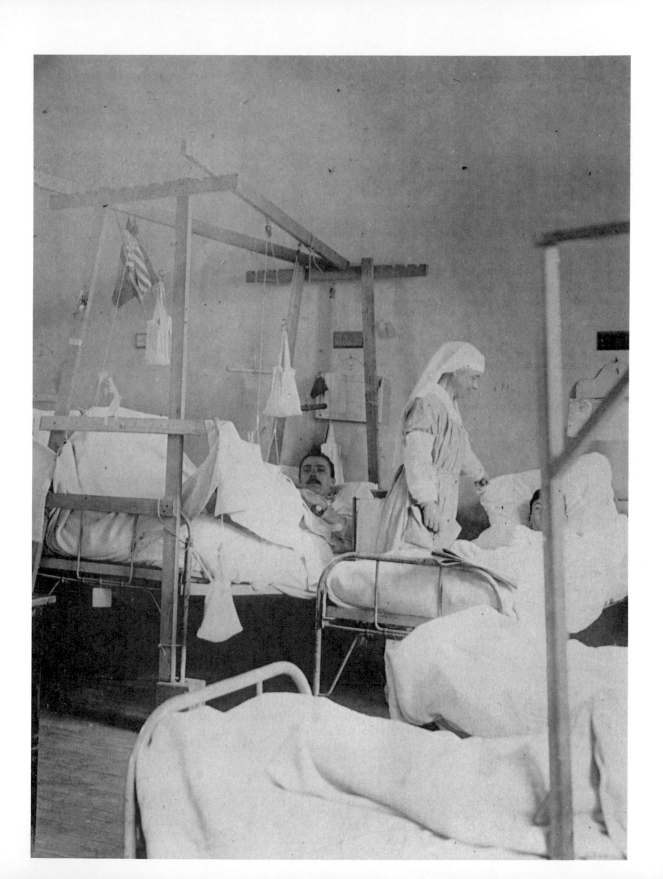

"You have confidence?"

"No," said the major.

There were three boys who came each day who were about the same age I was. They were all three from Milan, and one of them was to be a lawyer, and one was to be a painter, and one had intended to be a soldier, and after we were finished with the machines, sometimes we walked back together to the Café Cova, which was next door to the Scala.[3] We walked the short way through the communist quarter because we were four together. The people hated us because we were officers, and from a wine-shop someone called out, "A basso gli ufficiali!"[4] as we passed. Another boy who walked with us sometimes and made us five wore a black silk handkerchief across his face because he had no nose then and his face was to be rebuilt. He had gone out to the front from the military academy and been wounded within an hour after he had gone into the front line for the first time. They rebuilt his face, but he came from a very old family and they could never get the nose exactly right. He went to South America and worked in a bank. But this was a long time ago, and then we did not any of us know how it was going to be afterward. We only knew then that there was always the war, but that we were not going to it any more.

We all had the same medals, except the boy with the black silk bandage across his face, and he had not been at the front long enough to get any medals. The tall boy with a very pale face who was to be a lawyer had been a lieutenant of Arditi[5] and had three medals of the sort we each had only one of. He had lived a very long time with death and was a little detached. We were all a little detached, and there was nothing that held us together except that we met every afternoon at the hospital. Although, as we walked to the Cova through the tough part of town, walking in the dark, with light and singing coming out of the wine-shops, and sometimes having to walk into the street when the men and women would crowd together on the sidewalk so that we would have had to jostle them to get by, we felt held together by there being something that had happened that they, the people who disliked us, did not understand.

We ourselves all understood the Cova, where it was rich and warm and not too brightly lighted, and noisy and smoky at certain hours, and there were always girls at the tables and the illustrated papers on a rack on the wall. The girls at the Cova were very patriotic, and I found that the most patriotic people in Italy were the café girls—and I believe they are still patriotic.

The boys at first were very polite about my medals and asked me what I had done to get them. I showed them the papers, which were written in very beautiful language and full of *fratellanza* and *abnegazione*,[6] but which really said, with the adjectives removed, that I had been given the medals because I was an American. After that their manner changed a little toward me, although I was their friend against outsiders. I was a friend, but I was never really one of them after they had read the citations, because it had been different with them and they had done very different things to get their medals. I had been wounded, it was true; but we all knew that being wounded, after all, was really an accident. I was never ashamed of the ribbons, though, and sometimes, after the cocktail hour, I would imagine myself having done all the things they had done to get their medals; but walking home at night through the empty streets with the cold wind and all the shops closed, trying to keep near the street lights, I knew that I would never have done such things,

---

3. the Scala (ska′ la): An opera house in Milan.

4. "A basso gli ufficiali!" (a ba′ sō lye o͞o fē c̸ha′ lē): "Down with officers!" (Italian).

5. Arditi (ar dē′ tē): A select group of soldiers chosen specifically for dangerous campaigns.

6. *fratellanza* (fra tāl an′ za) **and *abnegazione*** (ab nä ga tzyō′ nä): "Brotherhood" and "self-denial" (Italian).

and I was very much afraid to die, and often lay in bed at night by myself, afraid to die and wondering how I would be when I went back to the front again.

The three with the medals were like hunting-hawks; and I was not a hawk, although I might seem a hawk to those who had never hunted; they, the three, knew better and so we drifted apart. But I stayed good friends with the boy who had been wounded his first day at the front, because he would never know now how he would have turned out; so he could never be accepted either, and I liked him because I thought perhaps he would not have turned out to be a hawk either.

The major, who had been the great fencer, did not believe in bravery, and spent much time while we sat in the machines correcting my grammar. He had complimented me on how I spoke Italian, and we talked together very easily. One day I had said that Italian seemed such an easy language to me that I could not take a great interest in it; everything was so easy to say. "Ah yes," the major said. "Why, then, do you not take up the use of grammar?" So we took up the use of grammar, and soon Italian was such a difficult language that I was afraid to talk to him until I had the grammar straight in my mind.

The major came very regularly to the hospital. I do not think he ever missed a day, although I am sure he did not believe in the machines. There was a time when none of us believed in the machines, and one day the major said it was all nonsense. The machines were new then and it was we who were to prove them. It was an idiotic idea, he said, "a theory, like another." I had not learned my grammar, and he said I was a stupid impossible disgrace, and he was a fool to have bothered with me. He was a small man and he sat straight up in his chair with his right hand thrust into the machine and looked straight ahead at the wall while the straps thumped up and down with his fingers in them.

"What will you do when the war is over if it is over?" he asked me. "Speak grammatically!"

"I will go to the States."

"Are you married?"

"No, but I hope to be."

"The more of a fool you are," he said. He seemed very angry. "A man must not marry."

"Why, Signor Maggiore?"[7]

"Don't call me 'Signor Maggiore.' "

"Why must not a man marry?"

"He cannot marry. He cannot marry," he said angrily. "If he is to lose everything, he should not place himself in a position to lose that. He should not place himself in a position to lose. He should find things he cannot lose."

He spoke very angrily and bitterly, and looked straight ahead while he talked.

"But why should he necessarily lose it?"

"He'll lose it," the major said. He was looking at the wall. Then he looked down at the machine and jerked his little hand out from between the straps and slapped it hard against his thigh. "He'll lose it," he almost shouted. "Don't argue with me!" Then he called to the attendant who ran the machines. "Come and turn this damned thing off."

He went back into the other room for the light treatment and the massage. Then I heard him ask the doctor if he might use his telephone and he shut the door. When he came back into the room, I was sitting in another machine. He was wearing his cape and had his cap on, and he came directly toward my machine and put his arm on my shoulder.

"I am so sorry," he said, and patted me on the shoulder with his good hand. "I would not be rude. My wife has just died. You must forgive me."

"Oh—" I said, feeling sick for him. "I am so sorry."

---

7. Signor Maggiore (sēn yôr′ maj jō′ rä): "Mr. Major" (Italian); a respectful way of addressing an officer.

He stood there biting his lower lip. "It is very difficult," he said. "I cannot resign myself."

He looked straight past me and out through the window. Then he began to cry. "I am utterly unable to resign myself," he said and choked. And then crying, his head up looking at nothing, carrying himself straight and soldierly, with tears on both his cheeks and biting his lips, he walked past the machines and out the door.

The doctor told me that the major's wife, who was very young and whom he had not married until he was definitely invalided out of the war, had died of pneumonia. She had been sick only a few days. No one expected her to die. The major did not come to the hospital for three days. Then he came at the usual hour, wearing a black band on the sleeve of his uniform. When he came back, there were large framed photographs around the wall, of all sorts of wounds before and after they had been cured by the machines. In front of the machine the major used were three photographs of hands like his that were completely restored. I do not know where the doctor got them. I always understood we were the first to use the machines. The photographs did not make much difference to the major because he only looked out of the window.

RESPONDING TO THE SELECTION

Your Response

1. How does the first sentence in the story make you feel?
2. Which of the story characters, if any, do you admire? Explain.

Recalling

3. Why does the narrator go to the hospital every afternoon?
4. (a) How had the narrator acquired his medals? (b) How does the attitude of the three boys toward the narrator change when they find out what he had done to get the medals?
5. (a) What advice does the major give the narrator toward the end of the story? (b) What has happened to the major's wife?
6. (a) What pictures are hanging on the wall when the major returns? (b) Why does the narrator think the pictures are deceptive?

Interpreting

7. What mood do the details of the setting convey?
8. (a) How is the narrator's attitude toward the war different from that of the three boys? (b) How might this difference in attitude be related to their nationalities?
9. What do you think is the significance of the major's interest in grammar?
10. In this story the machines come to symbolize the false hopes and promises of the modern age. What details convey the symbolic meaning of the machines?
11. Considering that the major waited until he was invalided out of the war to marry his wife, what is ironic about her death?

Applying

12. Gertrude Stein wrote, "You are all a lost generation." This epigraph has come to stand for the young people of Hemingway's time. In what way are the young men in this story "lost"?
13. Explain the two meanings suggested by the title of this story.
14. World War I left many people feeling disillusioned because it caused the death of thousands of people, though it seemed to have no purpose. How does this story reflect this sense of disillusionment?

ANALYZING LITERATURE

Understanding Modernism

Modernism was a literary movement in which writers attempted to capture the essence of modern life in both the form and content of their work. One of the themes of "In Another Country," for example, is that in the modern age people are often presented with false hopes and promises.

1. Like most other Modernist stories, "In Another Country" lacks an exposition and a resolution. What Modernist perception does the use of this technique reflect?
2. In this story the narrator makes no direct statements about the war, allowing us to draw our own conclusions. How does this reflect the Modernist belief in the uncertainty of modern life?

CRITICAL THINKING AND READING

Analyzing the Effect of Style

Hemingway's style is easily distinguished from that of most other writers. He wrote in journalistic style, relating events in a straightforward manner with little elaboration and using simple and direct yet rhythmic and precise language.

1. Considering the Modernists' desire to force readers to draw their own conclusions from their works, why is Hemingway's journalistic style appropriate?
2. The nineteenth-century poet Robert Browning wrote, "Less is more." This aphorism was picked up by the twentieth-century architect Ludwig Mies van der Rohe and came to stand for a style in which design was simplified and form was made to serve function. Explain how the aphorism "less is more" can be said to characterize Hemingway's writing style.

THINKING AND WRITING

Responding to a Statement

Hemingway once commented, ". . . I always try to write on the principle of the iceberg. There is seven-eighths of it under water for every part that shows." Write an essay relating this statement to "In Another Country." Start by reviewing the story, taking note of Hemingway's concise style and how he uses such techniques as symbolism and irony to convey meaning. Organize your notes into an outline. Then write your essay, using passages from the story to support Hemingway's statement. When you finish writing, revise your essay, making sure you have backed up your thesis with details from the story. Proofread your essay and share it with your classmates.

LEARNING OPTION

Writing. Consider what makes the first sentence from "In Another Country" memorable. Then write a memorable first line for a short story of your own. Share your opener with classmates. Based on its first line, would others like to read your future masterpiece?

Primary Source

Hemingway created realistic characters. In *Death in the Afternoon* (1932), he discussed how to create people in fiction. "When writing a novel a writer should create living people; people not characters. A *character* is a caricature. . . . If the people the writer is making talk of old masters; of music; of modern painting; of letters; or of science then they should talk of those subjects in the novel. If they do not talk of those subjects and the writer makes them talk of them he is a faker, and if he talks about them himself to show how much he knows then he is showing off. No matter how good a phrase or simile he may have if he puts it in where it is not absolutely necessary and irreplaceable he is spoiling his work for egotism. Prose is architecture, not interior decoration. . . ."

F. SCOTT FITZGERALD

1896–1940

During the 1920's many Americans lived with reckless abandon, attending wild parties, wearing glamorous clothing, and striving for personal fulfillment through material wealth. Yet this quest for pleasure was often accompanied by a sense of inner despair. In his short stories and novels, F. Scott Fitzgerald captured both the gaiety and the emptiness of the time.

Francis Scott Key Fitzgerald was born in St. Paul, Minnesota, into a family with high social aspirations but little wealth. He entered Princeton University in 1913. Being a romantic young man, he threw himself into the social life at Princeton, living the kind of life for which he became famous in the 1920's. He failed to graduate, and in 1917 he enlisted in the army. He was stationed in Montgomery, Alabama, where he fell in love with Zelda Sayre, a young southern belle. Shortly after being discharged from the army, Fitzgerald published his first novel, *This Side of Paradise* (1920). The novel earned him instant fame and wealth, which enabled him to persuade Zelda to marry him.

The Fitzgeralds soon became a part of the wealthy, extravagant, and hedonistic society that characterized the Roaring Twenties. Spending time in both New York and Europe, the glamorous couple mingled with rich and famous artists and aristocrats, attending countless parties and spending money recklessly. Despite his wild lifestyle, Fitzgerald remained a productive writer. During the twenties he published dozens of short stories and his most successful novel, *The Great Gatsby* (1925), the story of a self-made man whose dreams of love and social acceptance lead to scandal and corruption and ultimately end in tragedy. The novel displayed Fitzgerald's fascination with and growing distrust of the wealthy society he had embraced.

Following the stock market crash in 1929, Fitzgerald's life changed dramatically. His wife suffered a series of nervous breakdowns, his reputation as a writer declined, and financial difficulties forced him to seek work as a Hollywood screenwriter. Despite these setbacks, however, he managed to produce many more short stories and a second fine novel, *Tender Is the Night* (1934). Focusing on the decline of a young American psychiatrist following his marriage to a wealthy patient, the novel reflected Fitzgerald's awareness of the tragedy that can result from an obsession with wealth and social status.

Fitzgerald died of a heart attack in 1940. At the time he was in the midst of writing *The Last Tycoon* (1941), a novel about a Hollywood film mogul.

GUIDE FOR INTERPRETING

Writers' Techniques

Winter Dreams

Characterization. Characterization is the means by which a writer reveals a character's personality. Writers generally develop a character through one or more of the following methods: direct statements about the character, physical descriptions of the character, the character's actions, the character's thoughts and comments, or another character's reactions to or comments about the character. In "Winter Dreams" F. Scott Fitzgerald develops the two main characters using a variety of these methods. For example, he reveals an important aspect of Dexter Green's personality directly, when he comments that Dexter "wanted not association with glittering things and glittering people—he wanted the glittering things themselves."

Commentary

Written in 1922, "Winter Dreams" unfolds against the background of the Jazz Age. Focusing on Dexter Green's obsession with Judy Jones, a beautiful young woman from a prominent wealthy family, Fitzgerald explores the connection between love, money, and social status. Through Dexter he shows what life was like in the 1920's for an ambitious young man driven by the desire for "glittering things." A romantic at heart, Dexter idealizes Judy. Though she is selfish, arrogant, and erratic, he finds her exhilarating and desirable.

Fitzgerald wants to create sympathy for his two characters, despite their destructive fantasies and values. He explores what critic Lionel Trilling called "the power of love." According to Trilling, Fitzgerald was "the last notable writer to affirm the Romantic fantasy"—the nobility of giving your all for a romantic ideal, no matter what. We can criticize Dexter for being attracted to glamour and for wanting to be rich and to win over the richest girl in town, but Fitzgerald also wants us to be a little in awe of Dexter's devotion, which comes at the cost of his own happiness.

Focus

In Don Marquis's poem "Unjust," Archy the cockroach writes, "beauty gets the best of it/in this world." Freewrite, exploring your reaction to Archy's comment.

Winter Dreams

F. Scott Fitzgerald

I

Some of the caddies were poor as sin and lived in one-room houses with a neurasthenic[1] cow in the front yard, but Dexter Green's father owned the second best grocery store in Black Bear—the best one was "The Hub," patronized by the wealthy people from Sherry Island—and Dexter caddied only for pocket money.

In the fall when the days became crisp and gray, and the long Minnesota winter shut down like the white lid of a box, Dexter's skis moved over the snow that hid the fairways of the golf course. At these times the country gave him a feeling of profound melancholy—it offended him that the links should lie in enforced fallowness, haunted by ragged sparrows for the long season. It was dreary, too, that on the tees where the gay colors fluttered in summer there were now only the desolate sandboxes knee deep in crusted ice. When he crossed the hills the wind blew cold as misery, and if the sun was out he tramped with his eyes squinted up against the hard dimensionless glare.

In April the winter ceased abruptly. The snow ran down into Black Bear Lake scarcely tarrying for the early golfers to brave the season with red and black balls. Without elation, without an interval of moist glory, the cold was gone.

Dexter knew that there was something dismal about this Northern spring, just as he knew there was something gorgeous about the fall. Fall made him clinch his hands and tremble and repeat idiotic sentences to himself, and make brisk abrupt gestures of command to imaginary audiences and armies. October filled him with hope which November raised to a sort of ecstatic triumph, and in this mood the fleeting brilliant impressions of the summer at Sherry Island were ready grist to his mill. He became a golf champion and defeated Mr. T. A. Hedrick in a marvelous match played a hundred times over the fairways of his imagination, a match each detail of which he changed about untiringly—sometimes he won with almost laughable ease, sometimes he came up magnificently from behind. Again, stepping from a Pierce-Arrow automobile, like Mr. Mortimer Jones, he strolled frigidly into the lounge of the Sherry Island Golf Club—or perhaps, surrounded by an admiring crowd, he gave an exhibition of fancy diving from the springboard of the club raft. . . . Among those who watched him in open-mouthed wonder was Mr. Mortimer Jones.

And one day it came to pass that Mr. Jones—himself and not his ghost—came up to Dexter with tears in his eyes and said that Dexter was the —— best caddy in the club, and wouldn't he decide not to quit if Mr. Jones made it worth his while, because every other —— caddy in the club lost one ball a hole for him—regularly——

"No, sir," said Dexter decisively, "I don't want to caddy any more." Then, after a pause: "I'm too old."

"You're not more than fourteen. Why the devil did you decide just this morning that

---

1. **neurasthenic** (noor' əs then' ik) *adj.*: Here, weak, tired.

you wanted to quit? You promised that next week you'd go over to the state tournament with me."

"I decided I was too old."

Dexter handed in his "A Class" badge, collected what money was due him from the caddy master, and walked home to Black Bear Village.

"The best —— caddy I ever saw," shouted Mr. Mortimer Jones over a drink that afternoon. "Never lost a ball! Willing! Intelligent! Quiet! Honest! Grateful!"

The little girl who had done this was eleven—beautifully ugly as little girls are apt to be who are destined after a few years to be inexpressibly lovely and bring no end of misery to a great number of men. The spark, however, was perceptible. There was a general ungodliness in the way her lips twisted down at the corners when she smiled, and in

the—Heaven help us!—in the almost passionate quality of her eyes. Vitality is born early in such women. It was utterly in evidence now, shining through her thin frame in a sort of glow.

She had come eagerly out on to the course at nine o'clock with a white linen nurse and five small new golf clubs in a white canvas bag which the nurse was carrying. When Dexter first saw her she was standing by the caddy house, rather ill at ease and trying to conceal the fact by engaging her nurse in an obviously unnatural conversation graced by startling and irrelevant grimaces from herself.

"Well, it's certainly a nice day, Hilda," Dexter heard her say. She drew down the corners of her mouth, smiled, and glanced furtively around, her eyes in transit falling for an instant on Dexter.

Then to the nurse:

"Well, I guess there aren't very many people out here this morning, are there?"

The smile again—radiant, blatantly artificial—convincing.

"I don't know what we're supposed to do now," said the nurse looking nowhere in particular.

"Oh, that's all right. I'll fix it up."

Dexter stood perfectly still, his mouth slightly ajar. He knew that if he moved forward a step his stare would be in her line of vision—if he moved backward he would lose his full view of her face. For a moment he had not realized how young she was. Now he remembered having seen her several times the year before—in bloomers.

Suddenly, involuntarily, he laughed, a short abrupt laugh—then, startled by himself, he turned and began to walk quickly away.

"Boy!"

Dexter stopped.

"Boy——"

Beyond question he was addressed. Not only that, but he was treated to that absurd smile, that preposterous smile—the memory of which at least a dozen men were to carry into middle age.

"Boy, do you know where the golf teacher is?"

"He's giving a lesson."

"Well, do you know where the caddy master is?"

"He isn't here yet this morning."

"Oh." For a moment this baffled her. She stood alternately on her right and left foot.

"We'd like to get a caddy," said the nurse. "Mrs. Mortimer Jones sent us out to play golf, and we don't know how without we get a caddy."

Here she was stopped by an ominous glance from Miss Jones, followed immediately by the smile.

"There aren't any caddies here except me," said Dexter to the nurse, "and I got to stay here in charge until the caddy master gets here."

"Oh."

Miss Jones and her retinue now withdrew, and at a proper distance from Dexter became involved in a heated conversation, which was concluded by Miss Jones taking one of the clubs and hitting it on the ground with violence. For further emphasis she raised it again and was about to bring it down smartly upon the nurse's bosom, when the nurse seized the club and twisted it from her hands.

"You little mean old *thing!*" cried Miss Jones wildly.

Another argument ensued. Realizing that the elements of the comedy were implied in the scene, Dexter several times began to laugh, but each time restrained the laugh before it reached audibility. He could not resist the monstrous conviction that the little girl was justified in beating the nurse.

The situation was resolved by the fortuitous appearance of the caddy master, who was appealed to immediately by the nurse.

"Miss Jones is to have a little caddy, and this one says he can't go."

"Mr. McKenna said I was to wait here till you came," said Dexter quickly.

"Well, he's here now." Miss Jones smiled cheerfully at the caddy master. Then she dropped her bag and set off at a haughty mince toward the first tee.

"Well?" The caddy master turned to Dexter. "What you standing there like a dummy for? Go pick up the young lady's clubs."

"I don't think I'll go out today," said Dexter.

"You don't——"

"I think I'll quit."

The enormity of his decision frightened him. He was a favorite caddy, and the thirty dollars a month he earned through the summer were not to be made elsewhere around the lake. But he had received a strong emotional shock, and his perturbation required a violent and immediate outlet.

It is not so simple as that, either. As so frequently would be the case in the future, Dexter was unconsciously dictated to by his winter dreams.

II

Now, of course, the quality and the seasonability of these winter dreams varied, but the stuff of them remained. They persuaded Dexter several years later to pass up a business course at the State university—his father, prospering now, would have paid his way—for the precarious advantage of attending an older and more famous university in the East, where he was bothered by his scanty funds. But do not get the impression, because his winter dreams happened to be concerned at first with musings on the rich, that there was anything merely snobbish in the boy. He wanted not association with glittering things and glittering people—he wanted the glittering things themselves. Often he reached out for the best without knowing why he wanted it—and sometimes he ran up against the mysterious denials and prohibitions in which life indulges. It is with one of those denials and not with his career as a whole that this story deals.

He made money. It was rather amazing. After college he went to the city from which Black Bear Lake draws its wealthy patrons. When he was only twenty-three and had been there not quite two years, there were already people who liked to say: "Now *there's* a boy—" All about him rich men's sons were peddling bonds precariously, or investing patrimonies precariously, or plodding through the two dozen volumes of the "George Washington Commercial Course," but Dexter borrowed a thousand dollars on his college degree and his confident mouth, and bought a partnership in a laundry.

It was a small laundry when he went into it, but Dexter made a specialty of learning how the English washed fine woolen golf stockings without shrinking them, and within a year he was catering to the trade that wore knickerbockers. Men were insisting that their Shetland hose and sweaters go to his laundry, just as they had insisted on a caddy who could find golf balls. A little later he was doing their wives' lingerie as well—and running five branches in different parts of the city. Before he was twenty-seven he owned the largest string of laundries in his section of the country. It was then that he sold out and went to New York. But the part of his story that concerns us goes back to the days when he was making his first big success.

When he was twenty-three Mr. Hart—one of the gray-haired men who like to say "Now there's a boy"—gave him a guest card to the Sherry Island Golf Club for a weekend. So he signed his name one day on the register, and that afternoon played golf in a foursome with Mr. Hart and Mr. Sandwood and Mr. T. A. Hedrick. He did not consider it necessary to remark that he had once carried Mr. Hart's bag over this same links, and that he knew every trap and gully with his eyes shut—but he found himself glancing at the four caddies who trailed them, trying to catch a gleam or gesture that would remind him of himself, that would lessen the gap which lay between his present and his past.

It was a curious day, slashed abruptly with fleeting, familiar impressions. One minute he had the sense of being a trespasser—in the next he was impressed by the tremendous superiority he felt toward Mr. T. A. Hedrick, who was a bore and not even a good golfer any more.

Then, because of a ball Mr. Hart lost near the fifteenth green, an enormous thing happened. While they were searching the stiff grasses of the rough there was a clear call of "Fore!" from behind a hill in their rear. And as they all turned abruptly from their search a bright new ball sliced abruptly over the hill and caught Mr. T. A. Hedrick in the abdomen.

"By Gad!" cried Mr. T. A. Hedrick, "they ought to put some of these crazy women off the course. It's getting to be outrageous."

A head and a voice came up together over the hill:

"Do you mind if we go through?"

"You hit me in the stomach!" declared Mr. Hedrick wildly.

"Did I?" The girl approached the group of men. "I'm sorry. I yelled 'Fore!' "

Her glance fell casually on each of the men—then scanned the fairway for her ball.

"Did I bounce into the rough?"

It was impossible to determine whether this question was ingenuous or malicious. In a moment, however, she left no doubt, for as her partner came up over the hill she called cheerfully:

"Here I am! I'd have gone on the green except that I hit something."

As she took her stance for a short mashie shot, Dexter looked at her closely. She wore a blue gingham dress, rimmed at throat and shoulders with a white edging that accentuated her tan. The quality of exaggeration, of thinness, which had made her passionate eyes and down-turning mouth absurd at eleven, was gone now. She was arrestingly beautiful. The color in her cheeks was centered like the color in a picture—it was not a "high" color, but a sort of fluctuating and feverish warmth, so shaded that it seemed at any moment it would recede and disappear. This color and the mobility of her mouth gave a continual impression of flux, of intense life, of passionate vitality—balanced only partially by the sad luxury of her eyes.

She swung her mashie impatiently and without interest, pitching the ball into a sand pit on the other side of the green. With a quick, insincere smile and a careless "Thank you!" she went on after it.

"That Judy Jones!" remarked Mr. Hedrick on the next tee, as they waited—some moments—for her to play on ahead. "All she needs is to be turned up and spanked for six months and then to be married off to an old-fashioned cavalry captain."

"My God, she's good looking!" said Mr. Sandwood, who was just over thirty.

"Good looking!" cried Mr. Hedrick contemptuously, "she always looks as if she wanted to be kissed! Turning those big cow-eyes on every calf in town!"

It was doubtful if Mr. Hedrick intended a reference to the maternal instinct.

"She'd play pretty good golf if she'd try," said Mr. Sandwood.

"She has no form," said Mr. Hedrick solemnly.

"She has a nice figure," said Mr. Sandwood.

"Better thank the Lord she doesn't drive a swifter ball," said Mr. Hart, winking at Dexter.

Later in the afternoon the sun went down with a riotous swirl of gold and varying blues and scarlets, and left the dry, rustling night of Western summer. Dexter watched from the veranda of the golf club, watched the even overlap of the waters in the little wind, silver molasses under the harvest moon. Then the moon held a finger to her lips and the lake became a clear pool, pale and quiet. Dexter put on his bathing suit and swam out to the farthest raft, where he stretched dripping on the wet canvas of the springboard.

There was a fish jumping and a star shining and the lights around the lake were gleaming. Over on a dark peninsula a piano was playing the songs of last summer and of summers before that—songs from *Chin-Chin* and *The Count of Luxemburg* and *The Chocolate Soldier*[2]—and because the sound of a piano over a stretch of water had always seemed beautiful to Dexter he lay perfectly quiet and listened.

The tune the piano was playing at that moment had been gay and new five years before when Dexter was a sophomore at college. They had played it at a prom once when he could not afford the luxury of proms, and he had stood outside the gymnasium and listened. The sound of the tune precipitated in him a sort of ecstasy and it was with that ecstasy he viewed what happened to him now. It was a mood of intense appreciation, a sense that, for once, he was magnificently attuned to life and that everything about him was radiating a brightness and a glamor he might never know again.

A low, pale oblong detached itself suddenly from the darkness of the Island, spit-

---

2. *Chin-Chin* . . . *The Chocolate Soldier*: Popular operettas of the time.

ting forth the reverberate sound of a racing motorboat. Two white streamers of cleft water rolled themselves out behind it and almost immediately the boat was beside him, drowning out the hot tinkle of the piano in the drone of its spray. Dexter raising himself on his arms was aware of a figure standing at the wheel, of two dark eyes regarding him over the lengthening space of water—then the boat had gone by and was sweeping in an immense and purposeless circle of spray round and round in the middle of the lake. With equal eccentricity one of the circles flattened out and headed back toward the raft.

"Who's that?" she called, shutting off her motor. She was so near now that Dexter could see her bathing suit, which consisted apparently of pink rompers.

The nose of the boat bumped the raft, and as the latter tilted rakishly he was precipitated toward her. With different degrees of interest they recognized each other.

"Aren't you one of those men we played through this afternoon?" she demanded.

He was.

"Well, do you know how to drive a motorboat? Because if you do I wish you'd drive this one so I can ride on the surfboard behind. My name is Judy Jones"—she favored him with an absurd smirk—rather, what tried to be a smirk, for, twist her mouth as she might, it was not grotesque, it was merely beautiful—"and I live in a house over there on the Island, and in that house there is a man waiting for me. When he drove up at the door I drove out of the dock because he says I'm his ideal."

There was a fish jumping and a star shining and the lights around the lake were gleaming. Dexter sat beside Judy Jones and she explained how her boat was driven. Then she was in the water, swimming to the floating surfboard with a sinuous crawl. Watching her was without effort to the eye, watching a branch waving or a sea gull flying. Her arms, burned to butternut, moved sinuously among the dull platinum ripples, elbow appearing first, casting the forearm

back with a cadence of falling water, then reaching out and down, stabbing a path ahead.

They moved out into the lake; turning, Dexter saw that she was kneeling on the low rear of the now uptilted surfboard.

"Go faster," she called, "fast as it'll go."

Obediently he jammed the lever forward and the white spray mounted at the bow. When he looked around again the girl was standing up on the rushing board, her arms spread wide, her eyes lifted toward the moon.

"It's awful cold," she shouted. "What's your name?"

He told her.

"Well, why don't you come to dinner tomorrow night?"

His heart turned over like the flywheel of the boat, and, for the second time, her casual whim gave a new direction to his life.

III

Next evening while he waited for her to come downstairs, Dexter peopled the soft deep summer room and the sun porch that opened from it with the men who had already loved Judy Jones. He knew the sort of men they were—the men who when he first went to college had entered from the great prep schools with graceful clothes and the deep tan of healthy summers. He had seen that, in one sense, he was better than these men. He was newer and stronger. Yet in acknowledging to himself that he wished his children to be like them he was admitting that he was but the rough, strong stuff from which they eternally sprang.

When the time had come for him to wear good clothes, he had known who were the best tailors in America, and the best tailors in America had made him the suit he wore this evening. He had acquired that particular reserve peculiar to his university, that set it off from other universities. He recognized the value to him of such a mannerism and he had adopted it; he knew that to be careless in dress and manner required more confidence than to be careful. But carelessness was for his children. His mother's name had been Krimelich. She was a Bohemian of the peasant class and she had talked broken English to the end of her days. Her son must keep to the set patterns.

At a little after seven Judy Jones came downstairs. She wore a blue silk afternoon dress, and he was disappointed at first that she had not put on something more elaborate. This feeling was accentuated when, after a brief greeting, she went to the door of a butler's pantry and pushing it open called: "You can serve dinner, Martha." He had rather expected that a butler would announce dinner, that there would be a cocktail. Then he put these thoughts behind him as they sat down side by side on a lounge and looked at each other.

"Father and mother won't be here," she said thoughtfully.

He remembered the last time he had seen her father, and he was glad the parents were not to be here tonight—they might wonder who he was. He had been born in Keeble, a Minnesota village fifty miles farther north, and he always gave Keeble as his home instead of Black Bear Village. Country towns were well enough to come from if they weren't inconveniently in sight and used as footstools by fashionable lakes.

They talked of his university, which she had visited frequently during the past two years, and of the nearby city which supplied Sherry Island with its patrons, and whither Dexter would return next day to his prospering laundries.

During dinner she slipped into a moody depression which gave Dexter a feeling of uneasiness. Whatever petulance she uttered in her throaty voice worried him. Whatever she smiled at—at him, at a chicken liver, at nothing—it disturbed him that her smile could have no root in mirth, or even in amusement. When the scarlet corners of her lips curved down, it was less a smile than an invitation to a kiss.

Then, after dinner, she led him out on the dark sun porch and deliberately changed the atmosphere.

"Do you mind if I weep a little?" she said.

"I'm afraid I'm boring you," he responded quickly.

"You're not. I like you. But I've just had a terrible afternoon. There was a man I cared about, and this afternoon he told me out of a clear sky that he was poor as a church mouse. He'd never even hinted it before. Does this sound horribly mundane?"

"Perhaps he was afraid to tell you."

"Suppose he was," she answered. "He didn't start right. You see, if I'd thought of him as poor—well, I've been mad about loads of poor men, and fully intended to marry them all. But in this case, I hadn't thought of him that way, and my interest in him wasn't strong enough to survive the shock. As if a girl calmly informed her fiancé that she was a widow. He might not object to widows, but——"

"Let's start right," she interrupted herself suddenly. "Who are you, anyhow?"

For a moment Dexter hesitated. Then:

"I'm nobody," he announced. "My career is largely a matter of futures."

"Are you poor?"

"No," he said frankly, "I'm probably making more money than any man my age in the Northwest. I know that's an obnoxious remark, but you advised me to start right."

There was a pause. Then she smiled and the corners of her mouth drooped and an almost imperceptible sway brought her closer to him, looking up into his eyes. A lump rose in Dexter's throat, and he waited breathless for the experiment, facing the unpredictable compound that would form mysteriously from the elements of their lips. Then he saw—she communicated her excitement to him, lavishly, deeply, with kisses that were not a promise but a fulfillment. They aroused in him not hunger demanding renewal but surfeit that would demand more surfeit . . . kisses that were like charity, creating want by holding back nothing at all.

It did not take him many hours to decide

that he had wanted Judy Jones ever since he was a proud, desirous little boy.

IV

It began like that—and continued, with varying shades of intensity, on such a note right up to the dénouement. Dexter surrendered a part of himself to the most direct and unprincipled personality with which he had ever come in contact. Whatever Judy wanted, she went after with the full pressure of her charm. There was no divergence of method, no jockeying for position or premeditation of effects—there was a very little mental side to any of her affairs. She simply made men conscious to the highest degree of her physical loveliness. Dexter had no desire to change her. Her deficiencies were knit up with a passionate energy that transcended and justified them.

When, as Judy's head lay against his shoulder that first night, she whispered, "I don't know what's the matter with me. Last night I thought I was in love with a man and tonight I think I'm in love with you——" it seemed to him a beautiful and romantic thing to say. It was the exquisite excitability that for the moment he controlled and owned. But a week later he was compelled to view this same quality in a different light. She took him in her roadster to a picnic supper, and after supper she disappeared, likewise in her roadster, with another man. Dexter became enormously upset and was scarcely able to be decently civil to the other people present. When she assured him that she had not kissed the other man, he knew she was lying—yet he was glad that she had taken the trouble to lie to him.

He was, as he found before the summer ended, one of a varying dozen who circulated about her. Each of them had at one time been favored above all others—about half of them still basked in the solace of occasional sentimental revivals. Whenever one showed signs of dropping out through long neglect, she granted him a brief honeyed hour, which encouraged him to tag along for a year or so longer. Judy made these forays upon the helpless and defeated without malice, indeed half unconscious that there was anything mischievous in what she did.

When a new man came to town everyone dropped out—dates were automatically canceled.

The helpless part of trying to do anything about it was that she did it all herself. She was not a girl who could be "won" in the kinetic sense—she was proof against cleverness, she was proof against charm; if any of these assailed her too strongly she would immediately resolve the affair to a physical basis, and under the magic of her physical splendor the strong as well as the brilliant played her game and not their own. She was entertained only by the gratification of her desires and by the direct exercise of her own charm. Perhaps from so much youthful love, so many youthful lovers, she had come, in self-defense, to nourish herself wholly from within.

Succeeding Dexter's first exhilaration came restlessness and dissatisfaction. The helpless ecstasy of losing himself in her was opiate rather than tonic. It was fortunate for his work during the winter that those moments of ecstasy came infrequently. Early in their acquaintance it had seemed for a while that there was a deep and spontaneous mutual attraction—that first August, for example—three days of long evenings on her dusky veranda, of strange wan kisses through the late afternoon, in shadowy alcoves or behind the protecting trellises of the garden arbors, of mornings when she was fresh as a dream and almost shy at meeting him in the clarity of the rising day. There was all the ecstasy of an engagement about it, sharpened by his realization that there was no engagement. It was during those three days that, for the first time, he had asked her to marry him. She said "maybe some day," she said "kiss me," she said, "I'd like to marry you," she said "I love you"—she said—nothing.

The three days were interrupted by the arrival of a New York man who visited at her house for half September. To Dexter's agony, rumor engaged them. The man was the son of the president of a great trust company. But at the end of a month it was reported that Judy was yawning. At a dance one night she sat all evening in a motorboat with a local beau, while the New Yorker searched the club for her frantically. She told the local beau that she was bored with her visitor, and two days later he left. She was seen with him at the station, and it was reported that he looked very mournful indeed.

On this note the summer ended. Dexter was twenty-four, and he found himself increasingly in a position to do as he wished. He joined two clubs in the city and lived at one of them. Though he was by no means an integral part of the stag lines at these clubs, he managed to be on hand at dances where Judy Jones was likely to appear. He could have gone out socially as much as he liked— he was an eligible young man, now, and popular with downtown fathers. His confessed devotion to Judy Jones had rather solidified his position. But he had no social aspirations and rather despised the dancing men who were always on tap for the Thursday or Saturday parties and who filled in at dinners with the younger married set. Already he was playing with the idea of going East to New York. He wanted to take Judy Jones with him. No disillusion as to the world in which she had grown up could cure his illusion as to her desirability.

Remember that—for only in the light of it can what he did for her be understood.

Eighteen months after he first met Judy Jones he became engaged to another girl. Her name was Irene Scheerer, and her father was one of the men who had always believed in Dexter. Irene was light-haired and sweet and honorable, and a little stout, and she had two suitors whom she pleasantly relinquished when Dexter formally asked her to marry him.

Summer, fall, winter, spring, another summer, another fall—so much he had given of his active life to the incorrigible lips of Judy Jones. She had treated him with interest, with encouragement, with malice, with indifference, with contempt. She had inflicted on him the innumerable little slights and indignities possible in such a case—as if in revenge for having ever cared for him at all. She had beckoned him and yawned at him and beckoned him again and he had responded often with bitterness and narrowed eyes. She had brought him ecstatic happiness and intolerable agony of spirit. She had caused him untold inconvenience and not a little trouble. She had insulted him, and she had ridden over him, and she had played his interest in her against his interest in his work—for fun. She had done everything to him except to criticize him—this she had not done—it seemed to him only because it might have sullied the utter indifference she manifested and sincerely felt toward him.

When autumn had come and gone again it occurred to him that he could not have Judy Jones. He had to beat this into his mind but he convinced himself at last. He lay awake at night for a while and argued it over. He told himself the trouble and the pain she had caused him, he enumerated her glaring deficiencies as a wife. Then he said to himself that he loved her, and after a while he fell asleep. For a week, lest he imagined her husky voice over the telephone or her eyes opposite him at lunch, he worked hard and late, and at night he went to his office and plotted out his years.

At the end of a week he went to a dance and cut in on her once. For almost the first time since they had met he did not ask her to sit out with him or tell her that she was lovely. It hurt him that she did not miss these things—that was all. He was not jealous when he saw that there was a new man tonight. He had been hardened against jealousy long before.

He stayed late at the dance. He sat for an hour with Irene Scheerer and talked about books and about music. He knew very little about either. But he was beginning to be master of his own time now, and he had a

WINTER WONDERLAND
Rebecca Grutzik, Student, Stevens Point, Wisconsin
Courtesy of the Artist

rather priggish[3] notion that he—the young and already fabulously successful Dexter Green—should know more about such things.

That was in October, when he was twenty-five. In January, Dexter and Irene became engaged. It was to be announced in June, and they were to be married three months later.

The Minnesota winter prolonged itself interminably, and it was almost May when the winds came soft and the snow ran down

into Black Bear Lake at last. For the first time in over a year Dexter was enjoying a certain tranquillity of spirit. Judy Jones had been in Florida, and afterward in Hot Springs, and somewhere she had been engaged, and somewhere she had broken it off. At first, when Dexter had definitely given her up, it had made him sad that people still linked them together and asked for news of her, but when he began to be placed at dinner next to Irene Scheerer people didn't ask him about her any more—they told him about her. He ceased to be an authority on her.

---

3. priggish (prig' ish) *adj.*: Excessively precise.

May at last. Dexter walked the streets at night when the darkness was damp as rain, wondering that so soon, with so little done, so much of ecstasy had gone from him. May one year back had been marked by Judy's poignant, unforgivable, yet forgiven turbulence—it had been one of those rare times when he fancied she had grown to care for him. That old penny's worth of happiness he had spent for this bushel of content. He knew that Irene would be no more than a curtain spread behind him, a hand moving among gleaming teacups, a voice calling to children . . . fire and loveliness were gone, the magic of nights and the wonder of the varying hours and seasons . . . slender lips, down-turning, dropping to his lips and bearing him up into a heaven of eyes. . . . The thing was deep in him. He was too strong and alive for it to die lightly.

In the middle of May when the weather balanced for a few days on the thin bridge that led to deep summer he turned in one night at Irene's house. Their engagement was to be announced in a week now—no one would be surprised at it. And tonight they would sit together on the lounge at the University Club and look on for an hour at the dancers. It gave him a sense of solidity to go with her—she was so sturdily popular, so intensely "great."

He mounted the steps of the brownstone house and stepped inside.

"Irene," he called.

Mrs. Scheerer came out of the living room to meet him.

"Dexter," she said, "Irene's gone upstairs with a splitting headache. She wanted to go with you but I made her go to bed."

"Nothing serious, I——"

"Oh, no. She's going to play golf with you in the morning. You can spare her for just one night, can't you, Dexter?"

Her smile was kind. She and Dexter liked each other. In the living room he talked for a moment before he said good night.

Returning to the University Club, where he had rooms, he stood in the doorway for a moment and watched the dancers. He leaned against the doorpost, nodded at a man or two—yawned.

"Hello, darling."

The familiar voice at his elbow startled him. Judy Jones had left a man and crossed the room to him—Judy Jones, a slender enameled doll in cloth of gold: gold in a band at her head, gold in two slipper points at her dress's hem. The fragile glow of her face seemed to blossom as she smiled at him. A breeze of warmth and light blew through the room. His hands in the pockets of his dinner jacket tightened spasmodically. He was filled with a sudden excitement.

"When did you get back?" he asked casually.

"Come here and I'll tell you about it."

She turned and he followed her. She had been away—he could have wept at the wonder of her return. She had passed through enchanted streets, doing things that were like provocative music. All mysterious happenings, all fresh and quickening hopes, had gone away with her, come back with her now.

She turned in the doorway.

"Have you a car here? If you haven't, I have."

"I have a coupé."

In then, with a rustle of golden cloth. He slammed the door. Into so many cars she had stepped—like this—like that—her back against the leather, so—her elbow resting on the door—waiting. She would have been soiled long since had there been anything to soil her—except herself—but this was her own self outpouring.

With an effort he forced himself to start the car and back into the street. This was nothing, he must remember. She had done this before, and he had put her behind him, as he would have crossed a bad account from his books.

He drove slowly downtown and, affecting abstraction, traversed the deserted streets of the business section, peopled here and there where a movie was giving out its crowd or where consumptive or pugilistic youth lounged in front of pool halls. The clink of glasses and the slap of hands on the bars issued from saloons, cloisters of glazed glass and dirty yellow light.

She was watching him closely and the silence was embarrassing, yet in this crisis he could find no casual word with which to profane the hour. At a convenient turning he began to zigzag back toward the University Club.

"Have you missed me?" she asked suddenly.

"Everybody missed you."

He wondered if she knew of Irene Scheerer. She had been back only a day—her absence had been almost contemporaneous with his engagement.

"What a remark!" Judy laughed sadly—without sadness. She looked at him searchingly. He became absorbed in the dashboard.

"You're handsomer than you used to be," she said thoughtfully. "Dexter, you have the most rememberable eyes."

He could have laughed at this, but he did not laugh. It was the sort of thing that was said to sophomores. Yet it stabbed at him.

"I'm awfully tired of everything, darling." She called everyone darling, endowing the endearment with careless, individual camaraderie.[4] "I wish you'd marry me."

The directness of this confused him. He should have told her now that he was going to marry another girl, but he could not tell her. He could as easily have sworn that he had never loved her.

"I think we'd get along," she continued, on the same note, "unless probably you've forgotten me and fallen in love with another girl."

Her confidence was obviously enormous. She had said, in effect, that she found such a thing impossible to believe, that if it were true he had merely committed a childish indiscretion—and probably to show off. She

---

4. camaraderie (käm´ ə räd´ ər ē) *n.*: Warm, friendly feelings.

would forgive him, because it was not a matter of any moment but rather something to be brushed aside lightly.

"Of course you could never love anybody but me," she continued, "I like the way you love me. Oh, Dexter, have you forgotten last year?"

"No, I haven't forgotten."

"Neither have I!"

Was she sincerely moved—or was she carried along by the wave of her own acting?

"I wish we could be like that again," she said, and he forced himself to answer:

"I don't think we can."

"I suppose not. . . . I hear you're giving Irene Scheerer a violent rush."

There was not the faintest emphasis on the name, yet Dexter was suddenly ashamed.

"Oh, take me home," cried Judy suddenly; "I don't want to go back to that idiotic dance—with those children."

Then, as he turned up the street that led to the residence district, Judy began to cry quietly to herself. He had never seen her cry before.

The dark street lightened, the dwellings of the rich loomed up around them, he stopped his coupé in front of the great white bulk of the Mortimer Joneses' house, somnolent, gorgeous, drenched with the splendor of the damp moonlight. Its solidity startled him. The strong walls, the steel of the girders, the breadth and beam and pomp of it were there only to bring out the contrast with the young beauty beside him. It was sturdy to accentuate her slightness—as if to show what a breeze could be generated by a butterfly's wing.

He sat perfectly quiet, his nerves in wild clamor, afraid that if he moved he would find her irresistibly in his arms. Two tears had rolled down her wet face and trembled on her upper lip.

'I'm more beautiful than anybody else," she said brokenly, "why can't I be happy?" Her moist eyes tore at his stability—her mouth turned slowly downward with an exquisite sadness: "I'd like to marry you if you'll have me, Dexter. I suppose you think I'm not worth having, but I'll be so beautfiul for you, Dexter."

A million phrases of anger, pride, passion, hatred, tenderness fought on his lips. Then a perfect wave of emotion washed over him, carrying off with it a sediment of wisdom, of convention, of doubt, of honor. This was his girl who was speaking, his own, his beautiful, his pride.

"Won't you come in?" He heard her draw in her breath sharply.

Waiting.

"All right," his voice was trembling, "I'll come in."

V

It was strange that neither when it was over nor a long time afterward did he regret that night. Looking at it from the perspective of ten years, the fact that Judy's flare for him endured just one month seemed of little importance. Nor did it matter that by his yielding he subjected himself to a deeper agony in the end and gave serious hurt to Irene Scheerer and to Irene's parents, who had befriended him. There was nothing sufficiently pictorial about Irene's grief to stamp itself on his mind.

Dexter was at bottom hard-minded. The attitude of the city on his action was of no importance to him, not because he was going to leave the city, but because any outside attitude on the situation seemed superficial. He was completely indifferent to popular opinion. Nor, when he had seen that it was no use, that he did not possess in himself the power to move fundamentally or to hold Judy Jones, did he bear any malice toward her. He loved her, and he would love her until the day he was too old for loving—but he could not have her. So he tasted the deep pain that is reserved only for the strong, just as he had tasted for a little while the deep happiness.

Even the ultimate falsity of the grounds upon which Judy terminated the engagement that she did not want to "take him away" from Irene—Judy who had wanted nothing else—did not revolt him. He was beyond any revulsion or any amusement.

He went East in February with the intention of selling out his laundries and settling in New York—but the war came to America in March and changed his plans. He returned to the West, handed over the management of the business to his partner, and went into the first officers' training camp in late April. He was one of those young thousands who greeted the war with a certain amount of relief, welcoming the liberation from webs of tangled emotion.

VI

This story is not his biography, remember, although things creep into it which have nothing to do with those dreams he had when he was young. We are almost done with them and with him now. There is only one more incident to be related here, and it happens seven years farther on.

It took place in New York, where he had done well—so well that there were no barriers too high for him. He was thirty-two years old, and, except for one flying trip immediately after the war, he had not been West in seven years. A man named Devlin from Detroit came into his office to see him in a business way, and then and there this incident occurred, and closed out, so to speak, this particular side of his life.

"So you're from the Middle West," said the man Devlin with careless curiosity. "That's funny—I thought men like you were probably born and raised on Wall Street. You know—wife of one of my best friends in Detroit came from your city. I was an usher at the wedding."

Dexter waited with no apprehension of what was coming.

"Judy Simms," said Devlin with no particular interest; "Judy Jones she was once."

MANHATTAN TOPS
Herman Rose
Hirshhorn Museum and Sculpture Garden, Smithsonian Institution

"Yes, I knew her." A dull impatience spread over him. He had heard, of course, that she was married—perhaps deliberately he had heard no more.

"Awfully nice girl," brooded Devlin meaninglessly, "I'm sort of sorry for her."

"Why?" Something in Dexter was alert, receptive, at once.

"Oh, Lud Simms has gone to pieces in a way. I don't mean he ill-uses her, but he drinks and runs around——"

"Doesn't she run around?"

"No. Stays at home with her kids."

"Oh."

"She's a little too old for him," said Devlin.

"Too old!" cried Dexter. "Why, man, she's only twenty-seven."

He was possessed with a wild notion of rushing out into the streets and taking a train to Detroit. He rose to his feet spasmodically.

"I guess you're busy," Devlin apologized quickly. "I didn't realize——"

"No, I'm not busy," said Dexter, steadying his voice. "I'm not busy at all. Not busy at all. Did you say she was—twenty-seven? No, I said she was twenty-seven."

"Yes, you did," agreed Devlin dryly.

"Go on, then. Go on."

"What do you mean?"

"About Judy Jones."

Devlin looked at him helplessly.

"Well, that's—I told you all there is to it. He treats her like the devil. Oh, they're not going to get divorced or anything. When he's particularly outrageous she forgives him. In fact, I'm inclined to think she loves him. She was a pretty girl when she first came to Detroit."

A pretty girl! The phrase struck Dexter as ludicrous.

"Isn't she—a pretty girl, anymore?"

"Oh, she's all right."

"Look here," said Dexter, sitting down suddenly. "I don't understand. You say she was a 'pretty girl' and now you say she's 'all right.' I don't understand what you mean—Judy Jones wasn't a pretty girl, at all. She was a great beauty. Why, I knew her, I knew her. She was——"

Devlin laughed pleasantly.

"I'm not trying to start a row," he said. "I think Judy's a nice girl and I like her. I can't understand how a man like Lud Simms could fall madly in love with her, but he did." Then he added: "Most of the women like her."

Dexter looked closely at Devlin, thinking wildly that there must be a reason for this, some insensitivity in the man or some private malice.

"Lots of women fade just like *that*," Devlin snapped his fingers. "You must have seen it happen. Perhaps I've forgotten how pretty she was at her wedding. I've seen her so much since then, you see. She has nice eyes."

A sort of dullness settled down upon Dexter. For the first time in his life he felt like getting very drunk. He knew that he was laughing loudly at something Devlin had said, but he did not know what it was or why it was funny. When, in a few minutes, Devlin went he lay down on his lounge and looked out the window at the New York skyline into which the sun was sinking in dull lovely shades of pink and gold.

He had thought that having nothing else to lose he was invulnerable at last—but he knew that he had just lost something more, as surely as if he had married Judy Jones and seen her fade away before his eyes.

The dream was gone. Something had been taken from him. In a sort of panic he pushed the palms of his hands into his eyes and tried to bring up a picture of the waters lapping on Sherry Island and the moonlit veranda, and gingham on the golf links and the dry sun and the gold color of her neck's soft down. And her mouth damp to his kisses and her eyes plaintive with melancholy and her freshness like new fine linen in the morning. Why, these things were no longer in the world! They had existed and they existed no longer.

For the first time in years the tears were streaming down his face. But they were for himself now. He did not care about mouth and eyes and moving hands. He wanted to care, and he could not care. For he had gone away and he could never go back any more. The gates were closed, the sun was gone down, and there was no beauty but the gray beauty of steel that withstands all time. Even the grief he could have borne was left behind in the country of illusion, of youth, of the richness of life, where his winter dreams had flourished.

"Long ago," he said, "long ago, there was something in me, but now that thing is gone. Now that thing is gone, that thing is gone. I cannot cry. I cannot care. That thing will come back no more."

RESPONDING TO THE SELECTION

Your Response

1. Fitzgerald suggests that Dexter is destroyed by his "winter dreams." Do you think winter dreams are always harmful? Why or why not?
2. How might the story be different if Dexter had married Judy?

Recalling

3. (a) What happens when Dexter first meets Judy Jones? (b) What happens the second time they meet?
4. (a) Why does Dexter become engaged to another woman? (b) Why does he break the engagement?
5. How does Devlin shatter Dexter's image of Judy?

Interpreting

6. (a) Describe Judy's personality. (b) According to Devlin's description, how does Judy's personality change following her marriage?
7. (a) What does Judy represent to Dexter? (b) Why does he keep loving her even after he has lost her?
8. (a) What are Dexter's "winter dreams"? (b) What makes them *winter* dreams? (c) How does Judy fit into these dreams?
9. Fitzgerald came to believe that an obsession with wealth and social status ultimately leads to emptiness and dissatisfaction. How does this story reflect this belief?

Applying

10. Explain whether this story would be effective if it were set in contemporary American society.

ANALYZING LITERATURE

Understanding Characterization

Characterization is the means by which an author reveals a character's personality. Writers may use a variety of methods of characterization. For example, we learn a great deal about Judy Jones's personality from her behavior in Part I.
1. What other methods does Fitzgerald use to characterize Judy? Support your answer with examples.
2. What methods does Fitzgerald use to characterize Dexter? Support your answer.
3. (a) In what ways does Fitzgerald show Dexter and Judy to be alike? (b) In what ways does he show them to be different?

CRITICAL THINKING AND READING

Evaluating a Character's Behavior

Literature can often help us better understand ourselves and other people. Evaluating a character's behavior and its effect on the character's life and on other characters can sometimes have implications for our own behavior.
1. Toward the end of Part IV, Judy tells Dexter that she cannot be happy. How do you think her behavior throughout the story might have contributed to her unhappiness?
2. What do you think Dexter's experiences reveal about the potential dangers of an obsession with "glittering things"?

THINKING AND WRITING

Writing About Historical Context

As the biography of Fitzgerald (page 586) states, Fitzgerald's work "captured both the gaiety and the emptiness" of the 1920's. Write an essay in which you discuss how "Winter Dreams" captures the "gaiety and the emptiness" of the 1920's. Use passages from the story to support your argument. When you revise, make sure that you have not included any unnecessary information.

LEARNING OPTION

Cross-curricular Connection. Mah-jongg, anyone? Investigate the fads and crazes of the 1920's, including mah-jongg, crossword puzzles, electric trains, endurance contests, dance crazes, flappermania, and Tutmania. Choose a fad or craze that interests you, and bring the gaiety of the era to the classroom. For example, you might stage a rocking chair derby (rock till you drop), demonstrate how to shimmy, or play a medley of Twenties' hits.

KATHERINE ANNE PORTER

1890–1980

Katherine Anne Porter did not produce a great number of literary works during her long life. Yet the works she did produce were skillfully crafted, tightly structured, and written in a clear, elegant style.

Born in Indian Creek, Texas, Porter was raised in poverty. After becoming a journalist, she lived for several years in Mexico. There she developed an interest in writing fiction, and in 1922 she published her first story, "María Concepción," in *Century,* a highly regarded literary magazine. Eight years later she published her first book, *Flowering Judas* (1930). The book, a collection of six short stories, was praised by critics and earned Porter widespread recognition. *Flowering Judas and Other Stories,* an expanded edition containing ten stories, appeared in 1935 and was followed by several other major works, including *Noon Wine* (1937), *Pale Horse, Pale Rider* (1939), *No Safe Harbor* (1941), *The Leaning Tower and Other Stories* (1944), and *Ship of Fools* (1962)—Porter's only novel. In 1966 she received the Pulitzer Prize and the National Book Award for her *Collected Stories* (1965).

In his review of *The Leaning Tower,* critic Edmund Wilson tried to account for the "elusive" quality that made Porter an "absolutely first-rate artist": "These stories are not illustrations of anything that is reducible to a moral law or a political or social analysis or even a principle of human behavior. What they show us are human relations in their constantly shifting phases and in the moments of which their existence is made. There is no place for general reflections; you are to live through the experience as the characters do."

In her work Porter often explored the sense of uncertainty and disjointedness that results from changes in society. In many of her stories, including "The Jilting of Granny Weatherall," she portrayed families that were drifting apart and losing an awareness of their connection with the past, as the traditional sense of the family as a community disappeared with the coming of the modern age.

In an introduction to the 1940 edition of *Flowering Judas and Other Stories,* Porter offered this view of the meaning of art in an increasingly uncertain world: "All the conscious and recollected years of my life have been lived to this day under the heavy threat of world catastrophe, and most of the energies of my mind and spirit have been spent in the effort to grasp the meaning of those threats, to trace them to their sources, and to understand the logic of this majestic and terrible failure of the life of man in the Western world."

GUIDE FOR INTERPRETING

The Jilting of Granny Weatherall

Writers' Techniques

Stream of Consciousness. People's thoughts do not usually flow in a neat, organized manner. Instead, they usually proceed in an unorganized flow of insights, memories, and reflections. When a writer uses the stream-of-consciousness technique, he or she attempts to capture the way the mind works by showing the random movement and natural flow of a character's thoughts. In using this technique, the writer eliminates the transitions used in ordinary prose, instead connecting thoughts through the character's natural associations.

The stream-of-consciousness technique, which reflects the twentieth-century interest in psychology, was devised by the Modernists as part of their effort to capture the essence of the fragmented modern world in their work. The Modernists generally believed that there is no external order governing human existence and that, as a result, life is often splintered and disjointed. Their use of the stream-of-consciousness technique reflected this opinion and expressed their belief in the need for people to turn their thoughts inward.

The term "stream of consciousness" was actually coined by the American psychologist William James. He wrote, "Consciousness . . . does not appear to itself chopped up in bits. . . . A 'river' or a 'stream' are the metaphors by which it is most naturally described. In talking of it hereafter, let us call it the stream of thought, of consciousness, or of subjective life."

Flashback. In trying to re-create the natural flow of a character's thoughts, writers often use flashbacks—interruptions in the narrative in which an earlier event is recalled or described. In "The Jilting of Granny Weatherall," for example, flashbacks are used when Granny Weatherall's thoughts drift back to her younger days.

Focus

Try to capture your own "stream of consciousness." Start by thinking about a single person, place, or event. Then write down the various associations that flow through your mind.

Primary Source

Commenting on her schooling, Porter said that she received a "fragmentary, but strangely useless and ornamental education. . . ." Instead she was taught "by five writers: Henry James, James Joyce, W. B. Yeats, T. S. Eliot, and Ezra Pound." Porter described what a writer needs to write, as follows: "*first* a *theme,* and then a point of view, a certain knowledge of human nature and strong feeling about it, and style—that is to say, his own special way of telling a thing that makes it precisely his own and no one else's."

The Jilting of Granny Weatherall

Katherine Anne Porter

She flicked her wrist neatly out of Doctor Harry's pudgy careful fingers and pulled the sheet up to her chin. The brat ought to be in knee breeches. Doctoring around the country with spectacles on his nose! "Get along now, take your schoolbooks and go. There's nothing wrong with me."

Doctor Harry spread a warm paw like a cushion on her forehead where the forked green vein danced and made her eyelids twitch. "Now, now, be a good girl, and we'll have you up in no time."

"That's no way to speak to a woman nearly eighty years old just because she's down. I'd have you respect your elders, young man."

"Well, Missy, excuse me," Doctor Harry patted her cheek. "But I've got to warn you, haven't I? You're a marvel, but you must be careful or you're going to be good and sorry."

"Don't tell me what I'm going to be. I'm on my feet now, morally speaking. It's Cornelia. I had to go to bed to get rid of her."

Her bones felt loose, and floated around in her skin, and Doctor Harry floated like a balloon around the foot of the bed. He floated and pulled down his waistcoat and swung his glasses on a cord. "Well, stay where you are, it certainly can't hurt you."

"Get along and doctor your sick," said Granny Weatherall. "Leave a well woman alone. I'll call for you when I want you. . . .

Where were you forty years ago when I pulled through milk leg[1] and double pneumonia? You weren't even born. Don't let Cornelia lead you on," she shouted, because Doctor Harry appeared to float up to the ceiling and out. "I pay my own bills, and I don't throw my money away on nonsense!"

She meant to wave good-bye, but it was too much trouble. Her eyes closed of themselves, it was like a dark curtain drawn around the bed. The pillow rose and floated under her, pleasant as a hammock in a light wind. She listened to the leaves rustling outside the window. No, somebody was swishing newspapers: no, Cornelia and Doctor Harry were whispering together. She leaped broad awake, thinking they whispered in her ear.

"She was never like this, *never* like this!" "Well, what can we expect?" "Yes, eighty years old. . . ."

Well, and what if she was? She still had ears. It was like Cornelia to whisper around doors. She always kept things secret in such a public way. She was always being tactful and kind. Cornelia was dutiful; that was the trouble with her. Dutiful and good: "So good and dutiful," said Granny, "that I'd like to spank her." She saw herself spanking Cornelia and making a fine job of it.

---

1. **milk leg:** A painful swelling of the leg.

GARDEN OF MEMORIES, 1917
Charles Burchfield
Collection of The Museum of Modern Art,
New York

"What'd you say, Mother?"

Granny felt her face tying up in hard knots.

"Can't a body think, I'd like to know?"

"I thought you might want something."

"I do. I want a lot of things. First off, go away and don't whisper."

She lay and drowsed, hoping in her sleep that the children would keep out and let her rest a minute. It had been a long day. Not that she was tired. It was always pleasant to snatch a minute now and then. There was always so much to be done, let me see: tomorrow.

Tomorrow was far away and there was nothing to trouble about. Things were finished somehow when the time came; thank God there was always a little margin over for peace: then a person could spread out the plan of life and tuck in the edges orderly. It was good to have everything clean and folded away, with the hair brushes and tonic bottles sitting straight on the white embroidered linen: the day started without fuss and the pantry shelves laid out with rows of jelly glasses and brown jugs and white stonechina jars with blue whirligigs and words painted on them: coffee, tea, sugar, ginger, cinnamon, allspice: and the bronze clock with the lion on top nicely dusted off. The dust that lion could collect in twenty-four hours! The box in the attic with all those letters tied up, well, she'd have to go through that tomorrow. All those letters—George's letters and John's letters and her letters to them both—lying around for the children to find afterwards made her uneasy. Yes, that would be tomorrow's business. No use to let them know how silly she had been once.

While she was rummaging around she found death in her mind and it felt clammy and unfamiliar. She had spent so much time preparing for death there was no need for bringing it up again. Let it take care of itself now. When she was sixty she had felt very old, finished, and went around making farewell trips to see her children and grandchildren, with a secret in her mind: This is the very last of your mother, children! Then she made her will and came down with a long fever. That was all just a notion like a lot of other things, but it was lucky too, for she had once for all got over the idea of dying for a long time. Now she couldn't be worried. She hoped she had better sense now. Her father had lived to be one hundred and two years old and had drunk a noggin of strong hot toddy on his last birthday. He told the reporters it was his daily habit, and he owed his long life to that. He had made quite a scandal and was very pleased about it. She believed she'd just plague Cornelia a little.

"Cornelia! Cornelia!" No footsteps, but a sudden hand on her cheek. "Bless you, where have you been?"

"Here, mother."

"Well, Cornelia, I want a noggin of hot toddy."

"Are you cold, darling?"

"I'm chilly, Cornelia. Lying in bed stops the circulation. I must have told you that a thousand times."

Well, she could just hear Cornelia telling her husband that Mother was getting a little childish and they'd have to humor her. The thing that most annoyed her was that Cornelia thought she was deaf, dumb, and blind. Little hasty glances and tiny gestures tossed around her and over her head saying, "Don't cross her, let her have her way, she's

eighty years old," and she sitting there as if she lived in a thin glass cage. Sometimes Granny almost made up her mind to pack up and move back to her own house where nobody could remind her every minute that she was old. Wait, wait, Cornelia, till your own children whisper behind your back!

In her day she had kept a better house and had got more work done. She wasn't too old yet for Lydia to be driving eighty miles for advice when one of the children jumped the track, and Jimmy still dropped in and talked things over: "Now, Mammy, you've a good business head, I want to know what you think of this? . . ." Old. Cornelia couldn't change the furniture around without asking. Little things, little things! They had been so sweet when they were little. Granny wished the old days were back again with the children young and everything to be done over. It had been a hard pull, but not too much for her. When she thought of all the food she had cooked, and all the clothes she had cut and sewed, and all the gardens she had made—well, the children showed it. There they were, made out of her, and they couldn't get away from that. Sometimes she wanted to see John again and point to them and say, Well, I didn't do so badly, did I? But that would have to wait. That was for tomorrow. She used to think of him as a man, but now all the children were older than their father, and he would be a child beside her if she saw him now. It seemed strange and there was something wrong in the idea. Why, he couldn't possibly recognize her. She had fenced in a hundred acres once, digging the post holes herself and clamping the wires with just a negro boy to help. That changed a woman. John would be looking for a young woman with the peaked Spanish comb in her hair and the painted fan. Digging post holes changed a woman. Riding country roads in the winter when women had their babies was another thing: sitting up nights with sick horses and sick children and hardly ever losing one. John, I hardly ever lost one of them! John would see that in a minute, that would be something he could understand, she wouldn't have to explain anything!

It made her feel like rolling up her sleeves and putting the whole place to rights again. No matter if Cornelia was determined to be everywhere at once, there were a great many things left undone on this place. She would start tomorrow and do them. It was good to be strong enough for everything, even if all you made melted and changed and slipped under your hands, so that by the time you finished you almost forgot what you were working for. What was it I set out to do? she asked herself intently, but she could not remember. A fog rose over the valley, she saw it marching across the creek swallowing the trees and moving up the hill like an army of ghosts. Soon it would be at the near edge of the orchard, and then it was time to go in and light the lamps. Come in, children, don't stay out in the night air.

Lighting the lamps had been beautiful. The children huddled up to her and breathed like little calves waiting at the bars in the twilight. Their eyes followed the match and watched the flame rise and settle in a blue curve, then they moved away from her. The lamp was lit, they didn't have to be scared and hang on to mother any more. Never, never, never more. God, for all my life I thank Thee. Without Thee, my God, I could never have done it. Hail Mary, full of grace.

I want you to pick all the fruit this year and see that nothing is wasted. There's always someone who can use it. Don't let good things rot for want of using. You waste life when you waste good food. Don't let things get lost. It's bitter to lose things. Now, don't let me get to thinking, not when I am tired and taking a little nap before supper. . . .

The pillow rose about her shoulders and pressed against her heart and the memory was being squeezed out of it: oh, push down the pillow, somebody: it would smother her if she tried to hold it. Such a fresh breeze blowing and such a green day with no threats in it. But he had not come, just the same. What does a woman do when she has put on the white veil and set out the white cake for a man and he doesn't come? She tried to remember. No, I swear he never harmed me but in that. He never harmed me but in that . . . and what if he did? There was the day, the day, but a whirl of dark smoke rose and covered it, crept up and over into the bright field where everything was planted so carefully in orderly rows. That was hell, she knew hell when she saw it. For sixty years she had prayed against remembering him and against losing her soul in the deep pit of hell, and now the two things were mingled in one and the thought of him was a smoky cloud from hell that moved and crept in her head when she had just got rid of Doctor Harry and was trying to rest a minute. Wounded vanity, Ellen, said a sharp voice in the top of her mind. Don't let your wounded vanity get the upper hand of you. Plenty of girls get jilted. You were jilted, weren't you? Then stand up to it. Her eyelids wavered and let in streamers of blue-gray light like tissue paper over her eyes. She must get up and pull the shades down or she'd never sleep. She was in bed again and the shades were not down. How could that happen? Better turn over, hide from the light, sleeping in the light gave you nightmares. "Mother, how do you feel now?" and a stinging wetness on her forehead. But I don't like having my face washed in cold water!

Hapsy? George? Lydia? Jimmy? No, Cornelia, and her features were swollen and full of little puddles. "They're coming, darling, they'll all be here soon." Go wash your face, child, you look funny.

Instead of obeying, Cornelia knelt down and put her head on the pillow. She seemed to be talking but there was no sound. "Well, are you tongue-tied? Whose birthday is it? Are you going to give a party?"

Cornelia's mouth moved urgently in strange shapes. "Don't do that, you bother me, daughter."

"Oh, no, Mother. Oh, no. . . ."

LAVENDER AND OLD LACE
Charles Burchfield, ANA
From the Collection of the New Britain Museum of American Art

Nonsense. It was strange about children. They disputed your every word. "No what, Cornelia?"

"Here's Doctor Harry."

"I won't see that boy again. He just left five minutes ago."

"That was this morning, Mother. It's night now. Here's the nurse."

"This is Doctor Harry, Mrs. Weatherall. I never saw you look so young and happy!"

"Ah, I'll never be young again—but I'd be happy if they'd let me lie in peace and get rested."

She thought she spoke up loudly, but no one answered. A warm weight on her forehead, a warm bracelet on her wrist, and a breeze went on whispering, trying to tell her something. A shuffle of leaves in the everlasting hand of God, He blew on them and they danced and rattled. "Mother, don't mind, we're going to give you a little hypodermic." "Look here, daughter, how do ants get in this bed? I saw sugar ants yesterday." Did you send for Hapsy too?

It was Hapsy she really wanted. She had to go a long way back through a great many rooms to find Hapsy standing with a baby on her arm. She seemed to herself to be Hapsy also, and the baby on Hapsy's arm was Hapsy and himself and herself, all at once, and there was no surprise in the meeting. Then Hapsy melted from within and turned flimsy as gray gauze and the baby was a gauzy shadow, and Hapsy came up close and said, "I thought you'd never come," and looked at her very searchingly and said, "You haven't changed a bit!" They leaned forward to kiss, when Cornelia began whispering from a long way off, "Oh, is there anything you want to tell me? Is there anything I can do for you?"

Yes, she had changed her mind after sixty years and she would like to see George. I want you to find George. Find him and be sure to tell him I forgot him. I want him to know I had my husband just the same and my children and my house like any other woman. A good house too and a good husband that I loved and fine children out of him. Better than I hoped for even. Tell him I was given back everything he took away and more. Oh, no, oh, God, no, there was something else besides the house and the man and the children. Oh, surely they were not all? What was it? Something not given back. . . . Her breath crowded down under her ribs and grew into a monstrous frightening shape with cutting edges; it bored up into her head, and the agony was unbelievable: Yes, John, get the Doctor now, no more talk, my time has come.

When this one was born it should be the last. The last. It should have been born first, for it was the one she had truly wanted. Everything came in good time. Nothing left out, left over. She was strong, in three days she would be as well as ever. Better. A woman needed milk in her to have her full health.

"Mother, do you hear me?"

"I've been telling you—"

"Mother, Father Connolly's here."

"I went to Holy Communion only last week. Tell him I'm not so sinful as all that."

"Father just wants to speak to you."

He could speak as much as he pleased. It was like him to drop in and inquire about her soul as if it were a teething baby, and then stay on for a cup of tea and a round of cards and gossip. He always had a funny story of some sort, usually about an Irishman who made his little mistakes and

confessed them, and the point lay in some absurd thing he would blurt out in the confessional showing his struggles between native piety and original sin. Granny felt easy about her soul. Cornelia, where are your manners? Give Father Connolly a chair. She had her secret comfortable understanding with a few favorite saints who cleared a straight road to God for her. All as surely signed and sealed as the papers for the new Forty Acres. Forever . . . heirs and assigns[2] forever. Since the day the wedding cake was not cut, but thrown out and wasted. The whole bottom dropped out of the world, and there she was blind and sweating with nothing under her feet and the walls falling away. His hand had caught her under the breast, she had not fallen, there was the freshly polished floor with the green rug on it, just as before. He had cursed like a sailor's parrot and said, "I'll kill him for you." Don't lay a hand on him, for my sake leave something to God. "Now, Ellen, you must believe what I tell you. . . ."

So there was nothing, nothing to worry about any more, except sometimes in the night one of the children screamed in a nightmare, and they both hustled out shaking and hunting for the matches and calling, "There, wait a minute, here we are!" John, get the doctor now, Hapsy's time has come. But there was Hapsy standing by the bed in a white cap. "Cornelia, tell Hapsy to take off her cap. I can't see her plain."

Her eyes opened very wide and the room stood out like a picture she had seen somewhere. Dark colors with the shadows rising towards the ceiling in long angles. The tall black dresser gleamed with nothing on it but John's picture, enlarged from a little one, with John's eyes very black when they should have been blue. You never saw him, so how do you know how he looked? But the man insisted the copy was perfect, it was very rich and handsome. For a picture, yes, but it's not my husband. The table by the

---

2. **assigns:** Persons to whom property is transferred.

bed had a linen cover and a candle and a crucifix. The light was blue from Cornelia's silk lampshades. No sort of light at all, just frippery. You had to live forty years with kerosene lamps to appreciate honest electricity. She felt very strong and she saw Doctor Harry with a rosy nimbus around him.

"You look like a saint, Doctor Harry, and I vow that's as near as you'll ever come to it."

"She's saying something."

"I heard you, Cornelia. What's all this carrying on?"

"Father Connolly's saying—"

Cornelia's voice staggered and bumped like a cart in a bad road. It rounded corners and turned back again and arrived nowhere. Granny stepped up in the cart very lightly and reached for the reins, but a man sat beside her and she knew him by his hands, driving the cart. She did not look in his face, for she knew without seeing, but looked instead down the road where the trees leaned over and bowed to each other and a thousand birds were singing a Mass. She felt like singing too, but she put her hand in the bosom of her dress and pulled out a rosary, and Father Connolly murmured Latin in a very solemn voice and tickled her feet.[3] My God, will you stop that nonsense? I'm a married woman. What if he did run away and leave me to face the priest by myself? I found another a whole world better. I wouldn't have exchanged my husband for anybody except St. Michael[4] himself, and you may tell him that for me with a thank you in the bargain.

Light flashed on her closed eyelids, and a deep roaring shook her. Cornelia, is that lightning? I hear thunder. There's going to be a storm. Close all the windows. Call the children in. . . . "Mother, here we are, all of us." "Is that you, Hapsy?" "Oh, no, I'm Lydia. We drove as fast as we could." Their faces drifted above her, drifted away. The rosary fell out of her hands and Lydia put it back. Jimmy tried to help, their hands fumbled together, and Granny closed two fingers

---

3. **murmured . . . feet:** Administered the last rites.
4. **St. Michael:** One of the archangels.

around Jimmy's thumb. Beads wouldn't do, it must be something alive. She was so amazed her thoughts ran round and round. So, my dear Lord, this is my death and I wasn't even thinking about it. My children have come to see me die. But I can't, it's not time. Oh, I always hated surprises. I wanted to give Cornelia the amethyst set—Cornelia, you're to have the amethyst set, but Hapsy's to wear it when she wants, and, Doctor Harry, do shut up. Nobody sent for you. Oh, my dear Lord, do wait a minute. I meant to do something about the Forty Acres, Jimmy doesn't need it and Lydia will later on, with that worthless husband of hers. I meant to finish the altar cloth and send six bottles of wine to Sister Borgia for her dyspepsia. I want to send six bottles of wine to Sister Borgia, Father Connolly, now don't let me forget.

Cornelia's voice made short turns and tilted over and crashed. "Oh, Mother, oh, Mother, oh Mother. . . ."

"I'm not going, Cornelia. I'm taken by surprise. I can't go."

You'll see Hapsy again. What about her? "I thought you'd never come." Granny made a long journey outward, looking for Hapsy. What if I don't find her? What then? Her heart sank down and down, there was no bottom to death, she couldn't come to the end of it. The blue light from Cornelia's lampshade drew into a tiny point in the center of her brain, it flickered and winked like an eye, quietly it fluttered and dwindled. Granny lay curled down within herself, amazed and watchful, staring at the point of light that was herself; her body was now only a deeper mass of shadow in an endless darkness and this darkness would curl around the light and swallow it up. God, give a sign!

For the second time there was no sign. Again no bridegroom and the priest in the house. She could not remember any other sorrow because this grief wiped them all away. Oh, no, there's nothing more cruel than this—I'll never forgive it. She stretched herself with a deep breath and blew out the light.

RESPONDING TO THE SELECTION

Your Response

1. What is your opinion of Granny Weatherall and the life she led? Explain.
2. How might this story be different if Granny had confronted George after he jilted her?

Recalling

3. (a) As she drifts in and out of consciousness, what painful memory is "squeezed out" of Granny's heart? (b) With what thought does this memory become mingled?
4. (a) What realization does Granny come to after her children arrive? (b) How does she respond to this realization?
5. (a) What does Granny ask of God just before she blows "out the light"? (b) What happens "for the second time"?

Interpreting

6. Why is "Weatherall" an appropriate surname for Granny?
7. (a) What is ironic about Granny's desire to find George so she can tell him she has forgotten him? (b) What might be the "something not given back" that George took?
8. What detail indicates that Granny's sense of time has become distorted?
9. (a) Why does the jilting dominate Granny's thoughts as she approaches death? (b) How is the jilting related to what she experiences in the final paragraph?
10. What does the light referred to in the last two paragraphs symbolize?

Applying

11. Explain whether you think the thoughts and feelings Granny has in the story are typical for a person in her condition.

ANALYZING LITERATURE

Seeing Stream of Consciousness

When using the **stream-of-consciousness** technique, a writer re-creates the natural flow of a character's thoughts. The writer accomplishes this by eliminating the transitions used in ordinary prose and by allowing only the character's natural associations to link thoughts.

1. Find two examples from "The Jilting of Granny Weatherall" in which Granny's thoughts drift from one subject to another subject that is seemingly quite different.
2. What natural associations connect the thoughts in each of these examples?

Understanding Flashback

The stream-of-consciousness technique often includes **flashbacks,** or interruptions in the narrative in which an earlier event is recalled or described. For example, early in the story, Granny recalls a series of events that occurred when she was sixty.

1. Find three more examples of flashbacks. What do you learn from each of these flashbacks?
2. How do the flashbacks contribute to Porter's effective use of the stream-of-consciousness technique?

CRITICAL THINKING AND READING

Understanding the Sequence of Events

When the stream-of-consciousness technique is used in a story, events are organized according to a character's associations, rather than in chronological order. This means that the narrative jumps around in time. As a result, to understand the sequence you must be able to reorganize the events in the order in which they occurred.

Rearrange the events presented in "The Jilting of Granny Weatherall" in chronological order.

THINKING AND WRITING

Writing About Techniques

Write an essay in which you explain why the stream-of-consciousness technique is particularly appropriate for "The Jilting of Granny Weatherall." Start by thinking about the purpose of the stream-of-consciousness technique and about the subject of the story and noting the reasons why the technique is appropriate for the story. Then prepare a thesis statement and write your essay. When you finish writing, revise your essay, making sure that you have adequately supported your thesis.

THOMAS WOLFE

1900–1938

A man of tremendous energy, appetites, and size, Thomas Wolfe poured out thousands of pages of fiction during his brief career. Unlike such Modernist writers as Hemingway and Fitzgerald, who wrote concise, carefully structured prose, Wolfe wrote elaborate, loosely structured fiction that was often uneven in quality. His novels and short stories tended to be long and somewhat unpolished, yet they were filled with vivid imagery and lyrical language.

Born in Asheville, North Carolina, Wolfe grew up in a large, eccentric family whose members later served as models for characters in his fiction. He attended the University of North Carolina at Chapel Hill, where he developed an interest in playwriting. After a year of postgraduate study at Harvard, he moved to New York. There he taught composition at New York University and wrote plays in his spare time. Unable to find success as a playwright, he turned to fiction. With the assistance of Maxwell Perkins, the leading editor of the time, Wolfe published his first novel, *Look Homeward, Angel,* in 1929. The novel, based on his experiences in Asheville, was a critical and financial success and earned him widespread recognition.

Describing the day that Perkins paid him for the manuscript of *Look Homeward, Angel,* Wolfe wrote: "It was the first time . . . that anyone had concretely suggested to me that anything I had written was worth as much as fifteen cents, and I know that I left the publisher's office that day and entered into the great swarm of men and women who passed constantly along Fifth Avenue at Forty-eighth Street and presently I found myself at 110th Street, and from that day to this I have never known how I got there."

Inspired by the success of his first novel, Wolfe began working on a sequel. Once again Perkins helped him to shorten and shape the novel, which was published as *Of Time and the River* in 1935. The novel sold well, yet Wolfe was criticized for basing his work too closely on his own life and for his reliance on Perkins. Stung by this criticism, Wolfe switched publishers and vowed to abandon his autobiographical mode in his next novel. Unfortunately, he died of a brain infection before he could finish this novel. He did, however, leave several thousand pages of manuscript in the hands of another editor, Edward Aswell, who shaped them into two more books, *The Web and the Rock* (1939) and *You Can't Go Home Again* (1940).

Although he has been criticized for his lack of discipline, Wolfe was clearly a gifted writer. In his novels and short stories, including "The Far and the Near," he displayed a strong sense of time and place, an ability to create vivid, realistic descriptions, and a profound understanding of the human condition.

The Far and the Near

Writers' Techniques

Point of View. Point of view refers to the vantage point or perspective from which a narrative is told. Most stories are told from either a first-person or third-person point of view. In a narrative with a first-person point of view, one of the characters tells the story in his or her own words, using the first-person pronoun *I*. In a narrative with a third-person point of view, the narrator does not participate in the story and refers to characters using the third-person pronouns *he* or *she*. A third-person narrator may be either limited or omniscient. A limited third-person narrator focuses on the thoughts and feelings of only one character. An omniscient third-person narrator conveys the thoughts and feelings of all the characters.

During the Modern Age, fiction writers generally abandoned the use of omniscient narrators in favor of first-person and limited third-person narrators. This practice reflected the Modernist belief that "reality" and "truth" cannot be viewed objectively. Writers also frequently attempted to convey a sense of uncertainty by using a narrator who lacked an understanding or awareness of the nature of human existence.

Commentary

Writing about the way he remembers experiences, Thomas Wolfe once remarked:

> The quality of my memory is characterized, I believe, in a more than ordinary degree by the intensity of its sense impressions, its power to evoke and bring back the odors, sounds, colors, shapes, and feel of things with concrete vividness. . . . the look of an old iron bridge across an American river, the sound the train makes as it goes across it; the spoke-and-hollow rumble of the ties below; the look of the muddy banks; the slow, thick, yellow wash of an American river; an old flat-bottomed boat half-filled with water stogged in the muddy bank. . . .

"The Far and the Near" is filled with the vivid sensory impressions that have accumulated in an engineer's mind from more than twenty years of traveling the same route on the railroad. As you read, notice Wolfe's descriptions and how they appeal to the engineer's senses and imagination. Wolfe emphasizes the intensity of these images by showing how memory, imagination, and longing all spring from the passing impressions of life.

Focus

According to an old Russian proverb, "A toe of the star-gazer is often stubbed." Freewrite, exploring the meaning of this proverb.

The Far and the Near

Thomas Wolfe

On the outskirts of a little town upon a rise of land that swept back from the railway there was a tidy little cottage of white boards, trimmed vividly with green blinds. To one side of the house there was a garden neatly patterned with plots of growing vegetables, and an arbor for the grapes which ripened late in August. Before the house there were three mighty oaks which sheltered it in their clean and massive shade in summer, and to the other side there was a border of gay flowers. The whole place had an air of tidiness, thrift, and modest comfort.

Every day, a few minutes after two o'clock in the afternoon, the limited express between two cities passed this spot. At that moment the great train, having halted for a breathing space at the town nearby, was beginning to lengthen evenly into its stroke, but it had not yet reached the full drive of its terrific speed. It swung into view deliberately, swept past with a powerful swaying motion of the engine, a low smooth rumble of its heavy cars upon pressed steel, and then it vanished in the cut. For a moment the progress of the engine could be marked by heavy bellowing puffs of smoke that burst at spaced intervals above the edges of the meadow grass, and finally nothing could be heard but the solid clacking tempo of the wheels receding into the drowsy stillness of the afternoon.

Every day for more than twenty years, as the train had approached this house, the engineer had blown on the whistle, and every day, as soon as she heard this signal, a woman had appeared on the back porch of the little house and waved to him. At first she had a small child clinging to her skirts, and now this child had grown to full womanhood, and every day she, too, came with her mother to the porch and waved.

The engineer had grown old and gray in service. He had driven his great train, loaded with its weight of lives, across the land ten thousand times. His own children had grown up and married, and four times he had seen before him on the tracks the ghastly dot of tragedy converging like a cannon ball to its eclipse of horror at the boiler head[1]—a light spring wagon filled with children, with its clustered row of small stunned faces; a cheap automobile stalled upon the tracks, set with the wooden figures of people paralyzed with fear; a battered hobo walking by the rail, too deaf and old to hear the whistle's warning; and a form flung past his window with a scream—all this the man had seen and known. He had known all the grief, the joy, the peril and the labor such a man could know; he had grown seamed and weathered in his loyal service, and now, schooled by the qualities of faith and courage and humbleness that attended his labor, he had grown old, and had the grandeur and the wisdom these men have.

But no matter what peril or tragedy he had known, the vision of the little house and the women waving to him with a brave free motion of the arm had become fixed in the

---

1. **boiler head:** The front section of a steam locomotive.

mind of the engineer as something beautiful and enduring, something beyond all change and ruin, and something that would always be the same, no matter what mishap, grief or error might break the iron schedule of his days.

The sight of the little house and of these two women gave him the most extraordinary happiness he had ever known. He had seen them in a thousand lights, a hundred weathers. He had seen them through the harsh bare light of wintry gray across the brown and frosted stubble of the earth, and he had seen them again in the green luring sorcery of April.

He felt for them and for the little house in which they lived such tenderness as a man might feel for his own children, and at length the picture of their lives was carved so sharply in his heart that he felt that he knew their lives completely, to every hour and moment of the day, and he resolved that one day, when his years of service should be ended, he would go and find these people and speak at last with them whose lives had been so wrought into his own.

That day came. At last the engineer stepped from a train onto the station platform of the town where these two women lived. His years upon the rail had ended. He was a pensioned servant of his company, with no more work to do. The engineer

walked slowly through the station and out into the streets of the town. Everything was as strange to him as if he had never seen this town before. As he walked on, his sense of bewilderment and confusion grew. Could this be the town he had passed ten thousand times? Were these the same houses he had seen so often from the high windows of his cab? It was all as unfamiliar, as disquieting as a city in a dream, and the perplexity of his spirit increased as he went on.

Presently the houses thinned into the straggling outposts of the town, and the street faded into a country road—the one on which the women lived. And the man plodded on slowly in the heat and dust. At length he stood before the house he sought. He knew at once that he had found the proper place. He saw the lordly oaks before the house, the flower beds, the garden and the arbor, and farther off, the glint of rails.

Yes, this was the house he sought, the place he had passed so many times, the destination he had longed for with such happiness. But now that he had found it, now that he was here, why did his hand falter on the gate; why had the town, the road, the earth, the very entrance to this place he loved turned unfamiliar as the landscape of some ugly dream? Why did he now feel this sense of confusion, doubt and hopelessness?

At length he entered by the gate, walked slowly up the path and in a moment more had mounted three short steps that led up to the porch, and was knocking at the door. Presently he heard steps in the hall, the door was opened, and a woman stood facing him.

And instantly, with a sense of bitter loss and grief, he was sorry he had come. He knew at once that the woman who stood there looking at him with a mistrustful eye was the same woman who had waved to him so many thousand times. But her face was harsh and pinched and meager; the flesh sagged wearily in sallow folds, and the small eyes peered at him with timid suspicion and uneasy doubt. All the brave freedom, the warmth and the affection that he had read into her gesture, vanished in the moment that he saw her and heard her unfriendly tongue.

And now his own voice sounded unreal and ghastly to him as he tried to explain his presence, to tell her who he was and the reason he had come. But he faltered on, fighting stubbornly against the horror of regret, confusion, disbelief that surged up in his spirit, drowning all his former joy and making his act of hope and tenderness seem shameful to him.

At length the woman invited him almost unwillingly into the house, and called her daughter in a harsh shrill voice. Then, for a brief agony of time, the man sat in an ugly little parlor, and he tried to talk while the two women stared at him with a dull, bewildered hostility, a sullen, timorous restraint.

And finally, stammering a crude farewell, he departed. He walked away down the path and then along the road toward town, and suddenly he knew that he was an old man. His heart, which had been brave and confident when it looked along the familiar vista of the rails, was now sick with doubt and horror as it saw the strange and unsuspected visage of an earth which had always been within a stone's throw of him, and which he had never seen or known. And he knew that all the magic of that bright lost way, the vista of that shining line, the imagined corner of that small good universe of hope's desire, was gone forever, could never be got back again.

RESPONDING TO THE SELECTION

Your Response

1. What associations do you have with train travel? With other forms of travel?
2. What experiences have you had in which the reality of a situation failed to live up to your expectations?

Recalling

3. Describe the engineer's daily experience for more than twenty years.
4. What realization does he come to at the end of the story?

Interpreting

5. What does the house come to represent to the engineer?
6. (a) How do the engineer's observations in the final scene contrast with his expectations? (b) When does he first sense that his experience is unlikely to match his expectations?
7. In what ways does Wolfe use distance and physical movement to symbolize the passage of time in this story?
8. What is the meaning of the story's title?
9. Explain the story's theme.

Applying

10. If you had been in the engineer's place, would you have visited the cottage? Explain.

ANALYZING LITERATURE

Understanding Point of View

Point of view refers to the vantage point or perspective from which a narrative is told. "The Far and the Near" is told from a limited third-person point of view. The narrator does not participate in the story and focuses on the thoughts and feelings of one character, the engineer. The reader seems to step inside the shoes of this character and see the world through his eyes.

1. How would the story be different if Wolfe had used a first-person point of view?
2. How would it be different if Wolfe had used an omniscient third-person point of view?

CRITICAL THINKING AND READING

Recognizing Period Characteristics

Like "The Far and the Near," most modern short stories are told from a subjective point of view. The author uses either a first-person narrator or a limited third-person narrator.

1. What Modernist belief does the use of the limited third-person point of view reflect?
2. In many modern stories, the character from whose point of view the story is told is naive, lacking understanding of the nature of human existence. In what sense is the engineer naive?
3. How is the engineer's innocence shattered?
4. How does the engineer's loss of innocence reflect the Modernist belief in the uncertainty and confusion of modern life?

THINKING AND WRITING

Comparing and Contrasting Stories

Write an essay in which you compare and contrast Dexter's attachment to Judy Jones in Fitzgerald's "Winter Dreams" with the engineer's attachment to his vision of the little house in "The Far and the Near." Review both stories, noting similarities and differences between the two characters' attachments. Then write your essay. Organize it by corresponding points of contrast. Use passages from the stories for support.

LEARNING OPTIONS

1. **Cross-curricular Connection.** Throughout the late 1800's and the early 1900's, America had a love affair with the railroad. For millions of Americans, the railroad embodied freedom and adventure. Explore the evolution of the American railroad and how it has changed over the last several decades. Share your findings with the class in a brief oral report.
2. **Art.** Create a map or a three-dimensional diagram of the engineer's route. Include all the details mentioned in the story, and use your imagination to come up with additional details. Present your map or diagram to the class.

EUDORA WELTY

1909–

In her short stories and novels, Eudora Welty captures life in the deep South, creating vivid portraits of the landscape and conveying the shared attitudes and values of the people. She often confronts the hardships and sorrows of life in the poor rural areas. Yet despite her awareness of people's suffering, her outlook remains positive and optimistic.

Welty was born in Jackson, Mississippi, where she has spent most of her life. She attended Mississippi State College for Women before transferring to the University of Wisconsin, from which she graduated in 1929. Hoping to pursue a career in advertising, she moved to New York and enrolled at Columbia University School of Business. However, because of the worsening Depression, she was unable to find a steady job and returned to Jackson in 1931.

After accepting a job as a publicist for a government agency, she spent several years traveling throughout Mississippi, taking photographs and interviewing people. Her experiences and observations inspired her to write fiction, and in 1936 her first short story, "Death of a Traveling Salesman," was published in a small magazine.

Welty became a leading American writer of this century. Over the years she has published numerous collections of short stories, including *A Curtain of Green* (1941), *The Wide Net and Other Stories* (1943), *The Bride of Innisfallen and Other Stories* (1955), and *Thirteen Stories* (1965). She has also written several novels, including *Delta Wedding* (1946), *The Ponder Heart* (1954), and *Losing Battles* (1970). In 1973 she was awarded the Pulitzer Prize for her novel *The Optimist's Daughter* (1972).

Throughout her work Welty displays an acute sense of detail and a deep sense of compassion toward her characters. In "A Worn Path," for example, she paints a sympathetic portrait of an old woman whose feelings of love and sense of duty motivate her to make a long, painful journey through the woods.

Welty uses her fiction to explore people's private lives. In "Must the Novelist Crusade?" she answers critics who feel that a modern writer has to "better the world or go to his grave reproached for the mess it is in." Welty claims: "Writing fiction is an interior affair. Novels and stories always will be put down little by little out of personal feeling and personal beliefs arrived at alone and at firsthand over a period of time as time is needed. To go outside and beat the drum is only to interrupt, interrupt, and so finally to forget and lose. Fiction has, and must keep, a private address. For life is *lived* in a private place; where it means anything is inside the mind and heart. Fiction has always shown life where it is lived. . . ."

A Worn Path

Writers' Techniques

Ambiguity. Ambiguity refers to uncertainty of intention or meaning. An ambiguous statement is one that can be interpreted in two or more ways. Similarly, when a work of literature is ambiguous or contains ambiguous elements, the work or certain elements of the work can be interpreted in more than one way. Readers may find various possible meanings and look for details that support each interpretation.

During the Modern Age, literary works became increasingly ambiguous. Writers suggested meaning and presented possibilities instead of asserting or directly stating their points. This style reflected the Modernist belief that life in the modern world is confusing and filled with uncertainties rather than definite answers.

Focus

"A Worn Path" is about an old woman, Phoenix Jackson, who repeatedly makes a long, arduous journey into town to get medicine for her grandson. Make a list of journeys that you have made repeatedly during your life. Then jot down your reasons for making each of these journeys.

Primary Source

In her essay "Is Phoenix Jackson's Grandson Really Dead?" Welty answers a frequently asked question about "A Worn Path."

> It's *all right,* I want to say to the students who write me, for things to be what they appear to be, and for words to mean what they say. It's all right, too, for words and appearances to mean more than one thing—ambiguity is a fact of life. A fiction writer's responsibility covers not only what he presents as the facts of a given story but what he chooses to stir up as their implications; in the end, these implications, too, become facts, in the larger fictional sense. But it is not all right, not in good faith, for things *not* to mean what they say.
>
> The grandson's plight was real and it made the truth of the story, which is the story of an errand of love carried out. If the child no longer lived, the truth would persist in the 'wornness' of the path. But his being dead can't increase the truth of the story, can't affect it one way or the other. I think I signal this, because the end of the story has been reached before old Phoenix gets home again: she simply starts back. To the question 'Is the grandson really dead?' I could reply that it doesn't make any difference. I could also say that I did not make him up in order to let him play a trick on Phoenix. But my best answer could be: "*Phoenix* is alive."

A Worn Path

Eudora Welty

It was December—a bright frozen day in the early morning. Far out in the country there was an old Negro woman with her head tied in a red rag, coming along a path through the pinewoods. Her name was Phoenix Jackson. She was very old and small and she walked slowly in the dark pine shadows, moving a little from side to side in her steps, with the balanced heaviness and lightness of a pendulum in a grandfather clock. She carried a thin, small cane made from an umbrella, and with this she kept tapping the frozen earth in front of her. This made a grave and persistent noise in the still air, that seemed meditative like the chirping of a solitary little bird.

She wore a dark striped dress reaching down to her shoe tops, and an equally long apron of bleached sugar sacks, with a full pocket: all neat and tidy, but every time she took a step she might have fallen over her shoelaces, which dragged from her unlaced shoes. She looked straight ahead. Her eyes were blue with age. Her skin had a pattern all its own of numberless branching wrinkles and as though a whole little tree stood in the middle of her forehead, but a golden color ran underneath, and the two knobs of her cheeks were illumined by a yellow burning under the dark. Under the red rag her hair came down on her neck in the frailest of ringlets, still black, and with an odor like copper.

Now and then there was a quivering in the thicket. Old Phoenix said, "Out of my way, all you foxes, owls, beetles, jack rabbits, coons and wild animals! . . . Keep out from under these feet, little bobwhites[1]. . . . Keep the big wild hogs out of my path. Don't let none of those come running my direction. I got a long way." Under her small black-freckled hand her cane, limber as a buggy whip, would switch at the brush as if to rouse up any hiding things.

On she went. The woods were deep and still. The sun made the pine needles almost too bright to look at, up where the wind rocked. The cones dropped as light as feathers. Down in the hollow was the mourning dove—it was not too late for him.

The path ran up a hill. "Seem like there is chains about my feet, time I get this far," she said, in the voice of argument old people keep to use with themselves. "Something always take a hold of me on this hill—pleads I should stay."

After she got to the top she turned and gave a full, severe look behind her where she had come. "Up through pines," she said at length. "Now down through oaks."

Her eyes opened their widest, and she started down gently. But before she got to the bottom of the hill a bush caught her dress.

Her fingers were busy and intent, but her skirts were full and long, so that before she could pull them free in one place they were caught in another. It was not possible to allow the dress to tear. "I in the thorny bush," she said. "Thorns, you doing your appointed work. Never want to let folks pass,

---

1. bobwhites *n.*: Partridges.

no sir. Old eyes thought you was a pretty little *green* bush."

Finally, trembling all over, she stood free, and after a moment dared to stoop for her cane.

"Sun so high!" she cried, leaning back and looking, while the thick tears went over her eyes. "The time getting all gone here."

At the foot of this hill was a place where a log was laid across the creek.

"Now comes the trial," said Phoenix.

Putting her right foot out, she mounted the log and shut her eyes. Lifting her skirt, leveling her cane fiercely before her, like a festival figure in some parade, she began to march across. Then she opened her eyes and she was safe on the other side.

"I wasn't as old as I thought," she said.

But she sat down to rest. She spread her skirts on the bank around her and folded her hands over her knees. Up above her was a tree in a pearly cloud of mistletoe. She did not dare to close her eyes, and when a little boy brought her a plate with a slice of marble cake on it she spoke to him. "That would be acceptable," she said. But when she went to take it there was just her own hand in the air.

So she left that tree, and had to go through a barbed-wire fence. There she had to creep and crawl, spreading her knees and stretching her fingers like a baby trying to climb the steps. But she talked loudly to herself: she could not let her dress be torn now, so late in the day, and she could not pay for having her arm or her leg sawed off if she got caught fast where she was.

At last she was safe through the fence and risen up out in the clearing. Big dead trees, like black men with one arm, were standing in the purple stalks of the withered cotton field. There sat a buzzard.

"Who you watching?"

In the furrow she made her way along.

"Glad this not the season for bulls," she said, looking sideways, "and the good Lord made his snakes to curl up and sleep in the winter. A pleasure I don't see no two-headed snake coming around that tree, where it come once. It took a while to get by him, back in the summer."

She passed through the old cotton and went into a field of dead corn. It whispered and shook and was taller than her head. "Through the maze now," she said, for there was no path.

Then there was something tall, black, and skinny there, moving before her.

At first she took it for a man. It could have been a man dancing in the field. But she stood still and listened, and it did not make a sound. It was as silent as a ghost.

"Ghost," she said sharply, "who be you the ghost of? For I have heard of nary death close by."

But there was no answer—only the ragged dancing in the wind.

She shut her eyes, reached out her hand, and touched a sleeve. She found a coat and inside that an emptiness, cold as ice.

"You scarecrow," she said. Her face lighted. "I ought to be shut up for good," she said with laughter. "My senses is gone. I too old. I the oldest people I ever know. Dance, old scarecrow," she said, "while I dancing with you."

She kicked her foot over the furrow, and with mouth drawn down, shook her head once or twice in a little strutting way. Some husks blew down and whirled in streamers about her skirts.

Then she went on, parting her way from side to side with the cane, through the whispering field. At last she came to the end, to a wagon track where the silver grass blew between the red ruts. The quail were walking around like pullets, seeming all dainty and unseen.

"Walk pretty," she said. "This the easy place. This the easy going."

She followed the track, swaying through the quiet bare fields, through the little strings of trees silver in their dead leaves, past cabins silver from weather, with the doors and windows boarded shut, all like old women under a spell sitting there. "I walking in their sleep," she said, nodding her head vigorously.

In a ravine she went where a spring was silently flowing through a hollow log. Old Phoenix bent and drank. "Sweet gum² makes the water sweet," she said, and drank more. "Nobody know who made this well, for it was here when I was born."

The track crossed a swampy part where the moss hung as white as lace from every limb. "Sleep on, alligators, and blow your bubbles." Then the track went into the road.

Deep, deep the road went down between the high green-colored banks. Overhead the live-oaks met, and it was as dark as a cave.

A black dog with a lolling tongue came up out of the weeds by the ditch. She was meditating, and not ready, and when he came at her she only hit him a little with her cane. Over she went in the ditch, like a little puff of milkweed.³

Down there, her senses drifted away. A dream visited her, and she reached her hand up, but nothing reached down and gave her a pull. So she lay there and presently went to talking. "Old woman," she said to herself, "that black dog come up out of the weeds to stall you off, and now there he sitting on his fine tail, smiling at you."

A white man finally came along and found her—a hunter, a young man, with his dog on a chain.

"Well, Granny!" he laughed. "What are you doing there?"

"Lying on my back like a June bug waiting to be turned over, mister," she said, reaching up her hand.

He lifted her up, gave her a swing in the air, and set her down. "Anything broken, Granny?"

"No sir, them old dead weeds is springy enough," said Phoenix, when she had got her breath. "I thank you for your trouble."

"Where do you live, Granny?" he asked, while the two dogs were growling at each other.

"Away back yonder, sir, behind the ridge. You can't even see it from here."

"On your way home?"

"No sir, I going to town."

"Why, that's too far! That's as far as I walk when I come out myself, and I get something for my trouble." He patted the stuffed bag he carried, and there hung down a little closed claw. It was one of the bobwhites, with its beak hooked bitterly to show it was dead. "Now you go on home, Granny!"

"I bound to go to town, mister," said Phoenix. "The time come around."

He gave another laugh, filling the whole landscape. "I know you old colored people! Wouldn't miss going to town to see Santa Claus!"

But something held old Phoenix very still. The deep lines in her face went into a fierce and different radiation. Without warning, she had seen with her own eyes a flashing nickel fall out of the man's pocket onto the ground.

"How old are you, Granny?" he was saying.

"There is no telling, mister," she said, "no telling."

Then she gave a little cry and clapped her hands and said, "Git on away from here, dog! Look! Look at that dog!" She laughed as if in admiration. "He ain't scared of nobody. He a big black dog." She whispered, "Sic him!"

"Watch me get rid of that cur," said the man. "Sic him, Pete! Sic him!"

Phoenix heard the dogs fighting, and heard the man running and throwing sticks. She even heard a gunshot. But she was slowly bending forward by that time, further and further forward, the lids stretched down over her eyes, as if she were doing this in her sleep. Her chin was lowered almost to her knees. The yellow palm of her hand came out from the fold of her apron. Her fingers slid

---

2. **sweet gum:** A tree that produces a fragrant juice.
3. **milkweed:** A plant with pods which when ripe release feathery seeds.

down and along the ground under the piece of money with the grace and care they would have in lifting an egg from under a setting hen. Then she slowly straightened up, she stood erect, and the nickel was in her apron pocket. A bird flew by. Her lips moved. "God watching me the whole time. I come to stealing."

The man came back, and his own dog panted about them. "Well, I scared him off that time," he said, and then he laughed and lifted his gun and pointed it at Phoenix.

She stood straight and faced him.

"Doesn't the gun scare you?" he said, still pointing it.

"No, sir, I seen plenty go off closer by, in my day, and for less than what I done," she said, holding utterly still.

He smiled, and shouldered the gun. "Well, Granny," he said, "you must be a hundred years old, and scared of nothing. I'd give you a dime if I had any money with me. But you take my advice and stay home, and nothing will happen to you."

"I bound to go on my way, mister," said Phoenix. She inclined her head in the red rag. Then they went in different directions, but she could hear the gun shooting again and again over the hill.

She walked on. The shadows hung from the oak trees to the road like curtains. Then she smelled woodsmoke, and smelled the river, and she saw a steeple and the cabins on their steep steps. Dozens of little black children whirled around her. There ahead was Natchez[4] shining. Bells were ringing. She walked on.

In the paved city it was Christmas time. There were red and green electric lights strung and criss-crossed everywhere, and all turned on in the daytime. Old Phoenix would have been lost if she had not distrusted her

eyesight and depended on her feet to know where to take her.

She paused quietly on the sidewalk where people were passing by. A lady came along in the crowd, carrying an armful of red-, green- and silver-wrapped presents; she gave off perfume like the red roses in hot summer, and Phoenix stopped her.

"Please, missy, will you lace up my shoe?" She held up her foot.

"What do you want, Grandma?"

"See my shoe," said Phoenix. "Do all right for out in the country, but wouldn't look right to go in a big building."

"Stand still then, Grandma," said the lady. She put her packages down on the sidewalk beside her and laced and tied both shoes tightly.

"Can't lace 'em with a cane," said Phoenix. "Thank you, missy. I doesn't mind asking a nice lady to tie up my shoe, when I gets out on the street."

Moving slowly and from side to side, she went into the big building, and into a tower of steps, where she walked up and around and around until her feet knew to stop.

She entered a door, and there she saw nailed up on the wall the document that had been stamped with the gold seal and framed in the gold frame, which matched the dream that was hung up in her head.

"Here I be," she said. There was a fixed and ceremonial stiffness over her body.

"A charity case, I suppose," said an attendant who sat at the desk before her.

But Phoenix only looked above her head. There was sweat on her face, the wrinkles in her skin shone like a bright net.

"Speak up, Grandma," the woman said. "What's your name? We must have your history, you know. Have you been here before? What seems to be the trouble with you?"

Old Phoenix only gave a twitch to her face as if a fly were bothering her.

"Are you deaf?" cried the attendant.

But then the nurse came in.

"Oh, that's just old Aunt Phoenix," she

---

4. Natchez (nach'iz): A town in southern Mississippi.

said. "She doesn't come for herself—she has a little grandson. She makes these trips just as regular as clockwork. She lives away back off the Old Natchez Trace." She bent down. "Well, Aunt Phoenix, why don't you just take a seat? We won't keep you standing after your long trip." She pointed.

The old woman sat down, bolt upright in the chair.

"Now, how is the boy?" asked the nurse.

Old Phoenix did not speak.

"I said, how is the boy?"

But Phoenix only waited and stared straight ahead, her face very solemn and withdrawn into rigidity.

"Is his throat any better?" asked the nurse. "Aunt Phoenix, don't you hear me? Is your grandson's throat any better since the last time you came for the medicine?"

With her hands on her knees, the old woman waited, silent, erect and motionless, just as if she were in armor.

"You mustn't take up our time this way, Aunt Phoenix," the nurse said. "Tell us quickly about your grandson, and get it over. He isn't dead, is he?"

At last there came a flicker and then a flame of comprehension across her face, and she spoke.

"My grandson. It was my memory had left me. There I sat and forgot why I made my long trip."

"Forgot?" The nurse frowned. "After you came so far?"

Then Phoenix was like an old woman begging a dignified forgiveness for waking up frightened in the night. "I never did go to school, I was too old at the Surrender,"[5] she said in a soft voice. "I'm an old woman without an education. It was my memory fail me. My little grandson, he is just the same, and I forgot it in the coming."

---

5. **the Surrender:** The surrender of the Confederate army, ending the Civil War.

"Throat never heals, does it?" said the nurse, speaking in a loud, sure voice to old Phoenix. By now she had a card with something written on it, a little list. "Yes. Swallowed lye. When was it?—January—two-three years ago—"

Phoenix spoke unasked now. "No, missy, he not dead, he just the same. Every little while his throat begin to close up again, and he not able to swallow. He not get his breath. He not able to help himself. So the time come around, and I go on another trip for the soothing medicine."

"All right. The doctor said as long as you came to get it, you could have it," said the nurse. "But it's an obstinate case."

"My little grandson, he sit up there in the house all wrapped up, waiting by himself," Phoenix went on. "We is the only two left in the world. He suffer and it don't seem to put him back at all. He got a sweet look. He going to last. He wear a little patch quilt and peep out holding his mouth open like a little bird. I remembers so plain now. I not going to forget him again, no, the whole enduring time. I could tell him from all the others in creation."

"All right." The nurse was trying to hush her now. She brought her a bottle of medicine. "Charity," she said, making a check mark in a book.

Old Phoenix held the bottle close to her eyes, and then carefully put it into her pocket.

"I thank you," she said.

"It's Christmas time, Grandma," said the attendant. "Could I give you a few pennies out of my purse?"

"Five pennies is a nickel," said Phoenix stiffly.

"Here's a nickel," said the attendant.

Phoenix rose carefully and held out her hand. She received the nickel and then fished the other nickel out of her pocket and laid it beside the new one. She stared at her palm closely, with her head on one side.

Then she gave a tap with her cane on the floor.

"This is what come to me to do," she said. "I going to the store and buy my child a little windmill they sells, made out of paper. He going to find it hard to believe there such a thing in the world. I'll march myself back where he is waiting, holding it straight up in this hand."

She lifted her free hand, gave a little nod, turned around, and walked out of the doctor's office. Then her slow step began on the stairs, going down.

RESPONDING TO THE SELECTION

Your Response

1. What emotions does this story evoke in you?
2. What is your reaction to the ending of the story? Would you prefer to know if Phoenix Jackson's grandson is alive? Why or why not?

Recalling

3. Why does Phoenix make her journey?
4. What obstacles does Phoenix Jackson encounter on her journey?
5. (a) What does the nurse ask Phoenix? (b) How does Phoenix explain her inability to answer?

Interpreting

6. What details of the setting help to create a somber, mournful atmosphere?
7. How would you characterize the attitudes of the hunter, the attendant, and the nurse toward Phoenix?
8. Why do you think Phoenix does not immediately respond to the questions of the nurse and the attendant?
9. What is the significance of the story's taking place at Christmas time?
10. What does Phoenix's journey symbolize?

Applying

11. Like Welty's other works, "The Worn Path" is set in the deep South. Do you think the story would be different if the setting were changed? Why or why not?

ANALYZING LITERATURE

Interpreting Ambiguity

When a work of literature is **ambiguous** or contains ambiguous elements, the work or the elements of the work can be interpreted in more than one way. For example, in "A Worn Path" Eudora Welty leaves the question of whether Phoenix Jackson's grandson is still alive open to interpretation.

1. Find two details from the story that support the interpretation that Phoenix's grandson is alive.
2. Find two details that support the interpretation that he is dead.
3. Why do you think Welty chooses not to reveal whether he is alive or dead?

THINKING AND WRITING

Writing a Continuation of the Story

Write a continuation of the story in which Phoenix returns home bearing the medicine. List details you can use to describe the setting. When you write your story, try to use these details to create an appropriate atmosphere and to foreshadow what will be waiting for her when she arrives home. When you finish writing, revise your story, making sure you have maintained a consistent point of view.

LEARNING OPTIONS

1. **Cross-curricular Connection.** The name *Phoenix* refers to the mythical Egyptian bird that rose from the ashes of its own funeral pyre. Read about the phoenix in an encyclopedia or a dictionary of mythology. Then write a paragraph explaining what makes *Phoenix* an appropriate name for Welty's main character.
2. **Speaking and Listening.** In her essay "Is Phoenix Jackson's Grandson Really Dead?" Eudora Welty answers the question with this statement: "*Phoenix* is alive." Reread the excerpt from Welty's essay on page 621. Be prepared to explain her response in a class discussion.

JOHN STEINBECK

1902–1968

Reflecting the influence of the Naturalists, John Steinbeck generally portrayed working-class characters who were manipulated by forces beyond their understanding or control. Yet although many of his characters suffered tragic fates, they almost always managed to retain a sense of dignity throughout their struggles.

Steinbeck was born in Salinas, California, the son of a county official and a schoolteacher. The people and the landscape of the area in northern California where he grew up eventually inspired many of the characters and settings of his literary works. After graduating from high school, he enrolled at Stanford University. He left before graduating, however, and spent the next five years drifting across the country, reading, writing, and working at odd jobs.

Steinbeck had little success as a writer until 1935 when he published *Tortilla Flat,* his third novel. Two years later he earned widespread recognition and critical acclaim with the publication of *Of Mice and Men.* This novel, which portrays two drifters whose dream of owning their own farm ends in tragedy, became a best-seller and was made into a Broadway play and a motion picture. Steinbeck then went on to write what is generally regarded as his finest novel, *The Grapes of Wrath* (1939), the accurate and emotional story of the "Okies," Oklahoma farmers dispossessed of their land and forced to become migrant farmers in California. The novel won the National Book Award and the Pulitzer Prize and established Steinbeck as one of the most highly regarded writers of his day.

Steinbeck produced several more successful works during his later years, including *Cannery Row* (1945), *The Pearl* (1947), *East of Eden* (1951), and *The Winter of Our Discontent* (1961). In 1962 he was awarded the Nobel Prize for Literature.

When asked why he wrote, Steinbeck answered, "Like everyone, I want to be good and strong and virtuous and wise and loved. I think that writing may be simply a method or technique for communication with other individuals; and its stimulus, the loneliness we are born to. In writing, perhaps we hope to achieve companionship. What some people find in religion, a writer may find in his craft . . . absorption of the small and frightened and lonely into the whole and complete, a kind of breaking through to glory."

In nearly all of his works, including "Flight," Steinbeck created vivid portraits of the landscape and demonstrated how people are shaped and manipulated by their environments. At the same time, his works reflect his belief in the need for social justice and his hope that people can learn from the suffering of others.

GUIDE FOR INTERPRETING

Flight

Writers' Techniques

Setting. The setting is the time and place in which the events in a work of literature occur. Although it is not usually the most important element in a literary work, the setting can often shape and motivate the characters. In real life people are sometimes viewed as being, to some extent, products of their environments. Similarly, characters in many literary works may be viewed as products of the setting. While a character's attitudes, values, and behavior may be shaped by the long-term effect of the setting, the setting may also have a more immediate impact on a character's actions. For example, in Jack London's story "To Build a Fire," most of the character's actions result directly from his efforts to cope with the extreme cold of the Arctic wilderness.

John Steinbeck believed that people are often manipulated by forces of society and nature beyond their understanding or control. As a result, the setting usually plays an important role in his works, often having both an immediate and long-term effect on the characters. In most of his stories and novels, he describes the setting in exact detail and clearly conveys how it shapes and motivates the characters.

Commentary

In the following passage, critic Edmund Wilson explores the relationship between Steinbeck's characters and the natural world:

> The stories in *The Long Valley* are almost entirely about plants and animals; and Mr. Steinbeck does not give the effect . . . of romantically raising the animals to the stature of human beings, but rather of assimilating the human beings to animals. . . . In 'Flight,' a young Mexican boy, who has killed a man and run away into the mountains, is finally reduced to a state so close to that of the beasts that he is apparently mistaken by a mountain lion for another four-footed animal. . . .

What statement do you think Steinbeck is making about the effect of the environment on characters?

Focus

In "Flight" Steinbeck uses sensory details to paint a vivid portrait of the setting. Prepare a list of sensory details describing your environment. List them in a chart under the headings of *Sight, Smell, Taste, Touch, Hearing.*

Flight

John Steinbeck

About fifteen miles below Monterey, on the wild coast, the Torres family had their farm, a few sloping acres above a cliff that dropped to the brown reefs and to the hissing white waters of the ocean. Behind the farm the stone mountains stood up against the sky. The farm buildings huddled like little clinging aphids[1] on the mountain skirts, crouched low to the ground as though the wind might blow them into the sea. The little shack, the rattling, rotting barn were gray-bitten with sea salt, beaten by the damp wind until they had taken on the color of the granite hills. Two horses, a red cow and a red calf, half a dozen pigs and a flock of lean, multicolored chickens stocked the place. A little corn was raised on the sterile slope, and it grew short and thick under the wind, and all the cobs formed on the landward sides of the stalks.

Mama Torres, a lean, dry woman with ancient eyes, had ruled the farm for ten years, ever since her husband tripped over a stone in the field one day and fell full length on a rattlesnake. When one is bitten on the chest there is not much that can be done.

Mama Torres had three children, two undersized black ones of twelve and fourteen, Emilio and Rosy, whom Mama kept fishing on the rocks below the farm when the sea was kind and when the truant officer was in some distant part of Monterey County. And there was Pepé, the tall smiling son of nineteen, a gentle, affectionate boy, but very lazy.

Pepé had a tall head, pointed at the top, and from its peak, coarse black hair grew down like a thatch all around. Over his smiling little eyes Mama cut a straight bang so he could see. Pepé had sharp Indian cheek bones and an eagle nose, but his mouth was as sweet and shapely as a girl's mouth, and his chin was fragile and chiseled. He was loose and gangling, all legs and feet and wrists, and he was very lazy. Mama thought him fine and brave, but she never told him so. She said, "Some lazy cow must have got into thy father's family, else how could I have a son like thee." And she said, "When I carried thee, a sneaking lazy coyote came out of the brush and looked at me one day. That must have made thee so."

Pepé smiled sheepishly and stabbed at the ground with his knife to keep the blade sharp and free from rust. It was his inheritance, that knife, his father's knife. The long heavy blade folded back into the black handle. There was a button on the handle. When Pepé pressed the button, the blade leaped out ready for use. The knife was with Pepé always, for it had been his father's knife.

One sunny morning when the sea below the cliff was glinting and blue and the white surf creamed on the reef, when even the stone mountains looked kindly, Mama Torres called out the door of the shack, "Pepé, I have a labor for thee."

There was no answer. Mama listened. From behind the barn she heard a burst of laughter. She lifted her full long skirt and walked in the direction of the noise.

Pepé was sitting on the ground with his

---

1. **aphids** (ā′fĭdz) n.: Small insects that suck the juice from plants.

back against a box. His white teeth glistened. On either side of him stood the two black ones, tense and expectant. Fifteen feet away a redwood post was set in the ground. Pepé's right hand lay limply in his lap, and in the palm the big black knife rested. The blade was closed back into the handle. Pepé looked smiling at the sky.

Suddenly Emilio cried, "Ya!"

Pepé's wrist flicked like the head of a snake. The blade seemed to fly open in midair, and with a thump the point dug into the redwood post, and the black handle quivered. The three burst into excited laughter.

Rosy ran to the post and pulled out the knife and brought it back to Pepé. He closed the blade and settled the knife carefully in his listless palm again. He grinned self-consciously at the sky.

"Ya!"

The heavy knife lanced out and sunk into the post again. Mama moved forward like a ship and scattered the play.

"All day you do foolish things with the knife, like a toy baby," she stormed. "Get up on thy huge feet that eat up shoes. Get up!" She took him by one loose shoulder and hoisted at him. Pepé grinned sheepishly and came halfheartedly to his feet. "Look!" Mama cried. "Big lazy, you must catch the horse and put on him thy father's saddle. You must ride to Monterey. The medicine bottle is empty. There is no salt. Go thou now, Peanut! Catch the horse."

A revolution took place in the relaxed figure of Pepé. "To Monterey, me? Alone? *Sí*, Mama."

She scowled at him. "Do not think, big sheep, that you will buy candy. No, I will give you only enough for the medicine and the salt."

Pepé smiled. "Mama, you will put the hatband on the hat?"

She relented then. "Yes, Pepé. You may wear the hatband."

His voice grew insinuating, "And the green handkerchief, Mama?"

"Yes, if you go quickly and return with no trouble, the silk green handkerchief will go. If you make sure to take off the handkerchief when you eat so no spot may fall on it. . . ."

"*Sí*, Mama. I will be careful. I am a man."

"Thou? A man? Thou art a peanut."

He went into the rickety barn and brought out a rope, and he walked agilely enough up the hill to catch the horse.

When he was ready and mounted before the door, mounted on his father's saddle that was so old that the oaken frame showed through torn leather in many places, then Mama brought out the round black hat with the tooled leather band, and she reached up and knotted the green silk handkerchief about his neck. Pepé's blue denim coat was much darker than his jeans, for it had been washed much less often.

Mama handed up the big medicine bottle and the silver coins. "That for the medicine," she said, "and that for the salt. That for a candle to burn for the papa. That for *dulces*[2] for the little ones. Our friend Mrs. Rodriguez will give you dinner and maybe a bed for the night. When you go to the church say only ten Paternosters[3] and only twenty-five Ave Marias.[4] Oh! I know, big coyote. You would sit there flapping your mouth over Aves all day while you looked at the candles and the holy pictures. That is not good devotion to stare at the pretty things."

The black hat, covering the high pointed head and black thatched hair of Pepé, gave him dignity and age. He sat the rangy horse well. Mama thought how handsome he was, dark and lean and tall. "I would not send thee now alone, thou little one, except for the medicine," she said softly. "It is not good to have no medicine, for who knows when the toothache will come, or the sadness of the stomach. These things are."

"Adios, Mama," Pepé cried. "I will come back soon. You may send me often alone. I am a man."

"Thou art a foolish chicken."

He straightened his shoulders, flipped the reins against the horse's shoulder and rode away. He turned once and saw that they still watched him, Emilio and Rosy and Mama. Pepé grinned with pride and gladness and lifted the tough buckskin horse to a trot.

When he had dropped out of sight over a little dip in the road, Mama turned to the black ones, but she spoke to herself. "He is nearly a man now," she said. "It will be a nice thing to have a man in the house again." Her eyes sharpened on the children. "Go to the rocks now. The tide is going out. There will be abalones[5] to be found." She put the iron hooks into their hands and saw them down the steep trail to the reefs. She brought the smooth stone *metate*[6] to the doorway and sat grinding her corn to flour and looking occasionally at the road over which Pepé had gone. The noonday came and then the afternoon, when the little ones beat the abalones on a rock to make them

---

2. *dulces* (dool'sās) *n.*: Candy; sweets.

3. **Paternosters** (pät'ər nôs'tərz): Our Fathers (The Lord's Prayer).

4. **Ave Marias** (ä' vä mə rē' əz): Hail Marys.

5. **abalones** (ab'ə lō'nēz) *n.*: Large shellfish.

6. *metate* (mä tä' tä'): A stone used in the southwestern United States for grinding meal.

tender and Mama patted the tortillas[7] to make them thin. They ate their dinner as the red sun was plunging down toward the ocean. They sat on the doorsteps and watched the big white moon come over the mountain tops.

Mama said, "He is now at the house of our friend Mrs. Rodriguez. She will give him nice things to eat and maybe a present."

Emilio said, "Some day I too will ride to Monterey for medicine. Did Pepé come to be a man today?"

Mama said wisely, "A boy gets to be a man when a man is needed. Remember this thing. I have known boys forty years old because there was no need for a man."

Soon afterwards they retired, Mama in her big oak bed on one side of the room, Emilio and Rosy in their boxes full of straw and sheepskins on the other side of the room.

The moon went over the sky and the surf roared on the rocks. The roosters crowed the first call. The surf subsided to a whispering surge against the reef. The moon dropped toward the sea. The roosters crowed again.

The moon was near down to the water when Pepé rode on a winded horse to his home flat. His dog bounced out and circled the horse yelping with pleasure. Pepé slid off the saddle to the ground. The weathered little shack was silver in the moonlight and the square shadow of it was black to the north and east. Against the east the piling mountains were misty with light; their tops melted into the sky.

Pepé walked wearily up the three steps and into the house. It was dark inside. There was a rustle in the corner.

Mama cried out from her bed. "Who comes? Pepé, is it thou?"

"Sí, Mama."

"Did you get the medicine?"

"Sí, Mama."

"Well, go to sleep, then. I thought you would be sleeping at the house of Mrs. Rodri-

guez." Pepé stood silently in the dark room. "Why do you stand there, Pepé? Did you drink wine?"

"Sí, Mama."

"Well, go to bed then and sleep out the wine."

His voice was tired and patient, but very firm. "Light the candle, Mama. I must go away into the mountains."

"What is this, Pepé? You are crazy." Mama struck a sulphur match and held the little blue burr until the flame spread up the stick. She set light to the candle on the floor beside her bed. "Now, Pepé, what is this you say?" She looked anxiously into his face.

He was changed. The fragile quality seemed to have gone from his chin. His mouth was less full than it had been, the lines of the lips were straighter, but in his eyes the greatest change had taken place. There was no laughter in them any more, nor any bashfulness. They were sharp and bright and purposeful.

He told her in a tired monotone, told her everything just as it had happened. A few people came into the kitchen of Mrs. Rodriguez. There was wine to drink. Pepé drank wine. The little quarrel—the man started toward Pepé and then the knife—it went almost by itself. It flew, it darted before Pepé knew it. As he talked, Mama's face grew stern, and it seemed to grow more lean. Pepé finished. "I am a man now, Mama. The man said names to me I could not allow."

Mama nodded. "Yes, thou art a man, my poor little Pepé. Thou art a man. I have seen it coming on thee. I have watched you throwing the knife into the post, and I have been afraid." For a moment her face had softened, but now it grew stern again. "Come! We must get you ready. Go. Awaken Emilio and Rosy. Go quickly."

Pepé stepped over to the corner where his brother and sister slept among the sheepskins. He leaned down and shook them gently. "Come, Rosy! Come, Emilio! The mama says you must arise."

The little black ones sat up and rubbed their eyes in the candlelight. Mama was out

---

7. tortillas (tôr tē′əz) *n*.: Thin, flat cakes of cornmeal.

of bed now, her long black skirt over her nightgown. "Emilio," she cried. "Go up and catch the other horse for Pepé. Quickly, now! Quickly." Emilio put his legs in his overalls and stumbled sleepily out the door.

"You heard no one behind you on the road?" Mama demanded.

"No, Mama. I listened carefully. No one was on the road."

Mama darted like a bird about the room. From a nail on the wall she took a canvas water bag and threw it on the floor. She stripped a blanket from her bed and rolled it into a tight tube and tied the ends with string. From a box beside the stove she lifted a flour sack half full of black stringy jerky. "Your father's black coat, Pepé. Here, put it on."

Pepé stood in the middle of the floor watching her activity. She reached behind the door and brought out the rifle, a long 38-56, worn shiny the whole length of the barrel. Pepé took it from her and held it in the crook of his elbow. Mama brought a little leather bag and counted the cartridges into his hand. "Only ten left," she warned. "You must not waste them."

Emilio put his head in the door. " 'Qui 'st 'l caballo,[8] Mama."

"Put on the saddle from the other horse. Tie on the blanket. Here, tie the jerky to the saddle horn."

Still Pepé stood silently watching his mother's frantic activity. His chin looked hard, and his sweet mouth was drawn and thin. His little eyes followed Mama about the room almost suspiciously.

Rosy asked softly, "Where goes Pepé?"

Mama's eyes were fierce. "Pepé goes on a journey. Pepé is a man now. He has a man's thing to do."

Pepé straightened his shoulders. His mouth changed until he looked very much like Mama.

At last the preparation was finished. The loaded horse stood outside the door. The water bag dripped a line of moisture down the bay shoulder.

The moonlight was being thinned by the dawn and the big white moon was near down to the sea. The family stood by the shack. Mama confronted Pepé. "Look, my son! Do not stop until it is dark again. Do not sleep even though you are tired. Take care of the horse in order that he may not stop of weariness. Remember to be careful with the bullets—there are only ten. Do not fill thy stomach with jerky or it will make thee sick. Eat a little jerky and fill thy stomach with grass. When thou comest to the high mountains, if thou seest any of the dark watching men, go not near to them nor try to speak to them. And forget not thy prayers." She put her lean hands on Pepé's shoulders, stood on her toes and kissed him formally on both cheeks, and Pepé kissed her on both cheeks. Then he went to Emilio and Rosy and kissed both of their cheeks.

Pepé turned back to Mama. He seemed to look for a little softness, a little weakness in her. His eyes were searching, but Mama's face remained fierce. "Go now," she said. "Do not wait to be caught like a chicken."

Pepé pulled himself into the saddle. "I am a man," he said.

It was the first dawn when he rode up the hill toward the little canyon which let a trail into the mountains. Moonlight and daylight fought with each other, and the two warring qualities made it difficult to see. Before Pepé had gone a hundred yards, the outlines of his figure were misty; and long before he entered the canyon, he had become a gray, indefinite shadow.

Mama stood stiffly in front of her doorstep, and on either side of her stood Emilio and Rosy. They cast furtive glances at Mama now and then.

When the gray shape of Pepé melted into the hillside and disappeared, Mama relaxed. She began the high, whining keen[9] of the death wail. "Our beautiful—our brave," she

---

8. **'Qui 'st 'l caballo** (kēst'l kä bä'yō): Here is the horse (colloquial Spanish).

9. **keen:** A wailing for the dead.

cried. "Our protector, our son is gone." Emilio and Rosy moaned beside her. "Our beautiful—our brave, he is gone." It was the formal wail. It rose to a high piercing whine and subsided to a moan. Mama raised it three times and then she turned and went into the house and shut the door.

Emilio and Rosy stood wondering in the dawn. They heard Mama whimpering in the house. They went out to sit on the cliff above the ocean. They touched shoulders. "When did Pepé come to be a man?" Emilio asked.

"Last night," said Rosy. "Last night in Monterey." The ocean clouds turned red with the sun that was behind the mountains.

"We will have no breakfast," said Emilio. "Mama will not want to cook." Rosy did not answer him. "Where is Pepé gone?" he asked.

Rosy looked around at him. She drew her knowledge from the quiet air. "He has gone on a journey. He will never come back."

"Is he dead? Do you think he is dead?"

Rosy looked back at the ocean again. A little steamer, drawing a line of smoke sat on the edge of the horizon. "He is not dead," Rosy explained. "Not yet."

Pepé rested the big rifle across the saddle in front of him. He let the horse walk up the hill and he didn't look back. The stony slope took on a coat of short brush so that Pepé found the entrance to a trail and entered it.

When he came to the canyon opening, he swung once in his saddle and looked back, but the houses were swallowed in the misty light. Pepé jerked forward again. The high shoulder of the canyon closed in on him. His horse stretched out its neck and sighed and settled to the trail.

It was a well-worn path, dark soft leaf-mold earth strewn with broken pieces of sandstone. The trail rounded the shoulder of the canyon and dropped steeply into the bed of the stream. In the shallows the water ran smoothly, glinting in the first morning sun. Small round stones on the bottom were as brown as rust with sun moss. In the sand along the edges of the stream the tall, rich wild mint grew, while in the water itself the cress,[10] old and tough, had gone to heavy seed.

The path went into the stream and emerged on the other side. The horse sloshed into the water and stopped. Pepé dropped his bridle and let the beast drink of the running water.

Soon the canyon sides became steep and the first giant sentinel redwoods guarded the trail, great round red trunks bearing foliage as green and lacy as ferns. Once Pepé was among the trees, the sun was lost. A perfumed and purple light lay in the pale green of the underbrush. Gooseberry bushes and blackberries and tall ferns lined the stream, and overhead the branches of the redwoods met and cut off the sky.

Pepé drank from the water bag, and he reached into the flour sack and brought out a black string of jerky. His white teeth gnawed at the string until the tough meat parted. He chewed slowly and drank occasionally from the water bag. His little eyes were slumberous and tired, but the muscles of his face were hard set. The earth of the trail was black now. It gave up a hollow sound under the walking hoofbeats.

The stream fell more sharply. Little waterfalls splashed on the stones. Five-fingered ferns hung over the water and dripped spray from their fingertips. Pepé rode half over in his saddle, dangling one leg loosely. He picked a bay leaf from a tree beside the way and put it into his mouth for a moment to flavor the dry jerky. He held the gun loosely across the pommel.

Suddenly he squared in his saddle, swung the horse from the trail and kicked it hurriedly up behind a big redwood tree. He pulled up the reins tight against the bit to keep the horse from whinnying. His face was intent and his nostrils quivered a little.

A hollow pounding came down the trail,

---

10. cress: Watercress, an edible white-flowered plant.

and a horseman rode by, a fat man with red cheeks and a white stubble beard. His horse put down its head and blubbered at the trail when it came to the place where Pepé had turned off. "Hold up!" said the man and he pulled up his horse's head.

When the last sound of the hoofs died away, Pepé came back into the trail again. He did not relax in the saddle any more. He lifted the big rifle and swung the lever to throw a shell into the chamber, and then he let down the hammer to half cock.

The trail grew very steep. Now the redwood trees were smaller and their tops were dead, bitten dead where the wind reached them. The horse plodded on; the sun went slowly overhead and started down toward the afternoon.

Where the stream came out of a side canyon, the trail left it. Pepé dismounted and watered his horse and filled up his water bag. As soon as the trail had parted from the stream, the trees were gone and only the thick brittle sage and manzanita[11] and chaparral[12] edged the trail. And the soft black earth was gone, too, leaving only the light tan broken rock for the trail bed. Lizards scampered away into the brush as the horse rattled over the little stones.

Pepé turned in his saddle and looked back. He was in the open now: he could be seen from a distance. As he ascended the trail the country grew more rough and terrible and dry. The way wound about the bases of great square rocks. Little gray rabbits skittered in the brush. A bird made a monotonous high creaking. Eastward the bare rock mountaintops were pale and powder-dry under the dropping sun. The horse plodded up and up the trail toward a little V in the ridge which was the pass.

Pepé looked suspiciously back every minute or so, and his eyes sought the tops of the ridges ahead. Once, on a white barren spur,

____

11. **manzanita** (man'zə nēt'ə): Shrubs or small trees.
12. **chaparral** (chap'ə ral') n.: A thicket of thorny bushes or shrubs.

he saw a black figure for a moment, but he looked quickly away, for it was one of the dark watchers. No one knew who the watchers were, nor where they lived, but it was better to ignore them and never to show interest in them. They did not bother one who stayed on the trail and minded his own business.

The air was parched and full of light dust blown by the breeze from the eroding mountains. Pepé drank sparingly from his bag and corked it tightly and hung it on the horn again. The trail moved up the dry shale hillside, avoiding rocks, dropping under clefts, climbing in and out of old water scars. When he arrived at the little pass he stopped and looked back for a long time. No dark watchers were to be seen now. The trail behind was empty. Only the high tops of the redwoods indicated where the stream flowed.

Pepé rode on through the pass. His little eyes were nearly closed with weariness, but his face was stern, relentless and manly. The high mountain wind coasted sighing through the pass and whistled on the edges of the big blocks of broken granite. In the air, a red-tailed hawk sailed over close to the ridge and screamed angrily. Pepé went slowly through the broken jagged pass and looked down on the other side.

The trail dropped quickly, staggering among broken rock. At the bottom of the slope there was a dark crease, thick with brush, and on the other side of the crease a little flat, in which a grove of oak trees grew. A scar of green grass cut across the flat. And behind the flat another mountain rose, desolate with dead rocks and starving little black bushes. Pepé drank from the bag again for the air was so dry that it encrusted his nostrils and burned his lips. He put the horse down the trail. The hooves slipped and struggled on the steep way, starting little stones that rolled off into the brush. The sun was gone behind the westward mountain now, but still it glowed brilliantly on the oaks and on the grassy flat. The rocks and the hillsides still sent up waves of the heat they had gathered from the day's sun.

Pepé looked up to the top of the next dry withered ridge. He saw a dark form against the sky, a man's figure standing on top of a rock, and he glanced away quickly not to appear curious. When a moment later he looked up again, the figure was gone.

Downward the trail was quickly covered. Sometimes the horse floundered for footing, sometimes set his feet and slid a little way. They came at last to the bottom where the dark chaparral was higher than Pepé's head. He held up his rifle on one side and his arm on the other to shield his face from the sharp brittle fingers of the brush.

Up and out of the crease he rode, and up a little cliff. The grassy flat was before him, and the round comfortable oaks. For a moment he studied the trail down which he had come, but there was no movement and no sound from it. Finally he rode out over the flat, to the green streak, and at the upper end of the damp he found a little spring welling out of the earth and dropping into a dug basin before it seeped out over the flat.

Pepé filled his bag first, and then he let the thirsty horse drink out of the pool. He led the horse to the clump of oaks, and in the middle of the grove, fairly protected from sight on all sides, he took off the saddle and the bridle and laid them on the ground. The horse stretched his jaws sideways and yawned. Pepé knotted the lead rope about the horse's neck and tied him to a sapling among the oaks, where he could graze in a fairly large circle.

When the horse was gnawing hungrily at the dry grass, Pepé went to the saddle and took a black string of jerky from the sack and strolled to an oak tree on the edge of the grove, from under which he could watch the trail. He sat down in the crisp dry oak leaves and automatically felt for his big black knife

to cut the jerky, but he had no knife. He leaned back on his elbow and gnawed at the tough strong meat. His face was blank, but it was a man's face.

The bright evening light washed the eastern ridge, but the valley was darkening. Doves flew down from the hills to the spring, and the quail came running out of the brush and joined them, calling clearly to one another.

Out of the corner of his eye Pepé saw a shadow grow out of the bushy crease. He turned his head slowly. A big spotted wildcat was creeping toward the spring, belly to the ground, moving like thought.

Pepé cocked his rifle and edged the muzzle slowly around. Then he looked apprehensively up the trail and dropped the hammer again. From the ground beside him he picked an oak twig and threw it toward the spring. The quail flew up with a roar and the doves whistled away. The big cat stood up: for a long moment he looked at Pepé with cold yellow eyes, and then fearlessly walked back into the gulch.

The dusk gathered quickly in the deep valley. Pepé muttered his prayers, put his head down on his arm and went instantly to sleep.

The moon came up and filled the valley with cold blue light, and the wind swept rustling down from the peaks. The owls worked up and down the slopes looking for rabbits. Down in the brush of the gulch a coyote gabbled. The oak trees whispered softly in the night breeze.

Pepé started up, listening. His horse had whinnied. The moon was just slipping behind the western ridge, leaving the valley in darkness behind it. Pepé sat tensely gripping his rifle. From far up the trail he heard an answering whinny and the crash of shod hooves on the broken rock. He jumped to his feet, ran to his horse and led it under the trees. He threw on the saddle and cinched it tight for the steep trail, caught the unwilling head and forced the bit into the mouth. He

felt the saddle to make sure the water bag and the sack of jerky were there. Then he mounted and turned up the hill.

It was velvet dark. The horse found the entrance to the trail where it left the flat, and started up, stumbling and slipping on the rocks. Pepé's hand rose up to his head. His hat was gone. He had left it under the oak tree.

The horse had struggled far up the trail when the first change of dawn came into the air, a steel grayness as light mixed thoroughly with dark. Gradually the sharp snaggled edge of the ridge stood out above them, rotten granite tortured and eaten by the winds of time. Pepé had dropped his reins on the horn, leaving direction to the horse. The brush grabbed at his legs in the dark until one knee of his jeans was ripped.

Gradually the light flowed down over the ridge. The starved brush and rocks stood out in the half light, strange and lonely in high perspective. Then there came warmth into the light. Pepé drew up and looked back, but he could see nothing in the darker valley below. The sky turned blue over the coming sun. In the waste of the mountainside, the poor dry brush grew only three feet high. Here and there, big outcroppings of unrotted granite stood up like moldering houses. Pepé relaxed a little. He drank from his water bag and bit off a piece of jerky. A single eagle flew over, high in the light.

Without warning Pepé's horse screamed and fell on its side. He was almost down before the rifle crash echoed up from the valley. From a hole behind the struggling shoulder, a stream of bright crimson blood pumped and stopped and pumped and stopped. The hooves threshed on the ground. Pepé lay half stunned beside the horse. He looked slowly down the hill. A piece of sage clipped off beside his head and another crash echoed up from side to side of the canyon. Pepé flung himself frantically behind a bush.

He crawled up the hill on his knees and one hand. His right hand held the rifle up off the ground and pushed it ahead of him. He moved with the instinctive care of an animal. Rapidly he wormed his way toward one of the big outcroppings of granite on the hill above him. Where the brush was high he doubled up and ran, but where the cover was slight he wriggled forward on his stomach, pushing the rifle ahead of him. In the last little distance there was no cover at all. Pepé poised and then he darted across the space and flashed around the corner of the rock.

He leaned panting against the stone. When his breath came easier he moved along behind the big rock until he came to a narrow split that offered a thin section of vision down the hill. Pepé lay on his stomach and pushed the rifle barrel through the slit and waited.

The sun reddened the western ridges now. Already the buzzards were settling down toward the place where the horse lay. A small brown bird scratched in the dead sage leaves directly in front of the rifle muzzle. The coasting eagle flew back toward the rising sun.

Pepé saw a little movement in the brush far below. His grip tightened on the gun. A little brown doe stepped daintily out on the trail and crossed it and disappeared into the brush again. For a long time Pepé waited. Far below he could see the little flat and the oak trees and the slash of green. Suddenly his eyes flashed back at the trail again. A quarter of a mile down there had been a quick movement in the chaparral. The rifle swung over. The front sight nestled in the v of the rear sight. Pepé studied for a moment and then raised the rear sight a notch. The little movement in the brush came again. The sight settled on it. Pepé squeezed the trigger. The explosion crashed down the mountain and up the other side, and came rattling back. The whole side of the slope grew still. No more movement. And then a white streak cut into the granite of the slit and a bullet whined away and a crash sounded up from below. Pepé felt a sharp pain in his right hand. A sliver of granite was sticking out from between his first and second knuckles and the point protruded from his palm. Carefully he pulled out the sliver of stone. The wound bled evenly and gently. No vein nor artery was cut.

Pepé looked into a little dusty cave in the rock and gathered a handful of spider web, and he pressed the mass into the cut, plastering the soft web into the blood. The flow stopped almost at once.

The rifle was on the ground. Pepé picked it up, levered a new shell into the chamber. And then he slid into the brush on his stomach. Far to the right he crawled, and then up the hill, moving slowly and carefully, crawling to cover and resting and then crawling again.

In the mountains the sun is high in its arc before it penetrates the gorges. The hot face looked over the hill and brought instant heat with it. The white light beat on the rocks and reflected from them and rose up quivering from the earth again, and the rocks and bushes seemed to quiver behind the air.

Pepé crawled in the general direction of the ridge peak, zig-zagging for cover. The deep cut between his knuckles began to throb. He crawled close to a rattlesnake before he saw it, and when it raised its dry head and made a soft beginning whirr, he backed up and took another way. The quick gray lizards flashed in front of him, raising a tiny line of dust. He found another mass of spider web and pressed it against his throbbing hand.

Pepé was pushing the rifle with his left hand now. Little drops of sweat ran to the ends of his coarse black hair and rolled down his cheeks. His lips and tongue were growing thick and heavy. His lips writhed to draw saliva into his mouth. His little dark eyes were uneasy and suspicious. Once when a gray lizard paused in front of him on the parched ground and turned its head sideways he crushed it flat with a stone.

When the sun slid past noon he had not gone a mile. He crawled exhaustedly a last hundred yards to a patch of high sharp manzanita, crawled desperately, and when the patch was reached he wriggled in among the tough gnarly trunks and dropped his head on his left arm. There was little shade in the meager brush, but there was cover and safety. Pepé went to sleep as he lay and the sun beat on his back. A few little birds hopped close to him and peered and hopped away. Pepé squirmed in his sleep and he raised and dropped his wounded hand again and again.

The sun went down behind the peaks and the cool evening came, and then the dark. A coyote yelled from the hillside, Pepé started awake and looked about with misty eyes. His hand was swollen and heavy; a little thread of pain ran up the inside of his arm and settled in a pocket in his armpit. He peered about and then stood up, for the mountains were black and the moon had not yet risen. Pepé stood up in the dark. The coat of his father pressed on his arm. His tongue was swollen until it nearly filled his mouth. He wriggled out of the coat and dropped it in the brush, and then he struggled up the hill, falling over rocks and tearing his way through the brush. The rifle knocked against stones as he went. Little dry avalanches of gravel and shattered stone went whispering down the hill behind him.

After a while the old moon came up and showed the jagged ridge top ahead of him. By moonlight Pepé traveled more easily. He bent forward so that his throbbing arm hung away from his body. The journey uphill was made in dashes and rests, a frantic rush up a few yards and then a rest. The wind coasted down the slope rattling the dry stems of the bushes.

The moon was at meridian when Pepé came at last to the sharp backbone of the ridge top. On the last hundred yards of the rise no soil had clung under the wearing winds. The way was on solid rock. He clambered to the top and looked down on the other side. There was a draw like the last below him, misty with moonlight, brushed with dry struggling sage and chaparral. On

the other side the hill rose up sharply and at the top the jagged rotten teeth of the mountain showed against the sky. At the bottom of the cut the brush was thick and dark.

Pepé stumbled down the hill. His throat was almost closed with thirst. At first he tried to run, but immediately he fell and rolled. After that he went more carefully. The moon was just disappearing behind the mountains when he came to the bottom. He crawled into the heavy brush feeling with his fingers for water. There was no water in the bed of the stream, only damp earth. Pepé laid his gun down and scooped up a handful of mud and put it in his mouth, and then he spluttered and scraped the earth from his tongue with his finger, for the mud drew at his mouth like a poultice. He dug a hole in

tle square, soaked it in the water and put it in his mouth. Over and over he filled the cloth and sucked it.

Still the lion sat and watched him. The evening came down but there was no movement on the hills. No birds visited the dry bottom of the cut. Pepé looked occasionally at the lion. The eyes of the yellow beast drooped as though he were about to sleep. He yawned and his long thin red tongue curled out. Suddenly his head jerked around and his nostrils quivered. His big tail lashed. He stood up and slunk like a tawny shadow into the thick brush.

A moment later Pepé heard the sound, the faint far crash of horses' hooves on gravel. And he heard something else, a high whining yelp of a dog.

Pepé took his rifle in his left hand and he glided into the brush almost as quietly as the lion had. In the darkening evening he crouched up the hill toward the next ridge. Only when the dark came did he stand up. His energy was short. Once it was dark he fell over the rocks and slipped to his knees on the steep slope, but he moved on and on up the hill, climbing and scrabbling over the broken hillside.

When he was far up toward the top, he lay down and slept for a little while. The withered moon, shining on his face, awakened him. He stood up and moved up the hill. Fifty yards away he stopped and turned back, for he had forgotten his rifle. He walked heavily down, and poked about in the brush, but he could not find his gun. At last he lay down to rest. The pocket of pain in his armpit had grown more sharp. His arm seemed to swell out and fall with every heartbeat. There was no position lying down where the heavy arm did not press against his armpit.

With the effort of a hurt beast, Pepé got up and moved again toward the top of the ridge. He held his swollen arm away from his body with his left hand. Up the steep hill he dragged himself, a few steps and a rest, and a few more steps. At last he was nearing the

the stream bed with his fingers, dug a little basin to catch water; but before it was very deep his head fell forward on the damp ground and he slept.

The dawn came and the heat of the day fell on the earth, and still Pepé slept. Late in the afternoon his head jerked up. He looked slowly around. His eyes were slits of wariness. Twenty feet away in the the heavy brush a big tawny mountain lion stood looking at him. Its long thick tail waved gracefully, its ears were erect with interest, not laid back dangerously. The lion squatted down on its stomach and watched him.

Pepé looked at the hole he had dug in the earth. A half inch of muddy water had collected in the bottom. He tore the sleeve from his hurt arm, with his teeth ripped out a lit-

top. The moon showed the uneven sharp back of it against the sky.

Pepé's brain spun in a big spiral up and away from him. He slumped to the ground and lay still. The rock ridge top was only a hundred feet above him.

The moon moved over the sky. Pepé half turned on his back. His tongue tried to make words, but only a thick hissing came from between his lips.

When the dawn came, Pepé pulled himself up. His eyes were sane again. He drew his great puffed arm in front of him and looked at the angry wound. The black line ran up from his wrist to his armpit. Automatically he reached in his pocket for the big black knife, but it was not there. His eyes searched the ground. He picked up a sharp blade of stone and scraped at the wound, sawed at the proud flesh and then squeezed the green juice out in big drops. Instantly he threw back his head and whined like a dog. His whole right side shuddered at the pain, but the pain cleared his head.

In the gray light he struggled up the last slope to the ridge and crawled over and lay down behind a line of rocks. Below him lay a deep canyon exactly like the last, waterless and desolate. There was no flat, no oak trees, not even heavy brush in the bottom of it. And on the other side a sharp ridge stood up, thinly brushed with starving sage, littered with broken granite. Strewn over the hill there were giant outcroppings, and on the top the granite teeth stood out against the sky.

The new day was light now. The flame of the sun came over the ridge and fell on Pepé where he lay on the ground. His coarse black hair was littered with twigs and bits of spider web. His eyes had retreated back into his head. Between his lips the tip of his black tongue showed.

He sat up and dragged his great arm into his lap and nursed it, rocking his body and moaning in his throat. He threw back his head and looked up into the pale sky. A big black bird circled nearly out of sight, and far to the left another was sailing near.

He lifted his head to listen, for a familiar sound had come to him from the valley he had climbed out of; it was the crying yelp of hounds, excited and feverish, on a trail.

Pepé bowed his head quickly. He tried to speak rapid words but only a thick hiss came from his lips. He drew a shaky cross on his breast with his left hand. It was a long struggle to get to his feet. He crawled slowly and mechanically to the top of a big rock on the ridge peak. Once there, he arose slowly, swaying to his feet, and stood erect. Far below he could see the dark brush where he had slept. He braced his feet and stood there, black against the morning sky.

There came a ripping sound at his feet. A piece of stone flew up and a bullet droned off into the next gorge. The hollow crash echoed up from below. Pepé looked down for a moment and then pulled himself straight again.

His body jarred back. His left hand fluttered helplessly toward his breast. The second crash sounded from below. Pepé swung forward and toppled from the rock. His body struck and rolled over and over, starting a little avalanche. And when at last he stopped against a bush, the avalanche slid slowly down and covered up his head.

RESPONDING TO THE SELECTION

Your Response
1. Did this story sustain your attention? Why or why not?
2. Did you find the ending satisfying? Why or why not?

Recalling
3. What had Pepé inherited from his father?
4. (a) Why does Mama Torres send Pepé into town? (b) Why does he return home early?
5. (a) What does Mama give Pepé before he flees? (b) Whom does she tell him to avoid?
6. (a) How does Pepé lose his possessions? (b) How is he wounded?
7. What happens to Pepé at the end of the story?

Interpreting
8. (a) How does Pepé change during the course of the story? (b) What events bring about these changes?
9. How do the descriptions of Pepé's physical appearance during his flight reflect his state of mind?
10. What is the significance of the fact that Pepé never sees his pursuers?
11. During the course of his flight, Pepé is gradually stripped of his possessions. His behavior becomes more and more animal-like as he is forced to rely on his instincts. (a) Find three instances in which Steinbeck compares Pepé's actions to those of an animal. (b) What does Pepé do in the end to retain his sense of dignity as a human being?

Applying
12. Do you agree with Mama Torres's statement that "A boy gets to be a man when a man is needed"? Why or why not?

ANALYZING LITERATURE

Understanding Setting
The **setting** is the time and place in which the events in a work of literature occur. Like many of Steinbeck's other works, "Flight" is set in northern California during the late 1800's or early 1900's.

1. What do the details of the setting in the first paragraph suggest about humanity's relationship to nature?
2. How does the landscape change during the course of Pepé's flight?
3. The setting of a literary work sometimes reflects the writer's view of the world. What outlook might the setting of "Flight" reflect?
4. American writer Ayn Rand once wrote, "Man's unique reward, however, is that while animals survive by adjusting themselves to their background, man survives by adjusting his background to himself." On the basis of "Flight," do you think John Steinbeck would agree or disagree with this statement? Explain.

CRITICAL THINKING AND READING

Analyzing the Effect of Setting
The **setting** often influences the characters' personalities and behavior. For example, in "Flight" the setting directly affects Pepé's actions as he flees from his pursuers, forcing him to become more and more instinctive and animal-like in his behavior.
1. How have Pepé's and Mama Torres's personalities been shaped by the setting?
2. How do the changes in the landscape during Pepé's flight affect his chances of escape?

THINKING AND WRITING

Writing About Setting
Write an essay in which you discuss how the setting has shaped Pepé's personality and how it affects his behavior during the story. Use evidence from the story to support your argument. When you revise, make sure your essay is logically organized.

LEARNING OPTION

Speaking and Listening. Who are the "dark watching men" that Mama advises Pepé to avoid? Scan the story for references to the dark watchers and decide if they are real or imaginary. What do they represent? Defend your view in a class discussion.

WILLIAM FAULKNER

1897–1962

William Faulkner is generally regarded as the most innovative American novelist of his time. In his work he experimented with narrative chronology, explored multiple points of view, and delved deeply into the minds of his characters. Yet although he used a variety of forms and techniques in his novels and short stories, most of his works are linked through a common setting, the fictional world of Yoknapatawpha County, Mississippi.

Faulkner grew up in Oxford, Mississippi. Although he never finished high school, he read a great deal and developed an interest in writing at an early age. In 1918 he enlisted in the British Royal Flying Corps and was sent to Canada for training. However, World War I ended before he had a chance to see combat, and he returned to Mississippi. Several years later, longing for a change of scene, he moved to New Orleans. There he became friends with Sherwood Anderson, who offered encouragement and helped get Faulkner's first novel, *A Soldier's Pay* (1926), published.

In 1926 Faulkner moved back to Oxford and concentrated on his writing. He first earned critical acclaim in 1929 when he published *The Sound and the Fury,* a complex novel exploring the downfall of an old southern family as seen through the eyes of three different characters. A year later he published *As I Lay Dying,* a novel in which the point of view constantly shifts, as Faulkner delves into the varying perceptions of death.

Faulkner went on to write several more inventive novels, including *Light in August* (1932), *Absalom, Absalom* (1936), and *The Wild Palms* (1939). His later works, such as *The Unvanquished* (1938) and *The Hamlet* (1940), were more traditional in form. Yet in these novels, Faulkner continued developing the history of Yoknapatawpha County and its people. Faulkner had invented this imaginative county based on his own in his novel *Sartoris* (1929). It was during the writing of this novel that Faulkner "discovered that my own little postage stamp of native soil was worth writing about and that I would never live long enough to exhaust it, . . . I opened up a gold mine of other people, so I created a cosmos of my own."

Despite the critical success of some of his works, Faulkner did not earn widespread public recognition until 1946, when *The Portable Faulkner*—an anthology in which many of his writings about Yoknapatawpha County were presented in chronological order—was published. Four years later he was awarded the Nobel Prize following the publication of *Intruder in the Dust* (1948), a novel in which he confronted the issue of racism.

GUIDE FOR INTERPRETING

The Bear; Nobel Prize Acceptance Speech

Writers' Techniques

Symbols. A symbol is a person, place, or thing that has a meaning in itself and also represents something larger than itself. For example, gold may be used as a symbol of greed, whereas a rose may symbolize love.

In the aftermath of World War I, many writers came to believe that modern life was filled with uncertainty and lacked any definite meaning. To express this belief, these writers turned away from directly stating their themes, and they suggested rather than asserted meaning. As a result, modern writers frequently used symbols to express their themes.

Allusions. An allusion is a reference to another literary work or to a figure, place, or an event from history, religion, or mythology.

Allusions serve two important purposes in literature. Like symbols they can contribute to the theme of a literary work. At the same time, they provide writers with a way of maintaining a link to the cultural roots of the past.

Literary Forms

Oratory. Oratory is the art of skilled, eloquent public speaking. When planning a speech, a skilled orator carefully considers his or her audience and the purpose and occasion of the speech. The speaker focuses on choosing a topic that is appropriate for the occasion and purpose, then writes the speech using language that he or she feels is suited to the audience.

When writing a speech, an orator must also be sure to emphasize his or her main points. To accomplish this, a speaker will use a variety of oratorical devices. Three of these devices are restatement, repetition, and parallelism. When a speaker uses restatement, he or she restates the same idea a number of times in a variety of different ways. When a speaker uses repetition, he or she restates the same idea using the same words. Parallelism refers to the repeated use of phrases, clauses, or sentences that are similar in structure.

Focus

"The Bear" is a story about a boy whose experiences during a series of hunting expeditions gradually lead him to an understanding about life. The English novelist Charles Dickens once wrote, "There is a passion for hunting something deeply implanted in the human breast." Freewrite, exploring your reaction to this statement.

The Bear

William Faulkner

He was ten. But it had already begun, long before that day when at last he wrote his age in two figures and he saw for the first time the camp where his father and Major de Spain and old General Compson and the others spent two weeks each November and two weeks again each June. He had already inherited then, without ever having seen it, the tremendous bear with one trap-ruined foot which, in an area almost a hundred miles deep, had earned for itself a name, a definite designation like a living man.

He had listened to it for years: the long legend of corncribs rifled, of shotes[1] and grown pigs and even calves carried bodily into the woods and devoured, of traps and deadfalls[2] overthrown and dogs mangled and slain, and shotgun and even rifle charges delivered at point-blank range and with no more effect than so many peas blown through a tube by a boy—a corridor of wreckage and destruction beginning back before he was born, through which sped, not fast but rather with the ruthless and irresistible deliberation of a locomotive, the shaggy tremendous shape.

It ran in his knowledge before he ever saw it. It looked and towered in his dreams before he even saw the unaxed woods where it left its crooked print, shaggy, huge, red-eyed, not malevolent but just big—too big for the dogs which tried to bay[3] it, for the horses which tried to ride it down, for the men and the bullets they fired into it, too big for the

very country which was its constricting scope. He seemed to see it entire with a child's complete divination before he ever laid eyes on either—the doomed wilderness whose edges were being constantly and punily gnawed at by men with axes and plows who feared it because it was wilderness, men myriad and nameless even to one another in the land where the old bear had earned a name, through which ran not even a mortal animal but an anachronism, indomitable and invincible, out of an old dead time, a phantom, epitome and apotheosis of the old wild life at which the puny humans swarmed and hacked in a fury of abhorrence and fear, like pygmies[4] about the ankles of a drowsing elephant; the old bear solitary, indomitable and alone, widowered, childless and absolved of mortality—old Priam[5] reft of his old wife and having outlived all his sons.

Until he was ten, each November he would watch the wagon containing the dogs and the bedding and food and guns and his father and Tennie's Jim, the Negro, and Sam Fathers, the Indian, son of a slave woman and a Chickasaw chief, depart on the road to town, to Jefferson, where Major de Spain and the others would join them. To the boy, at seven and eight and nine, they were not going into the Big Bottom to hunt bear and deer, but to keep yearly rendezvous with the bear which they did not even intend

---

1. shotes n.: Young hogs.
2. deadfalls n.: Traps arranged so that a heavy weight is dropped on prey.
3. bay v.: Chase and corner.

4. pygmies (pig′ mēz) n.: Members of African and Asiatic races known for their small stature.
5. Priam (prī′ əm): The king of Troy whose wife and children were killed when the Greeks invaded Troy during the Trojan War.

to kill. Two weeks later they would return, with no trophy, no head and skin. He had not expected it. He had not even been afraid it would be in the wagon. He believed that even after he was ten and his father would let him go too, for those two November weeks, he would merely make another one, along with his father and Major de Spain and General Compson and the others, the dogs which feared to bay it and the rifles and shotguns which failed even to bleed it, in the yearly pageant of the old bear's furious immortality.

Then he heard the dogs. It was in the second week of his first time in the camp. He stood with Sam Fathers against a big oak beside the faint crossing where they had stood each dawn for nine days now, hearing the dogs. He had heard them once before, one morning last week—a murmur, sourceless, echoing through the wet woods, swelling presently into separate voices which he could recognize and call by name. He had raised and cocked the gun as Sam told him and stood motionless again while the uproar, the invisible course, swept up and past and faded; it seemed to him that he could actually see the deer, the buck, blond, smoke-colored, elongated with speed, fleeing, vanishing, the woods, the gray solitude, still ringing even when the cries of the dogs had died away.

"Now let the hammers down," Sam said.

"You knew they were not coming here, too," he said.

"Yes," Sam said. "I want you to learn how to do when you didn't shoot. It's after the chance for the bear or the deer has done already come and gone that men and dogs get killed."

"Anyway," he said, "it was just a deer."

Then on the tenth morning he heard the dogs again. And he readied the too-long, too-heavy gun as Sam had taught him, before Sam even spoke. But this time it was no deer, no ringing chorus of dogs running strong on a free scent, but a moiling[6] yap-

ping an octave too high, with something more than indecision and even abjectness in it, not even moving very fast, taking a long time to pass completely out of hearing, leaving even then somewhere in the air that echo, thin, slightly hysterical, abject, almost grieving, with no sense of a fleeing, unseen, smoke-colored, grass-eating shape ahead of it, and Sam, who had taught him first of all to cock the gun and take position where he could see everywhere and then never move again, had himself moved up beside him; he could hear Sam breathing at his shoulder and he could see the arched curve of the old man's inhaling nostrils.

"Hah," Sam said. "Not even running. Walking."

"Old Ben!" the boy said. "But up here!" he cried. "Way up here!"

"He do it every year," Sam said. "Once. Maybe to see who in camp this time, if he can shoot or not. Whether we got the dog yet that can bay and hold him. He'll take them to the river, then he'll send them back home. We may as well go back, too; see how they look when they come back to camp."

When they reached the camp the hounds were already there, ten of them crouching back under the kitchen, the boy and Sam squatting to peer back into the obscurity where they huddled, quiet, the eyes luminous, glowing at them and vanishing, and no sound, only that effluvium of something more than dog, stronger than dog and not just animal, just beast, because still there had been nothing in front of that abject and almost painful yapping save the solitude, the wilderness, so that when the eleventh hound came in at noon and with all the others watching—even old Uncle Ash, who called himself first a cook—Sam daubed the tattered ear and the raked shoulder with turpentine and axle grease, to the boy it was still no living creature, but the wilderness which, leaning for the moment down, had patted lightly once the hound's temerity.

"Just like a man," Sam said. "Just like folks. Put off as long as she could having to be brave, knowing all the time that sooner or

---

6. **moiling:** Confused.

IN THE DEPTHS OF THE TIMBER
W. Herbert Dunton
Courtesy Amon Carter Museum, Fort Worth

later she would have to be brave once to keep on living with herself, and knowing all the time beforehand what was going to happen to her when she done it."

That afternoon, himself on the one-eyed wagon mule which did not mind the smell of blood nor, as they told him, of bear, and with Sam on the other one, they rode for more than three hours through the rapid, shortening winter day. They followed no path, no trail even that he could see; almost at once they were in a country which he had never seen before. Then he knew why Sam had made him ride the mule which would not spook. The sound one stopped short and tried to whirl and bolt even as Sam got down, blowing its breath, jerking and wrenching at the rein while Sam held it, coaxing it forward with his voice, since he could not risk tying it, drawing it forward while the boy got down from the marred one.

Then, standing beside Sam in the gloom of the dying afternoon, he looked down at the rotted overturned log, gutted and scored with claw marks and, in the wet earth beside it, the print of the enormous warped two-toed foot. He knew now what he had smelled when he peered under the kitchen where the dogs huddled. He realized for the first time that the bear which had run in his listening and loomed in his dreams since before he could remember to the contrary, and which, therefore, must have existed in the listening and dreams of his father and Major de Spain and even old General Compson, too, before they began to remember in their turn, was a mortal animal, and that if they had departed for the camp each November without any actual hope of bringing its trophy back, it was not because it could not be slain, but because so far they had had no actual hope to.

"Tomorrow," he said.

"We'll try tomorrow," Sam said. "We ain't got the dog yet."

"We've got eleven. They ran him this morning."

"It won't need but one," Sam said. "He ain't here. Maybe he ain't nowhere. The only

other way will be for him to run by accident over somebody that has a gun."

"That wouldn't be me," the boy said. "It will be Walter or Major or—"

"It might," Sam said. "You watch close in the morning. Because he's smart. That's how come he has lived this long. If he gets hemmed up and has to pick out somebody to run over, he will pick out you."

"How?" the boy said. "How will he know—" He ceased. "You mean he already knows me, that I ain't never been here before, ain't had time to find out yet whether I—" He ceased again, looking at Sam, the old man whose face revealed nothing until it smiled. He said humbly, not even amazed, "It was me he was watching. I don't reckon he did need to come but once."

The next morning they left the camp three hours before daylight. They rode this time because it was too far to walk, even the dogs in the wagon; again the first gray light found him in a place which he had never seen before, where Sam had placed him and told him to stay and then departed. With the gun which was too big for him, which did not even belong to him, but to Major de Spain, and which he had fired only once—at a stump on the first day, to learn the recoil and how to reload it—he stood against a gum tree beside a little bayou[7] whose black still water crept without movement out of a canebrake[8] and crossed a small clearing and into cane again, where, invisible, a bird—the big woodpecker called Lord-to-God by Negroes—clattered at a dead limb.

It was a stand like any other, dissimilar only in incidentals to the one where he had stood each morning for ten days; a territory new to him, yet no less familiar than that other one which, after almost two weeks, he had come to believe he knew a little—the same solitude, the same loneliness through

---

7. bayou (bī′ ōo) *n*.: A sluggish, marshy inlet or outlet of a lake or river.
8. canebrake *n*.: An area overgrown with cane plants.

which human beings had merely passed without altering it, leaving no mark, no scar, which looked exactly as it must have looked when the first ancestor of Sam Fathers' Chickasaw predecessors crept into it and looked about, club or stone ax or bone arrow drawn and poised; different only because, squatting at the edge of the kitchen, he smelled the hounds huddled and cringing beneath it and saw the raked ear and shoulder of the one who, Sam said, had had to be brave once in order to live with herself, and saw yesterday in the earth beside the gutted log the print of the living foot.

He heard no dogs at all. He never did hear them. He only heard the drumming of the woodpecker stop short off and knew that the bear was looking at him. He never saw it. He did not know whether it was in front of him or behind him. He did not move, holding the useless gun, which he had not even had warning to cock and which even now he did not cock, tasting in his saliva that taint as of brass which he knew now because he had smelled it when he peered under the kitchen at the huddled dogs.

Then it was gone. As abruptly as it had ceased, the woodpecker's dry, monotonous clatter set up again, and after a while he even believed he could hear the dogs—a murmur, scarce a sound even, which he had probably been hearing for some time before he even remarked it, drifting into hearing and then out again, dying away. They came nowhere near him. If it was a bear they ran, it was another bear. It was Sam himself who came out of the cane and crossed the bayou, followed by the injured bitch of yesterday. She was almost at heel, like a bird dog, making no sound. She came and crouched against his leg, trembling, staring off into the cane.

"I didn't see him," he said. "I didn't, Sam!"

"I know it," Sam said. "He done the looking. You didn't hear him neither, did you?"

"No," the boy said. "I—"

"He's smart," Sam said. "Too smart." He looked down at the hound, trembling faintly and steadily against the boy's knee. From the raked shoulder a few drops of fresh blood oozed and clung. "Too big. We ain't got the dog yet. But maybe someday. Maybe not next time. But someday."

So I must see him, he thought. *I must look at him.* Otherwise, it seemed to him that it would go on like this forever, as it had gone on with his father and Major de Spain, who was older than his father, and even with old General Compson, who had been old enough to be a brigade commander in 1865. Otherwise, it would go on so forever, next time and next time, after and after and after. It seemed to him that he could see the two of them, himself and the bear, shadowy in the limbo from which time emerged, becoming time; the old bear absolved of mortality and himself partaking, sharing a little of it, enough of it. And he knew now what he had smelled in the huddled dogs and tasted in his saliva. He recognized fear. *So I will have to see him,* he thought, without dread or even hope. *I will have to look at him.*

It was in June of the next year. He was eleven. They were in camp again, celebrating Major de Spain's and General Compson's birthdays. Although the one had been born in September and the other in the depth of winter and in another decade, they had met for two weeks to fish and shoot squirrels and turkey and run coons and wildcats with the dogs at night. That is, he and Boon Hoggenbeck and the Negroes fished and shot squirrels and ran the coons and cats, because the proved hunters, not only Major de Spain and old General Compson, who spent those two weeks sitting in a rocking chair before a tremendous iron pot of Brunswick stew, stirring and tasting, with old Ash to quarrel with about how he was making it and Tennie's Jim to pour whisky from the demijohn[9] into the tin dipper from which he drank it,

_____

9. **demijohn:** A large bottle with a narrow neck and a wicker casing and handle.

but even the boy's father and Walter Ewell, who were still young enough, scorned such, other than shooting the wild gobblers with pistols for wagers on their marksmanship.

Or, that is, his father and the others believed he was hunting squirrels. Until the third day he thought that Sam Fathers believed that too. Each morning he would leave the camp right after breakfast. He had his own gun now, a Christmas present. He went back to the tree beside the little bayou where he had stood that morning. Using the compass which old General Compson had given him, he ranged from that point; he was teaching himself to be a better-than-fair woodsman without knowing he was doing it. On the second day he even found the gutted log where he had first seen the crooked print. It was almost completely crumbled now, healing with unbelievable speed, a passionate and almost visible relinquishment, back into the earth from which the tree had grown.

He ranged the summer woods now, green with gloom; if anything, actually dimmer than in November's gray dissolution, where, even at noon, the sun fell only in intermittent dappling upon the earth, which never completely dried out and which crawled with snakes—moccasins and water snakes and rattlers, themselves the color of the dappled gloom, so that he would not always see them until they moved, returning later and later, first day, second day, passing in the twilight of the third evening the little log pen enclosing the log stable where Sam was putting up the horses for the night.

"You ain't looked right yet," Sam said.

He stopped. For a moment he didn't answer. Then he said peacefully, in a peaceful rushing burst as when a boy's miniature dam in a little brook gives way, "All right. But how? I went to the bayou. I even found that log again. I—"

"I reckon that was all right. Likely he's been watching you. You never saw his foot?"

"I," the boy said—"I didn't—I never thought—"

"It's the gun," Sam said. He stood beside the fence, motionless—the old man, the Indian, in the battered faded overalls and the frayed five-cent straw hat which in the Negro's race had been the badge of his enslavement and was now the regalia of his freedom. The camp—the clearing, the house, the barn and its tiny lot with which Major de Spain in his turn had scratched punily and evanescently at the wilderness—faded in the dusk, back into the immemorial darkness of the woods. *The gun*, the boy thought. *The gun.*

"Be scared," Sam said. "You can't help that. But don't be afraid. Ain't nothing in the woods going to hurt you unless you corner it, or it smells that you are afraid. A bear or a deer, too, has got to be scared of a coward the same as a brave man has got to be."

The gun, the boy thought.

"You will have to choose," Sam said.

He left the camp before daylight, long before Uncle Ash would wake in his quilts on the kitchen floor and start the fire for breakfast. He had only the compass and a stick for snakes. He could go almost a mile before he would begin to need the compass. He sat on a log, the invisible compass in his invisible hand, while the secret night sounds, fallen still at his movements, scurried again and then ceased for good, and the owls ceased and gave over to the waking of day birds, and he could see the compass. Then he went fast yet still quietly; he was becoming better and better as a woodsman, still without having yet realized it.

He jumped a doe and a fawn at sunrise, walked them out of the bed, close enough to see them—the crash of undergrowth, the white scut,[10] the fawn scudding behind her faster than he had believed it could run. He was hunting right, upwind, as Sam had taught him; not that it mattered now. He had left the gun; of his own will and relinquishment he had accepted not a gambit, not a choice, but a condition in which not

---

10. scut *n.*: A short, stumpy tail.

only the bear's heretofore inviolable anonymity but all the old rules and balances of hunter and hunted had been abrogated. He would not even be afraid, not even in the moment when the fear would take him completely—blood, skin, bowels, bones, memory from the long time before it became his memory—all save that thin, clear, quenchless, immortal lucidity which alone differed him from this bear and from all the other bear and deer he would ever kill in the humility and pride of his skill and endurance, to which Sam had spoken when he leaned in the twilight on the lot fence yesterday.

By noon he was far beyond the little bayou, farther into the new and alien country than he had ever been. He was traveling now not only by the compass but by the old, heavy, biscuit-thick silver watch which had belonged to his grandfather. When he stopped at last, it was for the first time since he had risen from the log at dawn when he could see the compass. It was far enough. He had left the camp nine hours ago; nine hours from now, dark would have already been an hour old. But he didn't think that. He thought, *All right. Yes. But what?* and stood for a moment, alien and small in the green and topless solitude, answering his own question before it had formed and ceased. It was the watch, the compass, the stick—the three lifeless mechanicals with which for nine hours he had fended the wilderness off; he hung the watch and compass carefully on a bush and leaned the stick beside them and relinquished completely to it.

He had not been going very fast for the last two or three hours. He went no faster now, since distance would not matter even if he could have gone fast. And he was trying to keep a bearing on the tree where he had left the compass, trying to complete a circle which would bring him back to it or at least intersect itself, since direction would not matter now either. But the tree was not there, and he did as Sam had schooled him—made the next circle in the opposite direction, so that the two patterns would bi-

sect somewhere, but crossing no print of his own feet, finding the tree at last, but in the wrong place—no bush, no compass, no watch—and the tree not even the tree, because there was a down log beside it and he did what Sam Fathers had told him was the next thing and the last.

As he sat down on the log he saw the crooked print—the warped, tremendous, two-toed indentation which, even as he watched it, filled with water. As he looked up, the wilderness coalesced, solidified—the glade, the tree he sought, the bush, the watch and the compass glinting where a ray of sunlight touched them. Then he saw the bear. It did not emerge, appear; it was just there, immobile, solid, fixed in the hot dappling of the green and windless noon, not as big as he had dreamed it, but as big as he had expected it, bigger, dimensionless against the dappled obscurity, looking at him where he sat quietly on the log and looked back at it.

Then it moved. It made no sound. It did not hurry. It crossed the glade, walking for an instant into the full glare of the sun; when it reached the other side it stopped again and looked back at him across one shoulder while his quiet breathing inhaled and exhaled three times.

Then it was gone. It didn't walk into the woods, the undergrowth. It faded, sank back into the wilderness as he had watched a fish, a huge old bass, sink and vanish back into the dark depths of its pool without even any movement of its fins.

He thought, *It will be next fall.* But it was not next fall, nor the next nor the next. He was fourteen then. He had killed his buck, and Sam Fathers had marked his face with the hot blood, and in the next year he killed a bear. But even before that accolade he had become as competent in the woods as many grown men with the same experience; by his fourteenth year he was a better woodsman than most grown men with more. There was no territory within thirty miles of the camp that he did not know—bayou, ridge, brake, landmark tree and path. He could have led anyone to any point in it without deviation, and brought them out again. He knew game trails that even Sam Fathers did not know; in his thirteenth year he found a buck's bedding place, and unbeknown to his father he borrowed Walter Ewell's rifle and lay in wait at dawn and killed the buck when it walked back to the bed, as Sam had told him how the old Chickasaw fathers did.

But not the old bear, although by now he knew its footprint better than he did his own, and not only the crooked one. He could see any one of the three sound ones and distinguish it from any other, and not only by its size. There were other bears within those thirty miles which left tracks almost as large, but this was more than that. If Sam Fathers had been his mentor and the backyard rabbits and squirrels at home his kindergarten, then the wilderness the old bear ran was his college, the old male bear itself, so long unwifed and childless as to have become its own ungendered progenitor,[11] was his alma mater. But he never saw it.

He could find the crooked print now almost whenever he liked, fifteen or ten or five miles, or sometimes nearer the camp than that. Twice while on stand during the three years he heard the dogs strike its trail by accident; on the second time they jumped it seemingly, the voices high, abject, almost human in hysteria, as on that first morning two years ago. But not the bear itself. He would remember that noon three years ago, the glade, himself and the bear fixed during that moment in the windless and dappled blaze, and it would seem to him that it had never happened, that he had dreamed that too. But it had happened. They had looked at each other, they had emerged from the wilderness old as earth, synchronized to that instant by something more than the blood that moved the flesh and bones which bore them, and touched, pledged something, affirmed something more lasting than the frail web of bones and flesh which any accident could obliterate.

Then he saw it again. Because of the very fact that he thought of nothing else, he had forgotten to look for it. He was still-hunting with Walter Ewell's rifle. He saw it cross the end of a long blow-down, a corridor where a tornado had swept, rushing through rather than over the tangle of trunks and branches as a locomotive would have, faster than he had ever believed it could move, almost as fast as a deer even, because a deer would have spent most of that time in the air, faster than he could bring the rifle sights up to it, so that he believed the reason he never let off the shot was that he was still behind it, had never caught up with it. And now he knew what had been wrong during all the three years. He sat on a log, shaking and trembling as if he had never seen the woods before nor anything that ran them, wondering with incredulous amazement how he could have forgotten the very thing which Sam Fathers had told him and which the bear itself had proved the next day and had now returned after three years to reaffirm.

And he now knew what Sam Fathers had meant about the right dog, a dog in which size would mean less than nothing. So when he returned alone in April—school was out then, so that the sons of farmers could help with the land's planting, and at last his father had granted him permission, on his promise to be back in four days—he had the dog. It was his own, a mongrel of the sort called by Negroes a fyce, a ratter, itself not much bigger than a rat and possessing that bravery which had long since stopped being courage and had become foolhardiness.

It did not take four days. Alone again, he found the trail on the first morning. It was not a stalk; it was an ambush. He timed the meeting almost as if it were an appointment with a human being. Himself holding the fyce muffled in a feed sack and Sam Fathers

---

11. **ungendered progenitor:** Its own parent.

with two of the hounds on a piece of plowline rope, they lay down wind of the trail at dawn of the second morning. They were so close that the bear turned without even running, as if in surprised amazement at the shrill and frantic uproar of the released fyce, turning at bay against the trunk of a tree, on its hind feet; it seemed to the boy that it would never stop rising, taller and taller, and even the two hounds seemed to take a sort of desperate and despairing courage from the fyce, following it as it went in.

Then he realized that the fyce was actually not going to stop. He flung, threw the gun away, and ran; when he overtook and grasped the frantically pinwheeling little dog, it seemed to him that he was directly under the bear.

He could smell it, strong and hot and rank. Sprawling, he looked up to where it loomed and towered over him like a cloudburst and colored like a thunderclap, quite familiar, peacefully and even lucidly familiar, until he remembered: This was the way he had used to dream about it. Then it was gone. He didn't see it go. He knelt, holding the frantic fyce with both hands, hearing the abased wailing of the hounds drawing farther and farther away, until Sam came up. He carried the gun. He laid it down quietly beside the boy and stood looking down at him.

"You've done seed him twice now with a gun in your hands," he said. "This time you couldn't have missed him."

The boy rose. He still held the fyce. Even in his arms and clear of the ground, it yapped frantically, straining and surging after the fading uproar of the two hounds like a tangle of wire springs. He was panting a little, but he was neither shaking nor trembling now.

"Neither could you!" he said. "You had the gun! Neither did you!"

"And you didn't shoot," his father said. "How close were you?"

"I don't know, sir," he said. "There was a big wood tick inside his right hind leg. I saw that. But I didn't have the gun then."

"But you didn't shoot when you had the gun," his father said. "Why?"

But he didn't answer, and his father didn't wait for him to, rising and crossing the room, across the pelt of the bear which the boy had killed two years ago and the larger one which his father had killed before he was born, to the bookcase beneath the mounted head of the boy's first buck. It was the room which his father called the office, from which all the plantation business was transacted; in it for the fourteen years of his life he had heard the best of all talking. Major de Spain would be there and sometimes old General Compson, and Walter Ewell and Boon Hoggenbeck and Sam Fathers and Tennie's Jim, too, because they, too, were hunters, knew the woods and what ran them.

He would hear it, not talking himself but listening—the wilderness, the big woods, bigger and older than any recorded document of white man fatuous enough to believe he had bought any fragment of it or Indian ruthless enough to pretend that any fragment of it had been his to convey. It was of the men, not white nor black nor red, but men, hunters with the will and hardihood to endure and the humility and skill to survive, and the dogs and the bear and deer juxtaposed and reliefed against it, ordered and compelled by and within the wilderness in the ancient and unremitting contest by the ancient and immitigable rules which voided all regrets and brooked no quarter, the voices quiet and weighty and deliberate for retrospection and recollection and exact remembering, while he squatted in the blazing firelight as Tennie's Jim squatted, who stirred only to put more wood on the fire and to pass the bottle from one glass to another. Because the bottle was always present, so that after a while it seemed to him that those fierce instants of heart and brain and courage and wiliness and speed were concentrated and distilled into that brown liquor which not women, not boys and children, but only hunters drank, drinking not of the blood they had spilled but some condensation of the wild immortal spirit, drinking it moderately, humbly even, not with the pagan's base hope of acquiring thereby the virtues of cunning and strength and speed, but in salute to them.

His father returned with the book and sat down again and opened it. "Listen," he said. He read the five stanzas aloud, his voice quiet and deliberate in the room where there was no fire now because it was already spring. Then he looked up. The boy watched him. "All right," his father said. "Listen." He read again, but only the second stanza this time, to the end of it, the last two lines, and closed the book and put it on the table beside him. " 'She cannot fade, though thou hast not thy bliss, for ever wilt thou love, and she be fair,' "[12] he said.

"He's talking about a girl," the boy said.

"He had to talk about something," his father said. Then he said, "He was talking about truth. Truth doesn't change. Truth is one thing. It covers all things which touch the heart—honor and pride and pity and justice and courage and love. Do you see now?"

He didn't know. Somehow it was simpler than that. There was an old bear, fierce and ruthless, not merely just to stay alive, but with the fierce pride of liberty and freedom, proud enough of that liberty and freedom to see it threatened without fear or even alarm; nay, who at times even seemed deliberately to put that freedom and liberty in jeopardy in order to savor them, to remind his old strong bones and flesh to keep supple and quick to defend and preserve them. There was an old man, son of a Negro slave and an Indian king, inheritor on the one side of the long chronicle of a people who had learned humility through suffering, and pride through the endurance which survived the suffering and injustice, and on the other side, the chronicle of a people even longer in the land than the first, yet who no longer existed in the land at all save in the solitary brotherhood of an old Negro's alien blood and the wild and invincible spirit of an old bear. There was a boy who wished to learn humility and pride in order to become skillful and worthy in the woods, who suddenly found himself becoming so skillful so rapidly that he feared he would never become worthy because he had not learned humility and pride, although he had tried to, until one day and as suddenly he discovered that an old man who could not have defined either had led him, as though by the hand, to that point where an old bear and a little mongrel dog showed him that, by possessing one thing other, he would possess them both.

And a little dog, nameless and mongrel and many-fathered, grown, yet weighing less than six pounds, saying as if to itself, "I can't be dangerous, because there's nothing much smaller than I am; I can't be fierce, because they would call it just noise; I can't be humble, because I'm already too close to the ground to genuflect;[13] I can't be proud, because I wouldn't be near enough to it for anyone to know who was casting that shadow, and I don't even know that I'm not going to heaven, because they have already decided that I don't possess an immortal soul. So all I can be is brave. But it's all right. I can be that, even if they still call it just noise."

That was all. It was simple, much simpler than somebody talking in a book about a youth and a girl he would never need to grieve over, because he could never approach any nearer her and would never have to get any farther away. He had heard about a bear, and finally got big enough to trail it,

12. " 'She . . . fair' ": from John Keats's "Ode on a Grecian Urn."

13. **genuflect** (jen′ yə flekt′) v.: Bend the knee, as in reverence or worship.

and he trailed it four years and at last met it with a gun in his hands and he didn't shoot. Because a little dog— But he could have shot long before the little dog covered the twenty yards to where the bear waited, and Sam Fathers could have shot at any time during that interminable minute while Old Ben stood on his hind feet over them. He stopped. His father was watching him gravely across the spring-rife twilight of the room; when he spoke, his words were as quiet as the twilight, too, not loud, because they did not need to be because they would last, "Courage, and honor, and pride," his father said, "and pity, and love of justice and of liberty. They all touch the heart, and what the heart holds to becomes truth, as far as we know truth. Do you see now?"

Sam, and Old Ben, and Nip, he thought. And himself too. He had been all right too. His father had said so. "Yes, sir," he said.

MULTICULTURAL CONNECTION

The Bear as a Universal Symbol

Consider what the bear symbolizes in Faulkner's story. Around the world, bears have come to represent courage, endurance, strength, and often, a bad temper. Above all, the bear is considered to be a sacred animal in many cultures, with magical powers to cure and protect. In India, for example, children traditionally rode on bears to prevent disease.

Among Native Americans. Since ancient times, the bear has been an object of worship among many Native American groups. Medicine men imitate bears in special ceremonies and seek spiritual and supernatural guidance from them. When these bear-priests die, it is believed that they go to live with the bears in the afterworld. Many Native American peoples also practice "bear medicine," which involves calling for help from the animal through dances and ceremonies, and using plant roots believed to have been given to people by the bears to cure illness. The Pueblo, Auni, Chippewa, and Sioux people all consider the bear to be a great healer.

In Europe. The Finno-Ugric people (including the Finns and Lapps of northeastern Europe) also revere the bear in their folk traditions. They refer to the bear as "the master of the forest." Special feasts and prayers are held in the bear's honor. After a bear is killed for food, its forgiveness is asked and its bones are buried unbroken in the belief that it will come back to life. This belief may be connected with the bear's habit of hibernating all winter and rising again each spring, as if from the dead.

Among the Russians. The nation that may be most often associated with the bear is Russia. In fact, political cartoonists from other nations have sometimes used the bear as a symbol representing Russia. To the Russians themselves, the bear is seen as a powerful but friendly and helpful creature. Bears often appear in Russian fairy tales, proverbs, poems, and songs.

In African American folklore. The bear is also a part of the folklore and popular traditions of the American South. African-American folk wisdom in Louisiana says that to dream of fighting a bear means persecution. A dream of a running bear, however, means happiness and good luck.

Exploring and Sharing

Investigate mythology and different customs to find out more about the art of bear medicine and traditional beliefs in magical bear powers.

RESPONDING TO THE SELECTION

Your Response

1. If you had the opportunity, would you join the narrator, Sam Fathers, and the others on their yearly trip into the Big Bottom? Why or why not?
2. After reading this selection, would you like to read a longer version of the story? Why or why not?

Recalling

3. What had the boy "already inherited" before participating in his first hunt?
4. What does the boy realize for the first time when he sees the bear's paw print?
5. (a) Why does the boy finally leave his gun behind when he is tracking the bear? (b) What other objects does he relinquish? (c) When does he first see the bear?
6. (a) What does the boy do when the fyce charges the bear? (b) What comment does Sam Fathers make after the bear has gone?
7. How does the boy's father help him to comprehend his inability to shoot the bear?

Interpreting

8. Early in the story, the narrator comments that the wilderness is "being constantly and punily gnawed at by men with axes and plows who feared it because it was wilderness." How are the men who travel to the Big Bottom twice a year different from the "men with axes"?
9. Why does the bear fear a coward more than a brave person?
10. (a) How does the boy's relationship to the wilderness change when he abandons his gun and other "lifeless mechanicals"? (b) How does this set him apart from the "men with axes"?
11. What does the narrator mean by his comment that when the bear and the boy looked at each other they were "synchronized to the instant by something more than blood that moved the flesh and bones which bore them"?
12. What understanding does the boy reach at the end of the story?

Applying

13. (a) Why do you think that people often fear the wilderness? (b) What does this fear suggest about human nature?

ANALYZING LITERATURE

Understanding Symbols

A **symbol** is a person, place, or thing that has a meaning in itself and also represents something larger than itself. The bear, for example, symbolizes the wilderness.

1. Find two descriptions of the bear that help to convey its symbolic meaning.
2. As a symbol of the wilderness, what virtues does the bear embody?
3. Considering the bear's symbolic meaning, what is the significance of its mortality?
4. Who possesses the power to destroy it?

Understanding Allusions

An **allusion** is a short reference to another literary work or to a figure, place, or event from history, religion, or mythology. For example, Faulkner alludes to the poem "Ode on a Grecian Urn" by English Romantic poet John Keats.

1. In Keats's poem the speaker comments on the permanence of a pastoral scene depicted on an urn. In "The Bear" the boy's father repeats two lines describing the urn's portrayal of a young man pursuing a beautiful maiden. How do these lines reinforce the meaning of the story?
2. Keats's poem ends with the following lines: "'Beauty is truth, truth beauty,'—that is all/Ye know on earth, and all ye need to know." How are these lines related to the meaning of the story?

THINKING AND WRITING

Writing About Symbols and Allusions

Write an essay in which you discuss how Faulkner uses symbols and allusions to convey the theme of "The Bear." Reread the story, focusing on Faulkner's use of symbols and allusions. Prepare a thesis statement. Then write your essay, using passages from the story to support your thesis.

Nobel Prize Acceptance Speech

William Faulkner

Stockholm, Sweden
December 10, 1950

I feel that this award was not made to me as a man, but to my work—a life's work in the agony and sweat of the human spirit, not for glory and least of all for profit, but to create out of the materials of the human spirit something which did not exist before. So this award is only mine in trust. It will not be difficult to find a dedication for the money part of it commensurate with the purpose and significance of its origin. But I would like to do the same with the acclaim too, by using this moment as a pinnacle from which I might be listened to by the young men and women already dedicated to the same anguish and travail, among whom is already that one who will some day stand here where I am standing.

Our tragedy today is a general and universal physical fear so long sustained by now that we can even bear it. There are no longer problems of the spirit. There is only the question: When will I be blown up? Because of this, the young man or woman writing today has forgotten the problems of the human heart in conflict with itself which alone can make good writing because only that is worth writing about, worth the agony and the sweat.

He must learn them again. He must teach himself that the basest of all things is to be afraid; and, teaching himself that, forget it forever, leaving no room in his workshop for anything but the old verities and truths of the heart, the old universal truths lacking which any story is ephemeral and doomed—love and honor and pity and pride and compassion and sacrifice. Until he does so, he labors under a curse. He writes not of love but of lust, of defeats in which nobody loses anything of value, of victories without hope and, worst of all, without pity or compassion. His griefs grieve on no universal bones, leaving no scars. He writes not of the heart but of the glands.

Until he relearns these things, he will write as though he stood among and watched the end of man. I decline to accept the end of man. It is easy enough to say that man is immortal simply because he will endure: that when the last ding-dong of doom has clanged and faded from the last worthless rock hanging tideless in the last red and dying evening, that even then there will still be one more sound: that of his puny inexhaustible voice, still talking. I refuse to accept this. I believe that man will not merely endure: he will prevail. He is immortal, not because he alone among creatures has an inexhaustible voice, but because he has a soul, a spirit capable of compassion and sacrifice and endurance. The poet's, the writer's, duty is to write about these things. It is his privilege to help man endure by lifting his heart, by reminding him of the courage and honor and hope and pride and compassion and pity and sacrifice which have been the glory of his past. The poet's voice need not merely be the record of man, it can be one of the props, the pillars to help him endure and prevail.

RESPONDING TO THE SELECTION

Your Response

1. If you had a chance to address the world, what points would you make in your speech? Explain.
2. Based on his remarks in accepting the Nobel Prize and on his story "Race at Morning," is Faulkner someone whom you would have liked to meet? Why or why not?

Recalling

3. (a) According to Faulkner, what is "our tragedy today"? (b) What have today's young writers forgotten? Why?
4. What must young writers teach themselves?
5. Why does Faulkner believe that humanity will prevail? (b) What must the writer do to ensure humanity's survival?

Interpreting

6. Why is fear "the basest of all things"?
7. Faulkner writes, "I believe that man will not only endure, but will prevail." What do you think Faulkner sees as the difference between prevailing and enduring?
8. In your own words, restate Faulkner's message concerning a writer's duty.

Applying

9. Explain why you do or do not agree with Faulkner's opinion concerning a writer's duty.

ANALYZING LITERATURE

Understanding Oratory

Oratory is the art of skilled, eloquent public speaking. When preparing a speech, an orator considers the audience and the occasion and purpose of the speech. To emphasize his or her main points, the orator will use such oratorical devices as restatement, repetition, and parallelism.

1. What is the purpose of Faulkner's speech?
2. Why is it appropriate for the occasion?
3. Why is the language appropriate for an intelligent, educated audience?
4. Find one example of Faulkner's use of restatement in the speech.
5. Find one example of his use of repetition.
6. Find one example of his use of parallelism.

THINKING AND WRITING

Writing About Related Themes

Write an essay in which you discuss how Faulkner's speech echoes the theme of his short story "Race at Morning." Reread "Race at Morning," focusing on details that reveal its theme. Then reread Faulkner's speech, noting how it echoes the theme of the story. When writing your essay, use passages from both the speech and the short story for support. When you revise, make sure you have not included any unnecessary information.

LEARNING OPTIONS

1. **Writing.** In his address Faulkner records the ultimate question of the 1950's: "When will I be blown up?" Now that the cold war is over, what do you think is the question of the age? Work with a small group to generate a list of possibilities. Do you and your classmates have the same concerns?
2. **Speaking and Listening.** Each year the Swedish Academy in Stockholm awards a Nobel Prize in Literature. Nominate your favorite author for the next Nobel Prize. In a short address to Academy members, describe the literary contribution your candidate has made to the "good of humanity." Keep in mind that the Swedish Academy generally selects authors on the basis of their complete work, rather than on an individual book.

ZORA NEALE HURSTON

1891–1960

When Zora Neale Hurston died in January 1960, she was buried in an unmarked grave in the Garden of the Heavenly Rest, a segregated cemetery in Fort Pierce, Florida. Today she is hailed as the "dominant black woman writer" of the Harlem Renaissance, a cultural movement of the 1920's centered in New York City's community of Harlem.

Born in Eatonville, Florida, the first incorporated all-black town in America, Hurston was one of eight children. She was, by her own account, a spirited, curious child who "always wanted to go." Her mother explained her daughter's urge to wander by claiming that travel dust had been sprinkled around the door the day she was born.

Hurston's childhood came to an abrupt end with the death of her mother when Hurston was nine. Shifted from house to house of relatives and friends, Hurston went to school on and off, whenever she could. She was about fourteen years old when she began to support herself, eventually getting a job as a wardrobe girl for a visiting Gilbert and Sullivan company. After traveling with the company for a year and a half, she settled in Baltimore and returned to school.

Hurston went on to study at Howard University, where she began to write. Encouraged by Charles S. Johnson, editor of the Urban League's magazine, *Opportunity,* she decided to move to New York. She arrived the first week of January, 1925, with "no jobs, no friends, and a lot of hope." Winning a scholarship to Barnard College, Hurston studied anthropology under Franz Boas. After graduation she began her career as a folklorist, returning to Florida to collect black folk tales and research customs.

When funds for research dried up, Hurston returned to Eatonville to write *Mules and Men,* a compilation of Florida folk tales and Louisiana folk customs. She wrote her first novel, *Jonah's Gourd Vine,* in 1934 at a publisher's request. In 1937 she received critical acclaim for her second novel, *Their Eyes Were Watching God,* the story of a young black woman's struggle to understand herself and to find a man who will treat her as an equal.

Hurston displayed in her work a lively imagination, a keen ear for dialect, and an appreciation for black culture. In all, she published four novels, two books of folklore, a dozen short stories, two musicals, dozens of essays, and the prize-winning autobiography *Dust Tracks on a Road*. Nonetheless her career lapsed into obscurity during the 1950's. In August 1973 contemporary writer Alice Walker located and marked Hurston's grave, recording the experience in a 1975 *Ms*. magazine article ("In Search of Zora Neale Hurston") and restoring Hurston to her rightful place in American literature.

GUIDE FOR INTERPRETING

from Dust Tracks on a Road

Literary Forms

Autobiographies. All writers draw on their own experiences in their work. Autobiography, however, makes the author's life its central concern. An **autobiography** is an account of a person's life written by that person, generally in the first person. In an autobiography the writer presents a continuous narrative of significant events from his or her perspective. The reader sees events through the writer's eyes and comes to understand the writer's point of view.

Some writers are motivated to write autobiographies by a desire to relive the past. Others want to justify their beliefs or sort out emotional and philosophical conflicts. What most writers of autobiographies have in common is the belief that his or her life is interesting or important or can, in some way, serve as an example to others.

In her autobiography, *Dust Tracks on a Road,* Zora Neale Hurston was determined to show that African Americans did more than suffer. "I saw," she wrote, "that what was being written by Negro authors was all on the same thing—the race problem, and saturated with our sorrows. By the time I graduated from college, I had sensed the falsity of the picture, because I did not find that sorrow. We talk about the race problem a great deal, but go on laughing and striving like everybody else."

Focus

Even as a child, Hurston showed an interest in literature. Write briefly about how you first became involved in something that interested you—a sport, a hobby, or something else.

Primary Source

In his Afterward, Henry Louis Gates, Jr., characterizes Hurston's achievement in *Dust Tracks* as follows:

[Hurston] gives us a *writer's* life, rather than an account, as she says, of "the Negro problem." So many events in this text are figured in terms of Hurston's growing awareness and mastery of books and language, language and linguistic rituals as spoken and written both by masters of the Western tradition and by ordinary members of the black community. These two "speech communities," as it were, are Hurston's great sources of inspiration. . . .

Hurston moves in and out of these distinct voices effortlessly, seamlessly. . . . It is this usage of a *divided* voice, a doubled voice unreconciled, that strikes me as her great achievement, a verbal analogue of her double experiences as a woman in a male-dominated world and as a black person in a nonblack world. . . .

from **Dust Tracks on a Road**

Zora Neale Hurston

I used to take a seat on top of the gate-post and watch the world go by. One way to Orlando[1] ran past my house, so the carriages and cars would pass before me. The movement made me glad to see it. Often the white travelers would hail me, but more often I hailed them, and asked, "Don't you want me to go a piece of the way with you?"

They always did. I know now that I must have caused a great deal of amusement among them, but my self-assurance must have carried the point, for I was always invited to come along. I'd ride up the road for perhaps a half-mile, then walk back. I did not do this with the permission of my parents, nor with their foreknowledge. When they found out about it later, I usually got a whipping. My grandmother worried about my forward ways a great deal. She had known slavery and to her my brazenness was unthinkable.

"Git down offa dat gate-post! You li'l sow, you! Git down! Setting up dere looking dem white folks right in de face! They's gowine[2] to lynch you, yet. And don't stand in dat doorway gazing out at 'em neither. Youse too brazen to live long."[3]

Nevertheless, I kept right on gazing at them, and "going a piece of the way" whenever I could make it. The village seemed dull to me most of the time. If the village was singing a chorus, I must have missed the tune.

Perhaps a year before the old man[4] died, I came to know two other white people for myself. They were women.

It came about this way. The whites who came down from the North were often brought by their friends to visit the village school. A Negro school was something strange to them, and while they were always sympathetic and kind, curiosity must have been present, also. They came and went, came and went. Always, the room was hurriedly put in order, and we were threatened with a prompt and bloody death if we cut one caper while the visitors were present. We always sang a spiritual, led by Mr. Calhoun himself. Mrs. Calhoun always stood in the back, with a palmetto switch[5] in her hand as a squelcher. We were all little angels for the duration, because we'd better be. She would cut her eyes and give us a glare that meant trouble, then turn her face towards the visitors and beam as much as to say it was a great privilege and pleasure to teach lovely children like us. They couldn't see that palmetto hickory in her hand behind all those benches, but we knew where our angelic behavior was coming from.

---

1. Orlando (ôr lan′ dō): A city in Florida, about five miles from Eatonville, Hurston's hometown.
2. gowine: "Going."
3. "Git down . . . live long": Hurston's grandmother's fears reflect the belief of many people at the time that it was inappropriate for African Americans to be assertive toward whites.

4. the old man: A white farmer who had developed a friendship with Hurston.
5. palmetto (pal met′ ō): A switch whip made from the fan-shaped leaves of the palmetto, a type of palm tree.

THE MATHER SCHOOL
Jonathan Green
Courtesy of the Artist

Usually, the visitors gave warning a day ahead and we would be cautioned to put on shoes, comb our heads, and see to ears and fingernails. There was a close inspection of every one of us before we marched in that morning. Knotty heads, dirty ears and fingernails got hauled out of line, strapped and sent home to lick the calf over again.

This particular afternoon, the two young ladies just popped in. Mr. Calhoun was flustered, but he put on the best show he could. He dismissed the class that he was teaching up at the front of the room, then called the fifth grade in reading. That was my class.

So we took our readers and went up front. We stood up in the usual line, and opened to the lesson. It was the story of Pluto and Persephone. It was new and hard to the class in general, and Mr. Calhoun was very uncomfortable as the readers stumbled along, spelling out words with their lips, and in mumbling undertones before they exposed them experimentally to the teacher's ears.

Then it came to me. I was fifth or sixth down the line. The story was not new to me, because I had read my reader through from lid to lid, the first week that Papa had bought it for me.

That is how it was that my eyes were not in the book, working out the paragraph which I knew would be mine by counting the children ahead of me. I was observing our visitors, who held a book between them, following the lesson. They had shiny hair, mostly brownish. One had a looping gold chain around her neck. The other one was dressed all over in black and white with a pretty finger ring on her left hand. But the thing that held my eyes were their fingers. They were long and thin, and very white, except up near the tips. There they were baby pink. I had never seen such hands. It was a fascinating discovery for me. I wondered how they felt. I would have given those hands more attention, but the child before me was almost through. My turn next, so I got on my mark, bringing my eyes back to the book and made sure of my place. Some of the stories I had reread several times, and this Greco-Roman myth was one of my favorites. I was exalted by it, and that is the way I read my paragraph.

"Yes, Jupiter had seen her (Persephone). He had seen the maiden picking flowers in the field. He had seen the chariot of the dark monarch pause by the maiden's side. He had seen him when he seized Persephone. He had seen the black horses leap down Mount Aetna's fiery throat. Persephone was now in Pluto's dark realm and he had made her his wife."

The two women looked at each other and then back to me. Mr. Calhoun broke out with a proud smile beneath his bristly moustache, and instead of the next child taking up where I had ended, he nodded to me to go on. So I read the story to the end, where flying Mercury, the messenger of the Gods, brought Persephone back to the sunlit earth and restored her to the arms of Dame Ceres, her mother, that the world might have springtime and summer flowers, autumn and harvest. But because she had bitten the pomegranate[6] while in Pluto's kingdom, she must return to him for three months of each year, and be his queen. Then the world had winter, until she returned to earth.

The class was dismissed, and the visitors smiled us away and went into a low-voiced conversation with Mr. Calhoun for a few minutes. They glanced my way once or twice and I began to worry. Not only was I barefooted, but my feet and legs were dusty. My hair was more uncombed than usual, and my nails

were not shiny clean. Oh, I'm going to catch it now. Those ladies saw me, too. Mr. Calhoun is promising to 'tend to me. So I thought.

Then Mr. Calhoun called me. I went up thinking how awful it was to get a whipping before company. Furthermore, I heard a snicker run over the room. Hennie Clark and Stell Brazzle did it out loud, so I would be sure to hear them. The smart-aleck was going to get it. I slipped one hand behind me and switched my dress tail at them, indicating scorn.

"Come here, Zora Neale," Mr. Calhoun cooed as I reached the desk. He put his hand on my shoulder and gave me little pats. The ladies smiled and held out those flower-looking fingers towards me. I seized the opportunity for a good look.

"Shake hands with the ladies, Zora Neale," Mr. Calhoun prompted and they took my hand one after the other and smiled. They asked if I loved school, and I lied that I did. There was *some* truth in it, because I liked geography and reading, and I liked to play at recess time. Whoever it was invented writing and arithmetic got no thanks from me. Neither did I like the arrangement where the teacher could sit up there with a palmetto stem and lick me whenever he saw fit. I hated things I couldn't do anything about. But I knew better than to bring that up right there, so I said yes, I *loved* school.

"I can tell you do," Brown Taffeta gleamed. She patted my head, and was lucky enough not to get sandspurs in her hand. Children who roll and tumble in the grass in Florida are apt to get sandspurs in their hair. They shook hands with me again and I went back to my seat.

When school let out at three o'clock, Mr. Calhoun told me to wait. When everybody had gone, he told me I was to go to the Park House, that was the hotel in Maitland,[7] the next afternoon to call upon Mrs. Johnstone

---

6. **pomegranate** (päm' gran' it): A round fruit with many seeds.

7. **Maitland** (māt' land): A city in Florida, close to Eatonville.

SCHOOL BELL TIME, 1978
Romare Bearden
Kingsborough Community College,
The City University of New York

and Miss Hurd. I must tell Mama to see that I was clean and brushed from head to feet, and I must wear shoes and stockings. The ladies liked me, he said, and I must be on my best behavior.

The next day I was let out of school an hour early, and went home to be stood up in a tub full of suds and be scrubbed and have my ears dug into. My sandy hair sported a red ribbon to match my red and white checked gingham dress, starched until it could stand alone. Mama saw to it that my shoes were on the right feet, since I was careless about left and right. Last thing, I was given a handkerchief to carry, warned again about my behavior, and sent off, with my big brother John to go as far as the hotel gate with me.

First thing, the ladies gave me strange things, like stuffed dates and preserved ginger, and encouraged me to eat all that I wanted. Then they showed me their Japanese dolls and just talked. I was then handed a copy of *Scribner's Magazine*,[8] and asked to read a place that was pointed out to me. After a paragraph or two, I was told with smiles, that that would do.

I was led out on the grounds and they took my picture under a palm tree. They handed me what was to me then a heavy cyl-

inder done up in fancy paper, tied with a ribbon, and they told me goodbye, asking me not to open it until I got home.

My brother was waiting for me down by the lake, and we hurried home, eager to see what was in the thing. It was too heavy to be candy or anything like that. John insisted on toting it for me.

My mother made John give it back to me and let me open it. Perhaps, I shall never experience such joy again. The nearest thing to that moment was the telegram accepting my first book. One hundred goldy-new pennies rolled out of the cylinder. Their gleam lit up the world. It was not avarice that moved me. It was the beauty of the thing. I stood on the mountain. Mama let me play with my pennies for a while, then put them away for me to keep.

That was only the beginning. The next day I received an Episcopal hymn-book bound in white leather with a golden cross stamped into the front cover, a copy of *The Swiss Family Robinson*, and a book of fairy tales.

I set about to commit the song words to memory. There was no music written there, just the words. But there was to my consciousness music in between them just the same. "When I survey the Wondrous Cross" seemed the most beautiful to me, so I committed that to memory first of all. Some of them seemed dull and without life, and I pre-

---

8. *Scribner's Magazine*: A literary magazine no longer being published.

from *Dust Tracks on a Road*   665

tended they were not there. If white people liked trashy singing like that, there must be something funny about them that I had not noticed before. I stuck to the pretty ones where the words marched to a throb I could feel.

A month or so after the young ladies returned to Minnesota, they sent me a huge box packed with clothes and books. The red coat with a wide circular collar and the red tam[9] pleased me more than any of the other things. My chums pretended not to like anything that I had, but even then I knew that they were jealous. Old Smarty had gotten by them again. The clothes were not new, but they were very good. I shone like the morning sun.

But the books gave me more pleasure than the clothes. I had never been too keen on dressing up. It called for hard scrubbings with Octagon soap suds getting in my eyes, and none too gentle fingers scrubbing my neck and gouging in my ears.

In that box were *Gulliver's Travels*, *Grimm's Fairy Tales*, *Dick Whittington*, *Greek and Roman Myths*, and best of all, *Norse Tales*. Why did the Norse tales strike so deeply into my soul? I do not know, but they did. I seemed to remember seeing Thor swing his mighty short-handled hammer as he sped across the sky in rumbling thunder, lightning flashing from the tread of his steeds and the wheels of his chariot. The great and good Odin, who went down to the well of knowledge to drink, and was told that the price of a drink from that fountain was an eye. Odin drank deeply, then plucked out one eye without a murmur and handed it to the grizzly keeper, and walked away. That held majesty for me.

Of the Greeks, Hercules moved me most. I followed him eagerly on his tasks. The story of the choice of Hercules as a boy when he met Pleasure and Duty, and put his hand in that of Duty and followed her steep way to the blue hills of fame and glory, which she pointed out at the end, moved me profoundly. I resolved to be like him. The tricks and turns of the other Gods and Goddesses left me cold. There were other thin books about this and that sweet and gentle little girl who gave up her heart to Christ and good works. Almost always they died from it, preaching as they passed. I was utterly indifferent to their deaths. In the first place I could not conceive of death, and in the next place they never had any funerals that amounted to a hill of beans, so I didn't care how soon they rolled up their big, soulful, blue eyes and kicked the bucket. They had no meat on their bones.

But I also met Hans Andersen and Robert Louis Stevenson. They seemed to know what I wanted to hear and said it in a way that tingled me. Just a little below these friends was Rudyard Kipling in his *Jungle Books*. I loved his talking snakes as much as I did the hero.

I came to start reading the Bible through my mother. She gave me a licking one afternoon for repeating something I had overheard a neighbor telling her. She locked me in her room after the whipping, and the Bible was the only thing in there for me to read. I happened to open to the place where David[10] was doing some mighty smiting, and I got interested. David went here and he went there, and no matter where he went, he smote 'em hip and thigh. Then he sung songs to his harp awhile, and went out and smote some more. Not one time did David stop and preach about sins and other things. All David wanted to know from God was who to kill and when. He took care of the other details himself. Never a quiet moment. I liked him a lot. So I read a great deal more in the Bible, hunting for some more active people like David. Except for the beautiful language of Luke and Paul,[11] the New Testament still plays a poor

---

9. tam (tam) *n.*: A cap with a wide, round, flat top, and sometimes a center pompom.

10. David: In the Bible, the second king of Israel, the land of the Hebrews.

11. Luke and Paul: Two Christian Apostles, who wrote parts of the New Testament.

second to the Old Testament for me. The Jews had a God who laid about Him when they needed Him. I could see no use waiting until Judgment Day to see a man who was just crying for a good killing, to be told to go and roast. My idea was to give him a good killing first, and then if he got roasted later on, so much the better.

RESPONDING TO THE SELECTION

Your Response
1. What are your impressions of young Zora?
2. What do you think about her tastes in reading?

Interpreting
3. What do you learn about Hurston from her statement "If the village was singing a chorus, I must have missed the tune"?
4. How can you tell that the two visitors from Minnesota made a great impression on Hurston?
5. What do Hurston's tastes in reading reveal about her?

Applying
6. Based on this excerpt, what kind of future would you predict for Zora Neale Hurston?

ANALYZING LITERATURE

Appreciating Autobiography
An **autobiography** presents a writer's experiences from his or her own perspective.
1. Why do you suppose Hurston included her meeting with the Minnesotans in her autobiography?

2. What does this excerpt suggest about Hurston's self-image? Explain.

CRITICAL THINKING AND READING

Making Inferences About Attitudes
In her autobiography Hurston does not directly address the prejudice experienced by African Americans during her lifetime. By reading between the lines, however, you can make inferences about prevailing racial attitudes and social conventions in her hometown.
1. What does Mr. Calhoun's reaction to the white visitors suggest about the Southern social system at the time?
2. (a) How would you describe the Minnesotans' attitude toward the young Zora Neale Hurston? (b) What does their attitude suggest about the prevailing attitudes of Northerners at the time?

THINKING AND WRITING
Write an episode for your autobiography. Drawing on the writing you did before reading this selection, explain how you first developed one of your major interests. Like Hurston, make the experience into a story.

MULTICULTURAL CONNECTION

Gathering Folklore

Collecting folklore helps preserve the heritage of a people or culture. Most folklore is passed down orally from generation to generation. If the older people who know it die without passing the stories and songs along to their descendants, the folklore will die too—unless someone comes along to record it.

Grimm's Fairy Tales. The most celebrated European folklore collectors are the Grimm brothers of Germany. In the early 1800's they faithfully recorded folk tales told by German villagers and farmers. Today *Grimm's Fairy Tales* are familiar to nearly everyone.

Zora Neale Hurston. One of those most responsible for preserving African American folklore is Zora Neale Hurston. After establishing herself as a writer, Hurston returned to Florida to record the folklore of the rural African Americans she grew up with. To accomplish this, she had to "dress as [the locals] did, talk as they did, live their life." Her ability to immerse herself in the local culture enabled her to gather the stories for her collection *Mules and Men* (1935).

JOHN DOS PASSOS

1896–1970

Although he published numerous novels, essays, and biographical sketches, John Dos Passos is remembered mainly for his experimental trilogy, *U.S.A.* In this work Dos Passos blends fiction and nonfiction—interweaving biographies of both fictional characters and real historical figures, newspaper excerpts, passages from popular songs, and quotations from speeches—to paint a biting portrait of early twentieth-century America.

Dos Passos was born in Chicago. He attended private schools and eventually enrolled at Harvard, from which he graduated in 1916. When the United States entered World War I, he joined the United States Army Ambulance Corps. His experiences during the war provided him with the material for his first two novels, *One Man's Initiation—1917* (1920) and *Three Soldiers* (1921).

In 1925 Dos Passos published *Manhattan Transfer,* in which he delved into the complexities of New York City life. In this novel Dos Passos developed the experimental technique which he later perfected in the *U.S.A.* trilogy. He presented scattered fragments of many characters' lives, which combine to form a complete picture of urban life.

Dos Passos published *The 42nd Parallel,* the first novel of the *U.S.A.* trilogy in 1930. The second and third novels, *1919* and *The Big Money,* appeared in 1932 and 1936. In 1937 the trilogy was published in its entirety under the title *U.S.A.*

U.S.A. was admired for its new and dramatic presentation of American culture and history. Dos Passos regarded all writers as "architects of history." "What do you write for then?" he asked. "To convince people of something? That's preaching, and is part of the business of everybody who deals with words; not to admit that is to play with a gun and say you didn't know it was loaded. But outside of preaching I think there is such a thing as writing for writing's sake. A cabinetmaker enjoys whittling a dovetail because he's a cabinetmaker; every type of work has its own delight inherent in it. The mind of a generation is its speech. A writer makes aspects of that speech permanent by putting them in print. He whittles at the words and phrases of today and makes forms for the minds of later generations. That's history. A writer who writes straight is an architect of history."

Dos Passos went on to publish several more novels, including a second trilogy, *District of Columbia* (1952). However, critics generally agree that his later works lack the inventiveness and forcefulness of *U.S.A.*

GUIDE FOR INTERPRETING

Tin Lizzie

Literary Forms

Biographies. A biography is an account of a person's life written by another person. Most biographies focus on recounting the central events of the subject's life—the events that make that person's life worth reading about. Sometimes, however, a writer will focus on conveying his or her impressions of the subject's character, rather than merely presenting a factual account of the subject's life. The result is what is known as an impressionistic biography. In an impressionistic biography, the writer concentrates on presenting details that help to reveal the subject's personality, often intentionally omitting details that would be included in a factual biography.

In *U.S.A.* Dos Passos presents many short, impressionistic biographical sketches, including ones about Woodrow Wilson and Henry Ford. Together these sketches help to convey Dos Passos's overall impression of America during the first three decades of the twentieth century.

Commentary

In praising Dos Passos's *U.S.A.* trilogy, critic Alfred Kazin compares Dos Passos to the inventors and entrepreneurs of the early twentieth century about whom Dos Passos writes. "What Dos Passos created with [his novel] was in fact another American invention—an American *thing* peculiar to the opportunity and stress of American life, like the Wright Brothers' airplane, Edison's phonograph . . . , Frank Lloyd Wright's first office buildings."

What Kazin was responding to was the new and inventive style of Dos Passos's writing. As you read Dos Passos's impressionistic biography of Henry Ford, pay attention to the way he plays with such things as capitalization, punctuation, and spelling. You may also recognize what Kazin called "the 'poetry' behind the book that makes the 'history' in it live": the different styles of speech that Dos Passos uses to convey his impressions of Henry Ford. Dos Passos varies the rhythms and language in his work to mimic the way people talk in real life. He also imitates the stock phrases and popular writing that appeared in the advertisements and newspapers of his time.

What "poetry" do you hear in the language of your everyday life?

Focus

Imagine that you were writing an impressionistic biography about a public figure or a person you know. Prepare a list of facts about this person's life that contribute to your impressions of his or her character.

Tin Lizzie

John Dos Passos

"Mr. Ford the automobileer," the feature-writer wrote in 1900,

"Mr. Ford the automobileer began by giving his steed three or four sharp jerks with the lever at the righthand side of the seat; that is, he pulled the lever up and down sharply in order, as he said, to mix air with gasoline and drive the charge into the exploding cylinder. . . . Mr. Ford slipped a small electric switch handle and there followed a puff, puff, puff. . . . The puffing of the machine assumed a higher key. She was flying along about eight miles an hour. The ruts in the road were deep, but the machine certainly went with a dreamlike smoothness. There was none of the bumping common even to a streetcar. . . . By this time the boulevard had been reached, and the automobileer, letting a lever fall a little, let her out. Whiz! She picked up speed with infinite rapidity. As she ran on there was a clattering behind, the new noise of the automobile.

For twenty years or more,

ever since he'd left his father's farm when he was sixteen to get a job in a Detroit machineshop, Henry Ford had been nuts about machinery. First it was watches, then he designed a steamtractor, then he built a horseless carriage with an engine adapted from the Otto gasengine he'd read about in *The World of Science*, then a mechanical buggy with a onecylinder fourcycle motor, that would run forward but not back;

at last, in ninetyeight, he felt he was far enough along to risk throwing up his job with the Detroit Edison Company, where

he'd worked his way up from night fireman to chief engineer, to put all his time into working on a new gasoline engine,

(in the late eighties he'd met Edison at a meeting of electriclight employees in Atlantic City. He'd gone up to Edison after Edison had delivered an address and asked him if he thought gasoline was practical as a motor fuel. Edison had said yes. If Edison said it, it was true. Edison was the great admiration of Henry Ford's life);

and in driving his mechanical buggy, sitting there at the lever jauntily dressed in a tightbuttoned jacket and a high collar and a derby hat, back and forth over the level ill-paved streets of Detroit,

scaring the big brewery horses and the skinny trotting horses and the sleekrumped pacers with the motor's loud explosions,

looking for men scatterbrained enough to invest money in a factory for building automobiles.

He was the eldest son of an Irish immigrant who during the Civil War had married the daughter of a prosperous Pennsylvania Dutch farmer and settled down to farming near Dearborn in Wayne County, Michigan;

like plenty of other Americans, young Henry grew up hating the endless sogging through the mud about the chores, the hauling and pitching manure, the kerosene lamps to clean, the irk and sweat and solitude of the farm.

He was a slender, active youngster, a good skater, clever with his hands; what he liked was to tend the machinery and let the

others do the heavy work. His mother had told him not to drink, smoke, gamble or go into debt, and he never did.

When he was in his early twenties his father tried to get him back from Detroit, where he was working as mechanic and repairman for the Drydock Engine Company that built engines for steamboats, by giving him forty acres of land.

Young Henry built himself an uptodate square white dwellinghouse with a false mansard[1] roof and married and settled down on the farm,

but he let the hired men do the farming;

he bought himself a buzzsaw and rented a stationary engine and cut the timber off the woodlots.

---

1. **mansard** (man′ särd): A roof with two slopes on each of the four sides.

He was a thrifty young man who never drank or smoked or gambled, but he couldn't stand living on the farm.

He moved to Detroit, and in the brick barn behind his house tinkered for years in his spare time with a mechanical buggy that would be light enough to run over the clayey wagonroads of Wayne County, Michigan.

By 1900 he had a practicable car to promote.

He was forty years old before the Ford Motor Company was started and production began to move.

Speed was the first thing the early automobile manufacturers went after. Races advertised the makes of cars.

Henry Ford himself hung up several records at the track at Grosse Pointe and on the ice on Lake St. Clair. In his 999 he did the mile in thirtynine and fourfifths seconds.

But it had always been his custom to hire others to do the heavy work. The speed he was busy with was speed in production, the records records in efficient output. He hired Barney Oldfield, a stunt bicyclerider from Salt Lake City, to do the racing for him.

Henry Ford had ideas about other things than the designing of motors, carburetors, magnetos, jigs and fixtures, punches and dies; he had ideas about sales,

that the big money was in economical quantity production, quick turnover, cheap interchangeable, easilyreplaced standardized parts;

it wasn't until 1909, after years of arguing with his partners, that Ford put out the first Model T.

Henry Ford was right.

That season he sold more than ten thousand tin lizzies, ten years later he was selling almost a million a year.

In these years the Taylor Plan was stirring up plantmanagers and manufacturers all over the country. Efficiency was the word. The same ingenuity that went into improving the performance of a machine could go into improving the performance of the workmen producing the machine.

In 1913 they established the assemblyline at Ford's. That season the profits were something like twentyfive million dollars, but they had trouble in keeping the men on the job, machinists didn't seem to like it at Ford's.

Henry Ford had ideas about other things than production.

He was the largest automobile manufacturer in the world; he paid high wages; maybe if the steady workers thought they were getting a cut (a very small cut) in the profits, it would give trained men an inducement to stick to their jobs,

wellpaid workers might save enough money to buy a tin lizzie; the first day Ford's announced that cleancut properlymarried American workers who wanted jobs had a chance to make five bucks a day (of course it turned out that there were strings to it; always there were strings to it)

such an enormous crowd waited outside the Highland Park plant

all through the zero January night

that there was a riot when the gates were opened; cops broke heads, jobhunters threw bricks; property, Henry Ford's own property, was destroyed. The company dicks[2] had to turn on the firehose to beat back the crowd.

The American Plan; automotive prosperity seeping down from above; it turned out there were strings to it.

But that five dollars a day

paid to good, clean American workmen

who didn't drink or smoke cigarettes or read or think,

and whose wives didn't take in boarders,

made America once more the Yukon of the sweated workers of the world;

made all the tin lizzies and the automotive age, and incidentally,

made Henry Ford the automobileer, the admirer of Edison, the birdlover,

the great American of his time.

_____

2. company dicks: Armed guards.

RESPONDING TO THE SELECTION

Your Response

1. What is your opinion of Dos Passos's style of writing? Do you recognize the "poetry" in it, or do you find it confusing? Explain.
2. If Dos Passos were alive today, what current public figures might he include in an update of *U.S.A.*? Why?

Recalling

3. (a) What did the young Henry Ford like? (b) What did he dislike?
4. How did Ford think he could make "the big money"?

Interpreting

5. (a) What details in the excerpt at the beginning of the selection make it clear that the American public knew very little about automobiles in 1900? (b) How is the portrayal of Ford in this excerpt different from the way he is portrayed in the rest of the selection?
6. Find two examples of Dos Passos's use of repetition to emphasize important ideas.
7. (a) What is unconventional about the form of the final sentence? (b) How does the form help to strengthen our final impression of Ford?

Analyzing

8. Dos Passos suggests that a person's accomplishments may reveal little about his or her character. Explain why you do or do not agree with this suggestion.

ANALYZING LITERATURE

Understanding Biography

A **biography** is an account of a person's life written by another person. In an impressionistic biography, the writer focuses on conveying his or her impressions of the subject, rather than merely recounting the central events of that person's life. For example, in "Tin Lizzie" Dos Passos presents his impressions of Henry Ford.

1. What impression does Dos Passos convey of Ford as a young man?
2. How does Dos Passos suggest that Ford thought of his workers as little more than machines?

3. How is Ford's character reflected in his conception of the ideal worker?
4. Considering the impression of Ford conveyed in the selection, what is ironic, or surprising, about the final line?

CRITICAL THINKING AND READING

Recognizing the Writer's Attitude

Although Dos Passos mentions a number of Ford's achievements in this essay, the way in which they are presented and the way in which Ford's character is portrayed make it clear that Dos Passos actually has a very critical attitude toward Ford and his accomplishments. For example, Dos Passos conveys a negative impression of Ford when he writes that what Ford "liked to do was to tend the machinery and let the others do the heavy work."

Find three other passages that reveal Dos Passos's critical attitude toward Ford.

THINKING AND WRITING

Writing an Impressionistic Biography

Using the list of facts you prepared before reading the selection, write an impressionistic biography. As you are writing, focus on presenting details that convey your impressions of the subject's character. When you finish writing, reread your biography to make sure it conveys the proper impression. After making any necessary revisions, proofread your biography and share it with your classmates.

LEARNING OPTIONS

1. **Writing.** Imagine that you are a teenager in 1909 and your family is among the first to get a "tin lizzie." How does it change your life? In a brief letter to a friend, describe how it feels to cruise the street in your new set of wheels.
2. **Art.** Join Henry Ford and John Dos Passos's feature writer in touting the automobileer's "steed." Design an ad to promote the first Model T. In your ad try to create an image of the car (or the car buyer) that will appeal to the American public.

E. B. WHITE

1899–1985

Known for his precise, direct style, E(lwyn) B(rooks) White is generally regarded as one of the most important American essayists of the twentieth century. In fact, White's work is still the standard against which the work of many of today's essayists is judged.

After growing up in Mount Vernon, New York, White attended Cornell University. There, he studied literature and served as the editor of the Cornell *Daily Sun*. Several years after his graduation, White joined the staff of *The New Yorker* magazine. His humorous, topical essays helped to establish *The New Yorker* as one of the nation's most successful general-interest magazines.

White produced essays for *The New Yorker* on a weekly basis until 1938. In these essays, many of which are collected in his books *Every Day Is Saturday* (1934) and *Quo Vadimus?* (1939), White used his talents as a humorist to explore numerous social and political themes. Influenced by the teachings of Henry David Thoreau, he strongly believed in individualism and simplicity. In an effort to simplify his own life, he bought a farmhouse in Maine and began spending much of his time there.

While continuing to contribute editorial essays to *The New Yorker,* White wrote for other magazines and published a variety of works: essays, poems, stories, and novels. From 1938 to 1943, he wrote a column for *Harper's* magazine called "One Man's Meat," in which he explored the conflicts of modern life and his decision to move to the country. He published these essays in *One Man's Meat* in 1942. He went on to publish several other collections of his writing, including *The Wild Flag* (1946), *Here Is New York* (1949), *The Second Tree From the Corner* (1954), and *The Points of My Compass* (1962). He also wrote two beloved children's books, *Stuart Little* (1945) and *Charlotte's Web* (1952). Always interested in humor, White collaborated with his wife, Katherine, in compiling the popular anthology *A Subtreasury of American Humor* (1941). A brilliant stylist in writing, he revised *The Elements of Style,* the classic manual of writing by William Strunk, Jr.

"Walden," an essay from *One Man's Meat,* reflects White's interest in Thoreau and his concern regarding the increasing complexity of modern life. The essay also demonstrates how White's belief in simplicity is reflected in his writing style.

GUIDE FOR INTERPRETING

Walden

Literary Forms

Personal Essays. A personal essay is an informal essay that focuses on a subject that is, at least to some extent, autobiographical.
Personal essays are prose works written in a relaxed, intimate, conversational style. They are generally brief and focus on a limited
topic. Despite their narrow focus, personal essays are loosely organized, with the writer at times digressing from the topic to express
opinions or discuss related matters. Because of their autobiographical nature, personal essays generally reveal something about the
writer's personality. "Walden," for example, reveals White's belief in
simplicity.

Focus

"Walden" is written in the form of a letter addressed to Henry David
Thoreau, the writer who most influenced White's work. Think of a
writer whose work has had a powerful effect on you. Then jot down
thoughts you would include in a letter to this writer, discussing the
ways in which his or her work affected you.

Primary Source

Style is an important element in essays. White's style is a good guide
to his personality and beliefs. An advocate of a simple, clear, direct
style, White advised inexperienced writers not to try to impress readers with excessively elaborate ornamental prose. In a chapter he
added to *Elements of Style,* he wrote:

> Young writers often suppose that style is a garnish for
> the meat of prose, a sauce by which a dull dish is made
> palatable. Style has no such separate entity; it is nonde-
> tachable, unfilterable. The beginner should approach style
> warily, realizing that it is himself he is approaching, no other;
> and he should begin by turning resolutely away from all de-
> vices that are popularly believed to indicate style—all man-
> nerisms, tricks, adornments. The approach to style is by way
> of plainness, simplicity, orderliness, sincerity.

Walden

E. B. White

June 1939

Miss Nims, take a letter to Henry David Thoreau. Dear Henry: I thought of you the other afternoon as I was approaching Concord doing fifty on Route 62. That is a high speed at which to hold a philosopher in one's mind, but in this century we are a nimble bunch.

On one of the lawns in the outskirts of the village a woman was cutting the grass with a motorized lawn mower. What made me think of you was that the machine had rather got away from her, although she was game enough, and in the brief glimpse I had of the scene it appeared to me that the lawn was mowing the lady. She kept a tight grip on the handles, which throbbed violently with every explosion of the one-cylinder motor, and as she sheered around bushes and lurched along at a reluctant trot behind her impetuous servant, she looked like a puppy who had grabbed something that was too much for him. Concord hasn't changed much, Henry; the farm implements and the animals still have the upper hand.

I may as well admit that I was journeying to Concord with the deliberate intention of visiting your woods; for although I have never knelt at the grave of a philosopher nor placed wreaths on moldy poets, and have often gone a mile out of my way to avoid some place of historical interest, I have always wanted to see Walden Pond. The account which you left of your sojourn there is, you will be amused to learn, a document of increasing pertinence; each year it seems to gain a little headway, as the world loses ground. We may all be transcendental yet, whether we like it or not. As our common complexities increase, any tale of individual simplicity (and yours is the best written and the cockiest) acquires a new fascination; as our goods accumulate, but not our well-being, your report of an existence without material adornment takes on a certain awkward credibility.

My purpose in going to Walden Pond, like yours, was not to live cheaply or to live dearly there, but to transact some private business with the fewest obstacles. Approaching Concord, doing forty, doing forty-five, doing fifty, the steering wheel held snug in my palms, the highway held grimly in my vision, the crown of the road now serving me (on the righthand curves), now defeating me (on the lefthand curves), I began to rouse myself from the stupefaction which a day's motor journey induces. It was a delicious evening, Henry, when the whole body is one sense, and imbibes delight through every pore, if I may coin a phrase. Fields were richly brown where the harrow, drawn by the stripped Ford, had lately sunk its teeth; pastures were green; and overhead the sky had that same everlasting great look which you will find on Page 144 of the Oxford pocket edition.[1] I could feel the road entering me, through tire, wheel, spring, and cushion; shall I not have intelligence with earth

---

1. Oxford pocket edition: An edition of Thoreau's *Walden* published by the Oxford University Press.

too? Am I not partly leaves and vegetable mold myself?—a man of infinite horsepower, yet partly leaves.

Stay with me on 62 and it will take you into Concord. As I say, it was a delicious evening. The snake had come forth to die in a bloody S on the highway, the wheel upon its head, its bowels flat now and exposed. The turtle had come up too to cross the road and die in the attempt, its hard shell smashed under the rubber blow, its intestinal yearning (for the other side of the road) forever squashed. There was a sign by the wayside which announced that the road had a "cotton surface." You wouldn't know what that is, but neither, for that matter, did I. There is a cryptic ingredient in many of our modern improvements—we are awed and pleased without knowing quite what we are enjoying. It is something to be traveling on a road with a cotton surface.

The civilization round Concord today is an odd distillation of city, village, farm, and manor. The houses, yards, fields look not quite suburban, not quite rural. Under the bronze beech and the blue spruce of the departed baron grazes the milch[2] goat of the heirs. Under the porte-cochère[3] stands the reconditioned station wagon; under the grape arbor sit the puppies for sale. (But why do

---

2. **milch** *adj.*: Milk-giving.
3. **porte-cochère** (pôrt' kō shâr'): Carport.

men degenerate ever? What makes families run out?)

It was June and everywhere June was publishing her immemorial stanza; in the lilacs, in the syringa,[4] in the freshly edged paths and the sweetness of moist beloved gardens, and the little wire wickets that preserve the tulips' front. Farmers were already moving the fruits of their toil into their yards, arranging the rhubarb, the asparagus, the strictly fresh eggs on the painted stands under the little shed roofs with the patent shingles. And though it was almost a hundred years since you had taken your ax and started cutting out your home on Walden Pond, I was interested to observe that the philosophical spirit was still alive in Massachusetts: in the center of a vacant lot some boys were assembling the framework of a rude shelter, their whole mind and skill concentrated in the rather inauspicious helter-skeleton of studs and rafters. They too were escaping from town, to live naturally, in a rich blend of savagery and philosophy.

That evening, after supper at the inn, I strolled out into the twilight to dream my shapeless transcendental dreams and see that the car was locked up for the night (first open the right front door, then reach over, straining, and pull up the handles of the left rear and the left front till you hear the click, then the handle of the right rear, then shut the right front but open it again, remembering that the key is still in the ignition switch, remove the key, shut the right front again with a bang, push the tiny keyhole cover to one side, insert key, turn, and withdraw). It is what we all do, Henry. It is called locking the car. It is said to confuse thieves and keep them from making off with the laprobe. Four doors to lock behind one robe. The driver himself never uses a laprobe, the free movement of his legs being vital to the operation of the vehicle; so that when he locks the car it is a pure and unselfish act. I have in my life gained very little essential heat from laprobes, yet I have ever been at pains to lock them up.

The evening was full of sounds, some of which would have stirred your memory. The robins still love the elms of New England villages at sundown. There is enough of the thrush in them to make song inevitable at the end of day, and enough of the tramp to make them hang round the dwellings of men. A robin, like many another American, dearly loves a white house with green blinds. Concord is still full of them.

Your fellow townsmen were stirring abroad—not many afoot, most of them in their cars; and the sound which they made in Concord at evening was a rustling and a whispering. The sound lacks steadfastness and is wholly unlike that of a train. A train, as you know who lived so near the Fitchburg line, whistles once or twice sadly and is gone, trailing a memory in smoke, soothing to ear and mind. Automobiles, skirting a village green, are like flies that have gained the inner ear—they buzz, cease, pause, start, shift, stop, halt, brake, and the whole effect is a nervous polytone curiously disturbing.

As I wandered along, the toc toc of ping pong balls drifted from an attic window. In front of the Reuben Brown house a Buick was drawn up. At the wheel, motionless, his hat upon his head, a man sat, listening to Amos and Andy[5] on the radio (it is a drama of many scenes and without an end). The deep voice of Andrew Brown, emerging from the car, although it originated more than two hundred miles away, was unstrained by distance. When you used to sit on the shore of your pond on Sunday morning, listening to the church bells of Acton and Concord, you were aware of the excellent filter of the intervening atmosphere. Science has attended to that, and sound now maintains its intensity without regard for distance. Properly sponsored, it goes on forever.

---

4. syringa (sə riŋ′ gə) n.: A plant with large clusters of tiny white flowers.

5. Amos and Andy: A popular radio show in the 1930's and 1940's.

A fire engine, out for a trial spin, roared past Emerson's house, hot with readiness for public duty. Over the barn roofs the martins dipped and chittered. A swarthy daughter of an asparagus grower, in culottes, shirt, and bandanna, pedaled past on her bicycle. It was indeed a delicious evening, and I returned to the inn (I believe it was your house once) to rock with the old ladies on the concrete veranda.

Next morning early I started afoot for Walden, out Main Street and down Thoreau, past the depot and the Minuteman Chevrolet Company. The morning was fresh, and in a bean field along the way I flushed an agriculturalist, quietly studying his beans. Thoreau Street soon joined Number 126, an artery of the State. We number our highways nowadays, our speed being so great we can remember little of their quality or character and are lucky to remember their number. (Men have an indistinct notion that if they keep up this activity long enough all will at length ride somewhere, in next to no time.) Your pond is on 126.

I knew I must be nearing your woodland retreat when the Golden Pheasant lunchroom came into view—Sealtest ice cream, toasted sandwiches, hot frankfurters, waffles, tonics, and lunches. Were I the proprietor, I should add rice, Indian meal, and molasses[6]—just for old time's sake. The Pheasant, incidentally, is for sale: a chance for some nature lover who wishes to set himself up beside a pond in the Concord atmosphere and live deliberately, fronting only the essential facts of life on Number 126. Beyond the Pheasant was a place called Walden Breezes, an oasis whose porch pillars were made of old green shutters sawed into lengths. On the porch was a distorting mirror, to give the traveler a comical image of himself, who had miraculously learned to gaze in an ordinary glass without smiling. Behind the Breezes, in a sun-parched clearing, dwelt your philo-sophical descendants in their trailers, each trailer the size of your hut, but all grouped together for the sake of congeniality. Trailer people leave the city, as you did, to discover solitude and in any weather, at any hour of the day or night, to improve the nick of time; but they soon collect in villages and get bogged deeper in the mud than ever. The camp behind Walden Breezes was just rousing itself to the morning. The ground was packed hard under the heel, and the sun came through the clearing to bake the soil and enlarge the wry smell of cramped housekeeping. Cushman's bakery truck had stopped to deliver an early basket of rolls. A camp dog, seeing me in the road, barked petulantly. A man emerged from one of the trailers and set forth with a bucket to draw water from some forest tap.

Leaving the highway I turned off into the woods toward the pond, which was apparent through the foliage. The floor of the forest was strewn with dried old oak leaves and *Transcript*s.[7] From beneath the flattened popcorn wrapper (*granum explosum*) peeped the frail violet. I followed a footpath and descended to the water's edge. The pond lay clear and blue in the morning light, as you have seen it so many times. In the shallows a man's waterlogged shirt undulated gently. A few flies came out to greet me and convoy me to your cove, past the No Bathing signs on which the fellows and the girls had scrawled their names. I felt strangely excited suddenly to be snooping around your premises, tiptoeing along watchfully, as though not to tread by mistake upon the intervening century. Before I got to the cove I heard something which seemed to me quite wonderful: I heard your frog, a full, clear *troonk*, guiding me, still hoarse and solemn, bridging the years as the robins had bridged them in the sweetness of the village evening. But he soon quit, and I came on a couple of young boys throwing stones at him.

---

6. rice . . . molasses: The main components of Thoreau's diet at Walden Pond.

7. Transcripts: *The Evening Transcript,* a Boston newspaper that is no longer published.

Your front yard is marked by a bronze tablet set in a stone. Four small granite posts, a few feet away, show where the house was. On top of the tablet was a pair of faded blue bathing trunks with a white stripe. Back of it is a pile of stones, a sort of cairn[8] left by your visitors as a tribute I suppose. It is a rather ugly little heap of stones, Henry. In fact the hillside itself seems faded, brow-beaten; a few tall skinny pines, bare of lower limbs, a smattering of young maples in suitable green, some birches and oaks, and a number of trees felled by the last big wind. It was from the bole of one of these fallen pines, torn up by the roots, that I extracted the stone which I added to the cairn—a sentimental act in which I was interrupted by a small terrier from a nearby picnic group, who confronted me and wanted to know about the stone.

I sat down for a while on one of the posts of your house to listen to the bluebottles[9] and the dragonflies. The invaded glade sprawled shabby and mean at my feet, but the flies were tuned to the old vibration. There were the remains of a fire in your ruins, but I doubt that it was yours; also two beer bottles trodden into the soil and become part of earth. A young oak had taken root in your house, and two or three ferns, unrolling like the ticklers at a banquet. The only other furnishings were a DuBarry pattern sheet, a page torn from a picture magazine, and some crusts in wax paper.

Before I quit I walked clear round the pond and found the place where you used to sit on the northeast side to get the sun in the fall, and the beach where you got sand for scrubbing your floor. On the eastern side of the pond, where the highway borders it, the State has built dressing rooms for swimmers, a float with diving towers, drinking fountains of porcelain, and rowboats for hire. The pond is in fact a State Preserve,

and carries a twenty-dollar fine for picking wild flowers, a decree signed in all solemnity by your fellow citizens Walter C. Wardwell, Erson B. Barlow, and Nathaniel I. Bowditch. There was a smell of creosote where they had been building a wide wooden stairway to the road and the parking area. Swimmers and boaters were arriving; bodies plunged vigorously into the water and emerged wet and beautiful in the bright air. As I left, a boatload of town boys were splashing about in mid-pond, kidding and fooling, the young fellows singing at the tops of their lungs in a wild chorus:

> Amer-ica, Amer-i-ca, God shed his
>   grace on thee,
> And crown thy good with brother-
>   hood
> From sea to shi-ning sea!

I walked back to town along the railroad, following your custom. The rails were expanding noisily in the hot sun, and on the slope of the roadbed the wild grape and the blackberry sent up their creepers to the track.

The expense of my brief sojourn in Concord was:

Canvas shoes $1.95		
Baseball bat .... .25	}	gifts to
Left-handed fielder's		take back
glove 1.25		to a boy
Hotel and meals 4.25		
In all $7.70		

As you see, this amount was almost what you spent for food for eight months. I cannot defend the shoes or the expenditure for shelter and food: they reveal a meanness and grossness in my nature which you would find contemptible. The baseball equipment, however, is the kind of impediment with which you were never on even terms. You must remember that the house where you practiced the sort of economy which I respect was haunted only by mice and squirrels. You never had to cope with a shortstop.

---

8. **cairn** (kern) n.: A conical heap of stones built as a monument or landmark.
9. **bluebottles** n.: Blue-colored blowflies.

R ESPONDING TO THE SELECTION

Your Response

1. What do you like most about this "letter" to Thoreau? Explain.
2. Would you be interested in making a pilgrimage to Walden Pond? Why or why not?

Recalling

3. What is White's purpose in going to Concord?
4. According to White, what happens as "our common complexities increase" and "our goods accumulate"?
5. How does White describe the civilization around Concord?
6. (a) What marks Thoreau's "front yard"? (b) What shows where his house was located?
7. How does the expense of White's "brief sojourn in Concord" compare with the amount of money Thoreau spent on food while at Walden Pond?

Interpreting

8. (a) What does White's observation of the woman mowing her lawn indicate about humanity's relationship to machines? (b) What do the descriptions of the dead animals on the highway reveal about the effects of modernization on nature?
9. White writes, "Under the bronze beech and the blue spruce of the departed baron grazes the milch goat of the heirs." (a) Who is the departed baron? (b) Who are the heirs?
10. What does this selection reveal about the ways in which Concord and Walden Pond have changed since Thoreau's time?

Applying

11. In what ways would you imagine Concord and Walden Pond have changed since White's visit?

A NALYZING LITERATURE

Understanding Personal Essays

A **personal essay** is a type of informal essay that focuses on a subject that is at least to some extent autobiographical. Because of their autobiographical nature, personal essays generally reveal something about the writer's personality.

1. What does this essay reveal about White's attitude toward Thoreau?
2. What does the essay reveal about White's attitude toward the modern world?
3. List three writers you think White would admire. Explain the reasons for your choices.

T HINKING AND WRITING

Comparing and Contrasting Essays

Write an essay in which you discuss the ways in which Walden Pond changed from Thoreau's time to White's time. Start by reviewing the excerpt from Thoreau's *Walden* on page 254. Take note of any details describing the pond's appearance. Then review "Walden," taking note of the contrast in the way White describes the pond. When you write your essay, discuss how the contrasts in the pond's appearance reflect the changes that took place in society as a whole. After you finish writing, revise and proofread your essay.

L EARNING OPTIONS

1. **Writing.** If Thoreau could have dictated a response to E. B. White, what might he have said? Consider Thoreau's personality and philosophy as revealed through his biography and writings on pages 252–263; then "take a letter" to E. B. White. Comment on White's observations in his letter of June 1939.

2. **Speaking and Listening.** Try out for a one-person show about E. B. White. Audition for the starring (and only) role by reading aloud excerpts from "Walden." Try to capture White's wry tone in your reading.

3. **Art.** White's essays and editorials helped set the tone of *The New Yorker,* a magazine known for its literature, its columns, and its cartoons. Locate a current or past issue of the magazine and study the cartoons. Then, in the style of *The New Yorker,* illustrate your favorite line from "Walden." Either draw a cartoon or give detailed directions for an artist to follow.

JAMES THURBER

1894–1961

A noted humorist, James Thurber wrote essays and short stories that generally evolved from his own experiences. In his humorous autobiographical sketches, such as "The Night the Ghost Got In," Thurber embellished the facts and described events in an amusing manner. In his short stories, Thurber created characters who struggled awkwardly against the unpleasant realities of life.

Born in Columbus, Ohio, Thurber attended Ohio State University. Following his graduation, he began a career in journalism, accepting a job as a newspaper reporter in Columbus. In 1927 he joined the staff of the magazine *The New Yorker*. Thurber remained associated with *The New Yorker* for the remainder of his life, contributing stories, essays, and cartoons. At *The New Yorker* he also worked closely with the celebrated writer E. B. White, who influenced his writing. Thurber, White, and other *New Yorker* writers such as Frank Sullivan, Robert Benchley, and S. J. Perelman helped establish a grand tradition of modern American humor. Thurber has written of humor, "Humor is emotional chaos remembered in tranquility." He has also written, "As brevity is the soul of wit, form, it seems to me, is the heart of humor and the salvation of comedy."

During the course of his career, Thurber published a great many books. Some of his books, such as *The Owl in the Attic and Other Perplexities* (1931) and *The Seal in the Bedroom and Other Predicaments* (1932), contain a mixture of short stories, parodies, and cartoons. Other books, including *My Life and Hard Times,* are composed of sketches about his childhood. He also wrote children's stories and collaborated with Elliot Nugent in writing a successful play, *The Male Animal* (1940). Thurber's best-known work is his short story, "The Secret Life of Walter Mitty," which was first published in *The New Yorker* in 1939.

"The Secret Life of Walter Mitty" is characteristic of Thurber's humor. It is the story of a middle-aged man who, unhappy with his everyday life, quietly dreams a life of adventure and heroism for himself. In all of Thurber's most humorous pieces, unhappiness is never far away. Commenting on how humorists get their inspiration, Thurber said, "The little wheels of invention are set in motion by the damp hand of melancholy." The characters in Thurber's essays, stories, and drawings seem to accept the puzzling difficulties of their lives with resignation, even as they explore little escapes.

During the last twenty years of his life, Thurber's vision failed, and he eventually became completely blind. He continued to write and draw as well as he could. Yet his later work is often tinged with a sense of bitterness.

Writers' Techniques

The Night the Ghost Got In

Humor. In literature, humor refers to writing that attempts to evoke laughter. To accomplish this purpose, writers must have the ability to perceive the ridiculous, comical, or ludicrous aspects of an incident, situation, or personality and to depict them in an amusing manner. In "The Night the Ghost Got In," for example, Thurber captures the humorous idiosyncrasies of his family members in depicting an amusing, chaotic series of events.

Humorists often exaggerate details and embellish facts in their work. By using exaggeration, a writer can make an amusing event or character seem even more humorous, or a writer can use exaggeration to create humor in an otherwise unamusing situation. For example, in "The Night the Ghost Got In," Thurber uses exaggeration to accentuate the amusing character traits of his family members.

Another technique that is frequently used by humorists is malapropism—the humorous misuse of words. For example, instead of having a character say that someone "*instigated* a riot," a writer might have the character comment that someone "*insinuated* a riot."

Commentary

In narrating the chaotic events that take place in his house in "The Night the Ghost Got In," Thurber never seems to lose his head. In fact, in reading the story, you may find Thurber's responses to be humorously understated. A houseful of policemen, several mischievous ghosts, a hysterical mother, a grandfather who thinks he is being attacked by "Meade's army" and shoots in defense—these elicit no more emotional a comment than "When I got to the attic, things were pretty confused."

Writing about this typically Thurberesque response to upheaval, critic James D. Hart commented that Thurber's "fantastic people and animals move with sad persistence through incredible upsets, and are all misshapen and repressed, products of a malignant fate which they stoically survive or combat." Everyone in this story seems a little bizarre, but, as Thurber suggests, that is because life is very bizarre. The way to arrive at the position of calm and acceptance occupied by Thurber's narrator in this story is to learn to accept that, as the old saying goes, truth is stranger than fiction.

Do you know of true incidents that are "stranger than fiction"?

Focus

Why do we laugh when someone slips on a banana peel? Why do we find it funny when someone is hit in the face by a custard pie? Freewrite, exploring your ideas on what makes someone laugh.

The Night the Ghost Got In

James Thurber

The ghost that got into our house on the night of November 17, 1915, raised such a hullabaloo of misunderstandings that I am sorry I didn't just let it keep on walking, and go to bed. Its advent caused my mother to throw a shoe through a window of the house next door and ended up with my grandfather shooting a patrolman. I am sorry, therefore, as I have said, that I ever paid any attention to the footsteps.

They began about a quarter past one o'clock in the morning, a rhythmic, quick-cadenced walking around the dining-room table. My mother was asleep in one room upstairs, my brother Herman in another; grandfather was in the attic, in the old wal-

nut bed which, as you will remember, once fell on my father. I had just stepped out of the bathtub and was busily rubbing myself with a towel when I heard the steps. They were the steps of a man walking rapidly around the dining-room table downstairs. The light from the bathroom shone down the back steps, which dropped directly into the dining-room; I could see the faint shine of plates on the plate-rail; I couldn't see the table. The steps kept going round and round the table; at regular intervals a board creaked, when it was trod upon. I supposed at first that it was my father or my brother Roy, who had gone to Indianapolis but were expected home at any time. I suspected next

"The ghost got into our house on the night of November 17, 1915 and raised such a hullabaloo of misunderstandings. . . ."

that it was a burglar. It did not enter my mind until later that it was a ghost.

After the walking had gone on for perhaps three minutes, I tiptoed to Herman's room. "Psst!" I hissed, in the dark, shaking him. "Awp," he said, in the low, hopeless tone of a despondent beagle—he always half suspected that something would "get him" in the night. I told him who I was. "There's something downstairs!" I said. He got up and followed me to the head of the back staircase. We listened together. There was no sound. The steps had ceased. Herman looked at me in some alarm: I had only the bath towel around my waist. He wanted to go back to bed, but I gripped his arm. "There's something down there!" I said. Instantly the steps began again, circled the dining-room table like a man running, and started up the stairs toward us, heavily, two at a time. The light still shone palely down the stairs; we saw nothing coming; we only heard the steps. Herman rushed to his room and slammed the door. I slammed shut the door at the stairs top and held my knee against it. After a long minute, I slowly opened it again. There was nothing there. There was no sound. None of us ever heard the ghost again.

The slamming of the doors had aroused mother: she peered out of her room. "What on earth are you boys doing?" she demanded. Herman ventured out of his room. "Nothing," he said, gruffly, but he was, in color, a light green. "What was all that running around downstairs?" said mother. So she had heard the steps, too! We just looked at her. "Burglars!" she shouted intuitively. I tried to quiet her by starting lightly downstairs.

"Come on, Herman," I said.

"I'll stay with Mother," he said. "She's all excited."

I stepped back onto the landing.

"Don't either of you go a step," said mother. "We'll call the police." Since the phone was downstairs, I didn't see how we were going to call the police—nor did I want the police—but mother made one of her quick, incomparable decisions. She flung up a window of her bedroom which faced the bedroom windows of the house of a neighbor, picked up a shoe, and whammed it through a pane of glass across the narrow space that separated the two houses. Glass tinkled into the bedroom occupied by a retired engraver named Bodwell and his wife. Bodwell had been for some years in rather a bad way and was subject to mild "attacks." Most everybody we knew or lived near had *some* kind of attacks.

It was now about two o'clock of a moonless night; clouds hung black and low. Bodwell was at the window in a minute, shouting, frothing a little, shaking his fist. "We'll sell the house and go back to Peoria," we could hear Mrs. Bodwell saying. It was some time before mother "got through" to Bodwell. "Burglars!" she shouted. "Burglars in the house!" Herman and I hadn't dared to tell her that it was not burglars but ghosts, for she was even more afraid of ghosts than of burglars. Bodwell at first thought that she meant there were burglars in his house, but finally he quieted down and called the police for us over an extension phone by his bed. After he had disappeared from the window, mother suddenly made as if to throw another shoe, not because there was further need of it, but, as she later explained, because the thrill of heaving a shoe through a window glass had enormously taken her fancy. I prevented her.

The police were on hand in a commendably short time: a Ford sedan full of them, two on motorcycles, and a patrol wagon with about eight in it and a few reporters. They began banging at our front door. Flashlights shot streaks of gleam up and down the walls, across the yard, down the walk between our house and Bodwell's. "Open up!" cried a hoarse voice. "We're men from Headquarters!" I wanted to go down and let them in, since there they were, but mother wouldn't hear of it. "You haven't a stitch on," she pointed out. "You'd catch your death." I wound the towel around me again. Finally the cops put their shoulders to our big heavy

THE NIGHT THE GHOST GOT IN
*Copyright © 1933, 1961, James Thurber,
From* My Life and Hard Times, *published by
Harper & Row.*

front door with its thick beveled glass and broke it in: I could hear a rending of wood and a splash of glass on the floor of the hall. Their lights played all over the living-room and crisscrossed nervously in the dining-room, stabbed into hallways, shot up the front stairs and finally up the back. They caught me standing in my towel at the top. A heavy policeman bounded up the steps. "Who are you?" he demanded. "I live here," I said. "Well, whattsa matta, ya hot?" he asked. I was, as a matter of fact, cold; I went to my room and pulled on some trousers. On my way out, a cop stuck a gun into my ribs. "Whatta you doin' here?" he demanded. "I live here," I said.

The officer in charge reported to mother. "No sign of nobody, lady," he said. "Musta got away—whatt'd he look like?" "There were two or three of them," mother said, "whooping and carrying on and slamming doors." "Funny, said the cop. "All ya windows and doors was locked on the inside tight as a tick."

Downstairs, we could hear the tromping of the other police. Police were all over the place; doors were yanked open, drawers were yanked open, windows were shot up and pulled down, furniture fell with dull thumps. A half-dozen policemen emerged out of the darkness of the front hallway upstairs. They began to ransack the floor: pulled beds away from walls, tore clothes off hooks in the closets, pulled suitcases and boxes off shelves. One of them found an old zither[1] that Roy had won in a pool tournament. "Looky here, Joe," he said, strumming it with a big paw. The cop named Joe took it and turned it over. "What is it?" he asked me. "It's an old zither our guinea pig used to sleep on," I said. It was true that a pet guinea pig we once had would never sleep anywhere except on the zither, but I should never have said so. Joe and the other cop looked at me a long time. They put the zither back on a shelf.

"No sign o' nuthin'," said the cop who

1. **zither** (ziṭh'ər) *n.*: A musical instrument with thirty to forty strings stretched across a flat sound-board and played with the fingers.

had first spoken to mother. "This guy," he explained to the others, jerking a thumb at me, "was nekked. The lady seems historical." They all nodded, but said nothing; just looked at me. In the small silence we all heard a creaking in the attic. Grandfather was turning over in bed. "What's 'at?" snapped Joe. Five or six cops sprang for the attic door before I could intervene or explain. I realized that it would be bad if they burst in on grandfather unannounced, or even announced. He was going through a phase in which he believed that General Meade's men, under steady hammering by Stonewall Jackson, were beginning to retreat and even desert.

When I got to the attic, things were pretty confused. Grandfather had evidently jumped to the conclusion that the police were deserters from Meade's army, trying to hide away in his attic. He bounded out of bed wearing a long flannel nightgown over long woolen underwear, a nightcap, and a leather jacket around his chest. The cops must have realized at once that the indignant white-haired old man belonged in the house, but they had no chance to say so. "Back, ye cowardly dogs!" roared grandfather. "Back t' the lines, ye yellow, lily-livered cattle!" With that, he fetched the officer who found the zither a flat-handed smack alongside his head that sent him sprawling. The others beat a retreat, but not fast enough; grandfather grabbed Zither's gun from its holster and let fly. The report seemed to crack the rafters; smoke filled the attic. A cop cursed and shot his hand to his shoulder. Somehow, we all finally got downstairs again and locked the door against the old gentleman. He fired once or twice more in the darkness and then went back to bed. "That was grandfather," I explained to Joe, out of breath. "He thinks you're deserters." "I'll say he does," said Joe.

THE NIGHT THE GHOST GOT IN

The cops were reluctant to leave without getting their hands on somebody besides grandfather; the night had been distinctly a defeat for them. Furthermore, they obviously didn't like the "layout"; something looked—and I can see their viewpoint—phony. They began to poke into things again. A reporter, a thin-faced, wispy man, came up to me. I had put on one of mother's blouses, not being able to find anything else. The reporter looked at me with mingled suspicion and interest. "Just what the heck is the real lowdown here, Bud?" he asked. I decided to be frank with him. "We had ghosts," I said. He gazed at me a long time as if I were a slot machine into which he had, without results, dropped a nickel. Then he walked away. The cops followed him, the one grandfather shot holding his now-bandaged arm, cursing and blaspheming. "I'm gonna get my gun back from that old bird," said the zither-cop. "Yeh," said Joe. "You—and who else?" I told them I would bring it to the station house the next day.

"What was the matter with that one policeman?" mother asked, after they had gone. "Grandfather shot him," I said. "What for?" she demanded. I told her he was a deserter. "Of all things!" said mother. "He was such a nice-looking young man."

Grandfather was fresh as a daisy and full of jokes at breakfast next morning. We thought at first he had forgotten all about what had happened, but he hadn't. Over his third cup of coffee, he glared at Herman and me. "What was the idee of all them cops tarry-hootin' round the house last night?" he demanded. He had us there.

Commentary

People who do not write or draw are often curious about how writers and artists come up with ideas for their work. This amused Thurber a great deal, because often he did not come up with ideas for work but actually adjusted his ideas to match the work that appeared on the page. In a humorous essay called "The Lady on the Bookcase," Thurber described the role that accident and even confusion played in his creative process. He labeled this particular type of so-called inspiration the "Concept of the Purely Accidental and the Theory of Haphazard Determination." Under this category he put his famous drawing of a husband and wife in bed with a barking seal on the headboard.

In explaining how he came up with the drawing and caption, Thurber wrote, "The seal on top of the bed, then . . . started out to be a seal on a rock. The rock, in the process of being drawn, began to look like the head of a bed, so I made a bed out of it, put a man and wife in the bed, and stumbled onto the caption as easily and unexpectedly as the seal had stumbled into the bedroom."

"All right, have it your way—you heard a seal bark!"

RESPONDING TO THE SELECTION

Your Response

1. "The Night the Ghost Got In" is an autobiographical sketch. Does the main incident remind you even remotely of an event in your life? Are any of the characters reminiscent of anyone you know? Explain.
2. How do you react to "things that go bump in the night"?

Recalling

3. Describe what each character in the narrator's family does on the night that "the ghost" got into the house.

Interpreting

4. What role does the lack of communication among the characters play in precipitating the events described?
5. (a) What does the mother's desire to throw a second shoe through the neighbors' window reveal about her character? (b) What does her response to her son's explanation of the grandfather's actions reveal about her character?
6. (a) What is surprising about the question the grandfather asks at breakfast the next morning? (b) What does it reveal about his character?
7. How is Thurber's depiction of himself different from his depiction of the other characters?

Applying

8. Many of Thurber's stories are filled with eccentrics—people whose idiosyncrasies or peculiarities make them humorously unique. How do people react to eccentrics in real life? Explain your answer.

ANALYZING LITERATURE

Understanding Humor

In literature, **humor** refers to writing that attempts to evoke laughter. Humorists achieve this purpose by depicting comical incidents, situations, or personalities. For example, in "The Night the Ghost Got In," Thurber describes an improbable and humorous series of events involving a number of unusual characters.

1. What makes Thurber's mother an unusual and amusing character?
2. What makes Thurber's grandfather an unusual and amusing character?
3. What is comical about the behavior of the police officers?
4. What malapropism, or humorous misuse of words, does the policeman commit when he describes the mother's behavior?
5. (a) What is the usual reaction to hearing footsteps in the middle of the night? (b) How does the contrast between the usual reaction and the Thurber family's reaction add to the humor of the story?

CRITICAL THINKING AND READING

Recognizing Exaggeration

Humorists often exaggerate details and embellish facts in their work. For example, Thurber clearly exaggerates the number of police officers who showed up at his house.

1. Do you think the actions of the police officers are exaggerated? Why or why not?
2. Do you think the grandfather's personality and behavior are exaggerated? Why or why not?

THINKING AND WRITING

Writing a Humorous Essay

Write an essay describing a humorous incident that you experienced. (If you like, you may make up the incident.) Freewrite, describing an unusual predicament. Then write your essay, using exaggeration to add to the humor of your story. When you finish writing, revise your essay, making sure you have related events in chronological order. Proofread your essay and share it with your classmates.

LEARNING OPTION

Art. Study Thurber's cartoons in "The Night the Ghost Got In." Then draw a cartoon of your own to illustrate another incident from the story. In your drawing you might use exaggeration to visually convey Thurber's style of humor.

The Night the Ghost Got In 689

RICHARD WRIGHT

1908–1960

Early in his career, Richard Wright gained a reputation for the quality of his writing and the depth of his outrage at how whites treated African Americans in the United States. When he published his novel *Native Son* in 1940, it became an immediate bestseller. Reaching a broad audience that included thousands of white Americans, Wright shocked readers by relating the story of Bigger Thomas, an alienated black teenager from Chicago.

Unlike earlier black writers, Wright rejected the idea that literature must depict uplifting characters. It troubled him that his previous book, *Uncle Tom's Children,* had aroused pity in its readers. "I swore to myself," he said, "that if I ever wrote another book, no one would weep over it; that it would be so hard and deep that they would have to face it without the consolation of tears." Riveting and relentless, *Native Son* was a literary landmark, and Wright became the literary standard by which other black writers measured themselves.

The grandson of slaves, Wright was born in the Mississippi Cotton Belt. His childhood was bleak. After his father deserted the family, his mother was hard put to support her two children. Shifted from relative to relative, Wright was able to attend school regularly only for a period of three years. His hunger for reading was as great as his hunger for food, satisfied only when he left home in 1925 to work for an optical company in Memphis. There he borrowed a white coworker's library card and gained access to a public library that was closed to blacks. An avid reader, Wright particularly admired the novels of Theodore Dreiser and the social commentary of H. L. Mencken.

Wright made his way to Chicago in 1928, continuing to study on his own while supporting himself by working first in a cafeteria and then as a postal clerk. He began to establish himself as a writer with the publication of *Uncle Tom's Children* in 1938. Two years later *Native Son* appeared, and Wright became a national celebrity.

While his reputation grew with the publication of his autobiography, *Black Boy: A Record of Childhood and Youth* in 1945, fame and the wealth it brought did little to alter Wright's status as a "black boy" in white society. In 1947 he decided to move to Paris, where race posed fewer social obstacles. In France he wrote *The Outsider* and several other novels, but none of these quite matched his earlier work. He died an expatriate in 1960. An autobiographical account of his later years, *American Hunger,* was published after his death.

GUIDE FOR INTERPRETING

Writers' Techniques

from Black Boy: A Record of Childhood and Youth

Narration. Narration is writing that tells a story. Sometimes a story is so gripping that we never notice who is telling it. More often than not, the narrator, or speaker, helps determine just how effective the story is. "Call me Ishmael," commands the narrator of Herman Melville's *Moby-Dick,* immediately capturing our attention and drawing us into the story.

Like writers of fiction, writers of nonfiction also use narration—particularly to recount events and situations from their own lives. When a work focuses on describing a personal experience, it is sometimes referred to as a personal or **first-person narrative.** An autobiography is an example of a first-person narrative. In it the writer narrates his or her own life story, using the first-person pronoun *I.*

In Richard Wright's autobiography, *Black Boy,* the narrator is Wright himself, or, more correctly, the image of himself that he wishes to present to the reader. In narrating the story of his childhood and youth, Wright describes events as only he could, sharing what he felt and thought as a "black boy" in the Jim Crow South. For example, here is how he explains his decision to leave Memphis for a new life in Chicago:

> [T]he white South had never known me—never known what I thought, what I felt. The white South said that I had a 'place' in life. Well, I had never felt my 'place'; or, rather, my deepest instincts had always made me reject the 'place' to which the South assigned me. It never occurred to me that I was in any way an inferior being. And no word that I had ever heard fall from the lips of southern white men had ever made me really doubt the worth of my own humanity.

Focus

In this excerpt from *Black Boy,* Richard Wright recounts a critical event in his life. Write about something important that has happened to you. What happened? How did you feel about it? Would you consider it a turning point in your life?

from **Black Boy: A Record of Childhood and Youth**

Richard Wright

The eighth grade days flowed in their hungry path and I grew more conscious of myself; I sat in classes, bored, wondering, dreaming. One long dry afternoon I took out my composition book and told myself that I would write a story; it was sheer idleness that led me to it. What would the story be about? It resolved itself into a plot about a villain who wanted a widow's home and I called it *The Voodoo of Hell's Half-Acre.* It was crudely atmospheric, emotional, intuitively psychological, and stemmed from pure feeling. I finished it in three days and then wondered what to do with it.

The local Negro newspaper! That's it . . . I sailed into the office and shoved my ragged composition book under the nose of the man who called himself the editor.

"What is that?" he asked.

"A story," I said.

"A news story?"

"No, fiction."

"All right. I'll read it," he said.

He pushed my composition book back on his desk and looked at me curiously, sucking at his pipe.

"But I want you to read it *now,*" I said.

He blinked. I had no idea how newspapers were run. I thought that one took a story to an editor and he sat down then and there and read it and said yes or no.

"I'll read this and let you know about it tomorrow," he said.

I was disappointed; I had taken time to write it and he seemed distant and uninterested.

"Give me the story," I said, reaching for it.

He turned from me, took up the book and read ten pages or more.

"Won't you come in tomorrow?" he asked. "I'll have it finished then."

I honestly relented.

"All right," I said. "I'll stop in tomorrow."

I left with the conviction that he would not read it. Now, where else could I take it after he had turned it down? The next afternoon, en route[1] to my job, I stepped into the newspaper office.

"Where's my story?" I asked.

"It's in galleys,"[2] he said.

"What's that?" I asked; I did not know what galleys were.

"It's set up in type," he said. "We're publishing it."

"How much money will I get?" I asked, excited.

"We can't pay for manuscript," he said.

"But you sell your papers for money," I said with logic.

"Yes, but we're young in business," he explained.

---

1. en route (en root′): On the way.
2. galleys (gal′ ēz) *n.*: Preliminary prints taken from set type.

"But you're asking me to *give* you my story, but you don't *give* your papers away," I said.

He laughed.

"Look, you're just starting. This story will put your name before our readers. Now, that's something," he said.

"But if the story is good enough to sell to your readers, then you ought to give me some of the money you get from it," I insisted.

He laughed again and I sensed that I was amusing him.

"I'm going to offer you something more valuable than money," he said. "I'll give you a chance to learn to write."

I was pleased, but I still thought he was taking advantage of me.

"When will you publish my story?"

"I'm dividing it into three installments," he said. "The first installment appears this week. But the main thing is this: Will you get news for me on a space rate basis?"

"I work mornings and evening for three dollars a week," I said.

"Oh," he said. "Then you better keep that. But what are you doing this summer?"

"Nothing."

"Then come to see me before you take another job," he said. "And write some more stories."

A few days later my classmates came to me with baffled eyes, holding copies of the *Southern Register* in their hands.

"Did you really write that story?" they asked me.

"Yes."

"Why?"

"Because I wanted to."

"Where did you get it from?"

"I made it up."

"You didn't. You copied it out of a book."

"If I had, no one would publish it."

"But what are they publishing it for?"

"So people can read it."

"Who told you to do that?"

"Nobody."

"Then why did you do it?"

"Because I wanted to," I said again.

They were convinced that I had not told them the truth. We had never had any instruction in literary matters at school; the literature of the nation or the Negro had never been mentioned. My schoolmates could not understand why anyone would want to write a story; and, above all, they could not understand why I had called it *The Voodoo of Hell's Half-Acre*. The mood out of which a story was written was the most alien thing conceivable to them. They looked at me with new eyes, and a distance, a suspiciousness came between us. If I had thought anything in writing the story, I had thought that perhaps it would make me more acceptable to them, and now it was cutting me off from them more completely than ever.

At home the effects were no less disturbing. Granny came into my room early one morning and sat on the edge of my bed.

"Richard, what is this you're putting in the papers?" she asked.

"A story," I said.

"About what?"

"It's just a story, granny."

"But they tell me it's been in three times."

"It's the same story. It's in three parts."

"But what's it about?" she insisted.

I hedged, fearful of getting into a religious argument.

"It's just a story I made up," I said.

"Then it's a lie," she said. . . .

"Granny, please . . . Everybody knows that the story isn't true, but . . . "

"Then why write it?" she asked.

"Because people might want to read it."

"That's the Devil's work," she said and left.

My mother also was worried.

"Son, you ought to be more serious," she said. "You're growing up now and you won't be able to get jobs if you let people think that you're weak-minded. Suppose the superintendent of schools would ask you to teach here in Jackson, and he found out that you had been writing stories?"

I could not answer her.

"I'll be all right, mama," I said.

Uncle Tom, though surprised, was highly critical and contemptuous. The story had no point, he said. And whoever heard of a story by the title of *The Voodoo of Hell's Half-Acre*? Aunt Addie said that it was a sin for anyone to use the word "hell" and that what was wrong with me was that I had nobody to guide me. She blamed the whole thing upon my upbringing.

In the end I was so angry that I refused to talk about the story. From no quarter, with the exception of the Negro newspaper editor, had there come a single encouraging word. It was rumored that the principal wanted to know why I had used the word "hell." I felt that I had committed a crime. Had I been conscious of the full extent to which I was pushing against the current of my environment, I would have been frightened altogether out of my attempts at writing. But my reactions were limited to the attitude of the people about me, and I did not speculate or generalize.

I dreamed of going north and writing books, novels. The North symbolized to me all that I had not felt and seen; it had no relation whatever to what actually existed. Yet, by imagining a place where everything was possible, I kept hope alive in me. But where had I got this notion of doing something in the future, of going away from home and accomplishing something that would be recognized by others? I had, of course, read my Horatio Alger[3] stories, my pulp stories,[4] and I knew my Get-Rich-Quick Wallingford[5] series from cover to cover, though I had sense enough not to hope to get rich; even to my naïve imagination that possibility was too remote. I knew that I lived in a country in which the aspirations of black people were limited, marked-off. Yet I felt that I had to go somewhere and do something to redeem my being alive.

I was building up in me a dream which the entire educational system of the South had been rigged to stifle. I was feeling the very thing that the state of Mississippi had spent millions of dollars to make sure that I would never feel; I was becoming aware of the thing that the Jim Crow laws[6] had been drafted and passed to keep out of my consciousness; I was acting on impulses that southern senators in the nation's capital had striven to keep out of Negro life; I was beginning to dream the dreams that the state had said were wrong, that the schools had said were taboo.

Had I been articulate about my ultimate aspirations, no doubt someone would have told me what I was bargaining for; but nobody seemed to know, and least of all did I. My classmates felt that I was doing something that was vaguely wrong, but they did not know how to express it. As the outside world grew more meaningful, I became more concerned, tense; and my classmates and my teachers would say: "Why do you ask so many questions?" Or: "Keep quiet."

I was in my fifteenth year; in terms of schooling I was far behind the average youth of the nation, but I did not know that. In me was shaping a yearning for a kind of consciousness, a mode of being that the way of life about me had said could not be, must not be, and upon which the penalty of death had been placed. Somewhere in the dead of the southern night my life had switched onto the wrong track and, without my knowing it, the locomotive of my heart was rushing down a dangerously steep slope, heading for a collision, heedless of the warning red lights that blinked all about me, the sirens and the bells and the screams that filled the air.

---

3. **Horatio Alger** (hō rā′ sho al′ jər): An American writer (1832–1899), who wrote children's stories in which poor boys achieved fame and fortune.
4. **pulp stories:** Sensational stories about love, crime, and so on.
5. **Get-Rich-Quick Wallingford:** A character from a series of stories by George R. Chester.

6. **Jim Crow laws:** Laws that discriminated against African Americans.

RESPONDING TO THE SELECTION

Your Response

1. What are your impressions of the young Richard Wright?
2. What are your impressions of the environment in which he grew up?
3. What kind of reception do you think Wright's story would have received in your eighth-grade class?

Recalling

4. What led Wright to write a story when he was in the eighth grade?
5. (a) How did Wright think his classmates would react to the story? (b) How did they actually react? (c) How did his family react?
6. What did the North represent to Wright?

Interpreting

7. What does Wright's decision to approach the local Negro newspaper and his behavior at the office reveal about him?
8. In what ways was Wright "pushing against the current" of his environment in trying to write?
9. How did Wright gauge his chances for success in life in the South? Explain.

Applying

10. Wright never fully answers his question: "But where had I got this notion of doing something in the future, of going away from home and accomplishing something that would be recognized by others?" How would you explain his drive?

ANALYZING LITERATURE

Understanding Narration

Narration is writing that tells a story. In the autobiography, one kind of **first-person narrative,** the writer tells about a personal experience, using the first-person pronoun *I*.

1. What experience or incident does Wright relate in this episode from his autobiography?
2. How might this story be different if it had been told by Wright's grandmother?

3. What else would you like to know about this incident in Wright's life?

CRITICAL THINKING AND READING

Making Connections Among Literary Works

Comparing a literary work with another from the same genre may help you see elements in each that might not have been readily apparent. You might also notice the choices each writer made in presenting his or her material. Review the excerpt from Benjamin Franklin's autobiography, which begins on page 100. Then compare Franklin's account of his first literary effort with that of Richard Wright.

1. Under what circumstances did each writer submit his first piece to a newspaper?
2. What influenced his choice of subject?
3. How did his social environment help or hinder his first writing effort?

THINKING AND WRITING

Writing a First-Person Narrative

Using the first person, write a two- or three-page narrative about a turning point in your life or about a period that marked a new beginning for you. Use vivid details to present the experience and your feelings about it. Find a partner to review your work, and take his or her suggestions into consideration as you prepare your final draft.

LEARNING OPTION

Writing. Sixteen years after the editor at the *Southern Register* published Wright's first short story, the author took the literary world by storm with the publication of *Native Son*. Imagine that you are the newspaper editor who first published Wright in 1924. In 1940 you read *Native Son* and discover that Wright is an accomplished author. How do you feel about your discovery? Record your response either in a journal entry or in a letter to Richard Wright.

Poetry

BLACK AND WHITE, 1930
Georgia O'Keeffe
The Whitney Museum of American Art

EZRA POUND

1885–1972

More than any other poet, Ezra Pound was responsible for the dramatic changes that occurred in American poetry during the Modern Age. Urging writers to "make it new," Pound influenced many poets of his day to discard the forms, techniques, and ideas of the past and to experiment with new approaches to writing poetry.

Pound was born in Hailey, Idaho, and grew up in Philadelphia. After studying at the University of Pennsylvania and at Hamilton College, he traveled in Europe, where he spent most of his life. Settling in London and later moving to Paris, he became a vital part of the growing Modernist movement. He influenced the work of the noted Irish poet William Butler Yeats and that of many American writers, including T. S. Eliot, William Carlos Williams, H. D., Marianne Moore, and Ernest Hemingway. He was also responsible for the development of Imagism, a literary movement that included Williams, H. D., and Moore.

Despite Pound's preoccupation with originality and inventiveness, his poetry reflects a deep interest in the past. In his early work, he often drew upon the poetry of ancient cultures, including Chinese, Japanese, and Provençal French. His dense, complex poems tend to be filled with literary and historical allusions. Often his poems are difficult to understand, because they are void of explanations or generalizations.

After 1920 Pound focused his efforts on writing *The Cantos,* a long poetic sequence in which he expressed his beliefs, reflected upon history and politics, and alluded to a variety of foreign languages and literatures. He eventually produced 116 cantos, which are widely varied in quality.

In 1925 Pound settled in Italy. During World War II, he was an outspoken supporter of the Italian dictator Benito Mussolini, mistakenly believing that a country governed by a powerful dictator was the most conducive environment for the creation of art. In 1943 Pound was indicted by the American government for treason, and a year later he was arrested by American troops and imprisoned. After being flown back to the United States in 1945, he was judged to be psychologically unfit to stand trial and was confined to a hospital for the criminally insane. He remained there until 1958, when he was released largely because of the efforts of his friends in the literary community. After his release he returned to Italy, where he spent the remainder of his life.

GUIDE FOR INTERPRETING

In a Station of the Metro; The River-Merchant's Wife: A Letter; Canto 13

Literary Movements

Imagism. Imagism was a literary movement established in the early part of the twentieth century by Ezra Pound and other poets. As the name suggests, the Imagists concentrated on the direct presentation of images, or word pictures. An Imagist poem expressed the essence of an object, person, or incident, without explanations or generalizations. Through the spare, clean presentation of an image, the Imagists hoped to evoke an emotional response—they hoped to freeze a single moment in time and to capture the emotions of that moment. To accomplish this purpose, the Imagists used the language of everyday speech, carefully choosing each word and avoiding any unnecessary words. Avoiding traditional poetic patterns, they also attempted to create new, musical rhythms in their poetry.

Because they generally focus on a single image, Imagist poems tend to be short. In their length and focus, many Imagist poems reflect the influence of the Japanese verse forms *haiku* and *tanka*. The haiku consists of three lines of five, seven, and five syllables. The tanka is written in five lines of five, seven, five, seven, and five syllables. Like Imagist poems, haikus and tankas generally evoke an emotional response through a single image.

Focus

"In a Station of the Metro" captures an impression of a crowd of people waiting on a dark subway platform. Freewrite about the types of impressions you have when you glance at a large crowd of people.

Primary Source

In the March 1913 issue of *Poetry* magazine, Pound published a set of "rules" for poets. Consider how his rules apply to poetry and to other kinds of writing.

It is better to present one image in a lifetime than to produce voluminous words.

Use no superfluous word, no adjective, which does not reveal something.

Don't use such an expression as 'dim lands of peace.' It dulls the image. It mixes an abstraction with the concrete. It comes from the writer's not realizing that the natural object is always the *adequate* symbol.

Be influenced by as many great artists as you can, but have the decency either to acknowledge the debt outright, or to try to conceal it.

In a Station of the Metro[1]

Ezra Pound

The apparition of these faces in the crowd;
Petals on a wet, black bough.

---

1. Metro: The Paris subway.

RESPONDING TO THE SELECTION

Your Response
1. What image does this poem bring to mind?
2. How would you describe a crowded subway or train station?

Recalling
3. What is the setting of this poem?

Interpreting
4. Pound compares the faces of people on a subway platform with "petals on a wet, black bough." (a) What does this comparison suggest about the effect of society on individuality? (b) What does the comparison suggest about the frailty of human beings?

Applying
5. How does the image in the poem compare with your own image of the faces of people on a subway platform or at a train station?

ANALYZING LITERATURE

Understanding Imagism
Imagism was a literary movement that focused on evoking emotions through the spare, clean presentations of images, or word pictures. The Imagists also emphasized the creation of new rhythms, the use of common language, and precision in choosing words.

1. In "In a Station of the Metro," Pound juxtaposes, or puts together, two images to capture an impression of faces quickly glimpsed on a dark subway platform. What emotions does the combination of images evoke?
2. Considering the common meaning of *apparition* as a strange figure appearing suddenly and thought to be a ghost, why do you think Pound chose the word *apparition* rather than *appearance*?
3. How does this word contribute to the emotional impact of the image?

LEARNING OPTIONS

1. **Art.** Reread "In a Station of the Metro." Then close your eyes and capture the main image of the poem. Draw what you see. Share your drawing with classmates.
2. **Writing.** Capture the essence of an object, person, or incident in an Imagist poem of your own. You might try your hand at writing a haiku (consisting of three lines of five, seven, and five syllables) or a tanka (consisting of five lines of five, seven, five, seven, and five syllables). To freeze and capture the emotions of a single moment in time, make sure that your language is both precise and suggestive.

The River-Merchant's Wife: A Letter

Ezra Pound

While my hair was still cut straight across my forehead
I played about the front gate, pulling flowers.
You came by on bamboo stilts, playing horse,
You walked about my seat, playing with blue plums.
5   And we went on living in the village of Chokan:[1]
Two small people, without dislike or suspicion.

At fourteen I married My Lord you.
I never laughed, being bashful.
Lowering my head, I looked at the wall.
10   Called to, a thousand times, I never looked back.

At fifteen I stopped scowling,
I desired my dust to be mingled with yours
Forever and forever and forever.
Why should I climb the lookout?

15   At sixteen you departed,
You went into far Ku-to-yen,[2] by the river of swirling eddies,
And you have been gone five months.
The monkeys make sorrowful noise overhead.

You dragged your feet when you went out.
20   By the gate now, the moss is grown, the different mosses,
Too deep to clear them away!
The leaves fall early this autumn, in wind.
The paired butterflies are already yellow with August
Over the grass in the West garden;
25   They hurt me. I grow older.
If you are coming down through the narrows of the river
    Kiang,

---

1. **Chokan** (Chō′ kän′): A suburb of Nanking, a city in the People's Republic of China.
2. **Ku-to-yen** (kōō′ tō′ yen′): An island in the Yangtze (yäng′ tsē) River.

Please let me know beforehand,
And I will come out to meet you
    As far as Cho-fu-Sa.[3]

By Rihaku

---

3. Cho-fu-Sa (chō′ fōō′ sä′): A beach
along the Yangtze River, several hundred
miles from Nanking.

LANDSCAPE ALBUM IN VARIOUS STYLES
Ch'a Shih-piao
The Cleveland Museum of Art

RESPONDING TO THE SELECTION

Your Response

1. How does this poem make you feel?
2. Which image do you find most striking? Explain.

Recalling

3. Summarize the events in the life of the river-merchant's wife.

Interpreting

4. This poem is adapted from a Chinese poem by Li T'ai Po. When the original poem was written, marriages were arranged by parents according to Chinese custom. (a) How did the river-merchant's wife feel at the time of her marriage? (b) How are these feelings conveyed? (c) How have her feelings for her husband changed since the time of their marriage?
5. How do the details of the setting in the fifth stanza indicate the passage of time?
6. (a) How does the river-merchant's wife feel about her husband's absence? (b) How do the descriptions of the monkeys and butterflies reflect her feelings?

Applying

7. Many societies have believed in arranged marriages. What do you think are the benefits and the drawbacks of arranged marriages both for the individuals involved and for society as a whole?

THINKING AND WRITING

Writing About Imagism

Although "The River-Merchant's Wife" is not a pure Imagist poem, it does possess a number of the characteristics of Imagist poetry. Write an essay in which you discuss these characteristics. Review the poem, noting the simplicity and precision of its language, its use of imagery to evoke emotions, and its musical rhythm. Write a thesis statement, and organize your notes into an outline. Then write your essay using passages from the poem to support your argument. When you revise, add transitions to connect your ideas.

Canto 13

Ezra Pound

Kung[1] walked
    by the dynastic temple and into the cedar grove,
      and then out by the lower river,
And with him Khieu, Tchi
5   and Tian the low speaking
And "we are unknown," said Kung,
"You will take up charioteering?
    Then you will become known,
"Or perhaps I should take up charioteering, or archery?
10 "Or the practice of public speaking?"
And Tseu-lou said, "I would put the defenses in order,"
And Khieu said, "If I were lord of a province
I would put it in better order than this is."
And Tchi said, "I would prefer a small mountain temple,
15 "With order in the observances,
    with a suitable performance of the ritual,"
And Tian said, with his hand on the strings of his lute
The low sounds continuing
    after his hand left the strings,
20 And the sound went up like smoke, under the leaves,
And he looked after the sound:
    "The old swimming hole,
"And the boys flopping off the planks,
"Or sitting in the underbrush playing mandolins."
25   And Kung smiled upon all of them equally.
And Thseng-sie desired to know:
    "Which had answered correctly?"
And Kung said, "They have all answered correctly,
"That is to say, each in his nature."
30 And Kung raised his cane against Yuan Jang,
    Yuan Jang being his elder,
For Yuan Jang sat by the roadside pretending to
    be receiving wisdom.
And Kung said
35   "You old fool, come out of it,
Get up and do something useful."

---

1. Kung: Confucius (551?–479? B.C.), Chinese philosopher and
teacher. Confucius emphasized devotion to parents, family and
friends, ancestor worship, and the maintenance of justice and peace.
Khieu, Tchi, Tian, Tseu-lou, Thseng-sie, and Yuan Jang were his disciples.

And Kung said
"Respect a child's faculties
"From the moment it inhales the clear air,
40 "But a man of fifty who knows nothing
        Is worthy of no respect."
And "When the prince has gathered about him
"All the savants and artists, his riches will be fully
    employed."
And Kung said, and wrote on the bo leaves:
45   If a man have not order within him
He can not spread order about him;
And if a man have not order within him
His family will not act with due order;
        And if the prince have not order within him
50 He can not put order in his dominions.
And Kung gave the words "order"
and "brotherly deference"
And said nothing of the "life after death."
And he said
55   "Anyone can run to excesses,
It is easy to shoot past the mark,
It is hard to stand firm in the middle."

And they said: If a man commit murder
        Should his father protect him, and hide him?
60 And Kung said:
        He should hide him.

And Kung gave his daughter to Kong-Tch'ang
        Although Kong-Tch'ang was in prison.
And he gave his niece to Nan-Young
65   although Nan-Young was out of office.
And Kung said "Wang[2] ruled with moderation,
        In his day the State was well kept,
And even I can remember
A day when the historians left blanks in their writings,
70 I mean for things they didn't know,
But that time seems to be passing."
And Kung said, "Without character you will
        be unable to play on that instrument
Or to execute the music fit for the Odes.
The blossoms of the apricot
        blow from the east to the west,
75 And I have tried to keep them from falling."

---

2. Wang: The first emperor of the Chou Dynasty, ruling China from
1122 to 1115 B.C.

RESPONDING TO THE SELECTION

Your Response

1. What would you do to "become known"? How might Kung react to your proposal?
2. How important do you think it is to have order within yourself?

Interpreting

3. This poem presents a dialogue between Confucius, or Kung, and several of his disciples. Confucius first asks his disciples how they will "become known." When they have finished responding, he comments that each has answered correctly "in his nature." (a) What does this comment reveal about his attitude toward his disciples? (b) What does the fact that he "smiled upon them equally" reveal?
4. What attitude concerning youth and old age does Confucius express?
5. (a) What does Confucius mean when he speaks of a person who has "order within him"? (b) Why is it important for a person to have "order within him"?
6. (a) If the "blossoms of the apricot" symbolize the ancient Chinese culture and its traditions, what do you think Confucius means when he says that the blossoms are blowing "from the east to the west"? (b) What does he mean when he says that he has "tried to keep them from falling"?

Applying

7. What ideas does Confucius express that are applicable to life in our society?

LEARNING OPTION

Writing. Use Kung's statements as a model for writing a series of statements that reflect your philosophy of life. Like Kung, you might comment on order, brotherly deference, and moderation. Introduce each statement with the phrase *And _____ said,* filling in your name.

Primary Source

Unlike the letters in our alphabet, which generally have no meaning by themselves, each Chinese character stands for a complete concept or image. As such, the written Chinese language is particularly well suited to metaphor, the key element in Imagist poetry. Imagist Ezra Pound consequently regarded written Chinese as the ideal poetic language.

In "The Chinese Written Character as Medium for Poetry," written with Ernest Fenollosa, Pound explored the connection between metaphor, poetry, and the Chinese written language. He wrote:

"Metaphor, the revealer of nature, is the very substance of poetry . . . Poetry is finer than prose because it gives us more concrete truth in the same compass of words. Metaphor, its chief device, is at once the substance and nature of language. Poetry only does consciously what the primitive races did unconsciously. The chief work of literary men in dealing with language, and of poets especially, lies in feeling back along the ancient lines of advance.

. . . I have alleged all this because it enables me to show clearly why I believe that the Chinese written language has not only absorbed the poetic substance of nature and built with it a second world of metaphor, but has, through its very pictorial visibility, been able to retain its original creative poetry with far more vigor and vividness than any phonetic tongue. . . ."

T. S. ELIOT

1888–1965

Thomas Stearns Eliot's poetry received more critical acclaim than that of any other American poet of his time. At the same time, his poetry, along with his literary criticism, influenced other writers of the period.

Born into a prominent family in St. Louis, Missouri, Eliot grew up in an environment that promoted his intellectual development. During his years as an undergraduate at Harvard, Eliot published a number of poems in *The Harvard Advocate,* the school's literary magazine. Then, in 1910, the same year in which he earned his master's degree in philosophy, he completed "The Love Song of J. Alfred Prufrock," his first important poem.

When World War I broke out, Eliot settled in England. There he became acquainted with Ezra Pound, another young American poet. Recognizing Eliot's talent, Pound influenced the editor of the American magazine *Poetry* to publish "The Love Song of J. Alfred Prufrock," making Eliot's work available to the public for the first time.

The publication of "Prufrock," along with the other poems in his first book, *Prufrock and Other Observations* (1917), created a stir in the literary world. Eliot had used techniques that had never before been used. Focusing on the frustration and despair of life in modern urban societies, the poems in Eliot's first book also set the tone for the other poems he would produce during the early stage of his career.

In 1922 Eliot published *The Waste Land,* his most famous poem. The poem contrasts the spiritual bankruptcy that Eliot saw as the dominant force in modern Europe with the values and unity that governed the past. The impact of *The Waste Land* on other writers, critics, and the public was enormous, and it is regarded as one of the finest literary works ever written.

In 1928 Eliot became a devout member of the Church of England, after becoming a British citizen the previous year. These changes preceded radical changes in the focus of Eliot's writing, as evidenced by his exploration of religious themes in *Ash Wednesday* (1930) and *Four Quartets* (1943). These poems suggest that Eliot felt that religious belief could be a means for healing the wounds inflicted on a person by the spiritually bankrupt society he depicted in *The Waste Land*.

During his later years, Eliot also produced a sizable body of literary criticism and wrote several plays. His first major play, *Murder in the Cathedral* (1935), is based on the death of Thomas à Becket. His other plays include *The Cocktail Party* (1950), *The Family Reunion* (1939), *The Confidential Clerk* (1954), and *The Elder Statesman* (1958). In 1948 he received the Nobel Prize for Literature.

GUIDE FOR INTERPRETING

The Love Song of J. Alfred Prufrock

Writers' Techniques

Stream of Consciousness. Stream of consciousness is a term originated by American psychologist William James to describe the natural flow of a person's thoughts. James noted that people's thoughts do not flow together in a logical, organized manner, but rather take the form of an unorganized and seemingly unconnected series of insights, memories, and reflections. During the early 1900's, writers began incorporating the ideas of James into their work by trying to capture the random movements of a character's thoughts to recreate the natural flow of people's thoughts. In using the stream-of-consciousness technique, the writers abandoned transitions and other linking devices used in ordinary prose, instead connecting thoughts through the character's natural associations.

Focus

William James once wrote, "There is no more miserable human being than one in whom nothing is habitual but indecision." Freewrite, exploring the meaning of this quotation.

Primary Source

Many readers of poetry read to discover the thoughts and feelings of the poet. They consider poetry to be a highly personal expression of one particular poet's views. Eliot disagreed with this concept of poetry. In his classic essay "Tradition and the Individual Talent," he argued that "the emotion of art is impersonal." By this he meant that the poet should not write from personal experience or about his own emotions. Writing poetry is an impersonal act of creation involving material outside personal experience. Eliot believed that poetry was the interaction of a poet's individual talent and the tradition of poetry. As he explained:

> It is not in his personal emotions, the emotions provoked by particular events in his life, that the poet is in any way remarkable or interesting. . . . The business of the poet is not to find new emotions, but to use the ordinary ones and, in working them up into poetry, to express feelings which are not in actual emotions at all. And emotions he has never experienced will serve his turns as well as those familiar to him. Consequently, we must believe that 'emotion recollected in tranquility' is an inexact formula [for poetry]. For it is neither emotion, not recollection, nor, without distortion of meaning, tranquility. It is a concentration, and a new thing resulting from the concentration. . . .

The Love Song of J. Alfred Prufrock

T. S. Eliot

S'io credessi che mia risposta fosse
a persona che mai tornasse al mondo,
questa fiamma staria senza più scosse.
Ma per ciò che giammai di questo fondo
non tornò vivo alcun, s'i'odo il vero,
senza tema d'infamia ti rispondo.[1]

Let us go then, you and I,
When the evening is spread out against the sky
Like a patient etherized[2] upon a table;
Let us go, through certain half-deserted streets,
5   The muttering retreats
Of restless nights in one-night cheap hotels
And sawdust restaurants with oyster-shells:
Streets that follow like a tedious argument
Of insidious intent
10 To lead you to an overwhelming question . . .
Oh, do not ask, "What is it?"
Let us go and make our visit.

In the room the women come and go
Talking of Michelangelo.[3]

The yellow fog that rubs its back upon the window-panes,
15 The yellow smoke that rubs its muzzle on the window-
        panes,
Licked its tongue into the corners of the evening,

---

1. S'io credessi . . . ti rispondo: The epigraph is a passage from Dante's *Inferno* in which one of the damned, upon being requested to tell his story, says: "If I believed my answer were being given to someone who could ever return to this world, this flame (his voice) would shake no more. But since no one has ever returned alive from this depth, if what I hear is true, I will answer you without fear or disgrace."
2. etherized (ē' thə rīzd) *v.*: Anesthetized with ether.
3. Michelangelo (mī' kəl an' jə lō): A famous Italian artist (1475–1564).

Lingered upon the pools that stand in drains,
Let fall upon its back the soot that falls from chimneys,
Slipped by the terrace, made a sudden leap,
20   And seeing that it was a soft October night,
Curled once about the house, and fell asleep.

And indeed there will be time[4]
For the yellow smoke that slides along the street
Rubbing its back upon the window-panes;
25   There will be time, there will be time
To prepare a face to meet the faces that you meet;
There will be time to murder and create,
And time for all the works and days[5] of hands
That lift and drop a question on your plate;
30   Time for you and time for me,
And time yet for a hundred indecisions,
And for a hundred visions and revisions,
Before the taking of a toast and tea.

In the room the women come and go
35   Talking of Michelangelo.

And indeed there will be time
To wonder, "Do I dare?" and, "Do I dare?"
Time to turn back and descend the stair,
With a bald spot in the middle of my hair—
40   (They will say: 'How his hair is growing thin!')
My morning coat, my collar mounting firmly to the chin,
My necktie rich and modest, but asserted by a simple pin—
(They will say: "But how his arms and legs are thin!")
Do I dare
45   Disturb the universe?
In a minute there is time
For decisions and revisions which a minute will reverse.

For I have known them all already, known them all—
Have known the evenings, mornings, afternoons,
50   I have measured out my life with coffee spoons;
I know the voices dying with a dying fall
Beneath the music from a farther room.
        So how should I presume?

---

4. there will be time: Similar to the narrator's plea in English poet
Andrew Marvell's "To His Coy Mistress": "Had we but world enough
and time . . ."
5. works and days: Ancient Greek poet Hesiod wrote a poem about
farming called "Works and Days."

MOONLIGHT, DOVEHOUSE STREET, CHELSEA
Algernon Newton
Fine Art Society, London

And I have known the eyes already, known them all—
55   The eyes that fix you in a formulated phrase,
And when I am formulated, sprawling on a pin,
When I am pinned and wriggling on the wall,
Then how should I begin
To spit out all the butt-ends of my days and ways?
60   And how should I presume?
And I have known the arms already, known them all—
Arms that are braceleted and white and bare
(But in the lamplight, downed with light brown hair!)
Is it perfume from a dress
65   That makes me so digress?
Arms that lie along a table, or wrap about a shawl.

And should I then presume?
And how should I begin?

     . . . . .

Shall I say, I have gone at dusk through narrow streets
70 And watched the smoke that rises from the pipes
Of lonely men in shirt-sleeves, leaning out of windows?. . .

I should have been a pair of ragged claws
Scuttling across the floors of silent seas.[6]

     . . . . .

And the afternoon, the evening, sleeps so peacefully!
75 Smoothed by long fingers,
Asleep . . . tired . . . or it malingers,
Stretched on the floor, here beside you and me.
Should I, after tea and cakes and ices,
Have the strength to force the moment to its crisis?
80 But though I have wept and fasted, wept and prayed,
Though I have seen my head (grown slightly bald) brought
    in upon a platter,[7]
I am no prophet—and here's no great matter;
I have seen the moment of my greatness flicker,
And I have seen the eternal Footman[8] hold my coat, and
    snicker.
85 And in short, I was afraid.

And would it have been worth it, after all,
After the cups, the marmalade, the tea,
Among the porcelain, among some talk of you and me,
Would it have been worth while,
90 To have bitten off the matter with a smile,
To have squeezed the universe into a ball
To roll it towards some overwhelming question.
To say: "I am Lazarus,[9] come from the dead,
Come back to tell you all. I shall tell you all"—
95 If one, settling a pillow by her head,
      Should say: "That is not what I meant at all.
      That is not it, at all."

---

6. I should . . . seas: In Shakespeare's *Hamlet*, the hero, Hamlet,
mocks the aging Lord Chamberlain, Polonius, saying, "You yourself,
sir, should be old as I am, if like a crab you could go backward (II.ii.
205–206).
7. head . . . platter: A reference to the prophet John the Baptist,
whose head was delivered on a platter to Salome as a reward for her
dancing (Matthew 14:1–11).
8. eternal Footman: Death.
9. Lazarus (laz′ ə rəs): Lazarus is resurrected from the dead by
Jesus in John 11:1–44.

And would it have been worth it, after all,
Would it have been worth while,
100 After the sunsets and the dooryards and the sprinkled
     streets,
After the novels, after the teacups, after the skirts that trail
     along the floor—
And this, and so much more?—
It is impossible to say just what I mean!
But as if a magic lantern[10] threw the nerves in patterns on
     a screen:
105 Would it have been worth while
If one, settling a pillow or throwing off a shawl,
And turning toward the window, should say:
      "That is not it at all,
      That is not what I meant, at all."

      · · · · ·

No! I am not Prince Hamlet, nor was meant to be;
110 Am an attendant lord, one that will do
To swell a progress,[11] start a scene or two,
Advise the prince; no doubt, an easy tool,
Deferential, glad to be of use,
115 Politic, cautious, and meticulous;
Full of high sentence,[12] but a bit obtuse;
At times, indeed, almost ridiculous—
Almost, at times, the Fool.

I grow old . . . I grow old . . .
120 I shall wear the bottoms of my trousers rolled.

Shall I part my hair behind? Do I dare to eat a peach?
I shall wear white flannel trousers, and walk upon the
     beach.
I have heard the mermaids singing, each to each.

I do not think that they will sing to me.

125 I have seen them riding seaward on the waves
Combing the white hair of the waves blown back
When the wind blows the water white and black.

We have lingered in the chambers of the sea
By sea-girls wreathed with seaweed red and brown
Till human voices wake us, and we drown.

---

10. magic lantern: An early device used to project images on a
screen.
11. To swell a progress: To add to the number of people in a
parade or scene from a play.
12. Full of high sentence: Speaking in a very ornate manner, often
offering advice.

RESPONDING TO THE SELECTION

Your Response

1. What is your impression of J. Alfred Prufrock?
2. If you met Prufrock at a party, would you engage him in conversation? Why or why not?
3. What advice would you give Prufrock if he were a friend of yours?

Interpreting

4. Prufrock sees himself as being divided into two parts, with one part being eager to take action, while the other part struggles to hold him back. (a) How does the first line suggest that Prufrock sees himself as divided? (b) What do the images in lines 1–12 suggest about his outlook on life?
5. Throughout the poem Prufrock is on his way to an afternoon tea party and is trying to build up enough courage to tell a woman of his love for her. (a) How does Prufrock convey his apprehension and uncertainty in lines 22–47? (b) In what ways does he indicate that he feels that he is growing old? (c) How does the belief that he is growing old affect his decisions?
6. (a) What feelings about the other guests he expects to find at the party does Prufrock convey in lines 48–68? (b) How does he expect to be treated by the other guests? (c) What does he mean when he remarks, "I have measured my life with coffee spoons"?
7. (a) What fears does Prufrock express in lines 80–85? (b) In lines 86–108 how does he convey the fact that he has given in to his apprehension and has decided not to express his love to the woman? (c) How does he attempt to justify his decision?
8. (a) How do the questions Prufrock asks in line 121 contrast with the questions he had found so overwhelming earlier in the poem? (b) How do the images in lines 125–129 contrast with the images in the first stanza? (c) How does the final line suggest that reality has once again intruded upon his thoughts, leaving him

in the same condition as when the poem started?

Applying

9. T. S. Eliot felt that the Modern Age was a time of confusion and uncertainty. In what ways does Eliot use Prufrock as an embodiment of the general sentiments of society as a whole?
10. (a) In what ways are many of us similar to Prufrock? (b) In what instances might our behavior be similar to Prufrock's?

ANALYZING LITERATURE

Understanding Techniques

The **stream-of-consciousness technique** allows a writer to re-create the natural flow of a character's thoughts. When using this technique, a writer uses only the character's natural associations to link thoughts. For example, in lines 69–73 Prufrock's thoughts drift from a contemplation of what he will say to the woman to the philosophical observation that he "should have been a pair of ragged claws."

Find two other instances in which Prufrock's thoughts drift from his immediate concerns to general philosophical observations.

CRITICAL THINKING AND READING

Interpreting Allusions

Interpreting the meaning of an **allusion**—a reference to another literary work or a figure, place, or event from history, religion, or mythology—may involve research. For example, to interpret the meaning of Eliot's allusion to Shakespeare's *Hamlet* (lines 109–118), you would have to consult the play itself, a critical essay, or a plot summary.

1. (a) Find two other allusions used by Eliot in the poem. (b) Interpret the meaning of each.
2. Do you think the use of allusions enriches the poem? Explain your answer.

WALLACE STEVENS

1879–1955

Wallace Stevens believed that the goal of poetry is to capture the interaction of the imagination and the real world. As a result he spent his career writing poems that delve into the ways in which the physical world is perceived through the imagination.

Stevens was born and raised in Reading, Pennsylvania. After graduating from Harvard, he worked briefly as a journalist before attending law school. He practiced law for a short time, then took a job in the legal department of an insurance company in Hartford, Connecticut. Eventually he became the company's vice-president.

Stevens did not publish his first collection of poetry, *Harmonium* (1923), until he was over forty. Although the book received little recognition from the general public, it earned praise from critics and other poets. In the poems in this book, Stevens uses dazzling imagery to capture the beauty of the physical world, while expressing the dependence of this beauty on the perceptions of the observer.

During the second half of his life, Stevens published many more volumes of poetry, including *Ideas of Order* (1935), *Parts of a World* (1942), *Transport to Summer* (1947), *The Auroras of Autumn* (1950), and *Collected Poems* (1955), which earned him the Pulitzer Prize. Despite his success as a poet, however, Stevens continued his career in insurance. He rarely appeared in public and only began giving readings toward the end of his life.

While Stevens's early poems explore the ways in which the imagination shapes reality, his later work tends to be more abstract. He began focusing on such philosophical subjects as death and humanity's relationship with nature. Instead of exploring different ways of perceiving reality, he delved into different ways of contemplating and comprehending reality.

In *The Necessary Angel,* a slim book about poetry and reality, Stevens wrote, "There is, in fact, a world of poetry indistinguishable from the world in which we live, or, I ought to say, no doubt, from the world in which we shall come to live, since what makes the poet the potent figure that he is, or was, or ought to be, is that he creates the world to which we turn incessantly and without knowing it and that he gives to life the supreme fictions without which we are unable to conceive of it."

Throughout his career, however, Stevens's goal as a poet was "to help people live their lives." Stevens believed that life in the Modern Age was often uncertain and confusing, and that it was the duty of the poet to provide new ways of understanding the world. By writing poems that help us to see our role in shaping reality, he was able to accomplish his goal.

Disillusionment of Ten O'Clock; Anecdote of the Jar

Literary Movements

Symbolism. Like many other writers of his time, Stevens was influenced by Symbolism, a literary movement that originated in France in the last half of the nineteenth century. Because people perceive the physical world in different ways, the Symbolist poets believed that the ideas and emotions that people experience are personal and difficult to communicate. As a result these poets avoided directly stating their own ideas and emotions in their poetry. Instead they tried to convey meaning through clusters of symbols—people, places, objects, or actions that have meanings in themselves and also represent something larger than themselves. Because of this reliance on symbols, Symbolist poems can often be interpreted in a number of different ways. Similarly many of Stevens's poems can be interpreted in more than one way.

Commentary

As you read Wallace Stevens's poetry, you will notice that his symbols encompass what is real as well as what is not real. Dreams and the imagination are intermixed with concrete objects. Does concrete reality exist outside our imaginations? How does imagination shape our experience of the real world? These are questions Stevens considered. He wanted "not ideas about the thing but the thing itself," as he suggested in another poem. Poetry, he felt, joins imagination and the real world. Consider these ideas as you read "Disillusionment of Ten O'Clock" and "Anecdote of the Jar."

Focus

In "Disillusionment of Ten O'Clock" the subject is people's dreams. Freewrite about dreams and their meanings. How do dreams relate to a person's life? What can dreams reveal about a person? How can people be affected by their dreams?

Disillusionment of Ten O'Clock

Wallace Stevens

The houses are haunted
By white night-gowns.
None are green,
Or purple with green rings,
5   Or green with yellow rings,
Or yellow with blue rings.
None of them are strange,
With socks of lace
And beaded ceintures.
10   People are not going
To dream of baboons and periwinkles.
Only, here and there, an old sailor,
Drunk and asleep in his boots,
Catches tigers
15   In red weather.

RESPONDING TO THE SELECTION

Your Response

1. Has reading this poem affected the way you perceive your life? Explain.
2. How would you describe your dreams?
3. Would you like to dream of "baboons and periwinkles" or to catch "tigers in red weather"? Explain.

Interpreting

4. In this poem Stevens contrasts an interesting, imaginative way of life with a dull, unimaginative way of life. (a) How does Stevens develop this contrast through his description of night-gowns? (b) How does his description of dreams further develop the contrast?
5. (a) Considering the poem's title and the reference to the houses as "haunted," which way of life do you think Stevens favors? (b) What comment does he seem to be making about modern life?

Applying

6. (a) What are some other things Stevens could have used to symbolize an unimaginative way of life? (b) What are some other things he could have used to symbolize an imaginative way of life?

THINKING AND WRITING

Responding to a Statement

Stevens felt that the goal of a poet was "to help people live their lives." Write an essay in which you discuss Stevens's comment in relation to the poem you have just read. Does it help people to live their lives? If so, how? When you finish writing, revise your essay, making sure that you have included enough evidence to thoroughly support your argument.

Anecdote of the Jar

Wallace Stevens

I placed a jar in Tennessee,
And round it was, upon a hill.
It made the slovenly wilderness
Surround that hill.

5 The wilderness rose up to it,
And sprawled around, no longer wild.
The jar was round upon the ground
And tall and of a port in air.

It took dominion everywhere.
10 The jar was gray and bare.
It did not give of bird or bush,
Like nothing else in Tennessee.

RESPONDING TO THE SELECTION

Your Response

1. What type of painting or drawing would you select to illustrate "Anecdote of the Jar"? Explain.

Interpreting

2. In your own words, describe the jar's effect on the wilderness.
3. How is the impression of the jar that the speaker conveys in the third stanza different from that conveyed in the first two stanzas?

Applying

4. What types of objects do people create that have a dramatic effect on nature?

ANALYZING LITERATURE

Interpreting Symbolism

Symbolism was a literary movement that originated in France in the late nineteenth century and that influenced many English and American writers of the twentieth century. The Symbolist poets avoided directly stating ideas and emotions in their poetry. Instead they suggested meaning through the use of symbols.

How does this poem reflect the influence of the Symbolist poets?

CRITICAL THINKING AND READING

Supporting an Interpretation

Because of the Symbolists' reliance on symbols, their poetry can often be interpreted in several ways. Similarly, many of Wallace Stevens's poems can be interpreted in more than one way.

Find evidence in the poem to support each of the following interpretations.

1. The jar symbolizes the human imagination, and the poem points out how the appearance of nature is shaped by our perceptions. The poem also points out that our imaginations depend on the physical world for input.
2. The jar symbolizes human interference with nature, and the poem explores the effects of human creations on nature.

AMY LOWELL

1874–1925

A descendant of New England Renaissance poet James Russell Lowell, Amy Lowell was a strong-minded poet, whose determination helped her to establish herself as the leader of the Imagist movement.

Born in Brookline, Massachusetts, she received an excellent education and traveled extensively as a young girl. In 1913 she published her first volume of poetry, *A Dome of Many Colors,* but the book was not well received. A year later, after reading a poem by the Imagist poet H. D., she traveled to London, hoping to become part of the Imagist movement. She began focusing on creating vivid, precise images in her poetry. At the same time, she energetically promoted the Imagist movement in lectures and essays, and she eventually became the movement's leader. Unfortunately, however, Ezra Pound, the founder of the Imagist movement, found her poetry overly sentimental, and her emergence as the leader of the Imagist circle prompted him to sever his connection with the group.

An outspoken commentator on poets and poetry, Lowell worked hard at defining what were, for her, the ingredients of good poetry: fresh, new rhythms; the language of common speech; clear, concrete, and vivid images. "A demon saleswoman," Eliot called her for her crusade to advertise the new poetry. Reacting against the popular view of the poet as an inspired genius who writes poetry spontaneously—a view inherited from early nineteenth-century Romanticism—Lowell insisted that poetry was a trade like any other. The poet needed to learn and practice writing poetry to do it well. In the preface to her collection *Sword Blades and Poppy Seeds* (1914), she elaborated on this definition of poetry. "No one expects a man to make a chair without first learning how, but there is a popular impression that the poet is born, not made, and that his verses burst from his overflowing heart of themselves. As a matter of fact, the poet must learn his trade in the same manner, and with the same painstaking care, as the cabinetmaker. His heart may overflow with high thoughts and sparkling fancies, but if he cannot convey them to his reader by means of the written word he has no claim to be considered a poet."

Lowell published eleven volumes of poetry between 1913 and 1925, and three others appeared after her death in 1925. Her collection *What's O'Clock* (1925) won her the Pulitzer Prize.

"Patterns," one of her best-known poems, appeared in *Men, Women, and Ghosts,* published in 1916. In this poem she uses colorful images to reflect the emotions of a woman whose fiancé has just been killed in a war.

GUIDE FOR INTERPRETING

Patterns

Literary Forms

Dramatic Monologue. A dramatic monologue is a poem in which one character speaks to one or more silent listeners at a critical point in the speaker's life. The speaker's comments reveal the circumstances surrounding the conversation and offer insights into his or her personality. In T. S. Eliot's poem "The Love Song of J. Alfred Prufrock," for example, the speaker expresses his feelings of uncertainty and disjointedness while debating whether or not to declare his love for a woman.

Commentary

"Patterns" is famous for its rich and brilliant imagery. Writing about Amy Lowell, poet and critic Louis Untermeyer said, "She is, preeminently, the poet of the external world; her visual effects are as 'hard and clear' as the most uncompromising Imagist could desire. The colors with which her words are studded seem like bits of bright enamel; every leaf and flower has a lacquered brilliance. . . . [E]verything flashes, leaps, startles, and burns with dynamic, almost savage speed. . . ."

Through this dynamic imagery, Lowell creates the patterns in this poem. She begins with the concrete pattern of the garden path and moves on to "a pattern called war." Her poem, which tells a simple story of unfulfilled love, begins quietly enough but goes on to express a protest against unnatural, artificially imposed patterns that may prevent individuals from fulfilling their lives.

"What are patterns for?" cries the speaker of the poem. What are they for? When do they serve a positive purpose, and when do they restrain? Consider these questions as you read the poem.

Focus

"Patterns" focuses on a woman's reaction to her fiancé's death during a war. Freewrite about the types of emotions that might be evoked by the loss of a loved one during a war.

Patterns

Amy Lowell

I walk down the garden-paths,
And all the daffodils
Are blowing, and the bright blue squills.
I walk down the patterned garden-paths
5   In my stiff, brocaded gown.
With my powdered hair and jeweled fan,
I too am a rare
Pattern. As I wander down
The garden-paths.
10   My dress is richly figured,
And the train
Makes a pink and silver stain
On the gravel, and the thrift
Of the borders.
15   Just a plate of current fashion,
Tripping by in high-heeled, ribboned shoes.
Not a softness anywhere about me,
Only whalebone and brocade.
And I sink on a seat in the shade
20   Of a lime-tree. For my passion
Wars against the stiff brocade.
The daffodils and squills

Flutter in the breeze
As they please.
25 And I weep;
For the lime-tree is in blossom
And one small flower had dropped upon my bosom.

And the plashing of waterdrops
In the marble fountain
30 Comes down the garden-paths.
The dripping never stops.
Underneath my stiffened gown
Is the softness of a woman bathing in a marble basin,
A basin in the midst of hedges grown
35 So thick, she cannot see her lover hiding,
But she guesses he is near,
And the sliding of the water
Seems the stroking of a dear
Hand upon her.
40 What is Summer in a fine brocaded gown!
I should like to see it lying in a heap upon the ground.
All the pink and silver crumpled up on the ground.

I would be the pink and silver as I ran along the paths,
And he would stumble after,
45 Bewildered by my laughter.
I should see the sun flashing from his sword hilt and the
    buckles on his shoes.
I would choose
To lead him in a maze along the patterned paths,
A bright and laughing maze for my heavy-booted lover.
50 Till he caught me in the shade,
And the buttons of his waistcoat bruised my body as he
    clasped me
Aching, melting, unafraid.
With the shadows of the leaves and the sundrops,
And the plopping of the waterdrops,
55 All about us in the open afternoon—
I am very like to swoon
With the weight of this brocade,
For the sun sifts through the shade.
Underneath the fallen blossom
60 In my bosom,
Is a letter I have hid.
It was brought to me this morning by a rider from the
    Duke.[1]

---

1. the Duke: Probably John Churchill, Duke of Marlborough (1650–
1722), English general and statesman who commanded the united
English and Dutch armies during the War of the Spanish Succession
(1701–1714).

"Madam, we regret to inform you that Lord Hartwell
Died in action Thursday se'nnight."[2]
65   As I read it in the white, morning sunlight,
The letters squirmed like snakes.
"Any answer, Madam," said my footman.
"No," I told him.
"See that the messenger takes some refreshment.
70   No, no answer."
And I walked into the garden,
Up and down the patterned paths,
In my stiff, correct brocade.
The blue and yellow flowers stood up proudly in the sun,
75   Each one.
I stood upright too,
Held rigid to the pattern
By the stiffness of my gown.
Up and down I walked,
80   Up and down.

In a month he would have been my husband.
In a month, here, underneath this lime,
We would have broke the pattern;
He for me, and I for him,
85   He as Colonel, I as Lady,
On this shady seat.
He had a whim
That sunlight carried blessing.
And I answered, "It shall be as you have said."
90   Now he is dead.

In Summer and in Winter I shall walk
Up and down
The patterned garden-paths
In my stiff, brocaded gown.
95   The squills and daffodils
Will give place to pillared roses, and to asters, and to snow.
I shall go
Up and down,
In my gown.
100   Gorgeously arrayed,
Boned and stayed.
And the softness of my body will be guarded from embrace
By each button, hook, and lace.
For the man who should loose me is dead,
105   Fighting with the Duke in Flanders,
In a pattern called a war.
Christ! What are patterns for?

————————

2. Thursday se'nnight: A week ago Thursday.

Your Response

1. Which images in the poem do you find most effective? Explain.
2. What patterns give order to your life? Which, if any, would you like to break?

Recalling

3. (a) Where does the speaker walk? (b) What is she wearing?
4. (a) About what had a messenger informed the speaker that morning? (b) How had she replied to the message?
5. (a) What does the speaker reveal about Lord Hartwell in the fourth stanza? (b) What does she vow to do in the fifth stanza?

Interpreting

6. The poem's speaker is an upper-class woman living in the early eighteenth century, whose life follows a rigid, formal "pattern." (a) How do her walks in the garden echo the overall pattern of her life? (b) How does the appearance of her dress reflect the pattern of her life? (c) How would getting married have broken the pattern?
7. (a) In what sense is war a "pattern"? (b) What type of "war" seems to be going on in the speaker's mind?
8. How does the final line contrast with the rest of the poem?

Applying

9. Provide your own answer to the woman's final question.

ANALYZING LITERATURE

Understanding Dramatic Monologue

A **dramatic monologue** is a poem in which one character speaks to one or more silent listeners at a critical point in the speaker's life. The speaker's comments reveal the circumstances surrounding the conversation and offer insights into his or her personality. For example, in "Patterns" the speaker's response to her fiancé's death provides insight into her personality.

1. What does the speaker's immediate reaction to the news of her fiancé's death reveal about her personality?
2. What is the speaker's attitude concerning her life?

THINKING AND WRITING

Comparing and Contrasting Poems

Write an essay in which you compare and contrast "Patterns" with the Imagist poems of Ezra Pound (pages 700–704). Reread the poems, noting similarities and differences between Lowell's poem and Pound's poems. Organize your notes according to corresponding points of comparison and contrast. Then write your essay, using evidence from the poems to support your argument. When you finish writing, revise your essay, making sure you have quoted exactly. Proofread your essay and prepare a final draft.

LEARNING OPTIONS

1. **Writing.** Imagine that ten years have passed since the speaker received the letter of Lord Hartwell's death. Has the speaker broken the pattern of her life? If so, how? Visit the speaker in her garden. In a brief paragraph or two, describe your impression of her.
2. **Speaking and Listening.** Work with a classmate to dramatize the last conversation between the speaker and her lover, Lord Hartwell, before he departed for war. In your conversation you might express your hopes for the future and describe the pattern of the life you plan to share.
3. **Cross-curricular Connection.** Fashion in the early 1700's dictated that the speaker of the poem powder her hair, carry a jeweled fan, and wear a stiff, brocaded gown. What does fashion dictate today? Together with classmates generate a list of dos and don'ts for the fashion-conscious teenager. Then find or draw a picture of someone who might be described as "a plate of current fashion." What does his or her appearance tell you about the pattern of our times?

H. D. (DOOLITTLE)

1886–1961

In 1913 when Ezra Pound reshaped three of Hilda Doolittle's poems and submitted them to *Poetry* magazine under the name "H. D., Imagiste," the Imagist movement was born. At the same time, it marked the beginning of a successful career for the young poet, who continued to publish her work under the name H. D. throughout the course of her career.

H. D. was born in Bethlehem, Pennsylvania. When she was fifteen she met Pound, who was a student at the University of Pennsylvania. She entered Bryn Mawr College but left because of poor health. In 1911 she moved to London, where she renewed her acquaintance with Pound. She married English poet Richard Aldington, a close friend of Pound's, in 1913. Together they studied Greek and developed a deep affection for classical literature. Unfortunately, however, their marriage failed during World War I, when Aldington enlisted in the army and was sent to France.

H. D. remained for a short while in London, where she became one of the leaders of the Imagist group. In 1920 she returned to America and settled in California, where she remained for a year before returning to England. After 1921, she lived in Switzerland, where she died in 1961.

Like the Greek lyrics that she greatly admired, H. D.'s early poems were characteristically brief, precise, and direct. Often emphasizing light, color, and physical textures, she created vivid, emotive images. She also abandoned traditional rhythmical patterns, instead creating innovative musical rhythms in her poetry.

In 1925 almost all of H. D.'s early poems were collected in *Collected Poems.* This volume also contains her translations from the *Odyssey* and from the Greek poet Sappho. She also wrote a play, *Hippolytus Temporizes,* which appeared in 1927, and two prose works: *Palimpsest* (1926) and *Hedylus* (1928).

During the later stages of her career, H. D. focused on writing longer works, including *The Walls Do Not Fall* (1944) and *The Flowering of the Rod* (1946). She also wrote an epic poem, *Helen in Egypt.* Comparing her early and late poetry, critic Joseph N. Riddel wrote: "The major distinction . . . is that the [later] poem has become a process or act of discovery. No longer a closed form, a thing itself, it has become a generative act." Despite these later works, however, H. D. is remembered mainly for her early Imagist poetry.

GUIDE FOR INTERPRETING

Pear Tree; Heat

Writers' Techniques

Imagery. Imagery refers to words or phrases that create mental pictures, or images, that appeal to one or more of the five senses—sight, hearing, touch, smell, or taste. Most often images appeal to our sense of sight. For example, H. D. creates a visual picture in our minds in "Pear Tree," when she writes "no flower ever opened so staunch a white leaf." Sometimes, however, images do not appeal to our sense of sight, and in some cases a single image appeals to more than one sense.

Imagery was the most vital element of Imagist poems. The Imagists focused on presenting powerful and vivid images, while deleting unnecessary or abstract words and avoiding explanations and generalizations. As a result the Imagists depended on the power of their images to evoke emotions and to capture the readers' attention.

Focus

Think of an image that you find especially striking. For example, you might think of a raging fire, a cherry tree in full bloom, or a snow-covered pine tree swaying in the winter wind. Then prepare a list of sensory details you might use to capture this image.

Primary Source

According to poet and critic Louis Untermeyer, H. D. was the "most important member" of the group of Imagists, including Ezra Pound, with whom she worked.

> She was the only one who steadfastly held to the letter as well as the spirit of its *credo*. She was, in fact, the only true Imagist. Her poems are like a set of Tanagra figurines. Here, at first glance, the effect is chilling—beauty seems held in a frozen gesture. But it is in this very fixation of light, color, and emotion that she achieves intensity. What at first seemed static becomes fluent; the arrested moment glows with quivering tension.
>
> Observe the poem entitled "Heat." Here, in the fewest possible words, is something beyond the description of heat—here is the effect of it. In these lines one feels the weight and solidity of a midsummer afternoon. . . . Her efforts to draw the contemporary world are less happy. H. D. is best in her reflections of clear-cut loveliness in a quietly pagan world; in most of her moods, she seems less a modern writer than an inspired anachronism."

How H. D. uses vivid images to create the "effect" of heat, rather than simply describe it, marks her as one of the Imagists. What effect does she create in "Pear Tree"?

Pear Tree

H. D.

Silver dust
lifted from the earth,
higher than my arms reach,
you have mounted,
5 O silver,
higher than my arms reach
you front us with great mass;

no flower ever opened
so staunch a white leaf,
10 no flower ever parted silver
from such rare silver;

O white pear,
your flower-tufts
thick on the branch
15 bring summer and ripe fruits
in their purple hearts.

ORCHARD IN BLOOM, LOUVEÇIENNES, 1872
Camille Pissarro
National Gallery of Art, Washington, D.C.

Your Response

1. What image does this poem bring to mind?
2. What emotions does the image evoke?

Interpreting

3. (a) What is the "silver dust" referred to in the first stanza? (b) In what sense is the silver dust "lifted from the earth"?
4. (a) What time of year is the speaker describing? (b) How is this information conveyed?
5. In the final stanza, H. D. uses apostrophe, directly addressing the pear tree. How does her use of this technique help convey a sense of harmony between humanity and nature?

Applying

6. H. D. uses the color silver several times. What associations do you have with the color silver?

THINKING AND WRITING

Writing an Imagist Poem

Write a poem in which you focus on creating a single vivid and emotive image. Imagine that you are writing your poem for someone who has never seen what you are describing. Start by reviewing the list of sensory details you made before. Add any additional details that come to mind. Write your poem in free verse, trying to capture the natural rhythms of ordinary speech. When you finish writing, revise your poem and share it with your classmates.

Commentary

In "Pear Tree," H. D. writes about a pear tree blossoming in spring. In another poem about a pear tree, entitled "Orchard," H. D. describes the tree at another point in its cycle of nature—late summer. When she addresses the tree in "Pear Tree," she seems to convey a sense of continuity between humanity and nature that is full of beautiful and rich promise. Her address to the pear tree in "Orchard" suggests that the tree's beauty is too much to bear: "you have flayed us with your blossoms, / spare us the beauty / of fruit-trees!" Comparing "Pear Tree" with "Orchard" may help you understand how imagery works to convey different meanings and moods in H. D.'s poetry.

Orchard

I saw the first pear
as it fell—
the honey-seeking, golden-banded,
the yellow swarm,
was not more fleet than I,
(spare us from loveliness!)
and I fell prostrate,
crying:
you have flayed us with your blossoms,
spare us the beauty
of fruit-trees!

The honey-seeking
paused not;
the air thundered their song,
and I alone was prostrate.

O rough-hewn
god of the orchard,
I bring you an offering—
do you, alone unbeautiful,
son of the god,
spare us from loveliness:
these fallen hazel-nuts,
stripped late of their green sheaths,
grapes, red-purple,
their berries
dripping with wine;
pomegranates already broken,
and shrunken figs,
and quinces untouched,
I bring you as offering.

OVERHANGING CLOUD IN JULY
Charles Burchfield
The Whitney Museum

Heat

H. D.

O wind, rend open the heat,
cut apart the heat,
rend it to tatters.

Fruit cannot drop
5 through this thick air—
fruit cannot fall into heat
that presses up and blunts
the points of pears
and rounds the grapes.

10 Cut the heat—
plow through it,
turning it on either side
of your path.

RESPONDING TO THE SELECTION

Your Response
1. How does this poem make you feel?
2. What associations of your own do you bring to the poem?

Interpreting
3. (a) What impression of heat does the speaker express? (b) How do the descriptions of the heat's interactions with the wind and fruit convey this impression?
4. What specific type of heat is the speaker describing?

Applying
5. (a) What is your own dominant impression of heat? (b) How does this compare with your dominant impression of cold?

ANALYZING LITERATURE

Understanding Imagery
   Imagery refers to language that creates mental pictures, or images, that appeal to one or more of the five senses. For example, when H. D. writes, "Fruit cannot drop through this thick air," she creates an image that appeals to both our sense of touch and our sense of sight.
1. Find another image that appeals to both the sense of touch and the sense of sight.
2. Find an image that appeals only to our sense of touch.

CRITICAL THINKING AND READING

Analyzing the Effect of Imagery
   The Imagists relied on imagery to capture the reader's interest and evoke an emotional response. For example, H. D.'s images of a blooming tree in "Pear Tree" are likely to evoke a sense of harmony and beauty and a feeling of hope.
1. What types of feelings do H. D.'s images of heat evoke?
2. Why are H. D.'s images of heat likely to capture the reader's interest?

LEARNING OPTIONS

1. **Writing.** Poet and critic Louis Untermeyer claims that in "Heat," H. D. goes beyond describing heat; she presents "the effect of it." Write a poem that captures the effect of cold or some other sensation. Begin by brainstorming your impressions. Then use free verse to create an image that appeals to the senses. Like H. D. you might address your poem to a force of nature.
2. **Cross-curricular Connection.** What music makes you feel the weight and solidity of a midsummer afternoon? Consider how this poem makes you feel. Then find a piece of music that similarly evokes the effect of heat. Play the music for classmates.

WILLIAM CARLOS WILLIAMS

1883–1963

A close friend of Ezra Pound, William Carlos Williams was an important member of the Imagist movement. Opposing Pound's belief in using allusions to maintain a link to the past, Williams focused on capturing the common, everyday images of his time in an effort to create poetry with relevance to the lives of ordinary people.

Williams was born in Rutherford, New Jersey, where he spent most of his life. After graduating from the University of Pennsylvania Medical School, he became a pediatrician. In 1909 he published his first volume of poetry and began pursuing a double career as a poet and a doctor. Williams felt that his experiences as a doctor helped provide him with inspiration as a poet, crediting medicine for his ability to "gain entrance to . . . the secret gardens of the self."

While Williams's first book was modeled after the work of English Romantic poets, he soon developed his own distinctive voice. This voice emerged with the publication of *Spring and All* (1913), a book of mixed prose and poetry. In this book and in *In the American Grain* (1925), Williams made it clear that his aim was to capture the essence of modern American life by depicting a variety of ordinary people, objects, and experiences using up-to-date, everyday language. He avoided presenting explanations or making generalizations, commenting that a poet should deal in "No ideas but in things." By this he meant that a poet should present concrete images that speak for themselves, evoking emotions and stimulating thoughts and ideas.

In 1948 Williams suffered a heart attack, and three years later he had the first of a series of strokes. He was forced to abandon his medical practice, and writing became increasingly difficult. However, he still managed to produce *Paterson* (1946–1958), a five-part epic poem filled with observations about life in the city of Paterson, New Jersey, and two additional collections of poetry, *The Desert Music* (1954) and *Pictures from Breughel and Other Poems* (1962). In 1963 he received the Pulitzer Prize for *Pictures of Breughel.*

Despite his fame and popularity and the prestigious awards he won, Williams always encouraged the young poets who wrote him letters or arrived at his home. He seemed never to forget the loneliness and isolation he himself had felt as a young and struggling poet. "I think the artist, generally speaking, feels lonely," he remarked in 1950. "Perhaps his recourse to art, in any form, comes from his essential loneliness. He is usually in rebellion against the world."

GUIDE FOR INTERPRETING

The Locust Tree in Flower; The Red Wheelbarrow; This Is Just to Say

Writers' Techniques

Rhythm. William Carlos Williams believed that rhythm—the arrangement of stressed and unstressed syllables in a poem—is the essence of poetry. In writing his poems, he attempted to shape the language of everyday speech into rhythmic units—lines and stanzas—that reflect and reinforce the meaning of the poems. Because each line serves as a separate rhythmic unit, you should read his poetry line by line, pausing briefly at the end of each line and pausing a bit longer at the end of each stanza. These pauses reinforce meaning by adding emphasis to important words, ideas, and images.

Focus

William Carlos Williams's poems focus on ordinary people, objects, and experiences. For example, in this group of poems, he writes about a locust tree, a red wheelbarrow, and the experience of eating plums from the icebox. Prepare a list of other ordinary experiences about which he might have written.

Primary Source

Modernist poets often took modern, industrial America as their subject. Claiming an equal status with English poetry, they asserted that common American subjects and common American language were as appropriate to poetry as the elevated subjects and diction of traditional poetry. In so doing they also invented a new critical language. Calling a poem a "machine made of words," Williams used a modern, industrial image to refashion conventional ideas about poetry. He wrote in 1944:

> A poem is a small (or large) machine made of words. When I say there's nothing sentimental about a poem I mean that there can be no part, as in any other machine, that is redundant.
>
> Prose may carry a load of ill-defined matter like a ship. But poetry is the machine which drives it, pruned to a perfect economy. As in all machines its movement is intrinsic, undulant, a physical more than a literary character. In a poem this movement is distinguished in each case by the character of the speech from which it arrives. . . .
>
> There is no poetry of distinction without formal invention, for it is in the intimate form that works of art achieve their exact meaning, in which they most resemble the machine, to give language its highest dignity, its illumination in the environment to which it is native.

PINK LOCUSTS AND WINDY MOON, 1959
Charles Burchfield
Collection of the Chase Manhattan Bank

The Locust Tree in Flower

William Carlos Williams

Among
of
green

stiff
5   old
bright

broken
branch
come

10 white
sweet
May

again

RESPONDING TO THE SELECTION

Your Response

1. What do you associate with the month of May?
2. What "thing" captures the essence of spring for you?

Interpreting

3. How does the title help you to understand the poem?
4. (a) Which lines describe the locust tree before it blossoms? (b) Which lines describe the tree after it blossoms?
5. (a) What does this poem reveal about a locust tree's appearance? (b) How does the line arrangement add emphasis to the tree's important characteristics?
6. What is the significance of the final line?

Applying

7. How well does this poem support Williams's claim that poets should deal in "No ideas but in things"?

LEARNING OPTIONS

1. **Cross-curricular Connection.** Is the image Williams presents of the locust tree accurate? Use an encyclopedia or a book about horticulture to learn more about the flowering tree. Share your findings with classmates.
2. **Art.** Create your own image of spring. You might draw a picture, take a photograph, make a sculpture, write a poem, or simply bring to class an object symbolizing spring. Share your image with classmates. Does it speak for itself?

The Red Wheelbarrow

William Carlos Williams

so much depends
upon

a red wheel
barrow

5   glazed with rain
water

beside the white
chickens.

RESPONDING TO THE SELECTION

Your Response

1. How is this poem like a painting of a still life?
2. If you were to use words to paint a still life, what objects would you mention?

Interpreting

3. What do you think depends on the red wheelbarrow?
4. To what sense do the images in the poem appeal?

Applying

5. (a) What types of associations do you have with the images in the poem? (b) What types of feelings do the images evoke?

ANALYZING LITERATURE

Understanding Rhythm

In writing his poems, William Carlos Williams attempted to shape the language of everyday speech into rhythmic units—lines and stanzas—that reflect and reinforce the meaning of the poems. For example, in "The Red Wheelbarrow," Williams calls our attention to the image of the wheelbarrow by breaking up the word and presenting it on two separate lines. His presentation of the word also reflects its meaning, since a wheelbarrow is composed of two separate parts.

1. What rhythmic and visual pattern does Williams establish in "The Red Wheelbarrow"?
2. How does the pattern help to emphasize each separate image?

LEARNING OPTION

Speaking and Listening. Discussing "The Red Wheelbarrow," critic Roy Harvey Pearce comments: "At its worst this is togetherness in a chickenyard. At its best it is an exercise in the creation of the poetic out of the anti-poetic." How do you see it? Be prepared to defend your view in a class discussion.

This Is Just to Say

William Carlos Williams

I have eaten
the plums
that were in
the icebox
5 and which
you were probably
saving
for breakfast

Forgive me
10 they were delicious
so sweet
and so cold

RESPONDING TO THE SELECTION

Your Response
1. What is your reaction to this poem?
2. What philosophy of life do you think this poem expresses? Explain.

Interpreting
3. How does the title relate to the poem?
4. To what senses do the images in the poem appeal?
5. (a) Why is the incident described in the poem important to the speaker? (b) How do the last three lines help to reveal the incident's importance?

Applying
6. Why do you think Williams might have chosen to write a poem about such a seemingly insignificant incident?

THINKING AND WRITING

Writing an Apology
"This Is Just to Say" is, after all, a note of apology. However, the speaker doesn't seem to be at all sorry for what he did. Create a similar situation: A character does something he or she knows is incorrect but is actually glad to have done. For example, you might write about a sister borrowing a sweater without asking or a child giving into temptation and sneaking a piece of just-baked pie. Using Williams's poem as a model, write a note of apology. When you revise, make sure you have included details that appeal to the senses.

LEARNING OPTION

Writing. Make Williams's poem into your own. Choose another food to take the place of "the plums" (line 2) and revise the poem accordingly. Share your version with classmates. Is it as effective as the original? Why or why not?

CARL SANDBURG

1878–1967

No poet better captured the spirit of industrial America than did Carl Sandburg. In his poems he paints a vivid portrait of the American working class, capturing its energy and enthususiasm in the lively, accessible manner that made him one of the most popular poets of his day.

The son of Swedish immigrants, Sandburg was born and raised in Galesburg, Illinois. Forced to go to work at an early age, Sandburg attended school on an irregular basis. After spending six years working at a variety of jobs, he enlisted in the army in 1898 to fight in the Spanish-American War. When he returned from the war, he enrolled at Lombard College. He left school shortly before his graduation, however, and spent several years traveling around the country, again working at a variety of jobs.

In 1913 Sandburg settled in Chicago, where he worked as a newspaper reporter. He began publishing poetry in *Poetry* magazine, a highly regarded literary journal based in Chicago, and in 1916 he published his first book, *Chicago Poems*. The book sold well and was praised for its passion and vigor. Sandburg earned widespread recognition and helped establish Chicago as one of the country's leading literary centers. During the next ten years, Sandburg published three more successful collections of poetry, *Cornhuskers* (1918), *Smoke and Steel* (1920), and *Slabs of the Sunburnt West* (1922).

In 1928 Sandburg offered ten definitions of poetry, among them these two: "Poetry is a search for syllables to shoot at the barriers of the unknown and the unknowable" and "Poetry is the opening and closing of a door, leaving those who look through to guess about what is seen during a moment."

While continuing to write poetry, Sandburg then began touring the country delivering lectures on Walt Whitman and Abraham Lincoln—two men whom he greatly admired—and started a career as a folk singer. He also spent a great deal of time collecting material for a biography of Lincoln, and he prepared an anthology of American folk songs, *The American Songbook* (1927). His multivolume Lincoln biography won the Pulitzer Prize in 1940, and in 1951 he received a second Pulitzer Prize for his *Complete Poems*. Sandburg was also awarded the United States Presidential Medal in 1964, and he was asked to address a joint session of Congress on the 150th anniversary of Lincoln's birth. During his later years, he lived on a farm in North Carolina, where he continued to write poetry and work on his autobiography.

GUIDE FOR INTERPRETING

Grass; *from* The People, Yes; Chicago

Free Verse. Heavily influenced by the poetry of Walt Whitman, Carl Sandburg composed his poems using long open lines of free verse—verse that has irregular meter and line length. Written in simple, straightforward language, Sandburg's long free-verse lines capture the activity and energy of industrial America and mirror the natural rhythms of ordinary speech. Sandburg's use of simple language and natural rhythms reflects his interest in common people—who usually served as the subjects of his poems—and his desire to reach a wide audience.

Rather than creating a pattern through regular meter and line length, Sandburg generally establishes a pattern in his poems through the use of parallelism—the repetition of phrases or clauses that are similar in structure or meaning. His use of parallelism also helps to emphasize important ideas and contributes to the natural rhythm of his poetry.

Throughout his career Sandburg strove to capture in his poetry the distinctiveness of American life and language. To do this, he wrote from the perspective of ordinary men and women, using the idioms and slang of common speech and treating subjects from ordinary lives. As one critic put it, he "broadened the field" of poetic subjects by writing about industrial scenes, such as packing houses, mills, and factories. He also described and celebrated the lives of the people who worked in these jobs. Sandburg's populist point of view is clearly evident in "The People, Yes," in which he speaks in the voice of the working, struggling people. It is also evident in his poem "Grass," where he reminds us of the common soldier who fought and died in history's many wars.

These characteristics of Sandburg's poetry distinguished his work from that of many of the poets of his day. For example, the poetry of Ezra Pound and T. S. Eliot is filled with sometimes obscure allusions and difficult language. Such poets as Pound and Eliot did not see poetry as primarily a way to portray the thoughts and feelings of common people living their everyday lives. As you read, you may wish to keep in mind Sandburg's different poetic goals.

In his poem "The People, Yes," Carl Sandburg uses vivid imagery to capture the essence of the American people. Prepare a list of descriptive details you could use in describing the American people.

Grass

Carl Sandburg

Pile the bodies high at Austerlitz and Waterloo.[1]
Shovel them under and let me work—
    I am the grass; I cover all.

And pile them high at Gettysburg
5   And pile them high at Ypres and Verdun.[2]
Shovel them under and let me work.
Two years, ten years, and passengers ask the conductor:
    What place is this?
    Where are we now?

10   I am the grass.
    Let me work.

---

1. Austerlitz (ôs′ tər lĭts′) **and Waterloo:** Sites of battles of the Napoleonic Wars.
2. Ypres (ē′ pr) **and Verdun** (vər dŭn′): Sites of battles of World War I.

MARSHES, DUNES AND FIELDS
Jane Freilicher

RESPONDING TO THE SELECTION

Your Response

1. What did you see as you read this poem?
2. Based on this poem, how would you describe Sandburg's attitude toward war? Explain.

Interpreting

3. (a) What is the attitude of the grass toward the events referred to in the poem? (b) What does this attitude suggest about humanity's relationship to nature?

4. How do the questions asked by the passengers reflect the pointlessness of war?
5. (a) Is Sandburg suggesting that it is possible for the death and destruction of war to be covered over and easily forgotten? Support your answer. (b) What is the purpose of the poem?

Applying

6. (a) What types of people do you think might share the attitude of the grass toward war? (b) What types of people do you think might strongly object to this attitude?

from The People, Yes

Carl Sandburg

The people will live on.
The learning and blundering people will live on.
They will be tricked and sold and again sold
And go back to the nourishing earth for rootholds,
5 The people so peculiar in renewal and comeback,
You can't laugh off their capacity to take it.
The mammoth[1] rests between his cyclonic dramas.

The people so often sleepy, weary, enigmatic,
is a vast huddle with many units saying:
10 "I earn my living.
I make enough to get by
and it takes all my time.
If I had more time
I could do more for myself
15 and maybe for others.
I could read and study
and talk things over
and find out about things.
It takes time.
20 I wish I had the time."

. . .

The people know the salt of the sea
and the strength of the winds
lashing the corners of the earth.
The people take the earth
25 as a tomb of rest and a cradle of hope.
Who else speaks for the Family of Man?
They are in tune and step
with constellations of universal law.

. . .

In the darkness with a great bundle of grief the people
march.
30 In the night, and overhead a shovel of stars for keeps, the
people march:
"Where to? what next?"

---

1. **mammoth** (mam' əth) *n.*: An extinct elephant with hairy skin.

RESPONDING TO THE SELECTION

Your Response

1. Do you think that this poem captures the essence of the American people today? Why or why not?
2. Do you view survival in today's world as a victory? Why or why not?

Recalling

3. What will happen to the "learning and blundering people"?

Interpreting

4. (a) What details suggest that this poem is about working-class people? (b) What is the speaker's attitude toward these people?
5. What does the poem suggest are the reasons people "live on," while animals such as the mammoth become extinct?

Applying

6. What is the significance of the fact that this poem was written during the Great Depression?

THINKING AND WRITING

Writing a Poem Using Free Verse

Using free verse, write a poem that captures the essence of the American people. Start by reviewing the list of details you prepared before you began reading. Try to think of additional details to add to your list. When you write your poem, try to structure your verse to re-create the natural rhythms of ordinary speech and try to use parallelism to establish a pattern and to emphasize your important ideas. When you finish writing, revise your poem and share it with your classmates.

Commentary

Many critics of American poetry have noted that Sandburg wrote in the tradition of Walt Whitman. Both celebrated the common people in their verse; both used common, everyday language instead of literary language; and both gave great range to free verse.

Another American poet with whom Sandburg may be likened is Edwin Arlington Robinson. Both used the idiomatic language of local dialects, with Sandburg staying close to midwestern speech and Robinson using that of his native New England. Both were concerned with the everyday lives of ordinary people. And both wanted to portray the realities of life in America.

For Robinson this meant writing poetry that was completely unsentimental in its vivid portrayal of individual lives. His poetic portraits are psychologically accurate and clearsighted descriptions of the ironies of existence. He wrote about lonely outcasts and misfits sympathetically and objectively. For example, he recorded Miniver Cheevy's drinking and Richard Cory's suicide with wry bitterness, but he managed to evoke feelings of tenderness for these characters while exposing their degradation.

Sandburg's effort to portray the realities of life in America led him to take a different approach. He did not create vivid, psychological portraits of characters. To capture the variety of everyday life, he used an impressionistic poetic style, creating a collective image of the "common people." Although his poetry, like Robinson's, shows an awareness of the destructive nature of society, Sandburg's verse is a hymn to the indestructibility of the human spirit. It stresses the bonds between people and reminds us that human virtues will prevail amid the disorder and waste of industrial society.

Chicago

Carl Sandburg

Hog Butcher for the World,
Tool Maker, Stacker of Wheat,
Player with Railroads and the Nation's Freight Handler;
Stormy, husky, brawling,
5   City of the Big Shoulders:

They tell me you are wicked and I believe them, for I have seen
    your painted women under the gas lamps luring the farm
    boys.
And they tell me you are crooked and I answer: Yes, it is true
    I have seen the gunman kill and go free to kill again.
And they tell me you are brutal and my reply is: On the faces
    of women and children I have seen the marks of wanton
    hunger.
And having answered so I turn once more to those who sneer
    at this my city, and I give them back the sneer and say to
    them:
10   Come and show me another city with lifted head singing so
    proud to be alive and coarse and strong and cunning.
Flinging magnetic curses amid the toil of piling job on job,
    here is a tall bold slugger set vivid against the little soft
    cities;
Fierce as a dog with tongue lapping for action, cunning as a
    savage pitted against the wilderness,
      Bareheaded,
      Shoveling,
15   Wrecking,
      Planning,
      Building, breaking, rebuilding,

Under the smoke, dust all over his mouth, laughing with
    white teeth,
Under the terrible burden of destiny laughing as a young man
    laughs,
20   Laughing even as an ignorant fighter laughs who has never
    lost a battle,
Bragging and laughing that under his wrist is the pulse, and
    under his ribs the heart of the people,
        Laughing!
Laughing the stormy, husky, brawling laughter of Youth, half-
    naked, sweating, proud to be Hog Butcher, Tool Maker,
    Stacker of Wheat, Player with Railroads and Freight Handler
    to the Nation.

RESPONDING TO THE SELECTION

Your Response

1. How does Sandburg's depiction of Chicago compare with your image of the city?
2. Do you share the poet's pride in the city? Explain.

Interpreting

3. (a) What overall impression does this poem convey of the city of Chicago? (b) What human qualities does the speaker attribute to the city?
4. (a) Of what faults concerning his city is the speaker aware? (b) How do these faults seem to affect his attitude toward the city?
5. What details suggest that Chicago was still a young and rapidly developing city when this poem was written?

Applying

6. (a) In what ways is the city described in this poem similar to and different from other cities with which you are familiar? (b) What do the differences among American cities reveal about the nation's character?

ANALYZING LITERATURE

Understanding Free Verse

Carl Sandburg's poems were generally written in long lines of **free verse**—verse that is irregular in meter and line length.

1. How does Sandburg's use of long, open free-verse lines in "Chicago" help to convey the energy, activity, and immensity of the city?
2. How does he emphasize some of the city's important characteristics by varying line length?

EDNA ST. VINCENT MILLAY

1892–1950

Although she spent only a few years in the New York City community known as Greenwich Village, Edna St. Vincent Millay will always be associated with the unconventional lifestyle and artistic experimentation characteristic of Greenwich Village during the 1920's. An enormously popular poet of her day, Millay embodied the rebellious, questing spirit that emerged in the aftermath of World War I.

Millay was born in Rockford, Maine, and began writing poetry at an early age. "Renascence," the first of her poems to attract public attention, was written when she was still in high school, and it appeared in a literary anthology when she was only twenty.

After graduating from Vassar College in 1917, Millay moved to Greenwich Village and quickly became part of the New York City artistic scene. While supporting herself by working as an actress and a playwright, she published a number of short stories and several collections of poetry, including *Renascence and Other Poems* (1917), *A Few Figs from Thistles* (1920), and *Second April* (1921). Her collection, *The Harp-Weaver and Other Poems* (1923), was awarded the Pulitzer Prize.

In 1923 Millay married Eugen Boissevain and moved to a farm in upstate New York, where she spent the rest of her life. Although she continued to write poetry, she began turning away from the intensely personal lyric poems that had made her famous. Instead, deeply disturbed by the rise of fascism in Europe and the resulting war, she started focusing on current events.

In her earlier poetry, which is generally regarded as her best, Millay displayed an ability to express the primary concerns of her time in a readily accessible, lyrical style. Like the work of other modern writers, her poetry expresses a rebellious attitude and explores the uncertainty and disillusionment of modern life. Yet her work remains linked to the past through her use of traditional verse forms and poetic devices.

Millay expressed her generation's sense of the intense brevity and beauty of life in *A Few Figs from Thistles:* "My candle burns at both ends; / It will not last the night; / But, ah, my foes, and, oh, my friends— / It gives a lovely light."

GUIDE FOR INTERPRETING

Renascence

Theme. The theme is the central idea or insight about life that a writer hopes to convey in a literary work. Some themes are universal, occurring again and again in the literature of many eras. For example, the idea that nature is a powerful and wondrous force is a recurring theme in the literature of the Native Americans, the Transcendentalists, and the writers of our own century. Writers also frequently express themes that reflect specific concerns of the eras in which they lived. For example, because of rapid technological changes and the shattering effects of World War I, modern writers often focused on themes related to the uncertain, fragmentary, and confusing nature of life in the modern world.

In "Renascence" Edna St. Vincent Millay explores a universal theme—the idea that a person can be reborn or reawakened to discover a new understanding of the world. However, in describing the need to be reborn, she expresses concerns and attitudes that are characteristic of the modern period.

Critics were full of praise for "Renascence" and full of admiration for its young author. Critic and poet Louis Untermeyer described the poem as "[b]eginning like a casual rhyme, it proceeds to a set of climaxes. It is as if a child had, in the midst of ingenuousness, uttered some terrific truth." Harriet Monroe, who founded *Poetry: A Magazine of Verse* in 1912, the year "Renascence" appeared in *The Lyric Year,* praised the poem highly: "The surprise of youth over the universe, the emotion of youth at encountering inexplicable infinities—that is expressed in this poem, and it is a big thing to express. Moreover, it is expressed with a certain triumphant joy, the very mood of exultant youth; and the poet gets a certain freshness into a measure often stilted." Finally, one of Millay's early biographers, Miriam Gurko, wrote: "'Renascence' would have been a tremendous achievement for a poet of any age. For a young girl it was phenomenal. One reader was to call it 'part birdsong, part essay in philosophy.' It is the overture to all her later work, embodying what were to become her principal themes and techniques. It expresses her feelings about death and her joy at being alive. It is a lyrical rhapsody on nature. At the same time, it reveals her early awareness of suffering and injustice. . . ."

Do you know of any other writers who have achieved widespread recognition at an early age?

Freewrite, exploring why a person might feel the need to experience a rebirth.

Renascence

Edna St. Vincent Millay

All I could see from where I stood
Was three long mountains and a wood;
I turned and looked another way,
And saw three islands in a bay.
5   So with my eyes I traced the line
Of the horizon, thin and fine,
Straight around till I was come
Back to where I'd started from;
And all I saw from where I stood
10   Was three long mountains and a wood.

Over these things I could not see:
These were the things that bounded me.
And I could touch them with my hand,
Almost, I thought, from where I stand!
15   And all at once things seemed so small
My breath came short, and scarce at all.
But, sure, the sky is big, I said:
Miles and miles above my head.
So here upon my back I'll lie
20   And look my fill into the sky.
And so I looked, and after all,
The sky was not so very tall.
The sky, I said, must somewhere stop . . .
And—sure enough!—I see the top!
25   The sky, I thought, is not so grand;
I 'most could touch it with my hand!
And reaching up my hand to try,
I screamed, to feel it touch the sky.

I screamed, and—lo!—Infinity
30   Came down and settled over me;
Forced back my scream into my chest;
Bent back my arm upon my breast;
And, pressing of the Undefined
The definition on my mind.
35   Held up before my eyes a glass
Through which my shrinking sight did pass
Until it seemed I must behold
Immensity made manifold;
Whispered to me a word whose sound
40   Deafened the air for worlds around,

And brought unmuffled to my ears
The gossiping of friendly spheres,
The creaking of the tented sky,
The ticking of Eternity.

45   I saw and heard, and knew at last
The How and Why of all things, past,
And present, and forevermore.
The Universe, cleft to the core,
Lay open to my probing sense,
50   That, sickening, I would fain pluck thence
But could not,—nay! but needs must suck
At the great wound, and could not pluck
My lips away till I had drawn
All venom out,—Ah, fearful pawn:
55   For my omniscience paid I toll
In infinite remorse of soul.

All sin was of my sinning, all
Atoning mine, and mine the gall
Of all regret. Mine was the weight
60   Of every brooded wrong, the hate
That stood behind each envious thrust,
Mine every greed, mine every lust.

And all the while, for every grief,
Each suffering, I craved relief
65 With individual desire;
Craved all in vain! And felt fierce fire
About a thousand people crawl;
Perished with each,—then mourned for all!

A man was starving in Capri;[1]
70 He moved his eyes and looked at me;
I felt his gaze, I heard his moan,
And knew his hunger as my own.
I saw at sea a great fog bank
Between two ships that struck and sank;
75 A thousand screams the heavens smote;
And every scream tore through my throat.

No hurt I did not feel, no death
That was not mine; mine each last breath
That, crying, met an answering cry
80 From the compassion that was I.
All suffering mine, and mine its rod;
Mine, pity like the pity of God.

Ah, awful weight! Infinity
Pressed down upon the finite Me!
85 My anguished spirit, like a bird,
Beating against my lips I heard;
Yet lay the weight so close about
There was no room for it without.
And so beneath the weight lay I
90 And suffered death, but could not die.
Long had I lain thus, craving death,
When quietly the earth beneath
Gave way, and inch by inch, so great
At last had grown the crushing weight,
95 Into the earth I sank till I
Full six feet under ground did lie,
And sank no more,—there is no weight
Can follow here, however great.
From off my breast I felt it roll,
100 And as it went my tortured soul
Burst forth and fled in such a gust
That all about me swirled the dust.

Deep in the earth I rested now.
Cool is its hand upon the brow
105 And soft its breast beneath the head

---

1. **Capri** (kä prē'): An Italian island located near the entrance to the Bay of Naples.

Of one who is so gladly dead.
And all at once, and over all
The pitying rain began to fall;
I lay and heard each pattering hoof
110 Upon my lowly, thatchèd roof,
And seemed to love the sound far more
Than ever I had done before.
For rain it hath a friendly sound
To one who's six feet under ground;
115 And scarce the friendly voice or face,
A grave is such a quiet place.

The rain, I said, is kind to come
And speak to me in my new home.
I would I were alive again
120 To kiss the fingers of the rain,
To drink into my eyes the shine
Of every slanting silver line,
To catch the freshened, fragrant breeze
From drenched and dripping apple trees.
125 For soon the shower will be done,
And then the broad face of the sun
Will laugh above the rain-soaked earth
Until the world with answering mirth
Shakes joyously, and each round drop
130 Rolls, twinkling, from its grass-blade top.

How can I bear it, buried here,
While overhead the sky grows clear
And blue again after the storm?
O, multi-colored, multi-form,
135 Belovèd beauty over me,
That I shall never, never see
Again! Spring-silver, autumn-gold,
That I shall never more behold!—
Sleeping your myriad magics through,
140 Close-sepulchred away from you!
O God, I cried, give me new birth,
And put me back upon the earth!
Upset each cloud's gigantic gourd²
And let the heavy rain, down-poured
145 In one big torrent, set me free,
Washing my grave away from me!

I ceased; and through the breathless hush
That answered me, the far-off rush
Of herald wings came whispering

---

2. gourd (gôrd) *n.*: The dried, hollowed-out shell of a piece of fruit
from a gourd plant, often used as a dipper or drinking cup.

150 Like music down the vibrant string
Of my ascending prayer, and—crash!
Before the wild wind's whistling lash
The startled storm-clouds reared on high
And plunged in terror down the sky!
155 And the big rain in one black wave
Fell from the sky and struck my grave.

I know not how such things can be;
I only know there came to me
A fragrance such as never clings
160 To aught save happy living things;
A sound as of some joyous elf
Singing sweet songs to please himself,
And, through and over everything,
A sense of glad awakening.
165 The grass, a-tiptoe at my ear,
Whispering to me I could hear;
I felt the rain's cool finger-tips
Brushed tenderly across my lips,
Laid gently on my sealèd sight,
170 And all at once the heavy night
Fell from my eyes and I could see!—
A drenched and dripping apple-tree,
A last long line of silver rain,
A sky grown clear and blue again.
175 And as I looked a quickening gust
Of wind blew up to me and thrust
Into my face a miracle
Of orchard-breath, and with the smell,—
I know not how such things can be!—
180 I breathed my soul back into me.

Ah! Up then from the ground sprang I
And hailed the earth with such a cry
As is not heard save from a man
Who has been dead, and lives again.
185 About the trees my arms I wound;
Like one gone mad I hugged the ground;
I raised my quivering arms on high;
I laughed and laughed into the sky;
Till at my throat a strangling sob
190 Caught fiercely, and a great heart-throb
Sent instant tears into my eyes:
O God, I cried, no dark disguise
Can e'er hereafter hide from me
Thy radiant identity!
195 Thou canst not move across the grass
But my quick eyes will see Thee pass,

Nor speak, however silently,
But my hushed voice will answer Thee.
I know the path that tells Thy way
200　Through the cool eve of every day:
God, I can push the grass apart
And lay my finger on Thy heart!

The world stands out on either side
No wider than the heart is wide:
205　Above the world is stretched the sky,—
No higher than the soul is high.
The heart can push the sea and land
Farther away on either hand:
The soul can split the sky in two,

210　And let the face of God shine through.
But East and West will pinch the heart
That can not keep them pushed apart:
And he whose soul is flat—the sky
Will cave in on him by and by.

RESPONDING TO THE SELECTION

Your Response

1. How would you describe the poet's view of nature?
2. Do you share the poet's view? Explain.

Recalling

3. By what does the speaker feel confined?
4. What happens when the speaker screams?
5. (a) In stanza 4 what lies open to the speaker? (b) What "toll" does she pay for the knowledge she gains?
6. What happens when the earth gives way beneath the weight of infinity?
7. What brings the speaker back to life?

Interpreting

8. In what sense is the speaker "bounded" at the beginning of the poem?
9. (a) What does the action of touching the sky symbolize? (b) Of what does the speaker become aware as a result of this action? (c) How does her awareness affect her?
10. (a) What does the speaker's death symbol-
ize? (b) What realization does she come to that makes her want to be reborn?
11. (a) Restate the ideas presented in the final stanza in your own words. (b) How does the speaker's description of her experiences further develop this theme?

Applying

12. In what ways is the poem's theme reminiscent of Native American and Transcendentalist themes about humanity's spiritual relationship with nature?
13. How does the speaker's need to be reborn reflect the Modernists' sense of disillusionment with the world?

LEARNING OPTION

Writing. What do you think Edna St. Vincent Millay was like as a teenager? Reread her biography on page 749. Then write a brief profile of the young poet for her high-school yearbook. Use your imagination to invent details about her interests and activities.

BIOGRAPHIES

Archibald MacLeish (1892–1982)

A lawyer, teacher, editor, dramatist, and poet, Archibald MacLeish was born in Glencoe, Illinois. He attended Yale, where he distinguished himself in both academics and athletics. He earned a law degree but soon gave up the practice of law to devote himself to literature. His early poems, such as "Ars Poetica," reflect the influence of such Modernist poets as Ezra Pound and T. S. Eliot. However, he eventually changed his style and began using traditional poetic forms in an effort to make his work more accessible. In the 1930's, as fascism rose in Europe and social unrest grew in America, MacLeish became active in politics and began exploring social and political issues in his work. During his career, MacLeish produced more than thirty books and won three Pulitzer Prizes.

Marianne Moore (1887–1972)

Marianne Moore was born in St. Louis, Missouri, and attended Bryn Mawr College. As the editor of the highly regarded literary journal, *The Dial,* she encouraged many new writers by publishing their work. However, she was hesitant about publishing her own work, despite the fact that it had been read and admired by many noted poets. In fact, her first book, *Poems* (1921), was published without her knowledge.

As part of the Modernist movement, Moore wrote poems that were unconventional in form, precise, inventive, and often witty. However, unlike most other Modernists, she chose not to write about the state of modern civilization. Instead, she wrote poems about such subjects as animals and other elements of nature. "Poetry," one of her best-known poems, delves into the subject of poetry itself.

GUIDE FOR INTERPRETING

Writers' Techniques

Ars Poetica; Poetry

Similes. A simile is an explicit comparison between two seemingly dissimilar things. This comparison is clearly indicated by a connecting word such as *like* or *as.* For example, the word *like* signals the comparison in the following simile: The sound of the explosion echoed through the air *like* thunder.

Similes force us to use our imaginations to make connections that are not readily apparent. They enable us to see the world in a startling new way.

Commentary

Marianne Moore was one of the most original poets of her time. Like other Modernists, she sought for ways to break with conventional poetic forms. She experimented with mixing abstract ideas and concrete images and using unusual rhythms, surprising rhymes, and different levels of diction. Her vivid and original images frequently derived from her astonishing range of interests: popular magazines, movies, baseball, boxing, and zoology. Many of her poems, including "Poetry," are striking for the way she arranges long sentences on the page in irregular, unpredictable poetic lines. As you read "Poetry," notice the striking images, and pay attention to the form and meaning of the poem.

Focus

Both Marianne Moore and Archibald MacLeish have definite ideas about what poetry should be. What do you think? What is your definition of poetry?

Ars Poetica[1]

Archibald MacLeish

A poem should be palpable and mute
As a globed fruit,

Dumb
As old medallions to the thumb,

5   Silent as the sleeve-worn stone
Of casement ledges where the moss has grown—

A poem should be wordless
As the flight of birds.

A poem should be motionless in time
10   As the moon climbs,

1. The title is an allusion to Horace's "Ars Poetica," or "The Art of Poetry," which was composed about 20 B.C.

Leaving, as the moon releases
Twig by twig the night-entangled trees,

Leaving, as the moon behind the winter leaves,
Memory by memory the mind—

15 A poem should be motionless in time
As the moon climbs.

A poem should be equal to:
Not true.

For all the history of grief
20 An empty doorway and a maple leaf.

For love
The leaning grasses and two lights above the sea—

A poem should not mean
But be.

RESPONDING TO THE SELECTION

Your Response
1. What do you value in poems, images or words? Explain.
2. What images come to mind when you think of grief? Of love?

Recalling
3. To what does the speaker compare a poem?
4. How should a poem show (a) the history of grief, and (b) love?

Interpreting
5. What do you think the speaker means by saying that a poem should be (a) "palpable and mute" (line 1); (b) "wordless" (line 7); (c) "motionless in time" (line 9); and (d) "equal to: Not true" (lines 17–18)?
6. Why do you think MacLeish chose to focus on the emotions of love and grief?

7. How does the final line sum up the ideas expressed in the poem?

Applying
8. Do you agree with MacLeish's definition of poetry? Why or why not?

ANALYZING LITERATURE

Understanding Similes
A **simile** is an explicit comparison between two seemingly dissimilar things, clearly indicated by a connecting word such as *like* or *as*. For example, MacLeish presents a simile in lines 1 and 2 in which he compares a poem to a globed fruit.
1. What does "globed" suggest about a poem?
2. (a) What comparison is made in the simile in lines 9 and 10? (b) How is this simile developed in the next four lines?
3. What is the effect of the repetition of this simile in lines 15 and 16?

Poetry

Marianne Moore

I, too, dislike it: there are things that are important beyond
  all this fiddle.
    Reading it, however, with a perfect contempt for it, one
      discovers in
  it after all, a place for the genuine.
    Hands that can grasp, eyes
5   that can dilate, hair that can rise
      if it must, these things are important not because a

  high-sounding interpretation can be put upon them but
    because they are
    useful. When they become so derivative as to become
      unintelligible,
  the same thing may be said for all of us, that we do not
    admire what
10   we cannot understand: the bat
        holding on upside down or in quest of something to

  eat, elephants pushing, a wild horse taking a roll, a
    tireless wolf under
    a tree, the immovable critic twitching his skin like a
      horse that feels a flea, the base-
    ball fan, the statistician—
15   nor is it valid
        to discriminate against "business documents and

  schoolbooks"; all these phenomena are important. One
    must make a distinction
    however: when dragged into prominence by half poets,
      the result is not poetry,
  nor till the poets among us can be
20   "literalists of
      the imagination"—above
        insolence and triviality and can present

  for inspection, "imaginary gardens with real toads in
    them," shall we have
    it. In the meantime, if you demand on the one hand,
25   the raw material of poetry in
      all its rawness and
      that which is on the other hand
        genuine, you are interested in poetry.

UNTITLED
Alexander Calder
Solomon R. Guggenheim Museum,
New York

RESPONDING TO THE SELECTION

Your Response

1. Are you interested in poetry? Explain.
2. In your opinion, which word or phrase best describes this poem: "fiddle," "derivative," or "genuine"? Explain.

Recalling

3. What does the speaker say a person discovers when reading poetry "with a perfect contempt for it"?
4. What happens when poems "become so derivative as to become unintelligible"?
5. What happens when poetry is "dragged into prominence by half poets"?
6. What does the speaker say about a person who demands "on the one hand, the raw material of poetry in all its rawness and that which is on the other hand genuine"?

Interpreting

7. What type of poetry does the speaker dislike?

8. (a) What does the speaker mean when she says that poets should be "literalists of the imagination"? (b) What are "imaginary gardens with real toads in them"?
9. What qualities does the speaker believe good poetry should possess?

Applying

10. Do you agree with the speaker's ideas about poetry? Why or why not?
11. Explain the similarities and the differences between Moore's views of poetry and MacLeish's.

LEARNING OPTION

Art. Marianne Moore sees the poetry in real things: "the bat holding on upside down . . . ," "elephants pushing," and so on. In a photo essay, show some real things in which you see poetry. You might use either photographs that you take or pictures from books or magazines.

E. E. CUMMINGS

1894–1962

Although E. E. Cummings's poems tend to be very unconventional in form and style, they generally embody traditional thought. In his finest poems, Cummings explores such subjects as love and nature, while innovatively using capitalization, punctuation, and grammar to reinforce meaning.

Following the French poets Guillaume Apollinaire and Stéphane Mallarmé, who had experimented with the typography of their poetry, Cummings was a member of a group of poets within the Modernist movement who played with the visual appearance of their poems. His interest in the visual aspects of poetry may have been related to his gifts as a painter. His paintings and drawings are still shown in museums. However, the unpredictability of the printed page in a volume of Cummings's poetry also reflects his lifelong goal of upsetting the conventional expectations of his readers.

Edward Estlin Cummings was born in Cambridge, Massachusetts. He graduated from Harvard and served in the French ambulance corps during World War I. In France he was unjustly imprisoned for three months in a detention camp. His experiences as a prisoner later provided him with the material for a vivid war novel, *The Enormous Room* (1922).

After the war Cummings remained in Paris to study painting but soon returned to the United States and settled in Greenwich Village in New York City. There he began working full-time as an artist, devoting time to both writing and painting. He went on to produce four volumes of poetry. While some critics attacked his unconventional style, all of his collections were well received by the general public. People responded favorably to his playful use of language and his concern with the appearance as well as the content of his poems. He also became known for his concern for the individual, his ability to recognize life's ironies, his interest in human relationships and human emotions, and his humorous approach to many of the confusing aspects of modern life.

Although his most often anthologized poems are his most sentimental ones, Cummings's best and most characteristic works are satirical in their attitude toward the world. He challenged conformity and the comfortable notions of fixed beliefs.

Cummings received a number of awards for his work, including the Boston Fine Arts Poetry Festival Award and the Bollingen Prize in Poetry. In 1968, six years after his death, a complete volume of his poetry, *The Complete Poems, 1913–1962,* was published.

GUIDE FOR INTERPRETING

since feeling is first; anyone lived in a pretty how town; old age sticks

Writers' Techniques

Style. Style refers to the manner in which a writer puts his or her ideas into words. It involves the characteristics of a literary selection that concern form of expression rather than the thoughts conveyed. In poetry, style is determined by such factors as choice and arrangement of words, length and arrangement of lines, stanza length and format, use of punctuation and capitalization, and use of literary devices.

Because he was as concerned with the visual arrangement of his poems as he was with sound and meaning, E. E. Cummings's style is among the most distinctive of any American poet. Cummings strove to mold his poems into unconventional shapes through variations in line length and spaces between letters and lines. Frequently, Cummings used the shape of a poem to convey or reinforce its meaning. For example, his poem about a grasshopper, "r-p-o-p-h-e-s-s-a-g-r," forms the shape of a grasshopper hopping and re-forming itself. Cummings also used capitalization and punctuation to reinforce meaning. Many of his poems contain little punctuation. As a result the few marks that are used serve to highlight important ideas. Similarly Cummings rarely used capital letters, except for emphasis. In fact Cummings even used a small *i* when his speakers referred to themselves. This reflected his perception of the self as a small part of a mass society and his belief in the need for modesty.

Commentary

Cummings's typographical games affect his poetry and the way it conveys meaning. Because Cummings breaks the rules of grammar and syntax, he draws attention to the words on the page and gives them a life of their own. As one critic put it, "the poems are made to misbehave," like individuals fighting against conventional boundaries. Each poem, alive in its own way, affirms individual emotional experience. Cummings's view of what human beings are resembled his ideas about his poetry. Both poems and people should move beyond a machinelike expression of measurable, or restrained, emotions.

Focus

"since feeling is first" focuses on the role of emotions in our lives. Freewrite about the ways in which feelings can affect our lives and why they can have such an impact.

since feeling is first

E. E. Cummings

since feeling is first
who pays any attention
to the syntax of things
will never wholly kiss you;

5 wholly to be a fool
while Spring is in the world

my blood approves,
and kisses are a better fate
than wisdom
10 lady i swear by all flowers. Don't cry
—the best gesture of my brain is less than
your eyelids' flutter which says

we are for each other: then
laugh, leaning back in my arms
15 for life's not a paragraph

And death i think is no parenthesis

LOVERS WITH FLOWERS
Marc Chagall
The Israel Museum, Jerusalem

![R]ESPONDING TO THE SELECTION

Your Response

1. Do you agree that "feeling is first"? Explain.
2. What do you think of the way Cummings manipulates syntax in his poem?

Interpreting

3. (a) What point does the speaker make about the relationship between reason and emotion? (b) What is his attitude concerning the role of emotions?
4. (a) What does the speaker mean when he says, "life's not a paragraph"? (b) Considering the fact that a parenthesis temporarily interrupts a sentence, what do you think the speaker means when he says, "death i think is no parenthesis"? (c) How is the speaker's perception of death related to his attitude concerning the role of emotions?

Applying

5. Do you agree with the speaker's attitude concerning the role of emotions? Why or why not?

![L]EARNING OPTION

Writing. Paying attention to syntax, rewrite Cummings's poem using standard capitalization, punctuation, and word usage. Then share your work with classmates. What qualities of the poem are lost in your revision?

anyone lived in a pretty how town

E. E. Cummings

anyone lived in a pretty how town
(with up so floating many bells down)
spring summer autumn winter
he sang his didn't he danced his did.

5 Women and men(both little and small)
cared for anyone not at all
they sowed their isn't they reaped their same
sun moon stars rain

children guessed(but only a few
10 and down they forgot as up they grew
autumn winter spring summer)
that noone loved him more by more

when by now and tree by leaf
she laughed his joy she cried his grief
15 bird by snow and stir by still
anyone's any was all to her

someones married their everyones
laughed their cryings and did their dance
(sleep wake hope and then)they
20 said their nevers they slept their dream

stars rain sun moon
(and only the snow can begin to explain
how children are apt to forget to remember
with up so floating many bells down)

25 one day anyone died i guess
(and noone stooped to kiss his face)
busy folk buried them side by side
little by little and was by was

all by all and deep by deep
30 and more by more they dream their sleep
noone and anyone earth by april
wish by spirit and if by yes.

Women and men(both dong and ding)
summer autumn winter spring
35   reaped their sowing and went their came
sun moon stars rain

RESPONDING TO THE SELECTION

Your Response

1. Did you enjoy reading this poem? Why or why not?
2. How might Cummings describe your hometown?

Recalling

3. (a) What does "anyone" sing? (b) What does he dance?
4. (a) How do "women and men" feel about "anyone"? (b) Who loves him "more by more"?
5. In the eighth stanza, what happens to "anyone"?

Interpreting

6. This poem tells about the man named "anyone" and his wife named "noone." Why do you think Cummings chose to use these names?
7. (a) What type of town is suggested by the phrase "pretty how"? (b) What type of impression does the speaker convey of the people from this town? (c) How does he convey the impression that their lives are monotonous and dull?
8. (a) What does the speaker mean when he says that the townspeople "laughed their cryings"? (b) What does he mean when he says that they "slept their dream"?
9. (a) What two lines in the poem convey the passage of time? (b) Why does Cummings vary the order of the words in these lines?

Applying

10. How might this poem be different if it were set in a large city rather than a town?

LEARNING OPTION

Speaking and Listening. Join the New York artistic scene during the 1920's. Imagine yourself in a Greenwich Village cafe and take part in a poetry reading. Share your favorite poems from the modern period with fellow writers, artists, intellectuals, and bohemians.

Primary Source

In a series of lectures delivered at Harvard University in 1952 and 1953, Cummings commented on how he felt about the writing of poetry:

" . . . so far as I am concerned, poetry and every other art was and is and forever will be strictly and distinctly a question of individuality . . . poetry is being, not doing. If you wish to follow, even at a distance, the poet's calling (and here, as always, I speak from my own totally biased and entirely personal point of view) you've got to come out of the measurable doing universe and into the immeasurable house of being. . . . Nobody else can be alive for you; nor can you be alive for anybody else. Toms can be Dicks and Dicks can be Harrys, but none of them can ever be you. There's the artist's responsibility; and the most awful responsibility on earth. If you can take it, take it—and be. If you can't, cheer up and go about other people's business; and do (or undo) till you drop."

old age sticks

E. E. Cummings

old age sticks
up Keep
Off
signs)&

5 youth yanks them
down(old
age
cries No

Tres)&(pas)
10 youth laughs
(sing
old age

scolds Forbid
den Stop
15 Must
n't Don't

&)youth goes
right on
gr
20 owing old

RESPONDING TO THE SELECTION

Your Response
1. For whom do you think Cummings has greater sympathy, senior citizens or young people? Explain.
2. How would you characterize old age and youth?

Interpreting
3. How does youth contrast with old age in this poem?
4. What is ironic about the final stanza?

Applying
5. Why do you think the young and old often have very different attitudes toward life?

ANALYZING LITERATURE

Examining Style
Style refers to the way in which a writer expresses his or her thoughts. We can easily identify E. E. Cummings's poetry once we are familiar with his style.
1. How does Cummings's use of capitalization in "old age sticks" help to emphasize the contrast between youth and old age?
2. How does his use of parentheses in the poem highlight the contrast in the attitudes of the young and the old?
3. How does the shape of the poem reflect its content?

THINKING AND WRITING

Writing About Style
Write an essay in which you discuss how Cummings's style reinforces the meaning of his poems. Review the three poems you have just read, noting how the various elements of Cummings's style, such as his unusual use of punctuation and capitalization, reinforce the meaning of each poem. When you write your essay, use at least one passage from each of the three poems to support your argument. When you revise, make sure that you have clearly defined and thoroughly supported your thesis.

ROBERT FROST

1874–1963

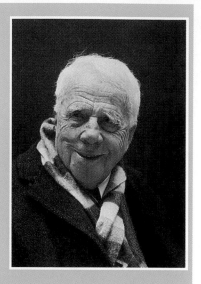

In becoming one of America's most loved and respected poets, Robert Frost displayed the same rugged persistence and determination exhibited by the rural New Englanders he depicted in his poems. Although he eventually received four Pulitzer Prizes and read at a presidential inauguration, Frost had a difficult time achieving success as a poet. Only after years of rejection by book and magazine publishers did he finally receive the acceptance for which he worked so hard.

Frost was born in San Francisco, but his father died when he was eleven, and his mother moved the family to Lawrence, Massachusetts. After graduating from high school, he briefly attended Dartmouth College. Disliking college life, he left school and spent time working as a farmer, a mill hand, a newspaper writer, and a schoolteacher. During his spare time, he wrote poetry and dreamed of someday being able to support himself by writing alone.

After marrying and tending a farm in New Hampshire for ten years, Frost moved to England in 1912, hoping to establish himself as a poet. While in England he became friends with a number of well-known poets, including Ezra Pound, and published two collections of poetry, *A Boy's Will* (1913) and *North of Boston* (1914). When he returned home in 1915, he discovered that his success in England had spread to the United States.

Frost went on to publish five more volumes of poetry, for which he received many awards. He also taught at Amherst, the University of Michigan, Harvard, and Dartmouth; lectured and read at dozens of other schools; and farmed in Vermont and New Hampshire. In 1960, at John F. Kennedy's invitation, Frost became the first poet to read his work at a presidential inauguration.

Frost's poetry was popular not only among critics and intellectuals, but also among the general public. In his poems he painted vivid portraits of the New England landscape and captured the flavor of New England life using traditional verse forms and conversational language. Despite their apparent simplicity, however, his poems are filled with hidden meanings, forcing us to delve beneath the surface to fully appreciate his work.

Writing about the effect a poem should have on the reader, Frost once said, "Like a piece of ice on a hot stove the poem must ride on its own melting. A poem may be worked over since it is in being, but may not be worried into being. Its most precious quality will remain its having run itself and carried away the poet with it. Read it a hundred times: it will forever keep its freshness as a petal keeps its fragrance. It can never lose its sense of a meaning that once unfolded by surprise as it went."

GUIDE FOR INTERPRETING

Robert Frost's Poetry

Symbols. A symbol is a person, place, or thing that has a meaning in itself and also represents something larger than itself. Frequently, an event or activity in a literary work may have a symbolic meaning. For example, the voyage of the *Pequod* in Herman Melville's *Moby-Dick* symbolizes humanity's quest to conquer everything in nature that seems paradoxical, unexplainable, and uncontrollable.

Symbols create different layers of meaning in a literary work. Because they generally contain symbols, Robert Frost's poems can usually be interpreted in more than one way. On the surface the poems seem straightforward and easy to grasp. Yet by analyzing Frost's use of symbols, we become aware of larger meanings that are hidden beneath the surface.

Narrative Poetry. A narrative poem is one that tells a story. Like a short story, a narrative poem describes an event or a series of events and has one or more characters, a setting, and a conflict. In a narrative poem, the story is told by a single speaker, which may be the voice of the poet or that of a fictional character. Many of Frost's poems are narratives.

Dramatic Poetry. Unlike narrative poetry, in which events are described in the words of the speaker, dramatic poetry re-creates an event using dialogue or monologue as well as description. In a dramatic poem we see the characters interacting with and talking to one another, and as a result it seems as if we are actually witnessing the event. Frost's "The Death of the Hired Man" is a dramatic poem.

In Frost's poem "Birches," the speaker fondly remembers swinging on the branches of birch trees during his childhood. List some of the activities you enjoyed during the early part of your childhood. Then write down some of your reasons for liking each of these activities.

NEW ENGLAND BIRCHES
Ernest Lawson
The Phillips Collection, Washington, D.C.

Birches

Robert Frost

When I see birches bend to left and right
Across the lines of straighter darker trees,
I like to think some boy's been swinging them.
But swinging doesn't bend them down to stay
5 As ice storms do. Often you must have seen them
Loaded with ice a sunny winter morning
After a rain. They click upon themselves
As the breeze rises, and turn many-colored
As the stir cracks and crazes their enamel.
10 Soon the sun's warmth makes them shed crystal shells
Shattering and avalanching on the snow crust—

Such heaps of broken glass to sweep away
You'd think the inner dome of heaven had fallen.
They are dragged to the withered bracken by the load,
15 And they seem not to break; though once they are bowed
So low for long, they never right themselves:
You may see their trunks arching in the woods
Years afterwards, trailing their leaves on the ground
Like girls on hands and knees that throw their hair
20 Before them over their heads to dry in the sun.
But I was going to say when Truth broke in
With all her matter of fact about the ice storm,
I should prefer to have some boy bend them
As he went out and in to fetch the cows—
25 Some boy too far from town to learn baseball,
Whose only play was what he found himself,
Summer or winter, and could play alone.
One by one he subdued his father's trees
By riding them down over and over again
30 Until he took the stiffness out of them,
And not one but hung limp, not one was left
For him to conquer. He learned all there was
To learn about not launching out too soon
And so not carrying the tree away
35 Clear to the ground. He always kept his poise
To the top branches, climbing carefully
With the same pains you use to fill a cup
Up to the brim, and even above the brim.
Then he flung outward, feet first, with a swish,
40 Kicking his way down through the air to the ground.
So was I once myself a swinger of birches.
And so I dream of going back to be.
It's when I'm weary of considerations,
And life is too much like a pathless wood
45 Where your face burns and tickles with the cobwebs
Broken across it, and one eye is weeping
From a twig's having lashed across it open.
I'd like to get away from earth awhile
And then come back to it and begin over.
50 May no fate willfully misunderstand me
And half grant what I wish and snatch me away
Not to return. Earth's the right place for love:
I don't know where it's likely to go better.
I'd like to go by climbing a birch tree,
55 And climb black branches up a snow-white trunk
Toward heaven, till the tree could bear no more,
But dipped its top and set me down again.
That would be good both going and coming back.
One could do worse than be a swinger of birches.

Mending Wall

Robert Frost

Something there is that doesn't love a wall,
That sends the frozen-ground-swell under it
And spills the upper boulders in the sun,
And makes gaps even two can pass abreast.
5 The work of hunters is another thing:
I have come after them and made repair
Where they have left not one stone on a stone,
But they would have the rabbit out of hiding,
To please the yelping dogs. The gaps I mean,
10 No one has seen them made or heard them made,
But at spring mending-time we find them there.
I let my neighbor know beyond the hill;
And on a day we meet to walk the line
And set the wall between us once again.
15 We keep the wall between us as we go.
To each the boulders that have fallen to each.
And some are loaves and some so nearly balls
We have to use a spell to make them balance:
"Stay where you are until our backs are turned!"
20 We wear our fingers rough with handling them.
Oh, just another kind of outdoor game,
One on a side. It comes to little more:
There where it is we do not need the wall:
He is all pine and I am apple orchard.
25 My apple trees will never get across
And eat the cones under his pines, I tell him.
He only says, "Good fences make good neighbors."
Spring is the mischief in me, and I wonder
If I could put a notion in his head:
30 "*Why* do they make good neighbors? Isn't it
Where there are cows? But here there are no cows.
Before I built a wall I'd ask to know
What I was walling in or walling out,
And to whom I was like to give offense.
35 Something there is that doesn't love a wall,
That wants it down." I could say "Elves" to him,
But it's not elves exactly, and I'd rather
He said it for himself. I see him there,
Bringing a stone grasped firmly by the top
40 In each hand, like an old-stone savage armed.
He moves in darkness as it seems to me,

Not of woods only and the shade of trees.
He will not go behind his father's saying,
And he likes having thought of it so well
45 He says again, "Good fences make good neighbors."

RESPONDING TO THE SELECTION

Your Response

1. What is your reaction to each poem?
2. In "Birches" the speaker maintains that "One could do worse than be a swinger of birches." Do you agree or disagree? Explain.
3. In "Mending Wall" how would you define the "something" that "doesn't love a wall"?

Recalling

4. (a) What does the speaker of "Birches" like to think when he sees birches "bend to the left and right"? (b) When does he dream of going back to be a "swinger of birches"?
5. (a) Why does the speaker of "Mending Wall" feel that the wall is unnecessary? (b) What is his neighbor's attitude?

Interpreting

6. (a) How would you characterize the boy described in "Birches"? (b) How would you describe his relationship with nature? (c) Whom do you think he represents?
7. (a) How would you characterize the speaker of "Mending Wall"? (b) How would you characterize his neighbor? (c) What is the speaker's attitude toward his neighbor?
8. In "Mending Wall" what is the significance of the fact that nature breaks apart the wall each winter?

Applying

9. (a) Why might a wall be unnecessary in the environment described in "Mending Wall"? (b) In what types of environments do you think a wall would be necessary?

ANALYZING LITERATURE

Interpreting Symbols

A **symbol** is a person, place, object, or action that has a meaning in itself and also represents something larger than itself. For example, in "Birches" the activity of swinging on birch trees symbolizes both a unity between humanity and nature and the notion of a temporary escape from reality.

1. Explain the following line: "One could do worse than be a swinger of birches."
2. What details in the poem suggest that the swinging on birches symbolizes the unity between humanity and nature?
3. What details suggest that the activity symbolizes a temporary escape from reality?

THINKING AND WRITING

Writing About a Symbol

Write an essay in which you discuss the symbolic meaning of the swinging on birches in Frost's poem "Birches." Review your answers from the Analyzing Literature activity. Prepare a thesis statement. Then write your essay, using passages from the poem to support your thesis. When you revise, make sure your body paragraphs are arranged in a logical order. Proofread your essay and share it with your classmates.

LEARNING OPTION

Art. Which line from "Mending Wall" captures your thoughts about walls? Choose the line that expresses your point of view and design a poster to illustrate it. Find a wall on which you can hang your poster.

The Death of the Hired Man

Robert Frost

Mary sat musing on the lamp-flame at the
    table,
Waiting for Warren. When she heard his
    step,
She ran on tiptoe down the darkened
    passage
To meet him in the doorway with the news
5 And put him on his guard, "Silas is back."
She pushed him outward with her through
    the door
And shut it after her. "Be kind," she said.
She took the market things from Warren's
    arms
And set them on the porch, then drew him
    down
10 To sit beside her on the wooden steps.

"When was I ever anything but kind to
    him?
But I'll not have the fellow back," he said.
"I told him so last haying, didn't I?
If he left then, I said, that ended it.
15 What good is he? Who else will harbor him
At his age for the little he can do?
What help he is there's no depending on.
Off he goes always when I need him most.
He thinks he ought to earn a little pay,
20 Enough at least to buy tobacco with,
So he won't have to beg and be beholden.
'All right,' I say, 'I can't afford to pay
Any fixed wages, though I wish I could.'
'Someone else can.' 'Then someone else will
    have to.'
25 I shouldn't mind his bettering himself
If that was what it was. You can be certain,
When he begins like that, there's someone
    at him
Trying to coax him off with pocket money—

In haying time, when any help is scarce.
30 In winter he comes back to us. I'm done."

"Sh! not so loud: he'll hear you," Mary said.

"I want him to: he'll have to soon or late."

"He's worn out. He's asleep beside the
    stove.
When I came up from Rowe's I found him
    here,
35 Huddled against the barn door fast asleep,
A miserable sight, and frightening, too—
You needn't smile—I didn't recognize him—
I wasn't looking for him—and he's
    changed.
Wait till you see."

          "Where did you say he'd been?"

40 "He didn't say. I dragged him to the house,
And gave him tea and tried to make him
    smoke.
I tried to make him talk about his travels.
Nothing would do; he just kept nodding
    off."

"What did he say? Did he say anything?"

45 "But little."

          "Anything? Mary, confess
He said he'd come to ditch the meadow for
    me."

"Warren!"
          "But did he? I just want to know."

"Of course he did. What would you have
    him say?
Surely you wouldn't grudge the poor old
    man
50 Some humble way to save his self-respect.
He added, if you really care to know,
He meant to clear the upper pasture, too.
That sounds like something you have heard
    before?
Warren, I wish you could have heard the
    way
55 He jumbled everything. I stopped to look
Two or three times—he made me feel so
    queer—
To see if he was talking in his sleep.
He ran on Harold Wilson—you remember—
The boy you had in haying four years
    since.
60 He's finished school, and teaching in his
    college.
Silas declares you'll have to get him back.
He says they two will make a team for
    work:
Between them they will lay this farm as
    smooth!
The way he mixed that in with other
    things.
65 He thinks young Wilson a likely lad, though
    daft
On education—you know how they fought
All through July under the blazing sun,
Silas up on the cart to build the load,
Harold along beside to pitch it on."

70 "Yes, I took care to keep well out of
    earshot."

"Well, those days trouble Silas like a dream.
You wouldn't think they would. How such
    things linger!
Harold's young college-boy's assurance
    piqued him.
After so many years he still keeps finding
75 Good arguments he sees he might have
    used.
I sympathize. I know just how it feels
To think of the right thing to say too late.
Harold's associated in his mind with Latin.

He asked me what I thought of Harold's
    saying
80 He studied Latin, like the violin,
Because he liked it—that an argument!
He said he couldn't make the boy believe
He could find water with a hazel prong—
Which showed how much good school had
    ever done him.
85 He wanted to go over that. But most of all
He thinks if he could have another chance
To teach him how to build a load of hay—"

"I know, that's Silas' one accomplishment.
He bundles every forkful in its place,
90 And tags and numbers it for future
    reference,
So he can find and easily dislodge it
In the unloading. Silas does that well.
He takes it out in bunches like big birds'
    nests.
You never see him standing on the hay
95 He's trying to lift, straining to lift himself."

"He thinks if he could teach him that, he'd
    be
Some good perhaps to someone in the
    world.
He hates to see a boy the fool of books.
Poor Silas, so concerned for other folk,
100 And nothing to look backward to with
    pride,
And nothing to look forward to with hope,
So now and never any different."

Part of a moon was falling down the west,
Dragging the whole sky with it to the hills.
105 Its light poured softly in her lap. She saw it
And spread her apron to it. She put out
    her hand
Among the harplike morning-glory strings,
Taut with the dew from garden bed to
    eaves,
As if she played unheard some tenderness
110 That wrought on him beside her in the
    night.
"Warren," she said, "he has come home to
    die:

You needn't be afraid he'll leave you this
    time."

"Home," he mocked gently.

           "Yes, what else but home?

It all depends on what you mean by home.
115 Of course he's nothing to us, any more
Than was the hound that came a stranger
    to us
Out of the woods, worn out upon the trail."

"Home is the place where, when you have
    to go there,
They have to take you in."

           "I should have called it
120 Something you somehow haven't to
    deserve."

Warren leaned out and took a step or two,
Picked up a little stick, and brought it back
And broke it in his hand and tossed it by.
"Silas has better claim on us you think
125 Than on his brother? Thirteen little miles
As the road winds would bring him to his
    door.
Silas has walked that far no doubt today.
Why doesn't he go there? His brother's
    rich,
A somebody—director in the bank."

130 "He never told us that."

           "We know it, though."

"I think his brother ought to help, of
    course.
I'll see to that if there is need. He ought of
    right
To take him in, and might be willing to—
He may be better than appearances.
135 But have some pity on Silas. Do you think
If he had any pride in claiming kin
Or anything he looked for from his brother,
He'd keep so still about him all this time?"

"I wonder what's between them."

               "I can tell you.
140 Silas is what he is—we wouldn't mind
    him—
But just the kind that kinsfolk can't abide.
He never did a thing so very bad.
He don't know why he isn't quite as good
As anybody. Worthless though he is,
145 He won't be made ashamed to please his
    brother."

"*I* can't think Si ever hurt anyone."

"No, but he hurt my heart the way he lay
And rolled his old head on that sharp-edged
    chair-back.
He wouldn't let me put him on the lounge.
150 You must go in and see what you can do.
I made the bed up for him there tonight.
You'll be surprised at him—how much he's
    broken.
His working days are done; I'm sure of it."

"I'd not be in a hurry to say that."

155 "I haven't been. Go, look, see for yourself.
But, Warren, please remember how it is:
He's come to help you ditch the meadow.
He has a plan. You mustn't laugh at him.
He may not speak of it, and then he may.
160 I'll sit and see if that small sailing cloud
Will hit or miss the moon."

              It hit the moon.
Then there were three there, making a dim
    row,
The moon, the little silver cloud, and she.

Warren returned—too soon, it seemed to
    her—
165 Slipped to her side, caught up her hand
    and waited.

"Warren?" she questioned.
           "Dead," was all he answered.

RESPONDING TO THE SELECTION

Your Response

1. What do you like best about this poem?
2. Why do you think the poet keeps Silas offstage?
3. How would you define *home:* "the place where, when you have to go there, [t]hey have to take you in" or "[s]omething you somehow haven't to deserve"? Explain.

Recalling

4. Why does Warren not want Silas back?
5. (a) In what condition is Silas? (b) What task does he say he has come to perform?
6. According to Warren what is "Silas's one accomplishment?"
7. What does Silas want to teach Harold Wilson?
8. (a) What does Mary believe is the reason Silas has come? (b) What does she believe is the reason Silas chose not to go to his brother's home?
9. What does Warren tell Mary after he has looked in on Silas?

Interpreting

10. How do the descriptions of the setting help to create a somber mood?
11. (a) How would you characterize Mary? (b) How would you characterize Warren?
12. (a) What do Silas's comments about Harold Wilson reveal about Silas's personality? (b) What do we learn about Silas's personality from his refusal to look to his brother for help?
13. (a) How are Mary's and Warren's definitions of home different? (b) How does this contrast reflect the differences in their personalities?

Applying

14. Do you think Mary and Warren would have been obligated to care for Silas? Why or why not?

ANALYZING LITERATURE

Understanding Dramatic Poetry

A **dramatic poem** is a poem that dramatizes an event using dialogue or monologue as well as description. For example, "The Death of the Hired Man" dramatizes Mary's and Warren's reactions to Silas's arrival.

1. How does Frost's use of dialogue make it seem as if we are actually witnessing the event?
2. Because it depends so much on dialogue, "The Death of the Hired Man" is similar to a scene from a play. What sets it apart from a play?

LEARNING OPTIONS

1. **Speaking and Listening.** Work with a classmate to bring Mary and Warren to life. Using the dialogue from "The Death of the Hired Man," act out the drama between husband and wife. Use the descriptive portions of the poem for guidance in setting the scene and planning your movements on the set. Rehearse your performance before presenting it to the class.
2. **Art.** Design a cross-stitch sampler that expresses your feelings about home. On your sampler you might include an original statement, an old adage, a line from this or another poem, or a quote from another source.
3. **Art.** In "The Death of a Hired Man," Frost does not present a physical description of Mary, Warren, or Silas. Nevertheless, he creates a clear portrait of the three characters. How do you see each one? Draw or find a picture to represent the farmer, his wife, or the hired hand. In your picture try to capture the personality of Frost's character.

"Out, Out—"

Robert Frost

The buzz saw snarled and rattled in the yard
And made dust and dropped stove-length sticks of wood,
Sweet-scented stuff when the breeze drew across it.
And from there those that lifted eyes could count

5 Five mountain ranges one behind the other
Under the sunset far into Vermont.
And the saw snarled and rattled, snarled and rattled,
As it ran light, or had to bear a load.
And nothing happened: day was all but done.

10 Call it a day, I wish they might have said
To please the boy by giving him the half hour
That a boy counts so much when saved from work.
His sister stood beside them in her apron
To tell them "Supper." At the word, the saw,

15 As if to prove saws knew what supper meant,
Leaped out at the boy's hand, or seemed to leap—
He must have given the hand. However it was,
Neither refused the meeting. But the hand!
The boy's first outcry was a rueful laugh,

20 As he swung toward them holding up the hand,
Half in appeal, but half as if to keep
The life from spilling. Then the boy saw all—
Since he was old enough to know, big boy
Doing a man's work, though a child at heart—

25 He saw all spoiled. "Don't let him cut my hand off—
The doctor, when he comes. Don't let him, sister!"
So. But the hand was gone already.
The doctor put him in the dark of ether.[1]
He lay and puffed his lips out with his breath.

30 And then—the watcher at his pulse took fright.
No one believed. They listened at his heart.
Little—less—nothing!—and that ended it.
No more to build on there. And they, since they
Were not the one dead, turned to their affairs.

---

1. ether (ē thər) *n.*: A chemical compound used as an anesthetic.

Your Response

1. How does this poem make you feel?
2. What do you find more disturbing, the boy's death or the onlookers' reaction to his death? Explain.

Recalling

3. (a) When does the accident occur? (b) How does it happen?
4. (a) What is the boy's immediate response to the accident? (b) What does he ask of his sister?
5. (a) What happens to the boy after the doctor comes? (b) How does the family respond?

Interpreting

6. What does the buzz saw represent? Support your answer.
7. How does the description of the setting contrast with the events in the poem?
8. What does the family's response to the incident suggest about the nature of rural life?
9. The poem's title comes from a scene in Shakespeare's *Macbeth* in which Macbeth laments the premature death of his wife with the following words:

   Out, out, brief candle!
   Life's but a walking shadow, a poor player,
   That struts and frets his hour upon the stage
   And then is heard no more.

   What does this quote reveal about the poem's theme, or main point?

Applying

10. How do you explain the family's response to the incident?

ANALYZING LITERATURE

Understanding Narrative Poetry

A **narrative poem** is a poem that tells a story. For example, "'Out, Out—'" tells the story of a tragic accident in Vermont.

1. The events in "'Out, Out—'" are described by a single speaker. What seems to be the speaker's attitude toward the events?
2. At what point in the poem does the speaker directly state his feelings?

THINKING AND WRITING

Writing a Dramatic Poem

Reshape "'Out, Out—'" into a dramatic poem. Review "The Death of the Hired Man," paying close attention to Frost's use of dialogue. Then begin writing your poem, using dialogue and description to dramatize the accident and the events surrounding it. When you revise, make sure that your poem will make the reader feel as if he or she is actually witnessing the events.

LEARNING OPTIONS

1. **Writing.** Reshape "'Out, Out—'" into a newspaper article. Building on the facts presented in the poem, write an account of the young boy's death. Be sure to answer the questions *who? what? when? where? why?* and *how?* in your lead paragraph. In subsequent paragraphs, you might include brief statements by both the boy's sister and his doctor.
2. **Speaking and Listening.** Take the role of a family friend and prepare a eulogy for the young boy in the poem. In your eulogy you might pay tribute to the boy who did "a man's work" and lament the tragedy of his premature death. Be prepared to deliver the eulogy at a "memorial service."
3. **Writing.** Consider what makes the last sentence in the poem memorable. Then write a memorable last sentence for a narrative poem of your own. Share your work with classmates. Is it harder to write a beginning line or an ending line?

Fire and Ice

Robert Frost

Some say the world will end in fire,
Some say in ice.
From what I've tasted of desire
I hold with those who favor fire.
5 But if it had to perish twice,
I think I know enough of hate
To say that for destruction ice
Is also great
And would suffice.

Nothing Gold Can Stay

Robert Frost

Nature's first green is gold,
Her hardest hue to hold.
Her early leaf's a flower;
But only so an hour.
5 Then leaf subsides to leaf.
So Eden sank to grief,
So dawn goes down to day.
Nothing gold can stay.

RESPONDING TO THE SELECTION

Your Response

1. Do you agree with the outlook expressed in each poem? Explain.
2. What do you think is likely to destroy the world: desire, hate, or something else? Explain.

Recalling

3. According to the speaker of "Fire and Ice," how will the world end?
4. What happens to each of the elements of nature mentioned in "Nothing Gold Can Stay"?

Interpreting

5. In "Fire and Ice," the speaker approaches a very serious subject in a seemingly casual manner. What might have been Frost's reasons for taking this approach?
6. (a) What emotion does each element in "Fire and Ice" represent? (b) What does the speaker suggest that these emotions have in common?
7. What is the meaning of the first line in "Nothing Gold Can Stay"?
8. (a) What is the theme, or main point, of "Nothing Gold Can Stay"? (b) How does the allusion, or reference, to Eden help to convey the theme?

Applying

9. Aside from desire and hate, what emotions do you think bring out destructive impulses in people?

Stopping by Woods on a Snowy Evening

Robert Frost

Whose woods these are I think I know.
His house is in the village though;
He will not see me stopping here
To watch his woods fill up with snow.

5   My little horse must think it queer
To stop without a farmhouse near
Between the woods and frozen lake
The darkest evening of the year.

He gives his harness bells a shake
10   To ask if there is some mistake.
The only other sound's the sweep
Of easy wind and downy flake.

The woods are lovely, dark and deep,
But I have promises to keep,
15   And miles to go before I sleep,
And miles to go before I sleep.

RESPONDING TO THE SELECTION

Your Response

1. What images does this poem bring to mind?
2. In this poem the speaker is torn between his desire to stay and his awareness of "promises" he has made. Do you think he makes the right choice? Explain.

Interpreting

3. (a) What do the speaker's actions in this poem reveal about his personality? (b) What internal conflict does the speaker experience? (c) How is the conflict resolved?
4. What difference between humans and animals is revealed through the horse's behavior?

5. (a) How does the repetition of the *d* sound in line 13 reinforce the meaning of the line? (b) What is the effect of Frost's use of repetition in the final two lines?
6. Explain the last three lines of this poem.

Applying

7. Just as swinging from birch trees provides the boy in "Birches" with a temporary escape from reality, pausing to observe nature provides the speaker with a temporary escape from reality in "Stopping by Woods on a Snowy Evening." Why do you think that people at times need to find this type of temporary escape?

Acquainted with the Night

Robert Frost

I have been one acquainted with the night.
I have walked out in rain—and back in rain.
I have outwalked the furthest city light.

I have looked down the saddest city lane.
5   I have passed by the watchman on his beat
And dropped my eyes, unwilling to explain.

I have stood still and stopped the sound of feet
When far away an interrupted cry
Came over houses from another street,

10   But not to call me back or say good-by;
And further still at an unearthly height
One luminary clock against the sky

Proclaimed the time was neither wrong nor right.
I have been one acquainted with the night.

RESPONDING TO THE SELECTION

Your Response
1. How does this poem make you feel?
2. What does it mean to be "acquainted with the night"?

Interpreting
3. What type of mood do the images in lines 1–4 create?
4. What is the speaker "unwilling to explain" in line 6?
5. What does the speaker's comment that "the time was neither wrong nor right" reveal about his life?
6. (a) What does night symbolize in this poem? (b) How does Frost use repetition to help convey the symbolic meaning of the night?

Applying
7. What does this poem suggest about Frost's attitude toward city life?

ANALYZING LITERATURE

Understanding Rhythm
   Rhythm is the arrangement of stressed and unstressed syllables in a poem. Poets vary the regular rhythm of a poem in a number of ways. Often poets interrupt the regular rhythm by introducing pauses, or caesuras, within lines. Another way poets vary rhythm is by using run-on lines—lines that flow naturally into the next line.
1. Find two caesuras in "Acquainted with the Night."
2. Find two run-on lines in the poem.

W. H. AUDEN

1907–1973

Although he was influenced by the Modernist poets, Wystan Hugh Auden managed to remain his own person. He adopted those aspects of Modernism with which he felt comfortable, while at the same time maintaining many elements of traditional poetry. Throughout his career he wrote with insight into the plight of people struggling to preserve their individuality in an increasingly conformist society.

Auden was born in York, England, and attended Oxford University. In 1930 he published his first collection of poetry, *Poems*. At about the same time, he became very active in politics. He spoke out about the plight of the poor in England and against the emergence of Nazism in Germany, and he actively supported the Republicans who were fighting against the Fascists in the Spanish Civil War. He also used his talents as a poet to express his political beliefs. As a result, many of his early poems focused on political issues.

In 1939 Auden moved to the United States, and in 1946 he became an American citizen. At the time of his move, he rediscovered his Christian beliefs, which grew increasingly stronger during his later years. He expressed his beliefs in *Double Man* (1941) and *For the Times Being* (1944), depicting religion as an effective way of coping with the disjointedness of modern society. In *The Age of Anxiety* (1947), a long narrative poem that earned him a Pulitzer Prize, he explored the confusion and isolation associated with post-World War II life. He went on to publish several more volumes of poetry, including *Nones* (1951), *The Shield of Achilles* (1955), *Homage to Clio* (1960), *About the House* (1967), and *City Without Walls* (1970), and he also produced a large body of literary criticism.

Despite being comforted by his religious beliefs, Auden became increasingly disillusioned with the modern world during his later years. Hoping to find comfort in a university community, he returned to England to teach at Oxford in the late 1950's. Several years later he moved to Austria, where he spent the remainder of his life.

Auden used his poetry and essays to explore the difficulties and responsibilities of being an artist in the modern age. As one who had turned to religious beliefs, he felt that the lack of faith in the modern age made it almost impossible to be an artist—in part, because he saw the absence of religious faith as being similar to an absence of faith in the values of art. If people no longer believed in universal truths, he reasoned, they could not believe in art, which deals with truth. "Poetry is not magic," he wrote in *The Dyer's Hand*. "Insofar as poetry, or any other of the arts, can be said to have an ulterior purpose, it is, by telling the truth, to disenchant and disintoxicate. . . ."

GUIDE FOR INTERPRETING

Who's Who; The Unknown Citizen

Satire. Satire is a kind of writing in which certain individuals, institutions, types of behavior, or humanity in general is ridiculed or criticized in a humorous manner. The purpose of satire is to promote changes in society or humanity. Satirists write about what they perceive to be the problems and flaws of the world. By poking fun at these problems and flaws or attacking them in a humorous manner, the satirists attempt to use the force of laughter to persuade us to accept their point of view and inspire us to take action to bring about change.

"Who's Who" explores some of the facts of a famous man's life. Of what types of facts concerning a famous person's life is the public usually aware? Of what types of facts is the public usually unaware? List the sources of the public's knowledge concerning a famous person's life.

Both "Who's Who" and "The Unknown Citizen" portray human beings as a collection of data in order to comment satirically upon the impact of modern society on humanity. "Who's Who" uses somewhat sordid and ordinary biographical facts to undercut our ideas about famous people. In "The Unknown Citizen" Auden shows how the data collected about people in a modern, bureaucratic society undermines our basic notions of what it means to be a human being.

As these poems suggest, Auden considered modern society to be basically hostile to human nature. He also thought that the concerns of this society—especially its focus on power and money—were directly opposed to the poet's interests. He made these comments in his essay "The Poet and the City":

> Poets are, by the nature of their interests and the nature of artistic fabrication, singularly ill-equipped to understand politics and economics. Their natural interest is in singular individuals and personal relations, while politics and economics are concerned with large numbers of people, hence with the human average (the poet is bored to death by the idea of the Common Man) and with impersonal, to a great extent, involuntary, relations. The poet cannot understand the function of money in modern society because for him there is no relation between subjective value and market value; he may be paid ten pounds for a poem which he believes is very good and took him months to write, and a hundred pounds for a piece of journalism which costs him but a day's work.

Who's Who

W. H. Auden

A shilling life will give you all the facts:
How Father beat him, how he ran away,
What were the struggles of his youth, what acts
Made him the greatest figure of his day:
5 Of how he fought, fished, hunted, worked all night,
Though giddy, climbed new mountains; named a sea:
Some of the last researchers even write
Love made him weep his pints like you and me.

With all his honors on, he sighed for one
10 Who, say astonished critics, lived at home;
Did little jobs about the house with skill
And nothing else; could whistle; would sit still
Or potter round the garden; answered some
Of his long marvelous letters but kept none.

▮ RESPONDING TO THE SELECTION

Your Response

1. How important do you think fame is to the poet? How important is it to you?
2. Do you think "all the facts" about any person's life should be public knowledge? Why or why not?

Recalling

3. What facts concerning the subject's life are mentioned?
4. (a) How did the one the subject "sighed for" spend her life? (b) What did this person do with his letters?

Interpreting

5. (a) What type of person is this poem about? (b) What do the facts suggest about his personality?
6. (a) What is surprising about the description of the woman whom he loved? (b) How do details in the poem suggest that she did not return his love?

7. (a) What is ironic, or surprising, about the fact that the subject of the poem weeped "pints like you and me"? (b) What does this suggest about the nature of happiness?
8. Explain the title of the poem.

Applying

9. Do you think that famous people are as likely to be unhappy as those who are not famous? Why or why not?

▮ LEARNING OPTION

Writing. You've been nominated for *Who's Who in American High Schools*. Supply "all the facts" that you think should be included in a brief entry about you. You might provide a list of standard biographical data, such as educational background, activities, interests, and accomplishments. You might instead choose to write a paragraph or poem that tells who you really are.

The Unknown Citizen

W. H. Auden

(To JS/07/M/378 This Marble Monument Is Erected by the State)

He was found by the Bureau of Statistics to be
One against whom there was no official complaint,
And all the reports on his conduct agree
That, in the modern sense of an old-fashioned word, he was
    a saint,
5 For in everything he did he served the Greater Community.
Except for the War till the day he retired
He worked in a factory and never got fired,
But satisfied his employers, Fudge Motors Inc.
Yet he wasn't a scab[1] or odd in his views,
10 For his Union reports that he paid his dues,
(Our report on his Union shows it was sound)
And our Social Psychology workers found
That he was popular with his mates and liked a drink.
The Press are convinced that he bought a paper every day
15 And that his reactions to advertisements were normal in
    every way.
Policies taken out in his name prove that he was fully
    insured,
And his Health-card shows he was once in hospital but left
    it cured.
Both Producers Research and High-Grade Living declare
He was fully sensible to the advantages of the Installment
    Plan
20 And had everything necessary to the Modern Man,
A phonograph, a radio, a car and a frigidaire.
Our researchers into Public Opinion are content
That he held the proper opinions for the time of year;
When there was peace, he was for peace; when there was
    war, he went.

---

1. scab *n.*: A worker who refuses to strike or takes the place of a striking worker.

25 He was married and added five children to the population,
    Which our Eugenist[2] says was the right number for a
      parent of his generation,
    And our teachers report that he never interfered with their
      education.
    Was he free? Was he happy? The question is absurd:
    Had anything been wrong, we should certainly have heard.

———————

2. Eugenist (ū jen′ ist) *n*.: A specialist in eugenics, the movement devoted to improving the human species through genetic control.

RESPONDING TO THE SELECTION

Your Response
1. Have you ever felt reduced to a number? Explain.
2. What do you think is the poet's attitude toward conformity?
3. What is your attitude toward conformity?

Recalling
4. Why is the unknown citizen remembered as a "saint"?
5. Which groups report on his activities?

Interpreting
6. (a) What is suggested by the numbers and letters used by the state in referring to the citizen? (b) In what sense is the citizen "unknown" to the state?
7. (a) What is the relationship of the state to the groups mentioned in the poem? (b) Why are these groups interested in the citizen? (c) What do the concerns of the groups and their relationship to the state reveal about the society as a whole?
8. (a) Why is it unlikely that the state would have heard anything about the citizen's freedom and happiness? (b) What seems to be the state's attitude toward his freedom and happiness?
9. How does Auden use capitalization to reinforce the meaning of the poem?

Applying
10. In what respects is the society portrayed in this poem similar to and different from our society?

ANALYZING LITERATURE

Interpreting Satire
   Satire is a kind of writing in which certain individuals, institutions, types of behavior, or humanity in general are ridiculed or criticized in a humorous manner. In "The Unknown Citizen," for example, Auden criticizes the increasingly impersonal and bureaucratic nature of modern society by presenting an exaggerated vision of a state in which people have been almost completely stripped of their individuality.
1. What is Auden's attitude toward the type of society he portrays in the poem?
2. How do the final two lines help to clarify Auden's attitude?
3. Considering Auden's attitude toward the society he portrays, what type of society do you think he supports?

LEARNING OPTION

Cross-curricular Connection. In "The Unknown Citizen," poet W. H. Auden speaks out against totalitarianism. Investigate the rise of totalitarian governments in Europe after World War I. Find out how accurately this poem portrays life in a totalitarian state. Share your findings in a brief oral report.

Harlem Renaissance Poetry

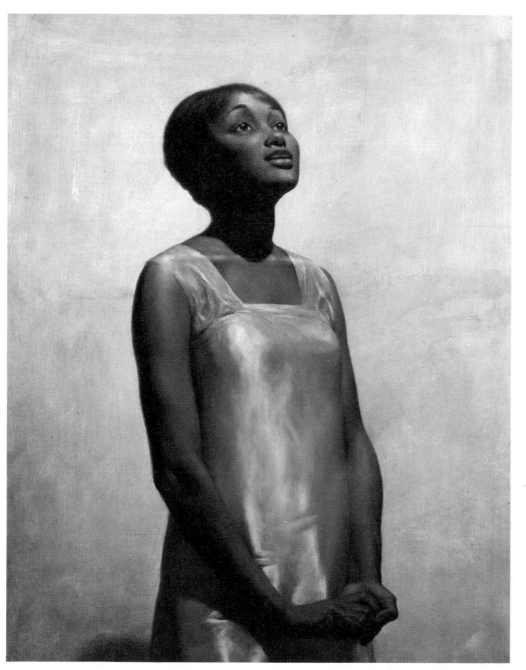

RUBY GREEN SINGING, 1928
James Chapin
Norton Gallery and School of Art, West Palm Beach, Florida

BIOGRAPHIES

Countee Cullen (1903–1946)

Unlike most other poets of his time, Countee Cullen used traditional forms and methods. However, no poet expressed the general sentiments of American blacks during the early 1900's more eloquently than Cullen.

Cullen was born in New York City. He graduated from New York University and later earned a master's degree from Harvard. His first collection of poetry, *Color,* was published in 1925. This was followed by *Copper Sun* (1927), *The Ballad of the Brown Girl* (1927), and *The Black Christ* (1929). In 1932 he published *One Way to Heaven,* a satirical novel about life in Harlem. During his later years he published two children's books, *The Lost Zoo* (1940) and *My Lives and How I Lost Them* (1942).

Cullen was one of the leaders of the movement to construct an intellectual and aesthetic culture for blacks in America, especially for those who had come from the South to New York City in the early 1900's. He claimed all of American and English literature as the literary heritage of blacks.

In "Any Human to Another," one of Cullen's best-known poems, he expresses the despair of black people.

Claude McKay (1890–1948)

In much of his work, Claude McKay evokes the rich colors and the rhythms of life on his native island of Jamaica. Yet although McKay considered Jamaica to be "home," he also regarded Harlem as his spiritual and psychic home, even though he frequently lived elsewhere. Writing to fellow Harlem Renaissance poet Langston Hughes from abroad in 1930, McKay said, "I write of America as home [although] I am really a poet without a country."

The son of poor farm workers, McKay moved to Kingston, the capital of the Caribbean island, when he was fourteen. While living in Kingston, he began writing poetry. When his collection *Songs of Jamaica* (1912) won an award from the Institute of Arts and Letters, he was able to emigrate to the United States.

McKay's poem "The Tropics in New York" is marked by a nostalgia for his homeland—a feeling echoed in the title of his autobiography, *A Long Way from Home* (1937).

GUIDE FOR INTERPRETING

Any Human to Another;
The Tropics in New York

Literary Movements

The Harlem Renaissance. During the late 1800's and early 1900's, many southern blacks moved north, hoping to find opportunities in the northern industrial centers. With this shift in population, the New York City community of Harlem developed into the cultural center for American blacks. There a cultural movement known as the Harlem Renaissance was established during the 1920's. The movement encompassed music, art, and literature, and included such writers as Countee Cullen, Claude McKay, Langston Hughes, Jean Toomer, and Arna Bontemps.

Although the literary forms and techniques used by the Harlem Renaissance writers varied widely, the writers all shared a common purpose: to prove that black writers could produce literature equal in quality to that of white writers. At the same time, the Harlem Renaissance writers focused on capturing the general sentiments of the American blacks of the time. In doing so they expressed their displeasure concerning their overall condition and articulated their cultural heritage.

Focus

In "The Tropics in New York, " Claude McKay presents a series of images, or word pictures, associated with the tropics. Prepare a list of the type of images you would expect to find in this series.

Commentary

One of the issues that the writers of the Harlem Renaissance debated among themselves and explored in their poetry was the relationship between race and poetry. Some viewed their poetry as primarily a vehicle for expressing what it means to be black in America; others regarded their works as dealing with more traditional poetic subjects: love, nature, childhood, home. These subjects were not considered to be exclusive of one another. But many black writers discovered a tension between writing poetry that dealt explicitly with black experiences and poetry that dealt more with universal experiences.

Countee Cullen, whose works have been compared with traditional British and American poetry, sometimes expressed a view that black writers should write within the broader literary tradition and transcend their own racial background. But at other times, he admitted how difficult this was to do. "Somehow or other I find my poetry of itself treating of the Negro, of his joys and his sorrows—mostly of the latter—and of the heights and depths of emotion which I feel as a Negro."

Which view do his poems express?

BIG MEETING, 1980
Varnette P. Honeywood
Black Lifestyles, Los Angeles

Any Human to Another

Countee Cullen

The ills I sorrow at
Not me alone
Like an arrow,
Pierce to the marrow,
5 Through the fat
And past the bone.

Your grief and mine
Must intertwine
Like sea and river,
10 Be fused and mingle,
Diverse yet single,
Forever and forever.

Let no man be so proud
And confident,
15 To think he is allowed
A little tent
Pitched in a meadow
Of sun and shadow
All his little own.

20 Joy may be shy, unique,
Friendly to a few,
Sorrow never scorned to speak
To any who
Were false or true.

25 Your every grief
Like a blade
Shining and unsheathed
Must strike me down.
Of bitter aloes wreathed,
30 My sorrow must be laid
On your head like a crown.

RESPONDING TO THE SELECTION

Your Response
1. What emotions does this poem arouse in you?
2. Do you agree with the speaker's assertion that people must share the sorrow of others? Why or why not?

Interpreting
3. How is the image presented in the first stanza echoed in the final stanza?
4. What is the meaning of the image presented in the third stanza?
5. Why does the speaker feel that joy is more difficult to share than sorrow?

Applying
6. Why do you think sharing feelings of sorrow with others often makes a person feel better?

ANALYZING LITERATURE

Understanding the Harlem Renaissance
The **Harlem Renaissance** was a cultural movement that emerged in Harlem during the 1920's. In their work the writers of the Harlem Renaissance tried to capture the essence of black life and communicate the general sentiments of the black people.
1. What do the emotions discussed in this poem suggest about the overall sentiments of the black people at the time?
2. How does the image presented in the first stanza suggest that the suffering of the black people is deeply rooted in the past?
3. What do you think is the poem's main purpose?

LEARNING OPTION

Cross-curricular Connection. The Harlem Renaissance encompassed music and art as well as literature. Explore the accomplishments of the musicians and artists involved in the movement. Choose one who interests you, and report on his or her achievements. Enhance your report by bringing in and sharing recordings or pictures.

The Tropics in New York

Claude McKay

Bananas ripe and green, and ginger-root,
    Cocoa in pods and alligator pears,
And tangerines and mangoes and grape fruit,
    Fit for the highest prize at parish fairs,

5 Set in the window, bringing memories
    Of fruit-trees laden by low-singing rills,
And dewy dawns, and mystical blue skies
    In benediction over nun-like hills.

My eyes grew dim, and I could no more gaze;
10   A wave of longing through my body swept,
And, hungry for the old, familiar ways
    I turned aside and bowed my head and wept.

RESPONDING TO THE SELECTION

Your Response

1. Have you ever longed for a place from your past? If so, which place? Why?
2. In this poem, the fruit in the window evokes memories of the poet's birthplace. What objects evoke memories of special places from your own past? Why?

Recalling

3. (a) What fruits are "set in the window"? (b) Of what do they bring memories?
4. (a) What emotion sweeps through the speaker's body in the final stanza? (b) How does he respond to this emotion?

Interpreting

5. How does the title contribute to the meaning of the poem?

6. What impression does the speaker convey of his homeland?
7. Which words create especially vivid images? Explain the reason for your choices.
8. How do the speaker's observations in the first stanza lead to the emotions he experiences in the third stanza?

Applying

9. Why do you think people often idealize and long for places from their past?

THINKING AND WRITING

Writing a Poem About a Special Place

Write a poem in which vivid, memorable images lead the speaker to recall a place for which he or she has very powerful feelings. Start by listing the images that lead to the speaker's rec-

ollections. Then list the speaker's emotions concerning the place he or she recalls. Present the speaker's observations in the first stanza; present his or her associations in the next stanza; and describe his or her emotions in the third stanza. When you finish writing, revise your poem and share it with your classmates.

LEARNING OPTIONS

1. **Art.** Put yourself in the place of a travel agent booking vacations to the tropical paradise McKay describes in his poem. Create a travel poster that you can hang in your window. Find pictures or create original drawings that correspond to the vivid images McKay uses to de-

scribe his native land. When you have finished your poster, present it to your classmates.

2. **Writing.** Imagine that the poet has returned to his native land after being away for more than twenty years. Tell the story of his return visit. Describe how he might have reacted. Would his former home live up to his memories of it? How might it have changed since he left?

3. **Cross-curricular Connection.** Explore the history and culture of Jamaica or one of the other Caribbean islands. Share your discoveries with your class. To give your classmates a better sense of what life is like on the island, bring in photographs, musical recordings, or native objects, such as tropical fruits and seashells.

LANGSTON HUGHES

1902–1967

Langston Hughes emerged from the Harlem Renaissance as the most prolific and successful black writer in America. Although he is best known for his poetry, he also wrote plays, fiction, autobiographical sketches, and movie screenplays.

Born in Missouri and raised in Illinois and Ohio, Hughes attended high school in Cleveland, where he contributed poetry to the school literary magazine. In 1921 he moved to New York City to attend classes at Columbia University, but a year later he left school to travel to Europe and Africa as a merchant seaman. When he returned to the United States, he met the poet Vachel Lindsay, who helped him publish his first volume of poetry, *The Weary Blues* (1926). The book attracted considerable attention and earned Hughes widespread recognition.

Although Hughes, like many of the Harlem Renaissance writers, was not born in Harlem and lived a large part of his life elsewhere, he identified Harlem as a source of inspiration and life for black artists. Harlem was where he felt at home and nourished, where he felt a sense of community. In his autobiography *Big Sea,* he described his arrival in Harlem in 1921. In his depiction of it, Harlem restores to him his life's breath. "At every subway station I kept watching for the sign: 135TH STREET. When I saw it, I held my breath. . . . I went up the steps and into the bright September sunlight. Harlem! I looked around. Negroes everywhere! . . . I took a deep breath and felt happy again."

Hughes went on to publish several other collections of poetry, including *The Dream Keeper* (1932), *Fields of Wonder* (1947), and *Montage of a Dream Deferred* (1951). In his poetry he experimented with a variety of forms and techniques and often tried to re-create the rhythms of contemporary jazz. Using his talents as a poet, he expressed pride in his heritage and voiced his displeasure with the oppression of blacks.

During the 1950's, Hughes helped to support himself by contributing a number of prose sketches to newspapers. Among the most popular was a series of tales about a fictional character named Jesse B. Semple, whom Hughes often referred to as "Simple." In 1963 Hughes developed these sketches into a musical play, *Simply Heaven*.

Hughes's work not only helped make the general public aware of black life, but it also inspired many other black writers. By eloquently chronicling the heritage of the black people and expressing their pride and determination, Hughes provided his people with a link to their cultural roots and a promise for a better future.

The Negro Speaks of Rivers

Writers' Techniques

The Speaker. The speaker is the voice of a poem. Although the speaker is often the poet himself or herself, the speaker may also be a fictional character, a group of people, or an inanimate object or another type of nonhuman entity. For example, in Carl Sandburg's poem "Grass," the speaker is the grass itself.

Focus

In "The Negro Speaks of Rivers," Hughes develops a comparison between rivers and black people. List some of the characteristics of rivers that you feel reflect certain aspects of the experience of black people.

Primary Source

Drawing on the populist example of Carl Sandburg's poetry, Hughes described his subject as being the entire community of American blacks: "Workers, roustabouts, and singers, and job hunters on Lenox Avenue in New York, or Seventh Street in Washington or South State in Chicago—people up today and down tomorrow, working this week and fired the next, beaten and baffled, but determined not to be wholly beaten, buying furniture on the installment plan, filling the house with roomers to help pay the rent, hoping to get a new suit for Easter—pawning that suit before the Fourth of July."

In his "documentary, journalistic, and topical" poems, as he called them, Hughes sought to capture the rhythms and resonances of the voices of black America. He also wanted to emphasize black America's connection to its own roots and tradition—in contrast to seeking connection to a European tradition or to whites in America. In "The Negro Speaks of Rivers," the rivers lead back to black Africa and to slavery in the South. The image of the river was common in the writings of the Harlem Renaissance as an image of the never-ceasing motion of life in Harlem. As critic Sidney H. Bremer writes: "Filled with children as well as adults, women as well as men, Harlem's streets are a neighborhood extension of family life and generation. That does not mean that the Harlem streets are happy—any more than families are always happy. But they are alive, generative. In explicit, repeated contrast to the deadening subway machines and dwarfing skyscraper streets of Anglo New York, Harlem's streets are defined by people walking. They are a 'stream of life.' . . . Even death confirms the generativity of life, as blues spawn the laughter of jazz and street life spills into the cabarets in Langston Hughes's first book of poems, *Weary Blues* (1925)."

The Negro Speaks of Rivers

Langston Hughes

I've known rivers:
I've known rivers ancient as the world and older than the
    flow of human blood in human veins.

My soul has grown deep like the rivers.

I bathed in the Euphrates when dawns were young.
5 I built my hut near the Congo and it lulled me to sleep.
I looked upon the Nile and raised the pyramids above it.
I heard the singing of the Mississippi when Abe Lincoln
    went down to New Orleans, and I've seen its muddy
    bosom turn all golden in the sunset.

I've known rivers:
Ancient, dusky rivers.

10 My soul has grown deep like the rivers.

▌RESPONDING TO THE SELECTION

Your Response

1. (a) What associations do you have with the places Hughes describes in the poem? Explain. (b) What places do you associate with your culture or your ancestors?
2. As in Hughes's poem, rivers are often used as symbols in literature. What do rivers symbolize, or represent, to you?

Interpreting

3. (a) Who is the speaker of "The Negro Speaks of Rivers"? (b) How does the title help to reveal the speaker's identity?

4. In this poem Hughes develops a comparison between rivers and black people. What does the age of rivers imply about the black race?
5. What do the references to specific rivers in lines 4–7 convey about the black experience?
6. (a) What do lines 3 and 10 suggest about how the black race has been affected by its experiences? (b) How do these two lines reflect the poem's theme, or main point?

Applying

7. In what respects can the human race as a whole be compared with rivers?

ONE WRITER'S PROCESS

Langston Hughes and "The Negro Speaks of Rivers"

Coming to Grips With History When Langston Hughes sat down to write a poem he had two histories to draw from—the history of poetry in America and the history of the African American people. Without his particular cultural background, he would have been a different kind of writer. As it was, whenever he put pen to paper he brought with him the history of a people and a determination to express something about that history through metaphor and lyric.

PREWRITING

The Poet's Process Hughes's poem "The Negro Speaks of Rivers" is an example of that determination. The idea for this poem came to Hughes while he was on a train to Mexico, where his father was living: "All day on the train I had been thinking about my father and his strange dislike of his own people. I didn't understand it, because I was a Negro, and I liked Negroes very much . . . I never tired of hearing them talk, listening to the thunderclaps of their laughter, to their troubles, to their discussions. . . ."

Listening to these discussions probably helped Hughes to discover the cadence of the language in "The Negro Speaks of Rivers." For a poet, the rhythms of speech can be more important than its content. It's not necessary to consciously study these rhythms; you can simply be open to the sounds of language as you would to music.

"I've known rivers" Hughes continued, "It was just sunset, and we crossed the Mississippi, slowly, over a long bridge. I looked out the window of the Pullman at the great muddy river flowing down toward the heart of the South, and I began to think what that river, the old Mississippi, had meant to Negroes in the past. . . . how Abraham Lincoln had made a trip down the Mississippi on a raft to New Orleans, and how he had seen slavery at its worst, and had decided within himself that it should be removed from American life. Then I began to think about other rivers in our past—the Congo, and the Niger, and the Nile in Africa—and the thought came to me: 'I've known rivers. . . .'"

DRAFTING

Getting It All Down Hughes wrote his poem "within the space of ten or fifteen minutes, as the train gathered speed in the dusk." He was eighteen years old, and he had written in a remarkably brief period what would become his first published poem.

Writing Aloud We don't know whether Hughes recited parts of "The Negro Speaks of Rivers" as he composed the poem. On other occasions, however, Hughes wrote "blues poems" in his head and sang them aloud as he wrote.

"One evening," he recalled, "I was crossing Rock Creek Bridge, singing a blues I was trying to get right before I put it down on paper. [Hughes confessed that he could "never carry a tune. But when I sing to myself, I think I am singing."] A man passing on the opposite side of the bridge stopped, looked at me, then turned around and cut across the roadway.

"He said, 'Son, what's the matter? Are you ill?'

"'No,' I said. 'Just singing.'

"'I thought you were groaning,' he commented. 'Sorry!' And went his way.

"So after that I never sang my verses aloud in the street anymore."

REVISING

In and Out of the Drawer Hughes changed "The Negro Speaks of Rivers" very little once it was on paper.

As Hughes went on to write more poems, however, it became his practice to put the finished poems away in a bottom drawer. Several weeks later, he would take them out to reread them. "If they seemed bad, I would throw them away. They would all seem good when I wrote them and, usually, bad when I would look at them again. So most of them were thrown away."

PUBLISHING

Help From Mentors Hughes, like many young writers, received help from mentors in getting his work published. One of these mentors was W.E.B. Du Bois, the prominent African American historian and social activist. Du Bois published "The Negro Speaks of Rivers" in the June 1921 issue of his magazine, *The Crisis.*

Another Literary Friendship Hughes also became friends with another prominent African American, Charles S. Johnson, editor of the magazine *Opportunity.* Hughes declared that Johnson "did more to encourage and develop Negro writers during the 1920's than anyone else in America. He wrote sympathetic letters, pointing out the merits of their work. He brought them together to meet and know each other. He made the *Opportunity* contests sources of discovery and help."

Hughes felt that Johnson was one of the people who helped bring about the "New Negro literature" by nursing young writers along until their books were "born."

A Chance Meeting The assistance that Hughes received from the well-known poet Vachel Lindsay came in an unusual and unexpected way. Hughes was working as a busboy at a Washington, D.C., hotel where Lindsay happened to be staying.

". . . I was thrilled the day Vachel Lindsay came. I knew him because I'd seen his picture in the papers that morning. He was to give a reading of his poems in the little theater of the hotel that night. I wanted very much to hear his poems, but I knew they did not admit colored people to the auditorium.

"That afternoon," Hughes goes on to say, "I wrote out three of my poems. . . . In the evening when Mr. Lindsay came down to dinner, quickly I laid them beside his plate and went away, afraid to say anything to so famous a poet, except to tell him I liked his poems and that these were poems of mine. I looked back once and saw Mr. Lindsay reading the poems as I picked up a tray of dirty dishes from a side table and started for the dumb-waiter."

The next morning Hughes bought a paper on his way to work and read that Vachel Lindsay had discovered "a Negro busboy poet." As a result of Lindsay's article, Hughes was met by reporters as he arrived at the hotel!

THINKING ABOUT THE PROCESS

1. Have you ever been inspired to write about something you saw while traveling? Explain.
2. What are the advantages and disadvantages of putting what you have written away for a time? Do you think this strategy could help you? Why or why not?
3. **Journal Writing** Hughes paid close attention to rhythms of speech and used them in his poetry. For several days, listen to the rhythms of the speech you hear around you and write your observations in a journal. Then share your findings with the class.

BIOGRAPHIES

Jean Toomer (1894–1967)

Like the other Harlem Renaissance writers, Jean Toomer had a deep interest in the cultural roots of the black people. In his work Toomer expressed his belief that maintaining an awareness of and a sense of pride in the black heritage was vital to the happiness and freedom of the black people.

Born in Washington, D.C., Toomer graduated from New York University in 1918. He then taught for several years in Georgia. His observations during his years as a teacher provided him with the material for *Cane* (1923), an unconventional book that consists of prose sketches, stories, poems, and a one-act play, all focusing on the concerns, interests, and experiences of American blacks.

Following the publication of *Cane,* Toomer was for a number of years considered to be the most talented writer of the Harlem Renaissance. During the early 1920's he published in such leading black journals as *The Crisis* and *Opportunity,* as well as in *The Little Review* (the leading journal of the Imagist movement). He was admired not only for his sensitive portrayals of black life, but, as one member of the group put it, for writing "without surrender or compromise of the artist's vision."

Toomer published few other works during the course of his life. After *Cane* fell into obscurity shortly after its publication, Toomer was virtually forgotten as a writer. In recent years, however, *Cane* has come to be recognized as one of the most important works to come out of the Harlem Renaissance and has influenced the work of a number of black writers.

Arna Bontemps (1902–1973)

A talented editor, novelist, dramatist, and poet, Arna Bontemps was one of the most scholarly figures of the Harlem Renaissance.

Bontemps was born in Louisiana and educated at the University of Chicago. He published his first novel, *God Sends Sunday,* in 1931. This book was followed by two novels about slave revolts, *Black Thunder* (1936) and *Drums at Dusk* (1939). Bontemps then went on to produce several volumes of nonfiction, including *The Story of the Negro* (1951) and *One Hundred Years of Negro Freedom* (1961). He also co-edited *The Poetry of the Negro* (1950), an anthology of black poetry, with Langston Hughes, and collaborated with Countee Cullen in writing *St. Louis Women* (1946), a musical play.

Bontemps also wrote poetry throughout his rich, varied literary career. Written in simple, direct language, using traditional forms and techniques, his poems are characterized by what Bontemps himself called "a certain simplicity of expression."

GUIDE FOR INTERPRETING

Storm Ending; A Black Man Talks of Reaping

Writers' Techniques

Metaphor. A metaphor is a comparison between two seemingly dissimilar things. This comparison is implied, rather than stated, and no connecting word is used. While metaphors are often brief, they may also be long, elaborate comparisons. This type of metaphor, in which details developing the comparison are presented throughout the poem, is known as an extended metaphor. For example, Langston Hughes uses an extended metaphor in "The Negro Speaks of Rivers," as he develops a comparison between rivers and the black people throughout the poem.

Commentary

Toomer and Bontemps, like other writers of the Harlem Renaissance, expressed the spirit and complicated rhythms of blues and jazz in their poetry. This was the music that came out of the black culture and became popular during the 1920's among whites, who would travel uptown to Harlem to hear blues and jazz in the Harlem clubs. Seeking to explain the source of the mood and poetic patterns of his poems, Langston Hughes wrote a note to his second volume of poetry in which he described how blues differed from traditional black spiritual music:

> The *Blues,* unlike the *Spirituals,* have a strict poetic pattern: one long line repeated and a third line to rhyme with the first two. Sometimes the second line in repetition is slightly changed and sometimes, but very seldom, it is omitted. The mood of the *Blues* is almost always despondency, but when they are sung people laugh.

> The mood of despondency that Hughes speaks of as being typical of the blues is one characteristic mood of the poetry of the Harlem Renaissance. Yet other Harlem Renaissance poets express moods derived from the energy and syncopations of jazz music. Which moods occur in "Storm Ending" and "A Black Man Talks of Reaping"?

Focus

In "Storm Ending" Jean Toomer describes a thunderstorm. Freewrite about the types of images you associate with thunderstorms and discuss the reasons why people have been captivated by thunderstorms.

BLACK PLACE II, 1944
Georgia O'Keeffe
The Metropolitan Museum of Art

Storm Ending

Jean Toomer

Thunder blossoms gorgeously above our heads,
Great, hollow, bell-like flowers,
Rumbling in the wind,
Stretching clappers to strike our ears . . .
5   Full-lipped flowers
Bitten by the sun
Bleeding rain
Dripping rain like golden honey—
And the sweet earth flying from the thunder.

RESPONDING TO THE SELECTION

Your Response

1. What did you see as you read this poem? What did you hear?
2. How would you describe the poem's mood?

Interpreting

3. (a) What natural event does the poem describe? (b) What is the speaker's attitude toward this event? (c) How is this attitude conveyed?

Applying

4. How would you describe your own attitude toward the natural event described in the poem?

ANALYZING LITERATURE

Understanding Metaphors

A **metaphor** is a comparison between two seemingly dissimilar things. An extended metaphor is a comparison that is developed throughout the course of a poem.

1. What two things are compared in the extended metaphor presented in "Storm Ending"?
2. How does Toomer establish this comparison in the first four lines?
3. How does he develop the comparison in the lines that follow?

THINKING AND WRITING

Creating an Extended Metaphor

Write a poem in which you present an extended metaphor. First decide on the two things you are going to compare. Then prepare a list of details developing this comparison. When writing your poem, establish the comparison in the first several lines; then develop it throughout the rest of the poem. After you finish writing, revise your poem, making sure that you have included enough details to adequately develop the comparison. When you finish revising, proofread your poem and share it with your classmates.

LEARNING OPTIONS

1. **Writing.** What was it like to live in Harlem during the 1920's among fellow writers, musicians, and artists? Ask Jean Toomer. Generate a list of questions that you would ask the poet if you had the opportunity. Then trade lists and try to answer the questions of a classmate.
2. **Cross-curricular Connection.** "Storm Ending" presents a poet's view of a thunderstorm. What is a meteorologist's view? Check an encyclopedia or a science textbook for a scientific explanation and description of thunder. Share your findings with classmates.

Primary Source

In his *Anthologies of Magazine Verse,* African American poet William Stanley Braithwaite published works of important American poets who had not yet received public recognition. Among the poets of the Harlem Renaissance, he reserved his highest praise for Jean Toomer. Of him he wrote:

". . . In Jean Toomer, the author of *Cane,* we come upon the very first artist of the race, who with all an artist's passion and sympathy for life, its hurts, its sympathies, its desires, its joys, its defeats and strange yearnings, can write about the Negro without the surrender or compromise of the artist's vision. So objective is it, that we feel that it is a mere accident that birth or association has thrown him into contact with the life he has written about. He could write just as well, just as poignantly, just as transmutingly, about the peasants of Russia, or the peasants of Ireland, had experience brought him in touch with their existence. *Cane* is a book of gold and bronze, of dusk and flame, of ecstasy and pain, and Jean Toomer is a bright morning star of a new day of the race in literature."

A Black Man Talks of Reaping

Arna Bontemps

I have sown beside all waters in my day.
I planted deep, within my heart the fear
that wind or fowl would take the grain away.
I planted safe against this stark, lean year.

5   I scattered seed enough to plant the land
in rows from Canada to Mexico
but for my reaping only what the hand
can hold at once is all that I can show.

Yet what I sowed and what the orchard yields
10 my brother's sons are gathering stalk and root;
small wonder then my children glean in fields
they have not sown, and feed on bitter fruit.

RESPONDING TO THE SELECTION

Your Response

1. What emotions does this poem evoke in you? Why?
2. What statement do you think the poet is making about the black experience in the United States?

Recalling

3. Why does the speaker plant "deep"?
4. (a) How much seed does the speaker scatter? (b) How much grain is he allowed to reap, or harvest?
5. Who reaps what the speaker has sown?

Interpreting

6. (a) Whom do you think the speaker calls his "brother's sons" (line 10)? (b) What do you think the "bitter fruit" (line 12) stands for?

7. What does the poem suggest about how black people are rewarded for their hard work?
8. How would you describe the tone of the poem?

Applying

9. What comment does this poem make about the Biblical statement (Galatians 6:7): "Whatsoever a man soweth, that shall he also reap"?

LEARNING OPTION

Art. Join the public relations department of the Harlem Chamber of Commerce. Together with classmates design a series of subway posters to create public awareness of the cultural contributions of black Americans during the 1920's. In your posters you might focus on writers, artists, musicians, or performers who took part in the Harlem Renaissance.

CROSS CURRENTS

Music in Harlem

Harlem during the 1920's was, for anyone interested in black American culture, the center of the world. "Harlem was like a great magnet for the Negro intellectual," Langston Hughes wrote in his autobiography, *The Big Sea*. Explaining how he felt when he first came to Harlem in 1921, Hughes said, "I really did not want to go to college at all. I didn't want to do anything but live in Harlem, get a job and work there. . . . " Not only did Harlem inspire and nurture such writers as Countee Cullen, Claude McKay, Jean Toomer, Arna Bontemps, Zora Neale Thurston, and Hughes, but it was the home of some of the most important figures in early jazz. Pianists and composers like Duke Ellington and Fats Waller; blues singers like Ethel Waters and Bessie Smith; entertainers like Josephine Baker, Florence Mills, and Bill Robinson were all part of the jazz age of the Harlem Renaissance. Even performers generally associated with other cities—such as Louis Armstrong with New Orleans—came to play in Harlem during the 1920's. "The world's most glamorous atmosphere!" exclaimed a young Duke Ellington upon his arrival in 1923. "Why it is just like the Arabian nights!"

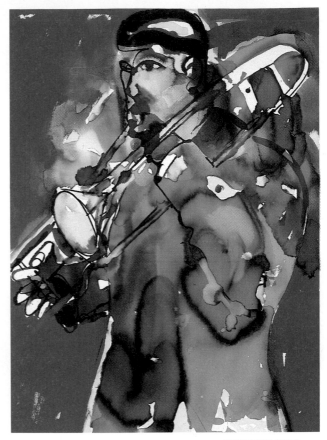

TROMBONE SOLO
Romare Bearden
Courtesy ACA Galleries

NIGHTLIFE IN HARLEM

It was, according to James Wendell Johnson, "a place where life wakes up at night." A booklet accompanying an early Columbia album called *The Sounds of Harlem* listed almost 125 entertainment spots between 125th and 135th Streets between Lenox and Seventh Avenues. These included at least forty clubs, among them the famous Cotton Club; more than seventeen cafés, speak-easies, cellars, lounges, bar and grills, and other places where blues and jazz were heard nightly; ten theaters and eight ballrooms where the jazz bands played and people danced all night. The most famous of these were the Apollo Theater and the Savoy Ballroom, which took up an entire city block between 140th and 141st Street. The interior of the Savoy reflected the glamour of

JAZZ VILLAGE
Romare Bearden
Courtesy ACA Galleries

the age: there were marble staircases; glass chandeliers; and a polished maple dance floor that had to be replaced every two years because of the wear of several thousand dancers, pounding the floor nightly.

Nightlife in Harlem was like jazz itself: full of energy, spirit, and surprise. People flocked to Harlem from all over the city to hear music and to dance. As the drummer Sammy Greer recalled: "The last show at the Cotton Club went on at two and the Club closed at three-thirty or four. Then everybody would go next door to Happy Roane's or to the breakfast dance at Smalls' Paradise, where the floor show went on at six o'clock in the morning. . . . It was the complete show with twenty-five or thirty people, including the singing waiters and their twirling trays. Show people from all over New York, white and colored, went there Sunday mornings. It's hard to imagine now, musicians coming out from the breakfast dance at eight or nine in the morning with their tuxedos on, and showgirls with evening dresses on. Or Charlie Johnson's band there, at six or seven in the morning, with maybe twenty-five musicians from the bands all over town, white and colored, playing at one time, all the top names in the music business."

BLUES AND JAZZ

Black performers of the Harlem Renaissance saw a close connection between their music and black America. "My men and my race are the inspiration of my work," Duke Ellington explained. "I try to catch the character and mood and feeling of my people. The music of my race is something more than the American idiom. It is the result of our transplantation to American soil and it was our reaction in plantation days, to the life we lived. The characteristic, melancholic music of my race has been forged from the very white heat of our sorrow and from our gropings."

The music of the Harlem Renaissance was dominated by two basic forms: blues and jazz. As Ellington suggested, the roots of blues and jazz were in the work songs, spirituals, and shouts of southern slaves, encouraged to sing by masters who thought that singing would keep up the morale of the slaves and make them work better. These slave songs, in turn, had their roots in the music of Africa. The pattern of theme and variation and the rhythmic counterpoint common in blues and jazz are elements in West African music. The blues, specifically, evolved as a folk music after the Civil War, expressing the hardships and struggles of blacks during Reconstruction. As Langston Hughes described the blues: "The music is slow, often mournful, yet syncopated, with a kind of marching bass behind it that seems to say, 'In spite of fate, bad luck, these blues themselves, I'm going on! I'm going to get there.' "

HARLEM AS INSPIRATION

Harlem itself inspired early jazz musicians and composers, much in the way it in-spired the writers of the age. In 1927 Fats Waller composed "Lenox Avenue Blues"; in 1928 songs with titles like "Harlem Drag" and "Harlem Twist" were recorded. Harlem seemed to be especially important to Duke Ellington, who recorded "Harlem Flat Blues" (1929), "Harlem Speaks" and "Drop Me Off in Harlem" (1933), and "Harmony in Harlem" (1938). Ellington's famous comment on his "Harlem Air Shaft" (1940) underlines the importance of life in Harlem to his work. It also eloquently describes what everyday life in black Harlem was like: "You get the full essence of Harlem in an air shaft. You hear fights, you smell dinner. . . . You hear intimate gossip floating down. You hear the radio. An air shaft is one great loudspeaker. You see your neighbor's laundry. You hear the janitor's dogs. The man upstairs' aerial falls down and breaks your window. You smell coffee. A wonderful thing, that smell. An air shaft has got every contrast. . . . You hear people praying, fighting, snoring. Jitterbugs are jumping up and down always over you, never below. That's a funny thing about jitterbugs. They're always above you. I tried to put it all down in 'Harlem Air Shaft'. . . . "

The music of blues and jazz that blacks created out of their experiences is considered to be the most important, if not the only, form of music indigenous to America. Begun as a form of expression for blacks amid hardships, blues and jazz were soon copied by prominent white songwriters of the twenties. But in their purest form, blues and jazz are born out of what Duke Ellington called the "dissonant" chord of black America's existence. "Dissonance is our way of life in America. We are something apart, yet an integral part."

YOUR WRITING PROCESS

WRITING A SELF-EVALUATION

Modern writers often describe places and characters with a few well-chosen words. Imagine that a job or college application requires you to describe yourself with just two or three adjectives and to explain why you chose those particular words. What words would you choose?

Focus

Assignment: Choose two or three adjectives to describe yourself and then explain your choices.

Purpose: To win a job or gain admission to a college.

Audience: A prospective employer or a college admissions committee.

Prewriting

1. I am . . . Make a list of as many adjectives as you can to describe yourself. Then circle the five that you think reflect your character most accurately.

2. Think of your audience. Sure, you might be shy or slovenly, but would an employer or a college admissions officer be pleased about these qualities? Keep your audience in mind and choose the traits that would appeal to them.

3. Cluster to get ideas. Make a cluster diagram using three to five adjectives as the central ideas. Think of experiences that show the qualities and specific reasons for your choices. What other associations do you have?

Student Model

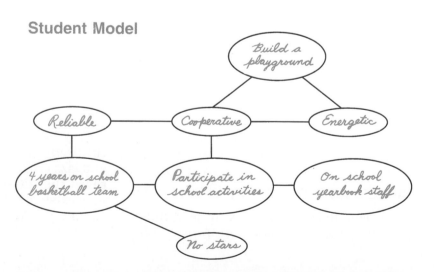

4. Show; don't tell. Narrow your choices down to three and think of several specific ways in which to *show* each adjective. Remember that it's not enough to tell; you must support each choice with lively and concrete details.

> **Student Model**
>
> Meticulous: I love to follow complicated recipes; I even iron my socks; my CD collection is in alphabetical order.

Drafting

1. Be yourself; be unique. Because your audience may read scores of these essays, make yours stand out from the crowd. Use precise words to describe experiences that could not have happened to anyone else.

> **Student Model**
>
> I was artistic even as a child. While other kids played hopscotch and dodge ball, I preferred finger painting and papier-mâché. My favorite sounds were the snipping of scissors and the screech of tape being pulled from its roll. My favorite smells were those of crayons and paste.

2. Use some imagination. Experiment with form. For example, you could cast your essay as a fairy tale, a campaign speech, or a poem. Use the voice of a friend or a teacher or a news anchorperson. Don't be afraid to try something weird. A good peer editor will tell you if you've gone too far.

Revising and Editing

1. Variety is spice. Avoid the temptation to begin every sentence with "I." Try participial and prepositional phrases, adjective and adverb clauses, and transitional words as sentence beginnings. Use both long and short sentences. Spice your essay with questions, quotations, and even exclamations.

2. Simplify, simplify, simplify. Eliminate anything that feels the least bit dishonest. Replace adjective-noun and adverb-verb combinations with more specific nouns and verbs. Avoid filler phrases such as "In my opinion" or "as a matter of fact." Reduce your language to its essential elements.

3. Ask a peer editor to respond. Have a classmate respond to your essay, noting its strengths and making suggestions for improvements. If you have experimented with the form of your essay, ask your classmate whether the novelty of your approach will work for or against you.

Grammar Tip

Your writing will be more emphatic and crisp if you use the **active** rather than the **passive voice.** In "Flight," for example, John Steinbeck could have written, "The valley was filled with cold blue light by the rising moon." He chose, however, to use the active voice: "The moon came up and filled the valley with cold blue light." [For more on active and passive voice, see the Handbook of Grammar and Revising Strategies, which begins on page 1136.]

Options for Publishing

• Seal your essay in an envelope, to be opened in a month. When you read it again, see whether or not your opinion of yourself has changed.

• Let a parent, relative, or good friend read your essay and ask them if they agree with the adjectives you have chosen.

• Use your writing as the basis of an actual essay for a college admission form or a job application.

Reviewing Your Writing Process

1. Would you use this piece or parts of it for a real college or job application? Explain.

2. Did you ask a peer editor to respond to your essay? If so, were his or her comments helpful? Why or why not?

GOLDEN GATE, 1955
Charles Sheeler
The Metropolitan Museum of Art

CONTEMPORARY WRITERS
1946–Present

Maria lay at night in the still of Beverly Hills and saw the great signs soar overhead at seventy miles an hour: *Normandie* 1/4 Vermont 3/4 Hollywood Fwy 1. Again and again she returned to an intricate stretch just south of the interchange where successful passage from the Hollywood to the Harbor required a diagonal move across four lanes of traffic.

Joan Didion

Maria Wyeth, the heroine of Joan Didion's novel *Play It As It Lays,* thinks about freeways, the central metaphor of the story. These freeways, like the Interstate Highway System begun in 1956, speed the movement of traffic. At the same time, however, they pose tricky driving problems. Survival requires skill.

Much of the new technology that has become widespread since 1945—television and computers in particular—can also have consequences beyond their obvious ones. The new technology does make life easier and pleasanter. Paradoxically, it also introduces complexities and problems that were unknown in earlier days.

The years from the end of the Second World War to the present day have been a time of change. Great strides have been made in civil rights and women's rights. Americans have fought in two Asian wars. Popular entertainment has changed dramatically, not just in presentation (from radio to television) but also in style (from big bands to rock music). These changes and others have had an effect on American literature. Their effect seems somehow less dramatic than the changes themselves, however. In general, contemporary writers have absorbed and extended earlier techniques but have introduced few startling innovations.

THE HISTORICAL SETTING

The United States emerged from the Second World War as the most powerful nation on earth. Proud of the part they had played in defeating the Axis, Americans now wanted life to return to normal. Soldiers and sailors came home, the rationing of scarce goods ended, and the nation prospered. But despite postwar jubilation, the dawn of the nuclear age and the ominous actions of the Soviet Union meant that nothing would be the same again.

In 1945, the United Nations was created amid high hopes that it would prevent future wars. Nonetheless, a Cold War between the Soviet Union and the West began as soon as the shooting war ended. In a speech in early 1946, Winston Churchill, Great Britain's wartime Prime Minister, said, "An iron curtain has descended across the continent" of Europe. It was in Asia, however, that the first armed conflict came. In 1950, President Harry S. Truman sent American troops to help anticommunist South Korean forces turn back a North Korean invasion.

From Quiet Pride to Activism

Americans of the 1950's are sometimes referred to as "the Silent Generation." Many of them had lived through both the Great Depression and the Second World War. When peace and prosperity finally arrived, they were only too glad to adopt a quiet, somewhat complacent attitude. They greatly admired President Dwight D. Eisenhower, one of America's wartime heroes.

Near the end of the 1950's, the Soviet Union launched Sputnik, the first artificial satellite to orbit the Earth. This Soviet space triumph spurred many people to call for changes in American science and education. President John F. Kennedy, elected in 1960, promised to "get the nation moving again." He had little time to do so, however, before his tragic assassination in 1963.

Kennedy's assassination was followed by an escalating and increasingly unpopular war in Vietnam. A wave of protest followed. Gone were the calm of the Eisenhower years and the high hopes of Kennedy's brief administration. In their place came idealistic but strident demands for rapid change: greater "relevance" in education, more progress on civil rights, an immediate end to the Vietnam War. It was a time of crisis and confrontations.

Real and lasting gains were made in civil rights after the Second World War. Astonishing as it may seem today, African Americans could not play baseball in the major leagues until Jackie Robinson broke the color barrier in 1947. Segregation in the public schools was outlawed by the Supreme Court in 1954. Tragedy struck in 1968, when black leader Martin Luther King, Jr., was assassinated in Memphis, Tennessee. Riots broke out in many cities across the nation.

One of the bright moments in a troublesome decade occurred in 1969. In July of that year, American astronaut Neil Armstrong became the first person to set foot on the moon.

SARABAND, 1959
Morris Louis
Solomon R. Guggenheim
Museum

A Quest for Stability

The upheavals of the 1960's brought a conservative reaction. Many Americans longed for a return to "the good old days." President Richard M. Nixon, elected in 1968, promised to end the Vietnam War and to restore order in the nation. Nixon's first-term achievements, especially in foreign policy, were soon overshadowed by his involvement in the Watergate affair. This scandal forced his resignation from the presidency in 1974. Vice President Gerald Ford took over, proclaiming, "Our long national nightmare is over."

Civil rights activism continued during these years, and another movement attracted growing attention—the women's liberation movement. Although the Nineteenth Amendment to the Constitution, ratified in 1920, had given women the right to vote, discrimination still existed. Women received lower pay than men for the same jobs, and promotion was more difficult. Betty Friedan's *The Feminine Mystique,* published in 1963, called for change. The women's movement grew steadily through the 1970's.

The final months of Jimmy Carter's one-term presidency were marred by high inflation and clouded by Iran's holding of more than fifty American hostages. The nation then sent Ronald Reagan to the White House. A former film star and two-term governor of California, Reagan proved to be a popular and persuasive President. His reelection in 1984 was one of the biggest landslide victories in American history. In 1988, George Bush, Reagan's vice president, was elected to the presidency.

The Changing Scene

Commercial television was still in its infancy at the end of the Second World War, but it was on the verge of spectacular growth. TV aerials soon sprouted on rooftops from coast to coast. Over the next few years, television changed the leisure habits of Americans. It even had an impact on presidential politics. John F. Kennedy's youthful but confident demeanor in the televised debates with Richard M. Nixon helped him win the election in 1960.

Contemporary Writers (A.D. 1946–Present)

Ralph Ellison

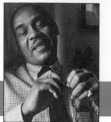

Flannery O'Connor

Fidel Castro

1946   **1956**   **1966**

AMERICAN EVENTS

- United States grants independence to the Philippines.
- **Carson McCullers** publishes *The Member of the Wedding.*
  - *Death of a Salesman* by **Arthur Miller** is first produced.
    - President Harry S. Truman sends troops to South Korea after North Korean invasion.
      - **Ralph Ellison** publishes *Invisible Man.*
        - Supreme Court rules public school segregation to be unconstitutional.
          - **Flannery O'Connor** publishes *A Good Man Is Hard to Find.*

- Alaska and Hawaii admitted to the Union as the 49th and 50th states.
  - **Robert Lowell's** *Life Studies* appears.
    - **John Updike** publishes *Rabbit Run.*
      - Joseph Heller publishes *Catch-22.*
        - Environmental protection movement spurred by Rachel Carson's book *Silent Spring.*
          - President John F. Kennedy assassinated in Dallas.
            - *Ariel,* **Sylvia Plath's** last collection of poems, appears.

- Martin Luther King, Jr., civil rights leader, murdered in Memphis.
  - Astronaut Neil Armstrong becomes the first person to set foot on the moon.
- **Joyce Carol Oates** publishes *Them.*
  - Last U.S. combat troops leave Vietnam; peace pact signed in 1973.
    - Toni Morrison publishes *Sula.*

WORLD EVENTS

- India-Pakistan: India and Pakistan granted independence from Great Britain.
  - Israel: United Nations establishes state of Israel.
  - Germany: Soviet Union blockades Allied sectors of Berlin.
    - England: Doris Lessing publishes *The Grass Is Singing.*
      - England: *Lord of the Flies* by William Golding appears.
        - Argentina: Jorge Luis Borges publishes *Extraordinary Tales.*

- Ghana: Ghana emerges as independent nation.
- USSR: *Doctor Zhivago* by Boris Pasternak appears.
  - Cuba: Fidel Castro comes to power.
    - Germany: East Germany erects Berlin Wall.
    - Australia: Patrick White publishes *Riders in the Chariot.*
      - USSR: *One Day in the Life of Ivan Denisovich* by Aleksandr Solzhenitsyn appears.

- Israel: Israel gains territory from Arab states in Six-Day War.
- South Africa: Dr. Christiaan Barnard performs first human heart transplant.
  - Northern Ireland: Long period of violence begins between Catholics and Protestants.
    - England: Iris Murdoch publishes *An Accidental Man.*
    - Mexico: Octavio Paz publishes *The Other Mexico.*
      - Middle East: Embargo on Middle East oil produces world shortages.

First Men on
the Moon

Violence Breaks
Out in Northern
Ireland

U.S. Soldier
in Vietnam

President Nixon
Resigns

1976   **1986**

- President Richard M. Nixon resigns.
  - Militant Iranian students take more than 50 Americans hostage in Teheran.
    - **Alice Walker** publishes *The Color Purple*.
      - Sally Ride becomes the first American woman to travel in space.

- Space shuttle *Challenger* explodes after launch from Cape Canaveral.
  - George Bush elected President.
  - Earthquake hits San Francisco.
    - American hostages released from Lebanon.
      - Bill Clinton elected president

- Vietnam: Hundreds of thousands of "boat people" flee Vietnam.
  - Trinidad: V. S. Naipaul publishes *A Bend in the River*.
    - Poland: Polish trade union movement Solidarity suppressed.

- USSR: Chernobyl nuclear disaster spreads radioactive cloud across Eastern Europe.
  - Eastern Europe: Berlin Wall comes down. Major changes occur in Eastern European governments.
    - Middle East: Unified forces led by United States defeat Iraq in Persian Gulf War.
    - Eastern Europe: Soviet Union dissolves.

The postwar period was a time of explosive suburban growth, made possible by the automobile. Despite the recent renewal of certain areas of older cities, the growth of suburbs continues today. At first, most suburban homeowners worked in the nearby city and commuted to their jobs by train, bus, or car. Later, major corporations began establishing suburban headquarters, and workers could live nearby or commute short distances from one suburb to another.

American industry changed rapidly during this period. Automation and foreign competition reduced the number of jobs in heavy industries like steel and automobile manufacturing. At the same time, the electronics industry was experiencing dynamic growth. Along with a sudden increase in the number of high-tech jobs came an increase in the number of service jobs. More leisure time and more money to spend brought a need for more employees to serve other people's needs.

The world has changed dramatically since 1945, and it is still changing. These changes have had an impact on the literature of the time, although this impact has not always been obvious.

UNTITLED, 1960–1961
Mark Rothko

LITERARY VARIETY AND PROMISE

The turbulence of contemporary times has not fostered a literary revolution of the kind that occurred in the 1920's, yet it has contributed to the development of a wide variety of literary movements that are often collectively referred to as Postmodernism. While many writers have been content to build on the experiments of the Modernists, others have sought to create works that stand apart from the past. Some writers have explored new literary forms and techniques, composing works from dialogue alone, creating works that blend fiction and nonfiction or fantasy and realism, and/or experimenting with the physical appearance of their work. Other writers have focused on capturing the essence of contemporary life in the content of their works, often expressing themes concerning the complex, impersonal, and commercial nature of today's world.

Authors for a New Era

Although contemporary writers have produced a wide variety of impressive works, it is all but impossible to predict which writers will achieve lasting fame and which will not. Time is needed to certify greatness. Modern readers and modern critics have their favorites, of course. Some of them will undoubtedly become part of America's enduring literary legacy.

Every writer owes a debt to those writers who have gone before. In that sense, literature is cumulative. The earliest American literature, except for that of the Native Americans, was based on European models. Writers in the United States today can look to a rich heritage of their own. Contemporary novelists are well aware of Nathaniel Hawthorne, Mark Twain, Ernest Hemingway, William Faulkner. Short-story writers know Edgar Allan Poe, Willa Cather, Eudora Welty. Poets study

Emily Dickinson, Walt Whitman, Langston Hughes. Playwrights are familiar with Eugene O'Neill and Thornton Wilder.

One of the literary giants to whom many modern writers look is not American but Irish: James Joyce. Although Joyce is difficult to read, his technical innovations and major themes have made an indelible mark on American fiction. The stream-of-consciousness technique, although not invented by Joyce, is strongly associated with him. Also influential is Joyce's fusing of the romantic and realistic traditions, achieving a middle ground between myth and reality.

Among the highly acclaimed novelists of our day is Saul Bellow, who won the Nobel Prize for literature in 1976. His novel *Herzog,* about an average man seeking truth in a world that overwhelms him, shows clear parallels with Joyce's *Ulysses.* Ralph Ellison's *Invisible Man,* about a young black man searching for identity, parallels Joyce's *Portrait of the Artist as a Young Man.*

Other contemporary novelists of stature include Carson McCullers, Robert Penn Warren, Norman Mailer, Bernard Malamud, John Updike, Flannery O'Connor, Joyce Carol Oates, Anne Tyler, and Alice Walker. Many of these novelists have written short stories as well. Flannery O'Connor and John Updike are modern masters of the short-story form. Joyce Carol Oates, winner of the National Book Award for her novel *Them,* has also won numerous awards for her short fiction. Other writers, such as Donald Barthelme and Ann Beattie, have written novels but are better known for their short stories. Isaac Bashevis Singer, a Polish-born New Yorker who wrote in Yiddish, was renowned for both his novels and his short stories. He won the Nobel Prize for Literature in 1978. John Cheever, a respected novelist, won the Pulitzer Prize for fiction in 1979 for his collected short stories, many of which concern suburban life.

Just as realism and romanticism have tended to merge in recent literature, so, curiously, have fiction and nonfiction. Truman Capote's *In Cold Blood,* published in 1966, was billed as a "nonfiction novel." Capote, primarily a novelist and short-story writer, used fictional techniques to analyze a real and seemingly senseless crime. Later authors, such as E. L. Doctorow in his novel *Ragtime,* combined historical figures with purely fictional characters. This technique has aroused considerable controversy.

Increasing attention has been paid recently to the place of nonfiction in the literary hierarchy. The essay has always been considered an important literary form, and some outstanding essays are published every year. James Baldwin and John McPhee are accomplished essayists. Among the many notable longer works of nonfiction are Paul Theroux's *The Great Railway Bazaar,* N. Scott Momaday's *The Names,* and Barry Lopez's *Arctic Dreams.*

Poetry Within the Tradition

A number of the famous prewar poets continued to publish extensively after the war. Robert Frost, Marianne Moore, Wallace Stevens, E. E. Cummings, William Carlos Williams, and Ezra Pound all produced major collections of their works. The younger poets, starting out in the shadow of these great names, were mostly content to work within the advances made in the 1920's and 1930's. One critic observed that to a beginning poet "the reassurance of sounding like something already acclaimed" was hard to resist.

The tumultuous 1960's brought great changes in social behavior, which affected the subject matter of all literature. In poetry, as in fiction, the resulting changes were often more personal and thematic than innovative. It seems ironic that out of the turmoil of the 1960's, the finest poetry to emerge follows older patterns.

One of the most respected contemporary poets is Robert Lowell. His *Lord Weary's Castle,* published in 1946, immediately established him as an important poet of his generation. Lowell, a great-nephew of the poet James Russell Lowell, is a writer to whom history and historical context are important. His poetry is traditional in form, but its range in theme, method, and tone is breathtaking.

Theodore Roethke, a master of poetic rhythm, was deeply influenced as a man and as a poet by his father, a strong-willed greenhouse owner in Saginaw, Michigan. Some of Roethke's most notable poems are attempts to come to grips with his fa-

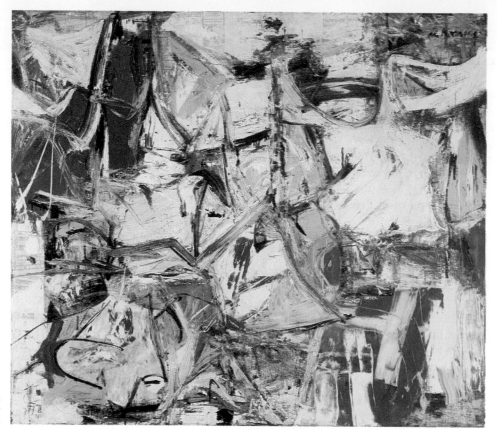

GOTHAM NEWS, 1955
Willem de Kooning
Albright-Knox Art Gallery

ther's death when Roethke was fourteen. The best of these are often referred to as his "greenhouse poems."

Georgia-born James Dickey is a poet and novelist whose southern heritage is of great importance in his work. Dickey was a decorated fighter pilot in the Second World War and later in Korea. He has also worked as a teacher and as an advertising executive. His novel *Deliverance* is perhaps his best-known work.

Two other poets of note are Elizabeth Bishop and Gwendolyn Brooks. Bishop, born in Massachusetts, traveled widely after graduating from Vassar College, finally settling in Brazil. Her poems are beautifully crafted, with precise and memorable descriptions. Brooks, a preeminent black poet, was born in Topeka, Kansas, but spent most of her life in Chicago. Her first collection, *A Street in Bronzeville*, published in 1945, assured her a reputation. This reputation was further enhanced by *Annie Allen*, published in 1949.

Many fine poets are at work today. Nowhere perhaps is America's pluralism displayed more vividly and to better advantage than in its poets. Although it is too early to assess these poets' achievements, it seems likely that some of their works will become the classics of tomorrow.

Beyond the Horizon

One of the features of literary history is its unpredictability. No one knows what will happen next. Of this, however, we can be reasonably sure: The novel is not dead, as some were proclaiming in the 1950's and 1960's. Poetry is not dead, nor is the short story. Literature has great resilience. While it may be profoundly influenced by other media—radio, television, film—it has not yet been replaced by them. Indeed, for sheer technical virtuosity, there has probably never been a more impressive group of American writers at work than at the present time.

AMERICAN VOICES

Quotations by Prominent Figures of the Period

Once or twice I have been asked what the peacock is "good for"—a question that gets no answer from me because it deserves none.
Flannery O'Connor, *"Peacocks Are a Puzzle"*

Ted Williams . . . had met the little death that awaits athletes. He had quit.
John Updike, "Hub Fans Bid Kid Adieu"

You know as well as I that when someone commits an injustice people make mincemeat of the victim, not of the culprit.
Isaac Bashevis Singer, "Advice"

The worst cynicism: a belief in luck.
Joyce Carol Oates, *Do With Me What You Will*

I discovered the difference between good writing and bad, and then made an even more alarming discovery: the difference between very good writing and true art; it is subtle, but savage.
Truman Capote, *Music for Chameleons*

Willy was a salesman. . . . He's a man way out there in the blue, rising on a smile and a shoeshine. . . . Nobody dast blame this man. A salesman is got to dream, boy. It comes with the territory.
Arthur Miller, *Death of a Salesman*

The road curved out and lay into the bank of rain beyond, and Abel was running. Against the winter sky and the long, light landscape of the valley at dawn, he seemed to be standing still, very little and alone.
N. Scott Momaday, *House Made of Dawn*

We will be ourselves and free, or die in the attempt. Harriet Tubman was not our grandmother for nothing.
Alice Walker, *You Can't Keep a Good Woman Down*

Every journey into the past is complicated by delusions, false memories, false namings of real events.
Adrienne Rich, *Of Woman Born*

READING CRITICALLY

The Literature of 1946–Present

In the years since World War II, American life has grown more and more diversified and complex. This diversity is reflected in the wide variety of different types of literary works that have been written in the past several decades.

HISTORICAL CONTEXT Soon after the United States dropped the first nuclear bomb on Hiroshima, it became clear that a new era had begun—an era unlike any previous period in the history of humanity. This era has been characterized by rapid change. Air travel has become commonplace, new methods of communication have been developed and old methods have been perfected, computers have become an integral part of American life, and several Americans have walked on the moon. The United States has participated in two wars in Asia and has passed through periods of stability and unrest. As a result of these changes, life in America today is dramatically different from what it was in 1946, and new technological advances make it clear that American life will continue to change.

LITERARY MOVEMENTS A number of small literary movements have developed since World War II. These movements are often referred to as Postmodernism. In fiction, some writers have continued to develop the fragmentary approach of the Modernists. Others have tried blending realism and fantasy in their works, and still others have experimented with radically different fictional forms and techniques. In poetry, many small regional movements have developed, and the poetry that has been written has varied dramatically in form, style, and content.

WRITERS' TECHNIQUES During the contemporary period, writers have continued to use many of the literary forms and techniques that were popular during the Modern Age. Free verse has remained a dominant poetic form, and many poets have continued to focus on creating vivid, striking images in their poems. In addition to using popular modern devices such as the stream-of-consciousness technique, fiction writers have experimented with a variety of new forms and techniques. For example, writers have composed works from dialogue alone, have created works that blend fiction with nonfiction, and have experimented with the physical appearance of their work.

Fiction

MORNING CALL, 1946
Milton Avery
Hirshhorn Museum and Sculpture Garden,
Smithsonian Institution, Washington, D.C.

BERNARD MALAMUD

1914–1987

In his novels and short stories, Bernard Malamud depicts the struggles of ordinary people, often focusing on their desire to improve their lives. He uses the Jewish people to represent all of humanity, capturing their attempts to maintain a link to their cultural heritage while trying to cope with the realities of the modern world. While some of Malamud's characters achieve success, others experience failure. By portraying people in both victory and defeat, Malamud captures the essence of the human experience and creates a delicate balance between tragedy and comedy in his work.

Malamud was born in Brooklyn, New York, the son of Russian immigrants. His father was a grocer who worked diligently in an effort to forge a better life for his family. After attending City College of New York and Columbia University, Malamud began publishing short stories in a number of well-known magazines. In 1952 he published his first novel, *The Natural,* which depicts the life of a gifted baseball player. After that he wrote several other novels, including *The Assistant* (1957), *A New Life* (1961), *The Tenants* (1971), and *Dubin's Lives* (1979). His novel about czarist Russia, *The Fixer* (1966), earned him the Pulitzer Prize and the National Book Award. He also received the National Book Award for *The Magic Barrel* (1958), a collection of short stories.

According to his own account, Malamud's boyhood was "comparatively happy." He grew up in a household where both Yiddish and English were spoken. The constant mingling of the two languages contributed to the writer's fine ear for characteristic spoken rhythms. His family's Judaism expressed itself more as culture than as religion, and through his family he gained a taste for Manhattan's Second Avenue Yiddish theater where two of his mother's relatives sometimes performed. Another favored boyhood pastime was listening to his father recount tales of Jewish life in czarist Russia. Young Bernard began to display his father's gift for telling stories by age nine when, recovering from pneumonia, he spent hours in the back room of the family store writing down the stories he'd made up to tell his friends. Malamud's fondness for his father's stories revealed itself later in the vast number of stories the author drew from Yiddish oral tradition.

Like most of Malamud's work, "The First Seven Years" focuses on the lives of common people. Depicting a Polish immigrant's desire to see his daughter achieve a better life, the story exposes the discrepancy that often exists between parents' dreams for their children and their children's actual desires.

GUIDE FOR INTERPRETING

The First Seven Years

Writers' Techniques

Epiphany. In a traditional short story, the plot moves toward a resolution, a point at which the conflict, or the struggle that the main character undergoes, is resolved and the final outcome of the action becomes clear. During the twentieth century, however, in an effort to capture the uncertainty and confusion of life in the modern world, most fiction writers have turned away from the traditional plot structure by ending their stories without a resolution. Instead, writers often construct plots that move toward an epiphany, a moment when a character has a flash of insight about himself or herself, another character, a situation, or life in general. For example, in "The First Seven Years," the main character, Feld, gains a sudden insight into his own life and his hopes for his daughter.

Focus

Like the main character in "The First Seven Years," many parents are deeply concerned with building better lives for their children. Freewrite about why parents often hope that their children's lives will be better than their own, discussing the types of actions that result from this desire.

Commentary

What determines the values of a person or a generation? Some people long for expensive sports cars and fine homes, whereas others value peace of mind or spiritual wealth. Often, the things most prized in life differ from one generation to the next, and frequently the difference involves a shift from material to spiritual poles. Bernard Malamud's story, "The First Seven Years," portrays the age-old generational shift as America experienced it in the 1950's. Here is how it is described in *American Writers*:

> The claim that our spiritual lives are being violated by our attachment to material goods and physical comforts is at least as old as the Old Testament. But in America these complaints probably were never so persuasively and variously made as in the late 1950's. . . . Since one of the primary human realities, if not the dominant one, has been material want, our sense of reality is being diminished to the degree that the new prosperity seems to be lessening our sharp responses to want.

The First Seven Years

Bernard Malamud

Feld, the shoemaker, was annoyed that his helper, Sobel, was so insensitive to his reverie that he wouldn't for a minute cease his fanatic pounding at the other bench. He gave him a look, but Sobel's bald head was bent over the last[1] as he worked and he didn't notice. The shoemaker shrugged and continued to peer through the partly frosted window at the nearsighted haze of falling February snow. Neither the shifting white blur outside, nor the sudden deep remembrance of the snowy Polish village where he had wasted his youth could turn his thoughts from Max the college boy, (a constant visitor in the mind since early that morning when Feld saw him trudging through the snowdrifts on his way to school) whom he so much respected because of the sacrifices he had made throughout the years—in winter or direst heat—to further his education. An old wish returned to haunt the shoemaker: that he had had a son instead of a daughter, but this blew away in the snow for Feld, if anything, was a practical man. Yet he could not help but contrast the diligence of the boy, who was a peddler's son, with Miriam's unconcern for an education. True, she was always with a book in her hand, yet when the opportunity arose for a college education, she had said no she would rather find a job. He had begged her to go, pointing out how many fathers could not afford to send their children to college, but she said she wanted to be independent.

As for education, what was it, she asked, but books, which Sobel, who diligently read the classics, would as usual advise her on. Her answer greatly grieved her father.

A figure emerged from the snow and the door opened. At the counter the man withdrew from a wet paper bag a pair of battered shoes for repair. Who he was the shoemaker for a moment had no idea, then his heart trembled as he realized, before he had thoroughly discerned the face, that Max himself was standing there, embarrassedly explaining what he wanted done to his old shoes. Though Feld listened eagerly, he couldn't hear a word, for the opportunity that had burst upon him was deafening.

He couldn't exactly recall when the thought had occurred to him, because it was clear he had more than once considered suggesting to the boy that he go out with Miriam. But he had not dared speak, for if Max said no, how would he face him again? Or suppose Miriam, who harped so often on independence, blew up in anger and shouted at him for his meddling? Still, the chance was too good to let by: all it meant was an introduction. They might long ago have become friends had they happened to meet somewhere, therefore was it not his duty—an obligation—to bring them together, nothing more, a harmless connivance to replace an accidental encounter in the subway, let's say, or a mutual friend's introduction in the street? Just let him once see and talk to her and he would for sure be interested. As for Miriam, what possible harm for a working girl in an office, who met only loud-mouthed

---

1. **last** *n.*: A block shaped like a person's foot, on which shoes are made or repaired.

salesmen and illiterate shipping clerks, to
make the acquaintance of a fine scholarly
boy? Maybe he would awaken in her a desire
to go to college; if not—the shoemaker's
mind at last came to grips with the truth—
let her marry an educated man and live a
better life.

When Max finished describing what he
wanted done to his shoes, Feld marked
them, both with enormous holes in the soles
which he pretended not to notice, with large
white-chalk *x*'s, and the rubber heels,
thinned to the nails, he marked with *o*'s,
though it troubled him he might have mixed
up the letters. Max inquired the price, and

the shoemaker cleared his throat and asked
the boy, above Sobel's insistent hammering,
would he please step through the side door
there into the hall. Though surprised, Max
did as the shoemaker requested, and Feld
went in after him. For a minute they were
both silent, because Sobel had stopped
banging, and it seemed they understood
neither was to say anything until the noise
began again. When it did, loudly, the shoemaker quickly told Max why he had asked to
talk to him.

"Ever since you went to high school," he
said, in the dimly-lit hallway, "I watched you
in the morning go to the subway to school,

and I said always to myself, this is a fine boy that he wants so much an education."

"Thanks," Max said, nervously alert. He was tall and grotesquely thin, with sharply cut features, particularly a beak-like nose. He was wearing a loose, long slushy overcoat that hung down to his ankles, looking like a rug draped over his bony shoulders, and a soggy, old brown hat, as battered as the shoes he had brought in.

"I am a business man," the shoemaker abruptly said to conceal his embarrassment, "so I will explain you right away why I talk to you. I have a girl, my daughter Miriam—she is nineteen—a very nice girl and also so pretty that everybody looks on her when she passes by in the street. She is smart, always with a book, and I thought to myself that a boy like you, an educated boy—I thought maybe you will be interested sometime to meet a girl like this." He laughed a bit when he had finished and was tempted to say more but had the good sense not to.

Max stared down like a hawk. For an uncomfortable second he was silent, then he asked, "Did you say nineteen?"

"Yes."

"Would it be all right to inquire if you have a picture of her?"

"Just a minute." The shoemaker went into the store and hastily returned with a snapshot that Max held up to the light.

"She's all right," he said.

Feld waited.

"And is she sensible—not the flighty kind?"

"She is very sensible."

After another short pause, Max said it was okay with him if he met her.

"Here is my telephone," said the shoemaker, hurriedly handing him a slip of paper. "Call her up. She comes home from work six o'clock."

Max folded the paper and tucked it away into his worn leather wallet.

"About the shoes," he said. "How much did you say they will cost me?"

"Don't worry about the price."

"I just like to have an idea."

"A dollar—dollar fifty. A dollar fifty," the shoemaker said.

At once he felt bad, for he usually charged two twenty-five for this kind of job. Either he should have asked the regular price or done the work for nothing.

Later, as he entered the store, he was startled by a violent clanging and looked up to see Sobel pounding with all his might upon the naked last. It broke, the iron striking the floor and jumping with a thump against the wall, but before the enraged shoemaker could cry out, the assistant had torn his hat and coat from the hook and rushed out into the snow.

So Feld, who had looked forward to anticipating how it would go with his daughter and Max, instead had a great worry on his mind. Without his temperamental helper he was a lost man, especially since it was years now that he had carried the store alone. The shoemaker had for an age suffered from a heart condition that threatened collapse if he dared exert himself. Five years ago, after an attack, it had appeared as though he would have either to sacrifice his business upon the auction block and live on a pittance thereafter, or put himself at the mercy of some unscrupulous employee who would in the end probably ruin him. But just at the moment of his darkest despair, this Polish refugee, Sobel, appeared one night from the street and begged for work. He was a stocky man, poorly dressed, with a bald head that had once been blond, a severely plain face and soft blue eyes prone to tears over the sad books he read, a young man but old—no one would have guessed thirty. Though he confessed he knew nothing of shoemaking, he said he was apt and would work for a very little if Feld taught him the trade. Thinking that with, after all, a landsman,[2] he would have less to fear than from a complete stranger, Feld took him on and within six

2. **landsman** *n.*: A fellow countryman.

weeks the refugee rebuilt as good a shoe as he, and not long thereafter expertly ran the business for the thoroughly relieved shoemaker.

Feld could trust him with anything and did, frequently going home after an hour or two at the store, leaving all the money in the till, knowing Sobel would guard every cent of it. The amazing thing was that he demanded so little. His wants were few; in money he wasn't interested—in nothing but books, it seemed—which he one by one lent to Miriam, together with his profuse, queer written comments, manufactured during his lonely rooming house evenings, thick pads of commentary which the shoemaker peered at and twitched his shoulders over as his daughter, from her fourteenth year, read page by sanctified page, as if the word of God were inscribed on them. To protect Sobel, Feld himself had to see that he received more than he asked for. Yet his conscience bothered him for not insisting that the assistant accept a better wage than he was getting, though Feld had honestly told him he could earn a handsome salary if he worked elsewhere, or maybe opened a place of his own. But the assistant answered, somewhat ungraciously, that he was not interested in going elsewhere, and though Feld frequently asked himself what keeps him here? why does he stay? he finally answered it that the man, no doubt because of his terrible experiences as a refugee, was afraid of the world.

After the incident with the broken last, angered by Sobel's behavior, the shoemaker decided to let him stew for a week in the rooming house, although his own strength was taxed dangerously and the business suffered. However, after several sharp nagging warnings from both his wife and daughter, he went finally in search of Sobel, as he had once before, quite recently, when over some fancied slight—Feld had merely asked him not to give Miriam so many books to read because her eyes were strained and red—the assistant had left the place in a huff, an incident which, as usual, came to nothing for he

had returned after the shoemaker had talked to him, and taken his seat at the bench. But this time, after Feld had plodded through the snow to Sobel's house—he had thought of sending Miriam but the idea became repugnant to him—the burly landlady at the door informed him in a nasal voice that Sobel was not at home, and though Feld knew this was a nasty lie, for where had the refugee to go? still for some reason he was not completely sure of—it may have been the cold and his fatigue—he decided not to insist on seeing him. Instead he went home and hired a new helper.

Having settled the matter, though not entirely to his satisfaction, for he had much more to do than before, and so, for example, could no longer lie late in bed mornings because he had to get up to open the store for the new assistant, a speechless, dark man with an irritating rasp as he worked, whom he would not trust with the key as he had Sobel. Furthermore, this one, though able to do a fair repair job, knew nothing of grades of leather or prices, so Feld had to make his own purchases: and every night at closing time it was necessary to count the money in the till and lock up. However, he was not dissatisfied, for he lived much in his thoughts of Max and Miriam. The college boy had called her, and they had arranged a meeting for this coming Friday night. The shoemaker would personally have preferred Saturday, which he felt would make it a date of the first magnitude, but he learned Friday was Miriam's choice, so he said nothing. The day of the week did not matter. What mattered was the aftermath. Would they like each other and want to be friends? He sighed at all the time that would have to go by before he knew for sure. Often he was tempted to talk to Miriam about the boy, to ask whether she thought she would like his type—he had told her only that he considered Max a nice boy and had suggested he call her—but the one time he tried she snapped at him—justly—how should she know?

At last Friday came. Feld was not feeling

particularly well so he stayed in bed, and Mrs. Feld thought it better to remain in the bedroom with him when Max called. Miriam received the boy, and her parents could hear their voices, his throaty one, as they talked. Just before leaving, Miriam brought Max to the bedroom door and he stood there a minute, a tall, slightly hunched figure wearing a thick, droopy suit, and apparently at ease as he greeted the shoemaker and his wife, which was surely a good sign. And Miriam, although she had worked all day, looked fresh and pretty. She was a large-framed girl with a well-shaped body, and she had a fine open face and soft hair. They made, Feld thought, a first-class couple.

Miriam returned after 11:30. Her mother was already asleep, but the shoemaker got out of bed and after locating his bathrobe went into the kitchen, where Miriam, to his surprise, sat at the table, reading.

"So where did you go?" Feld asked pleasantly.

"For a walk," she said, not looking up.

"I advised him," Feld said, clearing his throat, "he shouldn't spend so much money."

"I didn't care."

The shoemaker boiled up some water for tea and sat down at the table with a cupful and a thick slice of lemon.

"So how," he sighed after a sip, "did you enjoy?"

"It was all right."

He was silent. She must have sensed his disappointment, for she added, "You can't really tell much the first time."

"You will see him again?"

Turning a page, she said that Max had asked for another date.

"For when?"

"Saturday."

"So what did you say?"

"What did I say?" she asked, delaying for a moment—"I said yes."

Afterwards she inquired about Sobel, and Feld, without exactly knowing why, said the assistant had got another job. Miriam said nothing more and began to read. The shoemaker's conscience did not trouble him; he was satisfied with the Saturday date.

During the week, by placing here and there a deft question, he managed to get from Miriam some information about Max. It surprised him to learn that the boy was not studying to be either a doctor or lawyer but was taking a business course leading to a degree in accountancy. Feld was a little disappointed because he thought of accountants as bookkeepers and would have preferred "a higher profession." However, it was not long before he had investigated the subject and discovered that Certified Public Accountants were highly respected people, so he was thoroughly content as Saturday approached. But because Saturday was a busy day, he was much in the store and therefore did not see Max when he came to call for Miriam. From his wife he learned there had been nothing especially revealing about their meeting. Max had rung the bell and Miriam had got her coat and left with him—nothing more. Feld did not probe, for his wife was not particularly observant. Instead, he waited up for Miriam with a newspaper on his lap, which he scarcely looked at so lost was he in thinking of the future. He awoke to find her in the room with him, tiredly removing her hat. Greeting her, he was suddenly inexplicably afraid to ask anything about the evening. But since she volunteered nothing he was at last forced to inquire how she had enjoyed herself. Miriam began something noncommittal but apparently changed her mind, for she said after a minute, "I was bored."

When Feld had sufficiently recovered from his anguished disappointment to ask why, she answered without hesitation, "Because he's nothing more than a materialist."

"What means this word?"

"He has no soul. He's only interested in things."

He considered her statement for a long time but then asked, "Will you see him again?"

"He didn't ask."

"Suppose he will ask you?"

"I won't see him."

He did not argue; however, as the days went by he hoped increasingly she would change her mind. He wished the boy would telephone, because he was sure there was more to him than Miriam, with her inexperienced eye, could discern. But Max didn't call. As a matter of fact he took a different route to school, no longer passing the shoemaker's store, and Feld was deeply hurt.

Then one afternoon Max came in and asked for his shoes. The shoemaker took them down from the shelf where he had placed them, apart from the other pairs. He had done the work himself and the soles and heels were well built and firm. The shoes had been highly polished and somehow looked better than new. Max's Adam's apple went up once when he saw them, and his eyes had little lights in them.

"How much?" he asked, without directly looking at the shoemaker.

"Like I told you before," Feld answered sadly. "One dollar fifty cents."

Max handed him two crumpled bills and received in return a newly-minted silver half dollar.

He left. Miriam had not been mentioned. That night the shoemaker discovered that his new assistant had been all the while stealing from him, and he suffered a heart attack.

Though the attack was very mild, he lay in bed for three weeks. Miriam spoke of going for Sobel, but sick as he was Feld rose in wrath against the idea. Yet in his heart he knew there was no other way, and the first weary day back in the shop thoroughly convinced him, so that night after supper he dragged himself to Sobel's rooming house.

He toiled up the stairs, though he knew it was bad for him, and at the top knocked at the door. Sobel opened it and the shoemaker entered. The room was a small, poor one, with a single window facing the street. It contained a narrow cot, a low table and several stacks of books piled haphazardly around on the floor along the wall, which made him think how queer Sobel was, to be uneducated and read so much. He had once asked him, Sobel, why you read so much? and the assistant could not answer him. Did you ever study in a college someplace? he had asked but Sobel shook his head. He read, he said, to know. But to know what, the shoemaker demanded, and to know, why? Sobel never explained, which proved he read much because he was queer.

Feld sat down to recover his breath. The assistant was resting on his bed with his heavy back to the wall. His shirt and trousers were clean, and his stubby fingers, away from the shoemaker's bench, were strangely pallid. His face was thin and pale, as if he had been shut in this room since the day he had bolted from the store.

"So when you will come back to work?" Feld asked him.

To his surprise, Sobel burst out, "Never."

Jumping up, he strode over to the window that looked out upon the miserable street. "Why should I come back?" he cried.

"I will raise your wages."

"Who cares for your wages!"

The shoemaker, knowing he didn't care, was at a loss what else to say.

"What do you want from me, Sobel?"

"Nothing."

"I always treated you like you was my son."

Sobel vehemently denied it. "So why you look for strange boys in the street they should go out with Miriam? Why you don't think of me?"

The shoemaker's hands and feet turned freezing cold. His voice became so hoarse he couldn't speak. At last he cleared his throat and croaked, "So what has my daughter got to do with a shoemaker thirty-five years old who works for me?"

"Why do you think I worked so long for you?" Sobel cried out. "For the stingy wages I sacrificed five years of my life so you could have to eat and drink and where to sleep?"

"Then for what?" shouted the shoe-maker.

"For Miriam," he blurted—"for her."

The shoemaker, after a time, managed to say, "I pay wages in cash, Sobel," and lapsed into silence. Though he was seething with excitement, his mind was coldly clear, and he had to admit to himself he had sensed all along that Sobel felt this way. He had never so much as thought it consciously, but he had felt it and was afraid.

"Miriam knows?" he muttered hoarsely.

"She knows."

"You told her?"

"No."

"Then how does she know?"

"How does she know?" Sobel said, "because she knows. She knows who I am and what is in my heart."

Feld had a sudden insight. In some devious way, with his books and commentary, Sobel had given Miriam to understand that he loved her. The shoemaker felt a terrible anger at him for his deceit.

"Sobel, you are crazy," he said bitterly. "She will never marry a man so old and ugly like you."

Sobel turned black with rage. He cursed the shoemaker, but then, though he trembled to hold it in, his eyes filled with tears and he broke into deep sobs. With his back to Feld, he stood at the window, fists clenched, and his shoulders shook with his choked sobbing.

Watching him, the shoemaker's anger diminished. His teeth were on edge with pity for the man, and his eyes grew moist. How strange and sad that a refugee, a grown man, bald and old with his miseries, who had by the skin of his teeth escaped Hitler's incinerators,[3] should fall in love, when he had got to America, with a girl less than half his age. Day after day, for five years he had sat at his bench, cutting and hammering away, waiting for the girl to become a woman, unable to ease his heart with speech, knowing no protest but desperation.

"Ugly I didn't mean," he said half aloud.

Then he realized that what he had called ugly was not Sobel but Miriam's life if she married him. He felt for his daughter a strange and gripping sorrow, as if she were already Sobel's bride, the wife, after all, of a shoemaker, and had in her life no more than her mother had had. And all his dreams for her—why he had slaved and destroyed his heart with anxiety and labor—all these dreams of a better life were dead.

The room was quiet. Sobel was standing by the window reading, and it was curious that when he read he looked young.

"She is only nineteen," Feld said brokenly. "This is too young yet to get married. Don't ask her for two years more, till she is twenty-one, then you can talk to her."

Sobel didn't answer. Feld rose and left. He went slowly down the stairs but once outside, though it was an icy night and the crisp falling snow whitened the street, he walked with a stronger stride.

But the next morning, when the shoemaker arrived, heavy-hearted, to open the store, he saw he needn't have come, for his assistant was already seated at the last, pounding leather for his love.

---

3. Hitler's incinerators: During World War II, millions of Jews were murdered by the Nazis under the direction of German dictator Adolf Hitler (1889–1945).

R ESPONDING TO THE SELECTION

Your Response

1. With whom do your sympathies lie, Feld or Sobel? Explain.
2. If you were Sobel, would you have agreed to work two more years for Miriam? Why or why not?

Recalling

3. (a) Why does Feld respect Max? (b) How does Feld arrange to have Max meet Miriam?
4. Why is Miriam not interested in seeing Max again after their second date?
5. (a) What does Sobel reveal about his feelings for Miriam when Feld visits him? (b) How does Feld respond to this revelation? (c) What does he tell Sobel before he leaves his room?

Interpreting

6. How does Feld's belief that he "wasted his youth" relate to what he desires for his daughter?
7. (a) What does education represent to Feld? (b) What does it represent to Sobel?
8. What does Feld's inability to accept Miriam's assessment of Max's personality indicate about his own personality?
9. In what ways are Sobel and Feld similar?

Applying

10. "There are only two lasting bequests we can hope to give our children," wrote Hodding Carter. "One of these is roots; the other, wings." First discuss the meaning of this quotation. Then explain how it relates to the theme of this story.

A NALYZING LITERATURE

Understanding Epiphany

In many modern and contemporary stories, the action moves toward an **epiphany,** a moment in which a character has a flash of insight about himself or herself, another character, a situation, or life in general. Describe the epiphany that Feld experiences at the end of the story.

C RITICAL THINKING AND READING

Predicting Future Events

When a writer ends a story without a resolution, it is up to you to predict how the conflict will be resolved or whether it will be resolved at all. To make a valid prediction, you must consider what the story reveals about the characters' personalities and try to determine how they would be likely to act in the future.

1. How do you think Feld's relationship with Sobel will change following the incident at Sobel's rooming house? Support your answer.
2. Do you think Sobel will wait for two years? Explain your answer.
3. Do you think Feld will ever be able to completely accept Sobel as a son-in-law? Why or why not?

T HINKING AND WRITING

Writing About a Character

Write an essay in which you analyze Feld's personality. Start by rereading the story, focusing on Feld's feelings, actions, and desires. Then try to determine what his behavior reveals about his character. At some point in your essay, discuss Feld's revelation at the end of the story. Does he change? Do you sympathize with him? When you revise, make sure that you have used passages from the story to support your argument. When you finish revising, proofread your paper and share it with your classmates.

L EARNING OPTION

Speaking and Listening. Imagine that two years have passed since Sobel has returned to work. The time has come for him to claim his bride. Does Feld willingly relinquish his daughter? Together with a classmate, dramatize the conversation between Sobel and Feld in which the assistant reminds the shoemaker of his promise.

FLANNERY O'CONNOR

1925–1964

Flannery O'Connor's work reflects her intense commitment to her personal beliefs. In her exaggerated, tragic, and at times shockingly violent tales, she forces us to confront such human faults as hypocrisy, insensitivity, self-centeredness, and prejudice.

O'Connor was born in Savannah, Georgia, and was raised in the small Georgia town of Milledgeville. After receiving her undergraduate degree from the Georgia State College for Women, she went on to attend the University of Iowa Writers' Workshop. When she was twenty-seven, she published her first novel, *Wise Blood,* the story of a violent rivalry among the members of a fictional religious sect in the South. In 1955 she published her first collection of short stories, *A Good Man Is Hard to Find.* This was followed in 1960 by a second novel, *The Violent Bear It Away;* and in 1965 *Everything That Rises Must Converge,* another collection of her stories, was published.

Unfortunately, throughout most of her adult life, O'Connor suffered from lupus, a rare disease that eventually took her life. Because her disease set her apart from other people, O'Connor developed a deep sensitivity to misfits and outsiders. Not surprisingly, many of her most memorable characters are social outcasts or people who are in some way mentally or physically disabled. Although she portrays these characters in an unsentimental manner, there is an underlying sense of sympathy for their pain and suffering.

O'Connor's work reflects her strong Catholic faith, and she had this to say about the relationship between her faith and her writing: "When people have told me that because I am a Catholic, I cannot be an artist, I have had to reply, ruefully, that because I am a Catholic I cannot afford to be less than an artist." She lived in the true Bible Belt of the South and acknowledged readily that her people had a strong sense of the absolute. Whatever she viewed, she viewed from the standpoint of Christian orthodoxy, which is centered on the belief that sinfulness in humans must be redeemed through Christ. She strongly believed that humanity would be defeated unless people acknowledged their obligation to obey God. These beliefs permeate her work. In O'Connor's stories, violent or grotesque characters with moral deformities are headed toward damnation. Their only salvation is divine awareness and redemption.

"The Life You Save May Be Your Own" is a typical O'Connor story. A grim depiction of a group of outcasts, the story conveys a powerful moral message while capturing a number of the tragic realities of life in the modern world.

GUIDE FOR INTERPRETING

The Life You Save May Be Your Own

Writers' Techniques

Irony. Irony is a contrast or a difference between what is stated and what is meant, or between what is expected to happen and what actually happens. "The Life You Save May Be Your Own" is filled with situational irony—one of a number of different types of irony used in literature. This type of irony occurs when the actual result of an action or situation is quite different from the expected result. Much of the situational irony in O'Connor's story results from the contrast between the main character's comments and actions. This character, Mr. Shiftlet, complains that there is a lack of morality in the world and that people have no concern for others, yet his actions in the story make it clear that he himself lacks morality and has little concern for others.

Flannery O'Connor possessed a deep awareness of the irony and hypocrisy that exist in everyday life. A devoutly religious woman, O'Connor was disturbed by the fact that many people claim to have deep religious convictions yet behave in a manner that totally contradicts this claim. This type of hypocrisy is embodied in the character of Mr. Shiftlet, whose actions clearly contradict the beliefs he professes.

Focus

The title of the story is a slogan that commonly appeared on American highways a number of years ago. The slogan urged motorists to drive carefully to avoid killing themselves. Discuss the significance of this slogan. Whom else might a motorist's reckless driving affect? To what type of motives does the slogan appeal? What does it imply about human nature?

Primary Source

In her 1973 study of Flannery O'Connor, Dorothy Walters of Wichita State University discusses "the specific 'blend' of disparates which gives O'Connor's work its peculiar stamp of originality." These are her comments on irony in O'Connor's stories:

A background both Southern and Catholic, a view of the artist grounded on a firm moral base, an extreme sensitivity to the mixed tragicomic nature of experience—these are the forces which shape O'Connor's vision and lend color and direction to her work. As we might expect, these ingredients lead to an attitude highly ironic. Irony implies detachment and the ability to perceive meaning on multiple levels. Flannery O'Connor is acutely aware of such varied possibilities inherent in the life spectacle; and, as author-narrator, she consistently speaks through the voice of the *eiron*. . . .

The Life You Save May Be Your Own

Flannery O'Connor

The old woman and her daughter were sitting on their porch when Mr. Shiftlet came up their road for the first time. The old woman slid to the edge of her chair and leaned forward, shading her eyes from the piercing sunset with her hand. The daughter could not see far in front of her and continued to play with her fingers. Although the old woman lived in this desolate spot with only her daughter and she had never seen Mr. Shiftlet before, she could tell, even from a distance, that he was a tramp and no one to be afraid of. His left coat sleeve was folded up to show there was only half an arm in it and his gaunt figure listed slightly to the side as if the breeze were pushing him. He had on a black town suit and a brown felt hat that was turned up in the front and down in the back and he carried a tin tool box by a handle. He came on, at an amble, up her road, his face turned toward the sun which appeared to be balancing itself on the peak of a small mountain.

The old woman didn't change her position until he was almost into her yard; then she rose with one hand fisted on her hip. The daughter, a large girl in a short blue organdy dress, saw him all at once and jumped up and began to stamp and point and make excited speechless sounds.

Mr. Shiftlet stopped just inside the yard and set his box on the ground and tipped his hat at her as if she were not in the least afflicted; then he turned toward the old woman and swung the hat all the way off. He had long black slick hair that hung flat from a part in the middle to beyond the tips of his ears on either side. His face descended in forehead for more than half its length and ended suddenly with his features just balanced over a jutting steel-trap jaw. He seemed to be a young man but he had a look of composed dissatisfaction as if he understood life thoroughly.

"Good evening," the old woman said. She was about the size of a cedar fence post and she had a man's gray hat pulled down low over her head.

The tramp stood looking at her and didn't answer. He turned his back and faced the sunset. He swung both his whole and his short arm up slowly so that they indicated an expanse of sky and his figure formed a crooked cross. The old woman watched him with her arms folded across her chest as if she were the owner of the sun, and the daughter watched, her head thrust forward and her fat helpless hands hanging at the wrists. She had long pink-gold hair and eyes as blue as a peacock's neck.

He held the pose for almost fifty seconds and then he picked up his box and came on to the porch and dropped down on the bottom step. "Lady," he said in a firm nasal voice, "I'd give a fortune to live where I could see me a sun do that every evening."

"Does it every evening," the old woman said and sat back down. The daughter sat down too and watched him with a cautious sly look as if he were a bird that had come up very close. He leaned to one side, rooting in his pants pocket, and in a second he brought out a package of chewing gum and offered her a piece. She took it and unpeeled it and began to chew without taking her eyes off him. He offered the old woman a piece but she only raised her upper lip to indicate she had no teeth.

Mr. Shiftlet's pale sharp glance had already passed over everything in the yard—the pump near the corner of the house and the big fig tree that three or four chickens were preparing to roost in—and had moved to a shed where he saw the square rusted back of an automobile. "You ladies drive?" he asked.

"That car ain't run in fifteen year," the old woman said. "The day my husband died, it quit running."

"Nothing is like it used to be, lady," he said. "The world is almost rotten."

"That's right," the old woman said. "You from around here?"

"Name Tom T. Shiftlet," he murmured, looking at the tires.

"I'm pleased to meet you," the old woman said. "Name Lucynell Crater and daughter Lucynell Crater. What you doing around here, Mr. Shiftlet?"

He judged the car to be about a 1928 or '29 Ford. "Lady," he said, and turned and gave her his full attention, "lemme tell you something. There's one of these doctors in Atlanta that's taken a knife and cut the human heart—the human heart," he repeated, leaning forward, "out of a man's chest and held it in his hand," and he held his hand out, palm up, as if it were slightly weighted with the human heart, "and studied it like it was a day-old chicken, and lady," he said, allowing a long significant pause in which his head slid forward and his clay-colored eyes brightened, "he don't know no more about it than you or me."

"That's right," the old woman said.

"Why, if he was to take that knife and cut into every corner of it, he still wouldn't know no more than you or me. What you want to bet?"

"Nothing," the old woman said wisely. "Where you come from, Mr. Shiftlet?"

He didn't answer. He reached into his pocket and brought out a sack of tobacco and a package of cigarette papers and rolled himself a cigarette, expertly with one hand, and attached it in a hanging position to his upper lip. Then he took a box of wooden matches from his pocket and struck one on his shoe. He held the burning match as if he were studying the mystery of flame while it traveled dangerously toward his skin. The daughter began to make loud noises and to point to his hand and shake her finger at him, but when the flame was just before touching him, he leaned down with his hand cupped over it as if were going to set fire to his nose and lit the cigarette.

He flipped away the dead match and blew a stream of gray into the evening. A sly look came over his face. "Lady," he said, "nowadays, people'll do anything anyways. I can tell you my name is Tom T. Shiftlet and I come from Tarwater, Tennessee, but you never have seen me before: how you know I ain't lying? How you know my name ain't Aaron Sparks, lady, and I come from Singleberry, Georgia, or how you know it's not George Speeds and I come from Lucy, Alabama, or how you know I ain't Thompson Bright from Toolafalls, Mississippi?"

"I don't know nothing about you," the old woman muttered, irked.

"Lady," he said, "people don't care how they lie. Maybe the best I can tell you is, I'm a man; but listen lady," he said and paused and made his tone more ominous still, "what is a man?"

The old woman began to gum a seed.

"What you carry in that tin box, Mr. Shift-let?" she asked.

"Tools," he said, put back. "I'm a carpenter."

"Well, if you come out here to work, I'll be able to feed you and give you a place to sleep but I can't pay. I'll tell you that before you begin," she said.

There was no answer at once and no particular expression on his face. He leaned back against the two-by-four that helped support the porch roof. "Lady," he said slowly, "there's some men that some things mean more to them than money." The old woman rocked without comment and the daughter watched the trigger that moved up and down in his neck. He told the old woman then that all most people were interested in was money, but he asked what a man was made for. He asked her if a man was made for money, or what. He asked her what she thought she was made for but she didn't answer, she only sat rocking and wondered if a one-armed man could put a new roof on her garden house. He asked a lot of questions that she didn't answer. He told her that he was twenty-eight years old and had lived a varied life. He had been a gospel singer, a foreman on the railroad, an assistant in an undertaking parlor, and he come over the radio for three months with Uncle Roy and his Red Creek Wranglers. He said he had fought and bled in the Arm Service of his country and visited every foreign land and that everywhere he had seen people that didn't care if they did a thing one way or another. He said he hadn't been raised thataway.

A fat yellow moon appeared in the branches of the fig tree as if it were going to roost there with the chickens. He said that a man had to escape to the country to see the world whole and that he wished he lived in a desolate place like this where he could see the sun go down every evening like God made it to do.

"Are you married or are you single?" the old woman asked.

BLACK WALNUTS, 1945
Joseph Pollet
Collection of the Whitney Museum of American Art

There was a long silence. "Lady," he asked finally, "where would you find you an innocent woman today? I wouldn't have any of this trash I could just pick up."

The daughter was leaning very far down, hanging her head almost between her knees watching him through a triangular door she had made in her overturned hair; and she suddenly fell in a heap on the floor and began to whimper. Mr. Shiftlet straightened her out and helped her get back in the chair.

"Is she your baby girl?" he asked.

"My only," the old woman said "and she's the sweetest girl in the world. I would give her up for nothing on earth. She's smart too. She can sweep the floor, cook, wash, feed the chickens, and hoe. I wouldn't give her up for a casket of jewels."

"No," he said kindly, "don't ever let any man take her away from you."

"Any man come after her," the old woman said, " 'll have to stay around the place."

Mr. Shiftlet's eye in the darkness was focused on a part of the automobile bumper that glittered in the distance. "Lady," he said, jerking his short arm up as if he could point with it to her house and yard and pump, "there ain't a broken thing on this plantation that I couldn't fix for you, one-arm jackleg or not. I'm a man," he said with a sullen dignity, "even if I ain't a whole one. I got," he said, tapping his knuckles on the floor to emphasize the immensity of what he was going to say, "a moral intelligence!" and his face pierced out of the darkness into a shaft of doorlight and he stared at her as if he were astonished himself at this impossible truth.

The old woman was not impressed with the phrase. "I told you you could hang around and work for food," she said, "if you don't mind sleeping in that car yonder."

"Why listen, lady," he said with a grin of delight, "the monks of old slept in their coffins!"

"They wasn't as advanced as we are," the old woman said.

The next morning he began on the roof of the garden house while Lucynell, the daughter, sat on a rock and watched him work. He had not been around a week before the change he had made in the place was apparent. He had patched the front and back steps, built a new hog pen, restored a fence, and taught Lucynell, who was completely deaf and had never said a word in her life, to say the word "bird." The big rosy-faced girl followed him everywhere, saying "Burrttddt ddbirrrttdt," and clapping her hands. The old woman watched from a distance, secretly pleased. She was ravenous for a son-in-law.

Mr. Shiftlet slept on the hard narrow back seat of the car with his feet out the side window. He had his razor and a can of water on a crate that served him as a bedside table and he put up a piece of mirror against the back glass and kept his coat neatly on a hanger that he hung over one of the windows.

In the evenings he sat on the steps and talked while the old woman and Lucynell rocked violently in their chairs on either side of him. The old woman's three mountains were black against the dark blue sky and were visited off and on by various planets and by the moon after it had left the chickens. Mr. Shiftlet pointed out that the reason he had improved this plantation was because he had taken a personal interest in it. He said he was even going to make the automobile run.

He had raised the hood and studied the mechanism and he said he could tell that the car had been built in the days when cars were really built. You take now, he said, one man puts in one bolt and another man puts in another bolt and another man puts in another bolt so that it's a man for a bolt. That's why you have to pay so much for a car: you're paying all those men. Now if you didn't have to pay but one man, you could get you a cheaper car and one that had had a personal interest taken in it, and it would be a better car. The old woman agreed with him that this was so.

Mr. Shiftlet said that the trouble with the world was that nobody cared, or stopped and took any trouble. He said he never would have been able to teach Lucynell to say a word if he hadn't cared and stopped long enough.

"Teach her to say something else," the old woman said.

"What you want her to say next?" Mr. Shiftlet asked.

The old woman's smile was broad and toothless and suggestive. "Teach her to say 'sugarpie,'" she said.

Mr. Shiftlet already knew what was on her mind.

The next day he began to tinker with the automobile and that evening he told her that if she would buy a fan belt, he would be able to make the car run.

The old woman said she would give him the money. "You see that girl yonder?" she asked, pointing to Lucynell who was sitting on the floor a foot away, watching him, her eyes blue even in the dark. "If it was ever a man wanted to take her away, I would say, 'No man on earth is going to take that sweet girl of mine away from me!' but if he was to say, 'Lady, I don't want to take her away, I want her right here,' I would say, 'Mister, I don't blame you none. I wouldn't pass up a chance to live in a permanent place and get the sweetest girl in the world myself. You ain't no fool,' I would say."

"How old is she?" Mr. Shiftlet asked casually.

"Fifteen, sixteen," the old woman said. The girl was nearly thirty but because of her innocence it was impossible to guess.

"It would be a good idea to paint it too," Mr. Shiftlet remarked. "You don't want it to rust out."

"We'll see about that later," the old woman said.

The next day he walked into town and returned with the parts he needed and a can of gasoline. Late in the afternoon, terrible noises issued from the shed and the old woman rushed out of the house, thinking Lucynell was somewhere having a fit. Lucynell was sitting on a chicken crate, stamping her feet and screaming, "Burrddttt! bddurrddttt!" but her fuss was drowned out by the car. With a volley of blasts it emerged from the shed, moving in a fierce and stately way. Mr. Shiftlet was in the driver's seat, sitting very erect. He had an expression of serious modesty on his face as if he had just raised the dead.

That night, rocking on the porch, the old woman began her business, at once. "You want you an innocent woman, don't you?" she asked sympathetically. "You don't want none of this trash."

"No'm, I don't," Mr. Shiftlet said.

"One that can't talk," she continued, "can't sass you back or use foul language. That's the kind for you to have. Right there," and she pointed to Lucynell sitting cross-legged in her chair, holding both feet in her hands.

"That's right," he admitted. "She wouldn't give me any trouble."

"Saturday," the old woman said, "you and her and me can drive into town and get married."

Mr. Shiftlet eased his position on the steps.

"I can't get married right now," he said. "Everything you want to do takes money and I ain't got any."

"What you need with money?" she asked.

"It takes money," he said. "Some people'll do anything anyhow these days, but the way I think, I wouldn't marry no woman that I couldn't take on a trip like she was somebody. I mean take her to a hotel and treat her. I wouldn't marry the Duchesser Windsor," he said firmly, "unless I could take her to a hotel and giver something good to eat.

"I was raised thataway and there ain't a thing I can do about it. My old mother taught me how to do."

"Lucynell don't even know what a hotel is," the old woman muttered. "Listen here,

Mr. Shiftlet," she said, sliding forward in her chair, "you'd be getting a permanent house and a deep well and the most innocent girl in the world. You don't need no money. Lemme tell you something: there ain't any place in the world for a poor disabled friendless drifting man."

The ugly words settled in Mr. Shiftlet's head like a group of buzzards in the top of a tree. He didn't answer at once. He rolled himself a cigarette and lit it and then he said in an even voice, "Lady, a man is divided into two parts, body and spirit."

The old woman clamped her gums together.

"A body and a spirit," he repeated. "The body, lady, is like a house: it don't go anywhere; but the spirit, lady, is like a automobile: always on the move, always . . ."

"Listen, Mr. Shiftlet," she said, "my well never goes dry and my house is always warm in the winter and there's no mortgage on a thing about this place. You can go to the courthouse and see for yourself. And yonder under that shed is a fine automobile." She laid the bait carefully. "You can have it painted by Saturday. I'll pay for the paint."

In the darkness, Mr. Shiftlet's smile stretched like a weary snake waking up by a fire. After a second he recalled himself and said, "I'm only saying a man's spirit means more to him than anything else. I would have to take my wife off for the weekend without no regards at all for cost. I got to follow where my spirit says to go."

"I'll give you fifteen dollars for a weekend trip," the old woman said in a crabbed voice. "That's the best I can do."

"That wouldn't hardly pay for more than the gas and the hotel," he said. "It wouldn't feed her."

"Seventeen-fifty," the old woman said. "That's all I got so it isn't any use you trying to milk me. You can take a lunch."

Mr. Shiftlet was deeply hurt by the word "milk." He didn't doubt that she had more money sewed up in her mattress but he had already told her he was not interested in her money. "I'll make that do," he said and rose and walked off without treating with her further.

On Saturday the three of them drove into town in the car that the paint had barely dried on and Mr. Shiftlet and Lucynell were married in the Ordinary's office while the old woman witnessed. As they came out of the courthouse, Mr. Shiftlet began twisting his neck in his collar. He looked morose and bitter as if he had been insulted while someone held him. "That didn't satisfy me none," he said. "That was just something a woman in an office did, nothing but paper work and blood tests. What do they know about my blood? If they was to take my heart and cut it out," he said, "they wouldn't know a thing about me. It didn't satisfy me at all."

"It satisfied the law," the old woman said sharply.

"The law," Mr. Shiftlet said and spit. "It's the law that don't satisfy me."

He had painted the car dark green with a yellow band around it just under the windows. The three of them climbed in the front seat and the old woman said, "Don't Lucynell look pretty? Looks like a baby doll." Lucynell was dressed up in a white dress that her mother had uprooted from a trunk and there was a Panama hat on her head with a bunch of red wooden cherries on the brim. Every now and then her placid expression was changed by a sly isolated little thought like a shoot of green in the desert. "You got a prize!" the old woman said.

Mr. Shiftlet didn't even look at her.

They drove back to the house to let the old woman off and pick up the lunch. When they were ready to leave, she stood staring in the window of the car, with her fingers clenched around the glass. Tears began to seep sideways out of her eyes and run along the dirty creases in her face. "I ain't ever been parted with her for two days before," she said.

Mr. Shiftlet started the motor.

"And I wouldn't let no man have her but

you because I seen you would do right. Good-bye, Sugarbaby," she said, clutching at the sleeve of the white dress. Lucynell looked straight at her and didn't seem to see her there at all. Mr. Shiftlet eased the car forward so that she had to move her hands.

The early afternoon was clear and open and surrounded by pale blue sky. Although the car would go only thirty miles an hour, Mr. Shiftlet imagined a terrific climb and dip and swerve that went entirely to his head so that he forgot his morning bitterness. He had always wanted an automobile but he had never been able to afford one before. He drove very fast because he wanted to make Mobile by nightfall.

Occasionally he stopped his thoughts long enough to look at Lucynell in the seat beside him. She had eaten the lunch as soon as they were out of the yard and now she was pulling the cherries off the hat one by one and throwing them out the window. He became depressed in spite of the car. He had driven about a hundred miles when he decided that she must be hungry again and at the next small town they came to, he stopped in front of an aluminum-painted eating place called The Hot Spot and took her in and ordered her a plate of ham and grits. The ride had made her sleepy and as soon as she got up on the stool, she rested her head on the counter and shut her eyes. There was no one in The Hot Spot but Mr. Shiftlet and the boy behind the counter, a pale youth with a greasy rag hung over his shoulder. Before he could dish up the food, she was snoring gently.

"Give it to her when she wakes up," Mr. Shiftlet said. "I'll pay for it now."

The boy bent over her and stared at the long pink-gold hair and the half-shut sleeping eyes. Then he looked up and stared at Mr. Shiftlet. "She looks like an angel of Gawd," he murmured.

"Hitchhiker," Mr. Shiftlet explained. "I can't wait. I got to make Tuscaloosa."

The boy bent over again and very carefully touched his finger to a strand of the golden hair and Mr. Shiftlet left.

He was more depressed than ever as he drove on by himself. The late afternoon had grown hot and sultry and the country had flattened out. Deep in the sky a storm was preparing very slowly and without thunder as if it meant to drain every drop of air from the earth before it broke. There were times when Mr. Shiftlet preferred not to be alone. He felt too that a man with a car had a responsibility to others and he kept his eye out for a hitchhiker. Occasionally he saw a sign that warned: "Drive carefully. The life you save may be your own."

The narrow road dropped off on either side into dry fields and here and there a shack or a filling station stood in a clearing. The sun began to set directly in front of the automobile. It was a reddening ball that through his windshield was slightly flat on the bottom and top. He saw a boy in overalls and a gray hat standing on the edge of the road and he slowed the car down and stopped in front of him. The boy didn't have his hand raised to thumb the ride, he was only standing there, but he had a small cardboard suitcase and his hat was set on his head in a way to indicate that he had left somewhere for good. "Son," Mr. Shiftlet said, "I see you want a ride."

The boy didn't say he did or he didn't but he opened the door of the car and got in, and Mr. Shiftlet started driving again. The child held the suitcase on his lap and folded his arms on top of it. He turned his head and looked out the window away from Shiftlet. Mr. Shiftlet felt oppressed. "Son," he said after a minute, "I got the best old mother in the world so I reckon you only got the second best."

The boy gave him a quick dark glance and then turned his face back out the window.

"It's nothing so sweet," Mr. Shiftlet continued, "as a boy's mother. She taught him his first prayers at her knee, she give him love when no other would, she told him what was right and what wasn't, and she seen that he done the right thing. Son," he said, "I never rued a day in my life like the one I rued when I left that old mother of mine."

The boy shifted in his seat but he didn't look at Mr. Shiftlet. He unfolded his arms and put one hand on the door handle.

"My mother was a angel of Gawd," Mr. Shiftlet said in a very strained voice. "He took her from heaven and giver to me and I left her." His eyes were instantly clouded over with a mist of tears. The car was barely moving.

The boy turned angrily in the seat. "You go to the devil!" he cried. "My old woman is a flea bag and yours is a stinking pole cat!" and with that he flung the door open and jumped out with his suitcase into the ditch.

Mr. Shiftlet was so shocked that for about a hundred feet he drove along slowly with the door still open. A cloud, the exact color of the boy's hat and shaped like a turnip, had descended over the sun, and another, worse looking, crouched behind the car. Mr. Shiftlet felt that the rottenness of the world was about to engulf him. He raised his arm and let it fall again to his breast. "Oh Lord!" he prayed. "Break forth and wash the slime from this earth!"

The turnip continued slowly to descend. After a few minutes there was a guffawing peal of thunder from behind and fantastic raindrops, like tin-can tops, crashed over the rear of Mr. Shiftlet's car. Very quickly he stepped on the gas and with his stump sticking out the window he raced the galloping shower into Mobile.

▋RESPONDING TO THE SELECTION

Your Response

1. What emotions does this story evoke in you? Explain.
2. As the story ends, Mr. Shiftlet races into Mobile. What do you want to happen to him? Why?
3. What do you think this story suggests about the author's view of human nature? Do you share her view? Explain.

Recalling

4. What agreement do Mr. Shiftlet and the old woman reach at the end of the first scene?
5. (a) What arguments does the old woman use to persuade Mr. Shiftlet to marry Lucynell? (b) Why does Shiftlet say that he cannot marry her? (c) What causes him to change his mind?
6. What is the outcome of the story?

Interpreting

7. (a) What is the significance of Shiftlet's name? (b) What is the significance of the narrator's observation that Shiftlet's figure "formed a crooked cross"?
8. (a) What details in the first scene suggest that the old woman is not really listening to Shiftlet's comments? (b) With what is she preoccupied?
9. How does Shiftlet's comment that the spirit is "always on the move" foreshadow, or hint at, the outcome of the story?
10. (a) What is the cause of Lucynell's innocence? (b) Considering the cause of her innocence, what does the story imply about a person's ability to remain innocent in the modern world?
11. How does the incident with the hitchhiker relate to the rest of the story?
12. (a) In what ways are the characters in this story realistic? (b) In what ways are they exaggerated?
13. Explain the title of this short story.

Applying

14. Do you think this story could have been written during another period of American history? Explain your answer.

ANALYZING LITERATURE

Understanding Irony

This story is filled with situational irony—irony that occurs when the actual result of an action or situation is quite different from the expected result. Much of this irony results from the contrast between Mr. Shiftlet's comments and actions.

Explain how situational irony results from each of the following comments.

1. ". . . people don't care how they lie."
2. ". . . there's some men that some things mean more to them than money."
3. Mr. Shiftlet said that the trouble with the world was that nobody cared . . .
4. "Some people'll do anything anyhow these days, but the way I think, I wouldn't marry no woman that I couldn't take on a trip like she was somebody."

CRITICAL THINKING AND READING

Seeing Irony as a Key to Theme

The irony in this story plays a vital role in conveying its theme. For example, an important aspect of the theme—that people's actions often do not correspond to the beliefs they profess—is expressed through the contradictions between Mr. Shiftlet's comments and his behavior.

1. What is ironic about the statement at the end of the story that "Mr. Shiftlet felt that the rottenness of the world was about to engulf him"?
2. This statement, along with Mr. Shiftlet's comment, "The world is almost rotten," suggests that the world is in a state of deterioration. What do the events in the story suggest about the cause of this deterioration?
3. What is ironic about the way in which Shiftlet's prayer at the end of the story is answered?
4. What does this incident suggest will happen to people whose behavior contradicts the beliefs they profess?

THINKING AND WRITING

Writing a Story

Develop a popular slogan into a short story, as Flannery O'Connor did in "The Life You Save May Be Your Own." Start by thinking of a slogan that has implications that might not occur to most people. Then develop a plot that expresses these implications. Work the slogan into the story at some point, and use it as the story's title. When you finish writing your story, revise it to make sure that the situational irony is apparent. Proofread your story and share it with your classmates.

Primary Source

Flannery O'Connor was a consummate writer. Her teacher, Paul Engle, recalls his first meeting with Ms. O'Connor in 1946. She had come to his office to speak with him, and he was unable to understand a word of her native Georgian tongue. "Embarrassed, I asked her to write down what she had just said on a pad. She wrote: 'My name is Flannery O'Connor. I am not a journalist. Can I come to the Writer's Workshop?'. . . I told her to bring examples of her writing and we would consider her, late as it was. Flannery spoke a dialect beyond instant comprehension, but on the page her prose was imaginative, tough, alive: just like Flannery herself. . . . The stories were filled with insights, shrewd about human weakness, hard and compassionate. . . . She was shy about having them read, and when it was her turn to have a story presented in the Workshop, I would read it aloud anonymously. . . . The only communicating gesture she would make was an occasional amused and shy smile at something absurd. The dreary chair she sat in glowed."

JAMES BALDWIN

1924–1987

James Baldwin once told an interviewer that he "never had a child-hood." Because his stepfather worked long hours as both a preacher and a factory hand, Baldwin was given much of the responsibility of raising his eight stepbrothers and stepsisters. About the only leisure activity he was able to pursue was reading. He explained, "As [my stepbrothers and stepsisters] were born, I took them over with one hand and held a book with the other. . . . In this way I read *Uncle Tom's Cabin* and *A Tale of Two Cities* over and over again; in this way, in fact, I read just about everything I could get my hands on. . . ." Baldwin's early love for reading fueled his imagination, in-spiring ideas that served as seeds for his later success as a writer.

Baldwin was born in Harlem, the New York City community that served as a cultural center for African Americans during the 1920's and 30's. Even as a young boy, it was clear that he had a gift for words—he published a short story at age twelve—but both his mother and his stepfather were deeply religious and disapproved of his interest in literature. They wanted him to become a preacher like his stepfather. At age fourteen, he did.

At the same time, however, he continued to pursue his interest in literature. Encouraged by African American poet Countee Cullen, who taught in his junior high school, he began writing poetry and worked on his school's literary magazine. Inspired by the success of Richard Wright's novel *Native Son,* which proved to him that an African American could have a successful career as a writer, Baldwin even-tually decided to abandon preaching and devote his life to writing.

For several years Baldwin worked at odd jobs, while writing and reading in his spare time. When he was twenty-four, he won a fel-lowship that enabled him to travel to Europe and concentrate on his writing. In 1953 he published his first novel, *Go Tell It on the Moun-tain,* a semi-autobiographical story about a boy preacher. The novel marked the beginning of a distinguished literary career that included the novels *Giovanni's Room* (1956), *Another Country* (1962), and *Tell Me How Long the Train's Been Gone* (1968); a play set in the American South called *Blues for Mr. Charlie* (1964); and several suc-cessful collections of essays.

In his work Baldwin expresses the need for social justice, while delving into such universal concerns as the desire for love and the need for acceptance. Because his books dig deeply into contempo-rary life, they are sometimes painful to read, but the pain is always tempered by hope. In interviews throughout his life, he often repeated one phrase, and the simple idea it expresses is woven into every-thing he wrote: "People can be better than they are."

The Rockpile

Writers' Techniques

Setting. Just as real people are shaped to some extent by the environments in which they live, the characters in a work of fiction are often shaped by the setting, or the specific time and place in which the action occurs. The characters in a story set in a rural farming town at the turn of the century face dramatically different realities from the characters in a story set in the present in a large American city. As a result, their values, attitudes, and behavior are also likely to be quite different.

Drawn from Baldwin's childhood experiences, "The Rockpile" is set in Harlem during the 1930's. Life in this setting was influenced by the difficult economic and social realities that the people faced. Their beliefs and actions were often motivated by the need to cope with or overcome these realities. In addition, as you will see in this story, the physical features of the setting—the buildings, the streets, the vacant lots—at times had a direct impact on the characters' lives. As you read the story, try to imagine what it was like to live in Harlem at the time, and think about the impact of the setting on the characters' personalities and actions.

Focus

How would your life be different if you lived in Harlem in the 1930's? Freewrite, exploring your impressions of what your life would be like in this setting.

Primary Source

Commenting on how his personal experiences shaped his writing and on the unique challenges of being an African American writer, Baldwin wrote: "One writes out of one thing only—one's own experience. Everything depends on how relentlessly one forces from this experience the last drop, sweet or bitter, it can possibly give. This is the only real concern of the artist, to recreate out of the disorder of life that which is art. The difficulty then, for me, of being a Negro writer was the fact that I was, in effect, prohibited from examining my own experience too closely by the tremendous demands and the very real dangers of my social situation. . . . I have not written about being a Negro at such length because I expect that to be my only subject, but only because it was the gate I had to unlock before I could hope to write about anything else."

The Rockpile

James Baldwin

Across the street from their house, in an empty lot between two houses, stood the rockpile. It was a strange place to find a mass of natural rock jutting out of the ground; and someone, probably Aunt Florence, had once told them that the rock was there and could not be taken away because without it the subway cars underground would fly apart, killing all the people. This, touching on some natural mystery concerning the surface and the center of the earth, was far too intriguing an explanation to be challenged, and it invested the rockpile, moreover, with such mysterious importance that Roy felt it to be his right, not to say his duty, to play there.

Other boys were to be seen there each afternoon after school and all day Saturday and Sunday. They fought on the rockpile. Sure footed, dangerous, and reckless, they rushed each other and grappled on the heights, sometimes disappearing down the other side in a confusion of dust and screams and up- ended, flying feet. "It's a wonder they don't kill themselves," their mother said, watching sometimes from the fire escape. "You chil- dren stay away from there, you hear me?" Though she said "children" she was looking at Roy, where he sat beside John on the fire escape. "The good Lord knows," she contin- ued, "I don't want you to come home bleeding like a hog every day the Lord sends." Roy shifted impatiently, and continued to stare at the street, as though in this gazing he might somehow acquire wings. John said nothing.

THE BLOCK, 1971
Romare Bearden
Metropolitan Museum of Art

He had not really been spoken to: he was afraid of the rockpile and of the boys who played there.

Each Saturday morning John and Roy sat on the fire escape and watched the forbidden street below. Sometimes their mother sat in the room behind them, sewing, or dressing their younger sister, or nursing the baby, Paul. The sun fell across them and across the fire escape with a high, benevolent indifference; below them, men and women, and boys and girls, sinners all, loitered; sometimes one of the church-members passed and saw them and waved. Then, for the moment that they waved decorously back, they were intimidated. They watched the saint, man or woman, until he or she had disappeared from sight. The passage of one of the redeemed made them consider, however vacantly, the wickedness of the street, their own latent wickedness in sitting where they sat; and made them think of their father, who came home early on Saturdays and who would soon be turning this corner and entering the dark hall below them.

But until he came to end their freedom, they sat, watching and longing above the street. At the end of the street nearest their house was the bridge which spanned the Harlem River[1] and led to a city called the Bronx; which was where Aunt Florence lived. Nevertheless, when they saw her coming, she did not come from the bridge, but from the opposite end of the street. This, weakly, to their minds, she explained by saying that she had taken the subway, not wishing to walk, and that, besides, she did not live in *that* section of the Bronx. Knowing that the Bronx was across the river, they did not believe this story ever, but, adopting toward her their father's attitude, assumed that she had just left some sinful place which she dared not name, as, for example, a movie palace.

In the summertime boys swam in the river, diving off the wooden dock, or wading in from the garbage-heavy bank. Once a boy, whose name was Richard, drowned in the river. His mother had not known where he was; she had even come to their house, to ask if he was there. Then, in the evening, at six o'clock, they had heard from the street a

---

1. Harlem River: A river that separates Manhattan Island from the Bronx in New York City.

woman screaming and wailing; and they ran to the windows and looked out. Down the street came the woman, Richard's mother, screaming, her face raised to the sky and tears running down her face. A woman walked beside her, trying to make her quiet and trying to hold her up. Behind them walked a man, Richard's father, with Richard's body in his arms. There were two white policemen walking in the gutter, who did not seem to know what should be done. Richard's father and Richard were wet, and Richard's body lay across his father's arms like a cotton baby. The woman's screaming filled all the street; cars slowed down and the people in the cars stared; people opened their windows and looked out and came rushing out of doors to stand in the gutter, watching. Then the small procession disappeared within the house which stood beside the rockpile. Then, "*Lord, Lord, Lord!*" cried Elizabeth, their mother, and slammed the window down.

One Saturday, an hour before his father would be coming home, Roy was wounded on the rockpile and brought screaming upstairs. He and John had been sitting on the fire escape and their mother had gone into the kitchen to sip tea with Sister McCandless. By and by Roy became bored and sat beside John in restless silence; and John began drawing into his schoolbook a newspaper advertisement which featured a new electric locomotive. Some friends of Roy passed beneath the fire escape and called him. Roy began to fidget, yelling down to them through the bars. Then a silence fell. John looked up. Roy stood looking at him.

"I'm going downstairs," he said.

"You better stay where you is, boy. You know Mama don't want you going downstairs."

"I be right *back*. She won't even know I'm gone, less you run and tell her."

"I ain't *got* to tell her. What's going to stop her from coming in here and looking out the window?"

"She's talking," Roy said. He started into the house.

"But Daddy's going to be home soon!"

"I be back before *that.* What you all the time got to be so *scared* for?" He was already in the house and he now turned, leaning on the windowsill, to swear impatiently, "I be back in *five* minutes."

John watched him sourly as he carefully unlocked the door and disappeared. In a moment he saw him on the sidewalk with his friends. He did not dare to go and tell his mother that Roy had left the fire escape because he had practically promised not to. He started to shout, *Remember, you said five minutes!* but one of Roy's friends was looking up at the fire escape. John looked down at his schoolbook: he became engrossed again in the problem of the locomotive.

When he looked up again he did not know how much time had passed, but now there was a gang fight on the rockpile. Dozens of boys fought each other in the harsh sun: clambering up the rocks and battling hand to hand, scuffed shoes sliding on the slippery rock; filling the bright air with curses and jubilant cries. They filled the air, too, with flying weapons: stones, sticks, tin cans, garbage, whatever could be picked up and thrown. John watched in a kind of absent amazement—until he remembered that Roy was still downstairs, and that he was one of the boys on the rockpile. Then he was afraid; he could not see his brother among the figures in the sun; and he stood up, leaning over the fire-escape railing. Then Roy appeared from the other side of the rocks; John saw that his shirt was torn; he was laughing. He moved until he stood at the very top of the rockpile. Then, something, an empty tin can, flew out of the air and hit him on the forehead, just above the eye. Immediately, one side of Roy's face ran with blood, he fell and rolled on his face down the rocks. Then for a moment there was no movement at all, no sound, the sun, arrested, lay on the street and the sidewalk and the arrested boys. Then someone screamed or shouted; boys began to run away, down the street, toward the bridge. The figure on the ground, having caught its breath and felt its own blood, began to shout. John cried, "Mama! Mama!" and ran inside.

"Don't fret, don't fret," panted Sister McCandless as they rushed down the dark, narrow, swaying stairs, "don't fret. Ain't a boy been born don't get his knocks every now and again. *Lord!*" they hurried into the sun. A man had picked Roy up and now walked slowly toward them. One or two boys sat silent on their stoops; at either end of the street there was a group of boys watching. "He ain't hurt bad," the man said, "wouldn't be making this kind of noise if he was hurt real bad."

Elizabeth, trembling, reached out to take Roy, but Sister McCandless, bigger, calmer, took him from the man and threw him over her shoulder as she once might have handled a sack of cotton. "God bless you," she said to the man, "God bless you, son." Roy was still screaming. Elizabeth stood behind Sister McCandless to stare at his bloody face.

"It's just a flesh wound," the man kept saying, "just broke the skin, that's all." They were moving across the sidewalk, toward the house. John, not now afraid of the staring boys, looked toward the corner to see if his father was yet in sight.

Upstairs, they hushed Roy's crying. They bathed the blood away, to find, just above the left eyebrow, the jagged, superficial scar. "Lord, have mercy," murmured Elizabeth, "another inch and it would've been his eye." And she looked with apprehension toward the clock. "Ain't it the truth," said Sister McCandless, busy with bandages and iodine.

"When did he go downstairs?" his mother asked at last.

Sister McCandless now sat fanning herself in the easy chair, at the head of the sofa where Roy lay, bound and silent. She paused for a moment to look sharply at John. John stood near the window, holding the newspaper advertisement and the drawing he had done.

"We was sitting on the fire escape," he said. "Some boys he knew called him."

"When?"

"He said he'd be back in five minutes."

"Why didn't you tell me he was downstairs?"

He looked at his hands, clasping his notebook, and did not answer.

"Boy," said Sister McCandless, "you hear your mother a-talking to you?"

He looked at his mother. He repeated:

"He said he'd be back in five minutes."

"He said he'd be back in five minutes," said Sister McCandless with scorn, "don't look to me like that's no right answer. You's the man of the house, you supposed to look after your baby brothers and sisters—you ain't supposed to let them run off and get half-killed. But I expect," she added, rising from the chair, dropping the cardboard fan, "your Daddy'll make you tell the truth. Your Ma's way too soft with you."

He did not look at her, but at the fan where it lay in the dark red, depressed seat where she had been. The fan advertised a pomade[2] for the hair and showed a brown woman and her baby, both with glistening hair, smiling happily at each other.

"Honey," said Sister McCandless, "I got to be moving along. Maybe I drop in later tonight. I don't reckon you going to be at Tarry Service tonight?"

Tarry Service was the prayer meeting held every Saturday night at church to strengthen believers and prepare the church for the coming of the Holy Ghost on Sunday.

"I don't reckon," said Elizabeth. She stood up; she and Sister McCandless kissed each other on the cheek. "But you be sure to remember me in your prayers."

"I surely will do that." She paused, with her hand on the door knob, and looked down at Roy and laughed. "Poor little man," she said, "reckon he'll be content to sit on the fire escape *now*."

Elizabeth laughed with her. "It sure ought to be a lesson to him. You don't reckon," she asked nervously, still smiling, "he going to keep that scar, do you?"

---

2. **pomade** (päm ād') *n.*: A perfumed ointment.

JIM, 1930
William H. Johnson
National Museum of American Art, Washington, D.C.

"Lord, no," said Sister McCandless, "ain't nothing but a scratch. I declare, Sister Grimes, you worse than a child. Another couple of weeks and you won't be able to *see* no scar. No, you go on about your housework, honey, and thank the Lord it weren't no worse." She opened the door; they heard the sound of feet on the stairs. "I expect that's the Reverend," said Sister McCandless, placidly, "I *bet* he going to raise cain."[3]

---

3. raise cain: Slang for "cause trouble."

"Maybe it's Florence," Elizabeth said. "Sometimes she get here about this time." They stood in the doorway, staring, while the steps reached the landing below and began again climbing to their floor. "No," said Elizabeth then, "that ain't her walk. That's Gabriel."

"Well, I'll just go on," said Sister McCandless, "and kind of prepare his mind." She pressed Elizabeth's hand as she spoke and started into the hall, leaving the door behind her slightly ajar. Elizabeth turned slowly back into the room. Roy did not open his eyes, or move; but she knew that he was not sleeping; he wished to delay until the last possible moment any contact with his father. John put his newspaper and his notebook on the table and stood, leaning on the table, staring at her.

"It wasn't my fault," he said. "I couldn't stop him from going downstairs."

"No," she said, "you ain't got nothing to worry about. You just tell your Daddy the truth."

He looked directly at her, and she turned to the window, staring into the street. What was Sister McCandless saying? Then from her bedroom she heard Delilah's thin wail and she turned, frowning, looking toward the bedroom and toward the still open door. She knew that John was watching her. Delilah continued to wail, she thought, angrily, *Now that girl's getting too big for that,* but she feared that Delilah would awaken Paul and she hurried into the bedroom. She tried to soothe Delilah back to sleep. Then she heard the front door open and close—too loud, Delilah raised her voice, with an exasperated sigh Elizabeth picked the child up. Her child and Gabriel's, her children and Gabriel's: Roy, Delilah, Paul. Only John was nameless and a stranger, living, unalterable testimony to his mother's days in sin.

"What happened?" Gabriel demanded. He stood, enormous, in the center of the room, his black lunchbox dangling from his hand, staring at the sofa where Roy lay. John stood just before him, it seemed to her astonished vision just below him, beneath his fist, his heavy shoe. The child stared at the man in fascination and terror—when a girl down home she had seen rabbits stand so paralyzed before the barking dog. She hurried past Gabriel to the sofa, feeling the weight of Delilah in her arms like the weight of a shield, and stood over Roy, saying:

"Now, ain't a thing to get upset about, Gabriel. This boy sneaked downstairs while I had my back turned and got hisself hurt a little. He's alright now."

Roy, as though in confirmation, now opened his eyes and looked gravely at his father. Gabriel dropped his lunchbox with a clatter and knelt by the sofa.

"How you feel, son? Tell your Daddy what happened?"

Roy opened his mouth to speak and then, relapsing into panic, began to cry. His father held him by the shoulder.

"You don't want to cry. You's Daddy's little man. Tell your Daddy what happened."

"He went downstairs," said Elizabeth, "where he didn't have no business to be, and got to fighting with them bad boys playing on the rockpile. That's what happened and it's a mercy it weren't nothing worse."

He looked up at her. "Can't you let this boy answer me for hisself?"

Ignoring this, she went on, more gently: "He got cut on the forehead, but it ain't nothing to worry about."

"You call a doctor? How you know it ain't nothing to worry about?"

"Is you got money to be throwing away on doctors? No, I ain't called no doctor. Ain't nothing wrong with my eyes that I can't tell whether he's hurt bad or not. He got a fright more'n anything else, and you ought to pray God it teaches him a lesson."

"You got a lot to say *now,*" he said, "but I'll have *me* something to say in a minute. I'll be wanting to know when all this happened, what you was doing with your eyes *then.*" He turned back to Roy, who had lain quietly sobbing eyes wide open and body held rigid: and who now, at his father's touch, remembered the height, the sharp, sliding rock beneath his feet, the sun, the explosion of the sun, his plunge into darkness and his salty blood; and recoiled, beginning to scream, as his father touched his forehead. "Hold still, hold still," crooned his father, shaking, "hold still. Don't cry. Daddy ain't going to hurt you, he just wants to see this bandage, see what they've done to his little man." But Roy continued to scream and would not be still and Gabriel dared not lift the bandage for fear of hurting him more. And he looked at Elizabeth in fury:

"Can't you put that child down and help me with this boy? John, take your baby sister from your mother—don't look like neither of you got good sense."

John took Delilah and sat down with her in the easy chair. His mother bent over Roy, and held him still, while his father, carefully— but still Roy screamed—lifted the bandage and stared at the wound. Roy's sobs began to lessen. Gabriel readjusted the bandage. "You see," said Elizabeth, finally, "he ain't no- where near dead."

"It sure ain't your fault that he ain't dead." He and Elizabeth considered each other for a moment in silence. "He came mightly close to losing an eye. Course, his eyes ain't as big as your'n, so I reckon you don't think it matters so much." At this her face hardened; he smiled. "Lord, have mercy," he said, "you think you ever going to learn to do right? Where was you when all this happened? Who let him go downstairs?"

"Ain't nobody let him go downstairs, he just went. He got a head just like his father, it got to be broken before it'll bow. I was in the kitchen."

"Where was Johnnie?"

"He was in here."

"Where?"

"He was on the fire escape."

"Didn't he know Roy was downstairs?"

"I reckon."

"What you mean, you reckon? He ain't got your big eyes for nothing, does he?" He looked over at John. "Boy, you see your brother go downstairs?"

"Gabriel, ain't no sense in trying to blame Johnnie. You know right well if you have trouble making Roy behave, he ain't going to listen to his brother. He don't hardly listen to me."

"How come you didn't tell your mother Roy was downstairs?"

John said nothing, staring at the blanket which covered Delilah.

"Boy, you hear me? You want me to take a strap to you?"

"No, you ain't," she said. "You ain't going to taken no strap to this boy, not today you ain't. Ain't a soul to blame for Roy's lying up there now but you—you because you done spoiled him so that he thinks he can do just anything and get away with it. I'm here to tell you that ain't no way to raise no child. You don't pray to the Lord to help you do better than you been doing, you going to live to shed bitter tears that the Lord didn't take his soul today." And she was trembling. She moved, unseeing, toward John and took Delilah from his arms. She looked back at Gabriel, who had risen, who stood near the sofa, staring at her. And she found in his face not fury alone, which would not have surprised her; but ha- tred so deep as to become insupportable in its lack of personality. His eyes were struck alive, unmoving, blind with malevolence—she felt, like the pull of the earth at her feet, his long- ing to witness her perdition. Again, as though it might be propitiation, she moved the child in her arms. And at this his eyes changed, he looked at Elizabeth, the mother of his children, the helpmeet given by the Lord. Then her eyes clouded; she moved to leave the room; her foot struck the lunchbox lying on the floor.

"John," she said, "pick up your father's lunchbox like a good boy."

She heard, behind her, his scrambling movement as he left the easy chair, the scrape and jangle of the lunchbox as he picked it up, bending his dark head near the toe of his father's heavy shoe.

RESPONDING TO THE SELECTION

Your Response

1. Does this story call to mind any of your own childhood experiences? Explain.
2. If you were in Roy's place, would you have sneaked down to the rockpile? Explain. What would you have done if you were in John's place? Why?
3. Do you think that Gabriel overreacts to Roy's injury? Why or why not?

Recalling

4. What draws Roy to the rockpile?
5. (a) Whom does Gabriel blame for Roy's injury? (b) Whom does Elizabeth blame?

Interpreting

6. (a) What role does John serve in his family? Support your answer. (b) What evidence is there that his relationship with Gabriel is different from that of the other children?
7. (a) How would you characterize Gabriel? Support your answer. (b) Why is he so upset by Roy's injury? Explain.
8. (a) What conclusions can you draw about Gabriel's relationship with Elizabeth? Explain. (b) Why do his feelings toward Elizabeth soften at the end of the story?

Applying

9. What lessons could you learn from this story that you could apply to your own life? Explain.

ANALYZING LITERATURE

Understanding Setting

The setting of "The Rockpile"—Harlem during the 1930's—clearly plays a dominant role in the characters' lives, shaping both their attitudes and their behavior.

1. What can you infer, or conclude, about how the setting affects the way Gabriel and Elizabeth raise their children?
2. (a) What are some of the potential dangers that the setting presents? (b) What evidence is there that the rockpile symbolizes these dangers?

3. What evidence in the story shows that the conditions of the setting place a strain on the characters' relationships with one another?

CRITICAL THINKING AND READING

Linking Past and Present

More than half a century has passed since the time in which this story is set. Yet many of the complex problems in our nation's inner cities remain unsolved. Some of these problems have even intensified.

How do you think Baldwin's story might be different if it were set in the present? Support your answer.

THINKING AND WRITING

Writing a Story

Use the events in Baldwin's story as the basis for a story of your own. Brainstorm for types of places and activities that parents might forbid their children from going to or participating in. Then develop a story that, like Baldwin's, centers on a child's failure to obey his or her parents' wishes. Conclude your story by dramatizing the outcome of the child's actions. When you revise, make sure that you have clearly conveyed the child's motivations for disobeying his or her parents.

LEARNING OPTIONS

1. **Writing.** Imagine that you have been asked by a television producer to develop a series based on the characters in Baldwin's story. Write a proposal for the series, explaining the types of issues and events that will be presented in the weekly episodes. Share your proposal with your classmates.
2. **Art.** Create a cover design for the book jacket of a short-story collection featuring "The Rockpile." The design should include either a photograph or a piece of art you have found or an original drawing of yours. Present your work to the class, and explain the thinking behind your design.

JOHN UPDIKE

1932–

In his short stories and novels, John Updike vividly captures the essence of life in contemporary America. Through his depictions of ordinary situations and events, he explores many of the more important issues of our time and offers insights into the underlying significance of everyday life.

Updike was born in Reading, Pennsylvania, and was raised in the nearby town of Shillington. After graduating from Harvard, he spent a year at the Ruskin School of Drawing and Fine Art in England. When he returned to the United States, he joined the staff of *The New Yorker,* a magazine that has published many of his short stories.

Following the publication of his first collection of poetry, *The Carpentered Hen and Other Tame Animals* (1958), Updike published several other collections of poetry, many novels and short stories, numerous essays and book reviews, and a play. His novels include *The Poorhouse Fair* (1959), *Rabbit, Run* (1960), *Of the Farm* (1965), *Couples* (1968), *Rabbit Redux* (1971), *The Coup* (1978), *Rabbit Is Rich* (1981), and *Roger's Version* (1987). He earned the National Book Award for his novel *The Centaur* (1963), and his novel *The Witches of Eastwick* (1984) was made into a major motion picture. His collection of essays and criticism, *Hugging the Shore* (1983), was the winner of the 1983 National Book Critics Circle Award for criticism.

Updike has said, "I'm sure that my capacities to fantasize and to make coherent fantasies, to have patience to sit down day after day and to whittle a fantasy out of paper, all that relates to being an only child." He has coped with numerous personal drawbacks as well. In addition to enduring bouts of hay fever and psoriasis, a painful skin disease, he had a speech impediment as a child. The isolation he suffered from these ills compelled him toward the solitary occupations of drawing and writing. He excelled at both, but in early years focused his hopes on a career as a cartoonist, following in the path of James Thurber. As he matured, his interest shifted toward writing, and by age eighteen, he had decided to follow writing as a career. The aspiration may have been fostered by his mother, who had literary ambitions of her own.

"The Slump" reflects Updike's awareness of universal feelings and concerns that develop out of specific situations. By delving into the thoughts of a baseball player in the midst of an extended slump, he captures a sense of uncertainty and insecurity that all people experience at some point during their lives.

GUIDE FOR INTERPRETING

The Slump

Writers' Techniques

Diction. Diction refers to a writer's choice of words. When writing a short story or novel, a writer must carefully choose language that is appropriate for the characters and subject. For example, ornate, elevated language that is inappropriate in a story about uneducated factory workers would be suitable for a story about a group of scholars.

 Style. Until the contemporary period, stories were almost always told in the past tense. "He came, she said, they did," authors would write. John Updike was one of the first of the contemporary writers to employ the present tense. In his novel *Rabbit, Run,* Updike uses the present tense, a technique he called "a piece of technical daring in 1959," to "emphasize how thoroughly the zigzagging hero lived in the present. . . ."

Focus

Updike is one of many writers who have explored the world of sports and the experiences of athletes at work. Freewrite about the reasons sports are a common subject for literary works. Why do people enjoy reading about sports? What aspects of everyday life are embodied in the world of professional sports? What feelings and experiences do all people share with famous athletes? In what way does the field of sports serve as a metaphor for life?

Primary Source

In "The Slump" the ball player alludes to Søren Kierkegaard, a Danish philosopher who, among other things, expressed a unique view of the concept of repetition. Critic Northrop Frye explains: "By [the term] he apparently means, not the simple repeating of an experience, but the recreating of it which redeems or awakens it to life, the end of the process, he says, being the apocalyptic promise: 'Behold, I make all things new.' . . . we face the past: it may be shadowy, but it is all that is there. Plato draws a gloomy picture of man staring at the flickering shapes made on the wall of the objective world by a fire behind us like the sun. But the analogy breaks down when the shadows are those of the past, for the only light we can see them by is the Promethean fire within us. The substance of these shadows can only be in ourselves, and the goal of historical criticism, as our metaphors about it often indicate, is a kind of self-resurrection, the vision of a valley of dry bones that takes on the flesh and blood of our own vision. The culture of the past is not only the memory of mankind, but our own buried life, and study of it leads to a recognition scene, a discovery in which we see, not our past lives, but the total cultural form of our present life. It is not only the poet but his reader who is subject to the obligation to 'make it new.'"

The Slump

John Updike

They say reflexes, the coach says reflexes, even the papers now are saying reflexes, but I don't think it's the reflexes so much—last night, as a gag to cheer me up, the wife walks into the bedroom wearing one of the kids' rubber gorilla masks and I was under the bed in six-tenths of a second, she had the stopwatch on me. It's that I can't see the ball the way I used to. It used to come floating up with all seven continents showing, and the pitcher's thumbprint, and a grass smooch or two, and the Spalding guarantee in ten-point sans-serif,[1] and *whop*! I could feel the sweet wood with the bat still cocked. Now, I don't know, there's like a cloud around it, a sort of spiral vagueness, maybe the Van Allen belt,[2] or maybe I lift my eye in the last second, planning how I'll round second base, or worrying which I do first, tip my cap or slap the third-base coach's hand. You can't see a blind spot, Kierkegaard[3] says, but in there now, between when the ball leaves the bleacher background and I can hear it plop all fat and satisfied in the catcher's mitt, there's somehow just nothing, where there used to be a lot, everything in fact, because they're not keeping me around for my fielding, and already I see the afternoon tabloid has me down as trade bait.

The flutters don't come when they used to. It used to be, I'd back the convertible out of the garage and watch the electric eye put the door down again and drive in to the stadium, and at about the bridge turnoff I'd ease off grooving with the radio rock, and then on the lot there'd be the kids waiting to get a look and that would start the big butterflies, and when the attendant would take my car I'd want to shout *Stop, thief*, and walking down that long cement corridor I'd fantasize like I was going to the electric chair and the locker room was some dream after death, and I'd wonder why the suit fit, and how these really immortal guys, that I recognized from the bubble-gum cards I used to collect, knew my name. *They* knew *me*. And I'd go out and the stadium mumble would scoop at me and the grass seemed too precious to walk on, like emeralds, and by the time I got into the cage I couldn't remember if I batted left or right.

Now, heck, I move over the bridge singing along with the radio, and brush through the kids at just the right speed, not so fast I knock any of them down, and the attendant knows his Labor Day tip is coming, and we wink, and in the batting cage I own the place, and take my cuts, and pop five or six into the bullpen as easy as dropping dimes down a sewer. But when the scoreboard lights up, and I take those two steps up from the dugout, the biggest two steps in a ball-

---

1. ten-point sans-serif (san ser' if): The size and style of the lettering.
2. Van Allen belt: A belt of radiation that encircles the earth.
3. Kierkegaard (kir' kə gärd'): Søren (sö'rən) Kierkegaard (1813–1855), Danish philosopher and theologian.

player's life, and kneel in the circle, giving the crowd the old hawk profile, where once the flutters would ease off, now they dig down and begin.

They say I'm not hungry, but I still feel hungry, only now it's a kind of panic hungry, and that's not the right kind. Ever watch one of your little kids try to catch a ball? He gets so excited with the idea he's going to catch it he shuts his eyes. That's me now. I walk up to the plate, having come all this way—a lot of hotels, a lot of shagging—and my eyes feel shut. And I stand up there trying to push my eyeballs through my eyelids, and my retinas register maybe a little green, and the black patch of some nuns in far left field. That's panic hungry.

Kierkegaard called it dread.[4] It queers the works. My wife comes at me without the

---

4. dread: Kierkegaard believed that fear, or dread, is a natural part of the human condition.

gorilla mask and when in the old days, *whop!*, now she slides by with a hurt expression and a flicker of gray above her temple. I go out and ride the power mower and I've already done it so often the lawn is brown. The kids get me out of bed for a little fungo and it scares me to see them trying, busting their lungs, all that shagging ahead of them. In Florida—we used to love it in Florida, the smell of citrus and marlin, the flat pink sections where the old people drift around smiling with transistor plugs in their ears—we lie on the beach after a workout and the sun seems a high fly I'm going to lose and the waves keep coming like they've been doing for a billion years, up to the plate, up to the plate. Kierkegaard probably has the clue, somewhere in there, but I picked up *Concluding Unscientific Postscript*[5] the other day and I couldn't see the print, that is, I could see the lines, but there wasn't anything on them, like the rows of deep seats in the shade of the second deck on a Thursday afternoon, just a single ice-cream vendor sitting there, nobody around to sell to, a speck

of white in all that shade, old Søren Sock himself, keeping his goods cool.

I think maybe if I got beaned. That's probably what the wife is hinting at with the gorilla mask. A change of pace, like the time DiMaggio[6] broke his slump by Topping's[7] telling him to go to a night club and get plastered. I've stopped ducking, but the trouble is, if you're not hitting, they don't brush you back. On me, they've stopped trying for even the corners; they put it right down the pike. I can see it in his evil eye as he takes the sign and rears back, I can hear the catcher snicker, and for a second of reflex there I can see it like it used to be, continents and cities and every green tree distinct as a stitch, and the hickory sweetens in my hands, and I feel the good old sure hunger. Then something happens. It blurs, skips, fades, I don't know. It's not caring enough, is what it probably is, it's knowing that none of it—the stadium, the averages—is really there, just *you* are there, and it's not enough.

---

5. *Concluding Unscientific Postscript:* One of Kierkegaard's major works.

6. **DiMaggio:** Joe DiMaggio (1914–   ), New York Yankee center fielder from 1936 to 1951; now a member of the baseball Hall of Fame.
7. **Topping's:** Refers to Dan Topping, one of the Yankee owners from 1945 to 1964.

R ESPONDING TO THE SELECTION

Your Response
1. To what would you attribute the narrator's slump? Do you think that he really does not care enough? Explain.
2. In what situations have you felt the hunger that the narrator describes?

Recalling
3. (a) How do the coaches and newspapers explain the narrator's slump? (b) How does the narrator himself explain it?
4. (a) How did the narrator once feel when he saw "the kids" waiting outside the stadium?

(b) How does he now react when he sees them?
5. What now happens when the narrator takes "those two steps up from the dugout" and kneels "in the circle"?
6. What solution does the narrator come up with in the final paragraph?

Interpreting
7. Explain the significance of Kierkegaard's statement, "You can't see a blind spot."
8. (a) How has the narrator's attitude toward baseball changed during the course of his career? (b) How is this change in attitude conveyed?

9. Explain the meaning of the conclusion the narrator reaches in the final sentence.
10. (a) What does the story suggest about fame? (b) What does it suggest about aging? (c) What does it suggest about life in general?

Applying

11. The narrator complains, "They say I'm not hungry, but I still feel hungry, only now it's a kind of panic hunger, and that's not the right kind." (a) What does he mean by the word *hungry?* (b) What is the right kind of hunger? (c) Do you think it is necessary to be hungry to succeed? Explain.
12. What other types of situations might produce concerns and feelings similar to the ones experienced by the narrator?

ANALYZING LITERATURE

Appreciating Diction and Style

Diction refers to a writer's choice of words. In fiction a writer must use language that is appropriate for his or her subject and characters.
1. Why is the language in "The Slump" appropriate for the narrator and subject? Support your answer.
2. Would the story still be effective if Updike had used ornate, elevated language? Why or why not?
3. The narrator tells his story in the present tense. (a) How would the effect of this story be different if it were told in the past tense? (b) How effective is this technique? Explain your answer.

THINKING AND WRITING

Responding to Criticism

A critic has made the following comment about Updike's work: "Knowledgeable about the sports because he played them, Updike understands the difficulties of success and the poignancy of diminished prowess." Write an essay in which you discuss "The Slump" in relation to this comment. Before you start, make sure you understand the critic's comment in its entirety. What does he mean when he refers to "the poignancy of diminished prowess"? Include an explanation of the critic's comment in your essay. When you revise, make sure you have thoroughly supported your argument with passages from the story.

LEARNING OPTIONS

1. **Speaking and Listening.** Neither the coach nor the narrator's wife was able to help the narrator break out of his slump. See what you can do. Speak to the narrator as a friend, a fellow player, or a fan. You might offer your sympathy or chew him out—do whatever you think will help him regain his hitting stroke.
2. **Art.** Updike's anonymous narrator may well be one of the "really immortal guys" whom young rookies recognize from bubble-gum cards they used to collect. Flesh out the information Updike supplies about the narrator to give him a history and a name, and design a baseball card for him. Your card might include a brief profile of the player as well as his statistics.
3. **Language.** In "The Slump" Updike frequently uses baseball jargon—language that can be understood only by a person who knows the game. For example, when the narrator comments that he kneels "in the circle," he is referring to the on-deck circle in which the next batter awaits his or her turn. Help introduce a novice to the game by defining each of the following baseball terms from the story: *batting cage, dugout, shagging, fungo, beaned.*
4. **Writing.** Celebrate baseball in verse. Write an ode, a narrative poem, or a song in honor of America's favorite sport and national pastime. For inspiration you might watch a ball game, listen to a sportscast, or read an article about baseball.

JOYCE CAROL OATES

1938–

Joyce Carol Oates is one of the most prolific writers of our time. She has published many novels and collections of stories and has written numerous poems, plays, and critical essays, yet she has never sacrificed quality for productivity. As a result, nearly all of her work possesses a great amount of energy and intensity.

Oates was born in Lockport, New York. Located on the Erie Canal, Lockport was a town so small that Oates attended a one-room schoolhouse. There she had limited exposure to books, but that did not inhibit her from writing her own stories, which she bound with covers of her own design. In order to improve the presentation of her stories, she learned to type by age twelve. She later fictionalized life in Erie County, transforming it into Eden County, the setting for her first volume of stories as well as her first novel. As with Faulkner's Yoknapatawpha County, Oates's fictional Eden County is elaborately conceived and peopled with inhabitants who turn up in various ways from story to story. The practice of using a set cast of characters and familiar landmarks lends credibility and continuity to her fiction, enabling readers to move familiarly from volume to volume. But Eden County is not the paradise its name implies. In fact, it is at times insufferable to its inhabitants. As has been suggested, Oates may have chosen the name to remind readers how much we have lost.

Oates's first book, *With Shuddering Fall,* was published in 1964. Since then she has produced novels, collections of short stories, and volumes of poetry at an incredibly rapid pace. Her works of fiction include *Wheel of Love and Other Stories* (1970), *The Assassins* (1975), *Do With Me What You Will* (1978), *The Seduction and Other Stores* (1980), *Bellefleur* (1980), *A Bloodsmore Romance* (1982), and *Mysteries of Winterthurn* (1984). Oates's poetry collections include *Angel Fire* (1973), *The Fabulous Beasts* (1975), and *Love and Its Derangements and Other Poems* (1977). She has received numerous awards for her work, including the 1970 National Book Award for her novel *Them* (1968).

In her fiction Oates delves into the human mind. Her work often focuses on disturbed characters or characters who are anxiously searching for or struggling to come to terms with their identities. Oates has written, "We are stimulated to emotional response not by works that confirm our sense of the world, but by works that challenge it." "Journey" is the story of a symbolic quest for direction.

GUIDE FOR INTERPRETING

Journey

Point of View. Point of view refers to the vantage point from which a narrative is told. Most stories are told from either a first-person or a third-person point of view. In contemporary fiction, however, there are rare instances in which a writer uses a second-person point of view. In this type of narrative, the narrator does not participate in the story and refers to the story's protagonist, or main character, as *you*. Generally a second-person narrator is limited, focusing on the thoughts and feelings of only one character.

By using a second-person point of view, a writer can give his or her story a universal quality. Because the narrator refers to the main character as *you*, the reader actually assumes the role of the main character in the story. As a result, a second-person narrative may be viewed not as a story about a specific character, but as a story about human behavior in general.

How might a person's life be described as a journey? Freewrite about the ways in which life can be viewed as a journey.

In "Journey" Oates takes readers on a solitary and somewhat frightening journey, transforming each participant into an "Outsider." Here is how critic Carolyn Walker describes the role of the Outsider:

> Most interesting of all, perhaps, is Oates's treatment of the fear of being the Outsider. The Outsider is a person who perceives himself as somehow cut off from, shut out of, the human race. He suffers from being uncontrollably different, an aberration. . . .
>
> An important aspect of the Outsider's position is that he is locked out of love, which he sees as the needed path to salvation. . . . Ironically, the Outsider may discover that he is locked out of genuine, meaningful love, even if he has what appears on the surface to be a satisfactory love relationship. He may discover that he is actually locked into a hollow, unfulfilling "love."
>
> Given the horror of his situation, where does the Outsider in Oates's fiction look for comfort and solace? With genuine love unavailable, many of the characters look to art and the act of writing, . . . which results in some kind of spatially ordered pattern. . . . With the aid of the discovered pattern and order the characters hope to find a sense of personal meaning and sanity. . . .

Journey

Joyce Carol Oates

You begin your journey on so high an elevation that your destination is already in sight—a city that you have visited many times and that, moreover, is indicated on a traveler's map you have carefully folded up to take along with you. You are a lover of maps, and you have already committed this map to memory, but you bring it with you just the same.

The highway down from the mountains is broad and handsome, constructed after many years of ingenious blasting and leveling and paving. Engineers from all over the country aided in the construction of this famous highway. Its cost is so excessive that many rumors have circulated about it—you take no interest in such things, sensing that you will never learn the true cost anyway, and that this will make no difference to your journey.

After several hours on this excellent highway, where the sun shines ceaselessly and where there is a moderate amount of traffic, cars like your own at a safe distance from you, as if to assure you that there are other people in the world, you become sleepy from the monotony and wonder if perhaps there is another, less perfect road parallel to this. You discover on the map a smaller road, not exactly parallel to the highway and not as direct, but one that leads to the same city.

You turn onto this road, which winds among foothills and forests and goes through several small villages. You sense by the attitude of the villagers that traffic on this road is infrequent but nothing to draw special attention. At some curves the road shrinks, but you are fortunate enough to meet no oncoming traffic.

The road leads deep into a forest, always descending in small cramped turns. Your turning from left to right and from right to left, in a slow hypnotic passage, makes it impossible for you to look out at the forest. You discover that for some time you have not been able to see the city you are headed for, though you know it is still somewhere ahead of you.

By mid-afternoon you are tired of this road, though it has served you well, and you come upon a smaller, unpaved road that evidently leads to your city, though in a convoluted way. After only a moment's pause you turn onto this road, and immediately your automobile registers the change—the chassis bounces, something begins to vibrate, something begins to rattle. This noise is disturbing, but after a while you forget about it in your interest in the beautiful countryside. Here the trees are enormous. There are no villages or houses. For a while the dirt road runs alongside a small river, dangerously close to the river's steep bank, and you begin to feel apprehension. It is necessary for you to drive very slowly. At times your speedometer registers less than five miles an hour. You will not get to the city before dark.

The road narrows until it is hardly more than a lane. Grass has begun to grow in its center. As the river twists and turns, so does the road twist and turn, curving around hills that consist of enormous boulders, bare of all trees and plants, covered only in patches

MARTHA'S VINEYARD, 1925
Thomas Hart Benton
Collection of Whitney Museum of American Art

by a dull, brown lichen that is unfamiliar to you. Along one stretch rocks of varying sizes have fallen down onto the road, so that you are forced to drive around them with great caution.

Navigating these blind turns, you tap your horn to give warning in case someone should be approaching. But it is all unnecessary, since you come upon no other travelers.

Late in the afternoon, your foot numb from its constant pressure on the accelerator, your body jolted by the constant bumps and vibrations of the car, you decide to make the rest of your journey on foot, since you must be close to your destination by now.

A faint path leads through a tumble of rocks and bushes and trees, and you follow it enthusiastically. You descend a hill, slipping a little, so that a small rockslide is released; but you are able to keep your balance. At the back of your head is the precise location of your parked car, and behind that the curving dirt road, and behind that the other road, and then the magnificent highway itself: you understand that it would be no difficult feat to make your way back to any of these roads, should you decide that going by foot is unwise. But the path, though overgrown, is through a lovely forest, and then through a meadow in which yellow flowers are blooming, and you feel no inclination to turn back.

By evening you are still in the wilderness and you wonder if perhaps you have made a mistake. You are exhausted, your body aches, your eyes are seared by the need to stare so intently at everything around you. Now that the sun has nearly set, it is getting cold; evenings here in the mountains are always chilly.

You find yourself standing at the edge of a forest, staring ahead into the dark. Is that a field ahead, or a forest of small trees? Your path has long since given way to wild grass. Clouds obscure the moon, which should give you some light by which to make your way, and you wonder if you dare continue without this light.

Suddenly you remember the map you left back in the car, but you remember it as a blank sheet of paper.

You resist telling yourself you are lost. In fact, though you are exhausted and it is almost night, you are not lost. You have begun to shiver, but it is only with cold, not with fear. You are really satisfied with yourself. You are not lost. Though you can remember your map only as a blank sheet of paper, which can tell you nothing, you are not really lost.

If you had the day to begin again, on that highway which was so wide and clear, you would not have varied your journey in any way: in this is your triumph.

RESPONDING TO THE SELECTION

Your Response
1. The journey in the story is a metaphor for life. How would you describe the journey that represents your life?
2. If you had the day to begin again, how would your choices compare with the narrator's? Explain.
3. Do you think that it is possible to map out your life? Is it desirable? Why or why not?

Recalling
4. (a) Where does your journey begin? (b) What is your destination?
5. (a) Why do you turn off the highway? (b) Why do you turn onto an unpaved road? (c) Why do you decide "to make the rest of the journey on foot"?
6. (a) Where do you end up by evening? (b) What do you suddenly remember?
7. What do you conclude at the end of the day?

Interpreting
8. (a) Into what four stages can your journey be divided? (b) How does the appearance of the road or path that you follow change from stage to stage? (c) How does the appearance of the surrounding landscape change from stage to stage? (d) What other changes occur as you pass from stage to stage?
9. What is the significance of the fact that none of the places in the story are named?
10. In the beginning of the story, the narrator comments that "you are a lover of maps." (a) How does this attitude change during the course of the story? (b) What is the significance of the fact that in the end you remember the map "as a blank sheet of paper"?
11. What is the triumph felt at the end of the story?

Applying
12. Explain how this story relates to the following lines from Robert Frost's poem "The Road Not Taken": "Two roads diverged in the wood, and I— / I took the one less traveled by, / and that has made all the difference."

ANALYZING LITERATURE

Understanding Point of View

Point of view refers to the vantage point from which a narrative is told. Unlike most other stories, "Journey" is told from a second-person point of view.

1. How does Oates's use of a second-person point of view help make it clear that the story is meant to be interpreted symbolically?
2. Why would the story be less effective if Oates had used a first-person or third-person point of view?

CRITICAL THINKING AND READING

Supporting an Interpretation

When a story is meant to be interpreted symbolically, you must examine all the details in the story and determine how they fit together and what they represent.

The following is one possible interpretation of the symbolic meaning of "Journey." Support or refute this interpretation using details from the story:

The journey symbolizes a person's life, during which he or she passes from conformity to individuality. At first this person has his or her life carefully mapped out to follow a path that many others have taken. As the person's life progresses, however, he or she begins exploring new directions that fewer and fewer people have followed.

THINKING AND WRITING

Writing About Symbolic Meaning

Develop your answer from the Critical Thinking and Reading activity into an essay. Review your answer and try to think of additional details that support the interpretation. Organize your essay according to the stages of the journey. When you revise, make sure you have included enough details to thoroughly support your interpretation. After revising, proofread your essay.

LEARNING OPTIONS

1. **Art.** As a "lover of maps," draw or assemble a set of maps to show the route that the traveler in the story takes. Include at least four maps that show the transition from civilization to wilderness.
2. **Art.** In 1930, an unemployed engineer named Thomas Darrow designed the board game "Monopoly" based on a map he drew of Atlantic City. He became a millionaire. Give Thomas Darrow a run for his money. Design a board game based on a map you draw or a concept you develop for the story "Journey." Submit the game to classmates for evaluation.
3. **Speaking and Listening.** Do you think that there is a distinction between being lost and not knowing where you are? Take a position, and find a partner who does not agree with you. Together dramatize a conversation between a driver who claims that he or she is not lost and a passenger who is tired of riding around in circles. When is it time to stop and ask for directions?

DONALD BARTHELME

1931–1989

Donald Barthelme was one of the most innovative fiction writers of our time. Experimenting with a variety of radically different approaches to writing fiction, he frequently abandoned not only traditional forms but also the forms that characterize Modernist fiction.

Barthelme was born in Philadelphia, Pennsylvania, and raised in Houston, Texas. In 1964 he published his first book, *Dr. Caligari,* a collection of satirical and surrealistic stories. Three years later, he produced his first novel, *Snow White,* an elaborately structured work that explores the underlying emptiness of many contemporary ideologies and fads. He went on to publish several novels and numerous collections of short stories and to win a number of awards. He also produced a children's book, *The Slightly Irregular Fire Engine or the Hithering Thithering Djinn* (1971), which earned him the National Book Award for children's literature.

Having worked as a newspaper reporter, a museum director, and the managing editor of an art and literature review, Barthelme's experience was varied. He served in the United States Army in Korea and Japan, an epoch in his life to which he devoted some humorous attention in his fiction. He has been called "probably the most perversely gifted writer in the U.S.," a dubious distinction earned in part by his unyielding attempts to broaden both literary forms and the scope of human amusement. Critic Jack Kroll explains: "The world is hysteria but Barthelme doesn't get hysterical about it. He knows it's also funny." In fact, his work is often so humorous that readers may miss his serious intent. The often quirky and absurd nature of Donald Barthelme's work operates as a magnifying lens to focus attention directly on subjects worthy of a second look and reevaluation. Wanting to engage his reader intimately with his writing, he expressed his intention to write in a manner that leads readers to identify not just with characters or subjects but with the writer. He hoped to dupe the reader into feeling almost as if he or she were writing the story.

As in most Barthelme stories, both the form and the content of "Engineer-Private Paul Klee Misplaces an Aircraft Between Milbertshofen and Cambrai, March 1916" are unconventional. Barthelme uses a historical figure, Swiss abstract painter Paul Klee (1879–1940), as the story's main character. Loosely based on an incident that occurred during Klee's period of service with the German air corps during World War I, the story humorously examines the impersonal nature of military life.

Engineer-Private Paul Klee Misplaces an Aircraft Between Milbertshofen and Cambrai, March 1916

Literary Movements

Experimental Fiction. During the 1960's a number of writers began searching for ways to set their work apart from the literature of the past. This quest led to the development of new and radically different types of fiction in which conventional forms and structures were often completely abandoned. Some writers discarded the use of a narrator and began composing stories from dialogue alone. Others began experimenting with the physical appearance of their texts, at times even using blank pages as a part of a literary work. While basically adhering to conventional structures, other writers began exploring new and unconventional subjects. A number of writers turned their focus inward, writing stories about the process of writing and the forms and techniques of the story itself. Donald Barthelme's story "Sentence," for example, is, as the title suggests, one extremely long sentence about the peculiarities of sentences. Finally, some experimental writers turned to parodying ancient literary works, while others explored the use of historical figures as characters.

Commentary

Repetition is a tool writers use for various effects. As you read Barthelme's story, notice how he uses repetition to produce humor while presenting his view of military life. The Secret Police in the story are humorous bumblers who, by repeating the terms "secrets," "omnipresence," and "no one knows," show that they do not know what they are doing or why they are doing it. In his humorous characterization of the Secret Police, Barthelme suggests that they are absurd as is the military life that they represent. How do you feel about Barthelme's view of life in the military?

Focus

Barthelme's story focuses on the experiences of Swiss abstract painter Paul Klee during his period of service with the German air corps during World War I. List the reasons you think it might be difficult for an artist to adjust to life in the military.

Engineer-Private Paul Klee Misplaces an Aircraft Between Milbertshofen and Cambrai[1], March 1916

Donald Barthelme

Paul Klee said:

"Now I have been transferred to the Air Corps. A kindly sergeant effected the transfer. He thought I would have a better future here, more chances for promotion. First I was assigned to aircraft repair, together with several other workers. We presented ourselves as not just painters but artist-painters. This caused some shaking of heads. We varnished wooden fuselages, correcting old numbers and adding new ones with the help of templates. Then I was pulled off the painting detail and assigned to transport. I escort aircraft that are being sent to various bases in Germany and also (I understand) in occupied territory. It is not a bad life. I spend my nights racketing across Bavaria[2] (or some such) and my days in switching yards. There is always bread and wurst and beer in the station restaurants. When I reach a notable town I try to see the notable paintings there, if time allows. There are always unexpected delays, reroutings, backtrackings. Then the return to the base. I see Lily fairly often. We meet in hotel rooms and that is exciting. I have never yet lost an aircraft or failed to deliver one to its proper destination. The war seems interminable. Walden has sold six of my drawings."

The Secret Police said:

"We have secrets. We have many secrets. We desire all secrets. We do not have your secrets and that is what we are after, your secrets. Our first secret is where we are. No one knows. Our second secret is how many of us there are. No one knows. Omnipresence is our goal. We do not even need real omnipresence. The theory of omnipresence is enough. With omnipresence, hand-in-hand as it were, goes omniscience. And with omniscience and omnipresence, hand-in-hand-in-hand as it were, goes omnipotence. We are a three-sided waltz. However our mood is melancholy. There is a secret sigh that we sigh, secretly. We yearn to be known, acknowledged, admired even. What is the good of omnipotence if nobody knows? However that is a secret, that sorrow. Now we are everywhere. One place we are is here watching Engineer-Private Klee, who is escorting three valuable aircraft, B.F.W. 3054/16–17–18, with spare parts, by rail from Milbertshofen to Cambrai. Do you wish to know what Engi-

---

1. Milbertshofen (mil′ berts hof′ ən) **and Cambrai** (käm brā′): Milbertshofen is a town in Bavaria. Cambrai is a town in northern France.
2. Bavaria (bə ver′ ē ə): A state in southwest Germany.

neer-Private Klee is doing at this very moment, in the baggage car? He is reading a book of Chinese short stories. He has removed his boots. His feet rest twenty-six centimeters from the baggage-car stove."

Paul Klee said:

"These Chinese short stories are slight and lovely. I have no way of knowing if the translation is adequate or otherwise. Lily will meet me in our rented room on Sunday, if I return in time. Our destination is Fighter Squadron Five. I have not had anything to eat since morning. The fine chunk of bacon given me along with my expense money when we left the base has been eaten. This morning a Red Cross lady with a squint gave me some very good coffee, however. Now we are entering Hohenbudberg."[3]

The Secret Police said:

"Engineer-Private Klee has taken himself into the station restaurant. He is enjoying a hearty lunch. We shall join him there."

Paul Klee said:

"Now I emerge from the station restaurant and walk along the line of cars to the flatcar on which my aircraft (I think of them as *my* aircraft) are carried. To my surprise and dismay, I notice that one of them is missing. There had been three, tied down on the flatcar and covered with canvas. Now I see with my trained painter's eye that instead of three canvas-covered shapes on the flatcar there are only two. Where the third aircraft had been there is only a puddle of canvas and loose rope. I look around quickly to see if anyone else has marked the disappearance of the third aircraft."

The Secret Police said:

"We had marked it. Our trained policemen's eyes had marked the fact that where three aircraft had been before, tied down on the flatcar and covered with canvas, now there were only two. Unfortunately we had been in the station restaurant, lunching, at the moment of removal, therefore we could not attest as to where it had gone or who

had removed it. There is something we do not know. This is irritating in the extreme. We closely observe Engineer-Private Klee to determine what action he will take in the emergency. We observe that he is withdrawing from his tunic a notebook and pencil. We observe that he begins, very properly in our opinion, to note down in his notebook all the particulars of the affair."

Paul Klee said:

"The shape of the collapsed canvas, under which the aircraft had rested, together with the loose ropes—the canvas forming hills and valleys, seductive folds, the ropes the very essence of looseness, lapsing—it is irresistible. I sketch for ten or fifteen minutes, wondering the while if I might not be in trouble, because of the missing aircraft. When I arrive at Fighter Squadron Five with less than the number of aircraft listed on the manifest,[4] might not some officious person become angry? Shout at me? I have finished sketching. Now I will ask various trainmen and station personnel if they have seen anyone carrying away the aircraft. If they answer in the negative, I will become extremely frustrated. I will begin to kick the flatcar."

The Secret Police said:

"Frustrated, he begins to kick the flatcar."

Paul Klee said:

"I am looking up in the sky, to see if my aircraft is there. There are in the sky aircraft of several types, but none of the type I am searching for."

The Secret Police said:

"Engineer-Private Klee is searching the sky—an eminently sound procedure, in our opinion. We, the Secret Police, also sweep the Hohenbudberg sky, with our eyes. But find nothing. We are debating with ourselves as to whether we ought to enter the station restaurant and begin drafting our preliminary report for forwarding to higher headquarters. The knotty point, in terms of the preliminary report, is that we do not have

---

3. **Hohenbudberg** (hō ən bud′ berg): A village in northwestern Germany.

4. **manifest** (man′ ə fest′) *n*.: A cargo list.

the answer to the question 'Where is the aircraft?' The damage potential to the theory of omniscience as well as potential to our careers, dictates that this point be omitted from the preliminary report. But if this point is omitted, might not some officious person at the Central Bureau for Secrecy note the omission? Become angry? Shout at us? Omissiveness is not rewarded at the Central Bureau. We decide to observe further the actions of Engineer-Private Klee, for the time being."

Paul Klee said:

"I who have never lost an aircraft have lost an aircraft. The aircraft is signed out to me. The cost of the aircraft, if it is not found, will be deducted from my pay, meager enough already. Even if Walden sells a hundred, a thousand drawings, I will not have enough money to pay for this cursed aircraft. Can I, in the time the train remains in the Hohenbudberg yards, construct a new aircraft or even the simulacrum of an aircraft, with no materials to work with or indeed any special knowledge of aircraft construction? The situation is ludicrous. I will therefore apply Reason. Reason dictates the solution. I will diddle the manifest. With my painter's skill which is after all not so different from a forger's, I will change the manifest to reflect conveyance of *two* aircraft, B.F.W. 3054/16 and 17, to Fighter Squadron Five. The extra canvas and ropes I will conceal in an empty boxcar—this one, which according to its stickers is headed for Essigny-le-Petit.[5] Now I will walk around

town and see if I can find a chocolate shop. I crave chocolate."

The Secret Police said:

"Now we observe Engineer-Private Klee concealing the canvas and ropes which covered the former aircraft into an empty boxcar bound for Essigny-le-Petit. We have previously observed him diddling the manifest with his painter's skill which resembles not a little that of the forger. We applaud these actions of Engineer-Private Klee. The contradiction confronting us in the matter of the preliminary report is thus resolved in highly satisfactory fashion. We are proud of Engineer-Private Klee and of the resolute and manly fashion in which he has dealt with the crisis. We predict he will go far. We would like to embrace him as a comrade and brother but unfortunately we are not embraceable. We are secret, we exist in the shadows, the pleasure of the comradely/ brotherly embrace is one of the pleasures we are denied, in our dismal service."

Paul Klee said:

"We arrive at Cambrai. The planes are unloaded, six men for each plane. The work goes quickly. No one questions my altered manifest. The weather is clearing. After lunch I will leave to begin the return journey. My release slip and travel orders are ready, but the lieutenant must come and sign them. I wait contentedly in the warm orderly room. The drawing I did of the collapsed canvas and ropes is really very good. I eat a piece of chocolate. I am sorry about the lost aircraft but not overmuch. The war is temporary. But drawings and chocolate go on forever."

---

5. Essigny-le-Petit (es sē nyē′ lə pə tē′): A street or district of St. Quentin in northern France.

RESPONDING TO THE SELECTION

Your Response
1. What do you think of Klee's solution to his problem? Explain.
2. In explaining his actions, Paul Klee said, "The war is temporary. But drawings and chocolate go on forever." Do you agree? Why or why not?
3. After reading this selection, would you like to read more of Barthelme's fiction? Why or why not?

Recalling
4. What is Klee's primary duty as a member of the air corps?
5. (a) What is the Secret Police's "first secret"? (b) What is their "second secret"? (c) What is their goal?
6. What does Klee notice when he returns to the flatcar on which his aircraft are carried?
7. (a) How does Klee solve his problem? (b) How do the Secret Police react to Klee's solution?

Interpreting
8. (a) How do the duties of the Secret Police contrast with their desires? (b) What is their attitude toward their service? (c) How is this attitude revealed?
9. How can you tell that the Secret Police view themselves as gods?
10. (a) What concern do Klee and the Secret Police share? (b) What is the significance of the fact that they share this concern?
11. What is the significance of the mechanical fashion in which both Klee and the Secret Police speak in this story?
12. What is the meaning of Klee's comments about war, drawings, and chocolate?
13. (a) Who, or what, is Barthelme satirizing, or poking fun at, in this story? (b) What is the story's theme, or main point?

Applying
14. Explain why you do or do not think satire is an effective means of protesting war.

ANALYZING LITERATURE

Understanding Experimental Fiction
Barthelme's story is an excellent example of experimental fiction—a radically different type of fiction that developed during the 1960's as a result of the desire of writers to create work that stood apart from the literature of the past.
1. What is unconventional about the structure of Barthelme's story?
2. How does the structure reflect its meaning?

THINKING AND WRITING

Responding to Criticism
A critic has commented that despair is one of Barthelme's "favorite subjects for jest." Write an essay in which you discuss this comment in relation to the story you have just read. Reread the story, noting Barthelme's use of satire. Write your essay, using passages from the story to support your argument. When you revise, make sure your essay is logically organized.

LEARNING OPTIONS

1. **Writing.** If you were in Paul Klee's place, how would you have responded to the theft of the aircraft? Summarize the problem as Klee does; then share your solution with readers. Fill your name in the blank and write a short monologue that begins: _____ said:
2. **Cross-curricular Connection.** How might artist Paul Klee respond to the way he is characterized by author Donald Barthelme? Learn more about Klee's life, views, and art. View his pictures. Be prepared to share your impressions in a class discussion.
3. **Cross-curricular Connection.** Paul Klee has been called "one of the most varied, complex, and brilliant talents in the twentieth century." His art is uniquely his own; poetic, intellectual, and deceptively simple. Choose a picture by Paul Klee and present it to the class. Discuss your reaction to it and your interpretation of it.

ANNE TYLER

1941–

Inspired by the work of Eudora Welty, Anne Tyler devotes much of her fiction to exposing the unusual latent characteristics of outwardly ordinary people.

Born in Minneapolis, Minnesota, Tyler spent most of her childhood in Raleigh, North Carolina, and now lives with her family in Baltimore, Maryland. She studied Russian at Duke and at Columbia, at the same time developing her talents as a fiction writer. In 1964, when she was twenty-four, she published her first novel, *If Morning Ever Comes.* Since then, she has published several more novels, including *The Tin Can Tree* (1966), *The Clock Winder* (1973), *Earthly Possessions* (1977), *Dinner at the Homesick Restaurant* (1982), and *The Accidental Tourist* (1985). She has also written numerous short stories, many of which have appeared in *The New Yorker.*

As the wife of a child psychiatrist, the mother of two daughters, and a committed writer, Anne Tyler orchestrates a balance between family and work in the orderly and highly organized fashion that many of her characters long for. Monday through Thursday she works, seated on a daybed in her starkly plain study. There she writes with a pen in longhand so, as she explains, she can hear her characters speak. She reserves Fridays for errands and weekends for family matters. Her characters are not fictionalizations from her own life, but products of a fertile imagination that are drawn with her gift for fine, realistic detail. During recurrent hours of insomnia, she often records ideas in boxes of index cards.

When Tyler works on a novel, she follows a comfortable pattern that entails writing out a first draft and then reading it to "find out what it means." Then she revises the draft to unify it and to enhance the "subconscious intentions" she has discovered in the work. She keeps the goal of writing "serious" fiction firmly in sight as she revises. "A serious book," she has explained, "is one that removes me to another life as I am reading it. It has to have layers and layers, like life does. It has to be an extremely believable lie." A major satisfaction she derives from her writing comes through the connection she feels in sharing her created worlds with understanding readers. "They in their solitude, and I in mine, have somehow managed to touch without either of us feeling intruded upon. We've spent some time on neutral territory, sharing a life that belongs to neither of us."

"Average Waves in Unprotected Waters" displays Tyler's ability to create well-developed, realistic characters and evoke an emotional response through an unsentimental portrayal of the characters' tragic lives.

GUIDE FOR INTERPRETING

Average Waves in Unprotected Waters

Writers' Techniques

Foreshadowing. Foreshadowing is a technique that writers frequently use in short stories and novels to build **suspense,** or create tension about the outcome of events. When a writer uses foreshadowing, he or she presents details that hint at actions that will occur later on or suggest the story's outcome. For example, in her story "The Life You Save May Be Your Own," Flannery O'Connor hints at the tragic impact that Mr. Shiftlet will have on the lives of the Crater women when she writes that Mr. Shiftlet "paused and made his tone more *ominous* still."

Flashback. A flashback is an interruption in the sequence of narration in which an earlier event is related. Often a flashback takes the form of a reminiscence of one of the characters. For example, in her story "The Jilting of Granny Weatherall," Katherine Anne Porter presents numerous flashbacks as the main character's thoughts drift back to events that occurred in her younger days.

Commentary

Although "Average Waves in Unprotected Waters" concerns the lives of two characters, it focuses on Bet, the mother, whose fear of change reflects Tyler's own "utter lack of faith in change." As you read the story, notice how Tyler depicts the changeless nature of Bet's character. From childhood, when she stood staunch in waves that she could not ride, through adulthood, when she stayed on in a marriage that was grim, Bet remains steadfastly constant. Her resistance to change adds interest to the events of the day depicted in the story. How will Bet adjust to the change in her life? What shape will her life take hereafter? Look to the final sentence of the story for a clue.

What is your response to change? Do you willingly accept it, or do you resist?

Focus

In "Average Waves in Unprotected Waters," Anne Tyler explores a mother's attempts to cope with a severely handicapped child. Free-write about some of the difficulties that parents might have in dealing with a handicapped child. What types of emotions might parents experience in this situation? In what ways might a child's handicap affect the parents' lives? What actions might the parents take to make their child's life better?

Average Waves
in Unprotected Waters

Anne Tyler

As soon as it got light, Bet woke him and dressed him, and then she walked him over to the table and tried to make him eat a little cereal. He wouldn't, though. He could tell something was up. She pressed the edge of the spoon against his lips till she heard it click on his teeth, but he just looked off at a corner of the ceiling—a knobby child with great glassy eyes and her own fair hair. Like any other nine-year-old, he wore a striped shirt and jeans, but the shirt was too neat and the jeans too blue, unpatched and un-faded, and would stay that way till he out-grew them. And his face was elderly—pinched, strained, tired—though it should have looked as unused as his jeans. He hardly ever changed his expression.

She left him in his chair and went to make the beds. Then she raised the yellowed shade, rinsed a few spoons in the bathroom sink, picked up some bits of magazines he'd torn the night before. This was a rented room in an ancient, crumbling house, and nothing you could do to it would lighten its cluttered look. There was always that feeling of too many lives layered over other lives, like the layers of brownish wallpaper her child had peeled away in the corner by his bed.

She slipped her feet into flat-heeled loaf-ers and absently patted the front of her dress, a worn beige knit she usually saved for Sundays. Maybe she should take it in a little; it hung from her shoulders like a sack. She felt too slight and frail, too wispy for all she had to do today. But she reached for her coat anyhow, and put it on and tied a blue kerchief under her chin. Then she went over to the table and slowly spun, modeling the coat. "See, Arnold?" she said. "We're going out."

Arnold went on looking at the ceiling, but his gaze turned wild and she knew he'd heard.

She fetched his jacket from the closet—brown corduroy, with a hood. It had set her back half a week's salary. But Arnold didn't like it; he always wanted his old one, a little red duffel coat he'd long ago outgrown. When she came toward him, he started moaning and rocking and shaking his head. She had to struggle to stuff his arms in the sleeves. Small though he was, he was strong, wiry; he was getting to be too much for her. He shook free of her hands and ran over to his bed. The jacket was on, though. It wasn't buttoned, the collar was askew, but never mind; that just made him look more real. She always felt bad at how he stood inside his clothes, separate from them, passive, un-aware of all the buttons and snaps she'd fas-tened as carefully as she would a doll's.

She gave a last look around the room, checked to make sure the hot plate was off, and then picked up her purse and Arnold's suitcase. "Come along, Arnold," she said.

He came, dragging out every step. He

looked at the suitcase suspiciously, but only because it was new. It didn't have any meaning for him. "See?" she said. "It's yours. It's Arnold's. It's going on the train with us."

But her voice was all wrong. He would pick it up, for sure. She paused in the middle of locking the door and glanced over at him fearfully. Anything could set him off nowadays. He hadn't noticed, though. He was too busy staring around the hallway, goggling at a freckled, walnut-framed mirror as if he'd never seen it before. She touched his shoulder. "Come, Arnold," she said.

They went down the stairs slowly, both of them clinging to the sticky mahogany railing. The suitcase banged against her shins. In the entrance hall, old Mrs. Puckett stood waiting outside her door—a huge, soft lady in a black crêpe dress and orthopedic shoes. She was holding a plastic bag of peanut-butter cookies, Arnold's favorites. There were tears in her eyes. "Here, Arnold," she said, quavering. Maybe she felt to blame that he was going. But she'd done the best she could: babysat him all these years and only given up when he'd grown too strong and wild to manage. Bet wished Arnold would give the old lady some sign—hug her, make his little crowing noise, just take the cookies, even. But he was too excited. He raced on out the front door, and it was Bet who had to take them. "Well, thank you, Mrs. Puckett," she said. "I know he'll enjoy them later."

"Oh, no . . ." said Mrs. Puckett, and she flapped her large hands and gave up, sobbing.

They were lucky and caught a bus first thing. Arnold sat by the window. He must have thought he was going to work with her; when they passed the red-and-gold Kresge's sign, he jabbered and tried to stand up. "No, honey," she said, and took hold of his arm. He settled down then and let his hand stay curled in hers awhile. He had very small, cool fingers, and nails as smooth as thumbtack heads.

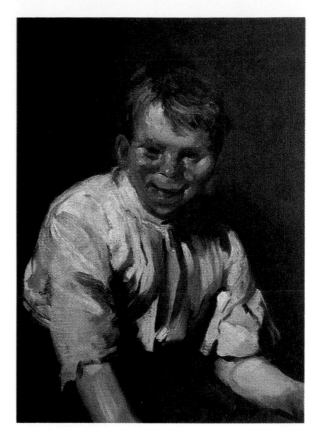

THE LAUGHING BOY
George Bellows
Hirschl & Adler Galleries, Inc.

At the train station, she bought the tickets and then a pack of Wrigley's spearmint gum. Arnold stood gaping at the vaulted ceiling, with his head flopped back and his arms hanging limp at his sides. People stared at him. She would have liked to push their faces in. "Over here, honey," she said, and she nudged him toward the gate, straightening his collar as they walked.

He hadn't been on a train before and acted a little nervous, bouncing up and down in his seat and flipping the lid of his ashtray and craning forward to see the man ahead of them. When the train started moving, he crowed and pulled at her sleeve. "That's right, Arnold. Train. We're taking a trip," Bet said. She unwrapped a stick of chewing gum and gave it to him. He loved gum. If she didn't watch him closely, he sometimes swallowed it—which worried her a little because she'd heard it clogged your kidneys; but at least it would keep him busy. She looked down at the top of his head. Through the blond prickles of his hair, cut short for practical reasons, she could see his skull bones moving as he chewed. He was so thin-skinned, almost transparent; sometimes she imagined she could see the blood traveling in his veins.

When the train reached a steady speed, he grew calmer, and after a while he nodded over against her and let his hands sag on his knees. She watched his eyelashes slowly drooping—two colorless, fringed crescents, heavier and heavier, every now and then flying up as he tried to fight off sleep. He had never slept well, not ever, not even as a baby. Even before they'd noticed anything wrong, they'd wondered at his jittery, jerky catnaps, his tiny hands clutching tight and springing open, his strange single wail sailing out while he went right on sleeping. Avery said it gave him the chills. And after the doctor talked to them Avery wouldn't have anything to do with Arnold anymore—just walked in wide circles around the crib, looking stunned and sick. A few weeks later, he left. She wasn't surprised. She even knew how he felt, more or less. Halfway, he blamed her; halfway, he blamed himself. You can't believe a thing like this will just fall on you out of nowhere.

She'd had moments herself of picturing some kind of evil gene in her husband's ordinary, stocky body—a dark little egg like a black jelly bean, she imagined it. All his fault. But other times she was sure the gene was hers. It seemed so natural; she never could do anything as well as most people. And then other times she blamed their marriage. They'd married too young, against her parents' wishes. All she'd wanted was to get away from home. Now she couldn't remember why. What was wrong with home? She

thought of her parents' humped green trailer, perched on cinder blocks near a forest of masts in Salt Spray, Maryland. At this distance (parents dead, trailer rusted to bits, even Salt Spray changed past recognition), it seemed to her that her old life had been beautifully free and spacious. She closed her eyes and saw wide gray skies. Everything had been ruled by the sea. Her father (who'd run a fishing boat for tourists) couldn't arrange his day till he'd heard the marine forecast—the wind, the tides, the small-craft warnings, the height of average waves in unprotected waters. He loved to fish, offshore and on, and he swam every chance he could get. He'd tried to teach her to bodysurf, but it hadn't worked out. There was something about the breakers: she just gritted her teeth and stood staunch and let them slam into her. As if standing staunch were a virtue, really. She couldn't explain it. Her father thought she was scared, but it wasn't that at all.

She'd married Avery against their wishes and been sorry ever since—sorry to move so far from home, sorrier when her parents died within a year of each other, sorriest of all when the marriage turned grim and cranky. But she never would have thought of leaving him. It was Avery who left; she would have stayed forever. In fact, she did stay on in their apartment for months after he'd gone, though the rent was far too high. It wasn't that she expected him back. She just took some comfort from enduring.

Arnold's head snapped up. He looked around him and made a gurgling sound. His chewing gum fell onto the front of his jacket. "Here, honey," she told him. She put the gum in her ashtray. "Look out the window. See the cows?"

He wouldn't look. He began bouncing in his seat, rubbing his hands together rapidly.

"Arnold? Want a cookie?"

If only she'd brought a picture book. She'd meant to and then forgot. She wondered if the train people sold magazines. If she let him get too bored, he'd go into one of his tantrums, and then she wouldn't be able

to handle him. The doctor had given her pills just in case, but she was always afraid that while he was screaming he would choke on them. She looked around the car. "Arnold," she said, "see the . . . see the hat with feathers on? Isn't it pretty? See the red suitcase? See the, um . . ."

The car door opened with a rush of clattering wheels and the conductor burst in, singing "Girl of my dreams, I love you." He lurched down the aisle, plucking pink tickets from the back of each seat. Just across from Bet and Arnold, he stopped. He was looking down at a tiny black lady in a purple coat, with a fox fur piece biting its own tail around her neck. "You!" he said.

The lady stared straight ahead.

"You, I saw you. You're the one in the washroom."

A little muscle twitched in her cheek.

"You got on this train in Beulah, didn't you. Snuck in the washroom. Darted back like you thought you could put something over on me. I saw that bit of purple! Where's your ticket gone to?"

She started fumbling in a blue cloth purse. The fumbling went on and on. The conductor shifted his weight.

"Why!" she said finally. "I must've left it back in my other seat."

"What other seat?"

"Oh, the one back . . ." She waved a spidery hand.

The conductor sighed. "Lady," he said, "you owe me money."

"I do no such thing!" she said. "Viper! Monger! Hitler!"[1] Her voice screeched up all at once; she sounded like a parrot. Bet winced and felt herself flushing, as if *she* were the one. But then at her shoulder she heard a sudden, rusty clang, and she turned and saw that Arnold was laughing. He had his mouth wide open and his tongue curled, the way he did when he watched "Sesame Street." Even after the scene had worn itself out, and the lady had paid and the conductor had moved on, Arnold went on chortling

---

1. Hitler: German dictator Adolf Hitler (1889–1945).

and la-la-ing, and Bet looked gratefully at the little black lady, who was settling her fur piece fussily and muttering under her breath.

From the Parkinsville Railroad Station, which they seemed to be tearing down or else remodeling—she couldn't tell which—they took a taxicab to Parkins State Hospital. "Oh, I been out there many and many a time," said the driver. "Went out there just the other—"

But she couldn't stop herself; she had to tell him before she forgot. "Listen," she said, "I want you to wait for me right in the driveway. I don't want you to go on away."

"Well, fine," he said.

"Can you do that? I want you to be sitting right by the porch or the steps or whatever, right where I come out of, ready to take me back to the station. Don't just go off, and—"

"I *got* you, I got you," he said.

She sank back. She hoped he understood.

Arnold wanted a peanut-butter cookie. He was reaching and whimpering. She didn't know what to do. She wanted to give him anything he asked for, anything; but he'd get it all over his face and arrive not looking his best. She couldn't stand it if they thought he was just ordinary and unattractive. She wanted them to see how small and neat he was, how somebody cherished him. But it would be awful if he went into one of his rages. She broke off a little piece of cookie from the bag. "Here," she told him. "Don't mess, now."

He flung himself back in the corner and ate it, keeping one hand flattened across his mouth while he chewed.

The hospital looked like someone's great, pillared mansion, with square brick buildings all around it. "Here we are," the driver said.

"Thank you," she said. "Now you wait here, please. Just wait till I get—"

"*Lady,*" he said. "I'll wait."

She opened the door and nudged Arnold out ahead of her. Lugging the suitcase, she started toward the steps. "Come on, Arnold," she said.

He hung back.

"Arnold?"

Maybe he wouldn't allow it, and they would go on home and never think of this again.

But he came, finally, climbing the steps in his little hobbled way. His face was clean, but there were a few cookie crumbs on his jacket. She set down the suitcase to brush them off. Then she buttoned all his buttons and smoothed his shirt collar over his jacket collar before she pushed open the door.

In the admitting office, a lady behind a wooden counter showed her what papers to sign. Secretaries were clacketing typewriters all around. Bet thought Arnold might like that, but instead he got lost in the lights—chilly, hanging ice-cube-tray lights with a little flicker to them. He gazed upward, looking astonished. Finally a flat-fronted nurse came in and touched his elbow. "Come along, Arnold. Come, Mommy. We'll show you where Arnold is staying," she said.

They walked back across the entrance hall, then up wide marble steps with hollows worn in them. Arnold clung to the bannister. There was a smell Bet hated, pine-oil disinfectant, but Arnold didn't seem to notice. You never knew; sometimes smells could just put him in a state.

The nurse unlocked a double door that had chicken-wired windows. They walked through a corridor, passing several fat, ugly women in shapeless gray dresses and ankle socks. "Ha!" one of the women said, and fell giggling into the arms of a friend. The nurse said, "*Here* we are." She led them into an enormous hallway lined with little white cots. Nobody else was in it; there wasn't a sign that children lived here except for a tiny cardboard clown picture hanging on one vacant wall. "This one is your bed, Arnold," said the nurse. Bet laid the suitcase on it. It was made up so neatly, the sheets might have been painted on. A steely-gray blanket was folded across the foot. She looked over at

Arnold, but he was pivoting back and forth to hear how his new sneakers squeaked on the linoleum.

"Usually," said the nurse, "we like to give new residents six months before the family visits. That way they settle in quicker, don't you see." She turned away and adjusted the clown picture, though as far as Bet could tell it was fine the way it was. Over her shoulder, the nurse said, "You can tell him goodbye now, if you like."

"Oh," Bet said. "All right." She set her hands on Arnold's shoulders. Then she laid her face against his hair, which felt warm and fuzzy. "Honey," she said. But he went on pivoting. She straightened and told the nurse, "I brought his special blanket."

"Oh, fine," said the nurse, turning toward her again. "We'll see that he gets it."

"He always likes to sleep with it; he has ever since he was little."

"All right."

"Don't wash it. He hates if you wash it."

"Yes. Say goodbye to Mommy now, Arnold."

"A lot of times he'll surprise you. I mean there's a whole lot to him. He's not just—"

"We'll take very good care of him, Mrs. Blevins, don't worry."

"Well," she said. " 'Bye, Arnold."

She left the ward with the nurse and went down the corridor. As the nurse was unlocking the doors for her, she heard a single, terrible scream, but the nurse only patted her shoulder and pushed her gently on through.

In the taxi, Bet said, "Now, I've just got fifteen minutes to get to the station. I wonder if you could hurry?"

"Sure thing," the driver said.

She folded her hands and looked straight ahead. Tears seemed to be coming down her face in sheets.

Once she'd reached the station, she went to the ticket window. "Am I in time for the twelve-thirty-two?" she asked.

"Easily," said the man. "It's twenty minutes late."

"What?"

"Got held up in Norton somehow."

"But you can't!" she said. The man looked startled. She must be a sight, all swollen-eyed and wet-cheeked. "Look," she said, in a lower voice. "I figured this on purpose. I chose the one train from Beulah that would let me catch another one back without waiting. I do not want to sit and wait in this station."

"Twenty *minutes*, lady. That's all it is."

"What am I going to do?" she asked him.

He turned back to his ledgers.

She went over to a bench and sat down. Ladders and scaffolding towered above her, and only ten or twelve passengers were dotted through the rest of the station. The place looked bombed out—nothing but a shell. "Twenty minutes!" she said aloud. "What am I going to do?"

Through the double glass doors at the far end of the station, a procession of gray-suited men arrived with briefcases. More men came behind them, dressed in work clothes, carrying folding chairs, black trunk-like boxes with silver hinges, microphones, a wooden lectern, and an armload of bunting. They set the lectern down in the center of the floor, not six feet from Bet. They draped the bunting across it—an arc of red, white, and blue. Wires were connected, floodlights were lit. A microphone screeched. One of the workmen said, "Try her, Mayor." He held the microphone out to a fat man in a suit, who cleared his throat and said, "Ladies and gentlemen, on the occasion of the expansion of this fine old railway station—"

"Sure do get an echo here," the workman said. "Keep on going."

The Mayor cleared his throat again. "If I may," he said, "I'd like to take about twenty minutes of your time, friends."

He straightened his tie. Bet blew her nose, and then she wiped her eyes and smiled. They had come just for her sake, you might think. They were putting on a sort of private play. From now on, all the world was going to be like that—just something on a stage, for her to sit back and watch.

RESPONDING TO THE SELECTION

Your Response
1. What do you think of Bet's new outlook on life? Explain.
2. Do you think Bet really has come to terms with her decision to institutionalize her son? Why or why not?

Recalling
3. (a) What turns out to be the purpose of Bet and Arnold's journey? (b) What does Bet hear just after she leaves Arnold?
4. (a) Why is Bet's train home delayed? (b) What happens while she is waiting for it?

Interpreting
5. When does it first become apparent that Arnold is in some way handicapped?
6. When Bet recalls how her father had tried to teach her to bodysurf, she remembers that she had "just gritted her teeth and stood staunch and let them [waves] slam into her." How does this response relate to her reaction to events occurring later in her life?
7. Why does Bet insist that the cab driver wait for her outside the hospital?
8. (a) What impression does Tyler convey in her description of the hospital? (b) What seems to be the nurse's attitude concerning Arnold's situation?
9. Explain the single, terrible scream that Mrs. Blevins hears as the nurse unlocks the doors for her.
10. What is ironic, or surprising, about the mayor's plans to speak in the train station for twenty minutes?
11. (a) What is the meaning of the story's final sentence? (b) How does the story's title relate to its meaning?

Applying
12. Do you think that most people would act as Bet does if they were in her place? Why or why not?

ANALYZING LITERATURE

Understanding Foreshadowing
Foreshadowing refers to the use of hints or clues in a narrative to suggest later events. For example, in the first paragraph of "Average Waves in Unprotected Waters," Tyler hints at a later event when she writes that Arnold "could tell something was up."
1. Find three other examples of foreshadowing in the story.
2. How does Tyler's use of foreshadowing help to build suspense?

CRITICAL THINKING AND READING

Ordering Events
A **flashback** is an interruption in the sequence of narration in which an earlier event is related. For example, a flashback occurs during the train ride when Bet reminisces about her past life. To fully understand a story that contains flashbacks, you must think about the order in which all the events occurred and be able to reorganize them in your own mind.
1. What prompts Bet's flashback?
2. What causes her flashback to end?
3. How does the flashback contribute to your understanding of the story?
4. Arrange all the events related in "Average Waves in Unprotected Waters" in chronological order.

THINKING AND WRITING

Responding to Criticism
A critic has commented that Anne Tyler "does not trivialize motives with rationalizations. She launches her imagined lives and describes their trajectories with an unpretentious sense of fate." Write an essay in which you discuss "Average Waves in Unprotected Waters" in relation to this statement. When you write your essay, use passages from the story to support your argument. Once you have finished writing, revise and proofread your essay.

ANN BEATTIE

1947–

Generally considered to be one of today's most accomplished young fiction writers, Ann Beattie has restlessly pursued innovations in narrative structure. Like many other contemporary writers, Beattie often composes works in the form of a broken, fragmented sequence of events, thoughts, emotions, and memories. This approach reflects Beattie's perceptions of the sense of aimlessness and disorder associated with contemporary life.

Born in Washington, D.C., Beattie achieved success as a writer at an early age. She has had numerous short stories published in *The New Yorker* and has produced several collections of stories. Her collections include *Distortions* (1976), *Secrets and Surprises* (1978), *The Burning House* (1982), and *Where You'll Find Me* (1986). Although she is known more for her short stories, she has also written a number of novels, including *Chilly Scenes of Winter* (1976), *Falling in Place* (1980), and *Love Always* (1985).

Chilly Scenes of Winter is a novel concerned with the people who came of age in the 1960's and have since found themselves disillusioned by society's changes. Ms. Beattie has said about it, "I was going out of my way in the novel to say something about the 60's having passed. It just seems to me to be an attitude that most of my friends and most of the people I know have. They all feel sort of let down, either by not having involved themselves more in the 60's . . . or else by having involved themselves to no avail. Most of the people I know are let down—they feel cheated—and these are the people I am writing about."

About the simple declarative style in which she writes, she says, "My stories are a lot about chaos . . . and many of the simple flat statements that I bring together are usually non sequiturs or bordering on being non sequiturs—which reinforces the chaos. I write in those flat simple sentences because that's the way I think. I don't mean to do it as a technique. It might be just that I am incapable of breaking through to the complexities underlying all that sort of simple statement you find in my work."

A typical Beattie story, "Imagined Scenes" captures a young woman's overwhelming sense of purposelessness. Using a detached narrator to present a series of seemingly distorted scenes, Beattie makes it seem as if we are actually witnessing events from the young woman's life, rather than being told a story.

GUIDE FOR INTERPRETING

Imagined Scenes

Literary Movements

Postmodernism. Postmodernism refers to the collection of literary movements that have developed in the decades following World War II. Like their predecessors, many of the Postmodernists have attempted to capture the essence of contemporary life in the form and content of their work. Others, however, have focused on creating works that stand apart from the literature of the past. To accomplish these purposes, writers have experimented with a variety of different approaches and used a wide range of literary forms and techniques. Many writers have continued to develop the fragmentary approach of the Modernists, omitting expositions, resolutions, and transitions, and composing stories in the form of a broken or distorted sequence of scenes, rather than in the form of a continuous narrative. Possessing the belief that reality is to some extent shaped by our imaginations, some writers have turned away from writing realistic fiction and begun writing fantasy or "magical realism"—fiction that blends realism and fantasy. Other writers have radically departed from traditional fictional forms and techniques, composing works from dialogue alone, creating works that blend fiction and nonfiction, and experimenting with the physical appearance of a work. Finally, a number of Postmodernist writers have confronted the problems they perceive in contemporary society through the use of satire and black humor.

Commentary

Setting is never accidental in a story, but in some stories, it is a central choice the author makes. In Ann Beattie's "Imagined Scenes," notice that the midwinter setting not only creates the frozen atmosphere of the story but also underscores the story's central points. That the story opens with a dream of a beach somewhere is significant. The relationship between David and his wife is being lived in the dead of midwinter, and her beach dream indicates dissatisfaction with the wintry state of things. Soon David mentions a trip to Greece, a country associated with warm weather and beaches. His wife muses to herself that she'd rather go to Spain, another warm country with beaches. Both seem unhappy with the present, but each sees in his or her future a different beach. Meanwhile, the snow grows deeper and deeper around them. As you read the story, consider what the winter, the snow, and the beaches represent in the lives of these people.

Focus

"Imagined Scenes" focuses on the life of a young woman who has been forced to pattern her life to accommodate her husband's career aspirations. Freewrite about the types of problems that you think might arise from this type of situation.

Imagined Scenes

Ann Beattie

"I've unlaced my boots and I'm standing barefoot on a beach with very brown sand, ocean in front of me and mountains in the distance, and trees making a pretty green haze around them."

"Pretty," David says.

"Where would that be?"

"Greece?"

When she wakes from a dream, David is already awake. Or perhaps he only wakes when she stirs, whispers to him. He doesn't sound sleepy; he's alert, serious, as though he'd been waiting for a question. She remembers last year, the week before Christmas, when she and David had gone out separately to shop. She got back to the house first, her keys lost—or locked in the car. Before she could look for them, headlights lit up the snowy path. David jumped out of his car, excited about his purchases, reaching around her to put the key in the door. Now she expects him to wake up when she does, that they will arrive home simultaneously. But David still surprises her—at the end of summer he told her he wouldn't be working in the fall. He was going back to college to finish the work for his Ph.D.

He sits in a gray chair by the fireplace and reads; she brings coffee to the table by his chair, and he turns off the light and goes up-

PLEASURES OF WINTER IN NEW YORK
Francis Peterson

stairs to bed when she is tired. By unspoken agreement, he has learned to like Roquefort dressing. He pokes the logs in the fireplace because the hot red coals frighten her.

"After I take orals in the spring we'll go to Greece to celebrate."

She wants to go to Spain. Couldn't the beach have been in Spain? No more questions—she should let him sleep. She shakes the thought out of her head.

"No?" he says. "We will. We'll go to Greece when I finish the orals."

The leaves of the plant look like worn velvet. The tops are purple, a shiny, fuzzy purple, and the underside is dark green. Suddenly the plant has begun to grow, sending up a narrow shoot not strong enough to support itself, so that it falls forward precariously, has to be staked. They agree it's strange that a plant should have such a spurt of growth in midwinter. David admires the plant, puts it in a window that gets the morning light and moves it into a side room late in the afternoon. Now when he waters the plant a little plant food is mixed in with the water. David is enthusiastic; he's started to feed the others to see if they'll grow. She comes home and finds him stretched by the fireplace, looking through a book about plants. Their plant isn't pictured, he tells her, but it may be mentioned in the text. She goes into the other room to look at the plant. The shoot appears to be taller. They bought the plant in a food store last winter—not very pretty then. It was in a small cracked pot, wrapped in plastic. They replanted it. In fact, David must have replanted it again.

She puts away the groceries and goes back to the living room. David is still on the rug reading the book. He's engrossed. The coffee would probably get cold if she brought it. She has to work that night. She goes upstairs to take a nap and sets the alarm. She rests, but can't fall asleep, listening to the quiet music downstairs. She pushes in the alarm button and goes back to the living

room. David is in his chair, reading the book, drinking coffee.

"I spent the most terrible winter in my life in Berlin. I don't know why, but birds don't leave Berlin in the winter. They're big, strong birds. They nest in the public buildings. I think the winter just comes too suddenly in Berlin, no plans can be made. The birds turn gray, like snowbirds. I think snowbirds are gray."

The old man is looking out the window. He is her patient. His daughter and son-in-law are away for a week, and his sister stays with him in the day. She has been hired to stay with him at night. He is not very ill, but old and unsteady.

She drinks tea with him, tired because she didn't nap.

"I don't sleep well," he tells her. "I want to talk all the time. My daughter doesn't sleep either. In the day we fight, or I worry her, but at night I think she's glad to have someone to talk to."

The snowplow is passing the house, slowly, the lights blinking against the newly plowed snowpiles. The lights illuminate a snowman on the next lawn—crudely made, or perhaps it's just not lit up from the right angle. She remembers her first snowman; her mother broke off the broom handle to give her and helped push the handle through the snowman. Her mother was impetuous, always letting her stay home from school to enjoy the snow, and her father had been surprised when he returned from work to see the broom head on the kitchen table. "Well, we couldn't get out. How could we go out in the snow to get anything?" her mother had asked her father. The snowplow has passed. Except for the wind, it is very quiet outside. In the room, the man is talking to her. He wants to show her his postcards. She's surprised; she hadn't realized she was being spoken to.

"Oh, not that kind of postcard. I'm an old man. Just pretty postcards."

He has opened a night-table drawer. Inside there is a box of tissues, a comb and brush, an alarm clock. He sits on the side of the bed, his feet not quite touching the floor, reaching into the drawer without looking. He finds what he wants: an envelope. He removes it and carefully pulls out the flap. He lets her look through the postcards. There is a bird's nest full of cherubs,[1] a picture of a lady elegantly dressed in a high, ruffled collar, curtseying beneath a flowering tree, and one that she looks at longer than the rest: a man in boots and a green jacket, carrying a rifle, is pictured walking down a path through the woods in the moonlight. Stars shine in the sky and illuminate a path in front of him. Tiny silver sparkles still adhere to the postcard. She holds it under the lamp on the night table: the lining of his jacket is silver, the edges of the rocks, a small area of the path. There is a caption: "Joseph Jefferson as Rip Van Winkle."[2] Beneath the caption is a message, ornately written: "Not yet but soon, Pa."

"Did your father write the postcard?"

"That's just one I found in a store long ago. I could make up a romantic story to tell you. I love to talk."

She waits, expecting the man's story. He leans back in bed, putting the envelope back in the drawer. His bedroom slippers fall to the floor, and he puts his legs under the covers.

"People get old and they can't improve things," he says, "so they lie all the time."

He waves his hand, dismissing something.

"I trust young people," he says. "I'd even tell you where my money is: in the dresser drawer, in the back of a poetry book."

The snowplow has returned, driving up the other side of the street. The lights cast patterns on the wall. He watches the shadows darken the wallpaper.

---

1. cherubs (cher' əbz) *n.*: Representations of heavenly beings as winged children with chubby, rosy faces.
2. Rip Van Winkle: A character who sleeps for twenty years without awakening in a story by Washington Irving.

"I have real stories," he says, pointing to a photograph album on a table by the chair. "Look through and I can tell you some real stories if you want to know."

He is ready to sleep. She arranges the quilt at the bottom of the bed and starts to leave.

"The light doesn't bother me," he says, waving her toward the chair. "Look through my album. I'm old and cranky. I'm afraid for my pictures to leave the room."

It's early afternoon and no one is in the house. There are dishes on the dining-room table, records and record-album covers. There's a plate, a spoon, two bowls, three coffee cups. How many people have been here? There's no one to ask. There's some food on the counter top—things she doesn't remember buying. An apple pie. She goes into the living room and sits in a chair, looking out the window. More snow is predicted, but now the day is clear and bright, the fields shining in the sun. She goes into the kitchen again to look for the note he hasn't left. On her way to the bedroom to sleep, she looks out the window and sees David coming up the road, only a sweater and scarf on, holding a stick at his side that the dog is jumping for. On the floor by the chair the plant book is open, and several others, books he's studying for his exams. The front door is open. The dog runs into the living room, jumps on her.

"You should be asleep. You can't work at night if you're not going to sleep in the day."

"I thought I'd wait for you to come back."

"You shouldn't have waited. I could have been anywhere."

"Where would you go?"

He's chilled. His knuckles are bright pink, untying the scarf at his throat. He's putting another log on the fire, pushing the screen back into place.

"How's the old man?"

"He's no trouble. Last night I fixed his photograph album for him. Some of the pictures had come loose and I glued them in."

"You look like you need sleep."

"Looks like you've been working," she says, pointing to the books by the chair.

"I've had trouble concentrating. The snow was so beautiful last night. I took the dog out for long walks in the woods."

David is stroking the dog, who lies curled by the fire, panting in his sleep.

"Get some rest," he says, looking at his watch. "I met the people who moved in down the hill and told them I'd help put a sink in. He's very nice. Katherine and Larry Duane."

David kisses her on his way out. The dog wakes and wants to go with him, but at the front door he's told to stay. The dog whines when the door closes, then waits a minute longer before going back to the living room to sleep by the fireplace.

"It's awful. When you get old you expect things to be the same. Sometimes I think the cold air could clear my head. My neighbor is ten years younger than me and he jogs every day, even through snow."

"I'm leaving now," his sister says. She puts on a blue coat and a blue velvet cap that ties under the chin. Her hair is white and copper. She has small, dainty hands. She repeats that she's leaving and pats him on the shoulder, more to make sure he's listening than out of affection. "There are oranges in the bag on your bureau. Linus Pauling says that a sufficient intake of vitamin C will prevent colds."

"How would I get a cold? Every day is the same. I don't go out."

Her coat is buttoned, her hat tied securely. "That's like asking where dust comes from," she says, and disappears down the stairs.

"She's very good to come every day. I forget to thank her. I take it for granted. Fifteen years makes so much difference. She's able to do so much more, but her hands hurt her. She does embroidery so they don't go stiff."

He is looking through a book of Currier and Ives prints.[3] "I suppose I'll have to eat her oranges. There'll be more from Florida when they get back."

She looks at a picture he holds up for her to see, offers to read him science-fiction stories.

"I don't think so. My sister read them this morning. I've had enough make-believe. No spaceships are coming to Earth today, only snow."

She looks at her watch to see if it's time for his medicine. Her watch isn't there. Did she forget to wear it? He asks for tea, and while the water is boiling in the kitchen she dials David, to see if the watch is on the night table. She hangs up and dials again, but there's still no answer. She looks out the window and sees that it has already begun to snow. Perhaps she lost the watch on the way in. The clasp was loose—she should have asked David to fix it. She turns off the burner and goes outside, looking quickly up and down the front walk before the snow begins to accumulate. She doesn't see it. The car? She looks, but it isn't there. She looks on the front steps and in the entranceway. No. It must be at home. She reheats the water, making tea, and carries the cup and saucer upstairs.

She puts it down quietly on the bureau. He's fallen asleep. She sits in a chair and watches the snow fall, and in a while she closes her eyes and begins imagining things: mountains, and blue, blue water, all the snow melted into water. This time the name of the country comes to her: Greece. She's been sent to Greece to find something on the beach, but she just stands there staring at the mountains in the distance, the water washing over her feet. Her feet are cold; she takes them out of the water, backing up onto the sandy beach. She's lifted her feet from the floor, waking up. She goes to the bureau and gets the tea, even though it's cold. The snow is falling heavily now. Everything is blanketed in whiteness; it clings to the trees, her car is covered with snow. She must have slept through the night. She hears his sister downstairs, closing the door behind her.

"I take her for granted," the old man

---

3. Currier and Ives prints: Nineteenth-century lithographs depicting the manners, people, and events of the times.

says. "Like snow. Every day I expect more snow."

The plant is gone. She looks in all the rooms and can't find it. Her watch is on the bathroom sink, where she put it when she showered. She showers again and washes her hair, blows it dry. The bathroom is steamy; she can't see her face in the glass.

"David?"

She thought she heard something, but it was only a branch brushing against the bathroom window. She walks naked up to the bedroom and puts on jeans and one of David's sweaters. She notices that some of the books he's been studying have been replaced in the bookcase. Now she's sure she hears him. The dog runs into the house. The front door bangs shut.

"Hi," she calls.

"Hi." David is climbing the steps. "I'm not used to you working for a whole week. I never see you." His cheeks are so cold they sting when he kisses her. "I was down at the Duanes'. They had puppies born this morning."

"What kind?"

"Collies."

"Take me to see them," she says.

"They were going out when I left."

"We could go later in the afternoon."

"They'll think I live there," he laughs.

"It's good for you to be out. You've been working so hard."

"I haven't done any work for a couple of days."

"Yes you have. I saw pages of notes on the dining-room table."

"Larry left his notes behind. He brought them down to read me an article he's working on. He teaches at the university, Botany."

"Botany?" she says. "Is that what happened to the plant?"

"They liked it so much I gave it to them. It was such a freak thing, to grow that way in the winter."

She calls early in the morning: 4 A.M.

The telephone rings, and there is no answer. The old man can tell that she's worried when he awakens.

"I tried to get my husband last night but there was no answer."

"Men are heavy sleepers."

"No," she says. "He'd wake up."

"All men are heavy sleepers. I can sleep when people are talking—I don't even hear the children talking on their way to school any more. I can sleep with the light on."

"I think school was canceled," she says, looking out the window.

It has snowed all night. It's still snowing.

"Call my sister and tell her not to come," he says. "If anything happens I can call."

She picks up the phone in the upstairs hallway and gives his sister the message, but the old lady is coming anyway. She has boots and an umbrella, and she's coming. He shakes his head.

"It's terrible to be old. You have no power."

He gets out of bed and opens a bureau drawer.

"Can I help you?"

"I'm putting on my things to go for a walk in the snow."

"You should stay inside. It's too cold today."

"I don't feel the cold any more. I can go out."

"Have breakfast first," she says.

"No. I want to go out before she comes."

She leaves the room while he dresses. He takes a long time. Maybe his sister will come early, before they go out. No. He opens the door and walks out without his cane, wearing a sweater and a silk scarf tucked into the neck.

"My jacket is in the hall closet," he says. "I need the air."

She helps him down the stairs. He doesn't weigh much. She asks if he'll take his cane, but he wants her arm instead. She gets his jacket and holds it for him to put on. She takes her own jacket out of the closet and zips it.

It's bright outside. They both stop, momentarily blinded by the glare. The snow is wet and deep.

"Just down the walk," she says.

"Yes. All right."

Children, off from school, are playing in the yards. Someone has already built a snowman. He likes it, wants a closer look. They go down the walk to the sidewalk. The children next door call hello. A little boy comes over to tell the old man about the snowman he's built. On another lawn some children are building a fort. Two little girls in snowsuits are carrying snow to the fort in buckets. She sees a big boy push a small boy into a snowbank. It's just fun. It's not just fun—he's kicking snow on him, kicking the little boy.

"Wait!" she says.

The big boy kicks snow in her face and runs. She pulls the younger boy out of the snow, brushing it out of his hair.

"What happened?" she asks him. He's crying, brushing himself and pointing to the boy who ran away at the same time. Now another boy is screaming. She turns and sees that the old man has slipped in the snow. She runs back. He's red in the face, but he's all right. He bent over to make a snowball and one of the children accidentally ran into him. She reaches down to help him up. He's light, but it's hard to get a good grip. The pavement is slippery, she's afraid she might slip. She sends one of the children home to get his mother. But a man walking down the sidewalk has already bent to help the old man up.

"What are you doing here?"

"I came to pick you up," David says. "Your car never would have made it up the hill. I had chains put on."

They help the old man into the house. In the hallway he brushes snow off his shoulders, embarrassed and angry. He thinks the child knocked him over on purpose. She hangs up his coat and David helps him upstairs. He goes up the stairs more quickly than he came down, talking about the boy who knocked into him. But he's forgotten about it by the time his sister arrives. He's telling David about Berlin in the winter, about the birds. He complains about his memory—Berlin must have been beautiful in the spring. When his sister arrives she's brought fruit for her, too, saying that she's a nurse, she must know about Dr. Pauling. It's her last day. The daughter and the husband will be coming home from Florida. But the sister comes every day, even when they're home—she has an umbrella and high boots. Wait. The old man has something for her: a postcard. He's giving her the postcard. The stars twinkle brightly in her hand.

The children are still playing when she goes outside with David. The big boy she spoke to earlier hides behind a car and tries to hit them with a snowball, but he misses. David's mad at her, mad that she took the old man out. He won't speak.

"We'll have to go back for my car," she says.

No answer.

"I called you last night and there was no answer."

He looks up. "You called?"

"Yes. You weren't there."

"I didn't know it was you. I was asleep. Why were you calling?"

The snow is very deep. He's driving slowly, concentrating so the car doesn't skid. On the radio, the weather forecast calls for more snow.

"I guess you were walking the dog in the woods," she says.

"I just told you," he says. "I was asleep."

She closes her eyes, imagines him sleeping, then imagines him with the dog, pulling a broken branch out of the snow, holding it high for the dog to jump up. The dog yelps, runs in circles, but the snow is too deep to jump out of. David is asleep, under the covers. He's walking up the hill, the dog barking, jumping for the stick. She tries to imagine more, but she's afraid that if she doesn't open her eyes she'll fall asleep in the car.

Back in the house, she closes her eyes again. He's drawn the curtains, and the room is a little less bright. She's very tired. The dog whines outside the door, wanting

David. David takes his trumpet off the night table and puts it in the case. He must be practicing again.

David leaves, saying that he's going downstairs to clean up. She hears some noise: cups and saucers? and much later, ringing. She's calling David, but there's no answer. David is calling her at the foot of the stairs.

"What?"

"Someone on the phone for you."

She goes downstairs to answer the phone. She sits at a chair by the table. The table is clear. Everything has been cleared away.

"Hello?"

The voice is soft. She can hardly hear. It's the old man's sister. She's tired of the old man and his sister, tired of work. She had already dismissed the old man from her mind, like last week's dreams, but now the old man's sister has called. His sister is upset. She's talking about the snow. Apparently she's snowed in, the snow is deeper than her boots, she's been trying to reach her husband to tell him. The planes from Florida won't land. No planes are landing. The old lady is thanking her for taking care of her brother. Why is she whispering?

"I come every day. I have my umbrella and my high boots so I can do my duty. I always try to bring him things that will please him so he won't think I only do it because I have to. My niece has to get away. He's so demanding. He wants her attention all day and night."

She's still half asleep, squinting against the glare, straining to hear. His sister is at the phone outside his bedroom in the hallway. The plane is still in Florida; it hasn't left because it can't land. His sister is asking if there's any way she can come back.

As she talks, the runway is buried deeper in snow. They're trying to clear it, but the snow is heavy, the planes can't land. The planes from Greece won't land. Now no one is on the beach in Greece, or at home in the United States; they're up in the air, up above the snow. She's sitting in a chair by the table. The table is clear. What was on the table when she came in? David has cleaned the room.

"You're so lucky," the woman whispers. "You can come and go. You don't know what it's like to be caught."

RESPONDING TO THE SELECTION

Your Response

1. How would you feel if you were in the place of the young woman in the story? Why?
2. (a) What are your feelings about each of the characters? (b) Which character do you like best? Why? (c) Which character do you like least? Why?

Recalling

3. (a) What is the young woman's occupation? (b) What is David's occupation? (c) How do their occupations prevent them from spending a great deal of time together?

4. Why does the old man's sister call the young woman at the end of the story?

Interpreting

5. How would you describe the story's mood?
6. (a) What hints does Beattie provide that the relationship between the young woman and David is somewhat strained? (b) What might be the main cause of this tension?
7. (a) How is the old man's attitude toward his sister similar to David's attitude toward the young woman? (b) In what sense is the young woman's situation similar to the sister's situation? (c) What is ironic, or surprising, about the sister's final comment?
8. What do you think the snow symbolizes, or represents, in the story?

Applying

9. Do you think it would be possible for the young woman to change her situation? Why or why not?

ANALYZING LITERATURE

Understanding Postmodernism

"Imagined Scenes" is an excellent example of a common type of Postmodernist fiction. Written in the form of a broken sequence of scenes, the story's structure reflects the disjointed, fragmentary quality of contemporary life. Using a detached narrator, Beattie pieces together a series of events without transitions or explanations, making the reader feel as if he or she is actually witnessing the events, rather than having them described.

1. How are the beginning and ending of the story unlike those used in traditional short stories?
2. Why is the overall structure of the story appropriate for its subject?
3. What does this story suggest about the ability of people in contemporary society to communicate with one another?

CRITICAL THINKING AND READING

Thinking Metaphorically

In her story Beattie captures the human tendency to think metaphorically, or to seek to understand and explain the world through the use of implicit comparisons. For example, the old man associates the onset of winter with the birds he remembers seeing during his winter in Berlin.

1. What do the postcards represent to the old man?

2. What do the scenes the young woman imagines represent to her?

THINKING AND WRITING

Writing About Structure

Write an essay in which you analyze the structure of "Imagined Scenes" and discuss its relationship to the subject of the story and its theme. Reread the story, focusing on its structure. Prepare a thesis statement. Then write your essay, using evidence from the story to support your thesis. When you finish writing, revise your essay, making sure you have supported your analysis with details from the story. Proofread your essay and share it with your classmates.

LEARNING OPTIONS

1. **Speaking and Listening.** How do you think the young woman really feels about her life? What would happen if she confronted her husband with these feelings? Pair up with a classmate and work together to create a script for a confrontation between the woman and her husband. Try to make the dialogue consistent with the way the characters speak in the story. When you have finished, act out the scene for your classmates.
2. **Writing.** What places might the young couple visit if they go to Greece? Create an itinerary for a two- or three-week vacation. Include the places that you think the young couple would most enjoy visiting. Present your itinerary to the class and explain why you have included each stop.

ALICE WALKER

1944–

In her essay "In Search of Our Mothers' Gardens," Alice Walker asks: "What did it mean for a black woman to be an artist in our grand-mothers' time? In our great-grandmothers' day? It is a question with an answer cruel enough to stop the blood." She goes on to mourn the loss of the creative souls driven mad by the constraints of slav-ery. "But," Walker continues, "this is not the end of the story. . . ." She describes the strength of those who survived and handed on their creative spark. This creative spark fuels Walker's stories and poetry.

Born in Eatonton, Georgia, halfway between Atlanta and the South Carolina border, Walker was the youngest child in a family of sharecroppers. Of her childhood she writes: "It was great fun being cute. But then, one day, it ended." Scarred and nearly blinded by a BB-gun pellet, Walker reports that she did not lift her head for six years. When the scar tissue on her eye was removed, her self-con-fidence returned. She left high school as valedictorian and most pop-ular student.

Walker attended Spelman College, an elite college for African American women in Atlanta, Georgia. After two years she transferred to Sarah Lawrence College in Bronxville, New York, where she wrote the poems that were to make up her first book, *Once.* Published in 1968, the collection is notable for both the poems in which Walker shares her impressions of a summer visit to Africa and those in which she describes the struggle for civil rights in her native Georgia.

After graduating from Sarah Lawrence, Walker moved to Mis-sissippi to work in the civil rights movement. Hired as a writer-in-residence and teacher of black studies at Jackson State University, she began a career of writing and teaching and soon earned a rep-utation as one of the nation's finest young writers. Her first novel, *The Third Life of Grange Copeland,* was published in 1970. It was followed by several volumes of poetry, two collections of stories, a number of essays and critical works, and a second novel, all within twelve years.

The 1982 publication of a third novel, *The Color Purple,* trans-formed "an intense reputation into a national one." This novel about an indomitable woman named Celie was both a critical and a pop-ular success. Awarded both a Pulitzer Prize and an American Book Award, it was later made into a successful motion picture.

Since *The Color Purple,* Walker has written two more novels and several popular collections of poems and essays, including "In Search of Our Mothers' Gardens" (1983). The publication of each new book has been a literary event.

GUIDE FOR INTERPRETING

Everyday Use

Writers' Techniques

Character. A character is a person (or an animal) in a literary work. To make a character believable and his or her actions understandable, a writer must provide **motivation**—a reason for the character's thoughts, feelings, actions, or speech.

Characters are motivated by their values and by their wants, desires, dreams, wishes, and needs. Sometimes the reasons for a character's actions are stated directly, as in "The First Seven Years" when Sobel reveals his love for Miriam, explaining why he sacrificed five years of his life working for her father. At other times a character's motivation is implied. For example, when Lucynell Crater, the old woman in "The Life You Save May Be Your Own," suggests that Mr. Shiftlet teach her daughter to say "sugarpie," you know what is on her mind. The more effectively a writer presents a character's motivation, the more convincing the character will be.

Focus

In the story "Everyday Use," Walker describes the homecoming of a young woman who informed her mother in a letter that "no matter where we [her mother and sister] 'choose' to live, she will manage to come see us. But she will never bring her friends." What do you think might have motivated the young woman to leave home? What do you think motivates her return?

Primary Source

The story "Everyday Use" has been described as a fictional illustration of Walker's essay "In Search of Our Mothers' Gardens." In the essay Walker explores her maternal heritage, describing the creative legacy of "ordinary" black Southern women. Here is how she describes the functional art created by someone's grandmother:

> [I]n the Smithsonian Institution in Washington, D.C., there hangs a quilt unlike any other in the world. In fanciful, inspired, and yet simple and identifiable figures, it portrays the story of the Crucifixion. It is considered rare, beyond price. Though it follows no known pattern of quilt-making, and though it is made of bits and pieces of worthless rags, it is obviously the work of a person of powerful imagination and deep spiritual feeling. Below this quilt I saw a note that says it was made by "an anonymous Black woman in Alabama, a hundred years ago."
>
> If we could locate this "anonymous" black woman from Alabama, she would turn out to be one of our grandmothers—an artist who left her mark in the only materials she could afford, . . .

Everyday Use

Alice Walker

I will wait for her in the yard that Maggie and I made so clean and wavy yesterday afternoon. A yard like this is more comfortable than most people know. It is not just a yard. It is like an extended living room. When the hard clay is swept clean as a floor and the fine sand around the edges lined with tiny, irregular grooves, anyone can come and sit and look up into the elm tree and wait for the breezes that never come inside the house.

Maggie will be nervous until after her sister goes: she will stand hopelessly in corners, homely and ashamed of the burn scars down her arms and legs, eying her sister with a mixture of envy and awe. She thinks her sister has held life always in the palm of one hand, that "no" is a word the world never learned to say to her.

You've no doubt seen those TV shows where the child who has "made it" is confronted, as a surprise, by her own mother and father, tottering in weakly from backstage. (A pleasant surprise, of course: What would they do if parent and child came on the show only to curse out and insult each other?) On TV mother and child embrace and smile into each other's faces. Sometimes the mother and father weep, the child wraps them in her arms and leans across the table to tell how she would not have made it without their help. I have seen these programs.

Sometimes I dream a dream in which Dee and I are suddenly brought together on a TV program of this sort. Out of a dark and soft-seated limousine I am ushered into a bright room filled with many people. There I meet a smiling, gray, sporty man like Johnny Carson who shakes my hand and tells me what a fine girl I have. Then we are on the stage and Dee is embracing me with tears in her eyes. She pins on my dress a large orchid, even though she has told me once that she thinks orchids are tacky flowers.

In real life I am a large, big-boned woman with rough, man-working hands. In the winter I wear flannel nightgowns to bed and overalls during the day. I can kill and clean a hog as mercilessly as a man. My fat keeps me hot in zero weather. I can work outside all day, breaking ice to get water for washing; I can eat pork liver cooked over the open fire minutes after it comes steaming from the hog. One winter I knocked a bull calf straight in the brain between the eyes with a sledge hammer and had the meat hung up to chill before nightfall. But of course all of this does not show on television. I am the way my daughter would want me to be: a hundred pounds lighter, my skin like an uncooked barley pancake. My hair glistens in the hot bright lights. Johnny Carson has much to do to keep up with my quick and witty tongue.

But that is a mistake. I know even before I wake up. Who ever knew a Johnson with a quick tongue? Who can even imagine me looking a strange white man in the eye? It seems to me I have talked to them always with one foot raised in flight, with my head turned in whichever way is farthest from them. Dee, though. She would always look anyone in the eye. Hesitation was no part of her nature.

"How do I look, Mama?" Maggie says, showing just enough of her thin body enveloped in pink skirt and red blouse for me to know she's there, almost hidden by the door.

"Come out into the yard," I say.

Have you ever seen a lame animal, perhaps a dog run over by some careless person rich enough to own a car, sidle up to someone who is ignorant enough to be kind to him? That is the way my Maggie walks. She has been like this, chin on chest, eyes on ground, feet in shuffle, ever since the fire that burned the other house to the ground.

Dee is lighter than Maggie, with nicer hair and a fuller figure. She's a woman now, though sometimes I forget. How long ago was it that the other house burned? Ten, twelve years? Sometimes I can still hear the flames and feel Maggie's arms sticking to me, her hair smoking and her dress falling off her in little black papery flakes. Her eyes seemed stretched open, blazed open by the flames reflected in them. And Dee. I see her standing off under the sweet gum tree she used to dig gum out of; a look of concentration on her face as she watched the last dingy gray board of the house fall in toward the red-hot brick chimney. Why don't you do a dance around the ashes? I'd want to ask her. She had hated the house that much.

I used to think she hated Maggie, too. But that was before we raised the money, the church and me, to send her to Augusta to school. She used to read to us without pity; forcing words, lies, other folks' habits, whole lives upon us two, sitting trapped and ignorant underneath her voice. She washed us in a river of make-believe, burned us with a lot of knowledge we didn't necessarily need to know. Pressed us to her with the serious way she read, to shove us away at just the moment, like dimwits, we seemed about to understand.

Dee wanted nice things. A yellow organdy dress to wear to her graduation from high school; black pumps to match a green suit she'd made from an old suit somebody gave me. She was determined to stare down any disaster in her efforts. Her eyelids would not flicker for minutes at a time. Often I fought off the temptation to shake her. At sixteen she had a style of her own, and knew what style was.

I never had an education myself. After second grade the school was closed down. Don't ask me why: in 1927 colored asked fewer questions than they do now. Sometimes Maggie reads to me. She stumbles along good-naturedly but can't see well. She knows she is not bright. Like good looks and money, quickness passed her by. She will

SUNSET AND MOONRISE WITH MAUDELL STREET, 1978
Romare Bearden
Courtesy of the Estate of Romare Bearden

marry John Thomas (who has mossy teeth in an earnest face) and then I'll be free to sit here and I guess just sing church songs to myself. Although I never was a good singer. Never could carry a tune. I was always better at a man's job. I used to love to milk till I was hooved in the side in '49. Cows are soothing and slow and don't bother you, unless you try to milk them the wrong way.

I have deliberately turned my back on the house. It is three rooms, just like the one that burned, except the roof is tin; they don't make shingle roofs any more. There are no real windows, just some holes cut in the sides, like the portholes in a ship, but not round and not square, with rawhide holding the shutters up on the outside. This house is in a pasture, too, like the other one. No doubt when Dee sees it she will want to tear it down. She wrote me once that no matter where we "choose" to live, she will manage to come see us. But she will never bring her friends. Maggie and I thought about this and Maggie asked me, "Mama, when did Dee ever *have* any friends?"

She had a few. Furtive boys in pink shirts hanging about on washday after school. Nervous girls who never laughed. Impressed with her they worshiped the well-turned phrase, the cute shape, the scalding humor that erupted like bubbles in lye. She read to them.

When she was courting Jimmy T she didn't have much time to pay to us, but turned all her faultfinding power on him. He *flew* to marry a cheap city girl from a family of ignorant flashy people. She hardly had time to recompose herself.

When she comes I will meet—but there they are!

Maggie attempts to make a dash for the house, in her shuffling way, but I stay her with my hand. "Come back here," I say. And she stops and tries to dig a well in the sand with her toe.

It is hard to see them clearly through the strong sun. But even the first glimpse of leg out of the car tells me it is Dee. Her feet were always neat-looking, as if God himself had shaped them with a certain style. From the other side of the car comes a short, stocky man. Hair is all over his head a foot long and hanging from his chin like a kinky mule tail. I hear Maggie suck in her breath. "Uhnnnh," is what it sounds like. Like when you see the wriggling end of a snake just in front of your foot on the road. "Uhnnnh."

Dee next. A dress down to the ground, in this hot weather. A dress so loud it hurts my eyes. There are yellows and oranges enough to throw back the light of the sun. I feel my whole face warming from the heat waves it throws out. Earrings gold, too, and hanging down to her shoulders. Bracelets dangling and making noises when she moves her arm up to shake the folds of the dress out of her armpits. The dress is loose and flows, and as she walks closer, I like it. I hear Maggie go "Uhnnnh" again. It is her sister's hair. It stands straight up like the wool on a sheep. It is black as night and around the edges are two long pigtails that rope about like small lizards disappearing behind her ears.

"Wa-su-zo-Tean-o!"[1] she says, coming on in that gliding way the dress makes her move. The short stocky fellow with the hair to his navel is all grinning and he follows up with "Asalamalakim,[2] my mother and sister!" He moves to hug Maggie but she falls back, right up against the back of my chair. I feel her trembling there and when I look up I see the perspiration falling off her chin.

"Don't get up," says Dee. Since I am stout it takes something of a push. You can see me trying to move a second or two before I make it. She turns, showing white heels through her sandals, and goes back to the car. Out she peeks next with a Polaroid. She stoops down quickly and lines up picture after picture of me sitting there in front of the house

---

1. Wa-su-zo-Tean-o (wä so͞o zō tēn′ ō): An African greeting.

2. Asalamalakim: *Salaam aleikhim* (sə läm′ ä lī′ kēm′), an Islamic greeting meaning "Peace be with you."

with Maggie cowering behind me. She never takes a shot without making sure the house is included. When a cow comes nibbling around the edge of the yard she snaps it and me and Maggie *and* the house. Then she puts the Polaroid in the back seat of the car, and comes up and kisses me on the forehead.

Meanwhile Asalamalakim is going through motions with Maggie's hand. Maggie's hand is as limp as a fish, and probably as cold, despite the sweat, and she keeps trying to pull it back. It looks like Asalamalakim wants to shake hands but wants to do it fancy. Or maybe he don't know how people shake hands. Anyhow, he soon gives up on Maggie.

"Well," I say. "Dee."

"No, Mama," she says. "Not 'Dee,' Wangero Leewanika Kemanjo!"

"What happened to 'Dee'?" I wanted to know.

"She's dead," Wangero said. "I couldn't bear it any longer, being named after the people who oppress me."

"You know as well as me you was named after your aunt Dicie," I said. Dicie is my sister. She named Dee. We called her "Big Dee" after Dee was born.

"But who was *she* named after?" asked Wangero.

"I guess after Grandma Dee," I said.

"And who was she named after?" asked Wangero.

"Her mother," I said, and saw Wangero was getting tired. "That's about as far back as I can trace it," I said. Though, in fact, I probably could have carried it back beyond the Civil War through the branches.

"Well," said Asalamalakim, "there you are."

"Uhnnnh," I heard Maggie say.

"There I was not," I said, "before 'Dicie' cropped up in our family, so why should I try to trace it that far back?"

He just stood there grinning, looking down on me like somebody inspecting a Model A car. Every once in a while he and Wangero sent eye signals over my head.

"How do you pronounce this name?" I asked.

"You don't have to call me by it if you don't want to," said Wangero.

"Why shouldn't I?" I asked. "If that's what you want us to call you, we'll call you."

"I know it might sound awkward at first," said Wangero.

"I'll get used to it," I said. "Ream it out again."

Well, soon we got the name out of the way. Asalamalakim had a name twice as long and three times as hard. After I tripped over it two or three times he told me to just call him Hakim-a-barber. I wanted to ask him was he a barber, but I didn't really think he was, so I didn't ask.

"You must belong to those beef-cattle people down the road," I said. They said "Asalamalakim" when they met you, too, but they didn't shake hands. Always too busy: feeding the cattle, fixing the fences, putting up salt-lick shelters, throwing down hay. When the white folks poisoned some of the herd the men stayed up all night with rifles in their hands. I walked a mile and a half just to see the sight.

Hakim-a-barber said, "I accept some of their doctrines, but farming and raising cattle is not my style." (They didn't tell me, and I didn't ask, whether Wangero (Dee) had really gone and married him.)

We sat down to eat and right away he said he didn't eat collards[3] and pork was unclean. Wangero, though, went on through the chitlins[4] and corn bread, the greens and everything else. She talked a blue streak over the sweet potatoes. Everything delighted her. Even the fact that we still used the benches her daddy made for the table when we couldn't afford to buy chairs.

"Oh, Mama!" she cried. Then turned to Hakim-a-barber. "I never knew how lovely

---

3. collards (käl′ ərdz) *n.*: The leaves of the collard plant, often referred to as "collard greens."

4. chitlins (chit′lənz) *n.*: Chitterlings, a pork dish popular among southern African Americans.

these benches are. You can feel the rump prints," she said, running her hands underneath her and along the bench. Then she gave a sigh and her hand closed over Grandma Dee's butter dish. "That's it!" she said. "I knew there was something I wanted to ask you if I could have." She jumped up from the table and went over in the corner where the churn stood, the milk in it clabber by now. She looked at the churn and looked at it.

"This churn top is what I need," she said. "Didn't Uncle Buddy whittle it out of a tree you all used to have?"

"Yes," I said.

"Uh huh," she said happily. "And I want the dasher, too."

"Uncle Buddy whittle that, too?" asked the barber.

Dee (Wangero) looked up at me.

"Aunt Dee's first husband whittled the dash," said Maggie so low you almost couldn't hear her. "His name was Henry, but they called him Stash."

"Maggie's brain is like an elephant's," Wangero said, laughing. "I can use the churn top as a centerpiece for the alcove table," she said, sliding a plate over the churn, "and I'll think of something artistic to do with the dasher."

When she finished wrapping the dasher the handle stuck out. I took it for a moment in my hands. You didn't even have to look close to see where hands pushing the dasher up and down to make butter had left a kind of sink in the wood. In fact, there were a lot of small sinks; you could see where thumbs and fingers had sunk into the wood. It was beautiful light yellow wood, from a tree that grew in the yard where Big Dee and Stash had lived.

After dinner Dee (Wangero) went to the trunk at the foot of my bed and started rifling through it. Maggie hung back in the kitchen over the dishpan. Out came Wangero with two quilts. They had been pieced by Grandma Dee and then Big Dee and me had hung them on the quilt frames on the front porch and

QUILT MADE BY AN UNKNOWN SLAVE
Courtesy of the MacIntosh Family

quilted them. One was in the Lone Star pattern. The other was Walk Around the Mountain. In both of them were scraps of dresses Grandma Dee had worn fifty and more years ago. Bits and pieces of Grandpa Jarrell's Paisley shirts. And one teeny faded blue piece, about the size of a penny matchbox, that was from Great Grandpa Ezra's uniform that he wore in the Civil War.

"Mama," Wangero said sweet as a bird. "Can I have these old quilts?"

I heard something fall in the kitchen, and a minute later the kitchen door slammed.

"Why don't you take one or two of the others?" I asked. "These old things was just done by me and Big Dee from some tops your grandma pieced before she died."

"No," said Wangero. "I don't want those. They are stitched around the borders by machine."

"That'll make them last better," I said.

"That's not the point," said Wangero. "These are all pieces of dresses Grandma used to wear. She did all this stitching by hand. Imagine!" She held the quilts securely in her arms, stroking them.

"Some of the pieces, like those lavender ones, come from old clothes her mother handed down to her," I said, moving up to touch the quilts. Dee (Wangero) moved back just enough so that I couldn't reach the quilts. They already belonged to her.

"Imagine!" she breathed again, clutching them closely to her bosom.

"The truth is," I said, "I promised to give them quilts to Maggie, for when she marries John Thomas."

She gasped like a bee had stung her.

"Maggie can't appreciate these quilts!" she said. "She'd probably be backward enough to put them to everyday use."

"I reckon she would," I said. "God knows I been saving 'em for long enough with nobody using 'em. I hope she will!" I didn't want to bring up how I had offered Dee (Wangero) a quilt when she went away to college. Then she had told me they were old-fashioned, out of style.

"But they're *priceless*!" she was saying now, furiously; for she has a temper. "Maggie would put them on the bed and in five years they'd be in rags. Less than that!"

"She can always make some more," I said. "Maggie knows how to quilt."

Dee (Wangero) looked at me with hatred. "You just will not understand. The point is these quilts, *these* quilts!"

"Well," I said, stumped. "What would *you* do with them?"

"Hang them," she said. As if that was the only thing you *could* do with quilts.

Maggie by now was standing in the door. I could almost hear the sound her feet made as they scraped over each other.

"She can have them, Mama," she said, like somebody used to never winning any-thing, or having anything reserved for her. "I can 'member Grandma Dee without the quilts."

I looked at her hard. She had filled her bottom lip with checkerberry snuff and it gave her face a kind of dopey, hangdog look. It was Grandma Dee and Big Dee who taught her how to quilt herself. She stood there with her scarred hands hidden in the folds of her skirt. She looked at her sister with something like fear but she wasn't mad at her. This was Maggie's portion. This was the way she knew God to work.

When I looked at her like that something hit me in the top of my head and ran down to the soles of my feet. Just like when I'm in church and the spirit of God touches me and I get happy and shout. I did something I never had done before: hugged Maggie to me, then dragged her on into the room, snatched the quilts out of Miss Wangero's hands and dumped them into Maggie's lap. Maggie just sat there on my bed with her mouth open.

"Take one or two of the others," I said to Dee.

But she turned without a word and went out to Hakim-a-barber.

"You just don't understand," she said, as Maggie and I came out to the car.

"What don't I understand?" I wanted to know.

"Your heritage," she said. And then she turned to Maggie, kissed her, and said, "You ought to try to make something of yourself, too, Maggie. It's really a new day for us. But from the way you and Mama still live you'd never know it."

She put on some sunglasses that hid everything above the tip of her nose and her chin.

Maggie smiled; maybe at the sunglasses. But a real smile, not scared. After we watched the car dust settle I asked Maggie to bring me a dip of snuff. And then the two of us sat there just enjoying, until it was time to go in the house and go to bed.

RESPONDING TO THE SELECTION

Your Response

1. What are your impressions of each character?
2. How do you feel about Dee's wanting nice things and leaving home? Explain.
3. Do you think that the narrator made the right choice at the end of the story? Explain.

Recalling

4. What dream does the narrator recall as she waits for Dee in the yard?
5. (a) What objects does Dee ask to have? (b) What does she intend to do with each one?
6. What is Dee's response when the narrator says that she has promised to give the quilts to Maggie?

Interpreting

7. (a) What do the narrator's remarks at the beginning of the story reveal about her relationship with each of her daughters? (b) How does her relationship with each one change during the course of the story?
8. (a) What is ironic about Dee's taking picture after picture of her family in front of the house? (b) What is ironic about her professed interest in her heritage?
9. (a) What do the quilts mean to Dee? (b) What do they mean to Maggie?
10. How well do you think the narrator understands her daughters? Explain.

Applying

11. Do you think that it would have been possible for Dee to embrace her African heritage without rejecting her American heritage? Explain.
12. (a) What heirlooms does your family treasure? (b) What makes them important?

ANALYZING LITERATURE

Understanding Character

To make the attitudes and actions of a character believable, a writer must directly or indirectly convey the reasons for the character's behavior. In "Everyday Use," for example, Maggie's hesitancy

clearly results, in part, from the terrible childhood accident that has left more than a physical scar.

1. What appears to motivate Dee's interest in her heritage?
2. Why would Dee assume that she could waltz into the house, ask for, and get the churn top, the dasher, and the quilts?
3. What motivates the narrator to snatch the quilts away from Dee?

CRITICAL THINKING AND READING

Contrasting Characters

Although Dee and Maggie are sisters, they have very little in common, aside from their mother and their interest in the two quilts. Contrast the two characters to learn about the essential differences between them.

1. How do Maggie and Dee differ (a) physically, (b) intellectually, and (c) emotionally?
2. What does each know about (a) her African heritage and (b) her American heritage?
3. (a) What is the relationship between the two sisters? (b) How do the family dynamics change when the narrator gives Maggie the quilt?

THINKING AND WRITING

Writing a Letter

Imagine Dee's sense of betrayal when her mother grabs the quilt from her and hands it to Maggie. Take Dee's part and write a letter to a friend in which you describe her thoughts and feelings about the incident and her impressions of her mother and sister. Write in character, keeping in mind that Dee "has held life always in the palm of one hand, that 'no' is a word the world never learned to say to her."

LEARNING OPTION

Performance. Bring the narrator's daydream to life. Dramatize a TV reunion between the narrator and Dee that takes place several years after Dee's visit. Assume that Dee, who has "made it" in some profession, has not been back home in the interim.

Nonfiction

PAINTED WATER GLASSES, 1974
Janet Fish
Collection Whitney Museum of American Art

CARSON McCULLERS

1917–1967

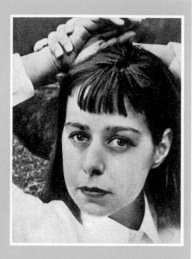

In her writing Carson McCullers captures the feelings of isolation and loneliness sometimes experienced by individuals living in a large, complex, and seemingly indifferent world. Although her works often express a bleak outlook, they also reflect her deep sense of compassion.

Born in Columbus, Georgia, McCullers displayed a great amount of musical talent as a young girl. When she was seventeen, she traveled to New York City to attend the Juilliard School of music, but she lost her tuition money on the subway. Unable to pursue her interest in music, she began taking writing courses at Columbia. She published her first story, "Wunderkind," when she was only nineteen, and her first novel, *The Heart Is a Lonely Hunter* (1940), was published when she was twenty-three.

McCullers went on to publish several more novels, including *The Member of the Wedding* (1945), *The Ballad of the Sad Cafe* (1951), and *Clock without Hands* (1961). Unfortunately, however, during her late twenties, she suffered a series of strokes that left her partially paralyzed and severely limited her ability to write. She remained steadfast in her efforts despite her physical difficulties. With the left side of her body partially paralyzed, it took her ten years to write *Clock without Hands.* She completed it by typing with one hand at the rate of one page a day.

Apart from her physical adversities, McCullers endured two difficult marriages to the same man, James Reeves McCullers. Reeves, a deeply troubled man, whom his wife's friends regarded as a delayed war casualty, eventually took his own life. McCullers wrote the play *The Square Root of Wonderful* to bring some understanding to his life and death.

McCullers's life held happy periods as well as troubled ones. Among the best were those spent in a rented brownstone in Brooklyn called February House with a group of writers and artists including Richard Wright, W. H. Auden, Christopher Isherwood, Louis MacNeice, and Gypsy Rose Lee. February House has been called a kind of a dream come true by McCullers. There, at least temporarily, she found the friendship and acceptance the heroines in her works often seek.

Four years after McCullers's death, *The Mortgaged Heart* (1971), an edition of her previously uncollected works, was published. In the following selection from this book, McCullers explores the causes of and possible solutions to the problem of loneliness.

GUIDE FOR INTERPRETING

Writers' Techniques

from The Mortgaged Heart

Argumentation. Argumentation is writing that attempts to convince the reader to accept a specific opinion or point of view. An argumentative essay, or an essay that focuses on presenting a convincing argument, can usually be divided into four parts: the introduction of the subject; the analysis of the subject; the presentation of the writer's opinion or point of view; and a brief summary of the writer's main points or ideas. In addition to following this type of logical organization, a writer must use facts and examples to support his or her opinion. The writer must also carefully consider his or her audience when writing the essay, making sure that the choice of facts and examples and the use of language are appropriate.

Focus

Carson McCullers's essay is about loneliness. What do you think are the main causes of loneliness in contemporary society? Prepare a list of reasons for people's loneliness; then list some possible solutions.

Primary Source

McCullers uses the essays in *The Mortgaged Heart* to discuss the methods and concerns of her own writing. In the essay "The Flowering Dream: Notes on Writing," she identifies the concern that is the basis of almost everything that she wrote: the problem of "spiritual isolation." Here are McCullers's observations:

> Spiritual isolation is the basis of most of my themes. My first book [*The Heart Is a Lonely Hunter*] was concerned with this, almost entirely, and all of my books since, in one way or another. Love, and especially love of a person who is incapable of returning or receiving it, is at the heart of my selection of grotesque figures to write about—people whose physical incapacity is a symbol of their spiritual incapacity to love or receive love—their spiritual isolation.

The Mortgaged Heart

Carson McCullers

This city, New York—consider the people in it, the eight million of us. An English friend of mine, when asked why he lived in New York City, said that he liked it here because he could be so alone. While it was my friend's desire to be alone, the aloneness of many Americans who live in cities is an involuntary and fearful thing. It has been said that loneliness is the great American malady. What is the nature of this loneliness? It would seem essentially to be a quest for identity.

To the spectator, the amateur philosopher, no motive among the complex ricochets of our desires and rejections seems stronger or more enduring than the will of the individual to claim his identity and belong. From infancy to death, the human being is obsessed by these dual motives. During our first weeks of life, the question of identity shares urgency with the need for milk. The baby reaches for his toes, then explores the bars of his crib; again and again he compares the difference between his own body and the objects around him, and in the wavering, infant eyes there comes a pristine wonder.

Consciousness of self is the first abstract problem that the human being solves. Indeed, it is this self-consciousness that removes us from lower animals. This primitive grasp of identity develops with constantly shifting emphasis through all our years. Perhaps maturity is simply the history of those mutations that reveal to the individual the relation between himself and the world in which he finds himself.

After the first establishment of identity there comes the imperative need to lose this new-found sense of separateness and to belong to something larger and more powerful than the weak, lonely self. The sense of moral isolation is intolerable to us.

In *The Member of the Wedding*[1] the lonely twelve-year-old girl, Frankie Addams, articulates this universal need: "The trouble with me is that for a long time I have just been an *I* person. All people belong to a *We* except me. Not to belong to a *We* makes you too lonesome."

Love is the bridge that leads from the *I* sense to the *We*, and there is a paradox about personal love. Love of another individual opens a new relation between the personality and the world. The lover responds in a new way to nature and may even write poetry. Love is affirmation; it motivates the *yes* responses and the sense of wider communication. Love casts out fear, and in the security of this togetherness we find contentment, courage. We no longer fear the age-old haunting questions: "Who am I?" "Why am I?" "Where am I going?"—and having cast out fear, we can be honest and charitable.

For fear is a primary source of evil. And when the question "Who am I?" recurs and is unanswered, then fear and frustration project a negative attitude. The bewildered soul can answer only: "Since I do not understand 'Who I am,' I only know what I am *not*." The corollary of this emotional incerti-

---

1. *The Member of the Wedding:* A novel and play by Carson McCullers.

NIGHT CITY
Richard Florsheim
Collection of Jane Golanty

tude is snobbism, intolerance and racial hate. The xenophobic individual can only reject and destroy, as the xenophobic nation inevitably makes war.

The loneliness of Americans does not have its source in xenophobia; as a nation we are an outgoing people, reaching always for immediate contacts, further experience. But we tend to seek out things as individuals, alone. The European, secure in his family ties and rigid class loyalties, knows little of the moral loneliness that is native to us Americans. While the European artists tend to form groups or aesthetic schools, the American artist is the eternal maverick—not only from society in the way of all creative minds, but within the orbit of his own art.

Thoreau took to the woods to seek the ultimate meaning of his life. His creed was simplicity and his *modus vivendi*[2] the deliberate stripping of external life to the Spartan[3] necessities in order that his inward life could freely flourish. His objective, as he put it, was to back the world into a corner. And in that way did he discover "What a man thinks of himself, that it is which determines, or rather indicates, his fate."

On the other hand, Thomas Wolfe turned to the city, and in his wanderings around New York he continued his frenetic and life-long search for the lost brother, the magic door. He too backed the world into a corner, and as he passed among the city's millions, returning their stares, he experienced "That silent meeting [that] is the summary of all the meetings of men's lives."

Whether in the pastoral joys of country life or in the labyrinthine city, we Americans are always seeking. We wander, question. But the answer waits in each separate heart—the answer of our own identity and the way by which we can master loneliness and feel that at last we belong.

---

2. *modus vivendi* (mō′ dəs vi ven′ dī): Latin for "manner of living."
3. Spartan (spär′ t'n) *adj.*: Characteristic of the people of ancient Sparta: hardy, stoical, severe, frugal.

RESPONDING TO THE SELECTION

Your Response

1. Do you agree with McCullers's premise that loneliness is the great American malady? Why or why not?
2. Can you relate to the sentiments that Frankie Addams expresses? Why or why not?
3. Where would you turn to seek "the ultimate meaning" of your life: to the woods, to the city, or somewhere else? Explain.

Recalling

4. According to the first paragraph, what is the nature of loneliness?

5. How does McCullers define maturity in the third paragraph?
6. What need develops after a person establishes his or her identity?
7. What difference between Europeans and Americans does McCullers point out in the eighth paragraph?
8. According to the final paragraph, what "waits in each separate heart"?

Interpreting

9. In the second paragraph, how does McCullers emphasize the urgency of the infant's search for identity?

10. How is Frankie Addams's age related to the statement she makes?
11. How is Wolfe's method of seeking the meaning of life different from Thoreau's?
12. (a) What does McCullers mean by the terms "moral isolation" and "moral loneliness"? (b) What does she mean when she comments that love "motivates the *yes* response"?

Applying

13. Do you think that today's Americans are more likely to be lonely than the early settlers? Why or why not?

ANALYZING LITERATURE

Understanding Argumentation

Argumentation is writing that attempts to convince the reader to accept a specific opinion or point of view. In her essay Carson McCullers attempts to convince readers to accept her conclusions about the causes of and possible solutions to the problem of loneliness.

1. Is McCullers's essay organized like a typical argumentative essay? Support your answer.
2. What is McCullers's opinion about the cause of loneliness in America?
3. What conclusion does she reach about the solution to the problem?
4. What examples does she use to support her conclusion?

CRITICAL THINKING AND READING

Understanding Paradoxes

A **paradox** is a statement that seems self-contradictory but in reality contains a possible truth. For example, McCullers presents a paradox in the first paragraph of her essay, stating that a friend of hers appreciated living in New York City because it enabled him to be alone.

1. Why does the paradox about life in New York City serve as an effective introduction to the essay?
2. What is paradoxical about a person's "dual motives" to claim his or her "identity and to belong"?

THINKING AND WRITING

Writing an Argumentative Essay

What opinions do you have that you would like to convince other people to accept? Think of a subject about which you have a strong opinion. Then write an argumentative essay focusing on this subject. Before you begin writing, decide on the audience you wish to address. When you write your essay, keep your intended audience in mind. Present your argument in the logical manner in which typical argumentative essays are organized. When you revise, make sure you have presented your opinions clearly and effectively.

LEARNING OPTION

Cross-curricular Connection. McCullers describes the American artist as "the eternal maverick." The word *maverick,* meaning a person who takes an independent stand, is of American origin: It can be traced back to Texas pioneer Samuel A. Maverick, who refused to brand his cattle. Together with classmates, generate a list of mavericks whom you admire. Is being a maverick an "American" quality?

RALPH ELLISON

1914–

In both his fiction and nonfiction, Ralph Ellison has confronted many of the problems faced by African Americans during the twentieth century. He has portrayed the quests of African Americans to discover and come to terms with their identities and has depicted their struggles against the obstacles of discrimination in American society.

Born in Oklahoma City, Ellison was educated at the Tuskegee Institute in Alabama, where he pursued his strong interest in music. Hoping to become a successful jazz musician, he moved to New York City. There he met Langston Hughes and Richard Wright, who helped inspire him to become a writer.

In 1952 Ellison published his first novel, *The Invisible Man.* The book, which recounts the often harrowing experiences of a nameless African American man, earned Ellison the National Book Award. Ellison's next book, a collection of essays and interviews called *Shadow and Act,* was published in 1964. This book includes "Hidden Name and Complex Fate," an essay in which he explores the relationship between his name and his identity.

Ralph Ellison is a writer of great magnitude. Since the publication of *The Invisible Man,* his work has enjoyed, for the most part, tremendous acclaim. In the late fifties, however, some African Americans decried the book for its moderate approach to race problems in America. Detractors felt that the book advocated sacrificing black culture to blend black America into white America. Ellison has discounted their objections as misinterpretations.

Ellison has noted that being both black and American has given definition to his work. The most valuable resource available to him, he feels, is his "double vision," his simultaneous position of being inside and outside American culture. It is a position, he says, of observation and perspective from which values can be studied in action. Ellison comments, "I've always written out of a sense of group experience as filtered through my individual experiences, talent, and vision." He goes on to say, "The problem of becoming an artist is related to that of becoming a man, of becoming visible. You need a discipline far more demanding than a loyalty to your racial group."

Those who know Ellison describe him as a stylistic perfectionist and "insanely ambitious" about his work. One old friend has said of Ellison's long-awaited second novel, it will not be released "until he is sure it is the greatest American novel ever written."

GUIDE FOR INTERPRETING

from Hidden Name and Complex Fate

Literary Forms

The Essay. An essay is a short prose work that generally focuses on a narrow topic. Essays can generally be divided into two categories: formal essays and informal essays. Formal essays are written using serious, dignified language and are carefully structured to inform, instruct, or persuade. At the beginning of the essay, the topic is clearly defined and an argument is presented. The writer then develops and supports the argument in the body of the essay and concludes with a brief summary or the presentation of an additional insight into the subject. In contrast, informal essays tend to be loosely organized and are generally written in a relaxed, intimate, conversational style. Less serious in purpose than formal essays, informal essays are usually written to amuse or entertain. Often informal essays attempt to evoke laughter, either by exploring an amusing subject or by treating a serious subject in an amusing manner.

Commentary

As you read "Hidden Name and Complex Fate," notice the power of names. Every person, object, or place is known by one or more words or names. The names we assign to represent things are symbols that take the place of things and thus allow people to communicate about them. For example, a young woman may be described repeatedly as a "dumb blonde." She will have no control over the name she has acquired, but it will affect her life greatly. People may pigeonhole her, feeling they know all about her through the derogatory epithet she unwillingly carries. They may not get to know her uniqueness any more than people talking about a tree will be likely to go outside and observe it for themselves. The greatest danger for the young woman, of course, is that she will accept the name applied to her. When that happens, language, one of man's greatest tools, has ceased to function in a positive way and has become a destructive club used for control. What are your feelings about names?

Focus

Freewrite about the relationship between people's names and their identities. How do you think most parents go about choosing names for their children? Why do you think parents often name their children after historical figures? Do you think that a person's name can in some way shape his or her development?

from Hidden Name and Complex Fate

Ralph Ellison

Once while listening to the play of a two-year-old girl who did not know she was under observation, I heard her saying over and over again, at first with questioning and then with sounds of growing satisfaction, "I am Mimi Livisay? . . . *I* am Mimi Livisay. I *am* Mimi Livisay . . . I am *Mimi* Li-vi-say! I am Mimi . . ."

And in deed and in fact she was—or became so soon thereafter, by working playfully to establish the unity between herself and her name.

For many of us this is far from easy. We must learn to wear our names within all the noise and confusion of the environment in which we find ourselves; make them the center of all of our associations with the world, with man and with nature. We must charge them with all our emotions, our hopes, hates, loves, aspirations. They must become our masks and our shields and the containers of all those values and traditions which we learn and/or imagine as being the meaning of our familial past.

And when we are reminded so constantly that we bear, as Negroes, names originally possessed by those who owned our enslaved grandparents, we are apt, especially if we are potential writers, to be more than ordinarily concerned with the veiled and mysterious events, the fusions of blood, the furtive couplings, the business transactions, the violations of faith and loyalty, the assaults; yes, and the unrecognized and unrecognizable loves through which our names were handed down unto us. . . .

Perhaps, taken in aggregate, these European names which (sometimes with irony, sometimes with pride, but always with personal investment) represent a certain triumph of the spirit, speaking to us of those who rallied, reassembled and transformed themselves and who under dismembering pressures refused to die. "Brothers and sisters," I once heard a Negro preacher exhort, "let us make up our faces before the world, and our names shall sound throughout the land with honor! For we ourselves are our *true* names, not their epithets! So let us, I say, Make Up Our Faces and Our Minds!"

Perhaps my preacher had read T. S. Eliot, although I doubt it. And in actuality, it was unnecessary that he do so, for a concern with names and naming was very much a part of that special area of American culture from which I come, and it is precisely for this reason that this example should come to mind in a discussion of my own experience as a writer.

Undoubtedly, writers begin their *conditioning* as manipulators of words long before they become aware of literature—certain Freudians[1] would say at the breast.[2] Per-

---

1. Freudians: People who believe in the theories and methods of Sigmund Freud (1856–1939), the founder of psychoanalysis.
2. at the breast: In infancy.

haps. But if so, that is far too early to be of use at this moment. Of this, though, I am certain: that despite the misconceptions of those educators who trace the reading difficulties experienced by large numbers of Negro children in Northern schools to their Southern background, these children are, in *their* familiar South, facile manipulators of words. I know, too, that the Negro community is deadly in its ability to create nicknames and to spot all that is ludicrous in an unlikely name or that which is incongruous in conduct. Names are not qualities; nor are words, in this particular sense, actions. To assume that they are could cost one his life many times a day. Language skills depend to a large extent upon a knowledge of the details, the manners, the objects, the folkways, the psychological patterns, of a given environment. Humor and wit depend upon much the same awareness, and so does the suggestive power of names.

"A small brown bowlegged Negro with the name 'Franklin D. Roosevelt Jones' might sound like a clown to someone who looks at him from the outside," said my friend Albert Murray, "but on the other hand he just might turn out to be a fireside operator. He might just lie back in all of that comic juxtaposition of names and manipulate you deaf, dumb and blind—and you not even suspecting it, because you're thrown out of stance by his name! There you are, so dazzled by the F.D.R. image—which you *know* you can't see—and so delighted with your own superior position that you don't realize that it's *Jones* who must be confronted."

Well, as you must suspect, all of this speculation on the matter of names has a purpose, and now, because it is tied up so ironically with my own experience as a writer, I must turn to my own name.

For in the dim beginnings, before I ever thought consciously of writing, there was my own name, and there was, doubtless, a certain magic in it. From the start I was uncomfortable with it, and in my earliest years it caused me much puzzlement. Neither could I understand what a poet was, nor why, exactly, my father had chosen to name me after one. Perhaps I could have understood it perfectly well had he named me after his own father, but that name had been given to an older brother who died and thus was out of the question. But why hadn't he named me after a hero, such as Jack Johnson,[3] or a soldier like Colonel Charles Young, or a great seaman like Admiral Dewey, or an educator like Booker T. Washington, or a great orator and abolitionist like Frederick Douglass? Or again, why hadn't he named me (as so many Negro parents had done) after President Teddy Roosevelt?

Instead, he named me after someone called Ralph Waldo Emerson, and then, when I was three, he died. It was too early for me to have understood his choice, although I'm sure he must have explained it many times, and it was also too soon for me to have made the connection between my name and my father's love for reading. Much later, after I began to write and work with words, I came to suspect that he was aware of the suggestive powers of names and of the magic involved in naming.

I recall an odd conversation with my mother during my early teens in which she mentioned their interest in, of all things, prenatal culture! But for a long time I actually knew only that my father read a lot, and that he admired this remote Mr. Emerson, who was something called a "poet and philosopher"—so much so that he named his second son after him.

I knew, also, that whatever his motives, the combination of names he'd given me caused me no end of trouble from the moment when I could talk well enough to respond to the ritualized question which grownups put to very young children. Emerson's name was quite familiar to Negroes in Oklahoma during those days when World

3. Jack Johnson (1878–1946): The world heavyweight boxing champion from 1908 through 1915.

MAN IN A VEST, 1939–1949
William H. Johnson
National Museum of American Art, Smithsonian Institution

War I was brewing, and adults, eager to show off their knowledge of literary figures, and obviously amused by the joke implicit in such a small brown nubbin[4] of a boy carrying around such a heavy moniker,[5] would invariably repeat my first two names and then to my great annoyance, they'd add "Emerson."

And I, in my confusion, would reply, "No, no, I'm not Emerson; he's the little boy who lives next door." Which only made them laugh all the louder. "Oh no," they'd say, "*you're* Ralph Waldo Emerson," while I had fantasies of blue murder.

For a while the presence next door of my little friend, Emerson, made it unnecessary for me to puzzle too often over this peculiar adult confusion. And since there were other Negro boys named Ralph in the city, I came to suspect that there was something about the combination of names which produced their laughter. Even today I know of only one other Ralph who had as much comedy made out of his name, a campus politician and deep-voiced orator whom I knew at Tuskegee,[6] who was called in friendly ribbing, *Ralph Waldo Emerson Edgar Allan Poe*, spelled Powe. This must have been quite a trial for him, but I had been initiated much earlier.

During my early school years the name continued to puzzle me, for it constantly evoked in the faces of others some secret. It was as though I possessed some treasure or some defect, which was invisible to my own eyes and ears; something which I had but did not *possess*, like a piece of property in South Carolina, which was mine but which I could not have until some future time. I recall finding, about this time, while seeking adventure in back alleys—which possess for boys a superiority over playgrounds like that

which kitchen utensils possess over toys designed for infants—a large photographic lens. I remember nothing of its optical qualities, of its speed or color correction, but it gleamed with crystal mystery and it was beautiful.

Mounted handsomely in a tube of shiny brass, it spoke to me of distant worlds of possibility. I played with it, looking through it with squinted eyes, holding it in shafts of sunlight, and tried to use it for a magic lantern. But most of this was as unrewarding as my attempts to make the music come from a phonograph record by holding the needle in my fingers.

I could burn holes through newspapers with it, or I could pretend that it was a telescope, the barrel of a cannon, or the third eye of a monster—*I* being the monster—but I could do nothing at all about its proper function of making images; nothing to make it yield its secret. But I could not discard it.

Older boys sought to get it away from me by offering knives or tops, agate marbles or whole zoos of grass snakes and horned toads in trade, but I held on to it. No one, not even the white boys I knew, had such a lens, and it was my own good luck to have found it. Thus I would hold on to it until such time as I could acquire the parts needed to make it function. Finally I put it aside and it remained buried in my box of treasures, dusty and dull, to be lost and forgotten as I grew older and became interested in music.

I had reached by now the grades where it was necessary to learn something about Mr. Emerson and what he had written, such as the "Concord Hymn" and the essay "Self-Reliance," and in following his advice, I reduced the "Waldo" to a simple and, I hoped, mysterious "W," and in my own reading I avoided his works like the plague. I could no more deal with my name—I shall never really master it—than I could find a creative use for my lens. . . .

If all this sounds a bit heady, remember that I did not destroy that troublesome mid-

---

4. **nubbin** *n.*: Anything small and undeveloped.
5. **moniker** *n.*: Slang for a person's name or nickname.
6. **Tuskegee** (tus kē′ gē): Tuskegee Institute, the Alabama college which Ellison attended.

dle name of mine, I only suppressed it. Sometimes it reminds me of my obligations to the man who named me.

It is our fate as human beings always to give up some good things for other good things, to throw off certain bad circumstances only to create others. Thus there is a value for the writer in trying to give as thorough a report of social reality as possible. Only by doing so may we grasp and convey the cost of change. Only by considering the broadest accumulation of data may we make choices that are based upon our own hard-earned sense of reality. Speaking from my own special area of American culture, I feel that to embrace uncritically values which are extended to us by others is to reject the validity, even the sacredness, of our own experience. It is also to forget that the small share of reality which each of our diverse groups is able to snatch from the whirling chaos of history belongs not to the group alone, but to all of us. It is a property and a witness which can be ignored only to the danger of the entire nation.

I could suppress the name of my namesake out of respect for the achievements of its original bearer but I cannot escape the obligation of attempting to achieve some of the things which he asked of the American writer. As Henry James[7] suggested, being an American is an arduous task, and for most of us, I suspect, the difficulty begins with the name.

---

7. **Henry James:** An American novelist (1843–1916).

Primary Source

Consciously or unconsciously, we all have private pictures of the people who answer to certain names. For their book *The Best Baby Name Book in the Whole Wide World*, Bruce and Vicki Lansky and their researchers have developed a list of names and their stereotypes. Try guessing the stereotypes before you look at them.

Amanda	cultured
Amy	active
Angela	pleasant-looking, somewhat wistful
Ann	ladylike and honest, but not pretty
Elizabeth	seductive
Emily	a sideline-sitter
Jennifer	youthful, yet old-fashioned
Jessica	ambitious and beautiful
Linda	utterly feminine, popular and energetic
Lisa	very frail, well-liked
Margaret	a bit dowdy
Mary	wholesome, womanly, active
Melissa	passive but graceful
Nicole	average on all counts
Patricia	plain
Peggy	spirited, cute
Vicky	very sexy, exceedingly well-liked and frisky
Anthony	tall, wiry, elegant
Benjamin	dishonest
Brian	superstar—macho, dynamic
Charles	masculine, popular, but not overly active
Christopher	diligent, intelligent
David	not quite as terrific as Dave, but still a winner
Eric	a big winner—very strong
Francis	passive, neuter
James	a big winner in all categories
Jason	hugely popular
John	trustworthy, surprisingly passive but manly
Justin	vigorous
Kevin	very popular, virile
Mark	spoiled
Michael	very, very popular
Nicholas	very strong
Richard	very good-looking
Stephen	a winner in all areas
Thomas	large, soft and cuddly
William	kind but not aggressive

RESPONDING TO THE SELECTION

Your Response

1. How has your name shaped your identity?
2. If you were to change your name, what name would you choose? Why?

Recalling

3. Why did Ellison's name puzzle him in his "earliest years"?
4. Of what does Ellison's middle name sometimes remind him?

Interpreting

5. What does Ellison mean when he comments that our names "must become our masks and our shields and the containers of all those values and traditions . . . of our familial past"?
6. What does Ellison mean when he refers to the "suggestive powers of names"?
7. How does Ellison relate his experiences with the photographic lens with his attempts to come to terms with his name?
8. In your own words, state the main point of Ellison's essay.

Applying

9. In *Romeo and Juliet*, Shakespeare wrote, "What's in a name? That which we call a rose/By any other word would smell as sweet." How does the idea about names expressed in these lines compare with the idea Ellison presents?
10. Do you think names play as important a role in people's lives as Ellison suggests? Why or why not?

ANALYZING LITERATURE

Understanding the Essay

Essays are short prose works that focus on a narrow topic. Generally an essay can be classified as either a formal essay or an informal essay. Ellison's essay, however, does not completely fit into either category, because it possesses characteristics of both formal essays and informal essays.

1. How is Ellison's essay organized?
2. What is the purpose of the essay?
3. How would you describe Ellison's use of language?

THINKING AND WRITING

Writing a Critical Response

Write a formal essay in which you respond to the opinions about names that Ellison expresses in his essay. Reread the essay, carefully noting the opinions Ellison expresses. Decide whether you agree or disagree with each of these opinions. Then begin writing your essay, using examples to support your argument. When you revise, make sure you structured your argument in a logical manner.

LEARNING OPTIONS

1. **Performance.** Couples who are expecting a child sometimes spend weeks, even months, trying to decide on a name. Pair up with a classmate and work together to create a humorous skit about a young couple trying to choose a name for a baby expected in the very near future. Act our your skit for the class.
2. **Language.** Find out the origin or meaning of your name—either your family name or your given name. The name *Smith,* for example, means "one who works in metals," and the name *Amanda* means "worthy to be loved." You might also learn the forms of your name in other languages; John, for instance, becomes Sean in Irish and Juan in Spanish.

JOAN DIDION

1934–

An innovative writer of both fiction and nonfiction, Joan Didion is known for her precise use of language and her ability to capture the essence of contemporary life using images from her own life.

Born and raised in California, Didion began writing at an early age. She earned a degree from the University of California at Berkeley and worked for a number of years as an editor for *Vogue* magazine. In 1963 she published her first novel, *Run River.* Five years later, she produced a volume of essays, *Slouching Towards Bethlehem,* which captured the flavor of life in San Francisco during the late 1960's. This book, along with a later collection of essays, *The White Album* (1979), earned Didion a reputation as one of the country's premier essayists. Since the publication of *The White Album,* she has published another work of nonfiction, *Salvador* (1983), and *Democracy* (1984), a novel that combines fiction with nonfiction.

Didion has written, "We tell ourselves stories in order to live. . . . We live entirely, especially if we are writers, by the imposition of a narrative line upon disparate images, by the 'ideas' with which we have learned to freeze the shifting phantasmagoria which is our actual experience."

In her essay "On the Mall," Didion displays her direct, precise style and her ability to transform a very ordinary subject into an interesting and entertaining work of literature.

Didion is fond of saying, "Everything you do counts," and she feels each image or gesture tells a story with moral implications. Her images are at times aching blends of elegance and despair, and her near tragic point of view shows the vulnerability she feels in her own life and in the lives we all live in our current world. She is particularly adept at depicting the harsh, nonhuman, or even anti-human extremes that surround us in our contemporary world. Her appeal comes from her ability to express a very personal despair in an almost universal way. One striking Didion image shows sunny California as Hell, with the hills of Malibu Beach engulfed in flame while happy surfers ride the waves below. Didion often shows such elements as fire or earthquake devastating people's lives while others not personally touched go about their business indifferently.

Ritual, she feels, holds one key to sustaining life by systematizing it and thus subduing its chaos. Often her works explore ritual as a means of survival. Her subjects, or characters, commonly carry on mundane little tasks and routines that give their lives shape and disguise the fact that things around them are, in actuality, falling apart.

GUIDE FOR INTERPRETING

On the Mall

Writers' Techniques

Exposition. Exposition is writing in which factual information is presented. Using exposition, the writer informs or educates the reader by presenting a series of facts, discussing their significance, and explaining how they relate to one another. In "On the Mall," for example, Didion uses exposition to inform the reader about the theories used in planning shopping malls.

Because it is vital to the reader's understanding of a literary work, exposition plays an important role in both fiction and nonfiction. In fact, many works of nonfiction are classified as expository essays because their primary purpose is to inform or educate the reader.

Focus

What sorts of impressions do you have of shopping malls? Freewrite about shopping malls, discussing the reasons for their popularity and your opinion of them.

Primary Source

There are shopping centers and then there is the West Edmonton Mall in Canada. Author Ian Pearson described it like this in an article for *Saturday Night* magazine:

> The world's largest collection of stores, restaurants, and funfair amusements, West Edmonton Mall is also the latest stage in high-pressure retailing. And it may be the future that awaits consumers everywhere. . . .
>
> West Edmonton Mall is eight city blocks long and three blocks wide, a two-level, yellow-brick structure that houses a miscellany of modern recreation. There's an indoor amusement park called Fantasyland with carousels, water rides, a miniature train, and a thirteen-story high, triple-loop roller coaster. There are hundreds of video games in two giant arcades which serve as social centers for thousands of teenagers. There's an NHL-sized rink on which the Edmonton Oilers occasionally practice. There's a fountain that shoots fire and water and another that squirts water in time to the themes from *Chariots of Fire* and *The Pink Panther.*
>
> Ficus trees and palm trees grow profusely under enormous skylights. Brass railings imbedded with tivoli lights line the edges of the rink, the submarine pond, and the upper level of the mall; . . . on Bourbon Street, a wing of the mall that is a copy of the New Orleans street, there are lifelike statues of jazz musicians. A shopper can traverse an international route from Hollywood West to Rodier of Paris to Casablanca and encounter tigers, bears, moray eels, tropical fish, toucans, flamingos, macaws, and spider monkeys.

Guide for Interpreting 915

On the Mall

Joan Didion

They float on the landscape like pyramids to the boom years, all those Plazas and Malls and Esplanades. All those Squares and Fairs. All those Towns and Dales, all those Villages, all those Forests and Parks and Lands. Stonestown. Hillsdale. Valley Fair, Mayfair, Northgate, Southgate, Eastgate, Westgate. Gulfgate. They are toy garden cities in which no one lives but everyone consumes, profound equalizers, the perfect fusion of the profit motive and the egalitarian ideal, and to hear their names is to recall words and phrases no longer quite current. Baby Boom. Consumer Explosion. Leisure Revolution. Do-It-Yourself Revolution. Backyard Revolution. Suburbia. "The Shopping Center," the Urban Land Institute could pronounce in 1957, "is today's extraordinary retail business evolvement. . . . The automobile accounts for suburbia, and suburbia accounts for the shopping center."

It was a peculiar and visionary time, those years after World War II to which all the Malls and Towns and Dales stand as climate-controlled monuments. Even the word "automobile," as in "the automobile accounts for suburbia and suburbia accounts for the shopping center," no longer carries the particular freight it once did: as a child in the late Forties in California I recall reading and believing that the "freedom of movement" afforded by the automobile was "America's fifth freedom." The trend was up. The solution was in sight. The frontier had been reinvented, and its shape was the subdivision, that new free land on which all settlers could recast their lives *tabula rasa.*[1] For one perishable moment there the American idea seemed about to achieve itself, via F.H.A.[2] housing and the acquisition of major appliances, and a certain enigmatic glamour attached to the architects of this newfound land. They made something of nothing. They gambled and sometimes lost. They staked the past to seize the future. I have difficulty now imagining a childhood in which a man named Jere Strizek, the developer of Town and Country Village outside Sacramento (143,000 square feet gross floor area, 68 stores, 1000 parking spaces, the Urban Land Institute's "prototype for centers using heavy timber and tile construction for informality"), could materialize as a role model, but I had such a childhood, just after World War II, in Sacramento. I never met or even saw Jere Strizek, but at the age of 12 I imagined him a kind of frontiersman, a romantic and revolutionary spirit, and in the indigenous grain he was.

I suppose James B. Douglas and David D. Bohannon were too.

I first heard of James B. Douglas and David D. Bohannon not when I was 12 but a dozen years later, when I was living in New York, working for *Vogue*, and taking, by correspondence, a University of California Extension course in shopping-center theory. This did not seem to me eccentric at the

---

1. **tabula rasa** (tab′yə lə rä′ sə): Clean slate.
2. **F.H.A.:** Federal Housing Administration.

time. I remember sitting on the cool floor in Irving Penn's studio and reading, in *The Community Builders Handbook*, advice from James B. Douglas on shopping-center financing. I recall staying late in my pale-blue office on the twentieth floor of the Graybar Building to memorize David D. Bohannon's parking ratios. My "real" life was to sit in this office and describe life as it was lived in Djakarta and Caneel Bay and in the great châteaux of the Loire Valley, but my dream life was to put together a Class-A regional shopping center with three full-line department stores as major tenants.

That I was perhaps the only person I knew in New York, let alone on the Condé Nast[3] floors of the Graybar Building, to have

3. **Condé Nast:** Company that publishes a variety of periodicals, including *Vogue* magazine.

memorized the distinctions among "A," "B," and "C" shopping centers did not occur to me (the defining distinction, as long as I have your attention, is that an "A," or "regional," center has as its major tenant a full-line department store which carries major appliances; a "B," or "community," center has as its major tenant a junior department store which does not carry major appliances; and a "C," or "neighborhood," center has as its major tenant only a supermarket): my interest in shopping centers was in no way casual. I did want to build them. I wanted to build them because I had fallen into the habit of writing fiction, and I had it in my head that a couple of good centers might support this habit less taxingly than a pale-blue office at *Vogue*. I had even devised an original scheme by which I planned to gain enough capital and credibility to enter the shopping-center game: I would lease warehouses in, say, Queens, and offer Manhattan delicatessens the opportunity to sell competitively by buying cooperatively, from my trucks. I see a few wrinkles in this scheme now (the words "concrete overcoat" come to mind), but I did not then. In fact I planned to run it out of the pale-blue office.

James B. Douglas and David D. Bohannon. In 1950 James B. Douglas had opened Northgate, in Seattle, the first regional center to combine a pedestrian mall with an underground truck tunnel. In 1954 David D. Bohannon had opened Hillsdale, a forty-acre regional center on the peninsula south of San Francisco. That is the only solid bio I have on James B. Douglas and David D. Bohannon to this day, but many of their opinions are engraved on my memory. David D. Bohannon believed in preserving the integrity of the shopping center by not cutting up the site with any dedicated roads. David D. Bohannon believed that architectural setbacks in a center looked "pretty on paper" but caused "customer resistance." James B. Douglas advised that a small-loan office could prosper in a center only if it were placed away from foot traffic, since people who want small loans do not want to be observed getting them. I do not now recall whether it was James B. Douglas or David D. Bohannon or someone else altogether who passed along this hint on how to paint the lines around the parking spaces (actually this is called "striping the lot," and the spaces are "stalls"): make each space a foot wider than it need be—ten feet, say, instead of nine—when the center first opens and business is slow. By this single stroke the developer achieves a couple of important objectives, the appearance of a popular center and the illusion of easy parking, and no one will really notice when business picks up and the spaces shrink.

Nor do I recall who first solved what was once a crucial center dilemma: the placement of the major tenant vis-à-vis the parking lot. The dilemma was that the major tenant—the draw, the raison d'être[4] for the financing, the Sears, the Macy's, the May Company—wanted its customer to walk directly from car to store. The smaller tenants, on the other hand, wanted that same customer to *pass their stores* on the way from the car to, say, Macy's. The solution to this conflict of interests was actually very simple: *two major tenants*, one at each end of a mall. This is called "anchoring the mall," and represents seminal work in shopping-center theory. One thing you will note about shopping-center theory is that you could have thought of it yourself, and a course in it will go a long way toward dispelling the notion that business proceeds from mysteries too recondite for you and me.

A few aspects of shopping-center theory do in fact remain impenetrable to me. I have no idea why the Community Builders' Council ranks "Restaurant" as deserving a Number One (or "Hot Spot") location but exiles "Chinese Restaurant" to a Number Three, out there with "Power and Light Office" and "Christian Science Reading Room." Nor do I know why the Council approves of enlivening a mall with "small animals" but specifically, vehemently, and with no further explanation, excludes "monkeys." If I had a center I would have monkeys, and Chinese restaurants, and Mylar[5] kites and bands of small girls playing tambourine.

A few years ago at a party I met a woman from Detroit who told me that the Joyce Carol Oates novel with which she identified most closely was *Wonderland*.

I asked her why.

"Because," she said, "my husband has a branch there."

I did not understand.

---

4. raison d'être (rā′zōn det′rə): Justification for existence.
5. Mylar (mī′ lär): Polyester made in extremely thin sheets of great strength.

"In Wonderland the center," the woman said patiently. "My husband has a branch in Wonderland."

I have never visited Wonderland but imagine it to have bands of small girls playing tambourine.

A few facts about shopping centers.

The "biggest" center in the United States is generally agreed to be Woodfield, outside Chicago, a "super" regional or "leviathan" two-million-square-foot center with four major tenants.

The "first" shopping center in the United States is generally agreed to be Country Club Plaza in Kansas City, built in the twenties. There were some other early centers, notably Edward H. Bouton's 1907 Roland Park in Baltimore, Hugh Prather's 1931 Highland Park Shopping Village in Dallas, and Hugh Potter's 1937 River Oaks in Houston, but the developer of Country Club Plaza, the late J. C. Nichols, is referred to with ritual frequency in the literature of shopping centers, usually as "pioneering J. C. Nichols," "trailblazing J. C. Nichols," or "J. C. Nichols, father of the center as we know it."

Those are some facts I know about shopping centers because I still want to be Jere Strizek or James B. Douglas or David D. Bohannon. Here are some facts I know about shopping centers because I never will be Jere Strizek or James B. Douglas or David D. Bohannon: a good center in which to spend the day if you wake feeling low in Honolulu, Hawaii, is Ala Moana, major tenants Liberty House and Sears. A good center in which to spend the day if you wake feeling low in Ox-

nard, California, is The Esplanade, major tenants the May Company and Sears. A good center in which to spend the day if you wake feeling low in Biloxi, Mississippi, is Edgewater Plaza, major tenant Godchaux's. Ala Moana in Honolulu is larger than The Esplanade in Oxnard, and The Esplanade in Oxnard is larger than Edgewater Plaza in Biloxi. Ala Moana has carp pools. The Esplanade and Edgewater Plaza do not.

These marginal distinctions to one side, Ala Moana, The Esplanade, and Edgewater Plaza are the same place, which is precisely their role not only as equalizers but in the sedation of anxiety. In each of them one moves for a while in an aqueous suspension not only of light but of judgment, not only of judgment but of "personality." One meets no acquaintances at The Esplanade. One gets no telephone calls at Edgewater Plaza. "It's a hard place to run in to for a pair of stockings," a friend complained to me recently of Ala Moana, and I knew that she was not yet ready to surrender her ego to the idea of the center. The last time I went to Ala Moana it was to buy *The New York Times*. Because *The New York Times* was not in, I sat on the mall for a while and ate caramel corn. In the end I bought not *The New York Times* at all but two straw hats at Liberty House, four bottles of nail enamel at Woolworth's, and a toaster, on sale at Sears. In the literature of shopping centers these would be described as impulse purchases, but the impulse here was obscure. I do not wear hats, nor do I like caramel corn. I do not use nail enamel. Yet flying back across the Pacific I regretted only the toaster.

MULTICULTURAL CONNECTION

Shopping Around the World

In her essay, Didion offers some humorous insights into the American love affair with shopping malls. The approach to shopping favored by Americans is not shared by people throughout the world, however. In fact, in many countries, most food and other goods are still sold by the people who produce them, either in specialty stores or in open markets held in main squares or on specific streets. Since farmers, fishermen, and craftsmen cannot do their jobs and go to the market at the same time, markets are usually held on certain days of the week.

Market day. In some places, everyone who has anything to sell goes to the same market. In other places, special days are set aside for different kinds of goods. The Tiv people of Nigeria, for instance, can tell what day it is by seeing what's in the marketplace: One day is devoted to items made of brass; another to objects made of wood.

Businesses grouped together. Unlike American malls, which consist of an array of unrelated businesses, cities and towns in many other countries feature districts in which similar specialty stores are grouped together. This allows buyers to go to a single area and find the best bargain when they are looking for a specific product or type of goods. Specialized shopping districts can be found in the Moroccan city of Marrakesh, in many European countries, and even in New York City, where almost every store on one part of 47th Street (known as "the diamond district") sells diamonds and jewelry.

The market as meeting place. Throughout the world, the "market" is more than just a place to buy goods. It is also a meeting place, and market days provide an opportunity for friends and neighbors to mix business and pleasure. This is as true in the villages of Asia and the trading posts of New Mexico as it is in suburban malls.

Sharing Your Experiences

Are there any ethnic specialty stores or markets where you live? What can one buy there that is not available in a supermarket?

RESPONDING TO THE SELECTION

Your Response

1. How important are shopping malls to you?
2. What do you think of Didion's dream of building a shopping mall? Explain.

Recalling

3. As a young girl, what was Didion's impression of developer Jere Strizek?
4. Why did Didion want to build shopping centers?
5. What does shopping-center theory dictate about (a) the width of parking spaces, and (b) the placement of major tenants?
6. What aspects of shopping-center theory "remain impenetrable" to Didion?
7. How would Didion's purchases at Ala Moana in Hawaii be described in the literature of shopping centers?

Interpreting

8. (a) What does Didion mean when she describes shopping malls as "pyramids to the boom years"? (b) In what sense are the malls "profound equalizers"?
9. What does Didion's description of her encounter with the woman from Detroit imply about the priorities of the American public?
10. How would you describe Didion's current attitudes toward both shopping centers and her early dreams of building them? (b) How are these attitudes conveyed?
11. What point does Didion's essay make about the role of shopping centers in American society?

Applying

12. Compare your own attitude toward shopping malls with Didion's current attitude.

ANALYZING LITERATURE

Understanding Exposition

Exposition is writing in which factual information is presented. For example, in the fifth paragraph of "On the Mall," Didion presents a series of facts about the "distinctions among 'A,' 'B,' and 'C' shopping centers."

1. What are the distinctions among "A," "B," and "C" shopping centers?
2. Find three more examples of factual information in Didion's essay.
3. Should this essay be classified as an expository essay? Why or why not?

CRITICAL THINKING AND READING

Separating Facts From Opinions

Didion's essay contains both facts and opinions. A **fact** is an objective statement that can be verified, or proved to be true. For example, Didion presents a fact when she writes, "Woodfield Mall, outside Chicago, is a two-million-square-foot center." In contrast, an **opinion** is a subjective statement that cannot be verified. For example, Didion states an opinion when she refers to the years immediately following World War II as a "peculiar and visionary time."

1. Find three more facts presented in the essay.
2. Find three more opinions presented in the essay.

THINKING AND WRITING

Writing About a Writer's Attitudes

Write an essay in which you discuss the attitudes that Didion conveys about shopping malls, shopping-center theory, and the role of shopping malls in American society. Reread the essay, focusing on Didion's attitudes and noting how these attitudes are conveyed. Prepare a thesis statement. Then write your essay, using passages from Didion's essay to support your thesis. When you revise, make sure you have varied the length and structure of your sentences.

LEARNING OPTION

Community Connections. Enter the "shopping-center game." Get together with several classmates to design a new shopping mall for your community. In developing your design, use your imagination, common sense, and shopping-center theory. How does your shopping center compare to the West Edmonton Mall described on page 915?

N. SCOTT MOMADAY

1934–

Proud of his Native American heritage, N. Scott Momaday has devoted his life to teaching and writing about Native American history, folklore, and mythology.

A Kiowa Indian, Momaday was born in Lawton, Oklahoma. After graduating from the University of New Mexico, he received a doctorate in literature from Stanford University. His first novel, *House Made of Dawn* (1968), an account of a young Indian torn between his ancestral roots and contemporary mainstream society, earned him a Pulitzer Prize. He then published what has become his best-known work, *The Way to Rainy Mountain* (1969), a collection of personal anecdotes and retellings of Kiowa myths and legends. Since then, he has produced several more books, including two volumes of poetry, *Angle of Geese and Other Poems* (1974) and *The Gourd Dancer* (1976), and a collection of anecdotes entitled *The Names* (1976).

Dr. Momaday is devoted to preserving his Kiowa heritage. As a boy he often visited his grandparents, both of whom shared their experiences with their grandson. His grandfather Mammedaty (whose name means "sky walker") "saw things other men do not," according to Momaday. His grandmother had attended the last Kiowa sun dance in the late 1880's. He explains that his grandmother "had a reverence for the sun, a holy regard that now is all but gone out of mankind. There was a warrior in her, and an ancient awe."

His grandparents' home served as a meeting place for aged Kiowas whom Momaday describes as people "made of lean leather" who "rubbed fat upon their hair and wound their braids with strips of colored cloth." He recalls that some "painted their faces and carried the scars of old and cherished enemies. They were old council warlords come to remind and be reminded of who they were."

N. Scott Momaday acknowledges that the current-day problems of Native American peoples have become generally more visible, but he feels that the increased awareness is not sufficient. In his writing he strives to preserve the oral tradition of Native American peoples as well as the significance of their legends.

Like Momaday's other works, "A Vision Beyond Time and Place" helps provide the reader with a better understanding of traditional Native American culture. In the essay Momaday recalls and discusses the significance of an old tribe member's daily prayers to the rising sun.

GUIDE FOR INTERPRETING

A Vision Beyond Time and Place

Writers' Techniques

Classification. Classification refers to the process of dividing a subject into categories, or classes. In nonfiction, writers sometimes use classification to clarify the meaning of an idea or a concept that may otherwise be difficult to grasp. For example, in "A Vision Beyond Time and Place," N. Scott Momaday uses classification to help define a specific type of "vision" with which most Americans are likely to be unfamiliar.

Focus

Discuss the different ways in which people view the world. Why do you think people from different cultures sometimes view the same thing in completely different ways? Why is it important for different cultures to share their views? How can this contribute to their abilities to understand one another?

Primary Source

The United States government policies toward Native American culture have long been suspect. Samuel Eliot Morison wrote in *The Oxford History of the American People*:

> The general assumption behind the federal government's policy [on Indians] was an anticipated disappearance of the Indians as a separate and distinct race. Hence it was a good thing to help the process—not, of course, by the earlier crude methods of starvation, disease, and extermination, but by promoting the breakup of reservations into individually owned allotments. Land ownership, it was believed, would make the redskins responsible citizens and assimilate them to the American Way of Life. The interior department speeded up this process through shortening by several years the time that an Indian had to occupy his allotment before [he could] sell it. In one year 60 percent of all Indians receiving titles to their allotments sold out, and most of them squandered the proceeds.
>
> This does not, however, apply to the Five Civilized Tribes of Oklahoma. They managed to retain much of their own culture, while adapting themselves to that of the Anglo-Saxon American; and many became eminent. Will Rogers, Senator R. L. Owen, and Admiral Joseph J. ("Jocko") Clarke, a great carrier group commander in World War II, were Cherokee; Charles Curtis, Vice President under Hoover, was an Osage, and the list might be extended indefinitely by including artists, professional singers, and ballerinas.

A Vision Beyond Time and Place

N. Scott Momaday

When my father was a boy, an old man used to come to [my grandfather] Mammedaty's house and pay his respects. He was a lean old man in braids and was impressive in his age and bearing. His name was Cheney, and he was an arrowmaker. Every morning, my father tells me, Cheney would paint his wrinkled face, go out, and pray aloud to the rising sun. In my mind I can see that man as if he were there now. I like to watch him as he makes his prayer. I know where he stands and where his voice goes on the rolling grasses and where the sun comes up on the land. There, at dawn, you can feel the silence. It is cold and clear and deep like water. It takes hold of you and will not let you go.[1]

I often think of old man Cheney, and of his daily devotion to the sun. He died before I was born, and I never knew where he came from or what of good and bad entered into his life. But I think I know who he was, essentially, and what his view of the world meant to him and to me. He was a man who saw very deeply into the distance, I believe, one whose vision extended far beyond the physical boundaries of his time and place. He perceived the wonder and meaning of Creation itself. In his mind's eye he could integrate all the realities and illusions of the earth and sky; they became for him profoundly intelligible and whole.

Once, in the first light, I stood where Cheney had stood, next to the house which my grandfather Mammedaty had built on a rise of land near Rainy Mountain Creek, and watched the sun come out of the black horizon of the world. It was an irresistible and awesome emergence, as waters gather to the flood, of weather and of light. I could not have been more sensitive to the cold, nor than to the heat which came upon it. And I could not have *foreseen* the break of day. The shadows on the rolling plains became large and luminous in a moment, impalpable, then faceted, dark and distinct again as they were run through with splinters of light. And the sun itself, when it appeared, was pale and immense, original in the deepest sense of the word. It is no wonder, I thought, that an old man should pray to it. It is no wonder . . . and yet, of course, wonder is the principal part of such a vision. Cheney's prayer was an affirmation of his wonder and regard, a testament to the realization of a quest for vision.

This native vision, this gift of seeing truly, with wonder and delight, into the natural world, is informed by a certain attitude of reverence and self-respect. It is a matter of extrasensory as well as sensory perception, I believe. In addition to the eye, it involves the intelligence, the instinct, and the imagination. It is the perception not only of objects

---

1. When my father . . . let you go: From N. Scott Momaday's *The Way to Rainy Mountain.*

THE MEDICINE ROBE
Maynard Dixon
Courtesy of the Buffalo Bill Historical Center, Cody, Wyoming

and forms but also of essences and ideals, as in this Chippewa song:

> *as my eyes*
> *search*
> *the prairie*
> *I feel the summer*
> *in the spring*

Even as the singer sees into the immediate landscape, he perceives a now and future dimension that is altogether remote, yet nonetheless real and inherent within it, a quality of evanescence and evolution, a state at once of being and of becoming. He beholds what is there; nothing of the scene is lost upon him. In the integrity of his vision he is wholly in possession of himself and of the world around him; he is quintessentially alive.

Most Indian people are able to see in these terms. Their view of the world is peculiarly native and distinct, and it determines who and what they are to a great extent. It is indeed the basis upon which they identify themselves as individuals and as a race. There is something of genetic significance in such a thing, perhaps, an element of being which resides in the blood and which is, after all, the very nucleus of the self. When old man Cheney looked into the sunrise, he saw as far into himself, I suspect, as he saw into the distance. He knew certainly of his existence and of his place in the scheme of things.

In contrast, most of us in this society are afflicted with a kind of cultural nearsightedness. Our eyes, it may be, have been trained too long upon the superficial, and *artificial*, aspects of our environment; we do not see beyond the buildings and billboards that seem at times to be the monuments of our civilization, and consequently we fail to see into the nature and meaning of our own humanity. Now, more than ever, we might do well to enter upon a vision quest of our own, that is, a quest after vision itself. And in this the Indian stands to lead by his example. For with respect to such things as a sense of heritage, of a vital continuity in terms of origin and of destiny, a profound investment of the mind and spirit in the oral traditions of literature, philosophy, and religion—those things, in short, which constitute his vision of the world—the Indian is perhaps the most culturally secure of all Americans.

As I see him, that old man, he walks very slowly to the place where he will make his prayer, and it is always the same place, a small mound where the grass is sparse and the hard red earth shows through. He limps a little, with age, but when he plants his feet he is tall and straight and hard. The bones are fine and prominent in his face and hands. And his face is painted. There are red and yellow bars under his eyes, neither bright nor sharply defined on the dark, furrowed skin, but soft and organic, the colors of sandstone and of pollen. His long braids are wrapped with blood-red cloth. His eyes are deep and open to the wide world. At sunrise, precisely, they catch fire and close, having seen. The low light descends upon him. And when he lifts his voice, it enters upon the silence and carries there, like the call of a bird.

RESPONDING TO THE SELECTION

Your Response

1. Based on his essay, what are your impressions of N. Scott Momaday?
2. What are your impressions of the old man whom Momaday describes? Is he someone you would have liked to know? Why or why not?
3. What feelings do you associate with watching the sun rise?

Recalling

4. (a) What did Cheney do every morning? (b) What special abilities does Momaday believe Cheney possessed?
5. According to Momaday, in what terms are most Native Americans "able to see"?
6. How does Momaday believe that the eyes of most Americans "have been trained"?

Interpreting

7. (a) How does the first paragraph tie together with the final paragraph? (b) What do these two paragraphs add to the rest of the essay?
8. What is the meaning of the Chippewa song Momaday quotes in his essay?
9. Why do some people believe that most people are unable to "see into the nature and meaning" of their "own humanity"?
10. What is Momaday suggesting that other people might learn from Native Americans?

Applying

11. Do you agree with Momaday's statement that most of us "might do well to enter upon a vision quest of our own"? Why or why not?
12. Do you agree with Momaday that "most of us in this society are afflicted with a kind of cultural nearsightedness"? Explain your answer.

ANALYZING LITERATURE

Understanding Classification

Classification refers to the process of dividing a subject into categories. In nonfiction, writers sometimes use classification to help clarify the meaning of difficult-to-grasp ideas or concepts.

1. What are the two types of visions Momaday describes in the essay?
2. How do these two types of visions contrast with each other?
3. How does Momaday use this contrast to help define a traditional Native American vision?

CRITICAL THINKING AND READING

Recognizing Cultural Attitudes

Momaday's attitude reveals a good deal about Native American attitudes and values. For example, toward the end of the essay, Momaday points out that Native Americans deeply value their oral tradition.

1. What do you think this selection reveals about the traditional Native American attitude toward nature?
2. How is this attitude revealed?

THINKING AND WRITING

Comparing and Contrasting Essays

In what ways are Native American beliefs similar to the ideas of the Transcendentalists? Write an essay in which you compare and contrast the Native American beliefs expressed in this essay with the Transcendentalist beliefs Ralph Waldo Emerson expresses in his essay *Nature.* Start by rereading both essays and reviewing the discussion of the Transcendentalist movement. Note the beliefs each essay conveys about humanity's spiritual relationship with nature. Organize your essay according to corresponding points of contrast, and use passages from each essay to support your argument.

LEARNING OPTION

Community Connections. Explore traditional Native American cultures in your region. Find out which groups live or have lived in or near your state. Choose one group and learn about its religious beliefs and ceremonies. What is the role of the sun? Share your findings with classmates.

SANDRA CISNEROS

1954–

As a young girl, Sandra Cisneros felt trapped and isolated. She felt a secret kinship to the American poet Emily Dickinson, who lived most of her life in solitude and hid her poetic talents. Unlike Dickinson, however, Cisneros emerged from her isolation and has become a popular contemporary writer.

Cisneros was born in Chicago into a large Mexican American family. Because her family was poor, they moved frequently and lived for the most part in small, cramped apartments. Recalling how she coped with these conditions, Cisneros comments, "Because we moved so much and always in neighborhoods that appeared like France after World War II—empty lots and burned out buildings—I retreated into myself." She also fueled her imagination by becoming an avid reader, devouring fairy tales and classic literary works.

After graduating from Loyola University in Chicago, Cisneros enrolled in the renowned Writer's Workshop at the University of Iowa. There she had an experience that changed her life. One of the other students was comparing the imagination to a huge house with many stairways and an attic. As Cisneros listened, she realized that the student actually *lived* in a house like that. Until then, she had never fully admitted how different her background was from that of the other students.

At first she felt sure she was going to have to give up writing. Then she realized that her Mexican American heritage and her childhood experiences provided her with something her fellow students lacked. What had at first seemed like a source of shame suddenly became a source of power.

After graduating from Iowa, she moved to Texas and wrote a group of connected stories about her childhood. In 1984 these stories were published as a collection entitled *The House on Mango Street.* The book was a modest success, but it produced little income for Cisneros. Running out of money, Cisneros left Texas in 1987 to accept a temporary teaching post in California.

Soon after reaching California, she received a grant from the National Endowment for the Arts. Feeling thrilled and vindicated, she plunged back into her writing. She also remembered that a few months earlier someone had given her the phone number of a literary agent in New York who had liked her book. She summoned up the courage to call, and the agent, Susan Bergholz, asked to see her new stories, even though they only amounted to thirty-nine pages. On the basis of this slim manuscript, Bergholz got Cisneros a contract with a major publisher for her next book, *Woman Hollering Creek.* Published in 1991, the book won critical acclaim and earned Cisneros widespread recognition.

Straw Into Gold: The Metamorphosis of the Everyday

**Writers'
Techniques**

Transforming Personal Experiences. The renowned American writer Isaac Bashevis Singer once commented, "In all my writing, I tell the story of my life, over and over again." This observation also applies to a multitude of other writers. Personal experiences are one of the richest sources of inspiration and material that writers can draw from. The most obvious use of personal experiences in writing is in nonfiction accounts, such as personal narratives and autobiographies. Often, however, writers use their imaginations to transform their personal experiences into works of fiction, drama, or poetry.

Although some works are clearly drawn from the writer's experiences, others are more loosely connected. For example, American writer Ernest Hemingway's novel *A Farewell to Arms* and his short story "In Another Country" (page 580) are obviously based on his experiences in Italy during World War I. Yet by fictionalizing the characters and events while grounding them in a true-to-life setting, Hemingway created literary works that convey truth and meaning that transcend the original experiences. On the other hand, the connection between British author Mary Shelley's life and her novel *Frankenstein* is much less obvious. Raised as an orphan, Shelley conveyed her childhood feelings of loneliness and rejection through the experiences of the monster in her novel.

In the following essay, Sandra Cisneros discusses how her work has been drawn from her personal experiences and her Mexican American heritage. Recognizing that there are still relatively few writers who have captured the Mexican American experience, she once told an interviewer, "I'm trying to write the stories that haven't been written. I feel like a cartographer; I'm determined to fill a literary void." With the widespread success of her recent work and the growing recognition of her literary importance, she has clearly achieved her goal.

Focus

What experiences have you had that might make good writing topics? Write a journal entry in which you explore some of the more memorable experiences you have had in the past several years. What makes these experiences memorable? How did you feel about the experiences at the time? How do you feel about them now?

Straw Into Gold: The Metamorphosis of the Everyday

Sandra Cisneros

When I was living in an artists' colony in the south of France, some fellow Latin-Americans who taught at the university in Aix-en-Provence[1] invited me to share a home-cooked meal with them. I had been living abroad almost a year then on an NEA[2] grant, subsisting mainly on French bread and lentils while in France so that my money could last longer. So when the invitation to dinner arrived, I accepted without hesitation. Especially since they had promised Mexican food.

What I didn't realize when they made this invitation was that I was supposed to be involved in preparing this meal. I guess they assumed I knew how to cook Mexican food because I was Mexican. They wanted specifically tortillas, though I'd never made a tortilla in my life.

It's true I had witnessed my mother rolling the little armies of dough into perfect circles, but my mother's family is from Guanajuato,[3] *provinciales*,[4] country folk. They only know how to make flour tortillas. My father's family, on the other hand, is

chilango,[5] from Mexico City. We ate corn tortillas but we didn't make them. Someone was sent to the corner tortilleria to buy some. I'd never seen anybody make corn tortillas. Ever.

Well, somehow my Latino hosts had gotten a hold of a packet of corn flour, and this is what they tossed my way with orders to produce tortillas. *Asi como sea.* Any ol' way, they said and went back to their cooking.

Why did I feel like the woman in the fairy tale who was locked in a room and ordered to spin straw into gold? I had the same sick feeling when I was required to write my critical essay for my MFA[6] exam—the only piece of noncreative writing necessary in order to get my graduate degree. How was I to start? There were rules involved here, unlike writing a poem or story, which I did intuitively. There was a step-by-step process needed and I had better know it. I felt as if making tortillas, or writing a critical paper for that matter, were tasks so impossible I wanted to break down into tears.

Somehow though, I managed to make those tortillas—crooked and burnt, but edible nonetheless. My hosts were absolutely ignorant when it came to Mexican food; they

---

1. Aix-en-Provence (eks äŋ prô väŋs'): A city in southeastern France.
2. NEA: National Endowment for the Arts.
3. Guanajuato (gwä' nä hwä' tô): A state in central Mexico.
4. *provinciales* (prô b̄ēn sē ä' läs): "Country folk."

5. *chilango* (chē län' gō): "City folk."
6. MFA: Master of Fine Arts.

thought my tortillas were delicious. (I'm glad my mama wasn't there.) Thinking back and looking at that photograph documenting the three of us consuming those lopsided circles I am amazed. Just as I am amazed I could finish my MFA exam (lopsided and crooked, but finished all the same). Didn't think I could do it. But I did.

I've managed to do a lot of things in my life I didn't think I was capable of and which many others didn't think me capable of either. Especially because I am a woman, a Latina, an only daughter in a family of six men. My father would've liked to have seen me married long ago. In our culture, men and women don't leave their father's house except by way of marriage. I crossed my father's threshold with nothing carrying me but my own two feet. A woman whom no one came for and no one chased away.

To make matters worse, I had left before any of my six brothers had ventured away from home. I had broken a terrible taboo. Somehow, looking back at photos of myself as a child, I wonder if I was aware of having begun already my own quiet war.

I like to think that somehow my family, my Mexicanness, my poverty all had something to do with shaping me into a writer. I like to think my parents were preparing me all along for my life as an artist even though they didn't know it. From my father I inherited a love of wandering. He was born in Mexico City but as a young man he traveled into the U.S. vagabonding. He eventually was drafted and thus became a citizen. Some of the stories he has told about his first months in the U.S. with little or no English surface in my stories in *The House on Mango Street* as well as others I have in mind to write in the future. From him I inherited a sappy heart. (He still cries when he watches the Mexican soaps—especially if they deal with children who have forsaken their parents.)

My mother was born like me—in Chicago but of Mexican descent. It would be her tough, streetwise voice that would haunt all my stories and poems. An amazing woman

BIOGRAPHY, 1988
Marina Gutierrez
Courtesy of the Artist

who loves to draw and read books and can sing an opera. A smart cookie.

When I was a little girl we traveled to Mexico City so much I thought my grandparents' house on La Fortuna, Number 12, was home. It was the only constant in our nomadic ramblings from one Chicago flat to another. The house on Destiny Street, Number 12, in the colonia Tepeyac,[7] would be perhaps the only home I knew, and that nostalgia for a home would be a theme that would obsess me.

My brothers also figured greatly in my art. Especially the oldest two; I grew up in their shadows. Henry, the second oldest and my favorite, appears often in poems I have written and in stories which at times only borrow his nickname, Kiki. He played a major role in my childhood. We were bunkbed mates. We were co-conspirators. We were pals. Until my oldest brother came back from studying in Mexico and left me odd-woman-out for always.

What would my teachers say if they knew I was a writer? Who would've guessed it? I

---

7. colonia Tepeyac (cô lō′ nēä tā pā′ yäc): A district of Mexico City.

wasn't a very bright student. I didn't much like school because we moved so much and I was always new and funny-looking. In my fifth-grade report card, I have nothing but an avalanche of C's and D's, but I don't remember being that stupid. I was good at art and I read plenty of library books and Kiki laughed at all my jokes. At home I was fine, but at school I never opened my mouth except when the teacher called on me, the first time I'd speak all day.

When I think how I see myself, it would have to be at age eleven. I know I'm thirty-two on the outside, but inside I'm eleven. I'm the girl in the picture with skinny arms and a crumpled shirt and crooked hair. I didn't like school because all they saw was the outside me. School was lots of rules and sitting with your hands folded and being very afraid all the time. I liked looking out the window and thinking. I liked staring at the girl across the way writing her name over and over again in red ink. I wondered why the boy with the dirty collar in front of me didn't have a mama who took better care of him.

I think my mama and papa did the best they could to keep us warm and clean and never hungry. We had birthday and graduation parties and things like that, but there was another hunger that had to be fed. There was a hunger I didn't even have a name for. Was this when I began writing?

In 1966 we moved into a house, a real one, our first real home. This meant we didn't have to change schools and be the new kids on the block every couple of years. We could make friends and not be afraid we'd have to say goodbye to them and start all over. My brothers and the flock of boys they brought home would become important characters eventually for my stories—Louie and his cousins, Meme Ortiz and his dog with two names, one in English and one in Spanish.

My mother flourished in her own home. She took books out of the library and taught herself to garden, producing flowers so envied we had to put a lock on the gate to keep out the midnight flower thieves. My mother is still gardening to this day.

This was the period in my life, that slippery age when you are both child and woman and neither, I was to record in *The House on Mango Street*. I was still shy. I was a girl who couldn't come out of her shell.

How was I to know I would be recording and documenting the women who sat their sadness on an elbow and stared out a window? It would be the city streets of Chicago I would later record, but from a child's eyes.

I've done all kinds of things I didn't think I could do since then. I've gone to a prestigious university, studied with famous writers, and taken away an MFA degree. I've taught poetry in the schools in Illinois and Texas. I've gotten an NEA grant and run away with it as far as my courage would take me. I've seen the bleached and bitter mountains of the Peloponnesus.[8] I've lived on a Greek island. I've been to Venice[9] twice. In Rapallo, I met Ilona once and forever and took her sad heart with me across the south of France and into Spain.

I've lived in Yugoslavia. I've been to the famous Nice[10] flower market behind the opera house. I've lived in a village in the pre-Alps[11] and witnessed the daily parade of promenaders.

I've moved since Europe to the strange and wonderful country of Texas, land of polaroid-blue skies and big bugs. I met a mayor with my last name. I met famous Chicana/o artists and writers and *políticos*.[12]

Texas is another chapter in my life. It brought with it the Dobie-Paisano Fellowship, a six-month residency on a 265-acre ranch. But most important Texas brought Mexico back to me.

---

8. Peloponnesus (pel′ ə pə nē′ səs): Peninsula forming the southeastern part of the Greek mainland.
9. Venice (ven′ is): A seaport in northern Italy.
10. Nice (nēs): A seaport and resort in southeastern France.
11. pre-Alps: The foothills of the Alps, a mountain range in south-central Europe.
12. políticos (pō lē′ tē cōs): "Politicians."

Sitting at my favorite people-watching spot, the snaky Woolworth's counter across the street from the Alamo,[13] I can't think of anything else I'd rather be than a writer. I've traveled and lectured from Cape Cod to San Francisco, to Spain, Yugoslavia, Greece, Mexico, France, Italy, and finally today to Seguin, Texas. Along the way there is straw for the taking. With a little imagination, it can be spun into gold.

---

13. the Alamo (al′ ə mō′): A mission in San Antonio, Texas, that was the scene of a famous battle between Texans and Mexican troops in 1836.

RESPONDING TO THE SELECTION

Your Response

1. What do you imagine it would have been like in Sandra Cisneros's place as a child? Explain.
2. Does Cisneros seem like someone you would enjoy meeting? Why or why not?

Interpreting

3. (a) What point is Cisneros trying to convey through her anecdote about preparing tortillas? (b) How is this anecdote connected to the rest of her essay?
4. What does this essay reveal about the obstacles that Cisneros overcame on the way to becoming a successful writer?
5. What does the essay suggest about Cisneros's imagination and eye for detail? Explain.
6. What is the main point of the essay? Support your answer.

Applying

7. How could you apply Cisneros's messages to your own life? Explain.

ANALYZING LITERATURE

Transforming Real-Life Experiences

Some writers refuse to comment on how their real-life experiences are reflected in their literary works. In this essay, however, Sandra Cisneros takes us "backstage" to meet some of the actual people who have shaped her work. For example, she explains how people she met when her family moved into a house in 1966 re-emerged years later as characters in the stories in *The House on Mango Street*.

1. What phase of Cisneros's life seems to have been most important in shaping her writing? Support your answer.

2. How has her family contributed to her writing?
3. What does Cisneros mean when she refers to spinning straw into gold?

THINKING AND WRITING

Writing a Story

In the stories in *The House on Mango Street*, Sandra Cisneros creates vivid portraits of the people and places in a neighborhood she lived in as a child. Write a short story or episode based on a memorable personal experience. Like Cisneros, focus on bringing to life the people and places involved in this experience. Feel free to use your imagination to make the characters and events more interesting and entertaining. After you have finished drafting your story, put it aside for a day or two. Then revise it with a fresh eye.

LEARNING OPTIONS

1. **Multicultural Activity.** How do Cisneros's experiences as a writer compare with those of writers from other cultural backgrounds? Find a writer with another cultural background whose work interests you. Then explore the writer's work and the experiences and influences that shaped it. Share your findings.
2. **Speaking and Listening.** What message might Sandra Cisneros convey in a speech to a group of aspiring young writers? Use your imagination to develop a segment of a speech that Cisneros might be likely to deliver to such an audience. Assume the role of Cisneros and deliver the speech to your classmates.
3. **Art.** Create a drawing or a collage that depicts your neighborhood or a place in your neighborhood. Present your drawing or collage to your classmates and explain its purpose.

BARRY LOPEZ

1945–

Although he also writes fiction, Barry Lopez is known mainly for his nonfiction about nature and the environment. Written in a vivid, poetic style, his works explore certain aspects of nature from a variety of perspectives, creating a well-rounded view that both informs and entertains readers.

Born in Port Chester, New York, Lopez was educated at the University of Notre Dame and the University of Oregon. In 1976 he published his first book, *Desert Notes: Reflections in the Eye of a Raven,* a collection of fictional narratives. Since then he has produced several more books and has contributed articles, essays, and short fiction to many major magazines. His most successful work, *Of Wolves and Men* (1978), a nonfiction work examining the relationships between wolves and men and between wolves and other animals, was praised by critics and earned Lopez a number of awards.

From his home in a remote part of Oregon, Lopez travels frequently to lecture on the esthetics of the Arctic and the "moral ambiguities" of killing seals for scientific study. He has become a coveted guest on the college lecture circuit and enjoys a tremendous popularity due in part to this country's renewed enthusiasm for nature.

A soft-spoken man with an affable temperament, Lopez spent his early years in California's San Fernando Valley among alfalfa fields, sheep, and horses. His abiding love of nature was apparent early on, and he recalls being "mesmerized by the Mojave Desert, summers at Grand Canyon, and at Lake Arrowhead."

His reverence for nature in all its forms is matched by his expertise with language. Reviewers are nearly unanimous in praise of his prowess as a writer, noting his "jewel-like prose," and his "magical, shimmering similes." If his written words dazzle, then his spoken ones do too. When he speaks, he chooses words carefully and feels somewhat embarrassed when his audience's attention becomes, as one observer put it, "almost a physical thing, every heart in the room seeming to beat in time with his own." He says, "I care about language and landscape, both separately and for the connection between them, which is what writing is to me."

Filled with clear, descriptive language, the following excerpt from *Arctic Dreams* paints a vivid portrait of the Arctic wilderness, while examining the reasons so many people have been drawn to this region despite the dangers it poses.

GUIDE FOR INTERPRETING

from Arctic Dreams

Writers' Techniques

Imagery. Lopez's writing has been described as poetic, because it is filled with vivid imagery—words or phrases that create mental pictures, or images, that appeal to one or more of the five senses. While most of Lopez's images appeal to the sense of sight, some of his images cannot be visualized, and others appeal to more than one sense. For example, Lopez creates an image that appeals to both the sense of sight and the sense of touch when he writes, "the late-night sun, small as a kite in the northern sky, poured forth an energy that burned against my cheekbones."

In *Arctic Dreams* Lopez uses imagery to create a clear, lasting impression of the Arctic wilderness—an impression that helps to enlighten readers about the reasons people are drawn to the Arctic wilderness.

Focus

What are your impressions of the Arctic wilderness? Freewrite about the physical appearance of the Arctic wilderness, the types of animals that inhabit it, and the dangers it poses to people who venture into it.

Primary Source

In March of 1989, the supertanker *Exxon Valdez* ran aground in Alaska's Prince William Sound, dumping almost 11 million gallons of petroleum into the pristine seas. The effect on Barry Lopez's beloved Alaska coastline was devastating. The following is a record from *Newsweek* magazine of what the spill left behind.

Drop by Drop: A Box Score

Oil spilled: **10,836,000 gallons**
Shoreline contaminated by oil: **1,090 miles**
Shoreline treated by Exxon: **1,087 miles**
Shoreline still needing cleaning, according to the state:
  At least 1,000 miles
Number of dead birds: **33,126**
  of dead eagles: **138**
  of dead otters: **980**
Cost of cleanup to Exxon: **$1.28 billion (after-tax cost; insurance companies will reimburse Exxon $400 million)**
People involved in cleanup: **12,000**
Vessels and planes used in cleanup: **12,000**
Oil recovered: **2,604,000 gallons (est.)**
Waste from oil cleanup: **24,000 tons**
Lawsuits filed against Exxon: **145**

from Arctic Dreams

Barry Lopez

One summer evening I was camped in the western Brooks Range of Alaska with a friend. From the ridge where we had pitched our tent we looked out over tens of square miles of rolling tundra along the southern edge of the calving grounds of the Western Arctic caribou herd. During those days we observed not only caribou and wolves, which we'd come to study, but wolverine and red fox, ground squirrels, delicate-legged whimbrels and aggressive jaegers, all in the unfoldings of their obscure lives. One night we watched in awe as a young grizzly bear tried repeatedly to force its way past a yearling wolf standing guard alone before a den of young pups. The bear eventually gave up and went on its way. We watched snowy owls and rough-legged hawks hunt and caribou drift like smoke through the valley.

On the evening I am thinking about—it was breezy there on Ilingnorak Ridge, and cold; but the late-night sun, small as a kite in the northern sky, poured forth an energy that burned against my cheekbones—it was on that evening that I went on a walk for the first time among the tundra birds. They all build their nests on the ground, so their vulnerability is extreme. I gazed down at a single horned lark no bigger than my fist. She stared back resolute as iron. As I approached, golden plovers abandoned their nests in hysterical ploys, artfully feigning a broken wing to distract me from the woven grass cups that couched their pale, darkly speckled eggs. Their eggs glowed with a soft, pure light, like the window light in a Ver-

meer[1] painting. I marveled at this intense and concentrated beauty on the vast table of the plain. I walked on to find Lapland longspurs as still on their nests as stones, their dark eyes gleaming. At the nest of two snowy owls I stopped. These are more formidable animals than plovers. I stood motionless. The wild glare in their eyes receded. One owl settled back slowly over its three eggs, with an aura of primitive alertness. The other watched me, and immediately sought a bond with my eyes if I started to move.

I took to bowing on these evening walks. I would bow slightly with my hands in my pockets, toward the birds and the evidence of life in their nests—because of their fecundity, unexpected in this remote region, and because of the serene arctic light that came down over the land like breath, like breathing.

I remember the wild, dedicated lives of the birds that night and also the abandon with which a small herd of caribou crossed the Kokolik River to the northwest, the incident of only a few moments. They pranced through like wild mares, kicking up sheets of water across the evening sun and shaking it off on the far side like huge dogs, a bloom of spray that glittered in the air around them like grains of mica.

I remember the press of light against my face. The explosive skitter of calves among grazing caribou. And the warm intensity of

---

1. Vermeer (vər mer′): Dutch painter Jan Vermeer (1632–1675).

the eggs beneath these resolute birds. Until then, perhaps because the sun was shining in the very middle of the night, so out of tune with my own customary perception, I had never known how benign sunlight could be. How forgiving. How run through with compassion in a land that bore so eloquently the evidence of centuries of winter.

During those summer days on Ilingnorak Ridge there was no dark night. Darkness never came. The birds were born. They flourished, and then flew south in the wake of the caribou.

The second incident is more fleeting. It occurred one night when I was being driven past a graveyard in Kalamazoo, Michigan. Among the gravestones was one marking the burial place of Edward Israel, a shy young man who sailed north in 1881 with Lieuten-

ant Adolphus Greely. Greely and his men established a base camp on Ellesmere Island, 450 miles from the North Pole, and explored the surrounding territory in the spring of 1882. A planned relief expedition failed to reach them that summer, and also failed again the next year. Desperate, Greely's party of twenty-five retreated south, hopeful of being met by a rescue party in 1884. They wintered at Cape Sabine, Ellesmere Island, where sixteen of them died of starvation and scurvy,[2] another committed suicide, and one man was executed for stealing food. Israel, the expedition's astronomer, died on May 27, 1884, three weeks before the others were

---

2. scurvy (skur′ vē) *n.*: A disease caused by vitamin-C deficiency.

rescued. The survivors remembered him as the most congenial person among them.

I remember looking out the back window of the car that evening and seeing Israel's grave in the falling light. What had this man hoped to find? What sort of place did he think lay out there before him on that bright June morning in 1881 when the *Proteus* slipped its moorings at Saint John's, Newfoundland?

No one is able to say, of course. He was drawn on by the fixations of his own imagination, as were John Davis and William Baffin before him and as Robert Peary and Vilhjalmur Stefansson[3] would be after him. Perhaps he intended to make his mark as a scientist, to set his teeth in that high arctic landscape and come home like Darwin[4] to a sedate and contemplative life, in the farmlands of southern Michigan. Perhaps he merely hungered after the unusual. We can only imagine that he desired something, the fulfillment of some personal and private dream, to which he pinned his life.

Israel was buried with great public feeling and patriotic rhetoric. His gravestone reads

IN LIFE A TRUE CHILD OF GOD

IN DEATH A HERO

These two incidents came back to me often in the four or five years that I traveled in the Arctic. The one, timeless and full of light, reminded me of sublime innocence, of the innate beauty of undisturbed relationships. The other, a dream gone awry, reminded me of the long human struggle, mental and physical, to come to terms with the Far North. As I traveled, I came to believe that people's desires and aspirations were as much a part of the land as the wind, solitary animals, and the bright fields of stone and tundra. And, too, that the land itself existed quite apart from these.

The physical landscape is baffling in its ability to transcend whatever we would make of it. It is as subtle in its expression as turns of the mind, and larger than our grasp; and yet it is still knowable. The mind, full of curiosity and analysis, disassembles a landscape and then reassembles the pieces—the nod of a flower, the color of the night sky, the murmur of an animal—trying to fathom its geography. At the same time the mind is trying to find its place within the land, to discover a way to dispel its own sense of estrangement.

The particular section of the Arctic I became concerned with extends from Bering Strait in the west to Davis Strait[5] in the east. It includes great, unrelieved stretches of snow and ice that in summer become plains of open water and an ocean that is the tundra, a tawny island beneath the sky. But there are, too, surprising and riveting sights: Wilberforce Falls on the Hood River suddenly tumbles 160 feet into a wild canyon in the midst of the Canadian tundra, and its roar can be heard for miles. Humboldt Glacier, a towering, 50-mile-long sea margin of the Greenland ice sheet, calves[6] icebergs into Kane Basin with gargantuan and implacable force. The badlands of east-central Melville Island, an eroded country of desert oranges, of muted yellows and reds, reminds a traveler of canyons and arroyos in southern Utah. And there are places more exotic, like the Ruggles River, which flows out of Lake Hazen on Ellesmere Island in winter and runs 2000 feet through the Stygian[7] darkness, wreathed in frost smoke, before it disappears underneath its own ice. South of Cape Bathurst and west of the

---

3. John Davis ... Vilhjalmur Stefansson: Arctic explorers.
4. Darwin: Charles Darwin (1809–1882), an English naturalist who formulated the theory of evolution.

5. Bering Strait ... Davis Strait: The Bering Strait separates Siberia and Alaska. The Davis Strait separates Greenland and Baffin Island, Canada.
6. calves *v.*: Releases.
7. Stygian (stij′ ē ən) *adj.*: Characteristic of the river Styx, the river encircling Hades, the land of the dead, in Greek mythology.

Horton River in the Northwest Territories, bituminous shale fires that have been burning underground for hundreds of years make those coastal hills seem like a vast, smoldering heap of industrial slag. South of the central Kobuk River, one hundred foot dunes rise above hundreds of square miles of shifting sand. In East Greenland lies an arctic oasis called Queen Louisa Land, a valley of wild grasses and summer wildflowers surrounded by the walls of the Greenland ice cap.

The Arctic, overall, has the classic lines of a desert landscape: spare, balanced, extended, and quiet. In the Queen Elizabeth Islands the well-drained tundra plains and low-lying bogs more familiar in the south give way to expanses of weathered rock and gravel, and the illusion of a desert is even more complete. On Baffin and Ellesmere islands and in northern Alaska, sharply pitched arctic mountain ranges, which retain their remoteness even as you stand within them, complete a pervasive suggestion of austerity. The apparent monotony of the land is relieved, however, by weather systems moving through, and by the activities of animals, particularly of birds and caribou. And because so much of the country stands revealed, and because sunlight passing through the dustless air renders its edges with such unusual sharpness, animals linger before the eye. And their presence is vivid.

Like other landscapes that initially appear barren, arctic tundra can open suddenly, like the corolla of a flower, when any intimacy with it is sought. One begins to notice spots of brilliant red, orange, and green, for example, among the monotonic browns of a tundra tussock. A wolf spider lunges at a glistening beetle. A shred of muskox wool lies inert in the lavender blooms of a saxifrage. When Alwin Pederson, a Danish naturalist, first arrived on the northeast coast of Greenland, he wrote, "I must admit to strange feelings at the sight of this godforsaken desert of stone." Before he left, however, he was writing of muskoxen grazing in lush grass that grew higher than the animals' heads in Jameson Land, and of the stark beauty of nunataks, the ice-free spires of rock that pierce the Pleistocene[8] stillness of the Greenland ice cap. I, like Pederson, when stooping to pick up the gracile rib bone of an arctic hare, would catch sudden and unexpected sight of the silken cocoon of an arctic caterpillar.

The wealth of biological detail on the tundra dispels any feeling that the land is empty; and its likeness to a stage suggests impending events. On a summer walk, the wind-washed air proves depthlessly clear. Time and again you come upon the isolated and succinct evidence of life—animal tracks, the undigested remains of a ptarmigan in an owl's casting, a patch of barren-ground willow nibbled nearly leafless by arctic hares. You are afforded the companionship of birds, which follow after you. (They know you are an animal; sooner or later you will turn up something to eat.) Sandpipers scatter before you, screaming *tuituek*, an Eskimo name for them. Coming awkwardly down a scree[9] slope of frost-riven limestone you make a glass-tinkling clatter—and at a distance a tundra grizzly rises on its hind legs to study you; the dish-shaped paws of its front legs deathly still, the stance so human it is unnerving.

Along creek washouts, in the western Arctic especially, you might stumble upon a mammoth tusk. Or in the eastern Arctic find undisturbed the ring of stones used by a hunter 1500 years ago to hold down the edge of his skin tent. These old Dorset camps, located along the coasts where arctic people have been traveling for four millennia, are poignant with their suggestion of the timeless determination of mankind. On rare occasions a traveler might come upon the more

---

8. Pleistocene (plīst' tə sēn): A geological era characterized by the spreading and recession of continental ice sheets and the appearance of modern man.

9. scree (skrē) *adj.*: A covering of rock fragments on a slope below a rock face.

imposing stone foundations of a large house abandoned by Thule-culture[10] people in the twelfth century. (The cold, dry arctic air might have preserved, even down to its odor, the remains of a ringed seal killed and eaten by them 800 years ago.) More often, one comes upon the remains of a twentieth-century camp, artifacts far less engaging than a scrap of worked caribou bone, or carved wood, or skewered hide at a Dorset or Thule site. But these artifacts disintegrate just as slowly—red tins of Prince Albert brand crimp-cut tobacco, cans of Pet evaporated milk and Log Cabin maple syrup. In the most recent camps one finds used flashlight batteries in clusters like animal droppings, and a bewildering variety of spent rifle and shotgun ammunition.

You raise your eyes from these remains, from whatever century, to look away. The land as far as you can see is rung with a harmonious authority, the enduring force of its natural history, of which these camps are so much a part. But the most recent evidence is vaguely disturbing. It does not derive in any clear way from the land. Its claim to being part of the natural history of the region seems, somehow, false.

It is hard to travel in the Arctic today and not be struck by the evidence of recent change. What is found at modern campsites along the coast points to the sudden arrival of a foreign technology—new tools and a new way of life for the local people. The initial adjustments to this were fairly simple; the rate of change, however, has continued to accelerate. Now the adjustments required are bewildering. And the new tools bring with them ever more complicated sets of beliefs. The native culture, from Saint Lawrence Island to Greenland, is today in a state of rapid economic reorganization and of internally disruptive social readjustment. In a recent article about the residents of Nunivak

Island, for example, a scientist wrote that the dietary shift from wild to store-bought foods (with the many nutritional and social complications involved) is proceeding so quickly it is impossible to pin down. "By the time this paper appears in print," he wrote, "much of the information in it will be of historical value only."

Industrial changes have also come to the Arctic, following the discovery of oil at Prudhoe Bay, Alaska, in 1968; the 800-mile-long trans-Alaska pipeline itself, with its recent Kuparuk extension; base camps for oil exploration on Canada's Melville Island and Tuktoyaktuk Peninsula; huge lead-zinc mining operations on northern Baffin and Little Cornwallis islands; hundreds of miles of new roads; and increased ship, air, and truck traffic. The region's normally violent and unpredictable weather, its extreme cold and long periods of darkness, the great distance to supply depots, and the problem of stabilizing permanent structures over permafrost (which melts and shifts in erratic ways) have made the cost of these operations astronomical—indeed, in Canada they could not even be contemplated without massive assistance from the federal government.

Seen as widely separated dots and lines on a map, these recent, radical changes do not appear to amount to very much. But their rippling effect in the settlements and villages of the North—their economic, psychological, and social impact—is acute. And their success, though marginal and in some instances artificial, encourages additional schemes for development. Of special concern to local residents is a growing concentration of power in the hands of people with enormous economic resources but a poorly developed geographic sense of the region. A man from Tuktoyaktuk, a village near the mouth of the Mackenzie River, told me a pointed story. In the 1950's he traveled regularly up and down the coast by dogsled. When a distant early warning (DEW) line radar station went up along his accustomed route, he decided to stop to see what it was. The military

---

10. Thule (tho͞o′ lē) **culture:** An ancient culture that inhabited the northernmost regions of the world.

men welcomed him not as a resident of the region but as a figure of arctic fable. They enthusiastically fed his dogs a stack of raw steaks. Each time the man came, they pounded him on the back and fed his dogs piles of steak. Their largess seemed so odd and his rapport with them so unrealistic he stopped coming. For months afterward, however, he had tremendous difficulty controlling the dogs anytime they passed near the place.

Passing through the villages, even traveling across the uninhabited land, one cannot miss the evidence of upheaval, nor avoid being wrenched by it. The depression it engenders, because so much of it seems a heedless imposition on the land and on the people, a rude invasion, can lead one to despair. I brooded, like any traveler, over these things; but the presence of the land, the sheer weight of it before the senses, more often drew me away from the contemporary is-

sues. What, I wondered, had compelled me to bow to a horned lark? How do people imagine the landscapes they find themselves in? How does the land shape the imaginations of the people who dwell in it? How does desire itself, the desire to comprehend, shape knowledge? These questions seemed to me to go deeper than the topical issues, to underlie any consideration of them.

In pursuit of answers I traveled with people of differing dispositions. With Eskimos hunting narwhals off northern Baffin Island and walruses in the Bering Sea. With marine ecologists on hundreds of miles of coastal and near-shore surveys. With landscape painters in the Canadian Archipelago. In the company of roughnecks, drilling for oil on the winter ice in high winds at −30°F; and with the cosmopolitan crew of a freighter, sailing up the west coast of Greenland and into the Northwest Passage. They each assessed the land differently—the apparent emptiness of the tundra, which ran out like a shimmering mirage in the Northern Ocean; the blue-black vault of the winter sky, a cold beauty alive with scintillating stars; a herd of muskoxen, pivoting together on a hilltop to make a defensive stand, their long guard hairs swirling around them like a single, huge wave of dark water; a vein of lead-zinc ore glinting like tiny mirrors in a damp, Mesozoic[11] wall beneath the surface of Little Cornwallis Island; the moaning and wailing in the winter sea ice as the ocean's crust warped and shattered in the crystalline air. All of it, all that the land is and evokes, its actual meaning as well as its metaphorical reverberation, was and is understood differently.

These different views make a human future in that northern landscape a matter of conjecture, and it is here that one encounters dreams, projections of hope. The individual's dream, whether it be so private a wish as that the joyful determination of nesting arctic birds might infuse a distant friend weary of life, or a magnanimous wish, that a piece of scientific information wrested from the landscape might serve one's community—in individual dreams is the hope that one's own life will not have been lived for nothing. The very much larger dream, that of a people, is a story we have been carrying with us for millennia. It is a narrative of determination and hope that follows a question: What will we do as the wisdom of our past bears down on our future? It is a story of ageless conversation, not only conversation among ourselves about what we mean and wish to do, but a conversation held with the land—our contemplation and wonder at a prairie thunderstorm, or before the jagged line of a young mountain, or at the sudden rise of ducks from an isolated lake. We have been telling ourselves the story of what *we* represent in the land for 40,000 years. At the heart of this story, I think, is a simple, abiding belief: it is possible to live wisely on the land, and to live well. And in behaving respectfully toward all that the land contains, it is possible to imagine a stifling ignorance falling away from us.

Crossing the tree line to the Far North, one leaves behind the boreal owl clutching its frozen prey to its chest feathers to thaw it. Ahead lies an open, wild landscape, pointed off on the maps with arresting and anomalous names: Brother John Glacier and Cape White Handkerchief. Navy Board Inlet, Teddy Bear Island, and the Zebra Cliffs. Dexterity Fiord, Saint Patrick Canyon, Starvation Cove. Eskimos hunt the ringed seal, still, in the broad bays of the Sons of the Clergy and Royal Astronomical Society islands.

This is a land where airplanes track icebergs the size of Cleveland and polar bears fly down out of the stars. It is a region, like the desert, rich with metaphor, with adumbration. In a simple bow from the waist before the nest of the horned lark, you are able to stake your life, again, in what you dream.

---

11. Mesozoic (mes' ə zō'ik) *adj.*: A geological era characterized by the development and extinction of dinosaurs.

Your Response

1. How has reading this essay affected your image of the Arctic?
2. Which images from the essay do you find most striking? Explain.
3. Would you be interested in hearing Barry Lopez speak about his Arctic dreams?

Recalling

4. (a) What two incidents does Lopez recount in the first several paragraphs? (b) Of what do these two incidents remind Lopez?
5. What is the particular section of the Arctic with which Lopez became concerned?
6. (a) By what is the monotony of the Arctic land relieved? (b) What dispels any feeling that the Arctic land is empty?
7. (a) What industrial changes have come to the Arctic since the discovery of oil in 1968? (b) What has become a special concern for local residents?

Interpreting

8. What do the two incidents Lopez initially recounts reveal about the relationship between people and nature in the Arctic?
9. Although the people who come to the Arctic perceive the landscape in a variety of ways, Lopez argues that they all share a common vision. What is this vision?
10. (a) What is the main point of this essay? (b) How is the title related to the main point?

Applying

11. What other types of dangerous, threatening environments have explorers ventured into during the course of history?

ANALYZING LITERATURE

Using Imagery

Imagery refers to words or phrases that create mental pictures, or images, that appeal to one or more of the five senses. Although most of the imagery in *Arctic Dreams* appeals to the sense of sight, Lopez also uses some images that cannot be visualized and others that appeal to more than one sense.

1. Find five images that appeal to the sense of sight.
2. Find two images that appeal to another sense.
3. Find two images that appeal to more than one sense.

CRITICAL THINKING AND READING

Appreciating the Effect of Imagery

Through the use of imagery, Lopez creates a vivid impression of the Arctic wilderness in his essay. This impression helps provide readers with an understanding of peoples' desires to venture into this dangerous and unforgiving region.

1. What is the dominant impression of the Arctic wilderness that Lopez conveys?
2. How does this impression relate to the main point of the essay?

THINKING AND WRITING

Responding to Criticism

A critic has commented that "A poet slips quietly out of Mr. Lopez's matter-of-fact prose, like an eye on a long nerve-string, to dance and feel." Write a brief essay in which you discuss this comment in relation to the excerpt from *Arctic Dreams.* Reread the essay, focusing on Lopez's use of language. Prepare a thesis statement. Then write your essay, using passages from *Arctic Dreams* to support your thesis. When you revise, make sure you have not included any unnecessary information.

LEARNING OPTION

Writing. Consider the images evoked by such Arctic place names as Brother John Glacier, Cape White Handkerchief, and Dexterity Fiord. Choose one of the places named in the essay, and use your imagination to invent a history that explains its name. In your history you might describe someone's Arctic dream.

AMY TAN

1952–

Throughout the early part of her life, Amy Tan rejected her Chinese heritage and embraced what she regarded as typical American values and ideals. She even explored ways of changing her appearance, once trying to reshape her nose by wearing a clothespin on it at night. It was not until she visited China with her mother at age thirty-five that she made peace with her Chinese roots and reconciled the Chinese and American aspects of her identity. Drawing from her experiences, Tan has written two novels about Chinese American life and has earned a place among America's most popular young novelists.

Amy Tan was born in Oakland, California, in 1952, three years after her parents had arrived in the United States from China. After attending college in Oregon and California, Tan earned a master's degree in linguistics. She soon began a successful career as a business writer, but she yearned to write fiction. At age thirty-three she set herself a goal: Within one year she would write a publishable story.

Although Tan failed to achieve her goal, her trip to China in 1987 strengthened her commitment to her fiction writing. Following her return she developed a story she had been working on into a novel about the lives of four Chinese American women of her mother's generation and their daughters. Published in 1989 as *The Joy Luck Club,* the novel became an immediate bestseller and garnered the types of reviews that all writers dream of. Tan became an overnight celebrity, receiving invitations to lecture at college campuses across the country and even being recruited to pose in an advertisement for blue jeans.

Faced with the challenge of writing a second novel that would live up to the reputation she had established, Tan struggled for months to overcome writer's block. After beginning six projected novels and abandoning each, she started work on *The Kitchen God's Wife.* Published in 1991, the novel won even more enthusiastic reviews than her first effort. One reviewer observed, "No doubt it was daunting to attempt to write a second book in the wake of the enormous success of *The Joy Luck Club,* but none of Ms. Tan's fans will be disappointed. *The Kitchen God's Wife* is a more ambitious effort, and, in the end, greatly satisfying."

GUIDE FOR INTERPRETING

Historical Context

Mother Tongue

The Immigrant Experience. The United States is a country deeply rooted in the immigrant experience. Its population is made up almost entirely of immigrants and descendants of immigrants from virtually every nation on earth. Although most immigrants are drawn to the United States by the promise of a better life, most face tough challenges when they arrive.

One of the greatest challenges for immigrants who are from non–English-speaking nations is overcoming the language barrier. The "mother tongues," or native languages, that immigrants bring with them are both a comfort and a limitation, a treasured connection to their previous homes and an impediment to acceptance in their new ones. Even after learning English, immigrants often discover that they are still discriminated against or treated differently because they speak with an accent.

The challenges of adapting to American life have led many immigrant groups—from Germans arriving in eighteenth-century Pennsylvania to today's refugees from Central America—to settle in communities in which people speak their language and share a cultural heritage. These communities continue to thrive in cities across America, representing a rich array of cultures and languages, from Chinese and Vietnamese to Armenian and Arabic.

In the following essay, Amy Tan relates how her mother's difficulties with the English language have shaped her mother's experiences in America. In addition, she explains how her writing has been shaped by her mother's attempts to master the language.

Focus

Write a journal entry in which you explore the obstacles that might be faced by someone who has a limited understanding of the English language.

Mother Tongue

Amy Tan

I am not a scholar of English or literature. I cannot give you much more than personal opinions on the English language and its variations in this country or others.

I am a writer. And by that definition, I am someone who has always loved language. I am fascinated by language in daily life. I spend a great deal of my time thinking about the power of language—the way it can evoke an emotion, a visual image, a complex idea, or a simple truth. Language is the tool of my trade. And I use them all—all the Englishes I grew up with.

Recently, I was made keenly aware of the different Englishes I do use. I was giving a talk to a large group of people, the same talk I had already given to half a dozen other groups. The nature of the talk was about my writing, my life, and my book, *The Joy Luck Club.* The talk was going along well enough, until I remembered one major difference that made the whole talk sound wrong. My mother was in the room. And it was perhaps the first time she had heard me give a lengthy speech, using the kind of English I have never used with her. I was saying things like, "The intersection of memory upon imagination" and "There is an aspect of my fiction that relates to thus-and-thus"—a speech filled with carefully wrought grammatical phrases, burdened, it suddenly seemed to me, with nominalized forms, past perfect tenses, conditional phrases, all the forms of standard English that I had learned in school and through books, the forms of English I did not use at home with my mother.

Just last week, I was walking down the street with my mother, and I again found myself conscious of the English I was using, the English I do use with her. We were talking about the price of new and used furniture and I heard myself saying this: "Not waste money that way." My husband was with us as well, and he didn't notice any switch in my English. And then I realized why. It's because over the twenty years we've been together I've often used the same kind of English with him, and sometimes he even uses it with me. It has become our language of intimacy, a different sort of English that relates to family talk, the language I grew up with.

So you'll have some idea of what this family talk I heard sounds like, I'll quote what my mother said during a recent conversation which I videotaped and then transcribed. During this conversation, my mother was talking about a political gangster in Shanghai[1] who had the same last name as her family's, Du, and how the gangster in his early years wanted to be adopted by her family, which was rich by comparison. Later, the gangster became more powerful, far richer than my mother's family, and one day showed up at my mother's wedding to pay his respects. Here's what she said in part:

"Du Yusong having business like fruit stand. Like off the street kind. He is Du like Du Zong—but not Tsung-ming Island people. The local people call putong, the river

---

1. **Shanghai** (shaŋ′ hī′): A seaport in eastern China.

east side, he belong to that side local people. That man want to ask Du Zong father take him in like become own family. Du Zong father wasn't look down on him, but didn't take seriously, until that man big like become a mafia. Now important person, very hard to inviting him. Chinese way, come only to show respect, don't stay for dinner. Respect for making big celebration, he shows up. Mean gives lots of respect. Chinese custom. Chinese social life that way. If too important won't have to stay too long. He come to my wedding. I didn't see, I heard it. I gone to boy's side, they have YMCA[2] dinner. Chinese age I was nineteen."

You should know that my mother's expressive command of English belies how much she actually understands. She reads the *Forbes*[3] report, listens to *Wall Street Week*,[4] converses daily with her stockbroker, reads all of Shirley MacLaine's[5] books with ease—all kinds of things I can't begin to understand. Yet some of my friends tell me they understand 50 percent of what my mother says. Some say they understand 80 to 90 percent. Some say they understand none of it, as if she were speaking pure Chinese. But to me, my mother's English is perfectly clear, perfectly natural. It's my mother tongue. Her language, as I hear it, is vivid, direct, full of observation and imagery. That was the language that helped shape the way I saw things, expressed things, made sense of the world.

Lately, I've been giving more thought to the kind of English my mother speaks. Like others, I have described it to people as "broken" or "fractured" English. But I wince when I say that. It has always bothered me that I can

think of no way to describe it other than "broken," as if it were damaged and needed to be fixed, as if it lacked a certain wholeness and soundness. I've heard other terms used, "limited English," for example. But they seem just as bad, as if everything is limited, including people's perceptions of the limited English speaker.

I know this for a fact, because when I was growing up, my mother's "limited" English limited *my* perception of her. I was ashamed of her English. I believed that her English reflected the quality of what she had to say. That is, because she expressed them imperfectly her thoughts were imperfect. And I had plenty of empirical evidence to support me: the fact that people in department stores, at banks, and at restaurants did not take her seriously, did not give her good service, pretended not to understand her, or even acted as if they did not hear her.

My mother has long realized the limitations of her English as well. When I was fifteen, she used to have me call people on the phone to pretend I was she. In this guise, I was forced to ask for information or even to complain and yell at people who had been rude to her. One time it was a call to her stockbroker in New York. She had cashed out her small portfolio and it just so happened we were going to go to New York the next week, our very first trip outside California. I had to get on the phone and say in an adolescent voice that was not very convincing, "This is Mrs. Tan."

And my mother was standing in the back whispering loudly, "Why he don't send me check, already two weeks late. So mad he lie to me, losing me money."

And then I said in perfect English, "Yes, I'm getting rather concerned. You had agreed to send the check two weeks ago, but it hasn't arrived."

Then she began to talk more loudly. "What he want, I come to New York tell him front of his boss, you cheating me?" And I was trying to calm her down, make her be

2. YMCA: Young Men's Christian Association.
3. *Forbes*: A magazine of business and finance.
4. *Wall Street Week*: A weekly television program that reports business and investment news.
5. Shirley MacLaine's (mək lānz'): Shirley MacLaine is an American actress who has written several books.

Amy Tan and her mother

quiet, while telling the stockbroker, "I can't tolerate any more excuses. If I don't receive the check immediately, I am going to have to speak to your manager when I'm in New York next week." And sure enough, the following week there we were in front of this astonished stockbroker, and I was sitting there red-faced and quiet, and my mother, the real Mrs. Tan, was shouting at his boss in her impeccable broken English.

We used a similar routine just five days ago, for a situation that was far less humorous. My mother had gone to the hospital for an appointment, to find out about a benign brain tumor a CAT scan[6] had revealed a month ago. She said she had spoken very good English, her best English, no mistakes. Still, she said, the hospital did not apologize when they said they had lost the CAT scan and she had come for nothing. She said they did not seem to have any sympathy when she told them she was anxious to know the exact diagnosis, since her husband and son had both died of brain tumors. She said they

would not give her any more information until the next time and she would have to make another appointment for that. So she said she would not leave until the doctor called her daughter. She wouldn't budge. And when the doctor finally called her daughter, me, who spoke in perfect English—lo and behold—we had assurances the CAT scan would be found, promises that a conference call on Monday would be held, and apologies for any suffering my mother had gone through for a most regrettable mistake.

I think my mother's English almost had an effect on limiting my possibilities in life as well. Sociologists and linguists probably will tell you that a person's developing language skills are more influenced by peers. But I do think that the language spoken in the family, especially in immigrant families which are more insular, plays a large role in shaping the language of the child. And I believe that it affected my results on achievement tests, IQ tests, and the SAT. While my English skills were never judged as poor, compared to math, English could not be considered my strong suit. In grade school I did moderately well, getting perhaps B's, sometimes

---

6. CAT scan: A method used by doctors to diagnose brain disorders.

B-pluses, in English and scoring perhaps in the sixtieth or seventieth percentile on achievement tests. But those scores were not good enough to override the opinion that my true abilities lay in math and science, because in those areas I achieved A's and scored in the ninetieth percentile or higher.

This was understandable. Math is precise; there is only one correct answer. Whereas, for me at least, the answers on English tests were always a judgment call, a matter of opinion and personal experience. Those tests were constructed around items like fill-in-the-blank sentence completion, such as, "Even though Tom was _____, Mary thought he was _____." And the correct answer always seemed to be the most bland combinations of thoughts, for example, "Even though Tom was shy, Mary thought he was charming," with the grammatical structure "even though" limiting the correct answer to some sort of semantic opposites, so you wouldn't get answers like, "Even though Tom was foolish, Mary thought he was ridiculous." Well, according to my mother, there were very few limitations as to what Tom could have been and what Mary might have thought of him. So I never did well on tests like that.

The same was true with word analogies, pairs of words in which you were supposed to find some sort of logical, semantic relationship—for example, "*Sunset* is to *nightfall* _____ is to _____." And here you would be presented with a list of four possible pairs, one of which showed the same kind of relationship: *red* is to *stoplight, bus* is to *arrival, chills* is to *fever, yawn* is to *boring.* Well, I could never think that way. I knew what the tests were asking, but I could not block out of my mind the images already created by the first pair, "*sunset* is to *nightfall*"—and I would see a burst of colors against a darkening sky, the moon rising, the lowering of a curtain of stars. And all the other pairs of words—red, bus, stoplight, boring—just threw up a mass of confusing images, making it impossible for me to sort out something as logical as saying: "A sunset precedes nightfall" is the same as "a chill precedes a fever." The only way I would have gotten that answer right would have been to imagine an associative situation, for example, my being disobedient and staying out past sunset, catching a chill at night, which turns into feverish pneumonia as punishment, which indeed did happen to me.

I have been thinking about all this lately, about my mother's English, about achievement tests. Because lately I've been asked, as a writer, why there are not more Asian Americans represented in American literature. Why are there few Asian Americans enrolled in creative writing programs? Why do so many Chinese students go into engineering? Well, these are broad sociological questions I can't begin to answer. But I have noticed in surveys—in fact, just last week—that Asian students, as a whole, always do significantly better on math achievement tests than in English. And this makes me think that there are other Asian-American students whose English spoken in the home might also be described as "broken" or "limited." And perhaps they also have teachers who are steering them away from writing and into math and science, which is what happened to me.

Fortunately, I happen to be rebellious in nature and enjoy the challenge of disproving assumptions made about me. I became an English major my first year in college, after being enrolled as pre-med. I started writing nonfiction as a freelancer the week after I was told by my former boss that writing was my worst skill and I should hone my talents toward account management.

But it wasn't until 1985 that I finally began to write fiction. And at first I wrote using what I thought to be wittily crafted sentences, sentences that would finally prove I had mastery over the English language. Here's an example from the first draft of a story that later made its way into *The Joy Luck Club,* but without this line: "That was my mental quandary in its nascent state." A terrible line, which I can barely pronounce.

Fortunately, for reasons I won't get into today, I later decided I should envision a reader for the stories I would write. And the reader I decided upon was my mother, because these were stories about mothers. So with this reader in mind—and in fact she did read my early drafts—I began to write stories using all the Englishes I grew up with: the English I spoke to my mother, which for lack of a better term might be described as "simple"; the English she used with me, which for lack of a better term might be described as "broken"; my translation of her Chinese, which could certainly be described as "wa-tered down"; and what I imagined to be her translation of her Chinese if she could speak in perfect English, her internal language, and for that I sought to preserve the essence, but neither an English nor a Chinese structure. I wanted to capture what language ability tests can never reveal: her intent, her passion, her imagery, the rhythms of her speech and the nature of her thoughts.

Apart from what any critic had to say about my writing, I knew I had succeeded where it counted when my mother finished reading my book and gave me her verdict: "So easy to read."

▌R ESPONDING TO THE SELECTION

Your Response
1. After reading this essay, what are your feelings about Tan and her mother? Explain.
2. Do you agree with Tan's conclusion that successful writing is "easy to read"? Why or why not?

Interpreting
3. How has Tan's mother shaped Tan's writing? Support your answer.
4. How has Amy Tan's attitude toward her mother changed as she has grown older? Support your answer.
5. How does the way Tan now views her mother's English differ from how others view it?
6. (a) What can you infer from this essay about Amy Tan's character? (b) What can you infer about her mother's character?

Applying
7. (a) What would it be like to live in a place where a language barrier made it difficult for you to communicate with others? (b) How would you try to overcome the language barrier?

▌A NALYZING LITERATURE

Appreciating the Immigrant Experience
In her essay Tan captures an important aspect of the immigrant experience—the struggle to overcome a language barrier.

1. What does Tan's essay suggest about how a limited mastery of the English language can affect the way people are treated by others?
2. What does the essay reveal about how language differences can lead to misconceptions or stereotypes? Support your answer.

▌T HINKING AND WRITING

Writing About Language
Imagine that you have been asked by a television producer to write a proposal for a television program focusing on the role of language in contemporary life. Begin by choosing the type of program you would like to create: a sitcom, a documentary, a game show, or another type of program. Decide what aspect of language you will focus on; for example, you might want to focus on street jargon. Then write a two-page proposal explaining your idea to network executives.

▌L EARNING OPTION

Art. To overcome potential language barriers, icons or symbols are often used in place of words on signs in public places. Create an icon or a series of icons to represent a place or a type of person. For example, you might create an icon to represent a school or a police officer.

Poetry

THEODORE ROETHKE

1908–1963

Throughout the course of his career, Theodore Roethke focused his poetry on various aspects of his own life. Although his style changed between the publication of his first book, *Open House* (1941), and the appearance of his posthumous collection, *The Far Field* (1964), Roethke continued to seek a sense of self by exploring his personal experiences in his poetry.

Roethke grew up in Saginaw, Michigan, where his family owned several large commercial greenhouses. In his family's greenhouses, he observed nature putting forth roots and blossoms, as well as falling into dormancy and death. These observations later provided him with ideas and inspiration for many of his poems.

His work was especially influenced by the Transcendentalist movement, and he expressed an abiding affinity for Emerson and Thoreau. His adolescence had been a "hell of bright awareness" as one critic put it. He felt odd in high school where possessing keen intelligence was equated with being a "sissy." Often frustrated because he didn't know what to do with his perceptions, Roethke viewed himself as "odious" and found relating to people a problem well into his university years. Following the Transcendentalist precepts, he took refuge in nature. "When I get alone out under the sky where man isn't too evident—then I'm tremendously exalted and a thousand vivid ideas and sweet visions flood my consciousness."

During much of his life, he lived dangerously close to madness. His mental struggles threatened to destroy both his teaching and poetic careers, and in 1943 he was hospitalized for manic-depressive psychosis, one of two events that formed the foundation for most of his later poetry. The other event that shaped his later work was the death of his father, who had been both a stern authoritarian and a sensitive, vulnerable soul. Although it had happened when Roethke was fourteen, the poet waited until his later years to sort out his ambiguous feelings toward Otto Roethke.

After receiving his education at the University of Michigan and Harvard, Roethke taught writing at Bennington College, Pennsylvania State University, and the University of Washington. A slow, diligent writer, Roethke spent many years assembling poems for his first book. He went on to publish several more volumes, including *The Lost Son* (1948), *The Waking* (1953), and *Words for the Wind* (1958). In 1954 he received a Pulitzer Prize for *The Waking,* and two years after his death he was awarded the National Book Award for *The Far Field*.

The Waking; Once More, the Round

Writers' Techniques

Rhyme. Rhyme refers to the repetition of sounds in the accented syllables of two or more words that appear close to each other. Rhyme that occurs at the ends of lines is called end rhyme, whereas rhyme that occurs within a line is called internal rhyme. When rhyme involves the repetition of identical sounds, it is called exact rhyme. For example, *snow-crow* is an exact rhyme. When the rhyme is not exact, it is called approximate rhyme or slant rhyme. For example, *dream-home* is an approximate rhyme.

Literary Forms

Villanelle. All poetry has form, but some poems are framed according to very structured "rules," or conventions. You are no doubt familiar with some formal poetry. Haiku, for instance, consists of seventeen syllables arranged in three lines of five, seven, and five syllables respectively. Sonnets each have fourteen lines and follow prescribed rhyme schemes and metrical arrangements. One of the most demanding forms of poetry is the villanelle. So difficult is it to write a good villanelle that poets seldom use this form. Theodore Roethke's "The Waking" is a villanelle. As you read it, notice how it fits the pattern.

A villanelle consists of six stanzas, the first five of which contain three lines each, with an end rhyme occurring between the first and third lines. The middle lines of all five stanzas rhyme with one another. The first and last lines of the first stanza form a unifying refrain throughout the poem. These lines are split after the first stanza and alternately repeated as the final line of each successive stanza until the sixth and final four-line stanza. In the sixth stanza, the two refrain lines are combined to form the two final lines of the poem. Further conventions govern the villanelle, but these serve to illustrate the constraints under which the poet labors when he or she creates a villanelle. Roethke follows the conventional formula in this poem except in line 15, where he breaks the convention, or "rule," by slightly altering the line. When a poet breaks a convention, he or she does so for important reasons, typically to call attention to the place where convention is breached. Why do you think Roethke wanted to call attention to line 15 in "The Waking"?

Focus

In Roethke's poem "The Waking," the speaker comments, "I learn by going where I have to go." Do you think this is the way most people learn? Freewrite about the ways in which people acquire knowledge during the courses of their lives.

The Waking

Theodore Roethke

I wake to sleep, and take my waking slow.
I feel my fate in what I cannot fear.
I learn by going where I have to go.

We think by feeling. What is there to know?
5   I hear my being dance from ear to ear.
I wake to sleep, and take my waking slow.

Of those so close beside me, which are you?
God bless the Ground! I shall walk softly there,
And learn by going where I have to go.

10   Light takes the Tree; but who can tell us how?
The lowly worm climbs up a winding stair;
I wake to sleep, and take my waking slow.

Great Nature has another thing to do
To you and me; so take the lively air,
15   And, lovely, learn by going where to go.

This shaking keeps me steady. I should know.
What falls away is always. And is near.
I wake to sleep, and take my waking slow.
I learn by going where I have to go.

Your Response

1. What is your reaction to the speaker's outlook on life? Explain.
2. The speaker implies that emotion is superior to intellect when he says: "We think by feeling. What is there to know?" Do you agree? Why or why not?

Interpreting

3. (a) What is paradoxical, or seemingly self-contradictory, about the statement, "I wake to sleep"? (b) What is the meaning of this paradox? (c) Find two other paradoxes in the poem. (d) Explain the meaning of each of these paradoxes.
4. What does the speaker mean when he says that he takes his "waking slow"?
5. What is the meaning of lines 3, 9, and 19?
6. (a) What is the other "thing" that Nature has "to do/To you and me"? (b) How does the speaker's reference to this "thing" help clarify the meaning of the poem?
7. Read this poem aloud. (a) What effect is created by the rhythm? (b) How is this effect appropriate for the subject matter?
8. What does this poem suggest about Roethke's attitude toward life?
9. Why is "The Waking" an appropriate title for this poem?

Applying

10. The American novelist Richard Wright has written, "Men can starve from lack of self-realization as much as they can from a lack of bread." Discuss the meaning of this quotation and its relation to "The Waking."

ANALYZING LITERATURE

Understanding Rhyme

Rhyme refers to the repetition of sounds in the accented syllables of two or more words that appear close to each other. Exact rhyme refers to the repetition of identical sounds. The use of the words *fear* and *ear* at the ends of lines 2 and 5 is an example of exact rhyme. When the rhyme is not exact, it is called approximate rhyme or slant rhyme. For example, Roethke uses slant rhyme in lines 5 and 8, when he rhymes the words *ear* and *there*.

1. Find two more examples of exact rhyme.
2. Find another example of slant rhyme.

Recognizing a Villanelle

A villanelle is a nineteen-line French verse form. It has two refrains formed by repeating line 1 in lines 6, 12, and 18 and by repeating line 3 in lines 9, 15, and 19. The three lines each of the first five stanzas rhyme *aba*. The final quatrain rhymes *abaa*.

1. What line of this poem is repeated in lines 6, 12, and 18?
2. What line is repeated in lines 9, 15, and 19?
3. What is the rhyme scheme, or the pattern of end rhymes, in the poem?
4. How is the form of this poem appropriate to the subject?

THINKING AND WRITING

Responding to Criticism

Critic Robert Boyers has commented that Roethke's "best poems permit us to embrace the principle of change as the root of stability." Write an essay in which you discuss this comment in relation to "The Waking." Reread the poem, noting what it suggests about the concepts of change and stability. Develop a thesis statement. Then write your essay, using passages from the poem to support your argument. When you finish writing, revise your essay, making sure that you have included enough supporting information.

LEARNING OPTION

Writing. As a teacher of poetry, Roethke advised beginners to "write like someone else." He followed his own advice; his villanelle "The Waking" shows the influence of his acknowledged mentor, Irish poet William Butler Yeats. Do as Roethke suggests. Choose a poet whose work you admire, analyze the poet's techniques, and write a poem using the same techniques. Acknowledge your mentor in a byline to the poem.

Once More, the Round

Theodore Roethke

What's greater, Pebble or Pond?
What can be known? The Unknown.
My true self runs toward a Hill
More! O More! visible.

5 Now I adore my life
With the Bird, the abiding Leaf,
With the Fish, the questing Snail,
And the Eye altering all;
And I dance with William Blake[1]
10 For love, for Love's sake;

And everything comes to One,
As we dance on, dance on, dance on.

---

1. William Blake: English poet (1757–1827).

WILD FLOWERS, 1978
Samuel Reindorf
Collections of George Williams

RESPONDING TO THE SELECTION

Your Response

1. What is your reaction to this poem? Explain.
2. How would you answer the speaker's first question, "What's greater, Pebble or Pond"? Explain.

Interpreting

3. What do the "Pebble" and "Pond" referred to in the first stanza represent?

4. Why does the speaker's "true self" run "toward a Hill"?
5. What does the speaker mean when he says that "the Eye" alters "all"?

Applying

6. In this poem Roethke compares life to a round dance, a type of dance in which groups of dancers move in a circle. To what other types of dances do you think life might be compared?

James Dickey (1923–   )

A lover of nature and a devoted outdoorsman, James Dickey is a man of great size (he is six foot three) and energy. Dickey's energy and affection for the outdoors are exhibited in his poetry. In his work he often shows people testing their survival instincts against the primitive elements of the natural world. This reflects his belief that maintaining contact with the world of nature can help people escape from the monotony of everyday existence.

Dickey was born in Atlanta, Georgia. He was a star football player in high school and served as a bomber pilot in World War II. After returning from the war, Dickey began writing poetry while studying at Vanderbilt University. During his senior year, one of his poems was published in *Sewanee Review*.

Dickey went on to publish several volumes of poetry, including *Into the Stone* (1960), *Buckdancer's Choice* (1965), *Poems 1957–1967* (1967), and *Puella* (1982). In 1966 he received the National Book Award for *Buckdancer's Choice*. In addition to poetry, he has written literary criticism and a bestselling novel, *Deliverance* (1970).

Denise Levertov (1923–   )

Denise Levertov has commented that she believes that the poem is the poet's means for discovering the divine in the real world. Acting upon this belief, Levertov writes original, inventive poetry that often explores the hidden meaning in ordinary events. Most of her poems stem from personal experience, but they are not merely personal treatments. She firmly believes a poet's aim should be greater than the narration of pictures, and through her work she strives to impart love of nature, faith in people, and the conviction that life must be fully experienced. Levertov feels the essence of life is paradox and that both communication and silence should be respected. Her poems often bring together the seeming polarities of activity and passivity, sound and silence.

Levertov was born in Essex, England. She began writing poetry at an early age, and in 1946 she published her first collection, *The Double Image*. A year later she married American writer Mitchell Goodman and moved to the United States. She became an American citizen in 1955, and her second book of poetry was published in 1957. Since then, she has written more than a dozen books of poetry, including *With Eyes at the Back of Our Heads* (1960) and *Relearning the Alphabet* (1970). She has also published two books of translations and a book of essays about writing poetry.

GUIDE FOR INTERPRETING

The Rain Guitar; Merritt Parkway

Literary Forms

Visual Poetry. Visual poetry refers to poems in which the letters, words, lines, and spaces are arranged to form a shape or create a visual effect. Often the shape of a visual poem in some way reflects or reinforces the poem's meaning. For example, seventeenth-century English poet George Herbert shaped his poem "The Altar" to look like a church altar and shaped his poem "Easter Wings" to resemble a pair of wings.

Commentary

As you read these two poems by Dickey and Levertov, notice that although they differ in many ways, they have more in common than their use of visual effects. Each confronts human isolation and connection and the way that connection between people enriches lives. "The Rain Guitar" brings two apparent strangers into the same place at the same time, though each has come for his own purpose. The speaker declaims, "It mattered to me not at all " about the other upon the bridge. And when we see that the second man has come to fish, the speaker again dissociates himself from the fisherman. "I had no line and no feeling. I had nothing to do with fish. . . . " But the poet suggests a link between the two that neither man yet acknowledges. The speaker's "threads were opening" and the second man "cast a fish thread" into the water. Poets use words precisely, and the repetition of *thread* implies a similarity between these men.

Denise Levertov offers a modern scene that, at first thought, would imply man's complete isolation. Indeed, she recounts the isolation of individuals within their separate cars. But she goes "above" that seclusion in several places and implies a connection between the drivers who share experiences so strikingly similar. She recognizes in "the dreamlike continuum . . ." that people are alike. With this line, "And the people—ourselves!" she expresses not only the link between people but their identity with one another. People, she implies, are not isolated, although they may appear to be except at "gasoline stops." She implies that the viewing of lives as unique and isolated from one another is an illusion we take as real, perhaps because of the speed with which we move "relentlessly" in our quickening world.

What feelings about connection and isolation do these poems evoke in you?

Focus

In "Merritt Parkway," Levertov writes about the experience of traveling along a crowded highway. Freewrite about the thoughts and feelings that you associate with highway travel.

The Rain Guitar

James Dickey

England, 1962

The water-grass under had never waved
But one way. It showed me that flow is forever
Sealed from rain in a weir. For some reason having
To do with Winchester, I was sitting on my guitar case
5   Watching nothing but eelgrass trying to go downstream with all the right motions
But one. I had on a sweater, and my threads were opening
Like mouths with rain. It mattered to me not at all
That a bridge was stumping
With a man, or that he came near and cast a fish
10   thread into the weir. I had no line and no feeling.
I had nothing to do with fish
But my eyes on the grass they hid in, waving with the one move of trying
To be somewhere else. With what I had, what could I do?
I got out my guitar, that somebody told me was supposed to improve
15   With moisture—or was it when it dried out?—and hit the lowest
And loudest chord. The drops that were falling just then
Hammered like Georgia railroad track
With E. The man went into a kind of fishing
Turn. Play it, he said through his pipe. There
20   I went, fast as I could with cold fingers. The strings shook
With drops. A buck dance settled on the weir. Where was the city
Cathedral in all this? Out of sight, but somewhere around.
Play a little more
Of that, he said, and cast. Music-wood shone,
25   Getting worse or better faster than it liked:
Improvement or disintegration
Supposed to take years, fell on it
By the gallon. It darkened and rang
Like chimes. My sweater collapsed, and the rain reached
30   My underwear. I picked, the guitar showered, and he cast to the mountain
Music. His wood leg tapped
On the cobbles. Memories of many men
Hung, rain-faced, improving, sealed-off
In the weir. I found myself playing Australian
35   Versions of British marching songs. Mouths opened all over me; I sang,
His legs beat and marched
Like companions. I was Air Force,
I said. So was I; I picked
This up in Burma, he said, tapping his gone leg

40   With his fly rod, as Burma and the South
          west Pacific and North Georgia reeled,
         Rapped, cast, chimed, darkened and drew down
           Cathedral water, and improved.

Responding to the Selection

Your Response

1. What kinds of music would you play on a "rain guitar"? Explain.
2. Do you feel a sense of kinship with the guitar player? Why or why not?

Interpreting

3. To what two senses do most of the images, or word pictures, in the poem appeal? Find examples to support your answer.
4. (a) What do the speaker's actions in the poem suggest about his state of mind? (b) What details in the poem indicate that his war experiences have had a powerful effect on him?
5. This poem is set in Winchester, England, the location of a famous cathedral, which the speaker refers to in the poem. (a) What is the relationship between the cathedral and the speaker's experiences in the poem? (b) What is the significance of the other places mentioned in the poem?

Applying

6. Why do you think music often reminds us of past experiences?

Analyzing Literature

Understanding Visual Poetry

Visual poetry refers to poems in which the letters, words, lines, and spaces are arranged to form a shape or create a visual effect. Often the shape of a visual poem reflects or reinforces the poem's meaning.

1. What is the visual effect of "The Rain Guitar"?
2. How is the visual effect related to the poem's meaning?

Thinking and Writing

Writing a Visual Poem

Imagine that you have been asked to write a visual poem for your school literary magazine. Start by choosing a subject for your poem. Then think about how you can shape the poem to reflect its meaning. Prepare a list of images, or word pictures, related to your subject. Then begin writing your poem, arranging the letters, words, and lines to form the appropriate shape. When you finish writing, revise and proofread your poem.

Learning Option

Cross-curricular Connection. What kinds of songs might be played by a guitarist in Winchester, England; Burma; the Southwest Pacific; or North Georgia? Investigate the music of one of these regions. Share your findings with classmates. If possible, bring in recordings to give other students a taste of the regional music you have chosen.

Merritt Parkway

Denise Levertov

As if it were
forever that they move, that we
keep moving—

Under a wan sky where
5   as the lights went on a star
pierced the haze & now
follows steadily
a constant
above our six lanes
10   the dreamlike continuum . . .

And the people—ourselves!
the humans from inside the
cars apparent
only at gasoline stops
15   unsure,
eyeing each other

drink coffee hastily at the
slot machines & hurry
back to the cars
20   vanish
into them forever, to
keep moving—

Houses now & then beyond the
sealed road, the trees / trees, bushes
25 passing by, passing
the cars that
keep moving ahead of
us, past us, pressing behind us
and
30   over left, those that come
toward us shining too brightly
moving relentlessly

in six lanes, gliding
north & south, speeding with
35 a slurred sound—

Your Response

1. What images does this poem bring to mind?
2. What associations and emotions do these images evoke?

Interpreting

3. Why might moving traffic seem like a "dream-like continuum"?
4. How do the details in lines 11–22 suggest that the people feel more comfortable in their cars than with other people?

5. In what sense is the road "sealed"?
6. In this poem Levertov uses highway travel as a metaphor for how people travel through life. Considering this fact, what does the poem suggest about the nature of people's lives in modern society?
7. How does the shape of "Merritt Parkway" reinforce its meaning?

Applying

8. How do the impressions of highway travel presented in the poem compare with your own impressions?

BIOGRAPHIES

Gwendolyn Brooks (1917–   )

In 1950 Gwendolyn Brooks became the first African American writer to win a Pulitzer Prize, receiving the award for her second collection of poetry, *Annie Allen* (1949). Since that time, Brooks's reputation as a writer has steadily grown, and she has become one of the most highly regarded poets of our time.

Brooks was born in Topeka, Kansas, and was raised in a section of Chicago known as "Bronzeville." This area provided her with the setting for her first book of poems, *A Street in Bronzeville* (1945). In this collection and in her other early works, Brooks focused on the suffering of city blacks, whom she saw as uprooted, often abused, untrained, and unable to compete for a living. In her later works, after having, as she put it, "rediscovered her blackness," she became more outspoken, openly expressing her support for the black movement.

Ms. Brooks's own early life differed from the lives of the poor speakers in her poems. Her home was warm and her parents loving and supportive. Of her childhood she recalls, "I loved poetry very early and began to put rhymes together at about seven, at which time my parents expressed most earnest confidence that I would one day be a writer."

Elizabeth Bishop (1911–1980)

Elizabeth Bishop's poetry reflects the influence of the work of Marianne Moore. Like Moore, Bishop is known mainly for her meticulously detailed descriptions of nature and her interest in discovering meaning in ordinary observations.

Bishop was born in Worcester, Massachusetts, and was educated at Vassar College. Following her graduation, she traveled extensively outside the United States, residing in Brazil for a number of years. Bishop's travels provided her with inspiration for many of her poems.

Bishop never confused the natural with the primitive or the elegant with the mannered; she showed the world through a truthful eye, without offering easy philosophical explanations. The critic Ann Stevenson said of her, "The best thing that can be said of her philosophy is that it is not philosophy at all but instinctive awareness." In her work she never told half-truths.

Although she published relatively few collections of poetry during her lifetime, Bishop received many honors and awards. Her awards include the 1956 Pulitzer Prize for *Poems: North and South—A Cold Spring* and the 1970 National Book Award for *Complete Poems*.

GUIDE FOR INTERPRETING

The Explorer;
Little Exercise; House Guest

Writers' Techniques

Rhythm. Rhythm is the arrangement of stressed and unstressed syllables in a poem. In poems with a regular rhythm, or meter, the arrangement of stressed and unstressed syllables forms a recurring pattern. However, poets usually introduce slight variations in the metrical pattern to avoid monotony or emphasize important words. Poets will also introduce pauses within lines to interrupt the regular rhythm. These pauses, called caesuras, are usually created by punctuation, though they may also be created by the meanings of words or the natural rhythms of language.

Another way poets can vary a regular rhythm is through the use of run-on lines. Unlike end-stopped lines, which end with a pause, run-on lines flow naturally into the next line. For example, in House Guest," line 1 ("The sad seamstress") flows into line 2 ("who stays with us this month").

Focus

In "Little Exercise" Elizabeth Bishop describes the arrival and passage of a thunderstorm as a sequence of scenes. Think of a similar natural event, such as a snowstorm or a landslide. Then describe the stages of this event in a sequence of scenes.

Primary Source

In her poetry, Gwendolyn Brooks fuses her deep awareness of her African American heritage with an appreciation for the conventions and traditions of Western poetry. One of her biographers, D. H. Melhem, has noted:

> [Brooks's] poetry marks the rich confluence and continuity of a dual stream: the black sermonic tradition and black music—the spiritual, the blues, and jazz; and white antecedents like the ballad, the sonnet, and conventional free forms. It suggests connections with Anglo-Saxon alliteration and strong-stressed verse, with the Homeric bard, and the African griot. Brooks's heroic and prophetic voice surfaces in what she calls "preachments." Brooks intends that her work "call to all black people."
>
> Guide and guardian to young talent, registrar of black needs and aspirations, Brooks presents a poetry of charity, of potential and actual black strength, community, and pride. Her memorable portraits of men, women, and children pose a general as well as specific validity. She is a major voice in American poetry, a heroic voice insisting on our mutual democratic heritage.

The Explorer

Gwendolyn Brooks

Somehow to find a still spot in the noise
Was the frayed inner want, the winding, the frayed hope
Whose tatters he kept hunting through the din.
A satin peace somewhere.
5 A room of wily hush somewhere within.

So tipping down the scrambled halls he set
Vague hands on throbbing knobs. There were behind
Only spiraling, high human voices,
The scream of nervous affairs,
10 Wee griefs,
Grand griefs. And choices.

He feared most of all the choices, that cried to be taken.

There were no bourns.
There were no quiet rooms.

RESPONDING TO THE SELECTION

Your Response

1. What did you see as you read this poem? What did you hear? Explain.
2. How do you feel about making choices? Explain.

Interpreting

3. To which sense do most of the images in this poem appeal? Find three examples to support your answer.
4. (a) What do the details indicate about the place in which the poem's subject lives? (b) What does this person's home symbolize, or represent? (c) What do his experiences in the poem symbolize?
5. (a) Why does the subject fear choices "most of all"? (b) What conclusions does he reach in the final two lines?

Applying

6. Why do you think people often fear having to make choices?

LEARNING OPTIONS

1. **Writing.** Who do you think is the subject of the poem? What life crisis does he face? Use your imagination to fill in the missing details. Then write a letter in his name to an advice columnist. In the letter, outline the choices "that cr[y] to be taken" and ask for help in resolving the dilemma. Sign the letter "The Explorer."
2. **Speaking and Listening.** Get together with a group of classmates to discuss decision making. Talk about how you approach making decisions or choosing among options. What should you do? Toss a coin? Listen to a friend? Listen to your heart? Work out a method or plan for making an important life decision, such as choosing a career or college. Share your plan with the class.

THE UNEXPECTED ANSWER
René Magritte
Patrimoine des Musées Royaux des Beaux-Arts de Belgique, Bruxelles

GREAT FLORIDA SUNSET, 1887
Martin Johnson Heade
Private Collection USA

Little Exercise

Elizabeth Bishop

Think of the storm roaming the sky uneasily
like a dog looking for a place to sleep in,
listen to it growling.

Think how they must look now, the mangrove[1] keys
5   lying out there unresponsive to the lightning
in dark, coarse-fibred families,

where occasionally a heron[2] may undo his head,
shake up his feathers, make an uncertain comment
when the surrounding water shines.

---

1. mangrove: A tropical tree with branches that spread and send
down roots, forming new trunks and causing a thick growth over a
large area.
2. heron (her′ ən) *n*.: A wading bird with a long neck, long legs,
and a long, tapered bill.

<pre>
10   Think of the boulevard and the little palm trees
     all stuck in rows, suddenly revealed
     as fistfuls of limp fish-skeletons.

     It is raining there. The boulevard
     and its broken sidewalks with weeds in every crack
15   are relieved to be wet, the sea to be freshened.

     Now the storm goes away again in a series
     of small, badly lit battle-scenes,
     each in "Another part of the field."[3]

     Think of someone sleeping in the bottom of a rowboat
20   tied to a mangrove root or the pile of a bridge;
     think of him as uninjured, barely disturbed.
</pre>

---

3. "Another . . . field": A stage direction used to designate different parts of a battlefield in several of William Shakespeare's plays.

![R]ESPONDING TO THE SELECTION

Your Response
1. Which image in the poem do you find most striking? Why?
2. What feelings do you associate with a thunderstorm?

Recalling
3. Describe the stages of the storm.

Interpreting
4. What details indicate that the poem is set in a tropical environment?
5. In what way is the speaker's description of the storm similar to a play?
6. Considering the way in which the storm is described in the first six stanzas, what is ironic, or surprising, about the scene described in the final stanza?
7. How does the title relate to the poem?

Applying
8. How does your image of a thunderstorm compare with the speaker's description?

![L]EARNING OPTIONS

1. **Art.** Follow the poet's instructions. Form a mental picture of each image in the poem. Either draw or write detailed instructions for an artist to use to create a series of pictures that illustrate the sequence of images.
2. **Writing.** Compose a "Little Exercise" of your own. In your poem describe a sequence of events as a series of images for the reader to visualize. Read your poem aloud to classmates, inviting them to close their eyes and form a mental picture of each image you describe.

House Guest

Elizabeth Bishop

The sad seamstress
who stays with us this month
is small and thin and bitter.
No one can cheer her up.
5   Give her a dress, a drink,
roast chicken, or fried fish—
it's all the same to her.

She sits and watches TV.
No, she watches zigzags.
10 "Can you adjust the TV?"
"No," she says. No hope.
She watches on and on,
without hope, without air.

Her own clothes give us pause,
15 but she's not a poor orphan.
She has a father, a mother,
and all that, and she's earning
quite well, and we're stuffing
her with fattening foods.

20 We invite her to use the binoculars.
We say, "Come see the jets!"
We say, "Come see the baby!"
Or the knife grinder who cleverly
plays the National Anthem
25 on his wheel so shrilly.
Nothing helps.

She speaks: "I need a little
money to buy buttons."
She seems to think it's useless
30 to ask. Heavens, buy buttons,

if they'll do any good,
the biggest in the world—
by the dozen, by the gross!
Buy yourself an ice cream,
35 a comic book, a car!

Her face is closed as a nut;
closed as a careful snail
or a thousand-year-old seed.
Does she dream of marriage?
40 Of getting rich? Her sewing
is decidedly mediocre.

Please! Take our money! Smile!
What on earth have we done?
What has everyone done
45 and when did it all begin?
Then one day she confides
that she wanted to be a nun
and her family opposed her.

Perhaps we should let her go,
50 or deliver her straight off
to the nearest convent—and wasn't
her month up last week, anyway?

Can it be that we nourish
one of the Fates in our bosoms?
55 Clotho, sewing our lives
with a bony little foot
on a borrowed sewing machine,
and our fates will be like hers,
and our hems crooked forever?

RESPONDING TO THE SELECTION

Your Response

1. Do you view the seamstress sympathetically or with contempt? Explain.
2. Is the fate of the seamstress sealed, or can she turn her life around? Express your opinion.
3. What advice would you give the seamstress if you were her host?

Interpreting

4. (a) What do the seamstress's actions reveal about her personality? (b) What do the descriptions of her appearance reveal about her personality?
5. (a) What is the speaker's attitude toward the seamstress? (b) How is this attitude conveyed? (c) How does the speaker's attitude change after the seamstress confides in her and her family?

Applying

6. In this poem the seamstress has a strong negative reaction to her inability to fulfill her goal in life. Do you think that most people would respond as negatively as the seamstress does if they were unable to achieve their goals in life? Why or why not?

ANALYZING LITERATURE

Understanding Rhythm

Rhythm is the arrangement of stressed and unstressed syllables in a poem. Poets vary the regular rhythm of a poem in a number of ways. Often poets interrupt the regular rhythm by introducing pauses, or caesuras, within the lines. Another way poets vary rhythm is by using run-on lines—lines that flow naturally into the next line.

1. Find two caesuras in "House Guest."
2. Find two run-on lines in the poem.

THINKING AND WRITING

Responding to Criticism

Critic Candace Stalter has commented that Elizabeth Bishop's "poetry reveals more diffuse sympathy for the oppressed than definite anger at the oppressor." Write an essay in which you discuss this comment in relation to "House Guest." Reread the poem, focusing on the attitude it expresses about the seamstress and her unhappiness. When you write your essay, use passages from the poem to support your argument. When you finish writing, revise and proofread your essay.

LEARNING OPTIONS

1. **Art.** In "House Guest," Bishop presents a psychological portrait of a young woman who is embittered by her fate. Her sorry appearance reflects her despair. What does she look like? Flesh out the details in the poem, and draw or locate a picture that represents the seamstress. In your picture try to capture her personality as it is presented in the poem.
2. **Writing.** Do you think the "house guest" is as indifferent to her surroundings as the speaker implies? Try to see things from the seamstress's perspective. Put yourself in her place, and write a diary entry in which you record her impressions of the speaker and the speaker's family. In your diary entry, you might focus on one of the incidents described in the poem.
3. **Cross-curricular Connection.** In the last stanza of the poem, the speaker asks: "Can it be that we nourish one of the Fates in our bosoms?" Answer her question. Using an encyclopedia or a book about Greek mythology, find out about the three Fates: Clotho and her sisters, Lachesis and Atropos. How would the ancient Greeks describe the role of the Fates in our lives?

BIOGRAPHIES

Robert Lowell (1917–1977)

Robert Lowell was a member of one of this country's oldest and most prominent families. His ancestors included two noted American poets, James Russell Lowell and Amy Lowell. Considering his background, it is not surprising that he was one of the most history-conscious and influential poets of his time.

Born in Boston, Lowell attended Harvard University for two years, then transferred to Kenyon College in Ohio, where he studied poetry under John Crowe Ransom. Lowell earned widespread recognition early in his career as a poet, winning a Pulitzer Prize for his collection *Lord Weary's Castle*. In the poems in this book and in those in his other early collections, Lowell relied on traditional poetic forms and techniques. During the late 1950's, however, Lowell abandoned his early style and began writing freer, more direct poems. This change first became evident when he published *Life Studies* (1959), a collection of confessional poems—poems in which Lowell openly and frankly explored his own personal life. The book had a tremendous impact on the literary world, giving rise to a school of confessional poets that included Sylvia Plath, John Berryman, and Anne Sexton.

Randall Jarrell (1914–1965)

Randall Jarrell was a talented poet, literary critic, and teacher. His poetry was praised by both writers and critics, including Robert Lowell, who called Jarrell "the most heartbreaking English poet of his day"; and his literary essays, many of which appear in his book *Poetry and the Age* (1953), have been credited with altering the dominant critical trends and tastes of his time.

Jarrell was born in Nashville, Tennessee. After graduating from Vanderbilt University, he became a teacher, a profession to which he remained dedicated for the rest of his life. During World War II, he served in the United States Air Force. His war experiences provided him with the material for the poems in his book *Losses* (1948). Many of his other poems, including those in *The Seven-League Crutches* (1951) and *The Lost World* (1965), focus on childhood and the sense of innocence with which it is associated. In contrast, the poems in *The Woman at the Washington Zoo* (1960) reflect Jarrell's concern with aging and loneliness.

GUIDE FOR INTERPRETING

Hawthorne; The Death of the Ball Turret Gunner; Losses

Writers' Techniques

Theme. The theme is the central idea or insight about life that a writer hopes to convey in a work of literature. In some literary works, the theme is stated directly. More often, however, the theme is implied, or revealed indirectly. When interpreting an implied theme, it is important to pay close attention to the writer's choice of details, portrayal of characters and events, and use of literary devices.

Commentary

War and poetry have gone hand in hand for as long as people have fought and written. As you read Randall Jarrell's affecting poems, "The Death of the Ball Turret Gunner" and "Losses," notice that they follow that tradition. Jarrell's poems echo the themes of sensitive men who fought before him. British poets Wilfred Owen and Siegfried Sassoon both fought in "The War to End All Wars," World War I, and saw their generation transformed by trench warfare and nerve-damaging mustard gas. Owen said, "My subject is War, and the pity of War. The Poetry is in the pity." His poetry became a monument to war's futility and waste. Passionately dedicated to humanity and to life, both Sassoon and Owen felt they had to understand battle in order to subdue it. They met briefly in a hospital for nervous disorders, fellow casualties of war. Sassoon, the established poet, encouraged young Owen to hone his sensitive poetic gifts and continue to illuminate the horror of young lives wasted to "the Cause," which grew more indistinct as the death tolls steadily climbed. Owen returned to the front to prove his courage under fire so that his protesting poetry would not seem mere cowardice, feeling he had to win medals to throw them away. He wrote to Sassoon but did not meet him again. Wilfred Owen was killed just before the war ended.

The cause of Owen and Sassoon and so many other poets who deplored the wasting of young life in war was taken up by Jarrell in World War II, the war that Owen and Sassoon's war was supposed to prevent. Do you feel war poetry serves a purpose?

Focus

"The Death of the Ball Turret Gunner" and "Losses" were inspired by Randall Jarrell's experiences in the United States Air Force. Why do you think writers often use war as a subject for their writing? Freewrite about the reasons war is such a common literary subject.

Hawthorne

Robert Lowell

Follow its lazy main street lounging
from the alms house to Gallows Hill[1]
along a flat, unvaried surface
covered with wooden houses
5   aged bv yellow drain
like the unhealthy hair of an old dog.
You'll walk to no purpose
in Hawthorne's Salem.

I cannot resilver the smudged plate.[2]

---

1. Gallows Hill: A hill in Salem, Massachusetts, where nineteen
people who were accused of practicing witchcraft were hanged.
2. resilver ... plate: Early photographs were taken on a metal
plate coated with silver.

CROWNINSHIELD'S WHARF
George Ropes
Peabody Museum of Salem

10   I drop to Hawthorne, the customs officer,[3]
    measuring coal and mostly trying to keep warm—
    to the stunted black schooner,
    the dismal South-end dock,
    the wharf-piles with their fungus of ice.
15   On State Street[4]
    a steeple with a glowing dial-clock
    measures the weary hours,
    the merciless march of professional feet.

    Even this shy distrustful ego
20   sometimes walked on top of the blazing roof,
    and felt those flashes
    that char the discharged cells of the brain.

    Look at the faces—
    Longfellow, Lowell, Holmes and Whittier!

---

3. customs officer: Hawthorne worked as a customs officer in Salem.
4. State Street: A street in the business district of Boston.

25 Study the grizzled silver of their beards.
    Hawthorne's picture,
    however, has a blond mustache
    and golden General Custer[5] scalp.
    He looks like a Civil War officer.
30 He shines in the firelight. His hard
    survivor's smile is touched with fire.

    Leave him alone for a moment or two,
    and you'll see him with his head
    bent down, brooding, brooding,
35 eyes fixed on some chip,
    some stone, some common plant,
    the commonest thing,
    as if it were the clue.
    The disturbed eyes rise,
40 furtive, foiled, dissatisfied
    from meditation on the true
    and insignificant.

---

5. General Custer: George Armstrong Custer (1839–1876), a general who served in the Civil War and was killed along with his troops by the Sioux at the Battle of Little Big Horn, had long blond hair.

Primary Source

Robert Lowell writes of Nathaniel Hawthorne's home. Critic Hyatt H. Waggoner, in his pamphlet *Nathaniel Hawthorne*, has the following to say about Hawthorne, his family, and his Salem:

"When Hawthorne was born in Salem, Massachusetts, in 1804 the town was already very old by American standards. The Hathornes had been there from the beginning. (Hawthorne added the *w* to the family name when he began to sign his stories.) By the 1690's one of them was prominent enough to be a judge in the witchcraft trials. His descendants' remarks on him in "The Custom House" introduction to *The Scarlet Letter* mix pride in his prominence and a sense of inherited guilt for his deeds as judge.

"Hawthorne is being a little whimsical in 'The Custom House,' protectively light in his tone, when he takes the judge's guilt on himself and offers to do penance that the family curse may be removed. But there is an undercurrent of seriousness. Salem is a part of him, for good and for ill. The 'mere sensuous sympathy of dust for dust' is perhaps all that is needed to bind town and man together. . . . Hawthorne admits to being haunted by the figure of the prominent but guilty ancestor who 'was present to my boyish imagination, as far back as I can remember.' . . .

"As he grew up, Hawthorne watched Salem decline. The Embargo of 1807 struck the town a heavy blow, and when the end of the War of 1812 made shipping possible again, Salem did not recover its importance as a seaport. The town was repeating the family history, it seemed. . . ."

RESPONDING TO THE SELECTION

Your Response

1. Based on the way he is portrayed in this poem, what is your opinion of Hawthorne? Explain.
2. If you were going to write a poem about one of your favorite writers, whom would you choose? Why?

Interpreting

3. (a) What type of impression is conveyed by the description of Salem in the first stanza? (b) How does line 9 relate to the description of Salem?
4. What is the significance of the allusion, or reference, to Gallows Hill?
5. (a) What impression of time is conveyed by the image, or word picture, in lines 15–17? (b) What impression of professional people does the image in line 18 convey?
6. (a) What do lines 19–22 reveal about Hawthorne? (b) What do the descriptions in lines 23–31 imply about the contrasts between Hawthorne's personality and the personalities of some of his literary contemporaries?
7. In the final stanza, what is Hawthorne seeking through his observations of common things?

Applying

8. (a) Why do you think Lowell might have chosen to write this poem? (b) What does the poem reveal about Lowell?
9. Proverbs 22:28 reads, "Remove not the ancient landmark, which the fathers have set." (a) In what way has Hawthorne served as a literary landmark for Lowell? (b) Think of your own field of interest. Who would serve as a "landmark" for you? Explain the reasons for your choice.

LEARNING OPTIONS

1. **Art.** The Peabody Museum in Salem, Massachusetts, houses the fifty-sequence mural *The Chronicle of Salem*. Add a panel to the mural. Based on Lowell's description of Hawthorne's Salem, either do a preliminary sketch or give detailed instructions for an artist's sketch.
2. **Cross-curricular Connection.** What happened to Salem after it lost its standing as a leading seaport? Did it fall into decline as both Hawthorne and Lowell suggest? What is it like today? Find out if the city was able to "resilver the smudged plate." Share your findings with classmates in a brief oral report.

The Death of the Ball Turret Gunner

Randall Jarrell

A ball turret was a small space, enclosed in plexiglass, on the underside of the fuselage of certain World War II bombers, that held a small man and two machine guns. When the bomber was attacked by a plane below, the gunner would fire his guns from an upside-down, hunched-up position.

From my mother's sleep I fell into the State,
And I hunched in its belly till my wet fur froze.
Six miles from earth, loosed from its dream of life,
I woke to black flak[1] and the nightmare fighters.
5 When I died they washed me out of the turret with a hose.

---

1. flak *n.*: Anti-aircraft fire.

RESPONDING TO THE SELECTION

Your Response
1. What emotions does this poem evoke in you? Why?

Interpreting
2. (a) To what does the word *State* (line 1) refer? (b) What does Jarrell mean when he writes that the gunner "fell into the State"?
3. (a) To what does Jarrell compare the ball turret gunner in the first two lines? (b) How does this comparison add to the impact of the poem?
4. Why might the gunner view life on earth as a "dream" (line 3)?
5. What does the final line reveal about the realities of war?

6. How does the brevity of this poem add to its impact?

Applying
7. Why do you think Jarrell chose to write about a ball turret gunner rather than a pilot or another type of soldier?

LEARNING OPTION

Speaking and Listening. Randall Jarrell based his poem "The Death of the Ball Turret Gunner" on his firsthand observations of World War II, a war that has been called "the good war." Do you think there is such a thing as a "good" war? Consider both the causes and effects of war and take a stand. Be prepared to defend your opinion in an informal class debate.

Losses

Randall Jarrell

It was not dying: everybody died.
It was not dying: we had died before
In the routine crashes—and our fields
Called up the papers, wrote home to our folks,
5 And the rates rose, all because of us.
We died on the wrong page of the almanac,
Scattered on mountains fifty miles away;
Diving on haystacks, fighting with a friend,
We blazed up on the lines we never saw.
10 We died like aunts or pets or foreigners.
(When we left high school nothing else had died
For us to figure we had died like.)

In our new planes, with our new crews, we bombed
The ranges by the desert or the shore,
15 Fired at towed targets, waited for our scores—
And turned into replacements and woke up
One morning, over England, operational.
It wasn't different: but if we died
It was not an accident but a mistake
20 (But an easy one for anyone to make).
We read our mail and counted up our missions—
In bombers named for girls, we burned
The cities we had learned about in school—
Till our lives wore out; our bodies lay among
25 The people we had killed and never seen.
When we lasted long enough they gave us medals;
When we died they said, "Our casualties were low."

RESPONDING TO THE SELECTION

Your Response

1. How does this poem make you feel? Explain.
2. Do you share the poet's attitude toward war? Why or why not?

Recalling

3. (a) What do the pilots bomb (line 14)? (b) At what do they fire (line 15)? (c) What do they burn (line 23)?

Interpreting

4. (a) Do the pilots really think that their missions are not difficult? Support your answer. (b) Do they really think that if they died "it was not an accident but a mistake"? Support your answer. (c) Who might be more likely to express these opinions?
5. What is ironic, or surprising, about the fact that the bombers are named for girls?
6. What is the significance of the fact the pilots never see the people they kill?
7. (a) Who is the *they* referred to in the final line? (b) What does their comment reveal about their attitude toward the pilots?

Applying

8. How is this poem similar to and different from some of the other literary works about war you have read?

ANALYZING LITERATURE

Understanding Theme

The **theme** is the central idea or insight about life that a writer hopes to convey in a work of literature. Most often, a theme is revealed indirectly through the writer's choice of details, portrayal of characters and events, and use of literary devices.

1. What is the theme of "Losses"?
2. What details play an important role in conveying the theme?
3. How does the use of irony also help convey the theme?

THINKING AND WRITING

Writing About a Writer's Attitude

Write an essay in which you discuss what "The Death of the Ball Turret Gunner" and "Losses" reveal about Jarrell's attitude toward war. Reread both poems, focusing on their themes. Create a chart, listing details from both poems that help convey the poet's attitude. Prepare a thesis statement. Then write your essay, using passages from the two poems to support your thesis. When you revise, make sure you have included enough supporting information. Check that you have quoted precisely and have punctuated your quotations accurately. Proofread your essay and share it with your classmates.

LEARNING OPTION

Writing. Develop a proposal for a movie or a television series based on the events described in "Losses." Create a group of fictional characters who could have participated in the events Jarrell describes. Drawing from the details in the poem, come up with a setting for your movie or series, and develop a rough outline of the plot. Then write a proposal for a network executive or the head of a movie studio. Focus on making your proposal clear and concise. When you have finished, share your proposal with your classmates.

BIOGRAPHIES

José García Villa (1914–   )

José García Villa's poetry reflects his concern for the individual. In fact, Villa himself has commented that his purpose as a poet is to find "man's selfhood and identity in the mystery of Creation."

Born in the Philippines, Villa came to the United States at the age of sixteen. While an undergraduate at the University of New Mexico, he established a reputation as a short-story writer. He began studying poetry while in college but did not have a collection published in the United States until 1942. This book, *Have Come, Am Here,* was followed by a second collection, *Volume Two,* in 1949. Since then Villa has published several more volumes of poetry and a collection of short stories.

Martín Espada (1957–   )

Martín Espada is one of the shining stars among the many emerging young Hispanic poets. One critic has remarked, "When one first hears the voice of Espada's poems, the determined dignity, the intense, quiet care, . . . one recognizes the presence of [his] power."

Born in Brooklyn, New York, Espada attended the University of Wisconsin at Madison and went on to receive a law degree from Northeastern University. His pursuit of a law career has not prevented him from establishing himself as a prolific writer. In addition to publishing his work in numerous journals and anthologies, he has published two critically acclaimed collections of poetry, *The Immigrant Iceboy's Bolero* (1982) and *Trumpets From the Islands of Their Eviction* (1987). His work has earned him fellowships from both the Massachusetts Artists' Foundation and the National Endowment for the Arts.

Victor Hernández Cruz (1949–   )

Victor Hernández Cruz uses vivid imagery and musical language to explore connections between his Puerto Rican roots and the realities of urban life his people experience in present-day America.

Born in Aguas Buenas, a small mountain village in Puerto Rico, Hernández Cruz moved to New York City with his family when he was five. Exhibiting a gift with language at an early age, he published *Papa Got His Gun! and Other Poems,* his first collection of poetry, when he was just sixteen. His subsequent collections, *Doing Poetry* (1968), *Snaps* (1969), and *Mainland* (1973), won raves from reviewers and earned him a reputation as one of the promising young American poetic voices.

GUIDE FOR INTERPRETING

Be Beautiful, Noble, Like the Antique Ant; We Live by What We See at Night; #1 Atmosphere; #2 Memory; Poem

Writers' Techniques

Sound Devices. One of the main characteristics of poetry that sets it apart from prose is its emphasis on sound. Many poems have a musical quality created by the use of sound devices. Often, sound devices also help to reinforce the meaning of a poem by adding emphasis to important words. Among the most common sound devices are alliteration, assonance, and consonance.

Alliteration is the repetition of similar consonant sounds at the beginnings of words or accented syllables. Notice the repetition of the *b* sound in the following lines from "We Live by What We See at Night": "when you cross the *b*ridge/*b*uilt *b*y your grandfather . . ."

Assonance is the repetition of vowel sounds. Look at José García Villa's repetition of the *o* sound in the second line of "Be Beautiful, Noble, Like the Antique Ant": "Who b*o*re the st*o*rms as he b*o*re the sun, . . . "

Consonance is the repetition of consonant sounds at the ends of words or accented syllables. For example, the *m* sound is repeated in the following lines from "We Live by What We See at Night": "loo*m*ing above the projects overwhel*m*ing Brooklyn."

Focus

In "Be Beautiful, Noble, Like the Antique Ant," José García Villa illustrates the importance of modesty. Freewrite about the value of modesty, exploring the reasons for it being an important virtue.

Be Beautiful, Noble, Like the Antique Ant

José García Villa

Be beautiful, noble, like the antique ant,
Who bore the storms as he bore the sun,
Wearing neither gown nor helmet,
Though he was archbishop and soldier:
5   Wore only his own flesh.

Salute characters with gracious dignity:
Though what these are is left to
Your own terms. Exact: the universe is
Not so small but these will be found
10 Somewhere. Exact: they will be found.

Speak with great moderation: but think
With great fierceness, burning passion:
Though what the ant thought
No annals reveal, nor his descendants
15 Break the seal.

Trace the tracelessness of the ant,
Every ant has reached this perfection.
As he comes, so he goes,
Flowing as water flows,
20 Essential but secret like a rose.

RESPONDING TO THE SELECTION

Your Response

1. What is your opinion of the speaker's advice? Explain.
2. Which animal or insect would you choose as a role model? Why?

Interpreting

3. (a) In what sense can an ant be thought of as "antique"? (b) In what sense is an ant like an "archbishop"? (c) In what sense is an ant like a "soldier"?
4. What does the speaker mean when he refers to the "tracelessness of the ant"?
5. In what sense is a rose "essential but secret"?
6. (a) What human virtues does the speaker attribute to the ant? (b) What does he feel that people can learn from ants?

Applying

7. What other human virtues might be attributed to ants?

8. From what other insects or animals do you think people might learn? Explain your answer.

LEARNING OPTIONS

1. **Cross-curricular Connection.** How well does the poet know ants? Use an encyclopedia to learn more about the insect. Does it, in fact, share the qualities of an archbishop and a soldier? If so, how? Be prepared to share your findings with classmates.
2. **Writing.** What might be learned from a cockroach? A pigeon? A skunk? Choose at least three animals or insects as the subjects for poems like those of José García Villa. Consider which qualities of each animal or insect are worth emulating. Then write the title for a poem about each one. Model your titles after Villa's: "Be _____, _____, Like the _____ _____."

We Live by What We See at Night

Martín Espada

When the mountains of Puerto Rico
flickered in your sleep
with a moist green light,
when you saw green bamboo hillsides
5 before waking to East Harlem[1] rooftops
or Texas barracks,
when you crossed the bridge
built by your grandfather
over a river glimpsed
10 only in interrupted dreaming,
the craving for that island birthplace
burrowed, deep
as thirty years' exile,
constant as your pulse.

15 This was the inheritance
of your son, born in New York:
that years before
I saw Puerto Rico,
I saw the mountains
20 looming above the projects,[2]
overwhelming Brooklyn,
living by what I saw at night,
with my eyes closed.

---

1. East Harlem: A section of northern Manhattan with a large
Hispanic population.
2. projects (prä′ jektz′) *n*.: Low-rent apartment complexes.

SPRING IN PUERTO RICO, 1976
Pedro Villarini
El Museo del Barrio

RESPONDING TO THE SELECTION

Your Response

1. What thoughts or memories does Espada's poem evoke in you? Why? Do any of the places he describes remind you of places from your own experience? Explain.
2. What places do you envision in your dreams? Why?

Interpreting

3. (a) What impressions does Espada convey of the place the speaker envisions in his dreams? Support your answer. (b) How does the place in the speaker's dreams contrast with the places he wakes to?
4. What evidence in the poem suggests that the "bridge" the speaker crosses symbolizes, or represents, a link to his Puerto Rican heritage?
5. In the second stanza, the speaker explains that his images of Puerto Rico came to him in his dreams "years before" he ever saw Puerto Rico. What do you see as the possible sources of the impressions that came to him in his dreams?

Applying

6. (a) What are your feelings about your cultural heritage? (b) What, if any, images do you have of the place or places your ancestors came from? (c) What is the source of these images?

ANALYZING LITERATURE

Understanding Sound Devices

Alliteration, assonance, and consonance are sound devices used by poets to create a musical effect and reinforce meaning. Alliteration is the repetition of similar consonant sounds at the beginnings of words or accented syllables. Assonance is the repetition of vowel sounds. Consonance is the repetition of consonant sounds at the ends of words or accented syllables.

1. Find two examples of alliteration in "We Live by What We See at Night."
2. Find two examples of assonance.
3. Find one example of consonance.
4. Read "We Live by What We See at Night" aloud, paying close attention to the use of sound devices. Then explain how the sound devices contribute to the poem's musical quality.

We Live by What We See at Night 987

Martín Espada and "We Live by What We See at Night"

PREWRITING

Mining the Memory What kinds of ideas make good material for poems? Poetry often depends on exploration—the writer's willingness to explore an idea or an image as fully as possible. The stimulus can come from anywhere: an argument overheard on a bus, a fragment of bright ribbon caught on a branch, the feel of a frigid gust of wind.

Memory is one of the poet's most useful tools. By activating real events or dreams from the past, the memory can yield the most interesting material for a poem. Espada used both his father's and his own memories as a source of inspiration for "We Live By What We See at Night." The poet's father, who came to the United States from Puerto Rico at a young age, had told him that he saw the mountains of his native country in his dreams each night, before he woke to the realities of the United States. "I remembered this snatch of conversation, connected it with my childhood images of mountains I had never seen, but had heard about and preferred to my real urban surroundings."

Using Remembered Images When Espada visited Puerto Rico as an adult, his first actual sight of the island brought back the early images his father had evoked. "[My father] always spoke of Puerto Rico as a beautiful place, in contrast with the surroundings of my early years in Brooklyn, which was urban and ugly," he says. It was this sharp contrast that provided the initial fertile ground for the poem.

Open-ended Plans Espada had originally planned to make this poem the first part of a longer three-part piece. After finishing the first draft, however, he decided that the poem stood well enough on its own.

"A poem is not an office building," he says. "I generally throw the blueprints away."

DRAFTING

Be Flexible No matter how carefully you plan a poem, you may find when you finish it that it has changed direction, or turned into something quite different from what you had planned. It helps to be flexible about the poems you write. Sometimes the evolving poem becomes its own best blueprint.

Writing in One Sitting Wonderful poems can emerge through long hours of writing and rewriting or through the labor of one sitting.

Although he usually spends a lot of time revising a poem, Espada says this poem "was written in a burst of energy, emerging as a complete thought." The poem was written on a single sheet of yellow legal paper, and Espada says the first draft took only a half-hour to complete.

Choosing a Title Espada chose the title of the poem after finishing the first draft. Many writers use the title as a vehicle to extend the meaning of the poem. Espada says, "The implication of the title is that we, as Puerto Ricans, survive in a hostile environment because of our strong cultural identity, which has its roots in the island." He adds, "More generally, the title speaks to the power of the imagination to transcend almost any conditions, granting human beings the will to go on with their lives."

REVISING

Work in Progress In general Espada says that he does not show his work in progress to other people; he tends to work alone, although he sees this as a peculiarity of his own character. He says, "I recommend that young writers share their work with others." He did read the poem in draft form to his wife, who responded positively. Says Espada, "She was also impressed by the fact that, in spite of all the pressures in my life to deny my Puerto Rican heritage, I still prize that heritage. This poem enabled her to understand me better, as well as the culture, which she has since embraced wholeheartedly."

A Few Key Changes Although Espada made very few changes to his first draft, he did add the word *burrowed* to the poem.

> the craving for that island birthplace
> *burrowed,* deep
> as thirty years' exile,
> constant as your pulse.

He says, "I needed an unusual word to describe the physical sensation attached to a strong feeling of loss, the deep digging of this emotion into the core of a human being." Because the success of a poem often depends on the ability of individual words to convey a symbol or image, changing even one word can have a great impact on a poem.

Writing Quickly According to Espada, the most difficult aspect of the poem arose from the ease in writing it. He says, "Since the poem was written so quickly and with so little revision, in contrast with most of my other work, I had difficulty accepting the poem as a quality piece." He almost omitted the poem from his book *Trumpets From the Island of Their Eviction* and included it only as an afterthought.

PUBLISHING

The Audience Reaction When you write, it is important to determine for whom you are writing. Can you imagine strangers reading your work, or is your work intended only for the eyes of the people you know? Espada's father read the poem when the book came out in 1987. Espada says, "His initial response was very favorable, though much later he indicated his discomfort with my description of the urban area where I spent my childhood."

Whether writers know their audience or not, they are not always able to predict the reaction of their readers to a particular piece of their work. Since Espada nearly omitted the poem from his book and included it only as an afterthought, he was surprised to find that the poem received more positive reaction from readers than any other poem in the book.

The concept embodied by Espada's poem is one that many people can relate to: Our dreams can console us for the disappointments of everyday life.

Espada's reaction to the poem six years after writing it is interesting. He says, "My use of language in poetry has changed since that time. Though I like the poem, I might write it differently today. Or I might not write it at all."

"Question, Celebrate, Condemn" Espada has inspirational advice for young writers. He says, "Your lives are the stuff of poetry. Try not to forget anything. Watch the faces around you and listen to the conversations." He adds, "Question, celebrate, condemn. Without the courage of young people, civilizations lose their integrity."

THINKING ABOUT THE PROCESS

1. Espada says, "I often rely on the power of memory for my poems, since I have relatively little time to write." How could keeping a daily journal enhance a writer's ability to remember details?
2. Espada says that his use of language in poetry has changed since he wrote the poem. How do you think a writer's ideas about language might change over a six-year period? What kinds of influences might affect a writer's use of language?
3. **Writing.** Espada's advice to young writers is to "watch the faces around you and listen to the conversations." Spend a day making notes about the people and conversations around you. Then write a poem based on some of the personalities or situations that you have observed.

#1 Atmosphere[1]
Victor Hernández Cruz

Don Arturo says:
You have to know
what the atmosphere
is creating
You have to know
Because if it's good
You can go somewhere
and make your own.

---

1. **#1 Atmosphere:** "#1 Atmosphere" and "#2 Memory" are part of a series of poems about a fictional character named Don Arturo.

#2 Memory
Victor Hernández Cruz

Don Arturo says:
You have to know
what you once said
Because it could
travel in the air
for years
And return in different
clothes
And then you have to
buy it.

Poem
Victor Hernández Cruz

Think with your body
And dance with your mind.

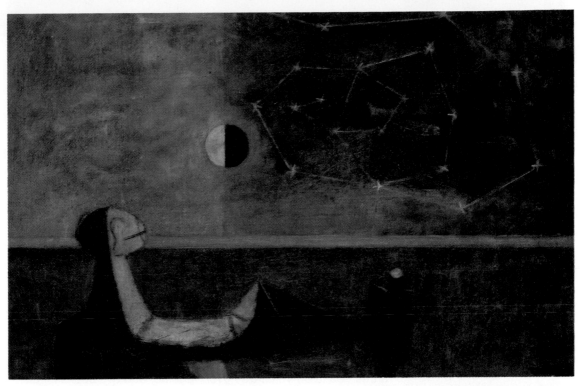

RESPONDING TO THE SELECTION

Your Response

1. What are your reactions to the three poems by Victor Hernández Cruz? Explain. Which of the poems did you most enjoy? Why?

Interpreting

2. (a) What is your interpretation of the advice Don Arturo offers in "#1 Atmosphere"? (b) Explain how it is possible to "go somewhere and make your own" atmosphere.

3. (a) What does Don Arturo mean when he says that "what you once said" can "return in different clothes"? (b) What does he mean when he says, "then you have to buy it"?

4. How do you interpret the advice that Cruz offers in "Poem"? Why?

Applying

5. (a) Can you apply any of the messages in these poems to your own life? If so, how? (b) Would you share anv of Cruz's insights with a friend? Explain.

THINKING AND WRITING

Writing a Poem

As Cruz's "Poem" demonstrates, a poem does not have to be long to be powerful. Follow Cruz's lead by writing a two-line poem conveying a message or insight that you feel is important. Like Cruz, try to capture your reader's attention by stating your message through an unusual or unexpected combination of words. When you revise, eliminate any unnecessary words that may dilute the power of your poem.

LEARNING OPTION

Performance. With a partner develop a rap song, using the two lines from Cruz's "Poem" as a refrain. Perform your song for the class, taking turns reciting the verses you have created.

BIOGRAPHIES

Richard Wilbur (1921–　　)

Like many other contemporary poets, Richard Wilbur is known for his elegant and imaginative use of language. Yet, unlike most of the other poets of our time, Wilbur uses traditional poetic forms and techniques in expressing an optimistic outlook toward life and an awareness of the world's beauty.

Wilbur was born in New York City but spent most of his childhood on a farm in rural northern New Jersey. After graduating from Amherst College, he served in the army infantry in Europe during World War II. He began writing poetry during the war and published his first book, *The Beautiful Changes and Other Poems* (1947), while he was a graduate student at Harvard.

Wilbur has gone on to publish many other volumes of poetry. His third book, *Things of This World* (1956), won both the Pulitzer Prize and the National Book Award. He has also published translations of a number of French dramas, a collection of essays, lyrics for an operetta based on Voltaire's novel *Candide,* and two books for children.

Robert Penn Warren (1905–1989)

Robert Penn Warren was one of the most versatile, prolific, and distinguished writers of our time. He wrote poetry, stories, novels, plays, criticism, essays, textbooks, and a biography, and he received three Pulitzer Prizes.

Warren was born in Guthrie, Kentucky. When he was sixteen, he entered Vanderbilt University, where he began to write poetry. After graduating from Vanderbilt in 1925, he studied at the University of California, Yale, and Oxford. In 1935 he became one of the founding editors of the literary magazine *The Southern Review*. Just over a decade later, he was awarded his first Pulitzer Prize for his novel *All the King's Men* (1947), which explores the subject of southern politics. He received his second Pulitzer Prize in 1958 for *Promises,* a volume of poetry; and in 1979 he won a third Pulitzer Prize for *Now and Then* (1979), another collection of poetry.

Warren consistently used southern settings and characters in both his poetry and fiction, but at the same time he focused on universal themes. In his work, he emphasized love of the land, continuity between generations, and the need for self-knowledge and fulfillment in an often violent world.

GUIDE FOR INTERPRETING

The Beautiful Changes; Gold Glade; Evening Hawk

Writers' Techniques

Imagery. Imagery refers to words or phrases that create mental pictures, or images, that appeal to one or more of the five senses—sight, hearing, touch, smell, or taste. Most often, images appeal to our sense of sight. For example, Warren creates a visual image in "Evening Hawk" when he writes, "From plane of light to plane, wings dipping through/Geometries and orchids that the sunset builds." Although visual imagery is the most common type of imagery, many images present sensations that we cannot visualize, and some images appeal to more than one sense. For example, in "Gold Glade," when Warren writes that there was "No breathing of air," he creates an image that appeals to our senses of hearing and touch but not to our sense of sight.

Commentary

Robert Penn Warren, one of America's most respected men of letters, died in September 1989. His friend, poet and novelist James Dickey, remembers him as " . . . a remarkable man, a wonderful writer. The main thing about Warren is that he had a powerful, primitive imagination that dealt with the basics of human existence, either personal, political, or religious. . . . And he did it to hell and gone. He was an all-out kind of a writer." Master of all traditional verse forms from lullabies to sonnets, Warren used them to express characteristically twentieth-century themes. Although his subjects came from his southern roots, he endowed them with universal appeal, offering anecdotes to illuminate concerns common to all. Critic Charles Bohner finds in Warren's work " . . . a gusto . . . reminiscent of the writer who, Warren said, has had the greatest influence on his life—Shakespeare."

In 1986 the United States Congress selected Robert Penn Warren as America's first poet laureate. The beauty of his images, language, and truth has enriched American literature and will be his lasting monument.

Focus

To what do you think the title of Richard Wilbur's poem "The Beautiful Changes" might refer? Explore the possible subjects of the poem by preparing a list of "beautiful changes" that occur in nature, in people's lives, and in people's behavior.

QUEEN ANNE'S LACE, 1957
Charles Burchfield
The Detroit Institute of Arts

The Beautiful Changes

Richard Wilbur

One wading a Fall meadow finds on all sides
The Queen Anne's Lace[1] lying like lilies
On water; it glides
So from the walker, it turns
5   Dry grass to a lake, as the slightest shade of you
Valleys my mind in fabulous blue Lucernes.[2]

---

1. Queen Anne's Laces: A weed with finely divided foliage and white flowers.
2. Lucernes (loo surnz'): The Lake of Lucerne, located in central Switzerland.

The beautiful changes as a forest is changed
By a chameleon's tuning his skin to it;
As a mantis, arranged
10   On a green leaf, grows
Into it, makes the leaf leafier, and proves
Any greenness is deeper than anyone knows.

Your hands hold roses always in a way that says
They are not only yours; the beautiful changes
15   In such kind ways,
Wishing ever to sunder
Things and things' selves for a second finding, to lose
For a moment all that it touches back to wonder.

RESPONDING TO THE SELECTION

Your Response

1. How do you react to seeing beautiful things? Do they bring to mind other beautiful things? Why or why not?
2. In which of the changes that occur in nature do you find the most beauty? Explain.

Recalling

3. What transformations does the speaker describe in the first two stanzas?

Interpreting

4. (a) What comparison does the speaker develop in the first stanza? (b) What type of "change" does this comparison represent?
5. (a) In what sense does the change of the mantis make the "leaf leafier"? (b) Why does the change prove that "any greenness is deeper than anyone knows"?
6. What is unusual about the speaker's use of the word *beautiful*?
7. (a) What does the speaker mean when he comments that change offers a "second find-

ing"? (b) Why does he believe that change can produce a sense of "wonder"?

Applying

8. Do you think that most people perceive changes in nature in the same way as the speaker does? Why or why not?

LEARNING OPTIONS

1. **Art.** Show how "the beautiful changes." Find or create a piece of artwork that illustrates the basic concept of Wilbur's poem. Use any visual medium; you might draw a picture, take a photograph, or make a collage.
2. **Cross-curricular Connection.** Does the chameleon "tun[e] his skin" to match the color of the forest as the poet suggests? Find out if Wilbur's description of the chameleon's activity is accurate. Check an encyclopedia or science book to learn how and when a chameleon changes color. Share your findings with classmates.

Gold Glade

Robert Penn Warren

Wandering, in autumn, the woods of boyhood,
Where cedar, black, thick, rode the ridge,
Heart aimless as rifle, boy-blankness of mood,
I came where ridge broke, and the great ledge,
5 Limestone, set the toe high as treetop by dark edge

Of a gorge, and water hid, grudging and grumbling,
And I saw, in mind's eye, foam white on
Wet stone, stone wet-black, white water tumbling,
And so went down, and with some fright on
10 Slick boulders, crossed over. The gorge-depth drew
    night on,

But high over high rock and leaf-lacing, sky
Showed yet bright, and declivity wooed
My foot by the quietening stream, and so I
Went on, in quiet, through the beech wood:
15 There, in gold light, where the glade gave, it stood.

The glade was geometric, circular, gold,
No brush or weed breaking that bright gold of leaf-fall.
In the center it stood, absolute and bold
Beyond any heart-hurt, or eye's grief-fall.
20 Gold-massy in air, it stood in gold light-fall,

No breathing of air, no leaf now gold-falling,
No tooth-stitch of squirrel, or any far fox bark,
No woodpecker coding, or late jay calling.
Silence: gray-shagged, the great shagbark[1]
25 Gave forth gold light. There could be no dark.

But of course dark came, and I can't recall
What county it was, for the life of me.
Montgomery, Todd, Christian—I know them all.
Was it even Kentucky or Tennessee?
30 Perhaps just an image that keeps haunting me.

------

1. **shagbark:** A hickory tree.

No, no! in no mansion under earth,
Nor imagination's domain of bright air,
But solid in soil that gave it its birth,
It stands, wherever it is, but somewhere.
35 I shall set my foot, and go there.

RESPONDING TO THE SELECTION

Your Response
1. What are some of your memories of autumn? How do they compare with the speaker's?
2. Do you think the glade is as golden as the speaker remembers it? Why or why not?

Recalling
3. How does the speaker describe the glade?
4. What is the speaker now unable to recall about the glade?
5. What does the speaker vow to do at the end of the poem?

Interpreting
6. At what point does the action of the poem shift from the past to the present?
7. (a) What does the speaker mean when he comments that the glade is "beyond any heart-hurt, or eye's grief-fall"? (b) What does he mean when he comments, "There could be no dark"?
8. (a) How many times is the word *gold* used in this poem? (b) What is the significance of this word?

Applying
9. (a) What does the gold glade represent to the speaker? (b) Why is he so anxious to return to the glade?

ANALYZING LITERATURE

Understanding Imagery
Imagery refers to words or phrases that create mental pictures, or images, that appeal to one or more of the five senses—sight, hearing, touch, smell, or taste. Although most of the imagery in "Gold Glade" appeals to our sense of sight, Warren also uses images that appeal to both our sense of hearing and our sense of touch.
1. Find one image that appeals to the sense of hearing and one image that appeals to the sense of touch.
2. How do the visual images used in describing the woods on the ridge (lines 1–5) contrast with the images used in describing the glade (lines 15–25)?

THINKING AND WRITING

Writing a Poem Using Imagery
Write a poem in which you use vivid imagery to re-create an important childhood experience. Start by thinking of an important experience you had as a child. Then prepare a list of concrete details describing the incident. When you write your poem, focus on creating vivid imagery and do not worry about rhythm or rhyme. After you finish writing, revise and proofread your poem, and share it with your classmates.

LEARNING OPTION

Language. In "Gold Glade" Warren experiments with language and coins a number of compound words: boy-blankness, gorge-depth, leaf-lacing, leaf-fall, grief-fall, light-fall, gold-falling, gray-shagging. What does each word mean? Create a "Robert Penn Warren dictionary" in which you define each word as it is used in the context of the poem. You might include a description of the word's connotation in addition to its explicit meaning, or denotation.

SUMMER LANDSCAPE WITH HAWK,
1901–06
Louis M. Eilshemius
The Phillips Collection,
Washington, D.C.

Evening Hawk

Robert Penn Warren

From plane of light to plane, wings dipping through
Geometries and orchids that the sunset builds,
Out of the peak's black angularity of shadow, riding
The last tumultuous avalanche of
5 Light above pines and the guttural gorge,
The hawk comes.

             His wing
Scythes[1] down another day, his motion

---

1. Scythes (sīthz) *v.*: Cuts as with a tool with a long single-edged
blade set at an angle on a long, curved handle.

Is that of the honed steel-edge, we hear
10   The crashless fall of stalks of Time.

The head of each stalk is heavy with the gold of our error.

Look! look! he is climbing the last light
Who knows neither Time nor error, and under
Whose eye, unforgiving, the world, unforgiven, swings
15   Into shadow.

Long now,
The last thrush is still, the last bat
Now cruises in his sharp hieroglyphics.[2] His wisdom
Is ancient, too, and immense. The star
20   Is steady, like Plato,[3] over the mountain.

If there were no wind we might, we think, hear
The earth grind on its axis, or history
Drip in darkness like a leaking pipe in the cellar.

---

2. hieroglyphics (hī' ər ə glif' ikz) *n*.: Pictures or symbols,
representing words, syllables, or sounds.
3. Plato (427?–347? B.C.): A Greek philosopher.

RESPONDING TO THE SELECTION

Your Response

1. What do you see as you read this poem?
2. Which image do you find most striking?
3. What is your reaction to the final stanza? Have you ever felt the type of connection to history that the speaker describes? Explain.

Interpreting

4. (a) What contrasting images, or word pictures, does Warren present in the first stanza? (b) How is this contrast developed throughout the rest of the poem?
5. (a) How does the speaker relate the hawk to darkness? (b) How does he relate its movement to time? (c) What does he mean when he comments that the "stalks of Time" are "heavy with the gold of our error"?
6. (a) Why might the speaker consider a bat to be wise? (b) Why might he compare a star to Plato?
7. What does the speaker mean when he describes history as dripping "in darkness like a leaking pipe in the cellar"?

Applying

8. What animals and other elements of nature, aside from the ones mentioned in the poem, do you associate with darkness?

BIOGRAPHIES

Sylvia Plath (1932–1963)

Despite her success as a poet, Sylvia Plath lived a very short, unhappy life. In many of her poems, she expresses her intense feelings of despair and her deep inner pain.

Born in Boston, Plath wrote poetry and received scholastic and literary awards as a child. Although she suffered a nervous breakdown during her junior year, she graduated with highest honors from Smith College. She went on to attend Cambridge University in England. In 1956 she married English poet Ted Hughes, and, after a year in the United States, the couple settled in England. Plath's first volume of poetry, *The Colossus* (1960), was the only collection of her work to appear during her lifetime. Two more books of her poetry and her novel, *The Bell Jar* (1963), were published posthumously.

Robert Hayden (1913–1980)

An extremely versatile poet, Robert Hayden used a variety of poetic forms and techniques and focused on a wide range of subjects. In addition to writing about his personal experiences, Hayden wrote about current and historical events, mythology, and folklore.

Born in Detroit, Hayden attended Wayne State University. He received a master's degree from the University of Michigan and taught there and at Fisk University in Tennessee. He published several collections of poetry, including *Heart-Shape in the Dust* (1940), *The Lion and the Archer* (1948), and *The Night-Blooming Cereus* (1972). His collection *A Ballad of Remembrance* received the Grand Prize for Poetry at the First World Festival for Negro Arts in 1966.

William Stafford (1914–   )

The poetry of William Stafford reflects his love for the natural world and his fear that modern technology will someday destroy the wilderness. Focusing on such subjects as the threat of nuclear war and the beauty of untamed nature, Stafford writes simply and directly about the causes in which he believes.

Born in Hutchinson, Kansas, Stafford attended the University of Kansas. Although he began submitting poems to poetry journals during the 1940's, he did not publish his first book, *West of Your City,* until he was forty-six. Since then he has published several more collections of poetry, including *Traveling Through the Dark,* which earned him the National Book Award in 1963.

GUIDE FOR INTERPRETING

Literary Forms

Mirror; Frederick Douglass; Those Winter Sundays; Traveling Through the Dark

Confessional Poetry. Confessional poetry is a type of poetry in which the poet speaks frankly and openly about his or her own life. This type of poetry was introduced by Robert Lowell, when he published his collection *Life Studies* in 1959. Lowell felt that the writing of poetry had become too intellectual and impersonal and needed a "breakthrough back into life." Traditionally, when writers used the first-person pronoun "I" in a poem, readers were taught to think of the "I" as the speaker of the poem, not the poet himself or herself. Even when the "I" clearly did refer to the poet, the poet tended to reveal little about his or her doubts, frustrations, and painful experiences. In *Life Studies,* however, Lowell openly expressed his thoughts and feelings concerning his family, his experiences, and his personal problems. Many other poets followed Lowell's example, and confessional poetry became a popular literary form. Other poets known for their confessional poetry include John Berryman, Sylvia Plath, and Anne Sexton.

Commentary

What makes a poem move a reader? The answer is not simple, but recognizable human truths and emotions are common to poetry that affects readers profoundly. As you read these four poems, you will notice that they contain those elements. Sylvia Plath's "Mirror" shows the inevitable human truth of aging and the devastation we all face with passing years. Plath observes the woman with a close sensitivity that makes the reader care for her and recognize himself or herself in her pain. In "Frederick Douglass," Robert Hayden evokes the memory of a founding figure in the struggle for African American rights and captures some of the realities of African American life today. In "Those Winter Sundays," Hayden frames a tribute to his father by narrating a simple story of a typical Sunday morning. The truth is evident in his words, but his father's caring eclipses all else. His quiet sacrifices are recognizable as a noble human quality—love. William Stafford's poem recounts a deer, dead on the road, and the dilemma faced by a man stopping to clear it away. The scene, once again, is recognizable even to one who has never experienced it, but even more affecting is the dilemma faced by the man. He must choose to do something, but nothing he does will seem completely satisfactory. We recognize his sadness, and we respond.

Focus

In "Those Winter Sundays," Hayden writes about the sacrifices his father made for his family. Freewrite about a person who has in some way tried to make your life easier and more pleasant.

Mirror

Sylvia Plath

I am silver and exact. I have no preconceptions.
Whatever I see I swallow immediately
Just as it is, unmisted by love or dislike.
I am not cruel, only truthful—
5   The eye of a little god, four-cornered.
Most of the time I meditate on the opposite wall.
It is pink, with speckles. I have looked at it so long
I think it is a part of my heart. But it flickers.
Faces and darkness separate us over and over.
10   Now I am a lake. A woman bends over me,
Searching my reaches for what she really is.
Then she turns to those liars, the candles or the moon.
I see her back, and reflect it faithfully.
She rewards me with tears and an agitation of hands.
15   I am important to her. She comes and goes.
Each morning it is her face that replaces the darkness.
In me she has drowned a young girl, and in me an old
    woman
Rises toward her day after day, like a terrible fish.

RESPONDING TO THE SELECTION

Your Response

1. How does this poem make you feel? Explain.
2. The speaker of the poem maintains: "I am not cruel, only truthful—." If the truth hurts, do you think that being truthful is cruel? Explain.

Interpreting

3. (a) Who is the speaker of the poem? (b) How is the speaker like a person? (c) How is the speaker like a lake?

4. In what way are the candle and the moon "liars"?
5. (a) Who is the "young girl" who has drowned? (b) Who is the "old woman"? (c) Why is the old woman "like a terrible fish"?
6. (a) How does the woman feel about aging? (b) How is her attitude revealed?

Applying

7. Do you think that most people share the woman's attitude toward aging? Why or why not?

GIRL IN A WHITE DRESS
Sir William Orpen
Private Collection

Frederick Douglass[1]

Robert Hayden

When it is finally ours, this freedom, this liberty, this
   beautiful
and terrible thing, needful to man as air,
usable as earth; when it belongs at last to all,
when it is truly instinct, brain matter, diastole, systole,[2]
5   reflex action; when it is finally won; when it is more
than the gaudy mumbo jumbo of politicians:
this man, this Douglass, this former slave, this Negro
beaten to his knees, exiled, visioning a world
where none is lonely, none hunted, alien,
10   this man, superb in love and logic, this man
shall be remembered. Oh, not with statues' rhetoric,
not with legends and poems and wreaths of bronze alone,
but with the lives grown out of his life, the lives
fleshing his dream of the beautiful, needful thing.

PART II, THE FREE MAN, NO. 30, THE
FREDERICK DOUGLASS SERIES
Jacob Lawrence
*Hampton University Museum, Hampton,
Virginia*

---

1. Frederick Douglass: An American abolitionist (1817?–1895).
2. diastole (dī as′ tə lē′), **systole** (sis′ tə lē′): Diastole is the usual
rhythmic dilation, or opening, of the heart. Systole is the usual
rhythmic closing of the heart.

RESPONDING TO THE SELECTION

Your Response
1. What do freedom and liberty mean to you? Do you believe that everyone living in present-day America is truly free? Why or why not?
2. How did this poem affect your impressions of Frederick Douglass? Explain.

Interpreting
3. (a) What is paradoxical, or self-contradictory, about the speaker's assertion that freedom is a "beautiful and terrible thing"? (b) How do you explain this statement?
4. What does the speaker mean when he says that Douglass will be remembered "with lives grown out of his life"?
5. (a) What does this poem suggest about the realities of life for African Americans in present-day America? Support your answer. (b) Do you think the poem conveys a positive vision of the future for African Americans? Explain.

Applying
6. How do you think Frederick Douglass would respond to this poem? Why?
7. Do you think there will ever come a time when everyone on earth will enjoy true freedom? Why or why not?

THINKING AND WRITING

Comparing and Contrasting Poems
Robert Hayden is not the first African American poet to pay tribute to Frederick Douglass. In his poem "Douglass" (page 534), the late-nineteenth-century poet Paul Laurence Dunbar evokes the memory of Frederick Douglass to help comfort African Americans in a difficult period of their history. Write an essay in which you compare and contrast Hayden's poem with Dunbar's, noting similarities and differences in the forms of the poems, the messages they convey, and the attitudes toward Douglass they reflect.

Those Winter Sundays

Robert Hayden

Sundays too my father got up early
and put his clothes on in the blueblack cold,
then with cracked hands that ached
from labor in the weekday weather made
5   banked fires blaze. No one ever thanked him.

I'd wake and hear the cold splintering, breaking.
When the rooms were warm, he'd call,
and slowly I would rise and dress,
fearing the chronic angers of that house,

10 Speaking indifferently to him,
who had driven out the cold
and polished my good shoes as well.
What did I know, what did I know
of love's austere and lonely offices?

RESPONDING TO THE SELECTION

Your Response

1. What are your childhood memories of winter Sundays?

Interpreting

2. What does the first stanza reveal about Hayden's father's dedication to his family?
3. What does Hayden mean when he says that he could "hear the cold splintering, breaking"?
4. What does Hayden mean when he refers to the "chronic angers" of his house?
5. How do you think Hayden eventually learned about "love's austere and lonely offices"?

Applying

6. Why do you think that some young people are unable to appreciate the sacrifices their parents make for them? (b) Why do you think young people sometimes have a difficult time communicating with their parents?

ANALYZING LITERATURE

Understanding Confessional Poetry

Confessional poetry is poetry that deals openly and frankly with a poet's personal life. Although confessional poems are autobiographical, the situations and problems on which they focus are often universal. For example, in "Those Winter Sundays," Hayden writes about his indifference toward the sacrifices his father made for his family—an attitude shared by many young people in contemporary society.

1. How has Hayden's attitude toward his father changed since his childhood?
2. How does he make it clear that he now regrets the way he reacted to his father?
3. What is his message to readers?

Traveling Through the Dark

William Stafford

Traveling through the dark I found a deer
dead on the edge of the Wilson River road.
It is usually best to roll them into the canyon:
that road is narrow; to swerve might make more dead.

5 By glow of the tail-light I stumbled back of the car
and stood by the heap, a doe, a recent killing;
she had stiffened already, almost cold.
I dragged her off; she was large in the belly.

My fingers touching her side brought me the reason—
10 her side was warm; her fawn lay there waiting,
alive, still, never to be born.
Beside that mountain road I hesitated.

The car aimed ahead its lowered parking lights;
under the hood purred the steady engine.
15 I stood in the glare of the warm exhaust turning red;
around our group I could hear the wilderness listen.

I thought hard for us all—my only swerving—,
then pushed her over the edge into the river.

RESPONDING TO THE SELECTION

Your Response

1. If you had been traveling "through the dark" with the speaker, what would you have suggested that he do? Explain.
2. What feelings does this poem evoke in you? Why?

Recalling

3. (a) Where does the speaker find the deer? (b) What does he observe about the deer "by glow of the tail-light"? (c) What does he discover when he touches the deer? (d) What does the speaker do with the deer at the end of the poem?

Interpreting

4. (a) How does the speaker personify, or attribute human qualities to, his car in the fourth stanza? (b) How does this image of the car relate to the speaker's discovery of the deer?
5. What does this poem reveal about the relationship between humanity and nature in the modern world?
6. In literature a journey is often used to symbolize, or represent, life. Assuming that this is the case in Stafford's poem, how might you interpret the poem's title?

Applying

7. Do you think the speaker makes the proper decision about what to do with the deer? Why or why not?

THINKING AND WRITING

Writing a Confessional Poem

Write a poem expressing your feelings of affection and appreciation for a person who has in some way tried to make your life easier or more pleasant. Start by reviewing the freewriting you did before you began reading this group of poems. When you write your poems, use concrete images, or word pictures, in describing your feelings. After revising your poem, share it with the person about whom it is written.

LEARNING OPTIONS

1. **Cross-curricular Connection.** In recent decades there has been a dramatic increase in the deer population. In some places the population has grown so large that deer can often be found roaming through city streets. Not surprisingly, a controversy has erupted about whether people should take additional measures to control the deer population. Investigate the recent growth in the deer population and the controversy over taking measures to control it. Then express your opinions about the issue in an informal class debate.
2. **Cross-curricular Connection.** Stafford's poem demonstrates one of the many ways in which humanity can come into conflict with nature. The relationship between people and nature has gained increased attention in recent years, as people become more and more concerned about the impact of human behavior on the environment. Choose an environmental issue that you consider important. For example, you might choose deforestation, air pollution, or global warming. Investigate the topic you have chosen. Take a position on the issue. Then design a persuasive billboard or advertisement expressing your position. Present your finished product to the class.

BIOGRAPHIES

Colleen McElroy (1935–   )

In her poetry Colleen McElroy delves into her African American heritage, exploring the connections between the experiences of the past, the realities of the present, and hope for the future.

Born in St. Louis, Missouri, McElroy received her undergraduate degree from Kansas State University and her doctorate from the University of Washington, where she now serves as a professor of English. A prolific writer, she has produced several collections of poetry, including *The Mules Done Long Since Gone* (1972) and *Music From Home: Selected Poems* (1976); numerous short stories; and a variety of educational books, articles, and film scripts.

Louise Erdrich (1954–   )

Although Louise Erdrich is known mainly for her popular and critically acclaimed fiction, she is also a gifted poet. Commenting on the poems in her collections, *Jacklight* (1984) and *Baptism of Fire* (1989), a critic has observed that "the virtuosity of Erdrich's acclaimed prose style is founded in the disciplined craft of her poetry. . . . "

A full-blooded Chippewa, Louise Erdrich was born in Little Falls, Minnesota. After receiving degrees from Dartmouth and Johns Hopkins, she settled in central New Hampshire with her husband, author Michael Dorris. Her first novel, *Love Medicine* (1984), the story of three Chippewa families living on a North Dakota reservation, enjoyed both critical and commercial success. Her reputation grew with the publication of her next effort, *Beet Queen* (1986). In 1991 she and her husband co-authored *The Crown of Columbus,* which offers a Native American perspective of American historical events.

James Wright (1927–1980)

In the introduction to his second book, *The Green Wall* (1957), James Wright wrote that his purpose as a poet was to say something that was "humanly important, instead of just showing off language." Throughout his career, Wright achieved this goal, while at the same time writing poetry that is filled with elegant language and rich, vivid imagery.

Wright was born in Martins Ferry, Ohio, and educated at Kenyon College and the University of Washington. During his brief life, he published five books of poetry, including *Saint Judas* (1959), *The Branch Will Not Break* (1963), and *Shall We Gather at the River* (1968). In 1972 he received the Pulitzer Prize for his *Collected Poems* (1971).

GUIDE FOR INTERPRETING

For My Children; Bidwell Ghost; Lying in a Hammock at William Duffy's Farm in Pine Island, Minnesota

Literary Forms

Lyric Poetry. A lyric poem expresses the personal thoughts and feelings of the speaker. One of the oldest and most popular forms of poetry, lyrics were originally sung to the accompaniment of a stringed instrument called a *lyre*. That is why such poetry is called *lyr*-ic and why we still refer to the words of songs as *lyrics.* Although most lyric poems are no longer set to music, they still tend to be brief and melodic, like songs. In addition, lyrics generally focus on producing a single, unified effect.

Virtually any subject is appropriate for a lyric, as long as it stirs the poet's thoughts and feelings. "Lying in a Hammock at William Duffy's Farm in Pine Island, Minnesota," for example, focuses on the thoughts that come to mind as the speaker relaxes in a tranquil and secluded setting.

Commentary

As you read the last line of James Wright's "Lying in a Hammock at William Duffy's Farm in Pine Island, Minnesota," notice that it makes this simple but affecting statement: "I have wasted my life." In contemplative repose the speaker is reflecting on the richness of nature's slow beauty. He is allowed respite from the busy world in which reflection plays no part. People often turn to nature for renewal. A solitary walk on the beach, a hike among the turning leaves of autumn, a rest in a hammock—these allow us to quiet the noise long enough to hear the silent voices of our souls. In our contemporary world it is difficult for us to stop and reflect about the choices we have made and the things that matter most. Does this poem remind us that it is important to do so?

Focus

In "Lying in a Hammock at William Duffy's Farm in Pine Island, Minnesota," the speaker presents his observations of a farm at sunset. What types of details do you think the speaker is likely to have observed? Prepare a list of images, or word pictures, that you associate with farms.

For My Children

Colleen McElroy

I have stored up tales for you, my children
    My favorite children, my only children;
Of shackles and slaves and a bill of rights.
But skin of honey and beauty of ebony begins
5   In the land called Bilad as-Sudan,[1]
So I search for a heritage beyond St. Louis.

My memory floats down a long narrow hall,
    A calabash[2] of history.
Grandpa stood high in Watusi[3] shadows
10 In this land of yearly rituals for alabaster beauty;
Where effigies of my ancestors are captured
    In Beatle tunes,
And crowns never touch Bantu[4] heads.

My past is a slender dancer reflected briefly
15   Like a leopard in fingers of fire.
The future of Dahomey[5] is a house of 16 doors,
The totem of the Burundi[6] counts 17 warriors—
    In reverse generations.
While I cling to one stray Seminole.[7]

20 My thoughts grow thin in the urge to travel
    Beyond Grandma's tale
Of why cat fur is for kitten britches;
Past the wrought-iron rail of first stairs
    In baby white shoes,
25 To Ashanti[8] mysteries and rituals.

Back in the narrow hallway of my childhood,
    I cradled my knees

---

1. Bilad as-Sudan (bē lād′ äs so͞o dan′): "Land of the blacks," an Arabic expression by which Arab geographers referred to the settled African countries north of the southern edge of the Sahara.
2. calabash (kal′ ə bash′) *n.*: A dried, hollow shell of a gourd, used as a bowl or a cup.
3. Watusi (wä to͞o′ sē): A people of east-central Africa.
4. Bantu (ban′ to͞o): A group of people from southern Africa.
5. Dahomey (də hō′ mē): Old name for Benin, in west-central Africa.
6. Burundi (bo͝o ro͝on′ dē): A country in east-central Africa.
7. Seminole (sem′ ə nōl′): A Native American people from Florida.
8. Ashanti (ə shän′ tə): A people of western Africa.

THE MADONNA AND CHILD, 1990
Momodou Ceesay

In limbs as smooth and long as the neck of a bud vase,
I began this ancestral search that you children yield now
30   In profile and bust
By common invention, in being and belonging.

The line of your cheeks recalls Ibo[9] melodies
    As surely as oboe and flute.
The sun dances a honey and cocoa duet on your faces.
35   I see smiles that mirror schoolboy smiles
    In the land called Bilad as-Sudan;
I see the link between the Mississippi and the Congo.

---

9. Ibo (ē′ bō′): An African people of southeastern Nigeria.

RESPONDING TO THE SELECTION

Your Response

1. What is your reaction to this poem? Does it stir up thoughts about your own ancestors and cultural traditions? Why or why not?

2. What tales will you "store up" for your children? Why?

Interpreting

3. Why do you think the speaker is so concerned with educating her children about the history of their people? Support your answer.

4. (a) What impressions does the speaker convey of her ancestors in the second and third stanzas? (b) Which images, or word pictures, contribute to these impressions? Explain.

5. What is the poem's theme, or central message? Support your answer.

Applying

6. How important do you think it is for parents to educate their children about their cultural heritage? Explain.

Bidwell Ghost

Louise Erdrich

Each night she waits by the road
in a thin white dress
embroidered with fire.

It has been twenty years
5 since her house surged and burst in the
    dark trees.
Still nobody goes there.

The heat charred the branches
of the apple trees,
but nothing can kill that wood.

10 She will climb into your car
but not say where she is going
and you shouldn't ask.

Nor should you try to comb the blackened
    nest of hair

or press the agates of tears
back into her eyes.   15

First the orchard bowed low and complained
of the unpicked fruit,
then the branches cracked apart and fell.

The windfalls sweetened to wine
beneath the ruined arms and snow.   20
Each spring now, in the grass, buds form
    on the tattered wood.

The child, the child, why is she so
    persistent
in her need? Is it so terrible
to be alone when the cold white blossoms
come to life and burn?   25

WINTER
Ozz Franca

Lying in a Hammock at William Duffy's Farm in Pine Island, Minnesota

James Wright

Over my head, I see the bronze butterfly,
Asleep on the black trunk,
Blowing like a leaf in green shadow.
Down the ravine behind the empty house,
5　The cowbells follow one another
Into the distances of the afternoon.

THE POET RECLINING 1915
Marc Chagall
The Tate Gallery, London

To my right,
In a field of sunlight between two pines,
The droppings of last year's horses
10 Blaze into golden stones.
I lean back, as the evening darkens and comes on.
A chicken-hawk floats over, looking for home.
I have wasted my life.

RESPONDING TO THE SELECTION

Your Response

1. Do you agree with the conclusion the speaker reaches at the end of the poem? Why or why not?
2. Would you like to lie in a hammock at William Duffy's farm in Pine Island, Minnesota? Why or why not?

Interpreting

3. Metonymy is a literary device in which something very closely associated with a thing is used to suggest or represent the thing itself. Wright uses this technique in line 5, using cowbells to represent cows. How does his use of this technique help him to create an image, or word picture, that appeals to both the sense of hearing and the sense of sight?
4. What overall impression do the images in the poem convey?
5. (a) Why might the speaker's observations of the farm lead him to the conclusion he reaches at the end of the poem? (b) Do you think the poet means his words to be taken at face value? Explain your answer.

Applying

6. How would you define a well-spent life?

ANALYZING LITERATURE

Understanding Lyric Poetry

"Lying in a Hammock at William Duffy's Farm in Pine Island, Minnesota" is an example of a lyric—a short, personal poem expressing the speaker's emotions and thoughts.

1. What emotions and thoughts does the speaker express in the poem?
2. What philosophy of life does the poem convey?

THINKING AND WRITING

Responding to Criticism

A critic has commented that in his poetry Wright focuses "not only on his experience but also on his response to that experience." Write an essay in which you discuss this statement in relation to "Lying in a Hammock at William Duffy's Farm in Pine Island, Minnesota." Use passages from the poem to support your argument. When you revise, make sure that you have adequately supported your opinion with details from the poem.

LEARNING OPTION

Writing. Imagine that you have just spent a week's vacation on William Duffy's farm in Pine Island, Minnesota. How have you spent the week? Have you enjoyed yourself? Write a postcard home in which you share your opinion of William Duffy, farm life, or James Wright, who suggested that you vacation on the farm.

Adrienne Rich (1929–   )

Adrienne Rich's career as a poet can be divided into two distinct stages. During the early part of her career, she wrote neatly crafted traditional verse. In contrast, her later poems are written in free verse and often explore her deepest personal feelings.

Born and raised in Baltimore, Rich began writing poetry at an early age. Her first volume of poetry, *A Change of World* (1951), was published just after she graduated from Radcliffe College. Since abandoning traditional poetic forms for free verse in the early 1960's, she has produced several collections of poetry. Her later books include *Snapshots of a Daughter-in-Law* (1963), *The Will to Change* (1971), and *Diving into the Wreck* (1973).

Simon Ortiz (1941–   )

An Acoma Pueblo Indian, Simon Ortiz carries on the Native American tradition of storytelling in his poetry. Not surprisingly, much of his poetry reflects his deep awareness of his cultural heritage.

Ortiz was born in New Mexico. After graduating from the University of New Mexico, he attended the University of Iowa Writers' Workshop. He has worked as a teacher, journalist, and public relations director and is currently a professor at the University of New Mexico. Possessing a strong belief in the importance of education, Ortiz devotes much of his free time to educating fellow Native Americans.

Diana Chang (1934–   )

Diana Chang, who spent most of her childhood in China, is another contemporary poet whose work reflects her cultural heritage. In fact, many of her poems, including "Most Satisfied by Snow" clearly exhibit the influence of ancient Oriental verse forms.

Born in New York City and raised in China, Chang settled in the United States following World War II. She attended Barnard College, graduating in 1955. In addition to writing poetry, she has written several novels, including *The Frontiers of Love* (1956), *The Only Game in Town,* and *Eye to Eye*. She has also served as the editor of *The American Pen,* a journal published by the international writers' association, P.E.N.

GUIDE FOR INTERPRETING

The Observer; Hunger in New York City; Most Satisfied by Snow

Writers' Techniques

Parallelism. Parallelism refers to the repeated use of phrases, clauses, or sentences that are similar in structure. Poets often use parallelism to create a sense of unity and establish a pattern in their poems, especially in poems written in free verse—verse that has irregular meter and line length. The use of parallelism also adds emphasis to certain words and phrases and helps to create a rhythm.

Commentary

As you read the three poems on the next few pages, notice that they all concern ways of nurturing the soul. Often in our fast-paced world, we remember to feed our bodies but forget to feed our souls. "The Observer" compares the lives of two people. The speaker envies the simplified, natural existence she envisions Dian Fossey living and implies that Fossey's life in the "pale gorilla-scented dawn" is richer than her own "in the old cell block." The richness she longs for is not material; it is the fullness of the soul.

"Hunger in New York City" addresses soul nourishment more directly. Ortiz expressly sees hunger "asking for food, words, wisdom, young memories. . . . " As you read the poem, notice what things the poem's speaker searches out and finds to feed himself in "the concrete of this city" where he finds little to "eat."

"Most Satisfied by Snow" ends with the words "I, too, flowering." How does a person flower? In the poem the speaker observes and is open to both the insubstantial fog and the very substantial snow. Perhaps, in comparing "us" to these things, she reminds us that the spiritual and the physical components of ourselves are both important and that we can grow, or flower, in soul as well as in body.

How do you nourish your hungry soul? What do you feed it to make it grow healthy and strong? Some people feed their souls nature, some tradition or memories, and some even feed it poetry.

Focus

In Adrienne Rich's poem "The Observer," the speaker contrasts her own life with the life of Dian Fossey, a scientist who studied gorillas by living among them in the African jungle. Freewrite about the type of life that you imagine Fossey might have led while living among the gorillas. Why do you think she chose to lead this sort of life? What dangers do you think she might have faced? Why might she have found the experience rewarding?

The Observer

Adrienne Rich

Completely protected on all sides
by volcanoes
a woman, darkhaired, in stained jeans
sleeps in central Africa.
5 In her dreams, her notebooks, still
private as maiden diaries,
the mountain gorillas move through their life term:
their gentleness survives
observation. Six bands of them
10 inhabit, with her, the wooded highland.
When I lay me down to sleep
unsheltered by any natural guardians
from the panicky life-cycle of my tribe
I wake in the old cellblock
15 observing the daily executions,
rehearsing the laws
I cannot subscribe to,
envying the pale gorilla-scented dawn
she wakes into, the stream where she washes her hair,
20 the camera-flash of her quiet
eye.

RESPONDING TO THE SELECTION

Your Response

1. What is your reaction to the lifestyle of the subject of the poem? Do you share the speaker's envy of her life? Why or why not?
2. Do you think that the poet has a realistic image of the subject's life? Why or why not?
3. Whose lifestyles do you envy? Why?

Interpreting

4. (a) What do the details in the poem suggest about the world in which the speaker lives? (b) How does her world contrast with the world in which the scientist lives? (c) What is the speaker's attitude toward her world? (d) How is this attitude revealed?
5. Why does the speaker envy the scientist?

Applying

6. Do you think that most people in contemporary American society would envy the scientist? Why or why not?

Primary Source

Dian Fossey lived among the gorillas while Jane Goodall, another scientist of great renown, chose a similar life among the chimpanzees of Africa. Here Goodall describes a day three months after her arrival. " . . . I set off alone one morning for the mountain I had climbed on my first afternoon—the mountain that rose directly above our camp. I left at my ususal time, when it was still cool, in the first glimmerings of dawn. After ten minutes or so my heart began to hammer wildly, I could feel the blood pounding in my head, and I had to stop to catch my breath. Eventually I reached an open peak about one thousand feet above the lake. It offered a superb view over the home valley, so I decided to sit there for a while and search for signs of chimpanzees through my binoculars.

"I had been there some fifteen minutes when a slight movement caught my eye. I looked around and saw three chimps standing there staring at me. I expected them to flee, for they were no farther than eighty yards away, but after a moment they moved on again, quite calmly, and were soon lost to sight in some thicker vegetation. . . .

"I remained on my peak, and later on in the morning a group of chimps . . . careered down the opposite mountain slope and began feeding in some fig trees that grew thickly along the streambanks in the valley below me. . . . Although they all stopped and stared and then hastened their steps slightly as they moved on again, the chimpanzees did not run in panic. . . .

"That day, in fact, marked the turning point in my study. The fig trees grow all along the lower reaches of the stream and that year the crop in our valley was plentiful, lasting for eight weeks. Every day I returned to my peak, and every day chimpanzees fed on the figs below. They came in large groups and small groups, singly and in pairs. Regularly they passed me. . . . And because I always looked the same, wearing similar dull-colored clothes, and never tried to follow them or harass them in any way, the shy chimpanzees began to realize, at long last, that after all I was not so horrific and terrifying."

Hunger in New York City

Simon Ortiz

Hunger crawls into you
from somewhere out of your muscles
or the concrete or the land
or the wind pushing you.

5   It comes to you, asking
for food, words, wisdom, young memories
of places you ate at, drank cold spring water,
or held somebody's hand,
or home of the gentle, slow dances,
10   the songs, the strong gods, the world
you know.

That is, hunger searches you out.
It always asks you,
How are you, son? Where are you?
15   Have you eaten well?
Have you done what you as a person
of our people is supposed to do?

And the concrete of this city,
the oily wind, the blazing windows,
20   the shrieks of automation cannot,
truly cannot, answer for that hunger
although I have hungered,
truthfully and honestly, for them
to feed myself with.

25   So I sang to myself quietly:
I am feeding myself
with the humble presence
of all around me;
I am feeding myself
30   with your soul, my mother earth;
make me cool and humble.
Bless me.

THE LONE TENEMENT
George W. Bellows

RESPONDING TO THE SELECTION

Your Response

1. In "Hunger in New York City," the speaker hungers for his home. What other kinds of hunger do people experience? What kinds have you experienced? Explain.
2. How would you describe the poet's view of city life? Do you share his view? Explain.

Interpreting

3. How does Ortiz personify hunger?
4. (a) What details indicate that the speaker has moved to the city from another place? (b) How is this place different from the city? (c) What details indicate that the speaker hungers for his original home?

Applying

5. This poem clearly reflects Ortiz's Native American heritage. What does it reveal about the traditional attitudes of his tribe?

THINKING AND WRITING

Writing a Poem Using Parallelism

Write a free-verse poem in which you use parallelism to establish a pattern. Start by thinking of a subject for your poem. You might want to write about a personal experience, an important event, or an element of nature. Prepare a list of details describing your subject. Arrange your details in logical order. Then write your poem. When you finish writing, revise and proofread your poem.

Most Satisfied by Snow

Diana Chang

Against my windows,
fog knows
what to do, too

Spaces pervade
5   us, as well

But occupied by snow,
I see

Matter
matters

10   I, too,
flowering

CHRISTMAS MORNING, ADIRONDACKS, 1946
Rockwell Kent

![R] ESPONDING TO THE SELECTION

Your Response

1. What emotions do the images, or word pictures, in this poem evoke in you? Explain.
2. By what aspect of nature are you "most satisfied"? Explain.

Interpreting

3. What does the speaker mean when she comments that "spaces pervade us"?

4. (a) What difference between fog and snow does this poem highlight? (b) How is this contrast embodied in humans?
5. (a) What is the meaning of the final two lines? (b) What is the poem's overall message?

Applying

6. This poem suggests that we can learn about ourselves by observing nature. Do you agree with this suggestion? Why or why not?

Lawson Fusao Inada (1938–   )

The first Asian American poet to have a book published by a major American publishing company, Lawson Fusao Inada has established himself as a widely respected member of the American literary community.

Born in Fresno, California, Inada graduated from Fresno State College and later received a master's degree from the University of Oregon. He has taught at several universities, served as a consultant for many literary organizations, and published a number of books, including *Before the War: Poems As They Happen* (1971). He was also responsible for editing *Aiiieeeee!: An Anthology of Asian-American Writers* (1974).

Lorna Dee Cervantes (1954–   )

A budding Mexican American literary voice, Lorna Dee Cervantes was born in San Francisco and continues to live in northern California. Educated at San Jose University and the University of California at Santa Cruz, she published her first collection of poems, *Emplumada,* in 1981. Her work has subsequently been included in numerous literary anthologies. She has also established her own small press and poetry magazine, *Mango.* In her work, she balances a concern for her cultural heritage with her keen awareness of the struggles faced by women—especially Hispanic women—in contemporary American society.

Rita Dove (1952–   )

Rita Dove has commented that "the events of the poem should never be more important than how that event is recreated." Considering this belief, it is not surprising that her poetry can be characterized by her vivid imagery and skillful use of language. She has also said that stock questions such as "What is poetry about?" are fruitless. Poetry, she believes, leads to personal experience and should awaken readers' feelings.

Dove was born in Akron, Ohio. She graduated with highest honors from Miami University in Oxford, Ohio, and later earned a master's degree from the University of Iowa. She has published several collections of poetry, including *The Yellow House on the Corner* (1980) and *Museum* (1983). In 1987 she received the Pulitzer Prize for her book, *Thomas and Beulah.* In 1993 she was nominated Poet Laureate by the Library of Congress.

GUIDE FOR INTERPRETING

Plucking Out a Rhythm; Freeway 280; This Life

Free Verse. The majority of contemporary poetry is written in free verse—verse that has irregular meter and line length. Though free verse lacks regular meter, it does not lack rhythm. Yet it does allow poets to experiment with new types of rhythms in their work. For example, Lawson Fusao Inada's use of free verse enables him to capture the natural rhythms of jazz in "Plucking Out a Rhythm."

Art communicates imagination and human experience through many forms. Painting, music, poetry, dance, and sculpture can all express similar things. The mediums change, not necessarily the messages. In "Plucking Out a Rhythm" and "This Life," the poets allude to art forms other than poetry to heighten the subjects expressed in the poems—they mix the arts. Lawson Inada builds an imaginative impression of a bass player creating jazz music piece by piece in a room, or in one's imagination, until the daylight and snow scatter it away. The sound and rhythm of the words play on the reader's imagination to build the impression of music. Finally, the reader hears music where there is none. The poetry and music have combined to create an imaginative experience.

Rita Dove uses a visual art form, a Japanese woodcut, in her poem to evoke a human experience for the reader. The scene conveyed in the woodcut is the scene shaped in the speaker's life and in the poem's words. The woodcut scene is static—a girl waiting—and there is no movement in the speaker's life either. By paralleling the experience of the girl in the woodcut to that of the poem's speaker, Ms. Dove doubles the impact of the experience on the reader.

Each of these poets has used hybrid art—that is, poem-and-music and poem-and-woodcut—to work upon the reader in more than one way. Inada, a Japanese American, and Dove, an African American, both embrace hybrid cultures within their own experiences. Do they suggest that adding one art to another, like adding one culture to another, enriches experience by allowing a multiple view of it?

In "Plucking Out a Rhythm," Lawson Fusao Inada explores how reality affects our imaginations. Freewrite about your own thoughts concerning the effect of reality on people's imaginations.

Plucking Out a Rhythm

Lawson Fusao Inada

Start with a simple room—
a dullish color—
and draw the one shade down.
Hot plate. Bed.
5 Little phonograph in a corner.

Put in a single figure—
medium weight and height—
but oversize, as a child might.

The features must be Japanese.

10 Then stack a black pompadour[1] on,
and let the eyes
slide behind a night of glass.

The figure is in disguise:

slim green suit
15 for posturing on a bandstand,
the turned-up shoes of Harlem . . .

Then start the music playing—
thick jazz, strong jazz—

and notice that the figure
20 comes to life:
sweating, growling
over an imaginary bass—
plucking out a rhythm—
as the music rises and the room is full,
25 exuding with that rhythm . . .

Then have the shade flap up
and daylight catch him
frozen in that pose

as it starts to snow—
30 thick snow, strong snow—

blowing in the window
while the music quiets,
the room is slowly covered,

and the figure is completely
35 out of sight.

---

1. pompadour (päm′pə dôr′) *n.*: A hairdo in which
the hair is swept up high from the forehead.

RESPONDING TO THE SELECTION

Your Response

1. In this poem, Inada creates a vivid image of a
musician playing jazz. (a) What images does
your favorite type of music evoke for you? (b)
What emotions does your favorite music
evoke?

Interpreting

2. What does the impact of the snow on the imaginary musician suggest about the effect of reality on the imagination?

Applying

3. In what way do people's imaginations set them
apart from one another?

ANALYZING LITERATURE

Understanding Free Verse

Free verse is verse that has irregular meter
and line length. Through the use of free verse,
poets are able to experiment with new types of
rhythms in their poetry.
1. Why is free verse an appropriate form for
"Plucking Out a Rhythm"?
2. How would the poem be different if it were written in verse with regular meter and line length?

VAUDEVILLE, 1951
Jacob Lawrence
Hirshhorn Museum and Sculpture Garden, Smithsonian Institution

Plucking Out a Rhythm 1027

Freeway 280

Lorna Dee Cervantes

Las casitas[1] near the gray cannery,
nestled amid wild abrazos[2] of climbing roses
and man-high red geraniums
are gone now. The freeway conceals it
5 all beneath a raised scar.

But under the fake windsounds of the open lanes,
in the abandoned lots below, new grasses sprout,
wild mustard remembers, old gardens
come back stronger than they were,
10 trees have been left standing in their yards.
Albaricoqueros, cerezos, nogales . . . [3]
Viejitas[4] come here with paper bags to gather greens.
Espinaca, verdolagas, yerbabuena . . . [5]

I scramble over the wire fence
15 that would have kept me out.
Once, I wanted out, wanted the rigid lanes
to take me to a place without sun,
without the smell of tomatoes burning
on swing shift in the greasy summer air.

20 Maybe it's here
en los campos extraños de esta ciudad[6]
where I'll find it, that part of me
mown under
like a corpse
25 or a loose seed.

---

1. **Las casitas** (lahs kah sē′ tahs): "The little houses."
2. **abrazos** (ah brah′ sohs): "Hugs."
3. **Albaricoqueros, cerezos, nogales** (ahl bahr rē koh′ keh′ rohs, seh reh′ sohs, noh gah′ lehs): "Apricot trees, cherry trees, walnut trees."
4. **Viejitas** (byeh hē′ tahs): "Old women."
5. **Espinaca, verdolagas, yerbabuena** (ehs pē nah′ kah, behr thoh lah′ gahs, yehr bah bweh′ nah): Spinach, purslane, peppermint."
6. **en los campos extraños de esta ciudad** (ehn lohs kahm′ pohs ehx trah′ nyohs deh ehs′ tah syōō thahth): "In the strange fields of this city."

UNTITLED
Peter Malone

Your Response

1. What do you imagine it might have been like to grow up in the little houses that the speaker recalls? Why?
2. Cervantes uses the freeway as a central image connected to both the abandoned lots and the speaker's personal experiences. What associations do you have with freeways? Explain.

Interpreting

3. What does the freeway symbolize?
4. (a) What impression of the now-vanished houses does the speaker convey in the opening stanza? (b) How are the abandoned lots rejuvenated, or reborn?
5. How do the personal experiences the speaker describes in the final two stanzas parallel the demise and rebirth of the little houses and the land around them?
6. What does the speaker seek to escape in the third stanza then rediscover in the final stanza?

7. How do the images in the final two lines connect to the rest of the poem?

Applying

8. What places are you familiar with that have been renovated after being neglected or abandoned?

LEARNING OPTIONS

1. **Community Connections.** Start a campaign to rebuild a neighborhood. Either write a persuasive letter to a local politician arguing for the need to fund the rebuilding of a neighborhood, or create a flyer for a rally in support of this cause. Present your letter or flyer to the class.
2. **Community Connections.** Find a place in your own community in need of renovation. With a group of your classmates, create a proposal for renovating or beautifying this place. For example, you might want to suggest planting trees or other vegetation. Share your proposal with the class.

This Life

Rita Dove

The green lamp flares on the table.
You tell me the same thing
as that one,
asleep, upstairs.
5 Now I see: the possibilities
are like golden dresses in a nutshell.

As a child, I fell in love
with a Japanese woodcut
of a girl gazing at the moon.
10 I waited with her for her lover.
He came in white breeches[1] and sandals.
He had a goatee[2]—he had

your face, though I didn't know it.
Our lives will be the same—
15 your lips, swollen from whistling
at danger,
and I a stranger
in this desert,
nursing the tough skin of figs.

---

1. breeches *n.:* Pants reaching to or just below the knees.
2. goatee (gō tē') *n.:* A small, pointed beard.

▉ RESPONDING TO THE SELECTION

Your Response

1. The speaker of Dove's poem recalls a Japanese woodcut that captured her interest as a child. What photographs or pieces of art stand out in your memory or have captured your imagination? Explain.

Interpreting

2. Who might the "one" mentioned in line 3 be?
3. What is the meaning of the simile, or comparison, in lines 5 and 6?
4. (a) What is the significance of the speaker's childhood memory? (b) How does it seem to relate to her present life?
5. What attitude does "whistling at danger" suggest?
6. What impression does the image of the "tough skin of figs" convey?

Applying

7. Why do childhood memories seem so vivid?

▉ THINKING AND WRITING

Responding to a Poem

Imagine that Rita Dove asked you to respond to "This Life." Reread the poem. What do you like about the poem? What do you dislike about it? Organize your thoughts. Then write your response, using passages from the poem to support your opinions. When you finish writing, revise and proofread your response.

▉ LEARNING OPTION

Art. Find or create a piece of art to accompany Dove's poem. The piece should connect to one or more of the poem's central images. Present the piece of art to the class and explain how it relates to the poem.

Drama

CLOSING SCENE, 1963
David Hockney
Courtesy of the Artist

ARTHUR MILLER

1915–

Considered among the finest American playwrights of the contemporary era, Miller has chronicled the dilemma of common people pitted against powerful and unyielding social forces. His plays have earned acclaim from both critics and the general public.

Miller was born in New York City in 1915. During the Depression, his father suffered severe financial losses that forced the family to move from Manhattan to more modest quarters in Brooklyn. In the aftermath of his family's financial downfall, Miller dropped out of high school and worked as a shipping clerk in an automobile parts warehouse—an experience that he later dramatized in *A Memory of Two Mondays* (1955). Despite his inability to complete high school, in 1934 he persuaded the University of Michigan to accept him as a student and used his savings from his warehouse job to finance the first year of his studies.

It was in college that Miller first began to write plays. After graduation, he continued to write while holding a variety of jobs, including one at the Brooklyn Naval Yard. In 1947 his play *All My Sons* opened on Broadway. The play, which focuses on a businessman whose actions during World War II bring about the disintegration of his family, earned immediate critical acclaim and established Miller as one of the country's most promising playwrights.

Miller fulfilled this promise as a writer two years later, when he completed *Death of a Salesman.* He created, in the character of Willy Loman, a deluded and tragic protagonist whose obsessive and futile quest for material success evoked an ambivalent reaction from the audience. *Death of a Salesman* won a Pulitzer Prize and catapulted Miller to international fame.

Departing from a contemporary milieu, Miller wrote *The Crucible* in 1953. Although it depicts the Salem witchcraft trials of 1692, the play was inspired by Miller's belief that the hysteria surrounding the witchcraft trials paralleled the contemporary political climate of McCarthyism—Senator Joseph McCarthy's obsessive quest to uncover communist infiltration of American institutions.

In 1956 the public spotlight became focused on Miller's personal life, when he married film star Marilyn Monroe. During his five-year marriage to Monroe, Miller did little writing, though he did write the screenplay for *The Misfits* (1961), a film that starred Monroe. After the marriage ended in divorce, Miller once again became a prolific writer. His later plays include *Vichy* (1964), *The Price* (1968), *The Creation of the World and Other Business* (1972), *The Archbishop's Ceiling* (1977), and *The American Clock* (1980).

GUIDE FOR INTERPRETING

Historical Context

The Crucible, Act I

The Salem Witchcraft Trials. In 1692 the colony of Massachusetts was plagued by a witchcraft hysteria that resulted in the death of at least twenty people and the jailing of at least 150 others. Although this event is considered by many to be one of the most tragic incidents in American history, it was actually only a small part of a much larger witchcraft hysteria that swept through the western world during the sixteenth and seventeenth centuries. In fact, historians estimate that between one and nine million alleged witches were either hanged or burned to death in Europe during this two-hundred-year period.

Despite the rampant hysteria in Europe at the time, there had been no mass accusations of witchcraft in Massachusetts prior to 1692. However, the extremely stressful nature of the lives of the Puritans who inhabited the colony made an outbreak such as the one that occurred in 1692 almost inevitable. The colonists endured harsh, cold winters; suffered through outbreaks of fatal diseases; struggled to save their crops in the face of such calamities as drought and insect infestation; experienced devastating fires; and lived through attacks by pirates and Indians, as well as French and Dutch warships. Finding themselves at the mercy of forces beyond their control, many of the colonists attributed their hardships to the Devil and were eager to strike back at the evil forces responsible for their suffering.

The witchcraft hysteria of 1692 originated in the small parish of Salem Village, now Danvers, Massachusetts. Most of the people of Salem Village were poor, uneducated, and superstitious; and they were quick to blame witchcraft when the minister's daughter and niece and several other girls became afflicted by a strange malady involving seizures and lapses into an unconscious state. After the minister, Reverend Samuel Parris, had questioned his daughter and niece for some time, the two girls accused the minister's slave, Tituba, and two other women of being responsible for their suffering. The three accused women were immediately taken into custody, and Tituba was coerced into confirming the girls' accusations. Eventually, other girls began naming people who were supposedly persecuting them, and dozens of people were jailed. Learning of the furor in Salem Village, the Governor of the Massachusetts Bay Colony appointed several of the colony's leading citizens to a court responsible for trying all those accused of witchcraft. It was at this point that the Salem witchcraft trials began.

Focus

Write a journal entry in which you explore your own perceptions of life in the Massachusetts Bay Colony and discuss how you think you would have fared if you had lived there.

The Crucible

Arthur Miller

CHARACTERS

Reverend Parris

Betty Parris

Tituba

Abigail Williams

Susanna Walcott

Mrs. Ann Putnam

Thomas Putnam

Mercy Lewis

Mary Warren

John Proctor

Rebecca Nurse

Giles Corey

Reverend John Hale

Elizabeth Proctor

Francis Nurse

Ezekiel Cheever

Marshal Herrick

Judge Hathorne

Deputy Governor Danforth

Sarah Good

Hopkins

ACT I
(An Overture)

A small upper bedroom in the home of REV-EREND SAMUEL PARRIS, *Salem, Massachusetts, in the spring of the year 1692.*

There is a narrow window at the left. Through its leaded panes the morning sunlight streams. A candle still burns near the bed, which is at the right. A chest, a chair, and a small table are the other furnishings. At the back a door opens on the landing of the stairway to the ground floor. The room gives off an air of clean spareness. The roof rafters are exposed, and the wood colors are raw and unmellowed.

As the curtain rises, REVEREND PARRIS *is discovered kneeling beside the bed, evidently in prayer. His daughter,* BETTY PAR-RIS, *aged ten, is lying on the bed, inert.*

At the time of these events Parris was in his middle forties. In history he cut a villainous path, and there is very little good to be said for him. He believed he was being persecuted wherever he went, despite his best efforts to win people and God to his side. In meeting, he felt insulted if someone rose to shut the door without first asking his permission. He was a widower with no interest in children, or talent with them. He regarded them as young adults, and until this strange crisis he, like the rest of Salem, never conceived that the children were anything but thankful for being permitted to walk straight, eyes slightly lowered, arms at the sides, and mouths shut until bidden to speak.

His house stood in the "town"—but we today would hardly call it a village. The meeting house was nearby, and from this point outward—toward the bay or inland—there were a few small-windowed, dark houses snuggling against the raw Massachusetts winter. Salem had been established hardly forty years before. To the European world the whole province was a barbaric frontier inhabited by a sect of fanatics who, nevertheless, were shipping out products of slowly increasing quantity and value.

No one can really know what their lives were like. They had no novelists—and would not have permitted anyone to read a novel if one were handy. Their creed forbade anything resembling a theater or "vain enjoyment." They did not celebrate Christmas, and a holiday from work meant only that they must concentrate even more upon prayer.

Which is not to say that nothing broke into this strict and somber way of life. When a new farmhouse was built, friends assembled to "raise the roof," and there would be special foods cooked and probably some potent cider passed around. There was a good supply of ne'er-do-wells in Salem, who dallied at the shovelboard[1] in Bridget Bishop's tavern. Probably more than the creed, hard work kept the morals of the place from spoiling, for the people were forced to fight the land like heroes for every grain of corn, and no man had very much time for fooling around.

That there were some jokers, however, is indicated by the practice of appointing a two-man patrol whose duty was to "walk forth in the time of God's worship to take notice of such as either lie about the meeting house, without attending to the word and ordinances, or that lie at home or in the fields without giving good account thereof, and to take the names of such persons, and to present them to the magistrates, whereby they may be accordingly proceeded against." This predilection for minding other people's business was time-honored among the people of Salem, and it undoubtedly created many of the suspicions which were to feed the coming madness. It was also, in my opinion, one of the things that a John Proctor would rebel against, for the time of the armed camp had almost passed, and since the country was reasonably—although not wholly—safe, the old disciplines were beginning to rankle. But, as in all such matters, the issue was not clear-cut, for danger was still a possibility, and in unity still lay the best promise of safety.

The edge of the wilderness was close by. The American continent stretched endlessly west, and it was full of mystery for them. It stood, dark and threatening, over their shoulders night and day, for out of it Indian tribes marauded from time to time, and Reverend Parris had parishioners who had lost relatives to these heathens.

The parochial snobbery of these people was partly responsible for their failure to convert the Indians. Probably they also preferred to take land from heathens rather than from fellow Christians. At any rate, very few Indians were converted, and the Salem folk believed that the virgin forest was the Devil's last preserve, his home base and the citadel[2] of his final stand. To the best of their knowledge the American forest was the last place on earth that was not paying homage to God.

For these reasons, among others, they carried about an air of innate resistance, even of persecution. Their fathers had, of course, been persecuted in England. So now they and their church found it necessary to deny any other sect its freedom, lest their New Jerusalem[3] be defiled and corrupted by wrong ways and deceitful ideas.

They believed, in short, that they held in their steady hands the candle that would light the world. We have inherited this belief, and it has helped and hurt us. It helped

---

1. shovelboard: A game in which a coin or other disk is driven with the hand along a highly polished board, floor, or table marked with transverse lines.

2. citadel (sit′ ə d′l) *n.*: A fortified place; stronghold.
3. New Jerusalem: In the Bible, the holy city of heaven.

them with the discipline it gave them. They were a dedicated folk, by and large, and they had to be to survive the life they had chosen or been born into in this country.

The proof of their belief's value to them may be taken from the opposite character of the first Jamestown settlement, farther south, in Virginia. The Englishmen who landed there were motivated mainly by a hunt for profit. They had thought to pick off the wealth of the new country and then return rich to England. They were a band of individuals, and a much more ingratiating group than the Massachusetts men. But Virginia destroyed them. Massachusetts tried to kill off the Puritans, but they combined; they set up a communal society which, in the beginning, was little more than an armed camp with an autocratic and very devoted leadership. It was, however, an autocracy by consent, for they were united from top to bottom by a commonly held ideology whose perpetuation was the reason and justification for all their sufferings. So their self-denial, their purposefulness, their suspicion of all vain pursuits, their hard-handed justice, were altogether perfect instruments for the conquest of this space so antagonistic to man.

But the people of Salem in 1692 were not quite the dedicated folk that arrived on the *Mayflower*. A vast differentiation had taken place, and in their own time a revolution had unseated the royal government and substituted a junta[4] which was at this moment in power. The times, to their eyes, must have been out of joint, and to the common folk must have seemed as insoluble and complicated as do ours today. It is not hard to see how easily many could have been led to believe that the time of confusion had been brought upon them by deep and darkling forces. No hint of such speculation appears on the court record, but social disorder in any age breeds such mystical suspicions, and when, as in Salem, wonders are brought

___
4. **junta** (hoon′tə) *n.*: An assembly or council.

forth from below the social surface, it is too much to expect people to hold back very long from laying on the victims with all the force of their frustrations.

The Salem tragedy, which is about to begin in these pages, developed from a paradox. It is a paradox in whose grip we still live, and there is no prospect yet that we will discover its resolution. Simply, it was this: for good purposes, even high purposes, the people of Salem developed a theocracy, a combine of state and religious power whose function was to keep the community together, and to prevent any kind of disunity that might open it to destruction by material or ideological enemies. It was forged for a necessary purpose and accomplished that purpose. But all organization is and must be grounded on the idea of exclusion and prohibition, just as two objects cannot occupy the same space. Evidently the time came in New England when the repressions of order were heavier than seemed warranted by the dangers against which the order was organized. The witch-hunt was a perverse manifestation of the panic which set in among all classes when the balance began to turn toward greater individual freedom.

When one rises above the individual villainy displayed, one can only pity them all, just as we shall be pitied someday. It is still impossible for man to organize his social life without repressions, and the balance has yet to be struck between order and freedom.

The witch-hunt was not, however, a mere repression. It was also, and as importantly, a long overdue opportunity for everyone so inclined to express publicly his guilt and sins, under the cover of accusations against the victims. It suddenly became possible—and patriotic and holy—for a man to say that Martha Corey had come into his bedroom at night, and that, while his wife was sleeping at his side, Martha laid herself down on his chest and "nearly suffocated him." Of course it was her spirit only, but his satisfaction at confessing himself was no lighter than if it had been Martha herself.

THE TRIAL OF TWO 'WITCHES' AT SALEM, MASSACHUSETTS, IN 1662
Howard Pyle

One could not ordinarily speak such things in public.

Long-held hatreds of neighbors could now be openly expressed, and vengeance taken, despite the Bible's charitable injunctions. Land-lust which had been expressed before by constant bickering over boundaries and deeds, could now be elevated to the arena of morality; one could cry witch against one's neighbor and feel perfectly justified in the bargain. Old scores could be settled on a plane of heavenly combat between Lucifer[5] and the Lord; suspicions and the envy of the miserable toward the happy could and did burst out in the general revenge.

REVEREND PARRIS *is praying now, and, though we cannot hear his words, a sense of his confusion hangs about him. He mumbles, then seems about to weep; then he weeps, then prays again; but his daughter does not stir on the bed.*

The door opens, and his Negro slave enters. TITUBA *is in her forties.* PARRIS *brought her with him from Barbados, where he spent some years as a merchant before entering the ministry. She enters as one does who can no longer bear to be barred from the sight of her beloved, but she is also very frightened because her slave sense has warned her that, as always, trouble in this house eventually lands on her back.*

TITUBA, *already taking a step backward:* My Betty be hearty soon?

PARRIS: Out of here!

TITUBA, *backing to the door:* My Betty not goin' die . . .

PARRIS, *scrambling to his feet in a fury:* Out of my sight! *She is gone.* Out of my— *He is overcome with sobs. He clamps his teeth against them and closes the door and leans against it, exhausted.* Oh, my God! God help me! *Quaking with fear, mumbling to*

---
5. **Lucifer:** The Devil.

himself through his sobs, he goes to the bed and gently takes BETTY's hand. Betty. Child. Dear child. Will you wake, will you open up your eyes! Betty, little one . . .

He is bending to kneel again when his niece, ABIGAIL WILLIAMS, *seventeen, enters—a strikingly beautiful girl, an orphan, with an endless capacity for dissembling. Now she is all worry and apprehension and propriety.*

ABIGAIL: Uncle? *He looks to her.* Susanna Walcott's here from Doctor Griggs.

PARRIS: Oh? Let her come, let her come.

ABIGAIL, *leaning out the door to call to* SUSANNA, *who is down the hall a few steps:* Come in, Susanna.

SUSANNA WALCOTT, *a little younger than* ABIGAIL, *a hurried girl, enters.*

PARRIS, *eagerly:* What does the doctor say, child?

SUSANNA, *craning around* PARRIS *to get a look at* BETTY: He bid me come and tell you, reverend sir, that he cannot discover no medicine for it in his books.

PARRIS: Then he must search on.

SUSANNA: Aye, sir, he have been searchin' his books since he left you, sir. But he bid me tell you, that you might look to unnatural things for the cause of it.

PARRIS, *his eyes going wide:* No—no. There be no unnatural cause here. Tell him I have sent for Reverend Hale of Beverly, and Mr. Hale will surely confirm that. Let him look to medicine and put out all thought of unnatural causes here. There be none.

SUSANNA: Aye, sir. He bid me tell you. *She turns to go.*

ABIGAIL: Speak nothin' of it in the village, Susanna.

PARRIS: Go directly home and speak nothing of unnatural causes.

SUSANNA: Aye, sir. I pray for her. *She goes out.*

ABIGAIL: Uncle, the rumor of witchcraft is all about; I think you'd best go down and deny it yourself. The parlor's packed with people, sir. I'll sit with her.

PARRIS, *pressed, turns on her:* And what shall I say to them? That my daughter and my niece I discovered dancing like heathen in the forest?

ABIGAIL: Uncle, we did dance; let you tell them I confessed it—and I'll be whipped if I must be. But they're speakin' of witchcraft. Betty's not witched.

PARRIS: Abigail, I cannot go before the congregation when I know you have not opened with me. What did you do with her in the forest?

ABIGAIL: We did dance, uncle, and when you leaped out of the bush so suddenly, Betty was frightened and then she fainted. And there's the whole of it.

PARRIS: Child. Sit you down.

ABIGAIL, *quavering, as she sits:* I would never hurt Betty. I love her dearly.

PARRIS: Now look you, child, your punishment will come in its time. But if you trafficked with spirits in the forest I must know it now, for surely my enemies will, and they will ruin me with it.

ABIGAIL: But we never conjured spirits.

PARRIS: Then why can she not move herself since midnight? This child is desperate! *Abigail lowers her eyes.* It must come out—my enemies will bring it out. Let me know what you done there. Abigail, do you understand that I have many enemies?

ABIGAIL: I have heard of it, uncle.

PARRIS: There is a faction that is sworn to drive me from my pulpit. Do you understand that?

ABIGAIL: I think so, sir.

PARRIS: Now then, in the midst of such disruption, my own household is discovered to be the very center of some obscene practice. Abominations are done in the forest—

ABIGAIL: It were sport, uncle!

PARRIS, *pointing at* BETTY: You call this sport? *She lowers her eyes. He pleads:* Abigail, if you know something that may help the doctor, for God's sake tell it to me. *She is silent.* I saw Tituba waving her arms over the fire when I came on you. Why was she doing that? And I heard a screeching and gibberish coming from her mouth. She were swaying like a dumb beast over that fire!

ABIGAIL: She always sings her Barbados songs, and we dance.

PARRIS: I cannot blink what I saw, Abigail, for my enemies will not blink it. I saw a dress lying on the grass.

ABIGAIL, *innocently:* A dress?

PARRIS—*it is very hard to say:* Aye, a dress. And I thought I saw—someone naked running through the trees!

ABIGAIL, *in terror:* No one was naked! You mistake yourself, uncle!

PARRIS, *with anger:* I saw it! *He moves from her. Then, resolved:* Now tell me true, Abigail. And I pray you feel the weight of truth upon you, for now my ministry's at stake, my ministry and perhaps your cousin's life. Whatever abomination you have done, give me all of it now, for I dare not be taken unaware when I go before them down there.

ABIGAIL: There is nothin' more. I swear it, uncle.

PARRIS, *studies her, then nods, half convinced:* Abigail, I have fought here three long years to bend these stiff-necked people to me, and now, just now when some good respect is rising for me in the parish, you compromise my very character. I have given you a home, child, I have put clothes upon your back—now give me upright answer. Your name in the town—it is entirely white, is it not?

ABIGAIL, *with an edge of resentment:* Why, I am sure it is, sir. There be no blush about my name.

PARRIS, *to the point:* Abigail, is there any other cause than you have told me, for your being discharged from Goody[6] Proctor's service? I have heard it said, and I tell you as I heard it, that she comes so rarely to the church this year for she will not sit so close to something soiled. What signified that remark?

ABIGAIL: She hates me, uncle, she must, for I would not be her slave. It's a bitter woman, a lying, cold, sniveling woman, and I will not work for such a woman!

PARRIS: She may be. And yet it has troubled me that you are now seven month out of their house, and in all this time no other family has ever called for your service.

ABIGAIL: They want slaves, not such as I. Let them send to Barbados for that. I will not black my face for any of them! *With ill-concealed resentment at him:* Do you begrudge my bed, uncle?

PARRIS: No—no.

ABIGAIL, *in a temper:* My name is good in the village! I will not have it said my name is soiled! Goody Proctor is a gossiping liar!

Enter MRS. ANN PUTNAM. *She is a twisted soul of forty-five, a death-ridden woman, haunted by dreams.*

PARRIS, *as soon as the door begins to open:* No—no, I cannot have anyone. *He sees her, and a certain deference springs into him, although his worry remains.* Why, Goody Putnam, come in.

MRS. PUTNAM, *full of breath, shiny-eyed:* It is a marvel. It is surely a stroke of hell upon you.

---

6. **Goody:** A title used to refer to a married woman; short for Goodwife.

PARRIS: No, Goody Putnam, it is—

MRS. PUTNAM, *glancing at* BETTY: How high did she fly, how high?

PARRIS: No, no, she never flew—

MRS. PUTNAM, *very pleased with it:* Why, it's sure she did. Mr. Collins saw her goin' over Ingersoll's barn, and come down light as bird, he says!

PARRIS: Now, look you, Goody Putnam, she never—*Enter* THOMAS PUTNAM, *a well-to-do, hard-handed landowner, near fifty.* Oh, good morning, Mr. Putnam.

PUTNAM: It is a providence the thing is out now! It is a providence. *He goes directly to the bed.*

PARRIS: What's out, sir, what's—?

MRS. PUTNAM *goes to the bed.*

PUTNAM, *looking down at* BETTY: Why, *her* eyes is closed! Look you, Ann.

MRS. PUTNAM: Why, that's strange. *To* PARRIS: Ours is open.

PARRIS, *shocked:* Your Ruth is sick?

MRS. PUTNAM, *with vicious certainty:* I'd not call it sick; the Devil's touch is heavier than sick. It's death, y'know, it's death drivin' into them, forked and hoofed.

PARRIS: Oh, pray not! Why, how does Ruth ail?

MRS. PUTNAM: She ails as she must—she never waked this morning, but her eyes open and she walks, and hears naught, sees naught, and cannot eat. Her soul is taken, surely.

PARRIS *is struck.*

PUTNAM, *as though for further details:* They say you've sent for Reverend Hale of Beverly?

PARRIS, *with dwindling conviction now:* A precaution only. He has much experience in all demonic arts, and I—

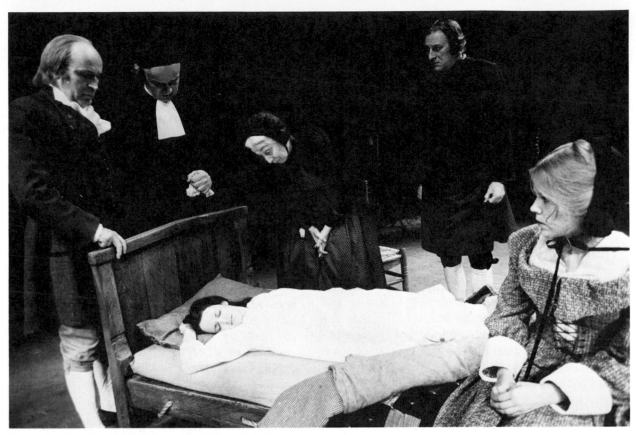

"*. . . the Devil's touch is heavier than sick.*"

MRS. PUTNAM: He has indeed; and found a witch in Beverly last year, and let you remember that.

PARRIS: Now. Goody Ann, they only thought that were a witch, and I am certain there be no element of witchcraft here.

PUTNAM: No witchcraft! Now look you, Mr. Parris—

PARRIS: Thomas, Thomas, I pray you, leap not to witchcraft. I know that you—you least of all, Thomas, would ever wish so disastrous a charge laid upon me. We cannot leap to witchcraft. They will howl me out of Salem for such corruption in my house.

A word about Thomas Putnam. He was a man with many grievances, at least one of which appears justified. Some time before, his wife's brother-in-law, James Bayley, had

been turned down as minister at Salem. Bayley had all the qualifications, and a two-thirds vote into the bargain, but a faction stopped his acceptance, for reasons that are not clear.

Thomas Putnam was the eldest son of the richest man in the village. He had fought the Indians at Narragansett, and was deeply interested in parish affairs. He undoubtedly felt it poor payment that the village should so blatantly disregard his candidate for one of its more important offices, especially since he regarded himself as the intellectual superior of most of the people around him.

His vindictive nature was demonstrated long before the witchcraft began. Another former Salem minister, George Burroughs, had had to borrow money to pay for his wife's funeral, and, since the parish was remiss in his salary, he was soon bankrupt.

Thomas and his brother John had Burroughs jailed for debts the man did not owe. The incident is important only in that Burroughs succeeded in becoming minister where Bayley, Thomas Putnam's brother-in-law, had been rejected; the motif of resentment is clear here. Thomas Putnam felt that his own name and the honor of his family had been smirched by the village, and he meant to right matters however he could.

Another reason to believe him a deeply embittered man was his attempt to break his father's will, which left a disproportionate amount to a stepbrother. As with every other public cause in which he tried to force his way, he failed in this.

So it is not surprising to find that so many accusations against people are in the handwriting of Thomas Putnam, or that his name is so often found as a witness corroborating the supernatural testimony, or that his daughter led the crying-out at the most opportune junctures of the trials, especially when—But we'll speak of that when we come to it.

PUTNAM—*at the moment he is intent upon getting* PARRIS, *for whom he has only contempt, to move toward the abyss:*[7] Mr. Parris, I have taken your part in all contention here, and I would continue; but I cannot if you hold back in this. There are hurtful, vengeful spirits layin' hands on these children.

PARRIS: But, Thomas, you cannot—

PUTNAM: Ann! Tell Mr. Parris what you have done.

MRS. PUTNAM: Reverend Parris, I have laid seven babies unbaptized in the earth. Believe me, sir, you never saw more hearty babies born. And yet, each would wither in my arms the very night of their birth. I have spoke nothin', but my heart has clamored intimations. And now, this year, my Ruth, my only—I see her turning strange. A secret child she has become this year, and shrivels like a sucking mouth were pullin' on her life too. And so I thought to send her to your Tituba—

PARRIS: To Tituba! What may Tituba—?

MRS. PUTNAM: Tituba knows how to speak to the dead, Mr. Parris.

PARRIS: Goody, Ann, it is a formidable sin to conjure up the dead!

MRS. PUTNAM: I take it on my soul, but who else may surely tell us what person murdered my babies?

PARRIS, *horrified:* Woman!

MRS. PUTNAM: They were murdered, Mr. Parris! And mark this proof! Mark it! Last night my Ruth were ever so close to their little spirits; I know it, sir. For how else is she struck dumb now except some power of darkness would stop her mouth? It is a marvelous sign, Mr. Parris!

PUTNAM: Don't you understand it, sir? There is a murdering witch among us, bound to keep herself in the dark. PARRIS *turns to* BETTY, *a frantic terror rising in him.* Let your names make of it what they will, you cannot blink it more.

PARRIS, *to* ABIGAIL: Then you were conjuring spirits last night.

ABIGAIL, *whispering:* Not I, sir—Tituba and Ruth.

PARRIS *turns now, with new fear, and goes to* BETTY, *looks down at her, and then, gazing off:* Oh, Abigail, what proper payment for my charity! Now I am undone.

PUTNAM: You are not undone! Let you take hold here. Wait for no one to charge you—declare it yourself. You have discovered witchcraft—

PARRIS: In my house? In my house, Thomas? They will topple me with this! They will make of it a—

---

7. abyss (ə bis′) *n.:* A deep crack in the earth.

Enter MERCY LEWIS, *the Putnams' servant, a fat, sly, merciless girl of eighteen.*

MERCY: Your pardons. I only thought to see how Betty is.

PUTNAM: Why aren't you home? Who's with Ruth?

MERCY: Her grandma come. She's improved a little, I think—she give a powerful sneeze before.

MRS. PUTNAM: Ah, there's a sign of life!

MERCY: I'd fear no more, Goody Putnam. It were a grand sneeze; another like it will shake her wits together, I'm sure. *She goes to the bed to look.*

PARRIS: Will you leave me now, Thomas? I would pray a while alone.

ABIGAIL: Uncle, you've prayed since midnight. Why do you not go down and—

PARRIS: No—no. *To* PUTNAM: I have no answer for that crowd. I'll wait till Mr. Hale arrives. *To get* MRS. PUTNAM *to leave:* If you will, Goody Ann . . .

PUTNAM: Now look you, sir. Let you strike out against the Devil, and the village will bless you for it! Come down, speak to them—pray with them. They're thirsting for your word, Mister! Surely you'll pray with them.

PARRIS, *swayed:* I'll lead them in a psalm, but let you say nothing of witchcraft yet. I will not discuss it. The cause is yet unknown. I have had enough contention since I came; I want no more.

MRS. PUTNAM: Mercy, you go home to Ruth, d'y'hear?

MERCY: Aye, mum.

MRS. PUTNAM *goes out.*

PARRIS, *to* ABIGAIL: If she starts for the window, cry for me at once.

ABIGAIL: I will, uncle.

PARRIS, *to* PUTNAM: There is a terrible power in her arms today. *He goes out with* PUTNAM.

ABIGAIL, *with hushed trepidation:* How is Ruth sick?

MERCY: It's weirdish, I know not—she seems to walk like a dead one since last night.

ABIGAIL, *turns at once and goes to* BETTY, *and now, with fear in her voice:* Betty? BETTY *doesn't move. She shakes her.* Now stop this! Betty! Sit up now!

BETTY *doesn't stir.* MERCY *comes over.*

MERCY: Have you tried beatin' her? I gave Ruth a good one and it waked her for a minute. Here, let me have her.

ABIGAIL, *holding* MERCY *back:* No, he'll be comin' up. Listen, now; if they be questioning us, tell them we danced—I told him as much already.

MERCY: Aye. And what more?

ABIGAIL: He knows Tituba conjured Ruth's sisters to come out of the grave.

MERCY: And what more?

ABIGAIL: He saw you naked.

MERCY, *clapping her hand together with a frightened laugh:* Oh, Jesus!

Enter MARY WARREN, *breathless. She is seventeen, a subservient, naive, lonely girl.*

MARY WARREN: What'll we do? The village is out! I just come from the farm; the whole country's talkin' witchcraft! They'll be callin' us witches, Abby!

MERCY, *pointing and looking at* MARY WARREN: She means to tell, I know it.

MARY WARREN: Abby, we've got to tell. Witchery's a hangin' error, a hangin' like they done in Boston two year ago! We must tell the truth, Abby! You'll only be whipped for dancin', and the other things!

ABIGAIL: Oh, *we'll* be whipped!

MARY WARREN: I never done none of it, Abby. I only looked!

MERCY, *moving menacingly toward* MARY: Oh, you're a great one for lookin', aren't you, Mary Warren? What a grand peeping courage you have!

BETTY, *on the bed, whimpers.* ABIGAIL *turns to her at once.*

ABIGAIL: Betty? *She goes to* BETTY. Now, Betty, dear, wake up now. It's Abigail. *She sits* BETTY *up and furiously shakes her.* I'll beat you, Betty! BETTY *whimpers.* My, you seem improving. I talked to your papa and I told him everything. So there's nothing to—

BETTY, *darts off the bed, frightened of* ABIGAIL, *and flattens herself against the wall:* I want my mama!

ABIGAIL, *with alarm, as she cautiously approaches* BETTY: What ails you, Betty? Your mama's dead and buried.

BETTY: I'll fly to Mama. Let me fly! *She raises her arms as though to fly, and streaks for the window, gets one leg out.*

ABIGAIL, *pulling her away from the window:* I told him everything; he knows now, he knows everything we—

BETTY: You drank blood, Abby! You didn't tell him that!

ABIGAIL: Betty, you never say that again! You will never—

BETTY: You did, you did! You drank a charm to kill John Proctor's wife! You drank a charm to kill Goody Proctor!

ABIGAIL, *smashes her across the face:* Shut it! Now shut it!

BETTY, *collapsing on the bed:* Mama, Mama! *She dissolves into sobs.*

ABIGAIL: Now look you. All of you. We danced. And Tituba conjured Ruth Putnam's dead sisters. And that is all. And mark this. Let either of you breathe a word, or the edge of a word, about the other things, and I will come to you in the black of some terrible night and I will bring a pointy reckoning that will shudder you. And you know I can do it; I saw Indians smash my dear parents' heads on the pillow next to mine, and I have seen some reddish work done at night, and I can make you wish you had never seen the sun go down! *She goes to* BETTY *and roughly sits her up.* Now, you—sit up and stop this!

But BETTY *collapses in her hands and lies inert on the bed.*

MARY WARREN, *with hysterical fright:* What's got her? ABIGAIL *stares in fright at* BETTY. Abby, she's going to die! It's a sin to conjure, and we—

ABIGAIL, *starting for* MARY: I say shut it, Mary Warren!

Enter JOHN PROCTOR. *On seeing him,* MARY WARREN *leaps in fright.*

Proctor was a farmer in his middle thirties. He need not have been a partisan of any faction in the town, but there is evidence to suggest that he had a sharp and biting way with hypocrites. He was the kind of man—powerful of body, even-tempered, and not easily led—who cannot refuse support to partisans without drawing their deepest resentment. In Proctor's presence a fool felt his foolishness instantly—and a Proctor is always marked for calumny therefore.

But as we shall see, the steady manner he displays does not spring from an untroubled soul. He is a sinner, a sinner not only against the moral fashion of the time, but against his own vision of decent conduct. These people had no ritual for the washing away of sins. It is another trait we inherited from them, and it has helped to discipline us as well as to breed hypocrisy among us. Proctor, respected and even feared in Salem, has come to regard himself as a kind of fraud. But no hint of this has yet appeared on the surface, and as he enters from the crowded parlor below it is a man in his prime we see, with a quiet confidence and an unexpressed, hidden force. Mary Warren, his servant, can barely speak for embarrassment and fear.

MARY WARREN: Oh! I'm just going home, Mr. Proctor.

PROCTOR: Be you foolish, Mary Warren? Be you deaf? I forbid you leave the house, did I not? Why shall I pay you? I am looking for you more often than my cows!

MARY WARREN: I only come to see the great doings in the world.

PROCTOR: I'll show you a great doin' on your arse one of these days. Now get you home; my wife is waitin' with your work! *Trying to retain a shred of dignity, she goes slowly out.*

MERCY LEWIS, *both afraid of him and strangely titillated:* I'd best be off. I have my Ruth to watch. Good morning, Mr. Proctor.

MERCY *sidles out. Since* PROCTOR's *entrance,* ABIGAIL *has stood as though on tiptoe, absorbing his presence, wide-eyed. He glances at her then goes to* BETTY *on the bed.*

ABIGAIL: Gad. I'd almost forgot how strong you are, John Proctor!

PROCTOR, *looking at* ABIGAIL *now, the faintest suggestion of a knowing smile on his face:* What's this mischief here?

ABIGAIL, *with a nervous laugh:* Oh, she's only gone silly somehow.

PROCTOR: The road past my house is a pilgrimage to Salem all morning. The town's mumbling witchcraft.

ABIGAIL: Oh, posh! *Winningly she comes a little closer, with a confidential, wicked air.* We were dancin' in the woods last night, and my uncle leaped in on us. She took fright, is all.

PROCTOR, *his smile widening:* Ah, you're wicked yet, aren't y'! *A trill of expectant laughter escapes her, and she dares come closer, feverishly looking into his eyes.* You'll be clapped in the stocks before you're twenty.

He takes a step to go, and she springs into his path.

ABIGAIL: Give me a word, John. A soft word. *Her concentrated desire destroys his smile.*

PROCTOR: No, no, Abby. That's done with.

ABIGAIL, *tauntingly:* You come five mile to see a silly girl fly? I know you better.

PROCTOR, *setting her firmly out of his path:* I come to see what mischief your uncle's brewin' now. *With final emphasis:* Put it out of mind, Abby.

ABIGAIL, *grasping his hand before he can release her:* John—I am waitin' for you every night.

PROCTOR: Abby, I never give you hope to wait for me.

ABIGAIL, *now beginning to anger—she can't believe it:* I have something better than hope, I think!

PROCTOR: Abby, you'll put it out of mind. I'll not be comin' for you more.

ABIGAIL: You're surely sportin' with me.

PROCTOR: You know me better.

ABIGAIL: I know how you clutched my back behind your house and sweated like a stallion whenever I come near! Or did I dream that? It's she put me out, you cannot pretend it were you. I saw your face when she put me out, and you loved me then and you do now!

PROCTOR: Abby, that's a wild thing to say—

ABIGAIL: A wild thing may say wild things. But not so wild, I think. I have seen you since she put me out; I have seen you nights.

PROCTOR: I have hardly stepped off my farm this seven-month.

"John—I am waitin' for you every night."

ABIGAIL: I have a sense for heat, John, and yours has drawn me to my window, and I have seen you looking up, burning in your loneliness. Do you tell me you've never looked up at my window?

PROCTOR: I may have looked up.

ABIGAIL, *now softening:* And you must. You are no wintry man. I know you, John. I *know* you. *She is weeping.* I cannot sleep for dreamin'; I cannot dream but I wake and walk about the house as though I'd find you comin' through some door. *She clutches him desperately.*

PROCTOR, *gently pressing her from him, with great sympathy but firmly:* Child—

ABIGAIL, *with a flash of anger:* How do you call me child!

PROCTOR: Abby, I may think of you softly from time to time. But I will cut off my hand before I'll ever reach for you again. Wipe it out of mind. We never touched, Abby.

ABIGAIL: Aye, but we did.

PROCTOR: Aye, but we did not.

ABIGAIL, *with a bitter anger:* Oh, I marvel how such a strong man may let such a sickly wife be—

PROCTOR, *angered—at himself as well:* You'll speak nothin' of Elizabeth!

ABIGAIL: She is blackening my name in the village! She is telling lies about me! She is a cold, sniveling woman, and you bend to her! Let her turn you like a—

PROCTOR, *shaking her:* Do you look for whippin'?

A psalm is heard being sung below.

ABIGAIL, *in tears:* I look for John Proctor that took me from my sleep and put knowledge in my heart! I never knew what pretense Salem was, I never knew the lying lessons I was taught by all these Christian women and their covenanted men! And now you bid me tear the light out of my eyes? I will not, I cannot! You loved me, John Proctor, and whatever sin it is, you love me yet! *He turns abruptly to go out. She rushes to him.* John, pity me, pity me!

The words "going up to Jesus" are heard in the psalm, and BETTY *claps her ears suddenly and whines loudly.*

ABIGAIL: Betty? *She hurries to* BETTY, *who is now sitting up and screaming.* PROCTOR *goes to* BETTY *as* ABIGAIL *is trying to pull her hands down, calling "Betty!"*

PROCTOR, *growing unnerved:* What's she doing? Girl, what ails you? Stop that wailing!

The singing has stopped in the midst of this, and now PARRIS *rushes in.*

PARRIS: What happened? What are you doing to her? Betty! *He rushes to the bed, crying, "Betty, Betty!"* MRS. PUTNAM *enters, feverish with curiosity, and with her* THOMAS PUTNAM *and* MERCY LEWIS. PARRIS, *at the bed, keeps lightly slapping* BETTY's *face, while she moans and tries to get up.*

ABIGAIL: She heard you singin' and suddenly she's up and screamin'.

MRS. PUTNAM: The psalm! The psalm! She cannot bear to hear the Lord's name!

PARRIS: No, God forbid. Mercy, run to the doctor! Tell him what's happened here! MERCY LEWIS *rushes out.*

MRS. PUTNAM: Mark it for a sign, mark it!

REBECCA NURSE, *seventy-two, enters. She is white-haired, leaning upon her walking-stick.*

PUTNAM, *pointing at the whimpering* BETTY: That is a notorious sign of witchcraft afoot, Goody Nurse, a prodigious sign!

MRS. PUTNAM: My mother told me that! When they cannot bear to hear the name of—

PARRIS, *trembling:* Rebecca, Rebecca, go to her, we're lost. She suddenly cannot bear to hear the Lord's—

GILES COREY, *eighty-three, enters. He is knotted with muscle, canny, inquisitive, and still powerful.*

REBECCA: There is hard sickness here, Giles Corey, so please to keep the quiet.

GILES: I've not said a word. No one here can testify I've said a word. Is she going to fly again? I hear she flies.

PUTNAM: Man, be quiet now!

Everything is quiet. REBECCA *walks across the room to the bed. Gentleness exudes from her.* BETTY *is quietly whimpering, eyes shut.* REBECCA *simply stands over the child, who gradually quiets.*

And while they are so absorbed, we may put a word in for Rebecca. Rebecca was the wife of Francis Nurse, who, from all accounts, was one of those men for whom both sides of the argument had to have respect. He was called upon to arbitrate disputes as though he were an unofficial judge, and Rebecca also enjoyed the high opinion most people had for him. By the time of the delusion, they had three hundred acres, and their children were settled in separate homesteads within the same estate. However, Francis had originally rented the land, and one theory has it that, as he gradually paid for it and raised his social status, there were those who resented his rise.

Another suggestion to explain the systematic campaign against Rebecca, and inferentially against Francis, is the land war he fought with his neighbors, one of whom was a Putnam. This squabble grew to the proportions of a battle in the woods between partisans of both sides, and it is said to have lasted for two days. As for Rebecca herself, the general opinion of her character was so high that to explain how anyone dared cry her out for a witch—and more, how adults could bring themselves to lay hands on her—we must look to the fields and boundaries of that time.

As we have seen, Thomas Putnam's man for the Salem ministry was Bayley. The Nurse clan had been in the faction that prevented Bayley's taking office. In addition, certain families allied to the Nurses by blood or friendship, and whose farms were contiguous with the Nurse farm or close to it, combined to break away from the Salem town authority and set up Topsfield, a new and independent entity whose existence was resented by old Salemites.

That the guiding hand behind the outcry was Putnam's is indicated by the fact that, as soon as it began, this Topsfield-Nurse faction absented themselves from church in protest and disbelief. It was Edward and Jonathan Putnam who signed the first complaint against Rebecca; and Thomas Putnam's little daughter was the one who fell into a fit at the hearing and pointed to Rebecca as her attacker. To top it all, Mrs. Putnam—who is now staring at the bewitched child on the bed—soon accused Rebecca's spirit of "tempting her to iniquity," a charge that had more truth in it than Mrs. Putnam could know.

MRS. PUTNAM, *astonished:* What have you done?

REBECCA, *in thought, now leaves the bedside and sits.*

PARRIS, *wondrous and relieved:* What do you make of it, Rebecca?

PUTNAM, *eagerly:* Goody Nurse, will you go to my Ruth and see if you can wake her?

REBECCA, *sitting:* I think she'll wake in time. Pray calm yourselves. I have eleven children, and I am twenty-six times a grandma, and I have seen them all through their silly seasons, and when it come on them they will run the Devil bowlegged keeping up with their mischief. I think she'll wake when she tires of it. A child's spirit is like a child, you can never catch it by running after it; you must stand still, and, for love, it will soon itself come back.

PROCTOR: Aye, that's the truth of it, Rebecca.

MRS. PUTNAM: This is no silly season, Rebecca. My Ruth is bewildered, Rebecca; she cannot eat.

REBECCA: Perhaps she is not hungered yet. *To* PARRIS: I hope you are not decided to go in search of loose spirits, Mr. Parris. I've heard promise of that outside.

PARRIS: A wide opinion's running in the parish that the Devil may be among us, and I would satisfy them that they are wrong.

PROCTOR: Then let you come out and call them wrong. Did you consult the wardens before you called this minister to look for devils?

PARRIS: He is not coming to look for devils!

PROCTOR: Then what's he coming for?

PUTNAM: There be children dyin' in the village, Mister!

PROCTOR: I seen none dyin'. This society will not be a bag to swing around your head, Mr. Putnam. *To* PARRIS: Did you call a meeting before you—?

PUTNAM: I am sick of meetings; cannot the man turn his head without he have a meeting?

PROCTOR: He may turn his head, but not to Hell!

REBECCA: Pray, John, be calm. *Pause. He defers to her.* Mr. Parris, I think you'd best send Reverend Hale back as soon as he come. This will set us all to arguin' again in the society, and we thought to have peace this year. I think we ought rely on the doctor now, and good prayer.

MRS. PUTNAM: Rebecca, the doctor's baffled!

REBECCA: If so he is, then let us go to God for the cause of it. There is no prodigious danger in the seeking of loose spirits. I fear it, I fear it. Let us rather blame ourselves and—

PUTNAM: How may we blame ourselves? I am one of nine sons; the Putnam seed have peopled this province. And yet I have but one child left of eight—and now she shrivels!

REBECCA: I cannot fathom that.

MRS. PUTNAM, *with a growing edge of sarcasm:* But I must! You think it God's work you should never lose a child, nor grandchild either, and I bury all but one? There are wheels within wheels in this village, and fires within fires!

PUTNAM, *to* PARRIS: When Reverend Hale comes, you will proceed to look for signs of witchcraft here.

PROCTOR, *to* PUTNAM: You cannot command, Mr. Parris. We vote by name in this society, not by acreage.

PUTNAM: I never heard you worried so on this society, Mr. Proctor. I do not think I saw you at Sabbath meeting since snow flew.

PROCTOR: I have trouble enough without I come five mile to hear him preach only hell-fire and bloody damnation. Take it to heart, Mr. Parris. There are many others who stay away from church these days because you hardly ever mention God any more.

PARRIS, *now aroused:* Why, that's a drastic charge!

REBECCA: It's somewhat true; there are many that quail to bring their children—

PARRIS: I do not preach for children, Rebecca. It is not the children who are unmindful of their obligations toward this ministry.

REBECCA: Are there really those unmindful?

PARRIS: I should say the better half of Salem village—

PUTNAM: And more than that!

PARRIS: Where is my wood? My contract provides I be supplied with all my firewood. I am waiting since November for a stick, and even in November I had to show my frostbitten hands like some London beggar!

GILES: You are allowed six pound a year to buy your wood, Mr. Parris.

PARRIS: I regard that six pound as part of my salary. I am paid little enough without I spend six pound on firewood.

PROCTOR: Sixty, plus six for firewood—

PARRIS: The salary is sixty-six pound, Mr. Proctor! I am not some preaching farmer with a book under my arm; I am a graduate of Harvard College.

GILES: Aye, and well instructed in arithmetic!

PARRIS: Mr. Corey, you will look far for a man of my kind at sixty pound a year! I am not used to this poverty; I left a thrifty business in the Barbados to serve the Lord. I do not fathom it, why am I persecuted here? I cannot offer one proposition but there be a howling riot of argument. I have often wondered if the Devil be in it somewhere; I cannot understand you people otherwise.

PROCTOR: Mr. Parris, you are the first minister ever did demand the deed to this house—

PARRIS: Man! Don't a minister deserve a house to live in?

PROCTOR: To live in, yes. But to ask ownership is like you shall own the meeting house itself; the last meeting I were at you spoke so long on deeds and mortgages I thought it were an auction.

PARRIS: I want a mark of confidence, is all! I am your third preacher in seven years. I do not wish to be put out like the cat whenever some majority feels the whim. You people seem not to comprehend that a minister is the Lord's man in the parish; a minister is not to be so lightly crossed and contradicted—

PUTNAM: Aye!

PARRIS: There is either obedience or the church will burn like Hell is burning!

PROCTOR: Can you speak one minute without we land in Hell again? I am sick of Hell!

PARRIS: It is not for you to say what is good for you to hear!

PROCTOR: I may speak my heart, I think!

PARRIS, *in a fury:* What, are we Quakers?[8] We are not Quakers here yet, Mr. Proctor. And you may tell that to your followers!

---

8. Quakers: The Quakers are members of a Christian religious sect that has no formal creed, rites, or priesthood. Parris is asserting his authority as a minister. Unlike the Quakers, the Puritans had a rigid code of conduct and were expected to heed the words of their ministers.

PROCTOR: My followers!

PARRIS—*now he's out with it:* There is a party in this church. I am not blind; there is a faction and a party.

PROCTOR: Against you?

PUTNAM: Against him and all authority!

PROCTOR: Why, then I must find it and join it.

There is shock among the others.

REBECCA: He does not mean that.

PUTNAM: He confessed it now!

PROCTOR: I mean it solemnly, Rebecca; I like not the smell of this "authority."

REBECCA: No, you cannot break charity with your minister. You are another kind, John. Clasp his hand, make your peace.

PROCTOR: I have a crop to sow and lumber to drag home. *He goes angrily to the door and turns to* COREY *with a smile.* What say you, Giles, let's find the party. He says there's a party.

GILES: I've changed my opinion of this man, John. Mr. Parris, I beg your pardon. I never thought you had so much iron in you.

PARRIS, *surprised:* Why, thank you, Giles!

GILES: It suggests to the mind what the trouble be among us all these years. *To all:* Think on it. Wherefore is everybody suing everybody else? Think on it now, it's a deep thing, and dark as a pit. I have been six time in court this year—

PROCTOR, *familiarly, with warmth, although he knows he is approaching the edge of Giles' tolerance with this:* Is it the Devil's fault that a man cannot say you good morning without you clap him for defamation? You're old, Giles, and you're not hearin' so well as you did.

GILES—*he cannot be crossed:* John Proctor, I have only last month collected four pound damages for you publicly sayin' I burned the roof off your house, and I—

PROCTOR, *laughing:* I never said no such think, but I've paid you for it, so I hope I can call you deaf without charge. Now come along, Giles, and help me drag my lumber home.

PUTNAM: A moment, Mr. Proctor. What lumber is that you're draggin', if I may ask you?

PROCTOR: My lumber. From out my forest by the riverside.

PUTNAM: Why, we are surely gone wild this year. What anarchy is this? That tract is in my bounds, it's in my bounds, Mr. Proctor.

PROCTOR: In your bounds! *Indicating* REBECCA: I bought that tract from Goody Nurse's husband five months ago.

PUTNAM: He had no right to sell it. It stands clear in my grandfather's will that all the land between the river and—

PROCTOR: Your grandfather had a habit of willing land that never belonged to him, if I may say it plain.

GILES: That's God's truth; he nearly willed away my north pasture but he knew I'd break his fingers before he'd set his name to it. Let's get your lumber home, John. I feel a sudden will to work coming on.

PUTNAM: You load one oak of mine and you'll fight to drag it home!

GILES: Aye, and we'll win too, Putnam—this fool and I. Come on! *He turns to* PROCTOR *and starts out.*

PUTNAM: I'll have my men on you, Corey! I'll clap a writ on you!

Enter REVEREND JOHN HALE *of Beverly.*

Mr. Hale is nearing forty, a tight-skinned, eager-eyed intellectual. This is a beloved errand for him; on being called here to ascertain witchcraft he felt the pride of the specialist whose unique knowledge has at last been publicly called for. Like almost all men of learning, he spent a good deal of time pondering the invisible world, especially since he had himself encountered a witch in his parish not long before. That woman, however, turned into a mere pest under his searching scrutiny, and the child she had allegedly been afflicting recovered her normal behavior after Hale had given her his kindness and a few days of rest in his own house. However, that experience never raised a doubt in his mind as to the reality of the underworld or the existence of Lucifer's many-faced lieutenants. And his belief is not to his discredit. Better minds than Hale's were—and still are—convinced that there is a society of spirits beyond our ken. One cannot help noting that one of his lines has never yet raised a laugh in any audience that has seen this play; it is his assurance that "We cannot look to superstition in this. The Devil is precise." Evidently we are not quite certain even now whether diabolism is holy and not to be scoffed at. And it is no accident that we should be so bemused.

Like Reverend Hale and the others on this stage, we conceive the Devil as a necessary part of a respectable view of cosmology. Ours is a divided empire in which certain ideas and emotions and actions are of God, and their opposites are of Lucifer. It is as impossible for most men to conceive of a morality without sin as of an earth without "sky." Since 1692 a great but superficial change has wiped out God's beard and the Devil's horns, but the world is still gripped between two diametrically opposed absolutes. The concept of unity, in which positive and negative are attributes of the same force, in which good and evil are relative, ever-changing, and always joined to the same phenomenon—such a concept is still reserved to the physical sciences and to the few who have grasped the history of ideas. When it is recalled that until the Christian era the underworld was never regarded as a hostile area, that all gods were useful and essentially friendly to man despite occasional lapses; when we see the steady and methodical inculcation into humanity of the idea of man's worthlessness—until redeemed—the necessity of the Devil may become evident as a weapon, a weapon designed and used time and time again in every age to whip men into a surrender to a particular church or church-state.

Our difficulty in believing the—for want of a better word—political inspiration of the Devil is due in great part to the fact that he is called up and damned not only by our social antagonists but by our own side, whatever it may be. The Catholic Church, through its Inquisition,[9] is famous for cultivating Lucifer as the arch-fiend, but the Church's enemies relied no less upon the Old Boy to keep the human mind enthralled. Luther[10] was himself accused of alliance with Hell, and he in turn accused his enemies. To complicate matters further, he believed that he had had contact with the Devil and had argued theology with him. I am not surprised at this, for at my own university a professor of history—a Lutheran,[11] by the way—used to assemble his graduate students, draw the shades, and commune in the classroom with Erasmus.[12] He was never, to my knowledge, officially scoffed at for this, the reason being that the university officials, like most of us, are the children of a history which still sucks at the Devil's teats. At this writing, only England has held back before the temptations of contemporary diabolism. In the countries of the Communist ideology, all resistance of any import is

---

9. Inquisition: The general tribunal established in the thirteenth century for the discovery and suppression of beliefs and opinions opposed to the orthodox doctrines of the Church.
10. Luther: Martin Luther (1483–1546), the German theologian who led the Protestant Reformation.
11. Lutheran: A member of the Protestant denomination founded by Martin Luther.
12. Erasmus: Desiderius Erasmus (1466?–1536), a Dutch humanist, scholar, and theologian.

linked to the totally malign capitalist succubi,[13] and in America any man who is not reactionary in his views is open to the charge of alliance with the Red hell. Political opposition, thereby, is given an inhumane overlay which then justifies the abrogation[14] of all normally applied customs of civilized intercourse. A political policy is equated with moral right, and opposition to it with diabolical malevolence. Once such an equation is effectively made, society becomes a congerie[15] of plots and counterplots, and the main role of government changes from that of the arbiter to that of the scourge of God.

The results of this process are no different now from what they ever were, except sometimes in the degree of cruelty inflicted, and not always even in that department. Normally, the actions and deeds of a man were all that society felt comfortable in judging. The secret intent of an action was left to the ministers, priests, and rabbis to deal with. When diabolism rises, however, actions are the least important manifests of the true nature of a man. The Devil, as Reverend Hale said, is a wily one, and until an hour before he fell, even God thought him beautiful in Heaven.

The analogy, however, seems to falter when one considers that, while there were no witches then, there are Communists and capitalists now, and in each camp there is certain proof that spies of each side are at work undermining the other. But this is a snobbish objection and not at all warranted by the facts. I have no doubt that people *were* communing with, and even worshiping, the Devil in Salem, and if the whole truth could be known in this case, as it is in others, we should discover a regular and conventionalized propitiation of the dark spirit. One certain evidence of this is the confession of Tituba, the slave of Reverend

Parris, and another is the behavior of the children who were known to have indulged in sorceries with her.

There are accounts of similar *klatches*[16] in Europe, where the daughters of the towns would assemble at night and, sometimes with fetishes,[17] sometimes with a selected young man, give themselves to love, with some bastardly results. The Church, sharp-eyed as it must be when gods long dead are brought to life, condemned these orgies as witchcraft and interpreted them, rightly, as a resurgence of the Dionysiac[18] forces it had crushed long before. Sex, sin, and the Devil were early linked, and so they continued to be in Salem, and are today. From all accounts there are no more puritanical mores in the world than those enforced by the Communists in Russia, where women's fashions, for instance, are as prudent and all-covering as any American Baptist would desire. The divorce laws lay a tremendous responsibility on the father for the care of his children. Even the laxity of divorce regulations in the early years of the revolution was undoubtedly a revulsion from the nineteenth-century Victorian[19] immobility of marriage and the consequent hypocrisy that developed from it. If for no other reasons, a state so powerful, so jealous of the uniformity of its citizens, cannot long tolerate the atomization of the family. And yet, in American eyes at least, there remains the conviction that the Russian attitude toward women is lascivious. It is the Devil working again, just as he is working within the Slav who is shocked at the very idea of a woman's disrobing herself in a burlesque show. Our

---

13. succubi (suk′ yoo bī): Female demons thought to lie on sleeping men.
14. abrogation (ab′ rə gā′ shən): Abolishment.
15. congerie (kän′ jə rē) *n*.: Heap; pile.

16. klatches (kläch′ əz) *n*.: Informal gatherings.
17. fetishes (fet′ ish əz) *n*.: Objects believed to have magical power.
18. Dionysiac (dī′ ə nis′ ē ak′) *adj*.: Wild, frenzied, and sensuous. Characteristic of Dionysus, the Greek god of wine and revelry.
19. Victorian: Of or characteristic of the time when Victoria was queen of England (1837–1901). The characteristics attributed to this period include respectability, prudery, and bigotry.

opposites are always robed in sexual sin, and it is from this unconscious conviction that demonology gains both its attractive sensuality and its capacity to infuriate and frighten.

Coming into Salem now, Reverend Hale conceives of himself much as a young doctor on his first call. His painfully acquired armory of symptoms, catchwords, and diagnostic procedures are now to be put to use at last. The road from Beverly is unusually busy this morning, and he has passed a hundred rumors that make him smile at the ignorance of the yeomanry in this most precise science. He feels himself allied with the best minds of Europe—kings, philosophers, scientists, and ecclesiasts of all churches. His goal is light, goodness and its preservation, and he knows the exaltation of the blessed whose intelligence, sharpened by minute examinations of enormous tracts, is finally called upon to face what may be a bloody fight with the Fiend himself.

He appears loaded down with half a dozen heavy books.

HALE: Pray you, someone take these!

PARRIS, *delighted:* Mr. Hale! Oh! it's good to see you again! *Taking some books:* My, they're heavy!

HALE, *setting down his books:* They must be; they are weighted with authority.

PARRIS, *a little scared:* Well, you do come prepared!

HALE: We shall need hard study if it comes to tracking down the Old Boy. *Noticing* REBECCA: You cannot be Rebecca Nurse?

REBECCA: I am, sir. Do you know me?

HALE: It's strange how I knew you, but I sup-

"We shall need hard study if it comes to tracking down the Old Boy."

pose you look as such a good soul should. We have all heard of your great charities in Beverly.

PARRIS: Do you know this gentleman? Mr. Thomas Putnam. And his good wife Ann.

HALE: Putnam! I had not expected such distinguished company, sir.

PUTNAM, *pleased:* It does seem to help us today, Mr. Hale. We look to you to come to our house and save our child.

HALE: Your child ails too?

MRS. PUTNAM: Her soul, her soul seems flown away. She sleeps and yet she walks . . .

PUTNAM: She cannot eat.

HALE: Cannot eat! *Thinks on it. Then, to* PROCTOR *and* GILES COREY: Do you men have afflicted children?

PARRIS: No, no, these are farmers. John Proctor—

GILES COREY: He don't believe in witches.

PROCTOR, *to* HALE: I never spoke on witches one way or the other. Will you come, Giles?

GILES: No—no, John, I think not. I have some few queer questions of my own to ask this fellow.

PROCTOR: I've heard you to be a sensible man, Mr. Hale. I hope you'll leave some of it in Salem.

PROCTOR *goes.* HALE *stands embarrassed for an instant.*

PARRIS, *quickly:* Will you look at my daughter, sir? *Leads* HALE *to the bed.* She has tried to leap out the window; we discovered her this morning on the highroad, waving her arms as though she'd fly.

HALE, *narrowing his eyes:* Tries to fly.

PUTNAM: She cannot bear to hear the Lord's name, Mr. Hale; that's a sure sign of witchcraft afloat.

HALE, *holding up his hands:* No, no. Now let me instruct you. We cannot look to superstition in this. The Devil is precise; the marks of his presence are definite as stone, and I must tell you all that I shall not proceed unless you are prepared to believe me if I should find no bruise of hell upon her.

PARRIS: It is agreed, sir—it is agreed—we will abide by your judgment.

HALE: Good then. *He goes to the bed, looks down at* BETTY. *To* PARRIS: Now, sir, what were your first warning of this strangeness?

PARRIS: Why, sir—I discovered her—*indicating* ABIGAIL—and my niece and ten or twelve of the other girls, dancing in the forest last night.

HALE, *surprised:* You permit dancing?

PARRIS: No, no, it were secret—

MRS. PUTNAM, *unable to wait:* Mr. Parris's slave has knowledge of conjurin', sir.

PARRIS, *to Mrs. Putnam:* We cannot be sure of that, Goody Ann—

MRS. PUTNAM, *frightened, very softly:* I know it, sir. I sent my child—she should learn from Tituba who murdered her sisters.

REBECCA, *horrified:* Goody Ann! You sent a child to conjure up the dead?

MRS. PUTNAM: Let God blame me, not you, not you, Rebecca! I'll not have you judging me any more! *To* HALE: Is it a natural work to lose seven children before they live a day?

PARRIS: Sssh!

REBECCA, *with great pain, turns her face away. There is a pause.*

HALE: Seven dead in childbirth.

MRS. PUTNAM, *softly:* Aye. *Her voice breaks; she looks up at him. Silence.* HALE *is impressed.* PARRIS *looks to him. He goes to his books, opens one, turns pages, then reads. All wait, avidly.*

PARRIS, *hushed:* What book is that?

MRS. PUTNAM: What's there, sir?

HALE, *with a tasty love of intellectual pursuit:* Here is all the invisible world, caught, defined, and calculated. In these books the Devil stands stripped of all his brute disguises. Here are all your familiar spirits—your incubi[20] and succubi, your witches that go by land, by air, and by sea; your wizards of the night and of the day. Have no fear now—we shall find him out if he has come among us, and I mean to crush him utterly if he has shown his face! *He starts for the bed.*

REBECCA: Will it hurt the child, sir?

HALE: I cannot tell, If she is truly in the Devil's grip we may have to rip and tear to get her free.

REBECCA: I think I'll go, then. I am too old for this. *She rises.*

PARRIS, *striving for conviction:* Why, Rebecca, we may open up the boil of all our troubles today!

REBECCA: Let us hope for that. I go to God for you, sir.

PARRIS, *with trepidation—and resentment:* I hope you do not mean to go to Satan here! *Slight pause.*

REBECCA: I wish I knew. *She goes out; they feel resentful of her note of moral superiority.*

PUTNAM, *abruptly:* Come, Mr. Hale, let's get on. Sit you here.

GILES: Mr. Hale, I have always wanted to ask a learned man—what signifies the readin' of strange books?

HALE: What books?

GILES: I cannot tell; she hides them.

HALE: Who does this?

---

20. incubi (iŋ′ kyə bī): Spirits or demons thought to lie on sleeping women.

GILES: Martha, my wife. I have waked at night many a time and found her in a corner, readin' of a book. Now what do you make of that?

HALE: Why, that's not necessarily—

GILES: It discomfits me! Last night—mark this—I tried and tried and could not say my prayers. And then she close her book and walks out of the house, and suddenly—mark this—I could pray again!

Old Giles must be spoken for, if only because his fate was to be so remarkable and so different from that of all the others. He was in his early eighties at this time, and was the most comical hero in the history. No man has ever been blamed for so much. If a cow was missed, the first thought was to look for her around Corey's house; a fire blazing up at night brought suspicion of arson to his door. He didn't give a hoot for public opinion, and only in his last years—after he had married Martha—did he bother much with the church. That she stopped his prayer is very probable, but he forgot to say that he'd only recently learned any prayers and it didn't take much to make him stumble over them. He was a crank and a nuisance, but withal a deeply innocent and brave man. In court, once, he was asked if it were true that he had been frightened by the strange behavior of a hog and had then said he knew it to be the Devil in an animal's shape. "What frighted you?" he was asked. He forgot everything but the word "frighted," and instantly replied, "I do not know that I ever spoke that word in my life."

HALE: Ah! The stoppage of prayer—that is strange. I'll speak further on that with you.

GILES: I'm not sayin' she's touched the Devil, now, but I'd admire to know what books she reads and why she hides them. She'll not answer me, y' see.

HALE: Aye, we'll discuss it. *To all:* Now mark me, if the Devil is in her you will witness

"I don't know, sir, but the Devil got him numerous witches."

some frightful wonders in this room, so please to keep your wits about you. Mr. Putnam, stand close in case she flies. Now, Betty, dear, will you sit up? PUTNAM *comes in closer, ready-handed.* HALE *sits* BETTY *up, but she hangs limp in his hands.* Hmmm. *He observes her carefully. The others, watch breathlessly.* Can you hear me? I am John Hale, minister of Beverly. I have come to help you, dear. Do you remember my two little girls in Beverly? *She does not stir in his hands.*

PARRIS, *in fright:* How can it be the Devil? Why would he choose my house to strike? We have all manner of licentious people in the village!

HALE: What victory would the Devil have to win a soul already bad? It is the best the Devil wants, and who is better than the minister?

GILES: That's deep, Mr. Parris, deep, deep!

PARRIS, *with resolution now:* Betty! Answer Mr. Hale! Betty!

HALE: Does someone afflict you, child? It need not be a woman, mind you, or a man. Perhaps some bird invisible to others comes to you—perhaps a pig, a mouse, or any beast at all. Is there some figure bids you fly? *The child remains limp in his hands. In silence he lays her back on the pillow. Now, holding out his hands toward her, he intones:* In nomine Domini Sabaoth sui filiique ite ad infernos.[21] *She does not stir. He turns to* ABIGAIL, *his eyes narrowing.* Abigail, what sort of dancing were you doing with her in the forest?

---

21. In nomine Domini Sabaoth sui filiique ite ad infernos (in nō′ mē nā dō′ mē nē Sab′ å ōt sōō′ ē fē′ lē ē kwā ē′ tä äd in fãr′ nōs): "In the name of the lord of hosts and his son get thee to the lower world."

ABIGAIL: Why—common dancing is all.

PARRIS: I think I ought to say that I—I saw a kettle in the grass where they were dancing.

ABIGAIL: That were only soup.

HALE: What sort of soup were in this kettle, Abigail?

ABIGAIL: Why, it were beans—and lentils, I think, and—

HALE: Mr. Parris, you did not notice, did you, any living thing in the kettle? A mouse, perhaps, a spider, a frog—?

PARRIS, *fearfully:* I—do believe there were some movement—in the soup.

ABIGAIL: That jumped in, we never put it in!

HALE, *quickly:* What jumped in?

ABIGAIL: Why, a very little frog jumped—

PARRIS: A frog, Abby!

HALE, *grasping* ABIGAIL: Abigail, it may be your cousin is dying. Did you call the Devil last night?

ABIGAIL: I never called him! Tituba, Tituba . . .

PARRIS, *blanched:* She called the Devil?

HALE: I should like to speak with Tituba.

PARRIS: Goody Ann, will you bring her up? MRS. PUTNAM *exits.*

HALE: How did she call him?

ABIGAIL: I know not—she spoke Barbados.

HALE: Did you feel any strangeness when she called him? A sudden cold wind, perhaps? A trembling below the ground?

ABIGAIL: I didn't see no Devil! *Shaking* BETTY: Betty, wake up. Betty! Betty!

HALE: You cannot evade me, Abigail. Did your cousin drink any of the brew in that kettle?

ABIGAIL: She never drank it!

HALE: Did you drink it?

ABIGAIL: No, sir!

HALE: Did Tituba ask you to drink it?

ABIGAIL: She tried, but I refused.

HALE: Why are you concealing? Have you sold yourself to Lucifer?

ABIGAIL: I never sold myself! I'm a good girl! I'm a proper girl!

MRS. PUTNAM *enters with* TITUBA, *and instantly* ABIGAIL *points at* TITUBA.

ABIGAIL: She made me do it! She made Betty do it!

TITUBA, *shocked and angry:* Abby!

ABIGAIL: She makes me drink blood!

PARRIS: Blood!!

MRS. PUTNAM: My baby's blood?

TITUBA: No, no, chicken blood. I give she chicken blood!

HALE: Woman, have you enlisted these children for the Devil?

TITUBA: No, no, sir, I don't truck with no Devil!

HALE: Why can she not wake? Are you silencing this child?

TITUBA: I love me Betty!

HALE: You have sent your spirit out upon this child, have you not? Are you gathering souls for the Devil?

ABIGAIL: She sends her spirit on me in church; she makes me laugh at prayer!

PARRIS: She have often laughed at prayer!

ABIGAIL: She comes to me every night to go and drink blood!

TITUBA: You beg *me* to conjure! She beg *me* make charm—

ABIGAIL: Don't lie! *To* HALE: She comes to me while I sleep; she's always making me dream corruptions!

TITUBA: Why you say that, Abby?

ABIGAIL: Sometimes I wake and find myself standing in the open doorway and not a stitch on my body! I always hear her laughing in my sleep. I hear her singing her Barbados songs and tempting me with—

TITUBA: Mister Reverend, I never—

HALE, *resolved now:* Tituba, I want you to wake this child.

TITUBA: I have no power on this child, sir.

HALE: You most certainly do, and you will free her from it now! When did you compact with the Devil?

TITUBA: I don't compact with no Devil!

PARRIS: You will confess yourself or I will take you out and whip you to your death, Tituba!

PUTNAM: This woman must be hanged! She must be taken and hanged!

TITUBA, *terrified, falls to her knees:* No, no, don't hang Tituba! I tell him I don't desire to work for him, sir.

PARRIS: The Devil?

HALE: Then you saw him! TITUBA *weeps.* Now Tituba, I know that when we bind ourselves to Hell it is very hard to break with it. We are going to help you tear yourself free—

TITUBA, *frightened by the coming process:* Mister Reverend, I do believe somebody else be witchin' these children.

HALE: Who?

TITUBA: I don't know, sir, but the Devil got him numerous witches.

HALE: Does he! *It is a clue.* Tituba, look into my eyes. Come, look into me. *She raises her eyes to his fearfully.* You would be a good Christian woman, would you not, Tituba?

TITUBA: Aye, sir, a good Christian woman.

HALE: And you love these little children?

TITUBA: Oh, yes, sir, I don't desire to hurt these children.

HALE: And you love God, Tituba?

TITUBA: I love God with all my bein'.

HALE: Now, in God's holy name—

TITUBA: Bless Him. Bless Him. *She is rocking on her knees, sobbing in terror.*

HALE: And to His glory—

TITUBA: Eternal glory. Bless Him—bless God . . .

HALE: Open yourself, Tituba—open yourself and let God's holy light shine on you.

TITUBA: Oh, bless the Lord.

HALE: When the Devil come to you does he ever come—with another person? *She stares up into his face.* Perhaps another person in the village? Someone you know.

PARRIS: Who came with him?

PUTNAM: Sarah Good? Did you ever see Sarah Good with him? Or Osburn?

PARRIS: Was it man or woman came with him?

TITUBA: Man or woman. Was—was woman.

PARRIS: What woman? A woman, you said. What woman?

TITUBA: It was black dark, and I—

PARRIS: You could see him, why could you not see her?

TITUBA: Well, they was always talking; they was always runnin' round and carryin' on—

PARRIS: You mean out of Salem? Salem witches?

TITUBA: I believe so, yes, sir.

Now HALE *takes her hand. She is surprised.*

HALE: Tituba. You must have no fear to tell

"I want to open myself!"

us who they are, do you understand? We will protect you. The Devil can never overcome a minister. You know that, do you not?

TITUBA, *kisses* HALE's *hand:* Aye, sir, oh, I do.

HALE: You have confessed yourself to witchcraft, and that speaks a wish to come to Heaven's side. And we will bless you, Tituba.

TITUBA, *deeply relieved:* Oh, God bless you, Mr. Hale!

HALE, *with rising exaltation:* You are God's instrument put in our hands to discover the Devil's agent among us. You are selected, Tituba, you are chosen to help us cleanse our village. So speak utterly, Tituba, turn your back on him and face God—face God, Tituba, and God will protect you.

TITUBA, *joining with him:* Oh, God, protect Tituba!

HALE, *kindly:* Who came to you with the Devil? Two? Three? Four? How many?

Tituba pants, and begins rocking back and forth again, staring ahead.

TITUBA: There was four. There was four.

PARRIS, *pressing in on her:* Who? Who? Their names, their names!

TITUBA, *suddenly bursting out:* Oh, how many times he bid me kill you, Mr. Parris!

PARRIS: Kill me!

TITUBA, *in a fury:* He say Mr. Parris must be kill! Mr. Parris no goodly man, Mr. Parris mean man and no gentle man, and he bid me rise out of my bed and cut your throat! *They gasp.* But I tell him "No! I don't hate that man. I don't want kill that man." But he say, "You work for me, Tituba, and I make you free! I give you pretty dress to wear, and put you way high up in the air, and you gone fly back to Barbados!" And I say, "You lie, Devil, you lie!" And then he come one stormy night to me, and he say, "Look! I have *white* people belong to me." And I look—and there was Goody Good.

PARRIS: Sarah Good!

TITUBA, *rocking and weeping:* Aye, sir, and Goody Osburn.

MRS. PUTNAM: I knew it! Goody Osburn were midwife to me three times. I begged you, Thomas, did I not? I begged him not to call Osburn because I feared her. My babies always shriveled in her hands!

HALE: Take courage, you must give us all their names. How can you bear to see this child suffering? Look at her, Tituba. *He is indicating* BETTY *on the bed.* Look at her God-given innocence; her soul is so tender; we must protect her, Tituba; the Devil is out and preying on her like a beast upon the flesh of the pure lamb. God will bless you for your help.

ABIGAIL *rises, staring as though inspired, and cries out.*

ABIGAIL: I want to open myself! *They turn to her, startled. She is enraptured, as though in a pearly light.* I want the light of God, I want the sweet love of Jesus! I danced for the Devil; I saw him; I wrote in his book; I go back to Jesus; I kiss His hand. I saw Sarah Good with the Devil! I saw Goody Osburn with the Devil! I saw Bridget Bishop with the Devil!

As she is speaking, BETTY *is rising from the bed, a fever in her eyes, and picks up the chant.*

BETTY, *staring too:* I saw George Jacobs with the Devil! I saw Goody Howe with the Devil!

PARRIS: She speaks! *He rushes to embrace* BETTY. She speaks!

HALE: Glory to God! It is broken, they are free!

BETTY, *calling out hysterically and with great relief:* I saw Martha Bellows with the Devil!

ABIGAIL: I saw Goody Sibber with the Devil! *It is rising to a great glee.*

PUTNAM: The marshal, I'll call the marshal!

PARRIS *is shouting a prayer of thanksgiving.*

BETTY: I saw Alice Barrow with the Devil!

The curtain begins to fall.

HALE, *as* PUTNAM *goes out:* Let the marshal bring irons!

ABIGAIL: I saw Goody Hawkins with the Devil!

BETTY: I saw Goody Bibber with the Devil!

ABIGAIL: I saw Goody Booth with the Devil!

On their ecstatic cries—

RESPONDING TO THE SELECTION

Your Response

1. How engaging did you find Act I of the play? Why? Are you eager to find out what happens next?
2. How important do you think it is to remember the Salem witchcraft trials? Explain.

Interpreting

3. (a) What do Reverend Parris's comments and actions in the first act reveal about his character? (b) What do Abigail Williams's comments and actions reveal about her character?
4. (a) What is revealed about Ann Putnam's personality? (b) What is revealed about Mary Warren's personality?
5. What seems to be the main motivation for Reverend Parris's concern about Abigail and Betty's behavior in the forest?
6. (a) When Reverend Parris leaves the room, Abigail, Mercy, Mary, and Betty briefly talk in private. What does this discussion reveal about their concerns? (b) How does this scene foreshadow, or hint at, events that will occur later in the play?
7. (a) How does Betty's reaction to the psalm support the assertion that there is "witchcraft afoot"? (b) What other incidents or situations do the various characters use to support this assertion?
8. What evidence is there that sharp divisions exist among the people of Salem Village?
9. (a) What role does Rebecca Nurse serve when she appears in the first act? (b) How would you describe the other characters' attitudes toward her?
10. (a) How would you characterize the manner in which Hale questions Tituba? (b) What causes Tituba to begin naming people whom she had supposedly seen with the Devil?

Applying

11. What types of situations might cause a contemporary American town to become afflicted by a general hysteria?

ANALYZING LITERATURE

Understanding the Historical Context

The Crucible is based on the Salem witchcraft trials of 1692. Considered one of the most tragic incidents in American history, the trials resulted in the death of at least twenty people and the jailing of at least 150 others.

1. Although the play is based on historical fact, some of the events and characters have been fictionalized. Why do you think Arthur Miller might have chosen not to strive for complete historical accuracy?
2. What evidence is there in the first act that Salem Village might be especially susceptible to an outbreak of witchcraft hysteria?

CRITICAL THINKING AND READING

Recognizing Cultural Attitudes

In *The Crucible* Arthur Miller conveys many of the dominant Puritan attitudes and beliefs. For example, during the initial discussion between Parris and Abigail, it is revealed that dancing was viewed as sinful and was strictly forbidden.

1. What evidence is there in the first act that the Puritans believed in severe punishments for those who had sinned?
2. What do the references to the frequent lawsuits and the squabbling over Reverend Parris's salary suggest about the Puritans' attitudes toward money and possessions?

THINKING AND WRITING

Writing About the Setting

Write a paper in which you discuss how the Puritans' attitudes, along with the stresses of their daily lives, may have increased the likelihood of an outbreak of witchcraft hysteria. Review the first act of *The Crucible,* noting what it reveals about the Puritans' ideals and concerns. Also note what it reveals about the stresses of Puritan life. Organize your ideas. Then write your paper.

GUIDE FOR INTERPRETING

The Crucible, Act II

Characterization. Characterization is the means by which a writer reveals a character's personality. Unlike a short story writer or novelist, a playwright usually cannot make direct statements about a character or reveal a character's thoughts. Instead, a dramatist must develop a character through the character's comments and actions and through other characters' comments about him or her. In fact, everything that the audience learns about the characters, including their names and occupations, must be revealed through the characters' comments and actions. Yet a playwright cannot write a dialogue with the sole intention of conveying details about the characters. The dialogue must seem natural and realistic, as if it were taken from real-life conversations.

In the published version of *The Crucible,* Arthur Miller has included information about historical background and commentary on the events and the actions of the characters. In this text Miller provides biographical information about many of the characters and offers valuable insights into their personalities. However, Miller's comments are meant only for readers of the play and would not be part of a dramatic presentation.

As you read or view a play, you begin to develop certain expectations about a character's behavior based upon what you have learned about his or her personality. Before you begin reading the second act, think about what you have already learned about each of the characters. For example, think about what Reverend Parris's comments and actions in the first act reveal about his personality. Considering what is revealed about Parris's personality in the first act, how do you expect him to conduct himself throughout the remainder of the play? How do you expect other characters, such as Abigail Williams, Mary Warren, John Proctor, Thomas Putnam, and Giles Corey, to conduct themselves?

Write a journal entry in which you predict what will occur in the second act. In your predictions explore each of the following questions: How rapidly will the witchcraft hysteria progress? Which characters will be accused of witchcraft? What will happen to the characters who are accused? What role will Reverend Hale play in the proceedings? What other types of characters might be introduced?

ACT II

The common room of Proctor's house, eight days later.

At the right is a door opening on the fields outside. A fireplace is at the left, and behind it a stairway leading upstairs. It is the low, dark, and rather long living room of the time. As the curtain rises, the room is empty. From above, ELIZABETH *is heard softly singing to the children. Presently the door opens and* JOHN PROCTOR *enters, carrying his gun. He glances about the room as he comes toward the fireplace, then halts for an instant as he hears her singing. He continues on to the fireplace, leaves the gun against the wall as he swings a pot out of the fire and smells it. Then he lifts out the ladle and tastes. He is not quite pleased. He reaches to a cupboard, takes a pinch of salt, and drops it into the pot. As he is tasting again, her footsteps are heard on the stair. He swings the pot into the fireplace and goes to a basin and washes his hands and face.* ELIZABETH *enters.*

ELIZABETH: What keeps you so late? It's almost dark.

PROCTOR: I were planting far out to the forest edge.

ELIZABETH: Oh, you're done then.

PROCTOR: Aye, the farm is seeded. The boys asleep?

ELIZABETH: They will be soon. *And she goes to the fireplace, proceeds to ladle up stew in a dish.*

PROCTOR: Pray now for a fair summer.

ELIZABETH: Aye.

PROCTOR: Are you well today?

ELIZABETH: I am. *She brings the plate to the table, and, indicating the food:* It is a rabbit.

PROCTOR, *going to the table:* Oh, is it! In Jonathan's trap?

ELIZABETH: No, she walked into the house this afternoon; I found her sittin' in the corner like she come to visit.

PROCTOR: Oh, that's a good sign walkin' in.

ELIZABETH: Pray God. It hurt my heart to strip her, poor rabbit. *She sits and watches him taste it.*

PROCTOR: It's well seasoned.

ELIZABETH, *blushing with pleasure:* I took great care. She's tender?

PROCTOR: Aye. *He eats. She watches him. I* think we'll see green fields soon. It's warm as blood beneath the clods.

ELIZABETH: That's well.

PROCTOR *eats, then looks up.*

PROCTOR: If the crop is good I'll buy George Jacob's heifer. How would that please you?

ELIZABETH: Aye, it would.

PROCTOR, *with a grin:* I mean to please you, Elizabeth.

ELIZABETH—*it is hard to say:* I know it, John.

He gets up, goes to her, kisses her. She receives it. With a certain disappointment, he returns to the table.

PROCTOR, *as gently as he can:* Cider?

ELIZABETH, *with a sense of reprimanding herself for having forgot:* Aye! *She gets up and goes and pours a glass for him. He now arches his back.*

PROCTOR: This farm's a continent when you go foot by foot droppin' seeds in it.

ELIZABETH, *coming with the cider:* It must be.

PROCTOR, *drinks a long draught, then, putting the glass down:* You ought to bring some flowers in the house.

ELIZABETH: Oh! I forgot! I will tomorrow.

PROCTOR: It's winter in here yet. On Sunday let you come with me, and we'll walk the farm together; I never see such a load of flowers on the earth. *With good feeling he goes and looks up at the sky through the open doorway.* Lilacs have a purple smell. Lilac is the smell of nightfall, I think. Massachusetts is a beauty in the spring!

ELIZABETH: Aye, it is.

There is a pause. She is watching him from the table as he stands there absorbing the night. It is as though she would speak but cannot. Instead, now, she takes up his plate and glass and fork and goes with them to the basin. Her back is turned to him. He turns to her and watches her. A sense of their separation rises.

PROCTOR: I think you're sad again. Are you?

ELIZABETH—*she doesn't want friction, and yet she must:* You come so late I thought you'd gone to Salem this afternoon.

PROCTOR: Why? I have no business in Salem.

ELIZABETH: You did speak of going, earlier this week.

PROCTOR—*he knows what she means:* I thought better of it since.

ELIZABETH: Mary Warren's there today.

PROCTOR: Why'd you let her? You heard me forbid her go to Salem any more!

ELIZABETH: I couldn't stop her.

PROCTOR, *holding back a full condemnation of her:* It is a fault, it is a fault, Elizabeth—you're the mistress here, not Mary Warren.

ELIZABETH: She frightened all my strength away.

PROCTOR: How may that mouse frighten you, Elizabeth? You—

ELIZABETH: It is a mouse no more. I forbid her go, and she raises up her chin like the daughter of a prince and says to me, "I must go to Salem, Goody Proctor; I am an official of the court!"

PROCTOR: Court! What court?

ELIZABETH: Aye, it is a proper court they have now. They've sent four judges out of Boston, she says, weighty magistrates of the General Court, and at the head sits the Deputy Governor of the Province.

PROCTOR, *astonished:* Why, she's mad.

ELIZABETH: I would to God she were. There be fourteen people in the jail now, she says. PROCTOR *simply looks at her, unable to grasp it.* And they'll be tried, and the court have power to hang them too, she says.

PROCTOR, *scoffing, but without conviction:* Ah, they'd never hang—

ELIZABETH: The Deputy Governor promise hangin' if they'll not confess, John. The town's gone wild, I think. She speak of Abigail, and I thought she were a saint, to hear her. Abigail brings the other girls into the court, and where she walks the crowd will part like the sea for Israel.[1] And folks are brought before them, and if they scream and howl and fall to the floor—the person's clapped in the jail for bewitchin' them.

PROCTOR, *wide-eyed:* Oh, it is a black mischief.

ELIZABETH: I think you must go to Salem, John. *He turns to her.* I think so. You must tell them it is a fraud.

PROCTOR, *thinking beyond this:* Aye, it is, it is surely.

ELIZABETH: Let you go to Ezekiel Cheever—he knows you well. And tell him what she said to you last week in her uncle's house.

---

1. **part like . . . Israel:** In the Bible God commanded Moses, the leader of the Jews, to part the Red Sea to enable the Jews to escape from the Egyptians into Canaan.

She said it had naught to do with witchcraft, did she not?

PROCTOR, *in thought:* Aye, she did, she did. *Now, a pause.*

ELIZABETH, *quietly, fearing to anger him by prodding:* God forbid you keep that from the court, John. I think they must be told.

PROCTOR, *quietly, struggling with his thought:* Aye, they must, they must. It is a wonder they do believe her.

ELIZABETH: I would go to Salem now, John— let you go tonight.

PROCTOR: I'll think on it.

ELIZABETH, *with her courage now:* You cannot keep it, John.

PROCTOR, *angering:* I know I cannot keep it. I say I will think on it!

ELIZABETH, *hurt, and very coldly:* Good, then, let you think on it. *She stands and starts to walk out of the room.*

PROCTOR: I am only wondering how I may prove what she told me, Elizabeth. If the girl's a saint now, I think it is not easy to prove she's fraud, and the town gone so silly. She told it to me in a room alone—I have no proof for it.

ELIZABETH: You were alone with her?

PROCTOR, *stubbornly:* For a moment alone, aye.

ELIZABETH: Why, then, it is not as you told me.

PROCTOR, *his anger rising:* For a moment, I say. The others come in soon after.

ELIZABETH, *quietly—she has suddenly lost all faith in him:* Do as you wish, then. *She starts to turn.*

PROCTOR: Woman. *She turns to him.* I'll not have your suspicion any more.

ELIZABETH, *a little loftily:* I have no—

PROCTOR: I'll not have it!

ELIZABETH: Then let you not earn it.

PROCTOR, *with a violent undertone:* You doubt me yet?

ELIZABETH, *with a smile, to keep her dignity:* John, if is were not Abigail that you must go to hurt, would you falter now? I think not.

PROCTOR: Now look you—

ELIZABETH: I see what I see, John.

PROCTOR, *with solemn warning:* You will not judge me more, Elizabeth. I have good reason to think before I charge fraud on Abigail, and I will think on it. Let you look to your own improvement before you go to judge your husband any more. I have forgot Abigail, and—

ELIZABETH: And I.

PROCTOR: Spare me! You forget nothin' and forgive nothin'. Learn charity, woman. I have gone tiptoe in this house all seven month since she is gone. I have not moved from there to there without I think to please you, and still an everlasting funeral marches round your heart. I cannot speak but I am doubted, every moment judged for lies, as though I come into a court when I come into this house!

ELIZABETH: John, you are not open with me. You saw her with a crowd, you said. Now you—

PROCTOR: I'll plead my honesty no more, Elizabeth.

ELIZABETH—*now she would justify herself:* John, I am only—

PROCTOR: No more! I should have roared you down when first you told me your suspicion. But I wilted, and, like a Christian, I confessed. Confessed! Some dream I had must have mistaken you for God that day. But you're not, you're not, and let you remember it! Let you look sometimes for the goodness in me, and judge me not.

ELIZABETH: I do not judge you. The magistrate sits in your heart that judges you. I never thought you but a good man, John—*with a smile*—only somewhat bewildered.

PROCTOR, *laughing bitterly:* Oh, Elizabeth, your justice would freeze beer! *He turns suddenly toward a sound outside. He starts for the door as* MARY WARREN *enters. As soon as he sees her, he goes directly to her and grabs her by the cloak, furious.* How do you go to Salem when I forbid it? Do you mock me? *Shaking her.* I'll whip you if you dare leave this house again!

Strangely, she doesn't resist him, but hangs limply by his grip.

MARY WARREN: I am sick, I am sick, Mr. Proctor. Pray, pray, hurt me not. *Her strangeness throws him off, and her evident pallor and weakness. He frees her.* My insides are all shuddery; I am in the proceedings all day, sir.

PROCTOR, *with draining anger—his curiosity is draining it:* And what of these proceedings here? When will you proceed to keep this house, as you are paid nine pound a year to do—and my wife not wholly well?

As though to compensate, MARY WARREN *goes to* ELIZABETH *with a small rag doll.*

MARY WARREN: I made a gift for you today, Goody Proctor. I had to sit long hours in a chair, and passed the time with sewing.

ELIZABETH, *perplexed, looking at the doll:* Why, thank you, it's a fair poppet.

MARY WARREN, *with a trembling, decayed voice:* We must all love each other now, Goody Proctor.

ELIZABETH, *amazed at her strangeness:* Aye, indeed we must.

MARY WARREN, *glancing at the room:* I'll get up early in the morning and clean the house. I must sleep now. *She turns and starts off.*

PROCTOR: Mary. *She halts.* Is it true? There be fourteen women arrested?

MARY WARREN: No, sir. There be thirty-nine now—*She suddenly breaks off and sobs and sits down, exhausted.*

ELIZABETH: Why, she's weepin'! What ails you, child?

MARY WARREN: Goody Osburn—will hang!

There is a shocked pause, while she sobs.

PROCTOR: Hang! *He calls into her face.* Hang, y'say?

MARY WARREN, *through her weeping:* Aye.

PROCTOR: The Deputy Governor will permit it?

MARY WARREN: He sentenced her. He must. *To ameliorate it:* But not Sarah Good. For Sarah Good confessed, y'see.

PROCTOR: Confessed! To what?

MARY WARREN: That she—*in horror at the memory*—she sometimes made a compact with Lucifer, and wrote her name in his black book—with her blood—and bound herself to torment Christians till God's thrown down—and we all must worship Hell forevermore.

Pause.

PROCTOR: But—surely you know what a jabberer she is. Did you tell them that?

MARY WARREN: Mr. Proctor, in open court she near to choked us all to death.

PROCTOR: How, choked you?

MARY WARREN: She sent her spirit out.

ELIZABETH: Oh, Mary, Mary, surely you—

MARY WARREN, *with an indignant edge:* She tried to kill me many times, Goody Proctor!

ELIZABETH: Why, I never heard you mention that before.

MARY WARREN: I never knew it before. I never knew anything before. When she come into

THE EXECUTION OF THE REVEREND STEPHEN BURROUGHS
FOR WITCHCRAFT AT SALEM, MASSACHUSETTS, IN 1692
19th-Century Engraving

the court I say to myself, I must not accuse this woman, for she sleep in ditches, and so very old and poor. But then—then she sit there, denying and denying, and I feel a misty coldness climbin' up my back, and the skin on my skull begin to creep, and I feel a clamp around my neck and I cannot breathe air; and then—*entranced*—I hear a voice, a screamin' voice, and it were my voice—and all at once I remembered everything she done to me!

PROCTOR: Why? What did she do to you?

MARY WARREN, *like one awakened to a marvelous secret insight:* So many time, Mr. Proctor, she come to this very door, beggin' bread and a cup of cider—and mark this: whenever I turned her away empty, she *mumbled.*

ELIZABETH: Mumbled! She may mumble if she's hungry.

MARY WARREN: But *what* does she mumble? You must remember, Goody Proctor. Last month—a Monday, I think—she walked away, and I thought my guts would burst for two days after. Do you remember it?

ELIZABETH: Why—I do, I think, but—

MARY WARREN: And so I told that to Judge Hathorne, and he asks her so. "Goody Osburn," says he, "what curse do you mumble that this girl must fall sick after turning you away?" And then she replies—*mimicking an old crone*—"Why, your excellence, no curse at all. I only say my commandments; I hope I may say my commandments," says she!

ELIZABETH: And that's an upright answer.

MARY WARREN: Aye, but then Judge Hathorne say, "Recite for us your commandments!"—*leaning avidly toward them*—and of all the ten she could not say a single one. She never knew no commandments, and they had her in a flat lie!

PROCTOR: And so condemned her?

MARY WARREN, *now a little strained, seeing his stubborn doubt:* Why, they must when she condemned herself.

PROCTOR: But the proof, the proof!

MARY WARREN, *with greater impatience with him:* I told you the proof. It's hard proof, hard as rock, the judges said.

PROCTOR, *pauses an instant, then:* You will not go to court again, Mary Warren.

MARY WARREN: I must tell you, sir, I will be gone every day now. I am amazed you do not see what weighty work we do.

PROCTOR: What work you do! It's strange work for a Christian girl to hang old women!

MARY WARREN: But, Mr. Proctor, they will not hang them if they confess. Sarah Good will only sit in jail some time —*recalling*—and here's a wonder for you; think on this. Goody Good is pregnant!

ELIZABETH: Pregnant! Are they mad? The woman's near to sixty!

MARY WARREN: They had Doctor Griggs examine her, and she's full to the brim. And smokin' a pipe all these years, and no husband either! But she's safe, thank God, for they'll not hurt the innocent child. But be that not a marvel? You must see it, sir, it's God's work we do. So I'll be gone every day for some time. I'm—I am an official of the court, they say, and I—*She has been edging toward offstage.*

PROCTOR: I'll official you! *He strides to the mantel, takes down the whip hanging there.*

MARY WARREN, *terrified, but coming erect, striving for her authority:* I'll not stand whipping any more!

ELIZABETH, *hurriedly, as* PROCTOR *approaches:* Mary, promise you'll stay at home—

MARY WARREN, *backing from him, but keep-*

ing her erect posture, striving, striving for her way: The Devil's loose in Salem, Mr. Proctor; we must discover where he's hiding!

PROCTOR: I'll whip the Devil out of you! *With whip raised he reaches out for her, and she streaks away and yells.*

MARY WARREN, *pointing at* ELIZABETH: I saved her life today!

Silence. His whip comes down.

ELIZABETH, *softly:* I am accused?

MARY WARREN, *quaking:* Somewhat mentioned. But I said I never see no sign you ever sent your spirit out to hurt no one, and seeing I do live so closely with you, they dismissed it.

ELIZABETH: Who accused me?

MARY WARREN: I am bound by law, I cannot tell it. *To* PROCTOR: I only hope you'll not be so sarcastical no more. Four judges and the King's deputy sat to dinner with us but an hour ago. I—I would have you speak civilly to me, from this out.

PROCTOR, *in horror, muttering in disgust at her:* Go to bed.

MARY WARREN, *with a stamp of her foot:* I'll not be ordered to bed no more, Mr. Proctor! I am eighteen and a woman, however single!

PROCTOR: Do you wish to sit up? Then sit up.

MARY WARREN: I wish to go to bed!

PROCTOR, *in anger:* Good night, then!

MARY WARREN: Good night. *Dissatisfied, uncertain of herself, she goes out. Wide-eyed, both, Proctor and Elizabeth stand staring.*

ELIZABETH, *quietly:* Oh, the noose, the noose is up!

PROCTOR: There'll be no noose.

ELIZABETH: She wants me dead. I knew all week it would come to this!

PROCTOR, *without conviction:* They dismissed it. You heard her say—

ELIZABETH: And what of tomorrow? She will cry me out until they take me!

PROCTOR: Sit you down.

ELIZABETH: She wants me dead, John, you know it!

PROCTOR: I say sit down! *She sits, trembling. He speaks quickly, trying to keep his wits.* Now we must be wise, Elizabeth.

ELIZABETH, *with sarcasm, and a sense of being lost:* Oh, indeed, indeed!

PROCTOR: Fear nothing. I'll find Ezekiel Cheever. I'll tell him she said it were all sport.

ELIZABETH: John, with so many in the jail, more than Cheever's help is needed now, I think. Would you favor me with this? Go to Abigail.

PROCTOR, *his soul hardening as he senses . . . :* What have I to say to Abigail?

ELIZABETH, *delicately:* John—grant me this. You have a faulty understanding of young girls. There is a promise made in any bed—

PROCTOR, *striving against his anger:* What promise!

ELIZABETH: Spoke or silent, a promise is surely made. And she may dote on it now— I am sure she does—and thinks to kill me, then to take my place.

PROCTOR'S *anger is rising; he cannot speak.*

ELIZABETH: It is her dearest hope, John, I know it. There be a thousand names; why does she call mine? There be a certain danger in calling such a name—I am no Goody Good that sleeps in ditches, nor Osburn, drunk and half-witted. She'd dare not call out such a farmer's wife but there be monstrous profit in it. She thinks to take my place, John.

THE HANGING OF A 'WITCH' AT SALEM, MASSACHUSETTS, IN 1692
19th Century Engraving

PROCTOR: She cannot think it! *He knows it is true.*

ELIZABETH, *"reasonably":* John, have you ever shown her somewhat of contempt? She cannot pass you in the church but you will blush—

PROCTOR: I may blush for my sin.

ELIZABETH: I think she sees another meaning in that blush.

PROCTOR: And what see you? What see you, Elizabeth?

ELIZABETH, *"conceding":* I think you be somewhat ashamed, for I am there, and she so close.

PROCTOR: When will you know me, woman? Were I stone I would have cracked for shame this seven month!

ELIZABETH: Then go and tell her she's a whore. Whatever promise she may sense— break it, John, break it.

PROCTOR, *between his teeth:* Good, then. I'll go. *He starts for his rifle.*

ELIZABETH, *trembling, fearfully:* Oh, how unwillingly!

PROCTOR, *turning on her, rifle in hand:* I will curse her hotter than the oldest cinder in hell. But pray, begrudge me not my anger!

ELIZABETH: Your anger! I only ask you—

PROCTOR: Woman, am I so base? Do you truly think me base?

ELIZABETH: I never called you base.

PROCTOR: Then how do you charge me with such a promise? The promise that a stallion gives a mare I gave that girl!

ELIZABETH: Then why do you anger with me when I bid you break it?

PROCTOR: Because it speaks deceit, and I am honest! But I'll plead no more! I see now your spirit twists around the single error of my life, and I will never tear it free!

ELIZABETH, *crying out:* You'll tear it free— when you come to know that I will be your only wife, or no wife at all! She has an arrow in you yet, John Proctor, and you know it well!

Quite suddenly, as though from the air, a figure appears in the doorway. They start slightly. It is MR. HALE. *He is different now— drawn a little, and there is a quality of deference, even of guilt, about his manner now.*

HALE: Good evening.

PROCTOR, *still in his shock:* Why, Mr. Hale! Good evening to you, sir. Come in, come in.

HALE, *to Elizabeth:* I hope I do not startle you.

ELIZABETH: No, no, it's only that I heard no horse—

HALE: You are Goodwife Proctor.

PROCTOR: Aye; Elizabeth.

HALE, *nods, then:* I hope you're not off to bed yet.

PROCTOR, *setting down his gun:* No, no. HALE *comes further into the room. And* PROCTOR, *to explain his nervousness:* We are not used to visitors after dark, but you're welcome here. Will you sit you down, sir?

HALE: I will. *He sits.* Let you sit, Goodwife Proctor.

She does, never letting him out of her sight. There is a pause as HALE *looks about the room.*

PROCTOR, *to break the silence:* Will you drink cider, Mr. Hale?

HALE: No, it rebels my stomach; I have some further traveling yet tonight. Sit you down, sir. PROCTOR *sits.* I will not keep you long, but I have some business with you.

PROCTOR: Business of the court?

HALE: No—no, I come of my own, without the court's authority. Hear me. *He wets his lips.* I know not if you are aware, but your wife's name is—mentioned in the court.

PROCTOR: We know it, sir. Our Mary Warren told us. We are entirely amazed.

HALE: I am a stranger here, as you know. And in my ignorance I find it hard to draw a clear opinion of them that come accused before the court. And so this afternoon, and now tonight, I go from house to house—I come now from Rebecca Nurse's house and—

ELIZABETH, *shocked:* Rebecca's charged!

HALE: God forbid such a one be charged. She is, however—mentioned somewhat.

ELIZABETH, *with an attempt at a laugh:* You will never believe, I hope, that Rebecca trafficked with the Devil.

HALE: Woman, it is possible.

PROCTOR, *taken aback:* Surely you cannot think so.

HALE: This is a strange time, Mister. No man may longer doubt the powers of the dark are gathered in monstrous attack upon this village. There is too much evidence now to deny it. You will agree, sir?

PROCTOR, *evading:* I—have no knowledge in that line. But it's hard to think so pious a woman be secretly a Devil's bitch after seventy year of such good prayer.

HALE: Aye. But the Devil is a wily one, you cannot deny it. However, she is far from accused, and I know she will not be. *Pause.* I thought, sir, to put some questions as to the Christian character of this house, if you'll permit me.

PROCTOR, *coldly, resentful:* Why, we—have no fear of questions, sir.

HALE: Good, then. *He makes himself more* comfortable. In the book of record that Mr. Parris keeps, I note that you are rarely in the church on Sabbath Day.

PROCTOR: No, sir, you are mistaken.

HALE: Twenty-six time in seventeen month, sir. I must call that rare. Will you tell my why you are so absent?

PROCTOR: Mr. Hale, I never knew I must account to that man for I come to church or stay at home. My wife were sick this winter.

HALE: So I am told. But you, Mister, why could you not come alone?

PROCTOR: I surely did come when I could, and when I could not I prayed in this house.

HALE: Mr. Proctor, your house is not a church; your theology must tell you that.

PROCTOR: It does, sir, it does; and it tells me that a minister may pray to God without he have golden candlesticks upon the altar.

HALE: What golden candlesticks?

PROCTOR: Since we built the church there were pewter candlesticks upon the altar; Francis Nurse made them y'know, and a sweeter hand never touched the metal. But Parris came, and for twenty week he preach nothin' but golden candlesticks until he had them. I labor the earth from dawn of day to blink of night, and I tell you true when I look to heaven and see my money glaring at his elbows—it hurt my prayer, sir, it hurt my prayer. I think, sometimes, the man dreams cathedrals, not clapboard meetin' houses.

HALE, *thinks, then:* And yet, Mister, a Christian on Sabbath Day must be in church. *Pause.* Tell me—you have three children?

PROCTOR: Aye. Boys.

HALE: How comes it that only two are baptized?

PROCTOR, *starts to speak, then stops, then, as though unable to restrain this:* I like it not that Mr. Parris should lay his hand upon my baby. I see no light of God in that man. I'll not conceal it.

HALE: I must say it, Mr. Proctor; that is not for you to decide. The man's ordained, therefore the light of God is in him.

PROCTOR, *flushed with resentment but trying to smile:* What's your suspicion, Mr. Hale?

HALE: No, no, I have no—

PROCTOR: I nailed the roof upon the church, I hung the door—

HALE: Oh, did you! That's a good sign, then.

PROCTOR: It may be I have been too quick to bring the man to book, but you cannot think we ever desired the destruction of religion. I think that's in your mind, is it not?

HALE, *not altogether giving way:* I—have—there is a softness in your record, sir, a softness.

ELIZABETH: I think, maybe, we have been too hard with Mr. Parris. I think so. But sure we never loved the Devil here.

HALE, *nods, deliberating this. Then, with the voice of one administering a secret test:* Do you know your Commandments, Elizabeth?

ELIZABETH, *without hesitation, even eagerly:* I surely do. There be no mark of blame upon my life, Mr. Hale. I am a covenanted Christian woman.

HALE: And you, Mister?

PROCTOR, *a trifle unsteadily:* I—am sure I do, sir.

HALE, *glances at her open face, then at* JOHN, *then:* Let you repeat them, if you will.

PROCTOR: The Commandments.

HALE: Aye.

PROCTOR, *looking off, beginning to sweat:* Thou shalt not kill.

HALE: Aye.

PROCTOR, *counting on his fingers:* Thou shalt not steal. Thou shalt not covet thy neighbor's goods, nor make unto thee any graven image. Thou shalt not take the name of the Lord in vain; thou shalt have no other gods before me. *With some hesitation:* Thou shalt remember the Sabbath Day and keep it holy. *Pause. Then:* Thou shalt honor thy father and mother. Thou shalt not bear false witness. *He is stuck. He counts back on his fingers, knowing one is missing.* Thou shalt not make unto thee any graven image.

HALE: You have said that twice, sir.

PROCTOR, *lost:* Aye. *He is flailing for it.*

ELIZABETH, *delicately:* Adultery, John.

PROCTOR, *as though a secret arrow had pained his heart:* Aye. *Trying to grin it away—to* HALE: You see, sir, between the two of us we do know them all. HALE *only looks at* PROCTOR, *deep in his attempt to define this man.* PROCTOR *grows more uneasy.* I think it be a small fault.

HALE: Theology, sir, is a fortress; no crack in a fortress may be accounted small. *He rises; he seems worried now. He paces a little, in deep thought.*

PROCTOR: There be no love for Satan in this house, Mister.

HALE: I pray it, I pray it dearly. *He looks to both of them, an attempt at a smile on his face, but his misgivings are clear.* Well, then—I'll bid you good night.

ELIZABETH, *unable to restrain herself:* Mr. Hale. *He turns.* I do think you are suspecting me somewhat? Are you not?

HALE, *obviously disturbed—and evasive:* Goody Proctor, I do not judge you. My duty is to add what I may to the godly wisdom of the court. I pray you both good health and good fortune. *To* JOHN: Good night, sir. *He starts out.*

"I do think you are suspecting me somewhat?"

ELIZABETH, *with a note of desperation:* I think you must tell him, John.

HALE: What's that?

ELIZABETH, *restraining a call:* Will you tell him?

Slight pause. HALE *looks questioningly at* JOHN.

PROCTOR, *with difficulty:* I—I have no witness and cannot prove it, except my word be taken. But I know the children's sickness had naught to do with witchcraft.

HALE, *stopped, struck:* Naught to do—?

PROCTOR: Mr. Parris discovered them sportin' in the woods. They were startled and took sick.

Pause.

HALE: Who told you this?

PROCTOR, *hesitates, then:* Abigail Williams.

HALE: Abigail.

PROCTOR: Aye.

HALE, *his eyes wide:* Abigail Williams told you it had naught to do with witchcraft!

PROCTOR: She told me the day you came, sir.

HALL, *suspiciously:* Why—why did you keep this?

PROCTOR: I never knew until tonight that the world is gone daft with this nonsense.

HALE: Nonsense! Mister, I have myself examined Tituba, Sarah Good, and numerous others that have confessed to dealing with the Devil. They have *confessed* it.

PROCTOR: And why not, if they must hang for denyin' it? There are them that will swear to anything before they'll hang; have you never thought of that?

HALE: I have. I—I have indeed. *It is his own suspicion, but he resists it. He glances at* ELIZABETH, *then at* JOHN. And you—would you testify to this in court?

PROCTOR: I—had not reckoned with goin' into court. But if I must I will.

HALE: Do you falter here?

PROCTOR: I falter nothing, but I may wonder if my story will be credited in such a court. I do wonder on it, when such a steady-minded minister as you will suspicion such a woman that never lied, and cannot, and the world knows she cannot! I may falter somewhat, Mister; I am no fool.

HALE, *quietly—it has impressed him:* Proctor, let you open with me now, for I have a rumor that troubles me. It's said you hold no belief that there may even be witches in the world. Is that true, sir?

PROCTOR—*he knows this is critical, and is*

striving against his disgust with HALE *and with himself for even answering:* I know not what I have said, I may have said it. I have wondered if there be witches in the world— although I cannot believe they come among us now.

HALE: Then you do not believe—

PROCTOR: I have no knowledge of it; the Bible speaks of witches, and I will not deny them.

HALE: And you, woman?

ELIZABETH: I—I cannot believe it.

HALE, *shocked:* You cannot!

PROCTOR: Elizabeth, you bewilder him!

ELIZABETH, *to* HALE: I cannot think the Devil may own a woman's soul, Mr. Hale, when she keeps an upright way, as I have. I am a good woman, I know it; and if you believe I may do only good work in the world, and yet be secretly bound to Satan, then I must tell you, sir, I do not believe it.

HALE: But, woman, you do believe there are witches in—

ELIZABETH: If you think that I am one, then I say there are none.

HALE: You surely do not fly against the Gospel, the Gospel—

PROCTOR: She believe in the Gospel, every word!

ELIZABETH: Question Abigail Williams about the Gospel, not myself!

HALE *stares at her.*

PROCTOR: She do not mean to doubt the Gospel, sir, you cannot think it. This be a Christian house, sir, a Christian house.

HALE: God keep you both; let the third child be quickly baptized, and go you without fail each Sunday to Sabbath prayer; and keep a solemn, quiet way among you. I think—

GILES COREY *appears in doorway.*

GILES: John!

PROCTOR: Giles! What's the matter?

GILES: They take my wife.

FRANCIS NURSE *enters.*

GILES: And his Rebecca!

PROCTOR, *to* FRANCIS: Rebecca's in the *jail!*

FRANCIS: Aye, Cheever come and take her in his wagon. We've only now come from the jail, and they'll not even let us in to see them.

ELIZABETH: They've surely gone wild now, Mr. Hale!

FRANCIS, *going to* HALE: Reverend Hale! Can you not speak to the Deputy Governor? I'm sure he mistakes these people—

HALE: Pray calm yourself, Mr. Nurse.

FRANCIS: My wife is the very brick and mortar of the church, Mr. Hale—*indicating* GILES—and Martha Corey, there cannot be a woman closer yet to God than Martha.

HALE: How is Rebecca charged, Mr. Nurse?

FRANCIS, *with a mocking, half-hearted laugh:* For murder, she's charged! *Mockingly quoting the warrant:* "For the marvelous and supernatural murder of Goody Putnam's babies." What am I to do, Mr. Hale?

HALE, *turns from* FRANCIS, *deeply troubled, then:* Believe me, Mr. Nurse, if Rebecca Nurse be tainted, then nothing's left to stop the whole green world from burning. Let you rest upon the justice of the court; the court will send her home, I know it.

FRANCIS: You cannot mean she will be tried in court!

HALE, *pleading:* Nurse, though our hearts break, we cannot flinch; these are new times, sir. There is a misty plot afoot so subtle we should be criminal to cling to old respects and ancient friendships. I have seen too many frightful proofs in court—the Devil is alive in Salem, and we dare not quail to follow wherever the accusing finger points!

PROCTOR, *angered:* How may such a woman murder children?

HALE, *in great pain:* Man, remember, until an hour before the Devil fell, God thought him beautiful in Heaven.

GILES: I never said my wife were a witch, Mr. Hale; I only said she were reading books!

HALE: Mr. Corey, exactly what complaint were made on your wife?

GILES: That bloody mongrel Walcott charge her. Y'see, he buy a pig of my wife four or five years ago, and the pig died soon after. So he come dancin' in for his money back. So my Martha, she says to him, "Walcott, if you haven't the wit to feed a pig properly, you'll not live to own many," she says. Now he goes to court and claims that from that day to this he cannot keep a pig alive for more than four weeks because my Martha bewitch them with her books!

Enter EZEKIEL CHEEVER. *A shocked silence.*

CHEEVER: Good evening to you, Proctor.

PROCTOR: Why, Mr. Cheever. Good evening.

CHEEVER: Good evening, all, Good evening, Mr. Hale.

PROCTOR: I hope you come not on business of the court.

CHEEVER: I do, Proctor, aye. I am clerk of the court now, y'know.

Enter MARSHAL HERRICK, *a man in his early thirties, who is somewhat shamefaced at the moment.*

GILES: It's a pity, Ezekiel, that an honest tailor might have gone to Heaven must burn in Hell. You'll burn for this, do you know it?

CHEEVER: You know yourself I must do as I'm told. You surely know that, Giles. And I'd as lief you'd not be sending me to Hell. I like not the sound of it, I tell you; I like not the sound of it. *He fears* PROCTOR, *but starts to reach inside his coat.* Now believe me, Proctor, how heavy be the law, all its tonnage I do carry on my back tonight. *He takes out a warrant.* I have a warrant for your wife.

PROCTOR, *to* HALE: You said she were not charged!

HALE: I know nothin' of it. *To* CHEEVER: When were she charged?

CHEEVER: I am given sixteen warrant tonight, sir, and she is one.

PROCTOR: Who charged her?

CHEEVER: Why, Abigail Williams charge her.

PROCTOR: On what proof, what proof?

CHEEVER, *looking about the room:* Mr. Proctor, I have little time. The court bid me search your house, but I like not to search a house. So will you hand me any poppets that your wife may keep here?

PROCTOR: Poppets?

ELIZABETH: I never kept no poppets, not since I were a girl.

CHEEVER, *embarrassed, glancing toward the mantel where sits* MARY WARREN'S *poppet:* I spy a poppet, Goody Proctor.

ELIZABETH: Oh! *Going for it:* Why, this is Mary's.

CHEEVER, *shyly:* Would you please to give it to me?

ELIZABETH, *handing it to him, asks* HALE: Has the court discovered a text in poppets now?

CHEEVER, *carefully holding the poppet:* Do you keep any others in this house?

PROCTOR: No, nor this one either till tonight. What signifies a poppet?

CHEEVER: Why, a poppet—*he gingerly turns the poppet over*—a poppet may signify—

Now, woman, will you please to come with me?

PROCTOR: She will not! *To* ELIZABETH: Fetch Mary here.

CHEEVER, *ineptly reaching toward* ELIZABETH: No, no, I am forbid to leave her from my sight.

PROCTOR, *pushing his arm away:* You'll leave her out of sight and out of mind, Mister. Fetch Mary, Elizabeth. ELIZABETH *goes upstairs.*

HALE: What signifies a poppet, Mr. Cheever?

CHEEVER, *turning the poppet over in his hands:* Why, they say it may signify that she—*he has lifted the poppet's skirt, and his eyes widen in astonished fear.* Why, this, this—

PROCTOR, *reaching for the poppet:* What's there?

CHEEVER: Why—*He draws out a long needle from the poppet*—it is a needle! Herrick, Herrick, it is a needle!

HERRICK *comes toward him.*

PROCTOR, *angrily, bewildered:* And what signifies a needle!

CHEEVER, *his hands shaking:* Why, this go hard with her, Proctor, this—I had my doubts, Proctor, I had my doubts, but here's calamity. *To* HALE, *showing the needle:* You see it, sir, it is a needle!

HALE: Why? What meanin' has it?

CHEEVER, *wide-eyed, trembling:* The girl, the Williams girl, Abigail Williams, sir. She sat to dinner in Reverend Parris's house tonight, and without word nor warnin' she falls to the floor. Like a struck beast, he says, and screamed a scream that a bull would weep to hear. And he goes to save her, and, stuck two inches in the flesh of her belly, he draw a needle out. And demandin' of her how she come to be so stabbed, she—*to* PROCTOR *now*—testify it were your wife's familiar spirit pushed it in.

PROCTOR: Why, she done it herself! *To* HALE: I hope you're not takin' this for proof, Mister!

HALE, *struck by the proof, is silent.*

CHEEVER: 'Tis hard proof! *To* HALE: I find here a poppet Goody Proctor keeps. I have found it, sir. And in the belly of the poppet a needle's stuck. I tell you true, Proctor, I never warranted to see such proof of Hell, and I bid you obstruct me not, for I—

Enter ELIZABETH *with* MARY WARREN. PROCTOR, *seeing* MARY WARREN, *draws her by the arm to* HALE.

PROCTOR: Here now! Mary, how did this poppet come into my house?

MARY WARREN, *frightened for herself, her voice very small:* What poppet's that, sir?

PROCTOR, *impatiently, points at the doll in* CHEEVER'S *hand:* This poppet, this poppet.

MARY WARREN, *evasively, looking at it:* Why, I—I think it is mine.

PROCTOR: It is your poppet, is it not?

MARY WARREN, *not understanding the direction of this:* It—is, sir.

PROCTOR: And how did it come into this house?

MARY WARREN, *glancing about at the avid faces:* Why—I made it in the court, sir, and—give it to Goody Proctor tonight.

PROCTOR, *to* HALE: Now, sir—do you have it?

HALE: Mary Warren, a needle have been found inside this poppet.

MARY WARREN, *bewildered:* Why, I meant no harm by it, sir.

PROCTOR, *quickly:* You stuck that needle in yourself?

MARY WARREN: I—I believe I did, sir, I—

"What poppet's that, sir?"

PROCTOR, *to* HALE: What say you now?

HALE, *watching* MARY WARREN *closely:* Child, you are certain this be your natural memory? May it be, perhaps that someone conjures you even now to say this?

MARY WARREN: Conjures me? Why, no, sir, I am entirely myself, I think. Let you ask Su-

sanna Walcott—she saw me sewin' it in court. *Or better still:* Ask Abby, Abby sat beside me when I made it.

PROCTOR, *to* HALE, *of* CHEEVER: Bid him begone. Your mind is surely settled now. Bid him out, Mr. Hale.

ELIZABETH: What signifies a needle?

HALE: Mary—you charge a cold and cruel murder on Abigail.

MARY WARREN: Murder! I charge no—

HALE: Abigail were stabbed tonight; a needle were found stuck into her belly—

ELIZABETH: And she charges me?

HALE: Aye.

ELIZABETH, *her breath knocked out:* Why—! The girl is murder! She must be ripped out of the world!

CHEEVER, *pointing at* ELIZABETH: You've heard that, sir! Ripped out of the world! Herrick, you heard it!

PROCTOR, *suddenly snatching the warrant out of* CHEEVER'S *hands:* Out with you.

CHEEVER: Proctor, you dare not touch the warrant.

PROCTOR, *ripping the warrant:* Out with you!

CHEEVER: You've ripped the Deputy Governor's warrant, man!

PROCTOR: Damn the Deputy Governor! Out of my house!

HALE: Now, Proctor, Proctor!

PROCTOR: Get y'gone with them! You are a broken minister.

HALE: Proctor, if she is innocent, the court—

PROCTOR: If *she* is innocent! Why do you never wonder if Parris be innocent, or Abigail? Is the accuser always holy now? Were they born this morning as clean as God's fingers? I'll tell you what's walking Salem— vengeance is walking Salem. We are what we always were in Salem, but now the little crazy children are jangling the keys of the kingdom, and common vengeance writes the law! This warrant's vengeance! I'll not give my wife to vengeance!

ELIZABETH: I'll go, John—

PROCTOR: You will not go!

HERRICK: I have nine men outside. You cannot keep her. The law binds me, John, I cannot budge.

PROCTOR, *to* HALE, *ready to break him:* Will you see her taken?

HALE: Proctor, the court is just—

PROCTOR: Pontius Pilate![2] God will not let you wash your hands of this!

ELIZABETH: John—I think I must go with them. *He cannot bear to look at her.* Mary, there is bread enough for the morning; you will bake, in the afternoon. Help Mr. Proctor as you were his daughter—you owe me that, and much more. *She is fighting her weeping. To* PROCTOR: When the children wake, speak nothing of witchcraft—it will frighten them. *She cannot go on.*

PROCTOR: I will bring you home. I will bring you soon.

ELIZABETH: Oh, John, bring me soon!

PROCTOR: I will fall like an ocean on that court! Fear nothing, Elizabeth.

ELIZABETH, *with great fear:* I will fear nothing. *She looks about the room, as though to fix it in her mind.* Tell the children I have gone to visit someone sick.

She walks out the door, HERRICK *and* CHEE-VER *behind her. For a moment,* PROCTOR *watches from the doorway. The clank of chain is heard.*

PROCTOR: Herrick! Herrick, don't chain her! *He rushes out the door. From outside:* Damn you, man, you will not chain her! Off with them! I'll not have it! I will not have her chained!

There are other men's voices against his. HALE, *in a fever of guilt and uncertainty, turns from the door to avoid the sight:* MARY WARREN *bursts into tears and sits weeping.* GILES COREY *calls to* HALE.

GILES: And yet silent, minister? It is fraud, you know it is fraud! What keeps you, man?

PROCTOR *is half braced, half pushed into the room by two deputies and* HERRICK.

PROCTOR: I'll pay you, Herrick, I will surely pay you!

HERRICK, *panting:* In God's name, John, I cannot help myself. I must chain them all. Now let you keep inside this house till I am gone! *He goes out with his deputies.*

PROCTOR *stands there, gulping air. Horses and a wagon creaking are heard.*

HALE, *in great uncertainty:* Mr. Proctor—

PROCTOR: Out of my sight!

HALE: Charity, Proctor, charity. What I have heard in her favor, I will not fear to testify in court. God help me, I cannot judge her guilty or innocent—I know not. Only this consider: the world goes mad, and it profit nothing you should lay the cause to the vengeance of a little girl.

PROCTOR: You are a coward! Though you be ordained in God's own tears, you are a coward now!

HALE: Proctor, I cannot think God be provoked so grandly by such a petty cause. The jails are packed—our greatest judges sit in

---

2. Pontius (pän′ shəs) **Pilate** (pī′ lət): The Roman leader who condemned Jesus to be crucified.

Salem now—and hangin's promised. Man, we must look to cause proportionate. Were there murder done, perhaps, and never brought to light? Abomination? Some secret blasphemy that stinks to Heaven? Think on cause, man, and let you help me to discover it. For there's your way, believe it, there is your only way, when such confusion strikes upon the world. *He goes to* GILES *and* FRANCIS. Let you counsel among yourselves; think on your village and what may have drawn from heaven such thundering wrath upon you all. I shall pray God open up our eyes.

HALE *goes out.*

FRANCIS, *struck by* HALE'S *mood:* I never heard no murder done in Salem.

PROCTOR—*he has been reached by* HALE'S *words:* Leave me, Francis, leave me.

GILES, *shaken:* John—tell me, are we lost?

PROCTOR: Go home now, Giles. We'll speak on it tomorrow.

GILES: Let you think on it. We'll come early, eh?

PROCTOR: Aye. Go now, Giles.

GILES: Good night, then.

GILES COREY *goes out. After a moment:*

MARY WARREN, *in a fearful squeak of a voice:* Mr. Proctor, very likely they'll let her come home once they're given proper evidence.

PROCTOR: You're coming to the court with me, Mary. You will tell it in the court.

MARY WARREN: I cannot charge murder on Abigail.

PROCTOR, *moving menacingly toward her:* You will tell the court how that poppet come here and who stuck the needle in.

MARY WARREN: She'll kill me for sayin' that! PROCTOR *continues toward her.* Abby'll charge lechery on you, Mr. Proctor!

PROCTOR, *halting:* She's told you!

MARY WARREN: I have known it, sir. She'll ruin you with it, I know she will.

PROCTOR, *hesitating, and with deep hatred of himself:* Good. Then her saintliness is done with. MARY *backs from him.* We will slide together into our pit; you will tell the court what you know.

MARY WARREN, *in terror:* I cannot, they'll turn on me—

PROCTOR *strides and catches her, and she is repeating, "I cannot, I cannot!"*

PROCTOR: My wife will never die for me! I will bring your guts into your mouth but that goodness will not die for me!

MARY WARREN, *struggling to escape him:* I cannot do it, I cannot!

PROCTOR, *grasping her by the throat as though he would strangle her:* Make your peace with it! Now Hell and Heaven grapple on our backs, and all our pretense is ripped away—make your peace! *He throws her to the floor, where she sobs, "I cannot, I cannot . . ." And now, half to himself, staring, and turning to the open door:* Peace. It is a providence, and no great change; we are only what we always were, but naked now. *He walks as though toward a great horror, facing the open sky.* Aye, naked! And the wind, God's icy wind, will blow!

And she is over and over again sobbing, "I cannot, I cannot, I cannot."

RESPONDING TO THE SELECTION

Your Response

1. At this point of the play, which character do you find most intriguing? Explain.
2. Ezekiel Cheever, court clerk, justifies arresting Martha Corey by stating: "You know yourself I must do as I'm told." How much personal responsibility do you think he bears for his role in the witchcraft proceedings?

Recalling

3. What evidence is used to support Abigail Williams's assertion that Elizabeth Proctor is guilty of witchcraft?

Interpreting

4. At one point John Proctor identifies revenge as the true evil that is afflicting Salem village. What evidence is there to support Proctor's assertion?
5. What does John Proctor mean when he alludes to Reverend Hale as Pontius Pilate?
6. (a) What is ironic about John Proctor's comment that the witchcraft trials are "a black mischief"? (b) Why is it ironic that Rebecca Nurse is charged with witchcraft? (c) What is ironic about the fact that Ezekiel Cheever is the one who arrests Elizabeth Proctor?

Applying

7. The American court system is based on the principle that a person is assumed to be innocent until proven guilty. Explain whether you think this principle applies to the proceedings in Salem.
8. If you were in Reverend Hale's position, how do you think you would react to the information you had gathered during your visit to the Proctors?

ANALYZING LITERATURE

Understanding Characterization

Characterization is the means by which a writer reveals a character's personality. Generally, playwrights must develop characters solely through dialogue and action.

1. What do Elizabeth Proctor's comments and actions reveal about her personality?
2. What do John Proctor's comments and actions reveal about his personality?
3. What is revealed about Hale's character during his questioning of the Proctors?
4. Review Miller's commentary in the first act and find at least three instances in which he offers insights into a character's personality. Then explain how each of the characters' comments and actions support Miller's insights.

CRITICAL THINKING AND READING

Appreciating Dialect

Dialect is the distinctive manner of speech of people living in a particular region. Writers often use dialect to capture the flavor of a specific region. In *The Crucible* Arthur Miller has the characters speak in the dialect of the early New England settlers. For example, note John Proctor's use of dialect in the following comment: "And why not, if they must hang for denyin' it? There are them that will swear to anything . . ."

1. Two of the characteristics of the dialect in this play are the lack of agreement between subjects and verbs and the use of double negatives. Find two examples of each of these characteristics in the second act.
2. Explain why the play would be less effective if Miller had not used dialect.

THINKING AND WRITING

Writing a Dialogue

Write a dialogue between two residents of Salem Village who are not portrayed in the play. The dialogue should focus on the growing witchcraft hysteria in the village, and it should be written in the appropriate dialect. Start by listing the incidents that you wish to have the characters discuss. Then list the character traits that you want each character to possess. When you write your dialogue, make sure the traits you have listed are revealed through their comments. After you have finished writing, revise your dialogue, making sure it seems natural and realistic.

GUIDE FOR INTERPRETING

Historical Context

The Crucible, Act III

The McCarthy Era. In a number of ways, the Salem witchhunt parallels another disturbing period of American history, the McCarthy era. Growing out of the existing fears concerning the spread of communism, the McCarthy era began in 1950, when Joseph McCarthy, a Republican senator from Wisconsin, charged that the State Department had been infiltrated by more than two hundred communists. McCarthy's accusation shook the entire nation, resulting in a pervasive atmosphere of fear and suspicion. Although a Senate committee determined McCarthy's claims to be unfounded, he refused to retract his charges, even though he had provided no evidence to support them. Instead, McCarthy appeared on a series of radio and television programs, reasserting his earlier charges and accusing other government officials of subversive activities.

When the Republicans gained control of the Senate in 1952, McCarthy was appointed chairman of the Senate permanent investigations committee. McCarthy exploited his new position by holding widely publicized hearings during which sweeping accusations were made and people were questioned in a hostile, inquisitorial manner. During the hearings, people's private lives were mercilessly scrutinized, with both their personal relationships and their affiliations with various organizations being brought into question. In addition, the members of the committee demanded that witnesses provide names of people who were involved in communist activities or who advocated principles that were remotely connected to communism. Although little concrete evidence was ever uncovered at the hearings, the careers of many government officials were ruined, and the nation lapsed into a state of near hysteria. In 1954, however, McCarthy himself came under investigation for improper conduct and alleged financial improprieties. As a result, McCarthy's influence in the Senate quickly dwindled, and the furor he had created eventually died out.

As you read the third act of *The Crucible,* look for the ways that the witchhunt of 1692 parallels the McCarthy era. For example, you might note that the hysteria that swept through Salem in 1692 parallels the atmosphere of fear and suspicion that dominated the McCarthy era.

Focus

How do you think you would respond if you were one of the characters accused of witchcraft? How would you respond if you were a character whose husband or wife had been accused of witchcraft? Freewrite, exploring your answers to these questions and discussing your reactions to the events in the first two acts.

ACT III

The vestry room of the Salem meeting house, now serving as the anteroom of the General Court.

As the curtain rises, the room is empty, but for sunlight pouring through two high windows in the back wall. The room is solemn, even forbidding. Heavy beams just out, boards of random widths make up the walls. At the right are two doors leading into the meeting house proper, where the court is being held. At the left another door leads outside.

There is a plain bench at the left, and another at the right. In the center a rather long meeting table, with stools and a considerable armchair snugged up to it.

Through the partitioning wall at the right we hear a prosecutor's voice, JUDGE HATHORNE'S, *asking a question; then a woman's voice,* MARTHA COREY'S, *replying.*

HATHORNE'S VOICE: Now, Martha Corey, there is abundant evidence in our hands to show that you have given yourself to the reading of fortunes. Do you deny it?

MARTHA COREY'S VOICE: I am innocent to a witch. I know not what a witch is.

HATHORNE'S VOICE: How do you know, then, that you are not a witch?

MARTHA COREY'S VOICE: If I were, I would know it.

HATHORNE'S VOICE: Why do you hurt these children?

MARTHA COREY'S VOICE: I do not hurt them. I scorn it!

GILES' VOICE, *roaring:* I have evidence for the court!

Voices of townspeople rise in excitement.

DANFORTH'S VOICE: You will keep your seat!

GILES' VOICE: Thomas Putnam is reaching out for land!

DANFORTH'S VOICE: Remove that man, Marshal!

GILES' VOICE: You're hearing lies, lies!

A roaring goes up from the people.

HATHORNE'S VOICE: Arrest him, excellency!

GILES' VOICE: I have evidence. Why will you not hear my evidence?

The door opens and GILES *is half carried into the vestry room by* HERRICK.

GILES: Hands off, damn you, let me go!

HERRICK: Giles, Giles!

GILES: Out of my way, Herrick! I bring evidence—

HERRICK: You cannot go in there, Giles; it's a court!

Enter HALE *from the court.*

HALE: Pray be calm a moment.

GILES: You, Mr. Hale, go in there and demand I speak.

HALE: A moment, sir, a moment.

GILES: They'll be hangin' my wife!

JUDGE HATHORNE *enters. He is in his sixties, a bitter, remorseless Salem judge.*

HATHORNE: How do you dare come roarin' into this court! Are you gone daft, Corey?

GILES: You're not a Boston judge, Hathorne. You'll not call me daft!

Enter DEPUTY GOVERNOR DANFORTH *and, behind him,* EZEKIEL CHEEVER *and* PARRIS. *On his appearance, silence falls.* DANFORTH *is a grave man in his sixties, of some humor and sophistication that does not, however, interfere with an exact loyalty to his position and his cause. He comes down to* GILES, *who awaits his wrath.*

DANFORTH, *looking directly at* GILES: Who is this man?

PARRIS: Giles Corey, sir, and a more contentious—

GILES, *to* PARRIS: I am asked the question, and I am old enough to answer it! *To* DANFORTH, *who impresses him and to whom he smiles through his strain:* My name is Corey, sir, Giles Corey. I have six hundred acres, and timber in addition. It is my wife you be condemning now. *He indicates the courtroom.*

DANFORTH: And how do you imagine to help her cause with such contemptuous riot? Now be gone. Your old age alone keeps you out of jail for this.

GILES, *beginning to plead:* They be tellin' lies about my wife, sir, I—

DANFORTH: Do you take it upon yourself to determine what this court shall believe and what it shall set aside?

GILES: Your Excellency, we mean no disrespect for—

DANFORTH: Disrespect indeed! It is disruption, Mister. This is the highest court of the supreme government of this province, do you know it?

GILES, *beginning to weep:* Your Excellency, I only said she were readin' books, sir, and they come and take her out of my house for—

DANFORTH, *mystified:* Books! What books?

GILES, *through helpless sobs:* It is my third wife, sir; I never had no wife that be so taken with books, and I thought to find the cause of it, d'y'see, but it were no witch I blamed her for. *He is openly weeping.* I have broke charity with the woman, I have broke charity with her. *He covers his face, ashamed.* DANFORTH *is respectfully silent.*

HALE: Excellency, he claims hard evidence for his wife's defense. I think that in all justice you must—

DANFORTH: Then let him submit his evidence in proper affidavit.[1] You are certainly aware of our procedure here, Mr. Hale. *To* HERRICK: Clear this room.

HERRICK: Come now, Giles. *He gently pushes* COREY *out.*

FRANCIS: We are desperate, sir; we come here three days now and cannot be heard.

DANFORTH: Who is this man?

FRANCIS: Francis Nurse, Your Excellency.

HALE: His wife's Rebecca that were condemned this morning.

DANFORTH: Indeed! I am amazed to find you in such uproar. I have only good report of your character, Mr. Nurse.

HATHORNE: I think they must both be arrested in contempt, sir.

DANFORTH, *to* FRANCIS: Let you write your plea, and in due time I will—

FRANCIS: Excellency, we have proof for your eyes; God forbid you shut them to it. The girls, sir, the girls are frauds.

DANFORTH: What's that?

FRANCIS: We have proof of it, sir. They are all deceiving you.

DANFORTH *is shocked, but studying* FRANCIS.

HATHORNE: This is contempt, sir, contempt!

DANFORTH: Peace, Judge Hathorne. Do you know who I am, Mr. Nurse?

FRANCIS: I surely do, sir, and I think you must be a wise judge to be what you are.

DANFORTH: And do you know that near to four hundred are in the jails from Marblehead to Lynn, and upon my signatures?

FRANCIS: I—

DANFORTH: And seventy-two condemned to hang by that signature?

---

1. **affidavit** (af′ ə dā′ vit) *n.*: A written statement made on oath.

FRANCIS: Excellency, I never thought to say it to such a weighty judge, but you are deceived.

Enter GILES COREY *from left. All turn to see as he beckons in* MARY WARREN *with* PROCTOR. MARY *is keeping her eyes to the ground;* PROCTOR *has her elbow as though she were near collapse.*

PARRIS, *on seeing her, in shock:* Mary Warren! *He goes directly to bend close to her face.* What are you about here?

PROCTOR, *pressing* PARRIS *away from her with a gentle but firm motion of protectiveness:* She would speak with the Deputy Governor.

DANFORTH, *shocked by this, turns to* HERRICK: Did you not tell me Mary Warren were sick in bed?

HERRICK: She were, Your Honor. When I go to fetch her to the court last week, she said she were sick.

GILES: She has been strivin' with her soul all week, Your Honor; she comes now to tell the truth of this to you.

DANFORTH: Who is this?

PROCTOR: John Proctor, sir. Elizabeth Proctor is my wife.

PARRIS: Beware this man, Your Excellency, this man is mischief.

HALE, *excitedly:* I think you must hear the girl, sir, she—

DANFORTH, *who has become very interested in* MARY WARREN *and only raises a hand toward* HALE: Peace. What would you tell us, Mary Warren?

PROCTOR *looks at her, but she cannot speak.*

PROCTOR: She never saw no spirits, sir.

DANFORTH, *with great alarm and surprise, to* MARY: Never saw no spirits!

GILES, *eagerly:* Never.

PROCTOR, *reaching into his jacket:* She has signed a deposition,[2] sir—

DANFORTH, *instantly:* No, no, I accept no depositions. *He is rapidly calculating this: he turns from her to* PROCTOR. Tell me, Mr. Proctor, have you given out this story in the village?

PROCTOR: We have not.

PARRIS: They've come to overthrow the court, sir! This man is—

DANFORTH: I pray you, Mr. Parris. Do you know, Mr. Proctor, that the entire contention of the state in these trials is that the voice of Heaven is speaking through the children?

PROCTOR: I know that, sir.

DANFORTH, *thinks, staring at* PROCTOR, *then turns to* MARY WARREN: And you, Mary Warren, how come you to cry out people for sending their spirits, against you?

MARY WARREN: It were pretense, sir.

DANFORTH: I cannot hear you.

PROCTOR: It were pretense, she says.

DANFORTH: Ah? And the other girls? Susanna Walcott, and—the others? They are also pretending?

MARY WARREN: Aye, sir.

DANFORTH: *wide-eyed:* Indeed. *Pause. He is baffled by this. He turns to study* PROCTOR'S *face.*

PARRIS, *in a sweat:* Excellency, you surely cannot think to let so vile a lie be spread in open court.

DANFORTH: Indeed not, but it strike hard upon me that she will dare come here with such a tale. Now, Mr. Proctor, before I decide

---

2. deposition (dep′ ə zish′ ən) *n.*: The testimony of a witness, made under oath but not in open court, and written down to be used during a trial.

whether I shall hear you or not, it is my duty to tell you this. We burn a hot fire here; it melts down all concealment.

PROCTOR: I know that, sir.

DANFORTH: Let me continue. I understand well, a husband's tenderness may drive him to extravagance in defense of a wife. Are you certain in your conscience, Mister, that your evidence is the truth?

PROCTOR: It is. And you will surely know it.

DANFORTH: And you thought to declare this revelation in the open court before the public?

PROCTOR: I thought I would, aye—with your permission.

DANFORTH, *his eyes narrowing:* Now, sir, what is your purpose in so doing?

"She never saw no spirits, sir."

PROCTOR: Why, I—I would free my wife, sir.

DANFORTH: There lurks nowhere in your heart, nor hidden in your spirit, any desire to undermine this court?

PROCTOR, *with the faintest faltering:* Why, no, sir.

CHEEVER, *clears his throat, awakening:* I— Your Excellency.

DANFORTH: Mr. Cheever.

CHEEVER: I think it be my duty, sir— *Kindly, to* PROCTOR: You'll not deny it, John. *To* DAN- FORTH: When we come to take his wife, he damned the court and ripped your warrant.

PARRIS: Now you have it!

DANFORTH: He did that, Mr. Hale?

HALE, *takes a breath:* Aye, he did.

PROCTOR: It were a temper, sir. I knew not what I did.

DANFORTH, *studying him:* Mr. Proctor.

PROCTOR: Aye, sir.

DANFORTH, *straight into his eyes:* Have you ever seen the Devil?

PROCTOR: No, sir.

DANFORTH: You are in all respects a Gospel Christian?

PROCTOR: I am, sir.

PARRIS: Such a Christian that will not come to church but once in a month!

DANFORTH, *restrained—he is curious:* Not come to church?

PROCTOR: I—I have no love for Mr. Parris. It is no secret. But God I surely love.

CHEEVER: He plow on Sunday, sir.

DANFORTH: Plow on Sunday!

CHEEVER, *apologetically:* I think it be evi- dence, John. I am an official of the court, I cannot keep it.

PROCTOR: I—I have once or twice plowed on Sunday. I have three children, sir, and until last year my land give little.

GILES: You'll find other Christians that do plow on Sunday if the truth be known.

HALE: Your Honor, I cannot think you may judge the man on such evidence.

DANFORTH: I judge nothing. *Pause. He keeps watching* PROCTOR, *who tries to meet his gaze.* I tell you straight, Mister—I have seen marvels in this court. I have seen peo- ple choked before my eyes by spirits; I have seen them stuck by pins and slashed by dag- gers. I have until this moment not the slight- est reason to suspect that the children may be deceiving me. Do you understand my meaning?

PROCTOR: Excellency, does it not strike upon you that so many of these women have lived so long with such upright reputation, and—

PARRIS: Do you read the Gospel, Mr. Proctor?

PROCTOR: I read the Gospel.

PARRIS: I think not, or you should surely know that Cain were an upright man, and yet he did kill Abel.[3]

PROCTOR: Aye, God tells us that. *To* DAN- FORTH: But who tells us Rebecca Nurse mur- dered seven babies by sending out her spirit on them? It is the children only, and this one will swear she lied to you.

DANFORTH *considers, then beckons* HATHORNE *to him.* HATHORNE *leans in, and he speaks in his ear.* HATHORNE *nods.*

HATHORNE: Aye, she's the one.

DANFORTH: Mr. Proctor, this morning, your wife send me a claim in which she states that she is pregnant now.

PROCTOR: My wife pregnant!

---

3. Cain . . . Abel: In the Bible Cain, the oldest son of Adam and Eve, killed his brother, Abel.

DANFORTH: There be no sign of it—we have examined her body.

PROCTOR: But if she say she is pregnant, then she must be! That woman will never lie, Mr. Danforth.

DANFORTH: She will not?

PROCTOR: Never, sir, never.

DANFORTH: We have thought it too convenient to be credited. However, if I should tell you now that I will let her be kept another month; and if she begin to show her natural signs, you shall have her living yet another year until she is delivered—what say you to that? JOHN PROCTOR *is struck silent.* Come now. You say your only purpose is to save your wife. Good, then, she is saved at least this year, and a year is long. What say you, sir? It is done now. *In conflict,* PROCTOR *glances at* FRANCIS *and* GILES. Will you drop this charge?

PROCTOR: I—I think I cannot.

DANFORTH, *now an almost imperceptible hardness in his voice:* Then your purpose is somewhat larger.

PARRIS: He's come to overthrow this court, Your Honor!

PROCTOR: These are my friends. Their wives are also accused—

DANFORTH, *with a sudden briskness of manner:* I judge you not, sir. I am ready to hear your evidence.

PROCTOR: I come not to hurt the court; I only—

DANFORTH, *cutting him off:* Marshal, go into the court and bid Judge Stoughton and Judge Sewall declare recess for one hour. And let them go to the tavern, if they will. All witnesses and prisoners are to be kept in the building.

HERRICK: Aye, sir. *Very deferentially:* If I may say it, sir. I know this man all my life. It is a good man, sir.

DANFORTH—*it is the reflection on himself he resents:* I am sure of it, Marshal. HERRICK *nods, then goes out.* Now, what deposition do you have for us, Mr. Proctor? And I beg you be clear, open as the sky, and honest.

PROCTOR, *as he takes out several papers:* I am no lawyer, so I'll—

DANFORTH: The pure in heart need no lawyers. Proceed as you will.

PROCTOR, *handing* DANFORTH *a paper:* Will you read this first, sir? It's a sort of testament. The people signing it declare their good opinion of Rebecca, and my wife, and Martha Corey. DANFORTH *looks down at the paper.*

PARRIS, *to enlist* DANFORTH'S *sarcasm:* Their good opinion! *But* DANFORTH *goes on reading, and* PROCTOR *is heartened.*

PROCTOR: These are all landholding farmers, members of the church. *Delicately, trying to point out a paragraph:* If you'll notice, sir— they've known the woman many years and never saw no sign they had dealings with the Devil.

PARRIS *nervously moves over and reads over* DANFORTH'S *shoulder.*

DANFORTH, *glancing down a long list:* How many names are here?

FRANCIS: Ninety-one, Your Excellency.

PARRIS, *sweating:* These people should be summoned. DANFORTH *looks up at him questioningly.* For questioning.

FRANCIS, *trembling with anger:* Mr. Danforth, I gave them all my word no harm would come to them for signing this.

PARRIS: This is a clear attack upon the court!

HALE, *to* PARRIS, *trying to contain himself:* Is every defense an attack upon the court? Can no one—?

PARRIS: All innocent and Christian people

are happy for the courts in Salem! These people are gloomy for it. *To* DANFORTH *directly:* And I think you will want to know, from each and every one of them, what discontents them with you!

HATHORNE: I think they ought to be examined, sir.

DANFORTH: It is not necessarily an attack, I think. Yet—

FRANCIS: These are all covenanted Christians, sir.

DANFORTH: Then I am sure they may have nothing to fear. *Hands* CHEEVER *the paper.* Mr. Cheever, have warrants drawn for all of these—arrest for examination. *To* PROCTOR: Now, Mister, what other information do you have for us? FRANCIS *is still standing, horrified.* You may sit, Mr. Nurse.

FRANCIS: I have brought trouble on these people; I have—

DANFORTH: No, old man, you have not hurt these people if they are of good conscience. But you must understand, sir, that a person is either with this court or he must be counted against it, there be no road between. This is a sharp time, now, a precise time—we live no longer in the dusky afternoon when evil mixed itself with good and befuddled the world. Now, by God's grace, the shining sun is up, and them that fear not light will surely praise it. I hope you will be one of those. MARY WARREN *suddenly sobs.* She's not hearty, I see.

PROCTOR: No, she's not, sir. *To* MARY, *bending to her, holding her hand, quietly:* Now remember what the angel Raphael said to the boy Tobias.[4] Remember it.

---

4. **Raphael . . . Tobias:** In the Bible Tobias is guided by the archangel Raphael to save two people who have prayed for their deaths. One of the two is Tobias's father, Tobit, who has prayed for his death because he has lost his sight; the other is Sara, a woman who is afflicted by a demon and has killed her seven husbands on their wedding day. With Raphael's assistance, Tobias exorcises the devil from Sara and cures his father of his blindness.

MARY WARREN, *hardly audible:* Aye.

PROCTOR: "Do that which is good, and no harm shall come to thee."

MARY WARREN: Aye.

DANFORTH: Come, man, we wait you.

MARSHAL HERRICK *returns, and takes his post at the door.*

GILES: John, my deposition, give him mine.

PROCTOR: Aye. *He hands* DANFORTH *another paper.* This is Mr. Corey's deposition.

DANFORTH: Oh? *He looks down at it. Now* HATHORNE *comes behind him and reads with him.*

HATHORNE, *suspiciously:* What lawyer drew this, Corey?

GILES: You know I never hired a lawyer in my life, Hathorne.

DANFORTH, *finishing the reading:* It is very well phrased. My compliments. Mr. Parris, if Mr. Putnam is in the court, will you bring him in? HATHORNE *takes the deposition, and walks to the window with it.* PARRIS *goes into the court.* You have no legal training, Mr. Corey?

GILES, *very pleased:* I have the best, sir—I am thirty-three time in court in my life. And always plaintiff, too.

DANFORTH: Oh, then you're much put-upon.

GILES: I am never put-upon: I know my rights, sir, and I will have them. You know, your father tried a case of mine—might be thirty-five year ago, I think.

DANFORTH: Indeed.

GILES: He never spoke to you of it?

DANFORTH: No, I cannot recall it.

GILES: That's strange, he gave me nine pound damages. He were a fair judge, your father. Y'see, I had a white mare that time, and this fellow come to borrow the mare— *Enter* PARRIS *with* THOMAS PUTNAM. *When* *he sees* PUTNAM, GILES' *ease goes; he is hard.* Aye, there he is.

DANFORTH: Mr. Putnam, I have here an accusation by Mr. Corey against you. He states that you coldly prompted your daughter to cry witchery upon George Jacobs that is now in jail.

PUTNAM: It is a lie.

DANFORTH, *turning to* GILES: Mr. Putnam states your charge is a lie. What say you to that?

GILES, *furious, his fists clenched:* A fart on Thomas Putnam, that is what I say to that!

DANFORTH: What proof do you submit for your charge, sir?

GILES: My proof is there! *Pointing to the paper.* If Jacobs hangs for a witch he forfeit up his property—that's law! And there is none but Putnam with the coin to buy so great a piece. This man is killing his neighbors for their land!

DANFORTH: But proof, sir, proof.

GILES, *pointing at his deposition:* The proof is there! I have it from an honest man who heard Putnam say it! The day his daughter cried out on Jacobs, he said she'd given him a fair gift of land.

HATHORNE: And the name of this man?

GILES, *taken aback:* What name?

HATHORNE: The man that give you this information.

GILES, *hesitates, then:* Why, I—I cannot give you his name.

HATHORNE: And why not?

GILES, *hesitates, then bursts out:* You know well why not! He'll lay in jail if I give his name!

HATHORNE: This is contempt of the court, Mr. Danforth!

DANFORTH, *to avoid that:* You will surely tell us the name.

GILES: I will not give you no name. I mentioned my wife's name once and I'll burn in hell long enough for that. I stand mute.

DANFORTH: In that case, I have no choice but to arrest you for contempt of this court, do you know that?

GILES: This is a hearing; you cannot clap me for contempt of a hearing.

DANFORTH: Oh, it is a proper lawyer! Do you wish me to declare the court in full session here? Or will you give me good reply?

GILES, *faltering:* I cannot give you no name, sir, I cannot.

DANFORTH: You are a foolish old man. Mr. Cheever, begin the record. The court is now in session. I ask you, Mr. Corey—

PROCTOR, *breaking in:* Your Honor—he has the story in confidence, sir, and he—

PARRIS: The Devil lives on such confidences! *To* DANFORTH: Without confidences there could be no conspiracy, Your Honor!

HATHORNE: I think it must be broken, sir.

DANFORTH, *to* GILES: Old man, if your informant tells the truth let him come here openly like a decent man. But if he hide in anonymity I must know why. Now sir, the government and central church demand of you the name of him who reported Mr. Thomas Putnam a common murderer.

HALE: Excellency—

DANFORTH: Mr. Hale.

HALE: We cannot blink it more. There is a prodigious fear of this court in the country—

DANFORTH: Then there is a prodigious guilt in the country. Are *you* afraid to be questioned here?

HALE: I may only fear the Lord, sir, but there is fear in the country nevertheless.

DANFORTH, *angered now:* Reproach me not with the fear in the country; there is fear in the country because there is a moving plot to topple Christ in the country!

HALE: But it does not follow that everyone accused is part of it.

DANFORTH: No uncorrupted man may fear this court, Mr. Hale! None! *To* GILES: You are under arrest in contempt of this court. Now sit you down and take counsel with yourself, or you will be set in the jail until you decide to answer all questions.

GILES COREY *makes a rush for* PUTNAM. PROCTOR *lunges and holds him.*

PROCTOR: No, Giles!

GILES, *over* PROCTOR's shoulder at PUTNAM: I'll cut your throat, Putnam, I'll kill you yet!

PROCTOR, *forcing him into a chair:* Peace, Giles, peace. *Releasing him.* We'll prove ourselves. Now we will. *He starts to turn to* DANFORTH.

GILES: Say nothin' more, John. *Pointing at* DANFORTH: He's only playin' you! He means to hang us all!

MARY WARREN *bursts into sobs.*

DANFORTH: This is a court of law, Mister. I'll have no effrontery here!

PROCTOR: Forgive him, sir, for his old age. Peace, Giles, we'll prove it all now. *He lifts up* MARY's *chin.* You cannot weep, Mary. Remember the angel, what he say to the boy. Hold to it, now; there is your rock. MARY *quiets. He takes out a paper, and turns to* DANFORTH. This is Mary Warren's deposition. I—I would ask you remember, sir, while you read it, that until two week ago she were no different than the other children are today. *He is speaking reasonably, restraining all his fears, his anger, his anxiety.* You saw her scream, she howled, she swore familiar spirits choked her; she even testified that Satan, in the form of women now in jail, tried to win her soul away, and then when she refused—

DANFORTH: We know all this.

PROCTOR: Aye, sir. She swears now that she never saw Satan; nor any spirit, vague or clear, that Satan may have sent to hurt her. And she declares her friends are lying now.

PROCTOR *starts to hand* DANFORTH *the deposition, and* HALE *comes up to* DANFORTH *in a trembling state.*

HALE: Excellency, a moment. I think this goes to the heart of the matter.

DANFORTH, *with deep misgivings:* It surely does.

HALE: I cannot say he is an honest man; I know him little. But in all justice, sir, a claim so weighty cannot be argued by a farmer. In God's name, sir, stop here; send him home and let him come again with a lawyer—

DANFORTH, *patiently:* Now look you, Mr. Hale—

HALE: Excellency, I have signed seventy-two death warrants; I am a minister of the Lord, and I dare not take a life without there be a proof so immaculate no slightest qualm of conscience may doubt it.

DANFORTH: Mr. Hale, you surely do not doubt my justice.

HALE: I have this morning signed away the soul of Rebecca Nurse, Your Honor. I'll not conceal it, my hand shakes yet as with a wound! I pray you, sir, *this* argument let lawyers present to you.

DANFORTH: Mr.Hale, believe me; for a man of such terrible learning you are most bewildered—I hope you will forgive me. I have been thirty-two year at the bar, sir, and I should be confounded were I called upon to defend these people. Let you consider, now— *To* PROCTOR *and the others:* And I bid you all do likewise. In an ordinary crime, how does one defend the accused? One calls up witnesses to prove his innocence. But witch-craft is *ipso facto*,[5] on its face and by its nature, an invisible crime, is it not? Therefore, who may possibly be witness to it? The witch and the victim. None other. Now we cannot hope the witch will accuse herself; granted? Therefore, we must rely upon her victims—and they do testify, the children certainly do testify. As for the witches, none will deny that we are most eager for all their confessions. Therefore, what is left for a law-yer to bring out? I think I have made my point. Have I not?

HALE: But this child claims the girls are not truthful, and if they are not—

DANFORTH: That is precisely what I am about to consider, sir. What more may you ask of me? Unless you doubt my probity?[6]

HALE, *defeated:* I surely do not, sir. Let you consider it, then.

DANFORTH: And let you put your heart to rest. Her deposition, Mr. Proctor.

PROCTOR *hands it to him.* HATHORNE *rises, goes beside* DANFORTH, *and starts reading.* PARRIS *comes to his other side.* DANFORTH *looks at* JOHN PROCTOR, *then proceeds to read.* HALE *gets up, finds position near the judge, reads too.* PROCTOR *glances at* GILES. FRANCIS *prays silently, hands pressed together.* CHEEVER *waits placidly, the sublime official, dutiful.* MARY WARREN *sobs once.* JOHN PROCTOR *touches her hand reassuringly. Presently* DANFORTH *lifts his eyes, stands up, takes out a kerchief and blows his nose. The others stand aside as he moves in thought toward the window.*

PARRIS, *hardly able to contain his anger and fear:* I should like to question—

DANFORTH—*his first real outburst, in which his contempt for* PARRIS *is clear:* Mr. Parris, I bid you be silent! *He stands in silence,*

---

5. ipso facto (ip′ sō fak′ tō): By that very fact.
6. probity (prō′ bə tē): *n.*: Complete honesty; integrity.

looking out the window. Now, having established that he will set the gait: Mr. Cheever, will you go into the court and bring the children here? CHEEVER *gets up and goes out upstage.* DANFORTH *now turns to* MARY. Mary Warren, how came you to this turnabout? Has Mr. Proctor threatened you for this deposition?

MARY WARREN: No, sir.

DANFORTH: Has he ever threatened you?

MARY WARREN, *weaker:* No, sir.

DANFORTH, *sensing a weakening:* Has he threatened you?

MARY WARREN: No, sir.

DANFORTH: Then you tell me that you sat in my court, callously lying, when you knew that people would hang by your evidence? *She does not answer.* Answer me!

MARY WARREN, *almost inaudibly:* I did, sir.

DANFORTH: How were you instructed in your life? Do you not know that God damns all liars? *She cannot speak.* Or is it now that you lie?

MARY WARREN: No, sir—I am with God now.

DANFORTH: You are with God now.

MARY WARREN: Aye, sir.

DANFORTH, *containing himself:* I will tell you this—you are either lying now, or you were lying in the court, and in either case you have committed perjury and you will go to jail for it. You cannot lightly say you lied, Mary. Do you know that?

MARY WARREN: I cannot lie no more. I am with God, I am with God.

But she breaks into sobs at the thought of it, and the right door opens, and enter SUSANNA WALCOTT, MERCY LEWIS, BETTY PARRIS, *and finally* ABIGAIL. CHEEVER *comes to* DANFORTH.

CHEEVER: Ruth Putnam's not in the court, sir, nor the other children.

DANFORTH: These will be sufficient. Sit you down, children. *Silently they sit.* Your friend, Mary Warren, has given us a deposition. In which she swears that she never saw familiar spirits, apparitions, nor any manifest of the Devil. She claims as well that none of you have seen these things either. *Slight pause.* Now, children, this is a court of law. The law, based upon the Bible, and the Bible, writ by Almighty God, forbid the practice of witchcraft, and describe death as the penalty thereof. But likewise, children, the law and Bible damn all bearers of false witness. *Slight pause.* Now then. It does not escape me that this deposition may be devised to blind us; it may well be that Mary Warren has been conquered by Satan, who sends her here to distract our sacred purpose. If so, her neck will break for it. But if she speak true, I bid you now drop your guile and confess your pretense, for a quick confession will go easier with you. *Pause.* Abigail Williams, rise. ABIGAIL *slowly rises.* Is there any truth in this?

ABIGAIL: No, sir.

DANFORTH, *thinks, glances at* MARY, *then back to* ABIGAIL: Children, a very augur bit will now be turned into your souls until your honesty is proved. Will either of you change your positions now, or do you force me to hard questioning?

ABIGAIL: I have naught to change, sir. She lies.

DANFORTH, *to* MARY: You would still go on with this?

MARY WARREN, *faintly:* Aye, sir.

DANFORTH, *turning to* ABIGAIL: A poppet were discovered in Mr. Proctor's house, stabbed by a needle. Mary Warren claims that you sat beside her in the court when she made it, and that you saw her make it and witnessed how she herself stuck the needle into it for safe-keeping. What say you to that?

ABIGAIL, *with a slight note of indignation:* It is a lie, sir.

DANFORTH, *after a slight pause:* While you worked for Mr. Proctor, did you see poppets in that house?

ABIGAIL: Goody Proctor always kept poppets.

PROCTOR: Your Honor, my wife never kept no poppets. Mary Warren confesses it was her poppet.

CHEEVER: Your Excellency.

DANFORTH: Mr. Cheever.

CHEEVER: When I spoke with Goody Proctor in that house, she said she never kept no poppets. But she said she did keep poppets when she were a girl.

PROCTOR: She has not been a girl these fifteen years, Your Honor.

HATHORNE: But a poppet will keep fifteen years, will it not?

PROCTOR: It will keep if it is kept, but Mary Warren swears she never saw no poppets in my house, nor anyone else.

PARRIS: Why could there not have been poppets hid where no one ever saw them?

PROCTOR, *furious:* There might also be a dragon with five legs in my house, but no one has ever seen it.

PARRIS: We are here, Your Honor, precisely to discover what no one has ever seen.

PROCTOR: Mr. Danforth, what profit this girl to turn herself about? What may Mary Warren gain but hard questioning and worse?

DANFORTH: You are charging Abigail Williams with a marvelous cool plot to murder, do you understand that?

PROCTOR: I do, sir. I believe she means to murder.

DANFORTH, *pointing at* ABIGAIL, *incredulously:* This child would murder your wife?

PROCTOR: It is not a child. Now hear me, sir. In the sight of the congregation she were twice this year put out of this meetin' house for laughter during prayer.

DANFORTH, *shocked, turning to* ABIGAIL: What's this? Laughter during—!

PARRIS: Excellency, she were under Tituba's power at that time, but she is solemn now.

GILES: Aye, now she is solemn and goes to hang people!

DANFORTH: Quiet, man.

HATHORNE: Surely it have no bearing on the question, sir. He charges contemplation of murder.

DANFORTH: Aye. *He studies* ABIGAIL *for a moment, then:* Continue, Mr. Proctor.

PROCTOR: Mary. Now tell the Governor how you danced in the woods.

PARRIS, *instantly:* Excellency, since I come to Salem this man is blackening my name. He—

DANFORTH: In a moment, sir. *To* MARY WARREN, *sternly, and surprised.* What is this dancing?

MARY WARREN: I—*She glances at* ABIGAIL, *who is staring down at her remorselessly. Then, appealing to* PROCTOR: Mr. Proctor—

PROCTOR, *taking it right up:* Abigail leads the girls to the woods, Your Honor, and they have danced there naked—

PARRIS: Your Honor, this—

PROCTOR, *at once:* Mr. Parris discovered them himself in the dead of night! There's the "child" she is!

DANFORTH—*it is growing into a nightmare, and he turns, astonished, to* PARRIS: Mr. Parris—

PARRIS: I can only say, sir, that I never found any of them naked, and this man is—

DANFORTH: But you discovered them dancing in the woods? *Eyes on* PARRIS, *he points at* ABIGAIL. Abigail?

HALE: Excellency, when I first arrived from Beverly, Mr. Parris told me that.

DANFORTH: Do you deny it, Mr. Parris?

PARRIS: I do not, sir, but I never saw any of them naked.

DANFORTH: But she have *danced*?

PARRIS, *unwillingly:* Aye, sir.

DANFORTH, *as though with new eyes, looks at* ABIGAIL.

HATHORNE: Excellency, will you permit me? *He points at* MARY WARREN.

DANFORTH, *with great worry:* Pray, proceed.

HATHORNE: You say you never saw no spirits, Mary, were never threatened or afflicted by any manifest of the Devil or the Devil's agents.

MARY WARREN, *very faintly:* No, sir.

HATHORNE, *with a gleam of victory:* And yet, when people accused of witchery confronted you in court, you would faint, saying their spirits came out of their bodies and choked you—

MARY WARREN: That were pretense, sir.

DANFORTH: I cannot hear you.

MARY WARREN: Pretense, sir.

PARRIS: But you did turn cold, did you not? I myself picked you up many times, and your skin were icy. Mr. Danforth, you—

DANFORTH: I saw that many times.

PROCTOR: She only pretended to faint, Your Excellency. They're all marvelous pretenders.

HATHORNE: Then can she pretend to faint now?

PROCTOR: Now?

PARRIS: Why not? Now there are no spirits attacking her, for none in this room is accused of witchcraft. So let her turn herself cold now, let her pretend she is attacked now, let her faint. *He turns to* MARY WARREN, Faint!

MARY WARREN: Faint?

PARRIS: Aye, faint. Prove to us how you pretended in the court so many times.

MARY WARREN, *looking to Proctor:* I—cannot faint now, sir.

PROCTOR, *alarmed, quietly:* Can you not pretend it?

MARY WARREN: I—*She looks about as though searching for the passion to faint.* I—have no *sense* of it now, I—

DANFORTH: Why? What is lacking now?

MARY WARREN: I—cannot tell, sir, I—

DANFORTH: Might it be that here we have no afflicting spirit loose, but in the court there were some?

MARY WARREN: I never saw no spirits.

PARRIS: Then see no spirits now, and prove to us that you can faint by your own will, as you claim.

MARY WARREN, *stares, searching for the emotion of it, and then shakes her head.* I—cannot do it.

PARRIS: Then you will confess, will you not? It were attacking spirits made you faint!

MARY WARREN: No, sir, I—

PARRIS: Your Excellency, this is a trick to blind the court!

MARY WARREN: It's not a trick! *She stands.* I—I used to faint because I—I thought I saw spirits.

DANFORTH: *Thought* you saw them!

MARY WARREN: But I did not, Your Honor.

HATHORNE: How could you think you saw them unless you saw them?

MARY WARREN: I—I cannot tell how, but I did. I—I heard the other girls screaming, and you, Your Honor, you seemed to believe them, and I—It were only sport in the beginning, sir, but then the whole world cried spirits, spirits, and I—I promise you, Mr. Danforth, I only thought I saw them but I did not.

DANFORTH *peers at her.*

PARRIS, *smiling, but nervous because* DAN-FORTH *seems to be struck by* MARY WARREN'S *story:* Surely Your Excellency is not taken by this simple lie.

DANFORTH, *turning worriedly to* ABIGAIL: Abigail. I bid you now search your heart and tell me this—and beware of it, child, to God every soul is precious and His vengeance is terrible on them that take life without cause. Is it possible, child, that the spirits you have seen are illusion only, some deception that may cross your mind when—

ABIGAIL: Why, this—this—is a base question, sir.

DANFORTH: Child, I would have you consider it—

ABIGAIL: I have been hurt, Mr. Danforth: I have seen my blood runnin' out! I have been near to murdered every day because I done my duty pointing out the Devil's people—and this is my reward? To be mistrusted, denied, questioned like a—

DANFORTH, *weakening:* Child, I do not mistrust you—

ABIGAIL, *in an open threat:* Let you beware, Mr. Danforth. Think you to be so mighty that the power of Hell may not turn *your* wits? Beware of it! There is—*Suddenly, from an accusatory attitude, her face turns, looking into the air above—it is truly frightened.*

DANFORTH, *apprehensively:* What is it, child?

ABIGAIL, *looking about in the air, clasping her arms about her as though cold:* I—I know not. A wind, a cold wind, has come. *Her eyes fall on* MARY WARREN.

MARY WARREN, *terrified, pleading:* Abby!

MERCY LEWIS, *shivering:* Your Honor, I freeze!

PROCTOR: They're pretending!

HATHORNE, *touching* ABIGAIL'S *hand:* She is cold, Your Honor, touch her!

MERCY LEWIS, *through chattering teeth:* Mary, do you send this shadow on me?

MARY WARREN: Lord, save me!

SUSANNA WALCOTT: I freeze, I freeze!

ABIGAIL, *shivering, visibly:* It is a wind, a wind!

MARY WARREN: Abby, don't do that!

DANFORTH, *himself engaged and entered by* ABIGAIL: Mary Warren, do you witch her? I say to you, do you send your spirit out?

With a hysterical cry MARY WARREN *starts to run. Proctor catches her.*

MARY WARREN, *almost collapsing:* Let me go, Mr. Proctor, I cannot, I cannot—

ABIGAIL, *crying to Heaven:* Oh, Heavenly Father, take away this shadow!

Without warning or hesitation, PROCTOR *leaps at* ABIGAIL *and, grabbing her by the hair, pulls her to her feet. She screams in pain.* DANFORTH, *astonished, cries, "What are you about?" and* HATHORNE *and* PARRIS *call, "Take your hands off her!" and out of it all comes* PROCTOR'S *roaring voice.*

PROCTOR: How do you call Heaven! Whore! Whore!

HERRICK *breaks* PROCTOR *from her.*

HERRICK: John!

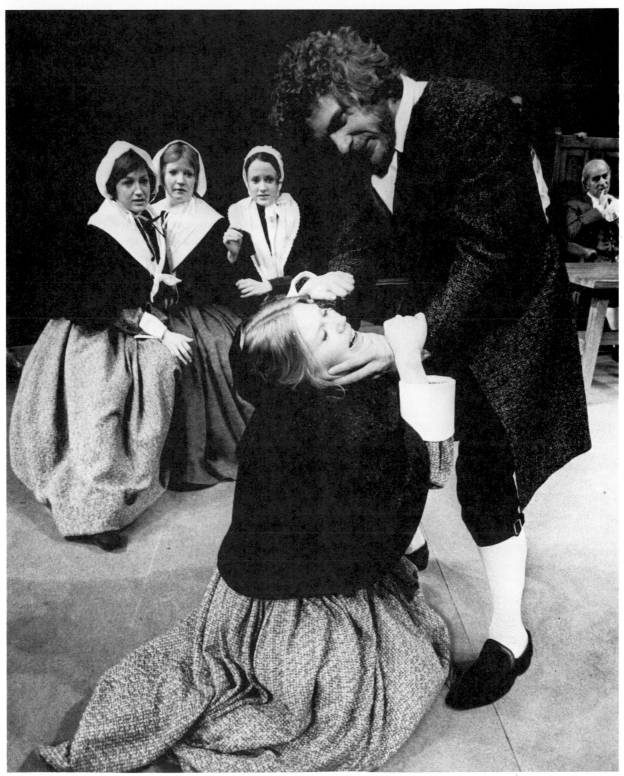

"How do you call Heaven!"

DANFORTH: Man! Man, what do you—

PROCTOR, *breathless and in agony:* It is a whore!

DANFORTH, *dumfounded:* You charge—?

ABIGAIL: Mr. Danforth, he is lying!

PROCTOR: Mark her! Now she'll suck a scream to stab me with, but—

DANFORTH: You will prove this! This will not pass!

PROCTOR, *trembling, his life collapsing about him:* I have known her, sir. I have known her.

DANFORTH: You—you are a lecher?

FRANCIS, *horrified:* John, you cannot say such a—

PROCTOR: Oh, Francis, I wish you had some evil in you that you might know me! *To* DAN-FORTH: A man will not cast away his good name. You surely know that.

DANFORTH, *dumfounded:* In—in what time? In what place?

PROCTOR, *his voice about to break, and his shame great:* In the proper place—where my beasts are bedded. On the last night of my joy, some eight months past. She used to serve me in my house, sir. *He has to clamp his jaw to keep from weeping.* A man may think God sleeps, but God sees everything. I know it now. I beg you, sir, I beg you—see her what she is. My wife, my dear good wife, took this girl soon after, sir, and put her out on the highroad. And being what she is, a lump of vanity, sir—*He is being overcome.* Excellency, forgive me, forgive me. *Angrily against himself, he turns away from the* GOVERNOR *for a moment. Then, as though to cry out is his only means of speech left:* She thinks to dance with me on my wife's grave! And well she might, for I thought of her softly. God help me, I lusted, and there *is* a promise in such sweat. But it is a whore's vengeance, and you must see it; I set myself entirely in your hands. I know you must see it now.

DANFORTH, *blanched, in horror, turning to* ABIGAIL: You deny every scrap and tittle of this?

ABIGAIL: If I must answer that, I will leave and I will not come back again!

DANFORTH *seems unsteady.*

PROCTOR: I have made a bell of my honor! I have rung the doom of my good name—you will believe me, Mr. Danforth! My wife is in-nocent, except she knew a whore when she saw one!

ABIGAIL, *stepping up to* DANFORTH: What look do you give me? DANFORTH *cannot speak.* I'll not have such looks! *She turns and starts for the door.*

DANFORTH: You will remain where you are! HERRICK *steps into her path. She comes up short, fire in her eyes.* Mr. Parris, go into the court and bring Goodwife Proctor out.

PARRIS, *objecting:* Your Honor, this is all a—

DANFORTH, *sharply to* PARRIS: Bring her out! And tell her not one word of what's been spoken here. And let you knock before you enter. PARRIS *goes out.* Now we shall touch the bottom of this swamp. *To* PROCTOR: Your wife, you say, is an honest woman.

PROCTOR: In her life, sir, she have never lied. There are them that cannot sing, and them that cannot weep—my wife cannot lie. I have paid much to learn it, sir.

DANFORTH: And when she put this girl out of your house, she put her out for a harlot?

PROCTOR: Aye, sir.

DANFORTH: And knew her for a harlot?

PROCTOR: Aye, sir, she knew her for a harlot.

DANFORTH: Good then. *To* ABIGAIL: And if she tell me, child, it were for harlotry, may God spread His mercy on you! *There is a knock. He calls to the door.* Hold! *To* ABI-

GAIL: Turn your back. Turn your back. *To* PROCTOR: Do likewise. *Both turn their backs*—ABIGAIL *with indignant slowness.* Now let neither of you turn to face Goody Proctor. No one in this room is to speak one word, or raise a gesture aye or nay. *He turns toward the door, calls:* Enter! *The door opens.* ELIZABETH *enters with* PARRIS. PARRIS *leaves her. She stands alone, her eyes looking for* PROCTOR. Mr. Cheever, report this testimony in all exactness. Are you ready?

CHEEVER: Ready, sir.

DANFORTH: Come here, woman. ELIZABETH *comes to him, glancing at* PROCTOR's *back.* Look at me only, not at your husband. In my eyes only.

ELIZABETH, *faintly:* Good, sir.

DANFORTH: We are given to understand that at one time you dismissed your servant, Abigail Williams.

ELIZABETH: That is true, sir.

DANFORTH: For what cause did you dismiss her? *Slight pause. Then* ELIZABETH *tries to glance at* PROCTOR. You will look in my eyes only and not at your husband. The answer is in your memory and you need no help to give it to me. Why did you dismiss Abigail Williams?

ELIZABETH, *not knowing what to say, sensing a situation, wetting her lips to stall for time:* She—dissatisfied me. *Pause.* And my husband.

DANFORTH: In what way dissatisfied you?

ELIZABETH: She were—*She glances at* PROCTOR *for a cue.*

DANFORTH: Woman, look at me? ELIZABETH *does.* Were she slovenly? Lazy? What disturbance did she cause?

ELIZABETH: Your Honor, I—in that time I were sick. And I—My husband is a good and righteous man. He is never drunk as some

are, nor wastin' his time at the shovelboard, but always at his work. But in my sickness—you see, sir, I were a long time sick after my last baby, and I thought I saw my husband somewhat turning from me. And this girl—*She turns to* ABIGAIL.

DANFORTH: Look at me.

ELIZABETH: Aye, sir. Abigail Williams—*She breaks off.*

DANFORTH: What of Abigail Williams?

ELIZABETH: I came to think he fancied her. And so one night I lost my wits, I think, and put her out on the highroad.

DANFORTH: Your husband—did he indeed turn from you?

ELIZABETH, *in agony:* My husband—is a goodly man, sir.

DANFORTH: Then he did not turn from you.

ELIZABETH, *starting to glance at* PROCTOR: He—

DANFORTH, *reaches out and holds her face, then:* Look at me! To your own knowledge, has John Proctor ever commited the crime of lechery? *In a crisis of indecision she cannot speak.* Answer my question! Is your husband a lecher!

ELIZABETH, *faintly:* No, sir.

DANFORTH: Remove her, Marshal.

PROCTOR: Elizabeth, tell the truth!

DANFORTH: She has spoken. Remove her!

PROCTOR, *crying out:* Elizabeth, I have confessed it!

ELIZABETH: Oh, God! *The door closes behind her.*

PROCTOR: She only thought to save my name!

HALE: Excellency, it is a natural lie to tell; I beg you, stop now before another is condemned! I may shut my conscience to it no more—private vengeance is working through this testimony! From the beginning this man has struck me true. By my oath to Heaven, I believe him now, and I pray you call back his wife before we—

DANFORTH: She spoke nothing of lechery, and this man has lied!

HALE: I believe him! *Pointing at* ABIGAIL: This girl has always struck me false! She has—

ABIGAIL, *with a weird, wild, chilling cry, screams up to the ceiling.*

ABIGAIL: You will not! Begone! Begone, I say!

DANFORTH: What is it, child? *But* ABIGAIL, *pointing with fear, is now raising up her frightened eyes, her awed face, toward the ceiling—the girls are doing the same—and now* HATHORNE, HALE, PUTNAM, CHEEVER, HERRICK, *and* DANFORTH *do the same.* What's there? *He lowers his eyes from the ceiling, and now he is frightened; there is real tension in his voice.* Child! *She is transfixed—with all the girls, she is whimpering, open-mouthed, agape at the ceiling.* Girls! Why do you—?

MERCY LEWIS, *pointing:* It's on the beam! Behind the rafter!

DANFORTH, *looking up:* Where!

ABIGAIL: Why—? *She gulps.* Why do you come, yellow bird?

PROCTOR: Where's a bird? I see no bird!

ABIGAIL, *to the ceiling:* My face? My face?

PROCTOR: Mr. Hale—

DANFORTH: Be quiet!

PROCTOR, *to* HALE: Do you see a bird?

DANFORTH: Be quiet!!

ABIGAIL, *to the ceiling, in a genuine conversation with the "bird," as though trying to talk it out of attacking her:* But God made my face; you cannot want to tear my face. Envy is a deadly sin, Mary.

MARY WARREN, *on her feet with a spring, and horrified, pleading:* Abby!

ABIGAIL, *unperturbed, continuing to the "bird":* Oh, Mary, this is a black art to change your shape. No, I cannot, I cannot stop my mouth; it's God's work I do.

MARY WARREN: Abby, I'm *here!*

PROCTOR, *frantically:* They're pretending, Mr. Danforth!

ABIGAIL—*now she takes a backward step, as though in fear the bird will swoop down momentarily:* Oh, please, Mary! Don't come down.

SUSANNA WALCOTT: Her claws, she stretching her claws!

PROCTOR: Lies, lies.

ABIGAIL, *backing further, eyes still fixed above:* Mary, please don't hurt me!

MARY WARREN, *to* DANFORTH: I'm not hurting her!

DANFORTH, *to* MARY WARREN: Why does she see this vision?

MARY WARREN: She sees nothin!

ABIGAIL, *now staring full front as though hypnotized, and mimicking the exact tone of* MARY WARREN'S *cry:* She sees nothin'!

MARY WARREN, *pleading:* Abby, you mustn't!

ABIGAIL AND ALL THE GIRLS, *all transfixed:* Abby, you mustn't!

MARY WARREN, *to all the girls:* I'm here, I'm here!

GIRLS: I'm here, I'm here!

DANFORTH, *horrified:* Mary Warren! Draw back your spirit out of them!

MARY WARREN: Mr. Danforth!

GIRLS, *cutting her off:* Mr. Danforth!

DANFORTH: Have you compacted with the Devil? Have you?

MARY WARREN: Never, never!

GIRLS: Never, never!

DANFORTH, *growing hysterical:* Why can they only repeat you?

PROCTOR: Give me a whip—I'll stop it!

MARY WARREN: They're sporting. They—!

GIRLS: They're sporting!

MARY WARREN, *turning on them all hysterically and stamping her feet:* Abby, stop it!

GIRLS, *stamping their feet:* Abby, stop it!

MARY WARREN: Stop it!

GIRLS: Stop it!

MARY WARREN, *screaming it out at the top of her lungs, and raising her fists:* Stop it!!

GIRLS, *raising their fists:* Stop it!!

MARY WARREN, *utterly confounded, and becoming overwhelmed by* ABIGAIL'S—*and the girls'—utter conviction, starts to whimper, hands half raised, powerless, and all the girls begin whimpering exactly as she does.*

DANFORTH: A little while ago you were afflicted. Now it seems you afflict others; where did you find this power?

MARY WARREN, *staring at* ABIGAIL: I—have no power.

GIRLS: I have no power.

PROCTOR: They're gulling you, Mister!

DANFORTH: Why did you turn about this past two weeks? You have seen the Devil, have you not?

HALE, *indicating* ABIGAIL *and the girls:* You cannot believe them!

MARY WARREN: I—

PROCTOR, *sensing her weakening:* Mary, God damns all liars!

DANFORTH, *pounding it into her:* You have seen the Devil, you have made compact with Lucifer, have you not?

PROCTOR: God damns liars, Mary!

MARY *utters something unintelligible, staring at* ABIGAIL, *who keeps watching the "bird" above.*

DANFORTH: I cannot hear you. What do you say? MARY *utters again unintelligibly.* You will confess yourself or you will hang! *He turns her roughly to face him.* Do you know who I am? I say you will hang if you do not open with me!

PROCTOR: Mary, remember the angel Raphael—do that which is good and—

ABIGAIL, *pointing upward:* The wings! Her wings are spreading! Mary, please, don't, don't—!

HALE: I see nothing, Your Honor!

DANFORTH: Do you confess this power! *He is an inch from her face.* Speak!

ABIGAIL: She's going to come down! She's walking the beam!

DANFORTH: Will you speak!

MARY WARREN, *staring in horror:* I cannot!

GIRLS: I cannot!

PARRIS: Cast the Devil out! Look him in the face! Trample him! We'll save you, Mary, only stand fast against him and—

ABIGAIL, *looking up:* Look out! She's coming down!

She and all the girls run to one wall, shielding their eyes. And now, as though cornered, they let out a gigantic scream, and MARY, *as though infected, opens her mouth and screams with them. Gradually* ABIGAIL *and the girls leave off, until only* MARY *is left there, staring up at the "bird," screaming madly. All watch her, horrified by this evident fit.* PROCTOR *strides to her.*

PROCTOR: Mary, tell the Governor what they—*He has hardly got a word out, when, seeing him coming for her, she rushes out of his reach, screaming in horror.*

MARY WARREN: Don't touch me—don't touch me! *At which the girls halt at the door.*

PROCTOR, *astonished:* Mary!

MARY WARREN, *pointing at* PROCTOR: You're the Devil's man!

He is stopped in his tracks.

PARRIS: Praise God!

GIRLS: Praise God!

PROCTOR, *numbed:* Mary, how—?

MARY WARREN: I'll not hang with you! I love God, I love God.

DANFORTH, *to Mary:* He bid you do the Devil's work?

MARY WARREN, *hysterically, indicating* PROCTOR: He come at me by night and every day to sign, to sign, to—

DANFORTH: Sign what?

PARRIS: The Devil's book? He come with a book?

MARY WARREN, *hysterically, pointing at* PROCTOR, *fearful of him:* My name, he want my name. "I'll murder you," he says, "if my wife hangs! We must go and overthrow the court," he says!

DANFORTH'S *head jerks toward* PROCTOR, *shock and horror in his face.*

PROCTOR, *turning, appealing to* HALE: Mr. Hale!

MARY WARREN, *her sobs beginning:* He wake me every night, his eyes were like coals and his fingers claw my neck, and I sign, I sign . . .

HALE: Excellency, this child's gone wild!

PROCTOR, *as* DANFORTH'S *wide eyes pour on him:* Mary, Mary!

MARY WARREN, *screaming at him:* No, I love God; I go your way no more. I love God, I bless God. *Sobbing, she rushes to* ABIGAIL. Abby, Abby, I'll never hurt you more! *They all watch, as* ABIGAIL, *out of her infinite charity, reaches out and draws the sobbing* MARY *to her, and then looks up to* DANFORTH.

DANFORTH, *to* PROCTOR: What are you? *Proctor is beyond speech in his anger.* You are combined with antichrist,[7] are you not? I have seen your power; you will not deny it! What say you, Mister?

HALE: Excellency—

DANFORTH: I will have nothing from you, Mr. Hale! *To* PROCTOR: Will you confess yourself befouled with Hell, or do you keep that black allegiance yet? What say you?

PROCTOR, *his mind wild, breathless:* I say— I say—God is dead!

PARRIS: Hear it, hear it!

PROCTOR, *laughs insanely, then:* A fire, a fire is burning! I hear the boot of Lucifer, I see his filthy face! And it is my face, and yours, Danforth! For them that quail to bring men out of ignorance, as I have quailed, and as you quail now when you know in all your black hearts that this be fraud—God damns our kind especially, and we will burn, we will burn together.

DANFORTH: Marshal! Take him and Corey with him to the jail!

HALE, *staring across to the door:* I denounce these proceedings!

PROCTOR: You are pulling Heaven down and raising up a whore!

HALE: I denounce these proceedings, I quit this court! *He slams the door to the outside behind him.*

DANFORTH, *calling to him in a fury:* Mr. Hale! Mr. Hale!

---

7. **antichrist:** In the Bible, the great antagonist of Christ expected to spread universal evil.

RESPONDING TO THE SELECTION

Your Response

1. Were you surprised by the dramatic response of Abigail and the other girls to the accusation that they were pretending? Why or why not?
2. At this point, what, if anything, do you think can stop the proceedings?

Interpreting

3. (a) How would you characterize Judge Hathorne? (b) How would you characterize Deputy Governor Danforth?
4. Why are Giles Corey's informant and the people who signed the first deposition afraid of being called to testify in court?
5. (a) How has Reverend Hale's character changed since the end of the second act? (b) Which of his comments and actions reveal this change? (c) What is the cause of the change in Hale's character?
6. (a) What is the significance of Reverend Hale's observation that "every defense is considered an attack upon the court"? (b) What is the significance of Danforth's assertion that "a person is either with this court or he must be counted against it"?
7. (a) Why does Elizabeth Proctor lie when she is questioned by Danforth? (b) How might the outcome of the witchcraft hysteria have been different if Elizabeth Proctor had told the truth?
8. Why does Mary Warren recant her admission and turn on John Proctor?

Applying

9. (a) What qualities do you think a judge should possess? (b) Which of these qualities do you think that Hathorne and Danforth are lacking?

ANALYZING LITERATURE

Understanding Historical Context

There are several parallels between the witchcraft hysteria of 1692 and the events that oc-curred during the McCarthy era in the twentieth century. For example, during both the witchcraft trials and the McCarthy hearings, people were questioned in a hostile, inquisitorial manner.

1. During the McCarthy era, people who questioned the authority of McCarthy's Senate committee soon found themselves under suspicion of guilt. What evidence is there in the third act of Miller's play that this also occurred during the Salem witchcraft trials?
2. McCarthy's committee displayed a disregard for legal rights, such as the right to counsel and the right not to be branded guilty by reason of association. What evidence is there in the third act that these rights were also ignored during the Salem witchcraft trials?

THINKING AND WRITING

Writing About Parallels

Write a paper in which you discuss the parallels between the Salem witchhunt and the events of the McCarthy era. Begin by reviewing the first three acts of the play and rereading the Guides for Interpreting on the Salem witchcraft trials and the McCarthy era. You may also want to consult outside sources to find additional information about these two events.

LEARNING OPTIONS

1. **Art.** An editorial cartoon can be a powerful tool for expressing a point of view and swaying public opinion. Make a statement about the Salem witch trials by drawing a cartoon that might have been circulated in 1692. You need not express your own opinion; you might voice outrage against or support for the proceedings.
2. **Writing.** How might you have responded in 1692 if your spouse were accused of witchcraft? Follow John Proctor's lead. Draw up a petition to serve as a testament on the accused's behalf. In your petition mount a defense of the accused.

GUIDE FOR INTERPRETING

Writers' Techniques

The Crucible, Act IV

Theme. The theme is the central idea or insight into life that a writer hopes to convey in a work of literature. In some literary works, the theme is directly stated. More often, however, the theme is implied, or revealed indirectly, through the portrayal of characters and events or through the use of literary devices such as irony or symbols.

While shorter literary works often have only one theme, longer works are likely to have several themes. *The Crucible,* for example, has many themes. One of these themes is that fear and suspicion are infectious and can produce a state of general hysteria that results in the destruction of public order and rationality. Another theme is that it is possible for people's conceptions of good and evil to become so corrupted that they commit irreversible misdeeds in the name of virtue. Still another theme of the play is that people who claim to be pious and virtuous may in fact be guilty of hypocrisy. This theme is evident in the actions of Reverend Parris, who pretends to be motivated by concerns about the moral health of the village, though in reality he is concerned only about himself.

As you read the fourth act, pay close attention to how each of these themes is conveyed through the comments and actions of the characters. Also look for other possible themes, and note how each of these themes is revealed.

Focus

Although Reverend Hale has realized that the witchcraft proceedings are a tragic mistake, he does not have the power to stop them. Imagine that you were in Reverend Hale's place. How would you feel about the situation in Salem? What would be your attitude toward Danforth and Hathorne? What actions might you take? Freewrite, exploring your responses to these questions and offering predictions about Reverend Hale's behavior in the final act.

Primary Source

When *The Crucible* was first published, Arthur Miller added a note about the play's historical accuracy: "This play is not history in the sense in which the word is used by the academic historian. Dramatic purposes have sometimes required many characters to be fused into one; the number of girls involved in the 'crying-out' has been reduced; Abigail's age has been raised; while there were several judges of almost equal authority, I have symbolized them in Hathorne and Danforth. However, I believe that the reader will discover here the essential nature of one of the strangest and most awful chapters in human history. The fate of each character is exactly that of his historical model, and there is no one in the drama who did not play a similar—and in some cases exactly the same—role in history."

ACT IV

A cell in Salem jail, that fall.

At the back is a high barred window; near it, a great, heavy door. Along the walls are two benches.

The place is in darkness but for the moonlight seeping through the bars. It appears empty. Presently footsteps are heard coming down a corridor beyond the wall, keys rattle, and the door swings open. MARSHAL HERRICK *enters with a lantern.*

He is nearly drunk, and heavy-footed. He goes to a bench and nudges a bundle of rags lying on it.

HERRICK: Sarah, wake up! Sarah Good! *He then crosses to the other bench.*

SARAH GOOD, *rising in her rags:* Oh, Majesty!

Comin', comin'! Tituba, he's here, His Majesty's come!

HERRICK: Go to the north cell; this place is wanted now. *He hangs his lantern on the wall.* TITUBA *sits up.*

TITUBA: That don't look to me like His Majesty; look to me like the marshal.

HERRICK, *taking out a flask:* Get along with you now, clear this place. *He drinks, and* SARAH GOOD *comes and peers up into his face.*

SARAH GOOD: Oh, is it you, Marshal! I thought sure you be the devil comin' for us. Could I have a sip of cider for me goin'-away?

HERRICK, *handing her the flask:* And where are you off to, Sarah?

TITUBA, *as* SARAH *drinks:* We goin' to Barba-

"Oh, it is you, Marshal! I thought sure you be the devil comin' for us."

dos, soon the Devil gits here with the feathers and the wings.

HERRICK: Oh? A happy voyage to you.

SARAH GOOD: A pair of bluebirds wingin' southerly, the two of us! Oh, it be a grand transformation, Marshal! *She raises the flask to drink again.*

HERRICK, *taking the flask from her lips:* You'd best give me that or you'll never rise off the ground. Come along now.

TITUBA: I'll speak to him for you, if you desires to come along, Marshal.

HERRICK: I'd not refuse it, Tituba; it's the proper morning to fly into Hell.

TITUBA: Oh, it be no Hell in Barbados. Devil, him be pleasureman in Barbados, him be singin' and dancin' in Barbados. It's you folks—you riles him up 'round here; it be too cold 'round here for that Old Boy. He freeze his soul in Massachusetts, but in Barbados he just as sweet and—*A bellowing cow is heard, and* TITUBA *leaps up and calls to the window:* Aye, sir! That's him, Sarah!

SARAH GOOD: I'm here, Majesty! *They hurriedly pick up their rags as* HOPKINS, *a guard, enters.*

HOPKINS: The Deputy Governor's arrived.

HERRICK, *grabbing* TITUBA: Come along, come along.

TITUBA, *resisting him:* No, he comin' for me. I goin' home!

HERRICK, *pulling her to the door:* That's not Satan, just a poor old cow with a hatful of milk. Come along now, out with you!

TITUBA, *calling to the window:* Take me home, Devil! Take me home!

SARAH GOOD, *following the shouting* TITUBA *out:* Tell him I'm goin', Tituba! Now you tell him Sarah Good is goin' too!

In the corridor outside TITUBA *calls on—* "*Take me home, Devil: Devil take me*

home!" *and* HOPKINS' *voice orders her to move on.* HERRICK *returns and begins to push old rags and straw into a corner. Hearing footsteps, he turns, and enter* DANFORTH *and* JUDGE HATHORNE. *They are in greatcoats and wear hats against the bitter cold. They are followed in by* CHEEVER, *who carries a dispatch case and a flat wooden box containing his writing materials.*

HERRICK: Good morning, Excellency.

DANFORTH: Where is Mr. Parris?

HERRICK: I'll fetch him. *He starts for the door.*

DANFORTH: Marshal. HERRICK *stops.* When did Reverend Hale arrive?

HERRICK: It were toward midnight, I think.

DANFORTH, *suspiciously:* What is he about here?

HERRICK: He goes among them that will hang, sir. And he prays with them. He sits with Goody Nurse now. And Mr. Parris with him.

DANFORTH: Indeed. That man have no authority to enter here, Marshal. Why have you let him in?

HERRICK: Why, Mr. Parris command me, sir. I cannot deny him.

DANFORTH: Are you drunk, Marshal?

HERRICK: No, sir; it is a bitter night, and I have no fire here.

DANFORTH, *containing his anger:* Fetch Mr. Parris.

HERRICK: Aye, sir.

DANFORTH: There is a prodigious stench in this place.

HERRICK: I have only now cleared the people out for you.

DANFORTH: Beware hard drink, Marshal.

HERRICK: Aye, sir. *He waits an instant for further orders. But* DANFORTH, *in dissatisfac-*

tion, turns his back on him, and HERRICK *goes out. There is a pause.* DANFORTH *stands in thought.*

HATHORNE: Let you question Hale, Excellency; I should not be surprised he have been preaching in Andover lately.

DANFORTH: We'll come to that; speak nothing of Andover. Parris prays with him. That's strange. *He blows on his hands, moves toward the window, and looks out.*

HATHORNE: Excellency, I wonder if it be wise to let Mr. Parris so continuously with the prisoners. DANFORTH *turns to him, interested.* I think, sometimes, the man has a mad look these days.

DANFORTH: Mad?

HATHORNE: I met him yesterday coming out of his house, and I bid him good morning—and he wept and went his way. I think it is not well the village sees him so unsteady.

DANFORTH: Perhaps he have some sorrow.

CHEEVER, *stamping his feet against the cold:* I think it be the cows, sir.

DANFORTH: Cows?

CHEEVER: There be so many cows wanderin' the highroads, now their masters are in the jails, and much disagreement who they will belong to now. I know Mr. Parris be arguin' with farmers all yesterday—there is great contention, sir, about the cows. Contention make him weep, sir; it were always a man that weep for contention. *He turns, as do* HATHORNE *and* DANFORTH, *hearing someone coming up the corridor.* DANFORTH *raises his head as* PARRIS *enters. He is gaunt, frightened, and sweating in his greatcoat.*

PARRIS, *to Danforth, instantly:* Oh, good morning, sir, thank you for coming. I beg your pardon wakin' you so early. Good morning, Judge Hathorne.

DANFORTH: Reverend Hale have no right to enter this—

PARRIS: Excellency, a moment. *He hurries back and shuts the door.*

HATHORNE: Do you leave him alone with the prisoners?

DANFORTH: What's his business here?

PARRIS, *prayerfully holding up his hands:* Excellency, hear me. It is a providence. Reverend Hale has returned to bring Rebecca Nurse to God.

DANFORTH, *surprised:* He bids her confess?

PARRIS, *sitting:* Hear me. Rebecca have not given me a word this three month since she came. Now she sits with him, and her sister and Martha Corey and two or three others, and he pleads with them, confess their crimes and save their lives.

DANFORTH: Why—this is indeed a providence. And they soften, they soften?

PARRIS: Not yet, not yet. But I thought to summon you, sir, that we might think on whether it be not wise, to—*He dares not say it.* I had thought to put a question, sir, and I hope you will not—

DANFORTH: Mr. Parris, be plain, what troubles you?

PARRIS: There is news, sir, that the court—the court must reckon with. My niece, sir, my niece—I believe she has vanished.

DANFORTH: Vanished!

PARRIS: I had thought to advise you of it earlier in the week, but—

DANFORTH: Why? How long is she gone?

PARRIS: This be the third night. You see, sir, she told me she would stay a night with Mercy Lewis. And next day, when she does not return, I send to Mr. Lewis to inquire. Mercy told him she would sleep in *my* house for a night.

DANFORTH: They are both gone?!

PARRIS, *in fear of him:* They are, sir.

DANFORTH, *alarmed:* I will send a party for them. Where may they be?

PARRIS: Excellency, I think they be aboard a ship. DANFORTH *stands agape.* My daughter tells me how she heard them speaking of ships last week, and tonight I discover my—my strongbox is broke into. *He presses his fingers against his eyes to keep back tears.*

HATHORNE, *astonished:* She have robbed you?

PARRIS: Thirty-one pound is gone. I am penniless. *He covers his face and sobs.*

DANFORTH: Mr. Parris, you are a brainless man! *He walks in thought, deeply worried.*

PARRIS: Excellency, it profit nothing you should blame me. I cannot think they would run off except they fear to keep in Salem any more. *He is pleading.* Mark it, sir, Abigail had close knowledge of the town, and since the news of Andover[1] has broken here—

DANFORTH: Andover is remedied. The court returns there on Friday, and will resume examinations.

PARRIS: I am sure of it, sir. But the rumor here speaks rebellion in Andover, and it—

DANFORTH: There is no rebellion in Andover!

PARRIS: I tell you what is said here, sir. Andover have thrown out the court, they say, and will have no part of witchcraft. There be a faction here, feeding on that news, and I tell you true, sir, I fear there will be riot here.

HATHORNE: Riot! Why at every execution I have seen naught but high satisfaction in the town.

PARRIS: Judge Hathorne—it were another sort that hanged till now. Rebecca Nurse is no Bridget that lived three year with Bishop before she married him. John Proctor is not Isaac Ward that drank his family to ruin. *To* DANFORTH: I would to God it were not so, Excellency, but these people have great weight yet in the town. Let Rebecca stand upon the gibbet[2] and send up some righteous prayer, and I fear she'll wake a vengeance on you.

HATHORNE: Excellency, she is condemned a witch. The court have—

DANFORTH, *in deep concern, raising a hand to* HATHORNE: Pray you. *To* PARRIS: How do you propose, then?

PARRIS: Excellency, I would postpone these hangin's for a time.

DANFORTH: There will be no postponement.

PARRIS: Now Mr. Hale's returned, there is hope, I think—for if he bring even one of these to God, that confession surely damns the others in the public eye, and none may doubt more that they are all linked to Hell. This way, unconfessed and claiming innocence, doubts are multiplied, many honest people will weep for them, and our good purpose is lost in their tears.

DANFORTH, *after thinking a moment, then going to* CHEEVER: Give me the list.

CHEEVER *opens the dispatch case, searches.*

PARRIS: It cannot be forgot, sir, that when I summoned the congregation for John Proctor's excommunication there were hardly thirty people come to hear it. That speak a discontent, I think, and—

DANFORTH, *studying the list:* There will be no postponement.

PARRIS: Excellency—

DANFORTH: Now, sir—which of these in your opinion may be brought to God? I will myself strive with him till dawn. *He hands the list to* PARRIS, *who merely glances at it.*

---

1. news of Andover: During the height of the terror in Salem village, witchcraft hysteria broke out in the nearby town of Andover. There, many respected people were accused of and confessed to practicing witchcraft. However, people soon began questioning the reality of the situation, and the terror quicky subsided.

2. gibbet (jib′ it) *n.:* A gallows.

PARRIS: There is not sufficient time till dawn.

DANFORTH: I shall do my utmost. Which of them do you have hope for?

PARRIS, *not even glancing at the list now, and in a quavering voice, quietly:* Excellency—a dagger— *He chokes up.*

DANFORTH: What do you say?

PARRIS: Tonight, when I open my door to leave my house—a dagger clattered to the ground. *Silence.* DANFORTH *absorbs this. Now* PARRIS *cries out:* You cannot hang this sort. There is danger for me. I dare not step outside at night!

REVEREND HALE *enters. They look at him for an instant in silence. He is steeped in sorrow, exhausted, and more direct than he ever was.*

DANFORTH: Accept my congratulatons, Reverend Hale; we are gladdened to see you returned to your good work.

HALE, *coming to* DANFORTH *now:* You must pardon them. They will not budge.

HERRICK *enters, waits.*

DANFORTH, *conciliatory:* You misunderstand, sir; I cannot pardon these when twelve are already hanged for the same crime. It is not just.

PARRIS, *with failing heart:* Rebecca will not confess?

HALE: The sun will rise in a few minutes. Excellency, I must have more time.

DANFORTH: Now hear me, and beguile yourselves no more. I will not receive a single plea for pardon or postponement. Them that will not confess will hang. Twelve are already executed; the names of these seven are given out, and the village expects to see them die this morning. Postponement now speaks a floundering on my part; reprieve or pardon must cast doubt upon the guilt of them that died till now. While I speak God's law, I will not crack its voice with whimpering. If retaliation is your fear, know this—I should hang ten thousand that dared to rise against the law, and an ocean of salt tears could not melt the resolution of the statutes. Now draw yourselves up like men and help me, as you are bound by Heaven to do. Have you spoken with them all, Mr. Hale?

HALE: All but Proctor. He is in the dungeon.

DANFORTH, *to* HERRICK: What's Proctor's way now?

HERRICK: He sits like some great bird; you'd not know he lived except he will take food from time to time.

DANFORTH, *after thinking a moment:* His wife—his wife must be well on with child now.

HERRICK: She is, sir.

DANFORTH: What think you, Mr. Parris? You have closer knowledge of this man; might her presence soften him?

PARRIS: It is possible, sir. He have not laid eyes on her these three months. I should summon her.

DANFORTH, *to* HERRICK: Is he yet adamant? Has he struck at you again?

HERRICK: He cannot, sir, he is chained to the wall now.

DANFORTH, *after thinking on it:* Fetch Goody Proctor to me. Then let you bring him up.

HERRICK: Aye, sir. HERRICK *goes. There is silence.*

HALE: Excellency, if you postpone a week and publish to the town that you are striving for their confessions, that speak mercy on your part, not faltering.

DANFORTH: Mr. Hale, as God have not empowered me like Joshua to stop this sun from rising,[3] so I cannot withhold from them the perfection of their punishment.

HALE, *harder now:* If you think God wills you to raise rebellion, Mr. Danforth, you are mistaken!

DANFORTH, *instantly:* You have heard rebellion spoken in the town?

HALE: Excellency, there are orphans wandering from house to house; abandoned cattle bellow on the highroads, the stink of rotting crops hangs everywhere, and no man knows when the harlots' cry will end his life—and you wonder yet if rebellion's spoke? Better you should marvel how they do not burn your province!

DANFORTH: Mr. Hale, have you preached in Andover this month?

HALE: Thank God they have no need of me in Andover.

DANFORTH: You baffle me, sir. Why have you returned here?

HALE: Why, it is all simple. I come to do the Devil's work. I come to counsel Christians they should belie themselves. *His sarcasm collapses.* There is blood on my head! Can you not see the blood on my head!!

PARRIS: Hush! *For he has heard footsteps. They all face the door.* HERRICK *enters with* ELIZABETH. *Her wrists are linked by heavy chain, which* HERRICK *now removes. Her clothes are dirty; her face is pale and gaunt.* HERRICK *goes out.*

DANFORTH, *very politely:* Goody Proctor. *She is silent.* I hope you are hearty?

ELIZABETH, *as a warning reminder:* I am yet six months before my time.

DANFORTH: Pray be at your ease, we come not for your life. We—*uncertain how to plead, for he is not accustomed to it.* Mr. Hale, will you speak with the woman?

HALE: Goody Proctor, your husband is marked to hang this morning.

Pause.

ELIZABETH, *quietly:* I have heard it.

HALE: You know, do you not, that I have no connection with the court? *She seems to doubt it.* I come of my own, Goody Proctor. I would save your husband's life, for if he is taken I count myself his murderer. Do you understand me?

ELIZABETH: What do you want of me?

HALE: Goody Proctor, I have gone this three month like our Lord into the wilderness. I have sought a Christian way, for damnation's doubled on a minister who counsels men to lie.

HATHORNE: It is no lie, you cannot speak of lies.

HALE: It is a lie! They are innocent!

DANFORTH: I'll hear no more of that!

HALE, *continuing to* ELIZABETH: Let you not mistake your duty as I mistook my own. I came into this village like a bridegroom to his beloved, bearing gifts of high religion; the very crowns of holy law I brought, and what I touched with my bright confidence, it died; and where I turned the eye of my great faith, blood flowed up. Beware, Goody Proctor—cleave to no faith when faith brings blood. It is mistaken law that leads you to sacrifice. Life, woman, life is God's most precious gift; no principle, however glorious, may justify the taking of it. I beg you, woman, prevail upon your husband to confess. Let him give his lie. Quail not before God's judgment in this, for it may well be God damns a liar less than he that throws his life away for pride. Will you plead with him? I cannot think he will listen to another.

---

3. **Joshua . . . rising:** In the Bible Joshua, the leader of the Jews after the death of Moses, asks God to make the sun and the moon stand still during a battle, and his request is granted.

ELIZABETH, *quietly:* I think that be the Devil's argument.

HALE, *with a climactic desperation:* Woman, before the laws of God we are as swine! We cannot read His will!

ELIZABETH: I cannot dispute with you, sir; I lack learning for it.

DANFORTH, *going to her:* Goody Proctor, you are not summoned here for disputation. Be there no wifely tenderness within you? He will die with the sunrise. Your husband. Do you understand it? *She only looks at him.* What say you? Will you contend with him? *She is silent.* Are you stone? I tell you true, woman, had I no other proof of your unnatural life, your dry eyes now would be sufficient evidence that you delivered up your soul to Hell! A very ape would weep at such calamity! Have the devil dried up any tear of pity in you? *She is silent.* Take her out. It profit nothing she should speak to him!

ELIZABETH, *quietly:* Let me speak with him, Excellency.

PARRIS, *with hope:* You'll strive with him? *She hesitates.*

DANFORTH: Will you plead for his confession or will you not?

ELIZABETH: I promise nothing. Let me speak with him.

A sound—the sibilance of dragging feet on stone. They turn. A pause. HERRICK *enters with* JOHN PROCTOR. *His wrists are chained. He is another man, bearded, filthy, his eyes misty as though webs had overgrown them. He halts inside the doorway, his eyes caught by the sight of* ELIZABETH. *The emotion flowing between them prevents anyone from speaking for an instant. Now* HALE, *visibly affected, goes to* DANFORTH *and speaks quietly.*

HALE: Pray, leave them, Excellency.

DANFORTH, *pressing* HALE *impatiently aside:*

Mr. Proctor, you have been notified, have you not? PROCTOR *is silent, staring at* ELIZABETH. I see light in the sky, Mister; let you counsel with your wife, and may God help you turn your back on Hell. PROCTOR *is silent, staring at* ELIZABETH.

HALE, *quietly:* Excellency, let—

DANFORTH *brushes past* HALE *and walks out.* HALE *follows.* CHEEVER *stands and follows,* HATHORNE *behind.* HERRICK *goes.* PARRIS, *from a safe distance, offers:*

PARRIS: If you desire a cup of cider, Mr. Proctor, I am sure I—PROCTOR *turns an icy stare at him, and he breaks off.* PARRIS *raises his palms toward* PROCTOR. God lead you now. PARRIS *goes out.*

Alone. PROCTOR *walks to her, halts. It is as though they stood in a spinning world. It is beyond sorrow, above it. He reaches out his hand as though toward an embodiment not quite real, and as he touches her, a strange soft sound, half laughter, half amazement, comes from his throat. He pats her hand. She covers his hand with hers. And then, weak, he sits. Then she sits, facing him.*

PROCTOR: The child?

ELIZABETH: It grows.

PROCTOR: There is no word of the boys?

ELIZABETH: They're well. Rebecca's Samuel keeps them.

PROCTOR: You have not seen them?

ELIZABETH: I have not. *She catches a weakening in herself and downs it.*

PROCTOR: You are a—marvel, Elizabeth.

ELIZABETH: You—have been tortured?

PROCTOR: Aye. *Pause. She will not let herself be drowned in the sea that threatens her. They come for my life now.*

ELIZABETH: I know it.

Pause.

"You are a—marvel, Elizabeth."

PROCTOR: None—have yet confessed?

ELIZABETH: There be many confessed.

PROCTOR: Who are they?

ELIZABETH: There be a hundred or more, they say. Goody Ballard is one; Isaiah Goodkind is one. There be many.

PROCTOR: Rebecca?

ELIZABETH: Not Rebecca. She is one foot in Heaven now; naught may hurt her more.

PROCTOR: And Giles?

ELIZABETH: You have not heard of it?

PROCTOR: I hear nothin', where I am kept.

ELIZABETH: Giles is dead.

He looks at her incredulously.

PROCTOR: When were he hanged?

ELIZABETH, *quietly, factually:* He were not hanged. He would not answer aye or nay to his indictment; for if he denied the charge they'd hang him surely, and auction out his property. So he stand mute, and died Christian under the law. And so his sons will have his farm. It is the law, for he could not be condemned a wizard without he answer the indictment, aye or nay.

PROCTOR: Then how does he die?

ELIZABETH, *gently:* They press him, John.

PROCTOR: Press?

ELIZABETH: Great stones they lay upon his chest until he plead aye or nay. *With a tender smile for the old man:* They say he give them but two words. "More weight," he says. And died.

PROCTOR, *numbed—a thread to weave into his agony:* "More weight."

ELIZABETH: Aye. It were a fearsome man, Giles Corey.

Pause.

PROCTOR, *with great force of will, but not quite looking at her:* I have been thinking I would confess to them, Elizabeth. *She shows nothing.* What say you? If I give them that?

ELIZABETH: I cannot judge you, John.

Pause.

PROCTOR, *simply—a pure question:* What would you have me do?

ELIZABETH: As you will, I would have it. *Slight pause:* I want you living, John. That's sure.

PROCTOR, *pauses, then with a flailing of hope:* Giles' wife? Have she confessed?

ELIZABETH: She will not.

Pause.

PROCTOR: It is a pretense, Elizabeth.

ELIZABETH: What is?

PROCTOR: I cannot mount the gibbet like a saint. It is a fraud. I am not that man. *She is silent.* My honesty is broke, Elizabeth; I am no good man. Nothing's spoiled by giving them this lie that were not rotten long before.

ELIZABETH: And yet you've not confessed till now. That speak goodness in you.

PROCTOR: Spite only keeps me silent. It is hard to give a lie to dogs. *Pause, for the first time he turns directly to her.* I would have your forgiveness, Elizabeth.

ELIZABETH: It is not for me to give, John, I am—

PROCTOR: I'd have you see some honesty in it. Let them that never lied die now to keep their souls. It is pretense for me, a vanity that will not blind God nor keep my children out of the wind. *Pause.* What say you?

ELIZABETH, *upon a heaving sob that always threatens:* John, it come to naught that I should forgive you, if you'll not forgive yourself. *Now he turns away a little, in great agony.* It is not my soul, John, it is yours. *He stands, as though in physical pain, slowly rising to his feet with a great immortal longing to find his answer. It is difficult to say, and she is on the verge of tears.* Only be sure of this, for I know it now: Whatever you will do, it is a good man does it. *He turns his doubting, searching gaze upon her.* I have read my heart this three month, John. *Pause.* I have sins of my own to count. It needs a cold wife to prompt lechery.

PROCTOR, *in great pain:* Enough, enough—

ELIZABETH, *now pouring out her heart:* Better you should know me!

PROCTOR: I will not hear it! I know you!

ELIZABETH: You take my sins upon you, John—

PROCTOR, *in agony:* No, I take my own, my own!

ELIZABETH: John, I counted myself so plain, so poorly made, no honest love could come to me! Suspicion kissed you when I did; I never knew how I should say my love. It were a cold house I kept! *In fright, she swerves, as* HATHORNE *enters.*

HATHORNE: What say you Proctor? The sun is soon up.

PROCTOR, *his chest heaving, stares, turns to* ELIZABETH. *She comes to him as though to plead, her voice quaking.*

ELIZABETH: Do what you will. But let none be your judge. There be no higher judge under Heaven than Proctor is! Forgive me, forgive me, John—I never knew such goodness in the world! *She covers her face, weeping.*

PROCTOR *turns from her to* HATHORNE; *he is off the earth, his voice hollow.*

PROCTOR: I want my life.

HATHORNE, *electrified, surprised:* You'll confess yourself?

PROCTOR: I will have my life.

HATHORNE, *with a mystical tone:* God be praised! It is a providence! *He rushes out the door, and his voice is heard calling down the corridor:* He will confess! Proctor will confess!

PROCTOR, *with a cry, as he strides to the door:* Why do you cry it? *In great pain he turns back to her.* It is evil, is it not? It is evil.

ELIZABETH, *in terror, weeping:* I cannot judge you, John, I cannot!

PROCTOR: Then who will judge me? *Suddenly clasping his hands:* God in Heaven, what is John Proctor, what is John Proctor? *He moves as an animal, and a fury is riding in him, a tantalized search.* I think it is honest, I think so; I am no saint. *As though she had denied this he calls angrily at her:* Let Rebecca go like a saint; for me it is fraud!

Voices are heard in the hall, speaking together in suppressed excitement.

ELIZABETH: I am not your judge, I cannot be. *As though giving him release:* Do as you will, do as you will!

PROCTOR: Would you give them such a lie? Say it. Would you ever give them this? *She cannot answer.* You would not; if tongs of fire were singeing you you would not! It is evil. Good, then—it is evil, and I do it!

HATHORNE *enters with* DANFORTH, *and, with them,* CHEEVER, PARRIS, *and* HALE. *It is a businesslike, rapid entrance, as though the ice had been broken.*

DANFORTH, *with great relief and gratitude:* Praise to God, man, praise to God; you shall be blessed in Heaven for this. CHEEVER *has hurried to the bench with pen, ink, and paper.* PROCTOR *watches him.* Now then, let us have it. Are you ready, Mr. Cheever?

PROCTOR, *with a cold, cold horror at their efficiency:* Why must it be written?

DANFORTH: Why, for the good instruction of the village, Mister; this we shall post upon the church door! *To* PARRIS, *urgently:* Where is the marshal?

PARRIS, *runs to the door and calls down the corridor:* Marshal! Hurry!

DANFORTH: Now, then, Mister, will you speak slowly, and directly to the point, for Mr. Cheever's sake. *He is on record now, and is really dictating to* CHEEVER, *who writes.* Mr. Proctor, have you seen the Devil in your life? PROCTOR'S *jaws lock.* Come, man, there is light in the sky; the town waits at the scaffold; I would give out this news. Did you see the Devil?

PROCTOR: I did.

PARRIS: Praise God!

DANFORTH: And when he come to you, what were his demand? PROCTOR *is silent.* DANFORTH *helps.* Did he bid you to do his work upon the earth?

PROCTOR: He did.

DANFORTH: And you bound yourself to his service? DANFORTH *turns, as* REBECCA NURSE *enters, with* HERRICK *helping to support her. She is barely able to walk.* Come in, come in, woman!

REBECCA, *brightening as she sees* PROCTOR: Ah, John! You are well, then, eh?

PROCTOR *turns his face to the wall.*

DANFORTH: Courage, man, courage—let her witness your good example that she may come to God herself. Now hear it, Goody Nurse! Say on, Mr. Proctor. Did you bind yourself to the Devil's service?

REBECCA, *astonished:* Why, John!

PROCTOR, *through his teeth, his face turned from* REBECCA: I did.

DANFORTH: Now, woman, you surely see it profit nothin' to keep this conspiracy any further. Will you confess yourself with him?

REBECCA: Oh, John—God send his mercy on you!

DANFORTH: I say, will you confess yourself, Goody Nurse?

REBECCA: Why, it is a lie, it is a lie; how may I damn myself? I cannot, I cannot.

DANFORTH: Mr. Proctor. When the Devil came to you did you see Rebecca Nurse in his company? PROCTOR *is silent.* Come, man, take courage—did you ever see her with the Devil?

PROCTOR, *almost inaudibly:* No.

DANFORTH, *now sensing trouble, glances at* JOHN *and goes to the table, and picks up a sheet—the list of condemned.*

DANFORTH: Did you ever see her sister, Mary Easty, with the Devil?

PROCTOR: No, I did not.

DANFORTH, *his eyes narrow on* PROCTOR: Did you ever see Martha Corey with the Devil?

PROCTOR: I did not.

DANFORTH, *realizing, slowly putting the sheet down:* Did you ever see anyone with the Devil?

PROCTOR: I did not.

DANFORTH: Proctor, you mistake me. I am not empowered to trade your life for a lie. You have most certainly seen some person with the Devil. PROCTOR *is silent.* Mr. Proctor, a score of people have already testified they saw this woman with the Devil.

PROCTOR: Then it is proved. Why must I say it?

DANFORTH: Why "must" you say it! Why, you should rejoice to say it if your soul is truly purged of any love for Hell!

PROCTOR: They think to go like saints. I like not to spoil their names.

DANFORTH, *inquiring, incredulous:* Mr. Proctor, do you think they go like saints?

PROCTOR, *evading:* This woman never thought she done the Devil's work.

DANFORTH: Look you, sir. I think you mis- take your duty here. It matter nothing what she thought—she is convicted of the unnat- ural murder of children, and you for sending

"Do what you will. But let none be your judge."

your spirit out upon Mary Warren. Your soul alone is the issue here, Mister, and you will prove its whiteness or you cannot live in a Christian country. Will you tell me now what persons conspired with you in the Devil's company? PROCTOR *is silent.* To your knowledge was Rebecca Nurse ever—

PROCTOR: I speak my own sins; I cannot judge another. *Crying out, with hatred:* I have no tongue for it.

HALE, *quickly to Danforth:* Excellency, it is enough he confess himself. Let him sign it, let him sign it.

PARRIS, *feverishly:* It is a great service, sir. It is a weighty name; it will strike the village that Proctor confess. I beg you, let him sign it. The sun is up, Excellency!

DANFORTH, *considers: then with dissatisfaction:* Come, then, sign your testimony. *To* CHEEVER: Give it to him. CHEEVER *goes to* PROCTOR, *the confession and a pen in hand.* PROCTOR *does not look at it.* Come, man, sign it.

PROCTOR, *after glancing at the confession:* You have all witnessed it—it is enough.

DANFORTH: You will not sign it?

PROCTOR: You have all witnessed it; what more is needed?

DANFORTH: Do you sport with me? You will sign your name or it is no confession, Mister! *His breast heaving with agonized breathing,* PROCTOR *now lays the paper down and signs his name.*

PARRIS: Praise be to the Lord!

PROCTOR *has just finished signing when* DANFORTH *reaches for the paper. But* PROCTOR *snatches it up, and now a wild terror is rising in him, and a boundless anger.*

DANFORTH, *perplexed, but politely extending his hand:* If you please, sir.

PROCTOR: No.

DANFORTH, *as though* PROCTOR *did not understand:* Mr. Proctor, I must have—

PROCTOR: No, no. I have signed it. You have seen me. It is done! You have no need for this.

PARRIS: Proctor, the village must have proof that—

PROCTOR: Damn the village! I confess to God, and God has seen my name on this! It is enough!

DANFORTH: No, sir, it is—

PROCTOR: You came to save my soul, did you not? Here! I have confessed myself; it is enough!

DANFORTH: You have not con—

PROCTOR: I have confessed myself! Is there no good penitence but it be public? God does not need my name nailed upon the church! God sees my name; God knows how black my sins are! It is enough!

DANFORTH: Mr. Proctor—

PROCTOR: You will not use me! I am no Sarah Good or Tituba, I am John Proctor! You will not use me! It is no part of salvation that you should use me!

DANFORTH: I do not wish to—

PROCTOR: I have three children—how may I teach them to walk like men in the world, and I sold my friends?

DANFORTH: You have not sold your friends—

PROCTOR: Beguile me not! I blacken all of them when this is nailed to the church the very day they hang for silence!

DANFORTH: Mr. Proctor, I must have good and legal proof that you—

PROCTOR: You are the high court, your word is good enough! Tell them I confessed myself; say Proctor broke his knees and wept like a woman; say what you will, but my name cannot—

DANFORTH, *with suspicion:* It is the same, is it not? If I report it or you sign to it?

PROCTOR—*he knows it is insane:* No, it is not the same! What others say and what I sign to is not the same!

DANFORTH: Why? Do you mean to deny this confession when you are free?

PROCTOR: I mean to deny nothing!

DANFORTH: Then explain to me, Mr. Proctor, why you will not let—

PROCTOR, *with a cry of his whole soul:* Because it is my name! Because I cannot have another in my life! Because I lie and sign myself to lies! Because I am not worth the dust on the feet of them that hang! How may I live without my name? I have given you my soul; leave me my name!

DANFORTH, *pointing at the confession in* PROCTOR's *hand:* Is that document a lie? If it is a lie I will not accept it! What say you? I will not deal in lies, Mister! PROCTOR *is motionless.* You will give me your honest confession in my hand, or I cannot keep you from the rope. PROCTOR *does not reply.* What way do you go, Mister?

His breast heaving, his eyes staring, PROCTOR *tears the paper and crumples it, and he is weeping in fury, but erect.*

DANFORTH: Marshal!

PARRIS, *hysterically, as though the tearing paper were his life:* Proctor, Proctor!

HALE: Man, you will hang! You cannot!

PROCTOR, *his eyes full of tears:* I can. And there's your first marvel, that I can. You have made your magic now, for now I do think I see some shred of goodness in John Proctor. Not enough to weave a banner with, but white enough to keep it from such dogs. ELIZABETH, *in a burst of terror, rushes to him and weeps against his hand.* Give them no tear! Tears pleasure them! Show honor now, show a stony heart and sink them with it! *He has lifted her, and kisses her now with great passion.*

REBECCA: Let you fear nothing! Another judgment waits us all!

DANFORTH: Hang them high over the town! Who weeps for these, weeps for corruption! *He sweeps out past them.* HERRICK *starts to lead* REBECCA, *who almost collapses, but* PROCTOR *catches her, and she glances up at him apologetically.*

REBECCA: I've had no breakfast.

HERRICK: Come, man.

HERRICK *escorts them out,* HATHORNE *and* CHEEVER *behind them.* ELIZABETH *stands staring at the empty doorway.*

PARRIS, *in deadly fear, to* ELIZABETH: Go to him, Goody Proctor! There is yet time!

From outside a drumroll strikes the air. PARRIS *is startled.* ELIZABETH *jerks about toward the window.*

PARRIS: Go to him! *He rushes out the door, as though to hold back his fate.* Proctor! Proctor!

Again, a short burst of drums.

HALE: Woman, plead with him! *He starts to rush out the door, and then goes back to her.* Woman! It is pride, it is vanity. *She avoids his eyes, and moves to the window. He drops to his knees.* Be his helper!—What profit him to bleed? Shall the dust praise him? Shall the worms declare his truth? Go to him, take his shame away!

ELIZABETH, *supporting herself against collapse, grips the bars of the window, and with a cry:* He have his goodness now. God forbid I take it from him!

The final drumroll crashes, then heightens violently. HALE *weeps in frantic prayer, and the new sun is pouring in upon her face, and the drums rattle like bones in the morning air.*

Your Response

1. What is your opinion of the play? Would you recommend it to a friend? Why or why not?
2. Do you think a tragedy like the Salem witchcraft trials could occur in an American community today? Why or why not?

Recalling

3. (a) Why is Reverend Parris worried when he meets with Hathorne and Danforth at the beginning of the act? (b) What proposal does Parris make to Danforth?
4. Why does Danforth arrange a meeting between John and Elizabeth Proctor?

Interpreting

5. (a) What might have motivated Abigail Williams to leave Salem? (b) How does Parris exhibit his self-centeredness when he relates the news of Abigail's disappearance to Hathorne and Danforth?
6. (a) What motivates Reverend Hale to seek confessions from the condemned prisoners? (b) What is ironic about Hale's comment that he has "come to do the Devil's work"?
7. What do Giles Corey's actions as he faces his death reveal about his character?
8. (a) Why is Elizabeth Proctor unable to offer her husband advice concerning his possible confession? (b) Why does Proctor decide to confess? (c) Why does Danforth respond so enthusiastically to Proctor's confession?
9. (a) Why does Proctor refuse to implicate others in his confession? (b) What factors lead him to retract his confession?

Applying

10. (a) Do you think that John Proctor makes the right decision? Why or why not? (b) If you were asked to write Proctor's epitaph, what would you say?

ANALYZING LITERATURE

Understanding Theme

The **theme** is the central idea or insight about life that a writer hopes to convey in a literary work. While shorter works often have only one theme, longer works are likely to have several themes. *The Crucible,* for example, has many themes.

1. One of the play's themes is that fear and suspicion are infectious and can produce a state of general hysteria that results in the destruction of public order and rationality. How does Miller convey this theme?
2. Another theme is that people who claim to be pious and virtuous may in fact be guilty of hypocrisy. How is this theme evident in the actions of Parris in the fourth act?
3. Another of the play's themes is that it is more noble to die with integrity than it is to compromise one's principles in order to live. How do the actions of John Proctor and Rebecca Nurse support this idea?

CRITICAL THINKING AND READING

Appreciating the Importance of Casting

Plays are generally written to be performed, not read. As a result, a person's response to a play usually depends to a great extent on the actors' portrayal of the various characters. For this reason, the casting of a dramatic production is extremely important.

Putting yourself in the role of casting director for a dramatic production of *The Crucible,* think of the specific actors or types of actors you would choose to play each of the following roles: Reverend Parris, Abigail Williams, Mary Warren, John Proctor, Elizabeth Proctor, Reverend Hale, Judge Hathorne, and Deputy Governor Danforth. Explain each of your choices.

THINKING AND WRITING

Writing About Theme

Choose one theme that you feel is important. Then write a paper in which you explain how this theme is conveyed. Begin by reviewing the play and noting details that relate to the theme. Organize your notes. Then write your essay, using passages from the play for support.

CROSS CURRENTS

Aaron Copland (1900–1990)

Considered America's most versatile, popular, and important composer, Aaron Copland wrote music to express what it feels like to be an American living in America. From his first jazz-influenced compositions of the 1920's to his great western folk ballets and his orchestral pieces echoing complex cityscapes, Copland's music is based on traditional melodies, harmonies, and rhythms that evoke the spirit of America's past and present.

AN AMERICAN COMPOSER

Born Aaron Kaplan to Russian immigrant parents in Brooklyn, New York, Copland decided as a teenager that he wanted to be a composer. Like other aspiring American artists of his generation, he went to Paris to study music. It was abroad—away from America—that Copland realized the importance of his American roots to the kind of music he wished to write. As he later recalled, "The idea that my personal expression in music ought somehow to be related to my own back-home environment took hold of me. The conviction grew inside me that the two things that seemed always to have been so separate in America—music and the life about me—must be made to touch. This desire to make the music I wanted to write come out of the life I had lived in America became a preoccupation of mine. . . . "

AMERICA'S HERITAGE

Copland's early pieces reflect America's jazz age of the twenties with its syncopated rhythms and ambiguous blues sounds. Soon, however, Copland began to search for what he later called a "vernacular music, which, as language, would cause no difficulties to my listeners." Out of this desire to write more simply and directly for the common listener, Copland developed a folksy American style that appealed to a wide audience. His most popular works are the ballets *Billy the Kid* (1938), *Rodeo* (1942), and *Appalachian Spring* (1944). Copland himself described these ballets as having a "musical naturalness" in keeping with America's pastoral heritage as opposed to Europe's classical culture. Based on American folk themes, they incorporate traditional cowboy songs, folk songs, and hymns to convey life on the prairie and in rural nineteenth-century

America. Recalling America's musical heritage, these works celebrate the American pioneer spirit, evoking the courage, struggle, and isolation of America's settlers. The ballets explore themes that are common in American literature. Both *Billy the Kid* and *Rodeo* are about the conflict between society and the outsider, the first a tragic version, the second a comic one. *Appalachian Spring* is about the domestic security and religious faith of a young newlywed pioneer couple.

Copland's music is a veritable course in American history and culture. His *A Lincoln Portrait* for narrator and orchestra, his suite based on John Steinbeck's *The Red Pony*, his musical settings of twelve poems of Emily Dickinson, and his opera *The Tender Land* reflect Copland's deep interest in America's roots. Copland also wrote the scores for several Hollywood films about small-town America, notably *Of Mice and Men* and *Our Town*. In his later works, Copland departed from the simple expressions of pastoral America to write music that catches the complex vigor of city life.

In addition to his contributions to modern music, Copland has devoted himself to the cause of American music and the advancement of American composers. He has also written books to promote wider acceptance of modern music. It is with good reason that Copland has been called the "Dean of American Composers."

YOUR WRITING PROCESS

WRITING A REVIEW

"I think of myself as a stylist, and stylists can become notoriously obsessed with the placing of a comma, the weight of a semicolon."

Truman Capote

That many of the writers in this unit make judgments about contemporary life should not be surprising. We all make judgments every day about people, food, television, music, and of course, the poems and stories we read in English class. Personal taste goes part way toward explaining our likes and dislikes, but is judgment only a matter of taste? Perhaps some programs, foods, and poems are simply better than others in an objective sense. What do you think?

Focus

Assignment: Write a review of one of the selections in this unit for your school newspaper.
Purpose: To evaluate the selection fairly.
Audience: Fellow students.

Prewriting

1. Look at reviews. Newspapers and magazines will provide models of book and performance reviews. Read two or three and make observations about point of view, tone, content, and style. Notice how good reviewers support their opinions by referring specifically to the work they are evaluating.

2. Make your choice. Flip through the unit and think about which selection you feel most strongly. Which one do you remember most clearly? Which one would you recommend to a friend? Which one would you eliminate if you could? About which selection do you have the most to say?

3. List the good and the bad. After you have made a choice, review the selection and list its strengths and weaknesses along with reasons for your judgments. You may find it helpful to use a graphic organizer to record your thoughts.

Student Model

Poem: "The Death of the Ball Turret Gunner" by Randall Jarrell

Strengths		Weaknesses	
	Reasons		*Reasons*
Poem has instant impact		First line is confusing	
	Brief		The image is not concrete
	Sensory images		Not clear what "state" means
	Exciting subject		Not clear what's happening
Powerful last line		Not rhymed	
	Surprising		Would be easier to recall if rhymed
	Shocking		Not as much verbal music

4. Bounce ideas around. After you have done some thinking on your own, discuss the selection with a classmate who is writing on a different topic. Have your classmate question you about the reasons behind your likes and dislikes.

Drafting

1. Use the chart to map your way. If you feel more comfortable knowing where you are headed, refer to your chart as you draft your review. You can discuss strengths and weaknesses alternately, or you can cover either one of these categories completely before you discuss the other.

2. Use quotations to back up your judgments. By occasionally quoting from the selection, you can give readers the flavor of the piece and help support the point you are making. (Don't overuse quotations, however.)

Student Model

"The Death of the Ball Turret Gunner" is effective because Randall Jarrell makes readers feel what it must be like to crouch in a gunner's turret. The second line, for instance, contains two vivid images that appeal to the sense of touch: "And I hunched in its belly till my wet fur froze."

---

3. Remember your audience. You are writing for your school newspaper. Some students have not read the selection you are evaluating. Be sure to include enough information to make those who haven't read the selection comfortable.

Revising and Editing

1. Look for loopholes in your logic. Be on the lookout for fallacies, or errors in reasoning.

2. A few literary terms can go a long way. Win your readers' confidence by replacing vague or fuzzy language with precise terms. For instance, replace awkward phrases like *the general vantage point from which the story is told* with crisp terms like *point of view.*

3. Stick to the text. Make sure every sentence is tied closely to your subject. Don't let yourself stray from the selection you are evaluating.

4. Have a peer editor evaluate your evaluation. Ask someone else to read your draft and answer questions like the following:
- Is it clear whether or not I like this selection?
- Do you think the evaluation is fair? Why or why not?
- Do I offer enough specific evidence to support my judgment?

Options for Publishing
- Submit your review to your school newspaper or literary magazine.
- Read your review aloud to the class and have them comment on it.
- Display your evaluation, with others, in the literature section of your school library, beside a copy of the selection being evaluated.

Reviewing Your Writing Process

1. How did you decide which selection to write about?

2. When you revised your essay, did you find any logical fallacies? Explain.

Writer's Hint

Following are two common fallacies:

Overgeneralization—making a statement that is too broad or too inclusive. Example: Sylvia Plath's "Mirror" is the only contemporary poem that deals with mirrors.

Begging the question—assuming what you want to prove without providing any evidence. Example: As everyone agrees, Lawson Fusao Inada's "Plucking Out a Rhythm" was influenced by jazz.

Roethke teaches

WASHINGTON

OREGON

Chief Joseph born

Chief Joseph's "I Will Fight No More Forever"

MONTANA

IDAHO

Ezra Pound born

WYOMING

NORTH DAKOTA

Sioux Territory

SOUTH DAKOTA

CALIFORNIA

NEVADA

Twain's *Roughing It*

Twain meets Artemus Ward

Amy Tan born

Twain's Calaveras County

Frost born

Steinbeck's "Flight"

UTAH

COLORADO

Katherine Ann Porter lives

NEBRASKA

Willa Cather's stories

KANSAS

G. Brooks born

W. Stafford born

ARIZONA

NEW MEXICO

Navajo Legends

Simon Ortiz lives, writes

OKLAHOMA

Ralph Ellison born

N. Scott Momaday born

Katherine Anne Porter born

Coronado's expedition

TEXAS

McMurtry's *Lonesome Dove*

Lopez's *Arctic Dreams*

London, Melville, Twain write

ALASKA

HAWAII

Literary Map of
the United States

HANDBOOK OF THE WRITING PROCESS
Lesson 1: Prewriting

Someone once remarked that easy writing makes difficult reading. Good writing always takes both time and effort. Understanding that writing a paper requires not one step but many can help you to have more realistic expectations of yourself as a writer. A writer does not simply sit down and produce a final version off the top of his or her head. Instead, a writer completes a number of stages that together make up the process of writing.

1. *Prewriting:* planning the piece of writing
2. *Drafting:* getting ideas down on paper in rough form
3. *Revising:* changing and improving the rough draft
4. *Proofreading:* correcting any errors in spelling or mechanics
5. *Publishing:* letting others read and share the writing

In this lesson you will learn about the steps that make up the prewriting stage.

STEP 1: ANALYZE THE SITUATION

You may feel that you should begin any paper by just sitting down and writing. However, a better way to begin is to think first about the entire context in which you will be working. To do so, ask the following questions about the writing situation:

1. *Topic* (the subject that you will be writing about): What, exactly, is this subject? Can you state it in a sentence? Is your subject too broad or too narrow?
2. *Purpose* (what you want your writing to accomplish): Is your purpose to tell a story? to describe? to explain? to persuade? to enter-tain? Will your writing serve some combination of these purposes?
3. *Audience* (the people for whom you are writing): What are the backgrounds of the people in your audience? Do these people already know a great deal about your topic? Will you have to provide basic background information?
4. *Voice* (the way the writing will sound to the reader): What impression do you want to make on your audience? What tone should the piece of writing have? Should your writing be formal or informal, objective or subjective, emotional or dispassionate?
5. *Content* (the subject and all the information provided about it): How much do you already know about your subject? What will you have to find out? Will you have to do some re-search? If so, what sources can you use? Can you use books, magazines, newspapers, ref-erence works, or interviews with other people? Can you draw on your own memories and experiences?
6. *Form* (the shape the writing will take, including its length and organization): What will the final piece of writing look like? How long will it be? Will it be written in one or more paragraphs? Will it have a distinct introduction, body, and conclusion? What method of organization or organizing principle will you use?

STEP 2: MAKE A PLAN

Ask the questions outlined in Step 1 to clarify the writing task. Answer any questions you can. Then make a plan of action for answering the questions that remain. You may find, for example, that you are unsure about your topic and that you need to do more thinking about it, or you may discover that you need to gather information for your paper and therefore will have to do some research.

STEP 3: GATHER INFORMATION

Ideas and information for writing can come either from within you or from outside sources. If you decide to use outside sources, you can try looking at books, magazines, films, television programs, or reference works of various kinds. You also might try using a computer information service or conducting interviews with people who are knowledgeable about your subject. If you decide to gather information from your own memories and experiences, you might try one of the following techniques:

1. *Analyzing:* Divide your topic into parts, think about these parts, and think about the relationships among the parts and between each part and the whole.
2. *Charting:* Make lists of key ideas or concepts related to your topic. List the parts of the topic, make a pros-and-cons chart, draw a tree diagram, or construct a timeline. Make any kind of list or chart that is relevant to your topic.
3. *Clustering:* Write your topic in the middle of a sheet of paper. Then think about the topic and jot down any related ideas that occur to you. Circle these related ideas and connect them, with lines, to the topic. Then think about the related ideas, jot down other ideas, and connect these lines. Continue in this way until you have filled the paper.
4. *Freewriting:* Without stopping to punctuate or to think about spelling or form, write down everything that comes into your mind as you think about the topic.
5. *Questioning:* Prepare a list of questions that deal with various aspects of your topic. Begin the questions with words such as *who, what, where, when, why,* and *how.*

These techniques also can be used to narrow a topic or to come up with a topic idea in the first place.

STEP 4: ORGANIZE YOUR NOTES

Your next step is to organize the information that you have gathered. If you have used note cards, you might organize them. If not, you might make a rough outline. In either case you need to choose an order in which to present your ideas and information. The order to use is one that grows logically from your materials. The following are some common methods of organization:

1. *Chronological order:* events arranged in order of occurrence in time
2. *Spatial order:* features or items arranged in a physical order or pattern, as from right to left
3. *Degree order:* points arranged from least to most or from most to least according to degree of presence or absence of some property such as complexity, familiarity, frequency, effectiveness, value, or importance

CASE STUDY: PREWRITING

Juanita's English class was studying mass communications. The teacher asked each student to choose one medium of mass communication and to write a paragraph on some topic related to that medium. At first Juanita couldn't think of a topic, so she made the tree diagram (on page 1128) in her notebook.

Juanita studied her diagram and decided that she wanted to write about school newspapers. However, she still needed a more narrow topic, so she did some freewriting and came up with this idea: She would write about the editorial policy of her school newspaper. This would be a good topic to write about because (1) Juanita worked on the school paper and knew something about its editorial policy and (2) because many of the students in Juanita's class probably didn't know what an editorial policy was, much less that the school paper had one.

Juanita then took the following notes:

- Topic: the editorial policy of our school newspaper

- Purpose: to explain the editorial policy to other students

- Audience: other students in my class (all readers of the school paper)

- Voice: relatively formal

- Content: information about the paper's editorial policy (but where am I going to find this information?)

- Form: one paragraph

Looking over her notes, Juanita recognized that she needed to make a plan for gathering information for her paragraph. She decided to interview the editor of the school paper, Colleen Ryan. First Juanita made a list of questions to ask Colleen, and then she arranged an interview. During the interview Juanita took notes, putting quotations around those comments that she got down word for word. Here are some of the notes that Juanita took:

- Does the school paper have an official editorial policy?
  "Yes." Policy is stated in a document called "The Editorial Policy of the Emerson High School Star Reporter"

- Who determines the editorial policy?
  "The editorial policy is determined by the editorial board, which is made up of the editor (that's me), the assistant editor, and the journalism advisor, Ms. Ortega."

- What, precisely, is the official editorial policy?
  Policy statement deals with lots of issues. Mostly, ensures that reporting will be fair, objective, unbiased.
  Also says that policy of paper is to print news of interest to students.
  Spells out what kinds of ads the paper can carry.
  Says who has the final word about what can go into the paper and what can't.

- Who does have the final word?
  Well, I suppose that the final word is Ms. Ortega's. She's the editor-in-chief. But the policy statement also says that the principal has the right to veto publication of any article if she considers doing so to be "in the best interest of the school."

- You mean that the principal can ask you not to print something? Doesn't that violate the freedom of the press?
  "In theory, perhaps it does. However, in practice, the principal never does stop pub-

lication of an article. Besides, every newspaper in the country has an editorial review board that turns thumbs up or thumbs down on particular articles."

• So having the materials in your paper be subject to review doesn't bother you?

No, because the principal is only going to reject an article if it is irresponsible, and "we simply don't allow irresponsible articles to be considered in the first place."

As the interview progressed, Juanita realized that she had found a much more interesting topic to write about than the newspaper's editorial policy. She decided to change her topic to the issue of whether the student press should be completely free or subject to review by the school administration. She knew that this meant changing her statement of purpose as well. Her purpose would be to present both sides of this complicated issue.

ACTIVITIES AND ASSIGNMENTS

A. Answer the following questions about the case study:
1. What method did Juanita use to come up with a topic?
2. When Juanita analyzed the writing situation, what did she realize that she needed to do?
3. How did Juanita change her writing plan during the interview? What other parts of her writing plan will this change affect?

B. Select your own topic, or choose a reading from this book about which you want to comment. Begin work on an informal paragraph by following the prewriting steps discussed in this lesson.

Lesson 2: Drafting and Revising

DRAFTING YOUR PAPER

Once your prewriting is finished, you are ready to begin the drafting stage. *Drafting* is the process of getting ideas down on paper in rough form. When you draft, keep the following points in mind:

1. Choose a drafting style that is right for you. Some people like to write a quick and very rough draft and then go back and rework this draft considerably. Other people prefer to write a slow, careful draft, revising as they go. Choose whichever method works best for you. The quick draft has the advantage of allowing you to get all your ideas down so that they can be manipulated easily. The slow draft has the advantage of reducing the amount of revision time required later on.

2. Bear in mind that your first version is a draft and need not be perfect. If you choose to do a slow, careful draft, don't work so slowly and carefully that you interrupt your stream of thought. Make getting your ideas down the main priority. You can go back and work on the details of sentence structure, organization, spelling, and mechanics during the revision and proofreading stages.

3. Keep your audience, purpose, and voice in mind as you write. As you work, try not to stray too far from your original plan. If you find that the original plan isn't workable, go back to the prewriting stage and make a new plan.

4. As you draft, keep yourself open to new ideas. Work from your prewriting notes and your rough outline. However, remember that some of the best ideas occur while people are actually writing. If a new idea occurs to you and it is a good one, then use it. Don't forget that you can revise your prewriting plan at any time if you feel the need to do so.

CHECKLIST FOR REVISION

Topic and Purpose
- [ ] Is my main idea clear?
- [ ] Does the writing achieve its purpose?

Content and Development
- [ ] Have I developed the main idea completely?
- [ ] Have I provided examples or details that support the statements I have made?
- [ ] Are my sources of information unbiased, up-to-date, and authoritative?
- [ ] Have I avoided including unnecessary or unrelated ideas?

Form
- [ ] Have I followed a logical method of organization?
- [ ] Have I used transitions to make the connections between ideas clear?
- [ ] Does the writing have a clear introduction, body, and conclusion?

Audience
- [ ] Will my audience understand what I have said?
- [ ] Will my audience find the writing interesting?
- [ ] Will my audience respond in the way I intend?

Voice and Word Choice
- [ ] Does the writing convey the impression I intended it to convey?
- [ ] Is my language appropriate?
- [ ] Have I avoided vague, undefined terms?
- [ ] Have I used vivid, specific nouns, verbs, and adjectives?
- [ ] Have I avoided jargon?
- [ ] Have I avoided clichés, slang, euphemisms, and gobbledygook except for humorous effect?

5. Allow yourself enough time to write. Do not try to do all your writing at the last minute. Give

yourself enough time to write a draft and then to revise and proofread it.

6. Write as many drafts as you need to write. One nice thing about writing is that you can do it over and over until you have a final product you are satisfied with.

REVISING YOUR DRAFT

Revising is the process of reworking a written draft to enhance its content and organization. After you finish your draft, use the checklist on the preceding page to identify ways to improve your paper.

CASE STUDY: DRAFTING AND REVISING

As you will recall from the preceding lesson, Juanita had decided to write a paper presenting two sides of a complicated issue: whether the student press should or should not be subject to review by academic administrators. As Juanita thought about this issue, she decided that she had firm personal opinions about it. She therefore decided to change her topic once again: She would write about why she believed that administrators should have the right to review articles before they appear in the student press.

Juanita wrote a first draft of her paper and then revised it. Here is her draft with the revisions that she made:

Recently,
~~Two days ago~~ I interviewed the editor of our   Colleen Ryan,

school newspaper, The Emerson High School

During our conversation   according to the
Ms. Ryan told me   paper's editorial
Star Reporter. ~~She said~~ that the Principal ~~had~~   policy,   has

the right to review any articles before they

could be printed in the paper. Initially I was

inscensed by
~~mad about~~ this ~~.~~ Because it seemed to violate

---

the students right to free press. As I thought   a   However,

about the issue I realised that their were good

the review policy. First,
reasons for ~~this.~~ High school journalists are not

experienced. They need guidance regarding

such matters as what can be published in a

newspaper and what cannot. No paper can

sort of material.   for example,
print just any ~~kind of stuff~~. The law says that

papers can be held accountable for ~~anything~~ .
materials with

ing
~~that they~~ (print ~~that is~~ libelous) The review policy
malice   a forethought ⊙

ensures that articles that violate the law will not
in the school paper. Second,
be published. All newspapers, including

professional ones, have review policies. The

Editor-in-Chief, and sometimes the Publisher,

ies ⊙
can veto publication of certain story. In the

case of the school paper, the journalism

sponser acts as the editor in chief, and the

Principal acts as the Publisher. They therefore

have the same right to accept or reject certain

articles as would thier counterparts in the world

of proffessional print journalism. Some

students might object to working under the

constraints of the review policy. However, these

students need to realise that they will be

working under the same constraints. When
become   ists.
they ~~enter the world~~ of proffessional journalism.

ACTIVITIES AND ASSIGNMENTS

A. Answer the following questions about the case study:

1. Why did Juanita change the phrase "Two days ago" to the word "Recently"?
2. What transitions did Juanita add to show the logical connections between her ideas?
3. In what places did Juanita replace informal language with language that is more formal?
4. What sentence fragments did Juanita correct? How did she correct these fragments?
5. What information did Juanita add to make her statements clearer?
6. What spelling, punctuation, and capitalization errors did Juanita not correct during revision? During what stage of the writing process should such errors be corrected?

B. Use your notes and outlines from the preceding lesson to draft and revise a paragraph. Follow the procedures described in this lesson.

Lesson 3: Proofreading and Publishing

USING EDITORIAL SYMBOLS

After you have revised your draft, you are ready to begin proofreading. *Proofreading* is the process of checking for errors in spelling, grammar, mechanics, and manuscript form. As you proofread, use the editorial symbols shown on the next page to mark corrections on your draft.

USING A PROOFREADING CHECKLIST

Try to allow time between revising and proofreading. Doing so will make it easier for you to notice minor errors that you might otherwise miss. Proofread carefully, since just a few minor mistakes can distract a reader from the many good ideas in your writing. Use the checklist at right to guide your proofreading.

When you have a question about some rule of spelling, grammar, mechanics, or manuscript form, check the rule in a dictionary, in a writing textbook, or in a grammar book. As you proofread, bear in mind the mistakes that you have made on papers in the past and try to avoid repeating them. After you proofread, make a neat final copy of your paper and check this copy as well.

PUBLISHING, OR SHARING, YOUR WORK

The neat final copy of your paper is ready for an audience. Most school papers are read by only your teacher, but you or your class can find other ways to share your writing. Here are some suggestions:

1. Share your writing with friends, parents, and other relatives.
2. Mail a copy of a paper you like to grandparents or to other relatives.
3. Read your paper aloud to a discussion group, to the whole class, or to a different class.
4. Trade papers with other students who sit nearby or who work with you on projects or in groups.
5. Create a publication that contains writing by all the students in your class.
6. Make your own "book" of papers that you have written during the year. Share this book with classmates, with friends, or with relatives.

CHECKLIST FOR PROOFREADING

Grammar and Usage
☐ Are all my sentences complete? That is, have I avoided sentence fragments?
☐ Do all my sentences express just one complete thought? That is, have I avoided run-on sentences?
☐ Do my verbs agree with their subjects?
☐ Did I use all the words in my paper correctly? Am I sure the meaning and connotation of each word fits the writing?
☐ Does each pronoun clearly refer to something?
☐ Have I used adjectives and adverbs correctly?

Spelling
☐ Is every word correctly spelled?
☐ Have I double-checked the spelling of proper nouns?

Punctuation
☐ Does each sentence end with a punctuation mark?
☐ Have I used commas, semicolons, colons, hyphens, dashes, parentheses, quotation marks, and apostrophes correctly?

Capitalization
☐ Have I eliminated unnecessary capital letters?
☐ Have I capitalized all words that need capital letters?

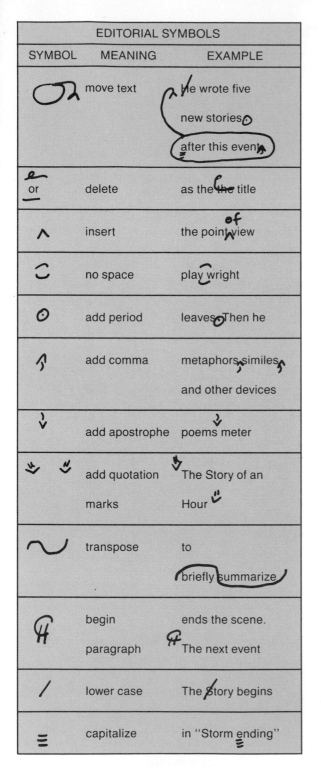

EDITORIAL SYMBOLS		
SYMBOL	MEANING	EXAMPLE
	move text	He wrote five new stories after this event
or	delete	as the the title
∧	insert	the point of view
⌒	no space	play wright
⊙	add period	leaves Then he
⌄	add comma	metaphors similes and other devices
⌄	add apostrophe	poems meter
	add quotation marks	The Story of an Hour
∼	transpose	to briefly summarize
ℋ	begin paragraph	ends the scene. The next event
/	lower case	The Story begins
≡	capitalize	in "Storm ending"

7. Submit some of your writing to the school literary magazine.
8. Start a school literary magazine.
9. Submit your writing to your school newspaper, to your community newspaper, or to another publication that prints works by young writers.
10. Enter your work in an essay or creative writing contest.

CASE STUDY: PROOFREADING AND PUBLISHING

Juanita used the Checklist for Proofreading to find and correct the errors that remained in her rough draft. Here is Juanita's proofread paragraph:

Recently I interviewed Colleen Ryan, the editor of our school newspaper, The Emerson High School Star Reporter. During our conversation Ms. Ryan told me that according to the paper's editorial policy, the principal has the right to review any articles before they are printed in the paper. Initially I was incensed by this policy because it seemed to violate the students' right to a free press. However, as I thought about the issue, I realized that there were good reasons for the review policy. First, high-school journalists are not experienced. They need guidance regarding such matters as what can be published in a newspaper and what cannot. No paper can print just any sort of material.

The law says, for example, that papers can be held accountable for printing libelous materials with malice aforethought. The review policy ensures that articles that violate the law will not be published in the school paper. Second, all newspapers, including professional ones, have review policies. The Editor-in-Chief, and sometimes the Publisher, can veto publication of certain stories. In the case of the school paper, the journalism sponsor acts as the editor-in-chief, and the Principal acts as the Publisher. They therefore have the same right to accept or reject certain articles as would their counterparts in the world of proffessional print journalism. Some students might object to working under the constraints of the review policy. However, these students need to realize that when they become proffessional journalists, they will be working under the same constraints.

After proofreading her paper, Juanita made a clean final copy. Then she checked this copy once again for errors and shared the paper with classmates in a small-group discussion. She and her classmates had a lively debate about the issue.

ACTIVITIES AND ASSIGNMENTS

A. Answer the following questions about the case study:
1. What errors did Juanita correct in spelling, punctuation, capitalization, and manuscript form?
2. Are there any changes that Juanita should have made in her draft that she didn't make?

B. Proofread and share the paragraph that you drafted in the last lesson. Follow these steps:
1. Check your revised draft for errors, using the Checklist for Proofreading, on page 1133. Use standard editorial symbols to make any necessary corrections.
2. Make a neat final copy of your paragraph. Check this copy carefully to make sure you have added all your final changes and have not made mistakes in copying.
3. Share your draft with your teacher and with your classmates.

HANDBOOK OF GRAMMAR AND REVISING STRATEGIES

Strategies for Revising Problems in Grammar and Standard Usage ... 1137

This section offers practical tips for revising your writing. Each topic includes an overall GUIDE FOR REVISING and one or more revising strategies. Strategies are illustrated by a first draft, a suggested revision, and sometimes a model sentence from a professional writer featured in *Prentice Hall Literature, The American Experience.* The GUIDES FOR REVISING address the following issues:

Problems of Sentence Structure 1137
- ■ Run-on Sentences
- ■ Fragments

Problems of Clarity and Coherence 1138
- ■ Effective Transition
- ■ Revising for Pronoun-Antecedent Agreement
- ■ Dangling Modifiers
- ■ Misplaced Modifiers

Problems of Consistency 1141
- ■ Subject-Verb Agreement
- ■ Confusion of Adjectives and Adverbs
- ■ Inconsistencies in Verb Tense
- ■ Faulty Parallelism

Problems With Incorrect Words or Phrases 1144
- ■ Nonstandard Pronoun Cases
- ■ Double Negatives

Problems of Readability 1145
- ■ Sentence Variety
- ■ Overuse of Passive Voice

Problems of Conciseness 1146
- ■ Deadwood and Wordy Phrases
- ■ Redundancy
- ■ Unnecessary Intensifiers
- ■ Vague or Obvious Statements

Summary of Grammar 1148

Summary of Capitalization and Punctuation 1150

Glossary of Common Usage 1152

STRATEGIES FOR REVISING PROBLEMS IN GRAMMAR AND STANDARD USAGE
Problems of Sentence Structure

■ Run-on Sentences

GUIDE FOR REVISING: A run-on sentence results when two or more independent clauses are not separated by punctuation or a coordinating conjunction. A run-on sentence also occurs when only a comma is used to join two or more independent clauses.

Strategy 1: Form two sentences by using a period to separate independent clauses.

First Draft E. B. White wrote weekly essays for the *New Yorker in* these short pieces he explored social and political themes, often with a dash of dry humor.

Revision E. B. White wrote weekly essays for the *New Yorker.* In these short pieces, he explored social and political themes, often with a dash of dry humor.

Strategy 2: Separate independent clauses with a semicolon.

First Draft The narrator in Poe's story tries to alleviate Usher's profound melancholy, the two friends paint and read together.

Revision The narrator in Poe's story tries to alleviate Usher's profound melancholy; the two friends paint and read together.

Strategy 3: Use a comma and a coordinating conjunction (*and, but, or, for, yet, so*) to join the two sentences.

First Draft Ezra Pound was born in Idaho he spent most of his adult life in Europe.

Revision Ezra Pound was born in Idaho, but he spent most of his adult life in Europe.

■ Fragments

GUIDE FOR REVISING: A fragment is a group of words that does not express a complete thought. Although a fragment may begin with a capital letter and end with a period, it is only part of a sentence because it lacks a subject, a verb, or both.

Strategy 1:	**Add the necessary sentence parts to make a phrase fragment into a complete sentence with a subject and verb.**
First Draft	The Fireside Poets focused on popular themes. Used traditional forms and techniques in most of their work.
Revision	The Fireside Poets focused on popular themes. They used traditional forms and techniques in most of their work.

Strategy 2:	**Always check to see that long series of words are in fact complete sentences. If necessary, add a subject, verb, or both.**
First Draft	In N. Scott Momaday's collection of personal anecdotes and retellings of Kiowa myths and legends, *The Way to Rainy Mountain* (1969).
Revision	In N. Scott Momaday's collection of personal anecdotes and retellings of Kiowa myths and legends, *The Way to Rainy Mountain* (1969), Momaday offers a sensitive view of Native American cultural traditions.

Problems of Clarity and Coherence

■ Effective Transitions

GUIDE FOR REVISING: Transitions are words or phrases that help the reader by signaling connections between words, sentences, and paragraphs.

Strategy 1:	**Use transitions to indicate chronological order. Transitions may be used to indicate frequency, duration, or a particular time.**
First Draft	Mrs. Mallard heard the news of her husband's death and burst into tears.
Revision	When Mrs. Mallard heard the news of her husband's death, she burst into tears.
Model From Literature	During the whole of a dull, dark, and soundless day in the autumn of the year, when the clouds hung oppressively low in the heavens, I had been passing alone, on horseback, through a singularly dreary tract of country, and at length found myself, as the shades of evening drew on, within view of the melancholy House of Usher. —*Poe, p. 194*

Strategy 2:	**Use transitions to indicate spatial relationships. Transitions may be used to show closeness, distance, or direction.**
First Draft	In his poem Longfellow describes the arms in the Arsenal.
Revision	At the opening of his poem, Longfellow describes the arms stacked from floor to ceiling inside the Arsenal.
Model From Literature	Deep, deep the road went down between the high green-colored banks. Overhead the live oaks met, and it was as dark as a cave. —*Welty, p. 624*

Strategy 3:	**Use transitions to indicate comparison or contrast, or cause and effect.**
First Draft	Barry Lopez's vivid imagery gives his writing an almost poetic quality; the scientific details in his work are scrupulously accurate.
Revision	Barry Lopez's vivid imagery gives his writing an almost poetic quality; the scientific details in his work, on the other hand, are scrupulously accurate.
Model From Literature	'Tis the business of little minds to shrink; but he whose heart is firm, and whose conscience approves his conduct, will pursue his principles unto death. —*Paine, p. 124*

■ Revising for Pronoun-Antecedent Agreement

GUIDE FOR REVISING: Personal pronouns must agree with their antecedents in number (singular or plural), person (first, second, or third), and gender (masculine, feminine, or neuter).

Strategy 1:	**Make sure that a pronoun used to stand for a noun that appears somewhere else in the sentence agrees in number (singular or plural) with that noun.**
First Draft	Athletes' experiences and the world of sports greatly interest John Updike, and it often appears in his novels and stories.
Revision	Athletes' experiences and the world of sports greatly interest John Updike, and they often appear in his novels and stories.

Strategy 2:	**When dealing with pronoun-antecedent agreement, take care not to shift either person or gender.**
First Draft	In John Steinbeck's story "Flight," Pepe flees from his pursuers in a setting that forces you to become more and more instinctive and animal-like.

Revision	In John Steinbeck's story "Flight," Pepe flees from `his` pursuers in a setting that forces `him` to become more and more instinctive and animal-like.

Strategy 3:	**(a) When you use a pronoun to stand for two or more nouns joined by *or* or *nor,* make sure that the pronoun is singular. Use a plural personal pronoun if any part of a compound antecedent joined by *or* or *nor* is plural.**
First Draft	`Neither T. S. Eliot nor Ezra Pound` seems to have regretted `their` decision to emigrate from America at an early age.
Revision	`Neither T. S. Eliot nor Ezra Pound` seems to have regretted `his` decision to emigrate from America at an early age.
	(b) When you use a pronoun to stand for two or more nouns joined by *and,* make sure that it is plural.
First Draft	The Delaware and the Navajo narrated `its` creation stories in myths.
Revision	The Delaware and the Navajo narrated `their` creation stories in myths.

Strategy 4:	**When you use a personal pronoun to stand for a singular indefinite pronoun, make sure that it is also singular. Use a plural personal pronoun when the antecedent is a plural indefinite pronoun.**
First Draft	Ezra Pound and William Carlos Williams were close friends; `each` used imagery in a distinctive way in `their` poetry.
Revision	Ezra Pound and William Carlos Williams were close friends; `each` used imagery in a distinctive way in `his` poetry.

Strategy 5:	**Avoid using a reflexive pronoun when its antecedent is not clearly stated and when it can be replaced by a personal pronoun.**
First Draft	Ben read Wallace Stevens's "Anecdote of the Jar" aloud to Maria and `myself.`
Revision	Ben read Wallace Stevens's "Anecdote of the Jar" aloud to Maria and `me.`

■ Dangling Modifiers

GUIDE FOR REVISING: A dangling phrase or clause either seems to modify the wrong word or no word at all, because the word it should logically modify has been omitted from the sentence.

Strategy:	**Fix a participial phrase by adding the word that the phrase should modify, usually right after or before the phrase.**
First Draft	Having lived with gusto to the age of ninety-six, many younger people failed to appreciate life.
Revision	Having lived with gusto to the age of ninety-six, Lucinda Matlock thought that many younger people failed to appreciate life.

■ Misplaced Modifiers

GUIDE FOR REVISING: A modifier placed too far away from the word it modifies is called a misplaced modifier. Misplaced modifiers may seem to modify the wrong word in a sentence. Always place a modifier as close as possible to the word it modifies.

Strategy:	**Move the modifying word, phrase, or clause closer to the word it should logically modify.**
First Draft	Destined for those sinners who fail to repent, Jonathan Edwards vividly describes the horrible torments.
Revision	Jonathan Edwards vividly describes the horrible torments destined for those sinners who fail to repent.

Problems of Consistency

■ Subject-Verb Agreement

GUIDE FOR REVISING: Subject and verb must agree in number. A singular subject needs a singular verb, and a plural subject needs a plural verb.

Strategy 1:	**If the subject is singular (it names only one thing), then the verb must also be singular. If the subject is plural (it names two or more things), then the verb must be plural.**
First Draft	An allegory are a tale with two or more levels of meaning.
Revision	An allegory is a tale with two or more levels of meaning.

Strategy 2:	**A phrase or clause that interrupts a subject and its verb does not affect subject-verb agreement.**
First Draft	The attitudes of the hunter, the nurse, and the attendant toward Phoenix Jackson is condescending.
Revision	The attitudes of the hunter, the nurse, and the attendant toward Phoenix Jackson are condescending.

Strategy 3:	**The antecedent of a relative pronoun determines its agreement with the verb.**
First Draft	Wallace Stevens and Robert Lowell are among the poets who has had the most significant impact on modern verse.
Revision	Wallace Stevens and Robert Lowell are among the poets who have had the most significant impact on modern verse.

Strategy 4:	**Use a singular verb with two or more singular subjects joined by *or* or *nor*. When singular and plural subjects are joined by *or* or *nor*, the verb must agree with the subject closest to it.**
First Draft	Many contemporary writers feel that neither Realism nor Romanticism fully capture the complexity of human experience.
Revision	Many contemporary writers feel that neither Realism nor Romanticism fully captures the complexity of human experience.

Strategy 5:	**A compound subject joined by *and* is usually plural and requires a plural verb.**
First Draft	Humor and brevity is characteristic of a successful anecdote.
Revision	Humor and brevity are characteristic of a successful anecdote.

Strategy 6:	**A collective noun takes a singular verb when the group it names acts as a unit. It takes a plural verb when the group act as individuals with different points of view.**
First Draft	From their consistently insensitive behavior, it is clear that the hospital staff in Eudora Welty's "A Worn Path," is unable to treat Phoenix Jackson as a person worthy of respect.
Revision	From their consistently insensitive behavior, it is clear that the hospital staff in Eudora Welty's "A Worn Path" are unable to treat Phoenix Jackson as a person worthy of respect.

■ Confusion of Adjectives and Adverbs

GUIDE FOR REVISING: Adjectives modify nouns and pronouns. Adverbs modify verbs, adjectives, or other adverbs; they may also modify phrases and clauses.

Strategy:	**Be careful to make the correct use of troublesome adjective and adverb pairs such as *bad/badly*, *fewer/less*, and *good/well*.**
First Draft	From Abigail Adams's "Letter to Her Daughter," we can conclude that the White House was rather bad furnished in 1800.

Revision   From Abigail Adams's "Letter to Her Daughter," we can conclude that the White House was rather badly furnished in 1800.

GUIDE FOR REVISING: Verb tenses should not shift unnecessarily from sentence to sentence or within a single sentence.

Strategy 1:   **Be sure that the main verbs in a single sentence or in a group of related sentences are in the same tense.**

First Draft   Before the man in Jack London's "To Build a Fire" sets out on his journey, an old-timer from Sulphur Creek warned him of the bitterly cold temperatures.

Revision   Before the man in Jack London's "To Build a Fire" sets out on his journey, an old-timer from Sulphur Creek warns him of the bitterly cold temperatures.

Strategy 2:   **In sentences describing two actions that occurred at different times in the past, the past perfect tense is used for the earlier action.**

First Draft   By the time Thoreau started his experiment at Walden Pond in 1845, Emerson wrote a number of important Transcendentalist works.

Revision   By the time Thoreau started his experiment at Walden Pond in 1845, Emerson had written a number of important Transcendentalist works.

■ **Faulty Parallelism**

GUIDE FOR REVISING: Parallel grammatical structures can be two or more words of the same part of speech, two or more phrases of the same type, or two or more clauses of the same type. Correct a sentence containing faulty parallelism by rewording it so that each parallel idea is expressed in the same grammatical structure.

Strategy 1:   **Check to see that the words, phrases, and clauses in a series are parallel.**

First Draft   In his speech Patrick Henry criticizes opposing arguments, denounces British government, and is in favor of the cause of liberty.

Revision	In his speech Patrick Henry criticizes opposing arguments, denounces British government, and favors the cause of liberty.

Strategy 2:	**Do not write a comparison that unnecessarily links different structures. Reword the comparison so that its elements are parallel.**
First Draft	Foreshadowing and the suspenseful are important elements in Nathaniel Hawthorne's fiction.
Revision	Foreshadowing and suspense are important elements in Nathaniel Hawthorne's fiction.

Problems With Incorrect Words or Phrases

■ Nonstandard Pronoun Cases

GUIDE FOR REVISING: Use the nominative case of a personal pronoun for the subject of a sentence, for a predicate nominative, and for the pronoun in a nominative absolute. Use the objective case for the object of any verb or preposition, or for the subject of an infinitive.

Strategy 1:	**Be sure to identify the case of a personal pronoun correctly when the pronoun is part of a compound construction. To confirm the cases of pronouns, try rewording the sentence mentally.**
First Draft	April's report gave Sally and I some helpful insights into Emily Dickinson's poetry.
Revision	April's report gave Sally and me some helpful insights into Emily Dickinson's poetry.

Strategy 2:	**The possessive case is also regularly used when a pronoun precedes a gerund.**
First Draft	Although the old woman distrusts Mr. Shiftlet at first, she seems to regard him repairing the car as a sign of his good faith.
Revision	Although the old woman distrusts Mr. Shiftlet at first, she seems to regard his repairing the car as a sign of his good faith.
Model From Literature	I shouldn't mind his bettering himself, If that was what it was. —*Frost, p. 770*

Strategy 3:	In elliptical clauses with *than* or *as,* use the form of the pronoun that you would use if the clause were fully stated.
First Draft	Diana has read more of the Fireside Poets than me.
Revision	Diana has read more of the Fireside poets than I.

■ Double Negatives

GUIDE FOR REVISING: A double negative is the use of two or more negative words in one clause to express a negative meaning.

Strategy:	Use only one negative word to give a clause or sentence a negative meaning.
First Draft	Before this year I had never read no poetry by Elizabeth Bishop.
Revision	Before this year I had never read any poetry by Elizabeth Bishop.

Problems of Readability

■ Sentence Variety

GUIDE FOR REVISING: Varying the length and structure of your sentences will help you to hold your readers' attention.

Strategy 1:	Combine short, related sentences by using compound subjects or verbs; phrases; or compound, complex, or compound-complex sentences.
First Draft	After 1836 Longfellow lived in Cambridge, Massachusetts. He lived near Harvard College. He was a professor at Harvard. He taught French and Spanish there for eighteen years.
Revision	After 1836 Longfellow lived in Cambridge, Massachusetts, near Harvard College, where he was a professor of French and Spanish for eighteen years.

Strategy 2:	Simplify rambling sentences by separating them into simpler sentences or by regrouping ideas.
First Draft	Edward Taylor first worked as a teacher in England, but then persecution of him for his Puritan beliefs brought this career to an abrupt end and forced him to emigrate, so he came to America, graduated from Harvard, and then served as a minister and physician in the town of Westfield, Massachusetts, where he spent the rest of his life.
Revision	When he was persecuted for his Puritan beliefs, Edward Taylor's career as a teacher in England came to an abrupt end.

Emigrating to America, he attended Harvard. He then spent the rest of his life in Westfield, Massachusetts, where he served as a minister and physician.

Strategy 3:	**Avoid a series of monotonous sentence openers or a series of sentences that overuse any one particular sentence structure. Vary the sentence openers in a passage.**
First Draft	The speaker in McKay's poem walks the streets of New York. He sees tropical fruits in the shop windows. He thinks of home. He becomes sad. Then he bows his head. A wave of longing overcomes him. He weeps bitterly.
Revision	As the speaker in McKay's poem walks the streets of New York, he sees tropical fruits in the shop windows. Reminded of home, he becomes sad. Then, after a wave of longing overcomes him, he bows his head, weeping bitterly.

■ Overuse of Passive Voice

GUIDE FOR REVISING: Strengthen your writing by using the active voice whenever possible. Passive verbs usually force the reader to wait until the end of the sentence to identify the doer of the action.

Strategy:	**Change passive verbs to active verbs whenever possible.**
First Draft	In Frost's "Out, Out—," wood is being cut by the boy when he is fatally injured by the saw.
Revision	In Frost's "Out, Out—," the boy is cutting wood when the saw fatally injures him.

Problems of Conciseness

■ Deadwood and Wordy Phrases

GUIDE FOR REVISING: Deadwood, or unnecessary words, can distract readers and weaken your writing. Eliminate empty or hedging words whenever you can. Also cut any additional words that create long phrases and clauses where shorter expressions might be stronger.

Strategy:	**Eliminate all nonessential words from your sentences to make them concise.**
First Draft	"The Red Wheelbarrow" exemplifies in a clear fashion William Carlos Williams's approach to the making of poetry.
Revision	"The Red Wheelbarrow" is a clear example of William Carlos Williams's approach to poetry.

■ Redundancy

GUIDE FOR REVISING: Redundancy is the unnecessary repetition of an idea. Redundancy makes writing heavy and dull.

Strategy:	**Eliminate redundant words, phrases, and clauses.**

First Draft The title of Robert Frost's poem "Out, Out—" is an oblique, indirect allusion to the final, concluding lines of a famous speech by Macbeth.

Revision The title of Robert Frost's poem "Out, Out—" is an allusion to the concluding lines of a famous speech by Macbeth.

■ Unnecessary Intensifiers

GUIDE FOR REVISING: Intensifiers such as *really, very, truly,* and *of course* should be used to strengthen statements. Overuse of these words may weaken a sentence.

Strategy:	**Eliminate any unnecessary intensifiers.**

First Draft Several scenes in Arthur Miller's *The Crucible* really offer a truly penetrating critique of religious hypocrisy.

Revision Several scenes in Arthur Miller's *The Crucible* offer a penetrating critique of religious hypocrisy.

■ Vague or Obvious Statements

GUIDE FOR REVISING: Vague statements frustrate or confuse readers by not making the meaning clear. Obvious statements may irritate readers by conveying a condescending impression.

Strategy:	**Make your sentences as clear and informative as possible by eliminating vague statements. Do not use obvious statements that "talk down" to the reader.**

First Draft The way Malamud describes things in his story is interesting.

Revision Malamud's use of setting in "The First Seven Years" helps the reader to visualize the predicaments of Feld, Sobel, and Miriam.

First Draft The setting for most of William Faulkner's novels and stories is Yoknapatawpha, a fictional county in Mississippi, which is a state in the Deep South.

Revision The setting for most of William Faulkner's novels and stories is Yoknapatawpha, a fictional county in Mississippi.

SUMMARY OF GRAMMAR

Nouns   A **noun** names a person, place, or thing.

A **common noun** names any one of a class of people, places, or things. A **proper noun** names a specific person, place, or thing.

Common nouns	Proper nouns
essayist	Joan Didion, E. B. White
city	Boston, New Orleans

Pronouns   **Pronouns** are words that stand for nouns or for words that take the place of nouns.

Personal pronouns refer to (1) the person speaking, (2) the person spoken to, or (3) the person, place, or thing spoken about.

	Singular	Plural
First Person	I, me, my, mine	we, us, our ours
Second Person	you, your, yours	you, your, yours
Third Person	he, him, his, she, her, hers	they, them, their, theirs

A **reflexive pronoun** ends in -self or -selves and adds information to a sentence by pointing back to a noun or pronoun near the beginning of the sentence.
> You resist telling *yourself* you are lost.
> —Oates, p. 862

An **intensive pronoun** ends in -self or -selves and simply adds emphasis to a noun or pronoun in the same sentence.
> A man can distinguish *himself* between temper and principle, . . .   —Paine, p. 122

Demonstrative pronouns direct attention to specific people, places, or things.
> *this* hat   *these* coats   *that* frame

A **relative pronoun** begins a subordinate clause and connects it to another idea in the sentence.
> Be beautiful, noble, like the antique ant,
> *Who* bore the storms as he bore the sun, . . .
> —Villa, p. 984
> I made a little book, in *which* I allotted a page for each of the virtues.   —Franklin, p. 104

Indefinite pronouns refer to people, places, or things, often without specifying which ones.
> *None* are green,
> Or purple with green rings, . . .
> —Stevens, p. 716

Verbs   A **verb** is a word or group of words that expresses time while showing an action, a condition, or the fact that something exists.

An **action verb** is a verb that tells what action someone or something is performing.
> I *found* the fresh Rhodora in the woods, . . .
> —Emerson, p. 249

A **linking verb** is a verb that connects its subject with a word generally found near the end of the sentence. All linking verbs are intransitive.
> Her name *was* Phoenix Jackson.   —Welty, p. 622

Helping verbs are verbs that can be added to another verb to make a single verb phrase.
> Sir, we *have done* everything that *could be done* to avert the storm which *is* now *coming* on.
> —Henry, p. 118

Adjectives   An **adjective** is a word used to describe a noun or pronoun or to give a noun or pronoun a more specific meaning. Adjectives answer these questions:

What kind?	*green* leaf, *tall* chimney
Which one?	*this* clock, *those* pictures
How many?	*six* days, *several* concerts
How much?	*more* effort, *enough* applause

The articles *the, a,* and *an* are adjectives. *An* is used before a word beginning with a vowel sound.

A noun may sometimes be used as an adjective.

Adverbs   An **adverb** is a word that modifies a verb, an adjective, or another adverb. Adverbs answer the questions *Where? When? In what manner? To what extent?*
> She came *yesterday.* (modifies verb *came*)
> Please sit *here.* (modifies verb *sit*)
> We departed *immediately.* (modifies verb *departed*)
> They were *completely* unaware. (modifies adjective *unaware*)
> It rained rather *often.* (modifies adverb *often*)

Prepositions   A **preposition** is a word that relates a noun or pronoun that appears with it to another word in the sentence. Prepositions are almost always followed by nouns or pronouns.
> *aboard* the train   *among* us   *below* our plane
> *into* view   *toward* them   *until* dark

Conjunctions   A **conjunction** is a word used to connect other words or groups of words.

Coordinating conjunctions connect similar kinds or groups of words.
> dogs *and* cats   friendly *but* dignified

Correlative conjunctions are used in pairs to connect similar words or groups of words.

both Prem and Sanjay   neither she nor I

Subordinating conjunctions connect two complete ideas by placing one idea below the other in rank or importance.

Even before they'd noticed anything wrong, they'd
    wondered at his jittery, jerky catnaps . . .
                                        —Tyler, p. 874

Conjunctive adverbs are adverbs used as conjunctions to connect complete ideas.

Flannery O'Connor portrayed social outcasts in an
    unsentimental way; nevertheless, her underlying
    sympathy for their suffering is evident.

Interjections   An **interjection** is a word that expresses feeling or emotion and functions independently of a sentence.

Ah, awful weight!   —Millay, p. 748

Subject-Verb Agreement   To make a subject and verb agree, make sure that both are singular or both are plural.

All of it, all that the land is and evokes, its actual
    meaning as well as its metaphorical reverberation,
    was and is understood differently.
                                        —Lopez, p. 942

Phrases   A **phrase** is a group of words, without a subject and verb, that functions in a sentence as one part of speech.

A **prepositional phrase** is a group of words that includes a preposition and a noun or pronoun.

beyond the horizon   inside the corral
in front of the store   throughout his life

An **adjective phrase** is a prepositional phrase that modifies a noun or pronoun by telling what kind or which one.

And the concrete of this city
the oil wind, the blazing windows,
the shrieks of automation cannot,
truly cannot, answer for that hunger . . .
                                        —Ortiz, p. 1020

An **adverb phrase** is a prepositional phrase that modifies a verb, an adjective, or an adverb by pointing out where, when, in what manner, or to what extent.

Along creek washouts, in the western Arctic especially, you might stumble on a mammoth tusk.
                                        —Lopez, p. 939

An **appositive phrase** is a noun or pronoun with modifiers, placed next to a noun or pronoun to add information and details.

I drop to Hawthorne, the customs officer,
    measuring coal and mostly trying to keep
    warm— . . .   —Lowell, p. 975

A **participial phrase** is a participle that is modified by an adjective or adverb phrase or that has a complement. The entire phrase acts as an adjective.

Two or three men, conversing earnestly together,
    ceased as he approached, . . .   —Harte, p. 452

A **nominative absolute** is a noun or pronoun followed by a participle or participial phrase that functions independently of the rest of the sentence.

The preparations being complete, the two private
    soldiers stepped aside and each drew away the
    plank upon which he had been standing.
                                        —Bierce, p. 465

An **infinitive phrase** is an infinitive with modifiers, complements, or a subject, all acting together as a single part of speech.

Some proposed to evade the order by changing the
    name of the paper; . . .   —Franklin, p. 109

wholly to be a fool
while spring is in the air
my blood approves . . .   —Cummings, p. 760

Clauses   A **clause** is a group of words with its own subject and verb.

An **independent clause** can stand by itself as a complete sentence. A **subordinate clause** cannot stand by itself as a complete sentence; it can only be part of a sentence.

An **adjective clause** is a subordinate clause that modifies a noun or pronoun by telling what kind or which one.

The sad seamstress
who stays with us this month
is small and thin and bitter.   —Bishop, p. 970

Subordinate adverb clauses modify verbs, adjectives, adverbs, or verbals by telling where, when, in what manner, to what extent, under what condition, or why.

Whenever Richard Cory went down town,
We people on the pavement looked at him.
                                        —Robinson, p. 542

A **noun clause** is a subordinate clause that acts as a noun.

What reverses may attend the remainder is in the
    hand of Providence; . . .   —Franklin, p. 18

SUMMARY OF CAPITALIZATION AND PUNCTUATION

CAPITALIZATION

Capitalize the first word in sentences, interjections, and incomplete questions. Also capitalize the first word in a quotation if the quotation is a complete sentence.

> And then I said in perfect English, "Yes, I'm getting rather concerned." —*Tan, p. 949*

Capitalize all proper nouns and adjectives.

T. S. Eliot	Mississippi River	Harvard College
Turkish	November	Puerto Rican

Capitalize a person's title when it is followed by the person's name or when it is used in direct address.

> Rev. Leonidas W. Smiley   Engineer-Private Klee

Capitalize titles showing family relationships when they refer to a specific person, unless they are preceded by a possessive noun or pronoun.

> Granny Weatherall   my grandfather Mammedaty

Capitalize the first word and all other key words in the titles of books, periodicals, poems, stories, plays, paintings, and other works of art.

> *Black Boy*   "Anecdote of the Jar"

Capitalize the first word and all nouns in letter salutations and the first word in letter closings.

> Dear Henry: Yours truly,

PUNCTUATION

End Marks   Use a **period** to end a declarative sentence, a mild imperative sentence, an indirect question, and most abbreviations.

> The sadness of sophistication has come to the boy. —*Anderson, p. 571*
>
> Pile the bodies high at Austerlitz and Waterloo. —*Sandburg, p. 738*
>
> Ask yourselves how this gracious reception of our petition comports with those warlike preparations which cover our waters and darken our land. —*Henry, p. 116*

Use a **question mark** to end an interrogative sentence, an incomplete question, or a statement that is intended as a question.

> "Who comes? Pepe, is it thou?" —*Steinbeck, p. 633*

Use an **exclamation mark** after an exclamatory sentence, a forceful imperative sentence, or an interjection expressing strong emotion.

> We wear the mask! —*Dunbar, p. 532*
>
> "Don't let him, sister!" —*Frost, p. 775*

Commas   Use a comma before the conjunction to separate two independent clauses in a compound sentence.

> From my mother's sleep I fell into the State,
> And I hunched in its belly till my wet fur froze. —*Jarrell, p. 979*

Use commas to separate three or more words, phrases, or clauses in a series.

> I spun, I wove, I kept the house, I nursed the sick, . . . —*Masters, p. 547*

Use commas to separate adjectives of equal rank. Do not use commas to separate adjectives that must stay in a specific order.

> As I approached, golden plovers abandoned their nests in hysterical ploys, artfully feigning a broken wing to distract me from the woven grass cups that couched their pale, darkly speckled eggs. —*Lopez, p. 936*

Use a comma after an introductory word, phrase, or clause.

> Finding Tom so squeamish on this point, he did not insist upon it, . . . —*Irving, p. 181*

Use commas to set off parenthetical and nonessential expressions.

> My poor aunt's figure, however, would have presented astonishing difficulties to any dressmaker. —*Cather, p. 482*

Use commas with places, dates, and titles.

> Boston, Massachusetts   November 17, 1915
> Dr. Martin Luther King, Jr.

Use commas after items in addresses, after the salutation in a personal letter, after the closing in all letters, and in numbers of more than three digits.

> Linden Lane, Princeton, N.J.   Dear Marian,
> Affectionately yours,   6,778

Use a comma to indicate words left out of an elliptical sentence and to set off a direct quotation.

> In T. S. Eliot's poetry, allusions are perhaps the most prominent device; in Ezra Pound's, images.
>
> "Well, Granny," he said, "you must be a hundred years old, and scared of nothing." —*Welty, p. 625*

Semicolons Use a semicolon to join independent clauses that are not already joined by a conjunction.

> The old woman didn't change her position until he was almost into her yard; then she rose with one hand fisted on her hip. —*O'Connor, p. 832*

Use semicolons to avoid confusion when independent clauses or items in a series already contain commas.

> Before these events, the day was glorious with expectancy; after them, the day was a dead and empty thing. —*Twain, p. 438*

Colons Use a colon before a list of items following an independent clause.

> The Arctic, overall, has the classic lines of a desert landscape: spare, balanced, extended, and quiet. —*Lopez, p. 939*

Use a colon to introduce a formal or lengthy quotation.

> In *The Member of the Wedding* the lovely twelve-year-old girl, Frankie Addams, articulates this universal need: "The trouble with me is that for a long time I have just been an *I* person." —*McCullers, p. 902*

Quotation Marks A **direct quotation** represents a person's exact speech or thoughts and is enclosed in quotation marks.

> "Good," he said. "You will be able to play football again better than ever." —*Hemingway, p. 580*

An **indirect quotation** reports only the general meaning of what a person said or thought and does not require quotation marks.

> One day I had said that Italian seemed such an easy language to me that I could not take a great interest in it, . . . —*Hemingway, p. 583*

Always place a comma or a period inside the final quotation mark.

> "Well, Missy, excuse me," Doctor Harry patted her cheek. —*Porter, p. 606*

Place a question mark or an exclamation mark inside the final quotation mark if the end mark is part of the quotation; if it is not part of the quotation, place it outside the final quotation mark.

> "Cornelia! Cornelia!" No footsteps, but a sudden hand on her cheek. "Bless you, where have you been?" —*Porter, p. 608*

Use single quotation marks for a quotation within a quotation.

> " 'All right,' I say, 'I can't afford to pay

Any fixed wages, though I wish I could.' 'Someone else can.' 'Then someone else will have to.' " —*Frost, p. 770*

Underline the titles of long written works, movies, television and radio shows, lengthy works of music, paintings, and sculptures.

> The Great Gatsby   Mary Poppins   Aida

Use quotation marks around the titles of short written works, episodes in a series, songs, and titles of works mentioned as parts of collections.

> "Winter Dreams"   "On the Mall"

Dashes Use dashes to indicate an abrupt change of thought, a dramatic interrupting idea, or a summary statement.

> She'd had moments herself of picturing some kind of evil gene in her husband's ordinary, stocky body—a dark little egg like a black jelly bean, she imagined it. —*Tyler, p. 874*

Use dashes to set off a nonessential appositive or modifier when it is long, when it is already punctuated, or when you want to be dramatic.

> You begin your journey on so high an elevation that your destination is already in sight—a city that you have visited many times and that, moreover, is indicated on a traveler's map you have carefully folded up to take along with you. —*Oates, p. 860*

Hyphens Use a hyphen with certain numbers, after certain prefixes, with two or more words used as one word, with a compound modifier coming before a noun, and within a word when a combination of letters might otherwise be confusing.

> fifty-four   daughter-in-law   up-to-date report

Apostrophes Add an apostrophe and *-s* to show the possessive case of most singular nouns.

> Taylor's poetry   a poet's career

Add an apostrophe to show the possessive case of plural nouns ending in *-s* and *-es*.

> the boys' ambition   the Cruzes' house

Add an apostrophe and *-s* to show the possessive case of plural nouns that do not end in *-s* or *-es*.

> the men's suits   the deer's antlers

Use an apostrophe in a contraction to indicate the position of the missing letter or letters.

> "You look like a saint, Doctor Harry, and I vow that's as near as you'll ever come to it." —*Porter, p. 612*

GLOSSARY OF COMMON USAGE

adapt, adopt

Adapt is a verb meaning "to change." *Adopt* is a verb meaning "to take as one's own."

> Washington Irving *adapted* many characters and situations from folk tales for his short stories.
>
> Ezra Pound's followers *adopted* a spare, almost lean style in their verse and put a high premium on clarity and immediacy in imagery.

advice, advise

Advice is a noun meaning "an opinion." *Advise* is a verb meaning "to give an opinion to."

> The man in Jack London's "To Build a Fire" ignores the *advice* of the old-timer from Sulphur Creek.
>
> How might Lucinda Matlock *advise* the younger generation of today's world?

affect, effect

Affect is almost always a verb meaning "to influence." *Effect* is usually a noun meaning "result." *Effect* can also be a verb meaning "to bring about" or "to cause."

> An understanding of T. S. Eliot's multiple allusions can *affect* one's appreciation of his poetry.
>
> In Willa Cather's story, the Wagner concert has a profound *effect* on the emotions of Clark's Aunt Georgiana.
>
> The aim of persuasive writing is often to *effect* a change in the attitudes of the audience.

among, between

Among is usually used with three or more items. *Between* is generally used with only two items.

> *Among* the writers of the Harlem Renaissance, Langston Hughes stands out for his mastery of many literary genres.
>
> At the end of Robert Frost's "Mending Wall," the speaker reports a conversation *between* himself and his neighbor.

as, because, like, as to

The word *as* has several meanings and can function as several parts of speech. To avoid confusion, use *because* rather than *as* when you want to indicate cause and effect.

> *Because* Anne Bradstreet firmly believed in God's Providence, she was able to console herself after the burning of her family's house.

Do not use the preposition *like* to introduce a clause that requires the conjunction *as*.

> The Puritans reacted to music and dancing *as* one might expect: They considered that such entertainments were dangerous occasions of sin.

The use of *as to* for *about* is awkward and should be avoided.

> Captain Ahab's bitter vehemence *about* the white whale must seem puzzling to the crew.

bad, badly

Use the predicate adjective *bad* after linking verbs such as *feel, look,* and *seem.* Use *badly* whenever an adverb is required.

> Although Granny Weatherall looks *bad,* she is not at all happy to see Doctor Harry at the beginning of Katherine Anne Porter's story.
>
> Elizabeth is *badly* shaken when Mr. Hooper refuses to remove the black veil.

because of, due to

Use *due to* if it can logically replace the phrase *caused by.* In introductory phrases, however, *because of* is better usage than *due to.*

> Peyton Farquhar's failure to recognize the trap of the Federal scout may be *due to* his eagerness to aid the Confederate cause.
>
> *Because of* Edgar Lee Masters's ability to sketch small-town characters accurately and accessibly, *Spoon River Anthology* became extremely popular.

being as, being that

Avoid using the expressions *being as* and *being that.* Use *because* or *since* instead.

> *Because* Walt Whitman believed that new styles were needed in American poetry, he consciously broke with traditional forms and experimented with free verse.
>
> *Since* Mr. Shiftlet is more interested in the car than in young Lucynell, it is hardly surprising that he abandons her at the roadside diner in Flannery O'Connor's "The Life You Save May Be Your Own."

beside, besides

Beside is a preposition meaning "at the side of" or "close to." Do not confuse *beside* with *besides,* which means "in addition to." *Besides* can be a preposition or an adverb.

> When Clark sits *beside* his Aunt Georgiana at the concert, he tries to imagine her emotions as she hears the music.
>
> *Besides* Mr. Oakhurst, which other characters are run out of town at the beginning of Bret Harte's "The Outcasts of Poker Flat"?
>
> Thomas Jefferson was the third President of the United States; he was a gifted architect and inventor, *besides.*

can, may

The verb *can* generally refers to the ability to do something. The verb *may* generally refers to permission to do something.

> One of Ralph Waldo Emerson's major themes is that human beings *can* acquire from nature a sense of their own potential and autonomy.

> William Faulkner's "The Bear" *may* seem difficult to read at first, but it is a profoundly rewarding story of a child's rite of passage.

different from, different than

The preferred usage is *different from.*

> In her powerful exploration of women's consciousness, Kate Chopin was *different from* the vast majority of her contemporaries.

due to the fact that

Replace this awkward expression with *because* or *since.*

> *Since* Miniver Cheevy spends much of his mental and emotional life in the past, it is hardly surprising that he is bitterly unhappy in the present.

farther, further

Use *farther* when you refer to distance. Use *further* when you mean "to a greater degree."

> The *farther* Phoenix Jackson travels in Eudora Welty's story "A Worn Path," the more her determination to reach her goal grows.

> In his speech Patrick Henry urges his countrymen to trust the British no *further.*

fewer, less

Use *fewer* for things that can be counted. Use *less* for amounts or quantities that cannot be counted.

> William Carlos Williams's poem "The Locust Tree in Flower" uses *fewer* words than any other poem I have ever read.

> The theme of Sherwood Anderson's short story "Sophistication" is that people would do better with *less* affectation and more genuine emotion.

good, well

Use the predicate adjective *good* after linking verbs such as *feel, look, smell, taste,* and *seem.* Use *well* whenever you need an adverb.

> At the end of F. Scott Fitzgerald's "Winter Dreams," Devlin implies to Dexter that Judy Jones does not look as *good* as she used to.

> Anne Tyler writes especially *well* about ordinary people and family relationships.

hopefully

You should not loosely attach this adverb to a sentence, as in "Hopefully, the rain will stop by noon." Rewrite the sentence so that *hopefully* modifies a specific verb. Other possible ways of revising such sentences include using the adjective *hopeful* or a phrase like *everyone hopes that.*

> In his Nobel Prize acceptance speech, William Faulkner wrote *hopefully* about mankind's ability to endure and prevail.

> Mai was *hopeful* that she could locate some more biographical information about Jean Toomer at her local library.

> Everyone *hopes* that Diane will win the oral interpretation contest with her rendition of Amy Lowell's "Patterns."

its, it's

Do not confuse the possessive pronoun *its* with the contraction *it's,* standing for "it is" or "it has."

> Perhaps the most memorable line in Emerson's poem "The Rhodora" is "Beauty is *its* own excuse for being."

> Wallace Stevens's "Anecdote of the Jar" suggests that *it's* impossible to mediate completely between the wilderness and the world of civilization.

kind of, sort of

In formal writing you should not use these colloquial expressions. Instead, use a word such as *rather* or *somewhat.*

> Robert Lowell's train of thought in "Hawthorne" is *rather* difficult to follow.

> When she describes the modern American shopping mall, Joan Didion's tone is *somewhat* satirical.

lay, lie

Do not confuse these verbs. *Lay* is a transitive verb meaning "to set or put something down." Its principal parts are *lay, laying, laid, laid. Lie* is an intransitive verb meaning "to recline." Its principal parts are *lie, lying, lay, lain.*

> Stream-of-consciousness narration *lays* a special responsibility on the reader to piece together the events in a story or narrative poem.

> Emily Dickinson argues paradoxically that the conquered foe, who *lies* "defeated" and "dying," can best appreciate the definition of success.

many, much

Use *many* to refer to a specific quantity. Use *much* for an indefinite amount or for an abstract concept.

Many of William Faulkner's novels deal with the themes of pride, guilt, and the search for identity.

Much of Donald Barthelme's fiction is concerned with the impersonality and mechanization of modern life.

may be, maybe

Be careful not to confuse the verb phrase *may be* with the adverb *maybe* (meaning "perhaps").

In some of Emily Dickinson's poems, the speaker *may be* the poet herself; in others, the speaker is clearly a different persona.

The most memorable, and *maybe* the most ineffectual, character in T. S. Eliot's poetry is J. Alfred Prufrock.

plurals that do not end in -s

The plurals of certain nouns from Greek and Latin are formed as they were in their original language. Words such as *criteria, media,* and *phenomena* are plural and should not be treated as if they are singular (*criterion, medium, phenomenon*).

In "Ars Poetica," Archibald MacLeish seems to deny that meaning is the most important *criterion* for the evaluation of poetry.

The *phenomena* discussed by the "learn'd astronomer" in Whitman's poem may have included planetary orbits and the influence of the moon on the tides.

raise, rise

Raise is a transitive verb that usually takes a direct object. *Rise* is intransitive and never takes a direct object.

Suspense *raises* readers' expectations and motivates them to continue reading a story to see how the plot will be resolved.

Some of Flannery O'Connor's best short stories can be found in her collection entitled *Everything That Rises Must Converge.*

set, sit

Do not confuse these verbs. *Set* is a transitive verb meaning "to put (something) in a certain place." Its principal parts are *set, setting, set, set. Sit* is an intransitive verb meaning "to be seated." Its principal parts are *sit, sitting, sat, sat.*

Phillis Wheatley's poem is so complimentary to Washington that it seems to *set* him on a pedestal.

As Mrs. Mallard *sits* upstairs alone, she suddenly realizes that the death of her husband has freed her to live for herself.

that, which, who

Use the relative pronoun *that* to refer to things or people. Use *which* only for things, and *who* only for people.

The modern poet *that* Lee liked best was Sylvia Plath.

The Romantic movement, which emphasized inner feelings and emotions, took place during the early 1800's.

The poet *who* was the first to read his work at a presidential inauguration was Robert Frost.

unique

Because *unique* means "one of a kind," you should not use it carelessly instead of the words "interesting" or "unusual." Avoid such illogical expressions as "most unique," "very unique," and "extremely unique."

Some critics have argued that its themes and style make Herman Melville's *Moby-Dick unique* in the history of the American novel.

who, whom

In formal writing remember to use *who* only as a subject in clauses and sentences and *whom* only as an object.

Walt Whitman, *who* grieved profoundly at Lincoln's assassination, rendered his tribute to the slain president in a long elegy entitled "When Lilacs Last in the Dooryard Bloom'd."

N. Scott Momaday, *whom* reviewers and literary critics have praised as one of our finest Native American voices, wrote about his Kiowa heritage in *The Way to Rainy Mountain.*

HANDBOOK OF LITERARY TERMS AND TECHNIQUES

ACT See *Drama.*

ALLEGORY An *allegory* is a story or tale with two or more levels of meaning—a literal level and one or more symbolic levels. The events, setting, and characters in an allegory are symbols for ideas or qualities. Many of Nathaniel Hawthorne's short stories, such as "The Minister's Black Veil," on page 268, are allegories.

ALLITERATION *Alliteration* is the repetition of consonant sounds at the beginning of words or accented syllables. Sara Teasdale uses alliteration in the second stanza of her poem "Understanding":

But you I never understood,
   Your spirit's secret hides like gold
Sunk in a Spanish galleon
   Ages ago in water cold.

Poets and other writers use alliteration to link and to emphasize ideas as well as to create pleasing, musical sounds.

ALLUSION An *allusion* is a reference to a well-known person, place, event, literary work, or work of art. Writers often make allusions to stories from the Bible, to Greek and Roman myths, to plays by Shakespeare, to political and historical events, and to other materials with which they can expect their readers to be familiar. In the selection from *Hidden Name and Complex Fate,* on page 908, Ralph Ellison alludes to Freudian psychology, to President Roosevelt's fireside chats, and to many famous Americans. By using allusions, writers can bring to mind complex ideas simply and easily.

ALMANAC An *almanac* is a magazine or book, published monthly, seasonally, or yearly, that contains weather forecasts, tide tables, important dates, lists of upcoming events, statistics, and other information of use or interest to readers. The selection on page 111 is from *Poor Richard's Almanack* by Benjamin Franklin. Franklin's almanac is famous for its humorous and wise sayings.

ANALOGY An *analogy* is a comparison between two unlike things. The purpose of an analogy is to describe something unfamiliar by pointing out its similarities to something that is familiar. In "A Noiseless Patient Spider," on page 407, Walt Whitman makes an analogy between a spider weaving its web and the soul seeking connections with things outside itself.
See *Metaphor* and *Simile.*

ANAPEST See *Meter.*

ANECDOTE An *anecdote* is a brief story about an interesting, amusing, or strange event. An anecdote is told to entertain or to make a point. In the excerpt from *Life on the Mississippi,* on page 438, Mark Twain tells several anecdotes about his experiences on the Mississippi River.

ANTAGONIST An *antagonist* is a character or force in conflict with a main character, or protagonist. In Jack London's "To Build a Fire," on page 490, the antagonist is neither a person nor an animal but is rather the extreme cold of the Yukon. Not all stories contain antagonists. However, in many stories the conflict between the antagonist and the protagonist is the basis for the plot.
See *Conflict, Plot,* and *Protagonist.*

APHORISM An *aphorism* is a general truth or observation about life, usually stated concisely and pointedly. Often witty and wise, aphorisms appear in many kinds of works. An essay writer may have an aphoristic style, making many such statements. Ralph Waldo Emerson was famous for his aphoristic style. His essay entitled "Fate" contains the following aphorisms:

> The book of Nature is the book of Fate.
> Men are what their mothers made them.
> Nature is what you may do.
> So far as a man thinks, he is free.
> A man's fortunes are the fruit of his character.

Used in an essay, an aphorism can be a memorable way to sum up or to reinforce a point or an argument.

APOSTROPHE   An *apostrophe* is a figure of speech in which a speaker directly addresses an absent person or a personified quality, object, or idea. Phillis Wheatley uses apostrophe in this line from "To the University of Cambridge, in New England":

> Students, to you 'tis given to scan the
>   heights

Apostrophe is often used in poetry and in speeches to add emotional intensity.
See *Figurative Language.*

ARGUMENTATION   *Argumentation* is discourse in which the writer presents and logically supports a particular view or opinion. Many critics and scholars distinguish argumentation, or reasoned discourse about opinions, from persuasion, or emotional discourse about opinions. However, some people use the two terms interchangeably.
See *Forms of Discourse* and *Persuasion.*

ASIDE   In a play, an *aside* is a speech delivered by an actor in such a way that other characters on the stage are presumed not to hear it. An aside generally reveals a character's inner thoughts. In Thornton Wilder's *Our Town,* for example, the Stage Manager uses many asides to communicate with the audience. In the same play, when the dead speak among themselves during the funeral, they are overheard by the audience but are presumed not to be heard by the living characters.

ASSONANCE   *Assonance* is the repetition of vowel sounds in conjunction with dissimilar consonant sounds. Emily Dickinson uses assonance in the line "The mountain at a g*i*ven d*i*stance." The *i* sound is repeated in the words *given* and *distance,* in the context of the dissimilar consonant sounds *g–v* and *d–s.*

ATMOSPHERE   See *Mood.*

AUTOBIOGRAPHY   An *autobiography* is a form of nonfiction in which a person tells his or her own life story. Notable examples of autobiographies include those by Benjamin Franklin and Frederick Douglass.
See *Biography* and *Journal.*

BALLAD   A *ballad* is a songlike poem that tells a story, often one dealing with adventure and romance. Most ballads have the following characteristics:
1. Simple language
2. Four- or six-line stanzas
3. Rhyme
4. A regular meter
    A *folk ballad* is one that originated in the oral tradition and was passed by word of mouth from generation to generation. Examples of folk ballads include "Yankee Doodle," "Casey Jones," and "John Henry." A *literary ballad* is one written by a specific person in imitation of the folk ballad. Henry Wadsworth Longfellow's "The Wreck of the Hesperus" is an example of a literary ballad. Here is its first stanza:

'Twas the schooner Hesperus,
   That sailed the wintry sea;
And the skipper had taken his little
   daughter,
   To bear him company.

BIOGRAPHY A *biography* is a form of nonfiction in which a writer tells the life story of another person. John Dos Passos's "Tin Lizzie," on page 670, is an example of biographical writing.
See *Autobiography*.

BLANK VERSE *Blank verse* is poetry written in unrhymed iambic pentameter. An *iamb* is a poetic foot consisting of one week stress followed by one strong stress. A *pentameter line* is a line of five poetic feet. Robert Frost's "Birches," on page 766, is written in blank verse.

CAESURA A *caesura* is a pause or break in the middle of a line of poetry. Double slanted lines (*ll*) have been used to mark the caesuras in these lines from Jean Toomer's "November Cotton Flower":

Boll weevil's coming,//and the winter's
   cold,
Made cotton stalks look rusty,//seasons
   old

CATALOG A *catalog* is a list of people, places, or things in a literary work. In the following example from "As I Ebb'd with the Ocean of Life," Walt Whitman records what he sees along the shore:

Chaff, straw, splinters of wood,
   weeds, and the sea-gluten.
Scum, scales from shining rocks, leaves
   of salt-lettuce, left by the tide.

Whitman often used catalogs in his verse to suggest the fullness, diversity, and scope of American life or of the human experience.

CHARACTER A *character* is a person or an animal who takes part in the action of a literary work. The following are some terms used to describe various types of characters:

The *main character* in a literary work is the one on whom the work focuses. *Major characters* in a literary work include the main character and any other characters who play significant roles. A *minor character* is one who does not play a significant role. A *round character* is one who is complex and multi-faceted, like a real person. A *flat character* is one who is one-dimensional. A *dynamic character* is one who changes in the course of a work. A *static character* is one who does not change in the course of a work.
See *Characterization* and *Motivation*.

CHARACTERIZATION *Characterization* is the act of creating and developing a character. There are two primary methods of characterization: direct and indirect. In *direct characterization,* a writer simply states a character's traits, as when the main character in "Flight," on page 630, is called "a gentle, affectionate boy." In *indirect characterization,* character is revealed by one of the following means:

1. By the words, thoughts, or actions of the character
2. By descriptions of the character's appearance or background
3. By what other characters say about the character
4. By the ways in which other characters react toward the character

See *Character*.

CINQUAIN See *Stanza*.

CLASSICISM *Classicism* is an approach to literature and the other arts that stresses reason, balance, clarity, ideal beauty, and orderly form in imitation of the arts of ancient Greece and Rome.

Classicism is often contrasted with *Romanticism,* which stresses imagination, emotion, and individualism. Classicism also differs from *Realism,* which stresses the actual rather than the ideal. See *Realism* and *Romanticism.*

CLIMAX   The *climax* is the high point of interest or suspense in a literary work. For example, William Faulkner's "The Bear," on page 646, reaches its climax when the boy finally meets the bear. The climax generally appears near the end of a story, play, or narrative poem.
See *Plot.*

CONCEIT   A *conceit* is an unusual or surprising comparison between two very different things. In Edward Taylor's "Huswifery," on page 68, the granting of grace is compared to spinning yarn, weaving and dyeing cloth, and making clothes. Such a far-fetched comparison is a conceit.

CONCRETE POEM   A *concrete poem* is one with a shape that suggests its subject.

CONFESSIONAL POETRY   *Confessional poetry* is verse that speaks of personal matters, often with great frankness, or candor. Famous American confessional poets include Maxine Kumin, Robert Lowell, Sylvia Plath, Anne Sexton, and John Berryman.

CONFLICT   A *conflict* is a struggle between opposing forces. Sometimes this struggle is internal, or within a character, as in Bernard Malamud's "The First Seven Years," on page 822. At other times this struggle is external, or between a character and an outside force, as in Jack London's "To Build a Fire," on page 490. Conflict is one of the primary elements of narrative literature because most plots develop from conflicts.
See *Antagonist, Plot,* and *Protagonist.*

CONNOTATION   A *connotation* is an association that a word calls to mind in addition to the dictionary meaning of the word. Many words that are similar in their dictionary meanings, or denotations, are quite different in their connotations. Consider, for example, José García Villa's line, "Be beautiful, noble, like the antique ant." This line would have a very different effect if it were "Be pretty, classy, like the old ant." Poets and other writers choose their words carefully so that the connotations of those words will be appropriate.
See *Denotation.*

CONSONANCE   *Consonance* is the repetition of consonant sounds at the ends of words or accented syllables. Emily Dickinson uses consonance in the following lines:

But if he ask where you are hi*d*
Until to-morrow,—happy letter!
Gesture, coquette, an*d* shake your hea*d*!

COUPLET   See *Stanza.*

CRISIS   In the plot of a narrative, the *crisis* is the turning point for the protagonist—the point at which the protagonist's situation or understanding changes dramatically. In Bernard Malamud's "The First Seven Years," on page 822, the crisis comes when Feld recognizes that Sobel loves Miriam.

DACTYL   See *Meter.*

DENOTATION   The *denotation* of a word is its objective meaning, independent of other associations that the word brings to mind.
See *Connotation.*

DENOUEMENT   See *Plot.*

DESCRIPTION A *description* is a portrayal, in words, of something that can be perceived by the senses. Writers create descriptions by using images, as N. Scott Momaday does in the following lines from "A Vision Beyond Time and Place," on page 924:

> His eyes are deep and open to the wide world. At sunrise, precisely, they catch fire and close, having seen. The low light descends upon him. And when he lifts his voice, it enters upon the silence and carries there, like the call of a bird.

Description is one of the major forms of discourse and appears quite often in literary works of all genres.
See *Image* and *Forms of Discourse*.

DEVELOPMENT See *Plot*.

DIALECT A *dialect* is the form of a language spoken by people in a particular region or group. Every dialect differs from every other dialect in the details of its vocabulary, grammar, and pronunciation. Writers often use dialect to make their characters seem realistic and to create local color. See, for example, Mark Twain's "The Notorious Jumping Frog of Calaveras County," on page 445.
See *Local Color* and *Vernacular*.

DIALOGUE A *dialogue* is a conversation between characters. Writers use dialogue to reveal character, to present events, to add variety to narratives, and to arouse their readers' interest. See *Drama*.

DICTION *Diction* is a writer's or speaker's word choice. Diction is part of a writer's style and may be described as formal or informal, plain or ornate, common or technical, abstract or concrete. In the selection from *The Mortgaged Heart,* on page 902, Carson McCullers uses formal diction suitable to her essay's serious purpose.
See *Style*.

DIMETER See *Meter*.

DRAMA A *drama* is a story written to be performed by actors. The playwright supplies dialogue for the characters to speak and stage directions that give information about costumes, lighting, scenery, properties, the setting, and the characters' movements and ways of speaking. The audience accepts as believable the many dramatic conventions that are used, such as soliloquies, asides, poetic language, or the passage of time between acts or scenes. An *act* is a major division in a drama. A *scene* is a minor division.
See *Genre*.

DRAMATIC CONVENTION See *Drama*.

DRAMATIC DIALOGUE A *dramatic dialogue* is a poem in which there are two speakers who converse with one another. An example in this text is Robert Frost's "The Death of the Hired Man," on page 770.
See *Dramatic Poem*.

DRAMATIC IRONY See *Irony*.

DRAMATIC MONOLOGUE A *dramatic monologue* is a poem or speech in which an imaginary character speaks to a silent listener. T. S. Eliot's "The Love Song of J. Alfred Prufrock," on page 708, is a dramatic monologue.
See *Dramatic Poem* and *Monologue*.

DRAMATIC POEM A *dramatic poem* is one that makes use of the conventions of drama. Such poems may be monologues or dialogues or may present the speech of many characters. Examples of dramatic poems in this anthology include those from Edgar Lee Masters's *Spoon*

River Anthology, on page 546, and Robert Frost's "The Death of the Hired Man," on page 770.

See *Dramatic Dialogue* and *Dramatic Monologue.*

DYNAMIC CHARACTER   See *Character.*

ELEGY   An *elegy* is a solemn and formal lyric poem about death, often one that mourns the passing of some particular person. Walt Whitman's "When Lilacs Last in the Dooryard Bloom'd," on page 408, is an elegy lamenting the death of President Lincoln.
See *Lyric.*

END-STOPPED LINE   An *end-stopped line* is one in which the end of the line coincides with a pause or with the end of a thought. End-stopped lines are often recognizable because of their end punctuation—a period, a comma, a dash, or some other mark. These lines from "Southern Mansion," by Arna Bontemps, are end-stopped:

> The years go back with an iron clank,
> A hand is on the gate,
> A dry leaf trembles on the wall.
> Ghosts are walking.

See *Run-on Line.*

EPIGRAM   An *epigram* is a brief, pointed statement, in prose or in verse, often characterized by use of some rhetorical device or figure of speech. Benjamin Franklin was famous for his epigrams, which include "Fools make feasts, and wise men eat them," and "A plowman on his legs is higher than a gentleman on his knees."

ESSAY   An *essay* is a short, nonfiction work about a particular subject. The term *essay* comes from the Old French word *essai,* meaning "a trial or attempt." As the history of the word suggests, an essay is meant to be exploratory. It is not meant to be an exhaustive treatment of a subject. Essays can be classified as formal or informal, personal or impersonal. They can also be classified according to purpose, as expository, argumentative, descriptive, persuasive, or narrative. See *Forms of Discourse.*

EXPOSITION   *Exposition* is writing or speech that explains, informs, or presents information. The main techniques of expository writing include analysis, classification, comparison and contrast, definition, and exemplification, or illustration. An essay may be primarily expository, as is Joan Didion's "On the Mall," on page 916, or it may use exposition to support another purpose such as persuasion or argumentation, as in the selection from Carson McCullers's *The Mortgaged Heart,* on page 902.

In a story or play, the exposition is that part of the plot that introduces the characters, the setting, and the basic situation.
See *Forms of Discourse* and *Plot.*

EXPRESSIONISM   *Expressionism* was an artistic movement of the early twentieth century. Expressionist painters, sculptors, and writers emphasized the inner experience of the individual rather than the time frame or physical objects of some absolute external reality. The Expressionist movement, exemplified by the works of artists like Van Gogh, influenced such writers as Eugene O'Neill and T. S. Eliot.

EXTENDED METAPHOR   See *Metaphor.*

FABLE   A *fable* is a brief story, usually with animal characters, that teaches a lesson, or moral. James Thurber was a famous American writer of fables.

FALLING ACTION   See *Plot.*

FICTION   *Fiction* is prose writing that tells about imaginary characters and events. Short stories and novels are works of fiction.
See *Genre, Narrative, Nonfiction,* and *Prose.*

FIGURATIVE LANGUAGE   *Figurative language* is writing or speech not meant to be taken literally. Writers use figurative language to express ideas in vivid and imaginative ways. For example, Emily Dickinson begins one poem with the following description of snow:

> It sifts from leaden sieves,
> It powders all the wood

   By describing the snow as if it were flour, Dickinson renders a precise and compelling picture of it.
See *Figure of Speech.*

FIGURE OF SPEECH   A *figure of speech* is an expression or a word used imaginatively rather than literally. Many types of figures of speech are used by writers in English, including apostrophe, hyperbole, irony, metaphor, metonymy, oxymoron, paradox, personification, simile, synecdoche, and understatement.
See *Figurative Language.* See also the entries for individual figures of speech.

FIRST-PERSON POINT OF VIEW   See *Point of View.*

FLASHBACK   A *flashback* is a section of a literary work that interrupts the chronological presentation of events to relate an event from an earlier time. A writer may present a flashback as a character's memory or recollection, as part of an account or story told by a character, as a dream or a daydream, or simply by having the narrator switch to a time in the past. A flashback occurs at the beginning of Ann Beattie's "Imagined Scenes," on page 882, when the protagonist remembers a time when she arrived home from shopping, was missing her keys, and was let in by David. Writers often use flashbacks as a dramatic way of providing background information.

FLAT CHARACTER   See *Character.*

FOIL   A *foil* is a character who provides a contrast to another character. In F. Scott Fitzgerald's "Winter Dreams," on page 588, Irene Scheerer is a foil for the tantalizing Judy Jones.

FOLK BALLAD   See *Ballad.*

FOLKLORE   *Folklore* is the body of stories, legends, myths, ballads, riddles, sayings, and other works that has arisen out of the oral traditions of peoples around the globe. The folklore traditions of the United States, including those of Native Americans and of the American pioneers, are especially rich.

FOOT   See *Meter.*

FORESHADOWING   *Foreshadowing* is the use, in a literary work, of clues that suggest events that have yet to occur.

FORMS OF DISCOURSE   The *forms of discourse* are the various modes into which writing can be classified. Traditionally, writing has been divided into the following modes:
1. *Exposition,* or expository writing, which presents information
2. *Narration,* or narrative writing, which tells a story
3. *Description,* or descriptive writing, which portrays people, places, or things
4. *Persuasion,* or persuasive writing, which attempts to convince people to think or act in a certain way

   Some people distinguish between *persuasion* and *argumentation,* defining the former as an attempt to move an audience by means of an emotional appeal and the latter as an attempt to move an audience by means of a reasoned or rational appeal.

Often, of course, several forms of discourse appear in a single work. A narrative, for example, may contain descriptive or expository passages. See *Argumentation, Description, Exposition, Narration,* and *Persuasion.*

FREE VERSE *Free verse* is poetry that lacks a regular rhythmical pattern, or meter. A writer of free verse is at liberty to use any rhythms that are appropriate to what he or she is saying. Free verse has been widely used by twentieth-century poets such as Leslie Marmon Silko, who begins "Where Mountain Lion Lay Down with Deer" with these lines:

> I climb the black rock mountain
> stepping from day to day
>   silently.

See *Meter.*

GENRE A *genre* is a division, or type, of literature. Literature is commonly divided into three major genres: poetry, prose, and drama. Each major genre can in turn be divided into smaller genres. Poetry can be divided into lyric, concrete, dramatic, narrative, and epic poetry. Prose can be divided into fiction (novels and short stories) and nonfiction (biography, autobiography, letters, essays, and reports). Drama can be divided into serious drama, tragedy, comic drama, melodrama, and farce.
See *Drama, Poetry,* and *Prose.*

GOTHIC *Gothic* refers to the use of primitive, medieval, wild, or mysterious elements in literature. Gothic elements offended eighteenth-century classical writers but appealed to the Romantic writers who followed them. Gothic novels feature places like mysterious and gloomy castles, where horrifying, supernatural events take place. Their influence on Edgar Allan Poe is evident in "The Fall of the House of Usher," on page 194.

HARLEM RENAISSANCE The *Harlem Renaissance,* which occurred during the 1920's, was a time of African American artistic creativity centered in Harlem, in New York City. Writers of the Harlem Renaissance include Countee Cullen, Claude McKay, Jean Toomer, Langston Hughes, and Arna Bontemps.

HEPTAMETER See *Meter.*

HEPTASTICH See *Stanza.*

HERO/HEROINE A *hero* or *heroine* is a character whose actions are inspiring or noble. The most obvious examples of heroes and heroines are the larger-than-life characters of myths and legend. More ordinary characters, however, can also act as heroes and heroines.

HEXAMETER See *Meter.*

HYPERBOLE A *hyperbole* is a deliberate exaggeration or overstatement. In Mark Twain's "The Notorious Jumping Frog of Calaveras County," on page 445, the claim that Jim Smiley would follow a bug as far as Mexico to win a bet is a hyperbole. As this example shows, hyperboles are often used for comic effect.

IAMB See *Meter.*

IAMBIC PENTAMETER *Iambic pentameter* is a line of poetry with five iambic feet, each containing one unstressed syllable followed by one stressed syllable ($\smile$ $'$). Iambic pentameter may be rhymed or unrhymed. Unrhymed iambic pentameter is called *blank verse.* These concluding lines from Anne Bradstreet's "The Author to Her Book" are in iambic pentameter:

And for thy, Mŏther, she ălăs ĭs pŏor,
Whĭch caúsed hĕr thús tŏ sénd theĕ óut
   ŏf dóor.

See *Blank Verse* and *Meter.*

IDYLL   An *idyll* is a poem or part of a poem that describes and idealizes country life. John Greenleaf Whittier's "Snowbound," on page 320, is an idyll.

IMAGE   An *image* is a word or phrase that appeals to one or more of the five senses—sight, hearing, touch, taste, or smell.
See *Imagery.*

IMAGERY   *Imagery* is the descriptive or figurative language used in literature to create word pictures for the reader. These pictures, or images, are created by details of sight, sound, taste, touch, smell, or movement. The following stanza, from Kuangchi C. Chang's "Garden of My Childhood," shows how a poet can use imagery to appeal to several senses:

> I ran past the old maple by the terraced hall
> And the singing crickets under the latticed
>   wall,
>
> And I kept on running down the walk
> Paved with pebbles of memory big and small
> Without turning to look until I was out of the
>   gate
> Through which there be no return at all.

IMAGISM   *Imagism* was a literary movement that flourished between 1912 and 1927. Led by Ezra Pound and Amy Lowell, the Imagist poets rejected nineteenth-century poetic forms and language. Instead, they wrote short poems that used ordinary language and free verse to create sharp, exact, concentrated pictures. "Oread," by H. D., illustrates how the Imagists concentrated on describing a scene or object without making abstract comments:

> Whirl up, sea—
> whirl your pointed pines,
> splash your great pines
> on our rocks,
> hurl your green over us,
> cover us with your pools of fir.

INCITING INCIDENT   See *Plot.*

INCONGRUITY   *Incongruity* is the combination or juxtaposition of incompatible or opposite elements. Many examples of incongruity can be found in T. S. Eliot's "The Love Song of J. Alfred Prufrock," on page 708. The speaker constantly shifts from grand pronouncements like "Do I dare/Disturb the universe?" to pathetic ones like "Do I dare to eat a peach?"

INVERSION   An *inversion* is a reversal or change in the regular word order of a sentence. For instance, Ezra Pound begins one poem with the line, "Sing we for love and idleness." This line reverses the usual subject-verb order, "We sing."

IRONY   *Irony* is a contrast between what is stated and what is meant, or between what is expected to happen and what actually happens. In *verbal irony* a word or a phrase is used to suggest the opposite of its usual meaning. In *dramatic irony,* there is a contradiction between what a character thinks and what the reader or audience knows to be true. In *irony of situation,* an event occurs that directly contradicts the expectations of the characters, of the reader, or of the audience.

IRONY OF SITUATION   See *Irony.*

JOURNAL   A *journal* is a daily autobiographical account of events and personal reactions. For example, Mary Chesnut's journal, on page 371, records events during the Civil War.

LEGEND   A *legend* is a traditional story. Usually a legend deals with a particular person—a hero, a saint, or a national leader. Often legends reflect a people's cultural values. American legends include those of the early Native Americans and those about folk heroes such as Davy Crockett and Daniel Boone.
See *Myth.*

LITERARY LETTER   A *literary letter,* or epistle, is a work of literature created for publication and meant to be read by a large general audience but written as though it were a personal letter to an individual. Ezra Pound's "The River-Merchant's Wife," on page 701, is a literary letter. See also the selection from de Crèvecoeur's *Letters from an American Farmer,* on page 148.

LOCAL COLOR   *Local color* is the use in a literary work of characters and details unique to a particular geographic area. Local color can be created by the use of dialect and by descriptions of customs, clothing, manners, attitudes, scenery, and landscape. Local-color stories were especially popular after the Civil War, bringing readers the West of Bret Harte, the Mississippi River of Mark Twain, and the New England of Sarah Orne Jewett.
See *Realism* and *Regionalism.*

LYRIC POEM   A *lyric poem* is a melodic poem that expresses the observations and feelings of a single speaker. Unlike a narrative poem, a lyric focuses on producing a single, unified effect. Types of lyrics include the elegy, the ode, and the sonnet. Among contemporary American poets, the lyric is the most common poetic form.

MAIN CHARACTER   See *Character.*

METAPHOR   A *metaphor* is a figure of speech in which one thing is spoken of as though it were something else. The identification suggests a comparison between the two things that are identified, as in "death *is* a long sleep" or "the sleeping dead."

A *mixed metaphor* occurs when two metaphors are jumbled together. For example, thorns and rain are illogically mixed in "the thorns of life rained down on him." A *dead metaphor* is one that has been overused and has become a common expression, such as "the arm of the chair" or "nightfall." Metaphors are used to make writing, especially poetry, more vivid, imaginative, and meaningful.

METER   The *meter* of a poem is its rhythmical pattern. This pattern is determined by the number and types of stresses, or beats, in each line. To describe the meter of a poem, you must *scan* its lines. *Scanning* involves marking the stressed and unstressed syllables, as follows:

> Sŏon ăs thĕ sún fŏrsóok thĕ eástĕrn máin
> Thĕ péalĭng thúndĕr shŏok thĕ héav'nlў
> plάin;
> —Phillis Weatley, "An Hymn to the Evening"

As the example shows, each strong stress is marked with a slanted line (´) and each weak stress with a horseshoe symbol (˘). The weak and strong stresses are then divided by vertical lines (|) into groups called *feet.* The following types of feet are common in poetry written in English:

1. *Iamb:* a foot with one unstressed syllable followed by one stressed syllable, as in the word "ăroúnd"
2. *Trochee:* a foot with one stressed syllable followed by one unstressed syllable, as in the word "brókĕn"
3. *Anapest:* a foot with two unstressed syllables followed by one stressed syllable, as in the phrase "ĭn ă flásh"

4. *Dactyl:* a foot with one stressed syllable followed by two unstressed syllables, as in the word "argument"

5. *Spondee:* a foot with two stressed syllables, as in the word "airship"

6. *Pyrrhic:* a foot with two unstressed syllables, as in the last foot of the word "imag|ining"

7. *Amphibrach:* a foot with an unstressed syllable, one stressed syllable, and another stressed syllable, as in the word "ungainly"

8. *Amphimacer:* a foot with a stressed syllable, one unstressed syllable, and another stressed syllable, as in "give and take"

Lines of poetry are often described as *iambic, trochaic, anapestic,* or *dactylic.*

Lines are also described in terms of the number of feet that occur in them, as follows:

1. *Monometer:* verse written in one-foot lines

Évĭl
Bĕgéts
Évĭl
   —Anonymous

2. *Dimeter:* verse written in two-foot lines

Thĭs ĭs | thĕ tíme
ŏf thĕ trág|ĭc mán
   —Elizabeth Bishop, "Visits to St. Elizabeth's"

3. *Trimeter:* verse written in three-foot lines:

Óvĕr | thĕ wín|tĕr glácĭĕrs
  Ĭ sée | thĕ súm|mĕr glów,
Ănd thróugh | thĕ wíld-|pĭled snówdrĭft
  Thĕ wárm | rósebŭds | bĕlów.
   Ralph Waldo Emerson, "Beyond Winter"

4. *Tetrameter:* verse written in four-foot lines:

Thĕ sún | thăt bríef | Dĕcém|bĕr dáy
Rŏse chéer|lĕss óv|ĕr hílls | ŏf gráy
   —John Greenleaf Whittier, *Snowbound*

5. *Pentameter:* verse written in five-foot lines:

Ĭ dóubt | nŏt Gód | ĭs góod, | wĕll-méan|ĭng, kínd,
Ănd díd | Hĕ stóop | tŏ quíb|blĕ cóuld | tĕll why
Thĕ lít|tlĕ búr|ĭed móle | cŏntín|ŭes blínd
   —Countee Cullen, "Yet Do I Marvel"

A six-foot line is called a *hexameter.* A line with seven feet is a *heptameter.*

A complete description of the meter of a line tells both how many feet there are in the line and what kind of foot is most common. Thus the lines from Countee Cullen's poem would be described as *iambic pentameter. Blank verse* is poetry written in unrhymed iambic pentameter. Poetry that does not have a regular meter is called *free verse.*

MINOR CHARACTER   See *Character.*

MONOLOGUE   A *monologue* is a speech delivered entirely by one person or character. See *Dramatic Monologue* and *Soliloquy.*

MONOMETER   See *Meter.*

MOOD   *Mood,* or atmosphere, is the feeling created in the reader by a literary work or passage. Elements that can influence the mood of a work include its setting, tone, and events. See *Setting* and *Tone.*

MOTIVATION   A *motivation* is a reason that explains a character's thoughts, feelings, actions, or speech. Characters are motivated by their values and by their wants, desires, dreams, wishes, and needs. Sometimes the reasons for a character's actions are stated directly, as in Willa Cather's "A Wagner Matinée," on page 480, when Clark explains his reception of his aunt by saying, "I owed to this woman most of the good that ever came my way in my boyhood." At other times the writer will just suggest a character's motivation.

MYTH   A *myth* is a fictional tale that explains the actions of gods or heroes or the causes of natural phenomena. Some myths are a kind of primitive science, explaining how and why natural phenomena came about. Other myths express the central values of the people who created them. The stories of the Navajo and the Delaware peoples included in this text are examples of Native American myths.

NARRATION   *Narration* is writing that tells a story. The act of telling a story is also called *narration.* The *narrative,* or story, is told by a storyteller called the *narrator.* A story is usually told chronologically, in the order in which events take place in time, though it may include flashbacks and foreshadowing. Narratives may be true, as are the events recorded in Mary Chesnut's journal, on page 371, or fictional, as are the events in Flannery O'Connor's "The Life You Save May Be Your Own," on page 832. Narration is one of the forms of discourse and is used in novels, short stories, plays, narrative poems, anecdotes, autobiographies, biographies, and reports.
See *Forms of Discourse, Narrative Poem,* and *Narrator.*

NARRATIVE   A *narrative* is a story told in fiction, nonfiction, poetry, or drama.
See *Narration.*

NARRATIVE POEM   A *narrative poem* tells a story in verse. Three traditional types of narrative verse are *ballads,* songlike poems that tell stories; *epics,* long poems about the deeds of gods or heroes; and *metrical romances,* poems that tell tales of love and chivalry. Examples of American narrative poems include Stephen Vincent

Benét's *John Brown's Body* and the ballad "John Henry."
See *Ballad.*

NARRATOR   A *narrator* is a speaker or character who tells a story. A story or novel may be narrated by a main character, by a minor character, or by someone uninvolved in the story. The narrator may speak in the first person, as in John Updike's "The Slump," on page 854, or in the third person as in Ann Beattie's "Imagined Scenes," on page 882. In addition, the narrator may have an omniscient or a limited point of view. The *omniscient narrator* is all-knowing, while the *limited narrator* knows only what one character does. Because the writer's choice of narrator helps determine the point of view, this decision affects what version of a story is told and how readers will react to it.
See *Point of View.*

NATURALISM   *Naturalism* was a literary movement among novelists at the end of the nineteenth century and during the early decades of the twentieth century. The Naturalists tended to view people as hapless victims of immutable natural laws. Early exponents of Naturalism included Stephen Crane, Jack London, and Theodore Dreiser.
See *Realism.*

NONFICTION   *Nonfiction* is prose writing that presents and explains ideas or that tells about real people, places, objects, or events. Essays, biographies, autobiographies, journals, and reports are all examples of nonfiction.
See *Fiction* and *Genre.*

NOVEL   A *novel* is a long work of fiction. A novel often has a complicated plot, many major and minor characters, a significant theme, and several varied settings. Novels can be classified in many ways, based on the historical periods in which they are written, on the subjects and themes that they treat, on the techniques that are used in them, and on the literary movements that inspired them. James Fenimore Cooper, author of *The Prairie,* was the earliest well-known American novelist. Classic nineteenth-century novels include *Moby-Dick,* by Herman Melville; *The Scarlet Letter,* by Nathaniel Hawthorne; *The Adventures of Huckleberry Finn,* by Mark Twain; and *Portrait of a Lady,* by Henry James. Well-known twentieth-century novels include *The House of Mirth,* by Edith Wharton; *O Pioneers!,* by Willa Cather; *An American Tragedy,* by Theodore Dreiser; *The Great Gatsby,* by F. Scott Fitzgerald; *The Sound and the Fury,* by William Faulkner; and *Invisible Man,* by Ralph Ellison. A *novella* is not as long as a novel but is longer than a short story. Ernest Hemingway's *The Old Man and the Sea* is a novella.

NOVELLA   See *Novel.*

OCTAVE   See *Stanza.*

ODE   An *ode* is a long, formal lyric poem with a serious theme that may have a traditional stanza structure. An ode may be written for a private occasion or for a public ceremony. Odes often honor people, commemorate events, respond to natural scenes, or consider serious human problems.
See *Lyric.*

OMNISCIENT POINT OF VIEW   See *Point of View.*

ONOMATOPOEIA   *Onomatopoeia* is the use of words that imitate sounds. Examples of such words are *buzz, hiss, murmur,* and *rustle.* Isabella Stewart Gardner uses onomatopoeia in "Summer Remembered":

> Sounds sum and summon the remembering of
> summers.

> The humming of the sun
> The mumbling in the honey-suckle vine
> The whirring in the clovered grass
> The pizzicato plinkle of ice in an auburn
>   uncle's amber glass.

ORAL TRADITION   *Oral tradition* is the passing of songs, stories, and poems from generation to generation by word of mouth. The oral tradition in America has preserved Native American myths and legends, spirituals, folk ballads, and other stories or songs originally heard and memorized rather than written down.
See *Ballad, Folklore, Legend, Myth,* and *Spiritual.*

ORATORY   *Oratory* is public speaking that is formal, persuasive, and emotionally appealing. Patrick Henry's "Speech in the Virginia Convention," on page 116, is an example of oratory.

ORNATE   *Ornate style* is a way of writing that uses long, complicated sentences with elaborate figures of speech, parallel structures, uncommon allusions, and unfamiliar word choices. This style was used during the seventeenth and eighteenth centuries by writers such as Cotton Mather. Because of its complexity and formality, writing in the ornate style is harder to follow than writing in the contrasting plain style.
See *Plain Style* and *Style.*

OVERSTATEMENT   See *Hyperbole.*

OXYMORON   An *oxymoron* is a figure of speech that combines two opposing or contradictory ideas. An oxymoron, such as "freezing fire" or the often used "conspicuous by his absence," suggests a paradox in just a few words.
See *Figurative Language* and *Paradox.*

PARABLE   A *parable* is a brief story, usually with human characters, that teaches a moral lesson. The most famous parables are those told by

Christ in the Bible. Some critics would classify Nathaniel Hawthorne's "The Minister's Black Veil," on page 268, as a parable.

PARADOX   A *paradox* is a statement that seems to be contradictory but that actually presents a truth. Marianne Moore uses paradox in "Nevertheless" when she says, "Victory won't come/to me unless I go/to it." because a paradox is surprising or even shocking, it draws the reader's attention to what is being said.
See *Figurative Language* and *Oxymoron.*

PARALLELISM   *Parallelism* is the repetition of a grammatical structure. Robert Hayden concludes his poem "Astronauts" with these questions in parallel form:

What do we want of these men?
What do we want of ourselves?

Parallelism is used in poetry and in other writing to emphasize and to link related ideas.

PARODY   A *parody* is a humorous imitation of a literary work, one that exaggerates or distorts the characteristic features of the original. American author Donald Barthelme was noted for his parodic style, which he used to point out absurd aspects of modern life.

PERSONIFICATION   *Personification* is a figure of speech in which a nonhuman subject is given human characteristics. In "April Rain Song," Langston Hughes personifies the rain:

Let the rain kiss you.
Let the rain sing you a lullaby.

Effective personification of things or ideas makes them seem vital and alive, as if they were human.
See *Figurative Language.*

PERSUASION   *Persuasion* is writing or speech that attempts to convince a reader to think or act in a particular way. During the Revolutionary War period, leaders such as Patrick Henry, Thomas Paine, and Thomas Jefferson used persuasion in their political arguments. Persuasion is also used in advertising, in editorials, in sermons, and in political speeches.
See *Argumentation* and *Forms of Discourse.*

PLAIN STYLE   *Plain style* is a type of writing in which uncomplicated sentences and ordinary words are used to make simple, direct statements. This style was favored by those Puritans who rejected ornate style because they want to express themselves clearly and directly, in accordance with the austerity of their religious beliefs. In the twentieth century, Ernest Hemingway was a master of plain style.
See *Ornate Style* and *Style.*

PLOT   *Plot* is the sequence of events in a literary work. In most novels, dramas, short stories, and narrative poems, the plot involves both characters and a central conflict. The plot usually begins with an *exposition* that introduces the setting, the characters, and the basic situation. This is followed by the *inciting incident,* which introduces the central conflict. The conflict then increases during the *development* until it reaches a high point of interest or suspense, the *climax.* The climax is followed by the end, or *resolution,* of the central conflict. Any events that occur after the resolution make up the *denouement.* The events that lead up to the climax comprise the *rising action.* The events that follow the climax comprise the *falling action.*
See *Conflict.*

POETRY   *Poetry* is one of the three major types of literature. In poetry, form and content are closely connected, like the two faces of a single coin. Poems are often divided into lines and stan-

zas and often employ regular rhythmical patterns, or meters. Most poems make use of highly concise, musical, and emotionally charged language. Many also make use of imagery, figurative language, and special devices such as rhyme.
See *Genre.*

POINT OF VIEW   *Point of view* is the perspective, or vantage point, from which a story is told. Three commonly used points of view are first-person, omniscient third-person, and limited third-person.

In the *first-person point of view,* the narrator is a character in the story and refers to himself or herself with the first-person pronoun *I.* "The Fall of the House of Usher," on page 194, is told by a first-person narrator.

The two kinds of third-person point of view, limited and omniscient, are called "third person" because the narrator uses third-person pronouns such as *he* and *she* to refer to the characters. There is no *I* telling the story.

In stories told from the *omniscient third-person point of view,* the narrator knows and tells about what each character feels and thinks. "The Devil and Tom Walker," on page 174, is written from the omniscient third-person point of view.

In stories told from the *limited third-person point of view,* the narrator relates the inner thoughts and feelings of only one character, and everything is viewed from this character's perspective. "An Occurrence at Owl Creek Bridge," on page 464, is written from the limited third-person point of view.
See *Narrator.*

PROSE   *Prose* is the ordinary form of written language. Most writing that is not poetry, drama, or song is considered prose. Prose is one of the major genres of literature and occurs in two forms: fiction and nonfiction.
See *Fiction, Genre,* and *Nonfiction.*

PROTAGONIST   The *protagonist* is the main character in a literary work. In "The Jilting of Granny Weatherall," on page 606, the protagonist is the dying grandmother.
See *Antagonist.*

PUN   A *pun* is a play on words. Robert Frost's "Mending Wall," on page 768, contains a pun in the lines "Before I built a wall I'd ask to know/ What I was walling in or walling out,/And to whom I was like to give offense." Of course, the word "offense" is meant to suggest, in addition to its normal meaning, the phrase "a fence."

PYRRHIC   See *Meter.*

QUATRAIN   See *Stanza.*

REALISM   *Realism* is the presentation in art of the details of actual life. Realism was also a literary movement that began during the nineteenth century and stressed the actual as opposed to the imagined or the fanciful. The Realists tried to write truthfully and objectively about ordinary characters in ordinary situations. They reacted against Romanticism, rejecting heroic, adventurous, unusual, or unfamiliar subjects. The Realists, in turn, were followed by the Naturalists, who traced the effects of heredity and environment on people helpless to change their situations. American realism grew from the work of local-color writers such as Bret Harte and Sarah Orne Jewett and is evident in the writings of major figures such as Mark Twain and Henry James.
See *Local Color, Naturalism,* and *Romanticism.*

REFRAIN   A *refrain* is a repeated line or group of lines in a poem or song. Most refrains end stanzas, as does "And the tide rises, the tide falls," the refrain in Henry Wadsworth Longfellow's poem on page 300; or "Coming for to carry me home," the refrain in "Swing Low, Sweet Chariot," on page 360. Although some refrains are nonsense lines, many increase suspense or emphasize character and theme.

REGIONALISM   *Regionalism* in literature is the tendency among certain authors to write about specific geographical areas. Regional writers, like Willa Cather and William Faulkner, present the distinct culture of an area, including its speech, customs, beliefs, and history. Local-color writing may be considered a type of Regionalism, but Regionalists, like the southern writers of the 1920's, usually go beyond mere presentation of cultural idiosyncracies and attempt, instead, a sophisticated sociological or anthropological treatment of the culture of a region.
See *Local Color* and *Setting.*

REPETITION   *Repetition* is the repeated use of any element of language—a sound, a word, a phrase, a clause, a sentence, a grammatical pattern, or a rhythmical pattern. For example, in "The Mortgaged Heart," on page 902, Carson McCullers repeats key words—*alone, lonely,* and *loneliness*—to connect and unify her arguments. Careless repetition bores a reader, but successful repetition links ideas and emphasizes main points.

RESOLUTION   See *Plot.*

RHYME   *Rhyme* is the repetition of sounds at the ends of words. Rhyming words have identical vowel sounds in their final accented syllables. The consonants before the vowels may be different, but any consonants occurring after these vowels are the same, as in *frog* and *bog* or *willow* and *pillow. End rhyme* occurs when rhyming words are repeated at the ends of lines. *Internal rhyme* occurs when rhyming words fall within a line. *Approximate,* or *slant, rhyme* occurs when the rhyming sounds are similar, but not exact, as in *prove* and *glove.*
See *Rhyme Scheme.*

RHYME SCHEME   A *rhyme scheme* is a regular pattern of rhyming words in a poem. To describe a rhyme scheme, one uses a letter of the alphabet to represent each rhyming sound in a poem or stanza. Consider how letters are used to represent the rhymes in the following example:

With innocent wide penguin eyes, three	a
large fledgling mocking-birds below	b
the pussywillow tree,	a
stand in a row.	b
—Marianne Moore, "Bird-Witted"	

The rhyme scheme of this section of Moore's poem is *abab.*
See *Rhyme.*

RHYTHM   *Rhythm* is the pattern of beats, or stresses, in spoken or written language. Prose and free verse are written in the irregular rhythmical patterns of everyday speech.

Consider, for example, the rhythmical pattern in the following free verse lines by Gwendolyn Brooks:

Lĭfe fŏr mȳ chĭld ĭs sĭmplĕ, ănd ĭs good.
Hĕ knŏws hĭs wĭsh. Yĕs, bŭt thăt ĭs nŏt áll.
Bĕcaúse Í knŏw mĭne tóo.

Traditional poetry often follows a regular rhythmical pattern, as in the following lines by America's first great female poet, Anne Bradstreet:

Ĭn crĭtĭc's hánds bĕwáre thŏu dóst nŏt cóme,
Ănd táke thȳ wáy whĕre yĕt thŏu árt nŏt knówn
    —"The Author to Her Book"

See *Meter.*

RISING ACTION   The *rising action* is that part of the plot in a story that leads up to the climax. During the rising action, suspense increases as the complications of the conflict develop.
See *Plot.*

ROMANCE A *romance* is a story that presents remote or imaginative incidents rather than ordinary, commonplace experiences. Although the events in a romance are improbable or impossible, the characters still reflect what Nathaniel Hawthorne calls "the truth of the human heart." Hawthorne considered his writings, such as *The House of the Seven Gables,* to be "romances" rather than "novels" because they were imaginative rather than realistic.
See *Novel* and *Romanticism.*

ROMANTICISM *Romanticism* was a literary and artistic movement of the nineteenth century that arose in reaction against eighteenth-century Neoclassicism and placed a premium on fancy, imagination, emotion, nature, individuality, and exotica. Romantic elements can be found in the works of American writers as diverse as Cooper, Poe, Thoreau, Emerson, Dickinson, Hawthorne, and Melville. Romanticism is particularly evident in the works of the New England Transcendentalists.
See *Classicism* and *Transcendentalism.*

ROUND CHARACTER See *Character.*

RUN-ON LINE A *run-on line* is one in which the thought continues, without pause, into the next line. Jean Toomer's "Song of the Son" illustrates how a line can run on to the next stanza as well as on to the next line:

> O Negro slaves, dark purple ripened plums,
> Squeezed, and bursting in the pine-wood air,
> Passing, before they stripped the old tree
> bare
> One plum was saved for me, one seed
> becomes
>
> An everlasting song, a singing tree,

Run-on lines change a poem's rhythm, adding variety and helping avoid monotony.
See *End-Stopped Line.*

SATIRE *Satire* is writing that ridicules or criticizes individuals, ideas, institutions, social conventions, or other works of art or literature. The writer of a satire, or satirist, may use a tolerant, sympathetic tone or an angry, bitter tone. Some satire is written in prose and some in poetry. Examples of satire in this text include Edwin Arlington Robinson's "Miniver Cheevy," on page 540, and W. H. Auden's "The Unknown Citizen," on page 783.

SCANSION *Scansion* is the process of analyzing a poem's metrical pattern. When a poem is scanned, its stressed and unstressed syllables are marked to show what poetic feet are used and how many feet appear in each line. The last two lines of Edna St. Vincent Millay's "I Shall Go Back Again to the Bleak Shore" may be scanned as follows:

> But Í | shall fínd | the súl | len rocks |
> and skíes
> Unchanged | from whát | they wére |
> when Í | was young.

See *Meter.*

SCENE See *Drama.*

SENSORY LANGUAGE *Sensory language* is writing or speech that appeals to one or more of the five senses.
See *Image.*

SETTING The *setting* of a literary work is the time and place of the action. A setting may serve any of a number of functions. It may provide a background for the action. It may be a crucial element in the plot or central conflict. It may also create a certain emotional atmosphere, or mood. The setting of Ernest Hemingway's "In Another Country," on page 580, is Milan, Italy, during World War I. The story centers on the hospital in which the protagonist receives physical ther-

apy for a war injury. The setting therefore provides a backdrop for the action and is central to the plot. Hemingway also uses his setting to suggest a mood of disillusionment and isolation.
See *Mood*.

SHORT STORY   A *short story* is a brief work of fiction. The short story resembles the novel but generally has a simpler plot and setting. In addition, the short story tends to reveal character at a crucial moment rather than develop it through many incidents. For example, Thomas Wolfe's "The Far and the Near," on page 616, concentrates on what happens to the engineer when he visits the people who waved to him every day. The American writers Washington Irving, Edgar Allan Poe, and Nathaniel Hawthorne were instrumental in creating and developing the short story genre. Other great American writers of short stories include Mark Twain, Bret Harte, Ambrose Bierce, Sarah Orne Jewett, Willa Cather, Jack London, O. Henry, Ernest Hemingway, Katherine Anne Porter, Eudora Welty, Flannery O'Connor, and John Updike.
See *Fiction* and *Genre*.

SIMILE   A *simile* is a figure of speech that makes a direct comparison between two subjects using either *like* or *as.* Here are two examples of similes:

> The trees looked like pitch forks against the sullen sky.

> Her hair was as red as a robin's breast.

See *Figurative Language.*

SOLILOQUY   A *soliloquy* in a play or prose work is a long speech made by a character who is alone and who reveals his or her private thoughts and feelings to the audience. By alternating the speeches of Paul Klee and of the Secret Police in his story on page 866, Donald Barthelme adapts the soliloquy to the short story.
See *Monologue.*

SONNET   A *sonnet* is a fourteen-line lyric poem focused on a single theme. Sonnets have many variations but are usually written in iambic pentameter, following one of two traditional patterns. The *Petrarchan,* or *Italian, sonnet* is divided into two parts, the eight-line octave and the six-line sestet. The octave rhymes *abba abba,* whereas the sestet generally rhymes *cde cde* or uses some combination of *cd* rhymes. The two parts of the Petrarchan sonnet work together: The octave raises a question, states a problem, or presents a brief narrative, and the sestet answers the question, solves the problem, or comments on the narrative.

The *Shakespearean,* or *English, sonnet* is made up of three quatrains and a concluding couplet and follows the rhyme scheme *abab cdcd efef gg.* Although the three quatrains may state and resolve a problem, as in the Petrarchan octave and sestet, each quatrain usually explores a different aspect of the main theme. The couplet then sums up the poem.
See *Lyric.*

SPEAKER   The *speaker* is the voice of a poem. Although the speaker is often the poet, the speaker may also be a fictional character or even an inanimate object or another type of nonhuman entity. Interpreting a poem often depends upon recognizing who the speaker is, whom the speaker is addressing, and what the speaker's attitude, or tone, is. In these lines from Sylvia Plath's "Mushrooms," the speaker is one (or perhaps all) of the mushrooms of the title:

> We shall by morning
> Inherit the earth.
> Our foot's in the door.

See *Point of View.*

SPIRITUAL A *spiritual* is a type of African American folk song dating from the period of slavery and Reconstruction. A typical spiritual deals both with religious freedom and, on an allegorical level, with political and economic freedom. For example, in some spirituals the Biblical river Jordan was used as a symbol for the Ohio River, which separated slave states from free states, and the Biblical promised land, Canaan, was used as a symbol for the free northern United States. The spirituals were developed on models derived from white American hymns and from African work songs and chants. Most spirituals contained Biblical allusions and made use of repetition, parallelism, and rhyme. Spirituals had a profound influence on the development of both poetry and song in the United States. See "Swing Low, Sweet Chariot," on page 360, and "Go Down, Moses," on page 361.

SPONDEE See *Meter.*

STAGE DIRECTIONS See *Drama.*

STANZA A *stanza* is a group of lines in a poem that are considered to be a unit. Many poems are divided into stanzas that are separated by spaces. Stanzas often function just like paragraphs in prose. Each stanza states and develops a single main idea.

Stanzas are commonly named according to the number of lines found in them, as follows:
1. *Couplet:* a two-line stanza
2. *Tercet:* a three-line stanza
3. *Quatrain:* a four-line stanza
4. *Cinquain:* a five-line stanza
5. *Sestet:* a six-line stanza
6. *Heptastich:* a seven-line stanza
7. *Octave:* an eight-line stanza

STATIC CHARACTER See *Character.*

STEREOTYPE See *Character.*

STREAM OF CONSCIOUSNESS *Stream of consciousness* is a narrative technique that presents thoughts as if they were coming directly from a character's mind. Instead of being arranged in chronological order, the events of the story are presented from the character's point of view, mixed in with the character's feelings and memories just as they might spontaneously occur in the mind of a real person. Katherine Anne Porter uses this technique in "The Jilting of Granny Weatherall," on page 606, to capture Granny's dying thoughts and feelings. Ambrose Bierce also uses the stream-of-consciousness technique in his short story "An Occurrence at Owl Creek Bridge," which appears on page 464. Stream-of-consciousness writing reveals a character's complex psychology and presents it in realistic detail.
See *Point of View.*

STYLE A writer's *style* is his or her typical way of writing. Style includes word choice, tone, degree of formality, figurative language, rhythm, grammatical structure, sentence length, organization—in short, every feature of a writer's use of language. Ernest Hemingway, for example, is noted for a simple prose style that contrasts with Thomas Paine's aphoristic style and with N. Scott Momaday's reflective style.
See *Diction, Ornate Style,* and *Plain Style.*

SUBPLOT A *subplot* is a second, less important plot within a story. A subplot may add to, contrast with, reflect, or vary the main plot.
See *Plot.*

SURPRISE ENDING A *surprise ending* is a conclusion that violates the expectations of the reader. Often a surprise ending is foreshadowed, or subtly hinted at, throughout the course of a work.

SUSPENSE *Suspense* is a feeling of growing uncertainty about the outcome of events in a liter-

ary work. Writers create suspense by raising questions in the minds of their readers. Because readers are curious or concerned, they keep reading to find out what will happen next. Suspense builds until the climax of the plot, at which point the suspense reaches its peak. Thereafter, the suspense is generally resolved.
See *Climax* and *Plot.*

SYMBOL   A *symbol* is anything that stands for or represents something else. A *conventional symbol* is one that is widely known and accepted, such as a voyage symbolizing life or a skull symbolizing death. A *personal symbol* is one developed for a particular work by a particular author. Examples in this text include Hawthorne's black veil, Melville's white whale, and Faulkner's bear.

SYMBOLISM   *Symbolism* was a literary movement during the nineteenth century that influenced many poets, including the Imagists and T. S. Eliot. Symbolists turned away from everyday realistic details, trying instead to express emotions by using a pattern of symbols.
See *Imagism* and *Realism.*

SYNECDOCHE   *Synecdoche* is a figure of speech in which a part of something is used to stand for the whole thing. In "Recuerdo," when Edna St. Vincent Millay says, "We hailed, 'Good morrow, mother!' to a shawl-covered head," the shawl-covered head stands for the woman being greeted.
See *Figurative Language.*

TERCET   See *Stanza.*

TETRAMETER   See *Meter.*

THEME   A *theme* is a central message or insight into life revealed by a literary work. An essay's theme is often directly stated in its thesis statement. The theme of a story, poem, or play, however, is usually not directly stated. For example, in "A Worn Path," on page 622, Eudora Welty does not directly say that Phoenix Jackson's difficult journey shows the power of love, but readers learn this indirectly by the end of the story.

THIRD-PERSON POINT OF VIEW   See *Point of View.*

TONE   The *tone* of a literary work is the writer's attitude toward his or her subject, characters, or audience. A writer's tone may be formal or informal, friendly or distant, personal or pompous. For example, William Faulkner's tone in his "Nobel Prize Acceptance Speech," on page 658, is earnest and serious, whereas James Thurber's tone in "The Night the Ghost Got In," on page 684, is humorous and ironic.
See *Mood.*

TRANSCENDENTALISM   *Transcendentalism* was an American literary and philosophical movement of the nineteenth century. The Transcendentalists, who were based in New England, believed that intuition and the individual conscience "transcend" experience and thus are better guides to truth than are the senses and logical reason. Influenced by Romanticism, the Transcendentalists respected the individual spirit and the natural world, believing that divinity was present everywhere, in nature and in each person. This last notion, that of an omnipresent divinity, or Over-Soul, shows the influence on Transcendentalism of the Hindu religion and of the Swedish mystic Emanuel Swedenborg. The Transcendentalists included Ralph Waldo Emerson, Henry David Thoreau, Bronson Alcott, W. H. Channing, Margaret Fuller, and Elizabeth Peabody.
See *Romanticism.*

TRIMETER   See *Meter.*

TROCHEE See *Meter.*

UNDERSTATEMENT *Understatement* means saying less than is actually meant, generally in an ironic way. An example of understatement is the description of a flooded area as "slightly soggy." See *Figurative Language, Hyperbole,* and *Irony.*

VERBAL IRONY See *Irony.*

VERNACULAR The *vernacular* is the ordinary language of people in a particular region. Instead of using a more formal literary language, writers may use the vernacular to create realistic characters or to approach readers informally.
See *Dialect.*

VILLANELLE A *villanelle* is a nineteen-line poem with only two rhymes that follows a strict pattern popular in traditional French poetry. It has two refrains formed by repeating line 1 in lines 6, 12, and 18 and by repeating line 3 in lines 9, 15, and 19. The three lines in each of the first five 3-line stanzas rhyme *aba;* the final quatrain rhymes *abaa.* An example of a villanelle in this text is Theodore Roethke's "The Waking," on page 954.

GLOSSARY

READING THE GLOSSARY ENTRIES

The words in this glossary are from selections appearing in your textbook. Each entry in the glossary contains the following parts:

1. Entry Word. This word appears at the beginning of the entry in boldface type.

2. Pronunciation. The symbols in parentheses tell how the entry word is pronounced. If a word has more than one possible pronunciation, the most common of these pronunciations is given first.

3. Part of Speech. Appearing after the pronunciation, in italics, is an abbreviation that tells the part of speech of the entry word. The following abbreviations have been used:

n. noun   **p.** pronoun   **v.** verb
adj. adjective   **adv.** adverb   **conj.** conjunction

4. Definition. This part of the entry follows the part-of-speech abbreviation and gives the meaning of the entry word as used in the selection in which it appears.

KEY TO PRONUNCIATION SYMBOLS USED IN THE GLOSSARY

The following symbols are used in the pronunciations that follow the entry words:

Symbol	Key Words	Symbol	Key Words
a	asp, fat, parrot	b	bed, fable, dub
ā	ape, date, play	d	dip, beadle, had
ä	ah, car, father	f	fall, after, off
		g	get, haggle, dog
e	elf, ten, berry	h	he, ahead, hotel
ē	even, meet, money	j	joy, agile, badge
		k	kill, tackle, bake
i	is, hit, mirror	l	let, yellow, ball
ī	ice, bite, high	m	met, camel, trim
		n	not, flannel, ton
ō	open, tone, go	p	put, apple, tap
ô	all, horn, law	r	red, port, dear
o͞o	ooze, tool, crew	s	sell, castle, pass
oo	look, pull, moor	t	top, cattle, hat
yo͞o	use, cute, few	v	vat, hovel, have
yoo	united, cure, globule	w	will, always, swear
oi	oil, point, toy	y	yet, onion, yard
ou	out, crowd, plow	z	zebra, dazzle, haze
u	up, cut, color	ch	chin, catcher, arch
ʉr	urn, fur, deter	sh	she, cushion, dash
		th	thin, nothing, truth
ə	a in ago	th	then, father, lathe
	e in agent	zh	azure, leisure
	i in sanity	ŋ	ring, anger, drink
	o in comply	'	[indicates that a
	u in focus		following l or n is a
ər	perhaps, murder		syllabic consonant,
			as in able (ā' b'l)]

FOREIGN SOUNDS

à This symbol, representing the a in French salle, can best be described as intermediate between (a) and (ä).

ë This symbol represents the sound of the vowel cluster in French coeur and can be approximated by rounding the lips as for (ō) and pronouncing (e).

ö This symbol variously represents the sound of eu in French feu or of ö or oe in German blöd or Goethe and can be approximated by rounding the lips as for (ō) and pronouncing (ā).

ō̇ This symbol represents a range of sounds between (ô) and (u); it occurs typically in the sound of the o in French tonne or German korrekt; in Italian poco and Spanish torero, it is almost like English (ô), as in horn.

ü This symbol variously represents the sound of u in French duc and in German grun and can be approximated by rounding the lips as for (ō) and pronouncing (ē).

kh This symbol represents the voiceless velar or uvular fricative as in the ch of German doch or Scots English loch. It can be approximated by placing the tongue as for (k) but allowing the breath to escape in a stream, as in pronouncing (h).

r This symbol represents any of various sounds used in languages other than English for the consonant r. It may represent the tongue-point trill or uvular trill of the r in French reste or sur, German Reuter, Italian ricotta, Russian gorod, etc.

ƀ This symbol represents the sound made by the letter v between vowels. It is pronounced like a b sound but without letting the lips come together.

A

abash (ə bash') *v.* To make ashamed

aberrations (ab' ər ā' shənz) *n.* Departures from what is right, true, or correct

abeyance (ə bā' əns) *n.* A temporary suspension

abiding (ə bīd' iŋ) *adj.* Enduring; lasting

abject (ab' jekt) *adj.* Wretched

ablution (ab lo͞o' shən) *n.* A washing or cleansing of the body as part of a religious rite

abrogated (ab' rə gāt' əd) *v.* Canceled

acclivity (ə kliv' ə tē) *n.* An upward slope

acquiesce (ak' wē es') *v.* To agree without protest

adamant (ad' ə mənt) *adj.* Unyielding

adhere (əd hir') *v.* To stick fast; stay attached

adieu (ə dyo͞o') *n.* "Farewell" (French)

adumbration (ad' um brā' shən) *n.* A shadowy outline

aesthetic (es thet' ik) *adj.* Of beauty

affliction (ə flik' shən) *n.* Pain or distress

agape (ə gāp') *adj.* Wide open

aggregate (ag' rə gət) *n.* The sum total

ague (ā' gyo͞o) *n.* A chill or fit of shivering

alacrity (ə lak' rə tē) *n.* Speed

albeit   (ôl bē′ it)   *conj.* Although

alburnum   (al bur′ nəm)   *n.* The soft wood between the bark and the heartwood where water is conducted

alderman   (ôl′ dər mən)   *n.* A member of a local council

amain   (ə mān′)   *adv.* At or with great speed

amalgam   (ə mal′ gəm)   *n.* An alloy of mercury used with silver as dental filling

ameliorate   (ə mēl′ yə rāt′)   *v.* Improve

anachronism   (ə nak′ rə niz′m)   *n.* Something that is or seems to be out of its proper time

analogy   (ə nal′ ə jē)   *n.* Similarity in some respects between things otherwise unlike

anarchy   (an′ ər kē)   *n.* The absence of government

anathema   (ə nath′ ə mə)   *n.* Curse

anomalous   (ə näm′ ə ləs)   *adj.* Abnormal; deviating from the regular arrangement, general rule, or usual method

antipodes   (an tip′ ə dēz′)   *n.* On the opposite side of the globe

aphid   (ā′ fid)   *n.* Small insect that sucks the juice from plants

apotheosis   (a pōth′ ē ō′ sis)   *n.* Glorification

apparition   (ap′ ə rish′ ən)   *n.* The act of appearing or becoming invisible

appellation   (ap′ ə lā shən)   *n.* A name or title

approbation   (ap′ rə bā′ shən)   *n.* Approval

apropos   (ap′ rə pō′)   *adv.* At the right time

ardor   (är′ dər)   *n.* Emotional warmth; passion

arduous   (är′ jōō wəs)   *adj.* Very difficult

arrest   (ə rest′)   *v.* To stop or check the motion

articulate   (är tik′ yōō lit)   *adj.* Able to express oneself easily and clearly

aspiration   (as′ pə rā′ shən)   *n.* Strong desire or ambition, as for advancement, honor

assail   (ə sāl′)   *v.* 1. To attack violently; assault 2. to have a forceful effect on

assent   (ə sent′)   *v.* To agree

assuage   (ə swāj′)   *v.* To lessen

astray   (ə strā′)   *adv.* Off the right path or way; wandering

asunder   (ə sun′ dər)   *adv.* Into parts or pieces

asylum   (ə sī′ ləm)   *n.* A place of refuge

attest   (ə test′)   *v.* To bear witness

audaciously   (ô dā′ shəs lē)   *adj.* Boldly

auger   (ô′ gər)   *n.* A tool used for drilling teeth

auroral   (ô rôr′ əl)   *adj.* Resembling the dawn

auspice   (ôs′ pəs′)   *n.* Approval and support

austere   (ô stir′)   *adj.* Showing strict self-discipline and self-denial

avarice   (av′ ər is)   *n.* Greed

aversion   (ə vur′ zhən)   *n.* An intense or definite dislike

avidly   (av′ id lē)   *adv.* Eagerly and enthusiastically

B

banshee   (ban′ shē)   *n.* In Scottish and Irish folklore, a female spirit believed to wail outside a house as a warning that a death will soon occur in the family

base   (bās)   *v.* Mean; contemptible

bastion   (bas′ chən)   *n.* A fortification

bayou   (bī′ ōō)   *n.* A sluggish, marshy inlet or outlet of a lake or river

beguile   (bi gīl′)   *v.* To charm; deceive

behold   (bi hōld′)   *v.* To look

beholden   (bi hōld′ ən)   *adj.* Owing thanks; indebted

beleaguered   (bi lē′ gərd)   *adj.* Encircled by an army

belie   (bi lī′)   *v.* To prove false

bellicose   (bel′ ə kōs)   *adj.* Quarrelsome

benevolent   (bə nev′ ə lənt)   *adj.* Kindly; charitable

benign   (bi nīn′)   *adj.* Doing little or no harm; not malignant

bereaved   (bi rēvd′)   *n.* The survivors of recently deceased people

bereavement   (bi rēv′ mənt)   *n.* The sadness resulting from the loss or death of a loved one

berserk   (bər surk′)   *adj.* In a frenzy, after a legendary Norse warrior who worked himself into a frenzy before battle

beseech   (bi sēch′)   *v.* To ask earnestly; implore

billet   (bil′ it)   *n.* A brief letter

binnacle   (bin′ ə k'l)   *n.* The case enclosing the ship's compass

blithe   (blith)   *adj.* Carefree

blunt   (blunt)   *v.* To make dull

brachycephalic   (brak′ i sə fal′ ik)   *adj.* Short-headed or broad-headed

brazenness   (brā′ zən nəs)   *n.* Shamelessness; boldness

brindled   (brin′ d'ld)   *adj.* Having a gray or tawny coat with streaks of darker color

brocaded   (brō kād′ id)   *adj.* Having a raised design woven into it

brood   (brōōd)   *v.* To ponder in a troubled or mournful way

C

cache   (kash)   *v.* To hide

cairn   (kern)   *n.* A conical heap of stones built as a monument or landmark

calamity   (kə lam′ ə tē)   *n.* A disaster

callow   (kal′ ō)   *adj.* Immature; inexperienced

calumny   (kal′ əm nē)   *n.* False accusation; slander

camaraderie   (käm′ ə räd′ ər ē)   *n.* Warm, friendly feelings

candid   (kan′ did)   *adj.* Impartial

caper   (kā′ pər)   *n.* A prank

capitulate   (kə pich′ ə lāt′)   *v.* To surrender conditionally

capstan   (kap′ stən)   *n.* A large cylinder, turned by hand, around which cables are wound

Carrara   (kə rä′ rə)   *n.* A fine, white marble

castanets   (kas′ tə nets′)   *n.* Small, hollowed out pieces of wood, held in the hand by a connecting cord and clicked together with the fingers

cataleptical (kat' 'l ep' tik 'l)   *adj.* In a state in which consciousness and feeling are suddenly and temporarily lost and the muscles become rigid

celestial (sə les' chəl)   *adj.* Of the heavens

chafe (chāf)   *v.* To rub to make warm

chaos (kā' äs)   *n.* The disorder of formless matter and infinite space, supposed to have existed before the ordered universe

chaparral (chap' ə ral')   *n.* A thicket of thorny bushes or shrubs

charnel (chär' n'l)   *adj.* Like a graveyard

cherub (cher' əb)   *n.* A representation of a heavenly being as a winged child with a chubby, rosy face

chronic (krän' ik)   *adj.* Continuing indefinitely

cipher (sī' fər)   *v.* To figure

cirrus (sir' əs)   *n.* High, detached wispy clouds

cleave (klēv)   *v.* Split

clematis (klem' ə tis)   *n.* A woody vine with bright-colored flowers

collateral (kə lat' ər əl)   *adj.* Descended from the same ancestors, but in a different line

commensurate (kə men' shər it)   *adj.* Corresponding in amount, magnitude, or degree

commissary (käm' ə ser' ē)   *n.* A person to whom some duty is given by authority

conceit (kən sēt')   *n.* A strange or fanciful idea

conciliatory (kən sil' ē ə tōr' ē)   *adj.* Tending to soothe the anger of

confederate (kən fed' ər it)   *adj.* United with others for a common purpose

conflagration (kän' flə grā' shən)   *n.* A big, destructive fire

congenial (kən jēn' yəl)   *adj.* Compatible; friendly; sympathetic

conjectural (kən jek' chər əl)   *adj.* Based on guesswork

conjecture (kən jek' chər)   *v.* To guess

connate (kän' āt)   *adj.* Having the same origin or nature

connivance (kə nī' vəns)   *n.* Secret cooperation

consanguinity (kän' saŋ gwin' ə tē)   *n.* Kinship

consecrate (kän' sə krāt')   *v.* To cause to be revered or honored

consternation (kän' stər nā' shən)   *n.* A great fear or shock that makes one feel helpless or bewildered

contemptuous (kən temp' chōō əs)   *adj.* Full of contempt; scornful

contentious (kän ten' shəs)   *adj.* Quarrelsome

continuum (ken tin' yōo wəm)   *n.* A continuous whole with parts that cannot be separated

contrive (kən trīv')   *v.* To scheme

convoluted (kän' və lōot' id)   *adj.* Intricate; complicated

copious (kō' pē əs)   *adj.* Very plentiful; abundant

cormorant (kôr' mə rənt)   *n.* A large, diving bird with a hooked beak and webbed toes

cornice (kôr' nis)   *n.* The projecting decorative molding along the top of a building

corollary (kôr' ə ler' ē)   *n.* An easily drawn conclusion

countenance (koun' tə nəns)   *n.* A facial expression

cozen (kuz' ən)   *v.* To cheat

crape (krāp)   *n.* A piece of black cloth worn as a sign of mourning

craven (krā' vən)   *adj.* Very cowardly

crescendo (krə shen' dō)   *adj.* Gradually increasing in loudness or intensity

crypt (kript)   *n.* An underground chamber or vault

cryptic (krip' tik)   *adj.* Having a hidden or ambiguous meaning

cunning (kun' iŋ)   *adj.* Skillful in deception; crafty; sly

curlew (kʉr' lōo)   *n.* A large, long-legged wading bird whose call is associated with the evening

cyclonic (sī klän' ik)   *adj.* Like a cyclone, a windstorm with violent, whirling movement

cynical (sin' i k'l)   *adj.* Denying the sincerity of people's motives and actions

cynicism (sin' ə siz'm)   *n.* The denial of the sincerity of people's motives or actions or of the value of living

D

declivity (di kliv' ə tē)   *n.* A downward slope

decorously (dek' ə rəs lē)   *adv.* Characterized by or showing decorum, propriety, good taste

deference (def' ər əns)   *n.* A courteous regard or respect

deferential (def' ə ren' shəl)   *adj.* Very respectful

degenerate (di jen' ər it)   *adj.* Deteriorated

deliberation (di lib' ə rā' shən)   *n.* Careful consideration

delusion (di lōo' zhən)   *n.* A false belief

demean (di mēn')   *v.* To behave; conduct

demiculverin (dem' ē kul' vər in)   A large cannon

demur (di mʉr')   *v.* To object

depravity (di prav' ə tē)   *n.* Corruption; wickedness

deprecating (dep' rə kāt' iŋ)   *adj.* Expressing disapproval

derivative (də riv' ə tiv)   *adj.* Arrived at through complex reasoning

desolate (des' ə lit)   *adj.* Forlorn; wretched

despotic (de spät' ik)   *adj.* Harsh; cruel; unjust

despotism (des' pə tiz'm)   *n.* Tyranny

detention (dē ten' shən)   *n.* A keeping in custody; confinement

diabolical (dī' ə bäl' ə k'l)   *adj.* Of the devil

dictum (dik' təm)   *n.* A statement or saying

digress (dī gres')   *v.* To depart temporarily from the main subject

dilapidated (di lap' ə dāt' id)   *adj.* In disrepair

diligence (dil' ə jəns)   *n.* A constant, careful effort; perseverance

diligent (dil' ə jənt)   *adj.* Hard-working; industrious

din (din)   *n.* A loud, continuous noise or clamor

discern (di sʉrn')   *v.* To perceive or recognize; make out clearly

discordant (dis kôr' d'nt)   *adj.* Not in harmony; clashing

dispatch   (di spach′)   *v.* To put an end to; kill

disposition   (dis′ pə zish′ ən)   *n.* An inclination or tendency

dissembling   (di sem′ bliŋ)   *n.* Pretense; hiding under false appearances

diverse   (də vʉrs′)   *adj.* Various

diversity   (də vʉr′ sə tē)   *n.* Difference

divine   (də vīn′)   *n.* A clergyman

docile   (däs′ 'l)   *adj.* Obedient

dolorous   (dō′ lər əs)   *adj.* Sad; mournful

dominion   (də min′ yən)   *n.* The power to rule

doubloon   (du blōōn′)   *n.* The gold coin Ahab offered as reward to the first man to spot the whale

dour   (door)   *adj.* Stern; severe

drayman   (drā′ mən)   *n.* The driver of a dray, a low cart with detachable sides

dubious   (dōō′ bē əs)   *adj.* Questionable

duodecimos   (dōō′ ə des′ ə mōz)   *n.* Books about five by eight inches

dusky   (dus′ kē)   *adj.* Dim; shadowy

dynastic   (dī nas′ tik)   *adj.* Of a period during which a certain family rules

dyspepsia   (dis pep′ sē ə)   *n.* Indigestion

E

eccentric   (ik sen′ trik)   *adj.* Peculiar

efface   (i fās′)   *v.* To wipe out; obliterate

effigy   (ef′ i jē)   *n.* A portrait, statue, or other likeness of a person

effluvium   (e flōō′ vē əm)   *n.* An aura

effrontery   (e frun′ tər ē)   *n.* Unashamed boldness

effuse   (e fyōōz′)   *v.* To spread out; diffuse

egalitarian   (i gal′ ə ter′ ē ən)   *adj.* Asserting, resulting from, or characterized by the belief in the equality of all people

eloquence   (el′ ə kwəns)   *n.* Expressiveness; persuasive power

elusive   (i lōō′ siv)   *adj.* Hard to grasp

embrasure   (em brā′ zhər)   *n.* An opening

eminence   (em′ ə nəns)   *n.* Greatness; celebrity

eminent   (em′ ə nənt)   *adj.* Distinguished

empirical   (em pir′ i kəl)   *adj.* Relying or based solely on experiment and observation rather than theory

engrossed   (en grōst′)   *adj.* Absorbed

enigmatic   (en′ig mat′ ik)   *adj.* Perplexing; baffling; mysterious

ephemeral   (i fem′ ər əl)   *adj.* Short-lived

equanimity   (ek′ wə nim′ ə tē)   *n.* Composure

equivocal   (i kwiv′ ə k'l)   *adj.* Having more than one possible interpretation

eschew   (es chōō′)   *v.* To abstain from

ether   (ē′ thər)   *n.* A chemical compound used as an anesthetic

etherize   (ē′ thə rīz)   *v.* To anesthetize as with ether

etiquette   (et′ i kət)   *n.* The rules for manners and ceremonies

evanescence   (ev′ ə nes′ 'ns)   *n.* A fading from sight

evanescently   (ev′ ə nes′ 'nt lē)   *adv.* Fleetingly

evitable   (ev′ ə tə b'l)   *adj.* Avoidable

exalt   (eg zôlt′)   *v.* To fill with joy, pride; elate

exigency   (ek′ sə jən sē)   *n.* A pressing need; demand

exile   (eks′ īl)   *v.* To banish

expatriated   (eks pā′ trē āt′ id)   *adj.* Deported; driven from one's native land

expedient   (ek spē′ dē ənt)   *adj.* Useful for effecting a desired result; convenient

expostulation   (ik späs′ chə lā′ shən)   *n.* Expression of objection

extort   (ek stôrt′)   *v.* To obtain by threat or violence

extricate   (eks′ trə kāt)   *v.* To set free

exude   (eg zōōd′)   *v.* To ooze, discharge

F

facetious   (fə sē′ shəs)   *adj.* Joking at an inappropriate time

facile   (fas′ 'l)   *adj.* Fluent

fallow   (fal′ ō)   *adj.* Left uncultivated or unplanted

fallowness   (fal′ ō nis)   *n.* Inactivity

fast   (fast)   *v.* To eat very little or nothing

fecundity   (fi kun′ də tē)   *n.* Productivity

feign   (fān)   *v.* To make a false show of

felicitate   (fə lis′ ə tāt)   *v.* To congratulate

felicity   (fə lis′ ə tē)   *n.* Happiness; bliss

festoon   (fes tōōn′)   *n.* A wreath of flowers or leaves

fettuccine   (fet′ ōō chē′ nē)   *n.* Broad, flat noodles

finite   (fī′ nīt)   *adj.* Having measurable or definable limits

flogging   (fläg′ iŋ)   *n.* A beating with a strap, stick, or whip, as punishment

flourish   (flʉr′ ish)   *v.* To grow vigorously; succeed; thrive; prosper

flume   (flōōm)   *n.* An artificial channel for carrying water to provide power and transport objects

folio   (fō′ lē ō′)   *n.* The largest regular size of books, over eleven inches in height

foppery   (fäp′ ər ē)   *n.* Foolishness

foreboding   (fôr bōd′ iŋ)   *n.* A prediction

foreknowledge   (fôr′ näl′ ij)   *n.* Knowledge of something before it happens or exists; prescience

forestall   (fôr stôl′)   *v.* To act in advance of

fortuitous   (fôr tōō′ ə təs)   *adj.* Fortunate

frippery   (frip′ ər ē)   *n.* A showy display of elegance

frugally   (frōō′ g'l ē)   *adv.* Thriftily

furtive   (fʉr′ tiv)   *adj.* Sneaky; shifty; secretive

G

gall   (gôl)   *n.* Bitterness

garret   (gar′ it)   *n.* An attic

garrulous   (gar′ ə ləs)   *adj.* Talking too much

gaudy   (gôd′ ē)   *adj.* Cheaply brilliant

genuflect   (jen′ yə flekt′)   *v.* To bend the knee, as in reverence or worship

gerfalcon   (jʉr′ fal′ k'n)   *n.* A large, fierce falcon of the Arctic

gesticulate   (jes tik′ yə lāt)   *v.* To gesture with hands or arms

glean (glēn) *v.* To collect the remaining grain after reaping

glee (glē) *n.* An unaccompanied song

gloaming (glō′ miŋ) *n.* The evening dusk; twilight

goatee (gō tē′) *n.* A small, pointed beard

gossamer (gäs′ ə mər) *n.* A very thin, soft, filmy cloth

gourd (gôrd) *adj.* The dried, hollowed-out shell of a piece of fruit from a gourd plant, often used as a dipper or drinking cup

gracile (gras′ 'l) *adj.* Slender; slim

grandeur (gran′ jər) *adj.* Magnificence

grave (grāv) *adj.* Serious; solemn

gripsack (grip′ sak) *n.* A small bag for holding clothes

guffaw (gə fô′) *v.* To laugh in a loud, coarse manner

guile (gīl) *n.* Craftiness

guise (gīz) *n.* A manner or way

guttural (gut′ ər əl) *adj.* Of the throat

H

hallow (hal′ ō) *v.* To honor as sacred

halyard (hal′ yərd) *n.* A rope for raising or lowering sail

harrow (här′ ō) *v.* To distress

herald (her′ əld) *n.* A messenger

heritage (her′ i tij′) *n.* Property that is or can be inherited

hernia (hʉr′ nē ə) *n.* The protrusion of part of the intestine through the abdominal muscles

heron (her′ ən) *n.* A wading bird with a long neck, long legs, and a long, tapered bill

hieroglyphic (hī′ ər ō glif′ ik) *n.* A picture or symbol representing a word, syllable, or sound

hoary (hôr′ ē) *adj.* Very old; ancient

hostler (häs′ lər) *n.* A person who tends horses at an inn or stable

humble (hum′ b'l) *adj.* Not proud; modest

husbandry (huz′ bən drē) *n.* Farming

hypnotic (hip nät′ ik) *adj.* Inducing a sleeplike condition

I

ideality (ī′ dē al′ ə tē) *n.* Something that is ideal and has no reality

illiterate (i lit′ ər it) *adj.* Unable to read or write

illumination (i lōō′ mə nā′ shən) *n.* The supplying of light

imbibe (im bīb′) *v.* To drink in

immemorial (im′ mə môr′ ē əl) *adj.* Extending back beyond memory or record

impalpable (im pal′ pə b'l) *adj.* Imperceptible to the sense of touch

impeccable (im pek′ ə bəl) *adj.* Without defect or error; flawless

imperceptible (im′ pər sep′ tə b'l) *adj.* Not plain or distinct to the senses or the mind

imperially (im pir′ ē əl ē) *adv.* Majestically

imperious (im pir′ ē əs) *adj.* Urgent

impertinent (im pʉr′ t'n ənt) *adj.* Not showing proper respect

impetuous (im pech′ oo wəs) *adj.* Acting or done suddenly with little thought; rash; impulsive; moving with great force or violence

impious (im′ pē əs) *adj.* Lacking reverence for God

implacable (im plak′ ə b'l) *adj.* Relentless

importunate (im pôr′ chə nit) *adj.* Insistent

importunity (im′ pôr tōōn′ ə te) *n.* A persistent request or demand

imprecation (im′ prə kā′ shən) *n.* A curse

impregnable (im preg′ nə b'l) *adj.* Unshakable; unyielding

improvident (im präv′ ə dənt) *adj.* Failing to provide for the future; lacking foresight or thrift

inanimate (in an′ ə mit) *adj.* Not endowed with life

inauspicious (in′ ôs pish′ əs) *adj.* Not boding well for the future

incessantly (in ses′ 'nt lē) *adv.* Unceasingly

incisor (in sī′ zər) *n.* A front tooth

incongruous (in käŋ′ grōō wəs) *adj.* Incompatible

inconsiderable (in′ kən sid′ ər ə bəl) *adj.* Not worth consideration; unimportant

incredulously (in krej′ ōō ləs lē) *adv.* Skeptically; doubtingly

incubus (iŋ′ kyə bəs) *n.* Something nightmarishly burdensome

inculcation (in′ kul kā′ shən) *n.* Teaching by repetition and insistent urging

incursion (in kʉr′ zhən) *n.* A sudden, brief invasion or raid

indecorous (in dek′ ər əs) *adj.* Improper

indigo (in′ di gō′) *n.* A blue dye

ineffable (in ef′ ə b'l) *adj.* Inexpressible

inert (in ʉrt′) *adj.* Motionless

infidel (in′ fə del′) *n.* A person who holds no religious belief

ingratiating (in grā′ shē āt′ iŋ) *adj.* Bringing into favor

iniquity (in ik′ wə tē) *n.* A sin

insidious (in sid′ ē əs) *adj.* Deceitful; secretly treacherous

insinuate (in sin′ yōō wāt′) *v.* To hint or suggest indirectly; imply

integrity (in teg′ rə tē) *n.* The adherence to a code of values

interminable (in tʉr′ mi nə b'l) *adj.* Seeming to last forever; without, or apparently without, end

intimacy (in′ tə mə sē) *n.* The state or fact of being intimate or familiar

intriguing (in trē′ giŋ) *adj.* Exciting interest or curiosity

intuitively (in tōō′ i tiv lē) *adv.* Instinctively

inviolable (in vī′ ə lə b'l) *adj.* Safe from danger

ipecacuanha (ip′ ə kak′ yōō wan′ ə) *n.* A plant with roots used for medicinal purposes

J

jauntily (jôn′ ti lē) *adv.* In a carefree fashion

javelin (jav′ lin) *n.* A light spear for throwing

jocularity (jäk′ yə lar′ ə tē)   *n.* A joking good humor

jubilant (jo͞o′ bə lənt)   *adj.* Joyful and triumphant; elated; rejoicing

juxtaposition (juk′ stə pə zish′ ən)   *n.* Placing side by side

L

laggard (lag′ ərd)   *adj.* Slow or late in doing things

lamentation (lam′ ən tā′ shən)   *n.* The outward expression of grief

lance (lans)   *n.* A long wooden stabbing weapon with a sharp metal spearhead

latent (lāt′ 'nt)   *adj.* Present but invisible or inactive; lying hidden and undeveloped within a person or thing, as a quality or power

legacy (leg′ ə sē)   *n.* The money or property left to someone by a will

levee (lev′ ē)   *n.* A landing place along the bank of a river

licentious (lī sen′ shəs)   *adj.* Disregarding accepted rules

limber (lim′ bər)   *adj.* Flexible

list (list)   *v.* To sway

literalist (lit′ ər əl ist)   *n.* One who insists on the exact meaning of words

loath (lōth)   *adj.* Reluctant; unwilling

loathsome (lōth′ səm)   *adj.* Causing loathing; disgusting; abhorrent; detestable

lubber (lub′ ər)   *n.* A slow, clumsy person

lucidity (lo͞o sid′ i tē)   *n.* Brightness

lugubrious (lə go͞o′ brē əs)   *adj.* Very sad or mournful

lull (lul)   *v.* To calm or soothe by gentle sound or motion

luminary (lo͞o′ mə ner′ ē)   *adj.* Giving off light

luminous (lo͞o′ mə nəs)   *adj.* Shining; bright

lurid (lo͝or′ id)   *adj.* Vivid in a harsh or shocking way

lustrous (lus′ trəs)   *adj.* Shining

lusty (lus′ tē)   *adj.* Strong; hearty

lye (lī)   *n.* Any strongly alkaline substance, usually sodium or potassium hydroxide, used in cleaning, making soap

M

magnanimity (mag′ nə nim′ ə tē)   *n.* Ability to rise above pettiness or meanness; generosity

magnanimous (mag nan′ ə məs)   *adj.* Noble in mind; rising above pettiness and meanness

mah-jongg (mä′ jôŋ′)   *n.* A game of Chinese origin, played with pieces resembling dominoes

malediction (mal′ ə dik′ shən)   *n.* A curse

malevolence (mə lev′ ə ləns)   *n.* The quality or state of being malevolent; malice; spitefulness

malevolent (mə lev′ ə lənt)   *adj.* Wishing evil or harm to others

malign (mə līn′)   *adj.* Evil

malinger (mə liŋ′ gər)   *v.* To pretend to be ill

mammoth (mam′ əth)   *n.* An extinct elephant with hairy skin

manifest (man′ ə fest′)   *n.* A cargo list

manifold (man′ ə fōld′)   *adj.* In many ways; plentiful and varied

mansard (man′ särd)   *n.* A roof with two slopes on each of the four sides

marrow (mar′ ō)   *n.* The soft tissue that fills the cavities of most bones

maverick (mav′ ər ik)   *n.* A nonconformist

meander (mē an′ dər)   *v.* To move lazily

meditate (med′ ə tāt′)   *v.* To think deeply

meditation (med′ ə tā′ shən)   *n.* A deep reflection

melancholy (mel′ ən käl′ ē)   *adj.* Gloomy

melee (mā′ lā)   *n.* A noisy, confused fight

mendicant (men′ di kənt)   *n.* A beggar

mesquite (mes kēt′)   *n.* A type of small thorny tree

metamorphosis (met′ ə môr′ fə sis)   *n.* A transformation

metate (mā tä′ tā)   *n.* A stone used in the southwestern United States for grinding meal

meticulous (mə tik′ yo͞o ləs)   *adj.* Extremely careful about details

miasma (mī az′ mə)   *n.* An unwholesome atmosphere

milieu (mēl yo͞o′)   *n.* The environment

minutia (mi no͞o′ shē ə)   *n.* The small and trivial details

mollify (mäl′ ə fī)   *v.* To soothe; calm

monotonous (mə nät′ 'n əs)   *adj.* Having little or no variation or variety; tiresome because unvarying

morose (mə rōs′)   *adj.* Gloomy, sullen

mundane (mun dān′)   *adj.* Commonplace; ordinary

munificent (myo͞o nif′ ə s'nt)   *adj.* Generous

musing (myo͞oz′ iŋ)   *v.* Thinking deeply and at length

myriad (mir′ ē əd)   *adj.* Countless

N

naive (nä ēv′)   *adj.* Unaffectedly, or sometimes foolishly simple, childlike; unsophisticated

nascent (nas′ ənt)   *adj.* Beginning to form, start, grow, or develop

nomadic (nō mad′ ik)   *adj.* Of, characteristic of, or like nomads or their way of life; wandering

nostalgia (näs tal′ jə)   *n.* A longing

O

obeisance (ō′ bā′ s'ns)   *n.* A gesture of respect

obscured (əb skyo͝ord′)   *adj.* Lacking light; dim; dark

obstinacy (äb′ stə nə sē)   *n.* Stubbornness

obstreperous (əb strep′ ər əs)   *adj.* Noisy or unruly

obtuse (äb to͞os′)   *adj.* Slow to understand or perceive

ominous (äm′ ə nəs)   *adj.* Threatening; sinister

omnipotent (äm nip′ ə tənt)   *adj.* All-powerful

omnipresence (äm′ ni prez′ 'ns)   *n.* A presence in all places at the same time

omniscience (äm nish′ əns)   *n.* A knowledge of all things

oppress (ə pres′)   *v.* To weigh heavily on the mind; rule harshly; tyrannize over

opprobrious (ə prō′ brē əs)   *adj.* Abusive; disrespectful

ornery (ôr′ nər ē) *adj.* Having a mean disposition

oscillation (äs′ ə lā′ shən) *n.* The act of swinging regularly back and forth

ostentation (äs′ tən tā′ shən) *n.* A boastful display

ostentatious (äs′ tən tā′ shəs) *adj.* Intended to attract notice

P

pacify (pas′ ə fī′) *v.* To make peaceful or calm; appease; tranquilize

paean (pē′ ən) *n.* A song of triumph

palisade (pal′ ə sād) *n.* A large pointed stake set in the ground to form a fence used for defense

palpable (pal′ pə b′l) *adj.* Able to be touched, felt, or handled

paradoxical (par′ ə däks′ i k′l) *adj.* Expressing an apparent contradiction

Parian (per′ ē ən) *adj.* Referring to a fine, white marble of the Greek city Paros

parochial (pə rō′ kē əl) *adj.* Narrow; limited

parsimony (pär′ sə mō′ nē) *n.* Stinginess

passion (pash′ ən) *n.* An extreme, compelling emotion

pathos (pā′ thäs′) *n.* The quality in something which arouses pity, sorrow, or compassion

patriarch (pā′ trē ärk) *n.* The father and ruler of a family or tribe

patrimony (pat′ rə mō′ nē) *n.* The property inherited from one's father

pelf (pelf) *n.* The money or wealth regarded with contempt

pensive (pen′ siv) *adj.* Thinking deeply or seriously

penumbra (pi num′ brə) *n.* The partly lighted area surrounding the complete shadow of a body in full eclipse

penury (pen′ yə rē) *n.* A lack of money, property, or necessities

perdition (pər dish′ ən) *n.* Complete and irreparable loss; ruin

peremptory (pə remp′ tər ē) *adj.* That cannot be denied, changed, delayed or opposed

perfidy (pur′ fə dē) *n.* A betrayal of trust; treachery

periodicity (pir′ ē ə dis′ ə tē) *n.* A recurrence at regular intervals

peroration (per′ ə rā′ shən) *n.* The concluding part of a speech

pertinaciously (pur′ tə nā′ shəs lē) *adj.* Holding firmly to some purpose

pertinence (pur′ t′n əns) *n.* Appropriateness; relevance

perturbation (pur′ tər bā′ shən) *n.* Agitation

perusal (pə rōō′ z′l) *n.* The act of reading

pervade (pər vād′) *v.* To pass through; to spread throughout

pestilential (pes′ tə len′ shəl) *adj.* Of, causing, or likely to cause pestilence or infection

petulantly (pech′ ōō lənt lē) *adv.* Impatiently or irritably

phantasmagoric (fan taz′ mə gôr′ ik) *adj.* Fantastic or dreamlike

piety (pī′ ə tē) *n.* A devotion to religious duties

pilfer (pil′ fər) *v.* To steal

pimiento (pi men′ tō) *n.* A red, bell-shaped fruit, used for stuffing green olives

pine (pīn) *v.* To have an intense longing or desire

pinnace (pin′ is) *n.* A small sailing ship

pinnacle (pin′ ə k′l) *n.* A lofty peak

pious (pī′ əs) *adj.* Dutiful

pique (pēk) *v.* To arouse resentment in

placid (plas′ id) *adj.* Tranquil; calm

plaguy (plā′ gē) *adj.* Disagreeable

poignant (poin′ yənt) *adj.* Sharply painful to the feelings

poise (poiz) *n.* Balance; stability

pompadour (päm′ pə dôr′) *n.* A hairdo in which the hair is swept up high from the forehead

portentous (pôr ten′ təs) *adj.* Ominous

portfolio (pôrt fō′ lē ō) *n.* A flat, portable case, usually of leather, for carrying loose sheets of paper; briefcase

posterity (päs ter′ ə tē) *n.* All succeeding generations

posture (päs′ chər) *v.* To pose

precept (prē′ sept) *n.* A rule of conduct

preconception (prē′ kən sep′ shən) *n.* An idea formed beforehand

predilection (pred′ ′l ek′ shən) *n.* Preference

preposterous (pri päs′ tər əs) *adj.* Ridiculous

prescient (prē′ shē ənt) *adj.* Having foreknowledge

preternatural (prēt′ ər nach′ ər əl) *adj.* Differing from or beyond what is normally expected from nature; supernatural

priggish (prig′ gish) *adj.* Excessively precise

pristine (pris′ tēn′) *adj.* Pure, uncorrupted

prodigious (prə dij′ əs) *adj.* Powerful; wonderful

profane (prō fān′) *adj.* Showing disrespect or contempt for sacred things

promenader (präm′ ə nād′ ər) *n.* A person walking in a leisurely manner

prophecy (präf′ ə sē) *n.* Prediction of the future

propitiation (prō pish′ ē ā′ shən) *n.* Appeasing

propitious (prə pish′ əs) *adj.* Favorably inclined or disposed

proscenium (prō sē′ nē əm) *n.* The area of the stage in front of the curtain, where action takes place when the curtain is closed

protrude (prō trōōd′) *v.* To jut out

psychology (sī köl′ ə jē) *n.* The science dealing with the mind and with mental and emotional processes

pugilistic (pyōō′ jə lis′ tik) *adj.* Like a boxer

purged (purjd) *v.* Cleansed or rid of impurities

Q

quail (kwāl) *v.* Draw back in fear

quandary (kwän′ də rē) *n.* A state of uncertainty; dilemma

quarto (kwôr′ tō) *n.* A book about nine by twelve inches

querulous (kwer′ ə ləs) *adj.* Complaining; inclined to find fault

questing (kwest′ iŋ) *adj.* Searching

quintessentially (kwin′ tə sen′ shə lē) *adv.* Purely

R

radiant (rā′ dē ənt) *adj.* Shining brightly

ramification (ram′ ə fi kā′ shən) *n.* A branchlike division

rampant (ram′ pənt) *adj.* Spreading unchecked

ravenous (rav′ ə nəs) *adj.* Extremely eager

reap (rēp) *v.* To cut or harvest grain from a field

recompense (rek′ əm pens′) *n.* A reward

recondite (rek′ ən dīt′) *adj.* Dealing with very profound, difficult, or abstruse subject matter

recumbent (ri kum′ bənt) *adj.* Resting

redolent (red′ ′l ənt) *adj.* Suggestive

redress (ri dres′) *n.* An atonement; rectification

refluent (ref′ lōō wənt) *adj.* Flowing back

refulgent (ri ful′ jənt) *adj.* Radiant; shining

rehearse (ri hʉrs′) *v.* To narrate

relent (ri lent′) *v.* To soften in temper, resolution; become less severe, stern, or stubborn

remuda (rə mōō′ də) *n.* A group of extra saddle horses kept as a supply of remounts

repose (ri pōz′) *n.* The state of being at rest

repression (ri presh′ ən) *n.* Restraint

repugnant (ri pug′ nənt) *adj.* Offensive; disagreeable

reverence (rev′ ər əns) *n.* A feeling or attitude of deep respect, love, or awe

reverential (rev′ ə ren′ shəl) *adj.* Showing or caused by a feeling of deep respect, love, and awe

rhetoric (ret′ ər ik) *n.* Artificial eloquence; language that is showy and elaborate but largely empty of clear ideas or sincere emotion

rigor (rig′ ər) *n.* A stiffness; rigidity

rude (rōōd) *adj.* Crude or rough in form or workmanship

rueful (rōō′ fəl) *adj.* Feeling or showing sorrow or pity

ruminate (rōō′ mə nāt) *v.* To meditate

S

sacrament (sak′ rə mənt) *n.* Something regarded as having a sacred meaning

sagacious (sə gā′ shəs) *adj.* Shrewd

sage (sāj) *n.* A person widely respected for his or her wisdom

salient (sāl′ yənt) *adj.* Standing out from the rest

sallow (sal′ ō) *adj.* Of a sickly, pale-yellow hue

sally (sal′ ē) *v.* To rush out or come out suddenly

sardonic (sär dän′ ik) *adj.* Bitterly sarcastic

saturnalia (sat′ ər nā′ lē ə) *n.* A period of unrestrained revelry

savant (sə vänt′) *n.* A learned person; scholar

scorn (skôrn) *v.* To refuse or reject as wrong or disgraceful

scurvy (skʉr′ vē) *n.* A disease caused by vitamin-C deficiency

scythe (sīth) *v.* To cut as with a tool with a long single-edged blade set at an angle on a long, curved handle

sedge (sej) *n.* A grasslike plant

semantic (sə man′ tik) *adj.* Of or pertaining to meaning, especially meaning in language

seminal (sem′ ə n′l) *adj.* Highly original and influencing the development of future events

semi-somnambulant (sem′ i säm nam′ byōō lənt) *adj.* Half sleepwalking

sentience (sen′ shəns) *n.* A capacity of feeling

sepulcher (sep′ ′l kər) *n.* A grave; tomb

sequester (si kwes′ tər) *v.* To withdraw; seclude

serenity (sə ren′ ə tē) *n.* Calmness

servile (ser′ v′l) *adj.* Humbly yielding or submissive

sexton (seks′ tən) *n.* A person in charge of the maintenance of a church

shackle (shak′ əl) *n.* A metal fastening for the wrist or ankle of a prisoner; manacle

shroud (shroud) *n.* A set of ropes from a ship's side to the masthead

sibilance (sib′ ′l əns) *n.* A hissing sound

simulacrum (sim′ yōō lā′ krəm) *n.* A vague representation

sinuous (sin′ yōō wəs) *adj.* Bending or winding in and out; wavy

sleeper (slē′ pər) *n.* A tie supporting railroad tracks

slovenly (sluv′ ən lē) *adj.* Untidy

smite (smīt) *v.* To kill by a powerful blow

somber (säm′ bər) *adj.* Dark and gloomy or dull

somnolent (säm′ nə lənt) *adj.* Sleepy; drowsy

spartan (spär′ t′n) *adj.* Characteristic of the people of ancient Sparta; hardy, stoical, severe, frugal

specious (spē′ shəs) *adj.* Seeming to be good or sound without actually being so

spurious (spyoor′ ē əs) *adj.* False; artificial

squander (skwän′ dər) *v.* To spend or use wastefully

stark (stärk) *adj.* Severe

staunch (stônch) *adj.* Strong; unyielding

stringency (strin′ jən sē) *n.* Strictness; severity

stupefaction (stōō′ pə fak′ shən) *n.* Stunned amazement or utter bewilderment

subjugation (sub′ jə gā′ shən) *n.* The act of conquering

sublime (sə blīm′) *adj.* Noble; majestic

subscribe (səb skrīb′) *v.* To give support, sanction, or approval

subservient (səb sʉr′ vē ənt) *adj.* Submissive; servile

subsistence (səb sis′ təns) *n.* The means of support

suffice (sə fīs′) *v.* To be enough

suffrage (suf′ rij) *n.* A vote or voting

suffusion (sə fyōō′ zhən) *n.* A fullness of color

sulfureous (sul fyoor′ ē əs) *adj.* Greenish-yellow

sullen (sul′ ən)   *adj.* Sulky; glum

sundry (sun′ drē)   *adj.* Various, different

supercilious (soo′ pər sil′ ē əs)   *adj.* Disdainful

superfluous (sə pur′ floo wəs)   *adj.* Not needed

supposititious (sə päz′ ə tish′ əs)   *adj.* Supposed

surmise (sər mīz′)   *v.* To guess

sylvan (sil′ vən)   *adj.* Characteristic of the forest

syntax (sin′ taks)   *n.* An orderly or systematic arrangement

T

tableau (tab′ lō)   *n.* A representation of a silent, motionless scene

tabloid (tab′ loid)   *n.* A newspaper with many pictures and short, often sensational, stories

tabula rasa (tab′ yə lə rä′ sə)   *n.* A clean slate

tantrum (tan′ trəm)   *n.* A childish fit of temper

tarn (tärn)   *n.* A small lake

temerity (tə mer′ ə tē)   *n.* Foolhardy or heedless disregard of danger; recklessness

tempest (tem′ pist)   *n.* A violent storm

teocallis (tē′ ə ka′ lis)   *n.* The ancient temples erected by Aztec Indians of Mexico and Central America

termagant (tur′ mə gənt)   *n.* A quarrelsome woman

terrestrial (tə res′ trē əl)   *adj.* Of this world

threshold (thresh′ ōld)   *n.* The entrance or beginning point of something

timorous (tim′ ər əs)   *adj.* Full of fear

tortilla (tor te′ ə)   *n.* A thin, flat cake of cornmeal

tow (tō)   *n.* The coarse and broken fibers of hemp or flax before spinning

transcribe (tran skrīb′)   *v.* To write out or type out in full

transient (tran′ shənt)   *adj.* Not permanent; passing away with time

translate (trans lāt′)   *v.* To transport

transmogrify (trans mäg′ rə fī′)   *v.* To transform in a grotesque manner

travail (trə vāl′)   *n.* Painfully difficult or burdensome work

tremulous (trem′ yoo ləs)   *adj.* Characterized by trembling; quivering

trepidation (trep′ ə dā′ shən)   *n.* A fearful anxiety; apprehension

tulle (tool)   *n.* A thin, fine netting used for scarves

tumultuous (too mul′ choo wəs)   *adj.* Wild and noisy; greatly agitated

turbulence (tur′ byə ləns)   *n.* A commotion or wild disorder

tyranny (tir′ ə nē)   *n.* An oppressive and unjust government

U

unalienable (un āl′ yən ə b'l)   *adj.* Not to be taken away

undulate (un′ doo lāt)   *v.* To move in waves

unobtrusively (un əb troo′ siv lē)   *adv.* Inconspicuously

unperverted (un′ pər vurt′ id)   *adj.* Uncorrupted

unscrupulous (un skroop′ yə ləs)   *adj.* Not restrained by ideas of right and wrong

unsheathed (un shēthd′)   *adj.* Removed from its case

unwonted (un wun′ tid)   *adj.* Unfamiliar

usurer (yoo′ zhoo rər)   *n.* A moneylender who charges very high interest

usurpation (yoo′ sər pā′ shən)   *n.* The unlawful seizure of rights or privileges

V

vagabonding (vag′ ə bänd′ iŋ)   *adj.* Moving from place to place, with no fixed abode; wandering

vagary (və ger′ ē)   *n.* An unpredictable occurrence; odd, unexpected action or notion

vagrant (vā′ grənt)   *n.* An idle wanderer

vagueness (vāg′ nis)   *n.* A lack of definition in shape or form

vanquished (vaŋ′ kwisht)   *adj.* Defeated

venerable (ven′ ər ə b'l)   *adj.* Commanding respect

venomous (ven′ əm əs)   *adj.* Spiteful; malicious

venturous (ven′ chər əs)   *adj.* Daring

veracious (və rā′ shəs)   *adj.* Honest, truthful

verity (ver′ ə tē)   *n.* The truth

vernacular (vər nak′ yə lər)   *n.* The native speech, language, or dialect of a country or place

vigilance (vij′ ə ləns)   *n.* Watchfulness

vigilant (vij′ ə lənt)   *adj.* Alert to danger

visage (viz′ ij)   *n.* A facial appearance

vituperative (vī too′ prə tiv)   *adj.* Spoken abusively

vociferation (vō sif′ ə rā′ shən)   *n.* A loud or vehement shouting

vociferous (vō sif′ ər əs)   *adj.* Loud, noisy, or vehement in making one's feelings known

votive (vōt′ iv)   *adj.* Dedicated in fulfillment of a vow or pledge

W

waggery (wag′ ər ē)   *n.* A mischievous humor

wampum (wäm′ pəm)   *n.* Small beads made of shells

wan (wän)   *adj.* Sickly pale

wanton (wän′ t'n)   *adj.* Senseless; unjustified

wily (wī′ lē)   *adj.* Sly; cunning

X

xenophobic (zen′ ə fō′ bik)   *adj.* Afraid of strangers or foreigners

Y

yearning (yurn′ iŋ)   *n.* Deep or anxious longing; desire

Z

zither (zith′ ər)   *n.* A musical instrument with thirty to forty strings stretched across a flat soundboard and played with the fingers

INDEX OF FINE ART

Abraham Lincoln, William Willard, 414

Abraham Lincoln's Address at the Dedication of the Gettysburg National Cemetery, 19 November 1863, Artist Unknown, 380

After the First Snow in Winter in Vermont, Charles Hughes, 297

After the Show, Waldo Pierce, 575

Afterglow, Florida, Martin Johnson Heade, xvi

All Right, Have It Your Way—You Heard a Seal Bark!, James Thurber, 688

American Bookseller's Announcement for *Uncle Tom's Cabin,* 229

An Expression of a Silktown in New Jersey, Oscar F. Bluemner, Cover

Andrew Jackson Encouraging His Riflemen at the Battle of New Orleans, January 8, 1815, Artist Unknown, 163

Armistice Day, Gifford Beal, 554

Arrival of the Englishmen in Virginia, The, Theodore de Bry, 43

Arthur Rackham, "I at length. . . ," 195

Artist Unknown, *Abraham Lincoln's Address at the Dedication of the Gettysburg National Cemetery, 19 November 1863,* 380

Artist Unknown, *Andrew Jackson Encouraging His Riflemen at the Battle of New Orleans, January 8, 1815,* 163

Artist Unknown, *Columbus Landing in the New World,* 33

Artist Unknown, *Conquistadors in the Americas,* 41

Artist Unknown, *The Execution of the Rev. Stephen Burroughs for Witchcraft at Salem, Massachusetts, in 1692,* 1067

Artist Unknown, *Frederick Douglass,* 534

Artist Unknown, *George Washington Addressing the Second Continental Congress,* 93

Artist Unknown, *The Hanging of a 'Witch' at Salem, Massachusetts, 1692,* 1070

Artist Unknown, *Housetops in Charleston During the Bombardment of Fort Sumter, The,* 373

Artist Unknown, *Jane Austen,* 164

Artist Unknown, *Nat Bacon's Rebellion,* 5

Artist Unknown, *Paddle Steamboat Mississippi,* 439

Artist Unknown, *Patrick Henry Speaking Against the Stamp Act in the Virginia House of Burgesses in 1765,* 94

Artist Unknown, *Poor Richard's Almanack,* 111

Artist Unknown, *Reading the Emancipation Proclamation,* 387

Artist Unknown, *The Place of Emergence and the Four Worlds,* 18

Artist Unknown, *The Surrender at Appomattox,* 351

Artist Unknown, *A Witch Trial in Salem, Massachusetts, in 1692,* 79

Artist Unknown, *A Witch Trial in Salem, Massachusetts, in 1692,* 81

Artist Unknown, *The Witchcraft Trial of Giles Corey at Salem, Massachusetts, 1692,* 1091

Artist's Garden, The, Blakelock, 538

At the Opera, Mary Stevenson Cassatt, 485

Avery, Milton, *Morning Call,* 819

Barn Dance, Grandma Moses, 546

Battle Abbey Murals: The Four Season of the Confederacy, The Summer Mural, The, Charles Hoffbauer, 378

Battle of Lexington at the Beginning of the Combat, The, Amos Doolittle and John W. Barber, 92

Beal, Gifford, *Armistice Day,* 554

Bearden, Romare, *The Block,* 844

Bearden, Romare, *Jazz Village,* 804

Bearden, Romare, *School Bell Time,* from the *Profile/Part I: The Twenties* series (Mecklenburg County), 665

Bearden, Romare, *Sunset and Moonrise With Maudell Sleet,* from the *Profile/Part I: The Twenties* series (Mecklenburg County), 893

Bearden, Romare, *Trombone Solo,* 803

Beginning of New England, The, After the painting by Clyde O. Deland, 3

Bellows, George, *Floating Ice,* 589

Bellows, George, *The Laughing Boy,* 873

Bellows, George, *The Lone Tenement,* 1021

Benares, Marshall Johnson, 505

Benjamin Franklin's Birthplace in Boston, Massachusetts, 1882, J. H. Buffords, 101

Benton, Thomas Hart, *Martha's Vineyard,* 861

Benton, Thomas Hart, *West Tisbury Fair,* 571

Beyer, Edward, *Harper's Ferry From Jefferson Rock,* 527

Big Meeting, Varnette P. Honeywood, 788

Biography, Marina Gutierrez, 931

Black and White, Georgia O'Keeffe, 697

Black Place II, Georgia O'Keeffe, 800

Black Walnuts, Joseph Pollet, 834

Blakelock, *The Artist's Garden,* 538

Block, The, Romare Bearden, 844–845

Bluemner, Oscar F., *An Expression of a Silktown in New Jersey,* Cover

Boisseau, Alfred, *Louisiana Indians Walking Along a Bayou,* 428

Boston Harbor, Fitz Hugh Lane, 222

Bowery at Night, The, W. Louis Sonntag Jr., 429

Bronco Buster, The, Frederic Remington, 460

Buffords, J. H., *Benjamin Franklin's Birthplace in Boston, Massachusetts, 1882,* 101

Building the First White House, N. C. Wyeth, 143

Burchfield, Charles, *Edge of Town,* 453

Burchfield, Charles, *Garden of Memories*, 607
Burchfield, Charles, *Lavender and Old Lace*, 610
Burchfield, Charles, *Overhanging Cloud in July*, 728
Burchfield, Charles, *Pink Locusts and Windy Moon*, 732
Burchfield, Charles, *Queen Anne's Lace*, 994
Calder, Alexander, *Untitled*, 757
Caldwell, Vivian, *California Suite*, 511
California Suite, Vivian Caldwell, 511
Cammilliri, Nicholas, *U.S. Frigate Constitution*, 308
Cassatt, Mary Stevenson, *At the Opera*, 485
Catlin, George, *Red Jacket*, 21
Ceesay, Momodou, *The Madonna and Child*, 1011
Chagall, Marc, *Lovers With Flowers*, 760
Chagall, Marc, *The Poet Reclining*, 1014
Chambers, Thomas, *Niagara Falls*, 160
Chapin, James, *Ruby Green Singing*, 785
Chapman, John Gadsby, *Landing at Jamestown* (Also
    called *Hope of Jamestown*), 6
Chief Joseph's Surrender to Colonel Nelson A. Miles, Olaf
    C. Seltzer, 394
Christmas Morning, Adirondacks, Rockwell Kent, 1023
Christy, Howard Chandler, *The Signing of the Constitution*,
    86
Church, Frederick E., *Sunset*, 240
Church, Frederick E., *Twilight in the Wilderness*, 342
City From Greenwich Village, The, John Sloan, 555
Closing Scene, David Hockney, 1031
Cole, Thomas, *The Notch of the White Mountains
    (Crawford Notch)*, 230
Coleman, Glen Oden, *Queensboro Bridge*, 430
Columbus Landing in the New World, Artist Unknown, 33
Coming of the Mayflower, The, N. C. Wyeth, 54
Conception Synchromy, Stanton Macdonald-Wright, 560
Conquistadors in the Americas, Artist Unknown, 41
Cornell Farm, Edward Hicks, 225
Crowninshield's Wharf, George Ropes, 974
Currier & Ives, *The Funeral of President Lincoln, New
    York, April 25, 1865*, 410
Currier & Ives, *A Home on the Mississippi*, 367
Currier & Ives, *The Whale Fishery—The Sperm Whale in a
    Flurry*, 233
Darley, Felix Octavius Carr, Illustration from an 1872
    Edition of James Fenimore Cooper's *The Last of the
    Mohicans*, 168
de Bry, Theodore, *The Arrival of the Englishmen in
    Virginia*, 43
de Bry, Theodore and Jacques Lemoyne de Morgues,
    Search for Gold in an Appalachian Pond, 38
de Kooning, Willem, *Gotham News*, 816
de Thulstrup, Thor, *Louisiana Purchase Ceremony at New
    Orleans, 20 December 1803*, 162
Declaration of Independence, The, 1786, John Trumbull,
    135
Deland, Clyde O., After the painting by, *The Beginning of
    New England*, 3
Delaware Indians, The Walam Olum, 14
Dixon, Maynard, *The Medicine Robe*, 925

Doolittle, Amos and John W. Barber, *The Battle of
    Lexington at the Beginning of the Combat*, 92
Drawing of Alfred Hitchcock Profile, 219
Dunn, Harvey, *In Search of the Land of Milk and Honey*,
    424
Dunton, W. Herbert, *In the Depths of the Timber*, 648
Durand, Asher B., *Kindred Spirits*, 169
Durrie, George Henry, *Farm Yard, Winter*, 245
Eakins, Thomas, *Hiawatha*, 234
Eakins, Thomas, *The Thinker (Portrait of Louis N. Kenton)*,
    542
Eastman, Seth, *Indian Village, River Gila*, 26
Edge of Town, Charles Burchfield, 453
Eilshemius, Louis M., *Summer Landscape With Hawk*, 998
Evening, Wanda Gág, 68
*Execution of the Rev. Stephen Burroughs for Witchcraft,
    The*, Artist Unknown, 1067
Faithful Troops Cheer General Lee, N. C. Wyeth, 354
Farm Yard, Winter, George Henry Durrie, 245
February, John Henry Twachtman, 332
Fischer, Anton Otto, *Worsening Weather*, 518
Fish, Janet, *Painted Water Glasses*, 899
Fisher, Alanson, *Harriet Beecher Stowe*, 228
Floating Ice, George Bellows, 589
Florsheim, Richard, *Night City*, 903
Ford, Nancy Vaughn, *Quilt made by a slave*, 896
*Founding the First Permanent English Settlement in
    America*, A. C. Warren, 49
Franca, Ozz, *Winter*, 1013
Fraser, Charles, *Seat of John Julius Pringle*, 470
Frederick Douglass, Artist Unknown, 534
Freilicher, Jane, *Marshes, Dunes and Fields*, 739
From Arkansas, George Schreiber, 481
*Funeral of President Lincoln, New York, April 25, 1865,
    The*, Currier & Ives, 410
Gág, Wanda, *Evening*, 68
Garden of Memories, Charles Burchfield, 607
Gaul, Gilbert, *Tidings From the Front*, 352
*George Washington Addressing the Second Continental
    Congress*, Artist Unknown, 93
Girl in a White Dress, Sir William Orpen, 1003
Gotham News, Willem de Kooning, 816
Grand Canyon of the Yellowstone, The, Thomas Moran,
    525
Great Florida Sunset, Martin Johnson Heade, 968
Green, Jonathan, *The Mather School*, 663
Grutzik, Rebecca (Student), *Winter Wonderland*, 597
Gutierrez, Marina, *Biography*, 931
Hanging of a 'Witch' at Salem, Massachusetts, 1692, The,
    Artist Unknown, 1070
Harper's Ferry From Jefferson Rock, Edward Beyer, 527
Harriet Beecher Stowe, Alanson Fisher, 228
Heade, Martin Johnson, *Afterglow, Florida*, xvi
Heade, Martin Johnson, *Great Florida Sunset*, 968
Hiawatha, Thomas Eakins, 234
Hicks, Edward, *Cornell Farm*, 225
Higgins, Eugene, *The Return Alone*, 300

Hockney, David, *Closing Scene,* 1031

Hoffbauer, Charles, *The Battle Abbey Murals: The Four Season of the Confederacy, the Summer Mural,* 378

Hombre Ante el Infinito (Man Before Infinity), Ruffino Tamayo, 991

Home on the Mississippi, A, Currier & Ives, 367

Homer, Winslow, *Young Soldier: Separate Study of a Soldier Giving Water to a Wounded Companion,* 385

Honeywood, Varnette P., *Big Meeting,* 788

Hopper, Edward, *Room in Brooklyn,* 562

Housetops in Charleston During the Bombardment of Fort Sumter, The, Artist Unknown, 373

Huck Finn, E. W. Kemble, 442

Hughes, Charles, *After the First Snow in Winter in Vermont,* 297

''I at length. . . ,'' Arthur Rackham, 195

Illustration from an 1872 Edition of James Fenimore Cooper's *The Last of the Mohicans,* Felix Octavius Carr Darley, 168

In a Shoreham Garden, Samuel Palmer, 720

In Search of the Land of Milk and Honey, Harvey Dunn, 424

In the Depths of the Timber, W. Herbert Dunton, 648

Independence (Squire Jack Porter), Frank Blackwell Mayer, 149

Indian Village, River Gila, Seth Eastman, 26

Jazz Village, Romare Bearden, 804

Jim, William H. Johnson, 848

Johnson, Eastman, *A Ride for Liberty—The Fugitive Slaves,* 349

Johnson, Eastman, *The Wounded Drummer Boy,* 405

Johnson, Frank Tenney, *The Miners During the Gold Rush 1849, in California,* 425

Johnson, Marshall, *Benares,* 505

Johnson, Oliver, *Man with a Horn,* 567

Johnson, William H., *Jim,* 848

Johnson, William H., *Man in a Vest,* 910

Juke Box, Jacob Lawrence, 564

Kemble, E. W., *Huck Finn,* 442

Kent, Rockwell, *Christmas Morning, Adirondacks,* 1023

Kindred Spirits, Asher B. Durand, 169

Landing at Jamestown (Also called *Hope of Jamestown*), John Gadsby Chapman, 6

Lane, Fitz Hugh, *Boston Harbor,* 222

Last Stand at the Alamo, N. C. Wyeth, 166

Laughing Boy, The, George Bellows, 873

Lavender and Old Lace, Charles Burchfield, 610

Lawrence Tree, The, Georgia O'Keeffe, 406

Lawrence, Jacob, *Juke Box,* 564

Lawrence, Jacob, *Part II, The Free Man, No. 30,* 1004

Lawrence, Jacob, *Vaudeville,* 1027

Lawson, Ernest, *New England Birches,* 766

Leader, Benjamin William, *Near Harlech, North Wales,* 334

Leigh, William R., *The Mystic* (detail), 30

Library, Bernard Boruchz Zakheim, 559

Lone Tenement, The, George Bellows, 1021

Louis, Morris, *Saraband,* 811

Louisiana Indians Walking Along a Bayou, Alfred Boisseau, 428

Louisiana Purchase Ceremony at New Orleans, 20 December 1803, Thor de Thulstrup, 162

Lovers With Flowers, Marc Chagall, 760

Low Branch, Scarlett, 314

Macdonald-Wright, Stanton, *Conception Synchromy,* 560

Madonna and Child, The, Momodou Ceesay, 1011

Magritte, René, *The Unexpected Answer,* 967

Malone, Peter, *Untitled,* 1029

Man in a Vest, William H. Johnson, 910

Man with a Horn, Oliver Johnson, 567

Manet, Edouard, *The Raven,* 209

Manet, Edouard, *The Raven,* 211

Manhattan Tops, Herman Rose, 601

Marin, John, *Quoddy Head,* 327

Mark Twain Riding the Celebrated Jumping Frog, Frederic Waddy, 448

Marsh, Henry, *The Parson Barnard House,* 62

Marshes, Dunes and Fields, Jane Freilicher, 739

Martha's Vineyard, Thomas Hart Benton, 861

Mather School, The, Jonathan Green, 663

Mayer, Frank Blackwell, *Independence (Squire Jack Porter),* 149

Medicine Robe, The, Maynard Dixon, 925

Meynell, Francis, Lt., *Slaves Below Deck,* 154

Miners During the Gold Rush 1849, in California, The, Frank Tenney Johnson, 425

Modighani, Amedeo, *Woman With a Black Tie,* 475

Moonlight, Dovehouse Street, Chelsea, Algernon Newton, 710

Moran, Thomas, *The Grand Canyon of the Yellowstone,* 525

Moran, Thomas, *Vernal Falls, Yosemite Valley,* 186

Morning Call, Milton Avery, 819

Moses, Grandma, *Barn Dance,* 546

Munch, Edvard, *The Sun,* 747

Mystic, The (detail), William R. Leigh, 30

Near Harlech, North Wales, Benjamin William Leader, 334

New England Birches, Ernest Lawson, 766

Newton, Algernon, *Moonlight, Dovehouse Street, Chelsea,* 710

Niagara Falls, Thomas Chambers, 160

Niblett, Gary, *Rabbit Stew,* 431

Night City, Richard Florsheim, 903

Night the Ghost Got In, The, Illustrations from, James Thurber, 684, 686, 687

Notch of the White Mountains (Crawford Notch), The, Thomas Cole, 230

Number 3, Jackson Pollack, 951

O'Keeffe, Georgia, *Black and White,* 697

O'Keeffe, Georgia, *Black Place II,* 800

O'Keeffe, Georgia, *The Lawrence Tree,* 406

Old Holley House, Cos Cob, John Henry Twachtman, 323

Orchard in Bloom, Louveciennes (detail), Camille Pissaro, 726

Orpen, Sir William, *Girl in White Dress,* 1003

Outlier, The, Frederic Remington, 461
Overhanging Cloud In July, Charles Burchfield, 728
Paddle Steamboat Mississippi, 439
Painted Water Glasses, Janet Fish, 899
Palmer, Samuel, *In a Shoreham Garden,* 720
The Parson Barnard House, Henry Marsh, 62
Part II, The Free Man, No. 30, Jacob Lawrence, 1004
Patrick Henry Speaking Against the Stamp Act in the Virginia House of Burgesses in 1765, Artist Unknown, 94
Peterson, Francis, *Pleasures of Winter in New York,* 882
Philip (Metacomet), American Wampanoag Indian Chief, Paul Revere, 11
Pierce, Waldo, *After the Show,* 575
Pink Locusts and Windy Moon, Charles Burchfield, 732
Pissaro, Camille, *Orchard in Bloom, Louveciennes* (detail), 726
Place of Emergence and the Four Worlds, The, Artist Unknown, 18
Pleasures of Winter in New York, Francis Peterson, 882
Poet Reclining, The, Marc Chagall, 1014
Pollack, Jackson, *Number 3,* 951
Pollet, Joseph, *Black Walnuts,* 834
Poor Richard's Almanack, Artist Unknown, 111
Proserpine, Dante Gabriel Rossetti, 217
Pyle, Howard, *The Trial of Two 'Witches' at Salem, Massachusetts, In 1662,* 8, 1037
Queen Anne's Lace, Charles Burchfield, 994
Queensboro Bridge, Glen Oden Coleman, 430
Quilt made by a slave, Nancy Vaughn Ford, 896
Quoddy Head, John Marin, 327
Rabbit Stew, Gary Niblett, 431
Raven, The, Edouard Manet, 209
Raven, The, Edouard Manet, 211
Reading the Emancipation Proclamation, Artist Unknown, 387
Reading Woman, Terborch, 61
Red Bridge, The, Julian Alden Weir, 464
Red Jacket, George Catlin, 21
Reindorf, S., *Wild Flowers,* 957
Remington, Frederic, *The Bronco Buster,* 460
Remington, Frederic, *The Outlier,* 461
Remington, Frederic, *Turn Him Loose, Bill,* 435
Return Alone, The, Eugene Higgins, 300
Revere, Paul, *Philip (Metacomet), American Wampanoag Indian Chief,* 11
Ride for Liberty—The Fugitive Slaves, A, Eastman Johnson, 349
Room in Brooklyn, Edward Hopper, 562
Room With a Balcony, Adolph von Menzel, 337
Ropes, George, *Crowninshield's Wharf,* 974
Rose, Herman, *Manhattan Tops,* 601
Rossetti, Dante Gabriel, *Proserpine,* 217
Rothko, Mark, *Untitled,* 814
Ruby Green Singing, James Chapin, 785
Saraband, Morris Louis, 811
Scarlett, *Low Branch,* 314

School Bell Time, from the *Profile/Part I: The Twenties* series (Mecklenburg County), Romare Bearden, 665
Schreiber, George, *From Arkansas,* 481
Search for Gold in an Appalachian Pond, Theodore de Bry and Lemoyne de Morgues, 38
Seat of John Julius Pringle, Charles Fraser, 470
Seltzer, Olaf C., *Chief Joseph's Surrender to Colonel Nelson A. Miles,* 394
Signing of the Constitution, The, Howard Chandler Christy, 86
Slaves Below Deck, Lt. Francis Meynell, 154
Sloan, John, *The City from Greenwich Village,* 555
Sonntag, Jr., W. Louis, *The Bowery at Night,* 429
Soyer, Raphael, *Waiting Room,* 874
Spring in Puerto Rico, Pedro Villarini, 987
Stone City, Iowa, Grant Wood, 617
Summer Landscape With Hawk, Louis M. Eilshemius, 998
Sun, The, Edvard Munch, 747
Sunset, Frederick E. Church, 240
Sunset and Moonrise with Maudell Sleet from the *Profile/Part I: The Twenties* series (Mecklenburg County), Romare Bearden, 893
Tamayo, Ruffino, *Hombre Ante el Infinito (Man Before Infinity),* 991
Terborch, *Reading Woman,* 61
Thinker (Portrait of Louis N. Kenton), The, Thomas Eakins, 542
Thurber, James, "All Right, Have It Your Way—You Heard a Seal Bark!" from *Men, Women and Dogs,* 688
Thurber, James, Illustrations from *The Night the Ghost Got In,* 684, 686, 687
Tidings From the Front, Gilbert Gaul, 352
Trial of Two 'Witches' at Salem, Massachusetts in 1692, The, Howard Pyle, 8, 1037
Trombone Solo, Romare Bearden, 803
Trumbull, John, *The Declaration of Independence,* 135
Turn Him Loose, Bill, Frederic Remington, 435
Twachtman, John Henry, *February,* 332
Twachtman, John Henry, *Old Holley House, Cos Cob,* 323
Twilight in the Wilderness, Frederick E. Church, 342
U.S. Frigate Constitution, Nicholas Cammilliri, 308
Unexpected Answer, The, René Magritte, 967
Unidentified Artist, *Winter Sunday in Norway, Maine,* 269
Untitled, Alexander Calder, 757
Untitled, Peter Malone, 1029
Untitled, Mark Rothko, 814
Vaudeville, Jacob Lawrence, 1027
Vernal Falls, Yosemite Valley, Thomas Moran, 186
Villarini, Pedro, *Spring in Puerto Rico,* 987
von Menzel, Adolph, *Room With a Balcony,* 337
Waddy, Frederic, *Mark Twain Riding the Celebrated Jumping Frog,* 448
Waiting Room, Raphael Soyer, 874
Warren, A. C., *Founding the First Permanent English Settlement in America,* 49
Weir, Julian Alden, *The Red Bridge,* 464

West Tisbury Fair, Thomas Hart Benton, 571

Whale Fishery—The Sperm Whale in a Flurry, The, Currier & Ives, 233

Wild Flowers, S. Reindorf, 957

Willard, William, *Abraham Lincoln,* 414

Winter, Ozz Franca, 1013

Winter Sunday in Norway, Maine, Unidentified Artist, 269

Winter Wonderland, Rebecca Grutzik (Student), 597

Witchcraft Trial of Giles Corey at Salem, Massachusetts, 1692, The, Artist Unknown, 1091

Witch Trial in Salem, Massachusetts, in 1692, A, Artist Unknown, 79, 81

Woman With a Black Tie, Amedeo Modigliani, 475

Wood, Grant, *Stone City, Iowa,* 617

Worsening Weather, Anton Otto Fischer, 518

Wounded Drummer Boy, The, Eastman Johnson, 405

Wyeth, N. C., *Building the First White House,* 143

Wyeth, N. C., *The Coming of the Mayflower,* 54

Wyeth, N. C., *Faithful Troops Cheer General Lee,* 354

Wyeth, N. C., *Last Stand at the Alamo,* 166

Young Soldier: Separate Study of a Soldier Giving Water to a Wounded Companion, Winslow Homer, 385

Zakheim, Bernard Boruchz, *Library,* 559

INDEX OF SKILLS

ANALYZING LITERATURE

Allegory, 267
Alliteration, 208, 213, 526, 529, 983, 987
Allusions, 216, 217, 645, 657
Ambiguity, 621, 627
Anti-Transcendentalism, 267, 277
Aphorisms, 110, 112, 121, 125
Apostrophe, 244, 250
Argumentation, 901, 905
Assonance, 208, 213, 526, 529, 983, 987
Autobiography, 99, 109, 363, 369, 661, 667
Biography, 669, 673
Blank Verse, 185, 191
Characterization, 479, 487, 587, 603, 1062, 1081
Characters, 569, 576, 577
    flat characters, 569, 576
    grotesque character, 569, 576
    motivation of, 577, 891, 898
    round characters, 569, 576
Cinquain, 299
Classification, 923, 927
Confessional Poetry, 1001, 1005
Conflict, 489, 501
Consonance, 208, 213, 526, 529, 983, 987
Constitution, recognition of, 20, 23
Couplet, 299
Diction, 381, 853, 857
Dramatic monologue, 719, 723
Dramatic poetry, 765, 774
End rhyme (*See* Rhyme of Poetry)
Epiphany, 821, 829
Epistles, 147, 151
Essay, 907, 913
Exact rhyme (*See* Rhyme of Poetry)
Experimental fiction, 865, 869
Exposition, 915, 921
Extended Metaphor (*See* Metaphor)
Fiction, experimental, 865, 869
Figurative Language, 67, 69
First-person narrative, 691, 696
Flashback, 605, 613, 871
Flat Characters (*See* Characters)
Folk Tales, 173, 183
Foreshadowing, 871, 879
Free Verse, 397, 407, 737, 741, 743, 1025, 1026
Grotesque Characters (*See* Characters)
Harlem Renaissance, 787, 789
Historical Context, 263, 377, 379, 1033, 1061, 1082, 1103
History, 45, 50
Humor, 444, 449, 683, 689

Imagery, 319, 325, 725, 729, 935, 943, 993, 997
Imagism, 699, 700
Immigrant Experience, 945, 950
Internal rhyme (*See* Rhyme of Poetry)
Irony, 473, 477, 537, 541, 831, 841
Journal, 35, 37, 370, 375
Language, figurative language, 67, 69
Lyric Poem, 60, 61
Lyric Poetry, 1009, 1015
Metaphor, 799, 801
    extended metaphor, 799, 801
Meter, 307, 311
Modernism, 579, 585
Modes of Discourse, 53, 59
Motivation, of characters, 577, 891, 898
Myths, 13, 17
Narration, 437, 441, 691, 696
Narrative poetry, 765, 776
Naturalism, 503, 521
Octave, 299
Oral Tradition, 25, 28
Oratory, 115, 119, 659
Parallelism, 133, 137, 1017, 1021
Personal Essays, 675, 681
Personification, 127, 131
Persuasive Speeches, 73, 77
Poetry
    blank verse, 185, 191
    confessional poetry, 1001, 1005
    dramatic monologue, 719, 723
    dramatic poetry, 765, 774
    free verse, 397, 407, 737, 741, 743, 1026
    imagery, 319, 325, 725, 729
    lyric poem, 60, 61
    lyric poetry, 1009, 1015
    meter, 307, 311
    narrative poetry, 765, 776
    parallelism in, 1017, 1021
    refrain, 359, 361
    rhyme of, 526, 953, 955
    rhythm of, 731, 734, 779, 965, 971
    scansion, 307, 311
    sound devices, 208, 213, 526, 983, 987
    speaker in, 545, 549, 793
    stanza forms, 299, 305
    villanelle, 953, 955
    visual, 959, 961
Point of view, 463, 471, 615, 619, 859, 863 (*See also* Narration)
Postmodernism, 881, 889
Puritan Plain Style, 65

Quatrain, 299
Realism, 503, 521
Real-life experiences, transformation of, 929, 933
Refrain, 359, 361
Regionalism, 451, 459
Rhyme of Poetry, 526, 529, 953, 955
    end rhyme, 953
    exact rhyme, 953, 955
    internal rhyme, 529, 953
    slant rhyme, 953, 955
Rhythm of poetry, 731, 734, 779, 965, 971
Romanticism, 185, 191
Round Characters (See Characters)
Satire, 781, 784
Scansion, 307, 311
Setting, 629, 643, 843, 851
Sextet, 299
Simile, 753, 755
Single Effect, 193, 207
Slant Rhyme (See Rhyme of poetry)
Slave Narrative, 152, 155
Songs, refrain, 359, 361
Sonnet, 531, 535
Sound Devices, 208, 213, 526, 529, 983, 987
    alliteration, 208, 213, 526, 529, 983, 987
    assonance, 208, 213, 526, 529, 983, 987
    consonance, 208, 213, 526, 529, 983, 987
Speaker in poetry, 545, 549, 793
Stanza, forms of, 299, 305
Stream of Consciousness, 605, 613, 707, 713
Style, 78, 83, 253, 261, 331, 335, 397, 403, 759, 763, 853,
    857
Style of writer, 78, 83, 261
Symbolism, 279, 296, 715
Symbols, 645, 657, 717, 765, 769
Tercet, 299
Theme, 745, 973, 981, 1104, 1119
Tone, 313, 393, 395
Transcendentalism, 239, 241
Villanelle, 953, 955
Visual Poetry, 959, 961

CRITICAL THINKING AND READING

Allusions, 713
Attitudes, 543
    author's, 145, 277, 403, 673
    comparing and contrasting, 277
    cultural, 183, 459, 927, 1061
    inference about, 59, 145, 667
Author
    attitudes of, 145, 277, 403, 673
    bias, 83
    inference about, 109
    purpose of, 51
Casting in play, 1119
Cause and Effect, 248

Characters
    behavior of, 603
    contrasting, 898
    motivation of, 577
Charged Words, 137
Comparing and Contrasting Attitudes, 277
Conflict and theme, 501
Connections among literary works, 696
Cultural Attitudes
    inference about, 183, 459, 927
    recognition of, 927, 1061
Cultural Perspectives, appreciation of, 37
Cultural Values, interpretation of, 17
Dialect, 449, 1081
Diction, 381
Effect of Imagery, appreciating, 943
Exaggeration, 689
Flashback, 879
Imagery, 729, 943
Inference
    about attitudes, 59, 145, 667
    about author, 109
    about cultural attitudes, 183, 459, 927, 1061
Irony
    recognizing details of, 477
    and theme, 841
Main Ideas, 375
Metaphorical Thinking, 889
Metaphors, 23
Motivation, of characters, 577
Opinion, supporting, 151
Paradox, 251, 905
Period Characteristics, 619
Personification, 131
Play, casting in, 1119
Prediction, 829
Sequence of Events, 471, 613
Setting, 643
Sound Devices, 529
Style, 261, 369, 585
Supporting an Interpretation, 717, 863
Supporting Statements of Theme, 207
Symbols, 296
Theme
    and conflict, 501
    and irony, 841
Time, 851
Understanding Persuasive Techniques, 119
Writing About Lyric Poetry, 65

LEARNING OPTIONS

Art, 65, 125, 131, 151, 191, 207, 241, 243, 329, 541, 619,
    673, 681, 689, 700, 733, 757, 769, 774, 791, 802,
    851, 857, 863, 933, 950, 969, 971, 977, 995, 1030,
    1103
Community Connections, 921, 927, 1029

Cross-curricular Connection, 42, 125, 145, 191, 243, 250, 296, 303, 329, 361, 375, 487, 522, 529, 533, 603, 619, 627, 723, 729, 733, 784, 789, 791, 801, 869, 905, 961, 971, 977, 985, 995, 1007
Language, 23, 145, 857, 913, 997
Multicultural Activity, 301, 477, 533, 933
Performance, 301, 898, 913, 991
Speaking and Listening, 29, 83, 119, 191, 243, 501, 529, 627, 643, 659, 681, 723, 734, 762, 774, 776, 829, 857, 863, 889, 933, 966, 979
Writing, 119, 125, 137, 145, 207, 250, 296, 303, 332, 375, 381, 405, 441, 471, 477, 487, 522, 539, 541, 543, 547, 577, 585, 659, 673, 681, 696, 700, 705, 723, 729, 735, 751, 760, 776, 782, 791, 801, 851, 857, 869, 889, 943, 955, 966, 969, 971, 981, 985, 1015, 1103

THINKING AND WRITING

Adapting a Folk Tale, 183
Comparing and Contrasting, 23
Comparing and Contrasting Accounts, 59
Comparing and Contrasting Arguments, 137
Comparing and Contrasting Attitudes, 277
Comparing and Contrasting Characters, 459
Comparing and Contrasting Essays, 261, 681, 927
Comparing and Contrasting Myths, 19
Comparing and Contrasting Poems, 723, 1004
Comparing and Contrasting Speeches, 381
Comparing and Contrasting Stories, 619
Comparing and Contrasting Tones, 317
Creating an Extended Metaphor, 801
Developing a Personification, 131
Evaluating Persuasive Techniques, 77
Exploring a Different Point of View, 471
Exploring Another Point of View, 39
Responding in Criticism, 879
Responding to a Statement, 213, 585, 716
Responding to a Statement About Style, 112
Responding to Criticism, 191, 339, 522, 857, 869, 879, 943, 955, 971, 1015
Responding to Dickinson's Poetry, 343
Responding to Poetry, 1030
Supporting an Opinion, 487
Supporting a Statement of Theme, 207
Symbolism, 717
Writing About a Writer's Attitude, 921, 981
Writing About Conflict and Theme, 501
Writing About Conformity, 243
Writing About Historical Context, 603
Writing About History, 248
Writing About Irony, 477

Writing About Language, 950
Writing About Parallels, 1103
Writing About Related Themes, 659
Writing About Revolutionary Literature, 125
Writing About the Role of Spirituals, 331
Writing About Setting, 643
Writing About Structure, 889
Writing About Style, 763
Writing About Symbolic Meaning, 863
Writing About Symbolism and Theme, 296
Writing About Symbols, 769
Writing About Symbols and Allusions, 657
Writing About Techniques, 613
Writing About Theme, 577, 1119
Writing About the Setting, 1061
Writing a Conceit, 71
Writing a Confessional Poem, 1007
Writing a Continuation, 37
Writing a Continuation of the Story, 627
Writing a Description, 145
Writing a Dialogue, 1081
Writing a Dramatic Poem, 776
Writing a First-Person Narrative, 696
Writing a Formal Essay, 913
Writing a Historical Account, 51
Writing a Humorous Essay, 680
Writing a Journal Entry, 83
Writing a Letter, 379, 898
Writing an Apology, 735
Writing an Argumentative Essay, 905
Writing a Narrative, 42
Writing an Autobiographical Account, 109
Writing an Autobiography, 369, 667
Writing a Critical Response, 913
Writing an Epistle, 151
Writing an Epitaph, 547
Writing an Extended Personification, 529
Writing an Imagist Poem, 727
Writing an Impressionistic Biography, 673
Writing a Poem, 991
Writing a Poem About a Special Place, 790
Writing a Poem in Free Verse, 407
Writing a Poem in Support of a Cause, 309
Writing a Poem Using Free Verse, 741
Writing a Poem Using Imagery, 329, 997
Writing a Report, 263
Writing a Song, 30
Writing a Sonnet, 535
Writing a Speech, 119, 395
Writing a Statement of Ambition, 441
Writing a Story, 841, 851, 933
Writing a Story Using Dialect, 449
Writing a Summary, 375
Writing a Visual Poem, 961

INDEX OF TITLES BY THEMES

AMERICA IN CRISIS

Beat! Beat! Drums!, 404
Concord Hymn, 247
Crisis, Number 1, The, from, 122
Crucible, The, 1034
Death of the Ball Turret Gunner, The, 979
Declaration of Independence, The, 134
Gettysburg Address, The, 380
Letter to His Son, 378
Losses, 980
Mary Chesnut's Civil War, from, 371
Old Ironsides, 308
Speech in the Virginia Convention, 116
To His Excellency, General Washington, 129
When Lilacs Last in the Dooryard Bloom'd, 408
Wonders of the Invisible World, The, from, 79

CHOICES AND CONSEQUENCES

Autobiography, The, from, 100
Average Waves in Unprotected Waters, 872
Bear, The, 646
Black Boy: A Record of Childhood and Youth, from, 692
Civil Disobedience, from, 262
Everyday Use, 892
Explorer, The, 966
Fiddler Jones, 548
Flight, 630
Imagined Scenes, 882
I Will Fight No More Forever, 394
Letter to His Son, 378
Life on the Mississippi, The Boys' Ambition, from, 438
Life You Save May Be Your Own, The, 832
Minister's Black Veil, The, 268
Moby-Dick, from, 280
Rockpile, The, 844
To Build a Fire, 490
Tropics in New York, The, 790
Wagner Matinée, A, 480
Walden, from, 254
When I Heard the Learn'd Astronomer, 406
Winter Dreams, 588

HUMANS IN CONFLICT

Arsenal at Springfield, The, 304
Beat! Beat! Drums!, 404
Concord Hymn, 247
Crisis, Number 1, The, from, 122
Crucible, The, 1034
Death of the Ball Turret Gunner, The, 979
Declaration of Independence, The, 134
Engineer-Private Paul Klee Misplaces an Aircraft Between
    Milbertshofen and Cambrai, March 1916, 866
Gettysburg Address, The, 380
Grass, 738
In Another Country, 580
Letter to His Son, 378
Losses, 980
Mary Chesnut's Civil War, from, 371
Occurrence at Owl Creek Bridge, An, 464
Old Ironsides, 308
Speech in the Virginia Convention, 116
To His Excellency, General Washington, 129
Wonders of the Invisible World, The, from, 79

INDIVIDUALS IN SOCIETY

anyone lived in a pretty how town, 761
Autobiography, The, from, 100
Bidwell Ghost, 1012
Black Boy: A Record of Childhood and Youth, from, 692
Civil Disobedience, from, 262
Devil and Tom Walker, The, 174
Fall of the House of Usher, The, 194
Fiddler Jones, 548
Flight, 630
For My Children, 1010
Hidden Name and Complex Fate, from, 908
How happy is the little Stone, 342
Iroquois Constitution, The, from, 21
Luke Havergal, 538
Lying in a Hammock at William Duffy's Farm in Pine
    Island, Minnesota, 1014
Merritt Parkway, 962
Minister's Black Veil, The, 268
Miniver Cheevy, 540
Mortgaged Heart, The, 902
Much Madness is divinest Sense—, 340
old age sticks, 763
On the Mall, 916
Outcasts of Poker Flat, The, 452
Patterns, 720
Rain Guitar, The, 960
Richard Cory, 542
River-Merchant's Wife: A Letter, The, 701
Self-Reliance, from, 242
since feeling is first, 760
Song of Myself, from, 399
Soul selects her own Society—, The, 341
There is a solitude of space, 342

This is my letter to the World, 343
Unknown Citizen, The, 783
Wagner Matinée, A, 480
Walden, from, 254
We Wear the Mask, 532
Who's Who, 782
Worn Path, A, 622

NEW BEGINNINGS

Beautiful Changes, The, 994
Black Boy: A Record of Childhood and Youth, from, 692
Crucible, The, 1034
Far and the Near, The, 616
First Seven Years, The, 822
General History of Virginia, The, from, 46
Hunger in New York City, 1020
Journal of the First Voyage to America, from, 36
Journey, 860
Letters from an American Farmer, from, 148
Letter to Her Daughter from the New White House, 142
Mother Tongue, 946
Narrative of the Expedition of Coronado, The, from, 40
Navajo Origin Legend, The, from, 18
Nothing Gold Can Stay, 777
Of Plymouth Plantation, from, 54
Relation of Alvar Nuñez Cabeza de Vaca, from, 38
Renascence, 746
Sophistication, 570
Tropics in New York, The, 790
Wagner Matinée, A, 480
Walam Olum, The, from, 14
When Lilacs Last in the Dooryard Bloom'd, 408
Wonders of the Invisible World, The, from, 79

OUR LIVING EARTH

Anecdote of the Jar, 717
Arctic Dreams, from, 936
Bear, The, 646
Beautiful Changes, The, 994
Birches, 766
Evening Hawk, 998
First Snowfall, The, 316
Flight, 630
From the Houses of Magic, 26
Gold Glade, 996
Grass, 738
Hampton Beach, 326
Heat, 728
Lying in a Hammock at William Duffy's Farm in Pine
    Island, Minnesota, 1014
Mending Wall, 768
Most Satisfied by Snow, 1022
Nature, from, 240
Navajo Origin Legend, The, from, 18

Noiseless Patient Spider, A, 407
Nothing Gold Can Stay, 777
Observer, The, 1018
Open Boat, The, 504
Pear Tree, 726
Rhodora, The, 249
Snowbound, from, 320
Snowstorm, The, 245
Song Concerning a Dream of the Thunderbirds, 30
Song of Myself, from, 399
Song of the Chattahoochee, 527
Spring Song, 29
Stopping by Woods on a Snowy Evening, 778
Storm Ending, 800
Tide Rises, The Tide Falls, The, 300
To a Waterfowl, 189
To Build a Fire, 490
Traveling Through the Dark, 1006
Vision Beyond Time and Place, A, 924
Walam Olum, The, from, 14
Walden, from, 254

SEARCH FOR MEANING

Auspex, 315
Bear, The, 646
Chambered Nautilus, The, 310
Canto 13, 703
Far and the Near, The, 616
First Snowfall, The, 316
From the Houses of Magic, 26
Huswifery, 68
In Another Country, 580
Jilting of Granny Weatherall, The, 606
Love Song of J. Alfred Prufrock, The, 708
Moby-Dick, from, 280
Nature, from, 240
Navajo Origin Legend, The, from 18
Nobel Prize Acceptance Speech, 658
Renascence, 746
Self-Reliance, from, 242
Sinners in the Hands of an Angry God, from, 74
Song Concerning a Dream of the Thunderbirds, 30
Sophistication, 570
Spring Song, 29
Thanatopsis, 187
To a Waterfowl, 189
To Helen, 217
To My Dear and Loving Husband, 61
Upon a Wasp Chilled with Cold, 70
Upon the Burning of Our House, July 10th, 1666, 62
Vision Beyond Time and Place, A, 924
Wagner Matinée, A, 480
Walam Olum, The, from, 14
Walden, from, 254
Winter Dreams, 588

SELF-REALIZATION

Auspex, 315
Autobiography, The, from, 100
Average Waves in Unprotected Waters, 872
Bear, The, 646
Black Man Talks of Reaping, A, 802
Chambered Nautilus, The, 310
Dust Tracks on a Road, from, 662
Fiddler Jones, 548
First Seven Years, The, 822
Hidden Name and Complex Fate, from, 908
How happy is the little Stone, 342
Journey, 860
Life on the Mississippi, The Boys' Ambition, from, 438
Lucinda Matlock, 546
Lying in a Hammock at William Duffy's Farm in Pine
    Island, Minnesota, 1014
Mirror, 1002
Mother Tongue, 946
Noiseless Patient Spider, A, 407
Observer, The, 1018
Preface to the 1855 Edition of Leaves of Grass, from, 398
Slump, The, 854
Song of Myself, from, 399
Sophistication, 570
Story of an Hour, The, 474
Straw Into Gold: The Metamorphosis of the Everyday, 930
There is a solitude of space, 342
This is my letter to the World, 343
Those Winter Sundays, 1005
Traveling Through the Dark, 1006
When I Heard the Learn'd Astronomer, 406

STRUGGLE FOR JUSTICE

Any Human to Another, 789
Black Boy: A Record of Childhood and Youth, from, 692
Black Man Talks of Reaping, A, 802
Civil Disobedience, from, 262
Crisis, Number 1, The, from, 122
Crucible, The, 1034
Declaration of Independence, The, 134
Douglass, 534
Dust Tracks on a Road, from, 662
Flight, 630
For My Children, 1010
Frederick Douglass, 1004
Go Down, Moses, 361
Interesting Narrative of the Life of Olaudah Equiano, The,
    from, 153
Iroquois Constitution, The, from, 21
I Will Fight No More Forever, 394
Moby-Dick, from, 280
Mother Tongue, 946
My Bondage and My Freedom, from, 364
Negro Speaks of Rivers, The, 795

Occurrence at Owl Creek Bridge, An, 464
Outcasts of Poker Flat, The, 452
Speech in the Virginia Convention, 116
Swing Low, Sweet Chariot, 360
We Live by What We See at Night, 986
We Wear the Mask, 532
Worn Path, A, 622

USES OF IMAGINATION

Ars Poetica, 754
As imperceptibly as grief, 340
#1 Atmosphere, 990
Be Beautiful, Noble, Like the Antique Ant, 984
Bustle in a House, The, 339
Devil and Tom Walker, The, 174
Disillusionment of Ten O'Clock, 716
Engineer-Private Paul Klee Misplaces an Aircraft Between
    Milbertshofen and Cambrai, March 1916, 866
Explorer, The, 966
Fall of the House of Usher, The, 194
Freeway 280, 1028
Hawthorne, 974
"Hope" is the thing with feathers—, 332
House Guest, 970
How happy is the little Stone, 342
Hunger in New York City, 1020
I felt a Funeral, in my Brain, 338
I heard a Fly buzz—when I died—, 337
In a Station of the Metro, 700
I never saw a Moor—, 334
Little Exercise, 968
Locust Tree in Flower, The, 733
#2 Memory, 990
Most Satisfied by Snow, 1022
Much Madness is divinest Sense—, 340
My life closed twice before its close—, 339
narrow Fellow in the Grass, A, 335
Night the Ghost Got In, The, 684
Notorious Jumping Frog of Calaveras County, The, 445
Observer, The, 1018
Once More, the Round, 956
Plucking Out a Rhythm, 1026
Poem, 990
Poetry, 756
Raven, The, 209
Red Wheelbarrow, The, 734
Soul selects her own Society—, The, 341
Storm Ending, 800
Straw Into Gold: The Metamorphosis of the Everyday, 930
Success is counted sweetest, 336
Tell all the Truth but tell it slant—, 336
There is a solitude of space, 342
There's a certain Slant of light, 333
This Is Just to Say, 735
This is my letter to the World, 343
This Life, 1030

Vision Beyond Time and Place, A, 924
Waking, The, 954
We Live by What We See at Night, 986

VALUES AND BELIEFS

Acquainted with the Night, 779
Arsenal at Springfield, The, 304
#1 Atmosphere, 990
Autobiography, The, from, 100
Bear, The, 646
Be Beautiful, Noble, Like the Antique Ant, 984
Birches, 766
Brahma, 251
Chicago, 742
Crucible, The, 1034
Death of the Hired Man, The, 770
Declaration of Independence, The, 134
Everyday Use, 892
Fire and Ice, 777
First Seven Years, The, 822
For My Children, 1010
From the Houses of Magic, 26
Grass, 738
Huswifery, 68
Iroquois Constitution, The, from, 20
Lucinda Matlock, 546
#2 Memory, 990
Mending Wall, 768

My Bondage and My Freedom, from, 364
Nature, from, 240
Nothing Gold Can Stay, 777
Outcasts of Poker Flat, The, 452
"Out, Out—", 775
People, Yes, The, from, 740
Poem, 990
Poor Richard's Almanack, from, 111
Psalm of Life, A, 302
Renascence, 746
Self-Reliance, from, 242
Sinners in the Hands of an Angry God, from, 74
Song Concerning a Dream of the Thunderbirds, 30
Song of Myself, from, 399
Spring Song, 29
Speech in the Virginia Convention, 116
Stopping by Woods on a Snowy Evening, 778
Success is counted sweetest, 336
Tell all the Truth but tell it slant—, 336
Thanatopsis, 187
Those Winter Sundays, 1005
Tide Rises, The Tide Falls, The, 300
Tin Lizzie, 670
To a Waterfowl, 189
To My Dear and Loving Husband, 61
Upon a Wasp Chilled with Cold, 70
Upon the Burning of Our House, 62
Walden, 676
Wonders of the Invisible World, The, from, 79
Worn Path, A, 622

INDEX OF AUTHORS AND TITLES

Page numbers in *italics* refer to biographical information

A

Abbey, Edward, 264
Acquainted with the Night, 779
Adams, Abigail, *140,* 142
Anderson, Sherwood, *568,* 570
Anecdote of the Jar, 717
Any Human to Another, 789
anyone lived in a pretty how town, 761
Arctic Dreams, from, 936
Arsenal at Springfield, The, 304
Ars Poetica, 754
As imperceptibly as grief, 340
#1 Atmosphere, 990
Auden, W. H., *780,* 782, 783
Auspex, 315
Autobiography, The, from, 100
Average Waves in Unprotected Waters, 872

B

Baldwin, James, *842,* 844
Barthelme, Donald, *864,* 866
Bear, The, 646
Beat! Beat! Drums!, 404
Beattie, Ann, *880,* 882
Beautiful Changes, The, 994
Be Beautiful, Noble, Like the Antique Ant, 984
Bidwell Ghost, 1012
Bierce, Ambrose, *462,* 464
Birches, 766
Bishop, Elizabeth, *964,* 968, 970
Black Boy: A Record of Childhood and Youth, from, 692
Black Man Talks of Reaping, A, 802
Bontemps, Arna, *798,* 802
Bradford, William, *52,* 54
Bradstreet, Anne, *60,* 61, 62
Brady, Mathew, 418
Brahma, 251
Brooks, Gwendolyn, *964,* 966
Bryant, William Cullen, *184,* 187, 189
Bustle in a House, The, 339

C

Cabeza de Vaca, Alvar Nuñez, *34,* 38
Canto 13, 703
Casteñada, Pedro de, *34,* 40
Cather, Willa, *478,* 480
Cervantes, Lorna Dee, *1024,* 1028
Chambered Nautilus, The, 310
Chang, Diana, *1016,* 1022

Chesnut, Mary, *370,* 371
Chicago, 742
Chippewa, *24,* 29
Chopin, Kate, *472,* 474
Cisneros, Sandra, *928,* 930
Civil Disobedience, from, 262
Columbus, Christopher, *34,* 36
Concord Hymn, 247
Copland, Aaron, 1120
Crane, Stephen, *502,* 504, 523
Crèvecoeur, Michel-Guillaume Jean, de, *146,* 148
Crisis, Number 1, The, from, 122
Crucible, The, 1034
Cruz, Victor Hernández, *982,* 990
Cullen, Countee, *786,* 789
Cummings, E. E., *758,* 760, 761, 763

D

Death of the Ball Turret Gunner, The, 979
Death of the Hired Man, The, 770
Declaration of Independence, The, 134
Delaware, *12,* 14
Devil and Tom Walker, The, 174
Dickey, James, *958,* 960
Dickinson, Emily, *330,* 332–43
Didion, Joan, *914,* 916
Dillard, Annie, 264
Disillusionment of Ten O'Clock, 716
Doolittle, Hilda, *724,* 726, 728
Dos Passos, John, *668,* 670
Douglass, 534
Douglass, Frederick, *362,* 364, *368*
Dove, Rita, *1024,* 1030
Dunbar, Paul Laurence, *530,* 532, 534
Dust Tracks on a Road, from, 662

E

Edwards, Jonathan, *72,* 74
Eliot, T. S., *706,* 708
Ellison, Ralph, *906,* 908
Emerson, Ralph Waldo, *238,* 240, 242, 245, 247, 249, 251
Engineer-Private Paul Klee Misplaces an Aircraft Between Milbertshofen and Cambrai, March 1916, 866
Equiano, Olaudah, *152,* 153
Erdrich, Louise, *1008,* 1012
Espada, Martín, *982,* 986, *988*
Evening Hawk, 998
Everyday Use, 892
Explorer, The, 966

F

Fall of the House of Usher, The, 194
Far and the Near, The, 616
Faulkner, William, *644, 646, 658*
Fiddler Jones, 548
Fire and Ice, 777
First Seven Years, The, 822
First Snowfall, The, 316
Fitzgerald, F. Scott, *586, 588*
Flight, 630
For My Children, 1010
Franklin, Benjamin, *98,* 100, 111
Frederick Douglass, 1004
Freeway 280, 1028
From the Houses of Magic, 26
Frost, Robert, *764, 766, 768, 770, 775, 777–79*

G

General History of Virginia, The, from, 46
Gettysburg Address, The, 380
Go Down, Moses, 361
Gold Glade, 996
Grass, 738

H

Hampton Beach, 326
Harte, Bret, *450, 452*
Hawthorne, 974
Hawthorne, Nathaniel, *266, 268*
Hayden, Robert, *1000,* 1004, 1005
H. D., *724, 726, 728*
Heat, 728
Hemingway, Ernest, *578, 580*
Henry, Patrick, *114,* 116
Hidden Name and Complex Fate, from, 908
Hitchcock, Alfred J., *218*
Holmes, Oliver Wendell, *306,* 308, 310
"Hope" is the thing with feathers—, 332
House Guest, 970
How happy is the little Stone, 342
Hughes, Langston, *792, 795, 796*
Hunger in New York City, 1020
Hurston, Zora Neale, *660, 662*
Huswifery, 68

I

I felt a Funeral, in my Brain, 338
I heard a Fly buzz—when I died—, 337
Imagined Scenes, 882
Inada, Lawson Fusao, *1024, 1026*
In Another Country, 580
In a Station of the Metro, 700
I Never saw a Moor—, 334
Interesting Narrative of the Life of Olaudah Equiano, The,
    from, 153
Iroquois, *20,* 21
Iroquois Constitution, The, from, 21

Irving, Washington, *172, 174*
I Will Fight No More Forever, 394

J

Jarrell, Randall, *972, 979, 980*
Jefferson, Thomas, *132,* 134, *138*
Jilting of Granny Weatherall, The, 606
Joseph, Chief, *392, 394*
Journal of the First Voyage to America, from, 36
Journey, 860

L

Lanier, Sidney, *526, 527*
Lee, Robert E., *376, 378*
Letters from an American Farmer, from, 148
Letter to Her Daughter from the New White House, 142
Letter to His Son, 378
Levertov, Denise, *958, 962*
Life on the Mississippi, The Boys' Ambition, from, 438
Life You Save May Be Your Own, The, 832
Lincoln, Abraham, *376,* 380
Little Exercise, 968
Locust Tree in Flower, The, 733
London, Jack, *488,* 490
Longfellow, Henry Wadsworth, *298, 300, 302, 304*
Lopez, Barry, *934, 936*
Losses, 980
Love Song of J. Alfred Prufrock, The, 708
Lowell, Amy, *718, 720*
Lowell, James Russell, *312, 315,* 316
Lowell, Robert, *972,* 974
Lucinda Matlock, 546
Luke Havergal, 538
*Lying in a Hammock at William Duffy's Farm in Pine
    Island, Minnesota,* 1014

M

MacLeish, Archibald, *752, 754*
Malamud, Bernard, *820, 822*
Mary Chesnut's Civil War, from, 371
Masters, Edgar Lee, *544, 546, 548*
Mather, Cotton, *78,* 79
McCullers, Carson, *900, 902*
McElroy, Colleen, *1008,* 1010
McKay, Claude, *786, 790*
Melville, Herman, *278,* 280
#2 Memory, 990
Mending Wall, 768
Merritt Parkway, 962
Millay, Edna St. Vincent, *744, 746*
Miller, Arthur, *1032, 1034*
Minister's Black Veil, The, 268
Miniver Cheevy, 540
Mirror, 1002
Moby-Dick, from, 280
Momaday, N. Scott, *922, 924*
Moore, Marianne, *752, 756*

Mortgaged Heart, The, 902
Most Satisfied by Snow, 1022
Mother Tongue, 946
Much Madness is divinest Sense—, 340
My Bondage and My Freedom, from, 364
My life closed twice before its close—, 339

N

Narrative of the Expedition of Coronado, The, from, 40
Narrow Fellow in the Grass, A, 335
Native American Voices Today, 31
Nature, from, 240
Navajo, 12, 18
Navajo Origin Legend, The, from, 18
Negro Speaks of Rivers, The, 795
Night the Ghost Got In, The, 684
Nobel Prize Acceptance Speech, 658
Noiseless Patient Spider, A, 407
Nothing Gold Can Stay, 777
Notorious Jumping Frog of Calaveras County, The, 445

O

Oates, Joyce Carol, 858, 860
Observer, The, 1018
Occurrence at Owl Creek Bridge, An, 464
O'Connor, Flannery, 830, 832
Of Plymouth Plantation, from, 54
old age sticks, 763
Old Ironsides, 308
Once More, the Round, 956
On the Mall, 916
Open Boat, The, 504
Ortiz, Simon, 1016, 1020
Outcasts of Poker Flat, The, 452
"Out, Out—", 775

P

Paine, Thomas, 120, 122
Patterns, 720
Pear Tree, 726
People, Yes, The, from, 740
Pima, 24, 26
Plath, Sylvia, 1000, 1002
Plucking Out a Rhythm, 1026
Poe, Edgar Allan, 192, 194, 209, 214, 217
Poem, 990
Poetry, 756
Poor Richard's Almanack, from, 111
Porter, Katherine Anne, 604, 606
Pound, Ezra, 698, 700, 701, 703
Preface to the 1855 Edition of Leaves of Grass, from, 398
Psalm of Life, A, 302

R

Rain Guitar, The, 960
Raven, The, 209
Red Wheelbarrow, The, 734

Relation of Alvar Nuñez Cabeza de Vaca, from, 38
Remington, Frederick, 460
Renascence, 746
Rhodora, The, 249
Rich, Adrienne, 1016, 1018
Richard Cory, 542
River-Merchant's Wife: A Letter, The, 701
Robinson, Edwin Arlington, 536, 538, 540, 542
Rockpile, The, 844
Roethke, Theodore, 952, 954, 956

S

Sandburg, Carl, 736, 738, 740, 742
Self-Reliance, from, 242
since feeling is first, 760
Sinners in the Hands of an Angry God, from, 74
Slump, The, 854
Smith, John, 44, 46
Snowbound, from, 320
Snowstorm, The, 245
Song Concerning a Dream of the Thunderbirds, 30
Song of Myself, from, 399
Song of the Chattahoochee, 527
Sophistication, 570
Soul selects her own Society—, The, 341
Speech in the Virginia Convention, 116
Spirituals, 358, 360, 361
Spring Song, 29
Stafford, William, 1000, 1006
Steinbeck, John, 628, 630
Stevens, Wallace, 714, 716, 717
Stopping by Woods on a Snowy Evening, 778
Storm Ending, 800
Story of an Hour, The, 474
Straw Into Gold: The Metamorphosis of the Everyday, 930
Success is counted sweetest, 336
Swing Low, Sweet Chariot, 360

T

Tan, Amy, 944, 946
Taylor, Edward, 66, 68, 70
Tell all the Truth but tell it slant—, 336
Teton Sioux, 24, 30
Thanatopsis, 187
There is a solitude of space, 342
There's a certain Slant of light, 333
This is Just to Say, 735
This is my letter to the World, 343
This Life, 1030
Thoreau, Henry David, 252, 254, 262
Those Winter Sundays, 1005
Thurber, James, 682, 684
Tide Rises, The Tide Falls, The, 300
Tin Lizzie, 670
To a Waterfowl, 189
To Build a Fire, 490
To Helen, 217

To His Excellency, General Washington, 129
To My Dear and Loving Husband, 61
Toomer, Jean, *798, 800*
Traveling Through the Dark, 1006
Tropics in New York, The, 790
Twain, Mark, *436*, 438, 442, 445
Tyler, Anne, *870, 872*

U
Unknown Citizen, The, 783
Updike, John, *852, 854*
Upon a Wasp Chilled with Cold, 70
Upon the Burning of Our House, 62

V
Villa, José García, *982, 984*
Vision Beyond Time and Place, A, 924

W
Wagner Matinée, A, 480
Waking, The, 954
Walam Olum, The, from, 14

Walden, 676
Walden, from, 254
Walker, Alice, *890, 892*
Warren, Robert Penn, *992, 996, 998*
We Live by What We See at Night, 986
Welty, Eudora, *620, 622*
We Wear the Mask, 532
Wheatley, Phillis, *126,* 129
When I Heard the Learn'd Astronomer, 406
When Lilacs Last in the Dooryard Bloom'd, 408
White, E. B., *674,* 676
Whitman, Walt, *396, 398, 399,* 404, 406–408
Whittier, John Greenleaf, *318,* 320, 326
Who's Who, 782
Wilbur, Richard, *992, 994*
Williams, William Carlos, *730,* 733, 734, 735
Winter Dreams, 588
Wolfe, Thomas, *614,* 616
Wonders of the Invisible World, The, from, 79
Worn Path, A, 622
Wright, James, *1008,* 1014
Wright, Richard, *690, 692*

and Women and Other Stories by John Updike. Excerpt from Willa Cather Living by Edith Lewis. Copyright 1953 by Edith Lewis. Reprinted by permission of Alfred A. Knopf, Inc.

Alfred A. Knopf, Inc., and Olwyn Hughes Literary Agency
Lines from "Mushrooms" copyright © 1960 by Sylvia Plath. Reprinted from The Colossus and Other Poems by Sylvia Plath, by permission.

Latin American Literary Review Press
"Freeway 280" by Lorna Dee Cervantes. Reprinted by permission of the publisher, Latin American Literary Review, Volume 15, No. 10, 1977, Pittsburgh, Pennsylvania. Reprinted by permission of the publisher.

Life Picture Sales
From "A Vision Beyond Time and Place" by N. Scott Momaday, published in Life Magazine, 1971, © 1971 Time Warner. Reprinted with permission.

Little, Brown and Company
"There is a solitude of space" from The Complete Poems of Emily Dickinson edited by Thomas H. Johnson. Copyright 1914, 1942 by Martha Dickinson Bianchi. By permission of Little, Brown and Company.

Liveright Publishing Corporation
"since feeling is first," "anyone lived in a pretty how town," and "old age sticks," reprinted from Complete Poems, 1913–1962 by E. E. Cummings, by permission of Liveright Publishing Corporation. Copyright © 1923, 1925, 1931, 1935, 1938, 1939, 1940, 1944, 1945, 1946, 1947, 1948, 1949, 1950, 1951, 1952, 1953, 1954, 1955, 1956, 1957, 1958, 1959, 1960, 1961, 1962 by the Trustees for the E. E. Cummings Trust. Copyright © 1961, 1963, 1968 by Marion Morehouse Cummings. Lines from "Astronauts" from American Journal, Poems by Robert Hayden. "Those Winter Sundays" reprinted from Angle of Ascent, New and Selected Poems by Robert Hayden, by permission of Liveright Publishing Corporation. Copyright © 1975, 1972, 1970, 1966 by Robert Hayden. "Storm Ending" and lines from "Song of the Son" reprinted from Crane by Jean Toomer, by permission of Liveright Publishing Corporation. Copyright 1923 by Boni & Liveright. Copyright © renewed 1951 by Jean Toomer. "Frederick Douglass" reprinted from Collected Poems of Robert Hayden, edited by Frederick Blaysher, by permission of Liveright Publishing Corporation. Copyright © 1985 by Erma Hayden.

The Sterling Lord Agency, Inc.
Selections from "The Crisis, Number 1" in The Selected Work of Tom Paine edited by Howard Fast. Copyright 1945 by Howard Fast. Reprinted by permission of The Sterling Lord Agency, Inc.

Macmillan Publishing Company
Lines from "Bird-Witted" from Collected Poems by Marianne Moore. Copyright 1941, and renewed 1969, by Marianne Moore. Lines from "Nevertheless" from Collected Poems by Marianne Moore. Copyright 1944, and renewed 1972 by Marianne Moore. "Poetry" reprinted from Collected Poems by Marianne Moore. Copyright 1935 by Marianne Moore, renewed 1963 by Marianne Moore and T. S. Eliot. Reprinted with permission of Macmillan Publishing Company.

Ellen C. Masters
"Fiddler Jones" and "Lucinda Matlock" from Spoon River Anthology by Edgar Lee Masters, published by Macmillan Publishing Company.

Archives of Claude McKay
"The Tropics in New York" from The Poems of Claude McKay by Claude McKay, Harcourt Brace, publisher, copyright © 1981. Reprinted by permission of Archives of Claude McKay, Carl Cowl, administrator.

William Morrow & Company, Inc.
"Plucking Out a Rhythm" from Before the War by Lawson Fusao Inada. Copyright © 1971 by Lawson Fusao Inada. Reprinted by permission of William Morrow & Company, Inc.

New Directions Publishing Corporation
"Heat" and "Pear Tree" by H. D., Collected Poems, 1912–1944. Copyright © 1982 by The Estate of Hilda Doolittle. "Oread" from H. D., Selected Poems. Copyright 1925, 1953, © 1957 by Norman Holmes Pearson. "Merritt Parkway" by Denise Levertov, Collected Earlier Poems, 1940–1960 of Denise Levertov. Copyright © 1959 by Denise Levertov Goodman. "Canto 13" by Ezra Pound, The Cantos of Ezra Pound. Copyright 1934 by Ezra Pound. "In a Station of the Metro" and "The River-Merchant's Wife: A Letter" by Ezra Pound, Personae. Copyright 1926 by Ezra Pound. "The Locust Tree in Flower," "The Red Wheelbarrow," and "This Is Just to Say" by William Carlos Williams, Collected Poems Volume I: 1909–1939. Copyright 1938 by New Directions Publishing Corporation. "Orchard" by H. D. from Modern American Poetry, edited by Louis Untermeyer. Copyright 1958 by Harcourt, Brace and World, Inc. Reprinted by permission of New Directions Publishing Corporation.

New York University Press
From the "Preface" to Walt Whitman: Leaves of Grass, Reader's Comprehensive Edition edited by Harold W. Blodgett and Sculley Bradley. Copyright © 1965 by New York University. Reprinted by permission of New York University Press.

W. W. Norton & Company, Inc.
"The Observer" reprinted from The Fact of A Doorframe, Poems Selected and New, 1950–1984, by Adrienne Rich, by permission of W. W. Norton & Company, Inc. Copyright © 1984 by Adrienne Rich. Copyright 1975, 1978 by W. W. Norton & Company, Inc. Copyright © 1981 by Adrienne Rich. From "Civil Disobedience" reprinted from Walden and Civil Disobedience by Henry David Thoreau, edited by Owen Thomas. By permission of W. W. Norton & Company, Inc.

Copyright © 1966 by W. W. Norton & Company, Inc. "The Bear" by William Faulkner from *Uncollected Stories of William Faulkner,* edited by Joseph Blotner. Copyright 1942 and renewed 1970 by Estelle Faulkner and Jill Faulkner Summers. An expanded version of this story appears in *Go Down, Moses* by William Faulkner.

Harold Ober Associates, Inc.
"A Black Man Talks of Reaping" and lines from "Southern Mansions" from *Personals* by Arna Bontemps. Copyright © 1963 by Arna Bontemps. Reprinted by permission of Harold Ober Associates, Inc.

Simon J. Ortiz
"Hunger in New York City" from *Going For the Rain: Poems* by Simon J. Ortiz. Published by Harper & Row. Reprinted by permission of Simon J. Ortiz.

Princeton University Press
From "Where I Lived, and What I Lived For" and from "The Conclusion" in *Walden: The Writings of Henry D. Thoreau,* edited by J. Lyndon Shanley. Copyright © 1971 Princeton University Press. Excerpt from "Rhetorical Criticism, Theory of Genres" from *Anatomy of Criticism* by Northrop Frye. Copyright © 1957 by Princeton University Press. All rights reserved. Reprinted with permission of Princeton University Press.

Random House, Inc.
Excerpt from "Hidden Name and Complex Fate" from *Shadow and Act* by Ralph Ellison. Copyright 1953, © 1964 by Ralph Ellison. "The Bear" (7000-word version) by William Faulkner, copyright 1942 and renewed 1970 by Estelle Faulkner and Jill Faulkner Summers. An expanded version of this story appears in *Go Down, Moses* by William Faulkner. "Evening Hawk" copyright © 1975 by Robert Penn Warren, and "Gold Glade" copyright © 1957 by Robert Penn Warren, reprinted form *Selected Poems, 1923–1975* by Robert Penn Warren. Excerpt from *The Dyer's Hand and Other Essays* by W. H. Auden. Copyright 1948, 1950, 1952, 1953, 1954, © 1956, 1957, 1958, 1960, 1962 by W. H. Auden. Excerpt from *The Eye of the Story: Selected Essays and Reviews* by Eudora Welty. Copyright © 1978 by Eudora Welty. Reprinted by permission of Random House, Inc.

Random House, Inc., and Faber and Faber Ltd.
"The Unknown Citizen" copyright 1940 and renewed 1968 by W. H. Auden and "Who's Who" copyright 1937 and renewed 1965 by W. H. Auden, reprinted from *W. H. Auden: Collected Poems* by W. H. Auden, edited by Edward Mendelson. Reprinted by permission of Random House, Inc., and Faber and Faber Ltd.

Russell and Volkening, Inc., as agents for the author
"Average Waves in Unprotected Waters" by Anne Tyler, published in *The New Yorker,* February 28, 1977. Copyright © 1977 by Anne Tyler. Reprinted by permission of Russell and Volkening, Inc., as agents for the author.

Charles Scribner's Sons, an imprint of Macmillan Publishing Co.
F. Scott Fitzgerald, "Winter Dreams" from *All The Sad Young Men.* Copyright 1922 by Frances Scott Fitzgerald Lanahan; copyright renewed 1950. Ernest Hemingway, "In Another Country" from *Men Without Women.* Copyright 1927 Charles Scribner's Sons; copyright renewed © 1955 Ernest Hemingway. "Song of the Chattahoochee" from *The Poems of Sidney Lanier.* Barry Lopez, excerpted from *Arctic Dreams.* Copyright © 1986 Barry Holstun Lopez. "Luke Havergal" and "Miniver Cheevy" from *Collected Poems* by Edwin Arlington Robinson, published by Charles Scribner's Sons. "Richard Cory" from *The Children of the Night* by Edwin Arlington Robinson, published by Charles Scribner's Sons. Thomas Wolfe, "The Far and the Near" from *From Death to Morning.* Copyright 1935 by International Magazine Company, Inc.; copyright renewed © 1963 Paul Gitlin. Two excerpts from *Death in the Afternoon* by Ernest Hemingway. Copyright 1932 by Charles Scribner's Sons, renewed 1960 by Ernest Hemingway. Reprinted with the permission of Charles Scribner's Sons, an imprint of Macmillan Publishing Co.

Leslie Marmon Silko
Lines from "Where Mountain Lion Lay Down With Deer" by Leslie Marmon Silko from *Voices of the Rainbow* edited by Kenneth Rosen. Reprinted by permission of Leslie Marmon Silko.

Simon & Schuster, Inc.
Pronunciation key from *Webster's New World Dictionary,* Second College Edition. Copyright © 1986 by Simon & Schuster, Inc. Reprinted by permission.

Smithsonian Institution Press
"Song Concerning a Dream of the Thunderbirds" from *Teton Sioux Music* by Frances Densmore. Bureau of American Ethnology Bulletin 61. Smithsonian Institution, Washington, D.C., 1918. "Spring Song" from *Chippewa Music II* by Frances Densmore. Bureau of American Ethnology Bulletin 53. Smithsonian Institution, Washington, D.C., 1913. Reprinted by permission of Smithsonian Institution Press.

William Stafford
"Traveling Through the Dark" from *Stories That Could Be True: New and Collected Poems* by William Stafford. Copyright © 1960 by William Stafford. Reprinted by permission of the author.

Donald E. Stanford
"Huswifery" and "Upon a Wasp Chilled with Cold" reprinted by permission from *The Poems of Edward Taylor* edited by Donald E. Stanford, copyright © 1960 Donald E. Stanford.

Sterling Lord Literistic, Inc.
Excerpts from "The Crisis, Number 1" from *The Selected Work of Tom Paine,* edited by Howard Fast. Copyright 1945 by Howard Fast. Reprinted by permission of Sterling Lord Literistic, Inc.

Syracuse University Press

From "The Iroquois Constitution" from Arthur C. Parker, "The Constitution of the Five Nations" in *Parker on the Iroquois,* edited with an introduction by William N. Fenton. Syracuse, NY: Syracuse University Press, 1968. By permission of the publisher.

Rosemary A. Thurber

"The Night the Ghost Got In" copyright 1933, © 1961 by James Thurber. From *My Life and Hard Times,* published by Harper & Row. Cartoon caption: "Well, if I called the wrong number, why did you answer the phone?" Copyright 1943 James Thurber; copyright © 1971 Helen Thurber and Rosemary A. Thurber. From *Men, Women and Dogs,* published by Harcourt Brace Jovanovich, Inc. Reprinted by permission.

Time-Life Books, Inc.

Excerpt from "The King's Men" from *This Fabulous Century: 1920–1930* by the Editors of Time-Life Books copyright © 1969 Time-Life Books, Inc. Reprinted by permission of Time-Life Books, Inc.

The University of North Carolina Press

"To His Excellency, General Washington" and lines from "An Hymn to the Morning" from *The Poems of Phillis Wheatley* edited by Julian D. Mason, Jr. Copyright © 1966 by The University of North Carolina Press. Reprinted by permission.

University Press of New England

"For My Children" from *What Madness Brought Me Here: New and Selected Poems, 1968–1988,* by Colleen J. McElroy. Copyright 1990 by Colleen J. McElroy. Reprinted by permission of University Press of New England.

Vanguard Press, a division of Random House, Inc.

"Journey" reprinted from *The Poisoned Kiss and Other Stories From the Portuguese* by Joyce Carol Oates. Copyright © 1975 by Joyce Carol Oates. Reprinted by permission.

Viking Penguin, a division of Penguin Books USA, Inc.

"Sophistication" from *Winesbourg, Ohio* by Sherwood Anderson. Copyright 1919 by B. W. Huebsch; copyright renewed 1947 by Eleanor Copenhaver Anderson. "Flight" from *The Long Valley* by John Steinbeck. Copyright 1938, renewed © 1966 by John Steinbeck. "Be Beautiful, Noble, Like the Antique Ant" (Poem #39) from *Have Come, Am Here* by José García Villa. Copyright 1942, renewed © 1969 by José García Villa. "The Crucible," *Arthur Miller's Collected Plays* by Arthur Miller. Copyright © 1957, renewed © 1985 by Arthur Miller. All rights reserved. Excerpt from *The Fall River Axe Murders* by Angela Carter. Copyright © Angela Carter, 1985, 1986. All rights reserved. Reprinted by permission.

Wesleyan University Press

"Lying in a Hammock at William Duffy's Farm in Pine Island, Minnesota" copyright © 1961 by James Wright. Reprinted from *Collected Poems* by James Wright, by permission of Wesleyan University Press.

Wylie, Aitken & Stone, Inc.

"Engineer-Private Paul Klee Misplaces an Aircraft Between Milbertshofen and Cambrai, March 1916" from *Sadness* by Donald Barthelme. Copyright © 1970, 1971, 1972 by Donald Barthelme. Reprinted with permission.

The H. W. Wilson Company

Excerpt from *Current Biography Yearbook 1984.* Copyright 1984, 1985 by The H. W. Wilson Company. Reprinted by permission of the publisher.

ART CREDITS

Boldface numbers refer to the page numbers on which the art is found.

Cover and Title Page: *An Expression of a Silktown in New Jersey,* c. 1915, Oscar F. Bluemner, Oil on canvas, 30 1/4 x 40″, Purchase, FA1976.19, New Jersey State Museum; **vii:** *The Place of Emergence and the Four Worlds* (detail), Navajo, Courtesy of the Wheelwright Museum of the American Indian; **viii:** Cover of Tom Paine's *Common Sense,* 1776, The Granger Collection, New York; **xi:** *Turn Him Loose, Bill,* Frederic Remington, Superstock; **xii:** *Man With a Horn,* detail, Oliver Johnson, Oil on canvas; **xiv:** *Spring in Puerto Rico,* Pedro Villarini, 1976, Oil on canvas, Courtesy of El Museo del Barrio, New York, Photo by John Lei/Omni-Photo Communications, Inc.; **xvi:** *Afterglow, Florida,* c. 1890–1900, Martin Johnson Heade, Oil on canvas 17″ x 36″, The Chrysler Museum, Norfolk, Virginia, Gift of Walter P. Chrysler, Jr., In memory of Edward Brickhouse; **ix:** *Boston Harbor,* Fitz Hugh Lane, American 1804–1865, Oil on canvas, 26 1/4″ x 32″ (66.8 x 106.7 cm), M. and M. Karolik Collection of American Paintings 1815–1865 by exchange, Courtesy, Museum of Fine Arts, Boston; **3:** *The Beginning of New England* (After the painting by Clyde O. Deland), The Granger Collection, New York; **4:** (left) *Mona Lisa,* Leonardo da Vinci, Superstock; (center) *Captain John Smith,* The Granger Collection, New York; (right) *The Mayflower,* The Granger Collection, New York; **5:** (left) *Nat Bacon's Rebellion,* The Granger Collection, New York; (center) *Accused of Witchcraft,* Douglas Volk, Superstock; (right) *Johann Sebastian Bach,* Elias Gottlob Haussmann, The Granger Collection, New York; **6:** *Good Times in the New World (The Hope of Jamestown),* John Gladsby Chapman, Virginia Museum of Fine Arts, Richmond, The Paul Mellon Collection; **8:** *The Trial of Two 'Witches' at Salem, Massachusetts in 1692;* Illustration by Howard Pyle, The Granger Collection, New York; **11:** *Philip (Metacomet) American Wampanoag Indian Chief,* Paul Revere, The Granger Collection, New York; **12:** (top) *Song of the Aspen* (detail), Bert G. Phillips, Harrison Eiteljorg Collection; (bottom) *The Place of Emergence and the Four Worlds* Navajo, (detail), The Wheelwright Museum of the American Indian; **14:** From *The Walam Olum,* Photo by John Lei/Omni Photo Communications, Inc.; **18:** *The Place of Emergence and the Four*

Worlds, (Navajo) Courtesy of the Wheelwright Museum of the American Indian; **20:** *Red Jacket* (detail), George Catlin, The Thomas Gilcrease Institute of American History and Art, Tulsa, Oklahoma; **21:** *Red Jacket,* George Catlin, The Thomas Gilcrease Institute of American History and Art, Tulsa, Oklahoma; **24:** (top) *Indian Village, River Gila* (detail), Seth Eastman, Museum of Art, Rhode Island School of Design, Gift of RISD Library; (center) *Chief Joseph's Surrender* (detail), Olaf C. Seltzer, The Thomas Gilcrease Institute of American History and Art, Tulsa, Oklahoma; (bottom) *The Mystic* (detail), William R. Leigh, The Thomas Gilcrease Institute of American History and Art, Tulsa, Oklahoma; **26:** *Indian Village, River Gila,* Seth Eastman, Museum of Art, Rhode Island School of Design, Gift of RISD Library; **30:** *The Mystic* (detail), William R. Leigh, The Thomas Gilcrease Institute of American History and Art, Tulsa, Oklahoma; **33:** *Columbus Landing in the New World,* Artist Unknown, Undated lithograph, The Bettmann Archive; **34:** (top) *Christopher Columbus,* Art Resource, New York; (bottom) *A. N. Cabeza de Vaca,* The Granger Collection, New York; **38:** *Search for Gold in an Appalachian Pond,* Theodore de Bry and Jacques Lemoyne de Morgues, Giraudon/Art Resource, New York; **41:** *Conquistadors in the Americas,* Courtesy of the Trustees of the British Library; **43:** *The Arrival of the Englishmen in Virginia,* Theodore de Bry, The Granger Collection, New York; **44:** *John Smith,* The Granger Collection, New York; **49:** *Founding the First Permanent English Settlement in America,* A. C. Warren, Print Collection, Miriam and Ira D. Wallach Division of Art, Prints and Photographs, The New York Public Library, Astor, Lenox and Tilden Foundations; **52:** *William Bradford,* The Granger Collection, New York; **54:** *The Coming of the Mayflower,* N. C. Wyeth, from the Collection of the Metropolitan Life Insurance Company, New York City, Photograph by Malcolm Varon; **56:** *The Landing of the Pilgrims at Plymouth, Massachusetts, December 22nd, 1620,* Currier & Ives, 1876, The Harry T. Peters Collection, Museum of the City of New York; **61:** *Reading Woman,* Terborch, Superstock; **62:** *The Parson Barnard House,* c. 1715, Henry Marsh, North Andover Historical Society; **68:** *Evening,* 1929, Wanda Gág, Collection of the Tamarind Institute, University of New Mexico; **72:** *Jonathan Edwards* (detail), Amos Doolittle, The National Portrait Gallery, Smithsonian Institution, Washington, D.C./Art Resource, New York; **75:** *The Puritan,* c. 1898, Frank E. Schoonover, Oil on canvas, Collection of The Brandywine River Museum, Gift of Mr. and Mrs. Jacob J. Foster; **78:** *Cotton Mather,* Peter Pelham, The Granger Collection, New York; **79:** *A Witch Trial in Salem, Massachusetts, in 1692,* The Granger Collection, New York; **81:** *A Witch Trial in Salem, Massachusetts, in 1692,* The Granger Collection, New York; **86:** *The Signing of the Constitution,* 1787, Howard Chandler Christy, The Granger Collection, New York; **89:** Embossed tax stamp issued by the British Government in 1765, The Granger Collection, New York; **90:** (left) *Benjamin Franklin Conducts His Experiment,* Currier & Ives, The Granger Collection, New York; (center) *Colonists Protest Stamp Act,* John Trumbull, The Granger Collection, New York; (right) *Phillis Wheatley,* The Granger Collection, New York; **91:** (left) *The British Surrender at Yorktown,* John Trumbull, The Granger Collection,

New York; (center) *James Boswell,* Thomas Rowlandson, The Granger Collection, New York; (right) *Napoleon Bonaparte,* Jean Auguste Dominique Ingres, Superstock; **92:** *The Battle of Lexington at the Beginning of the Combat,* line engraving, 1832, Amos Doolittle and John W. Barber, The Granger Collection, New York; **93:** *George Washington Addressing the Second Continental Congress,* Contemporary colored line engraving, The Granger Collection, New York; **94:** *Patrick Henry Speaking Against the Stamp Act,* The Granger Collection, New York; **95:** Title page of Volume I, *The Federalist,* New York, 1788, The Granger Collection, New York; **98:** *Benjamin Franklin,* c. 1790, Pierre Michel Alix, The National Portrait Gallery, Smithsonian Institution, Washington, D.C./Art Resource, New York; **101:** *Birthplace of Franklin in Milk Street,* J. H. Buffords, The Metropolitan Museum of Art, Gift of William H. Huntington, 1882, Copyright © by the Metropolitan Museum of Art; **103:** *Delaware River Front, Philadelphia,* Thomas Birch, M. and M. Karolik Collection of American Watercolors and Drawings, 1800–1875, Courtesy, Museum of Fine Arts, Boston; **105:** *Quaker Meeting,* British, fourth quarter 18th century or first quarter 19th century, Bequest of Maxim Karolik, Courtesy, Museum of Fine Arts, Boston; **111:** *Poor Richard's Almanack,* The Granger Collection, New York; **114:** *Patrick Henry* (detail), c. 1835, James Barton Longacre after Lawrence Sully, The National Portrait Gallery, Smithsonian Institution, Washington, D.C./Art Resource, New York; **117:** *Patrick Henry Before the Virginia House of Burgesses,* 1851, Peter F. Rothermel, Red Hill, The Patrick Henry National Memorial; **120:** *Thomas Paine,* John Wesley Jarvis, The Granger Collection, New York; **123:** *Recruiting for the Continental Army,* c. 1857–59, William T. Ranney, Oil on canvas, 53 3/4 x 82 1/4″, Munson-Williams-Proctor Institute, Museum of Art, Utica, New York; **126:** *Phillis Wheatley* (detail), Unidentified artist after Scipio Moorhead, The National Portrait Gallery, Smithsonian Institution, Washington, D.C./Art Resource, New York; **128:** *George Washington at the Battle of Princeton,* Charles Wilson Peale, © Yale University Art Gallery; **132:** *Thomas Jefferson,* The Granger Collection, New York; **135:** *The Declaration of Independence,* 1786, John Trumbull, © Yale University Art Gallery; **140:** *Abigail Smith Adams,* The Granger Collection, New York; **143:** *Building the First White House,* N. C. Wyeth, Copyright © The White House Historical Association, Photo by the National Geographic Society; **146:** *Michel-Guillaume Jean De Crèvecoeur,* The Bettmann Archive; **149:** *Independence (Squire Jack Porter),* 1858, Frank Blackwell Mayer, National Museum of American Art, Smithsonian Institution, Bequest of Harriet Lane Johnson; **152:** *Olaudah Equiano,* Unknown Artist, Bridgeman/Art Resource, New York; **154:** *Slaves Below Deck,* (detail) Lt. Francis Meynell, National Maritime Museum, Greenwich; **160:** *Niagara Falls,* about 1832–1840, Thomas Chambers, © Wadsworth Atheneum, Hartford, Ella Gallup Sumner and Mary Catlin Sumner Collection; **162:** *Louisiana Purchase Ceremony at New Orleans, 20 December 1803,* Thor de Thulstrup, The Granger Collection, New York; **163:** *Andrew Jackson Encouraging His Riflemen at the Battle of New Orleans, January 8, 1815,* 19th century colored engraving, The Granger Collection, New York; **164:** (left) *Lewis and*

Clark Expedition, Oscar E. Berninghaus, Superstock; (center) *Jane Austen,* Colored engraving, The Granger Collection, New York; (right) *The Battle of New Orleans,* The Granger Collection, New York; **165:** (left) *Alfred, Lord Tennyson,* The Granger Collection, New York; (center) *Samuel Morse Demonstrating Telegraph,* The Granger Collection, New York; (right) *The Trail of Tears,* Robert Lindneux, The Granger Collection, New York; **166:** *Last Stand at the Alamo,* N. C. Wyeth, Superstock; **168:** Illustration from an 1872 Edition of James Fenimore Cooper's *The Last of the Mohicans,* Felix Octavius Carr Darley, The Granger Collection, New York; **169:** *Kindred Spirits,* Asher B. Durand, New York Public Library; Astor, Lenox and Tilden Foundations; **172:** *Washington Irving* (detail), Daniel Huntington, The National Portrait Gallery, Smithsonian Institution, Washington, D.C./Art Resource, New York; **186:** *Vernal Falls,* Yosemite Valley, Thomas Moran, Superstock; **195:** ''I at length . . . ,'' Edgar Allan Poe's *Tales of Mystery and Imagination* (London: George G. Harrap, 1935), Arthur Rackham, Print Collection, Miriam and Ira D. Wallach Division of Art, Prints and Photographs, The New York Public Library; Astor, Lenox and Tilden Foundations; **209:** Illustration to E. A. Poe's *The Raven,* Edouard Manet, Gift of W. G. Russell Allen, Courtesy, Museum of Fine Arts, Boston; **211:** Illustration to E. A. Poe's *The Raven,* Edouard Manet, Gift of W. G. Russell Allen, Courtesy, Museum of Fine Arts, Boston; **217:** *Proserpine,* Dante Gabriel Rossetti, The Tate Gallery, London/Art Resource, New York; **219:** CBS/Photofest; **222:** *Boston Harbor,* Fitz Hugh Lane, M. and M. Karolik Collection of American Paintings, 1815–1865, By Exchange, Courtesy, Museum of Fine Arts, Boston; **225:** *Cornell Farm,* Edward Hicks, Superstock; **226:** (center) *First Postage Stamps,* The Granger Collection, New York; (left) *Abraham Lincoln,* The Granger Collection, New York; (right) *Charlotte Brontë,* The Granger Collection, New York; **227:** (left) *Gold Mining in California,* Currier & Ives, The Granger Collection, New York; (center) *Women's Rights Convention,* The Granger Collection, New York; (right) *Henry David Thoreau,* The Granger Collection, New York; **228:** *Harriet Beecher Stowe,* 1853, Alanson Fisher, The Granger Collection, New York; **229:** American Bookseller's Announcement for *Uncle Tom's Cabin,* The Granger Collection, New York; **230:** *The Notch of the White Mountains (Crawford Notch),* 1839, Thomas Cole, Andrew W. Mellon Fund, © 1993 The National Gallery of Art, Washington; **233:** *The Whale Fishery—The Sperm Whale in a Flurry,* Currier & Ives, The Granger Collection, New York; **234:** *Hiawatha,* c. 1871, Thomas Eakins, Hirshhorn Museum and Sculpture Garden, Smithsonian Institution, Photo by Joseph Martin, Art Resource/Scala; **240:** *Sunset,* Frederick E. Church, Oil on canvas, 24 x 36, Collection of Munson-Williams-Proctor Institute Museum of Art, Utica, New York, Proctor Collection; **245:** *Farm Yard, Winter,* 1862, George Henry Durrie, Courtesy of the New York Historical Society, New York City; **252:** *Henry David Thoreau,* The Granger Collection, New York; **266:** *Nathaniel Hawthorne* (detail), 1862, Emanuel Gottlieb Leutze, The National Portrait Gallery, Smithsonian Institution, Washington, D.C./Art Resource, New York; **269:** *Winter Sunday in Norway, Maine,* c. 1860, Unidentified Artist, New York State Historical Association, Coopers-

town; **274:** *Cemetery,* Peter McIntyre, Courtesy of the Artist; **278:** *Herman Melville,* Wyatt Eaton, The Granger Collection, New York; **297:** *After the First Snow in Winter in Vermont,* Charles Hughes, Superstock; **298:** *Henry Wadsworth Longfellow,* Thomas B. Read, The National Portrait Gallery, Smithsonian Institution, Washington, D.C./Art Resource, New York; **300:** *The Return Alone,* Eugene Higgins, © The Phillips Collection, Washington, D.C.; **308:** *U.S. Frigate Constitution,* 1823, Nicholas Cammillieri, Courtesy of The Mariner's Museum, Newport News, Virginia; **314:** *Low Branch,* 1968, Scarlett, Courtesy New York Graphic Society, all rights reserved; **323:** *Old Holley House, Cos Cob,* John Henry Twachtman, Cincinnati Art Museum, John J. Emery Endowment; **327:** *Quoddy Head,* 1933, John Marin, Art Resource; **330:** *Emily Dickinson,* The Granger Collection, New York; **332:** *February,* 1890–1900, John Henry Twachtman, The Hayden Collection, Courtesy, Museum of Fine Arts, Boston; **334:** *Near Harlech, North Wales,* Benjamin William Leader, Bridgeman/Art Resource, New York; **337:** *Room with a Balcony,* Adolph von Menzel, Staatliche Museen Preubischer Kulturbesitz, Nationgalerie, Berlin; **342:** *Twilight in the Wilderness,* Frederick E. Church, The Cleveland Museum of Art, Mr. and Mrs. William H. Marlatt Fund, 65.233; **346:** *Let Us Have Peace (Grant and Lee)* J. L. G. Ferris, Superstock; **349:** *A Ride For Liberty—The Fugitive Slaves,* c. 1862, Eastman Johnson, Brooklyn Museum, Gift of Miss Gwendolyn O. L. Conkling; **350:** (left) *Frederick Douglass,* Attributed to Elisha Hammond, The Granger Collection, New York; (center) *Charles Darwin,* John Collier, The Granger Collection, New York; (right) *John Brown,* P. H. Balling, The Granger Collection, New York; **351:** (left) *Bombardment of Fort Sumter,* Currier & Ives, The Granger Collection, New York; (right) *The Surrender at Appomattox,* The Granger Collection, New York; **352:** *Tidings From the Front,* Gilbert Gaul, Superstock; **354:** *Faithful Troops Cheer General Lee,* 1865, N. C. Wyeth, U. S. Naval Academy Museum; **362:** *Frederick Douglass,* c. 1844, Attributed to Elisha Hammond, The National Portrait Gallery, Smithsonian Institution, Washington, D.C./Art Resource, New York; **367:** *A Home on the Mississippi,* 1871, Currier & Ives, The Museum of the City of New York, Harry T. Peters Collection; **373:** *The Housetops in Charleston During The Bombardment of Fort Sumter,* Harper's Weekly, May 4, 1861, Courtesy of the Library of Congress; **376:** (top) *Robert E. Lee,* 1864–1865, Edward Caledon Bruce, The National Portrait Gallery, Smithsonian Institution, Washington, D.C./Art Resource, New York; (bottom) *Abraham Lincoln* (detail), 1887, George Peter Alexander Healy, The National Portrait Gallery, Smithsonian Institution, Washington, D.C./Art Resource, New York; **378:** *The Battle Abbey Murals: The Four Seasons of the Confederacy, The Summer Mural,* Charles Hoffbauer, Collection of the Virginia State Historical Society, Richmond, VA; **380:** *Abraham Lincoln's Address at the Dedication of the Gettysburg National Cemetery, 19 November 1863,* The Granger Collection, New York; **385:** *Young Soldier: Separate Study of a Soldier Giving Water to a Wounded Companion,* 1861, Winslow Homer, Oil, gouache, black crayon on canvas, 36 x 17.5 cm, United States, 1836–1910, Cooper-Hewitt, National Museum of Design, Smithsonian Institution, Gift of Charles Savage Homer, Jr., 1912–12–

110, Photo by Ken Pelka, Courtesy of Art Resource, New York; **387:** *Reading the Emancipation Proclamation,* Artist Unknown, The Granger Collection, New York; **392:** *Hinmaton Yalaktit, Chief Joseph,* 1878, Cyrenius Hall, The National Portrait Gallery, Smithsonian Institution, Washington, D.C./Art Resource, New York; **394:** *Chief Joseph's Surrender to Colonel Nelson A. Miles,* Olaf C. Seltzer, The Thomas Gilcrease Institute of American History and Art, Tulsa, Oklahoma; **396:** *Walt Whitman,* UPI/Bettmann Newsphotos; **405:** *The Wounded Drummer Boy,* Eastman Johnson, The Union League Club, New York City, Joseph Martin, Scala/Art Resource, New York; **406:** *The Lawrence Tree,* 1929, Georgia O'Keeffe, Wadsworth Atheneum, Hartford, The Ella Gallup Sumner and Mary Catlin Sumner Collection; **410:** *The Funeral of President Lincoln, New York, April 25, 1865,* Currier & Ives, Anne S. K. Brown Military Collection, Brown University Library; **414:** *Abraham Lincoln,* William Willard, Gift of Mr. and Mrs. David A. Morse, The National Portrait Gallery, Smithsonian Institution, Washington, D.C./Art Resource, New York; **422:** *The Adirondack Guide,* 1894, Winslow Homer, Bequest of Mrs. Alma H. Wadleigh, Courtesy, Museum of Fine Arts, Boston; **424:** *In Search of the Land of Milk and Honey,* Harvey Dunn, The original Dunn painting hangs in the Hazel L. Meyer Memorial Library, Desmet, South Dakota; **425:** *The Miners During the Gold Rush 1849, in California,* Frank Tenney Johnson, Superstock; **426:** (left) Mark Twain on Cigar Box Label, The Granger Collection, New York; (center) *Inauguration of the Statue of Liberty,* The Granger Collection, New York; (right) *Blizzard of 1888,* The Granger Collection, New York; **427:** (left) *Wright Brothers' First Flight at Kitty Hawk,* The Granger Collection, New York; (center) *Albert Einstein,* Tomassetti, Superstock; (right) *Ford Model T,* The Granger Collection, New York; **428:** *Louisiana Indians Walking Along a Bayou,* Alfred Boisseau, New Orleans Museum of Art, Gift of Mr. William E. Groves; **429:** *The Bowery at Night,* 1895, W. Louis Sonntag, Jr., Museum of the City of New York; **430:** *Queensboro Bridge,* Glen Oden Coleman, Hirshhorn Museum and Sculpture Garden, Smithsonian Institution, Gift of Joseph H. Hirshhorn; **431:** *Rabbit Stew, 1981,* Gary Niblett, Oil on canvas, 32 x 44"; Photo courtesy of the Gerald Peters Gallery, Santa Fe, New Mexico; **435:** *Turn Him Loose, Bill,* Frederic Remington, Superstock; **436:** *Samuel Langhorne Clemens (Mark Twain)* (detail), 1935, Frank Edwin Larson, The National Portrait Gallery, Smithsonian Institution, Washington, D.C./Art Resource, New York; **439:** *Paddle Steamboat Mississippi,* Shelburne Museum, Shelburne, Vermont, Photo by Ken Burris; **442:** *Huck Finn,* E. W. Kemble, The Granger Collection; **448:** *Mark Twain Riding the Celebrated Jumping Frog,* Frederic Waddy, The Granger Collection, New York; **450:** *Bret Harte,* John Pettie, The Granger Collection, New York; **453:** *Edge of Town,* Charles Burchfield, The Nelson-Atkins Museum of Art, Kansas City, Missouri, (Gift of Friends of Art) 41–52; **460:** *The Bronco Buster,* 1895, Frederic Remington, Amon Carter Museum, Fort Worth, Photograph by Linda Lorenz, 1984; **461:** *The Outlier,* 1909, Frederic Remington, The Brooklyn Museum; **462:** *Ambrose Bierce,* The Bettmann Archive; **464:** *The Red Bridge,* Julien Alden Weir, The Metropolitan Museum of Art, Gift of Mrs. John A. Rutherford,

1914, Copyright © 1982 by The Metropolitan Museum of Art; **470:** *Seat of John Julius Pringle,* 1800, Charles Fraser, Carolina Art Association, Gibbes Art Gallery; **475:** *Woman with a Black Tie,* Amedeo Modigliani, Private Collection; **481:** *From Arkansas,* George Schreiber, Sheldon Swope Art Gallery, Terre Haute, Indiana; **485:** *At the Opera,* Mary Stevenson Cassatt, The Hayden Collection, Courtesy, Museum of Fine Arts, Boston; **505:** *Benares,* Marshall Johnson, Peabody Museum of Salem, Photo by Mark Sexton; **511:** *California Suite,* Vivian Caldwell, Courtesy of the artist; **518:** *Worsening Weather,* Anton Otto Fischer, United States Coast Guard Museum; **525:** *The Grand Canyon of the Yellowstone,* 1893–1901, Thomas Moran, Art Resource; **527:** *Harper's Ferry From Jefferson Rock,* 1857, Edward Beyer, Virginia State Library and Archives; **530:** *Paul Laurence Dunbar,* The Granger Collection, New York; **534:** *Frederick Douglass,* Historical Picture Services, Stock Montage; **536:** *Edwin Arlington Robinson* (detail), 1933, Thomas Richard Hood, The National Portrait Gallery, Smithsonian Institution, Washington, D.C./Art Resource, New York; **538:** *The Artist's Garden,* c.1880, Blakelock, National Gallery of Art, Washington, Art Resource, New York; **542:** *The Thinker (Portrait of Louis N. Kenton),* 1900, Thomas Eakins, The Metropolitan Museum of Art, Kennedy Fund, 1917, © 1967, 1984 by The Metropolitan Museum of Art; **544:** *Edgar Lee Masters* (detail), 1946, Francis J. Quirk, The National Portrait Gallery, Smithsonian Institution, Washington, D.C./Art Resource, New York; **546:** *Barn Dance,* 1950, Grandma Moses, © 1989, Grandma Moses Properties Co., New York; **552:** *City Roofs,* 1932, Edward Hopper, Courtesy of Kennedy Galleries, Inc., New York; **554:** *Armistice Day,* 1918, Gifford Beal, William Lowe Bryan Memorial Collection, Indiana University Art Museum, Photo by Michael Cavanagh, Kevin Montaghe; **555:** *The City From Greenwich Village,* 1922, John Sloan, © 1993 National Gallery of Art, Washington, Gift of Helen Farr Sloan; **556:** (left) *The End of the Climb,* Rollin Kirby, The Granger Collection, New York; (center) *James Joyce,* Jacques Emile Blanche, Superstock; (right) *Langston Hughes,* Winold Reiss, The Granger Collection, New York; **557:** (left) *The Stock Market Crash,* Otto Soglow, The Granger Collection, New York; (center) *Adolf Hitler,* The Pentagon (U.S. Army Archives); (right) *Japanese Bomb Pearl Harbor,* The Granger Collection, New York; **559:** *Library,* Bernard Boruch Zakheim, Coit Tower Mural (WPA), Collection of the City and County of San Francisco, Public Works of Art Project, 1934; **560:** *Conception Synchromy,* 1914, Stanton MacDonald-Wright, Hirshhorn Museum and Sculpture Garden, Smithsonian Institution, Scala/Art Resource, New York; **562:** *Room in Brooklyn,* Edward Hopper, Oil on canvas, 29" x 34", The Hayden Collection, Courtesy, Museum of Fine Arts, Boston; **564:** *Juke Box,* 1946, Jacob Lawrence, Copyright © 1987 The Detroit Institute of Arts, Gift of Dr. D. T. Burton, Dr. M. E. Fowler, Dr. J. B. Greene, and Mr. J. J. White; **567:** *Man with a Horn,* Oliver Johnson, Oil on canvas, Courtesy of the artist; **571:** *West Tisbury Fair,* Thomas Hart Benton, Collection of Mr. Arthur Levitt, Jr., New York, Photo by John Lei/Omni-Photo Communications; **575:** *After the Show,* 1933, Waldo Pierce, Oil on canvas, 32 1/4" x 46", Collection of Whitney Museum of American Art, Purchase; **586:** *F. Scott Fitzgerald* (detail), David Silvette, The National Portrait Gallery, Smithsonian Institution, Washington, D.C./Art Resource, New York; **589:** *Floating Ice,* 1910, George Bellows, Oil on canvas, 45″ x 63″, Collection of Whitney Museum of American Art, Gift of Gertrude Vanderbilt Whitney; **597:** *Winter Wonderland,* Rebecca Grutzik, Student, Stevens Point, Wisconsin, Courtesy of the artist; **601:** *Manhattan Tops,* Herman Rose, Hirshhorn Museum and Sculpture Garden, Smithsonian Institution, Gift of Joseph H. Hirshhorn, 1966; **607:** *Garden of Memories,* 1917, Charles Burchfield, Collection, The Museum of Modern Art, New York, Gift of Abby Aldrich Rockefeller (by exchange); **610:** *Lavender and Old Lace,* Charles Burchfield (1893–1967), from the collection of the New Britain Museum of American Art, Charles F. Smith Fund, Photo by E. Irving Blomstrann; **614:** *Thomas Wolfe,* 1938, Soss Melik, The National Portrait Gallery, Smithsonian Institution, Washington, D.C./Art Resource, New York; **617:** *Stone City, Iowa,* Grant Wood, Joslyn Art Museum, Omaha, Nebraska, Gift of the Art Institute of Omaha; **644:** *William Faulkner,* Soss Melik, The National Portrait Gallery, Smithsonian Institution, Washington, D.C./Art Resource, New York; **648:** *In the Depths of the Timber,* W. Herbert Dunton, Courtesy Amon Carter Museum, Fort Worth; **663:** *The Mather School,* Jonathan Green, Courtesy of the artist; **665:** *School Bell Time,* 1978, from the *Profile/Part I: The Twenties* series (Mecklenburg County) Romare Bearden, Collection: Kingsborough Community College, The City University of New York; **684, 686, 687:** Illustrations from "The Night the Ghost Got In," © 1933, 1961, James Thurber, from *My Life and Hard Times*, Published by Harper & Row; **688:** Copyright © James Thurber, Copyright © 1971 Helen Thurber and Rosemary A. Thurber, from *Men, Women and Dogs,* published by Harcourt Brace Jovanovich, Inc.; **690:** *Richard Wright* (detail), 1949, Miriam Troop, The National Portrait Gallery, Smithsonian Institution, Washington, D.C./Art Resource, New York; **697:** *Black and White,* 1930, Georgia O'Keeffe, Oil on canvas, 36″ x 24″, Collection of Whitney Museum of American Art, Gift of Mr. and Mrs. R. Crosby Kemper; **698:** *Ezra Pound,* Wyndham Lewis, The Granger Collection, New York; **702:** *Landscape in Various Styles,* Ch'a Shih-piao, The Cleveland Museum of Art, Gift of Mr. and Mrs. Severance A. Millikin, 55.37; **706:** *T. S. Eliot* (detail), Sir Gerald Kelly, The National Portrait Gallery, Smithsonian Institution, Washington, D.C./Art Resource, New York; **710:** *Moonlight, Dovehouse Street, Chelsea,* Algernon Newton, Fine Art Society, London, Bridgeman/Art Resource, New York; **720:** *In a Shoreham Garden,* Samuel Palmer, By Courtesy of the Board of Trustees of the Victoria and Albert Museum; **726:** *Orchard in Bloom, Louveciennes,* (detail), 1872, Camille Pissaro, © 1993 National Gallery of Art, Washington, Alisa Mellon Bruce Collection; **728:** *Overhanging Cloud in July,* 1947–1959, Charles Burchfield, Watercolor on paper, 39 1/2″ x 35 1/2″, Collection of Whitney Museum of American Art, Purchase, with funds from the Friends of the Whitney Museum of American Art; **732:** *Pink Locusts and Windy Moon,* 1959, Charles Burchfield, Collection of the Chase Manhattan Bank; **736:** *Carl Sandburg,* Miriam Svet, The National Portrait Gallery, Smithsonian Institution, Washington, D.C./Art Resource, New

York; **739:** *Marshes, Dunes and Fields,* 1977, Jane Freilicher, The Herbert W. Plimpton Foundation, on extended loan to the Rose Art Museum, Brandeis University, Waltham, Massachusetts, Photo by Herb Gallagher; **744:** *Edna St. Vincent Millay* (detail), Charles Ellis, The National Portrait Gallery, Smithsonian Institution, Washington, D.C./Art Resource, New York; **747:** *The Sun,* Edvard Munch, Fotograf by O. Vaering; **757:** *Untitled,* 1964, Alexander Calder, Solomon R. Guggenheim Museum, New York, Gift of the artist, 1965, Photo by Myles Aronowitz, © The Solomon R. Guggenheim Foundation, New York; **758:** *E. E. Cummings* (detail), 1958, Self Portrait, The National Portrait Gallery, Smithsonian Institution, Washington, D.C./Art Resource, New York; **760:** *Lovers With Flowers,* 1927, Marc Chagall, The Israel Museum, Jerusalem, Gift of Baron Edmond de Rothschild, Paris, © 1993 ARS, New York/ADAGP, Paris; **766:** *New England Birches,* Ernest Lawson, © The Phillips Collection, Washington, D.C.; **785:** *Ruby Green Singing,* 1928, James Chapin, Norton Gallery and School of Art, West Palm Beach, Florida; **786:** *Countee Cullen* (detail), c. 1925, Winold Reiss, The National Portrait Gallery, Smithsonian Institution, Washington, D.C./Art Resource, New York; **788:** *Big Meeting;* Varnette P. Honeywood, Black Lifestyles, © 1980, Acrylic on canvas, 48″ x 48″; **792:** *Langston Hughes* (detail), c. 1925, Winold Reiss, The National Portrait Gallery, Smithsonian Institution, Washington, D.C./Art Resource, New York; **798:** *Jean Toomer* (detail), c. 1925, Winold Reiss, Gift of Laurence A. Fleischman and Howard Garfinkle with a matching grant from the National Endowment of the Arts, The National Portrait Gallery, Smithsonian Institution, Washington, D.C./Art Resource, New York; **800:** *Black Place II,* 1944, Georgia O'Keeffe, The Alfred Stieglitz Collection, 1959, © 1984/85 by The Metropolitan Museum of Art; **803:** *Trombone Solo,* 1984, Romare Bearden, Courtesy Romare Bearden Estate, ACA Gallery, New York, NY; **804:** *Jazz Village,* 1967, Romare Bearden, Courtesy Romare Bearden Estate, ACA Gallery, New York, NY; **808:** *Golden Gate,* 1955, Charles Sheeler, George A. Hearn Fund, 1955, Copyright © 1984 by The Metropolitan Museum of Art; **811:** *Saraband,* 1959, Morris Louis, The Solomon R. Guggenheim Museum, New York, Photo by David Heald, © The Solomon R. Guggenheim Foundation, New York; **814:** *Untitled,* 1960–61, Mark Rothko, Art Resource, New York; **816:** *Gotham News,* 1955, Willem de Kooning, Oil on canvas, 69 x 79″, Albright-Knox Art Gallery, Buffalo, New York, Gift of Seymour H. Knox, 1955; **819:** *Morning Call,* 1946, Milton Avery, Hirshhorn Museum and Sculpture Garden, Smithsonian Institution, Scala/Art Resource, New York; **834:** *Black Walnuts,* 1945, Joseph Pollet, Oil on canvas, 30″ x 40″, Collection of Whitney Museum of American Art, Purchase, Gift of Gertrude Vanderbilt Whitney, by exchange; **844–845:** *The Block,* Romare Bearden, Copyright © 1986 by The Metropolitan Museum of Art, Gift cf Mr. and Mrs. Samuel Shore, 1978, (1978.61.1–.6); **848:** *Jim,* 1930, William H. Johnson, National Museum of American Art, Washington, D.C., Art Resource, New York; **861:** *Martha's Vineyard,* 1925, Thomas Hart Benton, Oil on canvas, 16 x 20″, Collection of Whitney Museum of American Art, Gift of Gertrude Vanderbilt Whitney; **873:** *The Laughing Boy,* George Bellows, Private Collection, Photograph courtesy of Hirschl and Adler Galleries; **874:** *Waiting Room,* Raphael Soyer, Collection of the Corcoran Gallery of Art, Museum Purchase, William A. Clark Fund, 1943; **882:** *Pleasures of Winter in New York,* Francis Peterson, Superstock; **893:** *Sunset and Moonrise with Maudell Sleet,* 1978, from the *Profile/Part I: The Twenties* series (Mecklenburg County), Romare Bearden, Courtesy of the Estate of Romare Bearden; **896:** Quilt made by a slave illustration #56 from *Stitched from the Soul,* Nancy Vaughn Ford, Photo courtesy of Dutton Studio Books; **899:** *Painted Water Glasses,* 1974, Janet Fish, Oil on canvas, 53 3/4" x 60", Collection of Whitney Museum of American Art, Purchase, with funds from Susan and David Workman; **903:** *Night City,* Richard Florsheim, Collection of Jane Golanty; **910:** *Man in a Vest,* 1939–1949, William H. Johnson, Gift of the Harmon Foundation, National Museum of American Art, Smithsonian Institution, Washington, D.C./Art Resource, New York; **925:** *The Medicine Robe,* Maynard Dixon, Courtesy of The Buffalo Bill Historical Center, Cody, Wyoming, Gift of Mr. and Mrs. Godwin Pelissero; **931:** *Biography,* 1988, Marina Gutierrez, Courtesy of the artist; **951:** *Number 3,* 1949, Jackson Pollack, Hirshhorn Museum and Sculpture Garden, Smithsonian Institution, Joseph Martin/Scala/Art Resource, New York; **957:** *Wild Flowers,* 1978, S. Reindorf, Collection of George Williams; **967:** *The Unexpected Answer,* René Magritte, Patrimoine des Musées Royaux des Beaux-Arts de Belgique, Bruxelles, © C. Herscovici/ARS, New York; **968:** *Great Florida Sunset,* 1887, Martin Johnson Heade, Private Collection USA, Photo courtesy Acquavella Galleries, Inc.; **974:** *Crowninshield's Wharf,* George Ropes, Peabody Museum of Salem; **985:** *Martha's Vineyard,* 1925, Thomas Hart Benton, Oil on canvas, 16" x 20", Collection of Whitney Museum of American Art, Gift of Gertrude Vanderbilt Whitney; **987:** *Spring in Puerto Rico,* 1976, Oil on canvas, Pedro Villarini, Courtesy of El Museo del Barrio, New York, Photo by John Lei/Omni-Photo Communications, Inc.; **991:** *Hombre ante el Infinito (Man Before Infinity),* Ruffino Tamayo, Art Resource, New York; **992:** *Robert Penn Warren,* 1935, Conrad A. Albrizio, The National Portrait Gallery, Smithsonian Institution, Washington, D.C./Art Resource, New York; **994:** *Queen Anne's Lace,* 1957, Charles Burchfield, Watercolor, Copyright © 1987 The Detroit Institute of Arts, Gift of John S. Newberry; **998:** *Summer Landscape With Hawk,* 1901–1906, Louis M. Eilshemius, The Phillips Collection, Washington, D.C.; **1003:** *Girl in a White Dress,* Sir William Orpen, Private Collection, Bridgeman/Art Resource, New York; **1004:** *Part II, The Free Man, No. 30,* The Frederick Douglass Series, Jacob Lawrence, Hampton University Museum, Hampton, Virginia; **1011:** *The Madonna and Child,* 1990, Momodou Ceesay, Dialogue Systems, Inc.; **1013:** *Winter,* Ozz Franca, Oil, 24" x 18", Edition of 999 s/n, Courtesy of The Hadley Companies; **1014:** *The Poet Reclining,* 1915, Marc Chagall, The Tate Gallery, London, © 1993 ARS, New York/ADAGP, Paris; **1021:** *The Lone Tenement,* George Bellows, Superstock; **1023:** *Christmas Morning, Adirondacks,* 1946, Rockwell Kent, Courtesy of the Rockwell Kent Legacies; **1027:** *Vaudeville,* 1951, Jacob Lawrence, Hirshhorn Museum and Sculpture Garden, Smithsonian Institution, Gift of Joseph H. Hirshhorn, 1966; **1029:** *Untitled,* Peter Malone, Chen/Art Resource, New York; **1031:** *Closing Scene,* 1963 © David Hockney, Oil 48" x 48", Courtesy of the artist, Photo by John Lei/Omni-Photo Communications, Inc.; **1037:** *The Trial of Two 'Witches' at Salem, Massachusetts, in 1662,* Howard Pyle, The Granger Collection, New York; **1067:** *The Execution of the Reverend Stephen Burroughs for Witchcraft at Salem, Massachusetts, in 1692,* The Granger Collection, New York; **1070:** *The Hanging of a 'Witch' at Salem, Massachusetts, in 1662,* 19th century engraving, The Granger Collection, New York; **1091:** *The Witchcraft Trial of Giles Corey at Salem, Massachusetts, 1692,* 19th century engraving, The Granger Collection, New York

PHOTOGRAPH CREDITS

29: Jim Brandenburg/Woodfin Camp & Associates; **32:** Thomas Victor/*Time* Magazine; **71:** David Cavagnaro/DRK Photo; **156:** Harbron/Sygma; **157:** Chip Hires/Gamma-Liaison, Inc.; **184:** *William Cullen Bryant* (detail), Unidentified photographer, The National Portrait Gallery, Smithsonian Institution, Washington, D.C./Art Resource, New York; **189:** Frank Whitney/The Image Bank; **192:** UPI/Bettmann Newsphotos; **218:** Movie Still Archives; **219:** The Kobal Collection/Superstock; **238:** The Granger Collection, New York; **247:** Steve Dunwell/The Image Bank; **249:** Pat O'Hara/DRK Photo; **251:** Paolo Koch/Photo Researchers, Inc.; **256:** Brad Parker/Thoreau Lyceum: **260:** Robert Frerck/Odyssey Productions; **264:** Richard Howard; **265:** Jay Dusard/Little, Brown & Co.; **281:** Nantucket Historical Association; **284:** Culver Pictures, Inc.; **293:** Culver Pictures, Inc.; **302:** Stephanie Maze/Woodfin Camp & Associates; **306:** *Oliver Wendell Holmes,* James Notman, The National Portrait Gallery, Smithsonian Institution, Washington, D.C./Art Resource, New York; **310:** James Carmichael/The Image Bank; **312:** The Bettmann Archive; **316:** Ulrike Welsch; **318:** *John Greenleaf Whittier* (detail), 1881, William Notman, The National Portrait Gallery, Smithsonian Institution, Washington, D.C./Art Resource, New York; **388:** Library of Congress; **400:** Don Klumpp/The Image Bank; **418:** The Granger Collection, New York; **419, 478, 488:** The Bettmann Archive; **490:** Wayne Lynch/DRK Photo; **497:** Annie Griffiths/DRK Photo; **502:** UPI/Bettmann Newsphotos; **526:** The Granger Collection, New York; **568:** UPI/Bettmann Newsphotos; **578:** Larry Burrows/*Life* Magazine © Time Warner Inc.; **581:** American Red Cross; **604, 620:** Thomas Victor; **628:** UPI/Bettmann Newsphotos; **631:** Art Wolfe/The Image Bank; **637:** Timothy Eagan/Woodfin Camp & Associates; **640:** Dan McCoy/Rainbow; **660:** Courtesy of the Estate of Carl Van

Vechten, Joseph Solomon, EXECUTOR, The National Portrait Gallery, Washington, D.C./Art Resource, New York; **668:** *John Dos Passos,* The National Portrait Gallery, Smithsonian Institution, Washington, D.C./Art Resource, New York; **671:** Historical Picture Services/Stock Montage; **674:** AP/Wide World Photos; **677:** Brad Parker/Thoreau Lyceum; **682:** UPI/ Bettmann Newsphotos; **693, 694:** George Karger/*Life* Magazine, © 1945 Time Warner Inc.; **714:** The Granger Collection, New York; **718, 724:** The Bettmann Archive; **730:** *William Carlos Williams,* The National Portrait Gallery, Smithsonian Institution, Washington, D.C./Art Resource, New York; **742:** Historical Picture Services/Stock Montage; **752:** (top) The Bettmann Archive; (bottom) AP/Wide World Photos; **754:** Janeart LTD, The Image Bank; **764:** Dmitri Kessel/*Life* Magazine © Time Inc.; **768:** Dewitt Jones/Woodfin Camp & Associates; **771:** Bill Bridge/DPI; **780:** The Bettmann Archive; **786:** G. K. Hall and Company; **791:** Michael Skott/Image Bank; **794:** C. C. Lockwood; **798:** UPI/Bettmann Newsphotos; **812:** (left) Bob Adelman/Magnum Photos; (right) Andrew St. George/Magnum Photos; (center) Leviton-Atlanta/Black Star; **813:** (left) The Granger Collection; (center, left) M. Philippot/ Sygma; (center, right) Peter Garfield/Folio, Inc.; (right) Alex Webb/Magnum Photos; **820:** Nancy Crampton; **823:** Dan McCoy/Rainbow; **830:** Flannery O'Connor Collection, Ina Dillard Russel Library, Georgia College; **842, 852:** Thomas Victor; **855:** Ken Karp; **858, 864, 870, 880, 890:** Thomas Victor; **900:** The Granger Collection, New York; **906:** Nancy Crampton; **914:** Thomas Victor; **917:** William Rivelli/The Image Bank; **919:** David W. Hamilton/The Image Bank; **922:** Thomas Victor; **928:** Ruben Guzman; **934:** Thomas Victor; **937:** Johnny Johnson/DRK Photo; **941:** Chuck O'Rear/Woodfin Camp & Associates; **944:** Robert Foothorap, G.P. Putnam's Sons; **948:** Jim McHugh; **952:** AP/Wide World Photos; **958:** Thomas Victor; **963:** Harold Sund/The Image Bank; **964:** (top) UPI/Bettmann Newsphotos; (bottom) Thomas Victor; **972:** © Rollie McKenna; **978** Historical Picture Services/Stock Montage; **982:** (top) New York Public Library; (center) Shelley Rotner/Omni-Photo Communication, Inc.; (bottom) Naomi H. Quinonez; **985:** Jeff Foott/DRK Photo; **992:** (top) Thomas Victor; **1000:** (top) AP/Wide World Photos; (center) The Bettmann Archive; (bottom) Kit Stafford; **1008:** (top) Nihad Becirovic; (center) Thomas Victor; (bottom) Thomas Victor, *Time* Magazine; **1016:** (top) Thomas Victor; (center) Marlene Fostor; (bottom) © Rollie McKenna; **1018:** Peter G. Veit/DRK Photo; **1024:** (top) Helga Matley; (center) Georgia McInnis/ Courtesy of Arte Publico Press, University of Houston; (bottom) Thomas Victor; **1032:** Retna, LTD **1041, 1046, 1053, 1056, 1059, 1074, 1078, 1086, 1097, 1105, 1112, 1116:** Martha Swope; **1120:** Henri Dauman/Magnum Photos, Inc.; **1121:** Martha Swope

ILLUSTRATION CREDITS

pp: 10, 28, 172, 176, 179, 182, 1124–1125: The Art Source.